POWER AT GROUND ZERO

POWER AT GROUND ZERO

Politics, Money, and the
Remaking of Lower Manhattan

LYNNE B. SAGALYN

OXFORD
UNIVERSITY PRESS

OXFORD
UNIVERSITY PRESS

Oxford University Press is a department of the University of Oxford.
It furthers the University's objective of excellence in research, scholarship,
and education by publishing worldwide. Oxford is a registered trade mark of
Oxford University Press in the UK and certain other countries.

Published in the United States of America by Oxford University Press
198 Madison Avenue, New York, NY 10016, United States of America.

Library of Congress Cataloging-in-Publication Data
Names: Sagalyn, Lynne B., author.
Title: Power at ground zero : politics, money, and the remaking of lower Manhattan /
Lynne B. Sagalyn.
Description: New York : Oxford University Press, 2016.
Identifiers: LCCN 2016009574 (print) | LCCN 2016027366 (ebook) |
ISBN 9780190607029 (hardback) | ISBN 9780190607036 (E-book) |
ISBN 9780190607043 (E-book)
Subjects: LCSH: September 11 Terrorist Attacks, 2001. | Manhattan (New York,
N.Y.)—History—21st century. | City planning—New York (State) | Land
use, Urban—New York (State) | Public buildings—New York (State)—Design
and construction. | Economic assistance—New York (State)—New York. |
BISAC: SOCIAL SCIENCE / Sociology / Urban. | ARCHITECTURE / Urban & Land
Use Planning. | ARCHITECTURE / General.
Classification: LCC HV6432.7 .S224 2016 (print) | LCC HV6432.7 (ebook) | DDC
974.7/1044—dc23
LC record available at https://lccn.loc.gov/2016009574

1 3 5 7 9 8 6 4 2

Printed by Sheridan Books, Inc., United States of America

For all who worked to rebuild Ground Zero
and the citizens of the City of New York

CONTENTS

PROLOGUE

ON SEPTEMBER 21, 2006, Governor George E. Pataki of New York and Governor Jon S. Corzine of New Jersey with Mayor Michael R. Bloomberg of New York City gathered at Ground Zero for a hastily called celebratory news conference to announce that the Board of Commissioners of the Port Authority of New York and New Jersey had approved a series of agreements expected to "expedite the redevelopment process." "The time has come to build this," said the Port Authority's chairman, Anthony R. Coscia. The agreements set forth the most definitive blueprint to date after years of conflict and contention over every piece of the master plan for rebuilding the sixteen acres at Ground Zero. The moment marked a watershed. The process of getting to this point had not been easy. It followed months of negotiations among the three government stakeholders and real estate developer Larry A. Silverstein, acting as general manager of his investment partnership's ninety-nine-year lease on the World Trade Center site—still a "hole"—negotiations that could only be described as difficult, disputatious, and at times ugly. Money was the fundamental sticking point. The "Global Realignment," as the new deal was called, redefined who would build what on the site, dividing control over the development rights for the commercial program between Silverstein and the Port Authority, owner of the land on which the World Trade Center complex had been built in the 1960s. Silverstein's role was reduced to building three of the five planned towers, though he emerged with the three best development sites from a real estate perspective. The Port Authority would build the Freedom Tower, an uneconomical political statement promoted by Pataki, as well as a fifth office tower and the retail component of the plan. The bi-state agency remained responsible for building out the complex underground infrastructure, which had to be accomplished before construction could start on any other part of the rebuild, including the memorial and the Memorial Museum. Just six weeks before the 9/11 attack, the Port Authority had sold a long-term interest in the World Trade Center complex to Silverstein in a much-heralded historic transaction that transferred ownership of the iconic complex to private investors. With the 2006 deal, the Port Authority was back in the real estate business. From the first day forward after 9/11, the words used by all stakeholders to describe the rebuilding effort were framed in patriotic meaning and heartfelt commitment to the losses of 9/11—words that spoke to its symbolic mandates.

The driving forces at work in rebuilding Ground Zero—civic purpose, political opportunity, and commercial gain—mirrored both the optimism of recovery and the rough-and-tumble politics of power in New York City. These forces would define the constellation of issues swirling about the site for many more years to come until visible progress above ground began to give shape to a new district in lower Manhattan. The realignments of the 2006 deal created modest confidence in the task of rebuilding among the stakeholders standing in the open air around the podium on a blue-skies day whose clarity was all too reminiscent of the day two hijacked planes rammed into the twin towers. On both sides scars remained. And wariness. The difficulties in coming to terms on these agreements did not stop with the board vote but continued for ninety minutes afterward, with both parties engaging in "last-minute wrangling," according to the *Times*.[1] The announcement of the news conference just minutes before it started gave the media little time to get there. This "semisecret" aspect of the event turned out to be a portent of rough times ahead, as relations between the public agency developer and the private-sector developer of Ground Zero remained strained by lack of trust and a misalignment of interests.

Several years of high-profile debates about architectural vision and fierce battles between dueling designers had galvanized public attention. These were now settled. The program for memorializing the losses of 9/11 was in place. The actual work of rebuilding lay ahead, in the complicated challenge of figuring out how to turn ambitious vision into tangible reality. The stakes of succeeding were of psychological as well as economic importance to the city at large and its region and the country.

After the big design decisions had been made, it seemed possible to conclude that the task of executing the plans was not newsworthy—that is, not much different from a conventional, albeit, large development project—until controversy threatened to reopen those already-made decisions or propelled elected officials into outrage and open conflict. Though seemingly mundane and less newsworthy, the task of reconciling aspirations with economic reality was paramount. It impacted everything at Ground Zero: how the 9/11 Memorial would be experienced and how the Trade Center site would meld with the urban fabric of adjacent neighborhoods. It would shape the experience of commuters and shoppers traveling through the Transportation Hub. Most critically from the perspective of state and local officials, it would determine when the new towers at Ground Zero would repopulate the skyline of lower Manhattan and with what level of public financial support to assure that they do. In short, for years a lot was happening to shape decisions at Ground Zero that often did not make headline news and that most people could not learn about.

As the saga of rebuilding unfolded, it seemed to become a New York story, a New York project, a New York memorial. However, as was evident on 9/11 and in the theater of geopolitical events thereafter, the terrorist attack was a profoundly violent assault on the United States as a capitalist society and on Western cultural, social, and economic values. As witnessed by millions in real time on television, the destruction of the World Trade Center sent shock waves around the world. It became the most memorable moment shared by television viewers during the last fifty years, according to a 2012 study by Sony electronics and the Nielsen television research company that ranked TV moments for their impact. The attack connected global audiences in ways most natural disasters do not: It was not the typical type of damage—poorly built structures, poorly capitalized operations, underinsured, affecting individuals with few means—but rather a high-density, high-profile, heavily insured symbol of Western capitalism. The unprecedented drama of physical destruction and emotional trauma besetting the families of the victims and citizens of New York City touched populations at large in nations across the globe, creating empathy and interest in rebuilding. The nearly three thousand 9/11 victims were of many nationalities. The twin towers were a touchstone icon for millions of tourists visiting New York. Rebuilding in response to that violent provocation holds meaning beyond those sixteen acres in lower Manhattan. For what it symbolizes, the story of rebuilding Ground Zero is a story of global significance.[2]

Because it is a story of global significance, rebuilding has had to meet many symbolic aspirations. It needed to embody American values and speak to the world about America's resilience in the face of mass murder that at least in Western eyes was senseless. Simultaneously, the effort had to show that local decision makers could "do the right thing" as the world watched. It had to represent strength and determination and reflect deep sensitivity in recognition of the lives lost in the attacks. It had to create an economic future for lower Manhattan. And it had to protect New York City's status as "the capital of the free world" and assure its global leadership in the twenty-first century. That was what the mayor promised in his inaugural address on January 1, 2002, and throughout his twelve years in office, Michael R. Bloomberg would try to act in full accord with what he promised: "We will go forward. We will never go back."

Within the historical context of New York City's economic trajectory, rebuilding Ground Zero was fraught with strategic consequence. Just as the original World Trade Center complex represented the culmination of a decades-long series of efforts aimed at revitalizing the city's founding center of business, forty years later rebuilding those sixteen acres reprised history—with new meaning, in a new century, in a new geopolitical context brought forth by 9/11. The destruction of the massive complex created a rare opportunity for New York City to rethink its long-term economic needs, at least in the downtown area. With President George W. Bush's promise of $20 billion of federal resources, those with responsibility for Ground Zero and beyond could think about taking bold actions to rebuild all of lower Manhattan, while sending a message to the world that regardless of whatever al-Qaeda terrorists aimed to do, New York City would come back stronger than ever. It was an unparalleled opportunity in the city's history.

Opportunity quickened the pulse of ambition. All of the central players at Ground Zero harbored vaulting ambitions, especially Governor Pataki, who envisioned Ground Zero as a platform for his higher political aspirations. Ambition suffused every vision, threaded through every conflict, and shaped the scale of every achievement in the rebuilding of these sixteen acres in lower Manhattan. To rebuild in defiance of the terrorists, to assure New York's position as a global city, to rebuild the economic engine of lower Manhattan, to think big, plan right in a democratic fashion, and move quickly—these aims became drivers of decisions of how New York City rebuilt at Ground Zero.

There were more tangible ambitions as well, and they seemed to grow as the opportunity to rebuild brought forth aspirations long held and newly minted: the desire to build a project that demonstrated planners had learned from experience at the original complex and could design and execute a better way to use those sixteen acres; the desire to link transportation with development more effectively and enhance the accessibility of lower Manhattan; the desire to build a monumental gateway for commuters; the idea of adding new social and cultural functions that would help the long-term revival of lower Manhattan; the imperative of creating a place more secure from terrorist attacks; the desire to integrate the complex into the fabric of the city, especially the adjacent neighborhood of Battery Park City. All of these hopes might be aided or warped by the Port Authority's desire to maintain institutional dominance, the private developer's ingrained economic motives, and the city and state's desire to maximize the promised resources from the federal government in their quest for civic renewal.

Complexity prevailed on every level—political, economic, and emotional—and set up inevitable conflicts as public officials worked assiduously to implement the plans for rebuilding. September 11 transformed the human meaning of the Trade Center site. What was secular was now sacred, a graveyard for nearly three thousand souls as well as a commercial real estate opportunity. Those sixteen acres, achingly defined by past images of the iconic twin towers anchoring the skyline of lower Manhattan, were now unbearably painful ruins transformed into repositories of memory. "What is to be done with an immensely valuable piece of land that is crucial to the local economy, but which has also become hugely important—indeed almost spiritual—to the people in New York and around the world?" the widely admired architectural critic Ada Louise Huxtable wrote just days after the attack. The terrifying destruction caused not by natural disaster but by terrorists' calculated mass murder called for "a tribute to those who died needlessly and tragically in an act of unredeemed horror," a symbolism "designed in response to an eternal need."[3] Simply replacing what was lost or replicating past approaches to city building would constitute a pallid response to human loss and physical destruction of such magnitude. The rebuilding response demanded something beyond convention—a big, inspiring, physical presence that embodied the symbolic aspirations of American values.

How would the aspirations for symbolic meaning and opportunity for economic purpose come into focus? How would the rhetoric of defiance and resilience translate into concrete plans, architectural reality, political decisions, building priorities, and economic costs? How would the need to commemorate the loss of thousands of lives coexist on the site with the need to rebuild an economic future for lower Manhattan? Bring daily life to the lacerated sixteen acres? Most critically, who would have the power to execute the ideals and ambitions of rebuilding in a situation of split property ownership and fragmented political power? And where would the money come from to execute the grand ambitions of rebuilding Ground Zero?

Achieving the collective aspirations for rebuilding the Trade Center site depended on money, lots of money, billions and billions of dollars, yet the force of economic reality did not reveal itself until the intense emotional debates about architectural vision had exhausted all but the most patient and dedicated followers of what was going on at Ground Zero. Addressing the question of where the money to rebuild the ten million square feet of office space would come from was not uppermost in the minds of public officials in the first several years following the disaster. As presented in the media, the spotlight focused on three big episodes: the missteps of the planning process and winning vision of a master plan, the worldwide competition for a memorial design and the emergence of a young unknown architect paired with a master of landscaped public spaces, and the public brawl between competing world-class architects over the design of the Freedom Tower. Every principal player had been obsessed with design, each in pursuit of individual ambition. The public wanted a big vision for transforming Ground Zero as the site of unfathomable loss into one of inspiration. Governor Pataki wanted a new icon on the skyline as the centerpiece of his effort to see Ground Zero rebuilt as a commercial center. The families of the victims wanted eternal remembrance for their lost loved ones—and a small group of activist family members wanted nothing else but loss to be remembered on these sixteen hallowed acres. The Port Authority wanted to restore its vertical money machine and resuscitate its institutional legacy of engineering prowess. Silverstein wanted to rebuild as a profit-making venture the commercial real estate complex that he had owned for just six weeks and that briefly represented the crowning achievement of his fifty-year career as a New York real estate investor. Bloomberg wanted to assure his city's global position as economic and cultural powerhouse.

But the money question was at the heart of rebuilding. Important as the architectural phases of the process were for cauterizing the immediate trauma of 9/11 by engaging the public with forward-looking visions, the real coming to terms with competing ambitions—program adjustments, cost compromises, and financial deals—was being conducted behind the scenes, in the off-the-record negotiations between the Port Authority and Larry Silverstein, in the second-floor executive offices in Albany, in the boardroom of the Port Authority on Park Avenue South, and in the midtown offices of Silverstein Properties. It was always about money and the power to move it—and those behind-the-scenes actions revealed a truism of public real estate development: one cannot build large without politics.

At Ground Zero, politics intersected with economics in powerfully symbolic ways that reveal how cities in the United States get rebuilt. The commercial stakes in rebuilding Ground Zero were as high as they get on the real-estate-rich island of Manhattan. These particular sixteen acres on the West Side of lower Manhattan, positioned between the stylish Tribeca neighborhood and emergent hipster Brooklyn, represented enormously valuable real estate. And economic value was always a primary factor of consideration for both the Port Authority and Silverstein's private investment partnership that had funded acquisition of his ninety-nine-year lease on the World Trade Center.

The juxtaposition of opportunity and tragedy shaped an epic story. Particular elements of the experience touched universal hopes and connected to much larger worlds, be they the home geographies of those who perished, comparisons with other emotional catastrophes, design competitions of great historical significance, record-setting heights of symbolic skyscrapers, or a program of commemoration set in a comparative context of the world's most notable memorials. For more than a decade, rebuilding Ground Zero was the world's most visible redevelopment project. While modern city building is often dismissed as cold-hearted and detached from meaning, the opposite was true at Ground Zero, where every action was infused with symbolic significance and debated with emotional intensity.

Michael Bloomberg was the sole chief elected official whose continuity of public service marked New York City's traverse from cataclysmic tragedy to determined defiance to triumphant rebound as the global city of the twenty-first century. The Massachusetts-born businessman turned politician was a New Yorker, one of the many born somewhere else who "came to New York in quest of something," as E. B. White characterized the many who came to "the city of final destination, the city that is a goal" in his famous 1949 essay of amour, *Here Is New York*. "New York is to the nation what the white church is to the village—the visible symbol of aspiration and faith, the white plume saying the way is up." Ambition was what brought so many to New York, what accounted, as White proclaimed, for its "high-strung disposition, its poetical deportment, its dedication to the arts, and its incomparable achievements."[4] It was coded into the DNA of New York City.

Despite having no formal power to shape events at Ground Zero, the mayor became the decisive actor, belatedly, but decisively nonetheless. After 9/11 "he was at his boldest, stabilizing the city's finances, and reassuring an edgy business community that revival was at hand," Joyce Purnick wrote in her 2009 biography of the mayor.[5] But nearly four years would pass, almost the full duration of his first term, during which he was relatively silent on the issues of rebuilding, more focused on the development of Far West Midtown, at best a detached figure in the unfolding drama at Ground Zero despite the high profile of his powerful position. Like successful executives who had shifted the locus of their business to midtown Manhattan, Bloomberg did not understand or appreciate the dynamic of the city's historic downtown, even though he had spent the early part of his career working there. That attitude did not, ultimately, interfere with the instinctive desire of the mayor to control valuable city turf, owned since the 1960s by the Port Authority of New York and New Jersey. At first, the Bloomberg administration tried to get control of the site through a clever proposal to swap the land under the city's airports operated by the Port Authority for the sixteen acres of Ground Zero, but when that failed because the other, bigger, more powerful political player on the site— Governor Pataki—was not about to relinquish any control, the mayor and his team set about devising other strategic interventions to get around the governor's control of the reins of power at Ground Zero.

Pataki and Bloomberg were both Republicans, and allies. Though he was previously a Democrat, Bloomberg's affiliation reflected a more recent party choice made to advance his run for mayor of New York City. As chief executives, these men governed differently. Those governing differences—reactive versus offensive, diffident versus decisive—shaped the political narrative at Ground Zero. In the early years of rebuilding, these two men presided from above until each saw an opportune time to intervene. Pataki's responses during the first five years of rebuilding (2001–2006) amounted to belated, ineffective leadership; although Bloomberg did not take an active stance on Ground Zero until late 2005, his interventions eventually twice broke through bottlenecks toward progress, in mid-2006 and again in mid-2010. Although the political tensions that existed between the governor and the mayor, who personally liked one another, typified those that have historically shaped relations between the city and the state, the post-9/11 world with its need to rebuild the site and remember the victims of that mass murder added an unprecedented dimension to the relationship. In response to 9/11, the ambitions of both men played out in dramatically different ways, shaping the outcomes of what exists today on those sixteen acres.

In his position as governor, Pataki held most of the political playing cards: control over state entities with the ability to influence what would happen at Ground Zero. Yet how was it that he failed to lead rebuilding in a realistic fashion to timely fruition? How was it that Mayor Bloomberg, who controlled no part of the complex process for rebuilding the gaping sixteen-acre hole in the heart of lower Manhattan, repeatedly pushed the key stakeholders through bottlenecks toward solutions, and in the process, assured the city of visual progress and himself of a ribbon cutting at the opening of the memorial on the tenth anniversary of 9/11?

As the presumptive developer of Ground Zero's commercial program, Larry Silverstein was in a vulnerable position from the start because the proceeds from insurance payouts were never going to be sufficient to cover the full cost of what he was obligated to rebuild, though that fact would hardly dim his well-known perpetual optimism, especially about rebuilding the Trade Center site. The economic feasibility of replacing ten million square feet of office space was shaky at best, and his lease with the Port Authority required him to rebuild fully what had been there regardless of whether insurance funds were sufficient. The uncertainty of the situation challenged any rational reading of the economic ambition behind rebuilding. Yet both the Port Authority and Silverstein confronted these financial challenges absent the element of trust and mutual respect so essential to solving complex problems in public-private development, and this condition crucially exacerbated the problems of execution. It was the Achilles heel of rebuilding at Ground Zero. How did Silverstein, the ultimate economic actor, persist through continual controversy and conflict in controlling the commercial rebuilding agenda for Ground Zero, despite repeated calls from politicians and the press for him to step aside and let others take over, or at least cede part of the Trade Center site? How did he leverage position to capture favorable deals that assured his rebuilding ambitions and a steady stream of fee revenue, not once, but four times—in 2003, 2006, 2010, and 2015?

The ambitions of the Port Authority similarly exceeded the bucket of federal dollars allocated to build an iconic permanent terminal at Ground Zero for its PATH commuter train, labeled as the World Trade Center Transportation Hub.

Once the financial reality of rebuilding became a paramount political concern, the Port Authority's monumental and excessively costly transportation station, intended to serve as a tribute to its fallen colleagues, came under withering attack. Initially celebrated as an inspiring iconic structure for downtown that would rival midtown's Grand Central Terminal, the Transportation Hub became a pariah—a symbol of institutional hubris. The agency's inability to manage its own ambitions for its institutional phoenix-like project subjected its officials to continuous and unmitigated criticism from the city's editorial boards, City Hall, and critics and commentators.

Ambition quickly eroded civic cooperation and institutional coordination, as well as public and private accommodation. That was the dark side of big aspirations and big plans. Politics, large and small, repeatedly challenged the multidimensional ambitions of rebuilding, and the deep conflicts that ensued for years created chaos and triggered widespread uncertainty, not to mention intense frustration with the lack of progress. Delays, setbacks, slow progress, blown budgets, and missed deadlines populated news headlines. A press-driven narrative of delay fueled by frustration, skepticism, and, finally, despair contributed to the volatile mix. Only doubts were rising on the Trade Center site. Even news of progress was but a temporary diversion for the press, which could not let go of its long-running narrative of delay. New Yorkers began to doubt not just the big ambitions but the civic ideals of what so many had hoped could be achieved through the dual effort to rebuild and remember. Was this still the nation's largest and most prosperous city, a city that viewed itself as a global trendsetter, a city that had historically reinvented itself economically and socially when the times demanded reincarnation? What were the problems in delivering on these promises and executing those big plans in timely fashion? Why was the effort to rebuild these sixteen acres so contentious?

The telling of how these sixteen symbolic acres got rebuilt ties together the recollections of scores of players and a broad range of interests: elected officials, government decision makers, agency board members, architects and designers, developers, 9/11 family members, real estate specialists, attorneys, investment bankers, journalists, civic leaders, communication experts, city planners, finance professionals, and construction management specialists, among others.[6] Whether from the public, private, or civic sector, each brought to bear a particular passion or a particular personal or professional perspective on how the emotion-laden site in lower Manhattan should be rebuilt or a particular interpretation of why events unfolded as they did. Some were involved in big policy decisions while others made small technical decisions; few held a position from which they might see all sides of a single issue, even those at the highest levels of decision-making.

Individual and collective perspectives most assuredly shaped their recollections, the weave of how they told their particular part of the story. Every narrative contributed to the warp and weft of a balanced full story of rebuilding. At times, different accounts could seem contradictory, though equally plausible—a Rashomon effect.

Beyond the many personalities involved and the jousting among political officials, private developers, institutional bureaucracies, and special interests, the process of rebuilding the Trade Center site reveals why large-scale projects take so long in American cities where dispersed political influence is a common condition. The story illuminates the powerful role that symbolic politics plays in designing high-profile sites. It illuminates the pitfalls in public-private developments where demand is uncertain and there is little accountability for costs. It suggests caution in placing blind faith in the public-private approach to large-scale city building, especially when government entities are not united. When they are not united, developers are able to exploit the fissures among government agencies to their advantage. Similarly, a foundation of trust between the public sector and private developer is essential to resolving the inevitable problems that crop up continually in the development of complex large-scale city-building projects. It is essential to success.

Ambition worked against an identity of interests at Ground Zero. Though complicated and protracted, the struggles did bring forth a new urban precinct. Aspirations for revitalization of the city's historical business center had been on the forefront of city policymaking for decades. Ironically, it took tragedy and the opportunity it begat to transform the historic fundamentals of lower Manhattan. *Power at Ground Zero* chronicles the role of politics and money in rebuilding the Trade Center site after 9/11 and how the alliances, compromises, and personalities of those involved shaped the achievements (and disappointments) of this most significant challenge to the city of New York and the nation.

POWER AT GROUND ZERO

December 17, 2001.   GREGG BROWN/GETTY NEWS/GETTY IMAGES

PART I
PREDICATE TO ACTION

CHAPTER 1

Compelling Civic Mandates

FIGURE 1.1 *Still smoldering: A small portion of the scene where the World Trade Center collapsed following the September 11 attack, September 17, 2001.* Eric J. Tilford/U.S. Navy photo

WITH THE HAZY DAWN of daylight that ushered in September 12, the air suffused with heavy particulate and the stench of smoke and burn and death, city officials and business leaders faced a stark challenge to assure New York's competitive position in the global constellation of cities. At stake was the newly polished twenty-first-century image of America's largest and most dynamic city, a place its citizens proudly considered as resolute and as tough as the Manhattan schist forming the bedrock of its dense collection of skyscrapers. Immediately, recovery crews were at work on the "pile," the collapsed mountain of rubble the gigantic complex came to be known by, the fires still burning deep beneath the destruction (figure 1.1). Families and friends were frantically positioning hundreds of missing-persons posters near hospitals and rescue centers, and on the streets of lower Manhattan, pinning them onto trees and signposts and buildings and wherever else they could catch the eyes of passersby or neighboring residents, the posters and spontaneous offerings of meaning serving as makeshift rituals of individual grief that "transformed the cityscape into a space for remembrance."[1] New Yorkers everywhere found themselves at a loss for words that could capture the physical magnitude and emotional trauma of what had transpired, of what hitherto was unbelievable but replayed in continuous loops on every conceivable medium until the incredulity of what had happened became too painfully real: the giant twins, unmistakable in their towering iconic presence on the skyline, seemingly invulnerable, now lay in ruin, smoldering—a profound graveyard for some twenty-eight hundred civilians who perished inside. The losses were incalculable. Everyone seemed to be in a state of shock and disbelief.

There are moments in time when cities become natural experiments and the 9/11 terrorist attack on New York provided one of them.[2] Did corporations and businesses need to be in New York? Was Wall Street finished as the capital of international finance? Would the immediate trauma or anxiety about possible future attacks cause city residents to leave, move to places where terrorism seemed less of a threat? Fears of firms leaving the city in a mass exodus, fears of residents fleeing, fears of tourists staying away, fears of the end of skyscraper development and, by extension, the very self of the city were paramount, and news headlines in the weeks after 9/11 messaged the doubts: "In Wounded Financial Center, Trying to Head Off Defections," "Reaching for the Sky, and Finding a Limit; Tall Buildings Face New Doubt as Symbols of Vulnerability," "When the Towers Collapsed, So Did Their Desire to Live Here."

Like the fiscal crisis of the mid-1970s, the 9/11 attack on the World Trade Center shook New Yorkers' confidence in the future of their city. Uncertainties existed across the five boroughs and beyond. Was New York still the resilient city that had overcome so many post–World War II crises—deindustrialization, disinvestment and property abandonment, racial and ethnic change, white suburban flight, social and cultural conflict, and a near brush with bankruptcy? Based on well-founded and widespread fears prevalent at the time, no one was able to say for sure that the attack would *not* have a lasting negative economic impact on the city and the region. The city's sense of invulnerability had been shattered, yet as historian Mike Wallace reminded readers in a special section of the *Times* that appeared within a week of the attack, "that sense always rested on a truncated reading of history. While the particular form of the attack was fiendishly novel, New York, over nearly four centuries, has repeatedly been the object of murderous intentions. Through a combination of luck and power, we have escaped many of the intended blows, but not all of them, and our forebears often feared that worse might yet befall them." On 9/11, however, New York City's role as a symbolic target became too painfully apparent. The fantasies of urban destruction in popular culture, Wallace wrote, had been "horribly realized."[3] If the illusion of invulnerability had been shattered, not so the determination to rebound and reconstruct and emerge stronger and better than ever; that too was part of New York's cultural history, part and parcel of its grit and ambition.

It was a time of desperate loss, yet also a time of distinct possibility. Tragedy delivered an exceptional opportunity and the promise of an extraordinary amount of dollars from Washington, D.C., with which to plan and rebuild lower Manhattan, its transportation and infrastructure, office inventory, housing supply, and open space amenities to match the new needs of the twenty-first century. At the same time, rebuilding could renew the district's historic dynamic. Reinventing itself was part of lower Manhattan's history. And since the Port Authority won the legal challenge to its development in November 1963, the original World Trade Center had shaped that history. Thirty-eight years later, the mission to rebuild these sixteen acres, emotionally raw and newly endowed with intense sensitivity for the families of those who died there, patriotic fervor for the nation at large, and profound meaning for the city's future, history was in the making. As the weeks following 9/11 wore on, a very public dialogue among the city's many interests set out compelling civic mandates for rebuilding—mandates, of course, that were integral to the city's sense of itself as a premier global city and that would drive the actions of its elected officials at Ground Zero.

ASSURING GLOBAL POSITION

On September 11, Mayor Rudolph W. L. Giuliani "became the leader New York City needed in its worst moment," remarked the *Times* editorial board. "With little rhetoric and less poetry, he consoled a stunned populace trying to make sense through the smoke and beyond the jagged skyline. With phrases aimed at people rather than the history books, Mr. Giuliani rallied a city to 'go back to normal,' to start going to restaurants, to try to work or go to school as a way to show its unbroken spirit." That was the way to show confidence, he said. He was everywhere, soothing fears, holding back chaos, and rallying New Yorkers to the task of rebuilding, his compassionate voice understanding of the grief as he exercised unassailable leadership that seemed tailor-made to his persona. "We're going to rebuild," he promised at his morning briefing on September 12. "We're going to come out of this stronger than we were before. Emotionally stronger, politically stronger, economically stronger." He talked about how his city would never bow to mere terrorism. In taking orderly control of the city's response in those early months after the attack, he set the pace and delivered much-needed psychological strength to a "grief-stricken and terrified population." He was synonymous with 9/11—the face of it—and emotionally, the city's mourner-in-chief.[4]

This was a new Giuliani, not the mayor "who is known to explode over seemingly small slights." The defensiveness and combativeness of his identity displaced by sincere compassion and emotional sensitivity, he became a surprisingly calm and effective mayor in a period of crisis, totally in control. He was the "essential man" whose popularity "overflows" the city.[5] A love fest ensued, nationally as well as locally; *Time* magazine called Giuliani "Tower of Strength" and "Mayor of the World" in its profile of him as "Person of the Year." Still, no amount of popularity and triumph of leadership could push to fruition the calls by some advocates for a statutory extension of term, "four more years," for this already term-limited mayor as a means of coping in the 9/11 emergency situation. While the attack led to a two-week postponement of the primaries that had begun on that fateful morning with the regular 6 A.M. opening of polling places, the mayoral election, between Democrat runoff candidate Mark J. Green and Republican Michael R. Bloomberg, took place as scheduled on November 6, 2001.

Following an orderly succession of power, stewardship over the task of repairing the city, coping with the immediate fiscal crisis, and assuring its growth and prosperity belonged to New York City's 108th mayor, Michael R. Bloomberg. In his forty-minute inaugural mayoral address on January 1, 2002, the businessman turned politician promised: "We will rebuild, renew and remain the capital of the free world." Saying it was "an historic moment," he called out to corporate leaders, telling them, "This is no time to leave the Big Apple. Your future is New York. And New York's is better than ever." The city, his city by adoption, was ready "to lead the world in the 21st century." In the immediate months and years ahead, it would have to tighten its budget and everyone would have to make sacrifices, but he reassured all that "we are still a city of big dreams, of big ideas, big projects and a big heart. We must plan and develop for the long term. We can never abandon our future."[6] The new mayor and his administrative team unequivocally considered rebuilding essential to advancing the long-term trajectory of New York City as the world's global capital. London was competition at the time and others on the ascent—Chicago, Los Angeles, Singapore, Beijing, Shanghai—would be competition in the near future; New York had to assure itself of global position, preferably dominance. Global was the natural frame of reference for the fifty-nine-year-old billionaire mayor whose success was founded upon building a worldwide business platform based on information technology, Bloomberg L.P., and from which he personally possessed global name recognition. No amount of rhetorical optimism, however, could dispel the ever-present questions about the city's future and the hard times ahead.

The immediate impact of 9/11 was economically devastating to downtown. In regard to the physical capital destroyed, the hijacked planes ramming into one after the other of the twin towers eliminated nearly one-quarter of the modern class A office space in downtown, left much of the infrastructure damaged and disrupted, and dramatically interrupted the area's burgeoning transformation into a vibrant multifaceted community (plate 1). The sheer scale of replacing all that was lost while rebuilding the economic and social fabric of the community, as quickly as possible, appeared herculean. An early estimate by the Federal Reserve Bank of New York put these physical capital losses (cleanup and site restoration, destroyed Trade Center buildings, damaged buildings in the area, contents of buildings at the complex, and public infrastructure) at $21.6 billion, but this was a very early estimate of only built elements and full of uncertainties. The estimated loss impacts on the labor market (loss of human life, net job losses, net earnings losses, and attack-related productivity effects) totaled $11.4 billion to $14.2 billion. Combined, these early estimates of total loss impacts of the 9/11 attack on New York City as of June 2002 ranged from $33 billion to $36 billion.[7]

Lower Manhattan was a terribly difficult place to live after 9/11 and would remain so for years on end as excavators, backhoe loaders, cranes, and related equipment worked on cleanup and recovery, and, in time, reconstruction. The immediate impacts—phone and data services severed, residents having to show identification to pass through security barricades into lower Manhattan, travel outside the neighborhood complicated by disrupted transit service—upended the daily lives of thousands of residents in the surrounding neighborhoods of Battery Park City, Tribeca, Chinatown, SoHo, and Little Italy. Armed police and National Guard were an ever-present reminder of security concerns born of the trauma. For weeks, sometimes months, residents were unable to return to their apartments. Concerns about environmental toxins from the collapsed structures contaminating the outdoor areas persisted for years amid a lack of accurate information and disclosure. Small businesses, retail shops, and neighborhood restaurants that escaped destruction but were unable to survive the months and months of business interruption either disappeared or experienced extensive costs. A state of emergency in the area continued in force until June 2002. All of these losses hit hard on multiple levels, real and symbolic, economic and social, and shaped what recovery would mean to neighborhood residents, downtown businesses, the district's elected officials, and the city's economy.

Firms were leaving for the suburbs, near and far. The idea of the urban corporate campus, ascendant prior to 9/11, immediately disappeared from conversation as businesses sought protective diversification rather than concentrated locations.[8] Within days of the attack—as headlined in the *New York Post*: "N.Y. Urges Bizmen: Stay! Helping Do Deals to Sway Firms against Relocating"—the city had pledged to do everything it could to make sure that firms and people stayed in New York City. But deals were not enough for some, like American Express, after its headquarters in 3 World Financial Center across from the World Trade Center was heavily damaged in the attack; the building was not destroyed, but this was the second attack for company employees who also experienced the first terrorist attack on the World Trade Center in 1993. The board of directors wanted to leave lower Manhattan. After 9/11, the financial-services giant relocated most of its displaced five-thousand-person workforce to temporary locations in Connecticut and New Jersey. At the same time, it began discussions with officials in the Giuliani administration about returning to downtown. The firm was committed to returning its headquarters to the city, but had made no commitment whether it would locate in downtown or midtown. CEO Kenneth I. Chenault asked the city for special security measures, including a detail of mounted police and K-9 patrol units (an elite subunit of the New York Police Department [NYPD] Emergency Service of specially trained search and rescue dogs and officers), before it would agree to return to downtown.

Giuliani publicly lashed out at the firm for "demands that are entirely unrealistic" and would, in effect, amount to "a private contract" with the firm that would "tie the hands of the police department." Company executives were infuriated. At Governor Pataki's urging, talks between the two sides resumed, and by late November, Chenault was able to tell his employees that Mayor Giuliani and Mayor-elect Bloomberg had promised "an enhance[ed] police presence" around its headquarters as well as other security services. American Express planned to return to its tower in lower Manhattan in April—without the carrot of tax breaks or other financial incentives. This was a big win. A permanent departure might have led other high-profile businesses to follow suit. "Ken Chenault deserves enormous credit; this was a decision of symbolic importance," Governor Pataki told me in a 2015 interview. "People do not understand the economic crisis of the immediate weeks and months after 9/11. They understand the emotional and physical crises, but not the economic. The mantra then was decentralization, move out and decentralize corporate offices."[9]

As increasing numbers of firms retreated from Manhattan, city officials and real estate owners and business leaders whose interests were embedded in the city watched their fears materialize. The employment losses attributable to the 9/11 attacks were threatening, not just because the numbers were large and disruptive to the productive potential of the New York City economy, but because the bulk of the losses were concentrated in that portion of the city's economy closely linked with the global economy. By October 1, the immediate loss of jobs attributable to the September 11 attack as estimated by economists at the Federal Reserve Bank of New York was approximately 38,000 to 46,000. In February, the range grew to 49,000 to 71,000, then "eased" to between 28,000 and 55,000 by June 2002.[10] While losses were felt in all of the city's five boroughs, they were most pronounced in Manhattan in the area surrounding the Trade Center. A subsequent study of the employment impact of the attack by the New York Regional Office of the Bureau of Labor Statistics published in June 2004 put the total city tally at about 430,000 lost job months and wage losses of $2.8 billion, equivalent to approximately 143,000 jobs, each month, for three months. In line with the fears of city officials, these losses were centered on the city's "export" economy—finance and insurance; professional, scientific, and technical occupations; information; arts, entertainment, and recreation; management of companies; real estate; and what was left of the city's manufacturing base—which accounted for 68 percent of all lost job months and 86 percent of all lost wages.

In 2000, jobs in the "export" sector accounted for more than 42 percent of all jobs in Manhattan, or more than 1 million jobs. Nearly 26 percent of these were in high-paying finance and insurance and the professional, scientific, and technical sectors. "For years, the finance industry, and Wall Street in particular, has been Manhattan's 'hometown' industry and driving economic force," the Bureau of Labor Statistics economists noted. The size of its profits, bonuses, and employment opportunities had long been a magnet for talent, a clarion call to the financially ambitious. September 11 did not change the city's status as the world financial capital, but the 2004 report concluded that the 9/11 losses "clearly damaged and weakened Manhattan's economic linkages with the Nation and the international community, but more importantly, altered the borough's unique character" because "it was the 'export' sector that gave New York its special place among international cities—its appeal, its reputation, its glamour, and its wealth."[11] Facing such a big blow, city officials and business leaders were not about to sit passively in the face of such a potentially crippling threat to the city's preeminent status in the global economy.

Manhattan was the core of the city's global status. Long international in tone and style, the borough experienced growth and change that greatly accelerated in the second half of the 1970s with the emergence of an international movement toward a global economy. Although on the verge of bankruptcy in the first part of that decade, New York with its enormous concentration of resources and talent was poised for "supremacy" in the emerging global economy, along with London. Only these two among the world's many big cities were exceptionally well endowed to take advantage of the new global forces, according to leading sociologist Saskia Sassen, who pioneered research in 1991 that identified the now popular concept of *The Global City*. New York dominated in a distinctive way, she explained in a later article, "by offering market innovations and new financial markets. Wall Street—still the Silicon Valley of finance—has made U.S. investment firms leaders in the global market," and the strength of U.S. banks and equity markets and the size and quality of its domestic capital markets buttressed this.[12]

The emergent global economy being powered by complex international transactions raised the scale of economic growth, stirred the need for multinational headquarters functions, and spawned the demand for specialized business services: legal, accounting, marketing and telecommunication, insurance, information services, and management consulting. Even as the digitalization of information and decentralization of activity fueled by rapidly advancing technology was transforming the way business was being conducted, location still mattered. It mattered, Sassen argued, because the complex nature of information behind these transactions required a highly educated professional workforce to analyze data and interpret the intelligence of results, while the execution of deals required combinations of top talent in a broad range of professional fields. The "social infrastructure for global connectivity" reinforced the importance of location. As these economic crosswinds of change gathered increasing strength, so too did the economic sectors for which Manhattan always exerted a particularly strong location attraction: financial markets, corporate support services, communications, and the arts. The global economy was reshaping New York's fortunes, as would the emergent digital technology. These trends were the advance guard of a transition to an information economy and Manhattan held a unique position as the global hub for information. "What the city could do better than any other," remarked urban planner Mitchell Moss, "was harness its strengths in finance and entertainment to create new forms of electronic production and distribution."[13]

The original World Trade Center "symbolized the aggressiveness and the dominance of the New York region in worldly matters," wrote political scientist Jameson W. Doig in his definitive book on the Port Authority of New York, *Empire on the Hudson*.[14] Though it was a financial white elephant for many years, the push behind the original World Trade Center was a harbinger of the city's move toward an information economy. In 1960, David Rockefeller, president of the family-associated Chase Manhattan Bank and the Downtown–Lower Manhattan Association (DLMA), a business organization he founded to promote downtown's revitalization, put forth a proposal for a $250 million commercial complex devoted to world trade, on 13.5 acres of land on a site on the East River waterfront. The Port Authority was asked by the DLMA to study the plan, and once the bi-state agency became involved, the idea evolved into much more than a private real estate project to bolster the declining fortunes of downtown. In elevating the scope of ambition, the World Trade Center became a project Rockefeller, the DLMA, and the Port Authority's powerful executive director, Austin J. Tobin, believed would reflect advanced thinking on how New York City might further capitalize on its dominant business position. It was a speculative bet on the future.

The starting point for Rockefeller had been a new corporate headquarters to accommodate Chase's thousands of employees who were spread out in nine downtown buildings. After its merger with the Bank of Manhattan Company (and name change to Chase Manhattan Bank), the bank became a giant worldwide institution, the city's largest and the world's second largest bank. It needed a new building to promote its rising global stature as much as to house its growing home operations.[15] Rockefeller was chairman of the committee charged with deciding on a new location; the time was 1954, and he wanted to keep the bank in downtown—where no new skyscraper had been built since 1930—as preserving a location of historical importance and reflecting a commitment to his city. After the hiatus of the Great Depression and World War II, downtown was hard-pressed to stem the tide of corporate moves north to midtown Manhattan, which was fast becoming the city's corporate epicenter. Prompted by the irrepressible real estate entrepreneur William Zeckendorf Sr., who never thought in terms of small projects, and in need of assistance to execute Zeckendorf's complicated scheme for assembling a sufficiently large parcel for development from the city's redevelopment czar and master builder, Robert Moses, who similarly did not work in small projects, Rockefeller intertwined his plan for his Chase headquarters project with his other ambition for a world trade center. And as large as it was, his ambition for a world trade center would grow even larger once the Port Authority and Tobin became involved with the project.

Championing the idea and taking over its development, the Port Authority vastly increased the size of the project—setting forth a program of ten million square feet of rentable office space, double what Rockefeller had proposed. The power of bigness had defined its very birth—"catalytic bigness," as David Rockefeller later described its scale, "something so oversize that it would not only keep Lower Manhattan vibrant (and Rockefeller's property values high) but also inspire other development to follow—and thus ensure that New York remained a critical global hub for international trade," James Glanz and Eric Lipton wrote in "The Height of Ambition," their lengthy 2002 *New York Times Magazine* article on the rise of the World Trade Center. The complex, they concluded, became "a place that reconnected to the global economy; a place that expressed the global reach of New York and the United States"[16] and earned its builder-owner a global profile.

As an idea to promote world trade, its origins, actually trace back to the 1939 World's Fair in Flushing Meadows, Queens and Rockefeller's uncle, Winthrop W. Aldrich, then chairman of Chase and a leading promoter of international trade. In a segment of the World Trade Center story that often gets skipped in the retelling of its history, the idea was founded on the idealistic goal of international peace through international trade. Early efforts along these lines faltered during World War II, Glanz and Lipton later wrote in their book-length biography of the World Trade Center project, *City in the Sky*, but then came back to life in 1946, when Governor Thomas E. Dewey named Aldrich to a new state agency named the World Trade Corporation. "Expanding international trade, conducted on a basis of mutual confidence and for mutual profit, looms as one of the great hopes for permanent peace," the governor said in his announcement of an assignment to build a permanent World Trade Center in New York. This effort too collapsed, "a scant four months after the board was named."[17] The peace part may have been all but forgotten except for rhetorical purposes, but the Seattle-born American architect chosen by the Port Authority to design the twin towers, Minoru Yamasaki, espoused the "noble ideal" in his remarks at the opening of the towers' dedication on April 4, 1973: "The World Trade Center is a living symbol of man's dedication to world peace....[B]eyond the compelling need to make this a monument to world peace, the World Trade Center should, because of its importance, become a representation of man's belief in humanity, his need for individual dignity, his belief in the cooperation of men, and through this cooperation, his ability to find greatness."[18] September 11 put a definitive end to such idealism.

The record-breaking height of the twin towers reflected the global aspirations of the city and the Port Authority of New York (its name at the time) in the early 1970s when the city was close to bankruptcy, the pillars of its economy teetering, and its long-term future uncertain (figure 1.2). At the dedication ceremony,

Governor Nelson A. Rockefeller (brother of David) called the twin skyscrapers "a great marriage of utility and beauty."[19] That may have been, but they contained acre after acre of empty space despite the many government agencies subsidizing the project by occupying nearly half of all the space in the World Trade Center complex. The achievement of building the world's tallest skyscrapers, however, seemed to serve as something of an emotional salve healing the fiscal wounds the city had inflicted upon itself over years of questionable budget practices. Year after year, as the Port Authority desperately strived to fill the empty floors, its institutional quest for the grandiose was called into question. Even before the space finally filled up with tenants (in 1980), the symbolic importance of the twin towers became a life force unto itself, its steady presence, metaphorically speaking, a source of encouragement to the body politic throughout times of stress—indeed, this is what turned it into an icon. "Though displaced as the world's tallest building within a month of its dedication (the Sears Tower in Chicago took the title)," *Times* reporter David W. Dunlap wrote just days after the 9/11 attack, "it was a powerful emblem of the city's capacity to recover from the economic stagnation downtown in the 1960's, from a perilous brush with bankruptcy in the mid-70's and from international terrorism in 1993, when the center was previously attacked."[20]

FIGURE 1.2 *Aerial view of the twin towers of the World Trade Center with the "beach" at Battery Park City in the background, c. 1973.* THE PETER J. ECKEL COLLECTION/ART RESOURCE, N.Y.

What would it mean for the city to recover after 9/11? Would it mean rebuilding the sixteen acres of the Trade Center site? All of lower Manhattan? Would New York City rise or fall based on what was done on those sixteen acres? There were few clear-cut answers. A fundamental question hung out there: Was the city changed forever? "Maybe Not," the *Times* headlined in an October 2001 account of scholarship about how cities work in times of catastrophic tumult, recover, and rebuild. "The long-term momentum of a metropolis, as a collective human creation of ambition and energy, is a force that is far more powerful than the short-term chaos of disaster, however horrific or heartbreaking," Kirk Johnson wrote. Cities, history taught, tend to be "stubbornly resilient."[21] In the immediate aftermath of 9/11, with a fierce determination fueled by an attitude of defiance—it could not, would not, be intimidated by terror—New York City set out to write its own distinctive chapter on resilience for the book of history.

ASSERTING RESILIENCE

New Yorkers with clear memories of the past did not have to dig deep to remember how the city struggled to emerge from the murky miasma of the difficult 1960s and the scary brush with municipal bankruptcy in the 1970s. New York and its serial crises made the covers of national magazines and journals; it was the poster child for urban decay, the apotheosis of the demise of city life, Exhibit A of the big bad city. These dark and gloomy decades loomed as an ever-threatening reminder of what would be if the city did not recover—in strength—from the devastating terrorist attack. Successfully rebuilding the Trade Center site—cost not a consideration—was a civic imperative. Bricks and mortar would be the stand-in for that recovery, a test of the city's historic resilience.

City officials, elected representatives, and business and community leaders quickly rallied around a deeply felt narrative of civic renewal, as had been the case in Oklahoma City after the 1995 bombing of the Alfred P. Murrah Federal Building. Notwithstanding differences of opinion on the specifics of what and how to rebuild, differences that would consume barrels of newspaper ink for weeks on end, they aligned in their advocacy of revitalizing the office economy as an indispensable means to maintaining the city's premier status, the region's economic vitality, and the neighborhood's potential as a twenty-four-hour community. The clustering of business activity related to global financial functions transacted on floor above floor of the twin towers symbolized the heart of the city's economy. Lower Manhattan accounted for 25 percent of New York's gross city product and nearly 12 percent of its total jobs, according to a 2002 McKinsey report, statistics offering unambiguous evidence of the district's material importance to the city's fiscal health and prosperity. Although midtown Manhattan held a larger share of the city's global business transactions, the World Trade Center personified New York's premier global status. "Virtually everyone in New York City, and indeed most of the country, understands the importance and urgency of rebuilding downtown Manhattan," editorialized the *Times*, and affirming "the city's status as a premier financial capital." Days later the *Daily News* editorial board echoed the sentiment, and a week later, *Newsday* following suit, saying failure to "mend the damage to Lower Manhattan with skill, alacrity and discipline" would result in a region "diminished."[22] Far beyond the physical precinct of New York, the symbolism of the 9/11 attack on the heart of capitalism endowed the challenge of rebuilding with global significance.

Coping with changing fortunes brought about by external events was nothing new for the political and business leadership of New York City, even though the calamitous physical attack of 9/11 was unexpectedly sudden and unprecedented. The need to adapt to shifting economic and demographic forces beyond its control had underpinned the city's constant reinvention over two centuries from its rise as a commercial center for water-born shipping and evolution to a manufacturing hub and garment center and then to a global financial capital. The postwar economic shifts of the 1950s were particularly hard on older cities and presented acute fiscal and social challenges. Like many a central city in older metropolitan regions in the East and Midwest where the industrial and mercantile economy had created a troika of economic power, wealth, and prestige that gave rise to a great many institutions of cultural excellence and supported a great many nonprofit social-service institutions and philanthropic organizations, New York City during the 1960s experienced profound economic and social change that shook the foundations of its civic self. The forces of "deindustrialization, disinvestment, racial change, and suburbanization that began full force in the 1950s [and] culminated in the racial conflict of the late 1960s and the fiscal crisis of the mid-1970s" had profound impacts—white flight, property abandonment, arson, crime, deep social unrest—which devastated the physical and social fabric of New York City. "One might well have been excused for thinking, based on the evidence, that New York was headed over the same cliff from which Detroit had already plunged," remarked urban expert and political scientist John Mollenkopf.[23]

"This did not happen," he added. "After 1977, the city and its metropolitan region experienced a remarkable recovery." Despite all odds, New York City "has proved to be the most strongly performing of all major old cities in the Northeast and Midwest." This was in "stark contrast" to other major urban centers, Newark, Philadelphia, St. Louis, for example. By 2000, the city's population had reached a historic high: 8,008,278. Moreover, it was the only city (of the four other big

Northeast and Midwest cities: Chicago, Philadelphia, Baltimore, Boston) to have recovered from the population losses experienced between 1950 and 1980 (net losses of 820,000 residents) and then gained some (net increase of 116,000 residents). As impressive as this recovery was, population, Mollenkopf was quick to point out, "is only one measure of urban trajectories." On two important economic benchmarks, total earnings and earnings per capita the city's performance proved to be similarly robust. "Although the long-term employment cycle in New York City has been bounded by about 3.2 million jobs at the low points (1976, 1992) and 3.7 to 3.8 million jobs at the high points (1969, 1989, 2000)," he wrote, "the overall quality of the jobs has steadily shifted upwards and total real wages and especially real annual wages per worker have climbed strongly." In no small part, the strength of the city's employment and earnings profile tracked back to the growth and importance of the global "export" sector—financial services and related corporate and business services in the city's economy—and its high-paying jobs concentrated in Manhattan.[24] The question Mollenkopf sought to answer was the question central to the city's recovery after 9/11: "How and why did New York City prove to be so resilient when its 19th century rivals along the East Coast, Philadelphia and Baltimore, have continued to lose population steadily, as have Cleveland, Detroit, Milwaukee, and St. Louis?" What made it the resilient city?

During the nineteenth century the compelling explanation was economic, as historian Thomas Kessner wrote in his important book, *Capital City: New York City and the Men behind America's Rise to Economic Dominance, 1860–1900*: "What proved especially remarkable was [the city's] irrepressible ability to master the changes that so swiftly reshaped the American economy. Other cities passed from importance as their role in the national economy changed, but New York, putting to great advantage the momentum of its mighty commercial system, never relinquished its dominance."[25] The explanation for New York City's exceptional resilience during the latter part of the twentieth century in the face of three decades of disruptive social and economic change lies beyond initial advantage and momentum, indeed, beyond any single reason, even the emergence and growth of the city's "export" sector. These high-valued-added activities played a critical role in reestablishing a strong economic foundation during the city's 1980s growth spurt. To that extent the city benefited both from its historic role as the nucleus of the nation's capital markets and corporate service complex and from the increasing importance of these activities in the national economy. But the reasons behind the city's rebound—and the implications for the post-9/11 task that lay ahead—also reside in local forces that lent a distinctively new cast to the city, making it newly attractive to thousands of people for the same reasons thousands of others had historically been drawn to New York: its dynamism, its opportunities, its wealth, its tradition of tolerance, and its celebrated diversity. But that could only happen if the city was safe and secure and perceived as stable—in other words, much depended on the political capacity of local government and its elected officials to provide effective leadership and deliver the necessary goods and services for the regional economy to grow and prosper.

"New York City stands as a clear example of how government can promote economic stability and population growth," Mollenkopf said in his concluding analysis of the many possible explanations for what made the city resilient. It has long been a major source of employment and income for its residents and a generous provider of public services. Because of its big-government profile and in spite of its high taxes, city government succeeded in restoring confidence in the nation's dominant city by means of active intervention. With the strong support and engagement of the private sector and its business elites and public labor unions, key elected officials struck deals during the city's fiscal crisis that spread the short-term pain of cutbacks and tax revenue increases, and they enacted budgetary reforms that restored confidence in the fiscal system. This "political compact" enabled other actions essential to a strong recovery: a recapitalization of the region's public infrastructure (struggling to emerge from decades of neglect and lack of investment), key changes in policing practices that helped bring down crime (and make neighborhoods, parks, and open spaces safe), and a multibillion-dollar local program to rehabilitate and increase the supply of affordable housing that helped sustain social peace.

By these big actions and in many other small ways, New York City became more livable, again. Refreshed by a commercially driven cleanup, Times Square, once the city's defining civic embarrassment, had become a symbol of its comeback. By 1997, the press was full of turnaround stories on New York City: "Comeback City" and its "amazing turnaround" (*U.S. News & World Report*), "An Old Word Is Back: Prosperity" (*NYT*), "New York Is Boom Town after Years in Gutter, Apple Shining Anew" (*DN*), and the like. And on the humorous side: "Take My City. Please; Crime Is Down. Streets Are Clean. What's a New York Comedian to Do?" (*NYT*). The economy was powering forward on job growth and shaping up to deliver a "robust decade" (*Crain's*). This powerfully renewed economic trajectory was a part of the special role New York City has played in the economic development of the country. The determination to rebuild and recover after 9/11, not only to assure the city's own position in the global economy but as a statement of national resilience, was resolutely embedded in its public officials, business interests, and citizens.

The city's constant efforts to revive from whatever economic or social depression it was suffering often found expression in economic development projects, real estate visions of economic growth through the rebuilding of city districts: the original World Trade Center complex, Battery Park City, Times Square, Chelsea and the High Line, Hudson Yards on the West Side of midtown Manhattan, all are examples of district transformation. Although these projects reflect a heavy focus on Manhattan, under the Edward I. Koch administration in the 1980s the city adopted an "Other Borough" strategy aimed at stimulating the development of downtown business centers in Brooklyn, Queens, the Bronx, and Staten Island. That policy initiative relied on an array of financial incentives (tax abatements, moving allowances, and cut-rate electricity) to make development in these boroughs more competitive, especially with Jersey City, Stamford, Connecticut, and other nearby office centers courting banks, securities firms, and other Manhattan companies. Eventually, the initiative, which carried over into the administration of David N. Dinkins, brought into being the largest commercial project outside Manhattan, MetroTech in downtown Brooklyn, and stimulated the development of Citicorp at Court Square in Long Island City, Queens, Teleport II on Staten Island, and Fordham Plaza in the Bronx. A reliance on real estate as an economic development strategy is deeply rooted in the economic and political culture of the city, and so it would be in revisioning rebuilding at Ground Zero.

As an economic development project, the original World Trade Center was but the latest and most ambitious attempt to revive the business fortunes of the city's original business hub. The historical path of Manhattan's commercial center traces a trek northward, with firms moving up the island, the exodus leaving a diminished downtown. Efforts to spur revitalization first began in the 1920s. Decade after decade, city officials, civic leaders, and downtown business interests worked to revive the faltering fortunes of the city's historically distinguished downtown, developing plans, lobbying for incentives, and pushing for projects such as the original World Trade Center. Between 1929, when downtown first experienced competition from midtown Manhattan as a choice location for corporate business, and 1993, nine major studies analyzed downtown's competitive problems, seeking solutions to stem fears of a permanent eclipse.[26] As an office district, downtown was hard pressed to compete with midtown Manhattan's deep economic base, superior commuter transportation, and compelling social infrastructure of amenities—the restaurants, retail shops, pedestrian-filled streets, small public spaces, and entertainment venues facilitating business networks and an intense level of activity. Midtown was where the city's largest financial firms—Bear Stearns, Citigroup, J. P. Morgan, Morgan Stanley, and DLJ, among them—had been moving for decades. Many firms, including Merrill Lynch, Goldman Sachs, Lehman Brothers, AIG, Deutsche Bank, and Standard & Poor's, had remained downtown. The two business districts represented geographic poles of competition for corporate tenants, midtown being the preferred location except when the supply of office space tightened and its attendant rent spikes widened the rent differential between these two districts and gave downtown a temporary edge, especially among rent-sensitive tenants. Typically, when the midtown office market becomes pricey its counterpart downtown has flourished.

Even in decline, downtown remained the nation's third largest office district, lined up in rank after midtown Manhattan and Chicago, yet its diminished role in the regional economy was an uncomfortable reality, so downtown leaders adopted a more expansive view of the type of activities downtown should be able to accommodate. Beginning with the paradigm-shifting *Lower Manhattan Plan of 1966*, planners began to envision the district as a more diverse place, a place to live, a place with waterfront amenities, and a place for educational and health institutions, as well as a place of corporate businesses activity and government offices. At the time, however, the distance between plan and transformation spanned a chasm.

Like many a historic city center across the nation, downtown was viewed as a weak office market. Although it was the home of the city's first skyscrapers, midtown was clearly winning the competition for new skyscrapers. Of the dozen buildings of one million square feet or more developed citywide during the 1920s, only four were downtown, where large sites were difficult to assemble in the prime area of the historic financial district,[27] and for decades new towers would be slow in coming. Following the completion of the World Trade Center twin towers in 1972 and 1973, thirteen class-A-quality office towers had been added to the skyline of downtown by 1990. Four were completed between 1972 and 1974 (55 Water Street, 85 Broad Street, One Liberty Plaza, and 130 Liberty Street), but more than ten years passed before the first two of four office towers of Battery Park City opened in 1985, followed by another the year after, and the fourth in 1987. And it was only the Canadian-based developer Olympia & York's willingness to take on sizable financial risk (typically shunned by the city's real estate families) that delivered full occupancy of the World Financial Center (now known as Brookfield Place) in the mixed-use complex. Olympia & York (O&Y) acquired tenants for these new towers by cleverly buying (at an opportune time in the market) the older buildings occupied by the tenants they wanted and, in so doing, reduced the speculative risk of big development with big early leasing commitments before the start of construction; the firm had a robust balance sheet and was willing to use it to pioneer entrance into the New York office market. The high quality of the amenities at the public sector's planned development of Battery Park City further distinguished the World Financial Center from the World Trade Center built two decades earlier and attracted tenants to the complex.

The brothers Reichmann who founded O&Y, Paul, Alfred, and Ralph, were unlike the scions of New York's established real estate families. In financial deal-making, they did things that were far ahead of commercial real estate practice. Their willingness to take the risk of being the master developer for the eight-million-square-foot commercial complex and their ability to work cooperatively with the New York State public authority that spearheaded its development, the Battery Park City Authority, set a new standard for downtown—as a public-private development and as an award-winning, large-scale, mixed-use complex.[28] More than a decade after the twin towers opened and on land owned by the Port Authority across from the World Trade Center complex, Larry Silverstein built 7 World Trade Center. Number 7 opened in 1987, but the hulking two-million-square-foot box of a forty-seven-story building radiated "all the charm of a massive shoebox."[29] The tower was not on par, architecturally, and it lacked the open spaces and amenities that graced Battery Park City and helped make that public-private project a model for large-scale planning efforts.

On the eve of 9/11, momentum toward a diversified 24/7 downtown district had taken root. Tax-based initiatives designed by the Giuliani administration in the mid-1990s were driving a dramatic transformation of an old commercial down-town into a mixed-use neighborhood; they were tremendously successful in doing what they were supposed to do: spur the conversion of older obsolete banks and office buildings into distinctive residences (more than 3,800 new residential units) that would attract more people to live downtown close to their workplaces, gener-ate spin-off retail shops and restaurants (at least 110 new businesses), and reduce the downtown office vacancy rate (to 6.4 percent from 20.2 percent). Lower Manhattan was presenting itself as the evolving edge of downtown hip, a histori-cal neighborhood organically revitalizing itself through its adjacency to Tribeca and the burgeoning booms in Brooklyn. In the constantly evolving social and ec-onomic landscape of New York City, it was the newest reincarnation of a neighbor-hood. No longer was downtown the old diminished neighborhood at the southern tip of Manhattan (map 1.1); its social geography was being recast as the growing neighborhood wedged between two other vibrant centers of population growth, edgy entertainment, trendy restaurants, and a thriving arts scene. The transfor-mation epitomized the type of demographic and social change associated with a newfound appreciation for urban living that was an especially important dynamic fueling the city's population growth surge in the 1990s. None of the civic leaders, urban planners, and vested business interests could have predicted the specifics of this resurgence that had for so long been a desired city objective. These signs of progress were exciting markers for the future. They assured city officials and

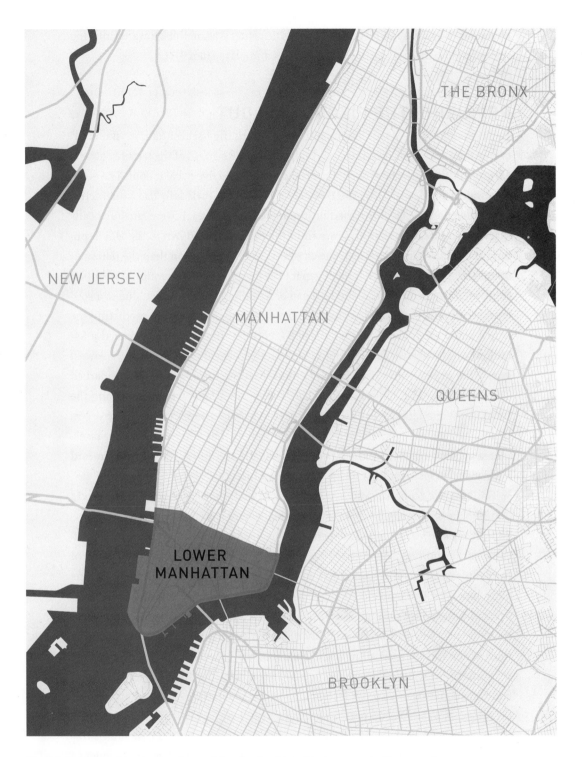

Map 1.1 Lower Manhattan's position in the New York metropolitan region.
CARTOGRAPHY: C&G PARTNERS FOR THE AUTHOR

downtown business interests that the historic center was on track toward fulfilling the vision of a diverse place to live and work and play. Then 9/11.

REPAIRING THE FISCAL FALLOUT

Newly inaugurated, Mayor Bloomberg faced a daunting fiscal situation. "Battered" is how the *Times* described the city's budget in the aftermath of the terrorist attack. "Frightful" was how the *Post* characterized the prospective fiscal fallout. The economy was in a "tailspin," said the *Daily News*. Each New York daily had a distinctive voice, but the bare facts reported on the news pages of each were unequivocally scary to all. Already under pressure from the midyear slowdown in the U.S. economy, the terrorist attack pushed the city into a deeper recession than the nation. It doubled the city's projected budget gap for the next fiscal year to roughly $4 billion from what had been expected to be a gap of $2 billion to $2.5 billion due to a softening economy. By the end of the year, city and state officials were predicting the deficit could range from $3.9 billion to $4.3 billion; Bloomberg anticipated a $4-billion gap. "Whatever it turns out to be, that is not good news; even at the lowest guess, the gap is nearly 10 percent of city taxpayer-financed revenues," remarked *Times* reporters Eric Lipton and Michael Cooper in a long article describing the fiscal challenge facing the city and its new mayoral administration. "The era in which the city taxpayers delivered so much money that a mayor could cut taxes, increase spending at twice the rate of inflation and still finish the year with record budget surpluses is, at least for now, a piece of history."[30]

Gauging the economic and fiscal impacts of such a strong shock to the city was bound to be somewhat fluid and open-ended. There were limits to what could be definitively known, given how dependent the city's revenue intake was on the outcome of location decisions made by hundreds of businesses and thousands of residents, as well as the economic trajectory of the U.S. economy. One thing was clear, however: The projected budget shortfalls were monumental and would trigger an immense reckoning: "New York City is a $40-billion enterprise, a government of such reach and responsibility that each year it spends more money than most states and some small nations," the reporters noted as means of putting the magnitude of the situation in perspective. Soon after the attack, Mayor Giuliani had signed an executive order freezing $1 billion in city spending and told almost every agency to look for 15 percent in cuts; the police and fire departments as well as the board of education faced smaller cuts of 2.5 percent cut. These cuts, however, would do little to soften the fiscal belt tightening required as a consequence of the terrorist attack on New York City, which was going to impact the Bloomberg administration's first budget for the fiscal year starting July 1—that's when the

$4-billion number would begin to impinge on whatever plans the new mayor had for the city prior to 9/11. The choices the new administration would have to make would be hard, but the new mayor was determined not to repeat the mistakes of the past. "We cannot drive people and business out of New York. We cannot raise taxes," he said. "We will find another way."[31]

If not taxes, the other options would be "doing cuts and finding ways to increase productivity," said the director of the city's Independent Budget Office (IBO), Ronnie Lowenstein.[32] Lowenstein was speaking from an analytically informed position; the IBO had recently issued a fiscal brief reporting on critical issues facing the city, and the agency's revenue model was predicting gloom ahead for the near-term revenue horizon.[33] Known for its objective, data-driven analyses, the independent publicly funded agency serves a unique role in the city's policy arena; created as part of the Charter Revision of 1989 (which guaranteed the agency at least 10 percent of the funds allotted to the Mayor's Office of Management and Budget), its primary responsibility has been to provide nonpartisan information about the city budget and tax revenues, for which the fiscal watchdog had gained a well-deserved reputation for objectivity and nonpartisanship.

Based on revised estimates to its December 2001 *Fiscal Outlook* report, the IBO's message to the new mayor foretold of unvarnished fiscal pain for several years: a projected shortfall of $3.4 billion in 2003, or 12.5 percent of city funds, widening to 15.9 percent of city funds in 2004, and to 16.8 percent of city funds in 2005. The only softening caveat of this harsh reality was relative: the fiscal facts were not as "bleak" for Mayor Bloomberg as they had been for Mayor David N. Dinkins when he was sworn in twelve years earlier and faced similar economic conditions. The next month, in February 2002, when Mayor Bloomberg outlined his plan for the coming year's budget, the projected gap had reached $4.8 billion. "The sheer enormity of the fiscal problem raises the question: Will Bloomberg ever get out from under these deficits? Will there ever be money for the big projects or new programs that all mayors desire, or will the defining task of his term be hacking from one budget to the next?" the *Daily News* asked. "Welcome to the Second Toughest Job in America, Mr. Bloomberg," the editorial board of the *Post* had chimed back in December while the number crunching was still ongoing.[34]

Bloomberg held big development aspirations for his adopted city. As mayor-elect, he had laid out an ambitious set of "prime candidates" for new development across all five boroughs.[35] In Manhattan, the agenda included redeveloping the city's waterfront, building a new stadium on the West Side of Manhattan, extending the Number 7 subway line to open up growth opportunities in the far west portion of midtown, and developing a new vision for lower Manhattan as a twenty-four-hour community refitted for the twenty-first century—and that included using the Trade Center site for economic development, something his predecessor had rejected as unfitting and inappropriate. "We shouldn't think about this site out there, right beyond us, right here, as a site for economic development," Mayor Giuliani said in his farewell address at St. Paul's Chapel, just a short distance from the Trade Center site. He thought the entire sixteen-acre site once occupied by the World Trade Center should be set aside as a patriotic shrine. A "soaring, monumental, beautiful" memorial should be pursued first. "And then if we do that part right, then the economic development will just happen," he added. Office space could be built "in a lot of different places."[36] Further endowing the site as one of overwhelming sadness was not what the Bloomberg administration thought best for the city's future; a sensitive memorial and museum of remembrance done in a tactful way to honor the tragedy, yes, absolutely, but it should not be the exclusive use of these sixteen acres. The mayor was viewing the city's future through a highly competitive global lens, Daniel L. Doctoroff, his first deputy mayor for economic development and rebuilding, told me in an interview. "His ambition was to repair the city and reimagine Manhattan. He's someone who doesn't look back, and this is an essential element of his character."[37]

Conquering the budget problems and delivering a balanced budget was the first order of business for the new mayor; the law required a balanced budget, as did the politics of maintaining local authority over the budget. "The City needs to control its own destiny," Bloomberg wrote in "My Economic Blueprint." "Currently, if the City incurs a deficit of $100 million or more, the Financial Control Board steps in to 'run the City.' This trigger has never changed since the fiscal crisis of the 1970s, even though our government budget has grown four fold. Should the economic impact of September 11 result in the 'worst case' scenario, a real possibility exists that this limit will be violated shortly after I take office." Bloomberg was focused, "in the interests of democracy," on finding "a legislative distinction between a one-time terrorist attack and profligate spending."[38] At this fragile juncture so soon after 9/11, Bloomberg needed to instill confidence by delivering a balanced budget; it would be the first test of his ability to lead the nation's largest city to a restored state of growth and prosperity.

This was an epic fiscal challenge on a scale not experienced since the early 1990s, the city's most difficult fiscal period since the 1970s fiscal crisis. Felix Rohatyn, a leading investment banker at Lazard Frères known for his skilled efforts as chair of the Municipal Assistance Corporation in negotiating budget reforms and rescuing the city from bankruptcy, argued as early as October 9, 2001, in a *Times* op-ed that this was a "fiscal disaster the city can't face alone"; he called on the federal government to help with a long-term federal program of assistance,[39] not just to New York City but to states and cities to "prevent what is likely to be a hard national recession from turning into a real depression." Many shared Rohatyn's well-founded concerns, yet the past was not prologue to the present. The city of New York of 2001 was not the city of New York of 1975. Fundamentally, it was a different and more prosperous place, forward-looking. The fiscal structure and controls that Rohatyn had helped put in place in 1975 (the Municipal Assistance Corporation and the Financial Control Board) had helped assure structural stability—"twenty consecutive balanced budgets, in good times and bad," he said.[40] The budget was monitored by numerous fiscal watchdogs: the state's Financial Control Board, the state comptroller's office, the city comptroller's office, and groups like the Independent Budget Office, the Citizens Budget Commission, and the Fiscal Policy Institute.

With the growth of the information technology sector, the city economy was becoming more diversified and less dependent on Wall Street and the financial-services industry. Crime remained under control. Most critically, New York City had become a highly attractive place to live as well as work, as attested to by its historic-high population count. The city's burgeoning information economy had occurred "without any major help from the state or federal government," wrote Mitchell Moss in his celebratory century-opening ode to the city, "Why New York Will Flourish in the 21st Century."[41] All of these positive distinctions promised to enhance New York's ability to recover quickly and benefit long-term from the opportunity born out of the tragedy of 9/11—an opportunity to rebuild the historic heart of the city and assure its central position in the global constellation of cities. How the rebuilding effort could meet the needs of the information economy and related social and economic trends was an open question.

A SITE WITH HISTORY

The World Trade Center was built as an emblem of government ambition and, in time, its twin towers came to be an icon of New York recognizable across the globe. Built on sixteen acres assembled out of a contentious condemnation of city plots and lots by the Port Authority, its violent destruction on 9/11 could not annihilate the civic pride of New Yorkers or personal experiences of all who walked its vast plaza, worked in its tall towers, dined in its Windows on the World restaurant, and visited its indoor and outdoor observatories on the 106th and 107th floors of the South Tower. The meaningful memories and symbolic legacy of what had been built on these sixteen acres proved far less destructible than the towering volumes of concrete and steel and glass that had collapsed so violently. The site at Ground Zero was layered with significant legacies, legacies that found new meaning as ideas about rebuilding these sixteen acres launched a wide-ranging public dialogue, as discussed in chapter 5.

For years these legacies hung in the shadows of policymaking, latent but potent reminders of the site's role in the economic, social, and political history of lower Manhattan. As planning efforts developed momentum throughout 2002, four legacies of the World Trade Center complex resounded in the ideas and ideals put forth in the public realm: its role as a catalyst to remediate downtown's economic stagnation; its iconic architectural contribution to the skyline of Manhattan; its failed superblock plan, a former symbol of modernity and economic efficiency intended to liberate the city from the constraints of the street grid;[42] and its institutional pedigree as an economically questionable megaproject of the Port Authority. Development of the complex had come about only through a grand bargain with the state of New Jersey for the Port Authority to take over the bankrupt Hudson & Manhattan Railroad (H&M, renamed as PATH), which carried some 140,000 commuters a day from Newark, Jersey City, and Hoboken to Manhattan. That the Port Authority had its headquarters in the North Tower, as all of the subsequent New York governors maintained offices there, became a piece of the historical legacy as well.

To assemble the site for the World Trade Center in the early 1960s, the Port Authority went the "taking" route, employing a hotly contested and controversial condemnation action to create two superblocks[43] (figure 1.3). The assemblage closed off parts of five streets (Cortlandt, Dey, Fulton, Washington, and Greenwich) of the city's historic street grid and eliminated twelve blocks of a neighborhood of small electronics shops known as Radio Row, displacing many small-scale store-owners (figure 1.4). "There were also two residential tenants in no hurry at all to depart," Edith Iglauer wrote in the *New Yorker* in 1972, "one of them a penthouse dweller who loved the river view from his eighty-five-dollar-a-month apartment atop a five-story building; the other, a monkey that escaped from a pet shop when it was about to be torn down, built a nest in a pile of beams, stole enough bananas daily from a nearby fruit stand to stay alive, and eluded workmen for months."[44] It took more than a year to clear the site of condemned buildings; when done, the demolition wiped out 164 buildings and produced a twenty-one-sided polygon of precisely 14.634 acres,[45] which figuratively grew in the colloquial tradition of real estate measurement to "16" acres and lodged into customary usage for at least forty years.

When fully tenanted, the World Trade Center complex housed a city within the city, complete with its own zip code: 10048. More than 42,000 people worked in a vertical commercial landscape of 10.5 million square feet of office space, 450,000 square feet of retail mall space, an 820-room hotel with conference facilities, and a vast seven-level underground of 2,000 parking spaces, storage vaults, and mechanical and loading facilities, as well as other supporting infrastructure, including the PATH station and a subway complex. In creating this vast commercial

FIGURE 1.3 *With a dummy in a coffin that represented Mr. Businessman, on July 13, 1962, merchants and clerks of Radio Row staged a protest against the condemnation proceeding by the Port of New York to build the World Trade Center.* © BETTMANN/ CORBIS

complex—at one and the same time a means to enhance its power and prestige as much as its coffers—the Port Authority had taken the unusual step of acting as the developer, a risky position typically left to the private sector that required authorizing legislation from both states, New York and New Jersey.

Its unprecedented scale created equally big problems. By the time of the World Trade Center's official ribbon-cutting ceremony in April 1973, Port Authority staff had been struggling for years to find enough tenants to fill the giant complex in a marketplace increasingly oversupplied with office space and on the verge of collapse. Not until 1980, ten years after the first tenants moved in, could the agency claim success in fully leasing out the office space, and even at that, only with a major assist from the state of New York, which had committed to sign a long-term lease for 1.9 million square feet of office space before construction even began. Together with the Port Authority and the U.S. Customs Service, government entities occupied 40 percent of the commercial office space in the complex, according to a 1981 audit prepared by the New York State deputy comptroller.[46]

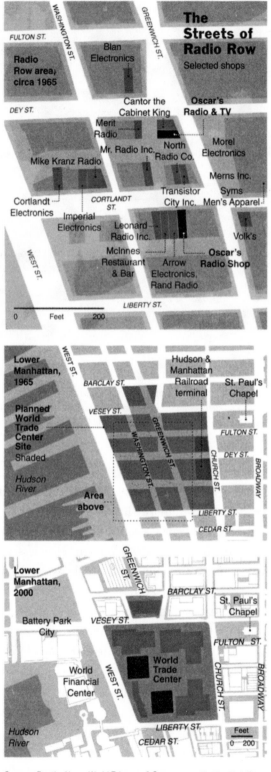

FIGURE 1.4 *The shops and street grid of Radio Row (1965), the planned site (1965), and the original site plan of the World Trade Center (2000).* THE NEW YORK TIMES

Much to the chagrin of the real estate community, the project immobilized the downtown office market. For years, private real estate owners and members of the powerful Real Estate Board of New York (REBNY) had raised their voices in unequivocal opposition to the project, fearing unfair competition with private developers from so much "subsidized" office space coming onto the market when vacancies already signaled a glut of space. Lawrence A. Wien, a leading real estate figure in the city, managing owner of the Empire State Building, and powerful opponent of the planned complex, organized a group of midtown Manhattan real estate owners into the Committee for a Reasonable World Trade Center and in early May 1968, the group ran a full-page ad in the *New York Times* (and other city newspapers)—"The Mountain Comes to Manhattan"—calling for a more "reasonable" height for the twin towers. The group, which claimed to represent the owners of 20 percent of the 157 million square feet of Manhattan office space, argued that the gigantism of the World Trade Center project was not just "economically unrealistic" but "flat-out dangerous," according to Glanz and Lipton.[47] Vividly illustrating the point, the ad, reproduced in figure 1.5, showed an artist's rendition of a large airplane about to crash into the towers, which appeared to stretch infinitely high in the sky.

Cost, too, drew public attention. Two years after the Port Authority had unveiled its architectural plans for the complex, by the time construction began on the site in 1966, the price tag for the complex had jumped to $575 million from $355 million (after an interim $470 million)—or more than $3.1 billion when converted to 2001 dollars—which, as Doig wrote, impelled the *New York Times* to pick up its editorial pen. The financial magnitude of the World Trade Center project would divert resources from other important regional transportation projects the Port Authority could undertake. In time, Doig wrote, the paper of record "joined the chorus of harsher critics," and argued that the project was "enormously expensive and grandiose" and should be cut down to "realistic and efficient size." Otherwise, the *Times* warned, the World Trade Center would only be a monument to "the city's former glories as a port and to the Authority's audacious ability to get its own way." But PA executive director Tobin and his aides "turned a deaf ear to those complaints, and the World Trade Center went forward, its costs rising year by year until they exceeded one billion dollars,"[48] or nearly $4 billion in 2001 dollars. The arrogance of that institutional attitude became a legacy, too.

Every aspect of the World Trade Center's construction spoke to scale and ambition. What made its gigantism so surprising was less the secrecy by which it came to be, for that was well known to be standard practice at the Port Authority, than the motive and ambition pushing the project to such a colossal scale. In 1961 during the early stages of planning when the project was being sited on the east

FIGURE 1.5 *On May 2, 1968, the Committee for a Reasonable World Trade Center ran an ad in the* New York Times *showing the risk of a commercial airliner flying into the World Trade Center towers. Letterhead for the committee came out of the stationery drawer of Lawrence A. Wien, leader of the committee and managing owner of the Empire State Building.* FROM THE NEW YORK TIMES, JANUARY 1, 2003 © 2003 THE NEW YORK TIMES

side of Manhattan below the Brooklyn Bridge, Tobin conceived of a trade center composed of several buildings (the tallest 72 stories and another of 30 stories), on the order of 5 to 6 million square feet, at least as large as the Pentagon, then the world's largest building in terms of office space with 6.5 million square feet configured in a signature low-density five-sided building. Months later, after the accommodation with the New Jersey side of the Port Authority led to a shift in the project's location to the West Side of Manhattan, where it could be combined with the rehabilitation of the H&M and would be closer to New Jersey, "Tobin and his trade-center planners broke free from the business-leaders' modest expectations and sharply recast the building plans," Doig wrote. The first phase of the project alone would contain 10 million square feet—nonnegotiable. Fearing criticism of the new scope of the project, the Port Authority "kept its decision largely to itself," according to Glanz and Lipton. When in January 1964 Tobin and the commissioners unveiled an entirely new design, described in the PA's annual report as "twin towers of gleaming metal, soaring 110 stories," the initial response was largely favorable, with the *Times* exclaiming, "No project has ever been more promising for New York." "What justifications were powerful enough for Tobin to accept the risks—in a dozen different political, fiscal, legal, technical, and cultural dimensions—that would surely come with a venture into unprecedented enormousness?" asked Glanz and Lipton. "His motives were straightforward" and protective of the institution's prerogatives. A giant World Trade Center would let Tobin invest the Port Authority's "skyrocketing" revenues and surpluses "in something other than the mass transit that he saw as a dangerous fiscal sinkhole." The 110-story twin towers that came to be along with the other structures of the vast complex were "of a scale like nothing of the kind that had ever been welded and bolted and hammered together before," Glanz and Lipton wrote.[49]

Even the site's archeological history mattered. During the foundation excavation, the engineers hoped to find the other half of the ship *Tijger*, purportedly sunk by the Dutch explorer Adriaen Block in 1613 after it burned; the first half had been found during the digging for the IRT subway line in 1916. Instead, the engineers found "garbage, animal carcasses, leather shoes, bottles, cannonballs, oyster shells, timber and other debris that had been dumped on the shore and used to extend the shoreline west over 300 years, to the other side of what is now West Street." But the 1.2 million cubic yards of material excavated for the World Trade Center foundation—"enough to make a pile about a mile high and seventy-five feet square," Iglauer wrote—was creatively recycled, dumped into "a great riverside cofferdam, or bulkhead" to create 23.5 acres of new landfill immediately west of the site on what would eventually become part of the 92-acre complex making up Battery Park City. It was Guy F. Tozzoli, the director of the project for the Port

Authority, who had made many such decisions, large and small, to address the problems of how to build what would be the two largest towers in the world.

This land expansion was yet another in a continuous historical pattern of extending lower Manhattan's boundaries into the waters off the island's east and west shores. Century after century since 1650, landfill projects had accommodated Manhattan's endless hunger for additional land. By 1972, approximately 643 acres of new waterfront had been added, nearly doubling that area of lower Manhattan (figure 1.6). Following prohibitions put in place by the federal government's Clean Water Act of 1972, which ended the practice of discharging into the

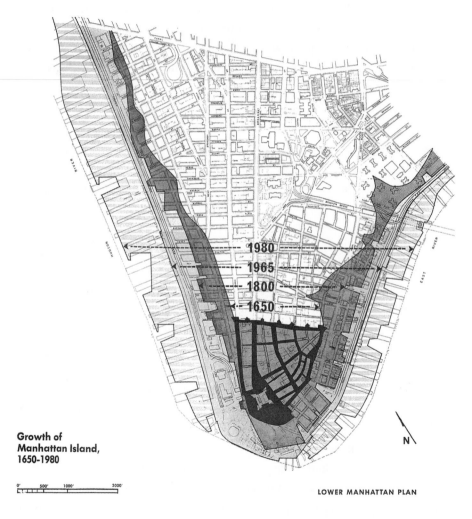

Growth of
Manhattan Island,
1650-1980

0'   500'   1000'   2000'

LOWER MANHATTAN PLAN

FIGURE 1.6 *The history of successive landfill expansions of lower Manhattan: 1650–1980; the 1980s line is a projection as of 1966. After the Clean Water Act of 1972 ended the practice of discharging into the waters of the United States, unless authorized by a permit issued by the U.S Army Corps of Engineers, Battery Park City became the city's last landfill expansion project.* THE LOWER MANHATTAN PLAN OF 1966

waters of the United States, unless authorized by a permit issued by the U.S Army Corps of Engineers, Battery Park City became the city's last landfill expansion project.

With the development of the World Trade Center, the Port Authority transformed the face of lower Manhattan: Its twin 110-story towers displaced the Empire State Building as the world's tallest skyscraper, and its site plan completely separated the project from the rest of Manhattan. "At the time, safe, clean, well-lighted superblocks, rather than traffic-congested streets, were considered good planning," Alexander Garvin, vice president for planning, design and development of the Lower Manhattan Development Corporation (LMDC), said of the superblock in his historical review of the context of rebuilding. "In order to increase efficiency and protect pedestrians from traffic accidents, the great plaza that provided access to all the buildings was connected to neighboring blocks on three sides by bridges (in the process removing customers from city streets and damaging local businesses). Unfortunately, the plaza had to be closed four to five months out of the year due to danger that falling ice posed to pedestrians."[50]

As one of the last of the massive urban renewal efforts in New York City, the World Trade Center complex was widely regarded as prima facie evidence of that era's brutal disregard for the humanistic fabric of a city. It wore this legacy boldly, just the way its domineering public developer had intended. The 1960s plan for the World Trade Center complex embodied a planning concept woefully out of date at the start of the twenty-first century: a superblock assemblage dominated by skyscrapers rising up out of a vast open plaza (figure 1.7). City planners and architects were no longer drawing up plans in the superblock fashion. The Battery Park City complex immediately west of the World Trade Center across West Street and a prized part of the fabric of lower Manhattan, symbolized the new planning approach of breaking a large-scale project into pieces that could be built out incrementally. Widespread understanding among planners, architects, and city officials of the failure of the World Trade Center planning vision had spawned a waiting list of errors to amend, the highest priority being reinsertion of the street grid into the site and elimination of the elevated open-air plaza that had walled off the sixteen acres from the rest of lower Manhattan. Restoring the street grid would connect the site to neighboring communities and recapture lost features of city life: pedestrian flow, street life, and view corridors.

The twin towers' collapse left the site in ruins, yet the so-called bathtub foundation held firm, aided by the massive piles of wreckage debris. Because of the site's origins—an area once beneath the Hudson River—clearing the 1.5 million tons of debris out of the seventy-foot deep hole vastly complicated the recovery effort. To keep those waters from finding their way back into the site, the dig-out had to be

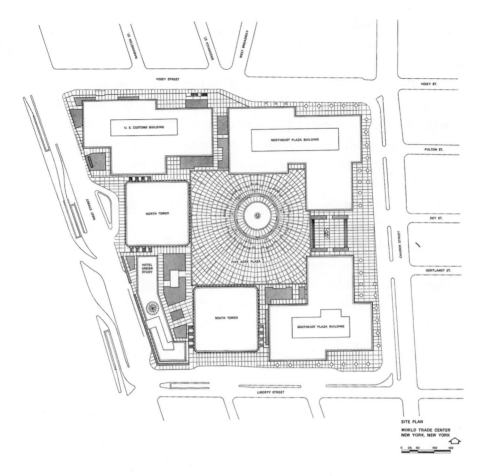

FIGURE 1.7 *The original superblock site plan of the World Trade Center.*

carefully choreographed for engineering safety lest the foundation walls shift or rupture, leading to flooding and destabilization of the buildings nearby (figure 1.8). Underground conditions were hazardous, and the recovery further complicated by damage to two PATH tunnels running through the site (flooded after the terrorist attack) as well as two subway lines (IRT No. 1 and No. 9) that had collapsed in several different places. Temporarily, the debris from the collapsed towers took the place of the underground floors of the complex that had provided the necessary lateral support for the slurry wall rimming the foundations of the twin towers, the Marriott Hotel, and 6 World Trade Center, home of the U.S. Customs House.

Imported technology from Italy, the World Trade Center's slurry wall foundation represented an innovative approach to constructing a foundation for the superblock site. It was only the third time the technique had been used in the United States, and the scale of use for the Trade Center was unprecedented.[51] Moreover, the approach typi-

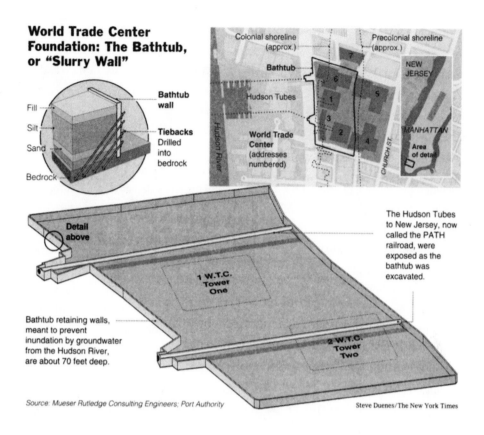

World Trade Center Foundation: The Bathtub, or "Slurry Wall"

Fill
Silt
Sand
Bedrock

Bathtub wall

Tiebacks Drilled into bedrock

Colonial shoreline (approx.)
Precolonial shoreline (approx.)

Bathtub
Hudson Tubes

World Trade Center (addresses numbered)

Hudson River
CHURCH ST.

NEW JERSEY
MANHATTAN
Area of detail

Detail above

1 W.T.C. Tower One

2 W.T.C. Tower Two

The Hudson Tubes to New Jersey, now called the PATH railroad, were exposed as the bathtub was excavated.

Bathtub retaining walls, meant to prevent inundation by groundwater from the Hudson River, are about 70 feet deep.

Source: Mueser Rutledge Consulting Engineers; Port Authority

Steve Duenes/The New York Times

FIGURE 1.8 *Post-9/11 hazardous "bathtub."* FROM THE NEW YORK TIMES, JANUARY 1, 2003 © 2003 THE NEW YORK TIMES

fied the type of engineering prowess that had given those who worked for the Port Authority rewarding status as "mandarins of public service."[52] Engineering the slurry wall foundation was one of the proud moments for the "below-grade guys," as George J. Tamaro referred to himself and the other foundation engineers of the Port Authority in a profile by PBS for its *America Rebuilds* series on Ground Zero. A young staff engineer and New Jersey native who grew up speaking Italian, Tamaro had been sent to Italy in 1964 to study reinforced concrete design with the well-known architect Pier Luigi Nervi, who was designing the Port's bus terminal at the George Washington Bridge. There he was introduced to the slurry-wall foundation technology, "la diaframma," he called it, which would become essential to the Port Authority as it went about developing the World Trade Center, and he would be put in charge of overseeing the construction of the slurry walls at the complex.

Though the stability of the underground was unpredictable after the towers collapsed, the bathtub wall—that three-foot-thick slurry wall of concrete, seventy feet deep, running thirty-one hundred feet around the rectangular perimeter and tied to bedrock with steel cables—had been sturdy under the earlier terrorist calamity,

Tamaro said. The 1993 attack on the World Trade Center had taken out two of the seven underground floors, yet the wall still held. It has a good degree of flexibility, he said, like a diaphragm. During the first week after the 9/11 attack, as Tamaro and his colleagues at Mueser Rutledge Consulting Engineers were figuring out how to empty out the basement with the necessary precautions, they had "no sense of the condition of the wall around the perimeter."[53] The technical feat of shoring up the slurry wall would become an important constraint on the practical reality of rebuilding, particularly as it affected the design of the 9/11 Memorial. Other encumbrances on the site included the PATH tracks and the need for security, truck access, and underground bus and car parking facilities, all of which would bedevil the design process by triggering conflict among the different interests with a stake at Ground Zero.

The twin towers gradually became a beloved icon of New York City, despite negative reviews and repeated disparagement by the community of architects and urban critics. Speaking a modern architectural language but referencing Gothic sensibility as cathedrals of commerce, the 110-story towers stood replete with symbolic meaning: They presented a compelling demonstration of technological possibility, yet soon this icon of imagination was brought down to human scale by the 1974 tightrope walk between the twins by twenty-four-year-old French citizen Philippe Petit (figure 1.9), a parachute jump from the roof of the North Tower by twenty-four-year-old New Yorker Owen Quinn the next year, and the 1997 ascent from base to rooftop by twenty-seven-year-old New Yorker George Willig.

FIGURE 1.9 *Philippe Petit walks between the twin towers, August 7, 1974.* JAMES MARCH/"MAN ON WIRE"

They carried forth the myth of the city in film after film, hundreds of them, the better known including a 1976 remake of *King Kong* (1933), *Superman: The Movie* (1978), *Escape from Manhattan* (1981), *Trading Places* (1983), *Wall Street* (1987), *Working Girl* (1998), and *The Cruise* (1998). They provided the architectural icon for downtown that so many urban designers had called for since the 1929 Regional Plan Association's "Plan for New York and Its Environs" (figure 1.10). Physically

FIGURE 1.10 *Proposed mural of shadows of the Empire State and Chrysler Buildings on the north sides of the World Trade Center towers, 1975.* COURTESY RICHARD HAAS

dominating the surrounding low-density neighborhood, the towers remained iconic even after other cities around the world built taller skyscrapers. This architectural legacy, along with the other three legacies—economic revitalization, institutional arrogance, planning ambition—would reemerge in the discourse about rebuilding the site.

THE ARC OF REBUILDING

On September 12, the site of the World Trade Center once again held forth New York City's aspirations for global preeminence, this time driven by defiance. Its fate rested in the hands of powerful clashing interests. Whose influence would prevail in the political contests over resources and power and why? Who would engage in the contest but fail to win standing and influence and why?

If the civic mandates of rebuilding Ground Zero were clear from the very beginning, what was needed to achieve them was not. For all stakeholders, that understanding evolved over time by way of a tortuous political process. Officials were figuring it out, inventing, as they went along, and contention was inevitable. Conceptually, "vision" was being asked to meet complex needs: repair an emotionally traumatized neighborhood, physically rebuild a large and devastated site, economically renew the city's downtown business district, and memorialize the personal losses experienced by thousands of family members and close friends of those who perished. Politicians could not set priorities among all of these noble but competing mandates. All of the major public players and private interests swirling about Ground Zero harbored big ambitions: Governor Pataki, Mayor Bloomberg, the Port Authority, Larry Silverstein. The victims' families commanded singular standing whenever they put forth deeply felt desires for specific forms of remembrance or objections to specific plans for Ground Zero. The press too wanted in. Consensus on a master plan emerged only through an orchestrated, seemingly democratic public process, but it was a fragile consensus, immediately and repeatedly challenged by a series of controversies that never seemed to end.

As became so evident in discussions about how to rebuild, New Yorkers were mourning the loss of the towers themselves and all they symbolized. "They were the biggest and brashest icons that New York has ever produced—physically magnificent, intimately familiar structures," Glanz and Lipton wrote in awe of the achievement. "Their builders were possessed of a determination that sometimes crossed the line into hubris: they refused to admit defeat before any problem that natural forces, economics, or politics could throw in their way."[54] The gigantic twins had physically defined economic power. They stood as the symbol of capitalism, for which they became a target of ideological terrorism, not once, but twice.

Would building replicas of the twin towers or a replacement equally iconic that again defined the skyline of lower Manhattan supply another target of terrorism? Who was to say whether this would be a wise and appropriate way to define defiance? Resilience?

In size and ambition the original World Trade Center set many a precedent, and when the time came to rebuild the site, distinctive episodes of the project's history reappeared in an almost predictable fashion. The messy brawls of the past came back into play because nothing big in New York gets built without serious opposition and passionate debate, and at Ground Zero interests many and varied, public and private, swirled about seeking power and influence. The option that government might exercise its right of eminent domain to take back the site from its private leaseholders though condemnation arose in public conversation and was seriously considered. Building all ten million square feet of commercial space lost on 9/11 in a depressed downtown office market reprised questions about the hubris of building at such a scale. Excessive costs again drew critical public attention. Archeological finds in need of preservation also resurfaced, and the newest artifacts of historical importance, remnants of the World Trade Center, would also need to be preserved.

Beyond these precursors, a condition unlike any other in the city's history directed the process of rebuilding these symbolic sixteen acres: a terrorist attack creating an unprecedented and emotionally compelling public interest that trumped prevailing property rights. Repeatedly, the legal prerogatives of the Port Authority, as landowner, and those of Larry Silverstein and his investor partnership, as owners of a long-term lease on the Trade Center site, were challenged by the politics of accommodating the civic mandates of rebuilding. Ultimately, these political dynamics precipitated an amendment to both stakeholders' property rights. But the process was terribly messy, terribly tangled, and, at times, terribly chaotic.

Generally overlooked or misunderstood, the roots of this decisive and divisive piece of the story can be traced to a contractual flaw in the July 2001 agreement between the Port Authority and the Silverstein investment partnership that privatized the ownership of the World Trade Center: The voluminous documents failed to provide for an unwinding of the ninety-nine-year lease, a "divorce." Providing for an exit, common in private real estate partnership agreements, would have lent greater clarity to the post-9/11 situation and given government officials greater power to execute the civic mandates. But no one contemplated total destruction of the complex. In the context of the 1993 terrorist attack, the omission was a fundamental if not fateful mistake, one that after 9/11 created an ambiguous situation of control and an immediate dysfunctional relationship between these two economic interests. The question "Who's in control?" became a constant refrain.

Divided ownership over the sixteen acres at Ground Zero seriously handicapped the power to execute the ambitions of rebuilding, public and private. Following the physical destruction of the World Trade Center, the Port Authority and Silverstein, who under the terms of his partnership agreement spoke for his investor group, were thrown into a joint endeavor to rebuild the site. The profile of this joint endeavor deviated from typical public-private developments for at least two reasons, both of which profoundly shaped the timeline and complexity of the rebuilding process: First, under the terms of his contract, the private developer already was in control of the publicly owned site, a reverse of the norm; existing site control gave Larry Silverstein far greater presumptive decision-making power early in the process than is typical in a public-private development. Second, the deep emotional trauma (unprecedented except for the attack on Pearl Harbor) of 9/11 added an unknown dimension to the politics of this public-private development; it defined the families of the victims as a political constituency, emotionally supercharged the situation, and created a unique planning challenge.

The compelling civic mandate to rebuild these sixteen acres at the heart of the downtown district created an epic opportunity for New York City. It represented an opportunity that otherwise would not have happened, or happened within the context of a broad-based public dialogue. Besides remediating the planning errors of the past, rebuilding the Trade Center site carried the promise of putting in place a cluster of cutting-edge, sustainable twenty-first-century office towers to rival those in competing global cities. It carried the promise of creating public open space that animated the area with hundreds of people, and bringing light and trees to what had been a vast barren plaza. Each one of these opportunities, however, would have to fit within *the* priority of priorities: creating an ever-lasting memorial to those nearly three thousand people who died in the 9/11 attack on lower Manhattan. So it would be that managing these competing claims of remembrance and rebuilding defined the political task at Ground Zero.

This emotion-laden task fell outside established institutional arrangements and planning protocols. Governor Pataki created an agency to manage a planning process for rebuilding Ground Zero and coordinate reconstruction throughout downtown, the LMDC. Throughout the highly visible first phase of planning during 2002, not the agency, not the Port Authority, not even the democratically elected steward of the body politic—the mayor—could successfully claim legitimate authority over the dual objectives of remembrance and rebuilding. No established procedure existed for this unprecedented task and ad hoc arrangements struck among the contending parties failed as substitutes. No clear structure would be put in place for making key decisions or resolving conflicts. Each public agent would bring its own statutory authority, administrative process, and political power to bear on parts of the process, but none could achieve mastery over the whole. The result was fragmentation and confusion. Public officials would initially try to fill this gap by charging designers with arriving at a master plan for the site, but while the designers could articulate possible alternatives, they could not resolve competing claims on the contested site; that responsibility belonged to elected officials. This structural flaw of the rebuilding process set in early.

In his position as governor, Pataki was in the position of power to guide the redevelopment of Ground Zero, yet he failed to lead rebuilding in a realistic fashion. He lacked the type of dynamic assertive leadership needed to manage the contentious politics of rebuilding after this national trauma. He was emotionally engaged, especially in dealing with the families of the victims, yet too disengaged to be an effective leader of the process, making decisions in reactive fashion when compelled by crisis or a conflict demanding a definitive resolution. He was a politician who viewed most things through the prism of his ambition. He firmly believed that the site should be rebuilt as the commercial center it was before to ensure the viability of lower Manhattan, which, he emphasized in an interview with me, was struggling before 9/11. Accordingly, he was not inclined to challenge the profit-making program of commercial uses that the Port Authority and its leaseholder, Larry Silverstein, similarly wanted to replace.

As owner of the site, the Port Authority had ultimate control of the site, legally, but it was unable to manage the scope of its ambition, be it the creation of an iconic transportation center or the centralized underground infrastructure system with its complicated development and construction schedule. As the holder of the long-term lease on the site, Silverstein was the ultimate economic actor, dogged and persistent with a bottom-line focus and an unwillingness to submerge these interests to a greater civic purpose; he was always holding out for the last dollar and did not have the moral agency to reconcile competing interests. Money explains a very big piece of the story at Ground Zero, but what the public wanted had nothing to do with the money ultimately driving decisions about what would be rebuilt. After "the veneer of public participation" in the many forums for discussion about the redesign of the site wore off, "the decision process revealed itself as a strikingly undemocratic contest among the governor, the mayor, the Port Authority, and the leaseholder."[55]

City Hall was in an especially weak position to influence decisions that would shape the physical and economic landscape of lower Manhattan for decades to come. It lacked formal rights to plan what would be built anew and formal powers to control the decisions of those who would take hold of the reins of planning. The Port Authority had owned the site for nearly forty years; by governing statute, it was free of New York City's regulatory and land-use powers, and it reported to two higher levels of government. After a heroic job of cleaning up and stabilizing the site in record time by the end of June 2002, the city was effectively shut out, control over the site returned to the Port Authority. The mayor, one journalist aptly quipped, "has more authority to suspend alternate side of the street parking regulations than in determining the course of what happens on the tract of land just south of City Hall."[56]

Yet these sixteen acres were an integral part of the city's territorial DNA, evermore so after 9/11. Whereas the Port Authority's city-within-a-city position gave the bi-state agency a governmental purpose on the site, the City of New York had no legal jurisdiction there, except for nearly forgotten control over two discontinued and closed street stubs running into the site that had somehow been left out of the Port Authority's original 1960s condemnation transaction, which did not amount to a lot of position from a real estate perspective. Its shadow position in the rebuilding process would irritate Mayor Bloomberg and Deputy Mayor Doctoroff, to no end. Politically, the situation was untenable. In the end, the mayor of New York City would be the one who would be judged by what happened at Ground Zero, and in an effort to recalibrate the dynamics of conflict and push the project forward through bottlenecks, the Bloomberg administration would make continuous strategic interventions, some successful, others not. The mayor also had his bully pulpit—and personal influence as an extraordinarily successful businessman in a town built on the profits of commercial success. And he would leverage both to become a force for progress in rebuilding.

The ambitions of these principal actors were constantly challenged by other players in the political orbit: federal government funding agencies, civic activists and preservationists, the families of the 9/11 victims, the New York Police Department, Goldman Sachs and other corporate interests, and New Jersey political interests across the Hudson River. Generally successful in asserting their interests into the plans for Ground Zero, these players had agendas that were nevertheless typically issue specific, for example, security or memorialization, and as such, their activist influence, temporary. The Port Authority, Mayor Bloomberg, and Larry Silverstein, in contrast, held commanding positions of power *throughout* the many years of rebuilding, the driving ambitions of their agendas exerting continuous influence over time.

Time played a hidden dimension in shaping the story of rebuilding Ground Zero, constantly reconfiguring the constellation of political power among the chief elected officials with a voice at Ground Zero and repositioning the influence of the direct stakeholders on the site. By the end of 2006, the mayor of New York City had gained some leverage in decision-making relative to the state's commanding influence during the first five years, and once the contentious issues surrounding the 9/11 Memorial were settled, the power of the activist families dissipated because they had little legitimacy when the issues of rebuilding shifted to the commercial arrangements between the Port Authority and Larry Silverstein. Still, as much as time diminished the intense political sensitivity to memorialization, it did not change the rhetoric of rebuilding because rhetoric framed the symbolic politics of what was at stake in rebuilding the Trade Center site.

The sweep of the rebuilding story traces a political path toward reconciling the many clashing interests with the emotional and economic realities of a post-9/11 environment. It is an arc with many tangents. The challenges of these tangents continually reshaped the storyline of rebuilding, adding to its complexity and fueling conflict. They reordered the conceptual vision of the master plan and winning memorial vision into what we see today on these sixteen acres. They added continual demands to the public sector for heavy subsidies to realize the ambitions of rebuilding Ground Zero.

This all played out within the context of the city's contemporary economic condition and Michael Bloomberg's ascension to City Hall shortly after 9/11. Context in all its forms—political, economic, historic, and institutional—shaped the decision-making at Ground Zero. It was a new era. Historic themes of the city's physical development would be ever present in the high-stakes debate about rebuilding Ground Zero, about what would replace the twin towers in the wake of their violent destruction and catastrophic loss of life. Ultimately, though, rebuilding involved an argument about urban political economy, about money and the power to control resources that could shape the city's trajectory. It scripted a story of how public and private decision-making actors harnessed the ambition that drives city officials and residents to constantly reinvent New York City's future.

The process of rebuilding the Trade Center site and how it turned out reflects uniquely on a New York way of doing development. The city's hard-charging, competitive culture foretold of contentious debate. It is a place of many voices, and not a place where consensus emerges easily, if at all. Although the city pioneered many planning innovations beginning with the nation's first citywide zoning ordinance in 1916, it is not a place of perfect city planning. It is a place where strong interests vie to shape the agenda of development through whatever means possible, abetted by being at the center of gravity of the nation's media industry. It is a place where power politics and unruly compromise ultimately produce results but only after much Strum und Drang. Messy and drawn out as the process can be, ultimately, the city, its business community, its civic groups, and its residents accommodate themselves to the results and build on them, moving forward in self-propelled fashion. Under normal conditions, the city's fractious development politics turn large-scale development projects into targets of opposition; in the aftermath of 9/11, hope was the only basis for thinking that an exception might hold sway under the extraordinary emotional conditions of revisioning the Trade Center site. Once the initial optimism that had inspired strong civic support hit the hard wall of reality and decisions had to be made about what to rebuild and how to remember, however, city politics reverted to form, which is to say, boisterous, contentious debate.

The story within this book is not about heroes and villains, rather about people and personalities with ambitions big and small, all wanting to put their mark on Ground Zero. It is about their clashes, egos, conflicts, and resolutions. It explains why, when the consensus to reassert the city's global position was so clear and strong, it was so hard to implement the ambitious vision of rebuilding focused on that goal. It tells the story of what it took to rebuild the sixteen acres at Ground Zero, from its ambitious plan through its tortuous execution and celebrated openings— who won and who lost in a relative sense—and in so doing the story offers readers a window on the issues that plague large-scale redevelopment projects—a window on the power and politics of money in American cities.

CHAPTER 2

Clashing Private Ambitions

FIGURE 2.1 Davies © 2002 The Journal News. Dist. by Universal UCLICK. Reprinted with permission. All rights reserved

WITHIN TWO DAYS OF THE ATTACK, his voice filled with emotion, Larry Silverstein vowed he would rebuild. The messaging set in place so soon after 9/11 framed his public position for years to come, even when his actions deviated from the lofty sentiments of that early script. Rebuilding in the same place would be the best memorial, he asserted. "It would be a tragedy of tragedies not to rebuild this part of New York. It would give the terrorists the victory they seek." He had a moral obligation, he said, to rebuild. "The city is not dead and cannot be allowed to die. We owe it to our children and grandchildren." That moral obligation morphed quickly into an "obligation" as well as a "right" to rebuild, which took on greater emphasis throughout the years of debate and contention. An "appropriate" memorial to honor the thousands who perished on 9/11 should be erected at Ground Zero, and "not be a footnote to a large development project," he said weeks later in a letter to the editor of the *Times*. "At the same time," he added, "it is imperative for our city, state and country that rebuilding go forward."[1] In these early days post 9/11, as he moved quickly to affirm his investor group's rights under their $3.2-billion lease with the Port Authority, it was not clear where such a memorial would fit into his aggressive plans for rebuilding the Trade Center site (figure 2.1).

His intention to build ten million square feet of office space, nearly all that was destroyed in the catastrophic attack, however, was quite clear. "We have an obligation to replace this," Silverstein said. "I don't believe that lower Manhattan can function as dynamically as it did without replacing" what was lost. He had "no doubt" that he would have the "cooperation of the port, the insurance carriers and the political leaders." The risks to the city's economic foundation from corporations fleeing to the suburbs and across the Hudson River was reason enough for Governor Pataki to support Silverstein's position for a full rebuild of the lost commercial space. Still, it was anything but clear how control over rebuilding decisions yet to be made would be shared with the bi-state Port Authority, as owner of the land; GMAC Commercial Mortgage, as lender of more than 90 percent of the funds he had needed to acquire the World Trade Center lease; government officials, as elected representatives of the people; and the families of the victims with their unassailable emotional claim on the still-smoldering site. Silverstein said his agreement with the Port Authority gave him control of the land for the next ninety-nine years, "meaning," as the *Daily News* reported, "he can rebuild if he wants to." But his assertion—"[w]e do have the right. That's what we negotiated for," quickly amended to we have the "right and obligation" to rebuild—was not about to go uncontested.[2] Before September had run its due course, the *Wall Street Journal* reported that the Port Authority Board of Commissioners had asked legal staff for an opinion on the complicated issue of who had the legal power to determine what was to be built on the site of the destroyed World Trade Center.

In the months immediately following the attack, no element of what anyone might envision as part of a plan for rebuilding was a foregone conclusion. Not only was there no clear process for how planning was to proceed, but it was already quite evident that rebuilding Ground Zero was going to be a monumental challenge fraught with complexity at every level: design, emotion, security, governance, control. In those intense early months, it was easy to see how the commercial claims made by Silverstein could seem too prosaic to fit within the more compelling public discourse about rebuilding with vision and memorializing with eternal meaning the thousands of lives lost. "Vision" was code for moving beyond the ordinary, beyond the business-as-usual approach to real estate development in the high-density, high-priced terrain of Manhattan. In this emotionally fluid context, the all-important complication of the leaseholder's right was nonetheless shaping up to be the all-powerful determinant of rebuilding—Silverstein's resolve to replace the ten million square feet of office space soon became a "given." Government officials ultimately could not get beyond the very real practical considerations of costly litigation and interminable delay that would come with a decision to regain full legal control over the sixteen-acre site, either through a condemnation action or negotiated buyout of Silverstein's position, though the PA board considered it at least twice.

The legal rights of property are dry, most understandable to real estate lawyers but opaque to most others. The language of law does not resonate emotionally and it does not communicate visually the way architecture did during the discourse of rebuilding in 2002 and 2003. In a most powerful way, though, it did not need to compete with those other elemental forces at Ground Zero because property rights held a position superior in law. Silverstein's rights were contractual, enforceable in the court of law, if need be. As an alternative force, moral authority to do the "right thing" for the greater civic good was unlikely to supplant the power of money interests in rebuilding on such valuable real estate terrain as at Ground Zero. On the other hand, the accommodation to moral authority would amend these property rights, in time. Before the test of his ability to rebuild all that he aspired to build came in 2006, however, Silverstein would persistently press forward in exercising the contractual rights that came with the real estate prize he had for decades sought to acquire from the Port Authority.

CAPTURING THE "PRIZE OF ALL PRIZES"

Acquiring the twin towers in July 2001 had been Silverstein's "dream come true," the crowning achievement of his forty-plus-year career as a successful and wealthy New York real estate investor known for his unrelenting negotiating style. Ever since completing the construction of 7 World Trade Center in 1987 on a superblock parcel immediately north of the World Trade Center (see bottom panel of figure 1.4), Silverstein had yearned to acquire the twin towers. "I remember looking up at the towers one day and thinking, that makes my building look like a peanut," he said. During the bidding process for the complex in January 2001, the day before bids were due, the wiry, silver-haired developer told the *New York Post*, "We're lusting for the World Trade Center, the prize of all prizes." Recovering from a broken pelvis, he was working on his bid's final details with business partners and advisors from his hospital bed at New York University Medical Center, where he had been admitted under a pseudonym so as not to cause rumors that might unsettle the bidding dynamics. "We had to play it very gingerly," said Silverstein's attorney for the negotiations and long time personal friend, Leonard Boxer, one of the city's most prominent real estate attorneys and chairman of Stroock & Stroock & Lavan's real estate practice. "We were so close to the finish line, and we didn't want people to know our quarterback was injured."[3] He had been hit by a drunk driver in a Ford sedan while crossing East Fifty-seventh Street on his way home after dinner at a midtown restaurant just five days before the deadline for submitting bids to the Port Authority, but injury from the hit-and-run accident did nothing to dim his ambition and determination to succeed. In an oft-repeated story, he asked the doctors to dial down the morphine so he was clear-headed.

Reviewing the numbers, Silverstein still did not think the prize was worth as much as did Vornado Realty Trust, a $6.8 billion New York–based public company, which won with a bid of $3.25 billion, superior to Silverstein's initial bid by approximately $600 million. When given a chance to rebid, as discussed later, Silverstein raised his bid to $3.22 billion, as did Boston Properties, another public company, which upped its bid to $3 billion; both fell short: The decimal-point difference involved hundreds of millions. Having lost, Silverstein nevertheless kept his team in place and waited quietly to see if Vornado's CEO Steven Roth and the Port Authority could reach agreement on final terms.

Understanding the magnitude of risk in a major real estate investment like the World Trade Center acquisition involves a detailed dive into every aspect of the proposed transaction. As the Vornado deal team got deeper into its diligence process a significant accounting issue surfaced: Because accounting standards consider a lease with a life that exceeds 75 percent or greater of the useful life of the asset akin to ownership of the asset, the real estate investment trust was going to have to carry the ninety-nine-year lease on its balance sheet, which would have impacted the firm's financial statements. To avoid the more burdensome accounting treatment, Vornado insisted upon changing the deal to a thirty-nine-year lease with six renewal options, which would have enabled the firm to treat the rental payments as an operating expense, which does not show up on a firm's balance sheet. Although the company's deal people did not see this as a problem and some staff at the Port Authority did not see it as an issue, the retrade became the Achilles heel of Vornado's bid. Other staff raised the question: Would the revised structure make it easier for Vornado not to renew at year forty? During the renegotiation, additional issues arose, and the deal became controversial for the Port Authority, whose board had been instructed by their governors to transact a ninety-nine-year lease. The parties were close to full agreement on the documents; about twelve points remained unresolved, according to a couple of insiders. A nonrefundable deposit of $100 million was due at the end of the exclusive twenty-day negotiating period even if the documents were not 100 percent complete. This would be money at risk, what the real estate industry calls "going hard."

The Port Authority had set up a timetable for the negotiations with its winning bidder, so Vornado faced a fish-or-cut-bait deadline. The company wanted more time to resolve the outstanding issues; the PA board gave the company an additional five days, but the agency refused to keep extending the timeline. Roth sent in a $100 million check after the five-day extension, during which long and hard negotiations resolved a lot of items, including the term of the lease, but ultimately, some of the things in the markup document were unacceptable to the Port Authority. Roth had a reputation for "bare-knuckled negotiations," and the retrading did not sit well with the agency's lawyers, who used a lengthy internal memo prepared by staff lawyers to push their position with the Port Authority Board of Commissioners, according to a well-informed insider to the transaction. The four commissioners on the subcommittee responsible for overseeing the sale—Peter S. Kalikow (NY), William J. Martini (NJ), Michael J. Chasanoff (NY), and Kathleen A. Donovan (NJ)—decided it was over and time to move on to the runner-up bidder. The board chairman told staff to start negotiations with Silverstein and his partner for the retail portion of the complex, Westfield America Inc., a publicly traded company listed on the New York Stock Exchange. However reluctant the agency might have been to move to the second-place bidder, it did not want to risk failing to execute on this high-profile privatization important to the governors of both states.

More than a month later after nerve-racking negotiations, on April 26, the Port Authority and Silverstein and Westfield finally signed contracts to acquire the ninety-nine-year leasehold for $3.211 billion. The date, close to the Port Authority's eightieth birthday, carried a touch of "historical elegance," said the agency's executive director, Neil D. Levin. Until the very last minute, it was a deal on the brink of collapse, anything but certain it could be completed. For much of the exclusive negotiating period (pre-set at twenty days plus five, the same as had been given to Vornado, but stretched to thirty-seven days), during which Silverstein's team and Port Authority staff worked through documents originating from the Vornado negotiations (which Silverstein was told gave him a "leg up" on getting the deal done), it had been touch and go. At the very end, Silverstein was still scrambling to resolve last-minute financing issues. He did not have all his equity in place for the deal; also, the agencies rating the debt securities that Silverstein's mortgage lender planned to sell raised technical issues that threatened higher costs.[4] When he asked for an additional extension, the Port Authority said "no." True to his reputation, at the last minute Silverstein sought to reopen several deal issues, including a reduction in his $800 million down payment, a concession the authority agreed to in exchange for higher yearly lease payments.[5]

Impatient and anxious that a second deal might crater at a time when the real estate market had passed its peak (which would have jeopardized the agency's ability to get top dollar for the complex from the third-place bidder), Port Authority staff on the day before the agency's annual meeting leaked to *Wall Street Journal* reporter Peter Grant that "[i]f there is no signed agreement by tomorrow, then we would expect the Board of Commissioners would instruct staff to terminate negotiations." The action would be taken, the Port Authority executive said, "as a result of Silverstein's inability to complete financing within the parameters of its proposal within the agreed upon time frame." When the leak hit the news wires, Silverstein lost no time putting in a telephone call to the Port Authority. At that next afternoon meeting, while the board of commissioners listened to other staff presentations for nearly an hour, Silverstein and his lead equity partner in the transaction, New York real estate scion Lloyd Goldman, age forty-three, head of the family-based real estate firm BLDG Management, were positioned in the agency's "war room" with Port Authority attorney Darrell Buchbinder. Tense negotiations the night before had failed to resolve all of the lease issues, and they were now all working to get last-minute closure on the deal. Just as Levin was about to pull the deal, the call came through from Buchbinder that the deal document was signed. "We got there at the 11th hour and 59th minute," said forty-two-year-old Peter S. Lowy, head of the large U.S. unit of the $6.8-billion Australia-based mall giant Westfield, whose branded shopping centers were known as Westfield Shoppingtowns. The acquisition was an "odyssey" involving months and months of work, Silverstein later told the celebrated nighttime TV host Charlie Rose.[6]

Following his patterned practice of using other people's money, the sixty-nine-year-old developer had brought in a group of investors who supplied the bulk of the equity required for the transaction. On the appointed day for signing the agreement with the Port Authority, Goldman and his low-profile investor group, which included Joseph Cayre, a wealthy investor whose fortune had been made in the entertainment industry, "began to get cold feet" because of last-minute financing changes. A savvy and experienced professional born into the world of New York commercial real estate, Goldman leveraged the situation to better his group's deal with Silverstein, extracting a larger share of the management fees and resolving some outstanding control issues, concessions Silverstein was pressured to make in order to hold on to his long-coveted prize.[7]

Throughout the negotiations, many real estate executives and Port Authority officials remained skeptical of Silverstein's financial capacity to succeed in his bid for the twin towers. People were waiting in the background, said one insider. Initially, even Silverstein did not know where the required $125 million of equity capital would come from. His typical equity raise from family, friends, and colleagues in increments of about a $1 million could not possibly aggregate to what he needed to capture the World Trade Center leasehold. Lloyd Goldman, as Alex Frangos and Peter Grant of the *Wall Street Journal* later reported, was "an unusual pick because he insisted on being involved in major decisions," unlike most of the passive investors who had joined in Silverstein's other deals. Silverstein hadn't personally known Goldman but Boxer, a power broker in the real estate industry who acted as a counselor and matchmaker, did and knew Goldman wanted in on the deal and had the capacity to round up other investors on relatively short notice. "Lloyd was integral to our bid for the World Trade Center," Silverstein told the business weekly, *Crain's New York Business*. That short acknowledgment reflected the fact that Goldman's investor group had put up the bulk of the $100 million deposit Silverstein needed to deliver to the Port Authority by 1 P.M. (an hour prior to the board meeting) that deadline day, April 26, in order to "go hard" on the deal.[8]

Silverstein was structuring a heavily leveraged transaction. To finance the greater part of the total $616 million down payment required by the Port Authority, he turned to GMAC, the lending arm of General Motors Corporation, which provided a $563 million mortgage and, for specific future capital improvements, an additional $200 million mezzanine loan. To control the $3.2-billion deal, Silverstein himself reportedly put up a mere $14 million, perhaps even less since some of his share may have come through another partnership with outside investors. Whatever obstacles came into play, Silverstein persisted—he was the "Eveready battery," said Boxer—and on July 24, the developer accepted a giant set of symbolic keys from the governors of the two states in an outdoor ceremony at the World Trade Center and closed on the loan with GMAC[9] (figure 2.2). Some six weeks later, the seasoned veteran of many a real estate crisis was looking at massive piles of twisted steel and concrete, rubble full of pain and unthinkable emotional loss, including the loss of four employees of his privately held company. The problem he then faced was like no other he had ever confronted.[10]

In what can be considered an ironic footnote of retrospective interest in a landmark transaction, Silverstein's investment exposure to the 9/11 attack on the World Trade Center turned out to be a matter of timing, of when he closed on the transaction. To legally seal the deal, both teams of professionals had worked long hours to complete the transaction as soon as possible. After the PA Board of Commissioners approved the deal on April 26, the governors of New York and New Jersey had, by statute, ten business days from the actual receipt of the board

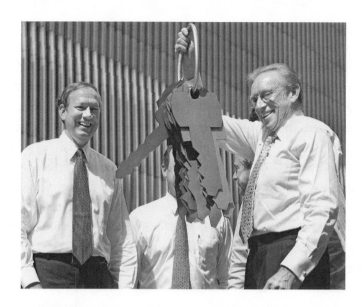

FIGURE 2.2 *On completion of the historic $3.2 billion transaction, Larry A. Silverstein proudly holds a giant set of keys to the World Trade Center, July 2001.* JEFF ZELEVANSKY/THE NEW YORK TIMES/REDUX

meeting minutes by the governors' offices during which they could exercise veto power and block any action of the Port Authority.[11] With that veto period past, Cherrie Nanninga, director of real estate at the Port Authority, signed the five separate "Agreements to Enter into Net Lease" documents (one for each of the four office towers and another for the retail complex); these contacts gave Silverstein ninety days plus one thirty-day extension during which to close the transaction. After two modifications to the closing schedule of the agreement, the last possible date for closing the transaction would be September 13, 2001.[12] They would close weeks before that final date because Silverstein wanted the assets, wanted the property transfer on record as soon as possible. There was a lot going on, Boxer told me: Mayor Giuliani was threatening a lawsuit over payment of property taxes to the city and the all-important GMAC bond offering was being prepared, among other issues. For the landmark transaction of his career, Silverstein and his firm's chief financial officer signed the agreement to lease dated as of July 16, 2001, and with the official closing on July 24, he took control of the complex that "identifies New York."[13]

During the bidding process Silverstein proved indefatigable. Time and time again, this characteristic personal and professional trait would define his quest to rebuild. He was "a dark horse bidder," wrote Andrew Rice in the *New York Observer*, even after he teamed up with Westfield America in an auction involving far bigger and more deeply experienced development firms, all highly capitalized and professionally run companies traded on the New York Stock Exchange. Silverstein ran a small family business whose capacity could not begin to match that of the other bidders, all of whom would have been on the short list of candidates for any of the nation's largest public-private development projects. But Silverstein had worked with the Port Authority before. He had built 7 World Trade Center on surplus land owned by the agency. And when the World Trade Center was bombed in February 1993, he immediately offered free space in his building to Port Authority staff. Friendly relations are what qualified him to bid, an insider told me.

After the Port Authority opened talks with Silverstein on March 21, veteran *Times* reporter Charles V. Bagli wrote, "some officials questioned whether his group had a large enough operation to run the Trade Center properly."[14] He wasn't a major player in the world of Manhattan real estate. As one inside source recalled, in the last day of intense negotiation before the deal would be presented to the board, when staff asked for the backup financial assumptions on his income projections to evaluate whether he could make the scheduled lease payments, they waited and waited until finally, with time fast closing in, they called Silverstein's office. The response—"We're waiting for the fax machine to warm up"—amazed them as it became all too apparent that not running the fax machine all the time was part of the home-grown character of the company's operations!

Silverstein, however, had a well-defined understanding of downtown and its market dynamics. He had entered the high-stakes investment arena of commercial real estate in 1980, with the purchase of his first big trophy building: 120 Broadway in the heart of the downtown financial district. Built as the headquarters of the Equitable Life Insurance Company in 1916, 120 Broadway at the time had a distinctive pedigree beyond being the largest office building in the world in total floor area—1.2 million square feet of office space built on less than an acre of land. Its outsized density and building design brought to the edge of the lot line without any setbacks cast shadows on the surrounding streets, roused tremendous controversy, and contributed to the adoption of the landmark 1916 New York City Zoning Resolution, the first citywide zoning resolution in the nation. Called "the old Equitable filing cabinets that had been the focus of real estate dreams in Manhattan," the downtown trophy now belonged to Silverstein, who set out to renew its original elegance.[15] That year he also brought 120 Wall Street, another notable downtown skyscraper.

Silverstein started buying older buildings and refurbishing them some two decades earlier. With his then partner and brother-in-law, Bernard Mendik, in 1957 they closed on their first investment property, a thirteen-story loft building on East Twenty-third Street. Acquiring investment property represented his second-level step into the world of commercial real estate, he having started out as a broker in his father's small leasing business in the loft district in lower Manhattan known today as SoHo. When asked by an interviewer for the *Real Deal* what he learned from his father, he revealed how brokerage shaped his career: "The rentals at that time were maybe 40 cents a foot, 50 cents a foot, 60 cents a square foot. It was all secondary, tertiary real estate. [It was] a difficult existence, but it showed me the value of a dollar. It showed me the art of negotiating." Buying and selling properties and trading up with successive transactions, he was old school real estate. His next step up the ladder of New York commercial real estate was ground-up development, and in that same year, 1980, he outbid others for the remaining site acquired by the PA in its development of the adjacent World Trade Center, on which stood only a small ConEdison substation. When his firm completed the forty-seven-story, 1.8-million-square-foot tower, 7 WTC, Manhattan's largest speculative office project of that decade, he "made his biggest imprint on the skyline in late 1986," the *Times* reported.[16]

Larry Silverstein is a New York story. Brooklyn-born, the broker-turned-investor-turned-developer spent his childhood years in Bedford Stuyvesant before his family moved to Washington Heights in Manhattan. He started his career in business with little more than his education as a 1952 graduate of New York University and later its law school, fierce determination, unshakable optimism, and long days of hard work, all of which he leveraged with other people's money to build an investment portfolio of hotels, apartment buildings, and office towers. By the mid-1980s, with the run-up in real estate values in Manhattan, he had amassed a sizable fortune, enough to have commissioned his first yacht, the 131-foot *Silver Shalis* (named after his daughters, Sharon and Lisa; he also has a son, Roger. All are in the family real estate business). By 1990, he controlled more than ten million square feet of space. The development exuberance of the 1980s, however, exacted a financial toll, and Silverstein's "empire shrank as he wrestled with high debt and falling rents that bedeviled other real estate giants like Donald Trump and Olympia & York's Paul Reichmann." Though "a bruised combatant in the Manhattan real estate slump" forced to relinquish properties to his creditors, Silverstein emerged a survivor.[17]

He fought hard to keep his buildings out of default, not wanting to lose them to his creditors, and his success in holding on to 7 World Trade Center during a period of severe market distress, in retrospect, enabled him to bid on the World Trade Center complex in 2001. When he began construction of the $300 million tower in 1984 without an anchor tenant and without permanent financing in place, it was a daring gamble, but a necessary gamble. "If I didn't break ground before July 1, I would have lost the lease," Silverstein told the *Wall Street Journal* at the time. "Sure, there are risks," he said. "But if you reach for the brass ring and grab it, the upside is enormous."[18] For the longest time, though, the economics of the project and any possible upside belonged to his lenders. Silverstein had expected to find a large tenant before the building, the largest speculative project in New York at the time, was complete, and by the end of 1985, after nearly a year of negotiations, he had finally landed the big deal with the investment banking firm Drexel Burnham Lambert, Inc., for occupancy of the entire tower for thirty years. The deal was signed in June 1986, but by the end of the year, Drexel had pulled out of the $3-billion deal, rocked by the Ivan Boesky insider-trading scandal (changes in federal tax law also unfavorably altered the economics and further eroded the logic of the deal).

Once again, the developer faced the problem of leasing a large empty building. This time, however, Silverstein's saving grace was a new lending relationship with Teachers Insurance and Annuity Association (TIAA). In 1987, Teachers made a commitment to provide Silverstein with a $385 million long-term mortgage on the completed tower, and in 1989, after Solomon Brothers had signed a lease for more than 50 percent of the building, it increased the financing by $50 million and the following year by another $55 million, thereby enabling the developer to carry the building and handle the high costs of leasing the space at a time when demand for office space was low and vacancies ever increasing. The $490 million financing was a strong and steady lifeboat, especially in light of the fact that at this time few lenders would put more than $100 million of their own funds in any one deal. Without that kind of financial support from a major institutional lender, Silverstein likely would have lost 7 World Trade, and if he lost 7 World Trade, would he have had a chance to bid for the World Trade Center brass ring in 2001?

Though "staggered by the real estate recession," by 1997 he was planning his comeback with what was then a $100 million project for the entire block between Eleventh Avenue and the West Side Highway between Forty-first and Forty-second Streets he had purchased for $20 million in 1984; Silver Towers, twin sixty-story luxury residential buildings containing 1,359 rental units was finally completed twenty-five years later in 2009 in the midst of a deep real estate slump, at a cost of approximately $600 million after many twists and turns along the way.[19] Over his fifty years in the business, Silverstein had seen enough real estate cycles to hold a firm conviction that New York always recovers from disaster, in time. From that perspective, it was prudent not to drop rental rates in an impatient response to fill vacant office space, and following that logic, he was not one to make big concessions in order to rent out his buildings on terms other than his own.

As a businessman, Silverstein walked into a deal with the reputation as a tough and tenacious negotiator fearful of leaving a dollar on the table, especially if that dollar was his. He took risks, but cared not to risk his own money; following a well-worn path of many developers, he formed project-based partnerships with other investors who supplied much if not all of the equity for his investments, as was the case for the World Trade Center. "He's one of the real gamblers in this business," said Steven Spinola, then president of the Real Estate Board of New York. "He's not afraid to take a chance. He'd never want to feel he didn't accomplish something or that he'd lost." He was a good but not distinguished builder, as were his competitors in the tight world of New York real estate—Mortimer Zuckerman of Boston Properties, Jerry Speyer of Tishman Speyer, John Zuccotti of Brookfield Properties, Richard LeFrak of the LeFrak Organization, to name a few. He was not like one of his well-known partners, William Zeckendorf Jr., son of legendary "Big" Bill, a man of big visions. The senior Zeckendorf assembled seventy-five parcels formerly housing smelly slaughterhouses on the East Side of Manhattan where the United Nations rose in 1947, and he built large-scale urban renewal projects in many cities (Century City in Los Angeles, Mile High Center in Denver, and Place Ville Marie in Montreal, among others) before his development company, Webb & Knapp, went bankrupt in 1965. Zeckendorf Jr. was more conservative than his father, but equally intense about building projects and of being in the game, although less focused than Silverstein on making the last dollar. "The idea of building and creating was more important to him than earning a lot of money from these buildings," Herbert Sturz, a former chairman of the New York City Planning Commission, told the *Wall Street Journal* during the bidding for the World Trade Center.[20]

Like others in the real estate industry, Silverstein became a philanthropist and a contributor to political campaigns. He served as a governor of the industry's powerful lobbying organization, the Real Estate Board of New York (REBNY), and as its chairman from 1983 to 1985, and as a trustee of his alma mater, New York University. He inherited his father's classical musical interests, plays the piano, and is a patron of the New York Philharmonic. Believing that real estate should be taught on a professional level, along with others he provided seed money and fundraising energy to help establish the NYU Real Estate Institute in 1967. Yet for all his wealth and his accomplishments, he was not a part of the real estate power elite that was rapidly reshaping the world of Manhattan real estate.

Then he captured the brass ring of the World Trade Center complex. He would steadfastly hold on to his prize through continued controversy and conflict, harsh personal criticism, and persistent questions about his financial capacity to carry through with his pledge to rebuild all that had been destroyed. "I simply decided to dedicate the next five years of my life to this," he said a few weeks after 9/11. "Given good health and cooperation from federal and city government, the governors of

New Jersey, New York, the Port Authority, we're going to rebuild this thing."[21] Throughout the rebuilding process, Silverstein would maintain a laser focus on the bottom line. The Trade Center deal was a business transaction, and that elemental characteristic would remain dominant throughout the debate about how to rebuild and whether his ambitious plans for the Trade Center complex would prevail. Whereas his experience with the Port Authority in building 7 World Trade had given him a taste of the bureaucracy, it was his decades of commercial real estate investing in New York, widely known as a contact sport, that armed him with the necessary mettle to manage the complex play of property rights issues surrounding the rebuilding of Ground Zero.

UNLOCKING AN AGGRESSIVE AGENDA

Silverstein had both short-term and long-term plans for capturing the complex's hidden economic value. Rents currently in place in the twin towers were substantially below average, about $33 a square foot in a submarket where asking rents for class A vacant space in the second quarter of 2001 were running $48 a square foot. This was a big spread with a lot of upside potential profit in releasing especially large blocks of space leased to investment-grade tenants such as Morgan Stanley (the towers' largest tenant, whose lease for 1.2 million square feet was due to expire in 2006), Empire Blue Cross, and Deutsche Bank. "Even without the rent hikes, Silverstein and his partners stand to make money right away," remarked Matt Sharp, associate director at Standard & Poor's, who evaluated Silverstein's economics on the twin towers for GMAC's sale of bonds backed by its mortgage.[22]

For years, the Port Authority had faced real problems in managing the complex to maximize value, as audit reports on the World Trade Center's occupancy and rentals going back in time as far as 1981 revealed.[23] As a private asset manager, Silverstein had the ability to cut the higher-than-average operating expenses, improve the efficiency of building operations, and produce bottom-line results; profits for the complex as a whole were pegged at nearly $40 million for 2001, based on Standard & Poor's analysis. Assuring the complex's competitive position was essential to producing those bottom-line results, and the Port Authority required Silverstein to invest at least $207 million of capital to improve fire alarm and other building systems, security systems, utility systems, common areas, and exterior public areas, as well as modernize elevators and escalators and rehabilitate building infrastructure. Moreover, in managing the transition of the office towers from a government-managed to privately managed asset, he had substantial flexibility because the lease agreement incorporated several measures to assure that decisions to streamline the property's operations could be made quickly, as the Fitch

Rating Report on the mortgage securitization emphasized. For example, he could retain or release PA employees during the property's transition to private operations.[24]

Westfield America had big plans, too. The five-acre Austin J. Tobin Plaza—an open space nearly twice as large as Piazza San Marco in Venice—presented a dollar-denominated vision of retail expansion for the mall giant, whose separate three-hundred-page lease with the Port Authority gave it rights to build on a part of the plaza (figure 2.3). Less than one month after closing on the deal, Westfield's ambitious plan for the outdoor place became public: 150,000 square feet of additional shopping space created by raising the plaza one level, opening up the concourse with a grand entrance to bring light into the underground areas, and making better connections with ramps and staircases to provide access to the new level. Below ground, the concourse was already filled with some seventy-five specialty stores, restaurants, and service suppliers that brought in more than $20 million in annual profits driven by the more than 150,000 people traveling though the Trade Center via five subways lines, PATH commuter trains, and several ferry lines, including the forty-two thousand workers in the World Trade Center towers who flowed through the space on a daily basis (figure 2.4). It ranked among the most profitable shopping malls in the United States with sales exceeding $900 a square foot, more than two and a half times the national average of $341 a square foot. Still, the capacity to produce even higher sales and profits awaited a strong private operator. "We really feel that the Port Authority went ahead and completely undervalued this property," Westfield's new head of leasing for the World Trade Center told the press just the day before the 9/11 attack.[25] To capture that value,

FIGURE 2.3 *The five-acre open plaza, officially called Austin J. Tobin Plaza, with* The Sphere, *a twenty-five-foot bronze sculpture by Fritz Koenig. Upon buying into the World Trade Center partnership with Larry Silverstein, Westfield America planned to create additional underground retail space in the World Trade Center mall by raising the plaza one level.* COURTESY THE VILLAGER

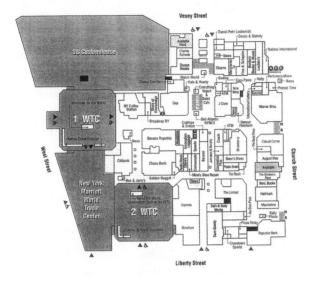

World Trade Center Mall
Concourse Level

FIGURE 2.4 *The maze of shops in the underground concourse level of the original World Trade Center.*

Westfield planned to fill the vacant mall space, raise rents when existing tenant leases came up for renewal, and replace middle-market retailers with higher-end stores.

Started in 1959 by Frank P. Lowy, who fled his home country of Czechoslovakia as a child to escape the Nazis, the highly successful Sydney-based company already owned an empire of thirty-nine shopping centers in the United States (plus managed the retail precincts at six airports) as a result of its ambitious expansion in the United States begun in 1977. Buying into the World Trade Center with Silverstein, who had brought the deal to the mall giant as a board member of Westfield America and a personal friend of Lowy, was the company's first foray into Manhattan. Westfield had been interested in the retail center since 1998, when the Port Authority announced it was planning to privatize the complex, and its successful joint-venture bid represented a marketing and money-making triumph for the global mall owner and operator—"incredible that an Australian company can own and manage one of the world's premier retail buildings," said Lowy's son, Peter S. Lowy.[26]

Silverstein wasted no time promoting his real estate vision for rebuilding the Trade Center site: four fifty-story towers, each with 2.5 million square feet of office space, along with a memorial. The project would be "predominantly commercial space," his public relations expert Howard Rubenstein told the press, with "the possibility of a hotel with condominiums above it." "Silverstein's instant rebuilding plan came to be seen as a publicity grab more than a serious notion, and he soon realized that he had no power to set a timetable," architectural critic Paul Goldberger wrote in mid-2002 in the first of several reports on rebuilding in the *New Yorker*. On the other hand, the developer had "a clear mission to rebuild 7 World Trade Center quickly," and he planned to break ground in 2002. "7 is going to be up first," he told the luncheon audience attending a conference on financing real estate deals sponsored by New York University at the Waldorf Astoria on November 7. "The site for 7 is cleared. It's done. Probably this time next year there'll be steel coming out of the ground."[27] He considered it a layup.

Expressed with deep emotion, Silverstein's determination to start rebuilding as soon as possible nevertheless served "as a way for him to stake out his claim early in a shifting landscape of loss, economic uncertainty, competition and clashing political interests," a *Times* reporter noted with a seasoned dose of New York skepticism. The pile was still burning. Rescue workers were still searching for bodies. People all over the world were still trying to understand what had happened beyond the obvious destruction, but Silverstein was mobilizing on all fronts, moving quickly, making plans, hiring architects, lobbying in D.C. for federal guarantees for construction loans and for protection from liability lawsuits brought by the victims or their families for structural weaknesses or management gaps at the World Trade Center. With his lawyers and PR people, he was strategically framing rebuilding as an insurance issue. Almost immediately, he started voicing his opinion that the attacks of 9/11 by two planes that hit the towers each represented a separate attack, or "occurrence," entitling him to twice his $3.55 billion insurance coverage.[28] This was a controversial position. Some thought the claim was "credible." Others in the real estate and law communities rolled their eyes or chatted among themselves in disbelief. The claim was audacious. As one well-placed real estate executive responded when I asked how industry veterans viewed the claim, "It was generally viewed as Larry Silverstein at his best."

To rebuild ten million square feet of office space Silverstein needed time to marshal resources, whatever additional billions he could command through his two-occurrence insurance claim. GMAC, his mortgage lender, had insisted on the $3.55 billion of insurance coverage, more than twice the $1.5 billion of coverage the Port Authority had required believing that was as much as the developer could get. Agency staff feared that if they asked for more than $1.5 billion and any of the parties balked, they might be accused of torpedoing the deal. The $1.5 billion was six times more than the largest claim the agency ever had after 1993, a former

CFO told me; $1.5 billion was also the limit per occurrence on the PA's policy for all its facilities at the time the lease was being negotiated. Still, financial documents connected with a 2001 World Trade Center bond issue warned that the leaseholder's casualty insurance policy amounted to "significantly less" than the cost of rebuilding. "With six or seven billion in insurance company proceeds, we have the opportunity to do something spectacular there," Larry Silverstein said. "Spectacular," he reiterated in a Public Lives interview with Robin Finn of the *Times*.[29] Speaking the language of public-spirited development, this skilled veteran of many a tough New York real estate brawl was prepared to doggedly pursue whatever litigation was necessary to succeed in his bold insurance claim.

The battle over how much the insurers had to pay out for the destruction of the World Trade Center complex, discussed in chapter 12, was only one of many major obstacles standing in the way of his aggressive push to rebuild. Moving rapidly to rebuild was Silverstein's desire, but his pace and assumptions annoyed Mayor Bloomberg, LMDC officials, and community and civic groups who wanted to see a fully vetted master plan for the Trade Center site before the start of any rebuilding, including 7 World Trade.

There was not much emotion on the site of 7; it was not hallowed ground—no one perished in the destruction of that building. It was physically separate from the sixteen acres and less legally complicated than the developer's rights at Ground Zero. Silverstein assumed he could rebuild what had been on the site before: nearly two million square feet of office space. But New Yorkers, especially residents living in the neighborhoods surrounding 7, hated the old 7 because, as most architectural critics were quick to point out, the forty-seven-story tower "seemed less like a building than a gargantuan wall" stretched all the way across Greenwich Street, blocking sightlines and light and isolating the neighborhood of Tribeca physically and visually from lower Manhattan[30] (figure 2.5).

If Silverstein wanted to build a new tower substantially different from the original 7, no public review process was necessary; he only needed the Port Authority's approval as owner of the land. "While Mr. Silverstein promises a 'spectacular' building, his ultimate goal should be a building that fits into a spectacular new plan for downtown Manhattan," the *Times* editorial board said. "While it is crucial to rebuild lower Manhattan without the long bouts of civic paralysis that dog most ambitious construction initiatives in New York City," *Newsday* editorialized, "the developer still is moving too fast. He at least needs to wait until broader plans take shape for the whole WTC site."[31] Rebuilding 7 WTC quickly, though, was being driven by a compelling outside force: The ConEdison electric substation upon which the original 7 WTC had been constructed had to be rebuilt as soon as possible because it supplied nearly two-thirds of all transformers operating

FIGURE 2.5 *A composite rendering of the original 7 World Trade Center tower designed by Emery Roth & Sons in 1987. SOM created this southward "before" condition to demonstrate how the old 7 WTC blocked access between Tribeca and the Financial District and beyond. It was always paired with a composite "after" design for 7 WTC that demonstrated how reopening Greenwich Street would change the experience of this part of the city.* COURTESY SOM

downtown. It could not wait for the emergence of that big vision. It was an immediate priority.

The big issue in rebuilding 7 was Greenwich Street. The idea of reestablishing the city street grid over the World Trade Center superblock lodged early in the public's perception of what had to be done to rebuild the site as a better urban place; it was in the earliest planning principles documents put out by several civic groups, as well as the adjacent property owner of World Financial Center, Brookfield Properties. Reopening Greenwich Street, often considered the "main street" for the residential neighborhood of Tribeca, from where 7 once stood on

Vesey Street to Liberty Street would "reunite the Tribeca area north of the Trade Center site with the office district to its south and relieve the heavy, north-south truck and bus traffic that passed through the area." It would also establish a north-south view corridor as had been in place before the Port Authority created the two superblocks for the complex. "If we put the street grids back in," said Madelyn G. Wils, chair of Community Board 1 and board member on the LMDC and a leading early advocate for opening up Greenwich Street, "you make it more like a cityscape at that point."[32]

"The elimination of Greenwich Street to make way for the World Trade Center represents what was wrong with an entire generation's work of architecture and planning." With these words, Paul Goldberger recited the mantra of a mistake few thought would ever be remedied. That superblock on which 7 had been built "destroyed every street, every relationship" to the rest of downtown, remarked the architect David M. Childs.[33] Partner and lead designer at Skidmore, Owings & Merrill (SOM), the influential architectural firm founded in 1936 by Louis Skidmore, Nathaniel Owings, and John O. Merrill, hired by Silverstein to design a new 7, Childs, age sixty-one, was in a position to influence the developer on Greenwich Street. He was passionate about restoring the historical street pattern by reconnecting streets with old New York names—Cortlandt, Fulton, and Dey—to the Trade Center site and its surrounding neighborhoods. It might even be possible to get back those river-to-river views you expect in New York, he thought. Because Greenwich Street was the historic western water edge of lower Manhattan, if it once again extended all the way down to the Battery, the street would echo the "grid of nature" (figure 2.6). And if successful in reinstating Greenwich Street on this parcel, the action would create the power of precedent to carry it through the whole Trade Center site.

This goal was not as easy to accomplish as the long-reigning planning logic suggested. Two stubby offcuts of the street were in the way: a short one running south of Liberty Street for a few blocks to Battery Place, and a second longer section just north of the World Trade Center that ran uptown to Gansevoort Street in the West Village. What exactly stood in the way? First, legal issues related to property title and second, overcoming bureaucratic hurdles in the many departments of city government that would have to weigh in on the change but did not consider the necessary land transfers involved in reconnecting Greenwich Street to its stubs a priority. It would take time and some well-placed behind-the-scenes phone calls to the office of Deputy Mayor Doctoroff. Just as critical, ConEdison would have to be persuaded that its replacement power substation could be accommodated on the smaller footprint resulting from the reinsertion of Greenwich Street. All of these parties—Silverstein Properties, ConEdison, Verizon (which had underground

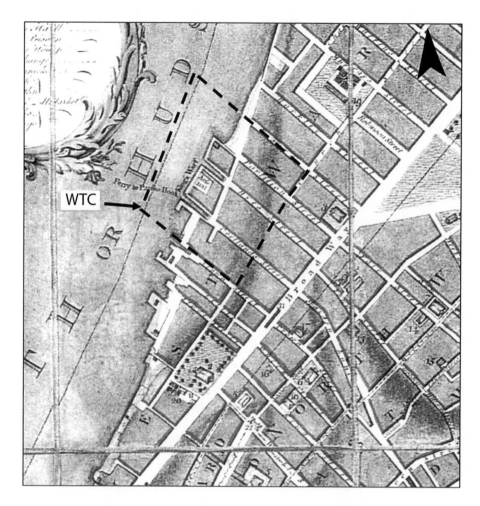

FIGURE 2.6 *Historical perspective of Greenwich Street as the western water line of lower Manhattan, 1767, superimposed with an outline of the World Trade Center site.* THE RATZEN PLAN 1776/HISTORICAL PERSPECITVES, INC./FINAL ENVIRONMENTAL IMPACT STATEMENT WORLD TRADE CENTER MEMORIAL AND REDEVELOPMENT PLAN

rights for its equipment in the bed of Vesey Street), and the city's Law Department and City Planning Department—would have to agree on the action, a not so common cooperative coming together. And for the land transfers (from the city to the Port Authority) to happen most expeditiously, a workaround needed to be found to transfer the land parcels involved without going through the city's regulatory Uniform Land Use and Review Process (ULURP), which would surely lengthen the process and open up every imaginable issue related to the site (and some not).

The credit for managing these bureaucratic hurdles goes to Alexander Garvin, director of planning, design, and development at the LMDC. A practicing city planner who taught at Yale University and had served as a member of the New

York City Planning Commission from 1970 to 1980, Garvin was two weeks on the job when he decided to visit Silverstein to talk about 7 World Trade and "get Greenwich back." He had never met the developer before, and he didn't have the power to say what he said—that the LMDC would not likely approve the design then being considered unless the building was reshaped to allow Greenwich Street to run through the 7 site to Vesey Street—but he said it anyway out of passion and conviction. Childs was at the meeting and when the architect pulled out a drawing of the rebuilt tower that exists on the site now, Garvin asked, why couldn't we do this? Childs responded, because we need twenty-three feet from Vesey Street (to assure the realignment of the streets). Childs and Garvin had studied architecture together at Yale, both graduating in 1967, and though their careers had gone in different directions, they took it upon themselves to get Greenwich Street back. "Planning in the city is not as simple as a set of urban-design principles," Garvin later told Goldberger. "Electric power in lower Manhattan is more important than a view corridor. But why can't we have both? If you push hard enough, you can find a way."[34] Garvin was determined to do that pushing.

The first drawings Childs had produced for the new 7 "called for a wide glass tower cantilevered over a narrower stainless-steel base," lighter in its footprint than the earlier massive stone building. But Childs began to change his mind about the cantilever design; "he didn't like the way the bulk of the tower projected outward, and how from a block or two uptown it would still seem to sit in the middle of the street, obstructing the view down Greenwich Street, just as the old No. 7 had," Goldberger wrote. "The more Childs thought about it, the less sure he became that simply opening up the bottom of the building solved the problem." Also, he was "uneasy about the effect that giving in to Silverstein's demands would have on his reputation." With a new slimmer design, he pushed Silverstein to see it his way, even though seeing things the way Childs envisioned meant accepting a downsized building by some 300,000 square feet, a not inconsiderable amount of valuable rental space. "I said, 'Larry, this building is your audition for the rest of the project,'" the diplomatic corporate architect told a *Crain's* reporter years later.[35] Behind the scenes then, Silverstein was being pushed to do things he would otherwise not have done.

Childs is a smooth, genial professional who enjoys the fray of large-scale, complex, city-building projects. After thirteen years in the Chicago home office of SOM, in 1984 he moved to New York City to rebuild the reputation and portfolio of the firm, which had lost some of the luster that had established its name as the nation's premier commercial design firm. As a designer, Childs eschewed a "signature" look. Raised as a Quaker, he was not interested in buildings as "egotistic big statements," he said. The six-foot-four-inch civic-minded design partner named the firm's first chairman in 1991 cut a different profile from the big-name architects who were increasingly taking front-and-center stage in cities around the globe. Called "the invisible architect" in a *Times* profile, Childs explained to architecture reporter Julie V. Iovine that he was most excited about making the fabric of a city—the pattern of streets and avenues that thread their way through places, the vistas created and neighborhoods defined by spatial arrangements. He was a savvy and pragmatic architect who understood how to work with commercial real estate developers, building trust and rapport. In Manhattan, his credits included Worldwide Plaza, Times Square Tower, Bear Stearns Headquarters, and Time Warner Center. "If his buildings sometimes tend to be over-polite, if not bland, that too is intentional," Iovine wrote.[36]

Silverstein had hired Childs to prepare plans for the renovation and improvement of the twin towers in August 2001, just two weeks after he closed on his historic acquisition, on the recommendation of his senior executive in charge of the World Trade Center redevelopment project, Geoffrey P. Wharton. Childs's career bridged the city's civic, government, and development communities, and this was just the type of professional commercial architect Silverstein needed to advise him on the World Trade Center. Then 9/11 happened. On September 12, he got a call from Silverstein saying, "Now I want you to rebuild these towers. You're going to be my Minoru Yamasaki." The whole complex that Childs "really disliked," as did so many New York architects, was reduced to a pile of rubble and the rebuilding task confronting Silverstein radically altered the assignment and Childs's approach: He would sign on with the rebuilding effort, he told Silverstein, if the developer agreed to three conditions: to reinsert the street grid to the extent possible; build so that the buildings came down to grade, down to the sidewalk like those around it; and hire multiple architects for the project. This last condition surprised Silverstein. But Childs believed it was essential "because that is the nature of New York and its scale"; architecture in New York is about building unique pieces on each block, building over time by multiple hands.[37]

Silverstein also retained Alexander Cooper of Cooper, Robertson & Partners to work on plans for the Trade Center site. Cooper was someone who "probably did as much as anyone to shift taste in the direction of doing things like restoring Greenwich Street," according to Goldberger. "His loyalty to customary ways of designing cities runs deep.... [He] feels that restoring street life is the first priority for any design in lower Manhattan." Like Childs and Garvin, Cooper studied architecture at Yale, graduating earlier than the others, in 1962. He began public sector work early in his career, first as a member of the New York City Planning Commission, then as director of the pioneering Urban Design Group of the Department of City Planning established under the administration of Mayor John V. Lindsay, and then as director of design for the city's Department of Housing and Development Administration (now the Department of Buildings). He had crafted the urban design guidelines for Battery Park City and the Forty-second Street Development Project, and designed numerous buildings. Cooper's approach to urban design involved "hunting for precedents and using them to create general guidelines for future development—but not dictating all the details." When first applied to Battery Park City in the late 1970s, this "was completely radical," he said, but by the late 1990s, it had become "conventional...just good city planning."[38]

Cooper was also working for John E. Zuccotti, chairman of Brookfield Office Properties, the largest landlord in the financial district, and the Toronto-based firm was most concerned with enhancing transportation connectivity in lower Manhattan. Since Brookfield was his primary client, Cooper's plan for the Trade Center site reflected this emphasis. It included the idea that the broad ten-lane West Street should be depressed underground and a new station built in lower Manhattan for the Long Island Railroad. Cooper's plan placed a row of bulky towers along Greenwich Street on the eastern side of the site because Brookfield considered the entire footprint of the twin towers off limits for a new building. "There is a certain power to this as a setting for the memorial: a wall of buildings around a memorial," he told Goldberger. After a few weeks of work, "Cooper and Childs discovered they had different ideas about what parts of the Trade Center site could be built on, so the two firms ended up producing separate plans."[39]

Although it was perhaps the one element on which a public consensus had coalesced, reinserting Greenwich Street into the grid took some doing. Garvin and Childs first had to convince ConEdison that the generators it had ordered could fit within a newly configured space. The required twenty-three-foot strip of land had to be acquired by friendly condemnation from the city through the state's urban development corporation and then transferred to the Port Authority and then made part of the 7 site (figure 2.7). Overcoming a big regulatory hurdle like this takes a lot of time, but once public officials relented on their objection and Childs's slimmer design satisfied the community board and Silverstein got the word that his insurance company would not contest his $861 million claim, the way was cleared for construction. Known to take risks, Silverstein made the decision—against the advice of his real estate lawyer, Robin Panovka, a partner at Wachtell, Lipton, Rosen & Katz—to go forward with construction before gaining formal control of the strip under the belief that the city would get him the property strip (which it did after construction was underway). In June 2002, the developer broke ground on the reconfigured site for the project; to its east, the city had gained a new fifteen-thousand-square-foot triangular park, but as Dunlap noted, the view down Greenwich Street would turn out to be but a "visual sliver"[40] (figure 2.8). Still, it

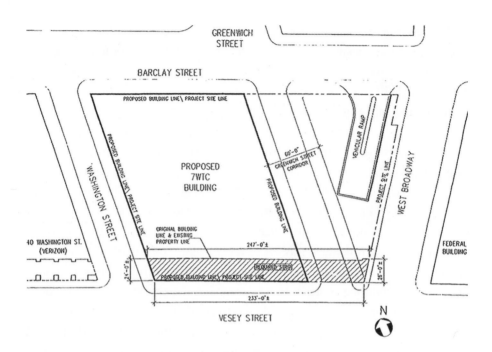

FIGURE 2.7 *Project site plan for 7 WTC with the twenty-three-foot strip needed for a smaller footprint.*
THE PORT AUTHORITY OF NEW YORK AND NEW JERSEY/LOWER MANHATTAN DEVELOPMENT CORPORATION

FIGURE 2.8 *The view down Greenwich Street after completion of the new 7 WTC. Though the view corridor was a "visual sliver," the reopening of Greenwich Street marked an important planning victory.* GARY HACK

was a planning win, a slightly narrower Greenwich Street between Barclay Street and Vesey Street being preferable to no Greenwich Street and no view corridor.

FALLING OUT OF ALIGNMENT

While Silverstein rejoiced with this physical marker of progress, all was not so well from Westfield's perspective. Tensions soon emerged from the partners' different business visions for the Trade Center site. The street-grid decision displeased the mall owner because it worked against the best interest of the company's tired-and-true retail concept. Reinserting Greenwich Street fragmented the retail space, making it disjointed and, from Westfield's perspective, less consumer friendly. And if it was less consumer friendly, it was less valuable as an investment. The seventy-two-year-old Frank Lowy had built his mall empire on the highly success-ful model of the suburban center; the design of this prototype—large, undivided pedestrian spaces without passing cars and trucks—was totally oriented to making it as easy as possible for consumers to spend money. The integrated nature of the stores, office space, and transportation at the World Trade Center was what drew Westfield into the transaction. When it came to rebuilding the retail center, Westfield assumed it would get "what we had before" the attack, Peter Lowy said, but when company officials later got their first look at Silverstein's tentative plans for the site as drawn up by Childs, they thought the design was "cut up like a birth-day cake." It put the site's street-level retail space on the eastern side in buildings separated by Fulton and Cortlandt Streets. As reported in the *Wall Street Journal*, Frank Lowy asked Childs to make new drawings without the streets. "Childs re-fused, saying his heart wasn't in it, and the idea wouldn't be politically feasible, according to a person at the meeting."[41]

After meeting with Zuccotti at Brookfield's offices, the Lowys resigned them-selves to Greenwich Street bisecting the entire site, but they continued to resist fully restoring the east-west Fulton, Cortlandt, and Dey Streets. Although the Port Authority was sympathetic to accommodating their views, the politics of the situ-ation ultimately convinced Westfield that the best solution would be for the com-pany to exit by selling back its interest to the Port Authority. The redevelopment process was likely to be lengthy and highly politicized. Even though Westfield le-gally controlled the rights to the surface areas of Tobin Plaza, from a corporate point of view, it would be hard to leverage this position in order to move forward with its expansion plan, and using its legal position to assert its rights was not something the company wanted to do. The decision to sell was a big decision for Westfield, a company executive told me. It was also symptomatic of the inherent conflict between Silverstein Properties as developer of the office towers and

Westfield America as the retail player and the Port Authority as the landowner. If an alignment of interests could not be found in the mission and ambition of redeveloping the commercial spaces at Ground Zero, ultimately, the landowner had the legal power to control planning for redevelopment.

Silverstein's alacrity about rebuilding every square foot of destroyed office space and his early aggressive moves in that direction put many on edge. In interviews only a couple of weeks after 9/11, the developer was telling news organizations of his plans, talking as if he was going to be making the decisions. Still obligated to make monthly rent payments of $10 million, he was promoting the argument that his ninety-nine-year, $3.2 billion lease agreement gave him "the right and the obligation" to redevelop the site. Public officials were saying, not so fast. First, nothing could be done on the site until the complex and costly job of clearing the rubble was complete; that would take anywhere from six months to a year. As to who would rebuild the Trade Center, the Port Authority chairman, business financier, and investor Lewis M. Eisenberg, went on record saying, "There will be a number of participants in that decision." When told of Silverstein's determination to rebuild, he added, "Different interests have different motivations," but declined to elaborate. "[The Port Authority] has to take the interests of the region and the public into account. In the end, we just don't know." This was just ten days after the attack. Two weeks later, the *Times* quoted a city official's words of caution: "It's still too early to talk about this in terms of real estate. Larry needs to be careful not to slide from civic pride to crass personal interests."[42]

Silverstein's "extraordinary combination of optimism and total shrewdness"—as Mary Ann Tighe, then vice chair of real estate brokerage firm Insignia/ESG, Inc., described her longtime friend—led some in government to see domination as his ultimate motive. Silverstein's plans for a 2002 rebuilding start were "a little optimistic," newly appointed chairman of the LMDC John C. Whitehead said at the end of November 2002. A year later Silverstein was still assuming he would be calling the shots at Ground Zero, but Port Authority vice chairman Charles A. Gargano was unambiguously direct. In a meeting with the *Daily News* editorial board, he said that Silverstein "can be adamant" about rebuilding all of the commercial space on the site, "but it's not his call."[43]

In these early weeks and months after 9/11 Silverstein was trying to consolidate control through as many channels as possible. All kinds of obstacles were steadily encroaching on his perceived degrees of freedom in aggressively pushing forward with his agenda as if this was a conventional real estate development project. Formidable obstacles, however, could not dim his perpetual confidence. He believed the market downtown would return and that he would have the best buildings to attract the strongest tenants. Of this, he was convinced. Critics contended otherwise. "No single developer has tried to complete a project of such scale in New York since the 1980's, when George Klein attempted to build four office towers in Times Square," Andrew Rice of the weekly *New York Observer* reminded readers. And at considerable length in *Times Square Roulette*, I explained the many setbacks Klein encountered and why and how that public-private development project took twists and turns not contemplated by any of the players over its twenty-plus-year saga. The complex rebuilding at Ground Zero would prove to be much, much harder—for everyone involved—and contrary to the narrative of delay that prevailed throughout, largely completed in a time frame that was acceptably short relative to similar urban megaprojects. Regardless, the first order of business would be to figure out who was in control of decision-making at Ground Zero.

A DYSFUNCTIONAL DOCUMENT

In signing ninety-nine-year leases with a developer who operated on the traditional model of family business that values holding real estate for generational benefit, the Port Authority had aligned its long-term economic interest with an investor group keyed to the same long-term investment horizon. This particular point of alignment meant that each party did not want the other party to be able to exit easily, and their lease agreement reflected that position. Once the towers fell into a pile of burning rubble, however, the implications of destruction defined a vastly different set of issues at once more complex and unfathomable than those the Port Authority and Silverstein inked in agreements on July 24, 2001.

There were two critical clauses in the leases, as Steven Brill, the author, lawyer, journalist, and founder of Court TV and *American Lawyer* magazine explained in *After: How America Confronted the September 12 Era*: "The first clause required Silverstein to use any insurance proceeds to rebuild in the event the Trade Center was destroyed. But the second clause required the Port Authority to *allow* Silverstein to rebuild the Trade Center exactly as it had been," as stated in the lease language, with the plans and specifications as they existed before the casualty or as otherwise agreed to with the Port Authority." These two clauses, he wrote, "all but required both Silverstein and the Port Authority to play an elaborate game of bluff." He was amazed that the contract said nothing more on this issue "except that in the event that it became impractical to rebuild, the two sides had to negotiate."[44] The contract did not provide for a "divorce" or buyout. Rebuilding the complex exactly as it had been rendered would become moot, politically, when Pataki declared the tower footprints sacred in June 2002 and then selected the Libeskind master plan in February 2003.

At the time of the 2001 transaction, Silverstein Properties (SPI) was still very much a family firm; it did not have the same deep organization and technical capacity as New York's largest and most experienced real estate development firms. Silverstein was known to have "a significant balance sheet and net worth but low liquidity," as the majority of his net worth was held in real estate, not unlike other developers. For that reason, when his lender on the 2001 transaction sold slices of the $563 million mortgage loan to investors through an offering of securities, a cash reserve of $25 million was required as part of the transaction, in addition to other measures to secure repayment of the loan.[45] As the process of rebuilding rolled forward, Larry Silverstein would build a large and sophisticated organization, but he had come to his position as presumptive developer of Ground Zero out of tragedy. He was not chosen to be *developer* by the type of deliberate choice and competitive process that adheres to large-scale public-private development projects such as the redevelopment of Forty-second Street at Times Square or Time Warner Center at Columbus Circle or the ground-up development of Battery Park City, all project bids he had responded to but failed to win. By default, he had become the presumptive developer of the Trade Center site.

The task of rebuilding the Trade Center site profoundly altered the agenda between the Port Authority and the Silverstein investor group. To begin with, what had been a straightforward transaction for the net lease of four operating office buildings (1 WTC, 2 WTC, 4 WTC, and 5 WTC) and the underground retail mall had by catastrophe turned into a multiple-building development project, and the property issues attached to development under a ground lease are wholly different in kind and scope from the issues both parties had resolved in their long-term lease agreement. The risks of a development project are far more complex and uncertain than the risks of operating existing properties. At a minimum, the owner of the land needs assurances that the developer has the financial resources and management capability to finish the project, and the lease must provide legal protections for the landowner to resume control in case there is a default prior to the completion of the improvements, because if the developer fails before the building is completed, the owner of the land is left with the burden of completion.

The Port Authority and Silverstein were now working with "a dysfunction document," said Anthony R. Coscia; "it's as if you are in the computer business and you're using a document for the automobile business," he told me. Coscia would become the longest continuous power player at the Port Authority, serving as chairman of the authority for nine years from 2003 to 2011, which also made him the longest-serving chairman in the Port's modern (post–Austin Tobin) history. "There was no way you can look at that site and operate under pre-9/11 conditions," he said in an interview reported in the New Jersey press.[46] For years, there would be no real attempt to renegotiate an agreement, yet another dimension of uncertainty in the slew of events rapidly engulfing the project.

In this interim of uncertainty, each partner was positioning for what was central to its interest in rebuilding. From September 12 onward, Silverstein worked single-mindedly to maintain a legal hold on "his right and obligation" to rebuild, which first and foremost depended on his ability to use the hundreds of millions in insurance advances parked in escrow to preserve his development rights by paying monthly debt service on the mortgage held by GMAC and monthly rent to the Port Authority. He also needed insurance funds to pay lawyers to fight his insurance battles, architects to prepare the design visions and construction documents for each tower, and communication consultants to carefully craft his public image and manage the media. Most importantly, he needed funds to pay lobbyists to position his investor partnership for low-cost tax-exempt Liberty Bonds, subsidies and favorable federal tax treatment of the investment losses incurred from the 9/11 destruction, and to win legislative protection for his investment partnership "so that from any liability he might have for structural or management gaps at the Trade Center (which had become his responsibility when he took over management of the center in July) would be capped at the approximately $1.5 billion in liability insurance he had."[47] These were immediate out-of-pocket cash costs necessary to maintain his position, and they would quickly mount into many hundreds of millions of dollars, and by steady depletion, the expected insurance recovery proceeds available for rebuilding would keep shrinking.

With site control and insurance funds (other people's money or OPM in the vernacular of real estate), Silverstein had the two prime elements of a developer's money equation, and both would initially play to his advantage when the time came to renegotiate his lease agreement with the Port Authority. Yet to the extent that the process dragged on or the insurers reduced the amounts they would advance before a final settlement, he ran the real risk of running out of money to stay in the game. Silverstein, however, was never one to doubt his personal abilities or professional resourcefulness. Optimism and optionality, the possibility of additional investment value, are the handmaidens of real estate development: All developers play the optionality of that kind of situation, believing a solution will be found for whatever constraint might arise. Silverstein was expert at the game.

As owner of the land, the quasi-autonomous Port Authority was constantly positioning to gain control over redevelopment of its home territory. The terrorist attack destroyed the second largest net-revenue-producing operating business in its portfolio (after the three regional air terminals). Although it did not fully control the rights to rebuild or the process of rebuilding as it had exercised those powers when first developing the World Trade Center complex in the early 1960s, unlike Silverstein, it had time on its side—as long as politics did not intrude to force it to do something that it did not want to do or spend money it did not want to spend. The staff-driven authority could patiently persevere, strategically prepare its own plans in detail to be on the ready, hire its own consultants, manage its own public relations and political personas, and proceed with its ambition to build an iconic transportation terminal. Also, unlike Silverstein, the agency had a big balance sheet, a steady source of income to carry these ongoing predevelopment costs, and the power to issue consolidated bonds to be able to pay off earlier bond issues on the basis of its income-producing assets. Eventually, Silverstein would have to sit down with the authority to negotiate a new lease agreement; if he held back, though, the Port Authority could always refuse to do things that would impact his position. It too knew how to play its version of the game.

CHAPTER 3

Commanding Political Opportunities

FIGURE 3.1 *Governor George E. Pataki and Mayor Michael R. Bloomberg, two of the most important arbiters of what would happen in lower Manhattan, overlooking dueling contenders at Ground Zero.* EDWARD SOREL

IF THE NEED FOR GOVERNMENT to play a commanding role in determining what was to happen at Ground Zero was unquestionable, the playbook for *how* that was going to happen was as clouded as the dense plumes of smoke shrouding those sixteen acres in the days and weeks following 9/11. As the chief elected officials, the governor and the mayor commanded natural positions of leadership. Leadership at Ground Zero called for the creation of a governing structure and planning process for making decisions over what was bound to be a messy and contentious and predictably political set of circumstances. The exigency and emotion associated with the task of rebuilding defined a heightened duty to engage the public in the planning process and assure a certain level of transparency over those decisions. An alignment of political interests in pursuit of these goals, however, was not a foregone conclusion in light of the historic tension between City Hall and Albany; still, the public expected government officials to act decisively to gain control over the resources necessary to carry out the twin mandates of memorialization and rebuilding. These responsibilities created an exceptional political platform, especially for George E. Pataki, then in the third year of his second term as governor. The eyes of the world were riveted on Ground Zero, and rhetorical speeches and real efforts at healing the pain of a nation commanded constant media attention. The governor, who easily won reelection in 1998 with more than 54 percent of the popular vote and harbored future ambitions for a higher elected office, held most of the cards in the political deck. But what would happen when other political interests—some elected by the voters and others structured by elected officials—each with a different agenda, different set of resources, and different command over the emotions swirling around Ground Zero, sought to play on the stage the governor was about to set? Who would win in the contests over resources and power (figure 3.1)?

THE STATE TAKES CHARGE

When the question of how to organize for recovery arose, turf issues erupted between the city and the state. Who was going to control the process? Who was going to get credit for managing the recovery? Ever aware of President George W. Bush's promise of $20 billion to help New York recover and rebuild, discussed in chapter 4, city officials moved quickly, seeking a way to directly control those funds. Within days, the Democratic leader of the City Council, who was also a candidate for mayor in the upcoming election, proposed a new mayoral reconstruction commission—with no state appointees—to oversee recovery. "We are the ones that have to rebuild, restructure and re-energize," said City Council Speaker Paul Vallone. "You start from the bottom up, and we are at the bottom of this situation, in a very figurative way."[1]

That logic had nary a chance of prevailing in the face of aligned Republican power calling the shots in Albany and Washington, D.C., but the mayoral election only eight weeks away in a city where registered Democratic voters outnumber Republicans by more than two to one injected just enough anxiety into the political landscape to heighten the debate about who was going to be in charge of rebuilding lower Manhattan—and, by logical extension of the psychology prevailing in those weeks and months after 9/11, the city's economy. In their quest for control, city officials reportedly tried to go around the Pataki administration and meet on their own with White House officials. However, they found themselves outmaneuvered when state officials were invited to the arranged meeting in late September, "where the White House officials chastised the city, saying that New York had to speak with one voice, and made it clear that federal money would flow through the state." After city officials consulted with aides of Governor Pataki, the Giuliani administration withdrew its earlier support for a mayoral commission. "If any [special] authority is created, it needs to be done in conjunction with the state of New York," Deputy Mayor Joseph J. Lhota said. "It's that's simple."[2] Even though Giuliani was thought to have stronger ties with Washington than Pataki, the compact between the states and the federal government embodied in the U.S. Constitution trumped the city's political influence, leaving in its wake a strategic question for the city: How does it become a more equal player? The general approach—try to get control of the money—was not in the cards in this case.

An alliance between the city and the state was necessary for reasons practical as well as political. The state has sway over the bi-state Port Authority through the governor of New York's customary appointment of the agency's executive director. Through its powerful Empire State Development Corporation (ESDC), the state also has the ability to override local zoning, flexibility in negotiating financial assistance packages, and legislative authority to create ESDC subsidiaries, such as the LMDC, able to exercise these powers. The state controls the Metropolitan Transit Authority (MTA). Also, the state's processes of environmental review are less stringent than those of the city. All of these comparative political advantages have for decades given the state a historically dominant role in New York City's large-scale development projects, from the redevelopment of Times Square in midtown to Battery Park City in lower Manhattan, the development of Roosevelt Island and Queens West in Queens, and Atlantic Yards and Brooklyn Bridge Park in Brooklyn, among others (map 3.1). Governor Pataki's chief economic development official, Charles A. Gargano, simultaneously chairman of the ESDC and vice chairman of the Port Authority, talked of a "partnership effort" with the city. At issue, of course, was what a partnership effort would mean in terms of control: "What gets done with a 50–50 commission?" Gargano asked in the weeks following 9/11. "When it comes to rebuilding, it's primarily the Port Authority and the state, working with the City of New York."[3]

"Power struggles between Albany and New York City are a standard part of local political life," a *Times* editorial reminded readers who might have momentarily forgotten that or reasonably believed, as did the Gray Lady, nickname for the

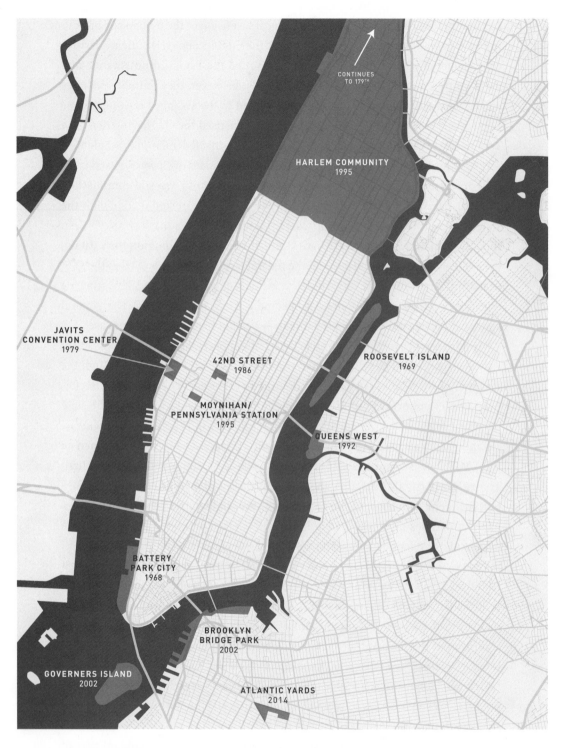

CONTINUES
TO 179TH

HARLEM COMMUNITY
1995

JAVITS
CONVENTION CENTER
1979

42ND STREET
1986

ROOSEVELT ISLAND
1969

MOYNIHAN/
PENNSYLVANIA STATION
1995

QUEENS WEST
1992

BATTERY
PARK CITY
1968

BROOKLYN
BRIDGE PARK
2002

GOVERNERS ISLAND
2002

ATLANTIC YARDS
2014

Map 3.1 Development corporations established by ESDC in NYC: 1968–2014. Cartography:
C&G Partners for the author

Times, that "political rivalries need to be set aside in service of the larger cause." In this instance, as in the past, the city and state would form an alliance because "no rebuilding plan can succeed without the enthusiastic participation of the next mayor." "The governor has a huge stake in New York City, but little foundation for action in the city," remarked Robert R. Douglass, the longtime politically savvy attorney and city leader and tireless advocate for lower Manhattan serving as the chairman of the Alliance for Downtown New York. "The city has home rule, and the state is not welcome except for the budget. The relationship gets political: Whose prerogative is it? The governor's pathway to the city depends heavily on a working relationship with the mayor." As in the past, the alliance would be built on mutuality of need: "The new mayor had to cope with a looming budget crisis, the general economic decline worsened by the September 11 attack, and the loss of finance and technology jobs that had begun with the collapse of the dot-com sector in late 2000," Bloomberg advisor Mitchell L. Moss wrote some years later. "The mayor needed the governor's support to help resolve the city's fiscal crisis, while the governor needed the mayor's cooperation to build at Ground Zero."[4]

The upcoming mayoral election complicated the control issue at Ground Zero. The two candidates were advocating different proposals: Democrat Mark J. Green proposed a new superagency accountable to the mayor and governor with input from other voices around the city; Republican Michael R. Bloomberg considered existing city and state agencies, plus the Port Authority and the MTA, sufficient to manage the city's reconstruction. He rejected the idea of a new state agency to oversee the rebuilding, believing instead that the mayor should be the point person on the city's downtown recovery. In the face of electoral uncertainty and anxiety over Green's front-runner status in a race widely anticipated to be too close to call, state officials favored holding off establishing a reconstruction entity until after the election on November 6, 2001.

In the meantime, the governor's staff floated proposals in the press for an ESDC subsidiary with the intent of minimizing the influence of the Democratic mayoral candidate. They were fearful Green might become the next mayor, and, as Pataki later put it, "we didn't have confidence that he and his team would understand the importance of doing this right."[5] Albany wanted to design a way to cut Green out of the picture. By creating the LMDC as a subsidiary of the ESDC and allocating a majority of the board seats to the state, the governor made sure all of the federal money pledged to New York would be under the state's control. Whether or not the Green fear was myth or rationale, Republicans could ensure their political control over rebuilding by declining to give the city equal representation on the LMDC board.

On the eve of the mayoral election, when the governor announced the establishment of the LMDC, his plan included a nine-person board with six members he would appoint and three the mayor would appoint. Following Bloomberg's upset victory (a win by the city's closest mayoral race in a century: 50 percent to 48 percent), Pataki refigured representation on the LMDC board. At first, he gave each government another appointment making for an eleven-person board; by March 2002, the board had grown to fourteen and finally settled in at sixteen in April, with equal representation for the city and state.[6] He wanted decision-making to be by consensus, he told me. These changes assured structural parity in representation, yet the design and governing structure of the organization charged with overseeing recovery in lower Manhattan mirrored the fact that the leading figures—Governor Pataki, Mayor Giuliani, Mayor-Elect Bloomberg, and President Bush—all Republicans, had a political stake in what happened at Ground Zero. Given that alignment, would the LMDC be able to operate above politics in the service of the larger—and nationally significant—civic cause (figure 3.2)? And how much control could the LMDC actually exercise over the Trade Center site in light of the legal interests of the Port Authority, Larry Silverstein and his investors, Westfield America, and the moral force of the families of the victims?

To head the LMDC, Governor Pataki appointed one of the city's most distinguished business professionals, a man revered on Wall Street and well known

FIGURE 3.2 Nick Anderson Editorial Cartoon used with permission of Nick Anderson, the Washington Post Writers Group and the Cartoonist Group. All rights reserved

among national Republicans, who would control the allocation of federal aid to New York City. The late John C. Whitehead had all the credentials needed to mediate among the many interests vying for influence and credit in the rebuilding effort: leading citizen of New York and loyal Republican; investment banker for thirty-seven years, culminating in his position as cochairman of Goldman Sachs; deputy secretary of state for four years in the Reagan administration; former chairman of the Federal Reserve Bank of New York, Securities Industry Association, Harvard University Board of Overseers, Brookings Institution, International Rescue Committee, and others too numerous to mention; philanthropist and fundraiser for many charitable causes; and friend to people from many walks of life all over the world. His was *A Life in Leadership*, as his autobiography described, *From D-Day to Ground Zero*.

Whitehead was seventy-nine at the time, and only thinking about retirement and the many things he wanted to do. He was reluctant to accept what he knew would be "an immense undertaking," what Governor Pataki told him would be a ten-year project. To rebut Whitehead's reluctance, the governor first turned the age issue inside out—"Everybody will know you have no personal agenda. You won't be looking ahead to your next job"; he also set up a "well-orchestrated sales effort" of calls from Whitehead's influential friends and colleagues and scheduled a press conference to announce the appointment before his offer was accepted. For almost the full forty-eight hours he had to decide, Whitehead waffled, but ultimately, his patrician sense of civic duty and distinguished years of service compelled him to accept; he felt he didn't have any right to say no given the significance of the task. "It was done," he said after hanging up on his telephone call with the governor. "The governor's problem—and with it the city's and even the nation's problem—had become my problem."[7]

Whitehead's appointment met with uniform praise. One person less than pleased, though, was Charles Gargano, head of the LMDC's parent organization, ESDC, "ostensibly" its boss. Gargano wanted a greater role for himself at Ground Zero, and Whitehead's appointment accompanied by his vow of a politically independent rebuilding effort "infuriated" him, according to at least one well-informed source. As detailed in an article in the *New York Observer* the following year, tensions between the two men prevailed from the beginning. Whitehead considered himself senior to Gargano, whom he had sworn in as ambassador to Trinidad and Tobago when he was deputy secretary of state during the Reagan administration. There was no love lost between these two, and Whitehead did all he could to keep Gargano out of the LMDC. Surprisingly, he was successful. Though politically conservative, Whitehead's predilections for speaking his mind, talking straight, and making crisp decisions were something of a risk for an administration that prized discipline and loyalty. His contacts in Washington and his ability to make news with announcements about Ground Zero that could "eclipse" not only Gargano but Pataki rankled some in the governor's office. He was "something of an unknown quantity in New York's political and real-estate circles."[8]

His success in the business world and his career as a high-level diplomat prepared him for the new challenges of LMDC chairman, yet by his own admission, he knew little of city planning or architecture and had little political experience in state or city government. At the time of his appointment in late November and for some time thereafter, little was certain about how the LMDC would function, what its powers would be, and how it would interface with the Port Authority. Initially, even its boundaries were unclear. In time, though, the LMDC's redevelopment responsibilities extended beyond Ground Zero to include all of the southern portion of the island, from Canal Street down to Battery Park and from the Hudson across to the East River—"some of the most valuable, most important, and most heavily populated real estate in the world," as Whitehead saw it.[9] The area of approximately twenty miles square traversed several distinctive neighborhoods: Chinatown, Tribeca, Battery Park City, and the financial district (see map 3.2).

The division of power between the state and the city is an age-old issue for mayors. For more than two decades during the era of ambitious federal support for revitalizing the nation's urban centers beginning with the federal highway and urban renewal programs of the 1950s, mayors succeeded in winning the fight for local control.[10] This victory, however, stands as an exception to the historical pattern. Under the U.S. Constitution, cities have no formal legal standing. Because of 9/11, Ground Zero was one place where this arrangement might have been different, remarked Carl B. Weisbrod. But from the start, the process of governing for rebuilding was structured in such a way that precluded the city's active involvement in rebuilding lower Manhattan; only through the mayor's appointments to the LMDC board did the city have some say over the distribution of an unprecedented pledge of federal dollars.

Due to Whitehead's concerted efforts and his reputation in Washington, federal dollars specifically and unusually were going *directly* to the LMDC, but only $2.7 billion, or approximately 13 percent of the total. "It was a curious way the federal government dealt with the state and the city on the Trade Center funds," remarked a seasoned political veteran. "HUD [U.S. Department of Housing and Urban Development] and DOT [U.S. Department of Transportation] probably did not want to send the money to the city or state, but rather wanted a third party—the LMDC. It was an awkward situation." As a result of this structural arrangement, "it was a must that the head of the LMDC would have the ear of the governor and the mayor, which was the case with Whitehead. Whitehead was chairman, but afterward that close connection to the governor was not clear." Awkwardness, he

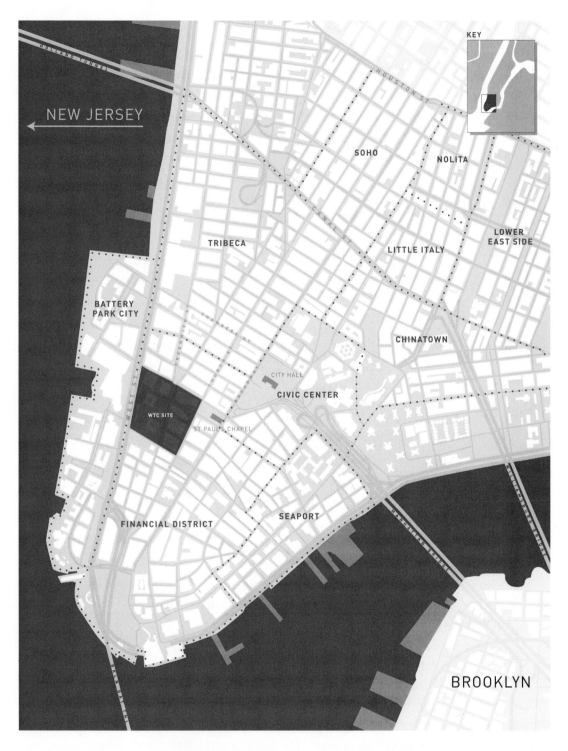

Map 3.2 The neighborhoods of lower Manhattan. CARTOGRAPHY: C&G PARTNERS FOR THE AUTHOR

added, "is an age-old problem: competition and jealousy, egos and political ambi-tion; it was not newly invented at Ground Zero."

Since the LMDC had been organized before Congress appropriated the money, it would have to abide by HUD rules because the money for economic recovery activities and long-term rebuilding programs was being funded through the agen-cy's Community Development Block Grant (CDBG) channel.[11] Setting up flexible rules for spending to assist the type of open-ended business and economic-development programs the LMDC might undertake was going to be tricky be-cause the CDBG funds were typically used to build low-income housing. After much debate and discussion and, reportedly, constant work on the part of New York's senators Charles E. Schumer and Hillary Rodman Clinton, Congress al-lowed a reluctant HUD to waive its low-income requirement and let the agency write the rules overseeing the lower Manhattan funds. The go-around allowed the LMDC to become a "creative dispenser of discretionary money,"[12] exercising a level of discretion atypical of federal-aid relationships. It was a structural advan-tage that gave the development agency financial leverage in rebuilding lower Manhattan, and over time it served to counter what would become a weak decision-making position when it came to rebuilding Ground Zero.

The issue of who had the most direct line to President Bush constantly came into play during the early months after 9/11, becoming "the subtext of many of the tussles between the LMDC and the Pataki administration," the New York Observer noted. "Mr. Pataki, of course, has access and clout with the White House, but as a major donor and former Reagan administration official, so does Mr. Whitehead." Closest of all, personally, was LMDC board member Roland W. Betts, the entre-preneurial cofounder of the Chelsea Piers Sports and Entertainment Complex. Called the "top New Yorker in Bush's White House," Betts had a "long-standing loyalty" to Bush that placed him in the "inner ring of the President's many circles of friends."[13] They started out as fraternity brothers at Yale, became closer friends following their graduation in 1968, and later became business partners, with Betts the lead owner in Bush's Texas Rangers Baseball Club partnership. Above all, Betts was a friend of the president's family.

Betts is a commanding physical presence of intense energy and determination. His pioneering development of Chelsea Piers on the West Side of Manhattan, what he called "just a huge historic accident" because he tired of taking his figure-skating daughter to 5 A.M. practices at a scruffy rink in midtown, was a risky bet in the early 1990s. "I tried to get 100,000 square feet at Pier 2 away from the state and ended up with 1.8 *million* square feet and four piers. It took a lot of imagina-tion to figure out what in God's name I was going to do with all of it." Also, as Robin Finn of the *Times* wrote in her Public Lives profile of Betts, it "required the acquisition of 27 state, city, and federal permits in less than four years, a political and urban miracle."[14] He was a Democrat appointed to the board by Pataki, another Yale classmate, whom he knew well from his Chelsea Piers project. At the helm of the LMDC site planning subcommittee, he was once again a man with a big task to do, and it fed his ego. Because of his close relationship with President Bush, whom he would keep "fully informed" of the LMDC's progress, Betts acquired an element of power.

Paper Tiger

From the start, Whitehead demanded independence: He did not want politics involved in the allocation of funds designed to assure recovery and rebuilding of lower Manhattan, including a memorial on the "near sacred site." "This was a big to-do. No one but John Whitehead could have pulled it together to become independent of ESDC," said Ira M. Millstein, LMDC's pro-bono counsel. One of America's top lawyers, a senior partner at Weil, Gotshal & Manages and leading international expert in corporate governance, the white-haired and bespectacled Millstein was also a longtime close friend of Whitehead's and had served with him on a number of commissions. He had accumulated a long list of credits in the way of public service, philanthropy, education, and authorship over five decades of a legendary legal career. Widely respected and often quoted, he was the attorney of choice corporations and public officials turned to when considering matters of regulatory strategy and reform of the practices and processes by which a corporation is directed and controlled. For decades he had been shaping the minds of law students as an adjunct professor at Columbia Law School, where he received his law degree and taught corporate governance. When Whitehead called him and asked for help in structuring the newly formed but amorphous LMDC, the seventy-five-year-old lifelong New Yorker did not hesitate to sign on. He would advise the group's directors "to oversee and monitor what the management's doing, to see that it's done right, and to see that it's done with all the constituents in mind." "With over $2 billion in funds to manage and distribute," he told me, "there had to be absolutely no hint of scandal, so we structured the organization with a real audit committee to establish the agency's independence."[15] That structure acted as a protective shield for Whitehead, allowing him to operate as a nonpartisan broker and engage with the competing groups vying for influence and grants at arms' distance from political interference.

"I would be surprised if the governor's office understood what Millstein had created as a governance structure," one LMDC board member told me in confidence. The Audit and Finance Committee does not appear in the LMDC's bylaws;

it is governed by a committee charter that makes it "responsible for overseeing the allocation of the Corporation's resources" and performing functions and activities "relating to the financial affairs" of the development corporation as may be assigned to it by the board.[16] The way the LMDC worked, the board allocated no funds unless the Audit and Finance Committee, whose members were loyal to Whitehead, had approved the action. "No one could serve on this committee who worked for government—that's the way Whitehead controlled the LMDC," the board member said. The committee was determined to "run clean," said one committee member. "Some of us didn't know about government appointments, and how typically people were expected to do what the governor expected, how he wanted them to respond." The Audit and Finance Committee effectively became the executive committee of the board. Since it was only making recommendations, not making board-level decisions, the "working group" was not subject to the state's sunshine law, which gives the public the right to attend meetings of public bodies, listen to the debates, and watch the decision-making process in action. The committee did not tell the city what it was doing in those early years. As a result, the LMDC functioned like no other public authority—independent not only of ESDC (which, as a fiduciary, the state parent found problematic) but also of city government. With his selection of Whitehead, "the governor got what he wanted: someone with an impeccable reputation—but he lost some control," remarked one well-placed source. "In that, there was an element of 'be careful what you wish for.'"

The LMDC board was different from other public-sector boards, remarked one board member with experience on many public boards. One of the things that made the LMDC board different was the extent to which the members did not necessarily feel beholden to the elected officials who appointed them. In its early days, the LMDC board consisted of independently powerful people who went into it wanting to make a difference. They were used to being heard and did not view themselves as subordinates. Unlike what was typical of public authority boards, where appointees were expected to vote in line with what the mayor wants, on the city side, Doctoroff and the mayor had meetings with city appointees at which they were told "here's our position," think about it. Not everyone agreed with the city's position, notwithstanding they had been appointed by the mayor. When interviewed by the mayor, one appointee was told to "do your best." Whether this was characteristic of the state side is unclear, but Whitehead treated the board as if it was a private-sector board. He wanted the full sense of the board in making decisions and believed those on the board acting together could come to good decisions. September 11 as an event also made the LMDC different from other public-sector boards; it was created only because of the event.

The LMDC was established with a threefold mission: to coordinate the revitalization of lower Manhattan south of Houston Street (see map 5.1), river to river; to create a "fitting" memorial to those lost in the 9/11 attack; and to work with the Port Authority to plan the future of the Trade Center site and surrounding areas. Whitehead viewed the task ahead as "not only a matter of repairing the physical and economic damage, but also of helping heal the trauma caused by this horrendous assault on our city and our nation." Translated into action, healing the trauma meant spending significant time listening to what others thought the LMDC should do. "There was no precedent for the rebuilding," he told me. "We faced problems no one had faced before. I had a very good board, good cross-section of society, and they were very helpful. I decided at the beginning that the days of being a czar had passed. The public input would be very important, though I didn't know exactly what had to be done. Long-range planning was going to take more time."[17]

As his first formal act, Whitehead instituted a two-month "period of listening" and created a series of eight advisory boards[18] to provide input on issues of concern to their respective constituencies as well as a general advisory council composed of federal, state, and city elected officials and business and civic leaders who would help formulate goals for the future of lower Manhattan. The advisory boards, members were told, would "make periodic recommendations to the LMDC board."[19] During the two-month listening period, the LMDC was constantly convening meetings, more than two hundred by the time the development corporation issued a five-year report in 2006. With hindsight, Whitehead came to the conclusion that there were too many hearings, too many subjects brought forth. Airing everything publicly created expectations and made some items more controversial than they needed to be, he told me. Whitehead took pride in bringing about consensus. Extensive public outreach was part of the LMDC's mandate, and the constant public hearings got the public interested. "I'm beginning to get the feeling there is a consensus," he told the *Wall Street Journal* in December shortly after he assumed the chairmanship. "It's when you get into the details that there might be differences."[20] The details were not long in coming to the fore.

To organize and manage the thorny details and head day-to-day operations of the LMDC Governor Pataki appointed Louis R. Tomson, a longtime ally and one of his closest advisors with a reputation for getting things done in Albany, an "Albany guy." Tomson, age sixty, was the one who would cut the deals and broker agreements with the Port Authority on rebuilding the site. He was a surrogate for the governor. Active in state Republican politics for three decades, he had served Pataki in many positions, as deputy secretary and later first deputy secretary to the governor with responsibility for the state's sixty public authorities, including the Port Authority and the Metropolitan Transportation Authority. He brought some private-sector business experience to his new position at the LMDC as well, as a senior executive at upstate energy company Plug Power prior to rejoining the public sector. His background as a lawyer and former managing partner at the governor's former law firm, Plunkett and Jaffe, and his heavyweight crew experience as an undergraduate at Columbia University would come into play as he pushed to make rebuilding happen at Ground Zero. Tomson, I was told, had wanted the Port Authority job, but the LMDC was a perfect fit, said a close Pataki loyalist. He was there to ensure that Pataki did not lose control of the LMDC. That being the case, the governor had set up in-house tension: After Pataki's signaling above-politics integrity with the appointment of Whitehead, Tomson was in place to assure the governor of state control of the agency.

Pataki's "go-to guy" was "a first-rate choice," said the *Daily News* editorial page. The newspaper called him a "reformer," on the basis of his labor to bring accountability to the state's vast public authorities. With "the solid backing" of Mayor Bloomberg as well as his LMDC board, Tomson "had the standing and political base needed to work with a galaxy of city, state, and federal agencies—and, just as significantly, private-sector partners—to rebuild." The *Times* said the choice gives the governor "more control over the corporation because Mr. Tomson has served as the governor's loyal troubleshooter in the past." He was a capable guy, a political operative, someone "you had to watch to protect your kneecaps," as one seasoned observer of New York politics put it. The *Times* worried about "whether he will make certain that the public's voice is heard" in the corporation's planning process.[21]

The LMDC was moving ahead with the planning process. From the visioning work of New York New Visions, formed after 9/11, as well as the other civic-group coalitions, the development corporation "deftly adapted the consensus platforms of the private sector planning agents."[22] Its *Blueprint for the Future of Lower Manhattan* set forth fourteen broad but specific public goals that addressed the revival of lower Manhattan, not just rebuilding the Trade Center site.[23] "These plans represent the best possible consensus we can find at the moment," said Alexander Garvin, the corporation's vice president in charge of planning. The principles seemed "benign," Pulitzer Prize-winning architectural critic Paul Goldberger wrote in his early review of how the future of Ground Zero was being resolved. "But is it possible to create an appropriate memorial and also increase the area's strength as a financial center? Is improving the neighborhood going to get in the way of developing Lower Manhattan as a tourist and cultural magnet? And if you create a 'comprehensive, coherent plan for transit access to Lower Manhattan'—in other words, a new station for the mess of disconnected subway and other transit lines downtown—will it cost so much that it will put other transit plans, like the Second Avenue subway [a project decades in planning], at risk?"[24]

These questions were uppermost in many conversations during the early months of 2002. "When people say they want something splendid in Lower Manhattan—and they say that repeatedly—they mean more than just the memorial itself," the *Times* editorialized. "They mean that the redevelopment of the larger World Trade Center site should be architecturally ambitious. They mean that it should have a culturally and physically responsive connection to the rest of downtown. What that also means, and this is more difficult, is that any commercial redevelopment of the World Trade Center site must also co-exist harmoniously with the memorial itself."[25]

The LMDC was ambiguous about how it would reconcile competing priorities. It would simultaneously respect the site "as a place of remembrance and reserve an area of the site for one or more permanent memorials" and push for new development that would "facilitate the immediate revitalization of Lower Manhattan to ensure its long-term viability."[26] These goals would have to be balanced against the leaseholder's demand for ten-million-plus square feet of office space and six hundred thousand square feet of high-yielding retail space, demands validated by the Port Authority's insistence for a full rebuild of the lost commercial space.

To the chagrin of many at large, the LMDC's key representatives for the planning process, Betts and Garvin, did not challenge the full-rebuild commercial program for the site: "It's the Port's site from an ownership standpoint, and what's the point of developing a whole plan and getting into a pissing contest with the Port because they don't like it?" Betts said. Both men started out believing that the Port Authority had the right to determine the program for the site—that is, what functions would occupy the land and how much space would be devoted to each—while the LMDC had the right to figure out what the whole thing would look like; the LMDC would also be in control of the memorial planning process. The city too accepted the Port Authority's position. "The economics of the Port Authority's position was never questioned and that dictated the program and control," said Josh Sirefman, point person on the Trade Center for Deputy Mayor Doctoroff and his chief of staff for two years until June 2006 (when he moved over to the Economic Development Corporation to serve as interim president).[27] Commercial development was going to dominate Ground Zero, which put the Port Authority and its leaseholder in the driver's seat.

The Port Authority's legal position and financial objectives in the rebuilding process posed an obvious problem for the development corporation. "The big issue for the LMDC was how to get the Port Authority to be cooperative; the Port wanted control over the site, as its owner," Millstein said. From the start, the jurisdictional issue clouded decision-making at Ground Zero. When asked in a "live-chat event" hosted by the public-service organization Gotham Gazette.com what was the "exact legal relationship" of the LMDC to the Port Authority and what it allowed him to do or not do, Tomson answered straight: "It has never been precisely defined." But, he added, "roughly, I believe the Port has ultimate legal authority over the site. And we, in conjunction with the City, have the power off the site." From the Port Authority's perspective, Executive Director Joseph Seymour told me, the LMDC was essential in the beginning because the Port Authority needed the LMDC "to arbitrate the process." These two Pataki appointees, Tomson and Seymour, had been close friends before they found themselves working together at Ground Zero. As agents of the state, they entered into a collaboration agreement "to avoid questions concerning whether the Port or LMDC has ultimate decision power," Tomson said.[28] The LMDC, same as the city, had no authority over the Port Authority, a state of affairs certain to create tensions. The LMDC did, however, have the one ingredient that might move the bi-state institution: money.

WOUNDED POWER

After 9/11, the Port Authority was a wounded institution. Devastated by the terrorist attack and the loss of its executive director, Neil D. Levin, who was killed on 9/11 and in office for barely six months; thirty-seven of its fifty-person police command; and forty-six of its operation staff, the agency was nearly paralyzed during those first weeks and months. It was "rudderless, its leadership gone and its soul pierced at its heart." Its thousands of employees were in shock. They lost family. The agency's signature headquarters in the North Tower lay in a mammoth pile of debris. Gone too were the records that told the story of its proud institutional legacy. Many employees walked down eighty-two flights of stairs before they knew they would survive the attack. Everyone was traumatized by the traumatizing event, and it took months before the agency started to operate as an organization once again. "The first two months were a difficult time," recalled Seymour, appointed by Pataki in mid-December 2001 to succeed Levin. "Staff was demoralized. Security at the airports, bridges, and tunnels was a constant concern; there were all kinds of threats. People didn't have offices or papers or any personal items. There were no pictures on the walls. Everything was gone."[29] The agency needed to find new offices and consciously sought not to lease space downtown; emotions were too raw. This affecting piece of the 9/11 story, underplayed in the media, tends to get forgotten, but it shaped the agency's actions, especially during the months immediately following the attack.

As owner of the sixteen-acre site, the quasi-autonomous regional power with a legendary bureaucracy was the most formidable and intractable player in the rebuilding dynamic, but a reluctant player at first. The shock to the institution kept it focused on internal concerns and affairs. "It didn't want to be out front," the Port Authority's long-serving chairman, Anthony R. Coscia, told me. "It had seen too many deaths, gone to too many funerals. It didn't want to make a name for itself." The tragedy of 9/11 "is not a hurt that works off."[30] Soon enough, however, the agency would seek to control rebuilding of the site by asserting the power of its property interests, as explained in chapter 6.

The Port Authority's losses created a tight emotional connection to rebuilding the site. Rebuilding became a passion, and its staff became determined do everything it could to maintain control over the process. Rebuilding was going to be the monument to their fallen brothers and sisters, and thus, it is hard to overstate the agency's drive for control and its ambition to recover its distinguished legacy. Rebuilding "was going to be a great opportunity for the Port Authority to reestablish itself as a great and majestic builder," said Christopher O. Ward, at the time chief of planning and external affairs and director of port development. It was "a glorious opportunity born out of unspeakable tragedy," the PA's corporate counsel told his peers in a published interview in May 2002.[31]

The Port Authority's distinctive and insular culture could only partially buffer the searing wounds of this most public of tragedies. Used to operating with little legislative oversight, the engineer-dominated authority was not accustomed to sharing its institutional turf, as would be demanded in the post-9/11 planning process. It was terrified of letting the public in, of losing control through public participation. Over decades of activity that reshaped the landscape of the New York–New Jersey region, it had earned an unshakable reputation as a strong-willed, autonomous, and arrogant institution. Although the halo of power had dimmed since the rule of its autocratic first director, Austin J. Tobin's larger-than-life legacy held sway within the institution and among its longtime staff. When the Port Authority developed the World Trade Center complex in the 1960s, the move into the realm of commercial real estate signaled aggressive risk taking beyond the conventional realm of a public transportation agency. How much of this legacy was it bound to repeat?

Financial considerations dominated the agency's strong desire to rebuild the site to its original scale. The $120 million in annual net lease revenues from the Trade Center represented 10 percent of the agency's 2001 net income, though that was only one measure of the complex's financial importance to the agency and not the most meaningful one at that. To feed its regional transportation mission, financial officials focused on a particular bottom-line metric: the amount of cash available to support debt service and reserves on the agency's bonds, and on this measure, the Trade Center lease revenues of 2001 accounted for a more significant 14.2 percent. After 9/11, increased security costs and related capital improvements forced the agency to scale back its recently approved five-year, $9 billion schedule of capital improvements to airports, bridges, tunnels, and PATH trains. These were fiscally strained times for the Port Authority. Demands to place open spaces and cultural facilities alongside the memorial space appeared as a threat to the revenue-producing potential of its site. "However that property is ultimately planned, the important thing from the PA's point of view is that we address the need to have a comparable revenue stream," one commissioner told the press.[32]

Considering Condemnation

Once the twin towers fell, the alignment between the Port Authority privatization of the complex and Silverstein's profit-making interests in operating the complex finalized just six weeks earlier collapsed as well. The public sector's interest in rebuilding in a post-9/11 environment and Silverstein's interest in making business profits were now out of sync, misaligned. During the next eighteen months as the planning process evolved, the misalignments only increased: The 9/11 families and the public wanted to build a memorial. The governor wanted to build out the vision of Studio Daniel Libeskind's master plan (plate 7), discussed in detail in a later chapter, complete with an iconic skyscraper, a Freedom Tower, as he would shortly name it. The Port Authority wanted to build its own institutional memorial in the form of a grand transportation terminal to rival Grand Central Terminal. Against these public ambitions, Silverstein was determined to rebuild the complete commercial complex as soon as possible in line with business dictates of the Manhattan real estate market.

Silverstein's property position was a big challenge for public officials. His ninety-nine-year lease agreement gave him control of the land, certain obligations, and a lot of rights. More than once, especially as conflicts with Silverstein became more apparent, the Port Authority considered employing government's power of eminent domain to condemn his lease and then pay to take it over. It would not have been unusual for a government entity to condemn the interest of one of its own tenants or lessees, remarked Gideon Kanner, a professor at Loyola Law School in Los Angeles and an expert on eminent domain.[33] If influential people in the downtown business community had been polled, the tally might well have shown support for condemnation, even though this would not take the project out of political hands. The site might have then been redeveloped in the same fashion as Battery Park City, with the Port Authority or a subsidiary of the ESDC operating in a semiautonomous fashion, developing the infrastructure and preparing individual sites for development, which would then be leased to different private developers. But semiautonomous decision-making was not a likely outcome at Ground Zero.

City officials discussed the condemnation idea. The Port Authority hired lawyers to look into how they might exercise the condemnation option and remove Silverstein from the rebuilding of Ground Zero. The governor's office considered it, but Governor Pataki did not want to go in that direction. "There were a lot of pluses to considering that," he said. "The negatives were to tie the site up in years of litigation." All came to the same conclusion: There was no practical way to do it. Condemnation would complicate resolution of the insurance casualty claim Silverstein was pursuing. The condemnation award would likely be years in determination and the cost unknown. The whole process would be too costly. You don't want to get into condemnation, the developer told PA executive director Seymour; it will go on for years. And Pataki wanted to move rebuilding forward as quickly as practical. "It was an important message to send to the city, the state, and the country," he said years later, "that this wasn't going to be something where legal impediments could prevent a vision from happening."[34]

Condemnation was just too big a political risk for both the Port Authority and the governor. In any kind of "friendly" deal short of condemnation, Silverstein would demand a big buyout number. The bi-state agency had just privatized its biggest asset to get out of the real estate business, and Silverstein was obligated to keep making lease payments to the agency or else forfeit his development rights, meaning the $120 million a year revenue flow to the agency would continue despite the destruction of the complex. On all sides, then, hard money considerations kept the threat of condemnation at bay. Money, of course, endows power and control, and each of the three big government stakeholders was constantly vying to maintain control or capture more. By keeping Silverstein's lease in place, the Port Authority could maintain its pivotal position in the rebuilding process taking place on land it owned. "They saw it as their key to hanging on to the site," said Robert D. Yaro, then president of the influential Regional Plan Association. "They were afraid of losing control to the city or the state."[35]

The notion that government could use its powers of eminent domain at Ground Zero surfaced in the press in July 2002, shortly after the LMDC's public humbling following the release of the first set of master plans prepared by Beyer Blinder Bell (chronicled in later chapters). In response to the severe criticism of the initial site plans as too dense, the LMDC was considering how it might move some of the ten million square feet of lost commercial space Silverstein intended to restore to nearby sites to be acquired by eminent domain. The possibility of condemning Silverstein's lease interests at Ground Zero surfaced as public officials talked through the press about enlarging the area for rebuilding. The notice was short-lived, however. Condemnation is "a perfect prescription for chaos," said

Silverstein's spokesman Howard Rubenstein in response to the press item; "this is something that is pure nonsense in terms of getting the job done."[36]

There are those who believe that had Nelson A. Rockefeller been governor at this time, in all likelihood things with Silverstein would have played out differently. Rockefeller would have had to deal with the same obstacles—Silverstein and his property rights and the New Jersey side of the Port Authority—but as a governor who loved to build and build big, Rockefeller would have been inclined to say to Silverstein, "You have been owner of the leasehold for only six weeks, and this is a national emergency. You are going to be condemned out." This would have put Silverstein in the position of having to make the argument in the press that rebuilding is a commercial venture, and that he has the right to make maximum profit—a different storyline than "I have the right as well as the obligation to rebuild." Condemning out Silverstein's leasehold interest could have changed the course of events; not doing so maintained the misaligned interests embedded in what had become a dysfunctional arrangement and made rebuilding Ground Zero dependent on Silverstein's continuing role, a condition the developer constantly leveraged to his business advantage.

The strong sense of civic unity immediately after 9/11 and the optimistic drive to rebuild seemed to discount or misunderstand how property rights would come to shape the politics of implementation. Property rights are powerful. They are complex. They are multifaceted. Law and common custom in the United States heavily protect them. They can be leveraged, politically as well as financially. At Ground Zero, they were the subtext of control, rarely played out publicly in speeches or in the press or in the courts, but always an underlying lever on the dynamics of decision-making, especially when conflict threatened litigation. In any discussion about how to recapture the leasehold interest of Larry Silverstein and his equity investors; how to manage the demands of their acquisition lender, GMAC Commercial Mortgage Corp.; or Westfield America's intense dissatisfaction with the Libeskind master plan, the power of property rights proved decisive. It enabled Silverstein to prevail in exercising his "right and obligation" to rebuild the office towers. The Port Authority was also able to regain ownership over the retail uses, thereby reducing the number of other potential players with rights to replace what they had lost when the complex was destroyed on 9/11. It also limited the opportunity to put in place a radically different vision of how these sixteen acres might reshape the urban fabric of downtown. When it was presented in February 2003, the Libeskind master plan put forth a new set of visual images but, aside from the acreage set aside for the memorial and an accompanying memorial museum, the new vision represented a reconfiguration of buildings dictated by property interests.

RIVALS IN OPPORTUNITY

From the start, power to preside over the rebuilding agenda at Ground Zero was imbalanced, split between two government entities with different powers, different resources, and different agendas. The differences were structural. As the landowner of those sixteen acres, the Port Authority held claim to a superior legal position when it came to rebuilding. Not only did it have the power of property rights behind its position, it was buttressed by a strong balance sheet, independent streams of revenue, and the statutory ability to issue bonds to finance its projects. Decades of legacy and tradition and a large veteran staff accustomed to doing things its own way filled out its determination to shape what got built at Ground Zero.

The LMDC controlled a big pot of federal dollars and the ability to distribute the money widely, seemingly without political interference. It commanded moral authority as the agency created to rebuild lower Manhattan because of the 9/11 event. As a newcomer, however, it was just organizing its staff and practices; it did not have "the web of relationships that other bureaucracies customarily rely on to ease communications and soften differences."[37] It had no property interests at Ground Zero. Most critically, it had no power to enforce decisions at Ground Zero. It was a paper tiger. It was never empowered to ride herd over the entire process, over the Port Authority and all the other agencies that would be involved in rebuilding. For the city, acting through the LMDC, this was the fundamental flaw. For the governor, the structure of the LMDC served a political function: The development corporation would oversee the planning and memorial processes yet allow him to step in and make dispositive decisions at Ground Zero.

The dynamic between the temporarily overwhelmed but powerful Port Authority seeking to restore control over its site and respect for its interest at Ground Zero and the mission-driven but legally powerless LMDC seeking to establish its legitimacy amid an intense and evolving political arena developed into distrust that played out in the planning process. Both government agents were on a mission. Both believed they would control the rebuilding process. Both sought power, rivals in an increasingly politicized environment.

Control over the planning process at Ground Zero was complicated by other conditions as well: the site's split ownership, the failure of public officials to set priorities, the inability of any principal or group to submerge its ambitions to the greater civic good, and the egos of those involved in making decisions. All of these forces played a role in explaining the contentious and complicated path of rebuilding. Above all, clear leadership was lacking. Rather than put his political capital on the line at the outset, Governor Pataki remained cautious and uncommitted during the planning debate, husbanding his political resources and exercising his powers "in a spirit of political opportunism rather than broad commitment to the public interest." How might an activist governor like Rockefeller have made decisions at Ground Zero? I asked civic leader Robert Douglass, whose inside knowledge of city-state relations was forged during the heady years of state government from 1965 to 1972 as counsel and later secretary to the governor, and longtime associate of the Rockefeller family. "Rockefeller would have been all over it," he replied.[38] Pataki, unlike Rockefeller, was not an urban-oriented governor; he was not a builder. He was an environmentalist and, by many accounts, left a good record in that area.

Pataki's actions and those senior staff were shaped by his immediate desire for a third term as governor and his future aspirations in national politics, his ongoing relations with President Bush (who faced reelection in November 2004), and the swirl of political loyalties around both men. The governor controlled the reins of power in the state; it was within his grasp to exercise formidable leadership. Despite his presumptive political ambitions—or perhaps because of them—he was slow and typically late to respond. His lack of hands-on attention created an obvious vacuum, and that vacuum created by the governor's political style became an opportunity for others to push forward their individual agendas of ambition. A certain level of confusion and conflict seemed "normal" in this unprecedented planning situation. The vacuum of leadership, however, compounded the situation. Many decisions seemed to reflect an ad hoc interplay of commanding personalities, fervent loyalties, powerful emotions, and strong individual interests. No one was in full control.

CHAPTER 4

Purse Power

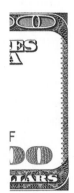

FIGURE 4.1 Author

ON SEPTEMBER 12, NEW YORK CITY regained its ambition for historic city build-ing. The city had a glorious heritage of thinking big, an innovative tradition of public construction that brought into being one remarkable project after another: Central Park (1857, 1873), the Brooklyn Bridge (1883), the New Croton Aqueduct (1890), the world's largest subway system (722 miles), and with the completion of the Holland Tunnel in 1927, the first mechanically ventilated underwater vehicu-lar crossing in history, to name a few. "No city on earth could match the energy New York displayed in remaking itself to meet the challenges of modern life—nor the brilliance, daring, and, in most cases, speed with which it carried out that re-making," the architect and writer James Sanders wrote in a *Times* op-ed near the first anniversary of 9/11.[1] Beginning in the mid-nineteenth century, a distinctive civic culture of ambition and expertise reshaped the physical landscape of New York City, as Keith D. Revell described in *Building Gotham: Civic Culture and Public Policy in New York City, 1898–1938*. Yet by the 1960s, the spirit of change and the cost-benefit calculus that made great public works possible was gone—dissipated in a reactionary wave of criticism to the autocratic methods of New York's greatest builder, Robert Moses. Urban renewal's wholesale destruction of neighborhoods, the shift to a community-based approach to development and new appreciation of preservation stimulated by Jane Jacobs's widely acclaimed *Death and Life of Great American Cities*, and the rise of the environmental movement profoundly changed the political calculus of thinking big. "New York seemed able to survive and even thrive without developing a new way" to build new big public works projects. On the morning of September 11, however, "the choice was taken out of the city's hands." The pendulum, Sanders believed, had begun to swing back to "the city's older tradition of daring and ambitious public works."[2]

Not everyone thought the legacy of difficult and contentious development projects—symbolized by the failure of Westway, the city's attempt to rebuild the collapsed West Side Highway into a six-lane artery as part of the Interstate Highway System on 234 acres of Hudson River landfill—caused the demise of ambitions for large-scale city building. Still, a broad consensus prevailed that it was not easy to build big in New York City, where a diffusion of power reduced the probabilities of making things happen, or happen in a reasonable time frame. The process of building major public works in the city was strangled in red tape, fractious politics, elaborate review processes, and inevitable litigation. For all the criticism of Robert Moses's autocratic methods, he "solved a crucial dilemma for democratic societies: how to build the large public works that were essential to modern urban life but whose daunting time frame and enormous human and economic costs made them anathema to public officials, who fear alienating any segment of the electorate."[3] To execute on their big ambitions, every player in the circle of influence surrounding Ground Zero would have to find a way to solve this dilemma. State officials, City Hall officials, New York's U.S. congressional representatives, Port Authority senior executives, LMDC executives, private-sector leaseholders and other development interests, the downtown business establishment, the 9/11 families—New York's governor and even New Jersey's—all would have to navigate the highly fragmented channels of power that bore on getting things done in New York City. Strategies would need to be formulated, alliances built, and political capital spent to push through ambitious agendas.

Thinking big engenders well-known problems: Building celebrated pieces of the city the size of Battery Park City or Rockefeller Center are massively expensive. If plans call for the use of eminent domain, the risk escalates exponentially. Guaranteed targets of litigation, large-scale projects typically play out over a two-decade time frame, sometimes longer, but well beyond a politician's normal time horizon. Legendary development hurdles further complicate execution. At Ground Zero, though, a large bundle of federal money was available, and eminent domain had been taken off the list of options precisely because it was too risky politically and certain to provoke lengthy and costly litigation by the leaseholder. A vision existed. A specially crafted development corporation had been put in place and powerful people appointed to its board. No legislative approvals for action were necessary since both the Port Authority and the LMDC were legally exempt from local land-use regulations. At an early forum to discuss issues and potential opportunities in rebuilding, Brookfield Properties executive and civic leader John E. Zuccotti remarked, "When you consider the problems with development, actually, it's fortuitous that both Battery Park City and the Port Authority are under public ownership. If the site had to be assembled, we'd never get anything done."[4] The political and economic challenges of rebuilding, nonetheless, remained daunting due to complications of property ownership, complexities of ambitious vision, and extraordinary costs, though costs would not even factor into the equation for years to come.

Testament to how New York City regained its will to think big and execute on an ambitious scale is the Forty-second Street Redevelopment Project at Times Square. As I detailed in *Times Square Roulette: Rebuilding the City Icon*, twenty years into what would become a thirty-year timeline of constant effort and major revisions to the initial plan, evidence of big success broke the curse of inhibition when it came to large-scale public development in New York. The achievement in Times Square offered a number of lessons about what it took to succeed with a high-profile symbolic project. Lesson one: Patience and perseverance. Lesson two: Opposition sometimes makes for a better project. Lesson three: Rebuilding must be symbolically consistent with the legacy of place. Lesson four: Leaders make things happen apart from market forces, political dynamics, and institutional context. Lesson five: Continuity of leadership is essential in the context of fragmented governmental power prevalent in American cities.

Rebuilding the Trade Center site differed from the Times Square project in two salient ways that vastly complicated the execution task at Ground Zero: The cast of players was much larger, especially on the intergovernmental front, and the emotional overlay of 9/11 created an unprecedented planning condition. For different reasons, both sites were overly endowed with symbolic meaning: If Forty-second Street–Times Square served as the symbolic soul of the city, the World Trade Center served as the symbolic pulse of the city economy, despite the fact that much of downtown's financial establishment had moved to midtown Manhattan. As in Times Square, the importance of symbolic politics loomed large at Ground Zero. The rhetoric deployed during fractious controversies might at times become hyperbolic. But by serving as a shield behind which intense disagreements yet to be resolved might persist, rhetoric helped to mediate the conflicted territory at Ground Zero.

Money was the crucible of rebuilding (figure 4.1). The mother lode of public resources needed not to just rebuild Ground Zero but to fulfill the city's ambitions for all of lower Manhattan was being routed through two often-clogged channels of intergovernmental power: Congressional vote getting in the chambers of the grand neoclassical U.S. Capitol building in Washington, D.C., and New York–New Jersey dealmaking in the Port Authority's mundane board room in midtown Manhattan. While money from Washington fueled the scope of New York's rebuilding ambitions, President George W. Bush's promise of $20 billion would only become reality when Congress appropriated the funds, and despite the unprecedented tragedy in lower Manhattan, the New York congressional delegation was going to have to fight hard to assure timely and complete delivery, as aptly captured by the editorial cartoon in figure 4.2.

For the two governors in control of the purse strings at the Port Authority, the political stakes involved in funding New York's rebuilding project were immediately evident and starkly different. Resolving their different priorities for tapping the agency's coffers created repeated obstacles in the path of progress at Ground Zero, obstacles that become paramount when it came time to craft a new deal with Larry Silverstein in 2006. That deal to restructure control over who would build what at Ground Zero became a predicate to a second deal in 2010 to support construction of his towers with deep subsidy dollars. In both instances, the New Jersey side of the PA weighed in to extract a major concession before it would agree to action at Ground Zero. The intense politicization of the bi-state agency,

FIGURE 4.2 *"$20 Billion? Sure, Maybe, and Not So Fast."* ©2002 ANDY RASH

nominally regional in its founding conception, and the twenty-year-long effort to privatize the World Trade Center complex heavily foreshadowed the politics of executing these successive deals with Silverstein. The struggles to break through bottlenecks in both money channels illustrate how political capital was used strategically and tactically behind the scenes to garner billions of dollars in public resources that could be funneled into the rebuilding effort.

MONEY FROM WASHINGTON

The state of emergency in New York City following the terrorist attack on 9/11 was unlike that following a natural calamity. The geopolitical forces behind the attack triggered security issues that threatened the city's dense and highly productive pattern of business activity and prompted immediate questions about its economic future. The scope of antiterrorist preparations and heightened security measures for the nation at large held particular salience for cities such as New York with high-density clusters of business activity, intricate infrastructure networks, and especially subway systems. Seen through the lens of 9/11, all were potential targets of mass attack. The city was not perceived as safe, though in the unshakable spirit that defined New York City, no official wanted to go on record with that thought.

The immediate economic losses from 9/11 were staggering: $26.1 billion in destroyed buildings and infrastructure; fifty-one thousand private-sector jobs lost in the first month after the attack; and a drop of $11.5 billion in gross city product, the most comprehensive measure of economic activity, in the quarter following the attack. Economic activity in lower Manhattan all but ceased for several weeks. City officials expected bad times ahead. Employment freezes and budget cuts were sure to follow. "The country is supportive," Joyce Purnick of the *Times* wrote, "but moral support will not make people want to rebuild or set up shop in New York or help a small business without the resources of a multinational company to find new offices. Nor will it make up for lost revenues, costly needs or understandable fears."[5]

In his disaster declaration President Bush promised, "We are prepared to spend whatever it takes to rescue victims, to help the citizens of New York City and Washington, D.C. to respond to this tragedy and to protect our national security." With bipartisan support Congress quickly passed a $40 billion emergency appropriation for immediate military expenses and recovery aid. New York City expected to get half, though just how much economic adrenaline the $20 billion would deliver remained unclear: The real costs of recovery and rebuilding were total unknowns (figure 4.3). The aid-package number seemed large—until the expenses involved were considered. And these expenses, Marcia Van Wagner, deputy research director and chief economist at the business-oriented Citizens

FIGURE 4.3 DAVIES ©2001 THE JOURNAL NEWS. DIST. BY UNIVERSAL UCLICK. REPRINTED WITH
PERMISSION. ALL RIGHTS RESERVED

Budget Commission, remarked at an academic meeting, would grow significantly when the goal changed from merely rebuilding to revitalizing lower Manhattan.[6]

The promise of federal aid fueled the city's ambition to rebuild in a fashion that would showcase its social and cultural resilience and, most importantly, provide for its long-term economic recovery. The goal was not just to rebuild the Trade Center site but reposition lower Manhattan for the twenty-first century. This $20 billion (not including additional appropriations for the Victims' Compensation Fund or first responders' health compensation) was money that would otherwise not have come into the city. As one of the nation's wealthiest states, New York had a balance of payments with Washington that was consistently negative; year after year as tracked by "The Federal Budget and the States," a report card initiated by the late U.S. senator Daniel Patrick Moynihan, New York sent proportionally more tax dollars to Washington than almost any other state and received much less back in benefits. In an updated balance-of-payments analysis for 2001, the Public Policy Institute of New York State estimated the payments deficit at $39.6 billion, second only to that of California with its $58 billion payments deficit. As the director of the government's office of federal affairs told United Press International, "George

Pataki makes a very persuasive argument to members of Congress when he tells them, 'New York has been there providing taxes for a long time to the country that has resulted in many, [sic] federally funded projects in the West and South and now New York, which took the hit for the whole country, needs help.'" The president's immediate pledge and initial outpouring of support created an initial optimism that at least "the city is not the enemy of the rest of the country anymore."[7] Very quickly, however, city and state officials realized that they were not about to get a carte-blanche check—no monetary limits, no conditions. And past negativism toward New York City, they correctly feared, remained an obstacle in the path of their efforts to assure delivery of the promised dollars.

New York City has never had an easy time getting money out of Washington; the nation's ambivalence toward its largest city has always made things a little harder. The memory of Washington's attitude during the 1975 fiscal crisis encapsulated in a now immortal *Daily News* headline—"Ford to the City: Drop Dead"—remains an ever-present scar. Some said it cost Ford the presidency the following year, though in his speech denying federal assistance that would spare New York City from bankruptcy, Ford never explicitly said "drop dead," as veteran *Times* reporter Sam Roberts explained in his report amending the record of Ford's speech. "Only two months after saying or meaning or merely implying 'drop dead'—or perhaps, resorting to tough love by holding the city's feet to the fire—Mr. Ford signed legislation to provide federal loans to the city, which were repaid with interest."[8]

Despite the unprecedented tragedy of 9/11, New York's U.S. senators, Charles Schumer and Hillary Rodman Clinton (both Democrats), and New York representatives John E. Sweeney and James T. Walsh in the House (both Republicans) had a fight on their hands to assure the promised $20 billion would actually come to the city. The White House promised funding "when you'll need it," but the New York lawmakers in Congress feared that if the money was not turned over immediately, Congress would take away the commitment to New York City should some other disaster or national emergency occur. "Washington 101," said Representative Gary Ackerman, Democrat from Queens: "You don't have the money until you have the money."[9]

Twenty billion was a big pot of money, and it would not come without political infighting. Only three days after the attack, the *Congressional Quarterly Weekly* reported on the "quiet tension" over how much control the president would have over the money Congress was about to appropriate.[10] What restrictions would apply on how the funds would be spent? How much money would go to immediate recovery efforts versus long-term rebuilding efforts? Downtown business interests wanted to know how much would go to lower Manhattan, not just to the Trade Center site. Protracted debate prevailed in both houses of Congress. Schumer said securing the full amount of promised aid would be a "very heavy lift." Conservatives in Congress were watching carefully to see that nobody took advantage of the crisis to fund their own pork projects. In other words, the aid packages to New York were going to get a lot of scrutiny in a legislative process well known to be unpredictable.[11]

In unified fashion, the thirty-three-member New York congressional delegation fought to get as much cash as possible as soon as possible before the "era of good feelings" ended, but, in time, fighting broke out within the delegation as competing agendas, partisan and personal, seemed to come into play. The inside political problems started with Governor Pataki's big ask—$54 billion in federal aid for recovery, his "Rebuild New York" plan—laid out in mid-October, just weeks after 9/11. The size of the request and the scope of items included in Pataki's wildly ambitious kitchen-sink-quality wish list—transportation projects clearly not related to the terrorist attack like a high-speed rail link between Schenectady and Manhattan, bridge repairs upstate, and modernizing crossings along the Canadian border—immediately pegged his hastily conceived ask as overreach. It was ridiculed. Pataki had risked his credibility. "It's a mistake... and could place legitimate funding requests at risk in the future," the *Daily News* editorialized. "Not surprisingly, the White House and both sides of the aisle in Congress have been decidedly cool to the add-ons. The state should revise its list." The *Times* editorial board offered the same advice. Pataki's "excessively ambitious wish" of public projects, including some that had been "sitting on the shelf," was "too diffuse to generate the kind of support that can be realistically expected from Washington"; the gaffe of "laying every possible option on the table as an opening bid," was "a tactic that works better in Albany than in Washington." And in Washington, the *Times* reported an advisor to the state as saying, "It landed like a lead balloon down there."[12]

Unhappy with the governor's position, Mayor Giuliani and other elected officials lost no time in distancing themselves from the governor's proposal. "The federal aid that we ask for should be honestly connected to the World Trade Center," said the mayor, who declined to lobby in Washington on behalf of the Pataki plan. "If we lose that principle in the debate then we're going to lose."[13] With input from city and state officials as well as business leaders in New York, Schumer and Clinton worked to put together a more modest $2 billion to $5 billion proposal, one that featured tax incentives for businesses and tax-exempt financing for reconstruction projects, forms of off-budget assistance that would cost the federal government more in lost revenues than pure cash outlays and, therefore, would have an easier time making its way through Congress.

Was the aid debate in Washington just a matter of timing or a matter of how much money the city really needed? Or was it getting caught in a bigger battle over federal spending? In his first visit to Washington as mayor-elect, newly minted Republican Michael R. Bloomberg urged the White House to reconsider its opposition to additional aid to New York in 2001. "I think what we are talking about is an issue of timing," he said. "But we need the money now." Many New York officials, including Giuliani, acknowledged that all of the $20 billion would not be needed immediately. "I don't quite understand why someone would limit it [the appropriation] to the end of this year," Giuliani said. "The city is going to need that help over the course of the next 12 to 18 months." In late October, city estimates put the cost of reconstruction at $8 billion to $15 billion. "Right now, we don't need $10 billion—we would put it in T[reasury]-bills if we got it," Giuliani said.[14] When he uttered those words, the fragile unity of the twelve GOP members in the New York delegation, who had banded together with Democrats to fight for aid for the city, crumbled. They had been threatening to hold up the defense spending bill to get almost $10 billion more in New York aid. Under intense lobbying from the White House, they agreed to drop their threat of an ugly congressional floor fight against their own party after the White House agreed to $1.5 billion in additional Community Development Block Grant money (shuffling money within the $20 billion of the president's pledge) to meet the needs of lower Manhattan.

The federal aid package stalled out in mid-December, "caught in a tug of war with Defense Secretary Donald Rumsfeld, who feels that some of the money earmarked by the Senate for the city should be going toward his military budget." The argument, the *Times* editorialized, "is part of a needlessly complex tussle over how to make the current year's deficit look as small as possible. The answer is obviously to concede to reality, and pass the New York aid as part of the $40 billion response to the terrorist attack, with the military money in a separate emergency appropriation." Finally, after weeks and weeks of debate and battle, negotiators for the House and the Senate agreed to provide New York with an additional $8.2 billion in emergency aid, including $2.7 billion in economic development money directed to the LMDC. This was in addition to $3 billion in federal assistance to cover the costs of rescue and recovery at Ground Zero. About the aid package, Schumer remarked, "Every day, we make a little progress. It's like the Battle of Stalingrad. You fight house by house, but eventually you win." And that was the way the city's protracted battle to collect on President Bush's $20 billion pledge would go.

The $11.2 billion was a down payment. The remainder would come in installments, for specific purposes. White House budget director Mitchell E. Daniels Jr., considered the pledge to New York a multiyear project. When, however, he tried to count $5 billion from a federal fund for victims of the attack against the president's $20 billion pledge, he stepped beyond the line of reason and respect. "Well, it's cash dollars going straight into the pockets—almost all, if not all New York, but the vast majority are people in the New York area," he said trying to justify his position. "And it would be preposterous not to count it. But you know, I'm just going to tell you: for us, this has never been—it seems strange to me to treat this as a money-grubbing game." New York's lawmakers pounced hard on Daniels's words. Immediately, both New York senators emphasized that these funds were explicitly not part of the $20 billion pledge and that the compensation funds were not related in any way to the cleanup, rebuilding, or economic recovery in New York.[15] Daniels quickly retracted his self-defined "poorly chosen" words and sought to affirm the administration's commitment to fulfilling the president's pledge. But the comment implied an attitude that would not be forgotten.

The nation's ambivalence toward New York remained a persistent, worrisome factor for local public officials. Much as some in Congress could not forget Pataki's oversized ask for federal aid, some in the New York delegation could not forget Daniels's money-grubbing comment. "By and large the White House has been calling the shots in determining how much aid New York will get and when it will get it, but powerful forces in Congress are beginning to assert themselves and influence the process," the Times reported in February 2002. With the country at war and budget hawks in Congress increasingly worried about the pace of federal spending, lawmakers from other parts of the country could be wavering or hostile toward the city and its call for federal aid. The brute force of "New York Drop Dead," said New Jersey's then senior senator, Democrat Robert G. Torricelli, had morphed into a somewhat subtler "New York, go away." It was just "a little harder," Schumer said "because we are from New York."[16]

Not long after, on March 8, 2002, in a ceremony in the White House Rose Garden, in what a Times editorial called "a startling love fest with some normally cantanker-ous New Yorkers," President Bush delivered fully on his pledge and then some, adding an additional $1.5 billion to the package of federal aid for New York City passed as part of the economic stimulus package. The additional funds "seemed intended to quell the suspicions that New York Democrats had been expressing about the Bush administration's commitment to helping the city rebuild," but love fest aside, the "bitterness engendered by the battle of the past few months," wrote Times reporter Raymond Hernandez, "was barely below the surface." Representative Charles B. Rangel, Democrat of Manhattan, took at jab at budget director Daniels when he thanked the president, "for making it easier" for New York lawmakers "not to have to worry about the Office of Management and Budget."[17]

This second-round package offered economic stimulus in the form of a $5.03 billion package of tax benefits intended to encourage businesses and residents to remain in New York, which Schumer and Clinton had pushed for long and hard. This $5 billion, a quarter of the total recovery package, was the estimated ten-year cost of foregone tax revenue to the federal Treasury from giving New York the authority to issue a special class of tax-free bonds—"Liberty Bonds"—and tax breaks to downtown businesses. Congress had never before passed a tax-benefits package in response to a disaster, according to the Internal Revenue Service, and targeting a specific geographic area had not generally been past practice either. The New York Liberty Zone Program, as it was known, consisted of several different types of tax benefits. Some would aid small businesses (work opportunity tax credits); others, private property owners and investors (special depreciation allowances, special treatment of leasehold improvement property, an extension of the replacement period for involuntarily converted property, tax-exempt bonds for private property investment activity); and another, the City of New York (advance refunding of municipal bonds).[18] Some of the benefits only applied to businesses and property in the Liberty Zone—defined as the area located on or south of Canal Street, East Broadway (east of its intersection with Canal Street), or Grand Street (east of its intersection with East Broadway), while others were available to taxpayers outside of the zone. Labeling the tax-exempt bonds "Liberty Bonds" dovetailed symbolically with their historic pedigree dating back to war bonds issued by the U.S. Treasury in 1917 to support the Allied cause in World War I.

Under the Job Creation and Worker Assistance Act of 2002, Congress authorized $8 billion in aggregate of Liberty Bonds to support the lower Manhattan rebuilding effort. Of the $8 billion, $6.4 billion was allocated for commercial projects and $1.6 billion for residential projects. The bonds could be used to finance the acquisition, construction, reconstruction, and renovation of property located primarily in the Liberty Zone, although exceptions for commercial projects outside the zone (up to $2 billion) were permitted—and controversial. The governor and the mayor were each given control over $4 billion of Liberty Bond authority. The decision to provide bond financing was discretionary, and the developers whose projects were approved under the program benefited from lower financing costs since interest on the bonds was exempt from income taxation at all three levels of government—federal, state, and city. The bonds were not obligations of the state or the city, but rather obligations of the entities established by the state (New York Liberty Development Corporation) or the city (New York City Industrial Development Agency) to issue the bonds, and they were secured by pledged project revenues, generally without recourse to the borrower, issuer, city, or state. Liberty Bonds would prove to be especially important to rebuilding lower Manhattan, although more than a year into the program with demand for residential buildings exceeding that for commercial projects, the city's Independent Budget Office was concerned about whether the city and state would be able to issue the full $8 billion before their bonding authority expired in seventeen months, at the end of 2004. Acceding to the reality of that concern, Congress would approve a five-year extension of the Liberty Bond program in September 2004; at that time, more than half of the appropriation, $5.2 billion, remained unused.[19]

The full $21.5 billion package would be paid out over time through a multiplicity of federal programs and disbursed to a wide variety of recipients, as was typical of historical federal urban-aid funding patterns: city government, state government, businesses, individuals, nonprofits, and other government entities, including federal agencies whose approval would be needed for specific projects. Because the full costs of emergency recovery were still unknown, as were the costs of the city's long-term rebuilding needs, some adjustment in these appropriations became inevitable. As those needs became apparent, New York's legislators moved quickly into a second round of intense lobbying to convince Congress to reappropriate funds and thereby help New York City gain programmatic flexibility through transfers that allowed reallocation of specific pots of federal dollars or conversion of tax benefits to other uses.[20]

Just months after President Bush's Rose Garden ceremony, the New York City Independent Budget Office (IBO) published a report that raised the question, "Is there a mismatch between the money available and what the city wants or needs it for?" In the September 2001 emergency aid bill, Congress had appropriated more money to the Federal Emergency Management Agency (FEMA) for cleanup, reconstruction of damaged facilities and equipment, police and fire overtime, and other such needs (approximately $9 billion) than subsequently appeared to be needed; the city had spent about $1 billion on such disaster relief, and estimates at the time indicated that the total city and state cleanup bill would not exceed $3 billion. That meant "roughly $6 billion may not be available for other than the currently defined purposes," the IBO concluded. At the same time, the price tag for revitalizing lower Manhattan "is large, much larger than the funding appropriated for such purposes."[21]

Coincident in timing with the report, the Bloomberg administration traveled to Washington hat in hand to make a case for using some of the federal aid earmarked for recovery to close the city's roughly $5 billion budget gap. In a letter to FEMA, Deputy Mayor Doctoroff sought compensation for lost tax revenues, at least $650 million of which the city argued was directly attributable to the 9/11 attack. This was a political stretch since in previous disasters, such as hurricanes or earthquakes, the federal government had not bailed out local governments for lost revenues. Over time, though, as the fluidity of spending needs evolved, the city succeeded in securing $1.7 billion of essentially unrestricted budget relief. This huge win came through two channels. The first was savings on the city's debt payments made possible by a federal tax bill passed in March 2002 allowing the city to refinance some outstanding debt at lower interest rates, at a cost to the federal government of $937 million (although the IBO noted the benefit to the city was less). The second was an "unprecedented transfer" of funds from the FEMA emergency-aid appropriation delivering $762.1 million in unrestricted budgetary relief. Years later, in 2011, in an accounting of 9/11 federal aid for New York City directed to general budgetary relief, the IBO's calculations totaled out at $1.9 billion.

Another transfer that marked a significant departure from federal policy was the reallocation of $2.75 billion of FEMA emergency funds to transportation rebuilding. This shift allowed disaster-relief money to be used to create something new, not just to rebuild what had been destroyed. For several months Schumer and Pataki lobbied hard for greater flexibility. After intensive negotiations between FEMA and the governor's office, federal, state, and city officials gathered at Ground Zero in mid-August to celebrate their cooperation in winning on this latest round of aid adjustments. Although the funds did not come without strings attached, meaning the various transportation agencies involved—the Port Authority, the Metropolitan Transportation Authority (MTA), and the State Department of Transportation—would have to apply to FEMA for funding of specific projects, the governor's office controlled the reins of power over these dollars, except for its shared power at the bi-state Port Authority.

"Transportation is the foundation of the revival of Lower Manhattan—the underpinning of any real renewal," the *Times* editorial board said at the start of the transportation reappropriation campaign, and downtown business interests, transit advocates, and public officials were perfectly aligned on this central policy principle.[22] The $1.8 billion Congress initially had appropriated could not begin to meet the city and state's ambitions for reconstructing and improving downtown's shattered transportation system. The wish list of projects for transportation infrastructure that New York officials; the chairman of the state-run MTA, Peter S. Kalikow; and Pataki loyal lieutenants PA executive director Joseph J. Seymour and LMDC president Louis R. Tomson presented to congressional leaders in April went far beyond rebuilding what was lost. "It was the first time that the city and state have delivered a definitive list of their transit plans, with price tags and priorities attached," the *Times* reported. At the top of that project list was $2 billion to build what the Port Authority wanted—a magnificent new transportation terminal that would rival midtown's Grand Central Terminal. The additional $2.75 billion transferred from FEMA went a distance to top the total funds allocated to transportation at $4.55 billion, yet that sum fell far short of the $7.3 billion government officials had been seeking to modernize downtown's labyrinthine transit system and fix other long-standing transportation problems in lower Manhattan.

The governor was gaining extraordinary reach into the affairs of the city. In telling public officials, "You figure out what is best for you and we are going to help fund that for you," FEMA officials had given the Pataki administration the discretion to set priorities for projects that would shape the city for the twenty-first century. The power embedded in the federal largess, one of the single largest sums ever available for city transportation (yet far short of the $8.55 billion federal gift to Boston for its Central Artery–Tunnel Project, aka the "Big Dig"),[23] presented a once-in-a-century opportunity. A pitched battle over how the money would be spent started almost immediately, waged largely out of public view. Should the money be spent only to improve the transit lines already there? Or should it also be used to bring in new service, for the first time making downtown as accessible to suburban commuters as midtown has always been because it has Grand Central Terminal and Penn Station?

Whereas a consensus had emerged on the importance of building a grand downtown transportation terminal and a Fulton Street subway station complete with concourse connections to the PATH station, it ended there. A contentious debate erupted over $700 million for other projects on the governor's $7.3 billion list—renovating the South Ferry Terminal, adding commuter ferries across the Hudson River, and building a concourse to connect four subway lines running beneath Rector Street. These projects had been proposed before 9/11, and Schumer tried to block them because they were not directly related to the 9/11 attack. Arguing that using disaster aid to finance these projects would violate the even more flexible rules that had been put in place for use of these FEMA funds, he nevertheless came under "withering attack from some of his own allies."[24] And perhaps unsurprisingly, it did not seem to matter that most of the potential projects did not add capacity to the downtown transportation system.

Extending commuter rail service into lower Manhattan to connect with Long Island and the region's airports, JFK and Newark Liberty International—a project known as the "train-to-plane"—was a high priority of downtown's most stalwart advocates. Schumer along with Doctoroff and Zuccotti of Brookfield Financial Properties and Weisbrod, president of the Alliance for Downtown New York, were pitching hard for it. Brookfield's consultants had figured out a way to actually build such a link, a super shuttle, though it was an exceedingly complex and costly proposition; estimates ranged from $1.9 billion to more than $5 billion. Continuous debate elevated the importance of the proposition. Advocates considered it a singular game-changing project able to reshape the basic nature of lower Manhattan. Some top state officials reportedly took a more "jaundiced view." "There's nothing wrong with it," one said. "But when the triage starts, what makes the cut?"[25]

Unsurprisingly, that depended on the politics behind who was making the cut. State officials, in consultation with several transportation agencies working under the umbrella of a "Transportation Working Group" comprising representatives of the state, the city, the state-run Metropolitan Transportation Authority, the Port Authority of New York and New Jersey, the New York State Department of Transportation, and the LMDC, made the cuts. Under the normal course of capital planning, the boards of the transportation authorities would prioritize and approve projects but state officials reportedly bypassed that process. The lapse in process angered then powerful State Assembly Speaker Sheldon Silver, lower Manhattan's longtime Democratic representative. In his speech before the Association for a Better New York on April 24, 2003, Governor Pataki laid out the transportation priorities that had made the cut: a permanent PATH Transportation Terminal at the World Trade Center to rival midtown Manhattan's Grand Central Terminal ($1.7 billion); a new and distinctive Fulton Street Transit Center that would reorganize the station's existing maze of narrow ramps, stairs, and platforms ($750 million); a new terminal at South Ferry Station to replace the functionally obsolete existing station under Battery Park serving Staten Island ($400 million). Beyond these three, the additional $1.7 billion would be spread among several downtown projects: a program to transform the wide expanse of concrete that defines West Street–Route 9A into a tree-lined promenade, with a new short tunnel from Vesey Street to Liberty Street to divert fast-moving traffic underground; direct rail service from lower Manhattan to Long Island and JFK Airport; and bus facilities and site infrastructure at Ground Zero. After more debate and adjustments over time in priorities (and cost estimates), federal officials announced grant awards totaling $4.23 billion for five projects on December 3, 2003, and July 12, 2005. As presented in table 4.1, the final list of projects included a WTC Vehicle Security Center and Tour Bus Facility ($478 million), and Route 9A–North and South Promenade ($287.3 million) at a much-reduced cost after Governor Pataki dropped the initial plan to bury West Street, as explained in a later chapter.[26]

The power to direct the scope of rebuilding downtown was not lodged in any one source of power; it was fragmented. The LMDC board, composed of powerful people appointed by the elected executives of state and local governments, lacked real power to make decisions impacting the rebuilding at Ground Zero, as explained in the previous chapter: unlike a typical public board, yet not powerful like a corporate board. In a relatively short time, it became the odd player out among the dueling forces at Ground Zero. But it had money: $2.7 billion of federal dollars in the form of relatively unrestricted Community Development Block Grant funds. Through that channel, the LMDC became a pivotal player in the resurgence of downtown. When the IBO tallied the fund allocations ten years after the 9/11 attack, long-term rebuilding and development had absorbed $11.34 billion, or 55 percent, of the $20.5 billion in aid coming from the federal government—$7.5 billion of which went directly to rebuilding the Trade Center site. True

Table 4.1 Federally Funded Transportation Grant Awards for Lower Manhattan, as Announced in July 2003 and December 2005

Project, Grantee, and Date	Funding Amount	Description
WTC Permanent PATH Transportation Terminal PANYNJ 2003, 2005	$2,201 million	Program to create a grand train terminal for lower Manhattan to rival Grand Central Terminal in midtown Manhattan; service the PATH rail service for commuters between New York and New Jersey and provide seamless pedestrian connections to multiple subway lines, bus systems, and ferry service for commuters; and provide for a large retail presence at the Trade Center. Called the transportation "Hub."
Fulton Street Transit Center MTA 2003, 2005	$847 million	Program for a new and distinctive multi-level facility to serve eleven subway lines; the project reorganizes the maze of narrow ramps, stairs, and platforms within the station itself and establishes a walkway under Dey Street connecting the Fulton Street Transit Center to the WTC transportation Hub.
South Ferry Terminal MTA 2003, 2005	$420 million	Program to replace the functionally obsolete station under Battery Park, which serves Staten Island Ferry riders. The new redesign accommodates the full length of a typical ten-car subway train, expanding the existing five-car platform.
Route 9A/WTC North/South Promenade NYS DOT 2005	$287.3 million	Landscaped promenade in the southern portion of Route 9A, also known as West Street, adjacent to the World Trade Center and Battery Park City. In addition to repairing the roadway, the project links the Trade Center site physically and visually to the southern tip of Manhattan, Ellis Island, and the Statute of Liberty.
WTC Vehicle Security Center/Tour Bus Facility PANYNJ 2005	$478 million	Central security conduit for the screening of vehicles to support operations of the World Trade Center commercial buildings, transportation terminal, memorial and other facilities. Also provides for substantial bus parking area and spaces for the Port Authority operations of the Trade Center.

Source: Federal Transit Administration (FTA).

to its name with the money it controlled, the LMDC spent $1.86 billion, or more than two of every three dollars, in lower Manhattan *beyond* Ground Zero. If a business or utility wanted assistance or local officials wanted housing, parks, streets, and educational facilities, or nonprofits and arts groups wanted cultural programming grants, the LMDC was the go-to place for funding with a downtown focus. In terms of assuring long-term sustainability, the LMDC's control over its pot of federal dollars was dispositive. It was the rare pool of discretionary money for lower Manhattan, and its impact was potent.

TWO STATES IN THE BOARD ROOM

The two states created the Port of New York Authority on April 30, 1921 (as an amendment to an 1834 compact between New York and New Jersey), as the nation's first bi-state agency established by interstate compact; the compact was approved by Congress in August of that year. Modeled after the London Port Authority, the agency was charged with developing the "terminal, transportation, and other facilities of commerce" in the New York–New Jersey region. It was, as urban historian Kenneth T. Jackson remarked in the foreword to Jameson W. Doig's *Empire on the Hudson*, "an institution unlike anything ever before seen in the United States." It was "founded as the very embodiment of the Progressive approach to politics—that is, to rely on experts, to insulate them from the narrow interests and patronage needs of elected office-holders, and to give them the power to get things done."[27] Neither its decision-making board of commissioners nor executive director were elected officials. Being given the statutory power to issue its own bonds allowed the Port Authority to get things done independently—following its own priorities. Moreover, it was able to protect its own priorities by incorporating them into bond resolutions—legal contracts with bondholders that cannot be impaired by legislatures—with legal effect over thirty- or forty-year periods. From the very start of its existence, the bond covenant proved to be a powerful tool that made possible financing the fledging institution's big regional projects. Though it did not have the power to tax, its borrowing capacity based on independent revenue sources from the heavily used bridges, tunnels, terminals, and associated transportation facilities it built endowed the Port Authority over time with great institutional power and commanding influence in shaping big-project infrastructure so essential to building the region's twentieth-century economic power.

Cooperative effort was structured into the bi-state compact. The Port Authority is governed by an unpaid board of twelve commissioners, six appointed by each governor (subject to approval by the respective state senate) for overlapping six-year terms; by custom, New York's governor has appointed the executive director and New Jersey's governor, the chairman of the board of commissioners. Neither governor commands individual power to control the spending decisions of the agency, which must be approved by its board with at least three commissioners of each state voting affirmatively. However difficult and irksome its institutional autonomy has proved to be, the Port Authority has been indispensable to achieving the ambitions of governor after governor of these two states facing each other across the deep and wide river named for Henry Hudson. Elected leaders desirous of building big and often risky growth-engine projects—projects of regional scope that span the New York–New Jersey territorial divide down the middle of the Hudson River splitting the natural unity of the great New York Bay—have turned to the Port for funding that in the ordinary course of more cumbersome democratic budget processes of legislative politics would be difficult to get. Securing funds for its big projects—interstate crossings (George Washington Bridge, Lincoln Tunnel, three bridge crossings between Staten Island and New Jersey), regional airports (LaGuardia, JFK, Newark Liberty International), marine and port facilities (Elizabeth, New Jersey, and Brooklyn, New York), and economic development projects, chief among them, the original World Trade Center—all called for bi-state agreement not so easily achieved. The governors needed one another to push through their priority projects, and no project was as illustrative of this structural tension as New York's push to build a World Trade Center and its subsequent rebuilding after 9/11.

Known as the Port of New York Authority or "PONYA" until 1972, the agency's original name understated the political power of New Jersey when it came to making resource-allocating decisions in the agency's board room. "To this smaller state," Doig wrote, "its demand for recognition is a matter of economic necessity, of political sovereignty. Above all, perhaps, it is a matter of pride."[28] Designed to tackle the problem of interstate coordination on a regional scale in the spirit of capitalism and the interests of economic efficiency, the Port has a domain that encompasses a geographic scope of gigantic proportions. As defined by the bi-state compact, the Port District extends roughly twenty-five miles in all directions from the Statue of Liberty across fifteen hundred square miles of land and water in two states; it includes the region's main waterways, the five counties of New York City, and portions of nine counties of New Jersey and of three counties in suburban New York State, as shown in figure 4.4. It takes in the most populous parts of both states. Yet as the original name proclaimed, the nation's largest city dominates the region as its magnetic force and center of economic gravity.

Structural parity in governance, however, has counterbalanced New York's economic dominance. It has allowed the smaller state—traditionally anxious about New York's economic and political power—time and time again to leverage its

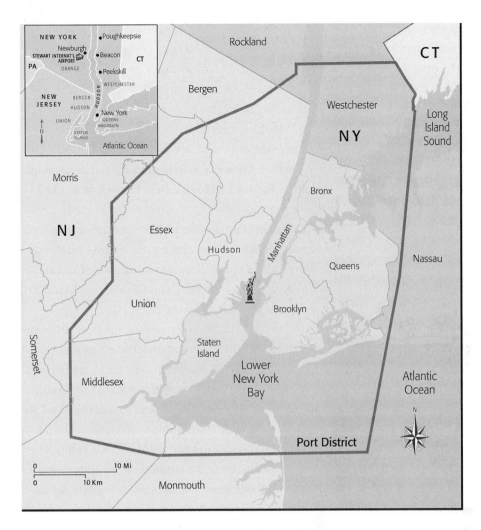

FIGURE 4.4 *The Port of New York district created in April 1921. The district includes the region's main waterways, the five counties of New York City, and portions of nine counties in New Jersey and of three counties in suburban New York State.* THE PORT AUTHORITY OF NEW YORK AND NEW JERSEY

position and push through its own priorities for capital spending by the Port Authority. Whereas the breadth of the Port District's geographic scope created the planning potential for long-range regional solutions to the area's vexing transportation problems, in terms of agency politics, regionalism has meant that nothing gets done without New Jersey's agreement, and that always involves the question: What's in it for New Jersey? In this regard, the historic deal that made possible the development of the World Trade Center in the 1960s represented the classic accommodation of interests, offering each state what it most desired at the time.

A world trade facility had first been proposed in 1960 in a report by the Downtown–Lower Manhattan Association (DLMA) as a means to revitalize the district. A year later, the Port Authority came out with its own report officially recommending construction of such a facility to be built along the East River. The site proposed by David Rockefeller's DLMA and strongly endorsed by Austin J. Tobin's Port Authority—a thirteen-and-a-half-acre stretch from Old Slip on its south boundary to Fulton Street on the north, near the site of the Fulton Fish Market on the East River—was "on the wrong side of Manhattan (or, perhaps, the Hudson) in the opinion of many in the New Jersey legislature" (map 4.1). New Jersey had been pushing for the Port Authority to help out with the decrepit and troubled Hudson and Manhattan Railroad (H&M), a line, James Glanz and Eric Lipton wrote in their authoritative biography of the original World Trade Center project, *City in the Sky*, that "had been operating under a bankruptcy agreement since 1954 and suffered from constant service outages and a tumbledown, rat-infested physical plant." If the Port Authority was going to spend millions of dollars on new infrastructure, they wrote, New Jersey governor Robert B. Meyner (Democrat, 1954–1962) "wanted the money to go toward saving the H&M."[29]

To push forward its ambition for the Trade Center project, the Port Authority broke with its long-adhered-to guideline that it should undertake a project only if it could be self-supporting in the long run and dropped its historical opposition to subsidizing rail transit—"an unloved visitor who would not leave," as Doig put it—and after years of debate and discussion, finally agreed to a takeover of the H&M, whose terminus was on the West Side of lower Manhattan. Over the objections of Tobin and New Jersey lawmakers, Governor Nelson A. Rockefeller first introduced legislation that linked the two projects, but in their separate East Side (trade center) and West Side (H&M) locations. The combined projects, he said, "reflect a recognition that the self-interest of each state will be advanced in a common effort in support of the great port, which is the prized asset of both states."[30] This legislative effort only produced stalemate.

In time, New York got its World Trade Center after an inspired accommodation moved its planned location from the East Side of lower Manhattan to the West Side, where it would "not face away from New Jersey," but "toward New Jersey." In this new location, the "handsome but shopworn H&M terminal buildings, twenty-two-story twin high-rises at 30 and 50 Church Street that had been the nation's largest office buildings at the turn of the century," would be demolished (figure 4.5). The new trade center would be built on top, after expanding the site through condemnation acquisitions of older buildings surrounding the H&M terminal.[31] With the two projects now linked in one location, New Jersey's legislators accepted the new plan, and in the spring of 1962, the two states enacted legislation permitting the agency to go forward both with the trade center and with the purchase and rehabilitation of the H&M. The agency's commissioners authorized the project

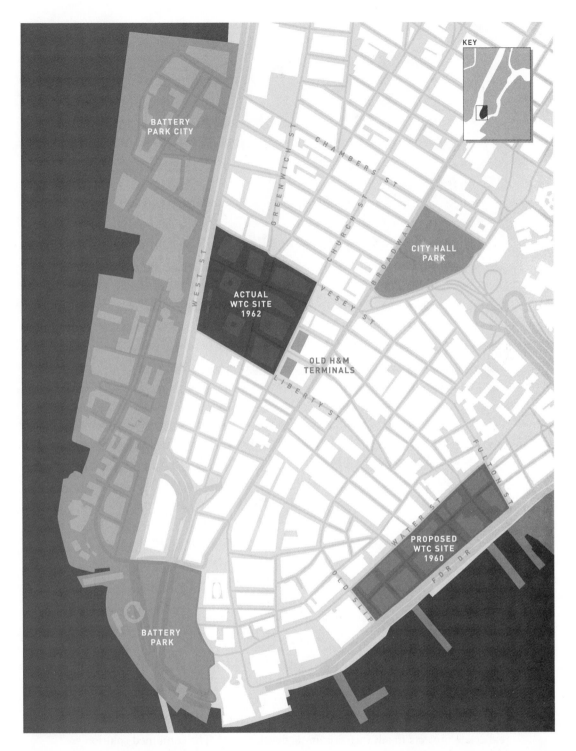

Map 4.1 Proposed and actual locations of the World Trade Center: 1960, 1962. CARTOGRAPHY: C&G PARTNERS FOR THE AUTHOR

FIGURE 4.5 *The twenty-two-story twin towers of the H&M terminal buildings at 30 and 50 Church Street (rear of the photo) before their demolition for construction of the World Trade Center, April 16, 1968.* AP PHOTO/ROBERT KRADIN

three years later and construction began in August 1966. Modernized, the commuter line was renamed the Port Authority Trans-Hudson Corporation, or PATH.

If the big World Trade Center project served the business-led economic development objectives of New York as a means to revitalize downtown, it was also a convenient, if unusual, means to deal with the Port Authority's problem of excess revenues, which as Doig explained, were filling the PA's coffers. Aiming to preserve its spending discretion and avoid getting sucked into the vortex of subsidizing money-losing commuter rail, the agency moved into new projects *outside* the rail-transit area. When it agreed to take over the troubled H&M commuter line, to the surprise of New Jersey, it did so subject to certain conditions, namely that the Port Authority would not become entangled in other large-scale rail programs. Through a cleverly constructed special bond covenant, a "statutory fence" originating with Tobin's most creative legislative bill drafter, Daniel Goldberg, the Port Authority protected itself and its bondholders from future open-tab subventions for rail transit.[32]

In linking New York's world trade center ambitions and New Jersey's H&M financial problem, the PA ushered in a new era of regional investments defined by real estate projects to advance economic development. The combined solution simultaneously ushered in a new notion of what it meant for the PA to support investments in the "region." Increasingly, regionalism came to be measured on a parity basis, dollars for a project in one state calling for a match in the other. That the Port Authority actually pays double for every capital investment on its agenda, as some longtime observers would say, might be an overstatement, but not that there was parity in commitments for capital projects each governor sought for his (or her) state. When in the mid-1950s the Port Authority invested heavily in Port Newark and then in container port development in Newark and Elizabeth, for example, New York governor W. Averell Harriman (1955–1958) complained and a little money went into the Staten Island piers, Doig told me.

In the thrust and parry of parity politics at the bi-state agency, the governors had an ultimate, if blunt, tool at their disposal: the ability to veto any action by the agency's board of commissioners. By virtue of existing legislation, this power gave each governor the right to approve or to disapprove the minutes of every meeting of the commissioners. By threatening to use the veto power to withhold resources for a particular project until the board gave into demands for a particular project on the other side of the Hudson, either governor could force the agency to allocate resources to that state's priority or, perhaps, live with nothing much getting done. Short of resorting to the veto, if the governors on both sides of the Hudson could not come to agreement on the agency's capital spending agenda, tabled resolutions, canceled meetings, stalemate and deferred agendas, and staff foot-dragging would result—as illustrated by the twenty years it took to execute on the idea of privatizing the World Trade Center, which was first put forth in 1981, and finally transacted in July 2001. Before Governor Pataki could claim success in moving the complex into private hands, a goal he espoused as part of his first election campaign in 1994, he had to navigate the shoals of Port Authority parity politics, eventually accommodating New Jersey governor Christine Todd Whitman's demand to subsidize her priority project, expansion of the big cargo hub at Elizabeth Marine Terminal in New Jersey. The long drawn-out episode to monetize the value of the PA's singular real estate asset aptly illustrates how the culture of parity politics would complicate and delay resolution of fundamental economic problems in the rebuilding saga at Ground Zero—and how the maneuvering of the agency reflects the political reality of bi-state regionalism across the Hudson.

"PART EVENT, PART SYMBOL, AND ALL REAL ESTATE"

With this direct opening to his April 1981 task-force report "The Future of the World Trade Center," John E. Zuccotti captured the complex dimensionality of successive political directives to transfer the publicly developed complex to the private sector. In the fall of 1980, Zuccotti and four others were tasked by Governor Hugh L. Carey (Democrat, 1975–1982) to assess the feasibility of disposition. The governor had been pushing for a sale since 1978, as a way of making possible "an increased

Port Authority–based comprehensive economic development program" with the proceeds of the World Trade Center transaction. A sale to a private operator also promised to boost New York City's property tax revenues at a time when the city was still coping with deep fiscal distress after its near brush with bankruptcy in the mid-1970s. "It's fine for a parachutist to draw attention to these buildings," the governor said referring to a recent stunt dive—and indirectly to the memorable and daring and illegal act of Frenchman Philippe Petit who walked, really danced, across the 130-foot gap separating the 110-story twin towers on a steel cable with only a balancing pole in the summer of 1974,"while the still-unfinished and largely unrented towers were courting financial disaster and facing a barrage of architectural and social criticism"—"but I want a 'For Sale' sign to draw attention to them now."[33]

After seven months of study, the task force concluded that "disposition of the Trade Center would generate substantially more public revenue annually than continued ownership by the Port Authority." In the transmittal letter to the governor, Zuccotti wrote that the members of his task force "unanimously agree that the case for disposition is clear and compelling. We believe that the public benefits from such a transaction would be substantial and that the timing is right to proceed now. In sum, it is doable and it is worth doing."[34] The task force did not see any legal impediment to the sale, either in the project's authorizing legislation or from the bondholders who had financed its construction. Although the fifty-page report noted that it had the potential for being the most expensive real estate transaction in the city or the world, the task force declined to put a price on what the complex was worth. Rather, it set out financial criteria for the Port Authority: a threshold price to make the agency "whole" on the public investment of $1.1 billion—a "bare bones figure"—and replacement of a net revenue stream generated by the asset (projected by the Port Authority to be $46.4 million in 1981, rising to $69.7 million in 1986).

The task force focused on the property itself, the real estate (to a large extent the complex had become a commercial real estate operation that had little to do with its original development premise, "world trade").[35] A disposition would not be "simple, even if price were no object" because "a variety of policy, financial, and legal decisions need to be made, coordinated, and effectuated," but the task force believed it could be accomplished and the World Trade Center put into private ownership by early 1983. "The mission of the Port Authority in developing the World Trade Center is over," Zuccotti told the press, and the Port Authority "should go on to other missions in the city."[36] Carey praised the report. His counterpart in New Jersey, Governor Brendan T. Byrne (also a Democrat), had taken a hands-off attitude toward Carey's task force and had no immediate comment on the report; he was already on record as saying if the complex was sold he would insist on some benefit for his state, such as the relocation of the Port Authority's headquarters to New Jersey.

A general consensus was growing that the World Trade Center was better off in private hands. Operationally, strategically, monetarily, it made sense for the Port Authority to divest the commercial complex. That was the pragmatic side of the equation. The World Trade Center was also a symbol of the proud institution, its glory days, and its regional power—meaning, it would not be so easy to execute on the real estate logic of a disposition. The powerful Port Authority staff was not in favor of a disposition; it was home base for thousands of employees. And, of course, the real estate calculus obscured the "fundamental governmental policy issue" of how the proceeds realized from a disposition of the giant office buildings should be used. That is another way of saying how parity politics would enter the equation. Governor Byrne saw "evident injustice" in the fact that "New Jersey has been given second-class treatment by the Port Authority."[37]

Over the next sixteen years, a blue-ribbon bi-state panel and three more comprehensive studies evaluated the disposition question, addressing every conceivable legal and financial transaction issue. The thorny political issue of who gets what, how the Port Authority, New York City, and New Jersey would benefit, however, remained unsettled at the same time as the economic stakes of a disposition grew higher—and as the gubernatorial administrations in both states turned over several times.

During the early years of debate about a possible sale, the value of the World Trade Center's contribution to the bottom line of the Port Authority grew rapidly. For 1981, net operating revenues from the complex were $69.2 million, up from $33.6 million in 1978, according to the data presented by a 1984 report by the investment bank Bear Stearns & Co, hired by Governors Mario M. Cuomo of New York (Democrat, 1983–1994) and Thomas H. Kean of New Jersey (Republican, 1982–1990) to study the options available for disposition of the complex. By 1983, the operating surplus from the World Trade Center had reached $106.9 million (growth at an average annual rate of 26.1 percent).[38] Stacked up against the Port Authority's other facilities (marine terminals, air terminals, tunnels and bridges, bus terminals and bus programs), the World Trade Center had succeeded in outdistancing tunnels and bridges as the second most significant operation, able to deliver a double-digit percentage to the agency's total net operating revenues—32.5 percent in 1983. Only the agency's operation of the region's three air terminals contributed a larger share, 53.8 percent. When the consulting team at the investment bank looked ahead five years to 1988, it projected World Trade Center revenues growing to $153 million and its contribution to the total holding steady at 32.3 percent.

Like Carey, both Governors Kean and Cuomo considered a sale as a way to generate funds for their capital spending needs, and as reported in the press, they reached an agreement on a range of projects the Port Authority should undertake. Kean was taking a more aggressive position on the issue than had his predecessor.

"For too long," Kean said in his message to New Jersey lawmakers in 1984 calling for enactment of legislation to expand the use of revenues from the agency, "both of our states have allowed the Port Authority to set its own agenda; for too long, we have failed to put its substantial resources to work in creating jobs for our people. But that era is over; we will fail no longer!" Kean added that he and Cuomo hoped to resolve the question of selling the World Trade Center that year. It is "a prime regional resource, one that could generate additional revenues for economic development, infrastructure improvements, and the creation of jobs in the region."[39]

Reading between these lines, it might have seemed that the die had been cast. In mid-June, however, the two governors announced that the World Trade Center would not be sold. Drawing on the results of the Bear Stearns study, which concluded that the complex "currently has greater value to the states and the port under continued public ownership than under private ownership," the governors said the big real estate asset should be used to generate $1.2 billion for major construction projects throughout the region. Reversing the recommendations of the earlier report and bi-state panel and angering New York City officials, the Bear Stearns report revealed a political reality: The Port Authority was still the only game in town when it came to funding big-ticket capital projects.

The process of harvesting value from the World Trade Center had begun the year earlier. PA executive director Peter C. Goldmark Jr., appointed by Governor Carey, for whom he had served as state budget director, was known not to be an advocate for disposition of the World Trade Center. Committed to public service, Goldmark had another idea about how to "harness the financial value of the World Trade Center to help meet the capital needs" of the region. He proposed the creation of a Bank for Regional Development financed by the flexible use of World Trade Center rental fees collected on the two million square feet of space being vacated by the State of New York. As the state vacated its below-market space in phases, the Port Authority would release that space to private tenants at market rates, and the captured incremental revenues would go to capitalize a regional development bank, thereby making "the capital capacity available to local governments in the area for reconstruction of their roads, bridges, and mass transit systems."[40] This was an inspired idea that came at a time when the action to sell the World Trade Center had stalled, and the political benefit was clear: The money in the development bank, as Goldmark said, "would be totally under the control of the two Governors" and could be used for a variety of purposes separate from the restrictions put on the Port Authority.[41] In January 1983, a Fund for Regional Development was set up to sublease the space held by the state of New York under long-term lease.[42] As a pot of discretionary money available to the two governors for economic development purposes (typically non-revenue-producing), the fund became a valuable off-budget money bucket each state used to independently support its priority projects.[43]

The World Trade Center with its substantial surplus funds had become an advantageous money-making asset the two governors could leverage for priority economic development and infrastructure spending. As such, its new role held sway over any further discussion of its disposition for ten years, until a conservative ideological shift took hold on both sides of the Hudson. Christine Todd Whitman, inaugurated in January 1994 as New Jersey's fiftieth governor, and George E. Pataki, inaugurated the year after as New York's fifty-third governor, both moderate Republicans with similar views on many things, especially reducing the role of government, had given the Port Authority a mandate to streamline operations and hold the line on bridge and tunnel tolls and PATH fares. Selling public assets and contracting out public services was part of the agenda, with privatization a new word in the political lexicon of both governors.

The call for efficiency in government and fiscal prudence was both pragmatic and apolitical, but when Pataki picked George J. Marlin to head the Port Authority in January 1995, the nomination took on a distinctly political cast.[44] With the Port facing "difficult financial and policy issues as the year opened," replacing the executive director, Doig wrote, offered Pataki and his advisors "an opportunity to gain control over an agency that he thought had been too independent of Albany interests. But that defensible goal was overwhelmed by the attraction of using the job to reward a crucial political supporter with a $170,000 annual salary, and no one was more deserving, in Pataki's view, than George J. Marlin, a bond salesman and a leader of the state's Conservative Party, which had helped Pataki win the governorship."[45] Marlin had no experience in government or in managing large bureaucratic organizations; his reputation was that of a conservative ideologue distrustful of big government.

Immediately, the political-payback nomination for this pivotal job, a job that traditionally called for a public role in meeting regional infrastructure needs, came in for sharp criticism. Marlin was a "mediocre choice," "a particularly offensive act of patronage," the *Times* said in at least two editorials. *Newsday* called him a political "gadfly." Historically, the Port Authority had been led by strong, independent figures with substantial public administrative experience, leaders able to stand a distance from both governors. Marlin's staunch advocacy of privatization, Pataki aides said, was part of his appeal to the governor. Alumni from the Port Authority leadership ranks saw the nomination as a troubling departure from the agency's professional culture. "If privatization is going to be honestly debated and thoroughly evaluated," said Richard C. Leone, a former chairman of the Port Authority (1990–1994) and head of the Twentieth Century Fund, "Mr. Pataki would do well to appoint an executive director who is well-versed and open-minded on the subject, rather than grease the skids by naming a privatization zealot." The agency's three most recent former executive directors—Peter Goldmark (1977–1985), Stephen Berger (1986–1990), and Stanley Brezenoff (1990–1995)—also publicly questioned the appointment.[46]

Commissioners of the Port Authority were unsettled by the choice, uneasy about Marlin's lack of hands-on administrative experience and by his political views. For a short while it seemed possible that the nomination might not garner sufficient support needed for approval, but after a month's delay, Whitman and a majority of the commissioners "succumbed," and Marlin was named executive director in February 1995.[47] Marlin's adversarial relations with Mayor Giuliani, whom he labeled "a fraud" in the 1993 mayoral campaign (Marlin ran as a candidate on the Conservative Party), certainly did not auger well for productive relations between the Port Authority and New York City, which had direct stakes in any transfer of interest to a private operator.

Choosing Marlin was a disastrous decision. It was not just Marlin's short resume and the appearance of political debt paying: The governor had twice violated Port Authority etiquette, first, by not consulting Governor Whitman in advance, and second, by informing her of the nomination by a fax communication. The faux pas and the antagonism it set in motion were harbingers of a deep rift that was to develop between the two Republican rivals. For eighteen months, it stalled the privatization of the World Trade Center, though not before the two governors agreed to hire Chemical Securities to study options for maximizing the value of the World Trade Center to the Port Authority.[48]

Chosen from a field of three investment bank contenders by the Port's chief financial officer and general counsel, Chemical was tasked with undertaking an evaluation of a range of options for maximizing the value of the World Trade Center to the Port Authority—from outright sale to partial sale to long-term lease to private management to status-quo retention. It was doing so, the draft executive summary said, against "a backdrop of declining WTC performance and increasing capital needs among the PA's businesses." This context was far from what had prevailed the last time the privatization issue had been studied by Bear Stearns. In 1984, "the WTC was one of the premier office buildings in Manhattan, the real estate market in Lower Manhattan was strong, and it was reasonable to conclude that the WTC's financial performance was likely to improve during the projection period."[49] In mid-1995, older office buildings faced a difficult market environment. The Manhattan office market had not fully recovered from the severe real estate recession of the late 1980s–early 1990s. Real estate professionals perceived its near-term future as uncertain and risky, especially the weaker lower Manhattan office market, where vacancy rates were higher, rents lower and constrained by limited demand, and leasing activity slower than in midtown, which continued to be the most desirable location in the city for office tenants. Asset values in downtown were still depressed. The vacancy rate at the twenty-four-year-old World Trade Center, a marginal class A asset, was 17.3 percent compared to a nearly negligible 1.1 percent across West Street at Brookfield's World Financial Center or 14.9 percent for all of the class A inventory in lower Manhattan. (Vacancy in class B office space was at 21.5 percent.) The World Trade Center was in need of substantial capital, approximately $500 million, to modernize its aging building infrastructure if it was to remain competitive within the lower Manhattan class A market. The 1993 terrorist bombing of the World Trade Center garage had materially compromised recent financial performance. Market perception of the complex was negative. All of these conditions, *Crain's New York Business* suggested, increased the odds of a sale.

Other considerations enhanced the disposition side of the decision ledger: The privatization concept was a growing national movement, institutional and private money was once again flowing into investment real estate, and even in its weakened state the World Trade Center was a unique property in size, worldwide name recognition, and public ownership. It would be attractive to a set of well-capitalized professional real estate investors who knew how to turn existing operating problems into profitable opportunities and could handle the scale of such a transaction. It had been a source of surplus revenues that fed the capital priorities of both governors. What was the iconic property now, a liability or an asset?

Chemical's answer: a liability with "substantial speculative risks that the PA would face as the continued owner" of the complex, but an asset whose current value the PA could "monetize and lock in all or a significant portion of the current value of the WTC" if it sold the office and retail complex either outright or on a long-term lease basis to a private-sector operator who could run the World Trade Center better than the Port Authority. The study draft completed in August was sharply critical of the agency's management of the World Trade Center, full of findings that would be difficult for agency staff to accept. The World Trade Center's contribution to PA net income had dropped 29 percent, from a high of $149.6 million in 1990 to $106 million in 1994. Its ability to continue as a "significant contributor" to the Port Authority's coffers and its essential investments and facilities had weakened. The operation of the complex was "suboptimal." Recent experience with tenant retention had "not been positive." Operating practices were not up to best practices in the private market, resulting in "higher-than-market-standard operating costs and inconsistent service delivery to current and prospective tenants." Potential still existed: prestige, proximity to transit, superior views, and a range of amenities were all "factors that should be an advantage in competing for tenants."[50] But wholesale change was required at the complex. Chemical's real estate experts concluded that the complex could not achieve its maximum value under the present ownership and operating strategy. After evaluating five different scenarios, the report recommended privatization—disposition through a leasehold sale—which they projected had the highest value, $1.4 billion.

The Chemical team was ready to present its findings, which it knew would be controversial, to the PA Board of Commissioners at its October 26, 1995, meeting. The report led off with a "loaded" title: *Options for Maximizing the Value of the World Trade Center to the Port Authority of New York and New Jersey.* Prior to the presentation, senior members of the team had gone around to Lewis M. Eisenberg, chair of the board, and Peter J. Kalikow, New York commissioner and real estate developer, among others, to brief them on the findings. They hadn't gotten very far into their presentation on that Thursday afternoon in the boardroom on the sixty-seventh floor of the Port's headquarters in the north tower of the twins, perhaps two or three slides, when "all bedlam broke out," according to a senior member of the Chemical team on the assignment. The team was asked to leave and never made the full twenty-five-slide presentation to the board.

Several weeks later, the team went over the presentation with Vice Chairman Charles A. Gargano. When news of the report eventually reached the papers in mid-November, agency officials would not comment on the draft and said they might not make the final version public. "Basically, the report is saying that [the authority] should get the hell out of the management business, and let someone else run it," one PA commissioner told the *Wall Street Journal.* Eisenberg planned to begin private discussions (in executive session) of the report at the commissioners' December 14, meeting, but that never happened; the material the Chemical team prepared for that meeting got filed away, again. The investment bank was never asked to finalize anything; all of the report documents say "draft." What was the issue? New Jersey kept asking, what are we going to get out of this? Governor Whitman was receptive to the idea of privatization, yet she had to be persuaded a sale would not hurt New Jersey, according to the *New Jersey Star-Ledger.*[51]

The Port Authority spent the following two years in further study and deliberation, next commissioning J. P. Morgan Securities for the work that might lead to the investment bank becoming the sales agent for the transaction.[52] Unsurprisingly, J. P. Morgan's analysis concluded, as had the Chemical study, that the best option for the Port Authority was disposition of the World Trade Center via a long-term lease. In April, the *Daily News* reported that the two governors agreed. Then the foot-dragging began. By the end of 1997, Gargano complained to the press, "We have to move forward. We've been dilly-dallying for a long time." His criticism, Peter Grant of the *Daily News* wrote, was "the most visible sign to date of long-simmering internal tension" within the PA boardroom over the fate of the complex—between New York commissioners who favored moving quickly and New Jersey commissioners who favored a go-slow approach.[53] For the rest of 1997, Eisenberg declined to put the privatization issue on the agenda for full board debate.

For New Jersey, the issue was cash—specifically, cash flow from the World Trade Center, which along with the surplus revenues from the airports, subsidized PATH and other facilities. In an interview with the editorial board of the *Star-Ledger*, Eisenberg said, "If we can't find a cash flow that doesn't [*sic*] replace the revenues of the World Trade Center, we don't do it."[54] What Eisenberg was saying, a former PA staffer emphasized, reflected the principle that governed all PA decisions going back decades, whenever staff considered the disposition of a revenue-producing asset. Since the revenues from these facilities were pledged to support the agency's consolidated bonds, to do otherwise than find replacement for these revenues would be irresponsible financial management.

The political question outstanding was whether the World Trade Center being in private hands might lead to pressure from the New York side to get rid of the PATH system, which in 1997 ran at an annual deficit of $166.8 million, or cut its subsidies. Any such action, though, would negatively impact the economy of New York, since PATH brings workers into Manhattan. What New York wanted was more parity in transit fares: It had long considered the differential in fares—the New York City subway fare had risen to $1.50 but the PATH fare had been kept at $1.00 since 1987—unfairly subsidized by the Port Authority with the surplus revenues from the World Trade Center and the region's airports, two of which (LaGuardia and JFK) were in New York. Meanwhile, the real estate market in midtown was heating up, rents were rising, and the cheaper rents in the downtown market were looking increasingly attractive since J. P. Morgan had finished its report a year earlier. The World Trade Center's large blocks of available space were filling up (occupancy had reached 94 percent), and the time to sell seemed better than ever; property values and rents in this office district had jumped dramatically. The World Trade Center was no longer looking like a difficult economic proposition, though it still needed significant upgrading.

By late September 1998, the PA board finally met in closed session to discuss a long-term lease proposal for the World Trade Center, and Eisenberg scheduled a vote on the proposal for its regularly scheduled meeting on September 24. Board members were ready to act—Pataki and Gargano had succeeded in taking it this far. Gargano had said that whoever leased the complex would have to pay full real estate taxes, which would probably cut the value of the transaction by some $300 million against the $1.5 billion figure for a leasehold transaction. The Giuliani administration was threatening to disrupt the deal, vociferously insisting the Port Authority surrender the complex's tax-exempt status if it was placed in the hands of a private real estate operator-investor; such a move would put the asset back on the city's tax rolls and deliver over $100 million in annual payments versus the $25 million the city was getting in payments in lieu of taxes at the time. On September 24, 1998, with the long-simmering dispute with the city over the tax issue remaining an open issue,[55] the PA board unanimously voted to offer the World Trade Center for ninety-nine-year lease to a private operator. A year later, the directors were formally briefed on the list of bidders culled from a list of two hundred prepared by J. P. Morgan and packages of offering documents were readied to send out to the qualified bidders (about thirty).

The action then came to a standstill—for eighteen months. It was caught in a very public tussle over how Port Authority capital spending was benefiting each state. Governor Whitman wanted board approval for a (subsidized) thirty-year lease deal with her state's two largest shipping lines, Sea-Land Service and Maersk Line, that would expand the big cargo hub at Elizabeth Marine Terminal in New Jersey[56] and until Governor Pataki approved it, her commissioners on the board would not be voting to approve mailing out the offering packages. Pataki refused to approve the Sea-Land–Maersk deal unless the New Jersey governor agreed to a major restructuring of the Port Authority that would give New York control of a greater, more equitable share of the agency's revenues. One reason Pataki balked, according to a senior financial official at the agency, was because the PA left a lot on the table. In any event, the New York governor's resistance was in many ways "a proxy battle in a larger war over control of the authority."[57] "In a bi-state agency whose interest is regional, all major projects are linked," Eisenberg said.[58] Indeed, the agency's historical regionalism was being redefined.

Political standoffs. Bitter bi-state feuds. Staff stalls. All seemed to be playing out behind the scenes, holding billions in bi-state authority projects hostage and undermining the privatization effort that ranked so high on Governor Pataki's to-do list. Staff started grumbling about the J. P. Morgan projections. They had questions about objectivity in light of the investment bank's potentially high transaction fee and lobbied to hire another set of consultants to evaluate its work. Gargano went along with this request, out of frustration and worry about missing the market, a circumstance of familiarity from his experience with the Forty-second Street Redevelopment Project. The new executive director, Robert E. Boyle (1977–early 2001), a longtime friend and fundraiser for Pataki and the governor's replacement for Marlin, who had been forced out by the end of 1996, spent a year pursuing the question whether the Port Authority should be dissolved. Whitman refused to hire more consultants. The all-too-familiar border war over whether the Port Authority—originally set up to prevent such wrangling—had helped New York or New Jersey more flared up again in highly publicized fashion. Board meetings were canceled. New York commissioners boycotted the December 1999 monthly meeting. It was, as the *Wall Street Journal* headline said on May 17, 2000, "How Not to Sell the Best-Known Office Complex."

The eighteen-month bi-state competitive rivalry finally exhausted itself by June 1, 2000, when the two governors reached agreement on a comprehensive package of Port Authority actions that offered something for everyone, but not before the boardroom tussle over the World Trade Center disposition and what was in it for New Jersey had ensnared more and more capital projects in a high-profile battle over resource allocation out of the Port Authority's coffers. The dispute's brinkmanship had drawn criticism from newspaper editorial boards and former governors in both states for embarrassing the agency and endangering its reputation. "The impasse took on a life of its own," an advisor to Governor Whitman told the *Times*, until "everything was on the table"—including otherwise routine expenditures. An earlier agreement reached by Gargano and Eisenberg in secret negotiations over a "global settlement" of disputes between the states disintegrated; Pataki would not approve the agreement and Whitman ordered Eisenberg "to pull everything," that is, table everything on the agency's agenda for approval, according to three New Jersey officials, the *Times* reported.[59] After Pataki reviewed the PA's operating results, he raised the ante: New York now wanted $400 million (up from $129 million) in a special allocation to offset port investments on the New Jersey side of the Hudson. When the governors announced their accord, the joint press release listed eighteen specific actions on Port Authority projects. Among them, New Jersey got approval of its Sea-Land–Maersk deal and New York got the go-ahead for the World Trade Center privatization, leasing to others of unused development rights over the Port Authority's Manhattan Bus Terminal in Times Square, and a special $250 million pool of money, a Regional Bank, to spend on port- and transportation-related items. Once again, parity politics—or what others commonly called "jelly beans" or the "cookie jar" for pet projects of the governors of the two states—ruled in the boardroom of the Port Authority.

The region's editorial pages celebrated the "Peace across the Hudson" and "End of a Stalemate," and "public officials pointed to ways in which their state had 'won.'"[60] Yet both Eisenberg and Gargano conceded that "philosophical differences persist between the states on the direction and approach of the agency." Because they persisted, those "philosophical differences" continued to challenge the needs and demands of the much longer journey ahead that would define rebuilding at Ground Zero. And throughout that journey, the boardroom of the Port Authority would remain a deep and uncertain channel of power for decision-making over those sixteen acres of lower Manhattan, especially when it came to dealing with Larry Silverstein and the original deal that gave him property power at Ground Zero.

March 26, 2003. STEPHEN CHERNIN/GETTY NEWS/GETTY IMAGES

PART II
TANGLED START
(2001–2004)

CHAPTER 5
"It's Our City"

FIGURE 5.1 *The crowd of forty-five hundred at the Javits Center "Listening to the City" event on July 20, 2002.* JACQUELINE HEMMERDINGER/THE CIVIC ALLIANCE

I T DID NOT TAKE long at all for the debate to begin, only the proverbial New York minute. The fires still burned deep within the debris of the World Trade Center site and the acrid smell still filled the air when the first news reports about the visions for rebuilding the "huge hole in the heart of New York and of every New Yorker" began to appear: "What to Do with the Hole in New York's Heart—Rebuild or Memorialize? Expect a Fierce Debate" (*WSJ*), "Conflicting Visions of How to Rebuild Lower Manhattan" (*NYT*), "Architects, Planners and Residents Wonder How to Fill the Hole in the City" (*NYT*). Early accounts reporting on the jockeying among city, state, and federal officials and developers, all with separate plans about what to build and who should guide the process, foretold of the cacophony of voices that would weigh in with views on rebuilding. "Even as the grief and mourning go on," two *Times* reporters wrote, "the city's wound is becoming a kind of repository of ideas about what the site, and the city around it, should become."[1] Optimism prevailed alongside grief—ambition alongside loss.

Traumatic events of physical destruction massive in scope—citywide fire conflagrations (Chicago, San Francisco), wartime bombings (London, Berlin, Hiroshima, Beirut, Manchester), earthquakes (Tokyo, Kobe), tsunamis (many from Japan's 2011 earthquake), and floods (New Orleans)—always present cities with fundamental planning questions of how and what to rebuild. In the face of such calamities, many cities have had to rebuild from the ground up, but how many have done so in a democracy, tried to do so through an open participatory process? How many have asked, what is the best way to involve the public at large in the planning and recovery process of their city?

No precedent existed in the United States for planning on such a public stage and under such traumatic emotional conditions. Responding to this terrorist attack was a more delicate matter than responding to damage caused by natural disasters because it implicitly involved a politics of balancing architectural vision, memory, and memorial—on the precise site of the attack in the dense heart of the city's downtown financial center on land that was among the most valuable in the nation. The sheer force of events created a palpable sense that time might handicap recovery. Public officials were being pressured from many directions to act quickly and rebuild straight away—move beyond the rhetoric of defiance toward tangible action.

By January, less than four months after 9/11, with progress on the massive cleanup of the site so unexpectedly rapid (plate 2), local officials had begun to worry about "pressure to have answers to questions about downtown's future faster than anyone ever expected."[2] How should New York spend the $20 billion in federal aid President Bush promised the city to rebuild? How should it use this tragic opportunity to develop lower Manhattan as a twenty-four-hour community of apartments, restaurants, and cultural activities? How much office and retail space should be replaced on the Trade Center site in light of the changing business landscape of financial services? What kind of memorial could best commemorate the senseless loss of thousands of unfinished lives on these sixteen acres that would have to accommodate other uses? Could New York find a way to create a meaningful place imbued with life for current generations, not a sad place, but a place sufficiently endowed with respectful remembrance capable of passing the test of time? These questions had no easy answers, but New Yorkers wanted to be consulted and involved in the process of determining answers to those questions (figure 5.1).

At the end of May 2002 workers removed the last girder at Ground Zero in a somber ceremony, the first of three major tributes marking the end of recovery efforts at the site. The heavy lift and agonizing dig of the cleanup were complete and the debris of the massive bathtub foundation emptied, but the physical site was far from tabula rasa. It was infused with intense memories of past planning mistakes and raw present anguish. Both the past and the present promised to shape the debate about how and what to rebuild, as would the site's physical, legal, and political encumbrances. The split public-private ownership of what was destroyed created layers of complexity bearing on the process for determining how rebuilding would proceed, complexities that did not exist when the Port Authority originally built the *City in the Sky*, as *Times* reporters James Glanz and Eric Lipton titled their definitive book on the World Trade Center.

Early on, some voices advocated for a powerful rebuilding czar, a modern-day Robert Moses who could overcome the conflicting imperatives and incessant pressures to "get things done." This was implausible. As understood by almost every planning professional and politician, including Governor Pataki, the idea of an all-powerful master builder was out of fashion. Moses's command-and-control strategy of urban renewal had been rejected decades earlier, so thoroughly discredited by experience that even the trauma and destruction of 9/11 could not bring it back. It had been replaced by the idea of consensus-oriented participatory planning empowered by the emergence of community activism in the late 1960s. "Few mourn the time when a handful of powerful people could shape a cityscape at will, as historians say the Rockefeller family did in the building of the World Trade Center in the 1960s," *Times* reporter Kirk Johnson wrote in "A Plan without a Master; Rebuilding by Committee? Robert Moses Would Cringe." "But many question whether the fractious but more democratic system that replaced it is any better in arriving at what is best for the most people, a measurement that used to be called 'the common good.'"[3] As the nation's largest and most closely watched project, rebuilding the Trade Center site, with its "intricately constructed" layers of government and private interests, would most surely test the efficacy of the more open consultative process. The enormousness of the project, and the countless, deep emotions it triggered, would make gaining consensus on its future difficult, if not impossible.

The unprecedented emotional context of Ground Zero required an especially deft planning response. Writing in the fall of 2008 after years of chaos had stymied rebuilding, architectural critic Ada Louise Huxtable pined for someone with the skills of an Edward J. Logue, "the planner who successfully rebuilt New Haven and Boston in the downbeat decades of the 1950s and 60s, and brought Roosevelt Island through conception to completion in New York in the 1970s." Logue was "a practical visionary," she wrote, "who knew how to implement a plan without rolling over to every political constituency and special interest. And he got things done."[4] Managing the many voices and shaping the many ideas into a coherent, productive whole in the context of raw emotion was the challenge of consensus planning. Were the players in charge of the formative decision-making up to the task? If skillful leadership did not emerge, what would happen at Ground Zero, a site symbolically central to the city's sense of self?

With the rebuilding enriched by the availability of $20 billion of federal funds, the opportunity to amend the mistakes of the past and build an economic foundation for the future of lower Manhattan brought out ambitions past and ambitions present. Before the end of 2001, even before the formal debates began, ad hoc hives of activity vigorously sought to focus attention on what each group considered the salient issues of rebuilding. The issues engaged everyone, and during the intense early years of planning for rebuilding the eyes of the world followed the debate at Ground Zero. In exhaustive daily coverage, the press chronicled every private action and every public event bearing on the vision debate. Countless hours were devoted to holding forums, public hearings, symposiums, and panels. Yet despite all the activity, "there was never any real public involvement in programming, in figuring out what to do with the site, only with the configuration of the master plan," architectural critic Paul Goldberger concluded. "So 99 percent of the ideas that were put out by the interested, eager parties after 9/11 were irrelevant because they didn't follow the Port Authority's commercial program."[5] Although they did not blueprint planning outcomes, the public debates about vision were essential to the process by which public officials and citizens came to understand the meaning of rebuilding in the immediate context of 9/11 loss and the historical trajectory of New York ambition.

City officials tried to alter the vision of the Port Authority and its leaseholder for the site by seeking a formal foothold on the decision-making over what would be built at Ground Zero. First, the newly elected mayor tried to alter the property condition at Ground Zero with a proposal to the Port Authority to swap city ownership of the land under LaGuardia and JFK Airports for those sixteen acres on its historic turf. The bold property exchange might have simplified the task of execution; it certainly would have altered the landscape of political opportunity at Ground Zero. Though it came to naught, Mayor Bloomberg would strike forth with other strategic interventions in the years to follow, all in an effort to shape what happened on this strategic piece of city turf.

HIVES OF ACTIVITY

Ideas about how to rebuild surfaced almost immediately. Out of emotional need to contribute to the effort or ambition to influence the agenda, suggestions poured forth. They came from established civic institutions, newly created coalitions, groups representing the downtown business community, residents of nearby neighborhoods, professional communities of design, special interests, and still other groups advocating a particular, singular focus, skyscraper safety, for example. They came in the form of generalized principles for rebuilding, specific planning proposals for rebuilding, and architectural visions of how to rebuild, as well as detailed blueprints for a broad-based renewal of lower Manhattan beyond the sixteen acres of the Trade Center site. They materialized through private discussions and research efforts of organized civic task forces and professional-group subcommittees, broad-based public-consultative processes, academic design studios, and solicitations for a gallery exhibit and news magazine feature story. The ideas filtered out to public audiences through many channels: reports and policy white papers, conferences and special participatory forums or workshops, and interactive websites, as well as public briefings and media campaigns. Some groups sought to mobilize public opinion, while others, to advocate specific positions or priorities, and still others, to shape the agenda through private briefings with government officials and other decision-makers. "What is emerging," *Times* beat reporter Edward Wyatt wrote, "is less chorus than cacophony—or, from another perspective, voices rising in rich intellectual ferment."[6]

New York's active interest groups were not waiting for the public sector to get organized. "We're in a rush because there's a window where maybe we can influence public policy, and we're afraid the window will close," said Raymond Gastil, head of the Van Alen Institute, one of sixteen design groups in a coalition called New York New Visions. "This can't be some biggies in a closed room. It has to be a public process," said Robert D. Yaro, president of the Regional Plan Association (RPA). "This is one of those times," said Carl B. Weisbrod, president of the city's largest business improvement district, the Alliance for Downtown New York, "when both speed and rationality are called for."[7] The ad hoc civic and business groups that were forming had no formal power, but they were trying to influence how government should organize to rebuild and the program for what should get built on the site. Many of those involved were skilled veterans of New York development battles, long on institutional memory and wise in the ways the city arrives at a plan of action. Some were friends of City Hall or might count themselves among the city's policy elite. Others were just impassioned professionals and citizens at large who wanted to engage in the process of rebuilding. The sound waves of debate and discussion among these ad hoc groups cast diverse vibrations of idealism, patriotic rhetoric, moral certitude, business pragmatism—but most of all, a dedication to the future well-being of New York City, even from the critics among them. And overcoming typically fierce professional competition, they acted in a more cooperative mode than might ordinarily have been expected.[8]

Within days of the calamity, meetings between commercial real estate people and city officials were being convened to figure out how to deal with the immediate needs of office tenants who were displaced from the district and to think about the long-term picture for lower Manhattan. The attack had destroyed 12.5 million square feet of office space, and an additional 13.8 million square feet had been damaged; together, the destruction had taken out nearly one-quarter of the downtown office inventory, and an even larger share, 44 percent, of its modern class A space, as tracked by Cushman & Wakefield in a *MarketBeat Special Report on the Manhattan Office Market after the World Trade Center Tragedy*. This was valuable space in the region's dueling office market hierarchy, critically important to Manhattan's ongoing battle to retain office jobs that could be lost to New Jersey waterfront cities (Jersey City, Hoboken, and Newark) and the northern suburbs of New York (White Plains, New York, and Stamford, Connecticut). The city had defined a fenced-in sector that encompassed the disaster site and its surrounding buildings, a "Red Zone." Uncertainty and a loss of confidence were pervasive. The psychology of the district was deeply shaken. Downtown real estate executives feared the viability of downtown as an employment center was at risk.

Tension between the need to rebuild quickly wherever development sites were available in the city, in lower Manhattan or elsewhere, and the need to rejuvenate the devastated financial district was inevitable. But they were not mutually exclusive options. "The real need," Weisbrod argued, was "to plan effectively for Lower Manhattan's future." In "Rebuild Downtown from Bottom Up," the *Daily News* captured the sentiment of many: "It is imperative to move forward decisively with the reclamation of the World Trade Center site—and to focus all available resources on creating a 21st century infrastructure to drive our 21st century economy.... New capacity. New transit services. New technology. In short, a new downtown rising like a phoenix from the ashes."[9]

Downtown Interests

Within two weeks of the attack, the New York City Partnership had moved into action. Founded in 1979 by David Rockefeller as a means of organizing business leaders to work directly with government and other civic groups in addressing social and economic problems in a "hands-on" way, the partnership had become the voice of New York City's business community on these issues. The nonprofit organization created Rebuild NYC and appointed an associated Long Range Infrastructure Task Force[10] to begin the work of assessing the economic impact and ramifications of September 11 on New York City. After six weeks of collaborative efforts with seven leading management consultant firms, all of whom contributed their services pro bono, the partnership and the Chamber of Commerce produced *Working Together to Accelerate New York's Recovery*, a 151-page report filled with tables and graphs that distilled its intensive analysis of the city's economy, more than two hundred interviews with leaders in the business community, and select in-depth consumer research into a six-step recovery plan.

As evident in the document's title, the emphasis was on accelerated action to "rapidly" develop a long-term plan for lower Manhattan. It called for "fast track" rebuilding of the downtown infrastructure to twenty-first-century standards, restoration of confidence by investing in comprehensive, innovative security measures, focus on the retention of financial-services jobs and income, quick repair of lower Manhattan as a functioning community and intensification of efforts to help small business, and promotion of the New York economy. Of the six priorities, it made fast track development of a long-term plan for downtown its top priority and urged setting a fixed end date to the planning process—by mid-2002—in order to avoid "the danger posed by years of debate and paralysis about what to do about downtown." Fast action was necessary, the partnership argued, because in cases of disaster recovery, "those cities that acted quickly to agree on a recovery plan, even though it may take years to implement, maintain their economic strength." It wanted assurances that the economic engine of lower Manhattan would be restored with a new type of prosperity, not just through traditional retention strategies, but with "an aggressive program to lure new knowledge-based industries that can drive economic growth," as its president, Kathryn S. Wylde, would later write in a *Times* op-ed.[11]

The partnership issued its report with a carefully calibrated media campaign that trumpeted a key finding: "WTC Attack to Result in Economic Output Loss of $83 Billion and 57,000 Jobs for the City." Put on its website just as Governor Pataki was considering the formation of what was to become the Lower Manhattan Development Corporation, the report's timing coincided with the uncertainty surrounding the issue of who was going to be in charge of rebuilding lower Manhattan. "You don't have to have 'the' plan," said a former aide to Mayors Edward I. Koch and David E. Dinkins. "But you do need a credible leadership, which can help you buy some time and help people feel that their interests will be reflected in this group and the subsequent plan for reconstruction." Business leaders from the partnership, the real estate industry, and the city's construction unions were forming a lobbying alliance to influence the structure of how decisions would be made in Washington as well as at home. "It's an attempt to resurrect the same kind of business-labor initiative that helped get us through the fiscal crisis of the 1970s," Wylde said. "Obviously, everybody thinks they're best equipped to recommend what the governor and the mayor should do," said Steven Spinola, president of the Real Estate Board of New York. "We believe we represent the people most affected, the owners and the tenants. When you add the Alliance for Downtown New York and labor, that's it."[12]

The Alliance for Downtown New York, formed in 1995 to enhance the quality of life in lower Manhattan, also moved into action immediately to help the traumatized community. "Obviously a physical rebuilding effort has to get underway expeditiously, but physical rebuilding is not simply a matter of getting office space built," said Weisbrod. "That's an important element of it," but only part of what the city needed to do. It was critical, he argued, for the city to address "those psychological and emotional barriers to companies and residents coming back, so that they have a sense that downtown will be not only as great a neighborhood as it was before all of this happened, but the greatest neighborhood in the city. That expectation," he said, "has to be provided very soon."[13]

The fragility of the community's sense of self could not be overstated. Restoring confidence in lower Manhattan was a high priority. The alliance worked behind the scenes to service its constituents, engage public and private decision-makers, and raise funds for recovery programs. Although it did not publish a formal agenda or set of principles as other groups did, staff members were active in a number of civic-group coalitions engaged in planning; Weisbrod, whom Mayor Bloomberg appointed to the board of the LMDC in April 2002, worked tirelessly to promote an eight-point agenda for rebuilding downtown. In an impassioned argument, "Downtown Must Be Rebuilt," he laid out the objectives that should guide the renewal effort, many of which would become part of an emerging consensus: maintain the financial core, improve the area's transportation infrastructure, nurture the residents (many of whom are affluent and have many options on where to live), advance the 24/7 community, redevelop the Trade Center site as part of a larger plan, connect Battery Park City to the east side of downtown, beautify the waterfront, and improve vehicular and pedestrian circulation.[14]

The most immediately affected downtown business entity was Brookfield Properties. Owner of three of the four buildings as well as the retail areas and Winter Garden in the adjacent complex then known as World Financial Center (renamed Brookfield Place) in Battery Park City and nearby 1 Liberty Plaza, the company had a lot riding on the recovery of lower Manhattan and the redevelopment of the Trade Center site, in particular. With eight million square feet of office space, the Toronto-based company was the largest landlord in the financial district, and 50 percent of its $2 billion equity base in New York City was in the World Financial Center complex, its U.S. headquarters. The New York market represented a significant portion of the publicly traded company's rental revenues from its commercial property operations.[15] The buildings, designed by César Pelli, had been acquired in 1996 following the collapse of the Canadian real estate giant Olympia & York, which had developed the commercial complex. Overextended by its enormous financial commitment to Canary Wharf in London, O&Y declared bankruptcy in May 1992. After the U.S. operations of the company were reorganized, Brookfield Properties controlled the new company that emerged. All four of the office towers in the complex suffered damage and were evacuated as the World Trade Center towers collapsed, then quickly repaired and readied for tenants.

"From a planning point of view, what we are left with is probably the most dramatic planning initiative that's ever been undertaken," Brookfield's chairman, John E. Zuccotti, remarked just nine days after the attack at a small meeting of people deeply involved in the aftermath of the attack. Zuccotti had become involved with O&Y in 1990 and had guided the company through bankruptcy and reorganization. An ardent advocate of lower Manhattan, he believed Battery Park City was "the greatest urban development project in the latter part of the 20th century in any place in the world." It had taken a long time and several plans to develop the ninety-two-acre community on the Hudson waterfront. "There were constraints because it wasn't planned originally in the context of the World Trade Center. It was a little bit ad hoc," he said. After 9/11, he believed that "as part of the efforts to restore confidence in Lower Manhattan, it's necessary to take a look at the 17 acres of upland that are there [at the Trade Center site] and look at Battery Park City to see how the two can be integrated in a way they should have been integrated a long time ago." Zuccotti was quietly asked by a close friend to consider the idea of doing a joint plan with Silverstein for the Trade Center site, and he agreed to think about it, but the next day's story in the *Wall Street Journal*, "Brookfield and Silverstein Hold Talks on Future of World Trade Center Site," likely based on a leak from Silverstein, raised Zuccotti's ire and the idea died at that moment.[16]

Wise and politically savvy, Zuccotti held a unique position in the recovery discussions following 9/11. His perspective on planning issues in New York stretched back in time and beyond his role in the creation of Battery Park City. Having served as the first deputy mayor of New York City (1975–1977) and chairman of the City Planning Commission (1973–1975), he was "one of the heroes who got the city out of the fiscal crisis of the 1970s." He understood the history behind New York State's efforts to privatize the World Trade Center, having headed the first task force to study its privatization in 1981. Much as his focus was on lower Manhattan, he saw rebuilding as "a great opportunity to address the other issues that were on the [city's] agenda and to plan for them at the same time." With substantial federal funding available, it was the right time to push for ambitious planning, but, he said, "it will take political leadership, compromise, planning and public-private cooperation at a pace unprecedented in the history of the city and state."[17] Keenly aware of the ways in which planning inherently involves politics, Zuccotti foresaw that the raw emotionalism of 9/11 presented a demanding planning situation: The task of rebuilding could be nothing other than emotionally charged because it was about managing the views of those whose loved ones—spouses, mothers, fathers, sons, daughters, lovers, friends—had been murdered, and murdered on a massive scale. It would create a temporary power base for the families of the victims. When the issues related to the memorial were settled, the influence of the families would pass, as Mayor Bloomberg candidly foretold, but in the interim, their politics would shape the politics of rebuilding.

Brookfield wanted to be a player in the process of rebuilding, and the post-9/11 situation was ripe for it to show leadership. On 9/11, its complete senior management team was downtown at the company's offices when a massive piece of steel shot into the east side of one building; almost all the glass panes of the complex's ten-story glass-vaulted Winter Garden Atrium were blown out by the dust clouds triggered by the collapse of the twin towers. On September 12, the team reconvened in midtown, where the firm was building 300 Madison Avenue, a thirty-five-story tower one block west of Grand Central Terminal. A week later, Zuccotti turned to his senior vice president responsible for the operations and management of the company's U.S. portfolio of eighteen million square feet, Lawrence F. Graham, and asked him what Brookfield's position should be.[18] Graham called in Alexander Cooper of Cooper, Robertson & Partners to develop a plan for the area and on the engineering professional services firm Parsons Brinkerhoff to develop a transportation plan.

Honored as a Fellow of the American Institute of Architects, the Yale-trained architect and urban designer held a special place in the architectural community as someone with an impact on the design of major pieces of cities. Along with Stanton Eckstut, Cooper had developed the revised master plan for the award-winning Battery Park City project by integrating the street grid into the original misdirected Corbusian master plan. Their new plan focused on the paramount importance of the public's needs for open space and public art. Their idea was to first design the streets, the parks, and the esplanade along the river, and then set the buildings along the street lines in the manner of the city's older neighborhoods. When called by Graham, Cooper did what planners do: He recalled the history of the site and the importance of restoring the street grid at the World Trade Center.

As part of the plan to unite Battery Park City with the rest of the Trade Center site and the rest of the city, Brookfield wanted to suppress West Street underground to about Barclay Street, an initiative that would also help quiet the area.[19] Viewing mass transit as key to restoring downtown Manhattan, Zuccotti was offering to link the Winter Garden, a grand public space that served as the center-piece of the Brookfield complex until on 9/11 it became an escape route for thousands of traumatized people, with a rebuilt mass-transit hub. The last piece of Brookfield's vision included extending commuter rail into lower Manhattan to link the district with nearby suburbs; this idea had been around for some time, but it was John Forman of Parsons Brinkerhoff who figured out a new way to do it.[20] Not every transportation group was convinced of the plan's merits. In particular, the RPA thought the project would serve relatively few riders for a high cost and would reduce subway service from Queens. RPA came out against the link and instead promoted connecting the PATH to Newark Airport by extending it along the Amtrak Northeast Corridor.

After six months of work, Brookfield had a plan, and its senior executives went on a "road show" with the tag line "$5 billion and five years—$3 billion for the railroad and $2 billion for the West Street underground." They showed the plan to everyone they could possibly influence: city officials, Governor Pataki and his people, LMDC officials, and the press. They did this quietly because they did not want it to be labeled the "Brookfield Plan"; they didn't want credit—just influence. They believed something needed to be done quickly to "normalize" lower Manhattan. Their plan was not really focused on rebuilding the Trade Center site with architecture. And they were agnostic about the memorial site, but understood that the footprints of the two towers had become a sensitive issue and should not be disturbed. In time, Cooper would also incorporate a cultural component into the plan. But in all their studies—and Brookfield had an entire room dedicated to these plans—Cooper resisted putting buildings on the site. From a commercial perspective, Brookfield, as well as many other office developers, believed no building should be taller than seventy stories because the required core of elevator banks in very tall towers eroded the rentable floor area and challenged project economics. Brookfield's proposal "ought to excite anyone who cares about the neighborhood," the *Times* said in an editorial in late November 2002. It's "the kind of transportation plan that we've been hoping to see from other sources—a cohesive and thoughtful program that is flexible about the sort of buildings that will ultimately be constructed, but gives enough detail to offer people an exciting vision of the possibilities. Most important, it focuses on the swiftest way to get people into, out of and around Lower Manhattan."[21]

The city's three downtown business groups—the Alliance for Downtown New York, the Association for a Better New York, and the Partnership for New York City—along with the Real Estate Board of New York were united behind the firm belief that transportation improvements were the highest priority for rebuilding and recovery. Without improved access to the region, downtown business leaders firmly believed the Trade Center site would be unmarketable. They wanted the two regional transportation giants—the Port Authority (typically opposed to mass transit) and the Metropolitan Transportation Authority—to move on their agenda. These government authorities had long time horizons and steady sources of funds. As engineering bureaucracies focused on serving current customers, they were pushed by demand and not pulled by development vision. They were slow moving, too.

Civic Voices

Galvanized into action by the partnership's Long Range Infrastructure Task Force, in January 2002, New York New Visions (NYNV) issued the first blueprint for rebuilding the Trade Center site. The result of a three-month voluntary collaboration of 350 professionals and civic leaders, *Principles for the Rebuilding for Lower Manhattan* set out "to inform the large-scale urban, economic and real estate decisions to be made in the coming months." This "unprecedented coalition" of twenty-one architecture, planning, and design organizations was "committed to honoring the victims of the September 11 tragedy by rebuilding a vital New York." It assumed Governor Pataki had given the newly established LMDC the authority to manage the rebuilding process and believed that through this report and subsequent reports and actions, it could influence the planning taking place in the LMDC's offices. For Alexander Garvin, LMDC vice president in charge of coordinating the formulation of comprehensive development plans for the Trade Center site and surrounding areas of lower Manhattan, the NYNV would become an especially important ally because he had no natural constituency for his work beyond the support of Deputy Mayor Doctoroff.[22]

The NYNV award-winning report was ambitious, substantive, and wise in the ways of city building. It set the task of rebuilding the site within the broader issue context of regional growth, transportation, and planning, reflecting an early and well-debated decision by NYNV professionals to focus on general principles for rebuilding and not on design. While acknowledging that "these principles and recommendations do not replace the broader public discourse about the future of our city that must and will take place among policy and decision makers," the report recommended an open memorial process, a flexible, mixed-use future for lower Manhattan, a more interconnected downtown, a renewal of lower Manhattan's relation to the region, and design excellence and sustainability. It called for a comprehensive plan for lower Manhattan to be accomplished through a participatory process involving government, the private sector, and the public. In the short term, it wanted to see a plan for temporary memorials, viewing places for visitors

Table 5.1 Downtown Interests and Civic Groups Active in Planning Discussions for Rebuilding Ground Zero: 2001–2003

Group	Description
New York City Partnership (Partnership for New York City)	Business group founded by David Rockefeller in 1979. Considered the voice of the business community on social and economic issues facing the city. Became the Partnership for the City of New York upon its merger with the Chamber of Commerce in 2002.
Alliance for Downtown	Organization of property owners, commercial tenants, residents, and elected officials focused on improving the quality of life in lower Manhattan. Established in 1995 as a business improvement district (BID), the city's largest.
Real Estate Board of New York (REBNY)	Special interest group representing the city's real estate owners and managers and brokers and salespeople. Founded in 1890, REBNY is a powerful voice in city affairs and strong lobbying force in Albany.
Brookfield Properties	Toronto-based developer, owner, and manager of commercial property. With holdings of eight million square feet of office space, it was the largest landlord in the financial district downtown in 2001.
New York New Vision (NYNV)	Coalition of twenty-one architecture, planning, and design organizations formed immediately after 9/11 in a pro-bono effort to address issues surrounding the rebuilding of lower Manhattan.
Civic Alliance	Coalition of more than eighty-five civic, business, environmental, community, university, and labor groups convened by the Regional Plan Association of New York (RPA) after 9/11 to provide a civic voice in rebuilding.
"Imagine New York" Municipal Art Society (MAS)	Coalition of academics, urban planners, architects, family members, and other concerned citizens organized under the umbrella of a forty-five-person steering committee by the MAS after 9/11.
Rebuild Our Town (R.Dot)	Coalition of representatives from approximately thirty lower Manhattan organizations that came together after 9/11 to represent the broad-based interests of residents, business, community advocates, artists, colleges, and academic and design professionals in lower Manhattan.
Labor Community Advocacy Network (LCAN)	Coalition of over fifty labor unions, community groups, research and advocacy organizations, and service providers formed by the Fiscal Policy Institute and the NYC Central Labor Council of the AFL-CIO after 9/11 to advocate for higher paying jobs and affordable housing.

Source: Author

and residents, and the needs of small businesses in the district addressed. When the LMDC issued its *Principles and Preliminary Blueprint for the Future of Lower Manhattan* several months later in April, NYNV's influence was apparent. The document "closely parallels and echoes" the *Principles* document, the coalition's leadership remarked in a letter to LMDC chairman John C. Whitehead.[23]

Several other private groups, often with overlapping memberships, emerged and embarked on parallel planning activities, as shown in table 5.1. The Civic Alliance to Rebuild Downtown New York, a coalition of more than eighty-five civic, business, environmental, community, university, and labor groups convened by the Regional Plan Association to provide a civic voice in rebuilding plans for lower Manhattan, was the most active and dominant of the other coalitions. With support from the Rockefeller Brothers Fund, the Ford Foundation, the W. K. Kellogg Foundation, and Con Edison, it organized innovative high-tech citywide citizen-participation efforts called "Listening to the City," which tested opinions of reconstruction and memorial. Following these large-scale public events in February and July 2002, the Civic Alliance moved deeper into detailed planning and policy development; based on the work of its eight working groups,[24] it released a forty-three-page document, *A Planning Framework to Rebuild Downtown New York*, filled with potential site plans and other images, as well as an animated version of its transportation recommendations.

As reflected in the title of its document, the Civic Alliance had looked beyond the Trade Center site to propose a plan for all of lower Manhattan, an area south of Canal Street river to river roughly one square mile in size (map 5.1). When it envisioned a future for lower Manhattan, it framed the opportunity in terms of the best practices of urban design, sustainability, transportation, and economic development, yet the thrust of its argument was that the fate of lower Manhattan rested on accessibility, which would be "largely determined by the quality of its transportation and communication infrastructure and its continued transformation to a vibrant 24-hour community." "What you want to do is shape a program leading to a master plan," said RPA president Yaro.[25]

Getting the ideas out into the public as well as to major decision makers was a paramount objective of all the civic coalitions. NYNV distributed ten thousand copies of *Principles*, the Civic Alliance distributed maps of *Around Ground Zero* and downtown, and website access to *Principles* and the partnership's *Working Together* allowed these ideas to spread widely through the civic and professional communities within a short few months.

Rebuild Downtown Our Town (R.Dot), a coalition of representatives from approximately thirty lower Manhattan organizations, came into being through the initiative of Beverly Willis, director of the Architecture Research Institute, and

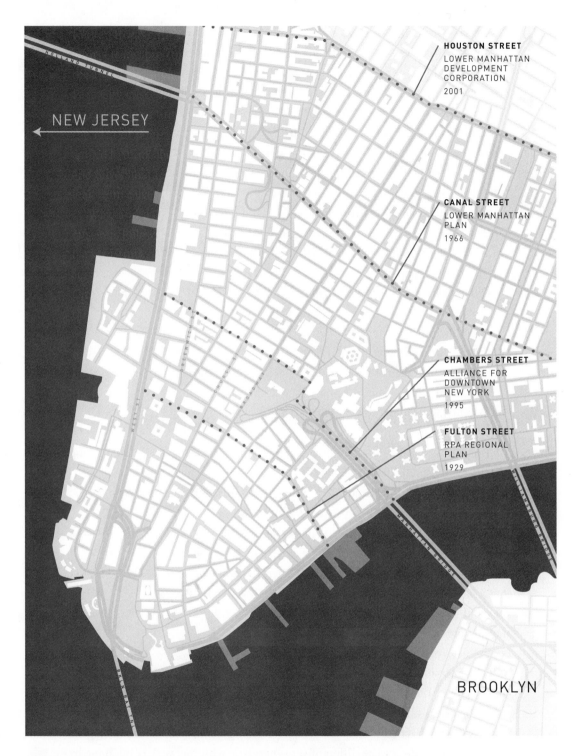

Map 5.1 Changing definitions of "downtown." Cartography: C&G Partners for the author

Susan Szenasy, editor in chief of *Metropolis* magazine, with the support of the Rockefeller Brothers Fund and the Alfred P. Sloan Foundation. It sought to represent the broad-based interests of lower Manhattan residents, business people and business associations, community advocates, artists, colleges, and academic and design professionals. Characterizing itself as the "voice of lower Manhattan"—the "thousands of people who have been directly affected by the destruction of the World Trade Towers"—R.Dot's primary interest was supporting "an imaginative, sustainable design that creates the possibility of a diverse, inclusive, 24-hour residential and business community." It shared many of the same goals and values as the Civic Alliance and New York New Visions and in its "Urban Design Armature for Rebuilding Lower Manhattan" recognized the primacy of a memorial on the Trade Center site, which it hoped would transform the planning vision beyond that of a development site.[26]

Although its members "shared the awareness of all the other coalition leaders that lower Manhattan's losses on 9/11 had citywide, national, and international levels of meaning," David W. Woods wrote in his analysis of civic leadership after 9/11, R.Dot worked hard "to make sure that its meaning for the most affected neighborhood would not be lost, and that local voices, needs, and visions would also be heard in the rebuilding process." Along with ensuring government accountability, its leaders were particularly concerned with how the Trade Center site would connect with the surrounding downtown area and believed that reestablishing the street grid through the site was critical in that regard. Speaking about the need for an overall plan for the area before individual projects (such as the rebuilding of 7 World Trade Center) went forward, R.Dot member Madelyn G. Wils, also chair of Community Board 1 and an LMDC board member, said, "This is an opportunity like no other that has ever come before us."[27] Savvy in the ways of getting out its message, R.Dot's organizers took a public relations approach to the distribution of the coalition's white paper, *Toward a Sustainable City*, releasing it at a press conference attended by NBC, the *Washington Post*, and the *Baltimore Sun* and getting it featured on a multisegment NPR program, in addition to making presentations to the LMDC, where it reportedly received an early and receptive hearing because of Wils's role on the LMDC Board.

The venerable Municipal Art Society (MAS), founded in 1893 to advocate for the quality of the city's built environment, organized a coalition of academics, urban planners and architects, family members, and other concerned citizens under the umbrella of a forty-five-person steering committee called "Imagine New York." Intending to be different yet synergistic with the work being done by other civic coalitions, Imagine New York focused its efforts on a project identifying the impact of the 9/11 terrorist attacks on the city, the state, and the region by eliciting expressions of individuals' hopes and dreams for New York's future, wherever they lived in the metropolitan region. Within a two-month period (March–April 2002), the coalition convened 230 public community-based visioning workshops throughout New York, New Jersey, and Connecticut, including thirty-five organized as planning and design charrettes, at which participants were invited to share their views on how 9/11 had affected them and what they imagined and hoped for through the rebuilding process.

In choosing extensive outlets for citizen participation, the key organizers were motivated by personal and professional commitments to participatory democracy, equity, and quality of life and environmental quality for all. Yet this approach came about only after younger staff members at the MAS essentially rebelled at the initial suggestion of the organization's president and executive director, put forth within days of the attack, that it would provide an opportunity to replan downtown. They "seemed shocked by this suggestion," wrote Arielle Goldberg in her study of how community and civic groups organized for action after 9/11. "Organized advocacy seems an inappropriate, almost blasphemous, response to the loss they had experienced on 9/11."[28]

Broader in scope than the Civic Alliance's Listening to the City, the Imagine New York workshops focused on "critical planning issues" impacting individuals and neighborhoods; they were "very much a normative experiment in 'imagining' how the city ought to look." Conducted in Cantonese, Spanish, and American Sign Language, as well as English, they were often in neighborhoods where participants lived and brought together individuals from different backgrounds and different interests to foster deliberation among them. Yielding some nineteen thousand ideas, the workshop output was consolidated (unedited except for grammar, consistency, and repetition) by the steering committee into forty-nine vision statements, and the Summary Report presented to governmental decision-makers for their use in the planning process for rebuilding lower Manhattan. The LMDC and the Port Authority, however, essentially ignored the Summary Report, as Goldberg explained in her essay on civic engagement.

Not every group sought to craft a planning blueprint for the Trade Center site. The Labor Community Advocacy Network (LCAN) comprising over fifty labor unions, community groups, research and advocacy organizations, and service providers, for example, was formed by the Fiscal Policy Institute and the New York City Central Labor Council of the AFL-CIO with support from the Rockefeller Foundation and the Open Society Institution to advocate for two main priorities: fostering high-paying jobs and building affordable housing. "LCAN viewed rebuilding in political, not design terms, arguing that it was an opportunity to break down the city's growing economic polarization," wrote planner Eugenie Birch.

"They focused less on specific projects for lower Manhattan and more on the city's low- and moderate-income workers and residents." Resource allocation was at the center of the coalition's concern; billions would be spent on rebuilding in the coming years, and LCAN wanted "an open and honest debate about those resource allocation decisions." After six months of meetings and discussion, in April LCAN issued a forty-eight-page "Policy Statement" that was consistent with its people-based (not place-based) emphasis; the five principles made no mention of the memorial, transit facilities, open space, or other planning goals. Although it took positions on planning decisions, Goldberg wrote, "LCAN was more focused on whether the rules governing development practices would be inclusive and whether they would include equity participation."[29]

Each of these private planning agents had its own agenda, purpose, membership, values and organizational culture, and priorities. Yet each saw in rebuilding an opportunity to push for big issues that could become part of a consensus vision for lower Manhattan's future: creation of a vibrant twenty-four-hour, mixed-use, mixed-income community; a diverse economic base anchored by a strong financial-services sector; an efficient transportation system that rationalized mass transit for all of downtown; concerted public funding for infrastructure and improved amenities, including open space, cultural facilities, and preserved historical areas; social equity and sustainable development. Most were not new aspirations, but rather recurrent thematic elements found in planning documents for downtown at least as far back as *The Lower Manhattan Plan of 1966*. The element unique to the post-9/11 articulation of these visions, of course, was a 9/11 memorial on the site—rebuilding the site could not be simply a real estate development project. The importance of these private planning agents extended beyond the particulars of plans for Ground Zero. "With fast-track responses," Birch concluded in her comprehensive post-9/11 analysis of proposals for downtown, "they telescoped the evolution of the ideas for downtown planning into a few months. In so doing, they brought broad attention to the definition of the 21st century downtown, the selection of appropriate actions to sustain it, and the use of new measures to insure broad and inclusive participation in planning for it."[30]

People, and not just New Yorkers, felt proprietary about Ground Zero. In taking the lead, the established civic organizations and newly formed coalitions played a powerful role in facilitating participatory processes and articulating ideas emerging from diverse communities. They provided a voice for the larger public, filling a void created when decision-making rebuilding principals, namely the Port Authority and Larry Silverstein, failed to provide venues for consultation with the public. Since they represented a large cross-section of citizen participation, including many with strong professional credentials and a long history of involvement in community issues in New York, the coordinators brought to the task organizational skills and networks of access to sources of funding for their work: foundation grants, professional and corporate contributions, and staff assistance from member organizations. Just how much influence they would ultimately have, however, would be tested when it came time for government officials to make planning decisions, allocate real resources, and set priorities (or not). As chair of the LMDC, Whitehead encouraged these ad hoc groups, and the LMDC soon formed ten advisory councils to gather input as part of the planning process. Input, even as part of a participatory planning process, did not necessarily link up to becoming a part of the agenda. Though government officials would ultimately adopt policies that differed from those put forth by these hives of activity, their activities still enriched the level and breadth of discussion about rebuilding than might otherwise have transpired. In particular instances, the Civic Alliance's role in organizing "Listening to the City" and NYNV's vigil over the LMDC's master plan design competition described in chapter 7, they did have an impact.

Architectural Fantasy

On January 17, 2002, longtime gallery owner Max Protetch opened the doors of his Chelsea art gallery for "A New World Trade Center," an exhibit featuring design proposals from more than fifty architects—well-known leading names as well as young inventive talent and avant-garde types—from around the world. After the *New York Times* and *Wall Street Journal* briefly covered the preopening and Protetch appeared on the *Today* show, the crush of people who waited in wrap-around-the-block lines for hours to see the exhibit shocked even Richard Ivy, editor in chief of *Architectural Record*, who helped Protetch with the planning of the event. "We witnessed something of an architectural feeding frenzy, as the crowds swelled into a sea and the media circled like sharks," he wrote of the opening. "To see the opening on the national news, you would never dream how quickly things had come together." Across the pond, design and architectural critic for the London-based *Observer* Deyan Sudjic wrote, "No architecture exhibit could have ever dreamt of such a response. For once, architects are not talking merely to themselves, they have the whole of New York looking over their shoulder."[31]

The visions at the show did not have much to do with real-world buildable architecture. They were, as Philip Nobel wrote in *Sixteen Acres*, a "fatal distance from public need." The designs were unbuildable and responded to problems "too conjectural, too personal, too obscure, too sensational...to be of much use when utility comes calling." On display were two-dimensional sketches, three-dimensional models and computer-generated images, video installations, memorial sketches, proposals for buildings designed with different technologies, and poetry. "In the absence of a client, property owners, a means of financing, or public approval, most of the exhibitors produced futuristic images without any indication of their use or who would be the occupants of whatever structures they proposed—nothing that dealt with the real issues of rebuilding," Garvin wrote years later in *The Planning Game: Lessons from Great Cities.*[32] "It was not the place to go to find 'the' solution," remarked Benjamin Forgey in his review of the show. "Rather, for the duration of the show, the Protetch Gallery is a territory of energy and suggestiveness. The challenge is to harness the passion and intelligence of architects like these to a sound and imaginative set of ground rules." Paul Goldberger was more direct in his assessment: "If you start with architects, you just get a bunch of their favorite shapes," he said in a speech at the Architectural Foundation of Cincinnati in May 2004. If it seems like "heresy" for an architectural critic to say don't start with architects, he went on to explain: "You start with some sort of consensus about what it is you want to do with a piece of land, and then you call in architects."[33]

This was the first full-scale exhibit of architectural ideas following September 11. It might have been one of the most widely attended gallery exhibitions in New York's history, as one commentary put it—if such statistics are actually collected. It filled a palpable void for meaning at a terribly vulnerable time in the city's history. It would go on tour to the National Building Museum in Washington, D.C., and to the Eighth International Biennale of Architecture in Venice—the first time the United States participated in this architectural exhibition. The show was published as a good-looking slim book by HarperCollins. The Library of Congress acquired the exhibition for $408,140 and made it available online for all to see. Architecture as a public passion appeared to have arrived in the twenty-first century as a consequence of tragedy.

In the wake of 9/11, Protetch was looking for a way to "do something positive and helpful" that would make a contribution. With this exhibit he was "the first individual to tap the well of public engagement."[34] An experienced art dealer who opened his first gallery in Washington, D.C., in 1969 at the age of twenty-three, while a graduate student in political science at Georgetown University, Protetch moved into the gallery scene in New York in 1978 and began showing architectural drawings long before others had taken up the idea. In mounting this exhibit, his idea was to present ideas 9/11 was generating in the architectural world. Great architecture could serve as a lasting monument, he believed; New York was a city of good buildings, not great ones, and the calamity afforded an "opportunity to present a grand vision for a renewed urban space."

Acting as an advocate for advanced design ideas, Protetch argued that forward thinking in design could become a growth imperative for New York. The idea was to use architecture as a catalyst for change, a catalyst for the city to think big and expand its horizons beyond the "business as usual" approach to city building. "The show is a conceptual show," he said, "the ideas are not meant to be built because first of all, there's no program. We don't know exactly what's going to be needed or permitted on the site, and there's no client"—which essentially meant no limits. What he aimed to do was to create a dialogue, expand the sense of architectural possibilities, speculate about future opportunities, muse how architecture could confer meaningful hope and optimism about the future. The impact on the American and international public at large of watching airplanes controlled by terrorists fly into the towers was, he said, "very possibly the first time in the history of the United States that the American public understood the symbolic, economic, political importance of architecture."[35]

Protetch was criticized by some for moving too fast before the transformed meaning of the Trade Center site could be absorbed. Of the 125 asked to participate, some architects hesitated. Others gently refused to take part in the exhibit because it was too soon or would look too self-promotional, opportunistic. Others might have thought it pointless, as Sudjic commented, because "the future of the site will be shaped not by the imaginations of the dozens of architects who did take part in the show, but by the room full of developers, insurance loss-adjusters and politicians even now carving up the area." Beyond the specific images of the Protetch exhibit, many detailed in language only architects could understand or clueless about what city building is all about, and others so audacious as to recall the sentiment the twin towers evoked in the sixties, this was the architecture community acting as a collective voice aiming to present visions to "lift the spirit, unite the city and speak to both the past and the future"—before great architecture "could easily get lost in the shuffle of competing claims."[36] In that sense, the show offered what the public wanted—something big and possibly inspiring—but the product was fantasy.

The next architectural fantasy presented to the public was curated by the *Times* architectural critic Herbert Muschamp in "Thinking Big: A Plan for Ground Zero and Beyond."[37] Offered as an exhibit of ideas from architects as "an incitement to the city to think big," the ideas came out in print on September 8, 2002, with a more elaborate interactive version posted on the Web. Muschamp was dissatisfied "that the official planning process was following a pattern conventionally used by real-estate developers," and he insisted that "it had to be broken." He was reacting to the highly embarrassing failure of the LMDC to present any kind of inspiring vision for rebuilding (described in chapter 7). In contrast to what he called "a privatized version of city planning," he gathered together twenty of his favorite architects in a collaborative "study project" to show how it could be done better, how architecture could "recast cultural identity for 21st century New York"[38] and provide "a revised mythology of our place in the era of globalization." He then added how "the entire framework is presented as a living memorial to those who died in last year's attack." "Don't Rebuild. Reimagine. Now is the time for New York to express its ambition through architecture and reclaim its place as a visionary city," Muschamp declared with typical hyperbolic enthusiasm for the ideas of those globally known architects he chose to showcase, ideas he hoped would tilt the focus at Ground Zero from commerce to culture.

Muschamp's study project did not aim to set out a comprehensive plan for Ground Zero or lower Manhattan; it was not about planning at all. Rather, each architect was assigned a specific site and asked to supply a corresponding image. In "The Blueprint," which the *New York Times Magazine* promoted on its front page as "The Masters' Plan," the architects' fashion show of images paraded down the West Street runway to Battery Place. In the fourteen-page spread illustrating in color and graphics each imagined design, there was no limit to the rhetorical claims for what the fantasy lineup of buildings by signature architects would achieve: "this plan would not only revitalize Lower Manhattan; it would also reassert New York's cosmopolitan identity. And it would re-establish New York's skyline as the most thrilling in the world."[39]

Muschamp and the *Magazine* were promoting culture as an end unto itself, as the Max Protetch exhibit that so enthralled the design world had promoted art. This was not city building. Architecture may be art and city building calls for artlike understanding of the fabric of a place, but a city is not a blank canvas to paint at will as Muschamp was advocating with his study project, most unrealistically. Physical circumstances make things possible or not. The heavy legacy of urban renewal reinforced through loss that the historic and cultural meaning of place matters and that social relationships need to be considered in fashioning new districts of a city.

Muschamp had issued his condemnation of the public planning process for bypassing cutting-edge architecture at Ground Zero months earlier, two days after the Port Authority and the LMDC announced the selection of the New York architecture firm Beyer Blinder Belle (BBB) to design a master plan for Ground Zero on May 21. The selection "confirms once again that architecture will play no more than a marginal role in the redevelopment of Lower Manhattan," he wrote. Viciously castigating this well-respected firm with an outstanding reputation based on its thirty-four years of professional practice, he begrudgingly acknowledged the firm's remodeling of historic structures (Grand Central Terminal and Ellis Island National Monument), but asserted, "its original work has been lackluster." BBB was his stalking horse, a means to let loose his anger at "the construction of mediocrity in Lower Manhattan," and "low level of architectural ambition sustained" by the public agencies in charge of the process.[40] Irresponsibly, Muschamp had preemptively pronounced his personal opinion of what was likely to result before BBB had even drawn a single line. Did this belong in the news section of the paper? Where does the press cross the line between presenting the news to inform the public and aiming to become a player by advocating a particular vision—other than on the editorial page?

WHAT ABOUT A SWAP?

In his collection of poetry, *Leaves of Grass*, New York's Walt Whitman wrote a prophetic ode to the "City of the world!":

> Proud and passionate city! mettlesome, mad, extravagant city!
> Spring up O city—not for peace alone, but be indeed yourself, warlike!
> Fear not—submit to no models but your own, O city!

More than 150 years later, Whitman's words evoked city government's poignant position in the three-way political struggle to rebuild at Ground Zero. From the start city officials fretted over their limited control of the redevelopment; it seemed logical that they should shoulder the mandate to rebuild Ground Zero. Yet without formal legal powers, they were left at a severe disadvantage in influencing decisions that would shape the physical and economic landscape of lower Manhattan for decades to come.[41]

Mayor Bloomberg disagreed with the central thrust of rebuilding ten million square feet of office space at Ground Zero. He wanted rebuilding to project more of a residential vision, perhaps because residential was the strongest prevailing demand at the time, and the site might get rebuilt fastest following that market direction. "Nobody was being honest about Lower Manhattan," Deputy Mayor Doctoroff told *Times* reporter Deborah Sontag. "The truth is, Lower Manhattan before 9/11 had a growing residential population, but it had been losing worker population since 1970." The problems of lower Manhattan "were swept under the rug in the wake of 9/11 by this kind of nostalgia for the World Trade Center and the tremendous emotion that existed."[42] Although he understood the city's ability to impact rebuilding was limited, Doctoroff thrived on confronting the big challenge: How could the Bloomberg administration play a critical role in defining the future of lower Manhattan? His answer: by maneuvering opportunistically and tactically—and repeatedly—to gain influence if not control.

Doctoroff was forty-three when he took a desk in the mayor's bullpen at City Hall as deputy mayor for economic development and rebuilding. New to the political game, he arrived with formidable analytical skills and a track record of success in the private sector. He had been an investment banker at Lehman Brothers for three years before going to work for Texas billionaire Robert W. Bass's Oak Hill Capital, where he managed the private-equity firm's investments in diverse industries, including information services, insurance, hotels, drug stores, and real estate. His fifteen years in private equity delivered the early wealth of his ambition that, he told the *Times*, would give him freedom to make unrestricted choices later. He had left the practice of law, finding greater interest and a quicker route to wealth though finance. Like the mayor, he was a $1-a-year man in City Hall. He had never thought about government before Nathan Leventhal, head of the mayor's postelection transition team and an early board member of an organization Doctoroff founded to try to bring the 2012 Olympics to New York City, recommended him for the economic development post. His first Olympics effort, for the 2008 games, he said, "was three years of on-the-job training" for the City Hall post.[43] Hard-charging with a strong ego, the new deputy mayor was used to doing things his own way; his entrance into politics would be bumpy at times. He was known to be a hothead who aimed to temper the tendency by counting the number of days he could go without losing his temper. He had an opinion on everything. "Reject, reconsider, accept, and own" was how one close staffer described the behavior paradigm best fitting the man. A determined high achiever, he would gain Bloomberg's complete confidence. The mayor liked risk takers, and Doctoroff fit the profile.

Doctoroff's first thrust at gaining control at Ground Zero was the bold proposal to swap the city ownership of the land beneath LaGuardia and JFK Airports, operated by the PA since 1947 under a series of leases, for the Trade Center site. The proposal, if successful, would simultaneously resolve a long-simmering dispute over the airports' lease agreement stymied for the full eight years of the Giuliani administration (Republican, 1994–2001). The city and the Port Authority had, in fact, been negotiating a deal for a new lease during the administration of David N. Dinkins (Democrat, 1990–1993); it was not quite at the signing stage when Dinkins lost the 1993 election, recalled Weisbrod, then president of the city's Economic Development Corporation. Negotiations under the new mayor resumed but quickly turned sour and in late 1994, broke down completely. Giuliani went on record saying the city would not extend the term of the lease, and his administration started to study privatization of the airports. As mayor, the former U.S. attorney for the Southern District of New York was using this vital link to the region's economic strength as a pawn in a bigger strategic attempt to wrest control from the agency by making it impossible for the Port Authority to issue long-term bonds to repay debt supported by revenues from the airports. Giuliani was unsuccessful in his war against the Port Authority, and the airports' lease issue remained outstanding.[44] When the Bloomberg team moved into City Hall, it marked a "real change," a senior Port financial official recalled. Doctoroff was said to have told PA staff he wanted the PA to run the airports and that there was "a lot of rhetoric from the past administration they would have to deal with."

Governments are in constant negotiation, always working with a package of issues that need to be resolved. Collateral issues like the airports' lease are out there as potential pivots that can break a political stalemate and resolve more than one policy objective. When Bloomberg came into office, the history of stalemate over the lease for the airports offered that potential. "What kind of negotiation [between the city and the Port Authority] goes on for ten years with no result?" PA chairman Anthony R. Coscia asked rhetorically when I interviewed him. "It was a good time to put a deal together, from both sides."[45] The city had been negotiating with the PA over extending the lease for about five months and simultaneously working on the Trade Center. The economics looked "eerily" similar. For New York City, the airports were purely an economic asset; for the PA, the Trade Center was purely an economic asset.

As Sontag relates the story, "One night in mid-2002, at a moment of simultaneous frustration about ground zero and about negotiations over the Port Authority's leases on the city airports," Bloomberg, Doctoroff, and his deputy, twenty-four-year-old Roy Bahat, "sat in the garden behind City Hall looking at spreadsheets. Flipping back and forth between the two sets of numbers," Bahat had "an epiphany." What the city was looking to collect from the Port Authority in rent and what the Port Authority was looking to collect from Larry Silverstein in rent were of the approximate same magnitude: $100 million. Bahat said, "Why not just trade?" Doctoroff thought about it for a week and had Bahat run some numbers, and he then sat down with Coscia. Doctoroff's staff reasoned they were in a strong position. A deal was certain to get done before the PA went back to the bond markets: Without the airports—the money-delivery machine providing the agency with nearly half of its operating budget—the PA "would cease to exist," and the closer it got to lease term, the better the city's position would get. Coscia was receptive to the idea. So too, the authority's executive director: "Although there is still a great deal of work to be done," Joseph Seymour told the press he "found the framework of this proposal to be credible and worth pursuing."[46]

The news of the informal swap proposal hit the papers in early August 2002, possibly a leak, in a flurry of articles, followed by editorials. The *Times* called it "the most creative idea to arise from the Lower Manhattan redevelopment process so far." The *Daily News* said it was "innovative" and "certainly intriguing." *Newsday* said the idea is "notable for its elegance and its potential." *Crain's* said the idea is "enormously attractive," and its "appeal is undeniable." The *Post* acknowledged the "superficial appeal" of the swap, offering "an innovative way to set in motion the rebuilding of lower Manhattan." However, the editorial went on to say, "In point of fact, it is no solution at all." Running through a list of potential hindrances to progress—"utmost strain on the resources of both the city and the state," questionable "judgment, courage and ability" of New York's elected leaders "to lead in ways that would get the job done," process impediments like reviews by community boards that would "slow meaningful reconstruction"—and calling themselves "cynics," the *Post* editors lacked faith in the city's capacity to manage rebuilding. And the *Post* was skeptical that the governor and the power structure in Albany "will stand idly by while City Hall takes control of reconstruction."[47] On this point, the editors were dead-on right, though officials at both the Port Authority and City Hall would work for months before Governor Pataki nixed the proposal.

The swap seems to offer a "win-win deal," the *Times* said, because it would "clarify the lines of authority and provide both the city and the Port Authority with managerial flexibility that neither has right now." It would also resolve what the *Daily News* said was "Hollywood accounting to cheat the city out of fair rents for the airports" that for years had been a high-profile source of controversy and arbitration between the city and the PA.[48] The Port Authority would gain control of its main revenue producer in perpetuity, remove any lease obligations, and clear the way for the issuance of long-term debt; it would remove the heavy responsibility for rebuilding the Trade Center site under terms and conditions growing increasingly uncomfortable for an agency used to calling all the shots without outside interference. The agency's powerful staff liked this potential package, a lot, and worked through the details with Bahat as both sides did the requisite legal due diligence.[49]

As a matter of policy, sentiment was strong that the city should control the Trade Center site as owner. After the major public review of plans for Ground Zero at the July "Listening to the City" event revealed revenue harvesting to be the PA's main concern, "permanently excising" the bi-state agency from the rebuilding process promised greater flexibility in planning the site's future uses. The implications of gaining control extended beyond the one-shot infusion of cash to the city treasury from the PA for payment of back rent on the airports' lease: It also meant being able to "develop the World Trade Center site in a way that best serves the interests of the entire city."[50] Translated—under city control, development at Ground Zero would proceed more in line with the mayor's desire to see housing, parks, and cultural institutions, along with office development—not the ten million square feet Silverstein and the Port Authority wanted to build.

The land swap enjoyed support from many quarters, including the downtown business community.[51] Nobody seemed to be against it, except perhaps Silverstein after rumors surfaced that the city was likely to try to remove him from the site either through a buyout or condemnation. Still, all of the editorials were quick to point out the many "issues," "questions," "tangle of loose ends," "potential problems"—not "insubstantial ones"—that would have to be worked out. As a land-to-land transaction, the swap was lopsided—4,930 acres at JFK plus 680 acres at LaGuardia for the 16 acres of the Trade Center. Economic value, though, not quantity of real estate was the metric of meaning, and if the swap did not constitute an even exchange, the city would be asking for a one-shot lump of cash to true-up the trade. New York City was facing multibillion dollar budget shortfalls in the years ahead, and potentially large budgetary impacts from giving up ownership of the airports and for taking ownership of the Trade Center site loomed menacingly. The cash from the PA for either the airports' back payments on the lease or the swap would be an important plug to the budget gap.

Figuring out the fiscal math of the potential transaction was complicated (weighing lost airport lease revenues, immediate and future, against commercial rents from a rebuilt Trade Center, all in the future) and did not look promising for the city. The thinking behind the land swap was political, not economic. The city would be trading long-term economics of the airports for long-term control over Ground Zero. Control is worth a premium, even if it is hard to value, and Bloomberg had repeatedly said he "wanted the city to be in control of its own destiny."[52] However, by exposing rebuilding to regulation from which the PA was largely exempt, the swap might delay the process. Not to be taken lightly were profound policy questions: Would it be wise to give the Port Authority total control of assets so vital to the economy of the city and Long Island when the bi-state agency hasn't been such a good steward of those airport assets? Would the agency end up favoring Newark Airport at the expense of LaGuardia and JFK Airports? For New Jersey, the concern was reversed: If the PA owned the two New York airports and merely leased the ground under Newark International, would it focus all its capital investments on LaGuardia and JFK?

The cautious optimism of the first week following its public airing segued to skepticism as additional questions accumulated about the swap's substantial financial and political complexity. Sources in Albany started to elaborate on its complications. By late fall the talks were in limbo; both sides recognized that they had to resolve the basic economic relationship between the city and the Port Authority—that is, settle the prolonged bitter battle over back airport lease payments—before getting to the conditions of a land swap.[53] Into the new year, the land swap discussions gained momentum. Doctoroff talked about an advisory board that would give the city some say in how the airports would be run, reflecting the mayor's view that any trade would not be a straight "land-for-land deal." As Bloomberg told the press, "With the swap, there would be lots of changes in regulations, lots of swapping of money streams, lots of agreements so that the city has some say in how its airports would be run." Absent those considerations, the business-minded mayor said, the swap "wouldn't make any sense, if you think about the economics"[54] (figure 5.2).

In April, the *Times* presumptively talked about the swap proposal as a "pending deal." The politics of any swap, though, required offering something to New Jersey, which would extract its "pound of flesh," as one insider to the city's deliberations put it. Governor James E. McGreevey (Democrat, 2002–2004) worried that his state would be shortchanged in the deal. "We couldn't be any clearer. Until we know this is beneficial for New Jersey, until we know what the numbers are…it's not moving," said the governor's spokesman.[55]

The idea was attractively simple. It was bold—a proposal bearing "all the hallmarks of a Doctoroff idea," said the *New York Observer*, but it was laden with technical complications and "politically sensitive just beneath the skin." PA vice chairman Charles A. Gargano, also chair of the Empire State Development Corporation and "a loyal Pataki soldier," was said to be riled by the swap proposal, a threat to his influence; he had already been "a loser in a bid to control the Lower Manhattan

Mike Sees City Taking Control At Ground Zero

But Where Does That Leave Larry Silverstein, Battered, Steadfast Holder of 99-Year Lease? City Would Get W.T.C. for Land Under Airports

FIGURE 5.2 *March 17, 2003,* The New York Observer

Development Corporation." In the end, it was a political decision—for Governor Pataki. Even if the PA, the city, and New Jersey could all be satisfied, the land swap promised to diminish Pataki's control over the site and the political benefits he derived from that control. After months of fitful discussion, Coscia got a call from Kenneth J. Ringler, another of the governor's loyal soldiers, telling him that Gargano and he were against the swap. Discussions cratered. "We were there," recalled Coscia when I spoke with him years later. "The governor [of New Jersey] would have supported the deal. Pataki was for it until he wasn't for it."[56] In late June 2003, Pataki publicly suspended the talks. The swap was dead.

As with other rebuilding stories, there are different versions of what happened to the swap proposal. The eleven months' passage between its first airing and its final demise suggests that it was not dismissed lightly. The swap proposal was real, Seymour told me; he was negotiating with Doctoroff, and they came to a land and financial memorandum of understanding. Then the deal went to the governor's chief of staff, where it was nixed. When I asked Seymour why it didn't happen, he answered: "The governor was leading the redevelopment of lower Manhattan and the WTC site after the horrific destruction of 9/11. Trading that leadership for the PANYNJ's ownership of the airport sites was not going to happen. Doctoroff and I should have recognized that." So why did the discussions for the land swap proceed? "Sometimes the governor will just sit back," he said, "and watch the turkeys dance."[57]

As often seemed to be the case at Ground Zero, there was more than one account of an episode. Bloomberg never even called Pataki to discuss it, the *Times* reported. One member of the city team said the talks never got to the point of "negotiation"; it was only a discussion, albeit a long discussion. Negotiation, he said, means that there is a general sense a deal can get done; this was not the case with the land swap, as time would reveal. A swap would have taken an act of both legislatures. As a legal matter, the Trade Center land would have had to be declared "surplus." The calculus from the city's perspective did not look good. Factoring in the New Jersey extraction, there wasn't enough economic value in a potential deal to be gained by either side and so the idea never got to the negotiation stage.

Still, in the aftermath, city officials were furious; it took five to six months for the administration not to be furious, according to one insider. The administration had considered the big picture of a deal. "I'm not sure at the end of the day that it would have been the best deal financially for the city," Doctoroff later told the *Times* reporter Sontag, "but the hope was that having a single government entity in charge would have been better." The obvious question, Doctoroff told me, was "Why not make a bigger deal out of the situation—yell and shout?" He went on to explain: A broad set of relationships conditions the city-state relationship. And he was not talking about any connection to the Hudson Yards project, referring to the mayor's interest in pushing forward the development of the far West Side of Manhattan. "Rather a bigger set of relationships tied to the budget, for example, MTA funds, is involved."[58] The reason was well known and not complex: The mayor and the City of New York need the governor; the mayor could not afford to antagonize the governor.

On his weekly radio show, Bloomberg commented on the land-swap proposal: "In the end, I think it should be up to the City of New York. It's part of our city. The [PA] was there for the WTC, but now tragically, that's no longer there.... While I understand New Jersey has an interest in what goes on in the region, I don't think the governor of New Jersey should have a big say, or the New Jersey Legislature, in what's developed there." As would any mayor, Bloomberg believed "the city should be in control of its own destiny." In mid-October, he announced that the city would extend its lease of LaGuardia and JFK Airports with the Port Authority until 2050, in exchange for a $700 million upfront payment and a steep increase in annual rents ($93.5 million or 8 percent of gross revenues). Whether the city could have gotten a better deal remains an open question that calls for a comprehensive analysis of the airports lease conflict. The formal agreement approved by the Port Authority Board of Commissioners in November detailed other items the city wanted: the creation of an airport advisory board composed of an equal number of representatives of the Port Authority and New York City (appointed by the mayor), a new arrangement on the taxation of the Trade Center, and feasibility studies of rail links between lower Manhattan and both JFK and Newark Airports.[59] Although the land swap was dead, the episode finally resolved the two other outstanding financial issues between the city and the Port Authority.

Four months after proposing the land swap, the city made a second strategic thrust for influence with the mayor's broad and expansive *New York City's Vision for Lower Manhattan*. This multifaceted $10.6 billion agenda covered all of lower Manhattan below Canal Street from the East River to the Hudson River. To make the area "a more vibrant global hub of culture and commerce," the city proposed three types of public investments: transportation initiatives to connect the district to the world around it, street improvement and open spaces to build new neighborhoods, and public places to create new amenities throughout the district. The vision emphasized new housing for thirty thousand people in keeping with a theme the mayor voiced early in his administration. Although the plan included office towers at the Trade Center site, the mayor's clear priority was to remake lower Manhattan into a twenty-four-hour residential and business community. Once floated, the plan was not immediately pushed hard by City Hall, which was focusing more of its attention on the Hudson Yards Project, its development priority.

The Bloomberg administration made a third thrust after the planned departure of the LMDC's first president, Lou Tomson. Tomson had been living alone in a Manhattan hotel, away from his family, and had finally served as president of the LMDC long enough to do what his friend, Governor Pataki, expected of him. One of his main assignments had been to lead the rebuilding effort through the governor's 2002 reelection campaign, keeping controversy away from the governor. For more than a year, he had been the Ground Zero lightning rod, a target of criticism for everyone—politicians, lower Manhattan residents, the media, and survivors who found fault with the pace and scale of rebuilding. "The job wore me out," he said. "It was the hours, as well as the need to accommodate many hostile opinions." He was in good health, but as the *Times* reported, had been bothered by the lingering effects of cancer treatment and was not fond of the weekly commute to and from his home on sixteen acres in the hills east of Albany.[60]

The city saw an opening for action. In a confidential letter to John P. Cahill, the governor's chief of staff, Mayor Bloomberg proposed to revamp the LMDC to give the city more authority over reconstruction of the Trade Center site and more control over the LMDC's remaining $1.25 billion of federal money. The proposal laid out shared decision-making over this pot of money consonant with the mayor's *Vision*. "The effect of having such an advisory board [for the Trade Center site consisting of the current LMDC site steering committee and reporting to the deputy mayor] giving approval," the *New York Post* reported, "would be much the same as in the city's proposed land swap with the Port Authority, giving the city control of the trade center site while keeping the development process exempt from the complicated review process the city would experience, a process from which the Port Authority is exempt."[61] The proposal went nowhere. Still pushing for an expanded role, city officials next attempted to refuse to approve the governor's choice to lead the LMDC, then operating with an interim president, until it received greater clarity on a wide variety of downtown building issues.

Many observers found Mayor Bloomberg's efforts to exert influence on Ground Zero surprisingly low-key in comparison with his forceful advocacy of the Hudson Yards Project. It was natural for them to ask whether the mayor and the governor had cut a deal for credit for and control over their respective development priorities that were also predictable competitors in the high-stakes real estate market of Manhattan. Had the governor's and the mayor's staffs come to a tacit agreement on who would do what work on each project? The agreement was not "formal," a close senior advisor of the governor told me, but an understanding did seem to exist. The mayor's interests were elsewhere at the time. It was well known that he had worked downtown and personally didn't care for the historic district. He saw the city's future and its growth as happening on the far West Side of midtown. Downtown's future, he believed, would be as a residential center; he didn't share the governor's unwavering conviction that downtown needed to remain a business center for the city. But Bloomberg's interest in downtown would change course and pick up momentum when the political landscape shifted course toward the end of Pataki's tenure in Albany. Anticipating a second term in City Hall, the mayor would move aggressively to gain position at Ground Zero.

CONTENTION AHEAD

Whatever consensus emerged in the first year of debate about rebuilding, conflict was in the making. It was predictable because it is part and parcel of New York City's distinctively fractious style of self-interested politics. The nation's biggest city is governed under a strong-mayor structure, but beyond what statutes can dictate, the city's political arena is shaped by numerous and diverse interests typically more focused on their own individual agendas than any citywide civic cause and guided by deep historical memories of development battles won and lost. Wielding rhetoric and alternative proposals, the city's interest groups are prone to challenge policies and plans, positioning themselves in an effort to shape the debate if not always win the argument. Coalitions form over individual issues and re-form as details evolve or new issues emerge. No New Yorker would place a bet on a consensual and uninterrupted process for a high-profile development project, not even at Ground Zero. The lower Manhattan constituency, its business and residential interests and elected representatives, in particular, is used to having a seat at the table, being empowered. It is knowledgeable of the city and how it works. It has a commitment to the city. Members of the fire department and police department have served the city from one generation to the next. Because the constituencies of interests are more sophisticated and affluent than those affected by more typical disasters such as the South Asian tsunami and Hurricane Katrina in New Orleans, the politics of rebuilding Ground Zero was guaranteed to differ from those types of natural disasters.

Large-scale development projects in New York are particularly prone to protracted controversy and extended timelines. The city's politics are the mirror of its commercial culture: aggressive and competitive. No influential elite hovers above the cacophony of special interests or commands the power of unified leadership to define an agenda for the city or convene principal stakeholders to forge a consensus of opinion and resolve high-level problems, as had come together during the

1970s fiscal crisis. New York City hadn't learned "team play," said Frank Macchiarola, then president of the New York City Partnership, a description that might equally apply to other cities—San Francisco, for example. New York has leading civic and business institutions engaged in the political environment such as the Partnership, but unlike Boston, no "Vault." The moniker for this group of twenty-five business leaders from downtown Boston who sought to rescue Boston from its deteriorating future in the 1960s and 1970s described its secretive meeting place: the basement vault of the Boston Safe Deposit & Trust Co. Formally known as the Coordinating Committee, it operated in a patently undemocratic manner but wielded great influence over public affairs until it disbanded in 1997.[62] During the lengthy process of depressing the Central Artery, a project known as "the Big Dig," and building a third-harbor tunnel, Boston's downtown leadership formed a separate committee, the Artery Business Committee, to push the project forward. Experienced developer and longtime Boston civic leader Norman Leventhal described its role simply: "To make sure it gets built and make sure it gets built right."[63]

During its formative postwar years, New York had Robert Moses—public servant turned controversial "power broker"—whose vast accumulated powers allowed him to exercise domineering control over the apparatus of redevelopment in New York City. With his fall from grace and devolution of his powers beginning in the mid-1960s, New Yorkers developed a deep distrust of centralized control over redevelopment. Moreover, the cacophony of interest-group voices, derived in part from numerous battles against the Moses redevelopment machine, established a new political pattern, one that brought forth more openly contentious dialogue and materially extended timelines for executing large-scale projects. It became hard, very hard, to execute large-scale visions for city building in New York City. Rebuilding Ground Zero, even more so than any other endeavor the city had faced in its history, needed strong leadership and a clear and consistent governing framework for making carefully deliberated decisions. However, the era of a powerful building czar had passed.

The early steps in the public planning process did not inspire confidence, but rather fell far short of widely held aspirations for such an achievement, to the great consternation of families of the victims and first responders, downtown residents, downtown business interests, and the ad hoc groups engaged in putting forth ideas for the future. No one reading the *Times* account of Ground Zero planning in late January 2002 would have disputed reporter Edward Wyatt's assessment: "The rebuilding of Lower Manhattan has the makings of a bitter New York struggle, a dialogue of disparate views of grief, money, power, politics and design, inflamed by differing passions, but with no framework to reconcile them."[64]

The raw emotion of 9/11 compounded the fragility of initial optimism and civic support, and it created a relatively short-term power base for the families of those who died in the terrorist attack. It would be very hard, if not impossible, to argue against the sacred (regardless of substantive merits), and the sacred dictated decisive early decisions about the nature of the site, such as Governor George Pataki's 2002 "footprints" declaration to the families that nothing would be built where the towers stood, discussed in chapter 7. The sacred similarly drove the political rhetoric that shaped not only the planning process but also decisions about how the chosen conceptual design for the memorial would translate to reality, what surviving artifacts would be preserved, and how culture and the performing arts would be (or not be) accommodated on the site. In his official farewell address delivered on the "thrice-hallowed ground" of the eighteenth-century St. Paul's Chapel of Trinity Church, a historic sanctuary that served as a place of rest and refuge for recovery workers at the Trade Center site, outgoing Mayor Rudolph Giuliani promised to push for a "soaring, monumental" memorial at the Trade Center site. "The place has to be sanctified," he said. It should not be thought about "as a site for economic development." He wanted the entire sixteen-acre site turned into a memorial "that would draw millions of people here that just want to see it." The mayor-elect thought differently: "Everybody thinks we will have a memorial and should have a memorial, and that is what we have the committee [the LMDC] for: to look and see what's the appropriate use of that space, and I think I'll sit back and let them come up with suggestions and give them my input." Bloomberg was "in favor of more of a mixed-use thing," and this initial idea of his would not vary over time.[65]

The tension between remembrance and rebuilding persisted throughout 2002 and 2003, the years of formal planning activity, and continued for years afterward as the actors in this epic drama debated and negotiated the master plan for rebuilding. The most powerful actor in this drama, the landowning Port Authority, had its own ideas about what was to happen at Ground Zero and about how those decisions would get made on its site. Though traumatized by the events of 9/11, the agency would soon enough act to assert control over its domain, and in the process trigger fierce institutional rivalry with the far weaker LMDC—and confusion about who was in charge at Ground Zero.

CHAPTER 6
"It's Our Site"

FIGURE 6.1 *On April 4, 1973, there was standing room only at the official dedication ceremonies for the World Trade Center.* New York Daily News Archive/Getty Images

O<small>N</small> M<small>AY</small> 30, <small>THE DATE THE NATION</small> had in the past reserved as a day to remember those who died while serving in the country's armed forces, a somber and quiet ceremony officially marked the end of the recovery operation at Ground Zero. The massive and mournful removal of 1.8 million tons of material from the collapse of the World Trade Center was complete, though for the families of those whose remains remained unidentified, some 1,815 of the 2,823 victims, the recovery would never be complete. The ceremony at Ground Zero ended the eight-and-a-half-month cleanup, expected to have taken at least a year but finished ahead of schedule and under budget, and marked a symbolic turning point, a "profound physical and psychological shift regarding a singular calamity." Earlier that month Mayor Bloomberg promised that those who lost their lives would not be forgotten, but the city, he said, had an "obligation to those left to continue the rebuilding that has already started."[1] The turn to renewal had begun.

One month later, on June 30, the City of New York, which had taken charge of the recovery efforts along with New York State, returned responsibility and control of the scarred sixteen-acre site to the Port Authority. No press release or fanfare accompanied this intergovernmental return of control. Although the physical heritage of its landmark towers, officially dedicated on April 4, 1973, at a widely attended ceremony evident in figure 6.1, was gone, "the pile" of concrete and twisted steel gone as well, the proud agency was determined to move forward with the rebuilding of its home territory. It wanted to set a tight deadline for proposals to redevelop its site in order "to fast-track" the process, its executive director, Joseph J. Seymour, said.[2]

Six weeks later, on August 12, the Port Authority issued a press release to celebrate the "historic announcement" that the Federal Emergency Management Agency (FEMA) would be providing $4.55 billion to fund "a world-class transportation system that will include a new PATH station, a downtown grand terminal, mass transit connections and underground concourses" linking PATH, six subway lines, and ferry connections—what the *Times* more pointedly called an "overhaul and update [of] the tangle of subway stations, commuter terminals and other transportation outlets in Lower Manhattan." FEMA deputy director Michael Brown was presiding over this press conference at Ground Zero because $2.75 billion of the transportation allocation represented surplus funds previously earmarked for use in the Trade Center site cleanup; state and local officials, including Senator Hillary Rodham Clinton, were on hand to applaud the effort that had made this transfer available for transportation upgrades (figure 6.2). Federal officials were giving state and local officials programmatic flexibility when they said, "You figure out what is best for you and we are going to help fund that for you." This grant of flexibility to a local jurisdiction was rare. Rarer still was the fact that federal officials were allowing FEMA funds, normally used only to replace what was destroyed in a disaster, to be used to expand and improve facilities that had been there before. Governor Pataki was on point when he said it was a "tremendous victory for New York."[3] With $2.2 billion, or almost 50 percent, of this federal grant that Pataki was about to allocate to the Port Authority for its dream transportation project, the Port Authority scored a victory as well: The agency could now build with ambition a grand transportation terminal using "free" billions from Washington. The timing of this event meshed nicely with the return of the site to the agency.

For the rest of 2002, 2003, and 2004, the Port Authority moved incrementally to regain as much control as possible over its sixteen acres, buying out all of the site's property interests except for the leases held by Larry Silverstein, planning a

FIGURE 6.2 *Mayor Michael Bloomberg at the microphone celebrates with federal, state, and local officials the federal aid package of $4.55 billion for overhauling transportation in lower Manhattan.* RICHARD PERRY/THE NEW YORK TIMES/REDUX

new underground city of infrastructure, bringing in outside consultants to develop a master plan of its own, and fashioning preliminary plans for a new transportation center stacked with retail stores. These building blocks toward control would better leverage the agency's position as it vied with the LMDC, Silverstein, and city officials to shape who would make what decisions at Ground Zero. It was the PA's site, but unlike in the 1960s when the agency took the audacious step to build the tallest towers in the world, in the post-9/11 rebuilding arena, the cast of contending political and civic interests claiming a part of this scarred and symbolic territory vastly complicated its institutional mission. Fortified by historical legacy, the agency was not going to be intimidated by institutional competition. Proceeding nearly unnoticed in the crush of press coverage of the drama over competing architectural visions for rebuilding Ground Zero, the Port Authority was taking action, quietly and strategically.

UNDERGROUND CONTROL

At some unknown but early date, staff at the Port Authority made a singular determinative decision—to rebuild an elaborate underground superblock that would provide all the air conditioning, utilities, sitewide vehicular access and security-screening operations, and bus parking needs of the "city within a city." Made unilaterally before a master plan had been selected by the LMDC, the PA's decision to re-create the same type of centralized servicing system as in the original World Trade Center complex meant that rebuilding Ground Zero would have to proceed as a single integrated project, and that concept fused with the notion that the complete site could be rebuilt all at once. Yet as many of those involved in the rebuilding process noted in conversation with me, the project could not be built all at once. "The all-at-once decision," said Robert R. Douglass, chairman of the city's largest business improvement district, the Alliance for Downtown New York, was like "building a Lego set without a table."[4]

To envision this underground city ask yourself the question, what do you see when you go to Disneyland? Only the clean and orderly arrangement of amusements, entertainment venues, restaurants, and streetscape furnishings all built around a carefully choreographed environment. The servicing to make that environment so consumer friendly and so carefree is underground, out of sight, contained in a single integrated complex a world apart from what goes on above ground. So it was at the original World Trade Center complex and so it would be again at Ground Zero—with consequences not fully apparent at the time agency staff moved forward with the underground superblock decision. "If there had been time, some alternatives to the underground superblock might have been discussed," an Engineering Department veteran remarked to me; "bus parking might have been placed off-site, but the servicing had to be underground." This irreversible decision, considered by many to be an early mistake, heavily affected the progress of rebuilding at Ground Zero in ways those in charge would not confront for years to come.

The Port Authority was responsible for replacing the blown-apart infrastructure at Ground Zero, and restoring PATH rail service to lower Manhattan from New Jersey, a conduit for some sixty-seven thousand passengers, was the first order of business. The PATH Terminal at the World Trade Center, opened in 1971, was located beneath the office and retail space of the complex in the "bathtub." The 9/11 attack on the twin towers destroyed the terminal and a seven-car PATH train, flooded the two PATH tunnels under the Hudson River, and damaged and rendered inoperable the system's Exchange Place Station in Jersey City. The last train to leave the World Trade Center station had rescued the last people on the platform and departed before the South Tower collapsed. Work on a temporary PATH station at the Trade Center site began in July 2002, after the board of commissioners in mid-December authorized the needed work to restore service as the first phase of its Downtown Restoration Program at an estimated cost of $544 million. During the sixteen months of construction, the press kept the public's attention focused on other activities at Ground Zero. "Wrangling over long-range master planning—commercial space, commuter rail links, the memorial itself,"

David W. Dunlap of the *Times* wrote, "has obscured the reality that the trade center site is being rebuilt now, without town hall meetings, architectural competitions or much public debate." When the no-frills station fitted out with corrugated metal ceiling, exposed beams, and concrete floors opened on November 23, 2003, at a cost of $323 million and another $106 million to restore the PATH tunnels (plus another $137 million for the Exchange Place Station), the same eight cars that had been the last to leave the station returned in the ceremonial first trip back across the mile-long journey from Exchange Place. The temporary station was the "first public portal to ground zero"[5] (figure 6.3). The Port Authority had gone about the most pressing engineering task at Ground Zero and finished the temporary station a month ahead of schedule. It was a real as well as symbolic milestone in the rebuilding effort, crucial for the economic recovery of lower Manhattan. The agency had bigger aspirations: The temporary station was but a stand-in for the grander Transportation Hub the Port Authority intended to build, and that ambition had moved a step closer in July when it selected the celebrated Spanish architect Santiago Calatrava to design a permanent $2 billion PATH station.

Creating an underground servicing system, including what became known as the Vehicle Security Center (VSC), increased the complexity of rebuilding the site

FIGURE 6.3 *Big sign at the newly opened temporary New Jersey commuter train PATH station at the World Trade Center site. Service resumed on November 23, 2003, after the station underwent a $566 million restoration program after being destroyed in the September 11 attack.* STAN HONDA/AFP/GETTY IMAGES

and made construction execution extraordinarily costly in time and money. The LMDC's planning documents for guiding the rebuilding of lower Manhattan made no mention of this integrated approach to rebuilding the site's all-important infrastructure: It was one of those decisions that had been made but not made—a silent power play preempting the formal planning process.

The extent of the agency's early planning activity for the underground revealed its strategic intent to reassert centralized control over the future functioning of the complex, and the development implications of its plans angered Silverstein, who worried about the commercial viability of his office towers. The decision to build an underground superblock went against the conventional practice of building and operating commercial buildings in Manhattan where individual owners controlled servicing. True, large-scale projects like Rockefeller Center developed in the late 1920s under a master plan operated in an integrated fashion with linkages through an underground commercial thoroughfare, but not so the 1980s award-winning development of Battery Park City. The 9/11 terrorist attack on New York changed the conventional development paradigm by inserting security into the planning process as a number-one priority, and centralized servicing spoke to that issue by channeling security screening of delivery trucks, tour buses, and other vehicles into a single point of entry. Security concerns appeared to justify a centralized system, yet the complications of the full-scale underground plan and what this would entail for the complete rebuilding of the sixteen-acre site and the associated costs went unquestioned.

With the rebuilding master plan conceived as an integrated venture sitting atop the underground superblock, no single element of it was separable from the whole; the centralized servicing system intricately linked all the elements together. Although different users would develop and operate the plan's office towers, memorial and memorial museum, performing arts center, and Transportation Hub, for the purposes of planning, design, and construction, the projects were inseparable. From a planning perspective, nothing could be built unless everything was built regardless of whether the buildings actually went up simultaneously because the placement of each structure and its supporting facilities had to be schematically detailed upfront, at the beginning, from the bottom up. The Port Authority could not build out the multilevel underground before configuring the private office towers and retail spaces in some detail since the underground structure had to accommodate the bedrock placement of the columns and elevator cores for Silverstein's buildings. The complex was akin to "a kids' game of pickup sticks"— they were all tied together through the connective hard elements of infrastructure making up the vast underground. "You can't touch one without touching everything else," remarked Christopher O. Ward, who was chief of planning and external affairs and director of port development at the authority at the time.[6]

The underground superblock fit the revenue-hungry agency's concept of re-building the site as a below-grade transportation project. A more urban view of a train-to-station-to-street circulation network was not something it was prone to consider; it wanted the high-traffic retail dollars within its turf. The transportation network it was designing would not work well without all the office buildings built at once. That the heavy upfront cost burden for the integrated underground superblock inevitably promised to generate conflict and controversy (and ultimately delays) over how the costs for building the vast interconnected public and private spaces would be allocated across the site's many users probably did not factor into the decision to re-create the centralized servicing system. But getting to grade, as they say in the development industry, to a ground-level platform on which the office towers, memorial, memorial museum, and cultural buildings could visibly rise, was going to be very costly; the price tag might easily exceed $2 billion, and depending upon what "up to grade" actually involved, the total cost could be much greater.

The upfront cost burden of the underground superblock would become an es-pecially vexing problem when the Lego-like, build-all-at-once scheme hit the inev-itable snags of implementation. Who was going to pay for the infrastructure allo-cated to each of the five speculative commercial towers if they were not built simultaneously? If the below-grade retail area got built first, how would construc-tion of the office towers proceed with that area already in place? These are the types of questions that bedevil negotiations among multiple parties in a large-scale development project and threaten interminable delays in construction until they are resolved. At Ground Zero, they would jeopardize the timetable Governor Pataki was setting for rebuilding in spring of 2003.

The scale and complexity of building the infrastructure in that seventy-foot-deep chasm, as noted earlier known colloquially as the "bathtub," would come to govern the real timetable of rebuilding. There was an added problem: to create development platforms for the permanent PATH terminal and three of the planned office buildings east of Greenwich Street, where most of the retail space would be located, a new bathtub had to be created, but this area had not been ex-cavated to the depth of the West Bathtub of the original World Trade Center com-plex. No clear priority existed for what would come first in the buildout of Ground Zero's sixteen acres; under the notion of a single integrated project, it would all come together at once. "This was a terrible mistake," remarked Avi Schick, a later chairman of the LMDC (April 2007–April 2015) appointed by Governor Eliot L. Spitzer. It "drove public opinion, drove design. It hardened in the public's mind and contributed to the perception of failure when the program could not be built all at once. Perhaps this was optimism—this was Ground Zero."[7]

It was a mistake—treating the site as a single integrated project—as the many problems linked to its execution would later reveal. Unlike the original World Trade Center arrangement, the rebuilt infrastructure at Ground Zero would have to thread through a tangle of complex property interests. "The buildings' foundations and underpinnings are seven levels deep, all knitted together, and in the future, as your walk around the concourse levels, you will constantly be changing jurisdictions, sometimes every few feet: in Port Authority territory here, on MTA turf there, entering privately developed space around the corner," wrote Christopher Bonanos in "The Complex." The new underground was laid out in four underground levels (plate 12), an adjustment from the original layering, but that did not change the new turf issues. Beyond the complications of shifting legal territories and conflicts over cost allocation, the Port Authority's success in imposing an underground superblock served a politically useful, if not especially productive, role. "By assuming rebuilding would all be done at once, there was no need to set priorities," Schick told me. From his perspective, the absence of a "sense of priorities" and the inability to set priorities was a fundamental mistake in the rebuilding process. The plan for a single integrated project was, in effect, "a plan with no losers. There was something for everyone; everyone wins. No tradeoffs."[8] That is, until conflict emerged.

BUYOUTS AND PAYOUTS

The Port Authority and Silverstein and his investor group shared at least one disruptive frustration: a near invisible but potent financial partner, GMAC Commercial Mortgage Corporation, the lender behind Silverstein's acquisition of the World Trade Center complex. With the physical collateral of its $563 million mortgage destroyed by the terrorist attack and its loan subsequently secured only by the insurance proceeds, the Horsham, Pennsylvania–based GM subsidiary quickly took an active role protecting the rights of bondholders it represented.[9] It had, Seymour said, "an expansive view of its rights."[10]

In mid-January 2002, the lender sued the Silverstein group seeking resolution to a dispute over the developer's desired use of insurance proceeds from the attack by having him place the funds in an escrow account controlled by GMAC. In its complaint, GMAC alleged that the Silverstein-related entities were seeking to use the proceeds as an "unfettered account" for expenses, including $700,000 a month for management of the now-destroyed complex, as well as expenses incurred in lobbying Congress in Washington, state officials in Albany, and City Hall in New York, after meeting its obligations to pay rent to the Port Authority and principal and interest to bondholders. For the rest of 2002, as the planning process for rebuilding moved spasmodically through the LMDC's public planning efforts and the Port Authority's independent behind-the-scenes planning exercise, no one really knew with certainty the size, uses, or configuration of what was going to be built at Ground Zero. When Studio Daniel Libeskind's *Memory Foundations* emerged as the chosen concept in February 2003, as discussed in chapter 7, the parameters of that conceptual plan opened up a Pandora's box of complaint and conflict not just from GMAC but from Silverstein, Westfield, and Host Marriott (which owned a hotel on the southwest corner of the Trade Center site, 3 WTC), all of whom saw in the master plan a violation of their property rights.

Two weeks after the Libeskind selection, Westfield made known its dissatisfaction, complete with an implied threat of litigation, in a letter to Seymour. Obtained by the *New York Post*, the March 14 letter stated, "We have reviewed the most recent version of the Libeskind plan and do not believe it is consistent with the Port Authority's obligations to us or, based on our expertise and experience, the type of retail that we believe is most appropriate for the site and its potential." As Westfield's chief executive Peter S. Lowy characterized it in the press, the letter was a last-ditch effort to be heard in the redevelopment process. Libeskind's master plan presented problems for the mall developer. It provided for approximately 800,000 square feet of retail space, half below ground and the other half above ground; this was considerably more than the roughly 430,000 square feet of retail space, all below ground, that had existed and more than the 650,000 square feet its lease with the Port Authority gave the mall developer in expansion rights. The problem was configuration: Westfield did not like the new arrangement with three or four levels of stacked retail—"It eliminates the ability for consumers to just walk by your store. That's a very big issue," said Westfield's vice chairman.[11]

That configuration, however, was what the city and community groups had been advocating from the very beginning of the planning process as a means to enliven the street scene around the site. Consistent with his graduate education in urban planning, Seymour personally believed in the street-level retail concept. Street-facing retail was part and parcel of the plan to reinsert the street grid into the superblock, which Westfield also disfavored because, in its view, that too was not in the best interests of retail profitability. The high-grossing retail spaces underground at the original World Trade Center had generated average annual sales of $900 a square foot at the time of the attack, and Westfield was not confident that the current proposal for retail space would meet that benchmark. "There's not great visibility...and the flow of the retail is more difficult now," Lowy said. The *Times* reported that Lowy "would not accept a design that might inadvertently diminish the value of one of the most lucrative retail franchises in the country."

The company wanted its differences with the landowner quickly resolved or, it said, "We will be forced to take appropriate steps to protect our interests."[12] Ten days later, the company filed a "freedom of information" request for documents from the Port Authority and the LMDC explaining the selection of the Libeskind design. When the PA allegedly refused to turn over that information, in mid-May the company brought into the fray a well-known litigator and former federal prosecutor for the Southern District of New York, Mary Jo White, to initiate legal action against the Port Authority. Westfield said it wanted its expertise recognized as an input into the development of the retail space, but it was increasingly looking like the mall giant wanted to be bought out of its property interest in the site.

Next up to remind the Port Authority about its property rights under its lease for 3 WTC was Host Marriott Corp., owner of World Trade Center Marriott Hotel, virtually destroyed in the attack. The publicly traded company owned 120 upscale and luxury hotels (Marriott, Ritz-Carlton, and the Four Seasons, among other brand names) and had been operating the 820-room hotel at the World Trade Center since 1995, after purchasing what had been the Vista Hotel for $141.5 million from the Port Authority. The sale of the Vista was the start of a politically driven process by the Port Authority to divest itself of assets unrelated to its core transportation mission. At the time, it was the Port Authority's biggest privatization sale, and it came shortly after the agency had completed a $65 million renovation-and-repair program for the "sleek and silvery" twenty-two-story hotel tucked between the twin towers atop the World Trade Center garage that had been heavily damaged in the 1993 terrorist bombing of the complex.[13] When it opened in 1981, the Vista was the first big new hotel built in lower Manhattan since the Astor House opened near City Hall in 1836—that is right, more than 145 years earlier! In a letter reportedly written in a conciliatory tone, Host Marriott said the company expected to rebuild a hotel on the site as large as the one that was destroyed in the 9/11 attack. Given its location on the southwest quadrant of the sixteen-acre site Governor Pataki had unexpectedly declared would be dedicated to the memorial a day before the site was returned to the Port Authority, it was obvious that the former location would not be available for commercial development. Coming on the heels of Westfield's public complaint, though, civic groups worried aloud about years of litigation and delay if these property right complaints had to wend their way through the courts for resolution.

The need to buy out these property interests seemed clear. From a practical and strategic perspective, buyouts would simplify implementing the Libeskind master plan, which the PA and the LMDC had formally committed themselves to do in a memorandum of understanding (MOU) signed May 10, 2002. Buyouts would also eliminate potential litigation over property rights in conflict with the master plan and the positions of those with powerful control rights to block redevelopment—both of which threatened to complicate increasingly tangled efforts to redevelop Ground Zero.

The Port Authority was already in negotiations with the U.S. General Services Administration (GSA) to relinquish its rights to redevelop its former building, 6 WTC (known as the Customs House building), in the location where it stood prior to its destruction on 9/11, and under the Libeskind master plan the building site for Pataki's icon, the 1,776-foot Freedom Tower. In lieu of being able to rebuild in this exact location, the GSA was given the option to occupy any equivalent amount of space in another building within the Trade Center site at the rental rates established in its 6 WTC lease. This noncash transaction, as the Port Authority's board meeting minutes of July 31, 2003, dryly noted, "provides the Port Authority and the WTC net leasees the ability to plan for the demands of the expedited reconstruction schedule that has been called for, without compromising the Port Authority's responsibility to the GSA."[14] In turn, the $345 million in insurance recovery money coming to the Port Authority from the building's destruction could be used as a source of funding for the construction of the Freedom Tower, in association with GSA's occupancy. One tenant taken care of.

Next up was Host Marriott. In October, the Port Authority and the hotelier reached a deal for the hotelier's exit from the Trade Center. Marriott agreed to surrender its obliterated premises and accelerate its remaining $65 million payment owed to the Port Authority for its original purchase, and for $1 million, the agency agreed to grant Marriott a valuable right of first offer (good for twenty years) for any future hotel development opportunity on the site. In December, Marriott received about $370 million in insurance payments, out of which it paid off the $65 million balance owed to the PA.

The control situation was growing turbulent. By rights of its agreements with the Port Authority leasing "substantially all of the Plaza and Concourse levels of the World Trade Center site," Westfield's approval was "required for any changes to the site or for any new redevelopment." As lender to the Silverstein investors, GMAC possessed consent rights, too. Following conventional arrangements for mortgage financing, any modification or amendment to the net lease agreement between the Port Authority and the Silverstein investors required its prior written consent, and consent was required for rebuilding of property put up as collateral that would differ from what existed prior to destruction. Those consent rights gave GMAC power to block plans or at least shape the terms of rebuilding, which made the PA, Westfield, and Silverstein all uncomfortable—exceedingly uncomfortable when shortly after Labor Day the lender filed suit in New York state court. GMAC's complaint alleged that the Silverstein group and the Port Authority had committed to a rebuilding plan without protecting bondholders, "engaging in a course of conduct that threatens to deplete the available insurance proceeds to a point where it impairs the security for the loan."[15] The lender also wanted to be consulted on building plans for Silverstein's towers. Landowner and leaseholder, the lawsuits made clear, were not free agents acting on their May MOU commitment to implement the master plan.

Silverstein had been dealing with the issue of a lender's consent rights since he started drawing up plans to redevelop 7 WTC in early 2002. On 7 WTC, the creditors interfering with his intentions were Blackstone Real Estate Advisors, a fund manager that had acquired the $449 million mortgage on the tower in October 2000, and Bank of America Securities, which financed Blackstone's investment through a private placement of $383 million in securities backed by the commercial mortgage. Together they held more than $475 million of debt on the property. Reinserting Greenwich Street into the street grid meant reducing the new 7 WTC by three hundred thousand square feet, as discussed in chapter 2. Creditors "want to be compensated" for the design changes, said Silverstein's public relations spokesperson, Howard Rubenstein. "Who would compensate them? It won't be the state or the city or the Port Authority or Silverstein."[16]

Reporting on this "friction at Ground Zero," Peter Grant of the *Wall Street Journal* backfilled the story: "But the creditors' frustrations go beyond their concern that design changes have reduced their collateral's value, say people familiar with their thinking. They have wanted to be involved in negotiations involving design, leasing and insurance but feel Mr. Silverstein has simply doled out incomplete progress reports." Blackstone did not even want the building to proceed in the especially weak downtown real estate market, but it could not very well protest the start since the first element of the new structure involved building a replacement for the Con Edison substation that had been destroyed in the 9/11 attack. The foundation work for the substation, financed with insurance proceeds, had already begun without a final agreement among the various parties over the plan to restore Greenwich Street through the site or a resolution of how the costs for the substation would be allocated. The creditors were "not objecting so far to decisions that legally affected their rights," but as construction moved forward and Silverstein's expenses increased dramatically, if the creditors were not satisfied, potential litigation loomed—unless they were bought out.[17]

Within a week of GMAC's lawsuit, Westfield "confirmed reports that it had commenced discussions and signed a non-binding letter of intent" with the Port Authority to sell its interest in the retail net lease for $140 million. The Port Authority was willing to buy out Westfield as long as it gained control of the retail operations and not Silverstein. "It makes no sense to let Silverstein buy out Westfield so he can profit and eliminate, scale back or enlarge the retailing based on his financial interest," said a PA executive. Westfield was selling its interests to the Port Authority, Chairman Frank Lowy said, "to help simplify the overall rebuilding process and expedite the rebuilding of the World Trade Center." It was allowing itself to be bought out, the press release went on to say, in recognition of "the conflict between the public and the needs of our commercial/net lease rights." The sale would "allow the public interest to take precedence."[18] Reading between the lines, Lowy was saying that the forces involved with the site were bigger than any one company, and he believed it was better for Westfield to move aside and bypass involvement. The project was going to take a long time, it was going to be very political, and it was going to go over budget. Westfield did not want to be in the middle of the politicized process. It did, however, want the legal option to come back into the project if in the future the Port Authority offered the retail premises to a third party: Nothing had changed about the company's ambition to control the retail opportunity in one of the country's most valuable locations.

The exit door had opened. At the same board meeting at which Port Authority commissioners discussed the Westfield buyout, the *Times* reported that they "quietly decided to begin discussions to buy out GMAC's mortgage so that the lender would not become an impediment." As long as the Port Authority was protected against a lower-than-expected insurance payout (still under heavy litigation over Silverstein's two-occurrence claim), the PA's vice chairman, Charles Gargano, was in fundamental agreement with a payoff of the GMAC loan. For the past nine months, GMAC had twice denied Silverstein's requests to pay his architects for design services out of the escrowed insurance proceeds. Silverstein and the Port Authority, GMAC said, had repeatedly refused its requests to set aside $563 million (plus interest) to protect bondholders. In its ongoing January 2002 lawsuit—an attempt to force the issue—GMAC proposed freezing all payments to the developer, a move the developer said would have "catastrophic" consequences on the rebuilding. Paying GMAC off is "the best solution here so we don't have people with their own agenda interfering," said Silverstein's lawyer and best friend since high school, Herbert Wachtell, cofounder of the prominent law firm Wachtell, Lipton, Rosen & Katz.[19]

If buyouts offered a way to reduce the number of interfering stakeholders, the cash required and funded out of the insurance proceeds was going to reduce the money available for rebuilding—still an unknown figure pending resolution of the developer's legal battles. Already, approximately $600 million of the $1.9 billion in the escrowed insurance account had been spent on ground rent to the Port Authority, loan payments on the GMAC loan, and losses and other items covered by business interruption insurance. Like Westfield, GMAC was not prepared to become involved in the politics of rebuilding the site: It just wanted repayment of its bondholders' money. At the urging of State Supreme Court justice Herman Cahn during a court conference in late September, the parties reached an interim arrangement: GMAC would release money for one month instead of the usual full quarterly payment while Silverstein came up with a loan-repayment plan that would allow the parties to work out a settlement. GMAC's bondholders were an important silent interest here, as GMAC's lawyer reminded the court: without their consent, Silverstein would not be able to pay off the mortgage early.

By the end of October, as requested by the court, Silverstein told Justice Cahn he had reached a tentative agreement with the Port Authority to buy out GMAC for approximately $570 million[20] and also, Westfield for $140 million. The "sweeping" tentative agreement reported in the press just before Thanksgiving resolved the dispute with something for everyone, including Larry Silverstein and his group of investors, who would get back $98.5 million,[21] or nearly 80 percent of the cash they put in to take control of the World Trade Center complex (the remainder of the cash equity would in time be released from an escrow account as well). At the same time, the investment partnership gained broad control over use of the funds held in the insurance escrow. This was an important strategic win for Silverstein. Control over the insurance escrow provided him with a ready pot of money he could tap to cover attorney fees and other professional expenses necessary to maintain his position as presumptive developer as he continued his litigation fight for double the insurance payout, $7.1 billion. The agreement also kept in place payment of management fees to Silverstein as provided for in "the existing Management and Leasing Agreement dated July 24, 2001" between the Silverstein investors and Silverstein's property management entity, which was consistent with post–September 11, 2001, practice.[22] Releasing the $98.5 million of reserves was something the PA's financial department wanted because the money could then be used for rebuilding. The PA got other things from the deal: carte blanche on the location of the Transportation Hub and the memorial, a limitation on the developer's professional fees, and the channeling of business interruption insurance proceeds back into the project.

The deal formally came together on December 1, 2003, when the Port Authority's director of real estate, Michael B. Francois, and Larry Silverstein signed a thirteen-page agreement for the GMAC payoff that the PA "had spent considerable time [on] and given substantial consideration [to] since October 2002." Even Governor Pataki's ambition was going to benefit, as the deal, an LMDC spokesperson said, "helps us to move forward [on the redevelopment process] to meet the Governor's aggressive timeline." The transaction was connected to settlement of the lawsuits. Of all the important agreements that were to come over the many years of working out the details of rebuilding, "each more detailed and voluminous than its predecessor," this thirteen-page agreement stood out among all the others. Called the "immediate swap" letter agreement, it resolved "what, at the time, seemed like an impossible deadlock," said Wachtell partner Robin Panovka, and "paved a path for rebuilding to proceed." The short agreement with its color-coded diagram exhibit "established the master plan for the site and created the blue print for all the agreements that followed."[23]

By the end of 2003, the buyout and payout transactions were all wrapped up, a holiday package so to speak: GMAC's bondholders had consented to the deal the lender had negotiated; the lender held "no grudge," but "learned a lot of lessons about financing high-profile properties," its chairman said.[24] After paying off its $100 million mortgage, Westfield recorded a gain of a couple of million above the $127 million it paid for its leasehold interest and a valuable right of first offer to come back into the project, for which it paid $1 million to the Port Authority, in parity with the precedent set by Marriott's buyout deal. The Port Authority regained 100 percent control of the valuable retail rights of the complex and Westfield's property damage and business interruption insurance claims related to the destruction of its retail space. Silverstein and his investors walked away with an early financial windfall as a byproduct of the deal.

"By paying off the GMAC loan, we have eliminated GMAC's ability to control rebuilding through its approval rights over the site plan and the individual towers," Silverstein's spokesman Howard Rubenstein told the press. This statement artfully avoided acknowledging the eye-opening beneficial gain to the Silverstein partnership that real estate professionals saw immediately: the optionality—meaning, the value of additional investment benefit—of the developer's new position. Two and a half years after acquiring the World Trade Center leasehold in a landmark transaction as a second-choice winner, Silverstein and his investors now had a big one-way option to go ahead and build ten million square feet of office space at Ground Zero, collecting fees for development and management all along the way—without equity at risk. The transaction left the developer in strategic and legal control with no downside. The Port Authority now had less control over Silverstein, fewer levers with which to align his interests with theirs. With this dysfunctional move, the agency made a big, irreversible mistake, and set in place irreversible perverse incentives. "Only in New York can a developer strike a deal with government to get his money back and still walk away with a prime piece of real estate," remarked Harvey Robins, a candid-speaking top city administrator in the late 1980s and early 1990s.[25] It was the developer's first, but not last, brilliant maneuver at Ground Zero. It was also the first but not the last dubious public deal from a policy perspective. The public landowner and private developer were now more fully in charge of their joint destiny—and all that it would entail in the years ahead—but their interests were not aligned, as the future would so plainly reveal.

NOT SO FAST

The institutional rivalry between the Port Authority and the LMDC was heating up. The LMDC's trusted and respected lawyer, Ira Millstein, had told the LMDC board that its mandate, at least on paper, was total planning control over the Trade Center site. Roland Betts, head of the site planning committee, asked himself how the LMDC could actually exercise this control given the fact that the Port Authority owned the site. When on its own the development corporation put out a request for proposals (RFP) for urban planning and transportation consulting services for the site and surrounding areas in April 2002, he found out: Port Authority officials "went crazy," according to a source for the *New York Observer*; they were livid. "It's our site," PA executive director Seymour told the press; issuing the RFP was "premature." His chairman, Jack G. Sinagra, said: "We can't lose sight of the fact that it's the Port Authority's property and the Port Authority's responsibility for what is eventually recreated on the site.'" LMDC chairman Whitehead responded that "both boards" would approve the plans for the site. "I think [PA chairman Sinagra] would agree that we must agree, too, with the final plan. There's no sign that there's disagreement on that."[26] Quickly, the LMDC pulled the RFP, and shortly afterward the agencies jointly issued a nearly identical RFP with the Port Authority listed as the lead agency on the cover page.

The PA was beginning to aggressively assert its grip on the planning process. The ambiguity of who was in control was now out in the open—unexpectedly during the New York gubernatorial campaign. Until this point, the Port Authority had not been vocally weighing in on the process. With the change in leadership and trauma the organization had experienced, Seymour had let the governor's troubleshooter at the LMDC take the lead. He was keeping the waters calm, so to speak. As Pataki loyalists, Seymour and Tomson presumably were in lockstep, yet a consensus prevailed in some camps that Seymour was deferring to Tomson, who was getting his orders from the governor. Now Seymour was saying, "The roles are for us to work together. It's no secret the governor wants the LMDC out there to manage the public process and get public input, and the Port will be doing the planning."[27] In beginning to aggressively advance the Port Authority's interests in rebuilding, Seymour had taken hold of the political maxim—"Where you stand depends upon where you sit."

Nominally, the uncertainty of who was in charge was formally addressed, if not resolved, with the announcement in May that the two government entities had signed a memorandum of understanding spelling out their respective roles in the rebuilding process, as Seymour had defined them. They would "cooperate and use their best efforts to prepare joint conceptual development plans and preliminary engineering designs" for the Trade Center site. Among principals (though not necessarily all LMDC board members until much later) it may have been informally understood that the LMDC would control the memorial design process and that the Port Authority would release some land for a memorial, allowing cultural facilities as well as commercial buildings on the site, but the document was silent on anything specifically relating to this essential priority of the LMDC mission. With the planning process for a permanent memorial clouded, the *Times* editorial board gave voice to a commonly held fear "that the memorial is going to be tacked on to a building rather than the focal point for the site," and the scant details of the MOU did little to resolve the question about the LMDC's power to make decisions.[28]

The priority given to master planning of the site over design planning for the memorial led the newly appointed chair of the City Planning Commission, Amanda M. Burden (2002–2013), to go public with criticism of the LMDC. If she were in charge, she said, the process of planning for the memorial would be well under way. "The only thing I can do is stress the urgency of this issue," she told the audience of an April forum sponsored by the Women's City Club. "Time cannot be wasted any longer. I don't think they [the family members] have an idea of what the process is yet, and we have to begin to design the process very soon."[29]

Burden's criticism brought to light her conspicuous absence in the planning process at Ground Zero. She was not among the cast of players pictured in a widely reviewed *New Yorker* piece by Paul Goldberger, "How the Future of Ground Zero Is Being Resolved," published in mid-May 2002 (figure 6.4). How much say would the city's regulatory steward have at Ground Zero in a planning arena growing ever more confused when it came to figuring out who was in charge? With the city lacking direct control over the Trade Center site, the planning commissioner's influence was limited. This was not the City Planning Commission of old, of pre-fiscal-crisis days, a time when it wielded power through its authority over the city's capital budget; that power had been taken away in the 1975 City Charter Revisions. Burden's leverage over the site was limited to the city's control of streets and sidewalks (ownership of two streets within the site linked to any proposal to reinsert Greenwich Street into the site) and review commentary on the project's overall master plan as formalized in the governing regulatory document, the *General Project Plan*. Other involvement would come from professional courtesies extended in design reviews, personal powers of influence, and collateral political considerations that might arise, especially when the state's agenda in the city

FIGURE 6.4 *The players at Ground Zero, April 12, 2002: Joseph Seymour, executive director, Port Authority; Peter Kalikow, chairman, Metropolitan Transportation Authority; Marilyn Jordan Taylor and David Childs, architects, Skidmore, Owings & Merrill; John Whitehead, chairman, Lower Manhattan Development Corporation; Monica Iken, founder, September's Mission; Madelyn Wils, chair, Community Board 1; Larry Silverstein, developer; Robert Yaro, president, Regional Plan Association.*
MARTIN SCHOELLER/AUGUST

needed mayoral support. Though they had served together on the City Planning Commission, relations between the two planning agents, Burden and Garvin, were strained at best; Burden had gotten the position Garvin wanted as chair of the commission.

In appointing Burden to chair the City Planning Commission, Mayor Bloomberg chose a top urban planning professional, an established New Yorker known for her meticulous attention to detail and design and careful threading of planning politics. She had been a member of the Planning Commission for more than a decade. She held a graduate degree in urban planning from Columbia University and had managed planning and design for the Battery Park City Authority, where she oversaw the development and implementation of design guidelines for the ninety-two-acre site, as well as the design of all open spaces and parks. When decisions at Ground Zero touched any element of open space or street-facing retail space, she would play a very strong role. Whether reviewing the design and construction of the 9/11 Memorial or overall streetscape design for the Trade Center site, she would do battle to ensure the city's positions were addressed in the development of the site.

The planning process was "completely ad hoc," Betts recalled. Although he believed the lack of specific enabling legislation made the LMDC's ad hoc planning process susceptible to legal challenge, he considered it critically important to move the process forward. To "organize" would have taken a year of precious time, and the LMDC faced heavy pressure to move fast, he told me. "Almost 11 weeks after the attack on downtown New York City, planning for the revival of Lower Manhattan has stalled," the *Times* editorial board complained. "The time for going slow is over." The Gray Lady kept up this pressure for months, arguing that "further delays will only encourage other agencies to start meddling" with the development corporation's business, that the city needs to be assured that plans for redeveloping the site are moving forward with "a sense of urgency," that the LMDC and its planners "begin working with all deliberate speed," that the focus of rebuilding seemed to be slipping and the LMDC "taking its time in devising a master plan."[30] The rush to action was understandable, but was it the wisest course of action?

Called the "most visionary member of the LMDC board" by Goldberger in his account of the early years of planning, *Up from Zero*, Betts was the man in charge of planning at the LMDC.[31] Close to Tomson, he kept the process moving along through the constant glare of high-profile press coverage. A working group met regularly to review many different plans that covered the walls in a big conference room in the Port Authority's reconstituted offices in lower Manhattan. The room was large because all the entities wanted to bring their own architects, lawyers, and staff. At high count, the number of attendees reached seventy. The large size of the meetings, Betts said, made them a circus. Reporters were supposed to be excluded, but sometimes they sneaked in, disguised in the crowd. To manage the process and plug the press leaks, Betts eventually set up a smaller steering committee that included LMDC chairman Whitehead; LMDC president Tomson; PA commissioners Charles Kushner and Anthony J. Sartor; PA executive director Seymour; a deputy secretary to Governor Pataki, Diana Taylor; and Deputy Mayor Doctoroff. Although it may have seemed obvious to this group that it needed to reduce the square footage built on the site, figuring out how to find money to make the Port Authority whole for the rent lost was not so obvious. The Port Authority kept asking where the money would come from and why it should have "to take a haircut." The option of expanding the site beyond the original boundaries of the Trade Center complex was always on the table but in these early meetings, Betts recalled, it was not yet part of the solution.

By New York standards, the sixteen-acre site was very large, equal to all of Rockefeller Center or the entire Grand Central Terminal district (figure 6.5). Still, it was not large enough to accommodate all of the ambitions for Ground Zero. Not much room was available to explore notions of city building that might move against the financial demands of the Port Authority and the rights of the leaseholders. This created the constant refrain in public discourse that planners were loading the site with densely packed commercial towers threatening to crowd out a meaningful memorial space. In time, the principal decision-makers came to realize that the only way out of this dilemma was to expand the site for rebuilding beyond Ground Zero. Adding the fifth office tower site south of the sixteen-acre site was "a no brainer," Seymour said some years later.[32]

The first report that "rebuilding may expand beyond the site" appeared in the *Times* in June 2002, before any visual plans for rebuilding had been presented to the public. Speaking to the New York Building Congress the next month, Tomson pointed out that additional land could be needed because a memorial might take up half the site while new office towers would probably be no taller than sixty stories. With an expanded site, "we can plan to accommodate the needs of the Port Authority, the wishes of the community and the mayor, the memorial, cultural institutions, residences and retail space."[33] Since nearly all the adjacent property was privately owned, by implication, the LMDC would have to exercise its powers of eminent domain if it could not reach a negotiated settlement with the owners on acquiring the parcel. Expanding the site to accommodate the consensus elements of rebuilding obviated a political situation that so far officials had been able to avoid—the need to make choices or set priorities.

For city officials, expanding the site could give them new leverage over the LMDC and PA. Although the Port Authority was exempt from city regulations, the city still

Comparative Scale

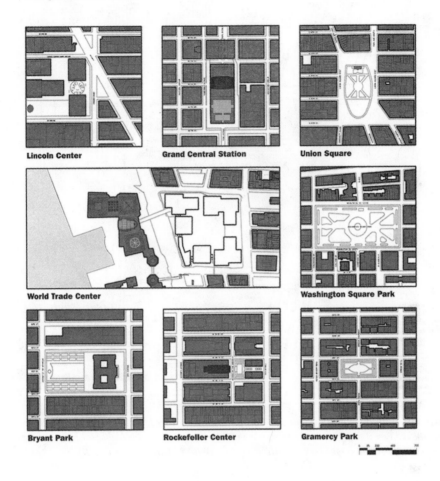

Lincoln Center · Grand Central Station · Union Square

World Trade Center · Washington Square Park

Bryant Park · Rockefeller Center · Gramercy Park

FIGURE 6.5 *The sixteen-acre World Trade Center site in scale relative to seven other major places in Manhattan.* COURTESY NEW YORK NEW VISIONS

controlled the streets and sidewalks surrounding the site, and when planning offi-cials proposed expanding the site to include two city blocks south of the Trade Center site, that control became a strategic lever for city officials. Formally incorporated in the LMDC's revised master plan, this "southern site" brought the severely damaged former Deutsche Bank property at 130 Liberty Street into the project area as the site of a fifth office tower (figure 6.6). The city's efforts to make a big point of this issue reflected its lack of formal influence. "I don't want to overemphasize the need to stake a claim to property rights. That's not what we're trying to do," remarked Doctoroff. "We're merely saying that's one of the issues that needs to be resolved."[34] The other issues outstanding revolved around control over the streets, operation of the public spaces, and provision of services like police patrol and fire protection, and Doctoroff

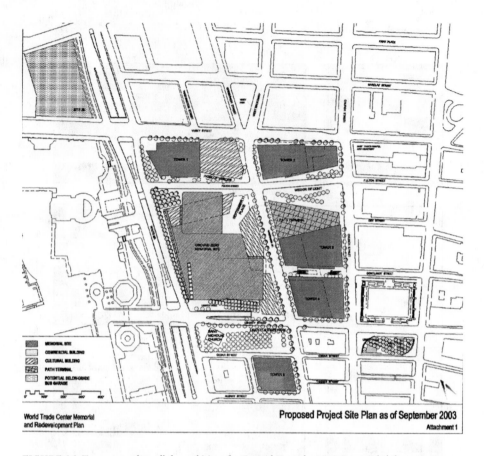

World Trade Center Memorial
and Redevelopment Plan

Proposed Project Site Plan as of September 2003

Attachment 1

FIGURE 6.6 *To accommodate all the ambitions for Ground Zero, the LMDC expanded the project area with the addition of two southern blocks, as seen in the proposed World Trade Center site plan as of September 2003.* COURTESY LOWER MANHATTAN DEVELOPMENT CORPORATION

would press hard on all of these issues as he sought to negotiate a formal agreement with the Port Authority governing redevelopment of the Trade Center site.

Executive Director Seymour's standing as a longtime loyal aide and friend of Governor Pataki notwithstanding, the Port Authority is a bi-state agency. Its decisions require approval of the governors of both New York and New Jersey. Since the governor of New Jersey could veto anything proposed for the site by vetoing the minutes of the board meeting or holding up decisions interminably, ironically, he had more power over rebuilding than the mayor of New York, a fact certain to make any mayor unhappy. In time, Betts brought the PA into an agreement about the amount of commercial square footage at Ground Zero. In time, Seymour recognized that the issue would not go away, that the site was too cluttered, and that the market might not support the planned volume of commercial office space. To get to this point, Betts recalled, Seymour had to go against his whole board—his commissioners who saw the rebuilding as just another real estate deal. A man on a mission and not one to let a hard-won concession slip away, Betts quickly grabbed a scrap of paper when the moment arrived, scrawled an outline of the agreed-upon terms reducing the square footage on the site, and had everyone in the room sign it. He held on to that paper.[35]

Three imperatives now shaped the planning process: memorializing the nearly three thousand persons who died there, rebuilding the site as a long-term public investment to assure New York's competitive global position, and recognizing the leaseholder's development rights and sustaining the lease income flowing to the Port Authority. "The fate of Ground Zero is, inevitably, a noisy political and aesthetic debate," Frank Rich wrote in "The De Facto Capital" in the fall of 2002 when the swirl of planning events and uncertainty continued to roil the atmosphere around lower Manhattan's future, "but whatever acrimony may attend it, it is also a classic American project: a battle between money and values, between commerce and art, between powerful interests and upstart citizenry, between past and future, all staged on an open 16-acre expanse that is urban America's largest frontier."[36] How prescient he was.

An intense struggle for control over site decisions at Ground Zero shadowed the planning process. Determining the configuration of the memorial, the commercial space, and the cultural facilities was equivalent to programming the financial equation for the site. If the LMDC maintained the lion's share of responsibility for planning, it would determine how much revenue the Port Authority could realize from its sixteen-acre land asset. When the LMDC launched the Innovative Design Study in mid-August following the failed first attempt at a master plan, discussed in the next chapter, PA executives were tellingly absent from the announcement. The two agencies, LMDC's Tomson remarked, "have different points of view on how to proceed."[37] Those differences meant the PA would be going its customarily independent way. At the end of September, just days before the LMDC was set to announce the seven new design teams, the PA hired Ehrenkrantz Eckstut & Kuhn (EEK) to do in-house transportation and infrastructure planning and urban design for "the Port Authority's land-use plan for the WTC site." In this second round of planning, the LMDC and the Port Authority—"separately and together"—would be "refining WTC site plan options based on public comment and other input," PA staff reported to the agency's board of commissioners.[38] Everyone was confused: Who was in charge? How were key decisions going to get made?

CHAPTER 7

Who's in Charge?

Pataki Grabs Center Stage As Zero Nero

Governor Casts Himself as Downtown Emperor, Lurching Over Bloomberg at W.T.C. Project; Architect Libeskind Weapon in Power Play

FIGURE 7.1 *April 28, 2003,* The New York Observer

THE EARLY PLANNING PROCESS at Ground Zero coincided with the 2002 gubernatorial race in which Governor Pataki faced two Democratic hopefuls: former secretary of the U.S. Department of Housing and Urban Development Andrew M. Cuomo and New York State comptroller H. Carl McCall. In this context, even seemingly technical site issues about rebuilding became high-profile political decisions. Often reticent on thorny political issues in normal times, Pataki seemed unusually quiet about what should happen at Ground Zero and how fast the planning process should proceed. Throughout 2002, the *Times* editorial board regularly criticized the project's snail-like pace. After Pataki was reelected to his third term in a landslide victory—a victory that made him "only the third Republican to win more than two terms in New York, putting him in a class with Thomas E. Dewey and Nelson A. Rockefeller"—it complained that "the debate over how a revived Lower Manhattan would work has been deadened by the benign neglect provided by election-year politics." Now, it was time for the mayor and the governor "to prove to the people and businesses already in Lower Manhattan or thinking of moving there that things are going to get better fast." Although the *Times* was the most insistent voice calling for more assertive leadership, *Crain's* joined in the chorus, asserting that "unless Pataki displays the leadership he has avoided, little progress would be made." The business weekly wanted the governor "to make it clear that he will make the final decisions, or he should cede control of the World Trade Center site to the city."[1]

Pataki made only one decision about Ground Zero before his reelection to a third term was secure. On June 29, 2002, to an audience of six hundred attending a day-of-remembrance ceremony for the families of the 9/11 victims at the Jacob K. Javits Convention Center, the governor unexpectedly announced, "We will never build where the towers stood. They will always be a lasting memorial for those that we lost. Their sacrifice must be remembered for all times to come, and I will do everything in my power to make sure that happens." By sealing an informal decision among rebuilding officials that the memorial would be placed on the southwest quadrant where the twin towers had stood, Pataki's "footprints statement" preempted the first set of master plans about to be unveiled in two weeks and reviewed by thousands of participants in a public town hall meeting format, "Listening to the City." The unexpected announcement surprised development officials, who discovered the commitment in the morning newspapers the next day, according to the *Times*.[2]

Whether or not his announcement represented a display of "assertive leadership," it was "good politics," the architectural critic Paul Goldberger wrote, somewhat cynically but not without good reason, "since by preempting that decision the governor probably helped convince many family members who had been opposed to construction anywhere on Ground Zero to mute their opposition to other uses on the site. After they knew that the footprints were to be protected, they could begin to accept the idea of commercial buildings on other portions of the site." Once again, a decision while seemingly subject to change had been "made but not made," wrote *Times* reporter Edward Wyatt, who was covering events at Ground Zero.[3] The governor's ultimate power to intervene and assertively insert himself into the planning process at Ground Zero was a harbinger of things to come (figure 7.1).

Months passed. The formal planning process started off poorly. Controversy ensued and then rejection of the first attempt at a master plan resulted in a second attempt to bring forth an inspiring vision for rebuilding. With global interest in events at Ground Zero at a peak and another assertive intervention by Governor Pataki, that process led to the selection of Studio Daniel Libeskind's *Memory*

Foundations master plan in late February 2003. Downtown business interests, however, were growing impatient with the governor's lack of leadership. Worried that political paralysis was jeopardizing downtown's prospects for recovery, the CEOs of three of downtown's biggest commercial tenants, American Express, Merrill Lynch, and the Bank of New York, threw down the gauntlet. In a strongly worded confidential memo dated March 17 addressed to the influential cochairs of the Partnership for New York City, Henry Kravis and Jerry Speyer, and made available to the *Post*, they said it is "difficult to overstate the damage that further silence and delay in decision-making [about redevelopment] will cause." Debris removal around the Trade Center site had made lower Manhattan a very difficult place to work in, and they warned that "if redevelopment tracks the kind of three-decade timetable that eventually produced the New Times Square," corporate departures were likely. They called for "a clear definition of accountability and responsibility" for Ground Zero and the rest of downtown, for clarification of "who is in charge."[4]

The governor got the message. Three weeks later, in a well-publicized speech to downtown business leaders at a luncheon of the Association for a Better New York (ABNY), Pataki laid out an ambitious plan for the revitalization of lower Manhattan with an "aggressive timetable."[5] The governor's response to the wake-up call detailed something for every constituency. For business interests focused on transportation, he suggested initiatives for subways, PATH, and ferry service and a study of how to provide new rail access from Long Island and JFK Airport. For downtown residents, he proposed a new high school, streetscape amenities on Broadway, and community parks throughout lower Manhattan; for the residents of the adjacent Battery Park City, he offered pedestrian bridges and improvements to West Street to link that neighborhood with the rest of lower Manhattan. For Wall Street interests, he suggested security improvements for the New York Stock Exchange. For the citywide civic groups, he said a start would be made on parts of Libeskind's master plan, including the 1,776-foot-tall "Freedom Tower." For the 9/11 families and the world at large, a memorial. Pataki slated sixteen of his initiatives for completion in 2003 and 2004, another six in the pipeline for 2005, another for the year after, and still more by 2009.

This "aggressive timetable" became Pataki's rebuilding agenda. He reiterated its pledges and updated its progress in speeches before ABNY later that fall and in May 2004. With that politically driven timetable he tied his legacy to rebuilding Ground Zero, and Ground Zero became a potent platform for his future political ambitions. Although his political aspirations would turn out to be as unrealistic as the aggressive timetable, they were formative in shaping decisions he would make, decisions that would prove to be costly and irreversible.

A FAILED BEGINNING

The Port Authority and the LMDC had started the formal planning process together in 2002 with a joint request for proposals for urban planning and transportation consulting services. Five weeks later, on April 23, 2002, the agencies selected Beyer Blinder Belle, in association with Parsons Brinckerhoff (and eleven other specialty and engineering firms), to provide consulting services on a $3 million contract. Both New York–based firms had strong credentials for creating an urban design and planning study for the Trade Center site. The well-regarded architecturally conservative BBB firm was known for its contextual approach to design and sensitive preservation of historic structures. It had worked in New York with government clients for more than thirty years on such notable restoration projects as Grand Central Terminal, the Ellis Island National Museum of Immigration, and on master plans for the Queens West Development at Hunters Point and Governors Island, as well as working on the U.S. Capitol. So too, Parsons Brinckerhoff, whose work in the city extended back more than one hundred years and included transportation planning for high-profile public projects such as Access to the Region's Core Project (a commuter rail project to increase passenger service between New Jersey and Manhattan) and Farley Post Office Building Redevelopment (conversion into a grand annex to Manhattan's Pennsylvania Station).

The selection proved to be controversial,[6] yet more to the point the very public debacle that eventually unfolded revealed how the planning intent and process of both agencies was terribly flawed. It was too quick, too narrow a directive, and underneath it all, too driven by politics. It was doomed to stumble, if not fail. If the two government entities got what they asked for, it was not what the public was demanding. A plan for the rebuilding of the Trade Center site called for visionary symbolism. That's what city officials, editorial boards, civic groups, and the public at large were clamoring for: inspirational vision to simultaneously heal the pain, uplift the spirit in memory of the 9/11 tragedy, and make the city of New York proud to a worldwide audience. The aspirations for something great were palpable. But what followed the selection of expert professional consultants "to assist" the two agencies in planning for the task at hand turned out to be bait-and-switch entrapment.[7] BBB became the sacrificial lamb as the agencies figured out how they should carry forth a meaningful planning process.

When issued, the request for proposals called for an "integrated urban design and transportation planning study for Downtown Manhattan and the World Trade Center Site." Contextual analysis—that is, taking into consideration the existing physical and architectural attributes of the area—was the goal: planning for the Trade Center site *within* the broad urban dynamic of lower Manhattan from

Chambers Street south. Comprehensive scope was the directive. Quickly, however, the job turned into something quite different—a programmatic exercise dictated by the Port Authority and unchallenged by the LMDC to arrange nearly 12 million square feet of commercial space on the sixteen-acre site (10 million square feet of office, 600,000 square feet for a hotel, and 600,000 square feet of retail). This was not what the consulting firm proposed to do in its response to the RFP. Almost immediately after its selection, BBB was told that the agencies did not have time for contextual comprehensive planning; the firm would not be working to visualize future possibilities, only a set of givens. The assignment was fraught with risk. If as they considered responding to the RFP any principals of the firm had worried about being involved, worried that they would be blasted by whatever happened because the situation was so emotionally charged, that pragmatic consideration, I am speculating, had obviously been pushed aside in the name of civic contribution, a deeply felt belief that this was their city, and they had to help.

Many times BBB partners told the agencies that there was too much square footage for the site and too much of one function, office space. Lower Manhattan was changing, becoming more residential. The consultants wanted to put additional uses on the site, but the Port Authority refused to endorse new planning work; agency officials and staff wanted a land-use plan that showed ways to accommodate all that had been on the site before. The only new requirement was that space be set aside for a memorial. Time was of the essence. Even before the firm had been selected, the LMDC at its April board meeting had discussed a detailed proposal for a July town meeting, a second "Listening to the City" (figure 7.2), and authorized partial funding of $500,000 for the event. The date for this event was firm, and Roland Betts, as chair of the LMDC site planning committee, was determined to stick to the schedule and deliver six site plans. It wasn't just working under pressure that caught BBB; that was often the way the firm worked for all kinds of clients who wanted work done immediately. It was the public process in combination with the emotion of 9/11 that made the time-driven push near impossible.

For phase 1 of the work, the firm was to deliver six concepts for land use on the site; phase 2 was "to further develop and define these options based on the public input received"; phase 3 would lead to a "preferred land-use and transportation plan." The work never got beyond phase 1. When the BBB plans were publicly unveiled in mid-July at Federal Hall, the historic landmark at Wall and Nassau Streets, built in 1700 as New York's first City Hall, almost everyone was underwhelmed by the plans, which shared "striking similarities." The firm had not been hired for architectural expression, as Frank Lombardi, the Port Authority's chief engineer and point person on this phase of rebuilding, told the press not long after the selection announcement: "There's a misperception out there that we are hiring a consultant to do architecture. We're

FIGURE 7.2 The Civic Alliance

not hiring an architectural firm. We're hiring an urban planner and a transportation consultant familiar with transport system." BBB had been told to render the six ideas in a planning sense, in massing models. "Both agencies explained that these six schemes were 'concept plans' intended to 'illustrate ideas for land use, infrastructure planning and building massing,' not architectural designs for proposed buildings," Alexander Garvin, the LMDC's director of planning, design, and development, wrote for an audience of Yale alumni.[8] That explanation, however, was irrelevant to the public at large and design professionals alike who wanted more than prosaic boxy representations of buildings presented in flat two-dimensional formats (plate 5).

Immediately, LMDC chairman Whitehead distanced himself from the soon-to-be-scorned plans, simply calling them a starting point. He went on record saying that if the LMDC concluded that it was not possible to preserve "those private-sector property rights" of the leaseholders and the Port Authority "and still build this as a beautiful place and a place of which we are proud...then we will change our plans." Mayor Bloomberg took critical aim at the plans, arguing that the balance between commercial space and housing should be rethought: "If you think about what would be the most appropriate ways to build for the future of those left behind," he said, "and to remember the sacrifice that those 2,800 people who died at the World Trade Center site [made] on Sept. 11, what could be better to memorialize them than to have housing and schools and cultural institutions and retail that all goes together to make it a vibrant place? They gave their lives so that we could live. Let's live there."[9] Thus began the period of public comment. Five days later, at the highly publicized meeting of some forty-five hundred people, shown in figure 5.1, the assembly unambiguously and emphatically rejected all six of the BBB plans presented at "Listening to the City II."

The event was organized by the Civic Alliance to Rebuild Downtown New York as a way of voicing its unease about the direction the project was taking. The coalition of eighty-five groups, aligned with private foundations and corporate donors contributing to the $2 million event, sought to develop consensus strategies for redeveloping lower Manhattan. The meeting used a technological format developed by America Speaks, a nonprofit organization specializing in facilitating consensus-building events, to project the alternative plans and gauge face-to-face responses to them. Quite dramatically, this event altered the trajectory of the planning debate, while being hailed by some as setting a new national standard for public participation. In the cavernous exhibition space of the Jacob K. Javits Convention Center, around hundreds of round tables seating ten, participants were asked to answer questions on electronic instant-polling devices. No one attending the meeting on that blistering hot summer Saturday would forget the overwhelmingly negative comments participants offered about the six plans variously described in the press as "dismal," "disappointing," "'uninspiring," "mediocre," "no soul," "lacking vision," and "not broad enough, bold enough, or big enough." Nor would participants forget the orderly but intense group dynamic that unambiguously told public officials that the plans were simply inadequate because they failed to meet the symbolic demands of this historic rebuilding task.

"Schemes not ambitious enough" was the complaint that got the most votes in the instant polling used to gauge responses. Second most troublesome was the excessive amount of office space. It was obvious to everyone in that skeptical and wary crowd that all of the schemes were preoccupied with arranging ten million square feet of office space around sixteen acres. New Yorkers are used to density, but a dense cluster of office towers, however configured on this emotion-filled site, came across as an inappropriate setting for remembering those who tragically perished on September 11. Participants recommended making every effort to cancel the Silverstein lease so that the Port Authority and the leaseholder's requirement for replacing all of the lost commercial space would not govern planning decisions. They called for proposals that were more clearly articulated, if not completely different, than those in the LMDC's *Revised Preliminary Blueprint for the Future of Lower Manhattan*: a suitable memorial as the centerpiece, restoring lower Manhattan's skyline, eliminating West Street as a barrier to the waterfront, restoring the street grid, emphasizing street-level activity, reducing the amount of office space, and providing memorable architecture. This was democratic input from a fully participatory process.

The press savaged the plans in ways no elected official could ignore. In "The Downtown We Don't Want," the *Times* editorial board called them "dreary, laden proposals that fall far short of what New York City—and the world—expect to see rise at ground zero." The editorial put the onus squarely on the mandate for "packing" the site with commercial square footage. It further questioned whether "some of the overcrowded designs may be posturing, with the aim of resolving complicated legal disputes involving" the leaseholders of the complex. And it put officials on notice that they would be held accountable for something visionary: "What these proposals demonstrate most conclusively is that nothing memorable can be done in Lower Manhattan if the Port Authority insists on reclaiming every inch of commercial space that it controlled before Sept. 11." Governor Pataki needed to "take the lead in negotiating with the companies that hold leases to the World Trade Center," it said a couple of days later in "Talk to the Man in Charge."[10]

Editors at the *Daily News* penned a sharper critique of the Port Authority, which they said was "flawed by design." "The LMDC, though filled with talented people, had been handcuffed by its boss, the Port Authority. It had to follow orders....As the design concepts prove, the PA still places its own needs first....It is accountable to no one. And that's the real problem." Over the next ten days, the tabloid followed up with two more editorials, upping its criticism of the Port Authority's "severe limitation on the land use," which made "a visionary plan impossible." The problem was structural: "This insulated agency is simply too self-centered, unimaginative and bureaucratic to handle such a sensitive project"[11] (figure 7.3).

Newsday told its readers "None of the WTC Proposals Is Good Enough." The editors similarly laid the blame squarely on the broad shoulders of the Port Authority and the requirement for putting the leaseholders first. They argued several positions: "forget about legalisms," "slow down," "creativity is key," and "hold Pataki responsible." Among the city's dailies, only the *Post* seemed to think the plans were a "fair first draft." "So far, so good," its editors said.[12] That was remarkable considering the near universal sentiment otherwise.

The fiasco of the "six variations on the same theme"—what architectural critic Ada Louise Huxtable called "six cookie-cutter losers"—can be traced to insider maneuvers as well as mistaken judgments by the officials in charge. Planning for the site had acquired byzantine complexity driven by competing interests and political loyalties. Betts was in charge of the site-planning process, convening weekly meetings to review plans being proposed. Garvin had hired another firm, Peterson-Littenberg, as in-house consultants to the LMDC planning staff. BBB was being paid by the Port Authority under the May MOU agreement with the LMDC. Tomson

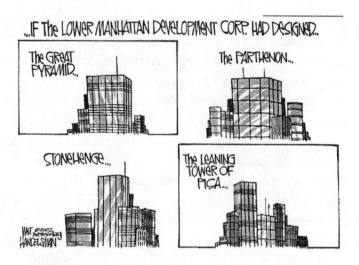

FIGURE 7.3 WALT HANDELSMAN ©2002

favored working with BBB; Betts and his site-committee colleague, minimalist architect Billy Tsien, were less enthusiastic. Caught in the middle of contending forces, Garvin decided that the way to survive was to bring other voices into the discussion, so he got permission from Brookfield executive John Zuccotti to have Cooper-Robertson (working for Brookfield) and Skidmore, Owings & Merrill (working for Silverstein) join in the planning; both firms were already engaged in studying the site. He was playing both ends against the center, and it proved deadly. When LMDC president Tomson was told the status of things, he let Garvin know he had made a mistake: Tomson did not want any plans shown but the BBB plans.[13]

What happened next amounted to design manipulation. By vote at a behind-closed-doors meeting of the joint agency task force to choose the designs that would be presented to the public at the Federal Hall presentation later in the month, officials at the Port Authority and the LMDC selected six schemes: two from among the nine BBB had prepared, the two created by Peterson-Littenberg, and the plans offered by the two private developers. BBB was told to render up all six plans in BBB "format"—in other words, to take authorship. Presumably, by attributing all the schemes to BBB, the two agencies would not have to explain why SOM and Cooper-Robertson were now engaged in the planning process. BBB made such significant changes, including eliminating major elements of each design, that the other architects found it difficult to recognize their work, according to Garvin. Garvin also said that the PA and the LMDC labeled the different schemes with names the authors never used and to which they would have objected, and that was why the architects' names (Peterson-Littenberg, Cooper-Robertson, SOM) were never printed or associated with those four of the six plans.[14]

All of this happened after the vote of the task force had been reversed (a switch reportedly agreed upon by Seymour and Tomson) and two of the rejected BBB plans substituted into the set of six. A member of the BBB team believed there was confusion about what actually had been voted on in the task-force meeting, "about whether they had literally meant the versions drawn up by the other developers or the BBB interpretations of them," the *Post* reported.[15] At a meeting for the governor to review the six plans (to which Garvin was not invited and at which the mayor was not present because he believed it was at a different time), Pataki asked if the plans had been approved by Betts's group; yes, he was told. When he heard about this, Garvin realized he was in trouble. Did the governor's people realize these six plans were problematic? That three of the six violated the tower footprints, "hallowed ground" the governor said just days before would never be built upon?

After the unequivocal rejection of the agencies' ideas for Ground Zero unveiled at the Javits Center big public meeting, the LMDC and the Port Authority contin-ued to publicly uphold the rhetoric of working collaboratively, but they were not in sync as each set out on an independent course to prepare a master plan for the site. And behind the scenes, with the fall gubernatorial election nearing, the Pataki administration was keeping a firm hand on the development process.

Garvin's handling of this first planning process would become his undoing at the LMDC after Paul Goldberger wrote of the BBB episode in "Designing Downtown" in the *New Yorker* in early January 2003. Garvin's position among Pataki's loyalists at the LMDC was somewhat suspect from the start because he was seen as an agent of the mayor, someone close to Doctoroff, with whom he had worked on New York City's bid for the 2012 Olympics. Shortly after Goldberger's article, the *Daily News* came out with an attack editorial, "No Room for Ego at Ground Zero." It savaged Garvin's decision-making and discredited his reputation as a top planner. Tomson fed the *Daily News* the information that led to that deadly editorial. "I dropped a dime on him," Tomson told others, as the story was related to me. (A few days later, Tomson formally announced he would step down as executive director of the LMDC, a decision the press had reported earlier in November.) For a few months afterward, Garvin continued to work on procedures for the next round of site planning and the memorial design process until April 15, 2003, when he announced his resignation. This is getting a bit ahead of the planning story, however.

STRIVING FOR LEGITIMACY

After being publicly humbled by an embarrassing opening act, the LMDC needed a second-act success. The development corporation was being called to task for not articulating clear priorities and for failing to manage a consensus-building process. News stories reported that "no one's home over there" and that the memorial design process was moving too slowly while the overall site planning was moving too quickly for so momentous a decision. Other reports charged that LMDC officials were meeting with private interests behind closed doors while keeping their own board in the dark over the planning process and the selection of a design firm. An insider put it this way: "Everyone thinks they are missing something going on in another room, even the governor."

The decision to make a master plan for the entire site before designing the memorial struck many citizens and professionals alike as proceeding in reverse gear. Shouldn't the memorial design come first and constrain the master plan? The master plan determined the territory reserved for a memorial, whereas the priority might logically have been how best to integrate an appropriate memorial design into the redevelopment of the site and the fabric of lower Manhattan. In short, the LMDC appeared opportunistic, uncoordinated, and confused. Even its president acknowledged in a breakfast speech at New York University Law School in January 2003 that "we've screwed up lots of times along the way." One of the biggest mistakes, Tomson said, was releasing the first set of rebuilding plans: "We did not convey to the public what we were trying to do with the plans we released in July." The mistake, said Betts, was in presenting plans as massing models, simple layouts that did not define what the buildings would look like when the public "thinks you've designed a building."[16]

To recover momentum, Betts decided to throw out the BBB plans and start all over. He now wanted to involve the world's best architects in the process.[17] Working in concert with Tsien, a well-known and respected minimalist architect, the two "soon emerged as the prime movers in an effort to shift the direction of the process," and with support of the site-planning committee, they encouraged the rest of the LMDC board to listen to Garvin, who would manage the new process.[18] They had "decided to play the architecture card," Paul Goldberger explained in his well-informed account of the inside maneuvering noted above, "to make the LMDC, at least for a few months at the end of 2002, into the most conspicuous architectural patron in the world. It was a shrewd decision, because it moved the planning process to an area that the Port Authority had traditionally shown little interest in."[19]

To sell this course of action to the Port Authority and the city, Tomson, who had a good relationship with Seymour, would work the Port Authority, while Betts, who had a long and close relationship with Doctoroff, would work the city. The eyes of the world were watching what they were doing, they would say. They would also mention that the website for the first set of rebuilding schemes (Planning 1.0) had received fifty million hits, that such a big project demanded world-class talent, and that they had to do it right this time around. Before they could launch their campaign, however, someone leaked their plans to the *Times*. As Betts recalled later, the task then became "very difficult."[20] Within the month the LMDC had launched a worldwide "Innovative Design Study" (Planning 2.0) with a request for qualifications to select as many as five architecture and planning firms to offer new ideas for the site. The LMDC emphasized the word "innovative" to signal how different this process (and presumably the product) would be.

The LMDC was not in a good position to manage its Innovative Design Study. It had planning expertise, but no design capability. To fill this gap, development corporation officials met regularly with New York New Visions members to provide a "kitchen cabinet of sorts" for Garvin, who asked them for advice on how to run a competition, input on the criteria to include in the Innovative Design Study request for qualifications, and a list of architects and planners to review the responses. Garvin initially asked NYNV to run the competition, but the group said no. Marcie Kesner, an experienced city planner who had worked in the Queens Borough president's office and cochaired the NYNV's executive committee, firmly believed that the LMDC should run the process. Like other "on-call advisers," she was concerned that the LMDC might just want them to provide political cover. The extent to which Garvin relied on the group was "flattering," she said, but always caused NYNV committee members to ask, "What is our role?"[21]

The group kept up a near vigil on the LMDC's actions. It regularly voiced distress about the corporation's lack of coordination, kept a sharp eye on procedural details, and pushed for openness and full participation in the planning exercise. It was constantly concerned about the integrity of the planning process and put forth a formal design critique at each stage on the way to a final master plan. NYNV saw itself as protecting the "immutable" planning principles put forth in its *Principles for Rebuilding Lower Manhattan*. The group believed its role was to keep the pressure on the LMDC; retiring from the field would send the wrong message to decision-makers. Ironically, NYNV was playing the role of the City Planning Department; just why this was so remained the unspoken open question among planning professionals. Neither Amanda Burden nor her department had been brought into the early planning process, and Doctoroff, whose relations with Burden were reportedly strained, took the heat for the planning department's exclusion. NYNV's advice, in short, offered the LMDC a needed source of legitimacy.

As the LMDC redrafted its message to the public and the design participants, two telling revisions appeared. The first revision seemed to suggest some softening of the Port Authority's position on the amount of commercial space that would have to be accommodated on the site. A few weeks after six teams (not five, as the LMDC site committee first intended) were chosen from a field of 407 submissions (with Garvin inserting the consultants he hired, Peterson-Littenberg, as a seventh team), the LMDC announced a downward revision of the office space component from 10 million square feet to 6.5 million. (This was the signed scrap-paper agreement Betts had secured from the four principal entities noted in chapter 6.) The Port Authority had not changed its position—"You can't assume the Port Authority is going to give up its real estate interests," a source for the agency was quoted as saying—but rather suggested that some of the space would be accommodated outside the sixteen-acre site. Since at this time the city and the Port Authority were still at loggerheads about where this might occur, "it was left purposely amorphous." The new revision also allowed for as much as two million additional square feet each of hotel and retail space. These revisions reflected the fluidity of the ongoing negotiations between the city and the Port Authority over a "raft of issues."[22]

Second, despite what the request for qualifications stated in boldface—"This is NOT a design competition and will not result in the selection of a final plan"—the Innovative Design Study would produce one winner. "Once the designs began to emerge," Goldberger wrote, Garvin "decided to give up on his notion of treating the architects' work like a smorgasbord, picking and choosing what was best." As Betts told the press, "It will be one central idea. Whatever plan survives is going to be subject to modifications, but it's far less likely that two plans would be combined. It's like combining two different artists whose style is completely different."[23] Given the prestige of the architects involved and the worldwide attention the competition attracted, could it have been otherwise, especially once the designs were unveiled to the public, whose comments were widely solicited? The process and the expectations it created could not be totally controlled; nothing remotely like that had been done before. Maybe it was naïve to have thought a coherent vision could be composed by the pick-and-choose-what-is-best approach, but from their perspective as owners of the site responsible for rebuilding the entire underground infrastructure, Port Authority officials held to the idea of a composite plan. Given their financial interests, they were not immediately endorsing the LMDC's evolution to a one-winner position.

Port Authority officials were not the only ones pushing back on the LMDC's ideas of how a site design would come into being. A few days before state and city officials were to meet and narrow the field of finalists to two, possibly three, architectural teams, Larry Silverstein went on record to assert his legal rights to the rebuilding of the Trade Center. In a nine-page letter sent to Whitehead, a letter *Wall Street Journal* reporters termed "uncharacteristically stern in tone for the normally discreet New York developer [and which] could signal a legal fight if Mr. Silverstein is bypassed in the process," the developer charged that rebuilding officials were ignoring his right to rebuild as he saw fit. The leases "expressly contemplate that in the event the complex was destroyed and it was not feasible, prudent or commercially reasonable to rebuild in accordance with the plans and specifications as they existed," his investor group has the "right to build substitute buildings," subject to the Port Authority's consent to the alternative rebuilding plan (and "consistent with the obligation of good faith implicit in every contract, that…the Port Authority cannot unreasonably withhold its consent"). He added that his group has "the right to select the architect responsible for preparing re-building plans."[24] Until this point, Silverstein had not said much on the issue of design, but consistently spoke of his determination to rebuild all ten million square feet of office space in buildings no greater than sixty to seventy stories in height.

With the choice of a master plan imminent, the developer went on the offen-sive. "None of the plans as currently configured presents a viable and safe vision for the redevelopment of the World Trade Center site," he wrote in the letter, copies of which were sent to the governors of New York and New Jersey, Mayor Bloomberg, officials of the Port Authority, and others. Pointedly, he reminded them that he controlled the insurance reimbursement funds from the destruction of the World Trade Center, "the only private source of funds for redevelopment." Since his in-vestor group had continued to make its rental payments "on the premise that our contract rights will be honored," he expected that the Port Authority and other governmental bodies "will not seek to interfere with or undercut our rights or con-strain us in our effort to build safe and desirable buildings." Neither the city nor the Port Authority publicly responded with much concern. "Mr. Silverstein's voice is important in the building process," the mayor's spokesman said, but "not the only voice." A Port Authority spokesman said the same, adding that the agency "will certainly take his views into account."[25] They would respect his opinions, but material disagreements between the parties existed on a number of significant points and were bound to expand as the public sector's rebuilding plans became more precise.

The Innovative Design Study Competition ran from August 2002 to February 2003, and culminated in the selection of Studio Daniel Libeskind's master plan *Memory Foundations*, discussed in this and later chapters. The six-month process attracted an unprecedented level of worldwide popular attention and generated extensive debate among design professionals and intense lobbying on all sides. As with Planning 1.0, the process for Planning 2.0 was fraught with controversy and reflected ongoing institutional rivalry between the Port Authority and the LMDC. Most notably, it left the conflicts inherent in the rebuilding process unresolved. This second attempt at site planning implicitly challenged the designers to resolve competing claims—in effect, to accomplish the political task that politicians were reluctant to do. The nine design schemes[26] unveiled in December produced praise for the LMDC (if not for the actual designs), crediting it with calling for a big vision and a standard of world-class design. Yet the bold ideas and visual clues of a new future at Ground Zero could not paper over the continuing confusion among civic groups, design professionals, and the public about how the critical decisions would be made. Nor did they mute the persistent call for less commercial space and criticism that wedging ten million square feet onto the site still amounted to an exercise in balance-sheet-based planning.

DOING ITS OWN THING

At first the Port Authority said its urban design consultant, Stanton Eckstut, the EEK principal in charge, would present his final concepts to officials along with the ideas from the LMDC teams in November. But little more than a month later, the PA said its master plan—the foundation for what would rise at the site— would not be ready to be shown to the public until February. "I hope it doesn't reflect a subversive planning effort," a New York official told the *Daily News.*[27]

The Port Authority was at work trying to rebuild the site's infrastructure. Its institutional authority over this realm was unchallenged. Indeed, the May 2002 memorandum of understanding with the LMDC gave the PA full responsibility for everything but managing the memorial design process and organizing public input, which, in turn, were the unchallenged mandates of the LMDC. Few observers, however, could be convinced that the efforts of the two agencies would converge in joint decision-making at some fuzzy point in the future, and signs of what was happening behind closed doors did nothing to diminish their skepticism.

To the Port Authority's way of thinking, the LMDC would supply the "vision" thing, the best elements of the LMDC's competition designs inserted into the PA site plan like a Lego toy. In other words, the LMDC's role in the decision-making for the master plan would keep it limited to "pretty building designs," as Eckstut reportedly said, adding that he alone was developing substantive plans for the site's streets, transportation facilities, and underground infrastructure. This infuriated Garvin, who had broader ambitions in mind when the LMDC commissioned the seven high-profile design teams. Skeptics and veterans of the city's development battles could not help wondering aloud whether the LMDC's Innovative Design Study was really just a sideshow while the PA made the final decisions. "It's a beauty contest and a distraction," said Robert D. Yaro, leader of the Civic Alliance. "Fundamentally it's a sideshow because none of these things will be built," said one LMDC director. The nine conceptual visions produced by the competition did, though, "show a variety of ways the site could have commercial development and a memorial without looking like a mess." Shortly after this second round of design visions was presented, the *Daily News* let go with force: "What a healthy, open process. And what a monumental waste of time," the editors complained. "One suspects the PA will dismiss the LMDC plans outright and selfishly plow ahead with what it wants. If that is not the intention, why does Eckstut's work continue in secret?" they asked.[28] Despite prevailing skepticism, the LMDC had gone too far down the road for the design competition to be a mere exercise. A master plan was going to result.

When Betts invited the Port Authority to exhibit its master plan alongside those commissioned by the LMDC, the answer was no. "It's a work in progress and doesn't lend itself to that kind of presentation," he was told.[29] When it came to its transportation agenda, however, the PA did not seem to have any problem revealing its work in progress. At the annual "Build Boston" architectural conference just a month before the LMDC's seven teams of architects were scheduled to show their nine conceptual master plans for the site, the PA's chief architect, Robert I. Davidson, showed preliminary designs for a permanent Transportation Hub with a soaring glass atrium. The PA released a second well-timed visual of its new transportation center stretching the block from Church to Greenwich Streets (figure 7.4) just days prior to the press conference announcing the LMDC's final selection of a master-plan design. The Port Authority had not selected an architect for the $2 billion downtown terminal it envisioned on the scale of Grand Central

FIGURE 7.4 *The Port Authority's initial concept for a retail-focused Transportation Hub, February 2003.* THE PORT AUTHORITY OF NEW YORK AND NEW JERSEY

Terminal, but it had laid out the underground engineering requirements for commuter and subway connections.

The work-in-progress excuse was disingenuous. Behind closed doors, the Port Authority was planning in a manner befitting its reputation of independence and bureaucratic opacity. Eckstut had been charged with working out detailed plans for the infrastructure below-grade. The PA was desperate to keep going with that work. In calling on Eckstut, PA officials did not put out an RFP, but hired a firm they had worked with in the past. EEK had competed against BBB for the LMDC work, narrowly missing out in nearly tied ratings. They were experts in large-scale innovative urban plans. Eckstut had designed the well-regarded master plan for Battery Park City with Alex Cooper in his former firm. To reconstruct the underground, the PA needed to understand what was going to be built above on the site, and Eckstut was asked to develop a transportation and infrastructure master plan that would allow the PA to connect what it was doing below with what would happen above.

His agenda was to connect the two levels and make them seamless. The work was driven by the idea of creating a new urban district, a strong pedestrian public realm that related to the streets surrounding the site. A sequence of public spaces would connect transit on and adjacent to the site, the Winter Garden at Battery Park City, and a potential new commuter rail connection by way of concourses and arcades lined with retail shops. He developed a full-scale model of the site, above and below ground, which the Port Authority insisted would yield far more specific and detailed engineering plans than those of the LMDC teams, even though those teams were also working with extensive models of the underground as a necessary tool to plan the retail shops, bus depots to accommodate the crowds expected to visit the memorial, and transportation terminal the Port Authority demanded.[30]

Those who saw Eckstut's plans reported that they resembled the rejected Beyer Blinder Bell schemes. The BBB massing plans were different, but in the arrangement of office space, not that different. Similarities existed because certain logic dictated how the office buildings could line up. Reestablishing Fulton and Greenwich Streets through the site carved the sixteen acres into quadrants (map 7.1). The reserved footprints' space defined a southwest memorial quadrant. Open space was best on the south side where sun prevailed. Given existing PATH train tracks, the transportation terminal could only go in a limited number of places, and the PA had placed it just east of Greenwich Street. Retail would go underground and adjacent to Church Street, away from the memorial and closest to where the vast majority of people would exit the transportation station at the eastern end of the site.

These relationships amounted to set pieces. Their similarity to the BBB plan "Memorial Plaza" again provoked some amount of nagging criticism when the

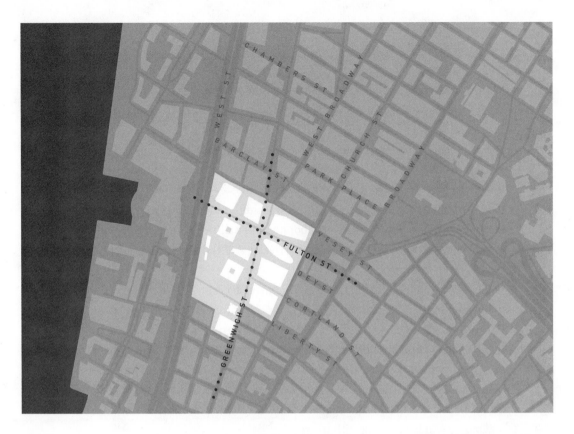

Map 7.1 Reinserting former streets into the World Trade Center superblock. The reserved footprints' space defined a southwest memorial quadrant. CARTOGRAPHY: C&G PARTNERS FOR THE AUTHOR

revised *Memory Foundations* master plan was made public in the fall of 2003, the implication being that the overwhelming consensus of those at the "Listening to the City" event had not been listened to. Yet months before that big meeting, "rebuilding officials knew that almost all the decisions about the site would be driven by the memorial...leaving few options for its basic design," wrote the *Times* beat reporter on rebuilding, Edward Wyatt. Though Libeskind and Garvin rejected the similarity as "coincidental at best," the set pieces, validated by the Port Authority's prerogatives to rebuild the maximum office space, produced the similarity. "When we roll it out," PA executive director Seymour said, "the land-use plan is going to be almost exactly what Beyer Blinder Bell proposed."[31]

Reports that intense interagency sparring was slowing the pace of the rebuilding efforts led Tomson and Seymour to acknowledge previous disagreements and clarify the messy and confused decision-making process for a second time. In a memo agreement dated December 5, 2002, little more than one page in length, the two officials signed on to "memorialize...a process that will lead to a single master plan for the World Trade Center site by February 2003"; the plan would identify transportation and infrastructure, land and parcel distribution, and land-use controls on the site. During the weeks in which design proposals from the seven design teams retained by the LMDC were on view in the Winter Garden at Battery Park City for public comment, Garvin and Eckstut were supposed to meet at least weekly to review the design work against a list of seven criteria. The intent was for the two urban designers, "in consultation with Silverstein Properties and Westfield America," to recommend a "single" master plan (reflecting implementation in phases) to the joint PA-LMDC working group by January 31, 2003.[32] To do so, they would have to work collaboratively—a difficult undertaking considering their well-known and long-standing rivalry and the problems of institutional rivalry. It never happened.

The Port Authority was making key technical decisions about the underground that would forever foreclose possibilities for changing what happened on the surface of the site. A $544 million program to design and construct a temporary PATH station at the Trade Center site was underway. "The LMDC is not ahead of the agenda," remarked one design insider. The *Daily News* was less kind in its assessment: "The LMDC has the good ideas and no power," it editorialized at the end of December. "The PA has rotten ideas and all the power. And poor, wounded downtown will have to live with the results."[33]

For the bi-state agency, restoration of its revenue stream trumped the interests of any other stakeholder. In one plan, it placed five structures within the foundation walls of the bathtub that encroached upon the footprints of the twin towers, considered "hallowed ground" by family members and placed off limits to development by Governor Pataki. An earlier design scheme had an underground transit concourse cutting through the North Tower footprint, but PA officials quickly backed off of that scheme and promised to move the concourse northward toward Vesey Street allowing it to skirt that footprint. It was a bit figurative to say that the footprints should be kept inviolate *down to bedrock*, because PATH trains had always run through this area, and Seymour said that the PATH trains were still likely to run along tracks that cross beneath the footprint of the South Tower. The families of the victims were nonetheless incensed at how insensitive the Port Authority was to their concerns.

Had they seen the never-released eighty-page final master plan, their ire would have been unfathomable because the PA had placed a "Grand Hall" for the new intermodal transportation and retail center that officials saw as an essential hub for lower Manhattan directly over the complete footprint of the North Tower. Pedestrians would have been diverted around the footprint by a circular colonnade that was part of an interior pedestrian street and public-space system providing access to the retail center and other on-site uses, including a memorial. From the circular central space, entrances and exits radiated outward connecting every street and open space within the site. It was about as far from a contemplative space as one could imagine—even in flat two-dimensional rendering it comes off as an intensely active central space uniting various pedestrian thoroughfares. The PA's plan portioned off a 6.5-acre memorial district in the southwest quadrant of the site and promised to "respect the footprints"—only as an *above-ground* constraint. Below the surface outline of the footprints at the lowest level, tour buses would be stacked up in two levels of parking along with service-area space and truck parking encroaching on the South Tower footprint below grade. No wonder the plan never saw the public light of day.[34]

The agency also evoked the intense ire of Silverstein, who persistently sought a free hand to do what he deemed necessary to meet his commercial interests. One underground plan for the southeast quadrant of the site detailed a pedestrian through-pass at multiple levels calculated to enhance the revenue-generating potential of an underground four-story interior mall, which the agency's retail lease-holder, Westfield America (not yet having been bought out of the site), was insisting upon. Intent on maximizing the marketability of his office space, Silverstein refused to consider this arrangement because it would dramatically alter the design of his office towers by pushing the entrance lobbies upward, to the third floor. He wanted elegant and spacious lobbies for his intended financial-services clientele, which he insisted could only be presented on the ground floor. An earlier Eckstut design put a truck access ramp and loading dock on Greenwich Street, which prevented the roadway from being fully restored through the former site of 7 World Trade Center. This so enraged the developer that he showed the PA's architects the door, telling them to pack up and leave his office. Silverstein had already given up three hundred thousand square feet of commercial space to permit reinstatement of the street grid, and he was not about to see the street cut off again.

The Port Authority quickly wrapped up its master planning work with Eckstut after the selection of the Libeskind master plan in February 2003, discussed in the next chapter. It next moved to advance its competitive position at Ground Zero by entering the architectural-vision game and seeking a world-famous architect to design an iconic Transportation Hub. The Hub would, in essence, become the Port Authority's individual identifiable 9/11 memorial to its lost employees. In late July 2003, after a quiet behind-the-scenes selection process, PA officials announced that they had selected Santiago Calatrava, a world-renowned Spanish architect and engineering poet of soaring stations and bridges, to design the permanent Transportation Hub. Widely praised, the selection reframed the Port Authority's reputation for being indifferent to aesthetics. This strategic choice simultaneously signaled the agency's unyielding position in the decision-making process and its intent to crown Ground Zero with its own icon, one that aimed to resuscitate its institutional prestige. It was not going to play second fiddle to the LMDC's architectural vision; as one insider put in, the PA was forced to "Calatrava" after the Libeskind decision.

THE GOVERNOR'S POWER

The selection of the Libeskind master plan generated worldwide attention (figure 7.5). The central site planning issues—whether to build four or five office towers, how to integrate the cultural facilities into the plan, how much of the historic street grid to reinstate, where to place underground security screening and bus parking facilities, and how much to expose of the slurry wall—still needed to be resolved. Teams of designers, planners, engineers, and associated professionals at the Port Authority and the LMDC debated these issues for weeks on end. Silverstein's architects and planners at SOM also put plans on the table; at one

FIGURE 7.5 *Architect Daniel Libeskind points out details of his master plan,* Memory Foundations, *to Mayor Michael Bloomberg and Governor George Pataki amid a crush of media at the press conference at the World Financial Center's Winter Garden, February 27, 2003.* NEW YORK DAILY NEWS ARCHIVE/ GETTY IMAGES

point, his team proposed three towers on the southeast quadrant and located the entrance to one tower in the middle of Libeskind's high-profile symbolic space, the "Wedge of Light." In this large open space, Libeskind said, "Each year on September 11th between the hours of 8:46 a.m., when the first airplane hit and 10:28 a.m., when the second tower collapsed, the sun will shine without shadow, in perpetual tribute to altruism and courage." This was one of two symbolically labeled public spaces in the plan, the other being the Park of Heroes. "Everyone was operating as if no master-plan scheme existed," recalled my husband, Gary Hack, urban designer on the Libeskind design team.[35] Eventually, even Silverstein concluded that the site could not hold ten million square feet and backed off.

The fact that no major stakeholder appeared to accept even a broadly conceptual master plan reflected an underlying reality: None were ready to relinquish the objectives of their ambition. Over time and over cycles of development, New York actors have been able to revive proposals through steady persistence. The possibility that the LMDC might not succeed in taking the accepted plan through the technical blocking and tackling of environmental impact review and other procedural hurdles kept other ideas alive. The possibility that the chosen plan might not succeed kept each stakeholder enmeshed in parallel planning, opportunism, false steps, and public retreats, all of which led to delays and confusion among players and the public at large. In other words, selection of a master plan did not ordain an easy or linear path forward. On the contrary, more conflict and political disarray was likely.

Betts's steering committee of eight principals representing the LMDC, the Port Authority, the city, and the state[36] met regularly to resolve the broad policy issues of site planning. Unless invited in for specific input, staff members were not included, although resolving all the technical details and problems of a site plan is typically a staff function. With the site's complex underground infrastructure and demands for high security unlike those in a conventional real estate project, the technical site-planning problems that had to be resolved were unusually complicated. Contentious issues bounced back and forth for weeks, even months, between these two government entities before a higher authority made a decision. The pattern of confused decision-making, with policymakers at times in disarray, prevailed because the governor typically demonstrated leadership only in response to some pressing political constituency—the families of the 9/11 victims or business constituencies in lower Manhattan—or in preparation for a ribbon-cutting event. He was letting the principal stakeholders work through the issues on their own, however noisy and conflicted this might get; that was his preferred style. "Pataki is not a micro manager," Seymour told me. "He lets his chief of staff work things out, and then he comes in and makes a decision."[37] His loyal aides heading both the Port Authority and the LMDC were watching out for his political inter-ests. He weighed in directly only when absolutely necessary to break deadlocks on critical planning decisions, when the public reaction promised to be favorable, or when symbolic gestures would afford him good publicity. His behavior, in other words, was consistent with the rational calculus of American politicians.

The power of the governor was never more apparent than when he made the decision to award the master plan to Studio Daniel Libeskind's *Memory Foundations* (plate 6) against the recommendation of the LMDC's site-planning committee, which had voted unanimously in favor of the other semifinalist, Rafael Viñoly's THINK team and its twin latticework scheme *Towers of Culture* (figure 7.6). The morning before the governor and the mayor were to be briefed on the two finalist plans, the *Times* ran an exclusive story on the basis of an insider leak from someone on the site committee. After a four-hour review of the architects' revi-sions to their master plans for the Trade Center site, the committee was going to recommend that the site be rebuilt on the basis of the THINK team's *Two Tall Towers*. In bold print, in standoff space in the middle of a column, the article re-ported that "rebuilding officials challenge the politicians who appointed them." Earlier, both the governor and the mayor had expressed support for the Libeskind plan. The article quoted one LMDC director as saying, "It's going to be a close one;

FIGURE 7.6 *THINK team* Towers of Culture *semifinalist concept entry in the Innovative Design Study competition, December 2003.* COURTESY RAFAEL VIÑOLY ARCHITECTS

it could simply come down to how the governor and the mayor feel." One committee member speaking on condition of anonymity said that the committee expected the governor and mayor to follow its recommendation: "We don't expect anyone to overrule us."[38] If this was a bold tactic by those who wanted the THINK team to win, it backfired; if it was a bold tactic by those who favored the Libeskind plan, it may have enhanced the outcome. Whichever the case, Betts, who was the strongest advocate for the THINK scheme and saw himself as the steward of the design process, was left standing alone, out on a limb, exposed to the governor's anger.

Betts and Garvin and other officials involved in the planning process had spent the previous three weeks in meetings with both architectural teams. They had given both teams a short time frame in which to refine the physical plans and engineering details so that their visions could be rendered feasible, as Goldberger described in detail in *Up from Zero*. Betts wanted to keep the design process moving forward. He had the THINK team focus hard on the tremendously challenging details of making the towers lighter and less expensive. (They would be built in eighty-foot modules off-site, then assembled like an erector set on-site; that way, Betts explained, no scaffolding would be needed.) He talked to corporate tenants, many of which saw Libeskind's design with the bathtub area exposed as a sunken plaza as more like a graveyard than a memorial, and they wanted something more uplifting. As these meetings progressed, Betts became more involved with the THINK team plan and less with Libeskind's plan. He constantly updated Doctoroff, who turned from skeptic to strong supporter of the twin latticework towers. In retrospect, Betts said, "I made a mistake by not involving many people in the process; if so, they too would have gotten excited" about the Viñoly vision.[39]

Up to this point, the governor and the mayor, who was more concerned with renewal of the larger canvas of lower Manhattan than specific issues at Ground Zero, had not been involved with the design process. When the nine designs[40] were on display in mid-December, Pataki had walked around the Winter Garden with Betts, Gargano, Tomson, Garvin, and PA senior officials for about an hour asking questions. When they were finished, the governor wanted to see the Viñoly and Libeskind plans again, though he didn't know the names of the architects. Meanwhile, dismayed by the cost of the THINK towers, which the *Times* reported were estimated at more than $800 million, compared to the much less costly $330 million for the Libeskind plan, Bloomberg asked, "How can we spend so much on the memorial?" according to two people present at a meeting after presentations of the two finalist designs. Just before the day of decision, LMDC president Lou Tomson told Betts that the governor was okay with both plans. Doctoroff told Betts that the mayor was okay with both plans. Betts did not foresee a problem with either selection.

The full site committee heard final presentations on both master plans only the evening before the vote. According to Betts, the committee liked both plans; his job was to persuade them to go with the Viñoly plan. He did not want the LMDC to dissent on the final formal vote of the steering committee, which was charged with making a decision about the master plan, so if something went awry, his sub-committee would support the Libeskind plan. The site committee voted unanimously for the Viñoly plan, though Tomson, who would go with whatever decision the governor made, abstained. "This should have told me something," Betts later remarked, but "I missed this, because Tomson did not care about the aesthetics of the decision," just the power and politics of the situation. At 5:30 A.M. the next day, Doctoroff called Betts to tell him of a report in the *Wall Street Journal* highlighting Viñoly's association with the Argentine junta (the military rulers installed after a right-wing coup d'état) prior to his immigration to the United States in 1978; the subcommittee had been worried about this issue and done its own research on it and was comfortable with the facts. The article was buried and supposedly harmless. However, Betts soon discovered that something else was brewing: the *Times* piece. "The phones started ringing incessantly," Betts recalled, "and the governor's press agent was yelling, who do you think you are? This introduced a new factor—pride and who calls the shots."[41]

There is an additional intriguing backstory to this episode. Early that morning the governor received a call from attorney Edward W. Hayes, "New York political infighter" and "go-to guy." Hayes had gone to law school with Pataki and was calling to check in on the whether the governor still liked the Libeskind plan, as he said he did after viewing the different proposals at the Winter Garden in December. At the viewing he told Hayes (according to Hayes), who was with him, "I think the Libeskinds will win. I like them. I like their proposal." Hayes had been introduced to Daniel and Nina Libeskind by Victoria Newhouse, an architectural historian and author and fan of Libeskind, who wanted Hayes to help Libeskind land this prize of a commission. Shortly thereafter, sometime in late November or early December, Nina Libeskind, the architect's business partner and wife, asked Hayes for help with the governor. When she saw the February 26 *Times* piece, she called Hayes at 7:30 A.M. and said, "We lost." Hayes hadn't yet seen the *Times* piece, and when he did, he wasn't about to leave it at that, as he explained in his autobiography *Mouthpiece*.[42]

Before he called the governor, Hayes worked the phones, calling people who knew selection committee members. "All the people I speak to are afraid to make a fuss or just feel it's simply too late: the committee has decided," he said. As Hayes tells the story, in back and forth telephone conversations, he worked to convince the governor that he still had a choice, despite the choice of his site committee. This is "the most important thing you'll ever do in public life," he argued. "No one even knows who's on your goddamned committee! But everyone knows who *you* are. Who are you comfortable with? That's who you have to go with." Pataki was always in favor of the Libeskind plan, he told me in an interview. "Viñoly's plan was a horrible plan; two skeletons. What did the others see in this plan? Did anyone ever build something like this? What would it cost?" So when Hayes called that morning and said, "We [Libeskind] lost," the governor said, "what do you mean, I was in favor of the Libeskind plan."[43]

The governor and the mayor met later that afternoon in a tiny room for an urgent final meeting to review the two plans. Betts still recalls the "steam" coming from Pataki, undoubtedly ballistic about the leaked story in the *Times.* "Pataki was really, really irked at us," he said. (When he spoke on the 2004 PBS show *Sacred Ground* about his thoughts when he read what was reported in the *Times* about the site committee's decision, the governor said: "Well, maybe it's not yet the decision.") The architects had not been scheduled to make another presentation to the governor and the mayor, but they were called in early that morning. By several accounts, Libeskind was said to have done a great job; Viñoly, not so good. Betts sat with the governor and the mayor and described the innovative engineering of the THINK towers; he was passionate about this aspect of the design concept, having spent so much time in the preceding weeks with Viñoly's team working through refinements of their plan and how the latticework towers could be fabricated and put in place at Ground Zero. Then bringing into play his long-standing personal relationship with President George W. Bush, he "underscored his views with a scarcely veiled threat," Philip Nobel wrote in *Sixteen Acres.* "Well, remember, there are three people in this room—the mayor, the governor, and the White House." Clearly irritated, Pataki's response sealed the decision: "I may just be a hick from Peekskill," he said, "but those towers look like death to me." Bloomberg reportedly likened them to the abandoned gas tanks along the Long Island Expressway in Elmhurst, Queens, that no one ever called beautiful (gigantic cylinders encased in a grid of steel on a site the city was spending $20 million to transform into Elmhurst Park at the request of the community). Calling them "skeletons of death," the governor told Betts "I will never build those skeletons."[44] The governor went out to talk to someone in the hall; the group thought he was going to come back. Five, ten minutes pass; thirty minutes pass. The mayor is getting upset. His cell phone rings; it's the governor—Pataki tells the mayor he's picked Libeskind.

After the governor's decision, there was never a formal vote by the LMDC steering committee. Later, when Betts called Pataki, the governor repeated his preference for the Libeskind plan. Maybe he had decided the twin towers were too risky, Betts told me. Betts thought Viñoly's plan was daring and bold; Libeskind's plan, safe and manageable, a plan that didn't make a commitment it couldn't fulfill and could be altered with a change in circumstances. Yet as one participant surmised, "Pataki is too much of a politician to say, 'I taught you a lesson,' but he had."

How was it that Betts came to favor the THINK twin-tower scheme and persuade his colleagues on the site committee of its symbolic merits, despite its difficult and costly and questionable constructability? Beyond the obvious differences in the architectural aesthetic visions of the two schemes, something bigger was being played out in the decision-making calculus of the LMDC site committee: a debate about who should have greater control over the site—the public sector under the governmental aegis of the LMDC or the private-sector leaseholder with legal rights to rebuild the site. Each proposal spoke to an underlying difference in orientation.

The THINK scheme came across as more symbolic than Libeskind's building ensemble, which was unquestionably commercial in intent even though the architect expressed the ideas behind *Memory Foundations* in highly symbolic and poetically florid terms: "Park of Heroes," "Wedge of Light," "deep indelible footprints," "foundations [that] withstood the unimaginable trauma of the destruction and stand as eloquent as the Constitution itself asserting the durability of Democracy and the value of individual life."[45] Betts wanted an extraordinary symbolic structure that would attract visitors from around the world. Viñoly's towers better fit his ambition for building the right symbol at Ground Zero, but not so the vast sunken memorial space at the bedrock foundation of the site that Libeskind conceived of as a "quiet, meditative and spiritual space."

The symbolic 1,776-foot tower topped by a spire evoking the raised arm of Lady Liberty in Libeskind's plan was but one tower of five, all of which would be built as a commercial venture, in phases over time as the market and financing demanded (plate 7). The pragmatic flexibility of that site plan drove a different set of development dynamics, one in which Larry Silverstein would be controlling the design decisions at the time when he had neither the organization nor the experience to develop a project of such scale. The future buildout of that proposal was far less certain than the THINK scheme. "Viñoly's latticework towers," Goldberger wrote in *Up from Zero*, "were to be an entirely public project," expensive but in the control of the LMDC. "The major statement of the plan was its commemorative aspect, not its commercial aspect, and Betts thought that was the right statement for the LMDC to be making."[46]

The LMDC and the PA had been moving forward with master plans for Ground Zero on parallel tracks, competitive and uncoordinated. At the Port Authority, consultants, engineers, and the director of priority capital projects, Anthony G. Cracchiolo, worked on technical issues, while Garvin and his consultants and staff did the same at the LMDC. Betts and his site-planning committee and steering committee of eight principals thrashed out the policy implications and execution issues. When decisions rose to the top, Tomson and the governor's people in Albany weighed in, as did senior officials in the Bloomberg administration. But on the day he chose Libeskind's *Memory Foundations* as the master plan for Ground Zero, Governor Pataki became the single arbiter of a highly politicized process. For the rest of 2003, he supported Libeskind's vision through a bitter struggle with Silverstein's architect, David Childs, over the design of the Freedom Tower, as detailed in a later chapter. The governor's support for Libeskind's vision, however, had its limits. It would not survive threats to his "aggressive timetable" for rebuilding Ground Zero, an agenda visibly calibrated to his ambition for a run at the Republican Party nomination for president.

POLITICAL DECISIONS

If there was any one decision that clearly revealed his ambitions, it was his promise of an iconic tower—a Freedom Tower. "Today we reclaim New York's skyline with a towering beacon to New York and our nation's resilience," Governor Pataki declared at the unveiling of the master plan's iconic visual landmark in mid-December 2003. "The Freedom Tower will be a proud new symbol of our country's strength—and a monument to our two lost icons." What the rhetoric promised, the architectural model put on view: a "unique geometrical torque of the building's tower" creating an asymmetrical form with a soaring offset 1,776-foot spire designed to "echo the profile of the Statue of Liberty's arm holding the Torch of Freedom."[47] Symbolism infused the iconic tower's tribute to the American creed of freedom in every dimension: in name, height, size, and location—at the northwest corner of the site to complete the spiraling composition of the master plan's towers. The model's formal unveiling at Federal Hall, the classical building where the first U.S. Congress met and wrote the Bill of Rights and George Washington was inaugurated as president, conferred additional historic meaning on this early act of political symbolism.

Even before its design formally came into view, the Freedom Tower was a difficult identifying skyline marker of the new Trade Center: a clear terrorist target built on the weakest of economic fundamentals. As a real estate investment, it was in the wrong location. Though never a fan of the Libeskind plan, Larry Silverstein was merely following conventional real estate wisdom when he objected to the Freedom Tower's location at the northwest corner of the site, where it would be farthest from the planned Transportation Hub. He tried to have it moved east, closer to the Transportation Hub and the shopping concourses that could favorably enhance the prospects for leasing the tower's more than two million square feet of office space. Doctoroff pushed back in a letter sent to the Port Authority opposing the developer's request, emphasizing that its planned location would provide signature visibility "separated from surrounding buildings ... not hemmed by nearby buildings." Government officials agreed. "The governor said all along that's where it should be," PA vice chairman Gargano said; "unless a problem develops, that's where it will be."[48]

"Skyscrapers in general are all about economics," remarked Carol Willis, architectural historian, author, and founder of the Skyscraper Museum in lower Manhattan. "This is different.... [T]his building transcends the simple equation—form follows finance," the title of one of her books. Willingness to rent space, especially among corporate tenants was uncertain from the start. "The simple question that no one could answer the day after 9/11," Frank Rich wrote in a *Times* op-ed—"What sane person would want to work in a skyscraper destined to be the most tempting target for aerial assault in the Western world?"—would remain unanswered for nearly a decade (until May 2011, when Condé Nast agreed to sign a lease for one million square feet of the tower renamed 1 World Trade Center). The commercial brokerage community was deeply skeptical: "The rationale for building it is all patriotism," said Mary Ann Tighe, one of the city's most respected commercial real estate brokers and chief executive officer for the New York Tristate Region at CBRE, a commercial real estate services firm. The Freedom Tower was a political statement, not a business proposition. And at least some Port Authority officials understood its symbolic role: "It's like building the Statue of Liberty," one said. "It's not an economic proposal. The Freedom Tower is a monument. That's what we're building."[49]

Governor Pataki responded to the Freedom Tower's highly tenuous economics by announcing that the offices of the governor of New York State would be the Freedom Tower's first tenant. Such a commitment was not unusual for a transformative public-private development project; for this project, however, it was déjà vu, an echo of the first lease commitment New York State made in 1967 to bolster the wobbly financial condition of the gigantic twin towers. As a practical matter, the 2.6-million-square-foot Freedom Tower was sure to absorb a very large share of the insurance proceeds available for rebuilding. This too would remain uncertain until Silverstein's ongoing litigation resolved whether the 9/11 attack on the World Trade Center towers was a one-event or two-event occurrence. This battle, Mortimer Zuckerman's *Daily News* editorial said, "dramatically sharpened" the economics of rebuilding. An eminently successful entrepreneurial real estate executive, Zuckerman knew a thing or two about high-profile development ventures. Without a big win in his quest for a $7.1 billion insurance payout, Silverstein's ability to build more than the Freedom Tower was dubious (after lease payments to the Port Authority, legal expenses, design fees, and related costs whittled away the amount available for rebuilding). "At risk are the other office towers that Mr. Silverstein hoped to build as rapidly as possible, and that may not be a bad thing," editorialized the *Times*. The critics pounced on the feasibility issue. "Outside the governor's office, there's near-universal agreement," one wrote, "that the tower—vast, expensive, iconic, incendiary (it's the architectural equivalent of a bright-red flag being waved at a charging bull), and thus possibly unrentable—is the biggest single obstacle to the rebuilding of ground zero. And yet not only is Pataki insistent that it be erected, he's insistent that it be erected first, placing a huge strain on Silverstein's limited resources."[50]

The governor's insistence that construction of the Freedom Tower was an absolute priority coupled with its tenuous economics cast an irrevocable die. The decision was dispositive, not just because it was early in the process of rebuilding but because it was politically impossible to reverse. (However, Pataki's successor in Albany, Eliot Spitzer, and his newly appointed executive director of the Port Authority, Anthony Shorris, very briefly considered doing so.) The fact that the Freedom Tower lacked economic viability created a predictable situation: As a private developer focused on the bottom line, Silverstein was not going to build an uneconomical building, a symbol, on his own dime. That much was clear from the beginning. And because it was predictable, the iconic tower would become a key element of the 2006 realignment agreement, which solved the problem by shifting full financial responsibility for and ownership of the Freedom Tower to the Port Authority.

Marching to the drumbeat of his presidential ambitions, Governor Pataki promised that "the rebirth of the World Trade Center site will move from 'paper to steel' on July 4, 2004—when ground will be broken on the Freedom Tower."[51] His announcement came the day after the LMDC adopted the *World Trade Center Memorial and Cultural Program General Project Plan*, the process-governing document that allowed the public sector to move forward with rebuilding work on the site. This was not the governor's first choice of dates. A year earlier, a remark by Silverstein to reporters and editors of the *Daily News* had pegged the groundbreaking event to coincide with the Republican presidential convention convening in Manhattan at the end of the summer, near the third anniversary of the terrorist attacks. The governor's office denied this report, which Silverstein's spokesman immediately disavowed, but the rumor persisted in the press. Though the new date skirted the charge of rank opportunism, critics quickly pointed out that the "groundbreaking" had more to do with Pataki's ambitions than any business considerations.

The emblematic cornerstone ceremony took place before anyone knew how high the tower would actually rise in relation to its symbolic 1,776-foot aspiration, what the building would look like, how much it would cost, who would finance it, and what tenants might be willing to sign leases for office space. "How do you break ground on ground that has already been shattered?" asked veteran *Times* reporter David W. Dunlap. "And how do you break ground when there really is no ground to break?" The answer: with reverence and symbolism. The Independence Day groundbreaking took place as planned, complete with the temporary placement of the cornerstone—a beautifully cut twenty-ton slab of Adirondack granite that the governor called "the bedrock of our state"—in the northwest corner of the site, seventy feet below street level. "Chiseled with a New York accent [a typeface named Gotham]" were the words "To honor and remember those who lost their lives on September 11, 2001 and as a tribute to the enduring spirit of freedom" (figure 7.7). After the hour-long ceremony full of symbolic flourishes and lofty rhetoric, a 150-ton crane replaced the stone on a concrete pedestal, where it would sit until transported away to Long Island as an artifact of a strictly ceremonial gesture. "As the first tangible element of the Freedom Tower—and, by extension, the trade center redevelopment—and as an image seen nationwide on Independence Day," Dunlap wrote after the event, "the cornerstone sent an aesthetic signal on intent."[52]

As long as determined optimism about rebuilding prevailed, perhaps this ceremonial gesture was not likely to matter much. Unattached to a permanent

FIGURE 7.7 *New York governor George Pataki, New Jersey governor James McGreevey, and Mayor Michael Bloomberg (third from the right) at the unveiling of the twenty-ton Adirondack granite cornerstone at the World Trade Center site, Sunday, July 4, 2004. After the hour-long ceremony, the symbolic cornerstone was transported away to Long Island, an artifact of a strictly ceremonial gesture.* AP PHOTO/GREGORY BULL

in-place foundation, the cornerstone was ready to move into place whenever a fully designed building went into construction. The real question lurking behind the ceremony was the same one that prevailed in the earliest days of the master-plan process: What would really be built? Reporting on the ceremony, Dunlap succinctly captured the spirit of the event: "Guessing the future of long-term mega-projects is a fool's game. Their momentum depends on an alignment of political will, popular support, market demand and economic conditions that shift constantly, beyond the ability of anyone to control or predict."[53] Putting those big-picture issues aside, the major principals at Ground Zero settled into the detailed process of creating a workable plan and, finally, focusing on the process for selecting a memorial design.

CHAPTER 8

A Master Plan Emerges

FIGURE 8.1 *"Tribute in Light," high-intensity searchlights projected skyward to form two violet columns of light where the twin towers had once been. Coproduced by Creative Time and the Municipal Art Society, Tribute became a memorable icon of the 9/11 terrorist attack on the World Trade Center.* CHRISTOPHER PENLER/SHUTTLESTOCK

WITH THE SELECTION OF STUDIO Daniel Libeskind's *Memory Foundations* in late February 2003, the work began. Much had yet to be determined—foremost, selection of a design for the memorial. Fears that the memorial might become a footnote to a large development project and frustration with the LMDC's decision to proceed with a master plan for the site ahead of a design for a memorial led outside interests to initiate a number of temporary memorials, the most memorable being Tribute in Light: high-intensity searchlights projected skyward to form "two violet columns of light where the towers had once been" (figure 8.1). First named the "Project for the Immediate Reconstruction of Manhattan's Skyline," Tribute turned into a powerful icon of the 9/11 attacks. It evocatively captured the sense of loss and projected rays of hope as city residents struggled to cope with a post-9/11 landscape. As trace shadows of the twin towers' memory, it simultaneously evoked "both their presence and absence," and hence, "life before September 11," which compellingly resonated with the public.[1] Coproduced by Creative Time and the Municipal Art Society, Tribute initially ran as a temporary installation from March 11 to April 14, 2002, yet every time it was to be the "final" year, popular sentiment demanded its replay, again and again, every year on September 11.[2] However sensitive and beloved this simple tribute was, it was temporary, ephemeral. The public clamored for a permanent memorial; the families especially wanted the process of selecting a design to begin straight away. The push to publicly memorialize became a rush, contravening the timeline of the historical practice of commemoration.

The master plan, unglamorous but essential, articulated in visual form how the many uses—memorial, commercial towers, cultural buildings, and transportation center—could fit on the sixteen-acre site and function together. Figuring out how these uses would actually mesh (or not) with the ambitions of stakeholders was an intricate task, messy and noisy, full of open struggles. Larry Silverstein wanted specific changes. Westfield wanted specific changes. The Port Authority wanted to make an iconic transportation terminal central to the sense of place at Ground Zero. The families of the victims wanted commemoration to take singular pride of place at Ground Zero. City officials, led by City Planning Commissioner Amanda Burden, wanted to assure active street life was structured into the mandate of the governing planning document for rebuilding the site. None of them wanted to compromise on their priority.

The intractability of finding common ground among different stakeholders triggered a series of high-profile controversies that shaped decisions about how the site would be rebuilt. That was typical of the way large-scale projects evolve in New York: Everything becomes negotiable. Although Studio Daniel Libeskind was tasked to provide design guidelines for the site, for example, they were never agreed upon since each actor believed it would do better by negotiating out the details case by case. "Zero-sum positions," remarked one seasoned developer who spoke off the record. "There's not a lot of respect for each other's voices, but with power politics and compromise, New York finds a way to do something good, and then what is produced is accepted as part of the city. The city is not visionary. It is not a consensus place. It is not about perfect planning." The political process is about forging compromise solutions that move a project forward. New York has long been a city that celebrates diversity and dissent, yet under the tragic circumstances of rebuilding Ground Zero, many undoubtedly hoped rebuilding would prove to be an exception to that norm. Not many, however, were likely to bet on it: The stakes—in memory and money—were simply too high.

DETERMINING THE MEMORIAL MISSION

The push for memorialization was coming soon, too soon by any historical benchmark, before anyone had really made sense of the horrific event. "People were still very much in the grief process," Nikki Stern explained at a joint meeting of the Memorial Competition Jury and the Families Advisory Council in the spring of 2003. Stern had lost her husband on 9/11 and would become a leading voice of reason and tolerance as executive director of Families of September 11, a national organization founded immediately after the terrorist attacks to provide support to those affected by the attacks and champion policies that respond to the threat of terrorism. "I can't think of a memorial that has been designed in such close proximity to an event as this one, and that freights your process with enormous baggage," she told jury members. "It gives the process itself special resonance, not just the outcome." A former public relations professional, Stern in her emotionally articulated words captured the intricacy of the memorializing task. "You cannot own it. And we don't own it. There may be concentric circles of loss or pain or experience. We may be in the center. But this memorial, while absolutely first and foremost [it] is a tribute to the dead, extends out in concentric circles to include other things that happened and other people it happened to. It resonates out to include the need to move forward...to include how future generations are going to feel....I think you need to find something that both resonates out and then pulls everything together."[3]

Being so close in time to 9/11, it would not be easy. The LMDC's Families Advisory Council, a group of eighteen family members and thirteen ex-officio clergy and government officials, had been grappling with hard questions since its first meeting early in 2002: What should be memorialized? The events or the attacks? The destroyed buildings? The people in the buildings and other victims of the attacks?

The complexity of the memorialization task embedded itself in the process—in the coming to grips with a statement of the mission and a program that would guide the selection of a memorial design and its execution as part of the redevelopment at Ground Zero. The emphasis on process was fundamental to recovery because the drive for a permanent memorial was so immediate in time. Even though too immediate, it was not practically feasible to delay because where the calamity happened was a living, working community that had been severely impacted physically and emotionally. Instead, a thoughtful process would have to serve as a substitute for the perspective of time. "[I]t is in the conversations, in the careful selection of people to think about this, that we in fact agonize and come to grips in certain ways with these massive, horrendous events," explained Edward Linenthal, a professor of religion and American culture and author of *The Unfinished Bombing: Oklahoma City in American Memory*.[4] The process could be nothing other than part and parcel of the design that would memorialize the 9/11 attacks and its victims, nothing other than part and parcel of rebuilding Ground Zero—not separate and apart—and it had to be understood as such.

The experience in Oklahoma City was the closest precedent in time. Though it was "not an exact template of the struggles awaiting those directly affected by the terrorism in New York City," Linenthal cautioned, "it was an appropriate road map to the dark and alien landscape that awaited"—"a microcosm of hindsight in advance," said a reviewer of his book.[5] The international impact of September 11, the scale of death, the nature of the city, the site's location within a dense urban district, and the custodianship of the Trade Center site all made the issues to be confronted in New York different, more complex, more challenging.

Still, the inclusive process of memorializing the bombing of the Alfred P. Murrah Federal Building in Oklahoma City on April 19, 1995, which took the lives of 186 people, offered LMDC officials and members of its Families Advisory Council emotional linkages and valuable insights into the daunting task of figuring out how to memorialize the 9/11 attacks: Allow process to take precedence. Enable all voices to be heard. Engage the community. Involve family members of the victims and survivors. Mount a professionally run open-call design competition with blind submissions judged by a jury. Recognize that the process itself would take time, that memorialization is active grief, and that it would be hard to get used to the rhythm of grief, the anger and pain-filled stories. Be mindful of the inevitable hierarchy of memorialization that exists between family members and survivors and first responders and that it must be sorted out. Understand that every agenda cannot be acted upon, but can be understood in terms of "the web of grief and conviction and concern." Accept that the media enfranchises the public to be part of the bereavement community. Value the process of developing a mission statement; beyond the struggle over each and every exacting word, it is a gentle way of moving "people over time from the sense of individual ownership of a commemorative idea...to a wider vision of what disaster meant," a larger civic function. The mission statement, Linenthal wisely wrote, "serves as an enduring orientation for the memorial process," an anchor in dealing with disagreements and resentments.[6]

These lessons extracted from the pain of the "unfinished" experience could not assure success or prevent the probable emergence of fault lines and conflicts because controversy was part of how memorials of significance become defined.

Rather, the lessons consistently spoke to the importance of a sensitive process for memorializing loss: Getting it right held the promise of revealing the true purpose of memorials, "not just to mourn the dead, but to actively reshape the moral conscience of people who come through."[7]

To guide the memorial process, in the beginning of July 2002, the LMDC selected Anita F. Contini, a deeply skilled and respected professional and downtown arts activist experienced in taking something that had no structure and creating a structure to assure success. This is what she had done with Creative Time, an innovative New York–based nonprofit arts organization she started in 1973 to bring art, performers, and the public together in vacant spaces of historical and architectural interest. She next brought that creativity to lower Manhattan, establishing the World Financial Center as a family-friendly cultural destination during her tenure as vice president and artistic director at Brookfield Properties/Olympia & York. When tapped to shepherd the delicate task of developing the process and procedures for the 9/11 memorial, and other cultural and civic programs for the LMDC, she was an executive at Merrill Lynch responsible for global sponsorships and events marketing.

With her long ties to both the downtown community and the New York arts community, Contini was a natural for the memorial task. Yet as she told me, "Could anyone possibly be prepared for this type of job?" The raison d'être was the most compelling mandate: "I didn't know how to say no to something like this. Sept. 11 changed everybody, and it changed me, too. I feared I had lost my son and my husband, but my fear turned into joy quickly, while others' didn't," she told *Times* reporter Robin Finn for a Public Lives profile. Characterized as genuine and unobtrusive, Contini believes in the power of diverse opinions as illustrative of the American way. "Diverse opinions are good. You need a dialogue with a lot of opinions to get a consensus. It doesn't mean you can actually make everybody happy in the end," she said realistically. "My job is to protect the integrity of the process. I really believe that we can count on something truly remarkable happening here, a superb creative vision that people will rally around. What I'm doing is putting the steps together so that the memorial makes sense for New York and this situation."[8] She would create a new process suited to the unique circumstances at Ground Zero.

While she was able to be "somewhat objective, it was harder for others whose personal loss was so emotional," she said. So much was laid on the trauma of it, the visual trauma as well. It affected her thinking all the time; she cautioned herself not to run with the first idea, to be very careful about each step of the process and to keep an open mind.[9] The first thing she did was enlist Kenneth T. Jackson, then president of the New-York Historical Society and an esteemed professor at

Columbia University well known for his many books on urban history (and his once-a-year midnight bike ride around the city with students) and editorship of the celebrated *The Encyclopedia of New York City*, to take members of the Families Advisory Council on a tour of New York City memorials and commemorative civic sculptures.[10] It proved to be revelatory. With there being little historical explanation to many of these memorials, Contini came away wondering how meaningful memorials are to future generations. "Maybe they shouldn't have long-term relevance—not everything should be remembered forever," she said. "Do we want to celebrate the culture of death, instead of the culture of the living? Do we want to have so much reminding us of the terror and the tragedy, or more of a living memorial about our culture? And do we give families respect without taking it away from the other people in the community and other needs?"[11]

Following the local tour of memorials, she took advisory committee members, LMDC board members, and staff on a five-day memorial research tour to Shanksville, Pennsylvania, Washington, D.C., Oklahoma City, and Montgomery, Alabama, to visit nineteen memorials representing a broad range of historical events. Some memorials were magnificent in scale, others powerful because of their intimacy; each reflected a unique event specific to time and place.[12] The trip and the talks with others engaged in creating, directing, and preserving memory tributes produced several important messages, all of which became important as Contini guided the memorial process at Ground Zero: The names would be the biggest challenge. Often people did not want to talk about the perpetrators, but this would have to happen. The approach and sight lines to a memorial are as much a part of the experience as the memorial itself, and how a memorial is constructed would be as important as the ideas it represents. The physical materials would count, so those managing the design process needed to focus on what would work and what would last and should not skimp on the materials. There would have to be a way to deal with the things people leave at the site. Ten years later, the number of people who would come to the memorial would be less. To be successful, a memorial has to have continued significance to future generations, endure over time as an active site, and serve to illuminate and inspire. As summarized in the LMDC's record of the tour, "Remembrance is not enough. Memorials are mandates to educate."[13]

The tour complete, Contini set about arranging for the writing of the mission statement that would establish goals for the memorial and a program statement that would provide "guiding principles" and identify "program elements," such as the inclusion of names, for how the mission of the memorial would be realized. This was, as Paul Goldberger detailed in *Up from Zero*, "the first step in laying the groundwork for the memorial competition, which Contini and her colleagues at the LMDC hoped to be ready to launch not long after the master plan was set early in 2003."[14] In mid-November, the LMDC announced the formation of the two drafting committees for the statements, carefully composed. The mix of family members, residents, survivors, first responders, arts and architectural professionals, community leaders, and representatives from the LMDC advisory councils[15] aimed to mediate the emergence of a hierarchy—family voices louder than others who also had ideas to contribute and stakes in memorialization. Each committee would take as a starting point the preliminary drafts prepared during the summer by committees of the Families Advisory Council.[16]

There were four fundamental questions the committees needed to address: Who is the memorial for? What does it commemorate? What will it say to the future? What will it include? To guide this piece of the process, Contini brought in Todd D. Jick, a social scientist specializing in leadership consulting, to serve as a facilitator among the many stakeholders involved with the memorialization process. He worked closely with the drafting committees, which were "struggling with the question of how to create a memorial that will take all of us through an arc of emotions ranging from the darkest moments of gloom and loss to heroic and life-affirming actions."[17]

Contini also put together a series of talks for the families and the community on memorial-related topics to provide insight into the process of commemoration and present for discussion a variety of historical, social, and artistic perspectives, "fabulous talks and open discussions that touched on sensitive issues," she said.[18] Paul Goldberger was among the six[19] asked to speak to the group, and his words, some of the most moving of his writings, addressed the paradoxes and contradictions and things that are not quite as they appear at Ground Zero. They spoke to the "arbitrary divide between sacred and everyday space" and the need to honor lives lost "exactly where it happened—the authenticity of the place." This is what makes what will be commemorated at the Trade Center site so different from other memorials, other than perhaps Gettysburg. "This is no small detail," he said. "It affects everything. But as we figure out how to make it clear that all of Ground Zero is sacred, we must at the same time accept the fact that its sacred nature might, paradoxically, be best expressed by celebrating the joy and the potential of everyday urban life. That is the real dilemma, and it is one for which no other memorial prepares us." His words resonated deeply. "A great memorial, like a great work of art, must be able to speak for itself," he said in closing. "It must be able to speak not only to those who have memories, but to those who do not. I know that this is painful to accept, but the main purpose of the memorial that is built is not to make those who have suffered loss feel better. It is to make sure that those who did *not* suffer loss begin to feel something of your pain, and to make them begin to understand and feel how catastrophic what happened was. It is to make them feel a sense of awe, and to make them resolve that it can never, never happen again."[20]

Drafting these statements was not going to be a long-drawn-out process. Contini put in place a time-condensed structured process: each committee would meet four times; each meeting, scheduled for two hours. She was working from a notion that had emerged in early discussions about the close-in-time nature of the memorialization process, that sometimes the need to move quickly leads to a sharper, more focused decision. Two months later, the LMDC released both statements to the public and then launched "an aggressive public outreach campaign to solicit public input," receiving some twenty-four hundred comments from public hearings, meetings with its advisory councils and Community Board 1, mailings to the families of victims and elected officials, and input from its official website, e-mail, and regular mail. The drafting committees convened again to review the public comments and make adjustments. During the process, Contini constantly went back to the Families Advisory Council to keep its members informed; there were always a few who didn't agree, but most agreed with what was being formulated. The memorial, she said, "had to be about the individual *and* about the larger event." The iterative process, Goldberger wrote, produced a final version "not nearly so genteel" as the initial attempt at a mission statement, which was "notable for its cautious, even hesitant language and sense of propriety." The final version was "short, simpler, and blunter":[21]

> Remember and honor the thousands of innocent men, women, and children murdered by terrorists in the horrific attacks of February 26, 1993, and September 11, 2001.
> Respect this place made sacred through tragic loss.
> Recognize the endurance of those who survived, the courage of those who risked their lives to save others, and the compassion of all who supported us in our darkest hours.
> May the lives remembered, the deeds recognized, and the spirit reawakened be eternal beacons, which reaffirm respect for life, strengthen our resolve to preserve freedom, and inspire an end to hatred, ignorance, and intolerance.

THE FOOTPRINTS

The task of selecting a memorial design floated above the institutional turf fights and political gray areas besetting the commercially sensitive decisions over density, land use, street patterns, pedestrian ways, and vehicular traffic. The mission of remembrance held sacred status at Ground Zero and that set it apart from the ground-level politics of the master plan debates. Nonetheless, the process for selecting a memorial design was, rhetorically at least, an integral part of the overall planning process for the site. "To be able to put on a memorial competition—or any competition for a monument or a work of public art or a museum building—you need to have a site designated. You need some definition for a competition," Contini told the press. This was the prevailing logic of proceeding with the master plan first, logic also in accord with the primacy of the commercial agenda the LMDC had accepted as a fait accompli (figure 8.2). "Accepting this order of things," Goldberger said, "had a subtle effect on the entire planning process, since it implicitly downgraded the memorial."[22] It was not the driving force of the plan—or so it seemed at the time in 2003. The politics of events unfolding over time, however, would demonstrate in ways other than planning sequence the memorial's priority claim.

The first formal articulation of the memorial's claim on Ground Zero came on June 29, 2002, when Governor Pataki declared the footprints of the twin towers to be sacred space, saying "We will never build where the towers stood." Though the

FIGURE 8.2 Davies ©2003 The Journal News. Dist. by Universal UCLICK. Reprinted with permission. All rights reserved

public announcement was unexpected, it reflected the informal consensus among LMDC officials. Not so, among their counterparts at the Port Authority, who were shocked by the governor's statement, I was told by an insider at the agency. When I interviewed the governor and asked what prompted him to make the footprints pronouncement when he did, he answered at length. "I had constant interaction with the families because their pain was so real. While I could not let them drive decisions, I had to be respectful of their feelings. It was important to show the sheer size of the attack, of the loss, and the footprints were a way to tell the story . . . and respect the enormous grief of the families. It was the logical and emotional thing to do," he said. "The scale of the footprints, each approximately one acre, was important. When you walk all around them, you can appreciate the physical magnitude of the loss and that helps to appreciate the magnitude of the emotional loss." The footprints, he said, "would help future generations understand not just the grief of the families, but the grief of all the first responders too."[23]

The timing of the governor's commitment may have surprised the public, but the idea of the footprints as sacred ground had gained immediate authenticity as a memorial, in particular, among the LMDC's Families Advisory Council. Quietly, the desired reintegration of the site into the city's street grid set up quadrants that seemed to confer exclusive status on what became the memorial quadrant even before the governor's footprints commitment.[24] Seen by some as an emotional IOU and by others as an obvious moral imperative, this commitment to the families of the 9/11 victims, once expressed, became politically unassailable. It was a formative decision with big implications for how the complex project would come into fruition. "The biggest issue at the time, which was somewhat overlooked, was the footprints," said Kevin M. Rampe, an executive at the development corporation since its inception who had worked for Tomson overseeing day-to-day operations of the LMDC as executive vice president and general counsel before becoming president (February 2003–May 2005), then chairman (May 2006–April 2007). "It was immediate, the question: Was the World Trade Center site going to be a sacred site? In the beginning of the planning process, commercial rebuilding was a given; from day one, the goal was to restore it. The sacred, however, would dictate the nature of the site—area, size of the program, location of transportation, and political rhetoric driving the process." The LMDC, he recalled, "would have to preserve the sacred nature of the site."[25] It would complicate rebuilding from day one.

Rampe took on the rebuilding mission as LMDC president soon after Pataki's selection of the *Memory Foundations* master plan, upon Tomson's retirement. "An accommodating ego, a thick skin, a Type A work ethic, an optimistic world view. If the traits, discordant as they may seem, make the man," Robin Finn wrote in a *Times* Public Lives profile, "Kevin M. Rampe appears to have the right stuff." The

9/11-mandated rebuilding mission, she added, "should come with a warning label. Danger: be prepared to get chewed out, worn out and burned out. P.S.: that's how you'll know you're doing the job right." Rampe was not well known outside of state government, where he served Governor Pataki in several positions, first assistant counsel handling banking, insurance, financial services, labor, and other issues, and then senior deputy superintendent and general counsel and first deputy superintendent of the New York State Insurance Department. A corporate attorney, the thirty-six-year-old had already proven to be a steady hand under demanding circumstances. As a litigator associate at Sherman & Sterling, he had been tapped to go to Kuwait to prepare $200 million in environmental and health claims against Iraq in the aftermath of the first Gulf war. "It was incredibly interesting and incredibly sad," he said.[26] It was a firsthand view of rebuilding that would unwittingly give him insight into the importance of resilience.

At the LMDC, his leadership skills enabled him to deal with the constant pressure of a planning process accelerated to accommodate intense pressure from voices across the political spectrum to get things done fast, to get past the 9/11 event, to heal fast. Even if he personally believed the whole planning process was too soon in time, he was pragmatic: The city could not wait. New Yorkers were not a patient lot. Plus, there were economic pressures to move fast: "Lower Manhattan businesses were suffering, and a real fear existed," he said, "that this would be the death of Manhattan." He wanted "to get it right." At Ground Zero, he said, "You can't apply any of the classic rules to this site. This is not just a development process; it's part of the healing process."[27]

What did preserving the footprints mean? "Families were struggling with the question of just what part of the 16-acre site should be treated as sacred ground," Christy Ferer wrote in an op-ed in the *Times*. Ferer was serving as Mayor Bloomberg's liaison between city government and the victims' families; she had lost her husband, Neil D. Levin, executive director of the Port Authority, in the attack. "Does it extend down 70 feet from ground level, the depth of the buildings' implosion? Does it extend 110 stories into the sky? Does sacred ground include the areas half a mile away where human remains were found atop neighboring buildings? Is it the part of the Fresh Kills landfill where forensic detectives painstakingly filtered 1.6 million tons of twisted wreckage and pulverized debris?"[28] These were questions for philosophers and religious leaders, but they had to be addressed on a practical level in the context of building out the vision of the master plan. Should the space be left hollow? Could you have in the space what was there pre-9/11, the PATH lines? Could it contain critical infrastructure? Could the memorial use the footprints?

There were many interpretations: perimeter boundary, physical floor or bedrock, or physical space up to the sky and down to the center of the earth?

Disagreement existed even among the families on what was meant by "the foot-prints." Everyone had their own distinctions, Rampe recalled. It was always contentious. For some family members, any definition other than preservation down to bedrock was less than authentic. "Artificial footprints" would deny the site historical relevance to future generations who they wanted to be able to "touch that bedrock and stand in that site and know the enormity of the attacks and always remember these people" who died there, said Anthony Gardner, one of the most activist of family members, chairman of WTC United Family Group, and a member of the Families Advisory Council.[29] For many of those who had nothing of their lost loved ones to bury, the raw power of bedrock footprints became all important, understandably so.

Was it inevitable that the footprints—"the offset square where the towers had stood"—be sanctified as inviolate? Politically, yes. The vast majority of the human remains had been found within the memorial quadrant, as made clear by the density of dots on the map prepared by the New York Fire Department detailing where human remains had been recovered from November 2001 through March 2002 (figure 8.3). "But the map," veteran *Times* reporter David W. Dunlap wrote in a 2005 article, "makes equally clear that bodies and body parts were found almost everywhere at and around the Trade Center site, including the site of the Freedom Tower." The dots on the NYFD map spilled out beyond the sixteen-acre site, "with outliers on distant blocks that had never seemed a part of the disaster," Philip Nobel wrote in *Sixteen Acres*. Unexpected discoveries of bones and bone fragments in places around the edges of the Trade Center site continued beyond the formal finish of the recovery effort. For many families, a call telling them that some remains of their relatives had been recovered did not come, even years later; five years after 9/11, this was the case for more than 40 percent of the victims' family members. The remains issue compounded the dilemma surrounding definition of the footprints; it could be nothing other than an exceptionally delicate issue. "New York's experience is not like that of Oklahoma City, where victims of terrorism were recovered and laid to rest. What survivors here need and expect from the trade center site…is very different. This is a burial ground, not just a location for a future national memorial," said Ferer.[30]

If the sanctity of the footprints derived from the fact that the 9/11 attacks made the site a graveyard, then the entire sixteen acres (as well as surrounding areas where thousands of remains were found), literally, would be a sacrosanct zone. This was the logic behind the early calls for making the entire site a sacred zone free of commercial development, as the then mayor Rudolph W. L. Giuliani had proposed. But declaring the entire Trade Center site sacred when remains were found distant from the footprints would have amounted to a symbolic, if well-intentioned,

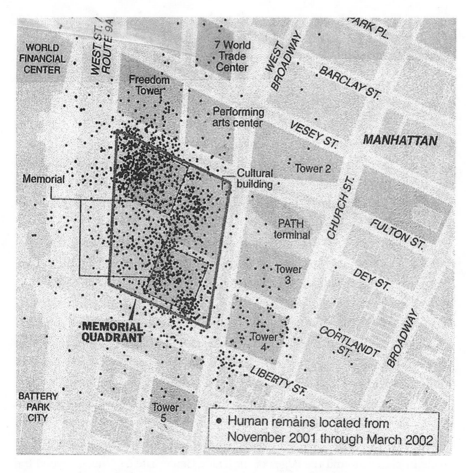

FIGURE 8.3 *Sacred ground: A burial ground as well as a place for a future national memorial. The New York Fire Department map of remains recovered from November 2001 through March 2002 around the World Trade Center site.* FROM THE NEW YORK TIMES, OCTOBER 6, 2005 © 2005 THE NEW YORK TIMES

gesture. The symbolism captured by the commitment to the footprints as sacred ground was more powerful—and, being contained to a specific portion of the site, more realistic, politically. "[T]he families had come to focus on the footprints only after having been denied everything else," Nobel wrote. "What had been born from emotional necessity was then codified by political necessity."[31] Thus, making visible the footprints of the twin towers became a requirement for the design of a 9/11 memorial at Ground Zero.

MEMORIAL ASSERTION

To select a memorial design, LMDC officials were determined to proceed above politics. They wanted to avoid the embarrassment of what had happened with the selection of a master plan, when the governor's decision openly countering the recommendation of Betts's site planning committee quashed its presumptive authority over the planning process. That is not to say the process would not be subject to delays or criticism, or that the chosen memorial design would be greeted with universal acclaim. The intent, however, was to avoid the political struggle that had plagued the process for selecting a site plan. Modeling what they would do on the carefully constructed process established to select a design for the Vietnam Veterans Memorial in Washington, D.C., and adopted by the Oklahoma City National Memorial, LMDC officials staged a worldwide open-design competition. "The impact was so wide in scope that the clear implication was that the competition should be an open call, not an invited call," Contini said.[32]

This was a big decision at an important junction, and Contini composed and shepherded the process at Ground Zero to protect it from political interference. The thirteen people on the independent memorial jury were carefully chosen. They represented an outstanding group of distinguished design and arts professionals, a single representative each for Mayor Bloomberg and for Governor Pataki, and, unlike the jury composed for the selection of a design for the Oklahoma City Memorial where family members demanded a majority of the votes, only one family member. "The whole structure took a lot of time," Contini said; "it was a major undertaking." LMDC officials had no idea of the number of entries that would come in from all over the world; the largest number in other competitions, they had been told, was 1,000. "When we heard that there were 3,000, then 4,000, and then 5,000 entries, we were amazed. So many submissions—some people may have just wanted to get their feelings out and to show their solidarity and support."[33] When the deadline for entries arrived on June 30, 2003, a total of 5,201 people (from sixty-two countries) had submitted a design, making the LMDC's memorial competition the largest architectural contest in history.

Design competitions are the exception rather than the norm in the contemporary United States. Competitions for major buildings, both public and private, were frequent and numerous in New York in the late nineteenth century and early twentieth century—for example, Central Park (1858), Washington Square Arch (1889–1892), and New York Public Library (1897). Soon thereafter not a single competition was held for the design of an American public building for fifty years, until the City of Boston announced a competition for a new city hall in 1960. Still, design competitions did not come back into fashion until the early 1980s. "With the help of a powerful multimedia focus, competitions have transformed planning from boring to sexy in the public mind," urban planner Karen Alschuler wrote in "The Competition Craze." "The jolt of intense, coordinated, creative thinking about challenging urban sites can stretch the concept of urban living in ways that public agencies may never achieve otherwise."[34] In the ideal, a design competition appeals to democratic sentiments in being open, civic minded, and public spirited. It appeals to citizens, draws the attention of the media, and stimulates young designers to devote their creative talents to developing innovative ideas, as was the case with Maya Lin and her award-winning design for the Vietnam Veterans Memorial. Lin was twenty-one and an undergraduate at Yale University when her design was selected from among 1,421 entries, which set the previous record for the largest design competition in history in 1981.

The strategic use of a competition as a public platform is not without its own political risks. Precisely because the process is open, relatively transparent, and a media-attracting event, a design competition creates big expectations among diverse constituencies. The danger is that the winning proposal might unrealistically raise public expectations about the ultimate outcome of the project. A competition develops a life of its own similarly uncontrollable by public officials and sponsor. Although design competitions are commissioned for many reasons, few of which have to do with design, all have to do political strategy. A political agenda always takes precedence over the important but ancillary search for new design possibilities, innovative solutions, or a compelling architectural or urban vision. Though political agendas vary quite a lot, all are lodged in the fundamental need to create or cultivate a strong constituency and garner the necessary resources to advance a desired project. Because they follow a competitive format and typically employ professional advisors, design competitions are a practical tool for avoiding charges of favoritism in selecting designers. Nevertheless, political considerations drive the decision to mount a competition and shape details of how a competition is structured and implemented, as is evident in how Contini went about her task at Ground Zero. Selecting an independent jury and endowing it with unquestioned authority to select a design establishes a mandate of trust. Yet shifting the risk of decision-making to a jury cannot reduce the heightened stakes for both sponsor and competitors, nor can it insulate sponsors from bureaucratic obstacles, politics within juries, and insufficient resources—in short, the conventional challenges of implementing a symbolically important design. This the LMDC would discover as it worked through the accommodations of integrating the chosen memorial design into the overall fabric of the master plan.

Contini and her LMDC colleagues succeeded in keeping politics at bay during the entire process for selecting a memorial design, in no small part, because Governor Pataki, Mayor Bloomberg, and former mayor Giuliani (not far removed from publicly commenting on 9/11 events) all agreed that the design decision should be the sole province of the jury. The remembrance element was too hot to touch. "We want to be very clear," Rampe said at the outset of the memorial process. "We will entrust the jury with the ultimate responsibility to select a design and once entrusted we must respect the jury's role in making the selection." Governor Pataki's voice was heard only at the final press conference, not before. The Port Authority was nowhere in the conversation, let alone the deliberations, on this most-sensitive element of rebuilding; it was not even represented on the memorial jury. The political calculus of this model was likely to work for the governor, regardless of the outcome. If it went well, the governor could take credit; if not, he was distanced from the result. "You can't have a memorial designed by politicians," Pataki remarked after the winning design had been unveiled.[35] Ironically, the LMDC's ability to shelter the memorial process from the Port Authority and the city also enabled it to alter important parts of the *Memory Foundations* master plan.

The rules set forth by the LMDC "Memorial Competition Guidelines"—which is to say, no rules—gave the jurors complete flexibility to alter the parameters of the Libeskind master plan in fulfilling the mandate of the Memorial Mission and Memorial Program. The "rules" specified that competitors could create a memorial "of any type, shape, height or concept" so long as it included five specifically enumerated physical elements essential for a fitting 9/11 memorial: recognition of each victim of the 9/11 attacks in New York, Virginia, and Pennsylvania and the victims of the 1993 terrorist bombing of the World Trade Center; an area for quiet visitation and contemplation; a separate area for visitation by the families and loved ones of the victims; a separate accessible area to serve as the final resting place for the unidentified human remains collected at the Trade Center site; and a way to make visible the footprints of the original World Trade Center towers. Other elements in the memorial program statement provided that the memorial or its surrounding areas might include surviving original elements and preservation of existing conditions of the Trade Center site. Design concepts needed only to be "sensitive to the spirit and vision of Studio Daniel Libeskind's master plan for the entire site." And the jury was not restricted in reviewing design concepts that "exceed the illustrated memorial site boundaries if in collaboration with the LMDC, they are deemed feasible and consistent with site plan objectives"[36] (plate 8).

The permissive flexibility of the competition guidelines reflected the jurors' input. In his firsthand account of the jury process, James E. Young explained that "it became clear almost immediately to the design professionals on the jury that the combination of mandatory program elements, Libeskind's site design, and the actual state of the site itself...would pose a daunting challenge to even the most experienced artists and architects." The 4.7-acre memorial site was "overdetermined." They feared potential designers would "throw up their hands and walk away from the competition." With permission from the other members of the jury, Young and several other jurors worked to expand the most constraining of the guidelines "to open up the site to the widest possible number of memorial designs." Still fearing that the invitation "to go beyond" the boundaries of the site plan would not come across as clearly as they wished, at the press-conference launch of the competition held at the Winter Garden in Battery Park City, the jurors announced that potential designers had permission to break the rules and challenge the site-plan design. Rampe endorsed the jury's words, reiterating the point by saying that if competitors were to express their creativity, "it may take going outside those guidelines." To attract the highest-caliber professionals, LMDC officials had given assurances that the jury would be the sole authority in this matter. The press repeatedly wrote of juror Maya Lin as someone who "broke some of the rules" to produce the spectacularly successful Vietnam Veterans Memorial.[37] By formal recognition as well as professional inclination, jury members were given license to disregard Libeskind's site plan if it created problems in selecting what they considered to be the most creative memorial design.

The LMDC set up a series of controlled forums where members of the design jury could listen to the views of different constituent groups. Confidentiality governed their activities. All signed agreements barring them from speaking to the press about the memorial selection process until the winner was announced. To head off the public relations battles that had poisoned the site-plan competition, these agreements included a clause prohibiting negative comments about peer designs that extended through December 31, 2005. The jurors' notebooks never left the office where they reviewed the 5,201 entries mounted on thirty-by-forty-inch boards and propped up on easels in rooms protected by a double-key system. The eight finalists were selected anonymously, in blind judging; they too signed confidentiality agreements, as did their model makers, illustrators, and computer animators.

The logic of the master plan was to first identify a space, "an empty canvas," Rampe said, for the symbolic memorial and to define the context—the height of the buildings that would surround the memorial and the approach to the memorial.[38] The "no-rules" memorial design competition brief, however, unambiguously defined the memorial selection as the planning priority to which the site plan would have to respond. Libeskind had himself incorporated into his vision for a memorial the unique surviving element of the 9/11 attack, the bathtub slurry wall. His site plan deliberately left it exposed as an ever-present reminder that the foundation held even as the seemingly invincible buildings crumbled. It also designated a memorial area depressed thirty (initially seventy) feet below the level of the street, which quickly acquired not-so-favorable tags: "the pit," "the commemorative pit," "the sunken pit," "the desolate pit." Libeskind's idea followed emotional logic—create a contemplative space sheltered from the bustle and noises of the surrounding streets—but it was overpowered by the negative labels being attached to it. To further shelter the memorial area from adjacent commercial activities, the site plan also included a place-holding museum and cultural buildings at the edges of the memorial area.

These conceptual elements created a specific physical template for the memorial, in effect predesigning the memorial. "The sunken area with its exposed slurry wall was such a powerful statement," Goldberger wrote, "that it seemed, at one point, to have all but been a memorial." The jury was free to reject Libeskind's "setting"—and did because of strong sentiments that a depressed memorial space would again isolate the site from its surrounding neighborhoods. Many jurors preferred a grade-level solution. "We saw pretty big problems with leaving large parts of the slurry wall depressed. It would be a big canyon, separated from the neighborhood," Young said. This feature also bothered downtown business interests and Battery Park City residents, who considered "the pit" an obstacle to pedestrian passage through the Trade Center site. Regardless of the logic or merit of the Libeskind vision, the jury wanted the memorial design to knit the site back into the neighborhood. It became an imperative—"the stark reality of reintegrating into the urban fabric a site that had been violently torn from it"—as expressed in the jury statement on the winning design.[39] The jury believed it was smarter than the others involved in the planning and removed some placeholders in the Libeskind plan, a juror later recalled at an academic meeting. "All memorials are negotiated. Nothing is set in stone." What was clearly being set in stone was the jury's assertion of its independence from the rest of the planning process.

Obvious as it was that this sophisticated jury would not want to cede even a small degree of its prerogative over the selection, more was at stake than professional independence. Safe haven from political interference allowed the thirteen jurors to resolve a salient ambiguity that had bedeviled the entire planning process—how to balance remembrance with rebuilding. It was one of the seemingly impossible paradoxes Goldberger spoke to at length in his talk to the Families Advisory Council. Using the moral authority of the memorial mission, the explicit encouragement of the competition guidelines, and its assured autonomy, the independent memorial-design jury defined remembrance as the centerpiece of the rebuilding endeavor. And it chose to do so in a way that brought the memorial back into relationship to the everyday life of the city, unified Ground Zero with the urban fabric of lower Manhattan, and healed the scar tissue of the original plan for the World Trade Center. This was no small achievement.

The eight finalists selected by the jury[40] all ignored the idea that the entire memorial should be depressed below street level. "Libeskind's big-hole-in-the-ground-as-memorial was a particularly cruel joke to perpetrate on the future of the city," recounted one juror. "It was uncivil and strangely inappropriate as a long-term urban element." The jury's chosen winner—*Reflecting Absence*—most eroded the meaning and substance of the memorial's position in the master plan. Michael Arad's memorial design only fit with the LMDC's criterion of being "consistent with site plan objectives" in the most permissive interpretation of those words. Before its ultimate designation, the jury insisted on refinements to Arad's initial memorial scheme. It required the hitherto unknown Israeli-American architect, age thirty-four, who held a modest post in the New York City Housing Authority designing police stations, to add an experienced landscape architect as a full member of the design team to shore up the minimalist design's evident deficiency: a barren landscape in desperate need of humanizing[41] (see figure 11.3). He enlisted one of the country's most celebrated landscape architects, Peter Walker, age seventy-one, of Berkeley, California.

When the finalist designs were put on display in the Winter Garden just before Thanksgiving, all of the city's three daily newspapers were underwhelmed. Judging from its editorial, "An Appropriate Memorial," the *Post* editorial board essentially didn't care about the process or the final design that would be chosen by "the connoisseurs...weighing in on the 'deeper meanings' of the eight final designs." Whichever design was chosen would be "controversial." Two things only mattered to the *Post* in the selection: the "memorial must not encroach on commercial development" and "the exhibit must recognize and identify the rescue workers—firefighters, cops, medical personnel and others—who died there as the heroes they were."[42] After this one editorial on the subject, it went silent on the memorial design selection.

The *Daily News* had a different idea: It wanted the public to judge whether any of the plans had "the sweep and majesty necessary to claim a place in the national soul—akin to Valley Forge, Gettysburg and Pearl Harbor." Its second editorial coming after a month of public review underscored the growing consensus that the eight designs being considered "fail to capture the horror and outrage, courage and grief of Sept. 11, 2001." Rather, the editorial board wanted the LMDC to look toward the "enormous, immutable power that emanates" from the "inanimate" artifacts being stored "below giant American flags hung on the walls of Hangar 17 at JFK airport," in particular the last steel column taken from Ground Zero, "bearing graffiti written by firefighters and ironworkers" (plate 3; the column is now installed in Founders Hall of the 9/11 Memorial Museum on the site). Whereas these artifacts had the power to cause "almost instantaneous discomfort and reflective pause," it was quite the opposite with the "rather bland memorial designs under consideration."[43]

In its first comment on "The Memorial Finalists" on November 20, the *Times* editorial board said, "Coming to terms with the eight memorial designs...will take a little time." It preferred a memorial that "encompasses light and renewal." Its next editorial noted that the public response to the designs of the eight finalists has been "generally tepid"; only two—*Passages of Light* and *The Memorial Cloud*—offered "the possibility" of achieving what it considered necessary for a 9/11 memorial: honoring the remembrance of those who perished and becoming a part of the very texture of lower Manhattan. The jury's announcement of the winning design concept by Michael Arad brought forth an editorial endorsement, albeit in modulated tones: "To many New Yorkers, including us, that choice came as something of a surprise." The editorial board's initial reaction to *Reflecting Absence* "was discomfort with its starkness. But initial reactions do not matter at this point," it said. With the "guidance" of the jury, the initial concept has "evolved significantly," and the involvement of Peter Walker was "encouraging," promising as it did to increase "the presence of nature and soften the starkness of what felt, in the original presentation, like an open plaza." The "real evocative power" of the plan, it believed, would come "from the emotional focus" of the two voids that were at the core of the design, voids that "movingly recall," it pointedly noted, "the work of sculptor Michael Heizer" (see figure 11.2). Two more editorials the next week unambiguously positive in tone declared that the "memorial design jury performed a great service to the city by encouraging revisions that produced a purity of design deserving strong protection."[44]

The *Times'* endorsement was uniquely important to public officials at the LMDC. It "salvaged" the memorial process, Rampe told me. No one liked the eight designs that been short-listed by the memorial competition jury, he said. When the governor and mayor were shown the designs, they did not like any of them, another insider confirmed. Pataki was not "inspired" by any. The voids themselves without the surrounding Freedom Tower (not shown in the design vision) did not assert their importance; they were not a symbol of strength and assertion of rebuilding. At first, Bloomberg only liked *Reflecting Absence* because it appeared to be the least costly to execute. The mayor did not want an excessively costly memorial, as became abundantly clear over time. The families started weeping, I was told, when they saw the designs, especially those that were literal; they did not like Arad's design either. If the memorial-selection process was not to devolve into political chaos, the LMDC needed a powerful advocate, so Rampe called Eleanor Randolph of the *Times* editorial board and asked flat out that the *Times* support the independent jury's ultimate selection of the memorial design, as the LMDC said it would. In time, the paper "wrote an editorial that became a good-housekeeping seal of approval of the process," Rampe said, and "after this the cognoscenti could not say anything."[45]

Op-ed commentators and architectural critics were lukewarm to hostile about Arad and Walker's *Reflecting Absence* and its twin "voids" of remembrance. A few defended the Libeskind plan by chronicling the erosions, while others bemoaned the architect's willingness to compromise so completely. The "revised memorial," remarked Martin C. Pedersen, executive editor of the widely read design magazine, *Metropolis*, "has resulted in the near-erasure of 'Memory Foundations.'" What remains, he added, "are its weakest elements: the 1776-foot Freedom Tower (designed by David Childs) and the massing of the future office buildings (dictated by the lease agreements)."[46]

The jury's decision put LMDC's Rampe in a bind. "Kevin Rampe couldn't reverse the independent jury, nor could he afford to alienate Libeskind, whose ideas for Ground Zero had been enthusiastically endorsed by Pataki, Rampe's boss," Goldberger wrote in the *New Yorker*. "The solution to this dilemma was, like everything else at Ground Zero, a delicately stitched together web of politics, policy, and disingenuous public statements." Viewed through the lens of interests competing for primacy on this contested ground, the LMDC's memorial design contest allowed its independent jury to make the first unassailable claim on the remembrance-versus-rebuilding conflict separate and apart from other forces that inevitably put the development corporation at a disadvantage relative to the Port Authority or the site's leaseholders. "We said from the beginning—and I think the selection by the jury shows that we didn't just say it, we meant it—that the memorial is the centerpiece," Rampe said with a touch of institutional self-congratulation soon after the agency had announced the winning design.[47]

ACCOMMODATION STRUGGLES

Almost no decision at Ground Zero was going unchallenged. However well considered and publicly vetted, the plans for rebuilding could not possibly satisfy everyone; that was a given. Powerful constituencies were always trying to influence decisions. At Ground Zero, even the smallest of decisions could become overly endowed with significance, both symbolic and real. New York City and its citizens were groping about to find post-9/11 equilibrium. And sometimes, the contentious groping wasn't all that pretty.

Going from a conceptual design to reality evoked much angst. A concept like the footprints, for example, was full of ambiguity and sparked many a battle between the Port Authority and the families, Silverstein and the families, and the LMDC and the residents of the adjacent community. Arad and Walker's memorial design endorsed the literal meaning of preserving the footprints as symbolic of representation of loss and remembrance—of individuals *and* the twin towers. "This design works," Maya Lin wrote in a letter to her jury colleagues, "because it has the strength to let the footprints be the memorial—not to try to upstage such a real and historic place with extra aesthetic form added to the site for arbitrary and additional meaning." The minimalist architect was persuasive in her advocacy of *Reflecting Absence*. The jury chose that vision based on its "powerful, yet simple articulation of the footprints of the Twin Towers," which "made the voids left by the destruction the primary symbols of our loss."[48]

The original competition guidelines had specified that the designers "make visible the footprints of the original World Trade Center towers," and all those making the final cut interpreted that to mean the simulated outlines; the LMDC later amended the brief, adding "access to the footprints at bedrock" to the program criteria. Just how much access to bedrock was necessary was left unspecified, in keeping with the jury's call for creativity unconstrained. Like the seven other finalists in the design competition, Arad and Walker's design made no provision for exposing the full extent of the tower columns at bedrock. "They are still there, row upon stubby row of rusting steel remnants, abandoned in the rubble. Barely visible, they appear thoroughly unremarkable. But this is ground zero rubble," Glenn Collins and Dunlap wrote. "And the remnants mark the footprints of the national wound."[49]

The symbolism of the bedrock concept could not be overstated. Although the towers' footprints rested upon a thick slab of concrete, not the real bedrock of Manhattan schist that provides structural stability and support for the city's skyscrapers, the distinction between the symbolic and literal did not hold meaning, especially for those many families who never received the remains of their lost ones. "A lot of people feel that the remains were fused with the earth, and others see it as more of a symbolic thing," remarked a spokesman for the Coalition of 9/11 families.[50] Access to the footprints was exceedingly important to many 9/11 family members, though there was no unanimity of opinion among them. "Fighting for the footprints" continued to generate controversy for more than two years and lawsuits aimed at stopping construction at Ground Zero. It became a preservation battle replete with multiple questions about what exactly constituted the "footprints."

The conflict engaged several preservation groups, including the well-respected nonprofit National Trust for Historic Preservation, which argued in a terse letter to the Port Authority that access to the footprints is "an absolutely fundamental historic preservation issue."[51] The LMDC believed it had been sensitive to the historical preservation process. In its view, the meaningful footprints were the perimeter columns themselves; the memorial space, exhibition galleries, and back-of-the-house functions (water pumps, water tanks, and electrical equipment) would be "within the perimeters formed by the truncated underground remnants of the columns that once supported the towers' facades." Building to the LMDC's plan, explained Dunlap in typical command of the physical details of a plan, "would require new walls inside the tower outlines and new floors over those parts of the original concrete foundation slabs that are heavily damaged or otherwise unusable." This was unacceptable to the preservationists who insisted that the footprints be considered "as a whole," that is, the perimeter columns and all of the original structural material within their outlines, including the box-beam column remnants. The then president of the development corporation, Stefan Pryor (2005–2006), responded that "the public mandate was to ensure that the footprints contained the memorial. Now what seems to have evolved is the point of view that they ought to contain nothing at all." This, he said, was a position "that goes too far."[52] Ultimately, reality dictated that symbolism prevail: The pool-filled voids of *Reflected Absence* reside within but do not define the footprints, and they are 31 percent smaller than the actual twin tower footprints. "Each pool," Dunlap explained, "will be a 176-foot square, centered within the original 211-foot-10-inch-square footprint," occupying 1.42 acres in contrast to the 2.06 acres occupied by the twin towers.[53]

The issue of "sacred ground" continually triggered heated debates, some more troublesome than others. Viewing Ground Zero apart from its context within the city at large and its position as a distinct realm in lower Manhattan led to conflicts between the families and neighboring residents. The fact that the terrorist attack did not just destroy a building, as in the case of the Federal Building in Oklahoma City, but tore a gigantic emotional hole in the heart of an urban neighborhood that was also the nation's third largest business district and had to be rebuilt made the memorialization of loss terribly complex. A dividing line existed between many of the 9/11 families and others who were part of the downtown residential neighborhood. Self-appointed spokespeople for the families wanted loss commemorated, memorialized, a cemetery-like experience. The community of residents, restaurant owners, architects, developers, and civic groups, on the other hand, mourned loss in general and those they knew who had died, but they wanted to revive the life of the community and build for the future. There was no right or wrong here; the concerns and desires of each group were legitimate but seemingly irreconcilable. The challenge of the memorialization process was to find commonalities where a shared solution could exist. This would come to be as Arad and Walker's design for the memorial evolved through difficult noisy public conflicts, as detailed in a later chapter.

The first set of plans prepared by the Port Authority proposed putting bus garages underneath what the Coalition of 9/11 Families called the "artificial footprints." Coalition members, by turns angry and increasingly vocal, wanted the areas beneath the towers to remain void of any construction. Absent those absolute conditions, its leader, Anthony Gardner, said "I don't think this site would have any historical relevance to future generations because future generations will stand on an artificial footprint and say, well, what was so incredible about this attack, why should I be moved when there is a bus garage on the true ground that this happened on."[54] Running interference for the family members, for whom he felt genuine sympathy, Governor Pataki went on record to define the "footprints" of the twin towers as extending from ground level all the way down to bedrock, some seventy feet below.

No one questioned the need for bus parking, just where it should go. Rebuilding officials believed bus parking for more than one hundred buses was necessary to accommodate the millions of people expected to visit the memorial each year, which they believed would be the most visited memorial in the United States. Its proximity to monuments like the Statue of Liberty, Ellis Island, or Federal Hall would further increase the demand for bus parking, so they reasoned. Downtown residents of Battery Park City and nearby neighborhoods had long been vocal about the environmental and safety issues of commuter buses that spent the day parked in lower Manhattan, sometimes idling for hours; they were understandably anxious about the volume of buses that would bring tourists to the site. "The operative word" was "home," said one resident member of Community Board 1; this neighborhood was their home, the home of their children, and they were concerned about neighborhood livability. As this particular discussion heated up at a forum organized by the LMDC to enable jurors for the design competition to hear ideas from members of the development corporation's advisory councils, one family member said she was being "honest" in "struggling with the request for lifestyle enhancements as far as connectivity [an above-grade memorial] and bringing the bus depot underground. The site is not a new land of opportunity.... [M]urder was committed there.... [I]t is a memorial."[55]

The amplitude of emotion was increasing. After consideration of an alternative site at Battery Park City for the underground garage, the issue was finally settled when officials from both the LMDC and the PA agreed to expand the area for rebuilding by acquiring two blocks south of the Trade Center; this allowed for the accommodation of the Port Authority's site infrastructure (other than the preexisting PATH train tracks) elsewhere than under the symbolically sacred footprints, as well as full restoration of ten million square feet of office space. The changes made as part of the revised master plan in September 2003 temporarily satisfied these family members; it was an early success that clearly revealed the temporal political power of the families and the difficulty of saying no to their heartfelt requests that the souls of their loved ones rest in peace on sacred ground. It was, however, but the beginning of future battles between the LMDC and the

Port Authority and the small set of activist family groups who fought to preserve bedrock access to the footprints, the box-beam column remnants, and the inclusive sanctity of the entire area within the slurry wall known as the bathtub within which the footprints sat. Time would differentiate these groups from the majority of families of the victims. A shared solution could be found for some of the sacred-ground arguments, but not all.

The footprints commitment presented LMDC officials with another sensitive site-planning issue: how to balance retailing and reverence. Retail shops could not be too close to the footprints, too close to commemoration. What, however, was far enough away? Retail space would help "reanimate a devastated precinct," but it needed to be done in "muted, respectful tones" a respectful distance from the memorial; it could not be too close to where "a horrific event occurred." This, Dunlap remarked, "poses planning challenges rivaling those faced by the memorial, the Freedom Tower, and the combined PATH terminal and transportation hub."[56] The challenges were simultaneously political. Retail space could be rebuilt underground, much like that in the former concourse on the site, or accommodated at street level in the two office towers aligned with Church Street where the shops would visually meet the memorial. The Port Authority's preliminary plans for rebuilding much of the retail space—along underground passageways connecting the PATH commuter line, various subway lines, and the Trade Center—ran afoul of the city's firmly held planning objectives for the site. And integrating retail shops into the commercial towers required pushing the lobbies of Silverstein's towers up to the third floor. The developer adamantly opposed such "sky lobbies," because he wanted visible elegant lobbies on the ground floor, accessible from the street, and believed that any other arrangement would hurt demand for his office space from his intended tenants, financial-services companies.

City officials had been pressing the LMDC for months on how the master plan would detail the treatment of retail frontage and through streets. These details were central to its planning agenda for reintegrating the site into lower Manhattan, creating pedestrian-friendly neighborhoods, and restoring the vitality of the streets surrounding the Trade Center. "The site must have a retail district that will be a regional destination while being respectful of the memorial," said Deputy Mayor Daniel L. Doctoroff. Downtown residents and civic groups also had been calling for retail shops to be rebuilt at ground level. The consensus around the city's position on retail clashed with that of the Port Authority and its retail leaseholder, Westfield America, both of which sought to create a robust revenue stream from a more extensive shopping mall, both below and above, than what had existed in the original complex. The city wanted almost two-thirds more ground-level retail space—nearly 187,000 square feet—than was being shown in the still-evolving "refined" master plan in the fall of 2003.[57]

Confident in their position, city officials persisted in demanding a role in how the Trade Center redevelopment plan would reshape the cityscape. "Currently, the most important unresolved issue," Doctoroff wrote in a detailed eight-page letter dated October 17, 2003, to PA executive director Seymour, "is the plan for the ground level: how retail, streets, open spaces, and sidewalks will work together to ensure that the site is full of people walking the streets, shopping in the stores and spilling over to the rest of Lower Manhattan." Making this happen, creating "the right public realm with the right kind of retail," could not be "decided by the number of square feet," but by the details of an urban design plan that specified where the retail space would be located and how it would connect to the area's public spaces and streets.[58]

The city wanted in on those details of the final site plan. The timing of his sixteen-point letter coming the day before Governor Pataki was scheduled to give a speech on the future of lower Manhattan hardly seemed coincidental, though Doctoroff said otherwise. The point of the letter, he argued, was to "crystallize in written form where we think we have to go from here."[59] On this point, the city had the power to press its position because it held regulatory power over streets and sidewalks surrounding the site. The LMDC's decision to expand the site for rebuilding by incorporating two blocks just south of Ground Zero into the master plan gave it a second point of leverage: In order to expand the site, the Port Authority and the LMDC needed the city's approval to discontinue use of Cedar Street and a portion of Washington Street.

The *World Trade Center Memorial and Cultural Program General Project Plan* (*GPP*) produced by the LMDC as the lead agency for the project established a broad framework for development over time, and by statute was subject to review by the City Planning Commission. Completed in early March 2004, the commission's full fourteen-page review "identified a small number" of changes to be made in the *GPP*, which were in line with the city's *Vision for Lower Manhattan* put forth by Mayor Bloomberg at the end of 2002. The Planning Commission asked the LMDC to restore Dey and Cortlandt Streets between Church and Greenwich Streets. Restoring these streets promised to knit the site back into the street grid but it would conflict with the Port Authority's ambitions for the site, as well as those of the developer, who was constantly pushing back on the master plan. The city further sought to insert language into the *GPP* that would give the Department of City Planning a role in adoption and modification of design guidelines for the site "commensurate with that of the LMDC and the Port Authority." This language putting the department on par with the LMDC and PA was not a mere bureaucratic piece of technical drafting but rather a political thrust to insert the city into the planning arena of Ground Zero. It would prove to be critical a couple of years later, when Planning Commissioner Burden became judge and jury on whether the Port Authority would be allowed to cover over Cortlandt Street as a mall contrary to the city's insistence for street-facing retail shops. City Planning's review and recommended modifications to the GPP carried "more than the power of positive persuasion," remarked David Karnovsky, then legal counsel for the Department of City Planning.[60] If the Planning Commission recommended disapproval or modification of the plan, state law required an override vote by two-thirds of the LMDC's board of directors for the GPP to take effect. Beyond that provision, the city could only get its way on its priority issues of open space, street retail space configuration, and design guidelines through persuasion or negotiation, since the GPP was not binding on the Port Authority, only on the LMDC.

The mayor's office questioned the situation's future implications: If the LMDC only had authority over managing the memorial project, overseeing public input, and managing the remaining federal funds, how long could the development corporation stay in existence? The LMDC, in other words, was an unlikely candidate to exercise long-term public stewardship over the rebuilding of Ground Zero. City officials wanted the three public bodies governing the redevelopment to forge an agreement not unlike the 1967 compact with the Port Authority. It did not want "required decisions and consents to be provided on an ad hoc basis," Doctoroff said. "We have a duty to the public to ensure that the redevelopment of the site is not delayed or hindered by a lack of coordination."[61]

Anxious to move the rebuilding plan forward for both substantive and political reasons—Pataki's administration had scheduled the cornerstone ceremony for the Freedom Tower for July 4—LMDC officials agreed to negotiate on the streets issue after signing the city's desired agreement, leaving open the possibility of restoring parts of Dey and Cortlandt Streets. The GPP was approved in early June, before a formal agreement on the roles of the PA, the LMDC, and the city had been definitively settled, but the twelve-page document now assured the city of "input" in the design guidelines to be adopted by the LMDC and the PA. More significantly, Burden had succeeded in inserting specific and detailed language on the scope of how the Department of City Planning would "participate in the drafting or modification" of such design guidelines. And the department continues to exercise this role at the Trade Center site.[62]

As formal codification of the master plan, the GPP (and its two subsequent amendments in May 2005 and February 2007) represented the first of several milestones toward resolving the "streets" issue between the city and the PA. This was a legacy issue rooted in the original development of the World Trade Center and the city's retained ownership of Cortlandt and Dey Streets as a "missed" part of the PA's land acquisition for the original development project (carried out pursuant to master agreements in 1967, 1968, and 1969). In a letter dated April 5, 2004, addressed to Seymour and Rampe, Doctoroff said, "Our research indicates that the city retains title to a significant interior portion of the former W.T.C. site, in addition to street and sidewalk widening areas that surrounded the building perimeters. The footprints of buildings proposed under the GPP are located within portions of this City property." Without denying the city's claim, the PA responded that the "ambiguities over ownership of miscellaneous strips of property…date back to the days when the streets were demapped [discontinued] in the 1960's and are not new."[63] The title ambiguities had not been enough of a cloud to prevent the original center from being built or to prevent Silverstein and his investors from signing a ninety-nine-year lease on the complex. But as Dunlap of the *Times* predictably pointed out in a detailed physical accounting, these strips of land added up to more than two and a half acres, a not inconsiderable portion of the site's sixteen acres (figure 8.4).

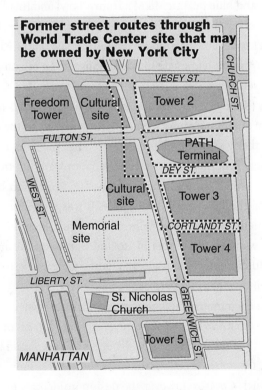

FIGURE 8.4 *The geography of New York City's ownership of streets within the PA-owned World Trade Center site, a means of leverage for the mayor's office to gain some traction on decision-making at Ground Zero.* FROM THE NEW YORK TIMES, APRIL 22, 2004 © 2004 THE NEW YORK TIMES

The parties achieved a second milestone in the political tussle over the streets when all of the co-dependent site stakeholders, Larry Silverstein included, finally hammered out the painstaking details of the project's commercial site dimensions. "The arduous process involved setting building heights, bulk and setback as well as the width of sidewalks and streets," Deborah Sontag reported in a five-year retrospective account of rebuilding. "Mr. Silverstein consistently wanted bigger floors and taller buildings, participants said, leading to such paralysis that Roland Betts stepped in to mediate. It took twelve weeks." It came down to a "three-foot battle," Betts told me; the program for the office towers on the eastern portion of the site (along Church Street) had to fit within the north-south distance—1,400 feet—but the program specification was 1,403 feet. "No one would give an inch, literally!" he said emphatically. "Not Silverstein. Not the city." Betts proposed to shrink the streets one foot (cumulatively), the sidewalks one foot (cumulatively), and the building cores one foot, which would mean each elevator of a bank of twelve would be one inch smaller. "That's one M&M out of an elevator," he said repeatedly. To make put his point about the minuscule size of the compromise, Betts took a fist full of red, white, and blue peanut M&M's from a bowl and lined them up against a ruler to literally show the M&M line was equivalent to one inch. "You can't tell me that you won't concede this amount of the M&M's out of each building," he said to Silverstein.[64] Betts had made his point; Silverstein relented. On November 24, officials representing the city (Daniel Doctoroff), the LMDC (Kevin Rampe), the Port Authority (Kenneth Ringler), and the private leaseholders (Larry Silverstein) signed the Design and Site Plan Agreement, the same day as the city and the Port Authority signed the WTC Redevelopment Agreement settling the streets issue.[65]

These agreements codified months of negotiations among the site's principal stakeholders. The World Trade Center Dimensioned Site Plan became the template for executing the Libeskind master plan. It was a significant enough milestone of achievement that framed copies of the signed graphic were evident on conference-room walls in the offices of Roland Betts and Silverstein Properties when I visited. Although it would undergo change for the next two years, this was the plan Silverstein would build to (plate 9).

The difficulties encountered in the months of struggle over defining the details of the site plan foretold the lack of alignment and buildup of an adversarial relationship between the Port Authority and Silverstein. This would make it difficult, if not impossible, for these direct stakeholders to find common ground in future situations of conflict. Controversy over the design guidelines prepared by Studio Daniel Libeskind intended to give three-dimensional form to Libeskind's master plan proved telling. Leaked to the press while in draft form before they had been finalized, the guidelines were not meant for circulation outside of the offices of the LMDC, the PA, and Silverstein Properties and his architect, SOM. They were quickly criticized as "restrictive" by one official and as "onerous" and "proscriptive" with "little room left...for anyone to exercise their originality and talent" by a couple of high-profile architects who had been asked to review them by the *New York Post*. The guidelines "dictated the shape and size of every office tower so precisely that other architects would have had little leeway to pursue significantly different designs of their own," Dunlap reported. *Times* architectural critic Herbert Muschamp jumped on the opportunity to display his dislike for "Libeskind's inflated ambitions for the World Trade Center site," asserting that the guidelines "reveal the extent to which such structures have dishonored the ground zero design process, which was supposed to be open and democratic." His critical attack, wrote Robert Ivy of *Architectural Record Magazine*, "outrageously relates the building forms to neo-Fascism." It was a superficial reading of history close to slander. In an op-ed for the *Times*, "A Houston On the Hudson?,"[66] Libeskind's team member on the project, Gary Hack, urban designer and dean of the School of Design at the University of Pennsylvania, argued from an experienced city planner's perspective why design guidelines were needed. By this time, after the leak-driven controversy played out in the press, design guidelines were likely to be negotiated on a case-by-case basis—a pattern of practice in New York City development.

More than two years later, after draft forms of the design guidelines had been circulating all that time, still no guidelines were in place. "How many commercial buildings will be designed at the World Trade Center site before the official World Trade Center Commercial Design Guidelines are issued?" Dunlap asked. The executive director of the New York chapter of the American Institute of Architects, Fredric M. Bell, complained that without design guidelines "Libeskind's site plan is but a poetic invocation to do the right thing." When Larry Silverstein was asked at a news conference in late December 2005 if the tower (200 Greenwich Street) being designed by architect Lord Norman Foster would follow the design guidelines, the developer replied that it would follow the master site plan, which was not exactly "an ironclad" commitment to follow the current guidelines.[67]

As a tool for guiding development in New York City, design guidelines have a history. They were first championed by the innovative Urban Design Group created in 1967 as part of Mayor John V. Lindsay's administration. The group became well known for implementing district urban design plans though special zoning districts and helped establish design in the city's approach to new development. It was an in-house consulting resource within the Department of City Planning, and urban designers were also added to the staffs of the five borough offices of the department. It continued under the administrations of Abraham D. Beame (1974–1977) and Edward I. Koch (1977–1989), but gradually diminished in importance under the later administrations until only a few urban designers remained on the department's central staff, although urban design continued to be a significant function of the department's borough offices. In 2007, during the Bloomberg administration, Amanda Burden reestablished a central Urban Design Group, and it has played an important role in reviewing development projects and producing standards for such city activities as streetscape design.

At Ground Zero the drive for a definitive set of design guidelines that the *GPP* asserted "will constitute a significant component of the land use plan and controls for the site" eventually came into being after three years of negotiations among the city, the PA, and Silverstein Properties. The 2006 agreement sets out six guidelines, all of which conform to the Libeskind master plan, *Memory Foundations*, even though they provide more flexibility for architectural expression in the selection of materials and architectural details. As stated in the 2007 amendment to the *GPP*, they were "flexible enough to accommodate design innovation and the need for adjustment and modification in response to changing conditions." Seasoned veterans of the New York development scene would not have been surprised. Based on his experience with the redevelopment of 4 Times Square, the first of the four new skyscrapers of the Forty-second Street Redevelopment Project put up in the second half of the 1990s, developer Douglas Durst predicted as much, telling *Times* reporter Charles V. Bagli that he had a pretty good idea how it would all work out at Ground Zero whether the towers were developed by Larry Silverstein or others. "The Times Square development guidelines [for the office towers] had been discarded," he said. "At the trade center, I would expect the developer will negotiate what the buildings will look like. Ultimately, it would resemble the conceptual plan only in spirit."[68]

If the ultimate outcome was similar, the driving condition at Ground Zero was not the same. The evolution of a set of design guidelines for the office towers at Ground Zero was another of the many struggles for control over the high-profile rebuilding project. Adhering to the timeline of the Design Guidelines Administrative Agreement it signed with the city on November 16, 2006, the Port Authority did have in its files a final *draft* of commercial design guidelines for the Trade Center (prepared by Studio Daniel Libeskind, dated February 2007), detailed in 230 pages. However, I was told by an agency insider that the Port Authority would not "adopt" them because it did not want to acknowledge control by the city. And if they were not adopted "in a form acceptable to the City," as called for in the *GPP* amended in early February 2007, there could be no "administration of the commercial design guidelines" as governed by the signed agreement. But that has not been the case in practice. Although the agreement has never been "formally adopted," the city and the PA have abided by it by bringing the designs for the Trade

Center towers to the Department of City Planning for review under a "gentleman's agreement."

The extensive debates about vision, countless public meetings, forums with stakeholders, noisy controversies over design, and press-saturated politics produced more progress in the three emotionally charged years following 9/11 than many New Yorkers were able to acknowledge. Workable plans for four elements central to rebuilding the Trade Center—a 9/11 Memorial design, a fully dimensioned site plan, a dramatic design for a place-making Transportation Hub, and an iconic 1,776-foot skyscraper—had been extracted from competing ambitions, contentious turf battles, and conflicts between the twin goals of remembrance and rebuilding that seemed to defy clean resolution. These pieces created a foundation for moving forward with the actual work of rebuilding. What ultimately emerged from these set pieces would depend on numerous design decisions, financial calls, technical challenges, and political considerations—in short, decisions about how to implement the ideas would redefine the conceptual visions that had been put before the public. These all-important implementation decisions would determine whether new cultural attractions revitalized lower Manhattan and whether costly new transportation investments linked it more directly with Long Island's commuters and rationalized the underground labyrinth of subway connections. These decisions would determine whether planned open spaces came about and whether market forces would ultimately determine the timing and number of office towers rising on the site.

Governor Pataki repeatedly promised rapid rebuilding, but veterans of large-scale development projects understood that in New York, ambitious city-building projects take decades and often, as in the case of Battery Park City, Forty-second Street at Times Square, and the Coliseum at Columbus Circle, they are implemented on the basis of a second (maybe third) plan, but rarely on the first—the first plan serving as a platform for debate and modification. Getting to the point of having a workable plan for advancing rebuilding had been a formidable challenge for a city known for its intense and fractious development politics. Challenges, however, were about to break open in the charged political arena of Ground Zero.

May 5, 2005. SPENCER PLATT/GETTY NEWS/GETTY IMAGES

PART III
CHALLENGES TO THE PLAN (2005–2006)

CHAPTER 9

Open to Revision

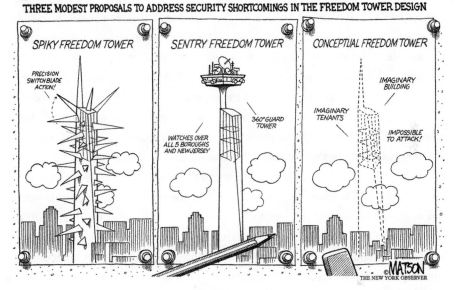

FIGURE 9.1 RJ Matson/The New York Observer

When LMDC officials announced Studio Daniel Libeskind's winning master plan *Memory Foundations* in late February 2003, it marked the moment of inspiration for rebuilding Ground Zero. After the controversies and conflicts of a contentious planning process, a general sense of optimism prevailed, and a worldwide public reasonably expected progress to follow. The moment of inspiration proved all too fleeting; the consensus behind the plan, all too fragile. As rebuilding moved from conceptual vision to detailed plans to building execution, conflicts erupted continually. Interventions and accommodations to the politics of each stakeholder on the site kept eroding the symbolic aspirations of Libeskind's vision, leaving but three signature elements: the 1,776-foot height of the Freedom Tower, the elusive "Wedge of Light," and a slice of the surviving seventy-foot-deep slurry wall that kept the subterranean waters of the Hudson River from pouring into the pit of total destruction. This was not totally unexpected. Doubts about the design vision's durability emerged immediately, called out in news headlines on the day of the winning announcement: "Design Decision Won't End Row at Ground Zero" (*WSJ*), "A Memorial, Yes, but Battle Lines Form for Everything Else at Ground Zero" (*NYT*), "Plan Picked, but Reborn Towers Won't Really Look like This" (*DN*). The rancorous conflict that followed, though, was especially bitter (figure 9.1).

Continuous accommodations revealed just how vulnerable Libeskind's vision was. Like most entries in a design competition, the vision "is more a sketch of the future than a final plan."[1] Any plan for Ground Zero would have been vulnerable for several reasons—prime among them, the overly endowed significance of the site and the balkanized reality that no single institution or person governed over decision-making, except perhaps Governor Pataki. Although *Memory Foundations* showed that the competing claims of the sacred and the secular could coexist on the site, what it could not do, what none of the other potential design plans could have done either, is solve the two-master problem: the dueling claims of control by the site's public entities and private interests—the PA as land owner with LMDC as public planning agent and Larry Silverstein as driver of the private profit-making interests. Tension between the political needs of the public sector and the commercial demands of the private investors permeated conflict after conflict. With the rebuilding lacking an overarching governance structure for clarifying the inevitable trade-offs and resolving the inevitable disputes, conflicts rose to the top before Governor Pataki swooped down into the fray of crisis to settle what he could. He held back by design. In general, he didn't push unless he was pushed by a constituency, be it the business community or the families of the victims. The governor followed the rhythms of his own agenda: his aggressive timetable for rebuilding, which prioritized a topping off of the Freedom Tower on the fifth anniversary of the attack—and before he finished his third term as governor at the end of 2006. For much of the next eighteen months, chaos reigned as politics overtook any sense of rational planning or architectural vision or political compromise.

RAPID DISILLUSIONMENT

Architecture was in the limelight as never before; some called it an architectural renaissance for New York City. "The debate that has unfolded over the rebuilding of the World Trade Center for the last year has brought New Yorkers as close as they have ever come to the ancient Florentine conviction that the most profound questions of urban design demand a public voice," James Traub wrote in the *New*

York Times Magazine. The competitive process by which *Memory Foundations* was selected—a second-try course of action brought about by "the sheer force of public scorn" for a "half-dozen unimaginative and practically indistinguishable proposals"—was a "fine triumph for democratic engagement (and inspired rhetoric)." Traub was not alone in believing it was "unprecedented." Even in the post–Robert Moses era, he wrote, "development remained an insider's game, sustained by public indifference and thus governed by the conflicting interests of various fractions. Very few of the development battles of the modern, putatively democratic era [in Manhattan]—Westway, Columbus Circle and Times Square, among others—actually vindicated the merits of public engagement." Unlike the Florentines who "thought of the physical city as a monument to their own glory," New Yorkers "think of it as a giant machine for the performance of work and the satisfaction of wishes." September 11 "marked a new moment in urban self-awareness," he argued. "The terrorist attack so profoundly sacralized the World Trade Center that many people seriously spoke of precisely rebuilding the towers, previously known as the most glaring possible example of anti-urban 60's gigantism."[2] That wasn't really what the public wanted, except for a special-interest group known as the Twin Towers Alliance.

The depth of engagement with architecture by a broad-based public and the intense coverage by the media reflected a moment of profound civic feeling. Architecture had become a matter of public discourse, a means through which the bigger body politic could embrace the creation of a "monument to collective experience" beyond the self of everyday life. Whichever one of the two semifinalists was selected, Studio Daniel Libeskind or the THINK team led by architect Rafael Viñoly with Shigeru Ban, Frederic Schwartz, and Ken Smith, "the city will be the winner," the *Times* editorial board said days before the selection. "It's not hard to see how either would transform Lower Manhattan. And the very process of arriving at this point has already changed the city....The tragedy of 9/11 gave the public a civic claim to that site."[3] Sustaining this civic claim would be difficult.

Libeskind's vision was able to convey the idea that, rebuilt, the site would be a great place inclusive of many different things; that idea made the plan acceptable and popular and drew consensus. It wrapped the political needs of constituents and money interests swirling around the site in symbolic icons: the spire crowning a tower evoking the Statue of Liberty, the fractured crystalline skyscrapers composing a striking skyline ensemble, the deep vast memorial space exposing the distressed concrete slurry walls of the complex, and the open spaces, particularly the "Wedge of Light."[4] In explaining his winning vision, the fifty-six-year-old architect was poetically skillful. At the formal announcement of the decision in the Winter Garden at Battery Park City on February 27, 2003, Libeskind "pulled together his complex ideas about architecture, democracy, and civic life" in an impressive performance that "won raves."[5] As a child of Holocaust survivors, he carried within him an emotional understanding of memorialization. He was a world-class architect who had taught all over the world, and at the time he won the Ground Zero design competition, Libeskind was the Paul Cret Professor of Architecture at the University of Pennsylvania's School of Design.

In choosing the Libeskind plan, the LMDC rejected many other ideas from signature architects: a minimalist checkerboard of five lattice-shaped towers rising to a height of 1,111 feet (Richard Meier & Partners); computer-generated shapes for a complex of five "united towers," the tallest at 1,620 feet, all connecting in ascent to form a "city in the sky" (United Architects); nine buildings interwoven forming a dense "vertical city" (Skidmore, Owings, & Merrill); two 1,450-foot twin towers centered around a formal public garden (Peterson-Littenberg); a twinned tower rising 1,764 feet, halves of which connected, or "kissed," at three points (Foster & Partners); and twin 1,665-foot latticework towers built over the footprints of the twin towers holding a "world cultural center" within which a museum, open amphitheater, conference center, and viewing platform would be built, seemingly suspended in space (THINK team). Imaginative architectural visions, bold ideas about vertical life, grand designs for the future, complex zeniths, and wonderland dreams of high ambitions—the proposals put forth for Ground Zero from these leading, globally recognized architects were inspiring to some and impractical to others. Architecture was having its public moment. Yet the gigantism, overemphasized attributes, lack of human scale, and inattention paid to the way these aspirational skyscrapers met the ground and meshed with the city (or not) failed to convince the public of their merits. The architectural community was ambivalent as well; no one was raving about these visions.

The Libeskind site plan was rational, prized for its flexibility as a development framework, and it won on that basis as well. It was, as one insider said, the linchpin of all the discordant voices; it stopped that noise. Skeptics of the planning process, however, were prominent. "The plans on view at the Winter Garden are placebos," Frank Rich wrote in an op-ed in the *Times*. "They're more compelling as an exercise in group therapy than as a window into the future."[6] Others thought the Libeskind design plan resembled the rejected Beyer Blinder Bell plans reviled by everyone at that tell-all public meeting "Listening to the City" of the previous July. Similarities to that scheme did exist, particularly to Memorial Plaza. They flowed from the program of the Innovative Design Study (the memorial quadrant, the insertion of Fulton and Greenwich Streets) and the Port Authority and Silverstein's insistence on replacing the ten million square feet. The Port Authority respected the plan for what the public could not see—the complexity of the technically demanding underground program; *this* is what the engineering-oriented agency cared about, and Studio Daniel Libeskind had spent weeks carefully working through the unheralded but essential technical issues.

Not long after the selection, by the spring, Libeskind's site plan was under heavy pressure. Conflicts inevitably arose in the process of reconciling the symbolism-laden design with a myriad of construction, financial, and political realities, giving rise to questions whether the LMDC had misrepresented the vision for design to the public. "[W]hen Libeskind's plan was chosen the public was given the impression that it was getting not just a site plan for Ground Zero but a fairly complete vision for the sixteen acres," wrote Paul Goldberger. That wasn't going to happen. At the end of the year, just before the LMDC was about to reveal the new design for the Freedom Tower replacing the Libeskind image that had been circulating for ten months, David W. Dunlap wrote, "There is, as the public will learn next week, a difference between a plan and a design, a design and a design concept. All the difference in the world." The final shape of the iconic skyscraper would have little resemblance to the competition-winning image. "No dream this large gets translated into physical reality without a thousand compromises and adjustments being made along the way," *Newsday*'s critic Justin Davidson had written earlier in the fall of 2003. Libeskind's plan "is not a static document; it's a proclamation of ideals."[7] True, but deep differences in interpreting those ideals were about to break out into the high-intensity limelight of a very public and acrimonious fight between Libeskind and Silverstein's architect David Childs over the controlling vision for the Freedom Tower design.

Libeskind's aspirations for full control over his master plan's aesthetic vision were dissolving. Earlier in the year, he had lost his bid to design the Port Authority's transportation terminal, partly because strict rules governing federal transportation officials' oversight of the project required bidders to have extensive experience in large infrastructure projects and to come through a competitive process. The Port Authority agreed to retain Studio Daniel Libeskind to develop design guidelines that, the *Times* reported, "will set the size of the terminal building, its prominent architectural features and other aesthetic elements that will make it look like the drawings that have been widely circulated."[8] The next month, however, when the Port Authority announced it had selected famed Spanish architect-engineer Santiago Calatrava to design the PATH terminal, the artistic prominence of the selection diminished the likelihood that Libeskind would have a role in this place-making element of the site plan. Six months later when the design was unveiled to widespread acclaim, Calatrava paid homage to Libeskind's "Wedge of Light" concept in the way he positioned the terminal obliquely on the block.

Libeskind said he was "very moved" when Calatrava showed him the direction for the station, "which not only is reinforcing the Wedge of Light but creating something wonderful as a civic building." His admiration was genuine, even though the new design obliterated the Wedge open space, appropriating it into the architecture of the building. Calatrava's orientation for the freestanding terminal materially shrank the grand public plaza on either side of Fulton Street as Libeskind had shown it in *Memory Foundations*. When the "bird in flight" opened its wings every September 11, Calatrava said, the "Wedge of Light" would shine through and preserve Libeskind's intended architectural expression. Over time, though, the plaza would morph into a mere landscaped sidewalk as out-of-control, financially driven changes pushed the Port Authority to eliminate the wings' opening movement.

Little more than a year after Libeskind's plan had been heralded, many of its signature place-making elements had been "altered, reduced or eliminated," Robin Pogrebin wrote from the *Times* cultural desk in "The Incredible Shrinking Daniel Libeskind." Despite repeated modification to his master plan, Libeskind's equanimity held, surprisingly. "I would be throwing myself off an elevation," said Nina Libeskind. "But Daniel had the capacity to look at something and find the good in it, to find the way it respected this or that element of his concept." Friends often suggested he walk away, she said. "They'd come in and say, 'Haven't you had enough? First the Freedom Tower, now the memorial?'"[9]

Similarly, voices in the architectural community believed he "should have understood that...the only leverage he had was to stand up and say, this is not my scheme anymore. I'm going to walk. And he never had the courage to do that," Nicolai Ouroussoff, the *Times'* architectural critic who moved into the position after the death of Herbert Muschamp in 2004, told Charlie Rose on his PBS show after the fact in late 2005. Contrary to what the *Times* critic wanted to believe or thought should have been the case, Libeskind had made it clear that he was prepared to walk off the project. Ouroussoff was on a riff about the marginalization of architecture as a driving force in rebuilding Ground Zero. Architecture was being used as "a cloak" to "legitimize what was happening there and give it this sense of being somehow enlightened when really nothing, none of the forces there were about that at all." The decisions of the competition "had nothing to do with architecture," he said. "They had everything to do with politics, economics, commercial interests, and also the kind of patriotic fervor and all the emotions that surround the site," which he believed had become "very dark in a lot of ways."[10]

Others in the community of architectural critics were equally, if not more, distressed as they watched the erosion of Libeskind's vision. "The death of the dream has come slowly, in bits and pieces, not as a sudden cataclysmic event," Ada Louise

Huxtable wrote in the spring of 2005. "It has not been a casualty of the more obvious debate over whether the replacement of the lost 10 million square feet of commercial space demanded by the developer is an economic necessity or the defilement of the land where so many died. This has been a subtler, more insidious sabotage, through the progressive downgrading and evisceration of the cultural components of Daniel Libeskind's competition-winning design," which she had seen as the hope for "the next great center of the city." Speaking on the *Charlie Rose Show* months before Ouroussoff, she pointed the finger at politics and money

FIGURE 9.2 *Urban Warriors: Daniel and Nina Libeskind.* MARY ELLEN MARK

interests as driving the process. New York is "a very difficult city to keep an ideal or a design alive [in]."[11]

Libeskind did fume over the way his plan was altered by the winning memorial design, and while he ultimately adopted a pragmatic attitude that fit his optimistic nature, the path toward acceptance was a rough one and came only after the bruising fight with Childs over the Freedom Tower design. The architect had forged his professional persona with his wife, strategist, and negotiator for the firm. Nina Libeskind had grown up in a family of Canadian politicians and worked as a labor arbitrator in Canada in the late seventies. She was a skillful, commanding force in her own right. Together they had persevered through nearly ten long years of political struggle with a "hostile city government" to move his vision for Berlin's Jewish Museum into built form—"pretty much as Libeskind had designed it: a zigzag form clad in zinc." That experience provided the groundwork for the process before them at Ground Zero—"urban warriors" Paul Goldberger called them[12]—but it would not fully prepare them for the particularly rough politics of New York (figure 9.2).

Libeskind was in a position to have a profound influence on what got built at Ground Zero—he had the plans; he had negotiated contracts with the Port Authority and the LMDC for work on the master plan, the design guidelines, and the memorial areas; and he had the backing of a strong patron in Governor Pataki. Together, the Libeskinds deployed the most resolute determination to protect the integrity of their studio's design concept, aided by their skilled and colorful attorney, Edward W. Hayes. Even though Libeskind himself would not get to design any building of his own at Ground Zero, the ambition behind their most resolute determination was out there. It was transparent. And easily understandable: This was the prize of prizes of design competitions in the new century just beginning to unfold.

DESIGNING AN ICON

In the spring of 2003, just two months after his selection of the Libeskind plan, Governor Pataki named the skyscraper at Ground Zero he ambitiously projected would become an icon. The branding was part of a package of promises the governor made to an audience of downtown business and civic leaders in an effort to inject new optimism into the process of rebuilding. Noting that the "black shroud over the Deutsche Bank building [severely damaged on 9/11] is an ever-present reminder of the darkest moment in our past," the governor told the audience he "had asked the LMDC to replace the shroud with a mural trumpeting a new symbol to rise at Ground Zero—the 1,776 Freedom Tower." The Freedom Tower, the governor said a year later in his cornerstone-laying speech on Independence Day, would "reclaim our glorious skyline, replicate that great lady liberty...honor the heroes we lost on that tragic day." The rhetoric of the day would only stretch so far. Twenty months later, with the roll of two big excavators down a ramp into the seventy-foot-deep pit of Ground Zero, the "cornerstone" was quietly removed when foundation work began in mid-2006, transported away—ultimately, never to be used because it appeared not to fit with the new tower that had been redesigned by Silverstein's architect, David Childs of SOM.[13]

The time had finally arrived for physical work to begin on the Freedom Tower, its footings and foundations. Much had changed since the public got its first vision of what might replace the twin towers on the skyline of lower Manhattan. In the more than four and a half years it had taken to advance to the start of construction, the design of the Freedom Tower had undergone radical transformation—three times. Childs and his team of designers and consulting experts at SOM were now the undisputed sole architects of the Freedom Tower. Libeskind's earlier association as "collaborating architect" with the rendered model of a hybrid building in December 2003 had essentially disappeared when, in response to the New York Police Department's security-driven concerns, Childs was told by the governor to rework the tower design, as discussed later in this chapter. That December 2003 design had, in turn, replaced Libeskind's February 2003 design concept, itself a modified version of the architect's original December 2002 proposal for Vertical World Gardens. Of the four symbolic elements that had defined Libeskind's concept for the world's tallest tower, only two were now recognizable: its height at 1,776 feet and its location at the northwest corner of the Trade Center site. The other two elements, the asymmetrical spire symbolically echoing the upraised torch of Lady Liberty and the alignment of the tower's western façade with the slurry wall marking the foundation of the original World Trade Center, were gone. Gone too were the "torqued form, parallelogram floor plan, energy producing windmills, suspension cables, lacy façade and open-air arcade" of the seventy-story December 2003 design produced by Childs—or as the LMDC described it, "an idea" by Libeskind "given form" by Childs.[14]

"With one eye on terrorism and another on what has already been lost to terrorists," Dunlap and Glenn Collins wrote, the redesigned (now) eighty-two-story Freedom Tower's "height and proportion, centered antenna and cut-away corners, tall lobbies and pinstripe façade evoke—both deliberately and coincidentally—the sky-piercing twins it is meant to replace." Its new shape also accentuated its stand-alone character, distinct from Libeskind's intention as the apex "in a spiraling crown of towers that would ascend in height from the south forming a kind of high-rise palisade around the memorial area." Libeskind's belief in creating a building composition reflected the way he interpreted New York: as a "city that is carved out, completely, as a composition," not a place of "solitary buildings," but as a place about the "composition of the whole." Childs, on the other hand, told talk-show host Charlie Rose that the redesigned shape of the Freedom Tower was a symbol of the event because it recalls the buildings that fell down. "I kept...all sides square, like the original buildings, so if you look at it in one direction, it has exactly the same profile, although it's glass"[15] (figure 9.3). Of course, the public was unlikely to get this subtle architectural message.

The Freedom Tower would stand as Governor Pataki's symbol of defiance. "We will build it to show the world that freedom will always triumph over terror and that we will face the 21st century with confidence," he said. "This is not just a building. This is a symbol of New York. This is a symbol of America. This is a symbol of freedom."[16] But what did it mean to design an icon of defiance? What did it mean to design an icon? Would this replacement for the twin towers automatically achieve icon status? What would, in other words, make the Freedom Tower an icon? Not identity alone as the nation's tallest tower. Supertall buildings were rising all over the globe, and before the steel of Ground Zero's entry into the twenty-first-century skyscraper race would top out—real estate parlance for structural steel reaching the full height of the building—in August 2012, the crown for the world's tallest tower would go to Dubai's Burj Khalifa, built to an architectural height of 2,717 feet. The spire of the Freedom Tower would reach 1,776 feet, easily surpassing the 1,250 feet height of New York's Empire State Building and Chicago's 1,451 feet Sears Tower, renamed Willis Tower.

There are other identities besides height by which bonding with a building confers icon status—cultural significance, historic importance, national ideals, civic pride of place. Whatever the identity, icons become icons because they have a meaningful claim on our emotions. In his influential book *Icons and Aliens*, John Costonis speaks of the environment as a "visual commons reinforcing the ties we share as members of the various communities to which we belong." He makes a compelling case that our sense of place—city, neighborhood, block—contributes to our sense of identity as individuals or members of distinctive groups. Associations in these environments engage thought and feeling; they serve as magnets, bonding people to icons. On a broader scale, "there is a sense in which the Eiffel Tower *is* Paris, the nation's Capitol *is* Washington, D.C., and the Statue of Liberty *is* America." Bonding with an icon provides reassurance, a sense of stability, he argued. After the catastrophe of 9/11, the need for reassurance was painfully evident—and so too, the call—from citizens, the civic organizations, the governor, and the mayor alike—to create a new icon at Ground Zero. "The restoration of the symbolic center of life is a matter of urgency [owing to the power of the] symbolic

Freedom Tower's Evolution

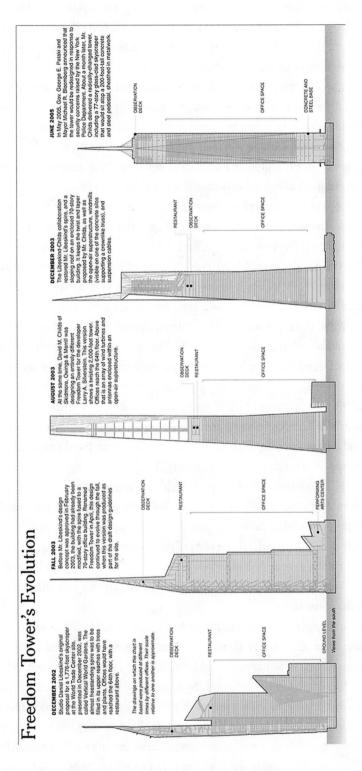

DECEMBER 2002

Studio Daniel Libeskind's original proposal for a 1,776-foot skyscraper at the World Trade Center site, presented in December 2002, was called Vertical World Gardens. The almost freestanding spire was to be filled in its upper reaches with trees and plants. Offices would have reached the 64th floor, with a restaurant above.

The drawings on which this chart is based were produced at different times by different offices. Their scale relative to one another is approximate.

Views from the south

OBSERVATION DECK

RESTAURANT

OFFICE SPACE

GROUND LEVEL

FALL 2003

Before Mr. Libeskind's design concept was approved in February 2003, the building had already been modified, with the spire fused to a 70-story office building. Renamed Freedom Tower in April, this design continued to evolve with revisions when this version was produced as part of the draft design guidelines for the site.

OBSERVATION DECK

RESTAURANT

OFFICE SPACE

PERFORMING ARTS CENTER

AUGUST 2003

At the same time, David M. Childs of Skidmore, Owings & Merrill was designing an entirely different Freedom Tower for the developer Larry A. Silverstein. This version shows a twisting 2,000-foot tower. Offices reach the 64th floor. Above that is an array of wind turbines and antennas enclosed within an open-air superstructure.

OBSERVATION DECK

RESTAURANT

OFFICE SPACE

DECEMBER 2003

The Libeskind-Childs collaboration restored Mr. Libeskind's spire, and a sloping roof on an enclosed 70-story building. It keeps the twist and taper proposed by Mr. Childs, as well as the open-air superstructure, windmills (visible on one of the concrete silos supporting a crownlike truss), and suspension cables.

RESTAURANT

OBSERVATION DECK

OFFICE SPACE

JUNE 2005

In May 2005, Gov. George E. Pataki and Mayor Michael R. Bloomberg announced that the tower would be redesigned in response to security concerns raised by the New York Police Department. About a month later, Mr. Childs delivered a radically-changed tower, including a 77-story glass-clad skyscraper that would sit atop a 200-foot-tall concrete and steel pedestal, sheathed in metalwork.

OBSERVATION DECK

OFFICE SPACE

CONCRETE AND STEEL BASE

FIGURE 9.3 MIKA GRÖNDAHL AND FRANK O'CONNELL/FROM THE NEW YORK TIMES, JANUARY 3, 2006 © 2006 THE NEW YORK TIMES

environment...to create a sense of stability," Kevin Lynch explained in his perceptive, oft-quoted book *Image of the City*.[17] The twin towers, reviled at first by architectural critics and the professional design community, became beloved as an icon of New York, a symbol of the city's economic power and a stand-in for the city's commercial history. The proposed Freedom Tower would become a signature new landmark on the skyline of lower Manhattan. Achieving status as an icon, however, is of a different order. A building becomes an icon by means of community support legitimizing it as such. How would the citizens of New York bond to this new skyscraper the governor promoted as a symbol of defiance? Was defiance sufficient as an enduring emotion to confer icon status? Only time would tell.

Designing the new skyscraping tower at Ground Zero was about the future, not the past. This "commission of the century" was about design credits for a tower promoted as the world's most symbolic, and the two architect egos went into battle for control of the design, no holds barred. "Neither of them really wants to give an inch, and neither really wants to share," Roland Betts said on the PBS *Frontline* show "Sacred Ground." Filmed during the contentious design process and aired in the fall of 2004, the show presented an "unvarnished, behind-the-scenes look at their forced collaboration on the skyscraper." The outright candor with which each side revealed its determination to prevail presents a sobering view of the warring competition missing from the polite protocol of testimonials delivered at press conferences or the restrained public statements given to newspaper reporters or spoken to other media, the *Charlie Rose Show*, for example. After months of professional and personal battle with no resolution, Governor Pataki ordered LMDC president Kevin M. Rampe to sort things out. The governor's aggressive timetable was at risk. Just months earlier when he laid out his ambitious plan for lower Manhattan, he had said there was "no room for error or delay, for parochial concerns or unnecessary legal battles."[18] The divisive differences of opinion between the architects threatened to delay the start of construction. Pataki had pledged that construction on the Freedom Tower would start in 2004, when Republicans gathered in New York City in August for their convention, and he was adamant about sticking to that timetable.

On July 15, Rampe called the architects to a meeting at LMDC headquarters on the twentieth floor of 1 Liberty Plaza in a room overlooking Ground Zero. Childs came with one of his SOM partners and John "Janno" Lieber, Silverstein executive in charge of the Trade Center project. Libeskind came with his lawyer, Edward W. Hayes, a hard-charging incisive veteran of political battles, who was a model for the lawyer Tommy Killian in Tom Wolfe's novel *The Bonfire of the Vanities*. Hayes understood the dynamic of power after being around the city's development battles for thirty-five years. His job, he said, was to lead Libeskind "though the jungles of

New York without getting ambushed and eaten alive." On what was ahead, he was razor-sharp: "There are people that reach positions of power, and as far as they're concerned, we're just players on a chessboard. And if we have to get run over, they run us right over. American history, that's it. They'll run you down in the street like a dog. And I think I can protect him. And I can protect him."[19]

The meeting that was supposed to last around two hours stretched on for eight before the two sides could say an agreement had been reached. The pressure from Albany was unmistakable: Senior advisors in Pataki's office were monitoring the progress of negotiations by telephone, and Rampe, the *Times* reported, was told that the meeting was not to break up until an agreement was reached. It was tough going, "grueling," Libeskind said; "[i]t felt like the Grand Inquisitor scene in 'The Brothers Karamazov.'" Speaking for the governor, Rampe had told both architects, "This project was bigger than either of them, and was better with both of them on this than without them."[20] For the first five hours, neither moved off position; each was afraid, Rampe said, of "being chewed up" by the other's "machine." After representatives of each side shuttled fruitlessly for hours between the warring parties in separate rooms, someone suggested that the two architects sit down in face-to-face discussion away from everyone else. Nearly two hours later the two came to an agreement each thought he could live with: Childs/SOM would be the official design architect of the Freedom Tower, and Libeskind/SDL would "meaningfully collaborate." The collaboration would "facilitate the development of the Freedom Tower in a manner consistent with the Libeskind vision," read the joint public statement. The key words were "manner consistent." Just what they really meant in terms of concessions each would have to make in practice was anyone's guess, but news of the agreement was greeted favorably by the editorial boards of the city's dailies anxious to applaud the hopeful prospect of forward progress.

Crain's New York Business had another view: "Skepticism is in order here. The fundamental issues that divide Larry Silverstein and his allies from Daniel Libeskind and his supporters have yet to be confronted or resolved—and they may be irreconcilable." Following its masthead mandate, *Crain's* was trying to inject practical business concerns into the debate. "[T]he entire planning process for rebuilding the site has lacked any economic framework," the editorial board complained; "downtown is not an architectural abstraction but an economic entity—and one of the largest business districts in the world."[21]

That was the way Larry Silverstein saw things too. "It's my absolute right to choose the architects," he said. "I signed the ground lease. I have the obligation to rebuild. I have the obligation to collect the insurance policy proceeds for purposes of rebuilding. Who's going to make the decisions? I've got to make them. No one else is equipped to make them. No one else can." In publicly praising Libeskind's selection, Silverstein had never said anything specific about Libeskind's design for the tower; he had just said it was the best site plan. The developer didn't believe the shape and size of Libeskind's proposed towers would provide enough rentable space, especially the right kind of space marketable to top-notch tenants who demanded unobstructed column-free floor space. Exercising what he believed to be his decision-making prerogative, Silverstein pushed public officials to move the location of the Freedom Tower closer to the transportation terminal to increase its convenience and appeal to tenants; he also pushed for the tower to be built last.[22] Libeskind pushed back, arguing that moving buildings around would upend the character of the site plan. "It's not just a matter of moving a building here or there," he said. "It can change the views, the light and wind conditions, the composition of the entire site." Doctoroff agreed. Officials in the Pataki administration agreed. Libeskind won the argument this time, but Hayes remained wary. "Silverstein is a traditional New York real estate operator," he told the narrator of *Frontline*'s "Sacred Ground." "They don't want to give you snow in a blizzard. They don't want to give you anything. I told everybody that from the beginning." He believed the developer would give lip service to being in agreement and then just not do it. "He wants to pretend he wants the master plan, but in fact, he doesn't want the master plan. He wants unilateral changes grossly unsuited to the master plan."[23]

Childs's work on a design for the Freedom Tower had started months before the mid-July meeting.[24] He had his own image for the tower, and it did not fit with Libeskind's. Neither did his idea of "collaboration" fit with Libeskind's concept of how the work would proceed. In their first meeting, Childs laid out the ground rules of "collaboration." As Nina Libeskind recalled, "I've never seen anyone so shocked when he walked out. He had no idea that this was going to happen. He thought David was a pretty reasonable person. And when he walked into that first meeting," according to Nina, "David said, 'I have no intention of working with you. I have no intention of doing your building. I have no intention of doing the Freedom Tower. I couldn't care less about the Statue of Liberty. I couldn't care less about how you feel about the site. It's nothing to do with what I'm going to do.' So Daniel said, 'Well then what are we collaborating on?' And he said, 'We're not.'" Libeskind could "comment" on Childs's design.[25]

For his design, Childs also had a partner, structural engineer Guy Nordenson, whose idea for a torque tower offered a solution to the irregular shape of the site for the Freedom Tower. Libeskind, according to insiders and the account in "Sacred Ground," had shown a greater willingness to compromise, using the more commercial floor plans from Childs's design for the lower half of the building while maintaining the asymmetrical spire at the top. But Childs didn't want help from

Libeskind, and he held to this position, unwaveringly. Why? Was something more than ego involved? More than his unquestioned technical skills in designing high-rise towers? More than his doubts about the structural soundness or cost-efficiency of Libeskind's asymmetrical tower design?[26] More fundamental than differences in architectural ideas? How much of SOM's time, money, and ego was at stake, beyond the point of design compromise? Could Childs have been way out in front of where he should have been, designing in greater detail than conventional practice would suggest at this stage of the process when so many of the project's economic parameters remained uncertain? There was no certainty about how much insurance money Silverstein would ultimately be able to claim for rebuilding ten million square feet of office space, especially since he lost the first-round battle of his two-occurrence legal claims that September, but his spending for upfront pre-development costs out of the pot of insurance dollars in escrow under his control kept reducing the amount that would remain available for rebuilding once the litigation was settled. The money question *Crain's* raised was real, but prominently absent from the public design dialogue.

Each architect believed he had the right to design the Freedom Tower based upon his client's position. Childs's client was Larry Silverstein, and Silverstein's views on Libeskind's qualifications to design a supertall tower were well known: The developer would say he was a brilliant academic architect who designed conceptual and emotional architecture, but his body of built work was small and low-scale museums. "He's never designed a high-rise in his life," Silverstein said repeatedly. "Tell me something. If you were needing neurosurgery, would you go to a general practitioner who has never done any kind of operating in his life?" (Libeskind's design for the Jewish Museum in Berlin was his first built architectural commission.) Along with much of the design community and civic groups, Libeskind was operating under the strong belief that the public was his client—the public had voted for his vision—and Governor Pataki supported building to that vision. All the same, his support did allow for something other than the literal vision Libeskind put forth: "The public spoke, and they want it to be a Freedom Tower that stands as a symbol of the strength, the confidence and the unity of the people in New York, and that's what we're going to see the people get." However expedient, the "forced marriage" was a tenuous way to begin. Hayes foresaw that there was just going to be a lot of conflict all the time. "Arranged marriages—sometimes they work and sometimes they don't," he said. "In my experience, they work when the alternative is sudden death. If you walk away from an arranged marriage, you're going to have a genuinely bad day after."[27]

It didn't take long for the collaboration to collapse. The design process was tied up in knots, the dueling designers locked in a private war with what seemed at the time to have profound public consequences. Each was working on his own version of the tower; there was no common design. Childs's design—a seventy-story symmetric structure that would twist and taper as it rose, culminating in an open-air lattice-like framework of cables, trusses, and windmill turbines—was markedly different from Libeskind's vision. The Port Authority was conveniently staying out of the fray, taking the position that making the two architects work together was not its responsibility. "We're not building the building," PA executive director Seymour told the *Daily News*. The editorial pages of the *Times* and the *Post*, rarely on the same wavelength when it came to public policy, were saying, "let the public see the plans," "there is no call for keeping any design secret."[28] Not only was Pataki's aggressive timetable at risk, the credibility of the still-young rebuilding process so carefully promoted as pathbreaking and transparent was pivoting on this increasingly rancorous conflict that only the governor could resolve.

"Libeskind could push only so far. Childs could push only so far. Nobody fully controlled it," was how Goldberger explained the situation on "Sacred Ground." "The governor couldn't get rid of either Childs or Libeskind. He couldn't afford to make either of them go away." Deadlines, however, have a way of focusing effort, and in his six-month progress report delivered at a breakfast meeting of ABNY at the end of October, Governor Pataki announced that the design for the Freedom Tower would be revealed on December 15. "That's the deadline I've set for the design," he said, taking the position as the tower's ultimate client. "I know everyone in this room wishes you the best of luck."[29]

More than luck was needed. Childs and Nordenson had been forging ahead with their design, planning to build their tower as high as possible. "I suggested this thing be 2,000 feet," Nordenson said, "because I knew that the higher it could be, the better it was in terms of broadcasting, and that the whole purpose of having something this tall was to create this platform for the antennas."[30] Incorporating broadcasting antennas was an important programmatic element for boosting the weak economics of an "iconic" tower, being built to satisfy political objectives. Broadcasters previously operating from the North Tower of the World Trade Center wanted to return, so Childs and Nordenson had been pushing for a higher structure on which to mount an antenna because height allows a wider customer reach. Libeskind too had been working on a tower design that incorporated an antenna, but there was no common ground in their designs. A rendering from SOM dated August 12, 2003, showed a twisting, but bulkier square two-thousand-foot structure with a large TV antenna centered in its top that bore little resemblance to Libeskind's asymmetrical and angular design. Everyone was putting up a good public front, saying that they expected the issues to get worked out, but the architects' feud was consuming valuable time. The feud dominated news headlines, yet the real story was difficult to ferret out from the public pleasantries being reported and from what emerged later after the dust-ups had settled.

Silverstein wanted to build, and he wanted to build the tower on time and meet the governor's timetable. He had grown impatient. On October 28, under pressure from LMDC officials, the developer "pounded his fist on the table" and demanded a resolution, telling the two, "There's no more time for personal or design differences. We need to come together on a consensus design in a couple of weeks." He outlined certain ground rules, according to a subsequent account by Dunlap: "Only one building was to be designed, not competing versions; the final design would have to make the most possible use of the technical work already performed by Skidmore; and Mr. Childs's design would have to reflect four principles outlined by Mr. Libeskind." For several weeks, they worked together, but with one week to go before the governor's deadline more bitter feuding led to another breakdown in relations and accusations that each was at fault. "[T]he press, the whole world is waiting for December 15th," Nina Libeskind said in conversation with Hayes over a restaurant lunch. "So we have three alternatives. One is that we agree to disagree, which is another stalemate. One is that you [we] go show your [our] buildings to the governor. If he decides he doesn't like what you're [we're] doing, then you'll [we'll] have to do it again. And the third alternative is that they [Silverstein and Childs] walk away."[31] Hayes did not believe the governor would back off; too much of his political legacy was riding on a resolution of the conflict.

Childs's tower had been growing taller. Libeskind worried that Childs's design was too massive and would completely overwhelm his plan's composition. This was where he would make his stand—the structure had to be 1,776 feet tall with a spire that abstractly echoed the upraised arm of the Statue of Liberty. That was the symbolic height. "If they don't reduce it by 200 feet, Daniel will not be standing there [at the unveiling of Childs's design], and he will have to call his own press conference or deliver a press release, and that'll be it," said Nina Libeskind. "We are not giving up." She was saying "we might fail, but we're not giving up. It ain't over til it's over." When Roland Betts found out about Childs's tallest iteration, he was aghast. "It looked ridiculous. And I know who holds the cards here, so I immediately called Pataki and said, 'Look, I just saw this thing, and you've got to get—somebody's got to get in there and bring the hammer down because you can't stand up in front of a crowded room of reporters—you, who's been the big champion of the Daniel Libeskind plan—and say, 'Here's the Childs Freedom Tower, and it's—I think it fits beautifully,' because it doesn't. And you'll look like a jerk.'"[32]

In the end, politics, not design, broke the deadlock. The deadlock had forged a crisis. By this point, it had become clear to at least one LMDC official that Childs and SOM had not intended to change their design. Libeskind's "involvement" had made no difference; there was not one element in the current design that reflected his input. "The governor has done everything but take family members as hostages to make sure that this project moves along," Hayes said. "Pataki is staking his whole place in history on this project. This is as large a historical project as anything in our history. The only one that compares is the building of Washington after the British burned it in 1812, at least in this country." Three days before the deadline, Pataki's men—PA vice chairman Gargano, PA executive director Seymour, LMDC president Rampe, and LMDC chief operating officer Matthew Higgins—met with Childs in the governor's midtown offices. They wanted Childs to reduce the tower's mass by bringing down the height of his open-air section. The governor also showed up and made the same request. "I do not want a compromise," he recalled telling Childs, Dunlap reported. "I want a consensus. The single most important thing is that both of you can look the harshest critic in the eye and say, 'I'm very proud of this building.'"[33]

A compromise did not emerge until shortly before the deadline. An offset spire found its way into Childs's tower design and the hybrid version of what was essentially Childs's tower was set at 1,100 feet enclosed and 400 feet open, with a 276-foot spire to claim the symbolic height and an antenna reaching beyond that. The "often spirited design effort" between the two skilled architects that was unveiled four days later at historic Federal Hall in lower Manhattan, turned out to be "a remarkably well-regarded design," better than "we had any right to expect," and the editorial pages gave Pataki credit "for making certain that the project did not dissolve into artistic squabbling along the way." Ada Louise Huxtable, for one, was far less forgiving: Libeskind and his tower were "aggressively co-opted by the more powerful duo [Silverstein and Childs], and the unfortunate result of the architectural arm-wrestling—an awkwardly torqued hybrid of the original offset, prismatic form—speaks more of ego and arrogance than art."[34]

Loving a good fight, the press avidly fed on the controversy. It covered the standoff between Childs and Libeskind extensively, framing it as a clash of personalities and styles—visionary designer of conceptual architecture (all dressed in black) best known for his brilliant and emotionally evocative Berlin Museum and "high-tech poetics" in angular shardlike shapes but who had never designed an office tower paired against the experienced, safe corporate architect (modest and well suited) without a distinctive signature style who excelled at maximizing the commercial value of high-rise buildings with many major buildings to his credit. These differences were real, but they masked the underlying fundamental tension prolonging the five-month effort to deliver a design for the Freedom Tower: the continuing struggle between public and private decision-makers for control over Ground Zero.

"The conflict between Libeskind and Childs reproduces the conflict between Pataki, who wants an iconic tower to echo the asymmetric salute of the Statue of Liberty, and Silverstein, who wants to maximize rentable floor space," said Hilary Ballon, professor and chair of the art history and archeology department at Columbia University at the time. "It makes sense for Libeskind and Childs to hold their ground until it's resolved who's in charge of Freedom Tower: the governor or the developer. Their power struggle is being displaced onto the architects. The idea that the architects can resolve their differences through a bargaining process, as if this were a labor negotiation, is misguided."[35] It was clear that the development corporation set up to manage the rebuilding process in lower Manhattan did not have the power to resolve issues at Ground Zero; only the governor did. Still, he was making decisions within a box marked out by Silverstein's property rights and the money the developer expected to claim from insurance proceeds. These were constraints set in place by the deliberate decision not to buy out Silverstein's interest or, at the time, to negotiate an alternative to his rights to rebuild all of the lost commercial space, and they would grow in influence in ways not yet foreseen. In the meantime, another crisis came into play and forced yet another redesign of the Freedom Tower.

A LETTER FROM THE NYPD

The Freedom Tower was going to be a natural terrorist target; its design had to be secure, blast-proof "robust" in the jargon of Ground Zero. The developer understood this. His architect understood this from doing the U.S. Embassy in Ottawa. The Port Authority understood this. The city understood this. "We tried many different things to solve the problem," Deputy Mayor Doctoroff told Charlie Rose. "We tried creating sort of a structure around the Freedom Tower. We discussed having a tunnel on West Street, which is the street immediately adjacent to the Freedom Tower." He emphasized that "standards for a skyscraper that would be sufficient in order to meet any conceivable threat" didn't exist. "The standards themselves had to be articulated."[36]

Silverstein's team at SOM had designed the tower to meet the standards of a federal courthouse and with the expectation that a tunnel would run under West Street, which would do double duty, functioning to contain damage to the Freedom Tower from a car or truck bomb and ease long-standing traffic issues on the roadway. By April 2005, the developer had what amounted to a conditional building permit from the Port Authority, the issuing (and only) agency that had to formally sign off on his building. Yet as he told Deborah Sontag for her *Times* recount of the first five years of rebuilding, "he was uneasy about proceeding without the Police Department's blessing." The Port Authority had represented to Silverstein that the security standards it had required for the building had the NYPD's sign off. Nevertheless, Silverstein asked the NYPD to take a look at the Freedom Tower's design from a security perspective, and sometime as early as June 2004, Silverstein executive Janno Lieber and the developer's consultants met with Commissioner Raymond W. Kelly's deputy commissioner for counterterrorism, Michael A. Sheehan, to take him through the standards the building had been designed to. According to Lieber, this led to the letters that went from the NYPD to the Port Authority. The developer, however, did not expect this review would blow up the Freedom Tower momentum.[37]

It hit like a bolt from the blue sky, the letter from Commissioner Raymond W. Kelly to public officials and Silverstein Properties, dated April 8, 2005, and made public, stating that the design of the Freedom Tower did not sufficiently address the police department's security concerns. This was some sixteen months after the unveiling of the much disputed Childs-SOM compromise tower design. As the visual landmark of Ground Zero, the symbolism of the Freedom Tower was exactly what troubled the NYPD. Based on its security analysis, the NYPD had concluded that the tower was vulnerable in the event of a large blast from a truck bomb, in part it said, because it was too close to West Street, a heavily traveled multilane state roadway, Route 9A. The original tower design placed the Freedom Tower twenty-five feet away from West Street, what the NYPD considered an "insufficient standoff distance." Based on security criteria used by the Department of Defense and other federal agencies, the NYPD wanted the tower set back as much as one hundred feet away, along with other changes that would "harden" the building against a major blast, although this approach would do little to protect the buildings at Ground Zero from more sophisticated attacks by terrorists with biological or chemical weapons.[38]

Arguing with Kelly on security was not an option. The NYPD's counterterrorist force is the nation's most sophisticated local one, second only to the federal force in D.C. Moreover, this was Ground Zero. Who was to say terrorists would not try for a third time to destroy this international symbol of capitalism? Who would say that New York City should not have the most secure tower that can be built? And practically speaking, once Kelly's letter came out, the Freedom Tower would have been uninsurable and unlikely to attract any tenants. The political disarray caused by this sudden unassailable objection seemed unreal. It was a "serious embarrassment for Pataki," the *Daily News* editorialized.[39]

The governor's office decided not to publicly gripe about the NYPD letter. With his downtown legacy in jeopardy, the governor was not about to back away from the tower. He wanted it built, he wanted it built tall, and he wanted it built fast. "My feeling was, first of all, you don't want to just blatantly contradict a security warning from the police department," Pataki later said. "And on the other hand, I wasn't about to emasculate Libeskind's plan by taking down the Freedom Tower." The official word from the Port Authority was that the project was two or three months behind schedule (others questioned this rosy assessment), held up by behind-the-scenes disputes about the positioning of the tower-top antenna and below-ground infrastructure. The governor was still counting on the tower being topped out in August 2006 and completed by 2009; this, however, was becoming more and more unlikely. Unresponsive to press requests for an interview on the security issue, an angry Pataki ordered Childs back to the drawing board to produce a new design. Silverstein, who had been given the report of the NYPD's counterterrorism experts, was "apoplectic," according to a rebuilding official. "It was an unmitigated disaster," a "gut wrenching moment," the developer later said. "We had wasted two years, and, as I pointed out to the governor, inflation was starting to take hold in the construction trades and everything was going to be more costly."[40] The governor wanted the design completed in two months, by the end of June, and Childs told him he could do it; this timeline was incredibly fast for a process that usually takes four to five months. In a luncheon speech before ABNY in mid-May, at another of his six-month progress reports on the status of rebuilding lower Manhattan, the governor noted that a preliminary redesign had been given a sign-off from the NYPD[41] (figure 9.4).

FIGURE 9.4 Davies ©2005 The Journal News. Dist. by Universal UCLICK. Reprinted with permission. All rights reserved

The redesign, in fact, turned into an intense, arduous effort by a team of SOM architects and engineers working full-stop to meet the governor's new June 29 deadline. When the NYPD demanded a change in the footprint of the Freedom Tower, it became a perfect opportunity for Childs to design the tower he had wanted to design all along. This would be his tower, unequivocally. Much to his chagrin, Silverstein realized that the December 2003 design for the estimated $1.5-billion Freedom Tower could not simply be "tweaked, revised, or otherwise modified to assuage terrorism"—something more had to be done. Moving the Freedom Tower back twenty-five feet at that critical time when construction would soon begin? "You don't move back the design for the biggest building in the U.S. without that being costly," said a well-known construction executive. The redesign cost an estimated $30 million, as reported in the *Times*.[42]

The major changes reconfigured the original 2003 design of the Freedom Tower by paring the parallelogram base of the original design to a smaller 200-foot square concrete and steel pedestal, to be draped in an ornamental facade. The new configuration resulted in a setback of 65 feet from West Street at its Fulton Street side and 125 feet from the highway at Vesey Street. SOM had designed many blast-resistant structures, but "no one had ever built such a secure building that tall before," said T. J. Gottesdiener, SOM partner on the project. "The design's evolution was annoyingly slow. There was never a eureka moment, just a series of confidence builders—ideas we knew would work, things that we could build upon." While Childs, Gottesdiener, and their design team worked away, the governor's point person at Ground Zero, John P. Cahill, and Stefan Pryor, who had succeeded Rampe as president of the LMDC, kept Libeskind, who was not engaged in this redesign, "in the loop"[43] (figure 9.5).

That the security issue had been quiescent comes off as counterintuitive, if not shocking; certainly, it suggests that links in a chain of coordination were missing: This was, after all, the site of two terrorist attacks. Security is a serious issue discussed quietly behind closed doors; it is not an issue for public broadcast, at least not in the planning stages of such a high-profile development. That it emerged at this time and in this way, however, spoke volumes about the jurisdictional politics and gaps in communication that had begun to chaotically sabotage progress toward rebuilding. Communication gaps in the security talks were widely rumored. As reported in the *Times*: "The police would say, 'Based on our intelligence, we think you can do more to make the building safer,' said one official involved in the security discussions. 'We would say, 'Tell us what.' The cops would say, 'We're not engineers.' We would say, 'O.K., tell us what we need to tell our engineers to protect against.' And it became this long, drawn-out back and forth." Concern about security issues worrying the police had been leaked by a member of the LMDC

FIGURE 9.5 *Governor George Pataki waits for the Freedom Tower at Ground Zero.* RJ MATSON/THE NEW YORK OBSERVER

board to the *New York Sun* in late fall 2004, but no further discourse appeared in public.[44] Long-prevailing friction between the city's police force and the "square shields" of the Port Authority police force did not help matters either. This dispute, in other words, had a history.

The timing of the NYPD's objections surprised everyone in the governor's office. Nine months earlier, on July 4, Governors Pataki and McGreevy and Mayor Bloomberg stood together, along with state and city officials, downtown community leaders, and 9/11 family members, to lay the cornerstone for the Freedom Tower, and no one raised objections to the tower at that point. It seemed inconceivable that this was happening now—however, this was Ground Zero. What was the context for this action? You had to ask, did the NYPD really want the tower built? It was such an obvious terrorist target.

"A storm of blame and accusations" broke out in the press, which was all over the issue, after months of behind-the-scenes bickering between the NYPD and the Port Authority and the LMDC, each of which had hired consultants to do a security analysis. "The NYPD blames the Port Authority for not responding to requests for information, the Port Authority says it provided all the necessary data and the Lower Manhattan Development Corp. says its didn't have the muscle to bring both agencies to heel," the *Daily News* editorialized in a tone of clear frustration. "I don't want to say the police have been irresponsible, but where were they until this month?" asked John C. Whitehead, a Pataki ally. "I wish they had called attention to the seriousness of the problem earlier, rather than at this late stage." "The Freedom Tower is going to be an iconic building on an incredibly complicated site. It is critical that we get the security absolutely right," Kelly said in a statement the following day. "Since the end of 2003, we have been working hard to make sure we do that. Some of our critics have little insight into this thorough and necessary process."[45] It took a while, one of Kelly's antiterrorism staff told NY1 News, but now the NYPD's suggestions had been accepted, and he was sure that the redesign would be safe. The design crisis was another public embarrassment. The editorial boards of the city's three daily newspapers placed the blame squarely on Governor Pataki.

While the police department had no formal security clearance system for a building, only an advisory role, it had communicated with Port Authority officials in two letters sent by its deputy commissioner for counterterrorism, Michael Sheehan, a professional military man, one at the end of August and the other in the beginning of October 2004. The letters asked the Port Authority to "expedite our discussions of these security and design issues before this construction proceeds any further." During the heat of the jurisdictional finger pointing, Port Authority officials said the August letter never reached them and that the meeting proposed in the October letter (sent when Sheehan received no response) was postponed because it fell on a religious holiday. They further defended their position by casting blame on the NYPD for not specifically identifying its security concerns until early April. An insider to the rebuilding effort explained to *Times* reporters that while city and state officials had responded to the correspondence in due course, "the bigger problem had been that the police were imprecise about their security concerns for months, and that they took months to provide clear standards for security of the building projects."[46] It was not a pretty picture, and everyone seemed to have a perspective on why this happened.

In 2015, Kelly wrote his own storyline on the episode in his autobiography, *Vigilance: My Life Serving America and Protecting Its Empire* City. "The minute I saw the building's design," he wrote, "two words entered my mind: *security nightmare.*" The NYPD had repeatedly "asked questions and requested additional information from the developer, the governor's office, and the Port Authority." Presumably this was after Silverstein reached out to Kelly, as Sontag reported after speaking with the developer. The problem, according to Kelly, seemed to rest with the Port Authority. "We got little more than boilerplate responses and thinly veiled brushoffs. Some of our responses were ignored completely," he said. So police officials decided to "press the Port Authority on this"—in writing, which, Kelly explained, "has a way of changing things. Suddenly people are on notice and at risk."[47] He copied Silverstein on the letter to Seymour and when that produced no action, he met with the developer in the company's old offices at 530 Fifth Avenue. My written query to Kelly twice asking for clarification on the episode elicited no response.

Behind the security-driven redesign lies a backstory confirmed by two highly placed sources that traces the roots of the NYPD's story to turf fighting between the NYPD and the Port Authority's police department. Since returning to the NYPD as police commissioner in 2002, Kelly reportedly had been fighting with the Port Authority and its police department. The bi-state agency had lost its police superintendent in the 9/11 attack, and the police chief had succeeded in getting one of his retired inspectors appointed as police superintendent of the Port Authority force. The appointment did not work out, and he was gone within two years, by May 1, 2004, after which Kelly brought him back to the NYPD as a deputy commissioner. The questions about security started thereafter, I was told. "Kelly has never forgotten a slight, whether real or imagined," wrote veteran policy reporter and author of *NYPD Confidential*, Leonard Levitt.[48] Like so much at Ground Zero, multiple storylines often converge on a single episode.

GOLDMAN SACHS BALKS

Security issues surrounding the Freedom Tower were also tied up with the West Street tunnel proposal and Goldman Sachs's announced plans to build a new headquarters in lower Manhattan. The inner connections between the investment bank's private development project and the public sector's big decisions over rebuilding Ground Zero illustrate how interwoven the politics of rebuilding became once hard-money decisions had to be made. The rough and tumble of New York's development politics typically were not this public, but, again, this was Ground Zero.

On Monday, April 4, 2005 (four days before news of the NYPD letter hit the press), Goldman Sachs announced it was suspending its plans to build a new forty-story headquarters in Battery Park City on West Street diagonally across from the Freedom Tower site. Goldman was one of lower Manhattan's largest employers, and one of its most prestigious. It planned to consolidate its eight thousand-plus employees in the new tower, which was being designed by the highly regarded architect Harry N. Cobb of the New York–based Pei Cobb Freed & Partners. The investment bank had resisted strong political pressure to establish a new headquarters in the Freedom Tower. Indeed, it would not move into any of Silverstein's towers at the Trade Center site, but instead chose to control its own destiny by building its own building. This was not an unusual decision for the firm. Goldman was following a corporate pattern that focused on protecting its employees and operations, and had recently completed a tower a mile away across the Hudson River in Jersey City. Owning rather than renting from a third-party landlord protected its cost structure; on its own dime, the investment bank installed very expensive communications infrastructure necessary for its business, and it did not want to be in a position of having to pay higher rents for a lease renewal. When it decided to suspend plans for the new headquarters, this crisis-inducing trigger exposed the underlying problematic state of city-state relations, the unresolved issue with the West Street tunnel, and the void in security planning for the area around Ground Zero, which could no longer be kept under wraps.

Goldman Sachs officials had lost confidence that continued government negotiations would produce a coherent security plan. The investment bank had been working with city and state officials, some of whom would not even meet in the same room, for about five months to develop such a plan for the Trade Center site and surrounding area. It had spent enormous time and money on schematic designs for security in the area surrounding the tower it planned to build, commissioned original research, and initiated a host of relationships with different national security interests. It was intently focused on the security of the Freedom Tower, so much so that it even tried to persuade Governor Pataki not to build the tower and considered a commercial proposal to buy out the development rights to the tower to prevent its construction, a source told me in confidence. But this was the governor's icon, and there would be no stepping away from his commitment.

Since initiating interest in building on this last commercial site at the award-winning Battery Park City complex, site 26, in December 2003, Goldman had engaged in more than a year of detailed internal planning activity. It had encouraged the police department to attend its building design meetings. It had conducted full discussions with government officials over security. Still, officials at the investment bank remained troubled not just by the lack of governmental coordination downtown and the absence of overall security measures for the area but by the still-pending decision about the proposed $860 million tunnel under West Street alongside the World Trade Center memorial and Freedom Tower sites.

The tunnel was a security issue. Goldman Sachs wanted an alternative to the tunnel, which as planned would have sent four lanes of express traffic through a bypass below West Street to surface at grade near the entrance of its building (figure 9.6). The *Times* reported that this would have been all too "daunting and forbidding for clients and visitors" and would have made crossing the street very difficult because of the ramps. The tunnel was not a new idea for mitigating prevailing traffic issues on West Street; it had been proposed several times years before and each time rejected for cost reasons. Believing he could justify the cost because it would connect Brookfield's World Financial Center across the way with

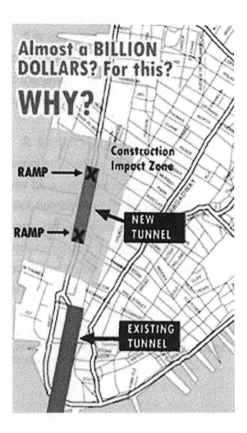

FIGURE 9.6 *The path of the proposed $860 million West Street tunnel with the northern ramp coming out in front of Battery Park City's site 26, where the financial-services firm Goldman Sachs planned to build a new headquarters.*

the Trade Center site and resolve a broader set of issues concerning the Freedom Tower, Governor Pataki two years earlier had endorsed the newest proposal for a West Street tunnel, saying it would "divert loud, fast-moving highway traffic underground to protect the dignity of the memorial, while also providing an elegant welcome at the front door of the World Financial Center"; West Street would "become downtown's signature boulevard—a distinguished stretch rather than a barren divide."[49] (The downside of the tunnel was that it would make a below-grade connection between the PATH terminal and the World Financial Center impossible.) The Port Authority's security experts believed that a tunnel would contain damage to the Freedom Tower from a car or truck bomb and reduce the need for fortress-type reinforcements and that the slurry wall would hold in such an event. The investment bank's research on security produced different findings and led the bank to conclude that the Freedom Tower was indefensible and that bottling up West Street in a tunnel would increase the security risk. A vehicle with a bomb exploding inside the tunnel could bring down Trade Center structures, producing an impact of greater force than if it had exploded at surface, and the all-important slurry wall would not hold. According to one government insider, the NYPD's position on this was not clear.

For Goldman officials, the decision logic was clear: Why should they locate their headquarters across from the main terrorist target in the country? Finding an alternative to the tunnel was the linchpin for their staying in lower Manhattan and building a new headquarters, and by several accounts, Goldman had been given a hard promise by the governor's office that there would be an above-grade solution on West Street. Politics would be involved in the process, they were told, but in the end there would be an above-grade solution. With the tunnel decision caught in a political holdup and an indication that Governor Pataki was leaning the other way as security concerns over the Freedom Tower became more pronounced, in November Goldman issued an ultimatum: nix the tunnel by April 1, or else there would be no new headquarters downtown. Goldman leaders were serious. When that Friday, April 1, deadline came and went without a solution, Goldman chairman and CEO Henry M. Paulson Jr. suspended the bank's plans. Stunned by the announcement, state and local officials thought Goldman was bluffing, but as one insider noted, as one of the most profitable investment banks on Wall Street, Goldman doesn't bluff. In two days it disbanded its downtown team of architects, construction managers, and engineers, canceled its contracts for the $2 billion tower, wrote off $46 million of expenditures, and hired Cushman & Wakefield to search for another site: It would consolidate its thousands of employees someplace else in Manhattan.

Goldman's seemingly abrupt decision was viewed by many, especially the business community with a vested stake in lower Manhattan, as a vote of no confidence in rebuilding. The headquarters announcement just a year earlier had been a watershed event. "As one of the largest and most prestigious businesses in the city," said Carl B. Weisbrod, then president of the influential Alliance for Downtown New York, "Goldman Sachs's decision to build and own property immediately adjacent to the trade center site will be an invitation to other firms to move to the site itself." It was a hard-won affirmation of downtown's commercial viability, and the investment bank had captured $1 billion of the $8 billion in tax-exempt Liberty Bonds authorized by the U.S. Congress for New York City's 9/11 recovery to finance its new headquarters. Now, fueled by governmental ineptitude, the impact of Goldman's reversal hit hard. "There's been a pullback on the part of companies considering downtown," said Mary Ann Tighe. "I think companies are responding to the uncertainty about redevelopment plans. Goldman really was the kickoff." Downtown's future also seemed uncertain because the market was sluggish compared with leasing activity in midtown Manhattan; moreover, adjacent to Ground Zero, Silverstein's fifty-one-story tower at 7 World Trade Center was nearing completion but had yet to sign on any tenants. "There's a sense, 'What does Goldman know that we don't know?'" remarked Tighe.[50]

Ten days after the Goldman announcement, Pataki abandoned the plan to rebuild West Street with a tunnel; in its place, the State Department of Transportation agreed to recommend an eight-lane surface boulevard. The above-ground plan, expected to cost about $700 million less than a tunnel, would take less time to build, and, in general, cause less disruption to the neighborhood. Businesses and residents alike were pleased in the belief that certainty would quell this controversy and enable efforts to restore vitality to lower Manhattan to move forward. "Everyone has been waiting for this decision," said William C. Rudin, chairman of the Association for a Better New York, adding that the recommendation would "solve a lot of pieces of the puzzle." "The situation was precarious," he recalled years later in an interview. "There had to be a balance and respectfulness on the part of the corporate commitment; it was important from a business perspective. The business community was encouraging both sides to work out a deal and make an important symbolic announcement. Negative sentiments still prevailed. A sense that the rebuilding project was viable had to be created. The first tenancy is very important, and Goldman was it. For every company that said yes to downtown, there were many, dozens that said no. The question was, will government be able to accomplish what it says?"[51]

About three weeks later in a major address at a *Crain's* Business Breakfast Forum, his first reappearance before this public audience in almost eighteen months, Senator Charles E. Schumer gave voice to this widespread sense of despair and alarm over the glacial pace of rebuilding lower Manhattan: "Unfortunately, a culture of inertia has infected downtown redevelopment and our city in general making large public projects like this one [Ground Zero] nearly impossible to complete." Criticism, he continued, "predominates over construction....[I]t doesn't matter how small a constituency or flawed an argument the critic possesses. He or she always seems to predominate in political circles, in the news media, and in the public debate." Unlike in profit-driven private projects, he argued, public pressure dominates big public projects and paralyzes the city's "can-do spirit." Schumer pressed for progress, asking, "Who lost Goldman Sachs?" Voicing concern that as "a statement of American resolve" construction of the Freedom Tower could not be delayed, he cautioned, "we can't let our security concerns leave us with a cement box." Perhaps more significantly, the U.S. senator warned his audience of business interests that $2 billion of federal funds would be lost if firm plans were not in place for the route and construction of a very costly rail link between downtown and JFK Airport.[52]

Plans for rebuilding were spiraling out of control. Confidence was vanishing. Political leadership was missing, and Pataki was being called to task for the serious and embarrassing setbacks and media fallout over delays at Ground Zero. "Nothing is being constructed except egos," remarked editorial writer Alfred P. Doblin of the New Jersey *Herald News*. "Pataki wants to write his legacy. Developer Larry Silverstein…wants to build structures he can make money from. NYPD wants a safe building. The rest of us want closure." The timing of expected delays was bad for the governor, who was trying to chart his political future and had tied his legacy to the reconstruction of the Trade Center site, now facing a series of setbacks. The day before Schumer's "Culture of Inertia" speech, Kevin Rampe announced he was resigning his post as president of the LMDC effective in late May to take a job as an executive at an international insurance company in Philadelphia. He was the second LMDC leader in three years to step down. He had disagreed with the abandonment of the tunnel and the redesign of the Freedom Tower, but said the security-driven events were unrelated to his decision; he had been considering a move for some time. He was seen as a "politically skillful ringmaster who had the confidence of the governor's office in day-to-day discussions, negotiations and planning," and his departure came "at a particularly sensitive moment for a rebuilding effort plagued by bad news," the *Times* reported.[53]

Pataki had to act, quickly. "Do Something, George" was the message from the *Post*. "Get Ground Zero Back on Track," said the *Daily News*. "The governor won't have a political future to worry about if he doesn't keep a clearer eye on the very complicated rebuilding of the World Trade Center site," warned the *Times*.[54] Pushed along by behind-the-scenes pressure from his business constituents, vocal criticism from leading public officials, and goading by frustrated editorial boards of the city's newspapers, Governor Pataki responded ten days later. In a luncheon speech before an audience of business leaders at ABNY, he announced the appointment of his top advisor and chief of staff, John P. Cahill, age forty-six, known to be fiercely loyal, trusted, and highly accessible, as rebuilding chief at the Trade Center site.

Cahill's appointment raised hopes of progress. "The message with Cahill is that he speaks for the governor," said Kathryn S. Wylde. Cahill had history with the governor; he had worked in Pataki's former law firm, Plunkett & Jaffee, and soon after being elected governor, Pataki had brought him to Albany as general counsel for the Department of Environmental Conservation and later appointed him commissioner; he had a master's degree in environmental law from Pace University. As secretary to the governor, the highest appointed position in state government, Cahill had dealt with many challenging and troublesome issues. He was involved with Ground Zero because everyone in the governor's office, he said, was involved with Ground Zero. Before he was appointed to the additional role of leading and coordinating the rebuilding at Ground Zero, he was being briefed "almost daily" by Rampe on events and strategy for rebuilding. He prided himself on being a good listener and trying to understand where the other side was coming from. "There will be no shortage of people with opinions downtown," he said. "That's a challenge, but it's also probably its greatest strength. At the end of the day, that's what's going to make this project a success."[55]

Cahill was tasked with providing hands-on leadership to coordinate the efforts of the many public stakeholders involved in rebuilding; everyone was to report to him, including the yet-to-be-appointed new president of the LMDC. His job was to get rebuilding back on track, to reestablish momentum. In his ABNY speech, the governor laid out Cahill's "five critical challenges": delivering a new design for the Freedom Tower incorporating NYPD security standards, managing the deconstruction of the Deutsche Bank Building, resolving negotiations with Goldman Sachs to return to lower Manhattan, assuring an on-schedule groundbreaking for the PA's Transportation Hub, and making sure that the all-important construction of the 9/11 Memorial was not impeded. Cahill also understood that it was his job to get a beam in the ground on the Freedom Tower and break ground on the 9/11 Memorial before his boss, unlikely to run for a fourth term, left office by the end of 2006.

Losing Goldman Sachs threatened the future of lower Manhattan. The investment bank represented U.S. financial power. Whereas the Freedom Tower was of iconic importance, the headquarters of Goldman Sachs was of singular economic importance to downtown's future as a financial-services capital. Without the investment bank, it would be near impossible to get other tenants downtown. It was a confidence issue. The press played on this, big time. And Goldman played hardball, doing what one would expect the investment bank to do: take full advantage of the situation—that they were wanted and needed downtown—to exact a big price to revoke its decision and go forward with building new headquarters in lower Manhattan. "They did what they do best, negotiate a great deal. Can't say I blame them," said Madelyn G. Wils, former chair of Community Board 1 and a director of the LMDC. Four months later (and about a week after release of the revised design for the Freedom Tower), state and local politicians lined up with Goldman's CEO to announce that they had reached an agreement that would allow the investment bank to move forward with its plans for a new headquarters in lower Manhattan. The cost of that renewed commitment was high: a sweetened retention deal that added more than $400 million of benefits to the investment bank's previous deal with government.[56] Count this as the price of incompetence.

The deal was among the largest ever offered by the city, and, in particular, by the Bloomberg administration, which had used retention benefits sparingly. The scope of economic incentives offered, though, conformed to the conventional

FIGURE 9.7 *Goldman Sachs's new headquarters at 200 West Street, across from 1 World Trade Center. Designed by Henry Cobb of the architectural firm Pei Cobb Freed & Partners, the forty-three-story $2 billion tower was completed in 2010.* GARY HACK

package of retention deals in New York: low-cost financing ($1.65 billion of Liberty Bonds), exemptions from paying sales tax on purchases, breaks on utility costs, cash grants for lower Manhattan employee head counts, and below-market payments in lieu of property taxes. Wanting and needing to remain competitive with others, Goldman Sachs also negotiated for and got a contractual agreement that granted it "most favored nation status." This guaranteed the investment bank additional economic incentives on par with new benefits made available to tenants or developers in the Trade Center area anytime for the next seven-plus years (until year end 2012). The Bloomberg administration took a lot of flak for the sweetened deal. "It was always going to cost something to persuade Goldman to build a $2 billion headquarters downtown," voiced the *Daily News* editorial, "but Pataki and Bloomberg broke the bank after bumbling by the governor's office over security issues prompted Goldman to say it would relocate elsewhere when the big bank really had nowhere else to go." The *Times* was more accepting of the "extremely sweet deal"; because it would "help revive Lower Manhattan's credentials as a global financial center…a price New York can't afford to refuse." The press and the politicians panicked, recalled then deputy mayor Doctoroff, and gave the firm "too good a deal"[57] (figure 9.7).

FINANCIAL TIES TO SECURITY

The extraordinary element of the Goldman Sachs deal was the government's commitment to a comprehensive security plan backed up by financial penalties. Documented in the investment bank's ground lease with the Battery Park City Authority and included in a public filing with the Securities and Exchange Commission, the security guarantee was part of an aggressive construction milestone schedule for eight specific downtown projects[58] that would have to be completed by December 31, 2009 (with a possible extension to March 31, 2010). Sales tax monies going to New York City and New York State and the lump-sum ground lease payment to the authority would be held in two escrow accounts until the construction milestones were reached. Should the state and city fail to meet the deadline, Goldman could recapture as much as $321 million in penalty payments. This was a banker's deal. "They wanted to make sure that there was a process for developing a security plan for the World Trade Center as well as for lower Manhattan generally," said Doctoroff, a former investment banker himself. The financial penalties were included to demonstrate the government's seriousness and promises on timeline and security. "The security plan," he explained, "involves the NYPD coming up with a more comprehensive approach to security than has been there, with the cooperation of Jim Kallstrom, the Governor's security adviser."[59]

The target completion date coincided with what was expected to be the end of Bloomberg's mayoral tenure, yet who knew how long it would take to finalize a comprehensive security plan. From its recent experience, Goldman knew that the task of coordination would be tough.

Established jurisdictional boundaries promised to make the security-planning process complex, politically. The turf for policing for lower Manhattan had been divided up by a security agreement between the Port Authority and the NYPD, with the PA police force responsible for the Trade Center site and the NYPD responsible for the rest of lower Manhattan. The city's police department had never had a role in the World Trade Center, though security for the rest of lower Manhattan was intricately connected to it. According to one insider, Kelly was always looking for a way in. The kerfuffle over the Freedom Tower security gave him a perfect opportunity, and he stepped into the void to gain position at the Trade Center site. The city and state's contractual obligation with Goldman Sachs, signed August 23, 2005, put Kelly in a commanding and possibly precedent-setting position: making the NYPD responsible for the success of the very expensive retention deal.[60] But working through the security-plan process would be complicated. The city-state joint responsibility for the security plan seemed to anticipate these tensions as evident in the language of the Goldman term sheet, which attempted to hold *each* government responsible for its share of the security plan. Nonetheless, the city specifically acknowledged that its responsibilities and obligations for the security plan were "in many respects indivisible" from those of the state.

It was going to be the state's security plan. In mid-May, during the heat of the chaos when all aspects of rebuilding seemed to be falling apart, Governor Pataki had appointed his senior advisor on counterterrorism, James K. Kallstrom, to oversee security matters for the building of the Freedom Tower and rebuilding of the Trade Center site and lower Manhattan. Kallstrom was a former assistant director of the FBI's New York City bureau, and had been there in 1993, when the World Trade Center was first bombed. Kallstrom, not Kelly, would also serve on the LMDC board. In a four-page letter to Goldman Sachs chief administrative officer Edward C. Forst written during the summer's intense negotiations, Kallstrom laid out a six-step process for developing the comprehensive security plan. Goldman would participate in the process with the right to comment. Given the history to date, the most daunting part of the process would undoubtedly be "fully" coordinating the "incident management and response plans that emerge" among the twelve stakeholder parties identified in the letter: the City of New York, the LMDC, the Port Authority (including its police department and PATH), the Lower Manhattan Construction Command Center, the NYPD, the NYFD, the

New York State and New York City Departments of Transportation, the MTA-NYCT, affiliates of Silverstein Properties, WTC Retail LLC, and the WTC Memorial Foundation, among others in the environs.[61]

Much would happen at Ground Zero in the ensuing years before, in May 2008, the *Daily News* broke the story that the city might be "on the hook to hand over $321 million" to the investment bank because the Port Authority, which did not sign the lease or benefits agreement with Goldman Sachs, was behind on its rebuilding obligations for the Transportation Hub and the memorial. An editorial of the same day as the news report chided Governor Pataki and Mayor Bloomberg for agreeing to such "huge penalties" and argued that the state and city could not afford such losses, which would provide a "windfall" to Goldman. During ensuing negotiations with Goldman Sachs, city officials claimed to be nearing completion of the comprehensive security plan for the Trade Center site and lower Manhattan, the one item for which the city was responsible, and they cast the blame for delay on the Port Authority and the administration of Governor Eliot L. Spitzer, who had come into office in January 2007. The *Daily News* did not relent on the issue, bullying the investment bank with two more editorials. It called upon Goldman's CEO to "be decent. Sign away your rights to the cash. And surrender the construction subsidies." Its campaign succeeded: The investment bank relented and ultimately let the "public off [the] hook for [the] $161M Ground Zero building penalty."[62]

The ambiguity of jurisdictional turf for security was finally and permanently resolved in July 2008, when Kelly succeeded in gaining broad operational control of policing for the Trade Center site. A deal between the city and the Port Authority established a dedicated NYPD police and security unit of about six hundred officers, which would develop a security plan for the site with the "concurrency of the Port Authority." According to the agreement, the NYPD Trade Center unit would manage "the security operations control center and oversight of security operations, personnel and technologies, including screening procedures and vehicular access." It would "interface" with the Port Authority, which would have "primary responsibility for all law enforcement and security activities at the World Trade Center Transportation Hub" and "would participate in and conduct police and security operations with respect to all office towers, and memorial and cultural facilities" at the World Trade Center in accordance with the Security Plan.[63] After months of negotiations involving many parties and concessions of additional jobs for the Port Authority police force, the long-simmering friction between the "real cops" and the "square shields" was settled. The city's police department was now indisputably in charge of security. Though this did not end controversy over security measures for the Trade Center site, now there was one point of accountability.

A NEW DESIGN AND A NEW NARRATIVE

On June 29, 2005, Governor Pataki, Mayor Bloomberg, Larry Silverstein, and David Childs assembled in the spacious Greek revival hall of the event space at Cipriani Wall Street, a New York landmark that had served as the home of the New York Merchants Exchange, the New York Stock Exchange, and the U.S. Customs House, to release the revised design for the Freedom Tower. They were returning to the same place where on May 12 the governor had pledged to deliver a new design. "It was a fulfillment of the pledge, in the place where the pledge was made," said LMDC president Stefan Pryor. But it was not an "unveiling"—that might draw attention to the jettisoned compromise design. And officials from the Port Authority did not attend. Reactions to the new tower design were mixed. Some deemed it better than what had been produced by the awkward forced marriage of Libeskind and Childs, but not great and not nearly inspired enough for the significance of the WTC site (figure 9.8). The redesign was consistent with Libeskind's concept only in its symbolic 1,776-foot height. "The chief Freedom Tower design change, driving other architectural considerations, was to harden the base of the tower against vehicle-borne explosives," wrote Dunlap and Collins.

FIGURE 9.8 *David Childs, of Skidmore, Owings & Merrill, explains the model of the redesigned Freedom Tower to Governor George Pataki and Larry Silverstein during a news conference to unveil the new plans for Ground Zero, June 29, 2005. Daniel Libeskind stands to Larry Silverstein's left. The Freedom Tower was redesigned to respond to security concerns raised by the NY Police Department.* AP Photo/Mary Altaffer

"The new building is to have a solid concrete core with walls more than 2 feet thick, and a robustly redundant braced steel frame." As one critic put it: "So this is what it comes down to: 20 stories of windowless fear. And a symbol of 'freedom' that, with its scared posturing and unprincipled self-interest, is everything that freedom should not be."[64]

Childs historically benchmarked the obelisk form of the building to the Washington Monument, but described it in terms of its New York DNA (two-hundred-foot block length), its relationship to the two missing buildings as something positive coming back against the void of loss, and its correlation to the two memorial pools, each two hundred feet by two hundred feet. The building had almost naturally assumed some dimension of the twin towers, he told *Times* reporters: "The building is simpler, architecturally. It is unique, yet it subtly recalls, in the sky, the tragedy that has happened here." The challenge, Gottesdiener said, had been "to build a great urban building that did not look like a concrete bunker."[65]

Although the initial rendering remained vague, the twenty-story concrete base presented a dull and frightfully unwelcoming new neighbor for the lively mixed-use district that had been in the process of evolving prior to 9/11. "New York is a city of vibrant street life and serendipitous sidewalk meetings, yet it's hard to imagine anything that casual happening alongside this brute base, at least as it's currently designed," wrote Blair Kamin, Pulitzer Prize–winning architectural critic for the *Chicago Tribune*. "For all the design's appealing clarity and simplicity, it does not turn out to be a persuasive synthesis of armor and aesthetics."[66]

If the security-driven redesign of the tower was lacking in inspiration when judged purely as architecture, it presented a more marketable image of hard-nosed practicality. "This is fundamentally a conventional office building sitting on the most traditional Manhattan units: a 200-by-200-foot city block," wrote Justin Davidson. "Its very squareness sends a comforting signal to companies hesitant about moving into downtown's unknowns. . . . Whether this lower chunk of the building will look like a squat refrigerator or have a textured, animated surface will depend on details that have yet to be worked out."[67]

Architectural critics blamed "bureaucratic bungling and political gutlessness." In "A Tower of Impregnability, the Sort Politicians Love," *Times* critic Nicolai Ouroussoff laid out his bitter disappointment. This obvious terrorist target needed to be made secure, yet as an expression of "the values of a particular time and era," the architecture was "sadly, fascinating" because "[t]he Freedom Tower embodies, in its way, a world shaped by fear." He complained about the "obsession with symbolism" and the "pandering to public sentiment," on the way to laying out his major grievance: "All of this could be more easily forgiven if it were simply due to bad design. But ground zero is not really being shaped by architects; it is being shaped by politicians."[68]

This was the common complaint of architectural critics. Most agreed that the tower could be improved with some tweaking, which the optimists expected would come about in due time because New Yorkers wanted more than a fortress overshadowing the 9/11 Memorial and because further modifications were almost inevitable at this site where so many competing interests and emotions reigned. Yet tweaking was unlikely to do much to alter the fundamental criticisms of these unenthusiastic reviews. Skeptically, the city's editorial voices wondered whether this design for the Freedom Tower would actually be what got built and who was going to pay for the added security enhancements. Design fatigue had set in.

The ramifications of the security-driven Freedom Tower episode were profound. To start with, the process for redesigning the tower to the security standards of an American embassy created significant delay, one year or more, and added perhaps as much as $250 million to the ever-increasing cost of what was now a $2.25 billion tower. Moreover, the precipitating cause of these increased costs presented Silverstein with an opportunity to call for financing assistance from government (one of many more to come), which irritated state and city officials no end; Port Authority commissioners once again discussed using eminent domain to oust the silver-haired developer whose continual demands annoyed them. As reported in the *Times,* "If Larry asks for too much money, the mayor and the governor will take him out of this project," said a top rebuilding official who attended a May 4 meeting of the two elected officials, who made it "very clear" to Silverstein that "we're not negotiating, we're building a building; Larry can be part of it or not."[69] Of course, they would negotiate over everything over the years to come.

The episode created a rift between the players and injected divisions within parties, public and private. Relations had been tenuous, but they were working, said Rampe. "Now, there [was] a series of questions: The city should have been in communication with its NYPD, right? Why not? The PA had gotten a letter from the NYPD about its security concerns, but the LMDC did not know anything about this! And there were five or six security consultants on the project."[70] Seeds of distrust were sown anew. The emphasis on security also jeopardized a core objective of redevelopment planning—the eradication of the superblock mistake and reknitting of the Trade Center site back into the neighborhood. This had been partially accomplished with the redevelopment of 7 World Trade Center and reinsertion of Greenwich Street into the street grid. Although this was still physically possible for other parts of the sixteen-acre site, from the resident community's perspective, the new set of security concerns made the achievement of this goal less likely.

Pandora's Box had been opened. "The minute the governor made the decision to redesign the Freedom Tower," remarked Rampe, "people said, 'Hey, if you can redesign that, why not rethink everything else?'" It would become open season for different interests to push for changes in other elements of the master plan. There was no disciplined way to resolve crises or enforce the parameters of the master plan, short of Governor Pataki stepping into the fray at the last minute, as he had shown was likely to be the case. Everything would be negotiated, the New York norm. Significantly, the security-driven redesign of the Freedom Tower raised the implication and charge that government was incompetent. It was "both astonishing and unacceptable," the editorialists of the *Daily News* wrote, that government let "one of the few major investments in downtown redevelopment" slip away for lack of a timely decision on the proposed West Street–Route 9A tunnel." "Everyone was in charge, so no one was in charge on the most important construction project in the country. And that hurts."[71]

It was another serious setback to the implementation process to rebuild Ground Zero, the first after controversy over the master plan had been settled. Beyond the obvious costs in time, money, and reputation for all government players, the disruption of momentum caused by the redesign of the Freedom Tower had a long-term impact as an unconstructive watershed. It framed the rebuilding process in a series of negative terms: a narrative of never-ending disputes, constant setbacks, and charges of ineptitude, which the press played upon for years to come. Recurrent refrains about the "slow pace of rebuilding" began in earnest at this time, in the spring of 2005. Three and a half years after 9/11, "the only things rising on the Ground Zero site are projected costs and tensions between the many interested parties," reported the *Wall Street Journal*.[72] Frustration from the lack of progress was evident in the editorial pages of the *Daily News* ("Adrift Downtown" and "Get Ground Zero Back on Track"), the *New York Times* ("Building on Ground Zero"), the *Wall Street Journal* ("Trump's Towers"), and *Crain's* ("To-do List for Fixing Downtown").[73] Op-ed columnists who closely followed events like the *Post*'s Steve Cuozzo took an ever-sharper tone in complaining that Ground Zero had "Ground to a Halt" because Governor Pataki and the Port Authority had not acted with a sense of urgency needed to overcome obstacles.[74] The early and impressive hallmarks of the city's achievement in rapidly clearing the site of the massive debris and the Port Authority's expeditious efforts to complete the temporary PATH terminal had been overtaken by a series of announcements that spelled D-E-L-A-Y. Momentum crashed. Business interests, politicians, and citizens alike all too keenly understood the signs of this worrisome slowdown of rebuilding progress. Throughout 2005 into 2006, chaos reigned at Ground Zero. The governor's appointment of Cahill was greeted by the press and others with renewed hope that the pace of rebuilding at Ground Zero would quicken. It could not, however, quell the next high-profile brutal controversy over the role of culture at Ground Zero that would soon eviscerate another core element of the vision for the site.

CHAPTER 10

Imbroglio over Culture

FIGURE 10.1 © DAILY NEWS, L.P. (NEW YORK). USED WITH PERMISSION

B RINGING ARTS AND CULTURE to Ground Zero as part of the rebuilding agenda
appeared to be an idea on which a consensus would readily emerge. Before
tragedy hit on 9/11, cultural activities had enlivened the everyday fabric of life in
lower Manhattan. The five-acre plaza in the center of the World Trade Complex
was a valued public space for the downtown community, however much dispar-
aged as barren and inhospitable by architectural critics and planners. Although it
"was not an ideal place," the president of the Lower Manhattan Cultural Council,
Liz Thompson, said at a public forum in mid-2002, "it did provide a town square";
it was a place "to gather a very diverse audience and introduce them to worthwhile,

exciting and sometimes challenging art." Since its founding in 1973 with support from David Rockefeller through the Chase Manhattan Bank and the New York State Council on the Arts, the nonprofit Cultural Council had been nurturing art and culture in and around the World Trade Center—humanizing the financial district with lunchtime concerts and evening performances on the plaza, outdoor sculptural exhibitions, and installations in bank lobby windows that otherwise tended toward dreary. It was filling a void left by the Port Authority, which had not given much thought to cultural amenities in its original development plans for the World Trade Center. After 9/11, the need for cultural institutions to spark rebirth in a place of so much death stood out. As a healing piece of the vision for rebuilding Ground Zero, the cultural program carried deep meaning: LMDC officials and planners wanted it to be a "living memorial," a way to celebrate life through the arts and "infuse the redevelopment with hope and energy drawn from the human spirit."[1] Everyone agreed on the ideal, even family members of the victims of 9/11.

All around the world, culture had taken on importance as a driver of economic transformation. It had become a well-established strategy. Museums were opening in all kinds of places, built as destinations; the celebrated Guggenheim Museum in Bilbao, Spain, designed by Frank Gehry brought worldwide attention to the phenomenon. Arts and culture were rooted in policymakers' ideas of what makes a strong and attractive urban district, and cities everywhere were investing heavily in culture. The logic of using arts needed little emphasis in New York. New York City, especially Manhattan, held uncontested primacy among American cultural centers. Culture was a defining element of the city's global profile and a point of pride among citizens and public officials. It was a calling card of the city's tourist economy. The diverse ethnicity of the city was itself a form of culture manifest in hundreds of cultural institutions, museums of religion and tradition, performance enterprises, and creative communities in every sector of the arts. Decades after its creation, Lincoln Center on the Upper West Side of Manhattan still exemplified the nation's pioneering example of a transformational urban cultural center.

"The quest for culture became an ideological demilitarized zone for local residents, artists, developers and their critics," noted *Times* culture writer Julie Salamon. As a countervailing force drawing residents, office workers, and tourists, cultural activities promised to relieve the unmitigated revenue focus of the commercial agenda by diversifying a district that would otherwise become even more overwhelmed by high-density office towers than before. "In some respects, it's a sacred site," said sociologist Herbert J. Gans, well known for his insightful analysis of the urban condition. "If it gets too commercial, it sounds too crass. You put some culture in there, it makes it more respectable and more community minded."[2] Culture was an essential ingredient in the mix planners and politicians alike were aiming for, and it fit especially well with their desire to add new social functions to the long-term goal of revitalizing lower Manhattan. In its being ostensibly neutral as a "living memorial," it was possible to believe that the cultural agenda at Ground Zero might be less contentious than the debate over its commercial agenda. That initial assumption turned out to be wrong—and politically naïve (see figure 10.1, discussed later).

Many months of public dialogue on rebuilding and editorial commentary had affirmed the cultural objective, to which the Dimensioned Site Plan of November 2004 allocated five hundred thousand square feet of space. Relative to the size of the overall rebuilding program, this was a modest amount of space.[3] In situating the cultural complex at Ground Zero in two proposed buildings—a Performing Arts Center and a Memorial Museum and Cultural Complex at respective northwest and southwest corners where Fulton and Greenwich Streets intersect (see plate 9)—Libeskind created a protective buffer between the memorial and the commercial and retail spaces of the program. Set on the corner of the southwest quadrant, the museum and Cultural Complex was positioned to play a transitional role, to create a sense of repose for the memorial, sheltering it from the thousands of people moving in and out of the PATH station day after day. It was the type of solution that distinguished the Libeskind master plan from the other five final entries as an urban design scheme, not just an architectural proposal. "This is not just an empty site of sadness," Libeskind said. "There has to be something that heals."[4]

In June 2003, a call went out to cultural institutions interested in locating or being a part of the cultural facilities at the Trade Center site. The LMDC had already been approached by several institutions bearing proposals to make a new home at Ground Zero; with its "Invitation to Cultural Institutions," the development corporation seemed to be sending "the message that decisions about a cultural element at ground zero will not be based on personal, political, or professional connections." The goals articulated in the "Invitation"—establish lower Manhattan as a world-class cultural destination, bring vitality to the neighborhood, and reinforce the burgeoning transformational trend toward downtown living that had begun to define the financial community south of Chambers Street—were as ambitious as the rest of the rebuilding agenda, yet not beyond reach. The brief for the "Invitation" emphasized that achieving these goals "would, in part, be dependent on the ability of cultural institutions to stimulate economic development. Commerce and creativity are interdependent economic drivers." In other words, the goals of the cultural agenda, like the entire effort of rebuilding, linked renewal with remembrance. This was no small burden, as *Times* culture reporter Robin Pogrebin emphasized by asking, "What artistic idea would be sufficiently bold and soul-stirring to lead ground zero into its future?"[5]

The widespread consensus on the constructive role culture could play in contributing to renewal and remembrance could not, however, shield the agenda from the inevitable tensions embedded in the duality of those goals. As soon as some of the families most actively engaged in the memorialization process saw the proposed design of the Cultural Center, the cultural program came under attack: Culture threatened to take away "their property." Ground Zero as a stolen possession was a powerful metaphor, and the claim of ownership became a sense of entitlement to authority over what would happen in the memorial quadrant. Once the issue of culture became politicized, getting the cultural program back on track became impossible. And the loss of what could have been destroyed an element of hope among many focused on the future of Ground Zero. The political theater of the cultural controversy promoted by the press highlights one of the most painfully contentious episodes of rebuilding and illustrates how a minority of vocal family members had taken over the process of rebuilding. It was an affront to the city's liberal tradition of tolerance. And it was also another example of how Governor Pataki swooped into a crisis and preempted the legitimacy of the LMDC.

PROCESS LESS THAN TRANSPARENT

The goals for cultural activity did not carry over in kind when it came to discussions about the type of programming best able to achieve them. On that disagreement reined, and no definitive guidelines existed for deciding how to meet the ambitions of serving several different constituencies for culture at Ground Zero. Should a new performing arts center provide entertainment designed to appeal to international tourists visiting the memorial, which the development corporation estimated could reach ten million annually? Neighborhood art facilities for lower Manhattan residents, who put entertainment and culture at the top of their redevelopment wish lists, especially a multipurpose cultural complex that could serve as a community and recreation center? Art that would honor the losses of the 9/11 families? Create a prestigious assembly of destination-worthy venues that would lure cultural New Yorkers downtown from their comfortable and convenient cultural options in midtown Manhattan, Lincoln Center, Carnegie Hall, City Center, and Radio City Music Hall? Should the LMDC select a major, well-established cultural institution that could bring both gravitas and fundraising capability, City Opera, for example, which was resident at Lincoln Center but eager for an alternative venue better able to meet its acoustical requirements and space needs than its current home at the New York State Theater? Or smaller, modest entities, still mainstream, that when clustered together would offer diverse programming? Or yet still, should it look toward the types of alternative culture that traditionally populated the downtown art scene? In other words, did the LMDC want something different and innovative but risky, or simply something that already existed in New York and that would move downtown? asked *Crain's New York Business*. It would be hard to satisfy all views. Large or small, established or start-up, the cultural entities would have to demonstrate strong business plans and an ability to raise their own funds because, as the "Invitation" call made clear, respondents should not assume "any financial contribution from LMDC toward the capital costs of construction or ongoing programming."[6] Although the development corporation was ultimately expected to provide the Performing Arts Complex between $200 million and $300 million from the pot of federal dollars it controlled, the self-sustaining message was unambiguous.

The nine-page "Invitation" call was not a formal request for proposals that would result in the awarding of contracts or grants. It was just the start of a process designed to help the LMDC figure out the scope and content of interest among cultural institutions and how best to accommodate the mixed goals of the cultural agenda. "It's a call for concepts," said LMDC president Kevin M. Rampe. "We want to be overwhelmed by the ideas." After an elaborate one-year process "that was criticized as opaque by some arts and community leaders and drawn out by a clash of interests over what constituency culture should serve at ground zero," the LMDC announced the four arts groups chosen from among the 113 submissions: the Joyce Theater Company (dance), the Signature Theater Company (theater), the Drawing Center (fine arts), and the Freedom Center (education). Early serious contenders like the New York City Opera (championed by LMDC chairman Whitehead but considered by many a doubtful choice even before the formal start of the process because it needed a twenty-two-hundred-seat theater, which did not fit on the site) as well as other reputation-solid cultural entities had been asked to develop more formal proposals that would evidence fundraising potential. The short list of fifteen institutions was pared down to seven finalists and then further pared to four in a "closely guarded" process. The designated four were not guaranteed spots at Ground Zero but rather an opportunity to further prove themselves by working with the development corporation over a six-month evaluation period "to conduct a detailed feasibility analysis of their proposed programming, funding capacity, and space requirements." As discussed in the LMDC's July board meeting, the LMDC would fund up to $1.5 million of combined expenses for planning and schematic design work, and retain the right to revisit the funding contract if any of the institutions did not meet the standards that were being proposed.[7]

Whatever institutions were chosen, criticism was bound to arise, and not just because New Yorkers are typically outspoken. People generally spend on the arts and entertainment out of a defined pocket of funds, and many institutions worried that new institutions brought into downtown might divert money and resources from those already there and struggling. When the proposed Freedom Center appeared to have an inside track, Robert M. Morgenthau, the Manhattan district attorney and chairman of the Museum of Jewish Heritage in Battery Park City, complained to the press about the competition: "You've got the Statue of Liberty down there, Ellis Island, Fraunces Tavern, Federal Hall, the American Indian Museum—they're all about some aspect of freedom. You're taking money out of other organizations and putting it into something that nobody knows anything about." Other organizations were grateful for LMDC support coming through its cultural grants program that had already set aside $4.7 million to help market ten downtown arts groups under the campaign slogan "History and Heritage in Downtown NYC." Anything that was going to get more people downtown was going to help the many museums, performing arts groups, and cultural institutions downtown. As was the case with other pieces of the planning process for rebuilding, it was hard for many outsiders to know what to expect in the way of transparency. "It's easy to be paranoid—you don't know who's deciding, you don't know what criteria they're using," said Alan J. Friedman, director of the New York Hall of Science in Queens.[8]

LMDC was unwilling to say why it chose those particular four cultural groups, other than to list seven general criteria for selection in its press release on the selection; the *Times* reported officials of the development corporation as saying they had aimed to meet the diverse interests of international tourists, neighborhood residents, and cultural aficionados, while seeking art that would honor those lost in the tragedy.[9] When the fifteen finalists were announced, one arts executive told *Crain's*, "We don't know any of the details of the criteria they're using to select projects. We were pleased to be finalized, but I couldn't tell you why we were and others weren't." Others too felt they were working in the dark without an exact deadline or guidance on how much of the overall costs they would be expected to cover. "They say they want to be inspired by what we submit, that they don't have a fixed idea," said Catherine De Zegher, executive director of the Drawing Center, a small nonprofit fine arts institution based in SoHo. "But it's very hard to put numbers on something that's not formulated."[10]

In defense of the development corporation's selection process, Rampe said, "We're trying to understand the seriousness of the institution and the ability it has for ongoing financial viability." Three months later and a week before announcing the final four, Rampe rejected a call by City Councilman Alan J. Gerson for transparency: "The right mix of cultural institutions on the site is not something that should be decided by public referendum." As chair of the council's Committee on Lower Manhattan Redevelopment, Gerson had issued a report strongly critical of the LMDC's selection process and its failure to involve residents, arts sector leaders, artists, and local elected officials in decisions about arts policy in lower Manhattan. He did not want "government to pick and choose our cultural fabric"; he was pushing a different idea for an arts renaissance downtown, advocating for the preservation of small arts organizations that represent the depth and diversity of New York's arts scene. He wanted the LMDC to support "an infrastructure that allows people in the arts to develop. That's what 'grass roots' means. It means creating workspaces, studio lofts, and theater rehearsal spaces. It means opening the doors and saying, 'Go to it.'"[11]

In an interview years later, Rampe told me the process was driven by City Hall under the aegis of a small selection committee: LMDC officials and representatives from the New York City Department of Cultural Affairs and the New York State Council on the Arts, though the individuals involved could not be identified (despite repeated attempts on my part to do so); business leaders, philanthropists, and arts executives were not enlisted in the selection process. The LMDC did not spend the time to build the kind of process it had developed for the memorial design competition; LMDC officials did not think culture would be controversial. That was naive. It was also a mistake. The committee composition and closely held character of the process left the cultural agenda vulnerable to the power of other interests, namely those self-designated activists who wanted the memorial to be the singular focus of Ground Zero. These activists, many organized under the advocacy platform Take Back the Memorial, did not speak for the thousands of 9/11 families nor were their priorities necessarily in line with those family members who decided to stay out of the political limelight and resume their lives best they could, quietly. Without powerful and vocal advocates, almost always necessary to survive bruising policy battles in New York, achieving the ambitions of the cultural agenda depended upon the LMDC and the influence of its chairman and the governor. That was a fatal flaw, as the ensuing months of controversy over the Freedom Center and the Drawing Center would soon reveal. A political coalition including the arts might not have been sufficient to counter the power of the vocal family members, but it most certainly would have influenced the dialogue and muted the power exerted by the media in shaping the controversy.

Fallout from the cultural community over the selections was immediate. The *Wall Street Journal*'s drama critic, Terry Teachout, had earlier in the year enthusiastically endorsed City Opera's proposal and now was caustic in his disappointment that the world-renowned institution had not been chosen. First, he dismissed the

Freedom Center as "one of those self-evidently silly ideas that only an underemployed committee could have conceived." He then complained that the collective impact of the other three institutions, although "serious and respectable," might "be minor to the point of invisibility." The choices were "modest and safe—the inverse of the magnificent cultural opportunity afforded by the reconstruction of Ground Zero," and "simply don't add up to anything remotely approaching a world-class center for the arts." Calling the selections a "hodgepodge of theaters and galleries of questionable worth in making downtown Manhattan a better place to live and do business," commentator Frederick M. Winship questioned whether "a cultural center so far removed from the major residential neighborhoods of the city will ever develop as a magnet for audiences for the performing arts, especially audiences for night performances." Whatever cultural program came into being at the Trade Center site by the time of the projected 2010–2011 opening season, it "is going to be of fairly modest size, with theaters of no more than 1,000 seats."[12]

Typically seen as a cultural arbiter, the *Times* came at the issue three ways. First, a news article from the cultural desk reported that rejection of a spot at Ground Zero would not stop City Opera's quest for a new home, given how dissatisfied it was with its venue at Lincoln Center. (In an editorial two weeks prior to the designation announcement, the *Times* editors acknowledged that as much as they loved the institution, City Opera's proposal seemed "too unwieldy" for the Ground Zero setting.) As to the other institutions, the *Times* offered praise for "a diversity and a quality of cultural imagination that fits Lower Manhattan and would galvanize culture life in that part of the city." Second, its longtime cultural critic, John Rockwell, expressed his lack of faith in the ultimate outcome in a review titled "What Impact Will Art Centers at Ground Zero Have (if Any)?" The downtown complex, he argued, "will be a medium-sized operation for medium-sized groups," not likely to shift the balance of cultural activity downtown or make much of an impact beyond itself. "What is clear is that the very name of the body that made these choices—a 'development corporation'—indicates the true rationale behind its selection.... The winners were picked not because anyone gave first thought to their worthiness as art, but because they represented a canny mix of institutions likely to make downtown a better place to live and do business."[13]

That same day, veteran reporters Robin Pogrebin (on the culture desk) and Edward Wyatt (on the Trade Center beat) reviewed the two-year storyline of what came to be, offering an explanation for how citywide considerations of financial and political significance exert a determinate, if indirect, influence on policy decisions seemingly far apart. In "Trade Center Cultural Decisions Affected by What's Best for Lincoln Center," they described how when it came to the cultural decisions at Ground Zero, the mayor's view on what was best for Lincoln Center prevailed. Culture was clearly a city issue, not a state issue. Whereas the governor had weighed in most other decisions about Ground Zero, he stepped aside and let the mayor's wishes prevail in this instance, which left City Opera's main champion, John Whitehead, nearly all alone. Although City Opera was not a perfect fit for Ground Zero for several reasons, Bloomberg's decision turned on money: If the City Opera was to vacate the Upper West Side cultural complex, Lincoln Center would lose an economic linchpin and the city would be left on the hook for the rent. Bloomberg was a well-known major philanthropist to the arts and had contributed $15 million to the Lincoln Center redevelopment project before becoming mayor, but he was convinced that "the hole...City Opera would leave at Lincoln Center was not fillable." He said no to the City Opera moving to the Trade Center site, and reportedly, he could not be lobbied on this issue.[14]

"Something has been terribly wrong with the approach to the cultural components from the start," wrote Ada Louise Huxtable. "A selection process that was to bring a significant representation of New York's creative institutions downtown ended as an exercise in bland cultural tokenism. What except fear of elitism and the determination to be incongruously evenhanded could have eliminated the New York City Opera, desperately in need of its own home and willing to devote energy and commitment to its funding and construction?" The small institutions the LMDC had selected could not provide "the strong cultural anchor required" to bring vibrancy to Ground Zero. "This was such a conscious leveling of art to the most acceptable common denominator," she wrote, "that it is impossible to divine any effort except the terminal safety of political correctness."[15]

While the critics went after the LMDC for not thinking big enough or bending to the desires of downtown residents, who did not think City Opera should be a priority of cultural development in lower Manhattan (based on a poll of eight hundred downtown residents reported in the *Times*), the arts community, represented by the chair of the New York City Arts Coalition, a broad-based advocacy group that promoted the role of the arts in the life of the city, criticized the selection process (City Opera versus the Joyce Theater) as a diversion from fundamental questions: What entity would ultimately be responsible for the cultural buildings? Was the publicly owned site going to be transferred to the cultural groups, and if so, how? If not, what entity would own these facilities? What financial commitments toward culture downtown would the city and state be making?

While these questions were being debated, the governor was struggling to find a prominent executive to head the Memorial Foundation and take on the responsibility for fundraising as much as $600 million for both a memorial and the two cultural buildings. This search delayed the decision on the cultural institutions, first expected in April and then in early May but not announced until mid-June. (The Memorial Foundation, the nonprofit private corporation formed to raise the funds for the memorial and cultural center, did not come into formal existence until six months after the cultural group selections were announced.) The cultural agenda at Ground Zero was tied to the memorial responsibility through the foundation's structure and mission. Although the planning relied on good intentions, the linkage of these two agendas would prove to be a difficult and, ultimately, unsustainable balancing act once controversy over the Freedom Center and Drawing Center erupted onto a page-one issue. At the time, though, the linkage appeared to make sense to those making the decisions at Ground Zero.

The Freedom Center, initially conceptualized as a Museum of Freedom and soon to be renamed the International Freedom Center (IFC), was an early strong contender in the selection process, considered by some as having an inside track. As a tribute to the idea of freedom and its struggles, the museum idea seemed to exemplify the notion of a "living memorial." The Freedom Center could be a springboard for current and future history, something to engage people in the next generations. "We see it as the intellectual and education complement to the emotional experience of the spiritual memorial," said its founder, Tom A. Bernstein, president of Chelsea Piers recreational complex, close business partner of Roland Betts, and a longtime human rights advocate. The idea was to give the event of 9/11 a continuing life, an educational narrative, and it had come out of a discussion with documentary filmmaker Peter W. Kunhardt, who founded the initiative with Bernstein. "We want to have some place that gives context and history and meaning to the whole thing. There is no one museum that tells the story of our freedom," said Bernstein. The Freedom Center, remarked Rampe, is "the one institution that was born of the events of Sept. 11 and links them into a broader theme."[16]

The tilt toward a freedom museum began early, Philip Nobel wrote in a long article in the *Times* titled "The Downtown Culture Derby." The LMDC's *Principles and Preliminary Blueprint for the Future of Lower Manhattan*, released in April 2002, identified a "museum of freedom and remembrance" as a proposal "under review that emerged during the listening process." Bernstein had discussed the idea of the museum with Whitehead and sent a proposal letter to the LMDC the month prior to issuance of the agency's rebuilding blueprint. American Express CEO Kenneth I. Chenault, whose children were friends with Bernstein's children, voluntarily offered to help, and the firm provided early corporate sponsorship. Bernstein's close connection to President George W. Bush was often cited in news accounts of the ICI process. Almost alone among the many early commentators, Nobel was sufficiently prescient to see not just high stakes for culture at Ground Zero but the looming political challenge when in late summer 2003, he wrote "emphasis on culture-as-commerce will be less popular with groups like the Coalition of 9/11 Families."[17] Art as controversial? Art without ideology? These have been enduring attributes of artistic expression. The selections of the Freedom Center and the Drawing Center were about to test whether tolerance could coexist with remembrance of the dead at Ground Zero.

GAME CHANGER

The simmering behind-closed-doors debate about the placement of cultural institutions at Ground Zero hit the national media with the *Wall Street Journal*'s publication of "The Great Ground Zero Heist," an op-ed by Debra Burlingame, the sister of one of the pilots whose hijacked American Airlines Flight 77 crashed into the Pentagon on 9/11. The op-ed was an open attack on culture at Ground Zero pressed forward with a larger ideological agenda. It came out June 7, 2005, a year to the day after the LMDC announced the selection of the four cultural institutions and just three weeks after Mayor Bloomberg, Governor Pataki, and other rebuilding officials unveiled the architects' design for the Cultural Center, one of the two cultural buildings planned for the site. The Cultural Center was intended to house a visitor's center, the International Freedom Center, and the Drawing Center. As the LMDC's fact sheets explained, the Freedom Center would serve as "the complement, and its building as the gateway" to the 9/11 Memorial, while the Drawing Center on the site was to "emerge as a catalyst of creativity, vibrancy, and new life for the community, the city, and the country" and "assume a civic role in restoring the social fabric of Lower Manhattan and in promoting cultural exchange and tolerance in the world at large"[18] (plate 10).

The Cultural Center was going to be a prominent building on Ground Zero with a multifaceted agenda—and that was the problem for Burlingame and a small set of activist 9/11 family members, who wanted nothing to interfere with the memorialization of their lost ones, and their aligned conservative supporters. "Ground Zero has been stolen, right from under our noses," she wrote at the end of the op-ed, unusually long by the *Journal*'s submission guidelines for opinion pieces. "How do we get it back?" (The op-ed guidelines of the *WSJ* as of January 1, 2000, suggest submissions of 600 to 1,200 "jargon-free words.") The sense of entitlement pervading the 1,682 words of Burlingame's op-ed went to the core question of rebuilding: Who did Ground Zero belong to? Burlingame and her coalition, including the newly launched Web-based organization Take Back the Memorial started by blogger Robert Shurbet, believed the site belonged, exclusively, to those who perished and to the events of that fateful, tragic day—and that day alone. "Words such as 'heist' and 'stolen' imply the crime of theft and suggest that TBM was created to rectify the injustice of this crime," wrote a scholar of communication, Theresa Ann Donofrio, in her careful analysis of the rhetoric of the activist group.[19] This sense of exclusivity was in diametric opposition to that of the 9/11 Memorial Foundation.

Burlingame was serving as a member of the Memorial Foundation board but she did not share her op-ed plans with her board colleagues. At the quarterly board meeting two months before, another family member, Monica Iken, reported that some 9/11 families had concerns about the placement of the cultural institutions on the site.[20] Burlingame's op-ed, however, was a shot fired out of the blue and against all the informal rules of board conduct, corporate board conduct. In the corporate world, discussion, however heated, stays within the board room; on the outside, all members speak in a single voice, typically. But the Memorial Foundation board was not a typical corporate board; its deeply emotional mission cast a distinctive profile. Because of its fundraising mandate, the initial thirty-two member board was still a "strongly traditional establishment cast: almost exclusively white (30 directors); preponderantly male (25); decidedly mature (21 directors are 60 or older); and oriented to big business (16 are financial, media, or real estate executives). Seven directors lost family members in the attack."[21] All of the family members on the foundation board except Burlingame were also members of the LMDC's Families Advisory Council. The public controversy Burlingame ignited with her op-ed triggered splits within the board room and, in time as the conflict unfolded, high-profile resignations.

"Everything I've done in my life has prepared me for this," Burlingame told Robin Finn for a Public Lives profile in the *Times*. "My acting made me comfortable with public speaking. Seven years as a flight attendant helped me understand what went on inside those planes. My legal background has been helpful all along, and it's going to be helpful when they try to kick me off the board!" (figure 10.2). Burlingame, age fifty-one, had practiced law for two years and spent five years at Court TV, where she covered dozens of civil and criminal proceedings ranging from the O. J. Simpson trial and the Clinton impeachment hearings to the Microsoft antitrust case. She understood the power of the media and the power of 9/11 politics. The "Great Ground Zero Heist" was not her first op-ed for the *Journal*; the paper had published three very long op-eds in 2004, all in different ways supportive of President Bush and his efforts against the war on terror and all highly critical of how the media stakes out an influential position on issues. She would use the same media for her campaign against the IFC, drawing on the same power of the "9/11 family members"—not a monolithic group, she told readers—who "retain a powerful weapon that they have learned to exploit to their advantage. They are '9/11 family members,'" she wrote, "and therefore enjoy the cloak of deference that has been

FIGURE 10.2 *Debra Burlingame, whose brother was piloting Flight 77 on 9/11, set off a storm of protest against the proposed International Freedom Center in a* Wall Street Journal *op-ed titled "The Great Ground Zero Heist."* AP PHOTO/CHRISTOF STACHE, POOL

graciously conferred upon them by the public, politicians and, most significantly, the media." She identified herself always as "the sister of Charles F. 'Chic' Burlingame III, captain of American Airlines flight 77, which was crashed at the Pentagon on September 11, 2001," and sometimes as "a life-long Democrat," or "co-founder of 9/11 Families for a Safe and Strong America." She was connected politically. She "had spoken at the Republican National Convention, appeared with President Bush on the campaign trail, and backed his use of 9-11 images in TV ads."[22]

Several of those closely involved in the cultural controversy questioned whether Burlingame had a broader agenda, though that idea did not emerge at first or directly. "Debra Burlingame came late to the game," said a family member I spoke with. "She had no emotional attachment to the WTC site; her brother was not killed on the site. She inserted herself into the process in the name of patriotism; she had become involved with the Republican National Committee. All of a sudden she had a sophisticated website, really fast. Where did this money come from? She used loaded language." Burlingame was political and partisan in her op-ed attack. She "derided the IFC's claims to Ground Zero by exposing the leftist leanings of some IFC supporters" and "mocked the possibility that lessons could be learned from 9/11" when she wrote: "Rather than a respectful tribute to our individual and collective loss, they will get a slanted history lesson, a didactic lecture on the meaning of liberty in a post-9/11 world." In attacking the "so-called lessons of September 11" as a way academics "promote their agenda," Burlingame was rejecting any intellectual claims to Ground Zero the academic community might make as part of a strategy for the families of the victims to claim sole authority to guide what would happen on the site.[23]

The sharply partisan caustic attack caught others off guard, including fellow family activists, according to Robert Kolker, who broke the story about the political power of the self-defined activist 9/11 families in a subsequent exposé "The Grief Police" in *New York Magazine*. Before they published the op-ed, editors at the *Journal* had insisted Burlingame visit with the IFC sponsors. The visit with cofounders Bernstein and Kunhardt and IFC president Richard J. Tofel, a respected former *Journal* executive, included family member and Memorial Foundation board member Lee Ielpi. During the meeting, Burlingame did not reveal that she had already submitted her op-ed to the *Journal*. She had "modest concerns about the IFC," Tofel told me years later. "It was a reasonable and emotional meeting; there was meaningful conversation about the whole event and the meaning of freedom. There were tears, as was common in these meetings with 9/11 family people." Overall, "it was a positive meeting; she raised none of the issues that were in the op-ed." In coming to his office, Burlingame was "checking the box," telling the *Journal* that she had spoken to the IFC for about an hour. All Tofel and the IFC sponsors knew was that the op-ed would be a tough piece, and they knew this only because of a courtesy call from the *Journal* editor.[24]

The first thrust of the ideologically driven op-ed was patently political: taking aim at the liberal goals of the Freedom Museum's ideals, its cofounder, Bernstein, and several members of its advisors. It was not just that she objected to their ideas for the museum; she objected to their politics and projected guilt by association, a lack of patriotism. This was paradoxical, as many accounts pointed out, because months earlier, the Freedom Center had been portrayed as too favorable to the Republicans since Bernstein and President Bush had been business partners. Plans and ideas for the Freedom Center were vague, as the *Times*' Robin Pogrebin, kept reporting.

The generality of the idea played to Burlingame's objective, which was to push for exclusive focus on the history and heroism of 9/11. She eschewed making an argument on actual substance and content in favor of bold assertions. Her argument followed a calculated ideological tangent. She charged that the organizers "have stated that they intend to take us on 'a journey through the history of freedom'—but do not be fooled into thinking that their idea of freedom is the same as those of those Marines." Her language was calculated to press historic hot buttons: "The public will have come to see 9/11 but will be given a high-tech, multimedia tutorial about man's inhumanity to man, from Native American genocide to the lynchings and cross-burnings of the Jim Crow South, from the Third Reich's Final Solution to the Soviet gulags and beyond. This is a history all should know and learn, but dispensing it over the ashes of Ground Zero is like creating a Museum of Tolerance over the sunken graves of the *USS Arizona*."[25]

For Burlingame, a broad view of what the value of freedom means in America could not share pride of place on Ground Zero, so the argument against the IFC was framed in the name of patriotism: "I fear that this is a freedom center which will not use the word 'patriot' the way our Founding Fathers did." These were conservatively charged words. The heavy rhetoric of the piece made Burlingame and the activist 9/11 families standing behind her an overnight conservative cause célèbre and fueled intense press and TV coverage. Her narrative strategy quickly put the IFC on the defense, in the difficult position of having to prove a negative— that it was not left-wing and anti-American.[26]

Burlingame's narrative strategy effectively succeeded in transforming the issue by giving it a national platform. "No one says the 9/11 families aren't entitled to their pain," Kolker wrote in "The Grief Police," whose subtitle read, "but Should a Small Handful of Them Have the Power to Reshape Ground Zero?" Until *New York Magazine* published the article in its November 2005 issue, the 9/11 families had been portrayed as one, despite differences of opinion on many issues. A short article "Victim Groups Don't Speak for Everyone," had appeared in the *New York Sun* near the first anniversary of 9/11, but it went virtually unnoticed. In reporting on the views of the many victim groups, Julia Levy had sought out some of the silent spouses, parents, and siblings "who did not want to dedicate themselves to affecting policy decisions." Some said, "it's not the buildings, but education that matters." Others noted that "some of these people may be trying to gather a moment for themselves in voicing their opinions." And still others believed it was time for the victims' families to "be grateful for [what] we've had in the way of attention" and, as Levy related the rest of the family member's remark, "let the politicians make the big decisions."[27]

What Kolker did was unmask the myth of "the families" in a way that crystallized the bigger politics at play. "Where the families had once simply laid claim to the moral high ground," he wrote, "Burlingame was showing them a new way: She'd tapped into culture politics, artfully associating the IFC with liberal intellectuals, the antiwar movement, and the p.c. police. This was no longer just a local development fight. Now it was a struggle between down-home blue-collar American values and the self-loathing predilections of the liberal cultural elites—a red-state–blue-state battle." As one activist family member explained, "She articulated the strategy, and we all participated in it, to let the public know about it so it would become a political issue."[28] Burlingame's campaign inspired the formation of Take Back the Memorial, which would continue advocating its singular position well after the IFC controversy ended.

The IFC was competition—for public attention, donations, size, and pride of place at Ground Zero. And the adage that a picture speaks a thousand words made that especially clear. Some of the family members serving on the LMDC Families Advisory Council didn't like the fact that the master plan for the site had preceded a plan for the memorial, and now with glossy visual images made public, the Cultural Center seemed further ahead in planning (notwithstanding the fact that, at best, programming for the IFC and the Drawing Center was vague) than the memorial, which was being guided by the newly created Memorial Foundation, whose board had met only twice. As unveiled at the press conference in May, the IFC and the Drawing Center would be housed in an elegant building designed by the international design firm Snøhetta, above ground and at the most likely and heavily trafficked pedestrian entrance to the site at the northeast corner of the memorial quadrant—the 100 percent intersection in real estate terms—whereas the Memorial Center would be below ground, out of sight, and as a result, might not be the first thing visitors would see on entering the site. Burlingame and her coalition wanted a larger, more prominent presence for the Memorial Center. The cultural building was to have 200,000 to 250,000 square feet of space, whereas the Memorial Center was at first only allocated 50,000 to 70,000 square feet (before it grew to more than 100,000 square feet)—this in a real-estate-centric city where power and priority is measured in square feet. "When you see how that Snøhetta building looks on a big screen next to the memorial, it really takes away from the memorial," remarked Monica Iken. "That's when we were like, 'Wait a minute, that's not what we wanted. I mean, first of all, you're encroaching on our memorial. Our memorial needs to stand alone. And then you're banking on *our* visitors to substantiate your institution going forward,' because they're gonna charge money to get in there. And that's when the chaos began."[29] The competition for physical prominence on Ground Zero was growing more crowded: first, it was the iconic 1,776-foot tower, then the birdlike Transportation Hub, and now the memorial. There were simply no modest ambitions at Ground Zero.

BOYCOTT POLITICS

The op-ed fueled a series of bitter attacks on the IFC and the Drawing Center as "unpatriotic distractions" and triggered a furious and intense summer of protests, defenses, and responses that eventually ended in the political eviction of the IFC from Ground Zero. The implications for rebuilding Ground Zero were lasting. The controversy became a litmus test for anything put on the Trade Center site. It distorted the discussion. Ignoring the active family organizations and their wishes was outside the bounds of political reality. "They're organized, they have voices, and what they say matters," political consultant Hank Sheinkopf said early in the process. "No politician can afford to upset the family members of the victims in any way, especially during an election cycle."[30] And that would be the case until all the issues surrounding the memorial and Memorial Museum were definitively resolved.

At the time, Tofel did not understand Burlingame's bigger agenda. A former assistant publisher of the *Wall Street Journal*, he countered Burlingame's accusations with reasoned explanations of the Freedom Center's intended programming in a response op-ed in the *Journal* two days later, but reason was a hard counter for deep-searing emotion, and some readers found his rhetoric condescending. The president and CEO of the Memorial Foundation, Gretchen Dykstra, wrote a letter to the editor of the *Journal* in support of the IFC, arguing that it would provide a "forum for important explorations of all freedoms: freedom from hunger, freedom from religious persecution, freedom from slavery, freedom from totalitarianism." Mayor Bloomberg responded in terms of the twin goals of rebuilding: "You are never going to please everybody," he said. "I don't think any memorial is going to do what they would really like to have; clearly, it's not going to bring back their loved ones. But we're trying to remember those who have passed and at the same time build for the future." Governor Pataki was supportive—at first: "We were attacked that day because of our values, because of our freedom," said the governor's point person on Ground Zero, John P. Cahill, who had recently been put in charge of overseeing hands-on coordination of rebuilding activities in lower Manhattan. "So to the extent the Freedom Center reflects those values and freedoms, it would be appropriate to have on the site."[31]

That perspective quickly dissipated once the opposition started to protest vehemently. First, approximately two hundred relatives of 9/11 victims gathered at Ground Zero to protest that the museum would, as reported in the *Times*, "dilute the purpose of the memorial and dishonor the memory of their relatives."[32] Protesters at the rally organized by the activist family group Take Back the Memorial said they did not want "a history lesson about tolerance" or discussions of world politics or civil rights on this hallowed ground (figure 10.3). Chanting "9/11 Memorial only, 9/11 Memorial only," they stood in steadfast opposition to anything that threatened their views on what was appropriate on the site that would memorialization the lives lost in the attacks on 9/11—especially these two cultural

FIGURE 10.3 *Family members of September 11 victims rally at Ground Zero to protest plans for cultural institutions at the site not related to the events of September 11.* SPENCER PLATT/GETTY NEWS/GETTY IMAGES

institutions. Their fierce political opposition was galvanized by Burlingame's *Wall Street Journal* op-ed "The Great Ground Zero Heist."

The political heat intensified dramatically a few days later, on June 24, when the *Daily News* published a front-page leader, "911 Outrage, DRAW THE LINE, NOW! Gov. Pataki is allowing a museum that exhibits anti-American art to display its works at Ground Zero. This is a disgrace, and THE NEWS demands action," and a photo of the Abu Ghraib prison with the caption "Is this what we need at Ground Zero?" (see figure 10.1). The news leader directed the reader to several pieces of artwork previously displayed at the Drawing Center's SoHo gallery. The relatively unknown Drawing Center had been spared the constant media attention focused on the IFC until the *Daily News*'s review of its post-9/11 exhibition catalogues revealed "numerous politically charged works" criticizing the country's war on terror. The *Daily News* also weighed in that day with a lead editorial—"Get the Picture, Governor?" and a news article, "'Violated...Again.' Kin Slap Art Center's 9-11 Pieces." Its intense campaign against the Drawing Center was set in place alongside the June 20 rally.

The issue had turned toxic. Hours after the *Daily News* disclosure, Governor Pataki distanced himself from the two cultural groups and delivered an ultimatum demanding "an absolute guarantee that as they proceed it will be with total respect for the sanctity of that site," that is, they would not program exhibits that would be offensive to 9/11 families and visitors to the memorial: "I view the memorial site as sacred ground, akin to the beaches of Normandy or Pearl Harbor," he told reporters, "and we will not tolerate anything on that site that denigrates America, denigrates New York or freedom or denigrates the sacrifice and courage that the heroes showed on Sept. 11th." The governor added, "If they do not meet that requirement, which to me is quite plain, that they show tremendous respect for this sacred site, they will not be at the memorial site. It's that simple, to the extent that I have the ability to do that." Burlingame was dismissive of the "absolute guarantee." "Pataki is out of his mind. He has his head in the sand," she said. "This is utter baloney. He's doing damage control. There is no such thing as an absolute guarantee."[33]

The apparent preemptive censorship did not sit well with numerous groups who viewed it as anti-American and contrary to the country's First Amendment principles. "The problem is, of course, that you can probably not find any reputable cultural institution any place in the world where some of what they display or do would be appropriate there, but not appropriate at this site," remarked Mayor Bloomberg, who was supportive on First Amendment grounds. "And so the balance has got to be, and the challenge for the curators is going to be: given the context of where these cultural institutions are, what's appropriate here?" Relatives started a letter-writing campaign to politicians calling for the removal of both cultural institutions from the Trade Center site, and fearing any type of exhibition on what they considered a cemetery, representatives of fourteen groups of 9/11 families traveled to Washington, D.C., to appeal to Congress and President Bush for help. Bernstein went on the defensive, vowing that his institution would never "blame America or attack the champions of freedom" and that the programming would be "appropriately celebratory of our nation." In a letter he wrote to LMDC president Stefan Pryor co-signed by his vice chair, Paula Grant Berry, Memorial Foundation board member and 9/11 family member, he said "we have taken a step back to examine how best to meet the high standards that all who are involved at Ground Zero remain committed to." To make their case stronger, Bernstein and Berry proposed to accommodate the so-called Family Room where victim's relatives come to mourn and remember privately. They also proposed a gallery "devoted to the international outpouring of sympathy and support for the U.S. and the victims," and relocation of the World Trade Center's Fritz Koenig sculpture, *Sphere for Plaza Fountain*, from its interim location in Battery Park to a spot outside the cultural building. "Do you know what the letter amounts to? Them saying 'trust us,'" said Burlingame.[34]

When the Memorial Foundation held its quarterly meeting on July 12, thirty of its forty-one members, including Bernstein and the seven 9/11 family members, were in attendance. Over the past month, the activist family groups had gotten more aggressive in their campaign against the IFC, which in concert with Burlingame's numerous media appearances and inflammatory newspaper quotes[35] increased the tension in the World Financial Center offices of American Express, where the meeting was being held. John C. Whitehead, whose outstanding service to the country in World War II and in government thereafter would meet everyone's definition of an American hero, had in his complementary role as chairman of the LMDC issued a three-page public statement three weeks earlier affirming the LMDC's priority commitment to the 9/11 Memorial and Memorial Museum as "the centerpiece, heart, and soul of our efforts" and the cultural complex as "the third element of our collective responsibility" as envisioned in the Libeskind master plan. In his role as chairman of the Memorial Foundation he addressed these priorities once again. But now the impact of public criticism of the cultural institutions was seriously threatening the foundation's fundraising campaign: Donors were hesitant to contribute given what they were reading about "the confusion and dissension in the press." Whitehead asked approval for a resolution laying out the priorities of the foundation: first, to ensure the $500 million of fundraising for the completion of the memorial and Memorial Museum, and second, to raise funds for the construction of the cultural components. The resolution passed, with four of the seven family member directors abstaining: Debra Burlingame, Lee Ielpi, Monica Iken, and Thomas S. Johnson. Two days later at the LMDC's monthly board meeting, Whitehead similarly addressed the "recent challenges and misconceptions" about the cultural component of the master plan faced by both the LMDC and the Memorial Foundation and reiterated his commitment to that conceptual blueprint and, "first and foremost, of the Memorial and the Memorial Museum."[36] Because of the "misconceptions" (others might have said misinformation), partisanship had come to dominate the substantive issues and politicize them beyond debate.

The "ever fiercer" political battle over what belonged on the site continued through the summer into September. The Drawing Center was reported to be considering withdrawing from the cultural complex at Ground Zero and the Joyce and Signature Theaters to have privately expressed their skepticism over whether the Performing Arts Center would become a reality. Whitehead announced he was going to ask the LMDC "to make one final effort" to find a site for the cultural complex farther removed from the memorial, possibly off-site; though he was doubtful a new site could be found, he wanted to make every effort to see if it was feasible. The political surrender had begun, unless you count the IFC's own defensive statement that the center would not "be used as a forum for denigrating the country we love."[37]

Even among victims' families the issue had become divisive. According to the *Washington Post*, a poll by "Families of September 11," one of many 9/11 family groups, found its fourteen hundred members evenly split on the issue. When Take Back the Memorial issued "An Open Letter to the American People" on its website calling for a boycott of the Memorial Foundation's fundraising efforts "until the I.F.C. and the Drawing Center are eliminated from the memorial plans," not all of the fourteen groups whose names were affixed to the letter actually had approved the use of their names. "I never signed off on anything like that," said Monica Iken, a founder of September's Mission, a Web-based, virtual project supportive of developing a living memorial. Was it a conflict of interest for board members to urge prospective donors to withhold support? As a foundation board member, Iken believed she had a responsibility to fundraise for the memorial. Not so Burlingame, who held firm to her orthodoxy: "You can't go out to the public and say, 'We're raising $500 million,' and not tell them they're building on the same site a building so large it will dwarf the memorial." Same with Lee Ielpi, who believed the Freedom Center "is a bad idea."[38] Both continued to serve on the foundation board, though. The family groups had begun to splinter.

The final political surrender unfolded quickly over the next month in a series of influential announcements that isolated the IFC. The first came from Whitehead reporting to the LMDC board at the mid-August meeting. In a departure from the norm, Whitehead announced his report would be given at the end of the meeting. Notwithstanding his steadfast support and the thorough process for selecting the cultural institutions, Whitehead reported that the development corporation "is asking the IFC to work with the victims' family members and other stakeholders to develop and present specific plans, program and governance structure." The report would be due no later than September 23, and at that time shared with the Families Advisory Council, made available to the public, and discussed "before the LMDC makes a final decision." He also reported that the board of the Drawing Center was finding it too difficult to comply with the new content restrictions laid down and had chosen to look at alternative sites, with support from the LMDC (which would at its next board meeting authorize an additional $150,000 in financial assistance for the task). There was no vote on the new procedural requirements. The LMDC did not issue a press release about the "next steps to ensure public participation in the International Freedom Center submission process" until September 21. Yet as *Times* reporter David W. Dunlap described in an article the day after the August board meeting, which he attended, the IFC "was all but shown the door by state officials." "If at the end of this process, the L.M.D.C. is not satisfied with the I.F.C.'s proposal," Whitehead reportedly said at the meeting, "we will find another use or tenant." The Freedom Center, Dunlap concluded, was being asked to "clear hurdles that have no evident dimensions," given that the LMDC chairman "declined to elaborate" on the process and criteria by which the IFC's submission would be judged.[39]

Acting for the mayor, Deputy Mayor Doctoroff immediately objected to the way the new review procedure had come about, and before Whitehead could adjourn the meeting he voiced his displeasure with the procedure: "To reach this conclusion without a significant amount—particularly within this body—of debate and public comment leading up to the debate is disappointing." Whitehead apologized for not having discussed the matter more with him, but added that "many weeks of discussion and consultation has taken place before this conclusion was reached." In September, the LMDC hired a conflict resolution specialist, Peter H. Woodin, to help mediate the dispute between the IFC and the 9/11 family members actively opposing its placement at Ground Zero. Woodin had served as deputy special master for the September 11th Fund, a not-for-profit organization created by the New York Community Trust and United Way of New York City[40] to provide the "broadest range of victims with the widest range of needs." The chances for a breakthrough to the impasse appeared dim, and nothing came of that mediation.

The surrender was nearly complete. Though he had forewarned of what he might do, the governor was now between a rock and a hard place: "If Mr. Pataki tries to eject the center himself, he can expect objections that he is repudiating a master plan he once embraced, buckling to political pressure and denying place for free speech at a site that is supposed to embody American values," Dunlap wrote. And yet, within the month, that is exactly what the governor did, without having reviewed the forty-seven-page IFC report, which was released to the public on September 22. In a short press release issued on September 28, just hours before a public forum to review the IFC's fate and before the LMDC had a chance to vote on it, Governor Pataki said, "Today there remains too much opposition, too much controversy over the programming of the IFC, and we must move forward with our first priority, the creation of an inspiring memorial. Therefore, the IFC cannot be located on the Memorial quadrant."[41]

It was all politics for the Pataki administration. The governor had until the end of 2006 to set in place his legacy, and this controversy threatened that ambition. Before the governor's final act banishing the IFC, the city's firefighters followed by its police union leaders, and then former mayor Giuliani, all came out against the IFC. Three New York Republican congressional representatives, John E. Sweeney, Peter T. King, and Vito J. Fossella, who had earlier threatened action against the LMDC if it did not kill plans for the IFC at Ground Zero, announced they were launching a congressional probe in a bid to block federal funds from being used to develop the IFC. The potential for nationally televised hearings on the Freedom

Center, remarked a former executive director of the Republican State Committee, Brendan Quinn, "would be a huge embarrassment" for the governor, who had recently traveled to Iowa as part of a National Governors' Association meeting and a test run of whether he had a chance of winning his party's presidential nomination.[42] And in what surely signaled final abandonment, just one day after the IFC submitted its report Senator Hillary Rodham Clinton voiced her opposition, which the *Post* blasted in big type on the front page on Saturday, September 24: "HILL NO! NIXES 9/11 FREEDOM CTR."[43] Then the mayor, who had up to this point been supportive of the IFC: "This is just not a normal location where you can put a cultural institution and have the cultural institution have total freedom to do anything they want."[44] Though his office did not want to let go, the issue had become a drag on memorial fundraising. It was over, ever so over.

COLLAPSED AMBITIONS

The reaction to Pataki's eviction of the IFC was swift. First, the IFC vanished, completely. Its intended work brought to an abrupt end. "There is no viable alternative place for the IFC at the World Trade Center site," the IFC said in a press release issued less than an hour later, because it "is the site for which the IFC was created, at the Lower Manhattan Development Corporation's request, and as an integral part of Daniel Libeskind's master site plan."[45] Bernstein resigned from the board of the Memorial Foundation over the loss of the visual arts at Ground Zero, as did two significant power players in the city, Agnes Gund (philanthropist, art patron, and president emerita of the Museum of Modern Art) and Henry R. Kravis (founding partner of leveraged buyout firm Kohlberg, Kravis Roberts & Co.); *ABC News* personality Barbara Walters had resigned earlier in August, reportedly frustrated over the lack of vision and progress.

For the "mess" at Ground Zero, the editorial pages of the *Times*, *Daily News*, and *Newsday* held the governor unequivocally responsible for his lack of leadership. The *Times* used its editorial page to reiterate support for what the Freedom Center meant to do, celebrate freedom. In an earlier editorial it had criticized the governor for abdicating his role as a leader in the controversy and, in effect, giving Burlingame his "proxy." "Pataki abandoned the center as if it were radioactive," wrote *Newsday*'s editors. "He didn't have the guts to defend his master plan. He couldn't even summon the courage to explain that the fight was a turf war and not a battle over disrespect to 9/11 heroes." Considering that the governor is accountable for all the decisions leading to this end, which the *Daily News* enumerated in its editorial, "Pataki's statement yesterday was astonishing in that he had the gall to blame the IFC for the fiasco." Only the *Post*, long on its castigation of placing the

IFC and the Drawing Center at Ground Zero, applauded the governor for "doing the right thing" and told "The Freedom Center: Good Riddance."[46]

The LMDC board had the most to say. The governor's sudden and preemptive intervention had publicly assaulted its institutional integrity and irrevocably damaged its institutional standing. Pataki had sided with the small set of hard-core, highly vocal 9/11 family activists (around thirty, according to Kolker), leaving his appointed agents for rebuilding to deal with the chaotic aftermath of his political tornado. It was not a pretty scene. Whitehead summed up the board's distress in his opening comments at the October meeting: "In all candor," he said as he opened the monthly meeting at One Liberty Plaza, its headquarters downtown nearby Ground Zero, "I must report that most of our board, including its chairman, was quite distressed that a process which we had established two years ago with full public approval was not allowed to work its way through to conclusion. It is hard for us to negotiate and settle many issues that will come before us in the months ahead unless we are seen by others to have the necessary ability to make the decisions, the necessary authority to make the decisions."[47]

"Distressed" is board polite. Whitehead was personally as well as professionally offended and angry. "Regrettable and dangerous rhetoric was thrown about irresponsibly," he was reported to have said at the time. "The names of people of good character and goodwill were unacceptably dragged through the mud." The meeting was intense. Every board member, whether attending in person or by phone, spoke publicly about the Freedom Center decision. It "amounted to remarkable political theater in a process where intramural disagreements are usually kept well hidden," Dunlap reported. "The willingness to speak openly about their frustration almost certainly reflects a high degree of discouragement and even anger." Pataki had not communicated with the LMDC board before making his decision. For the LMDC chairman, one of the governor's own appointees, to make such a public statement amounted to a rebuke. "[S]enior statesmen like him more often keep their own counsel, expressing disagreements behind closed mahogany doors," Dunlap wrote years later in February 2015 on the occasion of Whitehead's passing. Even though the principled objections Whitehead "raised at the time did not change the outcome, his willingness to raise them publicly served the process well." It was, Dunlap said in his moving tribute, "a bright moment of clarity in a perpetually muddied landscape." "The governor hired John because John was universally recognized as a man of integrity," Richard J. Tofel remarked during that week of remembrances for Whitehead. "And then, occasionally, Pataki had to be *reminded* that John was a man of integrity."[48]

The governor's decision was "a debacle," Betts told the press. "We have denied ourselves freedom of expression at ground zero."[49] Seeing that the LMDC's role had been "severely marginalized," Betts resigned from the board within days. "That was frankly the turning point for me and many others," he said. "We were running a process, and Pataki just blew it all away. He trashed the museum, he upstaged the L.M.D.C., he ceded to the victims, he let them portray Tom as a leftie nut and he made a parody of the process."[50] This was his second disheartening experience as an LMDC board member.

With the IFC's eviction, the ambitions of the cultural program collapsed. "Is Culture Gone at Ground Zero?" Pogrebin asked in the news lead of her *Times* article recounting the episode. Uncertainty set in, big time, as detailed in news reports year after year (2005: "Controversy Still Clouds Prospects at 9/11 Site"; 2006: "For Culture, a Clouded Future at Ground Zero"; 2007: "Ground Zero Arts Center Won't Have Theater Company, Only Dance"; 2008: "Proposal Would Relocate Arts Center to [Fulton Street] Transit Hub"; 2009: "Ground Zero Arts Center: Time Is Not on Its Side," "Moment of Truth for Ground Zero Arts Center"; 2010: "Culture Wilting at WTC"). The Drawing Center had already withdrawn, though not without financial compensation.[51] The city, which would take over responsibility for Ground Zero's performing arts center in 2006, dropped the Signature Theater from Ground Zero in early 2007 because of the cost and complicated logistics of having two culture institutions share a cramped space that also had to accommodate underground security elements related to transportation and safety. Some nineteen months later, in a decision culminating a "wearying five-year search" for space, the off-Broadway company announced it would set up a new $69 million home in the basement of a mixed-use building to be developed on Tenth Avenue in the heart of the Theater District, assisted by a $25 million contribution from the city.[52] From the four cultural institutions selected to bring energy and life to Ground Zero, only the Joyce Theater remained as a potential cultural presence at Ground Zero.

Snøhetta's founding partner, Craig Dykers, anticipated controversy. The firm had designed the Bibliotheca Alexandrina in Egypt and the Oslo Opera House in Norway, both very controversial and contentious projects. He was reluctant to respond to the request to design the September 11 Memorial Cultural Center because he believed the project belonged to the Americans. He is an American but he had lived in Europe over half of his life and was living in Norway at the time. It seemed out of place to interfere with the recovery effort organized by the city, state, and the LMDC. He didn't feel comfortable reading through the RFP sent to him, but after much urging by others and after saying no several times, he eventually read the LMDC document. In "a catharsis," Dykers told me, he realized he had to do it—for his father, who had spent thirty-five years in the U.S. Army—and to honor the efforts ongoing at the site. "It seemed empowering to place a cultural center to respect our daily lives amidst tragedy on the memorial site itself," he said; "it is very unusual and profound. The present is the messiest thing we have, but it is what makes life exceptional. We require things that allow us to understand dissonance—life is not hermitically sealed. This helps us understand the complex word around us."[53]

When the IFC and the Drawing Center were no longer a part of the cultural program for the site, family members and others came to Dykers, asking if the building could be made into a different kind of museum. He did not think so at first, but he felt he should meet once more with Governor Pataki, whom he had met with a couple of times before. He had twenty minutes to make a pitch to the governor—which he used to describe what he thought was missing from the site: "a place to give a sense of orientation to the site and empowerment, to connect to young people as well as adults, to widen the demographic and provide a mirror onto ourselves." Pataki listened for one and a half hours, and then he asked Dykers how much money he needed for the building. Dykers was surprised and said he wasn't completely sure, maybe $40 million? The next day Pataki's office called and said they would give $80 million. "It was an amazing moment," said Dykers. He believes "Pataki heard his point that we needed to honor the present and liked the idea that we must reflect presence as well as absence at this important place. The commercial skyscrapers could not do this," he said; "they were remote and about the future. And the memorial is about tragedy and the past." This building, Dykers believed, would be about the present.[54] The Snøhetta building would be dramatically reduced in size and radically redesigned as a memorial-related visitors center and entry pavilion to the underground Memorial Museum (renamed the Visitor Orientation and Education Center) (plate 11).

Two very different forces—the political power of a small vocal group of 9/11 families and the logistical problems of accommodating four performing arts theaters on a tight site—had strangled the cultural ambitions for the site, but the story was not over. The idea of a Performing Arts Center remained alive, on life support from the city under the Bloomberg administration and later under his successor, Mayor Bill de Blasio. A clear resolution of the cultural agenda, should there be one, was years away.

What happened? "The footprint decision was dictated by the political decision that the site was sacred," Rampe explained to me in an interview years later. "Once the footprints decision had been made, the mandate to preserve led to the question: How could you have the profane next to the sacred?" The LMDC did not view the cultural as "profane"; culture had a part in the rebuilding of downtown, and the involvement of the arts on the site was fundamental to the idea of a living memorial. Whereas the development corporation might have made an effort to put culture on the ground floors of other buildings, everyone just let it go, said one insider. No one knew how to address the issue, and they didn't want to anger the families. The cultural program—certainly the IFC—was just too soon in time because it did not resonate with the families. "It is very hard to fight the sacred," remarked Rampe. "This—the cultural as profane—had become a symbol and something the families felt they could win."[55]

In his preemptive and unilateral eviction of the Freedom Center, the governor may have wanted to shield Ground Zero from continuing controversy, as one of his advisors said, but the political stakes involved in this controversy were enormous. The controversy had gone national; it was all over selected international media as well. His people didn't want to be involved; they were into damage control. The IFC was offered $20 million (the same as had been given to the Drawing Center) and the landmarked former headquarters of J. P. Morgan & Co.—the "House of Morgan"—at 23 Wall Street (the target of a bombing nearly eighty-one years earlier that killed thirty-eight and injured four hundred) if the center would move off-site. "The IFC in the Morgan Bank, can you imagine how the symbolism of this would play right into the worse caricature of America! A Freedom Center Museum in the symbol of money grubbing capitalism?" Tofel remarked. But Bernstein and Tofel said this was not possible: "The idea only made sense having the power of the place," Bernstein told me.[56] He and his colleagues were trying to make something good come out of tragedy, and they believed the center's purpose was inextricable from the site itself.

For the governor, this was undoubtedly embarrassing after all these offers of money and space, and one can imagine he was angry. In the wake of the cultural imbroglio, Governor Pataki's "campaign" for a presidential nomination collapsed. The negative editorials attacking his lack of leadership said it all. Having used the rebuilding of Ground Zero as the centerpiece of his presidential ambitions, he had hitched his political future to its trajectory. When rebuilding at Ground Zero turned into a mess in the national limelight, his presumptive presidential campaign suffered in kind. So too, what the IFC would have brought to future generations visiting the Trade Center site.

LOSS HIERARCHY

For some 9/11 family members, Take Back the Memorial members in particular, the fight over the cultural institutions reprised a quest to have the entire sixteen-acre site sanctified as a memorial. Others accepted the master plan dedication of the footprints and surrounding plaza spaces as a memorial. Still others were simply confused about the titles and locations of the memorial, cultural buildings, and several symbolically named spaces (September 11 Plaza and Liberty Park) that made up that southwest quadrant of the WTC site. The decision to reinsert the street grid of the Trade Center site, one of the earliest and most consensual of planning decisions had reconfigured the former superblock into quadrants. This early decision aimed at knitting the site into the physical fabric of the surrounding community physically defined the "memorial quadrant" and, in retrospect, conferred upon it exclusive status. Pataki's 2002 footprints statement codified it as hallowed ground. But only with the expulsion of the IFC three years and three months later did the footprint of the memorial site expand beyond 4.7 acres defined by the Memorial Design Competition brief to include an additional one-acre public plaza north of what is now the Visitor Orientation and Education Center.

Was the decision to link the cultural agenda to the establishment of the Memorial Foundation an unsustainable balancing act? The linkage undoubtedly increased its political vulnerability once the controversy over the IFC and the Drawing Center erupted into page-one news. When some activist family members issued a call to boycott fundraising for the memorial, this became ever more so clear. Although the idea of a "living memorial" was considered central to bringing energy and spiritual renewal to the site, fundraising for the cultural buildings need not have been linked to the larger task of raising private funds for the memorial and Memorial Museum. In fact, the issue of how best to structure the Memorial Foundation had been debated for months prior to its formal creation in July 2004. The case for separation was made by John P. Cahill and Ira M. Millstein, the corporate-governance expert who played a formative role in the organizational set-up of the LMDC and the foundation. He served as the board's pro bono counsel in addition to being a board member of the Memorial Foundation and a long-time friend of Whitehead. In the end, Whitehead won out. He strongly believed that with only a memorial the site would be lacking in life, and the adjacent community did not want the site to be perceived as a cemetery. Tying the two together was Whitehead's way of assuring that the cultural program would complement the memorial, but as events turned out, the linkage handicapped fundraising.

The success of Burlingame's campaign against the IFC and the Drawing Center led some to wonder once again whether the master plan was really a master plan. What else in the master plan was open for revision? "If ground zero is too hallowed for a freedom museum," Dunlap asked, "how much longer will a performing arts center be considered appropriate? Or a million square feet of retail? Or four office towers? Especially if one of them is named Freedom?" As one 9/11 family member on the Memorial Foundation board remarked, "The I.F.C. and Drawing Center were the unfortunate targets this time but it probably won't end there."[57] The political power of a minority was a worrisome portent for progress at the site. In a larger historical sense, that "tyranny of a minority" was what James Madison worried about when he wrote Federalist No. 10 in 1787, published under the pseudonym Publius and printed within a few blocks of the Trade Center site.

The families' role in the rebuilding process was significant in framing the dialogue about the memorial mission and memorial program. The twenty-four members of the LMDC Families Advisory Council were involved month after month in defining planning and design issues, including artifact selection, site security, the interim viewing wall, and site connectivity with the surrounding communities. They were kept informed about other rebuilding issues beyond the memorial. They were not involved in the decisions about the cultural program, just given updates on the process. Reading through the minutes of these meetings, it becomes quite clear that family members held differing views on any number of remembrance and rebuilding issues. And there were many organized family groups. One member of the Families Advisory Council, Nikki Stern, said she counted eighteen different families' groups (including groups out of Boston and Washington, D.C.); the New York groups included Voices of September 11, Take Back the Memorial, Families of September 11, the Coalition of 9/11 (now called WTC United Family Group), World Trade Center Survivors, and September's Mission.[58] Years later, the number would clock in at twenty-three.

Some groups were divided within themselves; others, more like-minded, believed they owned the site and had a right to make decisions beyond the immediacy of the memorial. "Where is the entitlement thing coming from?" Stern asked. Stern lost her husband of eleven years, Jim Potorti, in the attack. The author of *Because I Say So: Moral Authority's Dangerous Appeal*, an impassioned essay written to explore why society believes victims are morally special, Stern questions the moral imperative that took over the debates about Ground Zero: "It's just another way of saying, 'I am certain' or a device that will give politicians cover for hard decisions—'you decide.'" While everyone is entitled to an opinion, is it appropriate for the opinion of family members to carry extra weight, for their voices to ring louder than others? The role of the families was not made clear or understood, she emphasized when I spoke with her. "I understand how this happened—a larger issue of how people deal with grief. They make hierarchies quickly and give moral authority to those most hurt. It's a weird dynamic." Stern was looking for a discussion about "sacred ground" to be led by religious leaders. "Families needed help discussing what sacred ground meant, and people were all over the map because they didn't get remains."[59]

Behind closed doors, no one made any effort to manage expectations of the families, another family member explained to me in confidence: "Leadership was unclear. Remember, this was going on very early in the process. It was also very clear that there was no way any politician would say anything in opposition to what a family member would say." In her first *Journal* op-ed "Our 9/11" in March 2004, Burlingame recounted how "[t]he leader of a lobbying group advised individuals at a 9/11 family meeting shortly after the attacks: 'Make no mistake, you have a lot of power. Politicians are more afraid of you than you know.'" No one wanted to get in their way, one Memorial Foundation board member recalled. "There were many touching stories, who could say no?" The families knew they could always go to Governor Pataki, who would support them. He had great sympathy for the families; he had gone to many of the funerals and was genuinely and deeply affected by the families' anguish, and had personal relationships with several of them. The family groups had access to other politicians, but by being responsible for pushing the Freedom Center off the site, the families' emotional claims made politicians anxious. "There was a level of caution and nervousness around the families among politicians and real estate people," said Stern.[60] How long would this political power last?

With 2,982 victims, the collective of 9/11 family members figured in the many thousands. Sheer numbers alone suggest that they would not all react to events in the same way. Divisions were defined by behavior as much as anything else, a participant involved in the episode explained. One division defined a group wanting to lead private lives against another wanting to live public lives. Burlingame was in the public-life group. She went on the *Today* show just a few days after her op-ed and built a professional life from her public platform as a 9/11 family member and an opponent to the Freedom Center; she was an available source for journalists who wanted a known opinion on the matter. A second division defined a group broadly sharing human suffering against others who did things that divided people into camps of good guys and bad guys. September 11 was a singular event in the lives of all 9/11 families—and for multiple reasons. The payout from the Victims Compensation Fund, according to the U.S. Department of Justice, averaged over $2.1 million per victim (depending upon income level and age, the high end of awards ranged from $3.2 to $7.1 million, after offsets for other factors). For many, it opened up the possibility of not needing to work for a living.

"How," Kolker asks, "did a group of 9/11 families go from being seen as the entirely sympathetic victims of perhaps America's greatest tragedy to being viewed as a self-interested obstructionist force that could hold up ground zero's progress for years, banishing any sign of cultural life downtown—except, perhaps, for the culture of mourning?" While the active family groups "dramatically narrow the options" for politicians, a political science professor at Baruch College pointed out, "they don't have a veto" over the ultimate decision.[61] The families were given a voice, and the press made it a more forceful voice. Knowing they could get a story in the papers anytime, many family groups used the press effectively, generating the controversial stories the press craved. The relationship was mutually reinforcing. The press and its rhetoric fed the activist families' false sense of entitlement—that they had the moral authority to shape decisions beyond the memorial. The symbiosis played a big role in the destruction of the Freedom Center and the Drawing Center at Ground Zero.

Was the idea of a Freedom Center too early for its time? Most likely. The Holocaust Museum, for example, opened in 1994, fifty years after the fact. During the debate about the Freedom Center, the shock was still so real, the emotions still so raw. Embracing a conceptually abstract idea when the pain of immediate loss cuts so close to the heart proved to be too difficult, even for many family members who believed in the ideals of the Freedom Center. Yet the cultural battle over its inclusion was one-sided because culture at Ground Zero had no strong advocate or political constituency, notwithstanding prominent members of the newly formed board of the Memorial Foundation and Whitehead's constant support. Some observers believed the sponsors did not do a good job of articulating what the museum would do, what exhibits it would mount, whether it would be a museum or a center of activism. "The families didn't understand what the museum was going to be about," said Stern, "so they were able to be swayed to be concerned about it. Those that were supporting the museum, which was evolving, had a terrible job" to do countering the assertions.[62] Without powerful advocates and with the press coalesced in one view (with the exception of the *Times*), the Freedom Center went down without much resistance.

"The idea was radioactive," reflected Bernstein years later when I interviewed him. "When you get irrational discourse, the problem is you can't diffuse it. And you get that when you have overheated emotions. Add to that the leadership factor—there was no political leadership. It was an emotional buzz saw. We were doomed," he said. He recalled Cahill asking him, "Can you move the auditorium out?"' Tofel asked, "Why?" When Cahill responded because someone might say things, Bernstein knew it was over. "For the Freedom Center to have happened it would have needed a political leader taking it on, dedicated to building an enduring institution," he said. "There's a reason these museums like the Holocaust and the Center for Civil and Human Rights in Atlanta take fifty years: It's a generational transfer that is delicate and can't be taken for granted."[63]

How can we use the whole experience to educate future generations? That is the most piercing question of the 9/11 trauma. Why not just identify a place for a memorial, a "strawberry fields forever?" a colleague of mine at Columbia University proposed in an informal discussion. The "strawberry-fields approach was problematic," he added, when the site is in a dense downtown district full of residents and commercial activity vital to the future economy of the city. "The impact of what was at stake in this and other decisions at Ground Zero confronted a unique hierarchy of loss not present in Oklahoma City after the bombing of the Murrah Building. To make sense of the tragic and world-unsettling event, the memorial needs a museum. A museum needs a storyline. A storyline needs a point of view, and a point of view is inherently political."[64]

The Memorial Center grew in size and significance as a consequence of the disassembling of the cultural program. The safer label of "museum" formally replaced "center," which implies dialogue and debate. The entrance to the Memorial Museum is through the Visitor Orientation and Education Center designed by Craig Dykers of Snøhetta and on the second floor is a 165-seat auditorium—for discussions on issues related to the museum's mission. Part of the museum's mission will, in time, overlap with what the Freedom Center aimed to do. As its mission evolves, it most likely will transcend 9/11; it will have to if it is to succeed over the decades. And it may grow to be positively provocative as an educational institution, as the Freedom Center aimed to do. Only time will tell.

PRESS POWER

The power of the press was paramount in the four-month vitriolic fight over inclusion of the Drawing Center and International Freedom Center at Ground Zero. Whereas the press played an outsized role in other high-profile conflict episodes, the six initial site plans for the site (2002), for example, it played a different role in the imbroglio over whether culture belonged at Ground Zero. It was different not just because the city's two tabloids aggressively pushed their answer—"No"—but because the *Daily News*'s front-page advocacy discredited any rational discourse on the issue as unpatriotic and unacceptable. By aiding and abetting the agenda of a small, select group of vocal 9/11 family members, the *Daily News* and the *New York Post* forced the rapid disappearance of both cultural institutions from Ground Zero. The politically charged campaign of removal turned the issue of the sacred versus the profane into a culture war and, in the process, made a mockery of the American ideal of tolerance and the First Amendment principle of freedom of speech.

The tabloids' war against the cultural institutions was waged with a steady barrage of rhetoric-heavy editorials so numerous as to rival the papers' reporting on the controversy's many other politically charged flash points.[65] During the sixteen weeks between the Burlingame op-ed and Governor Pataki's ouster of the IFC, the *Post* printed twenty editorials on the issue and the *News*, eleven; the *Times*, which was on the other side of the IFC controversy from tabloids, printed five. After

Pataki's ouster of IFC from Ground Zero, the total editorial tally, including post-mortem commentary, reached forty-two (and forty-nine, if op-eds are counted). For the tabloids, the editorial ink on this issue exceeded any other single episode of Ground Zero rebuilding; it was even greater than the editorial commentary on the controversial modifications to the competition-winning memorial design and the cost of both the memorial and its accompanying Memorial Museum. Over the course of more than seven years, between spring of 2006 and fall of 2012, on that episode the *News* printed eleven editorials and the *Post*, six.

The *News* and the *Post* went at the cultural controversy from different perspectives and with different degrees of angst and advocacy, disapproval and goading, partisan critique and personalized attack. The editorial board of the *News* concentrated its animus on the Drawing Center; it disapproved of art that appeared to criticize the Bush administration and the war in Iraq, considering it offensive to the memory of those who died in the 9/11 attack. It praised Pataki's demand for an "absolute guarantee," took credit for pointing out some of the "issues," and reiterated its judgment that the memorial sanctum was not "an appropriate showplace for the kind of political juvenilia that a SoHo gallery likes to mount." Initially, it withheld judgment on the Freedom Center "pending further information," but in succeeding editorials the paper became "uneasy" with the IFC's emerging ideas for a program of events that would "engage people in dialogue and debate on freedom." It did not believe that the IFC could "entertain intellectual free-for-alls and guarantee the sanctity of the site, as Pataki had demanded."[66] Ultimately, the editorial board allowed that the IFC had earned "the right to forge on," which was the editorial endorsement the IFC's leaders needed: The governor would support the institution, Tofel had been told, if the *Daily News* was behind them. In the end, it did not matter. Politics with a capital "P" overrode any substantive considerations.

"No Place for Politics," the *Post* announced in the first of its twenty-three editorials against the Freedom Center. "It was time to reach for the revolver. Because odds are that... this center won't focus on freedom's triumphs, so much as on its failures—particularly those in which America can be painted as the culprit." Only a "celebration of American values" was appropriate at Ground Zero. Repeatedly, the editorial board cited Burlingame's op-ed to rationalize its position and personalize its attack against left-leaning academics and the *New York Times* editorial page. The editorial board of the conservative, antigovernment *Post* held to its staunch support of Burlingame and her ideological arguments, actual facts versus false impressions about the IFC notwithstanding. It was going to be impossible from a First Amendment perspective to exercise censorship, and therefore, the IFC could not be trusted. The Drawing Center had to go too because Ground Zero "is just the wrong place for any museum or other institution that wants to have any sort of artistic freedom." If these institutions "won't relent," it advocated "a campaign aimed at slowing memorial fundraising." As it promised its readers, the *Post* kept at it with editorial after editorial, and as the September deadline neared for the IFC sponsors' report on specific plans and governance structure as the LMDC had requested, the editorials got longer and more insistent. From the earliest days of its editorial commentary on rebuilding, the *Post* had taken a position that rebuilding all of the lost office space was most important. It had rejected Mayor Giuliani's insistence that the entire sixteen-acre Ground Zero not be seen as a site for economic development. It wanted the site redeveloped quickly; it did not want a lot of public input, as that would delay the process. The paper had "paid little attention to the families during the site-planning process," Matthew Schuerman wrote in the *New York Observer*. "But once the fight was put in ideological terms," the paper owned by Rupert Murdoch "just couldn't say enough about it."[67]

In contrast to the tabloids, the editorial board of the *Times* made its argument in support of the IFC on the "character of freedom," against "censorship in advance" and letting "a handful of vocal family members, who may not have represented a majority of 9/11 families, change the dynamic of the World Trade Center site for the worse." The *Times* made the case that Ground Zero will have to "belong to the future" as well as "honor the memory of one terrible day in American history." It railed against what it saw as a "campaign about political purity—about how people remember 9/11 and about how we choose to read its aftermath, including the Iraq war." It chastised Pataki for failing to stand up for "the quintessentially American principle of free speech and the role of culture, in this most cultural of cities, in helping us understand 9/11," and concluded that he has "sacrificed any illusion of leadership." Culture at Ground Zero was being sacrificed because of political cowardice, and, as a result, the memorial precinct "may become nothing but a graveyard instead of a place where visitors are invested to both remember the victims of mass murder and celebrate the possibilities of life."[68]

Despite the differences in attitude, tone, and rhetoric, the cumulative force of the editorial boards of the three New York City dailies put extraordinary, unrelenting pressure on Governor Pataki to exercise leadership befitting his position. Week after week, sometimes multiple times each week, the negative editorials excoriated him for failing to act. Politicians don't want to be criticized, urban planner and mayoral advisor Mitchell Moss reminded me when we spoke about the politics of the Trade Center, and they love praise. He argued that negative editorials as a rule get dismissed and that positive editorials have a bigger impact. Yet in quantity and persistence, the editorials over the IFC controversy were of a different order, beyond the norm. They could not be ignored. They had an impact.

REVERBERATIONS

The cultural conflict and the politics of the activist families had a lasting impact on rebuilding. The high-profile controversy elevated the political symbolism of the rebuilding effort. As long as decisions were being made about the memorial complex, no politician could take a stand against the emotional claims of the families, though Mayor Bloomberg tried when he came out against Take Back the Memorial and spoke freely about the activist families' veto power. Inspired by their success with banishing the IFC and the Drawing Center, the core activists became more aggressive, filing lawsuits, making noises about the shape of retail development, questioning design issues and the burial placement of unidentified remains, and, in particular, prescribing how the names of the dead should be listed on the memorial parapets, as discussed in the next chapter. Take Back the Memorial decried any form of politics at Ground Zero, yet it used its advocacy platform in just that way, staging rallies, releasing press statements, and posting comments to its website. Moreover, notably absent from its arguments were critiques of conservative attempts to capitalize on 9/11. "The threat of a family veto—and more charges of anti-Americanism played out on editorial pages—hovers over every component of downtown's potential rebirth, threatening to scare off any politician who dares cross the families," was how Kolker explained the residual wariness and legacy of the IFC controversy. When Pataki emphasized the "memorial quadrant," in effect and perhaps by intent, he signaled the physical containment of the families' role in shaping decisions at Ground Zero. "I would say we have more definition now than we did prior to this controversy regarding the memorial quadrant," said Stefan Pryor.[69]

The families might still feel entitled to weigh in on decisions involving the Performing Arts Center, but when the territory of rebuilding issues shifted to the Port Authority and Larry Silverstein, as was the case for years thereafter, what standing would the families have to say anything about those disputes? Ultimately, the families' political power was time-bound, as Mayor Bloomberg foresaw it would be. When the issues related to the memorial were settled, their period of influence passed. Subsequent national events also eclipsed the singularity of their domestic political standing. "The 9/11 families were a special class within American politics for a period of time," said Tofel, who became president of ProPublica, an independent, award-winning, nonprofit newsroom that produces investigative journalism in the public interest. "They were unchallengeable, except with other 9/11 families. Time and events changed this. When Katrina hit, the families' time was up."[70]

The cultural conflict and its aggressive press coverage infected the public tenor of the entire rebuilding project. Most directly and immediately, it handicapped fundraising for the memorial, as Whitehead discussed more than once at board meetings of the Memorial Foundation during those tense months of conflict. Major donors and fundraisers were alienated, hesitant to contribute because of the intense discord chronicled in the press. No one wanted to contribute into a controversy. "When you get things sorted out," they told him, "come back to us, and we'll tell you what our gift will be."[71] Businesspeople on the foundation board who might otherwise have been involved were pushed away because they couldn't be involved in controversy, while the influential arts community, with one exception (the president of the Metropolitan Museum of Art, Emily K. Rafferty), was not involved with the foundation after the resignation of Agnes Gund. At that difficult October 2005 meeting, Whitehead, whose wisdom and calming influence had held things together, announced that the foundation had just surpassed the $100 million fundraising mark, the all-important point at which it would receive $100 million in matching funds for the memorial from the LMDC. At the April 2006 meeting he would report positive news that contributions had reached $130 million, but the pace of giving had slowed.

Fundraising for the Memorial was also bearing the burden of uncertainty surrounding unresolved conflicts between the Port Authority and Larry Silverstein over the economic feasibility of the commercial office towers. By October, the fundraising mark had increased a bit, to $145 million, but it was a slow climb toward the goal of raising $300 million from private sources (the LMDC would be contributing $200 million). The real pickup in fundraising would not come until fall 2006 when the board nominated Mayor Bloomberg to chair the foundation, and he took over leadership for its capital campaign. During the following three months, fundraising reached $253 million. Another $50 million would be raised before the next meeting in April 2007; by August 2008, the foundation reached its revised target goal, $350 million.

Pataki's abrogation of his own creation cost the LMDC whatever legitimacy it still had as a force in rebuilding Ground Zero. Not only did his "solution," as the *Times* news header framed it, contravene years of public process and a public vetting process for the Freedom Center, once again in the most abrupt way it made clear who was in charge of rebuilding. Speaking to a reporter for the *New York Observer*, a representative from Community Board 1 asked, "Do we really have to speak with the LMDC, or should we deal directly with the Governor? Do we really have to go to these public forums and spend hours at these presentations? Do they really care about residential input down there?" Or as one think-tank policy analyst put it: "The way that the Governor has chosen to pursue development at Ground Zero has been to hide behind the LMDC when it is convenient and to step out from behind when there is a cornerstone to be laid or an opportunity to look good. It really results in disarray, because no one knows who is really in charge."[72] Actually, by this time, it was quite clear who was in charge, but whatever confidence still existed that rebuilding would advance in a timely fashion or be responsive to a broad public interest had been eroded by Pataki's lack of leadership.

The last person to speak about the governor's action at that October board meeting of the LMDC was the late Edward J. Malloy, the politically savvy longtime president of the Building and Construction Trades Council of Greater New York and one of Governor Pataki's original appointees on the LMDC board. The meeting was open to the public and the news media in compliance with New York State's Open Meeting Law. Though he was attending via telephone, the gravitas of Malloy's remarks projected clearly: "If we as a board cannot marry the memories of those that perished on 9/11 with the expression and expansion of ideas of freedom, then I really wonder about our ability to achieve the vision that we were designated to fill."[73]

The LMDC had been marginalized in this brutal episode and the priority of the performing arts agenda orphaned. While the development corporation was not expected to turn off the lights anytime soon, it was no longer even nominally leading the rebuilding effort. Cahill, the governor's point person, was the one nominally in charge of rebuilding—for another fourteen months until the end of the Pataki administration. Headed by Bloomberg, the Memorial Foundation was moving to assert its position and ensure stewardship for the memorial agenda. One of the LMDC's fundamental roles was to mediate between agencies and set the agenda for rebuilding lower Manhattan. "Whether the governor and the mayor have the wherewithal to have L.M.D.C. continue that work," remarked Madelyn Wils, a longtime board member who spoke for the downtown community, "is not entirely clear."[74] The façade of power had shifted decisively. That was the most lasting impact of this most visible inflection point in the process of rebuilding at Ground Zero—until a proposal to build a mosque and cultural center on a site in lower Manhattan ignited a fierce political controversy.

In May 2010, when real estate developer Sharif El-Gamal proposed to build what became known as the "Ground Zero Mosque" two blocks north of the Trade Center site, an intense national debate erupted over whether an Islamic cultural center so close to Ground Zero was appropriate (figure 10.4). Protesters said its placement near Ground Zero was an insult to those who lost their lives there. Opposition "has become a call to arms for national Republicans," the *Wall Street Journal* reported. Fueled by Republican ideologues like former vice presidential candidate Sarah Palin, former House Speaker Newt Gingrich, and other conservatives who "have been shamelessly playing the politics of fear since 9/11," the rhetorical attacks surrounding the building of a Muslim complex near Ground Zero

FIGURE 10.4 Mike Keefe, InToon.com

quickly turned ugly. Overheated rhetoric filled the right-wing blogosphere. The attacks were full of "vitriol and outright bigotry," said the *Times* editorial board. Opponents of the Islamic complex had unsuccessfully tried to "derail" the development, the *Daily News* said, "under a subterfuge of landmarking" the 152-year-old building that had housed a Burlington Coat Factory. It was a "fool's errand," the editorial said. "The courts would surely overturn such an action as a transparently obvious violation of the First Amendment."[75] In an emotional and memorial speech, Mayor Bloomberg defended the project, citing religious freedom.

After the firestorm of protest, plans for the project known as Park 51 changed, repeatedly, as complications brought on by difficulties finding financing for the $140 million project, litigation delay, and movements in the real estate market downtown reshaped how El-Gamal decided to use the multiparcel site he had been assembling since 2009 (figure 10.5). Without controversy a small cultural center opened in September 2011 with a photographic exhibit of city children representative of 180 ethnicities from around the world in tribute to New York City's diversity, and prayer services were being held weekly in the building. Several years later, the developer announced that instead of a fifteen-story community center and prayer space, he would now build a three-story museum "dedicated to exploring the faith of Islam and its arts and culture" that would also include a sanctuary for prayer services and community programs, all to be designed by the Pritzker Prize–winning French architect Jean Nouvel.[76] Later that year, saying, "There's a new downtown that is coming to New York," El-Gamal

FIGURE 10.5 RJ Matson/St. Louis Dispatch

quietly refashioned his project, adding a thirty-nine-story forty-eight-unit condo-minium tower located at 45 Park. In the fall of 2015, with the luxury condominium market on a seemingly ever-increasing upward trajectory, his once-again revised condominium project would be built to seventy stories.

What was acceptable in the vicinity of "hallowed ground"? Did the plan to locate an institution with Islamic roots near the Trade Center site represent disrespect, an insult to the families of 9/11, or did it represent a symbol of national tolerance in the "freest city in the world," the world's greatest city of immigrants? Would this thirteen-story mosque building physically "outshine" the memorial itself? As had been the case in 2005 in the imbroglio over the Drawing Center and the International Freedom Center, the issue of what happened at Ground Zero had, once again, been heavily politicized. The political ideology infecting the debate surrounding the Ground Zero Mosque was the same, although the protagonists had changed. The 9/11 families (but for a few individuals) were not a voice in this controversy; they had moved on with their lives, forever impacted by the tragedy of their loss. Right-wing conservatives outside of New York City and some local Republican candidates for governor had hijacked the issue for partisan purposes.

CHAPTER 11

Memory Politics

FIGURE 11.1 *Memorial Pool, December 16, 2011, a few months after the opening of the Memorial Plaza on the tenth anniversary of 9/11.* PHOTO BY TOM STOELKER

THE "SOBERING, DISTURBING, HEARTBREAKING, and overwhelming master-piece...comes as a surprise to those of us who doubted that the chaotic and desultory reconstruction of Ground Zero could yield anything of lasting value." Succinctly, these words by architectural critic Martin Filler writing in the *New York Review of Books* captured the unanticipated emotional impact he and other architectural critics experienced at the opening of the National 9/11 Memorial at Ground Zero on the tenth anniversary of the terrorist attacks. Not every critic would wax so lyrically about the experience, but many were similarly taken by surprise. "I found the inky deepness of the pools and the sight of water being sucked into the earth, like the hopes and dreams of the dead, almost too much to bear, and I had to turn away," wrote Inga Saffron, architectural critic for the *Philadelphia*

Inquirer (figure 11.1). When it was first unveiled in 2004, Saffron had considered the nascent design of *Reflected Absence* to be deeply flawed—"so generic and so sanitized that it drains the site of its sound and fury, signifying nothing." The conceptual design had failed to "capture the raw horror of what happened," but the reality of the memorial design, she subsequently wrote, forced "a confrontation with the physical evidence of history."[1] Poetic as these evocations were, when they evaluated it as a serious work of architecture, the critics offered little more than muted praise for the Arad-Walker memorial. A near consensus held that true judgment would only come with the test of time. And the companion Memorial Museum, which would tell the story of the 9/11 attacks underneath the vast memorial quadrant, was years away from opening.

The intense emotional reality of the Memorial Plaza, opening on the tenth anniversary of the terrorist attacks on the United States and crowded with the families who experienced the most traumatic of losses ten years earlier, erased for a time the messy history of dissension that defined the tortuous path to this opening—the passionate controversies, the political disputes, the difficult architect, the personal animosities, the contentious preservation issues, the broken deadlines, and the quarrelsome cost overruns. "Without question, rebuilding the World Trade Center has had its challenges across every aspect of this project—be it financial, emotional, political, and otherwise," the president of the National September 11 Memorial and Museum, Joseph C. Daniels, would later say. "But the keys to the memorial and museum's success have been understanding our responsibility to act and recognizing that this is our sacred obligation. The question at every point has been, what is the right thing to do given the mission at hand?" Daniels recalled seeing thousands of family members reflecting at the pools, some whom foundation officials had never seen before, as evidence that the memorial succeeded in its mission.[2]

Doubt had been a constant companion to the ambitions of Michael Arad's *Reflecting Absence* ever since the closed-door jury deliberations imposed design changes on his pure (and stark) open plane. More changes followed before a "final" version presented to the public in January 2004 brought forth poisonous charges from many architectural critics that the meaning of the memorial design had been fatally compromised.[3] "The deck is stacked against the realization of anything but a fussy histrionic memorial at Ground Zero," wrote Philip Nobel, author of *Sixteen Acres: Architecture and the Outrageous Struggle for the Future of Ground Zero,* in *Metropolis,* a magazine of architecture and design. "A quick list of tricky demands on the thing might include: signaling defiance (as still befits the political moment), demonstrating respect for the dead (complicated by the fact that the memorial is also a graveyard), incorporating a repository for the unidenti-

FIGURE 11.2 *The voids of the Memorial Pools render absence visible. Arad's winning design (left) uses a language similar to Michael Heizer,* North, East, South, West, *1967/2002 (right top, detail; bottom, installation view).* PWP Landscape Architecture. Dia:Beacon, Riggio Galleries. © Michael Heizer/Triple Aught Foundation. PHOTO: TOM VINETZ. COURTESY DIA ART FOUNDATION, NEW YORK

fied remains (across the street from theaters and stores), and managing the expected onslaught of tourists that may very well make Ground Zero into what the *New York Post* has referred to as a 'Disneyland of Death.'"[4] These were not unreasonable concerns about a conceptual design that was being asked to bear the immense emotional burden of the 2001 attacks and the 1993 bombing of the World Trade Center on a contested site crowded with competing claims.

The enormity of the attack on the World Trade Center was given artistic form by the two voids–absences that borrowed their dimensions from the footprints of the twin towers—framed by cascading waters falling into pools thirty feet below street level, vanishing into nowhere, seemingly never to fill up. Using "a language similar to conceptual artist Michael Heizer's *North, East, South, West*," the voids render absence visible and "give the overwhelming losses of September 11 permanent presence"[5] (figure 11.2).

In reality, the size of the voids would be overwhelming, so overwhelming that Nobel (and others) wondered whether "visitors confronting the memorial, so much bigger at that moment than the memory of those who died all around," would confuse its meaning. "How will the dead compete with all this reverence for lost construction," he asked? "Even if it communicates nothing else, the design will immortalize the measure of the Twin Towers and the fact that they did once really stand. Architecture remembering architecture—that is beyond question something this memorial can do," he concluded. "Whether it will also distinguish between the site of the attack and its victims, whether it will 'respect this place made sacred through tragic loss,' whether it will redeem Ground Zero, only time will tell."[6]

To build out the memorial program the immediate principals would have to tackle tough issues, issues rooted in the complexity of the site in the fullest sense: its program of uses (and handmaiden, cost), its emotion (graveyard of mass murder), its engineering (underground infrastructure, river and slurry walls, man-made waterfalls of size unknown in North America), and its security (blast protection, public safety, suicide prevention). Technical design problems and engineering challenges would test the skills of experts. The design of the memorial would have to be amended to accommodate the technical demands of engineering and security, the emotional demands of 9/11's meaning (as those became apparent), and the aesthetic demands of a minimalist conceptual design that had not been fully worked out. Because no one was really making decisions within the real world of financial constraints, the cost estimates escalated exponentially— although that concern was not on anyone's worry list until Mayor Bloomberg blasted the financial alarm.

As overseer of the memorial design process with responsibility to ensure execution and construction, the LMDC faced the task of managing Michael Arad, thirty-four years old and technically inexperienced but aggressively pushing for total control of the multimillion budget. He quickly alienated everyone as he fought, resisted, and, at times, deviously maneuvered around others. He became angry and petulant at not being in full control of his design. Although winning the competition was incredibly empowering for Arad, the LMDC held domain over the bigger-picture issues such as the selection of the associate architects and the engineers, the allocation of money, and the decisions over scheduling, not to mention public relations and communication. The development corporation also had to manage the politics of the whole design team—Arad and landscape architect Peter Walker & Partners and Davis Brody Bond, the associate architects its officers had chosen to be responsible for the memorial's schedule, budget, and coordination. And it had to coordinate everything with the private not-for-profit Memorial Foundation, which was in charge of the memorial program and responsible for private fundraising to cover at least $300 million of the construction cost. Upon signing a project agreement with the Port Authority and the LMDC in early July 2006, the foundation became the "guardian of the design"; once the memorial was fully constructed, it would take possession of the site by way of an operating lease from the Port Authority and manage permanent operations of the memorial and Memorial Museum.

How did these defining conditions of the memorial program, each of which was complex in its own right, interface with the tension-prone dynamic between City Hall and Albany? With the Port Authority, formally beholden to two governors but effectively beholden to neither? How did the inevitable compromises and trade-offs of the design-development process shape the details of how the memorial concept was realized—and, significantly, at what cost? Was it at all possible for this process to go forward without being politicized by the victims' families, who had already proven to be powerfully influential in shaping the course of rebuilding at Ground Zero? Many years of contentious struggle over complicated core issues followed the burst of optimism accompanying the unveiling of *Reflecting Absence* at Federal Hall in lower Manhattan, that symbolic venue of our nation's history of democracy brought into twenty-first-century service as a statement of defiance in the face of terrorism. The storyline of answers to these questions travels from expectant beginnings to challenging design revisions to full-blown cost crisis threatening the realization of the memorial and its accompanying museum—before Mayor Bloomberg took on the chairmanship of the foundation and stewarded progress toward the tenth anniversary opening of the Memorial Plaza.

IMMEDIATE COMPROMISES

The mission of the Memorial was eloquently simple: "Remember and honor the thousands of innocent men, women, and children killed in the horrific attacks of September 11, 2001"; "respect this place made sacred through tragic loss"; "recognize the endurance of those who survived, the courage of those who risked their lives to save others, and the compassion of all who supported us in our darkest hours"; and "reaffirm respect for life, strengthen our resolve to preserve freedom, and inspire an end to hatred, ignorance and intolerance." In his design statement Arad confidently explained how *Reflecting Absence* responded to the destruction of the towers and loss of nearly three thousand lives. The ambition of designing an enduring commemoration so soon after mass tragedy, however, held perils, as the lessons of history had taught most professionals.[7]

"By their nature, memorials should be timeless," Martin C. Pedersen wrote in *Metropolis.* "Yet political pressures have dictated that we develop a memorial design two years after Sept. 11th's catastrophic morning. This is an invitation for aesthetic disaster. Even if all of the site's complications could be magically swept away, a powerful design would be difficult to achieve this soon. We don't know yet what the event or site means." Designing a memorial so soon in time was "an impossible burden."[8]

The underground galleries of the memorial so central to Arad's vision, another critic wrote, "may yet become what they must be: mournful and evocative spaces capable of moving those who remember and instructing those who do not. But for now they remain no more than a sincere but muffled homage, a vague gesture toward a history we do not yet understand." Even the memorial competition jury acknowledged that the politically driven fast-forward time frame was something of a liability: "The jury feels that if the memorial alone cannot address all the issues put forth in the mission statement, then together with the planned interpretive museum, all parts of the mission statement can be realized over time."[9]

Reflecting Absence's aesthetic approach of architectural minimalism embodied simplicity of expression. The guiding principle was nothing unnecessary. No ornamental details. No elaborate materials. Meaning would be conveyed through abstraction. The concept was all about loss. Yet the fierce minimalism of Arad's first images (figure 11.3) was too much for the jury, as well as for many of the families. By the time of its unveiling two weeks after the award announcement, at the jury's request, Arad's design had gained two significant elements that had not been a specific part of the design competition guidelines: a dense grove of trees to soften the stark open plane of the memorial plaza and a subterranean interpretive center located at bedrock where visitors would be able to view preserved artifacts

FIGURE 11.3 *Architect Michael Arad's design board for the 9/11 Memorial Design Competition. On it, Arad envisioned both "a sacred memorial ground" and "a large urban plaza." This large barren plaza was too much for the memorial jury, which required Arad to work with an accomplished landscape architect to humanize the plaza. Arad chose to partner with Peter Walker of Berkeley, California.* COURTESY MICHAEL ARAD/© HANDEL ARCHITECTS

from the twin towers: twisted steel beams, crushed ladder trucks, flattened police cars, squashed taxis, and personal effects of the victims, along with other artifacts held in storage in the cavernous Hangar 17 at JFK Airport. In a complementary voice, these artifacts would speak to what actually happened on 9/11 in a way that Arad's voids did not.

Except for the two 200-by-200-foot voids where the twin towers had stood, at street level Arad's design submission spoke of nothingness. The ground-level plane was so spare and minimal, "it almost seemed hopeless, nihilistic." The "lonely hard-paved plaza," was more than severely minimal, though. "Above ground, the plan was unfortunately reminiscent of the original plaza between the twin towers, a space almost universally derided for its lifelessness," Christopher Hawthorne wrote in *Slate*. "This design," Blair Kamin wrote for the *Chicago Tribune* "has real promise because it communicates not rhetorically, but physically, giving the visitor a visceral sense of absence. Yet its handling of the site is nothing short of brutal."[10]

Arad's severe treatment of the memorial plaza was unfathomable as a future vision for Ground Zero. The competition jury and residents of nearby neighborhoods alike believed the site had to be reconnected to the fabric of its surrounding urban community after so many decades of spatial isolation. The dense covering of deciduous trees Walker added, in place of Arad's sparse scattering of white pines—"some trees but they were practically dead," Walker remarked in an interview with Christopher Hawthorne—made a parklike setting for the memorial. The memorial design was now a hybrid: part memorial and part "urban forest," in the words of the designers' joint statement. The trees "punctuated" the surface of the memorial plaza, "forming informal clusters, clearings and groves." They symbolized the "annual cycle of rebirth."[11] Composing the memorial's continuation-of-life element was Walker's task. The challenge was to humanize the ground plane without losing the strength of the immense and empty plane, the sense of physical absence. Walker's humanistic landscape was the first improvement of aesthetic and emotional significance.

Internationally known for his expansive oeuvre, especially public spaces, civic landscapes, and corporate headquarters, Walker, age seventy-one, was bringing more than four decades of experience to the task. He had designed hundreds of projects all over the world, including Constitution Gardens at the National Mall in Washington, D.C.; the U.S. Embassy in Beijing; the Toyota Municipal Museum of Art in Toyota City, Japan; the Nasher Sculpture Center in Dallas; Barangaroo in Sydney, Australia; and Tanner Fountain at Harvard University in Cambridge, Massachusetts, to name a few. As one of the world's most accomplished landscape architects, he had served as consultant and advisor to numerous public agencies and institutions and on any number of prestigious panels, and been honored with numerous awards, including the highest medal of the American Society of Landscape Architects, the ASLA Medal. An influential practitioner educator, Walker had served as chair of the landscape architecture department at Harvard University and University of California, Berkeley, and became a leader of the renaissance of landscape architecture. "The thread that runs through all of my work is to make public space memorable, to make it the heart of the city," he said. "You have to make people aware of the space so that it sticks in their memory, and it is important to the community. It's not enough to just have open space. It has to have character and uniqueness." The memorial assignment—"a better-late-than-never role in 'improving' an austere design by a relative amateur"—was "a virtual crown on a career already crammed with renown," Robin Finn wrote in her Public Lives profile of the man.[12]

Arad's design presented a disciplined challenge. "Michael got it right," Walker said, "the artistic problem here is how to get people to see nothing as something." As a team, they would be trying "to make emptiness visible." And as a landscape architect, Walker's style was to "do a lot of things using as few elements as possible." At Ground Zero, he would spend a lot of time, he said, "explaining to everyone how trees work. That they play against the city. They are a contrast to the city. It has to do with shade. It has to do with them being alive and changing through the seasons. That's the nice thing about trees: They change in a way that humans tend not to pay attention to but like. I mean, when the leaves come out in the spring it's a big deal."[13] Walker's standards of design excellence are exacting and uncompromising, and he came into the project understanding the practical realities of working on a high-profile project in a city as complex as New York. Working on the 9/11 Memorial at the Trade Center in the thicket of several government entities, though, presented unique challenges and a need to study up on the Port Authority.

Unlike Walker's grove of trees, the addition of the underground interpretive center appeared to be motivated more by politics than aesthetics, as the guidelines for the competition did not call for another building element. The addition, Benjamin Forgey of the *Washington Post* suggested, might be viewed as an attempt "to satisfy the desires or criticisms of this or that faction in the memorial debate," in this case, "folks who want a literal, representational memorial, as opposed to Arad's abstraction." Intended as a "center" and not just a museum, it would contain "exhibition areas as well as lecture halls and a research library." With the addition of the underground interpretive center designed to serve the public and tell the story of 9/11, the revised conceptual design now provided family members access to a private space reserved for the unidentified remains and contemplation; this space at bedrock was where, in the words of the *Reflecting Abstraction* design statement, "a large opening in the ceiling would connect the space to the sky above."[14]

Arad's memorial, even at this early point, "had become a multifarious affair, its many elements tuned to the needs and tastes of the various process constituencies," grumbled Nobel years later. An architect by training, Nobel was disappointed with the process. With the memorial's list of names, healing waters, sanctity of the footprints, Arad had drawn upon "well-established" memorial elements. Arad's memorial "did not advance the conversation. It wasn't a critical work, leaning toward some future understanding; it was a summary of what was known," he concluded.[15] Was it not enough for the good architecture to be meaningful to the lay public? Or was his criticism that the appeal to popular desires was incapable of producing good architecture?

Immediately after the formal announcement and unveiling of *Reflecting Absence*, substantive concerns bordering on skepticism surfaced. "At this point, it's not entirely clear how it's all going to work below grade, how the two footprints will connect, and exactly how the spaces will relate to the museum of 9–11 artifacts now part of the plan. The vagueness here, I think, isn't particularly sinister," wrote Pedersen, "the design just hasn't been figured out." Justin Davidson, who had won a Pulitzer Prize for criticism in 2002 and was then *Newsday*'s arts critic, considered this version of *Reflecting Absence* "infinitely better than the bleak version" presented in the Winter Garden along with the seven other memorial finalists. But, he went on, "it is not thoroughly enough imagined to inspire much comfort or awe. Call it the 'trust us' approach: a theatrical announcement, filled with reassurances that one day all will be elegant and beautiful and right." It was, Davidson said, "a memorial design that, far from being final, is only two-thirds baked."[16] Others were not so generous in their assessment.

Further alterations (or compromises) to the design of *Reflecting Absence* only added to the angst of the critics, who all but ceased to comment after radical changes in mid-2006 eliminated the underground galleries central to Arad's idealization of a memorial space, discussed further on. As it made its way toward construction, evolving through three design iterations, *Reflecting Absence* became a much different memorial than the one Arad presented in his winning competition entry. Compromise upon compromise, or refinement upon refinement, or practicality upon practicality, had altered different elements of the design, notwithstanding the fact that the many changes did not violate Arad's signature evocative gesture of huge voids encompassing the footprints of the twin towers rimmed by cascading waters. The critics had nothing more to say before such time that the memorial was actually seen and experienced.

THE NAMES

Families of the 9/11 victims had much to say, however. They felt deeply about issues that would come to shape the final details of the memorial design, chief among them "the names" arrangement of those who died in the two attacks on the World Trade Center and the other attacks in Virginia and Pennsylvania on 9/11. In what order were the names to be listed? Were those killed to be listed by building, the area where they died? Should people be listed with their colleagues, friends, or relatives? Should their ages be listed next to their names? Should markers distinguish the first responders from those victims trapped inside the buildings or who died trying to escape? Should rank and affiliation define the first responders? What about the civilians who died helping others? Would any distinctions (or lack thereof) hold meaning twenty, thirty, or fifty years from the event? As a group, the families did not share a consensus view. Moreover, no solution was ever likely to satisfy everyone. Coalitions of families and firefighters advocated forcefully for particular arrangements; on a campaign, they organized protests, circulated petitions, and issued press releases. This was a noisy, divisive controversy. It went on for years, becoming almost more significant than the high-profile fight over the International Freedom Center—in this case, however, a solution was found that quieted all the noise.

In his original "Designer's Statement," Arad called for an arrangement of "no discernible order" in the belief that the multitude of names would underscore the vast scope of the tragedy. "The apparent randomness reflects the haphazard brutality of the deaths and allows for flexibility in the placement of names of friends and relatives in ways that permit for *meaningful adjacencies* [emphasis added]," he said. Two weeks later at the Federal Hall announcement, the idea of meaningful adjacencies was gone, replaced with a rationale for the random listing: "I have found that any arrangement that tried to impose meaning through physical adjacency will cause grief and anguish to people who might be excluded from that process, furthering the sense of loss that they are already suffering," read the revised "Official Designer's Statement" posted online. Following that logic, no attempt would be made "to impose order upon this suffering."

The LMDC had found the idea of meaningful adjacencies too complex for the nearly three thousand victims. The LMDC's position derived from a recommendation made by its Memorial Mission Statement Drafting Committee (comprising family members of victims, residents, survivors, first responders, design professionals, community leaders, and representatives of the LMDC's advisory councils) "to honor the loss of life equally and the contributions of all without establishing any hierarchies."[17] With the memorial jury aligned in opinion, the random listing of names with the only identifier being an agency insignia (police shield or the firefighters' Maltese cross) next to the names of the rescue workers (including emergency service workers and court officers) remained the official policy for nearly three years, despite persistent, unsettling, and, at times, dramatic protest from different coalitions of opponents.

Ever since Maya Lin's Vietnam Veterans Memorial on the Mall in Washington, D.C., broke conventional precedent and established a new paradigm for memorial remembrance, the listing of names had become a powerfully simple tribute mediating between the personal need to recognize individuals lost and the collective need to acknowledge national meaning. As at the Vietnam Veterans Memorial, an alphabetical listing was rejected as being meaningless, though recording names alphabetically had been a tradition of local war memorials as well as one of the most renowned, Sir Edward Lutyen's Thiepval Memorial to the 72,195 missing British and South African men who died in the Battles of the Somme of World War I between 1915 and 1918 with no known grave. "A name," explained Ai Weiwei, the Chinese contemporary artist and activist, "is the first and final marker of individual rights, one fixed part of the ever-changing human world. A name is the most basic characteristic of our human rights: no matter how poor or how rich, all living people have a name, and it is endowed with good wishes, the expectant blessings of kindness and virtue," he wrote in *Remembrance, 2010*.[18] Yet from the very moment Arad's random arrangement was announced, with the endorsement of Governor Pataki and Mayor Bloomberg, vocal dissension arose from many family members who would never accept that approach (figure 11.4).

The combination of randomness in the names arrangement and absence of hierarchy among the dead was turning out to be exceedingly controversial. A poll conducted by the Families of September 11 found that only 26 percent of the 2,225 responses favored the shield designation for uniformed rescue workers and only 5 percent favored the random arrangement. The firefighters and police wanted their special role recognized by a cohesive listing by unit and rank. "We did not die at random; we went in as rescuers," first responders would say in the paraphrase of one board member of the Memorial Foundation. "We want our engine company, our badges, our boys listed together." With that kind of compelling logic, who could be angry at a family member? But some families objected to this or any other type of hierarchy. "Everyone who was killed that day was attacked equally," said one family member. "If the naked name lies next to one with an insignia, what is signified?" another asked. "The memorial wall is no place for offense," he added. "It is a solemn reflective monument of what is common to all, not what makes them different." Cantor Fitzgerald thought otherwise. The financial firm lodged on the 101st to 105th floors of the North Tower suffered the largest number of losses, 685 employees; it wanted the arrangement to include an "affiliation"

FIGURE 11.4 *Family members of those killed at the World Trade Center on September 11 protest the current plans for a memorial there, January 9, 2005. Sally Regenhard, who lost her son, firefighter Christian Regenhard, speaks to reporters. Anthony Gardner, founder of the Coalition of 9/11 Families and advocate for preservation issues who lost his brother in the attack, stands to her left.* NEW YORK DAILY NEWS ARCHIVE/GETTY IMAGES

(typically, an employer), followed by ages and floor numbers and organized according to the tower in which they worked. "We're still looking for our loved ones," said Edith Lutnick, the executive director of the Cantor Fitzgerald Relief Fund, whose brother Gary died in the North Tower. "Now, you're forcing us to look again."[19]

Arad's conceptual design also was turning out to be far more complicated than it first appeared. As the names controversy filled headlines, the protest intersected with objections to where Arad had located the names' parapets: below the level of the Memorial Plaza in the underground galleries. Enormous halls far below street level, the underground galleries presented genuine security as well as safety concerns; visitors might have to go through an airport-security experience to reach bedrock. The noise of the waterfalls was likely to be deafening as well, a physical force that threatened to cancel out the design intent of creating a place for a contemplative memorial reflection. Technical advisors to the Skyscraper Safety Campaign, an organization founded by Sally Regenhard, whose probationary firefighter son perished on 9/11, raised concerns about the safety of the exit pathways in the underground galleries. Although there were some sixteen exits planned (not including escalators, elevators, and ancillary stairways), they were deep down—twenty-seven feet in the case of the eight exits from the main memorial level and sixty-nine feet for the eight exits from the main level of the museum. Regenhard's organization wanted what it called the "dangerous underground memorial" moved above ground. That too was compelling logic.

These and other issues about the status of the memorial were on the March 29, 2006, agenda of an oversight hearing of the City Council's Committee on Lower Manhattan Redevelopment chaired by Democrat Alan J. Gerson, elected in 2001 to represent downtown (District 1 in Manhattan). Though the City Council had no authority over Ground Zero, Gerson wanted to get the issues out in the open. The hearing was contentious. "What do the families want?" Regenhard asked at the hearing. "We want a memorial that's above the ground. We want the names above the ground. We want a safe and secure memorial that's built under the legal jurisdiction of the New York City building and fire codes. We don't want this convoluted multimillion- and billion-dollar, really meshuggeneh idea, O.K.?" In her short speech, Regenhard, *Times* reporter Deborah Sontag said, had "touched all the hot buttons: the perceived elitism and secretiveness of the process, safety and security, cost."[20] She was not alone in her objections. Other family member groups had standing objections to the underground location, in particular Anthony Gardner's World Trade Center United Family Group.

As the high-profile controversy intensified and a construction start for the memorial neared, the mayor came under great pressure, especially from first responders. The noise of intense opposition could be theatrical, which was not particularly unusual for New York City. At Gerson's daylong oversight hearing, firefighters walked into the City Council's ornate chamber of gilded moldings and polished mahogany dressed in full firefighting gear with the obvious intent of creating an indelible image of significance likely to appear on the nightly local newscasts. A month earlier several hundred police officers, firefighters, and emergency workers had rallied at Ground Zero with their union leaders and 9/11 family members to protest the memorial's underground location, citing security reasons and a strong belief that the underground location would disrespect the dead. "If you want to put people underground," said the president of the Detectives' Endowment Association, Michael J. Palladino, "go build a cemetery." Patrick J. Lynch, the president of the Patrolmen's Benevolent Association, was there to demand that uniformed victims be recognized separately: "We ask that the memorial see the light of day and not be hidden in the shadows."[21] This was powerful rhetoric, hard to disregard (figure 11.5).

The prominence and power of security objections really came to the fore after a confidential letter to LMDC president Stefan Pryor from Governor Pataki's senior

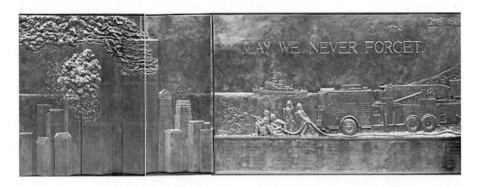

FIGURE 11.5 *Two segments of the fifty-six-foot-long and six-foot-high bronze bas relief bolted to the side of the Engine 10 Ladder 10 fire station—the command center of recovery operations on September 11—directly across from Ground Zero. The memorial was a gift from the national law firm Holland & Knight honoring the 343 firefighters and a Holland & Knight partner who perished on September 11.* GARY HACK

advisor for counterterrorism, James K. Kallstrom, was leaked to the press the following month, just weeks before bids from contractors for the memorial's structural foundation were due. "The Memorial Complex possesses an elevated level of risk and target attractiveness, as a result of its international symbolic stature and large public assembly capacity," Kallstrom wrote. "The very nature of its design encourages and engenders public interaction at both the Plaza level and below grade by providing visual and tactile connections between patrons, the structure the water features, and the architectural vistas. It is, however, these very elements, which constitute vulnerabilities from a security perspective, which are not adequately addressed in the current design documents."[22] Kallstrom's concerns focused on the threat of bombs or a chemical release on the ramps or in the two immense open-air voids at the heart of the memorial, and his six-page letter offered unusually detailed suggestions for mitigating the vulnerabilities such as minimizing the number of people on the ramps, partitioning the ramps to segregate exiting and entering personnel, and adding architectural design elements that would reduce the opportunity for explosions, airborne contamination, and suicides.

The disruptive controversy over the names continued to fester through the fall and into the winter. Also capturing the headlines were two other unsettling issues that touched on the politics of memory at the heart of remembrance: a national campaign of intense media attention to preserve the "Survivors' Staircase," the last above-ground remnant of the World Trade Center, which had provided an escape route for hundreds of people from the elevated open plaza, and the haunting emotional dilemma of where and how to place the unidentified remains of 1,123 of the victims, some 41 percent of the total at the time.[23] The 64-foot-long, 175-ton stairway, a symbol cherished by those who survived September 11, stood in partial ruin and in the way of one of Silverstein's commercial towers on the east side of the site.[24] Following on the heels of the security-driven redesign of the Freedom Tower, eviction of the International Freedom Center, and collapse of the cultural program at Ground Zero, the intense disputes related to the memorial agenda proved to be prima facie evidence of the overall chaos and confusion swirling around the rebuilding effort. It all had a chilling impact on fundraising for the memorial program.

The names controversy was in dire need of a solution. By year's end, Mayor Bloomberg in his new role as chairman of the Memorial Foundation settled the issue once and for all with a new arrangement acceptable to most, if not all, of the families and first responders. That arrangement, conceptually linked to Arad's original notion of meaningful adjacencies, had just about come full circle. "The idea for meaningful adjacencies," the Memorial Foundation's press release on the new arrangement explained, "has now been further developed into a design concept of ten identified groupings, which will tell the story of where people were during the September 11th attacks and grouping together the victims from the 1993 World Trade Center bombing." Adopting the original language of Arad's design statement, the foundation went on to explain that "the names of the deceased appear to be in no discernible order, reflecting the haphazard brutality of the deaths, but would nonetheless allow, for example, siblings and colleagues who perished together at the site to have their names listed side-by-side."[25]

Mayor Bloomberg had been politically attuned to the names issue from the very start. Upon seeing the new model of Arad and Walker's scheme the day before it was unveiled at Federal Hall in January 2004, he asked, "What about the names?" He understood, instinctively as most big-city mayors would, that this would be a most sensitive issue and that the uniformed personnel, the firefighters and police, would need to be recognized for making "the ultimate sacrifice" by rushing into those infernos to save others; they marched into hell. They were the heroes, the others were innocent victims. It had been the mayor's suggestion to place a service insignia beside their names. When the families' discontent with the hierarchy implicit in putting shields next to the uniformed responders surfaced soon after the Federal Hall viewing, the mayor remained firm in his support: "We'll never know what happened in some of those buildings," but as to the shields, he said, "it is exactly the right thing to do."[26]

The names issue had been one conflict that the Memorial Foundation could not get past, one board member told me. "All of us on the foundation board underestimated the implications of building a memorial on ground where lives were lost," said another. "The Vietnam, Holocaust, and other memorials were built on ground that was not sanctified as at Ground Zero. We learned the hard way— taking on the dynamic. None of us had experienced anything like this. We didn't anticipate that there would be a family-member reaction to design, the names, and every aspect of the memorial project. We had to be educated on what it took to build on sacred ground. Every single detail came under scrutiny; we didn't think the names would be such a big deal breaker." The memorial element "took a lot of delicate handling," said another board member close to the center of power at the foundation told me.

Soon after he was appointed chair of the foundation, the mayor engaged in the names issue, took it on as a serious matter. He's an engineer, remarked a former staffer, and he was looking for a solution. He didn't just decide by himself. He visited the Vietnam Veterans Memorial in Washington. He spoke with its designer, Maya Lin, who had been an influential member of the memorial jury and a strong advocate for Arad's design. In a move that was not planned, he reached out to the family members, who were touched and not expecting this. He listened to many people, including the president of the Uniformed Firefighters Association, Stephen J. Cassidy, who had been quietly lobbying city and state officials. He talked with Arad, who told the mayor his idea of "meaningful adjacencies" could capture the essence of whatever relationship was important to a family member—friend, co-worker, relation—without privileging some victims over others. A solution came out of that discussion, yet nothing they would have agreed upon would have happened without a review by his first deputy mayor, Patti Harris. Harris was the mayor's key trusted advisor, his loyal confidant, someone he had worked with since 1994 (at Bloomberg LP) and relied upon for sound judgment on everything from his philanthropy to his governance to his image. She oversaw his interests in the Trade Center memorial and cultural program. She had relationships with the families. Considered the most powerful person in the Bloomberg administration, she stayed out of the limelight, on the sidelines at the mayor's major events, but she was always a powerful force behind his actions.

At a December meeting of the executive committee of the Memorial Foundation, Bloomberg presented his plan and said, "This is what we're doing." He just said it, and that was that; no one said boo, recalled one committee member who spoke off the record. The mayor's plan for the names was adopted. In accordance with the board's governance procedures, there was a formal vote but the mayor, as chair of the board, made the decision. He told the family members that this is the way it would be. The depth of his knowledge and respectful consideration of the issue, in concert with his personal influence and political power, resolved the issue. "There is no 'right' answer," the mayor said in a public statement. "Nevertheless, it is time to move forward. I believe the solution we present today strikes the right balance and although I don't expect everyone to be happy with it, I can assure everyone that their views were heard as we struggled with this question."[27]

The mayor's plan for the names embodied the essence of a classic political compromise. It gave emotional value to each of the main coalitions opposed to the original names arrangement; each could see something of its views in the solution, and that made it acceptable. It pleased those who all along sought that the names' display be brought up to ground level: first responders, Coalition of 9/11 Families, and Put It above Ground Campaign. Also, in linking back to the architect's original flexible notion of meaningful adjacencies, it acknowledged the judgment of the competition jury and the LMDC and the politicians who had first endorsed that arrangement. The shield insignia next to first responders was dropped, meaning there would be no hierarchy, which pleased Thomas S. Johnson, a family member on the boards of the Memorial Foundation and the LMDC, who had been quietly talking with a small ad hoc group of about twenty from different family groups.[28] Among this group, there had been little support, if any, for the random listing, though they differed on how the names would be listed or grouped. In June 2006, a group of family members had publicly refused to endorse the memorial plan until Mayor Bloomberg and Governor Pataki gave up their insistence that the names be arranged randomly. "If ever there was a nonnegotiable issue, this is it," Johnson was quoted as saying. Six months later, as Dunlap reported, he could vote in favor of the plan: "With the adjacencies for victims whose families wish them to be listed together, and the removal of the shields, which were so objectionable to so many, this is an approach that I hope will be acceptable to the great majority of the families affected." Under the new plan, the uniformed victims would be grouped by command or precinct or company on the parapet ringing the south pool, where so many of the 343 firefighters perished. Even though they did not succeed in getting rank listed next to their victims' names, most firefighters and police agreed with the plan. "It's fitting," Cassidy said in meaningful words that reflected the culture of the firefighters, "that those who perished that day be listed together with their brothers who they went into battle with."[29]

Recording the names of those who died in the terrorist attacks of September 11, 2001, and February 26, 1993, in five rows on parapets surrounding each of the two pools stretching for more than fifteen hundred feet, almost a third of a mile, presented the next level of emotional complexity to be resolved. Extraordinary detail was involved in the exacting task of executing the new plan for meaningful adjacencies. Arad and his team spent roughly a year on the task, arranging and rearranging the names to meet the 1,200 "adjacency requests" made by victims' families. Many of the 2,982 names were arranged by hand using slips of paper printed with each victim's name and other meaningful relationships, and for the final quarter of names, a computer algorithm developed by the media firm Local Projects helped find the best matched location (figure 11.6). With each name there

FIGURE 11.6 *Printed scrolls of the names of the victims of the attacks on the World Trade Center, the Pentagon, and the plane that crashed in Shanksville, Pennsylvania, used by Michael Arad's team to review large sections of the arrangement at once. Clustered by "meaningful adjacencies" on the bronze parapets surrounding each memorial pool, the names run continuously for hundreds of feet.* COURTESY © HANDEL ARCHITECTS

is a story behind why it appears where it does. "These stories are very personal and human; you can relate to them on a personal level," Arad said. The stories brought meaning and clarity to the otherwise overwhelming impact of relating to nearly 3,000 names. The task of arranging the names was "incredibly laborious and emotional," he said. "If you move that name it triggers five other changes and so on." And the length of a name mattered in the composition of the parapet arrangement. The visual effect had to be "seamless," he added, "and it had to give every name its owner place, a physical, geographical specificity." The result presents something of a paradox: The names would "appear to be randomly arranged," Arad said, "when in fact they are very carefully arranged."[30]

The solution to cluster meaningful adjacencies meant that some affiliations such as the victims of the Pentagon attack, the 1993 attack, and the first responders would have their own names' panels (plate 18). The 658 victims who worked at Cantor Fitzgerald, for example, also comprised a self-contained adjacency. This result, however, still did not satisfy Edith Lutnick, a former labor lawyer who was the most outspoken and most often quoted and influential of critics of the random arrangement. (Her other brother, Howard W. Lutnick, chairman and chief executive of Cantor Fitzgerald and a member of the Memorial Foundation board, abstained when the vote came up for approval at the executive committee meeting.) The Lutnicks and their supporters did not get all they wanted, which was to have employees' affiliation listed, as well as their ages and the floors they worked on, and so, for them, the new plan was flawed. "You'll know from this memorial who died at the Pentagon, who died on Flight 175 and who was a firefighter," said Edith Lutnick. "Why do civilians not deserve the same respect and remembrance?"[31]

The dissatisfaction among a small group of family members continued, leading them once again to mount a public campaign against the mayor's compromise solution and to discourage contributions to the memorial until their demands were met. This time, though, they elicited little public sympathy. "It's hard to imagine a group of people who have been listened to more intently than this group of family members," emphasized the editorial board of the *Times*, which stood in strong support of the random arrangement as an expression of the victims' "stark and common fate." "Their views have helped to shape or reshape nearly every aspect of the redevelopment of ground zero—especially the memorial." In an explicit chastisement of Cantor Fitzgerald, the editorial board said, "ground zero cannot be turned into a private memorial. . . . [T]he public memorial must be more expansive." CEO Lutnick offered the Memorial Foundation $25 million on the condition that the names of those killed on the site would be grouped by their workplaces. "Thanks, but no thanks," said the *Daily News* editorial board to his "string-attached donation."[32]

The symbolism of the names' arrangement reflected in the meaningful adjacencies and set-aside panels identified by inscribed group affiliations bestowed emotional meaning, without the added weight of corporate affiliation unlikely to have public meaning thirty or fifty years hence. It was a pragmatic compromise aimed at breaking what the *Times* described as "an intensely emotional impasse that threatens the entire memorial project." The *Daily News* called it "an elegant solution," and the *New York Post* applauded the decision to single out the 9/11 rescuers for special recognition, calling it "one of the few things officials have gotten right at Ground Zero." That the names' solution garnered praise from all three editorial boards, which otherwise tended to see events at Ground Zero from quite different perspectives, was telling of its broad appeal. It was a turning-point achievement, a real and symbolic success with lasting implications. And one that every visitor would experience, especially at dusk, when "the names on the memorial are lit from within, transforming each letter from a void in bronze to a light amid darkness."[33]

MONEY ISSUES

The names issue had been fought out in a complicated environment of continual struggles at Ground Zero. One crisis followed after another, producing chaos and confusion throughout most of 2005 and 2006. When the shocking news of the bloated $972 million price tag for the memorial complex and its interwoven infrastructure hit the front page of the *Times* in May 2006, rebuilding officials conceded that the figure was "beyond reason." Just months earlier the Memorial Foundation spoke of estimates that pegged the cost of the memorial and Memorial Museum at $494 million, roughly on par with the $490 million figure given by the LMDC in November 2005 ($330 million for the memorial and $160 million for the museum), though this estimate did not include the entire cost of stabilizing the slurry wall ($25-plus million), the cost of designing and constructing museum exhibitions ($17-plus million), or most of the memorial's share of infrastructure costs ($110 million).[34] Still, this number was considerably more than the $350 million the LMDC reported to the press soon after the *Reflecting Absence* design had been unveiled in January 2004. The LMDC and the Memorial Foundation were working together, but in November 2005 Dunlap had reported on tensions between the two over design ambitions and cost consciousness on the memorial and Memorial Museum. Now in a confidential memorandum prepared for the Memorial Foundation by its construction manager (provided to the *Times*), Bovis Lend Lease put the cost of the memorial and Memorial Museum at $672 million, a stunning 36 percent increase from the previous $494 million figure. Moreover, none of these estimates included the $80 million budgeted for the Visitor Orientation and Education Center. New York State was funding this building separately, as compensating cover for Governor Pataki's decision to evict the International Freedom Center that would have occupied the structure.

The new estimate promised to make the National 9/11 Memorial at the Trade Center the most expensive memorial ever built in the United States, as both the *Times* and the *Wall Street Journal* emphasized by comparing the cost figure to the $182 million National World War II Memorial in Washington, D.C. (opened in 2004), the $29 million Oklahoma City National Memorial (opened in 2000), and the $7 million Vietnam Veterans Memorial in Washington D.C. (opened in 1982). (Adjusted for inflation in a conversion to 2006 dollars, the cost comparisons were slightly larger: $194.2 million, $34 million, and $14.6 million, respectively.) Though they could not supply a solution, the cost comparisons presented a wake-up perspective on the chaos of decision-making surrounding not just the memorial but the totality of rebuilding the Trade Center site. They called attention, and not for the first time, to the crisis in political leadership at Ground Zero.

The reign of chaos during this period brought forth more searing critiques from the editorial pages of the city's newspapers. They railed about the lack of progress, a morass they traced to the absence of clear and positive leadership. "Confusion reigns because Gov. Pataki has yet to display the savvy and leadership needed to guide creation of a viable replacement for the World Trade Center," opined the *Daily News*. Six weeks later, under the same headline, "Wanted: Leadership at Ground

Zero," it reiterated the complaint: "Here we are again, mired in incompetence and recriminations after someone finally had the good sense to put a dollar estimate to the cost of building the memorial and museum, as designed, approved and championed by Pataki and his aides. Golly, were they surprised to discover that the bills could be as high as $1 billion." The paper called for someone "with credible numbers and a clear process for trimming the memorial. For better or worse, this could be Pataki, or he could delegate responsibility to Bloomberg, whose term, after all, extends longer than the governor's. Either way, one ultimately accountable boss."[35]

The void in leadership advantaged Michael Bloomberg, who in his bid for a second term aggressively pushed forceful positions to intervene in the rebuilding process. To many observers, the mayor's welcomed intervention was belated, coming as it did only after his economic development aspirations for an Olympic bid and stadium on the far West Side of midtown Manhattan failed to materialize. Occupied with those priorities for most of his first term, the mayor had stayed in the shadows of the issues at Ground Zero, preferring instead to focus his actions on the broader canvas of lower Manhattan. Now, he was engaged, totally. Saying, "there's just not an unlimited amount of money that we can spend on a memorial," in early May 2006, he publicly called for responsible cost control on the memorial agenda, virtually mandating a spending cap of $500 million.[36]

This crisis marked a political watershed. A consensus of opinion over the out-of-bounds, uncontrollable costs of the memorial spilled across the editorial pages of each of the city's three daily newspapers, foretelling its untenable status. "The only thing a $1 billion memorial would memorialize is a complete collapse of political and private leadership in Lower Manhattan," lamented the *Times*. "It isn't merely the fact that the number is so high: $972 and rising. It's also the fact that the task of planning a buildable memorial has fallen into such disarray." The *Daily News* lectured the governor: "Here, too, we have a case in which this lamest of gubernatorial ducks charted a course for the site of the twin towers without paying attention to a mundane matter like economics, apparently believing all would work out if he made enough smiley promises. The *Post* pointed a figure at the "bitter *sub rosa* tussle over who'll pay for the memorial's infrastructure" as "bolstering the case for scaling back the grossly expensive undertaking." The new infrastructure estimate (based on data from both the Port Authority and Bovis) came in at $301 million, or nearly triple the previous estimate of $110 million by the foundation, the LMDC, and the Port Authority. Only a month had passed since the Port Authority agreed to contribute $100 million toward the construction costs for the memorial as part of an overall major realignment of public and private responsibilities for rebuilding the site, discussed in a later chapter. Now it was positioning to have the Memorial Foundation contribute $135.2 million to pay for specific common elements (structural systems, mechanical fit out of the central chiller plant, police and emergency operations centers, electrical service and site utilities, and relocation of river water lines out of the museum area). The foundation's position was clear: Neither it and by extension, its private donors, should have to pay for sitewide infrastructure costs. "The Port Authority, as overall owner of the site, or other governmental agencies will have to be responsible for general site-wide costs to provide the Foundation with a 'buildable site,'" the Bovis memo argued logically.[37]

The allocation of costs inevitably reflected the complexity of multiple users and property interests sharing the dense sixteen-acre site. It was derivative of the Port Authority's early deterministic decision to rebuild as a single integrated complex with a sitewide common infrastructure. The vast size of the seventy-foot-deep "pit" was also a big driver of costs. The engineering intricacy of the underground too was a definite factor in the equation. While construction experts would not find it difficult to determine the individual cost elements, in general, determining which use, what interest, would be responsible for what cost was never going to be a formulaic exercise. It was always going to be a negotiation. Allocation negotiations seek to resolve technical questions: I put this column in this place, now how much of the cost should be charged to each use benefiting from the fact that this column supports it? The chiller plant providing cooling capacity to the site, how much (if any) of the cost should be allocated to the memorial? There were hundreds, if not thousands, of similar allocation questions.

The struggle over shared infrastructure, as in any development project, becomes a fight over money. The concepts of the memorial design and the quality expectations for its buildout were bound to be costly. For example, no one had ever built fountains like those Arad called for in *Reflecting Absence*, and there was a myriad of other challenging technical issues to resolve in executing the design. To sustain the four hundred white swamp oak trees Walker specified, an extensive buried ecosystem needed to be built. And the New York construction market is the most expensive in the United States. Was it any wonder that with the project having gotten this far, with preparatory construction work on the memorial underway for just two months, costs became a prominent issue? The tumult that followed the shocking cost revelations and set in motion a series of events, however, was not as predictable.

The Memorial Foundation quickly came under intense fire for slow progress in raising its share of the cost burden. The first blast came from New York's no-nonsense mayor (not yet chairman of the Memorial Foundation), who believed the foundation was too focused on design and construction to the neglect of its fundraising responsibility. Foundation board members "bristled at Mr. Bloomberg's lectures over cost-cutting, saying they were the ones who first raised the alarm," the

Times reported. Two days after being blasted, the foundation announced it was indefinitely suspending fundraising activity "until complete clarity can be achieved with respect to the design and costs of the project." The next day, Governor Pataki's office—ever conscious of the clock running on the administration's tenure and intently focused on protecting the governor's legacy at Ground Zero during the remaining seven months—issued a rebuke, telling the foundation to "focus on their most important task—fund-raising." Three days later, Whitehead announced his resignation as chairman of both the LMDC and the Memorial Foundation effective at the end of May, though he would continue to serve as a member of the foundation. Apologizing for having to make the announcement "at such a challenging moment," he cited his four and a half years spearheading the post-9/11 rebuilding efforts, the passage of his eighty-fourth birthday, and the insistence of his family and his doctor that he step down. Moving quickly within the week, the governor appointed Kevin M. Rampe, the former president of the LMDC and a member of the Memorial Foundation board, as the new LMDC chairman. Next up event—the beleaguered foundation president and chief executive Gretchen Dykstra, "under tremendous and conflicting pressures," submitted her resignation after thirteen months on the job, notwithstanding a vote of confidence approved by the board via conference call three weeks earlier. The negatives of weak fundraising and slow progress in launching a strong national campaign had so frustrated many foundation board members that some spoke out publicly and strongly criticized her lack of leadership in moving the "ball forward."[38] Her departure presented further embarrassing evidence of chaos at the emotional core of Ground Zero (figure 11.7).

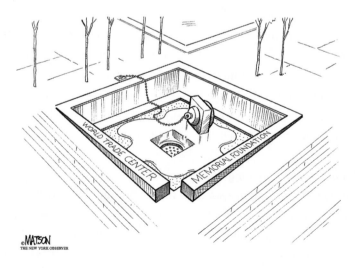

FIGURE 11.7 RJ Matson/The New York Observer

In its May 6 editorial "A Memorial Amiss," the *Times* pushed for two things to happen right away: "A competent entity needs to be put in charge of building the memorial. That should be the Port Authority, which has far and away the best track record among the concerned parties. Second, there needs to be a comprehensive analysis of Bovis's cost estimates." Both came to pass. The conflict over costs, which had been brewing for some time before the Bovis cost memorandum surfaced, created an opportunity for the Port Authority to step up its game and further muscle its way into total control of rebuilding. Months earlier in an announcement about its preliminary vision for a big shopping complex at the bases of three of the Silverstein towers (not yet designed), the Port said it could take on the memorial task. "We're very good at building things," said Kenneth J. Ringler Jr., the authority's successor to Seymour as executive director. "We've already got a $2 billion contract for the PATH terminal, we know the site better than anybody, and we think there would be a great benefit if we did this work for the foundation."[39] This was just two weeks before the Memorial Foundation would issue a request for proposals for a memorial construction manager.

The city had decided the Port Authority should take over construction of the memorial. Deputy Mayor Doctoroff, newly appointed to the LMDC board by Mayor Bloomberg (along with five other Bloomberg appointees), said, "From some perspectives, it makes a lot of sense.... [A] lot of work has to be done quickly to ensure what we do there really maximizes the efficiency of construction." In reality, it all came down to money. The mayor was direct: "One of the things that they have offered to do is to guarantee [that there would be] no cost overruns, which I will say does make it very attractive." Although Governor Pataki and Mayor Bloomberg were not always seeing eye to eye on issues at Ground Zero, the governor went on record with the same opinion. The proposal by the Port Authority to serve as construction manager for the Memorial Foundation merited serious consideration, the *Times* reported, if, Pataki said, the authority "can offer the ability to guarantee costs and provide greater efficiency."[40]

The setup was in place. There was no negotiation: The foundation was just told the Port Authority would take over construction. With its legacy of engineering expertise and an offer few if any politicians could refuse—to build the memorial at a fixed cost and cover any cost overruns—the PA and its staff, patiently waiting in the wings of this long-running drama, eventually (September 2006) got what it most likely figured would come sooner or later: consolidated control of the reconstruction of *its* site (and what went along with it: the ability to let more millions of dollars in contracts). The irony of the Port Authority taking over construction of the memorial when the agency's initial plan for the underground had violated the footprints had been long forgotten (figure 11.8).

FIGURE 11.8 *At its monthly meeting on July 6, 2005, the Board of Commissioners of the Port Authority announces that the agency will take over the building of the 9/11 Memorial and Memorial Museum.* CHRIS HONDROS/GETTY NEWS/GETTY IMAGES

REINING IN COSTS

In the meantime, more maneuvering was afoot. Bovis Lend Lease's track record as an experienced construction manager with more than a century of experience in construction services and skill in the complexities of large-scale complex projects spoke for itself. Yet its numbers were not being accepted uncritically by Governor's Pataki's office. For months, tensions between the mayor and governor had been building, as the mayor's posture on Ground Zero became aggressively interventionist. This was in sharp contrast to his stance during much of his first term when he took a position on Ground Zero second to the governor's. At a meeting hastily called by the governor's chief of staff and point person for rebuilding attended by officials of the Memorial Foundation, City Hall, the LMDC, and the Port Authority, Cahill "sharply criticized" the Bovis numbers.[41] The practical exigency of the situation demanded that the memorial design be modified in some material way. A convergence of issues—emergent security concerns, criticisms of the underground galleries by some victims' families, and a clear understanding that the costs of the memorial complex had become politically risky—made revisions mandatory. Concerned about the same set of facts, members of the foundation board's executive committee had met earlier in mid-April with representatives of family groups to discuss modifications to the original Arad-Walker design that would cut costs without violating the essential vision of the design. But if design changes threatened to trigger additional delays in construction, as was likely, it was not hard to see how state officials bent on protecting some kind of legacy for Pataki might resist efforts to radically revise the design.

In time-honored political fashion the chief elected officials called in another expert, Frank Sciame, CEO of F. J. Sciame Construction Company and Sciame Development, and asked him to assist in aligning the WTC memorial with the $500 million budget number. The company had installed a new president and Sciame was scheduled to take a personal three-month sabbatical and travel with his son to deeply research a longtime interest in prefabricated housing. When the calls from both the governor and the mayor came on May 16, the review became his sabbatical. "There was only one answer to give them," he told the press. "We started on May 17."[42]

Sciame saw this call to public service as a big task with big implications. The timeline for a report with recommendations was short: twenty-five days. Trained as an architect and operating as a developer, consultant, and construction executive, Sciame was widely respected and generally considered unbiased. He was also familiar with the memorial program, as his firm had teamed with Skanska USA in a bid to be the construction manager for the project, but failed to win the prize. He would only take on the task, he told Doctoroff and Cahill, if he had the authority to do it, that is, bring the budget in line without a veto for political reasons. Peter Walker said the designers viewed the exercise skeptically at first: "We were pretty deeply into working drawings when this happened—our portion was at 95 percent. We were fearful that Frank and his people were coming in at a late date."[43]

And so began the process leading to the next and final round of design revisions. The memorial, wrote *Times* reporters Charles V. Bagli and David W. Dunlap, "was supposed to be immune to the controversies that had engulfed the commercial rebuilding at the site, with its completion assured by an outpouring of good will and open checkbooks." Echoing the thoughts others shared, Dunlap kept up a steady flow of questioning reportage. "Will the fundamental design of the memorial have to be radically revised? And how did costs get so high in the first place?" Ever quick to catch the nuanced wording of a press release, he wrote that it was telling that Pataki and Bloomberg promised to remain committed to the Arad-Walker "vision"—not the "design." Using the word "vision" gave Pataki, the LMDC, and the Memorial Foundation "a lot of rhetorical maneuvering room. But how many revisions can the memorial sustain before that vision is diluted? Or lost?"[44]

The cost crisis over the memorial complex reflected a deeper set of issues stifling the promise of progress. Why was there no budget for the memorial? How much of the cost escalation could be pinned on what the experts called "scope creep," the uncontrolled and continuous growth in a project beyond already defined specifications? What were the underlying problems with fundraising? Why was it lagging? Was Whitehead being given all the support he needed in the effort to raise funds? And who was calling the shots? If the LMDC's job was to manage the memorial design process and the foundation's job was to raise the funds for its construction and operations, where did accountability reside? If clarity was lacking on this critical governance question, how would the political tensions between the Port Authority, the state of New York, and the city of New York resolve themselves in the cost crisis over the memorial? And how and why was it that Mayor Bloomberg took over the chairmanship of the foundation?

The divorce from budget consciousness started in the jury room of the memorial design competition. No consideration was given to a budget during the deliberations, said one jury member. "It was not part of our discussion when we were selecting the design. The only question asked, 'Was it possible to do this?'" This was not surprising as the guidelines for the memorial competition specified that "the budget for the memorial will depend upon the memorial design," and early in the review process the jury made a "very conscious decision not to consider issues of cost or budget, knowing that figuring out costs of various designs would have been a purely speculative exercise and a real distraction. The issue of costs and budget could only be addressed once a design was chosen and construction was planned," another jury member, memorial scholar James E. Young, told me.

From the beginning of the process, Mayor Bloomberg wanted cost to enter the equation, but he could not prevail against the emotionalism of the event: "When we asked about the various proposals' costs at the behest of the mayor, we got criticism," Rampe said. "It was like, 'How can you put a cost on the memorial?'" A budget for the memorial was still not a discussion item at LMDC board meetings until the issue was raised by Carl Weisbrod, one of the mayor's appointees to the board, at the November 2005 meeting (the first meeting after the Freedom Center had been evicted from the site). When a request for authorization to amend the agreements with the architects for the memorial by an additional $26.4 million came up for discussion, Weisbrod raised several questions: Was there an overall budget for planning and construction for the memorial and Memorial Museum? In response, President Stefan Pryor said "that the Corporation should be careful in releasing numbers that were raw and not yet value-engineered."[45] Weisbrod's next question was more fundamental: Was the LMDC trying to build to a budget at this time? The LMDC would be contributing millions to the memorial, so he wanted to understand what its contribution would represent as a percentage of the total. From the fiduciary perspective of a board member, if the LMDC was contributing funds without a budget in place, might it be expected to pay for the whole thing? And if the Performing Arts Center did not come to fruition, would the $100 million that the LMDC pledged to that use find its ways into the memorial?

Weisbrod is a politically savvy player who had been president of the City's Economic Development Corporation and before that president of the Forty-second Street Development Project. His experience in the arena of public-private development made him one of Mayor Bloomberg's first appointments to the LMDC board in 2002. He was widely respected and then president of the Alliance for Downtown New York, the city's largest business improvement district. Weisbrod knew it would be difficult to move along with plans for the overall project, which included the cultural spaces (Snøhetta building and the Performing Arts Center), if the budget for the memorial was a "constantly moving target."[46] When the Bovis estimates for the memorial complex hit the press in early May 2006, a couple of months after preparatory site work had started without a finalized budget in place, they revealed that increased scope for the Museum Entry Pavilion and cost estimates for the museum exhibit design and construction accounted for two of the four largest drivers of the cost differential—approximately $45 million, or 25 percent of the total.

Getting a firm handle on the construction budget of the memorial was precisely what Peter M. Lehrer, a well-known expert in construction management whose firm Lehrer/McGovern had managed the high-profile centennial restoration of the Statue of Liberty among many other high-profile projects, and Roland Betts had been working on for the past nine months, since August 2005. Serving without pay as cochairs of the joint design advisory review committee set up by the LMDC, they met weekly at noon in his conference room at Chelsea Piers (Pier 62 on the city's West Side waterfront, which Betts had developed with his partner Tom Bernstein). Working "bluntly," according to the *Times*, they intended "to bring certainty, clarity and momentum to a planning process that had been floundering"; they were not aiming to alter the memorial design, just make the design work.[47]

As early as October 2005, Lehrer reported to the foundation board that they were analyzing ways of controlling costs because the tight construction market was inflating prices. At this point, they still expected the memorial to open on September 11, 2009. In January, at the next quarterly board meeting, shortly after the first bid package for actual construction work had been issued, Lehrer described the complexity of the site and the challenges in coordinating the construction of the memorial and Memorial Museum with the other projects on the site; these included the reconstruction of the PATH and subway stations and the restoration of the utility infrastructure. While construction issues were still outstanding, all parties were working toward resolving them. The capital budget, he reported, was continuing "to be refined."

Alarm arose when in response to the January solicitation to contractors for pouring the concrete footings for the memorial, a job estimated at $12 million, they received bids ranging from $29 million to $61 million. This was two to four times above what they anticipated, the *Times* later reported in May when the cost crisis became public. Lehrer was first to blow the whistle that costs were running above the $500 million figure. At first some people thought he was being too conservative, according to one insider speaking off the record, so the foundation asked Bovis Lend Lease, which had won the construction management contract, to do a comprehensive review of the status of costs. The review was in progress when Lehrer reported to the board at its April meeting, after which he said that they expected to revisit the construction budget. The completion of that comprehensive review proved Lehrer was right. It was equally clear that value engineering, a process to find savings in building methods and materials that compromises neither safety nor design integrity, which to date had been productive, would no longer be sufficient to rein in costs. Meeting on a quarterly basis, the full board would be receiving reports a step behind the rapidly moving set of events that was shaping public perception of problems and a lack of forward progress.

Arad's Initiation to Reality

Infighting among the project's architects was another reason the Betts-Lehrer committee had been put in place. In relatively short order Michael Arad had alienated many professionals working on the memorial project. His relationships with all of the architects had eroded beyond repair. "It's shades of bad. I say that as someone who does respect Michael," LMDC president Stefan Pryor was quoted as saying in Joe Hagen's expose article in *New York Magazine*, "The Breaking of Michael Arad."[48] The tensions got so bad, an insider told me that Arad's father had to be called in to talk to Whitehead; the men knew each other from diplomatic circles; Moshe Arad had served as the Israeli ambassador to the United States (1987–1990) and before that as ambassador to Mexico (1983–1987).

Foundation board members too were frustrated with Arad. The "gray hairs" on the project team had tried to explain the reality of construction to him, but he was difficult, very difficult, and came to be seen as another source of contention on the already difficult cost issue. The conflict was between Arad and reality, one said. He did not have the knowledge to execute technically. He had never built anything, yet he was insistent that it had to be built his way; it was his design. He fought hard, as Hagen described in absorbing detail. He was not interested in cost pragmatism. At the end, he was angry.

The big decisions were being made by the foundation's Standing Committee for Design, Construction, and Real Estate cochaired by Lehrer, the "real adults" in the room as some put it. Day-to-day decisions were being made by the foundation's

FIGURE 11.9   New York *cover story "The Breaking of Michael Arad."* Photo by Michael O'Neil for New York Magazine

executive vice president for design, construction and capital planning, William H. Goldstein, and general counsel, Joseph C. Daniels. "Well you have to know that story [Hagen's expose on Arad's behavior] was planted," Peter Walker told architectural critic Christopher Hawthorne in an extensive interview for *Landscape Architecture Magazine.* Hawthorne asked, "By whom?" Walker thought it was probably someone on the elected side. "But it was a political thing, had nothing to do with the design. It was a political remedy. It was a way of disciplining us. And it worked a little because Michael came off badly in that."[49] The Hagen article was deliberate, another inside player told me; it was a way to take Arad down because he had become impossibly demanding, and the project needed to move forward (figure 11.9).

Moving to translate Michael Arad's conceptual ideas into schematic design and then construction detail laid bare the complexity of ambitions (and the elusiveness of the design ideal) for the memorial program held by all those involved: the design team, the 9/11 families, the LMDC, and the Memorial Foundation. For the demanding technical task of turning conceptual design into architectural reality, the LMDC had selected as the associated architects for the project Davis Brody & Bond Architects (DBB), a firm known for its practicality and its dedication to building structures of public purpose, as well as its knowledge of the ways of New York and how things got built there. "We're not coming in as critics," J. Max Bond Jr. said. "Our object is to take their concept and figure out how to realize it, to keep the design's integrity intact but also figure out all these problems, everything from infrastructure to security to lighting to fountains to the hardware on the doors. It's a wonderful opportunity to implement something that is going to carry great historical and emotional meaning."[50]

Those were the types of projects Bond excelled at and the ones that held significance for the sixty-eight-year-old influential African American, an eminence grise in architectural circles. He was responsible for the design of the Martin Luther King Jr. Center for Nonviolent Social Change in Atlanta and the Birmingham Civil Rights Institute in Alabama, as well as Harlem's Schomburg Center for Research in Black Culture. At DBB, he was the partner in charge of the Audubon Biomedical Science and Technology Park for Columbia University, which included the redevelopment of the Audubon Ballroom, where Malcolm X was assassinated. As an educator (former chair of the architecture department at Columbia University, and then dean of the School of Architecture and Environmental Studies at City College of New York) as well as a practitioner, he was always an influential role model for younger minority architects. Having served on the City Planning Commission from 1980 to 1986, and worked for the Port Authority on improving the public spaces of the original World Trade Center, he understood the inside game of New York development politics. He had served on the Memorial Program Drafting Committee of the LMDC. Gracious in manner, Bond held firm to strong principled positions. He was critical of the early ideas of the gardens and viewing platforms on high floors or at the tops of buildings, believing that any privately controlled space would come under strict scrutiny and, as a result, not be universally welcoming. The public realm was particularly important for "a city of immigrants," he said. "Architecture inevitably involves all the larger issues of society."[51] Until his untimely death, Bond would serve as the partner in charge of a team of twenty DBB professionals working with Arad and Walker and his DBB partner Steven M. Davis, who was the design partner on the project.

Early in its review of the plans, DBB proposed modifying *Reflecting Absence* to meet exacting engineering requirements and the competing demands of the many-layered site. The four ramps in Arad's conceptual design—one to enter and one to exit at each pool—were problematic; they were everywhere, said one member of the team. Arad wanted a long procession of ramps down to the memorial to serve as a transition from urban activity to private reflection; making their way by the series of ramps, visitors would descend gradually to bedrock where the names of those who died inscribed on low stone parapets surrounding the pools would be viewed through a curtain of cascading water falling from above. "He felt he was going to express himself through these passageways with the really beautiful image of standing behind these waterfalls and the water coming down and you'd see out," Walker said many years later.[52] When his vision was subjected to detailed tests of practical reality, however, engineering and security difficulties and the deadening roar of the waterfalls compounded one another.

In what was called "the war of the ramps," DBB proposed altering the placement of the pools, centering them in the footprints in a way that made Arad's scheme for four ramps untenable; in Arad's conceptual design, the pools were not centered in the footprints of the twin towers. Keeping the four ramps would have made it necessary to shift the alignment of the pools, and the misalignment would have been obvious because of the column stub remnants. Arad objected, aggressively and persistently: "It's not my vision." As he conceptualized the memorial, the four ramps were fundamental to the integrity of the original winning design. Reducing the ramps to two threatened to destroy "his notion of drawing visitors through a distinct walking narrative that focused on the experience of the pools, especially the initial breathtaking view at the bottom." More to the point, Hagen wrote, the change, "represented everything he had feared about losing control of the project."[53]

In violation of his contract, Arad went directly to LMDC board members to gain a final hearing on the ramps selectively using pieces of DBB's analysis to support his case. It didn't work, but it did elicit from Disney chairman Michael Eisner, a foundation board member and longtime patron of architecture, "some fatherly advice:" "If I were you, at this stage of my life," he was reported as saying by two witnesses to the scene, "I would get behind this thing and claim victory at the end. Let things move the way they need to move, and don't obstruct things."[54] In other words, Eisner was telling Arad it was time to wear long pants. After months of lost time causing further delays—LMDC officials said the war over the ramps put the project six months behind schedule—Arad lost out to DBB's solution for a two-ramp scheme. That was but the first alteration before the problematic ramps disappeared altogether when a committee Sciame formed recommended moving the name parapets to the ground plane of the Memorial Plaza. Once again it was a wise, older person, Robert R. Douglass, as a member of Sciame's committee and a former trustee of Dartmouth College, where Arad received a bachelor's degree, who had the task of delivering the message to Arad that the underground memorial could not be done. When Arad heard, he said, "That's not what I designed." Douglass responded: "You have two choices: adapt your design or walk away and disavow the design, becoming Michael who?"[55] After he lost the ramps episode, Arad was reduced to managing the names and the parapets.

The Only Option: Up

Sciame's charge was to "ensure a buildable World Trade Center memorial" in line with the politically mandated budget of $500 million. He was tasked to develop a set of "design refinement options" that would "be evaluated as to their consistency with *Reflecting Absence* and the Master Plan, Security Implications, Construction Costs, and Operations Cost." After the options were presented to the governor and mayor, the LMDC would solicit public input on the design refinements; then in consultation with the governor, the mayor, and the Memorial Foundation, the refinements would be submitted to the LMDC board for consideration and for adoption at its July board meeting. That was the careful process as laid out in the LMDC's press release of May 17, 2006. Sciame, however, had a broader view of what would be required; he was not going to confine his evaluation solely to the technical aspects of the cost dilemma. The political dimension of the task was equally important; he wanted to eliminate as much controversy as possible surrounding the beleaguered memorial. "If I didn't have enthusiastic support from everyone," he said, "I felt the task would have failed."[56]

He had been schooled on the political approach while studying architecture at City College of New York. In a course on the Politics of the Environment his professor required the class to read about Tammany Hall's powerful G. W. Plunkitt and the building of the Brooklyn Bridge, and from that class dialogue he came to understand how big a role politics played in how cities were shaped. Translated to the task at hand, he would meet with everyone: the designers (Arad, Walker, Bond, Libeskind, Dykers), the immediate stakeholders (LMDC, PA, Memorial Foundation), memorial-related interest groups (Families Advisory Council, the Memorial Mission Statement Drafting Committee, the Memorial Program Drafting Committee, and the Memorial Center Advisory Committee), as well as many members of the memorial jury, residential and commercial community leaders, and family members. "It was nonstop meetings," he told me. "We were listening and taking lots of notes." The extensive outreach was not expected. Sciame, though, wanted to understand what the families believed were the most important features of the memorial. For the design and technical issues, he assembled what he "thought was a really elite group of advisers"; no one refused the call, and all worked pro bono.[57] They worked off the already extensive analysis done by the Betts-Lehrer joint design-review advisory committee of the foundation and the LMDC. The cost numbers of that committee looked reasonable, but he had to understand the reasons why costs had escalated so; he did not believe the cost could be $972 million.

They set up a war room to review the data, with value engineering as a given. They established an evaluation matrix across three categories (design-layout, materials and value substitutions, and value engineering and construction methodology) and seven criteria (consistency with the *Reflecting Absence* vision; consistency with the master plan; security implications; dollar impact of construction cost savings; operational costs; schedule impact on September 11, 2009, opening; and practicality). They analyzed the impact of infrastructure shared across the site on the memorial and Memorial Museum and took issue with the Port Authority's position on the projected $301 million tab. That's what the Port claimed it would cost just to fill the seventy-foot hole from base to grade—to what Betts called "your windswept plaza." In what became a heated discussion, Sciame argued that this should not be a cost to the memorial, and he would not budge on this point. His team's analytical efforts shaved $123 million off the Port's infrastructure cost estimate and assumed the cost of the streets and sidewalks ($28 million) could be funded from other government entities.[58] The remaining $150 million, he argued, was the Port's responsibility. The agency had wanted a centralized underground it could control—and control carried a cost: it was going to have to accept the cost responsibility for getting to grade.

The time frame for their detailed eight-step process[59] was compressed. A few days prior to the June 15 deadline for the draft report, Sciame presented five options ranging in cost from $506 million to $614 million to the governor and mayor. The night before the presentation, the mayor's staff asked Sciame to include the operating costs of each memorial design in the presentation, which sent the team into an eleventh-hour crush. "The scary part of the task was that it needed to work," Sciame recalled. "It couldn't fail, or else the mayor and governor might abandon the memorial design and say, 'start again.'" One of the most contentious decisions—a critical break point—was whether to preserve the underground memorial galleries at the site and remove a waterfall structure or keep the waterfall. In a meeting that reportedly lasted about two hours, the political chief executives chose one option to include in the draft report—elimination of the underground galleries and retention of the waterfall. All thought this was in keeping with the original vision of *Reflecting Absence*.[60]

The underground galleries had been done in by a powerful confluence of forces: security vulnerabilities, vocal 9/11 family opposition, and high cost—security being the foremost determinant of the design alteration. At a savings of $162 million, the "refinement" significantly reconfigured the memorial experience without sacrificing what had become the touchstone of Arad's vision: the void absences within the footprints of the twin towers. With the bronze parapets surrounding the pools at grade on the Memorial Plaza, visitors reading the names would be able to look out over the falls of water and into the voids. At grade the names' parapets were immediate. The six underground galleries and ramps that had been a source of contention were no longer necessary since the plan was for visitors to

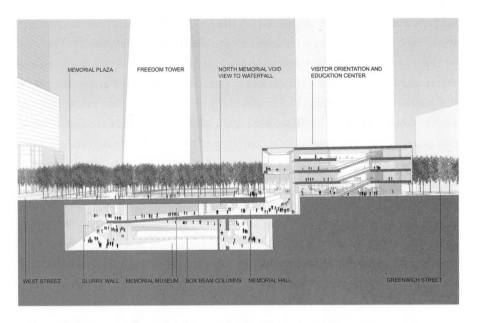

FIGURE 11.10 *Cross-section of the planned Memorial Museum entered from the plaza-level Museum Pavilion designed by Snøhetta.* RENDERING SNØHETTA/COURTESY 9/11 MEMORIAL

enter the memorial complex from a single screening point within the Visitor Orientation and Education Center (VOEC), from which they could access all elements of the memorial quadrant. They could choose to descend below grade to bedrock through the Memorial Museum, where they would still be able to see a symbolic section of the slurry wall and the truncated remains of the twin tower perimeter columns as well as other large 9/11 artifacts repositioned in the museum from Hangar 17 (figure 11.10).

The new arrangement also eliminated the issues with sound and noise as well as the need for the second entry pavilion that had been planned on the west side of the memorial quadrant. It scaled down other elements by cutting back the size of the Memorial Museum 20 percent, minimizing the memorial-related mechanical equipment located within the footprints, and consolidating spaces needed to run the museum's operations. Altogether, the memorial and the Memorial Museum now carried a $510 million cost tag. Counting the $80 million budget number for the VOEC—which was never included in cost figures for the memorial complex since it was being funded by the governor's 2006–2007 budget—and the $178 million for infrastructure (including $28 million to be covered by "appropriate grants" similarly not counted in the oft-cited cost figures), and a $90 million reserve fund for cost overruns, the full budgeted cost for building out the memorial complex totaled approximately $870 million (figure 11.11). The Sciame exercise reduced the cost estimate by $285.1 million, nearly 30 percent. The budget

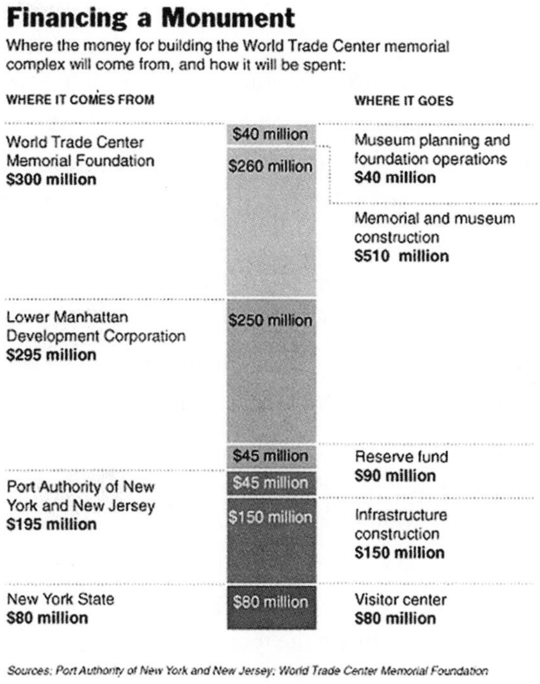

Financing a Monument

Where the money for building the World Trade Center memorial complex will come from, and how it will be spent:

WHERE IT COMES FROM		WHERE IT GOES
World Trade Center Memorial Foundation **$300 million**	$40 million	Museum planning and foundation operations **$40 million**
	$260 million	Memorial and museum construction **$510 million**
Lower Manhattan Development Corporation **$295 million**	$250 million	
Port Authority of New York and New Jersey **$195 million**	$45 million	Reserve fund **$90 million**
	$45 million	
	$150 million	Infrastructure construction **$150 million**
New York State **$80 million**	$80 million	Visitor center **$80 million**

Sources: Port Authority of New York and New Jersey; World Trade Center Memorial Foundation

FIGURE 11.11 FROM THE NEW YORK TIMES, JULY 7, 2006
© 2006 THE NEW YORK TIMES

figures, however, would soon be revised upward. The first revision came by the end of the year, after a reconciliation review by the Port Authority and the Memorial Foundation; with the new estimate at $530 million, the Foundation was charged with fundraising responsibility for the additional $20 million, the cost of closing the gap between the new cost figure ($530 million) and the Sciame cost figure ($510 million). Knowledge of what the memorial complex would ultimately actually cost would come only with time and audited costs, but costs would increase, inevitably, creeping up to the $1 billion-plus figure once again.

The announced simplification of the design was viewed by at least one critic as "likely to be an improvement." Writing for the *New York Sun*, arts and culture critic James Gardner lamented the fact that the memorial had to be expensive. "The problem with the memorial has never been the lack of money," he wrote. "Rather it was an unwieldy surfeit of dollars thrown at a design that would have profited from a far humbler conception." He praised the Firefighters' Memorial on Liberty Street "a 56-foot long bronze banner with a frieze and the names of the fallen," as an example of "simplicity itself" (figure 11.5). To his way of thinking, the need for value engineering of a project, which the press release on the World Trade Center Memorial on June 20 praised as "significant cost saving," was reflective of the fundamental problem, which "essentially means building on the cheap." Building on the cheap was not, however, how the memorial was going to be built.[61]

The single recommendation of the fourteen-page draft report—to move the parapets surrounding the pools up to the ground plane of the Memorial Plaza—justified what was going on in behind-the-scenes discussions with family members and others set in motion earlier by the foundation. By intent, the charge of the Sciame commission was to develop a set of "design refinement options" rather than look for wholesale major changes to be made, suggesting perhaps that the decision to remove the underground galleries was already in the works. These kinds of things were happening regularly, one insider said. Different players were constantly rendering opinions. It was chaotic, and from an outside perspective, incomprehensible.

Shortly before the change was made public, Sciame, Cahill, and Rampe met with Arad and "asked him if he would publicly challenge the decision to eliminate the underground galleries." Angry but resigned to what was coming, Arad decided that going public with his discontent "would satisfy nothing but my own feelings."[62] For the record, he said these were among the more "painful cuts" he was being asked to approve. "This change is the result of a difficult process that addressed the costs of this important endeavor. While I am disappointed by this change, I recognize the imperative to move forward and begin construction of the memorial as soon as possible." He pledged "to continue working to build a dignified memorial that remains true to the original objective—creating a place where we can all find the spaces to gather, reflect and share the memory of those lost." Walker told the press, "We like the majority of it, and we respect it," saying that Sciame "had to make decisions and choices among the competing interests in a way that doesn't destroy things." After the seven-day public-comment period during which 1,006 comments on the proposed changes were received,[63] the LMDC board unanimously adopted the scaled-back plans for the memorial complex.

THE MAYOR TAKES OVER

Reaction to what the *Times* editorial page labeled "9/11 Memorial, Version 2.0," was muted. The proposed resolution "should come as a relief to everyone who worried that the cost-cutting would turn the memorial into nothing more than a gloried city park." Restating concerns expressed earlier in the month, the editors took issue with the size and scope of the underground museum, "which has fairly taken over the underground galleries" and "been expanded out of proportion by those tinkering with the design since it was first approved." Just as problematic, "the Sciame redesign barely attempts to rein it in." The *Post* had no words of praise, only condemnation of the "Memorial Madness." It argued that "such astro-nomical figures demand more than a mere nip here and tuck there in the plans" that the Sciame proposal had offered.[64]

The path to resolution of the cost crisis masked underlying tensions between Albany and City Hall simmering since Mayor Bloomberg started campaigning for reelection. A lame-duck governor, Pataki was facing the likely prospect that a Democrat, New York's attorney general, Eliot L. Spitzer, would be the next person to occupy the governor's mansion come January 2007. Concerned about his legacy at Ground Zero, he wanted visual signs of progress by the time he left office at the end of 2006—a shovel in the ground before then. A stalled project was an obvious threat. Whitehead's resignation as chairman of both the LMDC and the founda-tion brought the power struggle into the public arena as each man vied to put his forces into position on the LMDC board. Each had eight seats, but the governor had final say over the selection of the LMDC chair since the development corpora-tion was a subsidiary of the state-chartered Empire State Development Corporation.

The Pataki camp reportedly favored ESDC chairman Charles Gargano, a long-time ally of the governor already on the LMDC board, but his adversarial relation-ship with the mayor's deputy for economic development, Daniel Doctoroff, was well known. With Mayor Bloomberg's agreement, Governor Pataki appointed Kevin Rampe as chairman and specifically charged him with coordinating the re-design and construction of the memorial by September 11, 2008. Although Rampe had become an executive at ACE Group of Companies in Philadelphia, he had re-mained very much engaged with the memorial as a member of the Foundation Board and its executive committee. Not long after these appointments, Spitzer, in full campaign mode, entered the fray, launching charges at the LMDC. "The LMDC—let me be very clear—the LMDC has been an abject failure, and those who were running the LMDC deserve an enormous piece of criticism," he pronounced.[65]

It was in this politically charged, volatile environment that the governor had tasked Sciame with cost control. Given Bloomberg's criticism of the foundation's lagging fundraising, the families' call for a fundraising boycott, and then the foundation's own decision to suspend fundraising, the governor undoubtedly wanted his own person in charge of the process for realigning the memorial to a realistic budget. Much as he did with earlier inflection-point decisions, Pataki took control in reactive fashion for political reasons. Inserting Sciame into the process directly challenged the leadership and competency of the private nonprofit foundation he did not control; it was a "slap at the foundation," wrote *Times* re-porter Charles V. Bagli.[66] If it was not resolved soon, the memorial cost crisis threatened not just more delays but the possibility of any positive legacy for the governor at Ground Zero.

In July, the Port Authority made good on its commitment to construct the memorial and signed a project agreement with the LMDC, the foundation, the city, and the state that laid out the design, development, construction, financing, and operation responsibilities of each player. In mid-August construction crews started work on 118 of the 142 foundation units, called footings, of the memorial complex from which the structure would rise from within the deep hole at Ground Zero. Construction progress was finally visible at Ground Zero, but the question of true and effective leadership still haunted the project—until Mayor Bloomberg took over as chairman of the Memorial Foundation a few months later in December 2006.[67]

The Memorial Foundation had been pointedly questioned on several fronts by the city's leading editorialists and sharply criticized by the mayor and by other stakeholders. It was a private nonprofit entity with a mission to raise funds from private donors for the 9/11 Memorial and Memorial Museum, so how would it be accountable for decisions that were going to shape the sacred ground of the memorial as a public place? As a private entity, it was exempt from the mandates for open meetings and records that apply to public agencies, so would there be disclosure? And would what was disclosed be "sufficient and timely" to satisfy transparency standards that went along with the importance of its mission and the millions of dollars in federal funds it would receive from the LMDC for construction of the 9/11 Memorial and Memorial Museum? The relationship between the foundation and the LMDC was vague. Having the same chairman for both entities was too conflicted, and the overlap of several board members further blurred the lines between the two entities. Was there duplication of effort in addition to unclear lines of decision-making between these two? During the big kerfuffle over costs, the *Times* editorial board questioned its reason for being, saying the task of building the memorial should be done by the Port Authority with the foundation's activities confined to private fundraising.

Internal dissension, weak management, and leadership disquiets further compounded the foundation's problems. Donors wanted to know that there was someone in charge making decisions. Fundraising had stalled out. With the negative press the foundation had been getting, it had been hard to raise money for the memorial. When Hurricane Katrina hit in August 2006, competition for private donations for this new calamity further handicapped fundraising. Constant press coverage of the foundation's fundraising troubles became self-reinforcing. The foundation had been late in getting to the task of fundraising, having started in 2005, nearly two years after a lengthy process of planning the memorial. Good intentions and a stellar high-profile board simply had not been enough to overcome the early problem in attracting star power to lead the fundraising effort, and the mayor's first-term focus on a bid for the 2012 Olympics and the development of the far West Side certainly had not helped. (Whitehead, I was told, complained of how hard it was for him to fundraise for the memorial because of the mayor's less than enthusiastic position on downtown.) Only when Bloomberg took over leadership did the fundraising picture change, quickly and dramatically. Within the next eighteen months, the foundation raised $217 million, reaching its revised $350 million fundraising goal for capital construction.

When three of its executive committee members—Russell L. Carson, Ira M. Millstein, and E. John Rosenwald Jr.—met with the mayor for breakfast at Gracie Mansion to convince him to take on the chairmanship of the foundation, the mayor did not hesitate when asked. "It was a seminal moment when he agreed to do it," said Rosenwald, vice chairman of J. P. Morgan Chase and cochair of the foundation's development committee.[68] As one of the city's premier philanthropists who chaired many a capital campaign for some of New York City's most important nonprofit organizations, Rosenwald would now have the strongest possible partner with a proven track record in philanthropy and unique access to others with the kind of money needed for this most civic of civic fundraising campaigns.

Bloomberg's business success and political power created a powerful fundraising platform for the foundation. "His profile was very important to his effectiveness in taking on the chairmanship," Rosenwald explained. "It was not just that he took on the responsibility, he also made a major contribution himself. As a result, we were able to arrange appointments with major corporate leaders in New York and all across the country. He was not asking them to do something he had not done himself, and this was very effective." That he had personally made one of the largest contributions to the memorial effort, at least $15 million, gave him a moral platform to ask others for money and reenergize the foundation's lackluster fundraising campaign. It made it hard for anyone, any corporation to say no. And, I was told, he enjoyed the challenge—going to the big offices, constantly shaking hands with security guards, administrative assistants, among others, and being greeted with smiles. The challenge of fundraising for the memorial became a major project for the mayor. "And it worked."[69]

And the "ask" was hardly awkward for the philanthropist mayor. Nor was hosting industry-specific events asking influential business leaders to contribute to the Memorial Foundation—a city purpose, not a Michael Bloomberg purpose—as he did at one such breakfast at Gracie Mansion attended by about a dozen of New York's major real estate leaders. The mayor wanted $5 million from each. It was an aspirational target in line with conventional wisdom of fundraising to aim high. The mayor scored success, with contributions ranging from $5 million to far less than $5 million. Asking for contributions for the memorial had been cleared by the city's Conflicts of Interest Board before the mayor assumed the chairmanship of the foundation. "The memorial is something different," said John Zuccotti.[70]

With his authority and influence, Mayor Bloomberg brought stability and leadership to the task. Amid the relief and applause, some family members angry at the mayor's position favoring the random listing of the victims' names protested his imminent chairmanship, and two foundation board members abstained from the voting while one voted against the resolution to appoint the mayor chairman of the foundation. The negative actions, however, did not register beyond the boardroom.

The mayor appeared to have clear reasons for taking on the chair of the foundation. For starters, the appointment validated his yearlong efforts to directly and strategically insert himself in the rebuilding process. He was the mayor and this was his city. He hoped to "break the logjams that have been victims' families at war with politicians and others over the design and other elements of the project." His new role also carried political implications, too: It seemed to settle any residual governmental tension between the mayor and the governor. Under the arrangement, Governor Pataki would become the foundation's honorary lifetime chairman. The governor, reported the *Times,* had been looking "to lock in a role in the future of Lower Manhattan past the end of his term this year,"[71] but according to Rampe, Pataki never wanted to chair the foundation. He wanted what all politicians want: credit and control. He just did not want to be in the position to have to raise funds.

After the intense turbulence of 2005 and 2006, the complex politics of rebuilding at Ground Zero appeared to have sorted itself out with clearer lines of authority and direct points of accountability, if not simplicity. The Port Authority was now responsible for delivering the memorial complex on an established budget by the eighth anniversary of the 9/11 attacks, and a $90 million project contingency budget had been set up to deal with the inevitable cost overruns. The mayor was now in charge of the foundation's fundraising efforts, and he had resolved the contentious issue of the names' arrangement. Also, just two weeks before the memorial cost crisis erupted in early May, Bloomberg in a behind-the-scenes collaboration with Port Authority chairman Coscia succeeded in pushing forward a deal that realigned public and private responsibilities for rebuilding the commercial program and reduced Larry Silverstein's role in the project. The deal did not come easily or readily, and the economic feasibility of replacing so much office space at the Trade Center site was questionable, as discussed in the next chapter.

It would be impossible to project exactly how events might have turned had Bloomberg not intervened so forcefully in each of the biggest conflicts of 2005 and

2006. Yet the prospects for spontaneous resolutions were hardly promising given the years of caustic conflict already logged. The mayor brought clarity of leadership to a fragile and fraught political arena. By leveraging the power of his political position and his considerable personal influence as a businessman, he shaped a path forward for rebuilding. His active leadership marked a deeply influential pivot point in the rebuilding at Ground Zero.

January 5, 2006.   CHRIS HONDROS/GETTY NEWS/GETTY IMAGES

PART IV
POLITICAL PIVOT (2006–2007)

CHAPTER 12

Larry's Quest

FIGURE 12.1 DAVID PASCAL

I N THE CONSTANT HEAT of conflict public officials repeatedly put forth a mantra that rebuilding Ground Zero was not just a real estate development project, it was something more. Certainly that was true. The developer said the same, repeatedly. Both wanted to impress upon the public the emotional significance and economic importance of rebuilding Ground Zero; the future of the city was at stake, they would say. At the same time, the commercial component of the rebuilding agenda was very much a real estate development project, and unlike any other in the city's history. Not for a moment, the record would have us believe, did Larry Silverstein entertain ambition any less than a total rebuild of the ten million square feet of commercial space that had been destroyed (figure 12.1). Fitting all that density in five towers on the sixteen-acre site, reduced by half with the set-aside of the memorial quadrant, had been deemed impossible by any rational standard. Although Silverstein and the Port Authority were firmly committed to building five enormous office towers, strong reservations prevailed in other quarters. Silverstein was counting on winning his insurance battles to assure his capacity to rebuild all he was obligated to rebuild under the terms of his lease agreement with the Port Authority, but the early losses in court added question mark after question mark to that scenario. Moreover, the financial feasibility of rebuilding all that commercial space had never been put to a market test—although that was about to change.

Everyone understood that the lease agreement had to be renegotiated. The question was, when would negotiations begin? And what would happen if it became impractical—that is financially questionable—for Silverstein to rebuild all ten million square feet of space? Before negotiations could begin in earnest, the convoluted legal battle over the insurance payout had to be resolved. This crucial element of surety would define the money equation. By the magnitude of insured property losses (including business interruption and aviation losses damaged beyond economic repair), the September 11 hijacked airliner attacks on the World Trade Center and the Pentagon, at $24.4 billion, ranked as the world's costliest acts of terror by a huge margin; the Bishopsgate Bombing on April 24, 1993, by the Irish Republican Army was the second costliest act, at $1.2 billion.[1] Although Silverstein's path through the insurance litigation was going to take a lot of time, at this early stage of rebuilding, time was not a real constraint: As most practitioners in the world of commercial real estate recognized, it was going to take years before anything would get built at Ground Zero.

Was the quest to rebuild ten million square feet of new office space in downtown commercially feasible—without public support? And if public support was necessary, how much subsidy would it take to make the commercial rebuilding agenda feasible? Throughout the many months of this first fierce battle between the developer and government officials, many observers were asking, why it was taking so long to come to a definitive development agreement that would finally ensure commercial construction of the office towers? Some were still asking the question, why five towers? On the market side of the rebuilding equation, a fundamental problem existed: Silverstein had purchased a largely leased complex—in a sea of vacant buildings in lower Manhattan. The economic recession begun prior to 9/11 had exacted a toll, as evident in the increasingly soft downtown office market; in the immediate submarket area known as World Financial, vacancy rates by year end 2002 hit 20.4 percent, despite the destruction of some thirty-one million square feet of office space (figure 12.2). The economics of replacing the ten million square feet without much market demand were obviously questionable.

FIGURE 12.2 *Even before 9/11, the economic recession had caused a softening of the office market downtown.* Cushman & Wakefield Research

The press chronicled the ongoing uncertainty of rebuilding, yet its ability to engage the general public with revealing stories about the complicated political economy of rebuilding all of the lost office space was limited. Gauging the interest of general readers, and the complexity of the feasibility equation at Ground Zero, paired with an ever-changing agenda of financial issues, could not easily be explained through conventional news reporting. If not already frustrated or turned off by the continual delays and conflict, an interested public would have found keeping track of the many moving parts and behind-the-scenes activity understandably difficult. As it was, little of it was made public; most of the action was taking place behind the scenes. It was all about money and the power to move it—and that was essential to understanding what was really going on at Ground Zero.

BATTLING FOR A DOUBLE PAYOUT

Immediately after 9/11, Silverstein claimed that the 9/11 hijackings sequentially ramming into the North Tower and then the South Tower of the World Trade Center amounted to two separate events, two occurrences, two fires, two building collapses. "It's probably incontrovertible from a planning, plotting, and scheming perspective that this was a single event," said the chief economist of the insurance industry's public-relations arm, the Insurance Information Institute.[2] It would, however, be up to the courts to determine whether the attacks amounted to one terrorist incident or two under the leasehold's insurance documents.

How much was "recoverable for the total destruction of the WTC that occurred after the buildings were struck by two fuel-laden aircraft that had been hijacked by terrorists?"—that was the central question to be decided by the federal court charged with adjudicating this dispute. When the towers fell, the insurance contracts were still being negotiated, and this threw a kink in the determination of the insurers' liability. Twenty-five carriers were needed to aggregate coverage for the enormous sum of $3.55 billion, and two different temporary contracts of insurance, or binders, were used to assure coverage until the formal policies were issued. The so-called WilProp policy form (issued by Silverstein's broker, Willis Group Holdings, Ltd.) included a special term that defined an "occurrence" to mean all losses attributable "directly or indirectly" to "one cause or to one series of similar causes"; this encompassing definition favored policyholders (and lowered premiums for Silverstein) because the more damage that could be combined into one occurrence (with occurrence defined broadly), the fewer deductibles the policyholder would have to pay.[3] (Silverstein's deductible on his $3.55 billion policy was $1 million.) The other insurance form used by Travelers Indemnity Company, which had come into the deal late in the transaction, did not specifically define "occurrence," so whether the September 11 attacks had been one or two occurrences was open to dispute. Typically, all carriers would use a single policy form but at the time of the attack, Silverstein's insurance broker had not yet reached such an agreement. As a result, the legal proceedings had to address several questions: First, which insurance language were the parties working from before and after the 9/11 attack? Second, for those insurers using the Travelers' form, was the destruction of the twin towers on 9/11 the result of one or two "occurrences"? And, third, since the thirty-year-old buildings were depreciated assets, what was the value of the towers as they stood at the time of destruction?

This last question on value would be determined through lengthy and inevitably contentious adversarial appraisal arbitration, with each side amassing the detailed data and professional expertise to prove the hypothetical replacement value of the twin towers down to the minutest level of cost, which would be decided by three arbitrators. (Replacement value is not the same as reproduction cost; the contractual obligation of the lease is to rebuild functionality, and the question of replacement value is not specific to design.) Determining how much it would cost, in current dollars, to replace the towers that had been brought down on 9/11 would establish the "replacement cost cap," which was the starting point for reckoning what the insurers would owe. This figure would then be adjusted by a hypothetical depreciation factor to account for the state of repair of the property and determine what insurers call the actual "cash value" of what was destroyed. The cash value is what the insurers would immediately owe Silverstein and the Port Authority, the co-insured. As spending on construction of the buildings proceeded over the many years of build-out and the cash value amount got depleted, Silverstein and the Port Authority would be able to claim additional amounts up to the replacement cost cap, assuming the towers were rebuilt.

A third piece to the appraisal proceeding was to determine what level of rents had been lost as a result of the destruction. The rent roll at the World Trade Center was $330 million, "and five years later, we've lost $1.6 billion of lost rents. So we have a claim in for those lost rents," attorney Marc Wolinsky, a partner at Wachtell, Lipton, Rosen & Katz, the firm representing the Silverstein partnership, said in his testimony at City Council hearings on the status of the insurance proceeds in October 2006. The appraisal proceedings presented the lawyers and their experts with plenty of opportunity to raise multiple points of contention, and given the magnitude of dollars at stake, each side presented its position as vigorously as possible. The process was lengthy and arduous. Wachtell partner Peter Hein "led a team through 100 days of hearings to determine that cost, down to the last screw." John Gross, a partner at Proskauer Rose, cocounsel with Wachtell on the appraisal portion of the litigation, described this part of the insurance battle as a "litigation within a litigation," and "an extraordinarily intense, detailed proceeding."[4]

"Silverstein's Army" was how the developer described his high-powered legal team on the 9/11 World Trade Center insurance matters (figure 12.3). "I had to find myself the best minds that I could find to get me two events, to provide $7 billion," Silverstein said in a speech delivered at a CEO summit at New York University in December 2001. The expertise he needed went beyond the legal representation he relied on for regular real estate business matters, and Silverstein knew exactly who he needed to represent him in his pursuit of resources to rebuild the Trade Center—Wachtell, Lipton, Rosen & Katz—the firm of his oldest and closest friend, Herbert Wachtell, head of its litigation department. Wachtell helped shape the two-occurrence argument. When they met on September 13, for an emergency counseling session, Wachtell told Silverstein that unless the insurance policies clearly stated otherwise, it was his opinion that prevailing law in New York State would define the terrorist attacks as two occurrences, two insurable events. This would be their position though other legal minds might disagree. "It wasn't a slam dunk for Silverstein, far from it," author and publisher Steven Brill wrote in *After: How America Confronted the September 12 Era*. "In fact, precedents from prior case law, in which there had been this kind of dispute over an occurrence clause where occurrence had not been defined, seemed to give Wachtell maybe a 40 percent chance of prevailing."[5]

Wachtell, Lipton, Rosen & Katz's expertise in large, complex, and demanding transactions is formidable. Founded in 1965, the firm built a powerhouse reputation

FIGURE 12.3 *Silverstein's legal team from Wachtell, Lipton, Rosen & Katz led by his oldest and closest friend, Herbert Watchell, head of the firm's litigation department. With Martin Lipton plus seventy of the firm's lawyers, they crafted Silverstein's two-occurrence strategy in an effort to gain $7.1 billion in insurance proceeds for rebuilding.* © MICHAEL JN BOWLES

on its specialized cutting-edge corporate practices (mergers and acquisitions, strategic investments, takeovers and takeover defense, corporate and securities law, and corporate governance). It served large and highly profitable clients, and was known for a business culture of deep partner engagement. Large in terms of its financial influence, not in terms of its size, Wachtell has a business strategy of selectively limiting the matters it undertakes to what one scholar described as "bet-the-company Brand-Name transactions" that has consistently made the firm one of the three most profitable legal firms in the nation; in fiscal 2001, profits per partner reached $3.3 million, according to the *American Lawyer*'s annual report on the nation's top-grossing law firms.[6]

The decision to represent Silverstein in his insurance claims was not an immediate decision, though the personal ties between Silverstein and Wachtell ran deep. They met as freshmen at New York City's High School of Music and Art, attended New York University together, and remained friends over the years as each pursued different careers. "This would be a mammoth drain on firm resources," Wachtell told reporter Alison Frankel of the *American Lawyer*. "It was a firm issue—could we afford to take this on?" After conferring with his partners in an impromptu meeting, they decided to do it for two reasons: "Larry is my closest and oldest friend," Wachtell said. "And this was a civic thing—we felt an obligation to be involved in the rebuilding of the city."[7] It would become the most demanding and "emotionally taxing representation" the firm had ever undertaken, according to a long profile of the firm's role in the insurance episode written by Ben Hallman for the *American Lawyer* after the litigation had ended. Beyond the legal expertise they contributed, the eight Wachtell partners (three on the real estate issues and five on the insurance litigation) acted as "advisers, strategists, and negotiators," remarked Silverstein's director for the Trade Center project, Janno Lieber. Before they would celebrate success, however, a difficult, and at times dispiriting, road lay ahead.

A String of Defeats

Over a fifteen-month period the math of rebuilding came into sharp public focus as the insurers captured increasing legal momentum in the litigation battle, winning a series of rulings favoring a one-occurrence scenario. In September 2002, federal judge John S. Martin ruled that the attack on the World Trade Center was a single occurrence under the terms of the WilProp insurance form used by three insurers. "This confirms what we've said all along," said Jacques E. Dubois, the chairman of the Swiss Reinsurance Co. "What happened on Sept. 11 was one occurrence. It points out the fiction in the Silverstein theory." This ruling brought to five (of twenty-five) the number of insurers whose liability would be based on a single occurrence; earlier in the year, two Bermuda-based insurers agreed to a cash payment for the full amount of their coverage, which totaled $365 million, also on the basis of binders they signed referencing the WilProp form. In damage-control mode, a spokesman for Silverstein said, "these three insurers' coverage amounts to a total of $112 million per occurrence, so that limiting these insurers to a single occurrence does not have a material effect on the overall amount of $6.7 billion to be recovered in the litigation."[8]

A year later, Silverstein lost his appeal on this ruling in a unanimous ruling by the U.S. Court of Appeals for the Second Circuit. Seven months after that September 2003 ruling, after ten weeks of testimony, the trial jury came to a partial verdict finding that eleven insurers were not liable for a double payout, cutting more than $1 billion from Silverstein's hoped for insurance recovery. It was a major victory for the insurers. The next week, on May 3, 2004, the same jury came back with a second verdict similarly ruling that London-based Swiss Re, the single largest carrier in the group of twenty-five providing nearly 25 percent of the $3.55

billion in coverage, or $877.5 million, was only liable for a single-occurrence payout. Together, these two verdicts eliminated $1.9 billion of potential liability for the insurance companies. With that elimination, the maximum potential insurance recovery was reduced to $4.675 billion. In other words, after the string of legal rulings, the magnitude of Silverstein's hoped-for recovery had shrunk from $7.1 billion to $6.6 billion to $5.6 billion to $4.675 billion—and the latter amount only if Silverstein won every subsequent round of the legal battle.

Barry R. Ostrager had won an important round for his big client, Swiss Re. The fifty-four-year-old veteran litigator from Simpson Thacher & Bartlett had quickened to the World Trade Center insurance fight. His big-dollar cases, as Brill put it, "typically involved more mundane matters than the high-profile corporate takeover battles that had made Wachtell a true legal superstar." And, according to Brill, Ostrager had a suspicion about Silverstein's insurance strategy: "that what Silverstein really wanted to do was to take his insurance money and not rebuild but instead realize a bonanza profit." It was a complicated theory: Simply put, from the $3.55 billion of insurance coverage, Silverstein might be able to walk away with more than $1 billion, after payments to the Port Authority ($1.5 billion), its mortgage lenders ($563 million), and other expenses—if he decided not to rebuild and was able to get out of his lease with the Port Authority. That scenario stemmed from Silverstein's contract with the Port Authority, which, Brill wrote, was "badly lawyered from the Port Authority side." However much Silverstein repeatedly declared he was going to rebuild, he was not going to walk away, to Ostrager that only meant that the developer "was playing chicken with the Port Authority." Under what conditions might Silverstein and his investors not rebuild? That is, what would cause the Port Authority to "blink first"? "The way Ostrager figured it," Brill wrote, "as long as Silverstein acted as if he was prepared to rebuild the same size Trade Center, he could get the Port Authority to blink first and say he couldn't, whereupon he could claim they had breached the contract and walk from the deal with that $1 billion—or more, if this litigation yielded a good settlement."[9]

The Silverstein team vehemently denied such a motive, asserting that Silverstein, who pledged to rebuild, would not be entitled to bank the money. Amid the insurance battle, Silverstein's team was running an intense and carefully orchestrated public relations campaign in which the developer was consistently portrayed as singularly dedicated to civic purpose in rebuilding New York. In the strategic thrust and counterthrust of legal maneuvers over the insurance payouts, Ostrager's hypothesis "might have seemed impossibly complicated" to a layperson or even to a reporter covering the Trade Center insurance story. But, as Brill noted, it would not be beyond John Martin, the federal judge handling the case. "As a lawyer in a sophisticated private practice he had been involved in complex business litigations earlier in his career," which was evident in his judicious understanding and detailed handling of the legal proceedings.[10]

After three major losses, it was now quite clear that the diminution in insurance recovery threatened Silverstein's ability to control the full set of development rights to rebuild the commercial spaces at Ground Zero. Everyone—public officials, civic groups, business interests, other real estate developers—immediately started to refigure the math of rebuilding. Costs for rebuilding ten million square feet of office space, plus retail space and four levels of underground infrastructure, as reported by several newspapers and an insider at the LMDC, were expected to run between $9 billion and $12 billion. As of 2004, decisions about who would pay for what part of the $2 billion underground infrastructure buildout had yet to be determined. But if it had appeared questionable whether the total buildout of office space could be financed from the insurance payouts before the jury decision, afterward it clearly seemed impossible. "You'd have to be blind not to realize that Larry losing the lawsuit changes his power in the overall equation," said one official active in the rebuilding process. "This has never been about Larry. It's about redeveloping the site."[11]

The press speculated whether Silverstein could hold on to his "obligation" to rebuild now that he clearly lacked sufficient funds. The headlines were telling: "Jury's Decision Leaves Rebuilding of WTC in Turmoil" (*WSJ*); "How a Verdict Could Alter the Shape of Lower Manhattan" (*NYT*); "Silverstein Retreat Looms at WTC" (*Crain's*); "Larry Loses Again—$$ Woes Spur WTC Jitters" (*NYP*); "Jury Decision Means Silverstein Must Explore Options" (*NYS*); "Is Silverstein Down to One at Zero Site?" (*NYO*).

At the Port Authority, redevelopment staff was at work considering a number of strategic options. If the projected insurance payout all but guaranteed that Silverstein could build the first and tallest tower (2.6 million square feet estimated to cost $1.5 billion), all else remained uncertain, other than the fact that the time had come to redefine the terms of the agency's agreement with Silverstein. With that in mind, would he be able to hold on to all ten million square feet of development rights? How much new space could the downtown market realistically absorb in the decade ahead? The Port Authority wanted all ten million square feet rebuilt, but the demand for that space had gone elsewhere after 9/11, so was it now practical to rebuild all that was lost? If development was phased in over time, how much would the developer have to pay the Port Authority in ground lease payments to continue to hold on to the development rights over the extended period of rebuilding?

"There's almost unanimous support on the board that we need to change his relationship," said a top Port Authority official. Some commissioners were thinking about how to take back the site. As they considered a range of real estate issues, the agency had at its side attorney Martin D. Polevoy, chair of the real estate practice of

DLA Piper. The *Wall Street Journal* reported, "the Port Authority has been quietly planning for a post-Silverstein Ground Zero for months and will now consider a mix of uses for the site." The *Times* graphically presented what this "coming up short" on insurance funds might mean in terms of bricks and mortar: one skyscraper, the $1.5-billion Freedom Tower, and three low-rise place-holding retail structures, the so-called podium scenario[12] (figure 12.4). In theory, the strategic option to buy out Silverstein still existed. Whether or not the board of commissioners would approve a move in that direction, Port Authority officials still could threaten to do so. In 2004 as in 2002, such a decision would turn on figuring out the optimal time for a buyout and factoring in the practical difficulties, political implications, and inevitable litigation that would come on the heels of a condemnation action. As long as the insurance case remained unsettled, the Port Authority had more to lose than to gain by attempting an early buyout of Silverstein's interests.

Silverstein's visibly weakened position in the overall rebuilding equation was no secret. The insurance verdicts brought to the fore the deep doubts many real estate professionals held about how much office space really needed to be replaced, and how much the Manhattan market could realistically absorb. The uncertain timing of new supply downtown made editorial boards nervous. "An endless delay

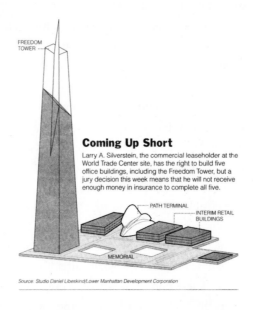

FIGURE 12.4 *The schematic of what might be built at Ground Zero if Silverstein came up short on funds to exercise his right to build five office towers: the Freedom Tower and three low-rise place-holding retail structures, the so-called podium scenario, 2004.* FROM THE NEW YORK TIMES, MAY 1, 2004 © 2004 THE NEW YORK TIMES

in commercial development at Ground Zero could thrust this massive project into direct competition with city plans for development of downtown Brooklyn and the rail yards of Manhattan west of Pennsylvania Station. There is a limit to how much new commercial office space the city can absorb," said the editors of *Newsday*. The lack of clarity on this point presented critics of the master plan with an opportunity to advocate for a fresh start. "The fundamental question now for Pataki, Bloomberg, and the Port Authority," editorialized the *Daily News*, "is whether the demand for office space downtown will be sufficient to justify faith that the Trade Center site will not become frozen as home to the world's tallest building and little else of consequence. The market suggests such an unappealing future while indicating that other uses, such as housing and expanded open space, would be a roaring success." The editorial argued that a "reconsideration of the master plan is in order." Editors at the *Times* took a milder position, noting that the four office towers scheduled to follow construction of the tallest tower might not be built as rapidly as possible but "will have to be developed in a manner that is more responsive to market conditions and—we hope—to the concerns of the public as well."[13]

The Port Acts

After that fateful May insurance verdict quashed Silverstein's two-occurrence claim from Swiss Re, the Port Authority sent a letter to Silverstein asking for a detailed financial-plan accounting of how he would pay to rebuild ten million square feet of office space on the site. Many observers of development politics might have considered this obvious response overdue—it was the Port's responsibility to question whether Silverstein and his investors had the necessary financial resources and sufficient staffing to develop on the scale called for under the master plan for the site. Nonetheless, the PA had finally begun to address the central economic question posed by the wholesale destruction of the World Trade Center complex. To respond to the Port, Silverstein hired Morgan Stanley to prepare the financials for the project. As in the case of any commercial real estate feasibility analysis, the financial test critically depended on many assumptions, but none more significant than the amount of projected rent revenue per square foot of office space. Rents in midtown for class A space in May 2005 averaged $53.98 a square foot compared to $34.18 a square foot downtown. At this time, according to Cushman & Wakefield data, the discount for going downtown amounted to a hefty 34 percent, a few points above the historical average, and it was trending upward. In mid-2005, the Manhattan office market was stuck in neutral, and Silverstein faced a losing string of insurance battles; nevertheless, the developer remained confident, convinced that the downtown market would be able to absorb the new buildings and generate high rents because it lacked the type of high-end class A office space he intended to build. Given the project's access to favorable tax-exempt financing with Liberty Bonds, which would lower the cost of construction, Silverstein's project manager, Janno Lieber, told the press, "We're in a position to capture the market that wants that space but doesn't want to pay the $70 to $80 a foot that midtown might command."[14]

The gap between rebuilding cost and available resources was obvious. The insurance payout alone was going to fall short of what it would take to replace the ten million square feet of office space called for in the redevelopment program, even if a successful two-event scenario yielded the new maximum payout of $4.675 billion. Developing A-quality office towers in Manhattan, as Silverstein was doing in the reconstruction of 7 World Trade Center across the way, cost roughly around $650 a square foot in 2005 (the official number for the cost of 7 WTC, rebuilt on leased land as before, was $700 million). Once the development sites were ready for construction, the feasibility equation needed to account for the costs of replacing the lost retail space and the complex infrastructure that would build up the site to grade and for the cost of leasing the land. Silverstein's own detailed cost estimate prepared by Tishman Construction in readiness for his first jury trial in February 2004 put construction costs for the ten million square feet of office space, eight hundred thousand square feet of retail space, and infrastructure and below-ground work at $7.4 billion to $7.8 billion. When factoring in his rent payments to the Port Authority and his legal costs, the construction figure balloons "to above $9 billion," the developer said in a letter accompanying the estimate, as reported by William Neuman of the *Post*.[15]

Inflation in construction costs in New York City in 2004 was running quite high, about 12.5 percent, according to the New York Building Congress, and though it had moderated some in 2005, inflationary cost pressures from worldwide demand for building materials were expected to continue on an upward trajectory. Accounting for inflation, the developer's 2004 construction cost estimate for the office towers would range from $8.3 to $8.8 billion in 2005. Inevitably, the cost of building out the commercial space at Ground Zero would only grow with time in line with three truisms about building in Manhattan: It always costs more to build in New York than in other cities, inflation runs higher in New York than other cities, and construction-cost inflation is more volatile than general inflation as measured by the Consumer Price Index.[16] The math spoke truth. And time was on no one's side when it came to cost control.

"Anyone who's in New York knows that how much we recover from this lawsuit will have an impact on the building," said LMDC president Kevin M. Rampe. Millions from insurance advance payments had gone to cover monthly rent payments to the Port Authority ($240 million), debt service on the GMAC mortgage ($64 million) and then its subsequent payoff ($563 million), the buyout of Westfield America's interest in the retail space ($140 million), and the nearly $126 million payback of the investor group's equity investment (approximately $27 million of which was being held in escrow). In addition, the developer was spending additional millions in design and engineering fees, and other ongoing expenses, including tens of millions in fees to his lawyers to fight the insurance battles to hold on to the development rights. By early 2004, more than $1.3 billion had already been paid out, according to the Port Authority's Annual Report; by year end, this number had grown to $1.6 billion (out of a total $2.1 billion of funds advanced before final settlement). The "harsh new math," editorialized the *Daily News*, is "chomping away at the resources for rebuilding Lower Manhattan, threatening to leave the city's fractured skyline in a state of permanent incompletion."[17]

If Silverstein's claim for a two-occurrence casualty failed, his ability to deliver on his full obligations to rebuild would be severely compromised without an alternative financing plan that included the new category of low-cost, tax-exempt Liberty Bonds authorized by Congress in 2002 as a 9/11 response to help revitalize lower Manhattan. And those bonds would need credit support to attract investors. "Larry was the first to say that the prospects of his financing the project without the extra insurance proceeds were very thin, and conventional wisdom agreed with him," said Kathryn Wylde of the Partnership for New York City. "The design and infrastructure requirements for this site are considerably more ambitious than the original Twin Towers, and I think there were real questions—questions that Larry was the first to raise—as to his ability to deliver without the additional insurance money." The Port Authority had its own insurance coverage for the underground improvements, which carried a maximum payout of $1.5 billion per occurrence,[18] but Silverstein would have to cover some portion of the infrastructure relating to his towers, and this material issue was still to be negotiated.

Victory, at Last

Silverstein could be nothing but disappointed about the string of defeats, yet he remained characteristically resolute in his determination to rebuild and fully confident in the skill of his high-powered legal team to carry the day in the second trial—and it did it to the amazement of many. This first big victory for Silverstein in his thirty-eight-month battle with the insurers came in early December 2004, when the jury ruled in favor of his claim for a two-occurrence attack. The win allowed him to collect up to $2.2 billion in coverage from nine insurers deemed to be using the Travelers' form for a maximum recovery of $4.675 billion. The celebration among the developer's litigation team was fulsome, a mixture of jubilation and relief. "It had been a very hard-fought matter," said Wachtell attorney Eric Roth at the triumphant dinner hosted by his colleague in charge of this phase of the battle, Bernard Nussbaum, a former White House counsel under President Bill Clinton, "and it wasn't always fought according to the Marquis of Queensbury rules" (a code of generally accepted rules in the sport of boxing).[19]

Silverstein had persisted in what some observers saw as an improbable quest for a two-occurrence claim, and his insurance victory marked a major change in circumstances with broad implications beyond the courtroom. News of the win not only increased the likelihood that a second tower would be constructed, but to proponents and opponents alike, the victory appeared to increase the momentum for the overall commercial development program. Beyond allowing Silverstein to hold on to his position, the trial achieved what had been a strategic public relations objective: promoting the prospect that a settlement larger than the one-occurrence claim of $3.55 billion was probable. News of his win quickly amended the prevailing perception of the developer's control over the site. The additional $1.1 billion from the two-occurrence verdict was "extra clout," said the *Times*, though just how much extra depended on what Silverstein would have to contribute for his share of common underground superstructure—the roadways, ramps, Vehicle Security Center, loading docks, and utilities. Some press reports surmised that the winning verdict would insulate the developer from further attacks, yet the die of financial uncertainty, firmly cast, was not easily broken. "The verdict," wrote reporters for the *Wall Street Journal*, "keeps the broader office-rebuilding program alive for now and helps solidify Mr. Silverstein's financial position as lead developer at Ground Zero." "It makes it less likely that those who would want to remove him from the site would be able to do so—because he's got a significant amount of money," said one official close to the rebuilding effort. Silverstein became the "resurgent developer, back in the catbird seat, no longer counted out...the single most important person in the redevelopment of Ground Zero, the only man with the presumptive right to build and the only one with the private funds to do it," wrote a reporter for the *New York Observer*.[20] It was, in short, a professional and personal watershed for Larry Silverstein; still, this hard-won and expensive victory did not guarantee his sure and certain survival as the master private developer of the Trade Center site. Not yet.

Many questions remained unanswered. Would the two-occurrence jury verdict stand upon appeal from the insurers? A shortfall still existed between the costs to rebuild the entire commercial project and the insurance funds available to do so. When it came time to actually start construction, how big would this gap have grown? If insurance was insufficient for a complete rebuild of the commercial program, how many towers could be built with what remained of the insurance payout? There appeared to be enough for the $1. 5-billion Freedom Tower, but what else? Would the capital markets support conventional financing for the remaining speculative towers? In other words, would Silverstein be able to attract the necessary credit tenants to secure financing and go forward with construction? How much of the financing gap could be filled with Liberty Bonds? Unanswered as well, how many more millions would Silverstein have to pull from the insurance bucket to pay his share of the site infrastructure? This intensely contested issue with the Port Authority, ongoing for quite some time, was nowhere near a resolution. But one thing was clear: Silverstein was determined to rebuild.

LARRY'S PR CAMPAIGN

Strategic communication was critically important for Larry Silverstein. In his determination to rebuild the Trade Center site, he faced an uphill public relations battle with his two-occurrence insurance claim, his reputation as a hard-nosed second-tier developer and manager of B class buildings in the intensely competitive world of New York commercial real estate, and public sentiment that the rebuilding task ahead demanded greater expertise and experience that could come with deliberate selection of a developer. No one was suggesting that the conventional rules of property rights governing his partnership's ninety-nine-year leasehold interest be abrogated. Rather, a condemnation action to take out the developer—who by default of tragedy was in control of the development rights for rebuilding this most sensitive of sites in the history of the city—might be in the best interest of the city and the public at large.

Managing these many challenges, Silverstein had the premier public relations firm in the business, Rubenstein Associates, and as his chief spokesman the maestro himself, who had already represented Silverstein for more than thirty-two years. "When it comes to the kind of messy New York fights that are likely to make their way not only into the business pages of the *New York Times* and *Wall Street Journal*, but also the tabloids and onto the nightly television newscasts," Brill wrote, "it was hard to match Howard Rubenstein's PR firm."[21]

Brooklyn-born and bred, the lawyer turned PR expert started his eponymous firm in 1954, and over the subsequent decades built a client roster that included many of New York's iconic organizations (including Bloomberg LP, Columbia University, the Metropolitan Opera, New York Philharmonic, and the Whitney Museum), many of its notables (including Leonard Lauder, George Steinbrenner, and Donald Trump), many of its politicians (as of 2001, the last six mayors and last three governors), and a good fraction of the city's real estate industry. It was apropos to say he had "served as a spokesman for nearly half the city, running interference for the likes of Ron Perelman and Leona Helmsley, sometimes by turning potentially toxic publicity to his clients' advantage," as the *New York Post* did on the celebratory occasion of his fifty years of spin. He could also count the newspaper's owner, Rupert Murdoch, among his long-term clients. Mayor Rudolph Giuliani called him the "dean of damage control" for New York's powerful,[22] and that moniker retained its ring of truth.

"The Fixer" is how the well-known business author Ken Auletta titled his *New Yorker* profile of Rubenstein; he was the one New Yorkers call when they have a problem. Rubenstein, he wrote, was "widely regarded as a public-relations expert, and that does describe much of his business, but he is perhaps above all a master of relationships, of making connections; he is a kind of lubricant of the city's gears—someone who searches for ways to make those gears mesh." "Politically ambidextrous," Auletta wrote, "Rubenstein's ubiquity was now a fact of New York life." Sage advisor and savvy strategist who used his confidences and confident understanding of the shades of gray to great effect, Rubenstein had "expertise at "dealing with the peculiarities of the New York press" that would be invaluable to Silverstein in the years ahead as the developer maneuvered to retain position at Ground Zero.[23] The longtime friend and counselor would also work in a larger context of creating a new image for the developer, an image suited to the legacy-creating mission he had in mind.

Rubenstein moved quickly on promoting the notion of two occurrences. Employing more elaborate wording than the dry language of insurance contracts, he reinforced the construed line of argument that Silverstein used repeatedly: "The separate crashes of two planes into two towers, starting two separate fires and two separate building collapses constitute two occurrences." Within two weeks, according to Brill, Silverstein was "eagerly telling friends that the combination of Wachtell's team and the PR people was going to get all the billions he needed to give New York the rebuilding of Ground Zero that the city deserved."[24]

The two-occurrence claim was much more than a legal battle to secure double the insurance payout. It was an elemental factor for creating the public perception that Silverstein would have the capacity to rebuild. Lacking capacity to rebuild was grounds for default on his recently signed leasehold with the Port Authority, and on September 12, he had neither the organization nor the balance sheet to meet that test of capacity—had the Port Authority evaluated it at that time. It was going to take years before the anticipated complex insurance battle would be resolved and still more years before actual tower construction could begin. Silverstein was facing an extended period of unknown duration during which there would be lots of public pressures: questions about whether he had the capacity to do what his deal with the Port Authority now required him to do, questions about whether the Port Authority would use its powers of eminent domain to take him out of the re-development equation completely or reduce his role in the project by bringing in other developers, questions about whether his construed two-occurrence strategy would prevail in the court of law, and questions about whether his architect's master plan for rebuilding the sixteen acres would prevail or, as seemed more likely, would be subordinated to the priorities of the public sector's planning process, which put off limits the footprints of the twin towers.

These were the early-on challenging questions; others would rapidly material-ize as the profound scope of what had to be done to rebuild these emotionally scarred acres unfolded and the problems of proceeding in a political fishbowl with the world watching became ever more complicated. Silverstein had to sell the public and public officials that he was properly capitalized and had the develop-ment capability to rebuild. Yet how would this match up against the hard-fisted insistence on the bottom line that had long defined his real estate persona?

Rubenstein and Silverstein wasted no time setting out the themes of their com-munication strategy, which appeared in news headlines in that first traumatic week and many weeks thereafter: "Trade Center Leaseholder Is Determined to Rebuild, but Will Wait to Make Plans" (*WSJ*), "Silverstein: 'If We Don't Rebuild It, We Give In'" (*Globe St.com*). He was fighting to "Rebuild and Honor" (*NYT*). In 2002, Rubenstein said his client was tenacious and "had no intention of backing out of this"–"Hell No, He Won't Go—Developer Silverstein Will Keep WTC Lease" (*NYP*), "Trade Center Leaseholder Braces for Battle" (*NYT*), "Silverstein Asserts His Rights in Project at Twin Towers Site" (*WSJ*). He was "Undaunted and Planning the Next Great Skyline" in a *Times* Public Lives profile. Next, the *Wall Street Journal* profiled "The Importance of Being Larry," and the *Economist*, in "Onwards and Upwards," wrote, "Larry Silverstein hopes to redraw the world's most famous sky-line." The well-positioned profiles kept coming for years thereafter, among the many: "At the Helm of Trade Center Site, as He Always Planned to Be" (*NYT*), "No Greater Legacy" (*Slatin Report*), "In Rebuild, Silverstein's 'Challenge of Ten Lifetimes'" (*Real Deal*), "Silverstein Preps for Golden Age at WTC" (*Crain's*), "Master of Slow and Deliberate at Ground Zero" (*NYT*), "Larry Takes a Bow on Ground Zero" (*NYO*), "Developer Creates Tower of Strength" (*Crain's*).

Silverstein was taking on a new persona, reinventing himself and creating a personal legacy at Ground Zero strikingly different from that of his professional past—business interests for private profit—with the Rubenstein PR machine crafting the new, more public-minded image. It was done through the press for the court of public opinion. The themes repeated themselves over time, shaping a narrative that took on a life of its own without challenge or critique: gritty fighter determined to prevail over all woes—begrudging insurance companies, foot-dragging bureaucrats at the Port Authority, difficult politicians, name-calling special interests, and so on—all for the honor of bringing glory to the city. In his seventies, he is in a hurry; he does not buy "green bananas" because he has no time for them to ripen. He is the plucky underdog.

There were set pieces of his narrative: He battled against all odds to win the leasehold over larger, better-capitalized competitors. Struck by a car, he framed the final pieces of his 2001 bid for the acquisition of the World Trade Center complex from his hospital bed after instructing his doctors to turn down the morphine being administered to minimize the excruciating pain from the many breaks to his body from the accident because he needed to be sharp, alert, not drugged. On the morning of 9/11, at the absolute insistence of his wife, Clara, he kept a dermatologist appointment, which he had canceled more than once; if not for that, he would have been at the World Trade Center that fateful morning because he had been going there every day since capturing the keys to his long-desired twin-tower prize. He lost four of his employees on 9/11, and is rebuilding with their memory in mind. As befitting his eternally optimistic personality, he will prevail.

When on the 2007 anniversary of the attack, the *Financial Times* published another such profile of Silverstein—"Cometh the Tower, Cometh the Man"—adding nothing new to the storyline, The Audit of *Columbia Journalism Review* let go with a searing two-part critique of the business press for presenting the same "stale story…as though it were original." In it, Elinore Longobardi said that coverage was "the object of much consternation" for "violating basic journalism standards," for failing to increase the depth and analysis of the problems at Ground Zero as more information became available over the years, and for failing to hold Silverstein accountable for his share of the problems at Ground Zero. Repeating the myth that he was "a victim of the state, rather than an extraordinary beneficiary" was a serious mistake, she argued. The narrative had misled the public as to what had really been going on in the rebuilding at Ground Zero.[25]

The PR-oriented profiles did not change over time, and they were problematic because they were one-sided: They omitted the business side of Silverstein's motivations and actions at Ground Zero. Those business motivations were fundamental drivers of what was going on at Ground Zero, the missing pieces of the big story. While it might be hard to separate Silverstein's self-interests from his sincere intent and efforts to rebuild, both sets of motivations needed to be explored by the press as a means of telling a full-sided story of what was going on at Ground Zero. Despite not being a conventional real estate development, rebuilding Ground Zero was as much a business story about money and the power of commercial real estate in New York as it was a civic story of historic rebuilding for New York's future as a global city in the twenty-first century. A full and true account of what was going on at Ground Zero, by definition, had to cover both sides of this complicated historic undertaking. But it did not.

THE DOWNTOWN OFFICE GAMBLE

The feasibility questions challenged the economic vision behind rebuilding. Although the Freedom Tower was a symbolic political gesture, the same could not be said for the four other planned office towers. Downtown boosters and government officials alike saw the replacement of this office space as essential to the viability of the downtown office market, the nation's fourth largest commercial district—fourth only because of the 9/11 destruction—behind third-place Washington, D.C., and Chicago in second place; midtown Manhattan was, of course, in the top slot. It was the newest wedge in a long-running war between the city's two competing office markets: midtown Manhattan and lower Manhattan. Although the seven buildings of the original World Trade Center represented a mere 2 percent of the office stock of the region (10 percent of the total inventory of New York City), they represented 12.5 percent of the downtown office market and an even more significant 20 percent of the post-1960s generation of office buildings in lower Manhattan. "While the region's very broad office base is only marginally affected by the physical loss of the twin towers' space," economist Hugh Kelly concluded based on an in-depth analysis of the New York office market in the aftermath of 9/11, "there was a major proportional loss of space for Lower Manhattan tenants whose requirements were for large floor-plate configurations in modern office buildings." Taking into account perimeter buildings damaged and destroyed more than doubled the 9/11 impact, pushing the loss tally to more than 31 million square feet, or nearly 30 percent of the district's pre-9/11 inventory of 107.7 million square feet, the equivalent of Atlanta's or Miami's inventory of office space.[26]

Kelly believed that it would be "difficult to envision employers committing to a district where more than 30 percent of its most modern space had been destroyed and not replaced." He cautioned that "the absence of an adequate office stock to accommodate job growth will retard or even reverse downtown's resurgence as a residential community."[27] Kelly's knowledgeable views mirrored those of many in the downtown business community when he made the argument that because of its location and transportation attributes, the Trade Center site was "highly suitable" for developing the kinds of top-quality office buildings needed to maintain the district's vitality as an employment center. Yet how much new space was "adequate" to meet this objective was less clear. Did ten million square feet need to be replaced, or would a lesser though still critical mass of five to seven million square feet be enough? Building ten million square feet of new space when seventeen million square feet already stood empty downtown made many business executives, especially landlords, extremely nervous.

The optimistic view of downtown's future was not uniformly shared among economists who considered the impact of 9/11 on the Manhattan office market and the city's economy. In fact, there was no clear consensus on the full longer-term impact of the terrorist attacks; it was still too early for most who analyzed the data to draw definitive conclusions. Some found reason for optimism in the behavior of firms dislocated from downtown: 80 percent chose to settle in the core markets of downtown or midtown Manhattan (Franz Fuerst). Others found reasons for optimism in the lack of any clear signs of lasting economic damage to Manhattan's strong historic draw as a prime office location (Jason Bram, Andrew Haughwout, and James Orr). Still others saw no viable economic future for the downtown office district.

Writing in 2002, Harvard economists Edward L. Glaeser and Jesse L. Shapiro considered Manhattan's downtown financial district, even before 9/11, as an "anachronism," artificially "propped up by government subsidies, most spectacularly in the building of the World Trade Center itself." They were "gloomy" about downtown's future prospects relative to the stronger midtown business district. For decades beginning in the 1950s, midtown Manhattan had steadily gained in relative dominance; its office space inventory was three times as large as downtown, it had three times as many employees as downtown, and it had a stronger competitive advantage in all those lifestyle attributes that made firms cluster near one another in dense big cities: proximity to residential areas, cultural institutions, entertainment, restaurants, and nightlife. Short of additional massive government subsidies, which they considered unwise (and spent more effectively elsewhere), downtown in their view had a limited economic future because of its many competitive disadvantages relative to midtown. What they discounted or missed in the data was the evolving character of lower Manhattan as a mixed-use neighborhood and the conversion of older, obsolete class B and class C office buildings into thousands of apartments.[28] Events, in time, would reveal the fault lines of their reasoning as thousands of young professionals and families continued to settle in lower Manhattan, drawing with them nightlife, restaurants, and the kind of avant-garde art scene that had long been a fixture of the area and was making it one of the city's fastest-growing residential districts (figure 12.5).

In 2002, the stakes for the future viability of lower Manhattan, not just as an office district but as a 24/7 community, were high. The sudden loss of one hundred thousand jobs and the destruction or damage to a large part of its office

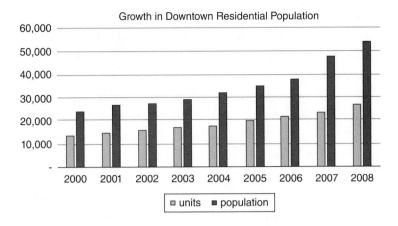

Growth in Downtown Residential Population

FIGURE 12.5 *Growth in downtown as a place to live: 2000–2008.* ALLIANCE FOR
DOWNTOWN NEW YORK

inventory propelled the area into a severe economic crisis. News headlines in the
early fall captured the uncertainty all too clearly: "Downtown, an Exodus That
Cash Can't Stop" (*NYT*), "Sept. 11's Shadow Darkening Outlook" (*Crain's*), "How
Damaged Is Downtown?" (*WSJ*). It was not all doom and gloom. Lower Manhattan
was showing substantial progress in coping with the events of 9/11; during the first
two years of recovery, for example, it had retained nearly 50 percent of the office
tenancy displaced in the 9/11 attacks, though this was seen as merely a short-term
achievement. Those observers holding a long-term view believed residential development was the growth strategy for the 24/7 mixed-use community, that it would
stimulate more economic growth downtown. The experience at Battery Park City
and the spontaneous residential boom in other neighborhoods in lower Manhattan,
SoHo and Tribeca, in particular, had proved so much. Still, in the short term, an
exodus of residents from lower Manhattan caused occupancy rates to drop sharply,
and in an effort to stabilize the residential market downtown, the LMDC made an
early allocation of $280.5 million for cash grants to households that made a two-
year commitment to stay or move into the area.

Spurred by the massive growth of office-based jobs for two decades, by mid-
2001, downtown had begun to acquire the attribute of the nation's best twenty-
four-hour communities. While it had not "fully matured in this respect," Kelly
argued that the amenities for the area flow from market forces created by the emerging "walk-to-work" opportunities. The transformation of Tribeca also was bringing CEOs and the professional class downtown, which was important to the future
revitalization of the downtown office market. Residential and commercial worked
in tandem with one another. "What will drive lower Manhattan is the business community and the number of workers—and, particularly, major companies—that stay

and grow here," said Carl Weisbrod, as president of the business-advocacy group Alliance for Downtown New York. "It would be a mistake, I think, to see residential crowd out commercial growth."[29]

The dislocation and deterioration of the office market experienced immediately after the 9/11 attack appeared to have stabilized by the end of 2003, yet the recovery trajectory for downtown was still unclear. The real estate risk of building all five towers at once was evident: What if they rebuild and nobody comes? It could take years for the market to absorb all that space, as had been the case with the original complex. That "giant white-elephant" legacy loomed as a haunting specter of the type of market risk that could overtake speculative skyscraper development, especially at the scale contemplated at Ground Zero. In 1974 when the Port Authority delivered the twin towers to the market the nation was in the throes of an economic recession brought on by soaring fuel prices triggered by the OPEC fuel embargo, and the city, coping with a fiscal crisis brought on by its own fiscal mismanagement, hovered on the brink of a municipal bankruptcy. Real estate markets in Manhattan hit their deepest lows since the Great Depression; "an awesome 29 million square feet of office space sat vacant, more than the combined total inventory of Los Angeles and Detroit," as landlords hoped and waited for tenants to materialize. With weak tenant demand and high vacancy rates, it took ten years for the World Trade Center to reach an acceptable level of occupancy, the largest portion of which housed employees of the Port Authority and various governmental agencies. The many years it took for the downtown market to absorb the supply shock of the World Trade Center's scale was a white-elephant legacy that the real estate community never lost sight of. In the intervening years, the red ink flowed; an audit in 1981 by the New York State comptroller revealed that after accounting for debt service costs, between 1972 and 1979, the Port Authority's complex had racked up a deficit of $125.7 million, and "based on current projections 1983 will be the first year the WTC breaks even."[30]

To real estate professionals, the true test of demand for office space in lower Manhattan in the twenty-first century would come from private-sector tenants making an elective decision to go downtown. And despite positive headlines in the *Wall Street Journal*—"Lower Manhattan Shows Signs of Recovery" and "Leases Boost Lower Manhattan Office Market"—the downtown office market faced serious short-term challenges: Leases covering approximately thirty-six million square feet, or about 30 percent of the district's post-9/11 inventory, would expire in 2004–2005; stretching the lease-expiration time frame to 2007, one economist projected that some two hundred thousand jobs were at risk of leaving the area.[31] Relatively low rents compared to midtown office space were the main draw for many tenants. Still, despite all the leasing activity in 2003, the vacancy rate for downtown office space stayed stubbornly close to 13 percent throughout 2004 into early 2005, dropping only to 12.3 percent by midyear, while in midtown vacancy dropped significantly from 12 percent to 9.7 percent during the same period, as tracked by Cushman & Wakefield.

The Bloomberg administration's support for the use of $650 million of Liberty Bonds to finance a new $915 million, fifty-one-story skyscraper for Bank of America's New York headquarters to be built by the Durst Organization—in midtown—increased the angst among downtown property owners and business organizations such as the Alliance for Downtown New York. "It sends the wrong message," one major real estate executive told Charles V. Bagli of the *Times*. "It looks like they're more focused on Midtown than down here." City and state officials had tried unsuccessfully to persuade the Charlotte, N.C.–based bank to move downtown, where it had more than four hundred employees at the World Trade Center, as well as another two thousand-plus in midtown. The new 2.1-million-square-foot tower, city officials argued, was not feasible without the favorable tax-exempt bonds, and the bank was "an exceptional tenant" in the depressed office market of the time. It would be expanding its presence with the new building on West Forty-second Street when other financial institutions were cutting their payrolls and reducing office space and other corporations were leaving town for Westchester, Jersey City, or places outside the region. The city was being pragmatic in the face of a shrinking financial-services industry, downtown's mainstay. Andrew M. Alper, president of the city's issuing agent for the bonds, the Industrial Development Agency, said the city did not see the demand downtown for all $8 billion of Liberty Bonds. The prospect of a state-of-the-art twenty-first-century office tower was a beacon in an otherwise cloudy economic landscape. It was "proof that New York, despite the recession, has intrinsic strengths that no major bank can ignore," said urban planner Mitchell Moss, director of the Urban Research Center at New York University.[32]

That in no way endeared the midtown development to the LMDC. In a full-house public hearing on the project's bond issuance before the board of the city's Industrial Development Agency in September 2003, LMDC chairman Whitehead issued a strong statement in opposition: "I believe the proposals for allocation of Liberty Bonds to incentivize large-scale commercial development outside of Lower Manhattan's Liberty Zone runs counter to our city's, state's and nation's rebuilding objective," he said. "Such a deployment of resources to areas beyond the Downtown erodes space in Lower Manhattan and thereby adversely impacts the pace of revitalization." Whitehead's opposing testimony marked "an unusual breach" among government officials overseeing development at Ground Zero.[33] It was highly unusual for a public board appointed by the mayor and the governor to publicly disagree—in writing—with the Liberty Bond decision. "It reflected Whitehead's independence and integrity," remarked Carl Weisbrod, "and, also, despite a weak hand, that the LMDC, at least in the Whitehead era, played it reasonably well."[34] What the city was doing fit within the pragmatic policy considerations of the time and legislative use of the Liberty Bond program—$2 billion could be used for projects outside the Liberty Zone—it just did not sit right with downtown interests, especially property owners and the Alliance for Downtown. They thought it was outrageous, a subsidy for the bank to move *out* of lower Manhattan, another lost opportunity.

The dire situation downtown galvanized State Assembly Speaker Sheldon Silver, who had been representing much of lower Manhattan since 1976, to vigorously push for "a comprehensive plan—a vision—for Lower Manhattan, not merely an economic strategy but more, a Marshall Plan." Until his political demise (on a corruption conviction) in 2015, Silver was the most powerful Democrat in Albany, and anything the city or state wanted to do had to go through his office. Even if he could not always get what he wanted, he was enormously powerful. And he was always an advocate for Larry Silverstein and his commercial agenda for rebuilding Ground Zero. Speaking at a breakfast meeting on Wall Street, Silver called upon government leaders to take dramatic steps to restore downtown's status as a world-class business center. The Pataki administration and the Port Authority, he argued, should pledge to lease an entire new tower at Ground Zero, and state and city governments should put in place incentives strong enough to lure businesses to Ground Zero and lower Manhattan, plus use all of the remaining $3.5 billion of commercial Liberty Bonds for developing Ground Zero. "It is my duty to constructively criticize the actions of government when such criticism is due," he said as a preface to his ardent pitch that "no other building project can take a higher priority," and "no public incentives for commercial development should be provided for Hudson Yards." This was a stinging rebuke, as Bagli phrased it, to the mayor's steady focus on building a stadium on the West Side of Manhattan and winning the 2012 bid for the Olympic Games. Silver's approval would be required for the stadium project, and if New York was to have any chance for the games, approval for the stadium needed to be in place prior to the July 6 meeting of the International Olympic Committee. The politics of this particular interplay of events was dicey and highly uncertain at the time Silver demanded the state and city enact his "Marshall Plan."[35]

The package of incentives passed by the state legislature in summer 2005 and signed into law by Governor Pataki did not appear to be luring businesses downtown as it was intended to do, at least not immediately. The subsidy package was a generous one, including multiple tax exemptions and rent subsidies that could significantly lower rent and make downtown even more highly competitive with midtown than it already was. The rent discount for going downtown compared to midtown (for existing buildings) had reached a historical high of 46 percent (plate 13, top). The average age of buildings downtown was ten years older than in midtown and there had been little new construction in downtown for nearly twenty years. The incentives were available to any firm that met the legislation's qualifications without special application. They were bound to make the Trade Center site with its high level of quality office buildings ever more attractive to tenants who were finding rents in midtown too expensive, according to a *World Trade Center Feasibility Study* prepared by the real estate services firm CBRE in October 2005 for Silverstein, who was being pressured by the media and commercial brokers to drop his rents at 7 World Trade Center. Total occupancy costs at the Trade Center, the real estate firm estimated, would be roughly half of those at a comparable new midtown building[36] (plate 13, bottom).

This was the long-term view of what would lure tenants to Ground Zero over time. The mayor supported the subsidy package even though the city would bear much of the cost. The downtown business community had pushed hard for these incentives to counter the host of negatives facing potential tenants for the Trade Center towers: concerns about construction delays on the site, the prospect of operating in a construction zone for years on end, confusion over the schedule for rebuilding, and controversial litigation brought by the families over the memorial and their opposition to the cultural program at Ground Zero. The business community's concern about the district's economic future was strategic. The volatility of the financial-services sector loomed as a worrisome factor in the area's long-term economic stability. "We have an overdependence of the financial industry that has to change over the next years, or we're going to be in real trouble," said Partnership for New York City president Wylde.[37]

The litmus test of market demand for new top-quality space was 7 World Trade Center, and the evidence of the time was not encouraging. Silverstein began construction on the speculative office tower in October 2003, after construction of the urgently needed ConEdison electrical substation destroyed on 9/11 was complete. He had gone ahead with 7 World Trade before many of the legal agreements and economic issues with his creditors holding the mortgage debt had been firmly resolved.[38] The developer's leasing agents began listing space for rent in fall 2003, but almost two years later, "Larry Silverstein's 52-Story Vacancy Problem" was a feature story in *New York Magazine*.

Silverstein's "stubborn insistence" on asking for rents that were substantially above what was typical in the downtown market was putting the "whole site at risk," was how *Crain's* described the situation in early May.[39] By year end 2005,

Silverstein still hadn't found any major tenants willing to pay his asking rents of $50 to $55 per square foot—easily the highest prices in downtown. The generous package of incentive subsidies available to firms leasing space in 7 World Trade should have been altering the decision-making calculus of firms seeking office space in the newest class A towers in Manhattan, according to the CBRE analysis of the relative impact of these incentives on occupancy downtown. Yet other than the developer and possibly his broker taking space in the building, tenants ready to sign leases were scarce. Prospective tenants would come and go, and some like Beijing Vantone/China Center, a much-hailed likely anchor tenant, came very close to the finish line. One broker called the leasing situation in Manhattan akin to "the scenario in *A Tale of Two Cities*"; activity in midtown (which historically filled up first before downtown) was robust. "If he can't rent space in 7 World Trade Center, how, critics asked, can he expect to fill almost six times that much?" wrote Alex Frangos and Christine Haughney in the *Wall Street Journal*.[40] Indeed. It would take more than five years until Silverstein Properties was able to issue a press release on September 19, 2011, announcing that 7 World Trade Center, the first office tower in New York to receive the U.S. Green Building Council's designation as a Leadership in Energy and Environmental Design (LEED) at the gold level, was 100 percent leased. He did not drop his rents.

By holding out for the highest possible rents and not renting as soon as he might have at lower rents, Silverstein was playing the optionality card of real estate. Rents dictate value. Landlords will often do a lot to get high rents, offer a big package of tenant improvements and months of free rent, for example, as inducements to tenants to sign at rents that will enhance a lender's assessment of a building in underwriting a mortgage loan. Silverstein, however, was not one to drop rents in order to get tenants. He had showed that moxie before. In the late 1980s when suffering a lengthy vacancy problem with his original 7 World Trade building, he had played "a waiting game," "pegging rents high," waiting for the "right tenants." He was not in a hurry, the *Times* reported, "thanks to an unusually structured deal that involved tax breaks and favorable financing, including a waiver on interest payments for a number of years." The structuring of his deal with the Port Authority and his lenders was such that he could break even by charging roughly $33 a foot. But he did not rent at that rate. Charging just $1 more would earn the developer "about $2 million a year on a building for which his own investment is virtually nil." He was not budging: "I have the staying power and the ability to do what I need to do," he said at the time. "We have a superior commodity—superior space at a first-class location."[41] Employing the same logic, he did the same in 2005 with his new and vastly better 7 World Trade tower.

Silverstein's brokers courted many but few firms were willing to sign on when class A space in downtown could be gotten for much less, around $35 a square foot. His high asking rent had turned off at least one prominent large-space user, downtown law firm Fried Frank Harris Shiver & Jacobson, which considered moving from its longtime home at 1 New York Plaza to 7 World Trade. The developer believed he was competing with midtown, not downtown buildings. "We don't believe (the rent is) too high, and we have no plans to reduce (it)," a spokesman for the developer told *Crain's*. "Seven World Trade Center is equal to the New York Times Building and the Bank of America Building," where asking rents were reportedly at least $75 a square foot and $100, respectively.[42] As before, Silverstein could afford to hold out for the higher rents he believed his state-of-the-art office building warranted, letting patience deliver greater profits because he had no cash in the deal: He was building 7 World Trade with insurance proceeds and the special congressionally authorized, low-cost, tax-exempt Liberty Bonds, which could be tapped to enhance the feasibility of constructing the commercial towers.

The labeling of these bonds, as noted earlier, dovetailed symbolically with their historic pedigree dating back to war bonds issued by the U.S. Treasury in 1917 to support the Allied cause in World War I. The governor and the mayor each controlled $4 billion of Liberty Bond allocations to induce projects as each saw fit. Silverstein's 7 World Trade had at first been approved for $400 million of Liberty Bonds in January 2003, but facing higher interest costs and a smaller payout from his insurers than he anticipated, two years later he had gone back to the city to request an additional $75 million of Liberty Bonds for the project, which was granted. With the project having to satisfy existing financial obligations related to the original building ($699 million), as well as development costs for the 1.7-million-square-foot tower ($671 million), the total refinancing for this tower adjacent to but not part of the Trade Center site came to $1.37 billion. Seven World Trade moved from blueprints into actual construction, said the Industrial Development Agency president Alper, "thanks in large part to the Liberty Bond program."[43] The bonds made the project feasible. The value they added to the project—$106 million, according to the financing appraisal—served as a public endowment. By my calculations, the $475 million in Liberty Bonds would save the developer some $2.4 million in annual debt service.

If strictly a private venture, rebuilding speculative office towers at Ground Zero would have been postponed until market conditions were favorable because conventional financing simply would not have been forthcoming in the absence of anchor tenants willing to commit to significant amounts of space—bankable leases from credit tenants in lender jargon. But this was a public-private undertaking of enormous political symbolism and importance to New York City.

OPEN ATTACK

To build the five speculative towers of the rebuilding program, Silverstein needed all the financial help the Liberty Bonds could provide. Predictably, in mid-2005, he went to the New York City Economic Development Corporation (EDC), which acts as an investment banker and advisor for the city and administrator of the city's portion of Liberty Bonds, and asked for all of the remaining yet-unallocated $3.35 billion in Liberty Bonds. City officials could not have been surprised at the ask, but the sheer size of Silverstein's request raised doubts about his capacity to do what he'd been saying all along he could do: rebuild all ten million square feet of commercial space at Ground Zero. "The city thought Silverstein's ask was too big, ridiculous," recalled Josh Sirefman, Deputy Mayor Doctoroff's chief of staff during this period. EDC president Seth Pinsky recalled, "For the first time we were seeing numbers."[44] They both questioned Silverstein's numbers and whether he needed all of the remaining Liberty Bonds. Because 7 World Trade was largely empty, EDC staff questioned Silverstein's ability as a developer. And the fact that the developer and his investment partnership had no money at risk because they had recaptured their equity investment as part of the December 2003 buy-out transaction with the Port Authority (discussed in chapter 6)—yet still controlled how the insurance proceeds could be used—incensed city officials, I was told. Silverstein, they believed, was playing for "the ups—the profits in development and management fees at the expense of what could get built," one insider explained, and this added further doubts to Silverstein's claim that a full buildout of the commercial program was economically feasible.

The developer's behavior just didn't make sense to city officials—until they asked the Socratic question: "What if Larry Silverstein isn't acting irrationally and there is an economic explanation for why this project isn't moving forward?" Years later in an interview Pinsky candidly admitted to me that it set them to thinking that maybe they were missing a piece of the picture. What looks irrational might be rational with new information.[45] The things Silverstein pushed for, market rents, for example, might have been right. Beyond the numbers, something else was going on, though: Silverstein's brash style clashed with the equally brash but different style of the city's top economic development policymakers, both of whom were former investment bankers. "There was a collision of Silverstein's style that undermined the perception of his real estate expertise," said one insider speaking off the record. "His style eroded instead of enhanced confidence in his ability to rebuild." He was not liked by several public players. Stories floated about that no one could do a deal with him. City officials considered Silverstein difficult to deal with: He was always reluctant to agree to deal points; instead, he would hang on and on; meetings ended without resolutions, with the principals walking out.

Silverstein's big ask for the remaining Liberty Bonds marked a turning point in the relations between City Hall and the developer and triggered the city's decisive move for a formal full-scale financial analysis of the feasibility issue. The feasibility issue had always been a concern among city policymakers. To test his supposition about Silverstein's capacity to rebuild, Doctoroff turned to the real estate experts at Lehman Brothers for hard numbers. Doing the numbers in his head, Doctoroff said he understood that the insurance funds were insufficient for Silverstein to build more than one building, which is what the Port Authority had been talking about as well, but he wanted an intensive, independent analysis of the economic feasibility and financial math of rebuilding the ten million square feet of office space. He and the mayor feared a walk-away scenario in which Silverstein would complete one tower (possibly two), default on his lease, and then walk away with millions in profit from fees, leaving the Port Authority without a way to finish the other buildings.[46]

This was fall 2005. Lehman Brothers' pro bono work on the financials opened the city's eyes to how truly complicated the project was. Acting as mediator in negotiations between the Port Authority and the developer, Doctoroff and his team shared the Lehman Brothers analysis with the Port Authority, which several insiders confirmed was on the cusp of making a deal with Silverstein. Governor Pataki's people were behind an "old" deal with Silverstein that city officials considered inferior to what they thought was in the best interests of the city. Years later as he first related the story to me, Doctoroff remained more than a little irritated about what almost happened. City officials wanted Silverstein to commit to at least two core conditions: equity in the deal and certainty on the timing of construction. Though the latter would come back to haunt the course of future events (as had happened before in the case of the redevelopment of Forty-second Street at Times Square when the real estate market went into a tailspin), Silverstein eventually conceded on the timing condition. Agreeing to a hard timing condition puts a developer in an economic straitjacket, eliminating degrees of freedom needed to manage the market risk of leasing up speculative space. That Silverstein agreed on this point was notable, though if it proved economically suicidal to proceed on such a course, he could, of course, always go back and attempt to renegotiate the deal, as so often happens in complex public-private development projects. And this he would do, aggressively—more than once.

All of these behind-the-scenes maneuvers were about to break out in public. With his reelection campaign in full swing that fall, Mayor Bloomberg went on record with a vow to take a bigger role in rebuilding at Ground Zero. Using his powerful bully pulpit, the mayor opened a blunt public offensive against the developer. "It would be in the city's interest to get Silverstein out," Bloomberg told the

Daily News editorial board, "[but] nobody can figure out how to do it yet. And can you imagine the stink if you gave him half a billion dollars or a billion dollars in profit to get him out?" It was "an unusually candid sit-down," noted a related story in the paper, in which the mayor "also expressed concern over the priorities of the Port Authority" and the "growing 'power'" of the 9/11 families, whose success at getting Governor Pataki to kill the proposed International Freedom Center for the site had complicated the task of fundraising for the memorial. Bloomberg's more expansive *Vision for Lower Manhattan* called for more residential buildings and other uses such as schools and hotels. "They are trying to force a kind of construction which maybe the marketplace doesn't want," he said about the ten million square feet of office space planned for Ground Zero.[47] He wanted to see residential uses on the site, but the PA claimed (correctly) that its statutory authority would not allow it to do housing. "Oh come on," the mayor said in response to a question. "If they have a building, all they have to do is sell the land to the private developer and then it's no problem to build—that's a technicality which literally would not slow anybody down two minutes."[48]

Saying the mayor "is right," the *Daily News* strongly criticized the plan for rebuilding ten million square feet of office space. After lightly acknowledging the "determination" to rebuild on the part of Governor Pataki, the Port Authority, and Silverstein, the editorial argued "one inescapable fact needs facing: There is not now, and there likely will never be, demand for such a huge block of offices downtown. Inexorably, that area of the city is shifting to a residential community as prime business tenants have decided they far prefer midtown." Moreover, Silverstein "is set on building regardless of whether he has a single tenant—a state of affairs unthinkable in the real estate community, where the rules of the game say you do not commit money, and you cannot raise money, for a project until tenants have signed on the dotted line.... The bottom line is that New York faces the terrible prospect of having a ghost town around Ground Zero for decades."[49]

Janno Lieber, Silverstein's point person, his right-hand man on the Trade Center project, and the face of the company's efforts to develop the office towers, was with his family in upstate New York over the weekend when he heard of the mayor's interview. He was shocked. "We made an exchange," he told me, referring to the November 2004 Design and Site Agreement between the Port Authority, the LMDC, the city, and Larry Silverstein; that agreement specified in excruciating detail the site plan's parameters of development. "We gave the Port Authority the memorial quadrant in exchange for receiving development sites ready to go, and we weren't able to move because the Port Authority hadn't delivered the sites," he said. To get to that agreement, Lieber, Doctoroff, Betts, and City Planning Commissioner Amanda Burden had wrestled about dimensions to ensure sufficient space for the core and lobby of Silverstein's towers. Lieber's recall of the event was still fresh in his mind years later because the next day he was scheduled to appear at an event at the construction site of a new building for the Brooklyn Children's Museum, a cause he's involved with, which the mayor would also be attending. "I think Larry would like to talk with you," he said to the mayor at that construction site of the Brooklyn Children's Museum. "What you said is not factual; we're ready to build but we have no sites," to which the mayor responded, "Tell Larry to call." The developer followed up, but that conversation and subsequent meeting did nothing to change the mayor's resolve, though Lieber believed that the mayor did not seem to understand that they had no sites at Ground Zero because the Port Authority was not delivering them on time.[50]

Lieber's job was to oversee the planning, design, and construction processes and to handle the economics involved in the business of development, including management of the insurance proceeds and tax-exempt Liberty Bonds, as well as all the legal matters involved; the high-profile nature of the project also brought marketing and public relations under his domain. It was the range of issues, not just the design, and not just the politics and government affairs, not just the details of a conventional real estate development project, that attracted him to the job when Silverstein hired him into the position in the spring of 2003. At forty-one, he had all the right credentials to tackle this particular long-term endeavor: a background in law (associate attorney specializing in litigation and governmental matters at Patterson, Belknap, Webb & Tyler), policy experience in transportation and familiarity with the halls of Congress (deputy assistant secretary for policy, then acting assistant secretary for transportation policy in the Clinton administration), New York City bona fides (Manhattan–Upper West Side born, resident of Brooklyn, stints in city government after graduating from Harvard University), and experience with complex large-scale public-private development projects (the proposed development of the Port Authority Bus Terminal and work as a consultant on the financial and legal structure for the conversion of the James A. Farley Post Office Building into Moynihan Station). Most critical was his immediate rapport with the developer: "Larry and I kind of hit it off, and when you're working for Larry, it's a very personal relationship," he told the *Real Deal*, a must-read industry rag for New York real estate professionals. "That's probably the single-most important qualification for this job"[51] (figure 12.6).

Lieber brought the skills of a tactician to the job, along with a personality "able to smooth over some of Silverstein's blunt angles." Like his boss, he had a clear sense of mission, cared passionately about the future of downtown, and had the thick skin of a tough negotiator. Yet he also harbored a light sense of humor. At this sensitive time when the city was working to oust Silverstein from the Trade

FIGURE 12.6 *Janno Lieber (left), senior executive at Silverstein Properties in charge of the company's rebuilding effort at the Trade Center site, and developer Larry Silverstein (right) at a design meeting for Tower 2, March 1, 2012.* JOE WOODHEAD, COURTESY SILVERSTEIN PROPERTIES INC.

Center site and the *Daily News* was penning editorials in support of the mayor's position, one evening at 5:00 P.M., Lieber got a call from Arthur Browne, editor of the paper's editorial page; it was obvious, Lieber told me, that the editorial had already been written. Answering the call, he said: "Lamb reporting for slaughter!" Browne wanted a comment from him. "Is this going to change the story?" Janno asked. Browne responded: "Unlikely, our in-house real estate expert [Mortimer Zuckerman] has spoken."[52]

In a statement released to the media on October 22, Silverstein said, "The Mayor's remarks are confusing. Over the last four years, the Mayor and his representatives on the LMDC have participated at every stage in the development of the World Trade Center master site plan, which calls for rebuilding the office space destroyed by terrorists on 9/11. Together with the Governor, the Mayor has frequently urged us to proceed as quickly as possible. I believe that New Yorkers want to see rapid rebuilding and not yet another exercise in planning and re-planning. I am confident in downtown's future as a great business center, and I remain committed to getting it done."[53] The Silverstein team members thought of themselves as heroes because, just months before, they had gotten rebuilding going again by quickly responding to an order from Governor Pataki to redesign the Freedom Tower after the NYPD's commissioner Kelly raised security issues about its location too close to West Street. They were taken aback by the mayor's sharp out-of-left-field attack.

At the same time, they had heard rumors that PA chairman Coscia wanted the agency to reclaim some of the Trade Center sites to give it a freer hand to develop retail space without waiting for the office towers on sites 3 and 4 to be built. Those rumors had surfaced months earlier in the press, and then again just weeks before the mayor's sudden outburst. With the bickering at Ground Zero ongoing in public and the distrust between the parties continuing to fester, Coscia announced the Port's intentions of building on its own 200,000 square feet of retail shops and restaurants in the Transportation Hub as the first phase of a retail program that called for an additional 300,000 square feet along the Church Street corridor of the site: "We're off to the races; we're doing this. By the first quarter of 2006, we'll have [a] fairly detailed design."[54] In fact, the Port Authority unveiled preliminary illustrations of the transit-hub retail a week after the mayor's attack on Silverstein hit the press.

None of this shook Silverstein's confidence in his development plan or his financing strategy. Following the conventions of commercial real estate, he planned to use insurance funds to build the Freedom Tower and a second tower and then borrow against the equity in the first two towers to finance the others. Intent upon a faster timetable of construction, city officials opposed this approach. Silverstein's timetable with its 2015 completion date and his phased tower delivery did not make officials in the Pataki administration happy either. Still, the mayor's comment incensed the governor and his aides, who reportedly fumed at the mayor's public about-face. "He has been a great partner from day one," Pataki said of Bloomberg. "But I'm perplexed that the city now thinks that Lower Manhattan cannot support the commercial space envisioned in the site plan." Pataki was running interference for the developer, but Bloomberg was not budging from his position: "The market's changed and there's no reason for us to feel obligated to build exactly what we talked about before," he told the *Post*'s editorial board.[55] The mayor wanted to get the site filled sooner than Silverstein's ten-year buildout.

The mayor's "outburst" caused something of a backlash from New York politicians. Sheldon Silver attacked the mayor's comments as "inconsistent and absurd." "Your new position will undoubtedly hurt efforts to re-establish the Lower Manhattan community as a strong commercial center," he said in a letter, as reported by the *Daily News*. The mayor's office issued a sharp response: "If Mr. Silver has any questions about the mayor's commitment to Lower Manhattan, he can pick up the phone and ask him instead of issuing bizarre press releases," said Bloomberg spokesman Edward Skyler. U.S. senator Charles E. Schumer also disagreed with the mayor's push for a rebuild that included residential units or a hotel, believing Ground

Zero was too valuable as a commercial hub. But Schumer also "took a tough line with Silverstein, saying the developer needs to prove his mettle by fully renting 7 World Trade Center," which was only about 20 percent rented because of the developer's above-market asking prices.[56]

Frustration was running deep and patience wearing thin for real action to begin at Ground Zero. In the stew of volatile emotions that defined Ground Zero, the perception, among insiders at the PA and in the governor's office that Silverstein was "an inflexible steward who has largely failed to move Ground Zero forward" was coming into sharp focus.[57] Even if the mayor and his officials did not believe Silverstein could be totally taken out of his leasehold position as presumptive re-builder of the Trade Center site, the mayor's blunt statement served a tactical purpose: to push Silverstein into a restructured deal that reduced his role in rebuilding at the same time it pushed forward the possibility of the mayor's alternative vision for the Trade Center site. City Hall had entered the fray, finally. Events were about to pivot at Ground Zero.

CHAPTER 13

Political Pivot

The New York Times

Mayor Seeking Major Changes at Ground Zero

October 24, 2005

NEW YORK POST

Mike: WTC Larry Can't Fini$h Job

February 7, 2006

DAILY NEWS

Silverstein, See Ya In Court. 'I'm not going to negotiate anymore,' Bloomberg says

New York Daily News, April 22, 2006

FIGURE 13.1 Author composite

Following a resounding reelection mandate—the mayor won by a twenty-percentage-point margin, the widest margin ever for a Republican mayor of New York—Bloomberg looked downtown to expand his legacy, to assert himself as he pushed to expand the city economy. This successful businessman turned politician was not one to look back, only forward—and he was frustrated: Pataki was not being decisive, a mayoral aide told me. Though the city lacked formal control over the Trade Center site, the mayor and his team were not bereft of political tools with which to exercise authority and intervene to steer the process of redevelopment in ways they thought would better meet the city's long-term needs for growth and prosperity (figure 13.1). The mayor controlled the city's $4 billion allocation of tax-exempt Liberty Bonds, and he was going to use that authority as a lever to push his vision for Ground Zero.

When Silverstein's application for the remaining $3.35 billion of Liberty Bonds towers came up for review at an Industrial Development Agency public hearing in December 2005, city officials laid out their conditions for approval. They wanted to impose strict timelines on construction to advance a more aggressive timetable for the towers. They wanted the ability to reassign the bond authorization, what finance people call a "clawback," to other developers if rebuilding did not progress in timely fashion or was slowed by a lack of market demand for office space. They wanted to preserve a small amount of Liberty Bonds for retail development purposes to assure the city's retail vision for downtown. And they wanted to prevent the developer from taking "excessive fees" out of the project. Both sides were said to "remain far apart" on several sticking points.[1] The tussle that ensued over the last Liberty Bond allocations became the wedge in the mayor's crusade to wrest certain control from the state over the future of rebuilding at Ground Zero.

The mayor's natural constituency, the business and real estate communities, believed they were "hostages to the mess at Ground Zero," remarked Kathryn S. Wylde, head of the influential Partnership for the City of New York. "The heavyweights in the business community looked to the mayor for action,"[2] as did a majority of New Yorkers, according to repeated polls. Moreover, regardless of legal position, the mayor was likely to be the one judged for what happened at Ground Zero, and his term of office now extended four years beyond Governor Pataki's exit at the end of 2006. Bloomberg's intervention in 2006 proved to be essential to addressing the feasibility question: Does Silverstein have the financial ability to meet the agenda for rebuilding ten million square feet of office space at Ground Zero?

POWER POLITICS

Deep strategic issues were at play at Ground Zero throughout 2005 and well into 2006. All sides were positioning themselves for an intense battle about to break out full force over the economics of rebuilding, a battle that was, in essence, an all-out tussle for political control. Even as the Port Authority and Silverstein stood aligned in the developer's push for a maximum insurance payout, their financial interests in rebuilding led to divergent paths on a number of fundamental issues, including how much retail space should be replaced on the site and how responsibility for the cost of building the complex multistory infrastructure necessary to support the commercial towers should be shared. With the insurance litigation seemingly settled by the end of 2004—after Silverstein had won his partial victory in his quest for a double insurance payout—the time had come for the Port Authority and Silverstein to sit down and discuss a new lease agreement, one that acknowledged the changed circumstances of what was commercially feasible for Silverstein to accomplish with what remained of the much-diminished insurance payout.

That did not happen. It was not yet time, politically. Yet by fall 2005, problems with the security-driven redesign of the Freedom Tower and the additional capital costs involved finally drove the start of discussions that would lead to negotiations. Redesigning the Freedom Tower was going to delay its completion by some eighteen months and increase costs by some yet-to-be-determined number. The collapse of the cultural agenda on the heels of the Freedom Tower redesign episode added to the ever-heightened uncertainty and lack of progress continually bedeviling progress at Ground Zero. The longer the project went without clear moves toward construction, the farther away that goal appeared. Pressure for progress was mounting on all parties. On December 8, the Port Authority and Silverstein signed an unusual two-page "Pre-Negotiation Agreement" in which the two parties affirmed that they "wish to facilitate open discussions and exchanges of ideas" with regard to negotiations on their "respective roles, rights and responsibilities in the redevelopment of the World Trade Center."[3]

Time had entered the equation of rebuilding. The sunset date for the Liberty Bond program, already extended once by Congress for five years, was closing in: The bonds had to be issued by year end 2009, and the likelihood of that happening was increasingly questionable. Other conditions were beyond the control of the negotiators. The timetable for the commercial program, for example, would, in part, be dictated by engineering realities in constructing the retaining walls on the commercial portion of the site, the so-called East Bathtub where the utilities, mechanical facilities, and underground circulation and vehicle security screening systems would be woven into the huge concrete basin.

Engineering the underground superblock was remarkably complicated, as Scott Raab skillfully detailed in a series of exclusive reports chronicling its construction published in *Esquire* in 2005 and 2006. The Port Authority was saying it would take eighteen to twenty-four months to build the bathtub, and other than work on the Transportation Hub, it had not yet moved forward with anything else; it was just finalizing the underground's engineering and design work. Port Authority staff, however, made at least one significant seemingly technical decision that materially affected Silverstein's tower plans: It shrank the size of its chiller plant (providing cooling to the 9/11 Memorial, Memorial Museum, and PATH Hub), thereby cutting off the new commercial office towers from its central air-conditioning and water-cooling system that would draw water from the Hudson River. On the one hand, the Port Authority's decision meant greater complexity and cost for Silverstein, who would have to construct his own chillers to service the Freedom Tower and other office buildings on the site with cooled air using city water. On the other hand, that decision released the commercial towers from the tether of the Port Authority's operations, and in that one sense would create a conventional, divisible development site for each of the Silverstein towers built above the East Bathtub.[4]

In agreeing to commit to the city's demand for an aggressive timetable for re-building of the commercial space at Ground Zero, Janno Lieber chose his words carefully when he said the savings in finance costs generated from the Liberty Bonds would permit Silverstein Properties to build "as fast as engineering can allow," that is, "as soon as the government provided the sites." If the city and Port Authority shared a distrust of Silverstein's ability to execute his plan to build the five towers consecutively, Silverstein's associates were equally distrustful of the Port Authority's capacity to manage the highly complicated underground project, its cost and budget, and, most critically from their perspective, its ability to deliver within a scheduled time frame. They did not believe the agency understood the physical and financial complexities of the project. The lack of trust was mutual—and a bottleneck to progress. Silverstein's executives might have trusted the Port Authority more had the agency put its chief engineer (a legendary position at the PA), Frank J. Lombardi, in charge rather than lodging the project in a separate WTC Construction Department run by Steven P. Plate. Plate was an engineer as well and dedicated to the task of rebuilding, though several players on both sides of the public-private project I spoke with believed his career experience did not seem that well suited to the technical demands of the assignment. Having started work on the Calatrava Transportation Hub in September 2005, the Port Authority needed to collaborate with Silverstein on the infrastructure for the site, but found itself "'butting heads' with him on a daily basis."[5] This increasingly antagonistic relationship full of mutual suspicion and weighed down by the baggage of past disputes and disagreements was the antithesis of what a public-private develop-ment relationship was all about.

Although he had site control, by the end of 2005, Silverstein was under growing public pressure to give up a portion of his development rights. With the critical path of rebuilding driven by the Port Authority's engineering and construction of underground infrastructure, taking Silverstein out of the project was unlikely to speed up the start of commercial redevelopment. The business press, however, agreed with the joint effort by the city and the Port Authority to cut back the devel-oper's role in rebuilding: "In the end, too much is at stake to be entrusted only to Mr. Silverstein," *Crain's New York Business* editorialized. "A deal under which he would put up the Freedom Tower and a second office building, then compete for the right to construct more office buildings, is best for this city."[6] Something of a consensus was building.

The political calendar was an ever-present factor in the power calculus that ruled at Ground Zero. Rebuilding Ground Zero had become a top priority for the reelected mayor in no small part, I was told, because Deputy Mayor Daniel L. Doctoroff had built a platform for him to become interested in lower Manhattan and the Trade Center site and had educated him on the issues. This was a new-found mission for the mayor, a longtime resident of the Upper East Side who had built his Bloomberg LP corporate headquarters on the Upper East Side as well. At the other end of the electoral calendar, Governor Pataki was facing the lame-duck year of his three-term administration, and he and his close associates desperately sought to accelerate rebuilding. If he was to leave a legacy at Ground Zero, the governor had to accomplish something meaningful by the end of 2006. In the aftermath of the chaos and continual delays throughout 2005, this was looking harder and harder to outside observers, but on the second floor in Albany, "[i]t was critical to get a beam in the ground before the Pataki administration left office," said one influential insider in a position to drive events.

The governor was pushing for visible hard-wired progress, and on December 14, he made a surprise announcement at a news conference on Long Island saying the state would provide Silverstein with $1.67 billion in Liberty Bonds, all of its remaining allocation, for construction of the Freedom Tower and a second office tower. Pataki's move, as Charles V. Bagli of the *Times* noted, aimed to mitigate the risk of a postponement of the groundbreaking for the Freedom Tower scheduled for the coming spring. His financing gift, however, came with a sharp directive and a specific timetable: Silverstein and the Port Authority had to work out their differences over a wide range of financial issues, including the Port Authority's proposal for the developer to cede a portion of the site back to the authority—in ninety days. The state, according to Bagli, "could withdraw the bond approval if the two sides reach an impasse."[7] Although Bloomberg had tried to use the city's allocation of Liberty Bonds as a lever to force Silverstein out of the rebuilding process, in a classic state-city power struggle Pataki played his trump card. His unilateral decision to bypass the city in a preemptive move once again displayed the superior power of the gubernatorial position.

And once again City Hall was blind-sided, said one deputy who sat in the mayor's bullpen, a sea of desks with low partitions, where Bloomberg placed his own cubicle in the center of the room, "within arm's reach and a shout's distance of his top lieutenants" (figure 13.2). The bullpen arrangement functioned in a distinctive fashion. "The inability to hide behind closed doors and the fact that the mayor could see everything made it possible to get answers from people, even when they would have preferred not to talk to you," recalled Ester Fuchs, a professor at Columbia University who sat in the bullpen as special advisor to the mayor for governance and strategic planning. "I think the mayor used the open space to play a brilliant mind game. You never really knew when he was paying attention to what you were doing or not doing."[8] That tradition-breaking arrangement in the old Board of Estimate chamber on the second floor of City Hall, the symbol of his

FIGURE 13.2 *Mayor Michael Bloomberg standing in the middle of his bullpen on the second floor in the former Board of Estimate chamber of City Hall within arm's reach of his top lieutenants, March 22, 2013. The open-communication model imported from Bloomberg's days on Wall Street served as the center of his administration's bureaucracy for his three terms in office.* HIROKO MASUIKE/THE NEW YORK TIMES/REDUX

Wall Street–influenced management style, had been an immediate harbinger of Bloomberg's determination to establish a new mayoral style of sharing information and being open and accessible.

Though not as openly public until this preemptive move, tensions between Governor Pataki and Mayor Bloomberg had been mounting since 2003. Power struggles over rebuilding had broken out before, over the structure and role of the LMDC, as well as the selection of its leadership; over the governor's last-minute attempt to shift the federal formula for homeland security money going to vulnerable states and cities in ways that would disadvantage New York City; and when the governor similarly "blind-sided" city officials with his announcement of a timetable for rebuilding Ground Zero in a speech to a prominent business group at a time the mayor was trying to assert influence over the site through his proposal for a land swap with the Port Authority. Both self-disciplined and successful, Pataki and Bloomberg operated with very different public personas. Pataki "rarely airs his innermost thoughts in public and almost never acts without a long-term political goal in mind," wrote *Times* political reporters Jennifer Steinhauer and James C. McKinley Jr. Bloomberg's style as mayor had been to keep things private and behind closed doors, but gradually he learned that politics differs from business, and "if you air things in public, the public becomes your ally. You can bring them to the negotiating table."[9] At a personal level, Pataki and Bloomberg were known to be friendly, to share private dinners and general good will. Nonetheless, competitive pressures and power tensions between New York's two highest elected officials are rooted in the governing priorities of state and local politics.

"Mayors want more money than Albany is ever willing to give, and governors have to juggle the political interests of the city, the suburbs and upstate communities as well as their own ambitions. As such, the two are always bickering. Especially if they are in the same political party," wrote Steinhauer and McKinley. Historically, differences in political mission have transcended the personal; at times, though, the edge of competition could become highly personal, as in the difficult relationship between Governor Nelson A. Rockefeller and Mayor John V. Lindsay. "The job of mayor is to take as much of the whole pie as he can get for his 36 or 37 or 38 percent of the population of the state," said former governor Mario M. Cuomo. "But that slice comes out of the rest of the pie that belongs to the larger part of the population and that's the governor's mission, to make sure it's distributed fairly."[10] As the economic powerhouse of the state, New York City, or "downstate" in the political lexicon, has always pressed hard against that political reality, but still, it has always been vulnerable to the state's higher-order actions. Although the ebb and flow of the political dynamic varies with the strength or weakness of each elected chief official, the governor holds far more prerogatives and power.

The city and the state were operating within different spheres of influence. Directly thwarted by Pataki's government machinery at Ground Zero, Bloomberg and Doctoroff had taken to focusing on a broad canvas of policy initiatives designed to assure growth and 24/7 vitality for all of lower Manhattan that were less subject to gubernatorial control. They invested in parks, housing, schools, transportation, and streetscapes. When it came to events taking place—or not, as was often the case—at Ground Zero, they pursued a series of strategic interventions, assiduously exercising the city's political capital in ways calibrated to push redevelopment forward faster, toward tangible progress. In his 2006 State of the City address, Mayor Bloomberg followed on point by publicly calling the question of the developer's financial capacity to meet his responsibility to rebuild all five office towers. In unmistakably clear language, he upped the rhetorical volume by calling on Silverstein Properties "to do the right thing—and hand off responsibility for building Towers 3 and 4, in exchange for a reduction of its rent." It was time, in other words "to push aside individual financial interests, and focus on what's best for our city." The mayor wanted "to pick up the pace of commercial construction" at Ground Zero and "to build for uses that reflect the realities of the market and the needs of Lower Manhattan—like the retail development that is so crucial to linking the site back into the life of the city." The Port Authority as well, he said, needed to commit "to occupying one of the towers and working quickly to identify a developer for the other, so that all projects can proceed simultaneously at the same, quick pace."[11]

The mayor's aggressive campaign to shrink Silverstein's role at Ground Zero was acquiring the power of action from an alliance with the New Jersey side of the Port Authority, an alliance built on mutual interests in the issue at hand as well as personal affinities. PA Chairman Coscia had been moving behind the scenes ever since late summer 2004, after a presentation by Silverstein and his financial consultants from Morgan Stanley to PA commissioners on the developer's financial plan planted deep seeds of doubt about its feasibility. Concerned about the downside risk of building without tenants lined up to fill the buildings within a reasonably short time frame, the commissioners worried that speculative construction would compromise Silverstein's ability to pay rent to the agency and to secure further financing as well. In the fall of 2005, in a personal meeting with Silverstein, Coscia, age forty-six, had advanced an informal proposal in which Silverstein would relinquish a portion of his development rights to build ten million square feet of commercial space in exchange for a reduction in his annual ground rent (due to increase by eighteen million dollars in August 2006): "Let's divide the work and do it faster," Coscia said. After being rebuffed with polite words from the septuagenarian developer—"You're a very nice young man and you probably have good things in your future, but you're very naive. Have a nice day"—Coscia found a receptive audience for his pitch with Doctoroff and City Hall.[12]

In terms of strategy, the pivotal meeting was held in Coscia's office sometime before Mayor Bloomberg's State of the City speech. The group included Doctoroff; his chief of staff, Josh Sirefman; his point person for lower Manhattan, EDC executive vice president Seth Pinsky; and PA deputy executive director James P. "Jamie" Fox. They had the city's financial analysis in hand, and the questions were, what to do with it, how to proceed? "The objective was to force Governor Pataki's hand, pressure him to do something, take action leading to a renegotiation of the lease, and the way to do it was to make Larry the target," one participant told me in confidence. "City Hall agreed to the strategy." Designed to pressure Pataki's office, the alliance between City Hall and the New Jersey side of the Port Authority played on the proven perception that Governor Pataki was prone to give Silverstein more latitude. The interpersonal glue to the alliance was a relationship of mutual respect and professional friendship between Coscia and Doctoroff that grew out of these months of strategizing and negotiations.

Seth Pinsky was the other key player in these negotiations. At thirty-four, he had become the quarterback of the city's negotiations with Larry Silverstein. In 2003, he joined the economic development agency as a vice president, after working a number of years as an associate in the law firm Cleary Gottlieb, Steen & Hamilton's real estate practice at One Liberty Plaza, where "he would monitor the recovery and cleanup efforts at Ground Zero, watching as workers searched for remains and stopped to salute as bodies were driven out of the site covered in an American flag." Before law school at Harvard University, he had worked as a financial analyst at James D. Wolfensohn Inc. He was "hired sort of into the bowels of EDC," remarked Doctoroff, and distinguished himself by an uncanny facility with financing and structuring deals. "You know in city government there is not a wide range of those sorts of skills that are available, particularly when you're dealing with commercial parties on the other side." Pinsky's private-sector experience proved invaluable in the public sector, as did his love of cities and what makes them tick—he used to design cities when he was in middle school, mapping out where businesses and residences should go. Because he had done transactions in the private sector and knew how private-sector counterparties think about transactions, "I couldn't be fooled with jargon," Pinsky told me, and as a result, "dealings with the public sector were more balanced." He developed a reputation as a fearsome negotiator for whom "there are no permanent obstacles," said Doctoroff with more than a touch of pride in his protégée. Affable and mild-mannered yet persistent, he became a closer, someone who got deals done. He understood that compromises were necessary to get things done in New York. He was smart and savvy. On the Trade Center situation, he had a goal in mind and insight into what the analysis of the situation would show, and he would use that to help break the logjam by seeing what it was that Silverstein really wanted. After the 2006 deal, Doctoroff saw to it that Pinsky was promoted to head EDC's Real Estate Transactions group, and in 2008 Mayor Bloomberg appointed him president of EDC.[13]

FIGHTING THROUGH NUMBERS

Shortly after the mayor's 2006 State of the City speech, city officials went public with their financial analysis of the commercial rebuilding program at Ground Zero. "We're not going to allocate Liberty Bonds today to buildings that are never going to be built," Doctoroff told the *Daily News*.[14] Assembled by a dozen officials at EDC, the Law Department, and City Hall, with the Lehman Brothers' real estate group acting as an outsourced analytical service, city officials had arrived at a straightforward conclusion confirming the mayor's previously stated fear of a walk-away scenario: Silverstein would exhaust his money for the project after building the Freedom Tower and possibly a second of the five towers planned for the site and default on his lease in 2009, even if all remaining Liberty Bonds were allocated to the project. They claimed the developer had underinsured the site, evidence of which had come out in the pretrial discovery papers of the insurance battle.[15] What most worried the city was the fact that the $4.675 billion in insurance proceeds had already been depleted by more than $1.7 billion spent on buyout payments, ground rent, lender and investor repayments, legal fees, design and consulting services, and other expenses, including management fees and additional amounts to Silverstein and his investors for "lost profits" from the interruption of business as a consequence of 9/11. The way these funds were being spent was eroding an ability to use the insurance proceeds to rebuild. Silverstein would still have to allocate some portion of the already depleted insurance funds to rebuild the underground infrastructure as well as the retail portion of the commercial program, leaving that much less (only $2.9 billion) for construction of ten million square feet of office, which the city estimated would cost $7.3 billion or more. Since demand for office space in new towers was at the time highly questionable, the city's analysis predicted that the developer would be unlikely to secure the additional necessary debt capacity unless rents for prime space rose to about $70 per square foot by 2011.[16]

The financial analysis prepared by the Lehman team helped the city understand the optionality of the situation. Two central questions were addressed: What could be done on a market basis, and what had to be subsidized? When would Silverstein have an economic motive to default? The team modeled out the fees to Silverstein from ongoing asset management and development. It did a net present value analysis of the benefit stream to each stakeholder, using its own assumptions about future rents and related variables; the city did not tell the Lehman team what assumptions to use in its modeling. The team made the case on the question of break-even rents. The ground lease was a major factor in the analysis; that expense, at $12 a square foot, relative to "ambitious" rents at $60 a square foot and after taking into account expenses for operations and third-party debt, made the equation uneconomic. The math made no sense, recalled one of the Lehman analysts. Although Silverstein had the rights to rebuild, his ability to support ground rents for the entire buildout was not sustainable. A cross-default provision in the lease tied the full buildout together in one financial package. That is, if the Silverstein partnership failed to meet the terms and conditions of any one lease, that default would trigger a default under all of the other leases. City officials spent a lot of time analyzing the cross-default provision of the ground lease: Was the cross default providing the force that would lead to a Silverstein default or was it the driver for why the ground-lease payments, as the first lien on the property, were unsustainable?

In a fourteen-page summary presentation, city officials argued that once insurance monies ran out, building any remaining office buildings would be uneconomical because the costs would exceed market value, and Silverstein would have no rational choice but to default on his lease obligations. Port Authority officials had hired their own experts, the real estate consulting firm Jones Lang LaSalle, to assess the financial viability of the project and based on that report, they realized their agency was in the same "financial space" as the city. It was, Seth Pinsky recalled, "an aha-moment for the Port."[17] "The build-out of the site, based on the current plan, is extremely questionable in terms of Silverstein's ability to go beyond the Freedom Tower," Port chairman Coscia told the press. "We are unconvinced it is a viable plan."[18] Default would leave the Port Authority to complete the remaining three towers, yet, according to the city's calculations, Silverstein and his investors would still profit handsomely from their investment, walking away with some $106 million if the developer defaulted on the entire site and as much as $565 million in fees, commissions, and equity if he was able to hold on to the Freedom Tower and one other building. The optionality of the existing situation did not give the developer much incentive to negotiate—stalemate was predictable.

The huge variability of purported profits city officials believed would result if Silverstein defaulted on his obligation to rebuild traced back to a particular feature of the original 2001 lease agreement, the cross-default provision. This critical contractual condition was designed to protect the security interests of the Port Authority as the owner of the ground. When the Port Authority and the Silverstein investor group finalized the lease deal in 2001, they actually signed separate lease agreements for each of the four towers Silverstein would manage and operate for the next ninety-nine years. Under the cross-default provision of these leases, the group would have to perform on every lease; if one building became unprofitable to operate, it could not just walk away without incurring a severe penalty because in doing so it would lose all property rights on the other towers. It was an all-or-nothing type of penalty provision, and only under certain cases would these cross-default provisions not apply. "The cross," as it would become known, was in place to align the economic interest in operating each existing tower with equal business effort. Once the attack on 9/11 destroyed those towers, it destroyed the intended functionality of that contractual provision of the lease. The Port Authority and the Silverstein group were now facing off in tense and difficult negotiations to define a new set of roles, responsibilities, and construction schedules that would govern the development of a complex multitower commercial project, and in this context, "the cross" took on a wholly different risk profile, for both parties.

In pushing for a speedy and comprehensive rebuilding effort, Doctoroff wanted a new cross-default provision in the development agreement. He believed it to be a very important tool for assuring completion of the office program for the site, and that made it a strategic chip in the city's effort to get some amount of control over the rebuilding agenda. Coscia too believed in rebuilding all the commercial space: "Our belief is that if a great amount of the site is put into development sooner rather than later, it will make it easier to lease Freedom Tower," he said. "We think that by building that critical mass, the likelihood of success is enhanced."[19] (Critical mass is always an important consideration in large-scale development, yet given the prevailing weak market conditions of the downtown office market, the logic was a bit of a stretch.) Yet even if "the cross" appeared to be in line with city objectives, would this singular provision tie the knot of performance too tight? From a policy perspective, aiming to simultaneously rebuild ten million square feet of office space in lower Manhattan may have been desirable, but from a real estate market perspective, was it realistic, practical, or wise? At this point, city officials were intent on reducing Silverstein's role to three towers, still more than six million square feet of space, so the same question about how much commercial space could responsibly be brought onto the market still hung out there.

The build-all-at-once approach contradicted the phased schedule laid out in the environmental impact statement (EIS) for the project, which followed the logic behind the master plan. As approved by the LMDC on April 13, 2004, the final EIS anticipated a buildout in several phases over eleven years: The first phase, scheduled for completion by 2009, would include the memorial, the Memorial Center, and cultural buildings, the below-grade levels across the project site, the Freedom Tower, up to 1 million square feet of retail space, streets, and all the proposed open space. Remaining phases, principally the additional office towers and hotel, were expected to be completed by 2015.

Assumptions supporting the city's financial analysis of the Trade Center commercial plan created plenty of opportunity for a rebuttal, and the developer did so almost immediately in a two-page public statement and counterattack issued by his firm's PR representative, Rubenstein Communications. At this time, Silverstein may have been the only one to believe he had the financial wherewithal to build all five towers. It was imperative for him to defend that position for tactical reasons, though he had implicitly (though in no way formally) relinquished his exclusive right to build all ten million square feet during the course of ongoing negotiations with the Port Authority over a new lease arrangement, in particular over which of the five development sites on the overall site he would actually develop. In late January, when the mayor called upon Silverstein "to do the right thing—and hand off responsibility for building Towers 3 and 4," Janno Lieber said publicly that the firm would build the three Church Street towers (Towers 2, 3, and 4)—the most valuable of the five sites from a real estate perspective. The Port Authority, meanwhile, was proposing that Silverstein continue to develop the Freedom Tower and a second building, in return for which it would adjust his annual rent; it would find other developers for the three other buildings. The industry's powerful Real Estate Board of New York rallied to the developer's defense, Bagli wrote. "I'm not convinced that the Port Authority is better equipped to build an office tower than my members are," said REBNY president Steven Spinola. "And I'm not sure there is a deal to be made if the Port wants Larry to drop what may be the best two office sites."[20]

The developer's rebuttal to the city's analysis was correct on some points where the city's logic was faulty, short on financial support for his strong counterassertions, and long on catch-phrase rhetoric that upped the stakes in the political arena and intensified the distrust the parties held for one another. "Silverstein Properties wishes to set the record straight on what it considers to be a series of misleading and at times outright wrong statements from City officials and offices over the past weeks," began the rebuttal. Seeking the high ground of public interest, it went on to state that these "unfortunate statements hurt all of Downtown," which, in light of the desperate fears of the downtown business community, spoke truth. Silverstein was also correct in claiming that bringing in other developers would do nothing to speed up rebuilding and just might slow it down further. Not only was the timetable for a start dictated by the building of the East Bathtub, which was not due to be finished until 2008, but any other developer, he pointed out, would likely proceed more slowly. "Without insurance proceeds that developer would have to borrow more money and raise equity…and would be unlikely to start construction before tenant commitments are in hand, which would further delay build-out."[21] What went unsaid, however, was the fact that the public award of Liberty Bonds would be available to other developers. Moreover, even though they could assist economically, nobody could figure out whether the Liberty Bonds would lower costs sufficiently to make the projects market feasible.

The clarity of the rest of the rebuttal was at best diffuse, revealing only partial facts. Silverstein argued that he had "demonstrated his financial commitment by long ago agreeing to allocate business interruption insurance (on top of property insurance) to the rebuilding effort," yet the city's analysis was sufficiently detailed in pointing out that Silverstein and his investors were being compensated for lost profits from business interruption, even though the team of professionals on the task did not have sufficient information to calculate the precise dollar amount. Silverstein similarly claimed that he had "continued to pay approximately $10 million in rent to the Port Authority every month since 9/11, even though the buildings that he leased are gone," a well-known fact; these payments, however, were part and parcel of the insurance funds being used to support his economic hold on the development rights at Ground Zero. He also took strong exception to the city's projection of his walk-away "profits," asserting that any such projected windfall was "illusionary" because three-quarters of the so-called profits was "not cash in

Mr. Silverstein's pocket, but the hypothetical 'value' of the buildings when they are leased." The logic of this position skillfully elided over the millions in development fees, management fees, and leasing commissions that most surely represented cash payouts. To call an estimate of building value "hypothetical," even if leased up at rents lower than what the developer would have underwritten in his financial analysis, was a conveniently disingenuous position for Silverstein to stake out: By convention, commercial real estate investors routinely estimate "value" in the absence of truly comparable market sales. Silverstein's fallback argument was that if Towers 3 and 4 were financeable, he would have no reason to walk away. Perhaps. In a final flourish of rhetoric, he called the city's attempt to wrest away his control of the site a "Soviet-style *confiscation*."[22]

The pivotal assumption of financial feasibility, the one variable more important than any other and that each side claimed the other got wrong, was the projection of future office rents. The city's analysis assumed rents of $35 to $40 a square foot based on recent lease agreements at the adjacent twenty-year-old World Financial Center complex owned by Brookfield Properties. In his rebuttal, Silverstein claimed that "the City's projected rent levels are at least 30 percent below the initial leases secured at 7 WTC," and he put forth as the right number $50 to $55 per square foot, which was what he was asking for at 7 WTC. Seven WTC did set a new standard for class A office towers in Manhattan, and though directly comparable in quality and state-of-the-art office space to the three towers he planned to build on the Trade Center site, his asking rent figure was just that, an asking rent. It did not reflect the value of the multiple incentive subsidies Governor Pataki had signed into law in fall 2005 to lure tenants to the Ground Zero area, subsidies available to tenants leasing space at 7 WTC, which when accounted for pushed those $50 to $55 rents down into the $40s.[23]

Despite these generous subsidies, tenant interest in downtown office space was weak. Overall vacancy downtown for the first three months of 2006 hovered around 11.6 percent compared to 7.8 percent in midtown Manhattan. Asking rents in downtown were moving up compared to those in 2005, mainly due to the addition of 7 WTC to the building inventory, yet as of February 2006, Silverstein had not yet lined up any major tenants for 7 WTC. His first lease, for 40,000 square feet with the prestigious not-for-profit New York Academy of Sciences, had only been signed in December 2005, and doubts about the developer's ability to fill this 1.7-million-square-foot building, yet alone an additional ten million square feet, were widespread, not even hushed over in whispers. Industry professionals were publicly pressuring him to make concessions on his asking rents—to no avail.

No one had a crystal ball to forecast the future of the office market. Office rents in Manhattan do not follow a predictable trajectory of straight-line growth. Rather, the Manhattan office market works in cycles because development activity runs in cycles. It takes three years or more to build a high-density tower, and between the decision point when a developer can justify the economics of building a speculative tower (and secure the necessary financing) and the date at which it comes onto the market, rents in existing class A buildings typically jump in a sudden and dramatic step fashion as the supply of office space gets increasingly squeezed before new buildings in quantity sufficient to satisfy demand are ready for occupancy. That at least has been the historical pattern of rent behavior in Manhattan for real estate cycles during the past thirty-five years. Real estate professionals anticipate such sudden rent spikes on the upswing in every real estate cycle, and they understand that the imbalance can persist beyond the rental peak.

The logic of that pattern is what fueled the argument Silverstein's longtime leasing broker, CBRE executive Mary Ann Tighe, and economist Hugh Kelly both made, rather ardently, at the City Council hearing in March 2006 in support of the full-rebuild scenario of ten million square feet: The space needs to be there, available to accommodate the demand as the cycle occurs, they each pointed out. That market pattern is also why Kelly found the city's conclusion that future downtown rents would have to rise dramatically to $70 per square foot in 2011—the tipping point in order for Silverstein not to default after completing the Freedom Tower and a second tower—"just utterly false." The quality of space, not just the quantity, was what mattered. "Downtown's ability to absorb that volume of space has been underestimated many, many times in the past," he said.[24] The future of a downtown office market was a subject on which well-informed people could, and did, disagree, often.

The hearing called by the City Council's Committee on Lower Manhattan Redevelopment chaired by Alan Gerson was the first substantive public airing of the economic issues surrounding rebuilding. Although the City Council had no power to decide anything at Ground Zero, not even the city's allocation of the Liberty Bonds, the public hearing provided a platform for Deputy Mayor Doctoroff and Project Director Janno Lieber to set out their positions. The Port Authority—"thumbing their nose at the New York City government," as Gerson phrased his disapproval—did not attend, submitting written testimony instead.[25] About the only point of agreement in the nearly six hours of testimony and questioning came on a clarion call for the Port Authority to get busy on the complex infrastructure for the site and fill the big hole so commercial construction could begin. Several councilmen pushed back vigorously on the city's analysis with reason, skeptical of its logic: Would putting another developer in place really speed up rebuilding? What could the Port Authority accomplish if building out the site is uneconomical for a private developer? Could the city really expect the Port Authority to build out Towers 3 and 4 itself? Just because the Port Authority is not driven by bottom-line profit, would it be able to build any less expensively? Was the release of two towers the only alternative? Isn't the real thing that's at stake here is whether the city is ready to release Liberty Bonds so we can get going?

In the midst of the public dispute that "seems headed for a protracted stalemate," Manhattan Borough president Scott M. Stringer called upon the city's Independent Budget Office, as a neutral voice, to examine the "real financial and economic scenarios at the center of the debate over rebuilding." The IBO focused on the critical economic issue it believed, accurately so, was being overlooked in the debate over the competing financial analyses: Would there be sufficient demand to fill the 10 million square feet of office space planned for the site at a time when the city was sponsoring two major office initiatives—Hudson Yards (with 28 million square feet) and downtown Brooklyn at Atlantic Yards (with 4.5 million square feet)—and likely other office development elsewhere in the city? The IBO reviewed new employment data and information about expected sources of new office space to update an earlier 2004 report on long-term trends in office employment in New York City and analyzed the implications of those trends for the future demand for office space in the city. Its tepid conclusion: "If historic trends in office employment are replicated in the coming decades, it now appears more likely that the demand could line up reasonably well with the expected supply." The agency qualified its assessment of a modest match-up with a caveat that timing of individual projects would be critical to their success or failure. Its assessment of historic real estate dynamics in the downtown market was similarly reserved. Newly constructed class A office buildings, generous subsidies, a large price differential from office space in midtown, improving neighborhood amenities, and strong transportation links, however, gave the IBO "reasons to be optimistic concerning the downtown market." Downtown would likely become more competitive with midtown, especially for the newer type of class A buildings with the necessary large floor plates and technological infrastructure. (The IBO's rent number, $45 a square foot, was what Doctoroff used in his City Council testimony.) Although this was not a rip-roaring endorsement of either player's position, the agency's conclusion—that the impact of 9/11 on future demand for office space at the Trade Center site remained an open question—captured the essence of the unknown future. It simply was not possible to discern whether Silverstein's rent assumptions would prove too optimistic or the city's rent projections too pessimistic. Only changes in market conditions in the years ahead and the ability of the eventual new buildings at Ground Zero to command a premium over other competitive downtown buildings would prove the case.[26]

On the surface, the dispute over the differing rent projections comes across as an out-and-out debate about the future economic viability of downtown as a business district. But in the ever-present strategic game of control at Ground Zero, city officials were using the financial math of their feasibility analysis as a cudgel to push for political control over the rebuilding agenda. As brought out so clearly in the City Council public hearing and the IBO letter report, in opposing assumptions and presumptions with no definitive answer, more analysis or better data was not going to settle the debate. Silverstein's views reflected decades of experience, professional intuition rooted in that experience, and the inborn optimism of a developer who must look years out into the future when betting on the risks of speculative development. In 1984, for example, he projected rents for his original 7 World Trade Center at $37 per square foot; the notion that thirty-plus years later rents for a new twenty-first-century office tower would only garner $35 per square foot must have seemed incredible to him. The city's rent assumptions were true to prevailing market data for existing buildings as of late 2005, and its views on the downtown office market were not as pessimistic as some critics had it.

Though conservatively low and unusually cautious for a growth-hungry city, those assumptions meshed with the mayor's political agenda for realigning Silverstein's role and his policy agenda for more residential development at Ground Zero. Years later, $35 had become an inside joke between Janno Lieber and Seth Pinsky: How was your day, they would ask one another? "I had 35 meetings," one would say. "I had 35 problems to solve," the other would say. "I had 35 things to do!" It was always "35" whatever. The joke was tantamount to how ridiculous it was for the mayor to say that that the developer would not command rents above $35 per square foot. "To this day, we all joke back and forth about who was right about that," Pinsky said.[27]

Six months later, just days before the realignment agreement was signed in September, Silverstein confirmed the "open secret in real estate circles"—he had finally landed his first big tenant for 7 World Trade: The credit-rating agency Moody's Corporation had signed a twenty-year lease for fifteen floors at $41.50 per square foot (with a bump to $46.50 after five years, $51.50 after ten years, and $56.50 after fifteen years).

CAMPAIGNING FOR PUBLIC SUPPORT

Negotiations between the Port Authority and Silverstein—bitter and full of the type of hard language one would expect from parties distrustful of one another but caught in a high-stakes showdown of money and politics—had hit an impasse. Saying there might be no "legal way to do certain things that the city would like to get done or the state or the Port Authority," Mayor Bloomberg was forthright about the city's right to allocate Liberty Bonds anywhere in lower Manhattan: "We're certainly not going to put our Liberty Bonds into anything that doesn't have the potential, with some reasonable assumptions by real estate experts, that this is going to work out." As he said that, the city's economic development machinery was moving a step closer toward allocating $50 million in Liberty Bonds to developer Joseph Moinian for a fifty-three-story hotel and condominium project a few blocks south of Ground Zero.[28]

The city took its case to the press, creating "some noise," as Doctoroff put it. "What we are doing is calling attention to the economic reality that requires a restructuring of the relationship between the Port Authority and Larry." The editorial page of the *Daily News* was first out with an opinion: "The numbers crunched by City Hall add up to one conclusion: Redevelopment at Ground Zero is all but guaranteed to fail unless Gov. Pataki and Mayor Bloomberg force developer Larry Silverstein to accept a much diminished role in this most crucial project." Pointing to the conclusion that Silverstein "has the dough to build, at most, two of the buildings planned for the WTC site," the editorial endorsed the mayor's position with a call to restrict Silverstein to two towers and add hotel and residential components to the project.[29]

Silverstein's office had given an exclusive to Bagli of the *Times*, which first broke the news of the city's analysis, but the paper of record took a week before publishing an editorial goading the governor to action: "The mayor's voice here is certainly needed, but Governor Pataki holds the key to these negotiations. Mr. Pataki controls $1.7 billion in Liberty Bonds that Mr. Silverstein needs to continue building commercial space on the site. The bonds are Mr. Pataki's leverage, but at this point, the governor seems to be tiptoeing around Mr. Silverstein," who controls the clock on rebuilding. Pointing to the governor's presidential aspirations as a motivating force for why he "desperately wants to break ground on the tower before he leaves office at the end of the year," the editorial criticized such a groundbreaking as a "hollow event," and instead pushed for Pataki to focus on the groundbreaking for the September 11 Memorial (expected in March) and couple that "genuine achievement with a demonstration that he is setting the rest of the redevelopment of Lower Manhattan on the best track possible"—meaning "settling matters now with Larry Silverstein." Even the *Post*, which tended to see the developer's point of view more often than not, saw merit in the mayor's position: "Surely Hizzoner [the *Post*'s frequent corruption of the title 'His Honor'] is doing New York a service by raising these issues—and seeking to light a fire under the key players in the noble hope of speeding up a positively shameful timetable." Still, the editorial board wanted to see proof that the mayor's plan "will actually work" before it endorsed any change in plans.[30]

The mayor's business acumen was not in doubt, but once again, the reaction to his increasingly combative intervention threw off political sparks. The reactions were somewhat predictable. Distressed at the standoff in negotiations between the developer and mayor, the downtown business community saw its greatest fears resurface: The continuing uncertainty of rebuilding threatened to scare away potential office tenants so desperately needed to reinvigorate downtown. Downtown business leaders understood Silverstein's legal ability to tie the project up for years. The continued uncertainty threatened fundraising for the 9/11 Memorial, which had barely gotten off to a start. Downtown interests were wringing their hands wondering if the bickering was ever going to stop and an agreement reached that would propel rebuilding forward. The way the business community looked at the messy situation brought about by the mayor's push was aptly captured by *Crain's New York Business* in a showdown story headline: "Politicking Imperils Progress at Site." As the mayor's point person on the intervention, Doctoroff was unapologetic: "We could all continue to put our heads in the sand and continue on our merry way. But in four or five years, we will have to confront a major, major problem that will inhibit the successful rebuilding of the site. It is essentially pay me now," he said, "or pay me a lot more later."[31]

The proposal that Silverstein cede development rights to at least two buildings had found common cause among the various government factions; yet at the same time, it reopened the long and hard-fought debate over competing visions for Ground Zero. Building more residences was the pivot point of dispute. The mayor wanted 7 percent of the site, or seven hundred thousand square feet of space in Towers 3 and 4 set aside for residential purposes (and another 7 percent for a hotel). He was aiming to build on the explosion in the residential market in lower Manhattan that was changing the character of the area. "It's very simple," Doctoroff explained. "With seven percent residential, this gets built very quickly, and you have eight million square feet of commercial space. Without the residential, you get five million square feet of commercial space, and the rest sits around while we wonder where the resources are going to come from." Shifting a small percentage of the site to residential (and a small percentage to hotel) "is the price you pay for getting the site built out four or five years earlier."[32] The city was unambiguously after "speed." Like a clock ticking, the more time passed, the greater the depletion of funds from the insurance payout, a good chunk of which was annual rent payments to the Port Authority.

The hurry-up part of rebuilding was not the agenda driver for the fiscally minded Port Authority, though. "Forty years ago, the original World Trade Center was built with the intent that New York City and the region would dominate the national and global economy," Coscia said. "We want to put back what was taken from us." Other forces arrayed in continuous support of the full commercial program included downtown's advocates such as the Alliance for Downtown, which deeply feared that the mayor's push to build residential space would undermine the future economic resurgence of downtown. Senator Schumer was particularly agitated by the turn of events and highly critical of the mayor's proposal to build apartments and a hotel in place of a full office buildout at Ground Zero, saying it reflected a "lack of confidence in downtown." Speaking at a breakfast meeting of the Association for a Better New York, he framed the issue in terms of job-generating growth. "We have only a limited chance to return Lower Manhattan to its place as a world-class business district, and we must seize it....[M]y fear is that the 10 million new square feet of space planned for the site won't be nearly enough to compensate for the millions of square feet we have lost to residential conversions and to fill the growing demand for office space downtown." Indirectly citing his pre-9/11 leadership of a 2001 blue-ribbon panel (informally known as the Group of 35) that recommended building sixty million square feet of new office space over the course of twenty years for three hundred thousand new workers, Schumer warned that the shrinking supply of commercial space would continue on its downward trajectory without new construction at Ground Zero. "If we don't act at Ground Zero, downtown and our city will be the lesser for it."[33] Trying to insert himself into a solution, he laid out a three-point compromise approach that called upon each party—the Port Authority, Silverstein Properties, and Mayor Bloomberg—to make specific concessions. It was a rare public display of tension between these two powerful politicians.

Politics, not economics, was going to determine the feasibility issue at Ground Zero. And in this extraordinarily emotional and symbolic place, where money mattered as much as memorialization (and more so as time moved on), the realignment of who would build what on the site would come about through the power and leverage each party wielded in closed-door negotiations, as all parties undoubtedly knew from the start. In their varying feasibility assessments, public statements to the press, and testimonies at the public hearings, each side was campaigning for public advantage. In a final pitch the day before Governor Pataki's March 14 deadline for a deal, Silverstein ran a full-page ad on the op-ed page of the *Times* putting forth four reasons why he should retain full development rights to rebuild at Ground Zero: "For America, It's About Resilience and Resolve. For New York City, It's About Time" (figure 13.3). The promotional piece served to restate his long-standing claim that it was his obligation as well as his right to rebuild what had been destroyed on 9/11, but that claim was now decisively weakened by the unusual and powerful political alliance between the New Jersey side of the Port Authority and the city's influential mayor.

FOR AMERICA,
IT'S ABOUT RESILIENCE AND RESOLVE.
FOR NEW YORK CITY, IT'S ABOUT TIME.

Rebuilding lower Manhattan isn't just our job, it's our obligation. For centuries, this City has been a symbol of hope, opportunity and freedom all over the world. Which is exactly why rebuilding this vital, growing part of it is an obligation we have—not just to New York, but to America. Rebuilding Downtown will restore and reclaim our City's skyline by creating new places and new traditions. In the process, it will create tens of thousands of jobs, and the finished buildings will attract the companies and opportunities New York needs to grow—not just for a few more years, but for generations to come.

We must rebuild the office space at the World Trade Center that was destroyed on 9/11. New York City needs new first-class office space to create and retain the good jobs that are so important to our economy. The City has lost almost 30 million square feet of office space Downtown since the late 1990s. We are proposing to restore 10 million square feet at the WTC, on sites with the right size footprint for first-class office buildings, located next to the best mass transit connections, beautiful parks, the finest restaurants, extensive retail and amazing culture. Further, they can be built—and offered to market—at rates that make them highly attractive to major office employers, and at a 40% discount to Midtown, which is a huge plus for the City and its economic development.

Not only should we do our best, we should do more than we ever imagined we could. In the days after September 11, 2001, Larry Silverstein vowed to rebuild. In the months and years that followed, we built 7 WTC, the first building to rise again at Ground Zero. In the weeks ahead, our work at the rest of the WTC site will begin. In April, we will start foundation work on the Freedom Tower. In May, we will join our new tenants as we move into 7 WTC. This summer, we will unveil designs for 200 Greenwich Street, the third new building at the WTC site. When completed, Ground Zero will be transformed into the Rockefeller Center of the 21st century—a spectacular, world-class, 24/7 mixed-use community.

Silverstein Properties is ready. Let's get the job done. New York's future is happening right now. Thanks to an unprecedented public process, we have the right plan for the WTC site. So let's do it. With our insurance proceeds, and assuming the City and State administrations honor their commitment to make Ground Zero a priority in the allocation of Liberty Bonds, Silverstein Properties has the resources and the passionate commitment to get the entire job done. New York City, we are ready to rebuild. We know you are too.

www.wtc.com
www.silversteinproperties.com

SILVERSTEIN PROPERTIES

FIGURE 13.3 *In a final pitch to retain his full development rights to rebuild five commercial towers at Ground Zero, Larry Silverstein ran a full-page ad on the op-ed page of the* New York Times, *March 13, 2006.* COURTESY SILVERSTEIN PROPERTIES INC.

Focused on the big-picture goal of a realignment of Silverstein's role at Ground Zero, Coscia and Bloomberg and Doctoroff had successfully defined the negotiating agenda by publicly issuing a clarion warning of financial impediments that would prevent Silverstein's investment partnership from fulfilling its construction commitments. This particular strategic intervention—not the city's first and not its last—was the first financial watershed of rebuilding (the second would come in 2010). It was the first programmatic setback in Larry Silverstein's determined quest to rebuild at Ground Zero. City officials may not have been among those seated at the negotiating table as the property principals and lawyers for the Port Authority and the Silverstein investor group went back and forth on many deal issues that had to be resolved within the governor's ninety-day time frame, but no deal would get done unless they were convinced that it made financial sense for the city's long-term future. In finally taking on the role that New Yorkers had long sought of him, Mayor Bloomberg began to shape the future path of redevelopment at Ground Zero, a path that nevertheless would remain highly contentious, delayed by new conflicts, and defined by unexpected reversals. But the principals first had to get to a deal, presumably by the mid-March deadline Governor Pataki had imposed.

CHAPTER 14
The Squeeze

FIGURE 14.1 *Governor George Pataki of New York (left) and Governor Jon Corzine of New Jersey followed by Mayor Michael Bloomberg and Trade Center developer Larry Silverstein as they walk by construction equipment at the Freedom Tower site on April 27, 2006. After months of debate and wrangling over control of development rights and money at Ground Zero, they were heading toward a groundbreaking for the tower's footings and foundation.* AP Photo/Jason DeCrow

O N THE EVE OF GOVERNOR PATAKI's deadline for a deal between the Port Authority and Larry Silverstein, Port Authority officials abruptly walked away from the negotiating table. Silverstein Properties had come back with a "bad-faith" counter-proposal, according to the governor's advisors, and public officials reacted swiftly, with anger and high emotion. "Get the hell out of here. The deal is dead," Port Authority executive director Kenneth J. Ringler said according to several people present. "Pay your goddamn rent," he added.[1] Several times, talks had nearly blown up before both sides returned to the negotiating table, but the intense acrimony of failure that evening cut short any mention of when the talks might resume. Each side had a different explanation for why the talks broke down, and before an agreement was finally reached six weeks later (figure 14.1), each would accuse the other of bringing up new issues. Blame was all around—on the governor for his long-standing lack of leadership, on the Port Authority for its bureaucratic sluggishness and complicated internal politics, and on Silverstein Properties for its bottom-line emphasis and never-ending demand for financial concessions when a favorable deal for the developer was already on the table.

The attacks on Larry Silverstein were personal and vituperative and became culturally insensitive when Charles A. Gargano, the Port Authority's vice chairman and New York State's chief economic development official, evoked the narrative of the avaricious developer, accusing Silverstein of wanting to "get as much money out of the project as possible" and describing him as "greedy." It was a heat-of-the-moment comment he soon thereafter sought to retract. Embarrassed and angry, Governor Pataki let off steam in a public rebuke of the developer he had consistently supported: Silverstein Properties "has betrayed the public's trust and that of all New Yorkers. We cannot and will not allow profit margins and financial interests to be put ahead of public interest in expediting the rebuilding of the site on the greatest tragedy on American soil." He challenged the developer to start building the $2.3-billion Freedom Tower the next month, or "move out of the way"—an implicit threat that the Port Authority would find him in default on his lease. It was an ugly moment for Silverstein, who too felt angry; he was insulted by the governor's remarks but remained silent until late afternoon the next day, when he stood in the lobby of 7 World Trade Center, addressed the press, and blamed the Port Authority. "We were all shocked. We felt we were making progress. A basic framework of a deal was at hand," he said before adding, "Nothing we had proposed was a departure from what had been discussed previously." The talks had run through the weekend and all day Monday and Tuesday. With two cups of coffee and his lawyer, the legendary New York dealmaker Martin Lipton and cofounding partner of Wachtell, Lipton, Rosen & Katz, at hand, he had been prepared to stay as long as it would take to reach an agreement. On NY1 TV the next evening, he said he was a victim of "personal slander."[2]

The failure to come to terms on a new alignment for rebuilding the commercial site had moved beyond mere frustration with the lack of progress. Among the public at large and the business community, in particular, it signaled a much deeper malaise. "The delay and the various controversies have created a crisis of confidence," said the head of the city's leading business group, Kathryn S. Wylde.[3] Dysfunctional was the best way to describe the state of affairs at Ground Zero. So little progress was visible since the rapidly concluded recovery efforts on the site nearly four years earlier and so much serial conflict and controversy had bedeviled rebuilding in the past twelve months alone that Governor's Pataki's ninety-day ultimatum to the parties to resolve a series of disputes and find a solution to the economic question of feasibility—or lose $1.67 billion in Liberty Bonds (and most likely an equal amount the city was withholding)—though belated, was viewed as a final effort, hopefully, leading to progress. The economics of rebuilding ten million square feet of office space were marginal at best; without the $3.35 billion of tax-exempt bonds, the five buildings would remain just blueprints. It was mid-March, and the governor's April calendar date for breaking ground on the $2.3-billion Freedom Tower—a second time (the first ceremony on July 4, 2004, was symbolic)—suddenly was also in jeopardy. Paralysis appeared to be the order of the day.

"THE TOOTHPASTE IS OUT OF THE TUBE"

Exasperated by the behavior of all parties, the city's daily papers slammed everyone involved in a series of fierce editorials—thirty-one in total starting the day talks imploded and ending only when a deal was finally reached some six weeks later: The *Times* printed six; the *Daily News*, eleven; and the *Post*, fourteen. In "Greed vs. Good at Ground Zero," the *Times* editorial board admonished the developer: "It is time for Mr. Silverstein to think beyond the already well-fed bottom line here and consider the public good....[He] may think he has the lease on his side, but the governor and the Port Authority negotiators have a moral and political leverage of their own. Unless Mr. Silverstein wants to be remembered as the man who ruined the legacy of the World Trade Center, he needs to reduce his demands."[4]

"Larry Silverstein has his rights and he has his nerve—and he is exercising both to the detriment of New Yorkers," said the *Daily News*, arguing that the developer's "strictly monetary focus" clashed with the public interest. The failed talks "left Silverstein exactly what he's been for too long—the key figure in a building scheme that's doomed to fail." The editorial offered faint praise for the governor: "Pataki's stand was a rare show of clear thinking in the muddle he made of Ground Zero with a master plan that took scant note of economic realities."[5]

The *Post*, which could find little to praise in the governor's actions by his third term, generally assailed his lack of leadership and rammed the governor for his "sorry legacy" at Ground Zero: "[L]ast week's overwrought theatrics—including the governor's ad hominem attacks on Silverstein's character and integrity—served no constructive purpose whatsoever." In an oft-repeated theme on its editorial page, Ground Zero was "Pataki's Permanent Pit": "Every mistake, every delay, every lapse in Ground Zero's pathetic 4 1/2-year history of stagnation can be traced to him. With only nine months left to his tenure, you'd think he'd want to get this project at least started pretty soon."[6]

A lone voice in this high-profile instance, the *Wall Street Journal* supported Silverstein as the most credible of the players, "not the least because he's the only one who has actually built something downtown since 9/11," 7 World Trade Center. Government was to blame for the "Zeros": "Four and a half years later, Ground Zero remains just that—a hole in the ground. The failure to even begin rebuilding," the paper editorialized, "is a disgrace, but it's also a classic display of New York's dysfunctional political culture." Leadership "has been in pathetic and short supply." All that was hoped for and not yet realized amounted to "a case study in government incompetence and buck-passing."[7]

There was no place to hide from the political fallout as it played out in the media for nearly two weeks until all parties agreed to a go-silent period during which they would not speak to the press. Because permanent failure was not an option, the suspended state of affairs was not sustainable. Both sides would have to rejoin the effort when cooler tempers prevailed. In a letter to the governor sent to reporters as well, Silverstein implored Pataki to use his "leadership right now and get talks back on track so this temporary setback does not become permanent." Pataki refused to take the developer's calls and his people refused to engage on the question of how or when talks could resume: "The toothpaste is out of the tube," one insider remarked privately to another. They were waiting, said Gargano, for Silverstein to make "a proposal that does not put the Port Authority at risk for over a billion dollars."[8]

The next day, Silverstein delivered a proposal to the Port Authority, which after seven hours was rejected as "unacceptable." In a "tersely worded statement," the agency said it would unveil its own proposal for the site the next week.[9] After weeks of intense cycles of back-channel talks, just before the scheduled April board meeting of the Port Authority, the outline of a "Conceptual Framework" finally emerged. How, in this toxic environment of acrimony and distrust, where nasty name-calling and shallow rhetoric reigned, did an agreement come into being? What political dynamic and combination of government horse-trading, institutional compromises, and economic inducements produced a deal? And how was it that a deal was possible six weeks later but not before?

The fundamental deal issues were well known: The sites for the five skyscrapers planned for Ground Zero were not equivalent in real estate value, so which sites would Silverstein give back and which sites would the Port agree to take over? In return for his giving up two sites, the developer's ground rent would be recalibrated, but by how much? How much of the remaining $2.9 billion of insurance proceeds would go to the Port, to Silverstein, and to the retail portion of the commercial program now controlled by the authority after its 2003 buyout of Westfield America? How much money would the developer put toward the infrastructure necessary to complete the redevelopment of the Trade Center site? With Silverstein having gotten back all of the funds he and his investors put into the project, how much skin-in-the-game equity would go back into the towers? Would they make a contribution toward the memorial?

Before talks broke off, the basic framework of who would build what seemed to have been resolved, and it unambiguously favored the developer: Silverstein would retain the three prime-value tower sites running east-west from Church to Greenwich Streets between Vesey and Liberty Streets, and the Port Authority would build the symbolic and increasingly expensive Freedom Tower, which all players acknowledged would be difficult to lease; it would also take control of a second building site where the heavily damaged but still standing Deutsche Bank Building had yet to be deconstructed. For the Port Authority to agree to take on the risk of the Freedom Tower, however, its New Jersey–appointed chairman, Anthony R. Coscia, said "it would have to be done in a way that would ensure that the entire site would be fully rebuilt, including the memorial."[10] This was good policy speak and a genuine issue of concern, but it also served as code for balancing the spending equation for New Jersey; it was a position to protect the bi-state agency from carrying too much of the financial burden for rebuilding these sixteen acres in lower Manhattan, which many on the New Jersey side of the Port Authority Board of Commissioners viewed as a New York project.

As noted earlier, there's a saying in politics that aptly captures the prevailing dynamic of the bi-state authority: "Where you stand depends on where you sit." Commonly called Miles's law after federal cabinet official Rufus E. Miles Jr., who coined the phrase, it speaks to the notion that officials' attitudes and beliefs tend to conform to the organizations they represent. It is how politically wise people describe entrenched institutional issues that extend beyond the tenure of any governor or mayor and color public-private negotiations. When it came to setting priorities, the independent and regional vision of the Port Authority that defined its early years and the legendary era of Austin J. Tobin seemed a distant historical memory; it had gradually eroded following Tobin's departure in 1972, and disappeared completely with the "disastrous decisions of 1995," wrote political historian Jameson W. Doig, author of the definitive book on the Port Authority, *Empire on the Hudson: Entrepreneurial Vision and Political Power at the Port of New York Authority*. One of those disastrous decisions by the newly inaugurated Governor Pataki, as described in chapter 4, was the appointment of George J. Marlin, a bond salesman, former mayoral candidate, and the leader of the state's Conservative Party, which had helped Pataki win the governorship.

Under Marlin, the Port Authority lost most of its top career staff—"a brain drain" one commissioner told a reporter, "that I think would cripple any organization"[11]—

and morale definitely dropped during the two years under Marlin, though it rose again under later executive directors. (While patronage appointees could always be found at the PA, the appointments beginning in 2010 under the administration of New Jersey governor Chris Christie, remarked Jameson Doig, "show patronage at work.")[12] The two statehouses with their short-term political concerns exerted commanding influence on the Port's spending decisions. The agency had turned into "an ATM machine" for each state's priorities, said a former senior staffer. In 2006, the New Jersey side of the Port wanted the Trans-Hudson Express Tunnel, or "Access to the Region's Core" (ARC) as it came to be known, which would add sorely needed new tunnel capacity under the Hudson and double the flow of trains from New Jersey into midtown Manhattan at an estimated cost of $6 billion. New Jersey also wanted the PATH train system expanded. With these capital-hungry transportation priorities, it did not want the bi-state agency's financial position compromised by a deal on the Trade Center.

Money was the basic sticking point in the eleventh-hour negotiations, especially as it involved the tenuousness of building the 2.6-million-square-foot Freedom Tower, which all but perhaps the governor understood to be a pivotal economic obstacle to rebuilding Ground Zero. There were other financial issues as well, including several that did not involve Silverstein. Yet if the Port Authority was to take over the Freedom Tower, what would Silverstein give in exchange for being relieved of such a white elephant, as it was commonly viewed at the time? Silverstein, ever astute, had not publicly offered to relinquish the Freedom Tower but rather consistently said he would deliver all ten million square feet of office space. Even with the Freedom Tower removed from the equation, the math of building office towers on the three most valuable sites still would not pencil out without public subsidies. The only way the economics of rebuilding the commercial space could pencil out was if more real estate value could be put into the site, and that could only happen if the public sector dipped into its tool kit of assistance—which it would end up doing twice, first in 2006, and again in 2010 in a much deeper dip.

Government commands access to a robust set of tools to make a real estate project feasible. The tool kit is full of off-budget devices, which most public officials deploy first because doing so will avoid a direct call on cash and protect existing priorities while minimizing taxpayer pain. The craft of political feasibility is figuring out which tools to select and how they should be deployed. To come to a politically feasible deal for the commercial towers at Ground Zero, New York City's mayor, New York's governor, and New Jersey's governor would have to resolve their competitive tensions. New Jersey's commissioners worried about Governor Pataki; they did not want to sacrifice the Port Authority's balance sheet for his future political ambitions. Pataki's people had been negotiating with Silverstein for months and, reportedly, were close to bringing a deal to the PA board, but at least two of New York's six commissioners believed the deal to be too favorable to Silverstein, so the governor faced the not-so-easy task of rounding up support among his state's own appointees as well. And even though the city was not sitting at the negotiating table, no deal would be forthcoming unless the mayor's top officials were convinced it made financial sense. The alliance with the New Jersey side of the Port was central to the city's influence in this high-profile episode. So quite literally, the meaning behind the formal labeling of the 2006 deal—"United Financial Agreement"—was spot-on.

WORKING BACK CHANNELS

"He has a reputation in the industry for being a great partner after you've made a deal with him, but for being extremely difficult to make a deal with, of being extremely stubborn, of being terrified of leaving any money on the table," remarked Wylde of the Partnership for New York City, which had counted Silverstein as one of its members since 1994. "He's a tenacious negotiator. He's also an optimist about his ability to consummate a transaction. But he doesn't give anything away," said Jonathan L. Mechanic, one of the city's most influential real estate attorneys, who represented Moody's Corporation and the Academy of Sciences in their lease at the new 7 World Trade.[13] Silverstein's business style—single-minded on his position, relentless in pursuit, ceaseless in bargaining—was hard to separate from a sincere intent and unshakable determination to rebuild Ground Zero, as a New Yorker and as a family-based businessman affected by the loss of four of his employees on 9/11. That sincere intent, however, did not change the developer's deeply preconditioned approach to evaluating the risks of rebuilding from a business-as-usual perspective. His interest was hard-wired to making money. That was his role as a profit-oriented developer, and he had been at it for fifty years, by his own calculation. He would continuously evaluate the money-making calculus and financial risk of bringing onto the market three huge towers of office space, doggedly pursuing whatever subsidy resources he believed were needed to do so, and carefully crafting a public relations strategy to manage whatever negative public approbation might come his way. By experience and style, he was thick-skinned to the reality of New York's real estate battles, which real estate pros considered a contact sport.

Developers are a breed apart. Many populate the real estate industry, but how do those who really make it, make it big—not just in the financial sense, but in a broader, personal sense? Extremely successful developers like Larry Silverstein possess something that not every developer has: an extraordinary degree of confidence in their own decisions and an opportunistic willingness to be a contrarian and take enormous risks based upon that vision. In their view, the question is, how long will it take for the rest of the world to figure out what I know will be? Would it occur to developers like Larry Silverstein to worry about what others think? To think his judgment may be wrong? Not likely. "In his mind, he's not guilty. It's a Teflon sense that he's never wrong," said one veteran market player. Taking on the risks of high-density development in the tough and competitive environment of Manhattan real estate requires Teflon resilience, an attribute Silverstein consistently demonstrated in his long career. "To be a developer on a grand scale you need to be born with no fear of heights and no memory of disaster," is how policy-wise and real-estate-savvy George Sternlieb described developers who think big.[14] Sharp elbows are necessary, as is a strong grip. "Don't stand a chance to get the bone out of the dog's mouth," is how one veteran player described the strong grip of a successful developer.

When Silverstein returned to the negotiating table that evening of the eleventh-hour talks with the marked-up version of what became the Conceptual Framework, the hours-long time lapse moved against him. The agreement had been favorable to the interests of his investment partnership even before he left to review the document with his team of executives and lawyers—and, most critically, the lead investor of the partnership, Lloyd Goldman, whose investor group held the majority equity position in the partnership. Whatever assessment he had made of the negotiating situation, it backfired. As a tactical calculation, Silverstein likely figured it would be more important for the Port Authority to make a deal, that PA officials would agree to his marked-up terms at the eleventh hour (or however many hours more he was prepared to sit at the negotiating table) rather than negotiate further about details, however significant. Real estate people want to make a deal; they do not like *not* making a deal because with so much time invested in diligence and working through the complexities of what passes for even a conventional transaction, they want to leave the negotiating table with a done deal. It's not over until it's over, however long it takes. And Silverstein is of the old school of real estate professionals who bargain long and hard up to the very end.

Silverstein was operating in the grand old tradition of what all real estate players do and all claim they don't do: retrade. Retrading is a description of what the *other* side does in a negotiation. "Everyone does it," remarked one consummate New York real estate attorney. "Everyone in real estate finds a way, some ways being more obvious than others, to retrade. It is almost a time-honored tradition in commercial real estate." Seasoned real estate professionals understand that there is no deal until there is a deal, signed. Because of the complexity in real

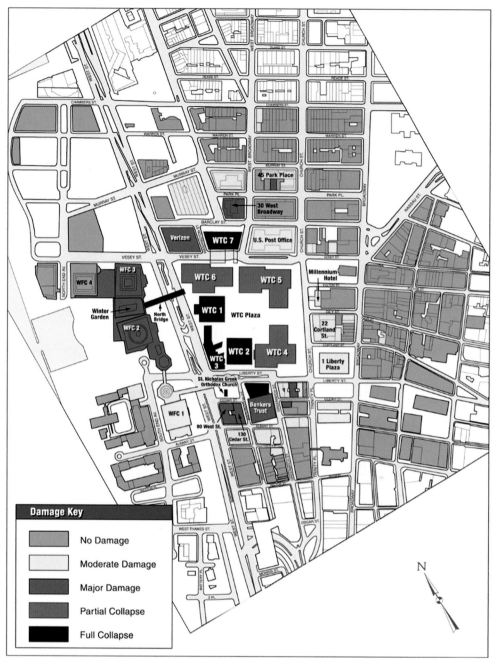

PLATE 1 *Damage areas at Ground Zero, September 2001.* FEDERAL EMERGENCY MANAGEMENT AGENCY

PLATE 2 *Recovery operations at the World Trade Center site, nearly complete in March 2002.* New York State Education Department

PLATE 3 *The "Last Steel Column" is removed from the World Trade Center site, May 2002.* Gil Gillen/OSHA

PLATE 4 *Relatives of those lost at Ground Zero stand on the ramp during the first anniversary memorial service, September 11, 2002.* DAVID L. POKRESS/AFP/GETTY IMAGES

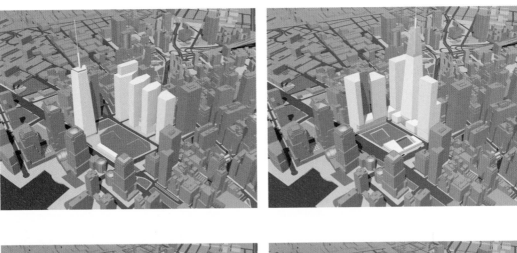

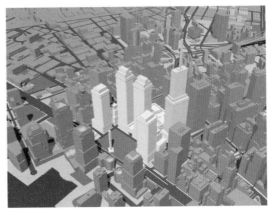

PLATE 5 *Renderings of the six master plans prepared by Beyer Blinder Bell unveiled at Federal Hall, July 2002. Left: Memorial Plaza, Memorial Square, Memorial Triangle. Right: Memorial Garden, Memorial Park, Memorial Promenade.* COURTESY LOWER MANHATTAN DEVELOPMENT CORPORATION

PLATE 6 *Architect Daniel Libeskind's concept sketch for the Innovative Design Study, December 2002.* © Daniel Libeskind

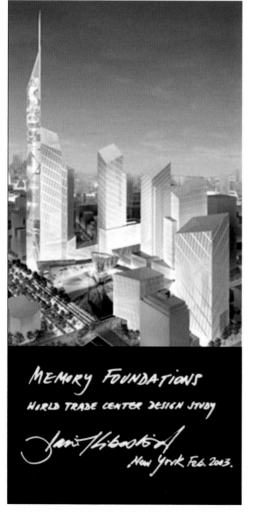

MEMORY FOUNDATIONS
WORLD TRADE CENTER DESIGN STUDY

New York Feb. 2003.

PLATE 7 *The winning design: Studio Daniel Libeskind's* Memory Foundations, *February 2003.* © Studio Daniel Libeskind

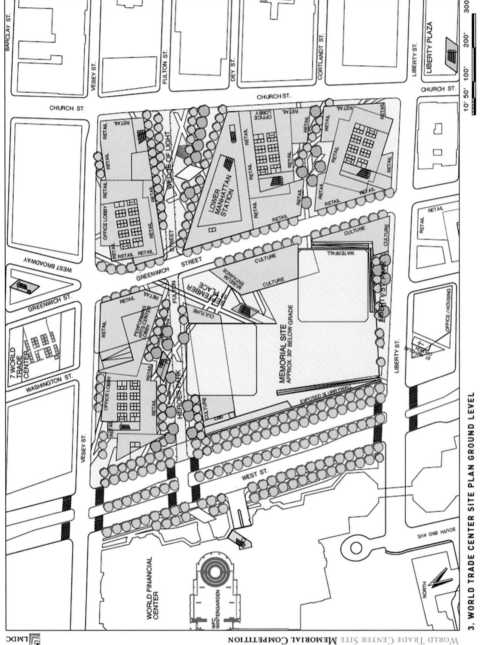

PLATE 8 *Site for the memorial on the World Trade Center site shown in the Memorial Competition Guidelines, April 2003.* COURTESY LOWER MANHATTAN DEVELOPMENT CORPORATION

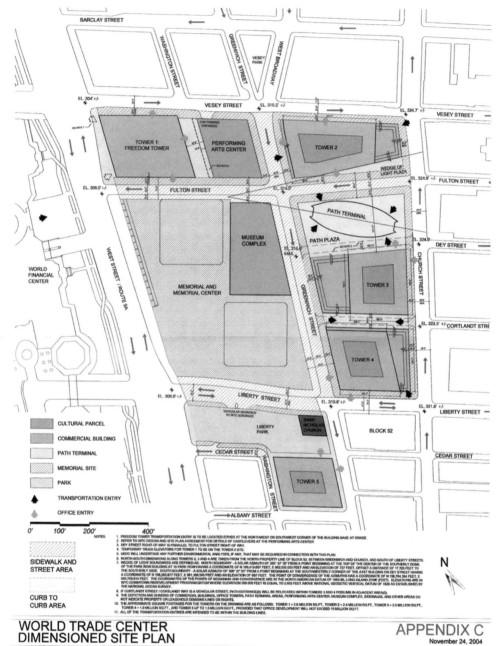

PLATE 9 *Dimensioned Site Plan for rebuilding the World Trade Center site, signed November 24, 2004.* COURTESY LOWER MANHATTAN DEVELOPMENT CORPORATION

PLATE 10 *Rendering of the first design for the Cultural Center presented by Craig Dykers of the Norwegian architectural firm Snøhetta, July 2005. The building was intended to house the International Freedom Center and the Drawing Center.* Snøhetta

PLATE 11 *Rendering of the Visitors Center and Memorial Museum entrance designed by Snøhetta, September 2008.* Image by Squared

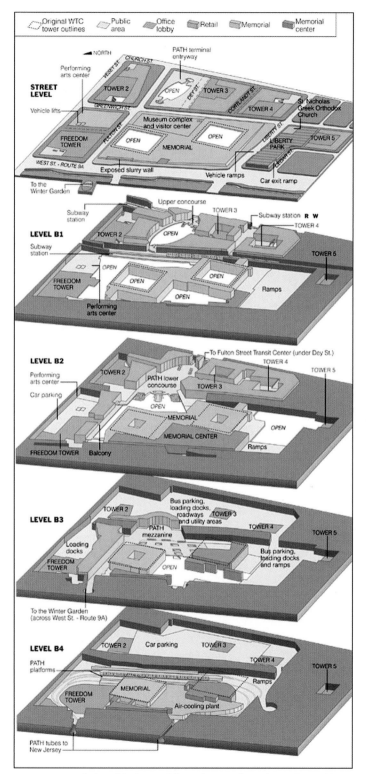

PLATE 12 *Rendering of the layers of the underground complex at the World Trade Center site, December 2004.* JOHN PAPASIANO/FROM THE NEW YORK TIMES, DECEMBER 16, 2004 © 2004 THE NEW YORK TIMES

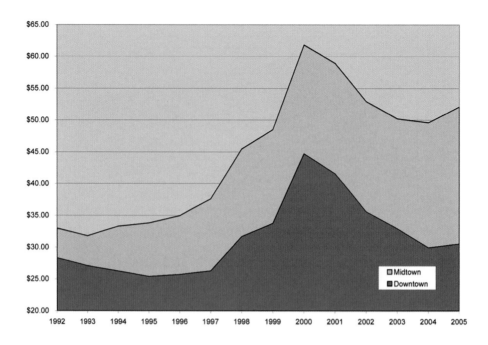

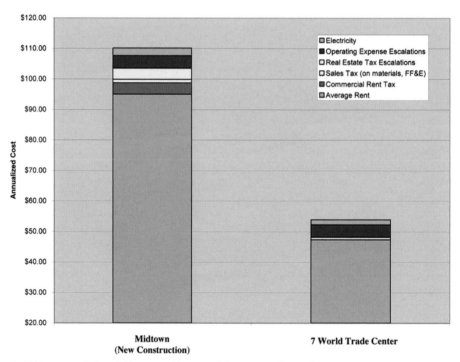

PLATE 13 *Rent differential between midtown and downtown office markets: 1992–2005 (top). How financial incentives impact the cost of supplying office space, 2005 (bottom). CBRE*

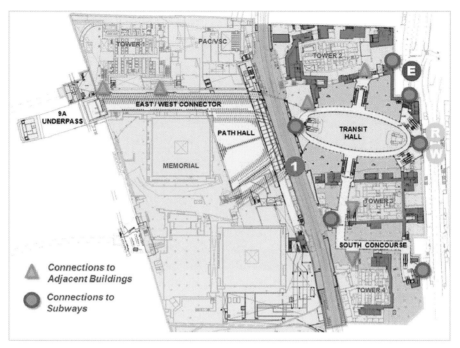

PLATE 14 *Rendering of the connections to adjacent buildings and to subways in the WTC Transportation Hub, 2007.* THE PORT AUTHORITY OF NEW YORK AND NEW JERSEY

PLATE 15 *Silverstein Properties installed a countdown clock in the tenth floor design studio in early 2006 that counted down each design milestone—concept design, schematic design, design development, and construction documents. The final deadline was reached in April 2008.* COURTESY SILVERSTEIN PROPERTIES, INC.

PLATE 16 *Construction workers installing steel reinforcing bars in preparation for a major concrete pour for the Freedom Tower, February 2009. The concrete is the strongest ever used in a New York City commercial office building.* THE PORT AUTHORITY OF NEW YORK AND NEW JERSEY

PLATE 17 *1 World Trade Center under construction, at 200 feet above street level (in addition to 60 feet below grade), March 2010.* THE PORT AUTHORITY OF NEW YORK AND NEW JERSEY

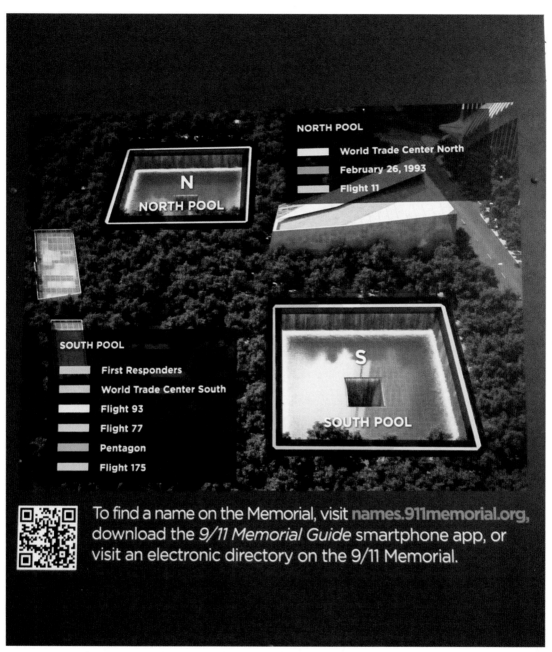

NORTH POOL

World Trade Center North

February 26, 1993

Flight 11

SOUTH POOL

First Responders

World Trade Center South

Flight 93

Flight 77

Pentagon

Flight 175

To find a name on the Memorial, visit names.911memorial.org, download the *9/11 Memorial Guide* smartphone app, or visit an electronic directory on the 9/11 Memorial.

PLATE 18 *Key to finding a name on the parapets of the Memorial Pools.* GARY HACK

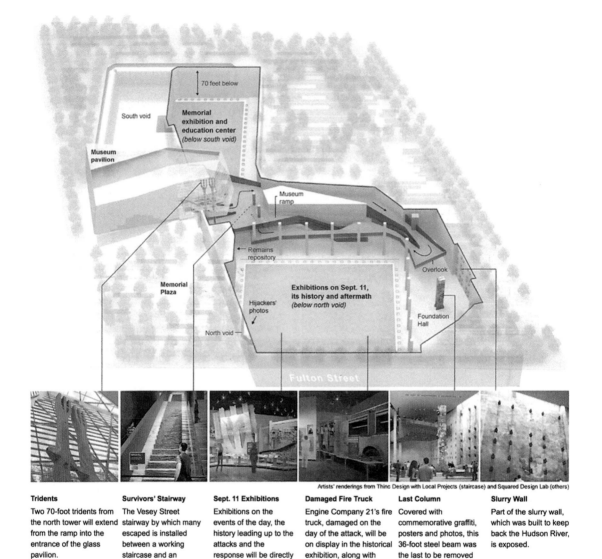

Tridents
Two 70-foot tridents from the north tower will extend from the ramp into the entrance of the glass pavilion.

Survivors' Stairway
The Vesey Street stairway by which many escaped is installed between a working staircase and an escalator.

Sept. 11 Exhibitions
Exhibitions on the events of the day, the history leading up to the attacks and the response will be directly below the north void.

Damaged Fire Truck
Engine Company 21's fire truck, damaged on the day of the attack, will be on display in the historical exhibition, along with hundreds of other artifacts and photographs.

Last Column
Covered with commemorative graffiti, posters and photos, this 36-foot steel beam was the last to be removed from Ground Zero during the cleanup.

Slurry Wall
Part of the slurry wall, which was built to keep back the Hudson River, is exposed.

Artists' renderings from Thinc Design with Local Projects (staircase) and Squared Design Lab (others)

PLATE 19 *Layout of the National 911 Memorial Museum opened in May 2014.* GRAHAM ROBERTS/FROM THE NEW YORK TIMES, JUNE 2, 2012 © 2012 THE NEW YORK TIMES

TOWER 3 FACILITY CASH MANAGEMENT WATERFALL

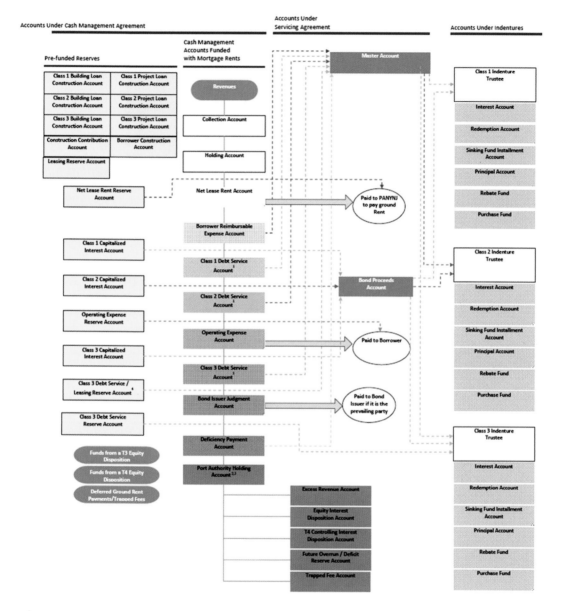

[1] Funded monthly only to the extent insufficient funds are available in the Capitalized Interest Reserve Account.
[2] Funds go to Port Authority Holding Account until the Tower 3 Tenant Support Agreement has been terminated.
[3] These accounts will be held at Wells Fargo and subject to a security interest in favor of the Port Authority only.
[4] Also subject to draws for Leasing Commissions and TI Allowances pursuant to a requisition

PLATE 20 *Flow chart of the cash management arrangement for Tower 3.* 3 WTC PROJECT LIBERTY BONDS PROSPECTUS, NEW YORK LIBERTY DEVELOPMENT CORPORATION

PLATE 21 *Transportation Hub near completion, February 2016.* GARY HACK

PLATE 22 *Much needed open space in lower Manhattan.* GARY HACK

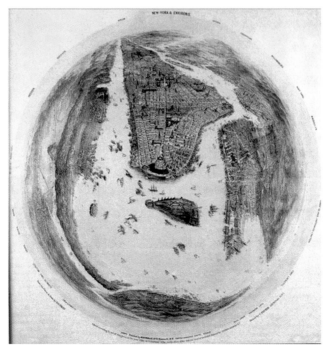

PLATE 23 *New York as the center of the world.* JOHN BACHMANN, *NEW YORK AND ENVIRONS*, 1859

estate and the constant search for balance in a negotiation, the possibility of a retrade is always on the horizon. Time is the element that triggers retrading. Time conditions the flow of a negotiation—time in which a deal must get done to meet a preset deadline, time at any one sitting of a round of negotiation, and time intervals between rounds of negotiation. "If you are in a room for seventy-two hours, and you can't leave, then there's not likely to be retrading. It's the flow and speed of a deal that allows one to understand the impermanence of any one element," the attorney said. "Every time something changes in a round of negotiations, it can be called "retrading" or a "counterproposal" by the other side.

Dealmaking in a public-private project is not the same as in a private-to-private transaction. Public officials tend to view things as a more rigid process, especially if they are unfamiliar with the conventions in the world of commercial real estate, as was the case with Pataki's Albany-accustomed loyalists. Typically, government officials have to get approval from their principals, the governor, mayor, or board of directors' chair, on the deal they are negotiating; once there is an understanding on what is acceptable in a deal, if something changes, they are faced with a problem: undoing what they have just secured agreement on. Such was the case when Ringler walked into the negotiation room at the Port Authority's headquarters near Union Square in Manhattan that March evening and shortly thereafter walked out after emphatically voicing his unyielding position. "Quite honestly, this was an example of Larry waiting until the last minute to cut a deal, and probably viewing that he could extract more from us because we were under the gun. So I said, 'It's over.' And I may have uttered profanities."[15]

Ringler had a tendency to be hot-headed, a man with a "well-disguised 'Irish temper,'" according to "Pataki's Point Man," the Public Lives profile the *Times* ran soon after the collapse of talks. His sole business experience was as a small-scale owner of his hometown bowling alley. In a succession of government positions, he had served as a two-term Republican supervisor in the upstate town of Bethlehem in Albany County and as first deputy at the Department of State and executive deputy commissioner of the State Department of Motor Vehicles. Just before Governor Pataki tapped him, at age fifty-six, to become the executive director of the Port Authority succeeding Joseph J. Seymour, he had a three-year run as the state commissioner of the Office of General Services. As with so many of the Pataki's appointees, his trajectory in government service was one of unstinting loyalty. "I never say no to the governor," Ringler told the *Times*. "And I'm going to make sure he never comes to the conclusion that he misplaced his trust in me." His twenty-seven-month tenure at the helm of the Port Authority was nearly consumed by the conflicts, controversies, and setbacks of the rebuilding process; 2006 was the toughest year. "What does Larry bring to the negotiations? Color," he said. "Color and an entourage. Larry is an enigma to me in many instances. I remember looking at him as he looked out the window during one of our meetings downtown by ground zero and thinking he really does care. That's one Larry. The other Larry is a businessman. Sometimes it seems like that Larry is more concerned with the bottom line than anything. The fact is," he said, "ground zero is not a normal business enterprise."[16]

When Port Authority officials' unwillingness to engage in further negotiations did not match up to his expectation, Silverstein lost his seat at the bargaining table. He had overplayed his hand with a political crowd whose culture as loyalists to their governor made it difficult if not impossible to accept any last-minute changes that could expose them to the charge of caving in to demands for further economic concessions. Some at the agency believed Silverstein had already been given everything in a Pataki-driven attempt to move the project forward before the governor left office at the end of 2006. As a tough and seasoned bargainer, Silverstein undoubtedly read the cards as such and tried to play them for further benefit. But further favorable concessions were not likely to pass the "smell test" of political acceptability at the eleventh hour of the deadline of negotiations. Although the government had been treating Silverstein's lease as "sacrosanct," the pillars of that support were cracking.[17] The collapse of talks left Silverstein fully exposed to the powerful alliance between Mayor Bloomberg and the New Jersey side of the Port Authority.

Governor Pataki too had overplayed his hand. Despite his long support of Silverstein and their many personal meetings since 9/11, he underestimated the developer's ceaseless bargaining for monetary advantage. During Pataki's tenure as governor, a series of weak New Jersey governors (in a state with a strong-governor structure) had offered him unusual power over the bi-state Port Authority, yet he failed to take full advantage of the situation. His post-9/11 executive director appointments to the authority were not viewed as the strongest of possible choices, but their loyalty was crucial to the governor. This was the "upstate factor" mentioned by several players. In interviews, I was repeatedly told that Pataki's people were not up to the task of negotiating with the hard-bargaining Silverstein team. "The PA was overmatched from day one," remarked Doctoroff in an interview years later.[18] If that was so at the staff level—"outgunned," was the way one longtime PA staffer put it—it was not so at the board level with Coscia at the helm, and as the story unfolded, New Jersey's newly inaugurated governor, Jon S. Corzine, would turn out to be an important player.

As political operatives, Pataki's team had never transacted a big project, and as a consequence, Pataki had "no juice" at the staff-dominated Port Authority, said Kevin M. Rampe. In addition, he didn't have control over his commissioners, who rarely spoke with one voice, in sharp contrast to the more organized and politically coordinated New Jersey commissioners. None of this was unknown. The New York appointments were "chaotic," said Janno Lieber. "The short-hand language for selection of New York's directors was '516 versus 914'"—the respective telephone area codes for Nassau and Westchester Counties. "Though it may not be factually correct, a perception existed that the New Jersey side ran the project."[19]

The question of how enriched Silverstein would be by a deal was an ever-present political dread for all players in the public sector. Speaking on his weekly radio show Friday after talks imploded, Mayor Bloomberg said: "I thought the deal the governor offered Larry Silverstein was a better deal than I would have offered, I'll tell you that." When he then said Governor Pataki, Governor Corzine, and the Port Authority would lay out a plan telling Silverstein, "Look, this is a fair deal; let's do this one, and Larry will agree," he was signaling the nonnegotiable politics of what would transpire, though he could not control the timetable for how long this would take to come about. Behind the scenes, the alliance was moving aggressively to shape an agreement that would definitively realign responsibilities for rebuilding with "a real set of deadlines with financial consequences, the 'stick,' in order to unlock the project and move toward progress," explained Deputy Mayor Doctoroff.[20] Those deadlines would apply to the Port Authority as well, because any deal depended upon the agency building out the East Bathtub, that area east of Greenwich Street abutting Church Street where three commercial towers and the Transportation Hub would be built.

In the weeks immediately following the breakdown of negotiations, Corzine was brought into secret talks with the mayor's team. The "handshake across the Hudson" between regional competitors typically "squabbling over everything from development rights and sports franchises to state boundaries and jobs" was an "intriguing alliance," wrote Diane Cardwell and Charles V. Bagli of the *Times* in a political analysis that later brought to light the secret alliance. Bloomberg and Corzine shared a lot of common ground from their professional business careers; they spoke the same language of business and investment banking, and understood how deals come about. Their "intriguing alliance" reflected mutual political interests in pushing to recast Silverstein's role at Ground Zero. "There's a common perspective on where things are headed absent intervention," said Doctoroff. "To the extent that the Port Authority's resources are threatened, the mayor sees it as a negative thing for New York, and clearly Governor Corzine sees the Port Authority in the same way. I think in this case there's a very natural symmetry of interest."[21]

This was true. Corzine, former CEO of Goldman Sachs who had worked in lower Manhattan, did not see rebuilding the site as a New York project. He understood its importance to the region, therefore to New Jersey, and he understood policy, said his former communications director, Stephen Sigmund, who also served as chief of public affairs and government affairs at the Port Authority during these negotiations. The power of the alliance between City Hall and New Jersey was about to back Governor Pataki into a wall. While this was in the making, Pataki's office was carrying on with Silverstein independent of the other top elected officials to get to a deal and cover his embarrassment by the eleventh-hour breakdown and move ahead with the scheduled groundbreaking for the Freedom Tower. That potential deal failed to pass muster with the City Hall and Trenton teams. After negotiations broke down, talks toward a deal were actually proceeding on parallel tracks: Pataki's office with Silverstein's representatives and Bloomberg's team with Coscia and Corzine's office, in secret.

When it came to reporting on deal negotiations, Bagli was exceptionally good at getting firsthand information from insiders; he had a direct line to many direct stakeholders. Widely respected for his understanding of the Trade Center story as an intersection of politics and real estate, he could see through an argument, and he understood the numbers. He had been reporting critically on corporate retention deals and public subsidies being given to developers and for stadium projects for years since coming to the *Times* in 1996 from the *New York Observer*, where he covered real estate, always with a sharp critical focus. He had been writing about the rebuilding of the Trade Center site from the very earliest days of debate and knew more about the project than many other reporters, and the *Times* gave him the space to write about the story. He listened carefully. Despite what several people characterized as a difficult relationship with Doctoroff, in February 2006 when the city was ready to air its analysis of Silverstein's questionable feasibility of rebuilding all five towers, Bagli was given the exclusive on the story: "5 Weeks Left for Decisions on Rebuilding." In the eyes of some, the *Times* reporter was becoming a player by his access and willingness to trade information—a "poster board for communication" that cannot be said directly to a party, said one insider speaking off the record, voicing what several others had told me.

The first news to emerge about a possible deal broke in the *Times* when Bagli reported that after two weeks of intensive bargaining, the Pataki administration and Silverstein were close to a deal that could be "remarkably lucrative" for the developer, according to state and city officials and authority executives. The next day Paul D. Colford, who was on the Ground Zero beat for the *Daily News*, reported that Governor Pataki was ready to put $250 million of funds originally marked for transportation toward the Freedom Tower, funds that had come from money set aside for New York from 2001 bridge and tunnel tariff hikes.[22] Bloomberg and Pataki met that day in the state's Manhattan offices on Third Avenue in an effort to resolve their differences over the tentative agreement that would transfer control of the Freedom Tower to the Port Authority—to no avail.

The New York governor was being squeezed on the deal's financial details from officials on both sides of the Hudson. Corzine, who had largely stayed out of the public fray over the negotiations (reportedly preoccupied with tense budget negotiations in Trenton), broke his silence on the issue in late March. The financial plans "aren't encouraging to me," he said.[23] Echoing Coscia's position, he repeated that any deal with the developer should consider funding for the memorial as "absolutely essential as part of an overall structuring of the financial package associated with the World Trade Center"; he wanted the final deal to provide about $100 million for the memorial, which was over budget and for which the foundation was experiencing difficulty raising sufficient funds.[24]

On the New York side, PA vice chairman Gargano was trying to bring his delegation of commissioners into line with his governor's position. "The pressure was direct," one New York commissioner speaking anonymously told Bagli. After a ninety-minute meeting at the offices of the Port Authority on March 30, Pataki's "last-ditch effort to strike a deal with the developer" crashed. Neither Mayor Bloomberg nor Governor Corzine would go along with the deal; it wasn't strong enough. They believed "it would enrich the developer at public expense, while putting the project itself in jeopardy."[25] Governor Pataki had anticipated an agreement in time for the Port Authority board meeting at the end of March, and now he was forced to pull the item from the meeting agenda. Strike two: another failure to close; another embarrassment for Governor Pataki.

THE BLAME GAME

Growing blame for the impasse was spread all around: Silverstein blamed the Port Authority and government's ineptitude, in general. Coscia blamed Silverstein. Sheldon Silver blamed the mayor and the governor. Pataki's aides blamed New Jersey officials for "nickel and diming New York on the most important redevelopment project in the world [while] at the same time they've managed to come up with $100 million in funding to keep New York's teams in New Jersey." The city's fiscal watchdogs, City Comptroller William C. Thompson and State Comptroller Alan G. Hevesi, added their voices to this most recent episode of border-war politics in a joint letter to Coscia in which they questioned the timing of new concerns about financial risks to the bi-state agency "on the eve of potentially concluding negotiations." The entire New York congressional delegation of twenty-nine took aim at New Jersey's governor in a bipartisan effort in a letter that asked him to put aside his "desire to maximize fiscal benefits" to his state and promote a "prompt rebuilding of the World Trade Center." The decisions at Ground Zero, they wrote, "first and foremost should be made by New Yorkers."[26]

"Corzine's Blackmail" is what the *Post* editorial page screamed on one day and on the next, "Bi-State Bandits"; on the day after that, it questioned what was really behind the Port's quest for $100 million for the memorial, pointing to its news report that "Jersey was holding out for a separate agreement on a commuter tunnel" across the Hudson. The *Daily News* blamed Pataki, who had "yet to display the savvy and leadership needed to guide creation of a viable replacement for the World Trade Center." If Pataki could not start leading, the editorial argued, "he should step aside for someone who knows how to get business done while protecting the public interest. Someone like Bloomberg." Mayor Bloomberg defended his ally on the Ground Zero talks, saying the idea that New Jersey officials were holding back their support of a Ground Zero deal for a "tunnel" was the work of "clever p.r."[27]

Public rumors that the New Jersey delegation was holding up a deal in a power play to secure funding for its priority rail link, the Trans-Hudson Tunnel project, persisted. The week before talks broke down, Port Authority officials denied any such linkage to the Ground Zero negotiations; after weeks of the blame game, Coscia and Corzine flatly denied that the delay in reaching an agreement had anything to do with the ARC project. But that funding of the trans-Hudson tunnel was a feature of the internal trading at the Port. The $100 million supposedly separating the Port Authority and Silverstein from coming to a comprehensive agreement, though significant in absolute terms, especially for funding the rapidly escalating cost of the memorial, was a small number in the big financial picture of a $7 billion project. It was not the obstacle.

Major policy decisions in the political arena often are not independent events; rather they relate in time to a broad and diverse set of collateral considerations shadowing what government officials are constantly working out with one another. In May 2005, for example, Governor Pataki agreed to support the New Jersey rail link, and he tied his decision to the Port Authority's future support of a rail link from lower Manhattan to JFK Airport, one of his priority projects that came to feature large in the post-9/11 planning for the district's revitalization. By bringing more New Jersey commuters into New York, ARC was of strategic importance to the economic growth of both states; as a regional transportation agenda item for the Port Authority, it was very much within the agency's statutory framework of action, its core mission. Although ARC was not discussed publicly, according to one inside New Jersey player, it was a part of the strategy all along: To get the Trade Center project done, there would be funding for ARC to go forward. According to at least two of the agency's former executive directors, the understanding that the Port would fund ARC to the level of $3 billion came out of the 2006 agreement,[28] and when financial problems with the 2006 Trade Center deal resurfaced in 2008, that understanding held implications for how the next set of financial problems at Ground Zero would be resolved.

Coscia passed over the governor's latest sinkhole at Ground Zero and artfully articulated a united front: "The issues we find with the Silverstein proposal are equally of concern to New York, New Jersey, Governor Pataki and Mayor Bloomberg," he said. "My expectation is that there is a growing unanimity of opinion among two governors and the mayor, and that is likely to enhance the chance of having an agreement." But the politicians' path toward a "unified" proposal to Silverstein was not smooth sailing. The political background of fragmented, separate negotiations—the mayor's officials and the New Jersey team in one set of discussions and Pataki aides and the Silverstein team in another—over the past several months had left a trail of misunderstandings and a lack of trust among all parties. The past would have to be overcome to move forward. These principals had not been around the same bargaining table for months. Since the past December, the Pataki administration had been in negotiations with Silverstein, which left the PA chairman and the mayor "without seats at the bargaining table," according to Bagli. "Even after the impasse on March 14, Silverstein executives complained that they were making concessions to Mr. Pataki's negotiators, while reading in the newspapers about new demands by City Hall or New Jersey."[29] The next meeting of the PA board was scheduled for April 26, and four long weeks lay ahead until a deal—acceptable to each side of the political equation—finally emerged.

Each direct stakeholder—Governor Pataki, Governor Corzine, Mayor Bloomberg, the Port Authority, and Silverstein Properties—held "an important piece of the puzzle needed to resolve the deadlock at the World Trade Center site," New York's senior U.S. senator, Charles E. Schumer, wrote in an op-ed putting forth his views on how to end the impasse. The parties, however, were unmatched in the power levers they could pull and the public support on which they might draw. Among the three elected officials, the New Jersey governor had the longest political horizon and the tightest control of his Port Authority delegation of commissioners, but he was late to the scene; among New Yorkers, he was widely perceived as butting into local city affairs. In a Quinnipiac poll conducted between April 4 and April 10, two-thirds of the 1,316 registered voters in New York City surveyed thought the New Jersey governor should avoid discussions involving redevelopment at the Trade Center site. Governor Pataki was a lame duck with loose, if any, control over his Port Authority commissioners, and weak to negligible public support on this issue. A large majority of the Quinnipiac poll respondents favored Mayor Bloomberg having a "major role in decisions" about the development of Ground Zero. The highly popular mayor, viewed as having played the most positive role at Ground Zero compared to Pataki or Silverstein, voiced a rare political defense of New Jersey interests: "They have half of the Port Authority; they have half of the responsibility. They get half of the benefits, and in a partnership both sides have to work on projects that are on both sides of the Hudson River."[30]

Bloomberg's team had been working with the New Jersey side of the Port Authority for more than six months in an alliance seeded much earlier. The men on these teams got along personally; they genuinely liked one another. The hard-charging Doctoroff related well to the well-liked and politically skillful Coscia. In contrast, several sources noted that the cultural clash with Pataki's people was substantial. Some of the strain reflected personal friction, some of it reflected the traditional tensions between City Hall and Albany, and some of it, the unique stakes involved at Ground Zero. "These were tough negotiations," recalled Seth Pinsky. "First, it was tough getting everyone to the table. Second, the negotiations were starting with a project that didn't make economic sense. Third, it was tough, but businesslike round-the-clock."[31]

Although these three government parties commanded the tools and political power to make the economics of rebuilding the office program work, the project needed "someone at the table who had skin in the game," remarked Rampe. It needed a developer "who will assure commercial success. If the Port Authority was left to its own decision making, it could be a redo of its first poor track record of commercial success with the World Trade Center."[32] This was what most of the real estate community believed as well. Although online polls conducted by *Crain's* indicated that Larry Silverstein had lost substantial public support after the talks on rebuilding broke down, he was the essential economic player if there was to be a revived future for downtown's commercial center, despite the reluctance of many professionals to admit this was the case. The reality of the developer's position was tilting the field in his favor. At this point, though, he would not have a say in the two deal options that the three government leaders were going to offer him, on a nonnegotiable basis.

BOXED-IN ACCEPTANCE

The three political principals finally sat down face-to-face on the afternoon of April 5 to work out their differences, differences on financial arrangements and a timetable that had largely hampered progress in rebuilding at Ground Zero not just for the last four months but arguably for much longer. The summit, called by Governor Pataki and held in his midtown Manhattan offices, lasted two hours. The press had little to report as all sides were sworn to secrecy, but one state official who spoke on the condition of anonymity said the discussions would continue for the next few days, "aimed toward advancing a joint detailed proposal to Silverstein."[33]

Progress on the talks could only be construed by the lack of any news for two weeks. After pressure was brought to bear on Pataki, the separate negotiations collapsed into a "unified" agreement reached on the evening of April 19. The governor called the developer, after which the plan for a global restructuring and realignment of roles was personally delivered to Silverstein by the PA's leadership, Coscia and Ringler; they asked the developer to consider it carefully. When details of the governments' joint proposal to Silverstein became public—after dashed hopes that it could be kept private as word began leaking—Mayor Bloomberg delivered a blunt message: "I think we have gotten to the point where the negotiations are, as far as I'm concerned, over," the mayor told the press. "This is it. We've offered two very generous proposals to Larry which will reduce the risks that Silverstein Properties would have and would maximize their ability to make money at the same time." The mayor was prepared to take the dispute to court, though it would take "an awful long time," he said holding firmly to his position. "If it stays a hole for a while and we fight it out in court, that's what it's going to be. We're not going to make a bad deal," he told the press.[34]

The proposed financial details were in fact quite favorable to Silverstein, as explained shortly. New Jersey's call for $100 million for the memorial, the talisman item that sparked the highly public interstate tussle, was finessed by changes in the developer's rent payments and other concessions that allowed the Port Authority to commit to the memorial contribution. The "Conceptual Framework," as the officials labeled the tentative unified plan, was an agreement in principle on a rebuilding plan, a blueprint ambitiously intended to assure buildout of the entire sixteen-acre site by 2012. With the final completion and documentation process still to come, public officials were not issuing celebratory press releases; they would wait until the series of definitive agreements documenting the transactions were signed five months later in September. As had become the norm, there would be more squabbling and more thorny issues to resolve before that event came to pass. In the meantime, on April 27, Pataki, "who was contemplating a presidential bid, left for a two-day trip to New Hampshire."[35]

Six days passed before the press was able to report, "Developer Takes a Financial Deal for Ground Zero, Accepts a Smaller Role," a decision significant enough for the *New York Times* to place the story on its front-page right-hand column. Silverstein had been given take-it-or-leave-it options: The first outlined a new partnership arrangement reallocating development rights for the five office towers between the developer, who would get the three sites with the most real estate value (Towers 2, 3, and 4 with buildable space amounting to 62 percent of the 10 million square feet of office space), and the Port Authority, which would take control of the unloved and uneconomic Freedom Tower project (though the plan at the time would pay Silverstein to build it). In a planned three-way swap, the PA would, in addition, gain title to the site of the former Deutsche Bank Building (Tower 5 site) from the LMDC and, in turn, transfer title to the memorial quadrant to the 911 Memorial Foundation. In exchange for Silverstein's giving up 3.8-million buildable square feet in two towers, the developer's rent payments were reduced on a proportional basis.[36] Several other economic terms underpinned the proposal.[37] Most significantly, the proposal required Silverstein to adhere to a specific development schedule for construction of Towers 2, 3, and 4, and if he failed to perform on that schedule, the authority could foreclose on the Silverstein investors' ownership interests. In short, "the cross" was back in the development agreement; city officials had insisted upon it. If Silverstein declined to accept the realignment proposal for whatever reasons, the alternative walk-away option was a flat payment of $50 million and ownership of Tower site 5, valued at $300 million, which once its deconstruction was complete could be developed by Silverstein for residential or office use, whichever offered the higher development value.[38]

After nearly a week of silence—what the *Daily News* editorial page called an "all too" typical response that left "New Yorkers hanging"—Silverstein decided to accept all of the Port's economic terms for a "new partnership approach" to rebuilding the site. Just two days before, he had told the state's economic development chief that "several issues were problematic." The developer's insistence "on treating every wrinkle at Ground Zero as a hard-fought negotiation point" was making "everything problematic and thus impossible," the *Daily News* said in its sharply critical editorial. The tabloid's frustration with Silverstein's maneuvering and delays in the interest of his "real estate enterprise" had hit a boiling point—he was "rapidly morphing into Public Enemy No. 1" and he had "to go."[39]

In a four-page letter dated April 25, addressed to Coscia and Ringler, the developer said he and his investors wanted "clarifications" on four major issues:[40]

Approvals: Prompt and definitive PA board approval of the Conceptual Framework, "now"; he and his investors could not wait until September for all of the approvals (by the states of New York and New Jersey, the City of New York, and the LMDC) as contemplated in the proposal. They wanted these approval contingencies removed because they were not willing to "take the chance that the project will be further delayed by inter-governmental disagreements that have nothing to do with us."

No penalties: Assurances that if events out of their control—specifically, construction-ready delivery of the individual sites—resulted in delays to the construction timetable, he and his investors would incur no penalties.

Fixed infrastructure payment: The Port Authority should stand by the prior formula for allocating the costs of common infrastructure components (buildings and systems) agreed upon during discussions leading up to the PA board meeting on March 29. "That formula was based on the *PA's own analysis* of what portion of these costs are SP's responsibility. The new proposal in your Conceptual Framework," Silverstein wrote, "departs from this agreement"; an open-ended liability for infrastructure costs, he argued, "would make it impossible for us to set a clear budget for the project, which is essential to obtaining the necessary financing." This was less a clarification than a key economic issue; they wanted a definitive and final settlement of the shared-site infrastructure costs.

Profit sharing: The PA would receive a 15 percent share "of the profits from any sale, refinancing, or other capital event," which Silverstein said "goes far beyond anything ever discussed before in out negotiations." He said the projected sum involved—"almost $200 million as valued by the PA's own proposal"—"seems to be without precedent" among other developers seeking to qualify for Liberty Bonds or other economic development programs.[41] Such "equity kickers," as they are called in real estate jargon, however, were not unprecedented in the city's economic deals; the earliest had surfaced in 1978 in the public-private development of the Times Square Marriott Hotel and in later transactions for the several project sites of the Forty-second Street Development Project.

The letter ended by noting that "there are a number of other finer points that will need to be addressed in connection with the definitive documentation for the transactions," including among others, "the proposed limitation on our use of our business interruption insurance"; he wanted clarity that "the other terms of our business interruption insurance arrangement would continue through the construction phase." As explained in a previous chapter, this insurance for lost rental income was an item of no small importance to Silverstein's ability to continue to draw upon the dollars parked in the insurance escrow to fund rent payments to the Port Authority and similar payment obligations for legal, consulting, and other fees and expenses pertaining to the Trade Center and its redevelopment—as well as significant "management fees" to the Silverstein lessees. There were no longer existing assets for Silverstein to manage, but he would continue to receive these fees as provided for in the December 2003 agreement between the PA and the Silverstein lessees. At this point, Silverstein and his company executives were managing what is called "the pre-development" process.

Within twenty-four hours the Port Authority sent back a revised Conceptual Framework, and in his response letter of April 26, "accepting all of your key terms," Silverstein wrote, "We understand each other's positions clearly, including the need for reasonable certainty of completion and financeability." He wanted to proceed immediately, he said, toward the documentation of the transaction rather than focus any longer on the Conceptual Framework and its seventeen specific elements.[42]

The Port Authority commissioners were tentatively scheduled to consider approval of the transaction in September, and the amount of work to be done before then was huge. Every one of the eleven items on a joint to-do list would have to be resolved on a mutually satisfactory basis to the Silverstein lessees and the PA. That was going to involve continuous dialogue between teams of professionals from both sides working through details upon details.[43] The seven items on the PA's to-do list were subject to its sole discretion, but to meet these conditions, the agency had to negotiate with other government entities to secure firm commitments to lease at least one million square feet of space in the 2.6-million-square-foot Freedom Tower, while also negotiating with Silverstein on its own commitment in principle to occupy 600,000 square feet or 50 percent of the space in Tower 4.[44] With the PA taking on the Freedom Tower, it was Pataki's job to come up with the government leases. Silverstein's job was to deliver drawings, said Janno Lieber.[45] The city's commitment to lease 600,000 square feet in Tower 4 was also on the to-do agenda.

All of these complex and detailed agreements would have to be formally documented by teams of lawyers. Furthermore, the status of insurance claims under Silverstein's insurance policies had to be clarified, and this was not as straightforward as might have been expected because less than a month after the April Conceptual Framework agreement, seven of the insurers attempted to use the new financial plan as a lever to delay, if not evade, their responsibility to pay the full $4.6 billion for rebuilding. Those insurance policies, as the *Times* editorialized, "have provoked enough charges, countercharges and court documents to fill a bank vault."[46] Another item yet to be definitively settled was whether Silverstein could get rights to the retail portion of the site, rights that were subject to a resolution clarifying the intent of the PA and Westfield America, which now held a right of first offer to redevelop the retail spaces. From the twelve-page Conceptual Framework, the realignment transaction would balloon into twelve volumes of agreements, hundreds of thousands of words diligently documenting the complex duality of an intergovernmental political arrangement and hard-fought business deal.

"The 'deal' is contingent on a host of legal steps and government actions that may *or may not* happen. And on the successful resolution of several key issues," said the *Post* in its second editorial that week on Ground Zero. Continuing its campaign against government officials and its pro-Silverstein stance, the editorial hit smacking clear: "This is, after all, Pataki's Pit—where anything that *can* go wrong because of inattention to detail or flagging seriousness of purpose *will* go wrong. No wonder officials aren't calling it a deal, but a 'conceptual framework'." The *Times*, more moderate in tone, also condemned "how badly blocked the redevelopment effort in Lower Manhattan has been in the last two years," though from a different perspective: "There have been many obstructions, including Mr. Silverstein himself. After months of negotiations, the mayor and the governors of New York and New Jersey lined up solidly against the developer last week and offered him two good options and one solid deadline. Mr. Silverstein did the right thing by accepting one of these options, which should turn out to be a profitable deal, not only for his own company, but also for the public." The amount of money the public was committing to make the Conceptual Framework a reasonable thrust at rebuilding—and ultimately would have to pump into Ground Zero—made the *Times'* last concluding phrase suspect from a financial perspective. From a political perspective, however, the *Daily News* editorial said it all: "The terms aren't pretty.... But there's no choice. You put the money in, or nothing gets built."[47]

The interim between the April Conceptual Framework agreement and the September document signing was fraught with tension. PA officials told Silverstein Properties they would not take the deal to their board without schematic designs. Schematics typically take a year to complete, so "schematics" became the level of development detail necessary to get to a point where the PA would bring the deal to its board, Lieber said.[48] Silverstein's development team felt put upon by a hard deadline, yet completing the design for the East Bathtub in a matter of four months became a point of pride for him; the push created momentum (see plate 15).

Just before the transaction was scheduled to come before the Port Authority board for consideration and formal approval, once again, the Pataki administration was forced to cancel the special meeting it had tentatively scheduled. The special meeting had been set two weeks earlier than the Port's regular monthly meeting, timing that would have coincided with the fifth anniversary of 9/11. "It would have been," Bagli of the *Times* reported, "a public relations coup when combined with the developer Larry A. Silverstein's unveiling of designs for three of the towers by world-renowned architects." Considerable differences over money but also over timing of when the eastern portion of the site along Church Street could be excavated and ready for building office towers still divided the developer and the Port Authority. The timing issue was a thorny one. Silverstein's team held long-standing reservations about the Port Authority's ability to manage the complexity of the site's reconstruction in a timely manner, and by early September the team did not believe the Port could meet the terms of the Conceptual Framework's strict schedule and deliver the first sites by mid-2007; sometime in 2008 was more likely. Silverstein wanted to be protected from any such delay that could expose his investor group to penalties for missing the completion dates on its "crossed" development schedule, but he also argued that any delay would entitle him to a compensatory rent reduction, which officials estimated could be worth as much as $50 million.[49] Once again, the developer was pushing on money terms.

The really big money issue had to do with the "market" rent New York City and the Port Authority would pay the developer for the six hundred thousand square feet of office space each had committed, in principle, to lease in Tower 4. Silverstein wanted $78 per square foot, which was a great deal more than the $50 per square foot officials assumed in April and $20 more than government officials had recently offered, according to Bagli. On a fifteen-year lease, the minimum term under the Conceptual Framework, the financial chasm between the parties amounted to $360 million. City officials considered the developer's number exorbitant, though not inconsistent with his earlier aggressiveness on asking rents for 7 WTC or on numbers he supplied in his application for Liberty Bonds. According to Bagli's reporting, officials complained that Silverstein "tried to use the governor's eagerness for a deal to extract concessions worth tens of millions of dollars, something Silverstein executives denied vehemently."[50] It was, dispiritingly, a familiar pattern of acrimonious conflict and predictable rhetoric.

In a speech on the resurgence of lower Manhattan Doctoroff offered light humor on the situation: "Larry Silverstein is so confident in the future that he's already raising the rent for the space the city will take in Tower 4." At the news conference to unveil the new tower designs a few days later, he said, "What we are unveiling today is a true testament, Larry, to you and to your vision, to your perseverance, which we all wish sometimes you didn't have as much of."[51] Joking aside, the average rent for first-class space in the submarket of World Financial Center–World Trade Center in September 2006 was $56.56 a square foot, according to Cushman & Wakefield, and it had been trending upward since May when it was just under $50 a square foot. Across the whole of downtown, the average rent for first-class office space was lower, $41.76 a square foot, and, as laid out in the Conceptual Framework, this was the intended benchmark for government leases in Tower 4. (These average rents, of course, did not reflect state and city tax incentives that would substantially reduce the cost of occupancy to commercial tenants and that would be accounted for in the deal for government tenants.)[52] The most direct comparable rent was the long-term lease Moody's Investor Service signed in September for six hundred thousand square feet in Silverstein's 7 WTC at $41.50 a square foot, a rent that was contractually set to rise to $46.50 by 2012.[53] Optimistic as ever, Silverstein's view in September 2006 was focused forward, and market conditions downtown firming up since April seemed to partially support his ambition for higher rents.[54]

The government commitments to lease more than 20 percent of the total planned office space at Ground Zero were critical to reducing the financial gap that would propel rebuilding forward. Although the project's long-term viability still depended upon attracting large private-sector tenants, these long-term secure occupancy agreements fueled the momentum for construction. They created value for the developer, bankable value that would enhance his ability to secure mortgage financing for the towers necessary to supplement the steadily depleting pot of insurance proceeds. The only way the site would get rebuilt was if more value could be put into the site, Pinsky told me.[55] A commitment to occupy space in Tower 4, the first of Silverstein's towers slated to go up, was one of the few things the city could offer, and it did so early, even though at the time city officials did not know precisely how they would make it happen.

Using government leases to prime the pump of economic development was nothing new, in New York or elsewhere across the nation; it was a tried and true tool of public-private development, and in the case of the World Trade Center, one that stretched back in time to the original complex, which too needed a political boost to assure its financial footing.[56] While the Port and the city were negotiating rent deals with Silverstein for Tower 4, another set of rent negotiations was proceeding in parallel as the Pataki administration worked to line up firm commitments from the federal government and state agencies to lease space in the Freedom Tower. In taking over ownership responsibility for the $2.3 billion Freedom Tower, the Port expected to get $973 million in insurance proceeds as part of the realignment transaction, as well as $250 million from the Pataki administration for the tower's construction, but acting much the same way as a private developer, it wanted a secure cash flow stream from government leases to assure the iconic tower's financial stability on a self-sustaining basis. As long as rent negotiations for Tower 4 were ongoing, whatever rent was set for the Freedom Tower would become an important benchmark.

When the long-awaited announcement of the Freedom Tower lease commitments made the front page of the *Times* on Sunday, September 17, the initial rents tentatively agreed upon by the New York State Office of General Services and the federal General Services Administration came in at $58.50 a square foot and $59.05 a square foot, respectively. These commitments were far from a formal lease, but Bagli reported Cahill's confident remark that Governor Pataki had gotten a "firm commitment from the [Republican in the] White House" that the U.S. Customs and Border Protections Agency along with the Department of Homeland Security would return to the site.[57] "This is clearly not an economic decision, but a political decision. It really is about symbolism and politics," said Robert D. Yaro, president of the Regional Plan Association, the independent and influential not-for-profit civic organization that has advocated transportation initiatives and monitored land use and development in the tri-state region encompassing New York, New Jersey, and Connecticut since 1922. "When the World Trade Center was built almost 40 years ago, the government was a growth industry and you could fill up the trade center with government offices, but clearly we're not in a period like that," he added.[58]

As with the original World Trade Center, the Freedom Tower was seen by some in the real estate industry as a threat to the market. Developer Douglas Durst (who years later would buy into equity ownership of the Freedom Tower) was publicly skeptical of the announcement: "It's going to be one of the most expensive buildings ever built in Manhattan." Holding constant to the family real estate firm's long-held philosophical stand against government assistance to real estate, he added, "To saddle already overburdened taxpayers of New York with the rent necessary to pay for it makes no sense at all."[59] And like his father, who was part of a committee that did the same in 1968, he took out an advertisement opposing the project, as he had done against the Forty-second Street Redevelopment Project (see figure 20.5).

On September 20, the *Wall Street Journal* reported on the Trade Center deal in its weekly real estate page, The Property Report, with the headline "Agencies May Overpay for Freedom Tower Space." As expected, the Freedom Tower rent number benchmarked the Tower 4 rent number: $59 a square foot was the initial rent the Port Authority would pay for its occupancy of approximately six hundred thousand square feet in Tower 4. The city's initial rate of $56.50 a square foot was 5 percent lower than the PA's deal because the space was for lower floors. The city's commitment was structured as an option for the developer, so if Silverstein could find corporate tenants willing to pay higher rates, he was free to do so. The deal was done.

REALIGNED ROLES

Just days after the news of these lease commitments, officials announced the conclusion and signing of a series of agreements formalizing the Conceptual Framework worked out in April. The WTC Global Realignment Agreements, as they were termed in the LMDC press release, redefined the net lease arrangement between the Port Authority and Silverstein investor group and established new milestones that aimed to speed up the redevelopment process and make certain a full buildout of the site "as early as 2012."

Governor Pataki called the deal "an historic event" that "moves us toward a swift completion date." Focused on what could be accomplished before he departed Albany at the end of 2006, the governor continued to project unrealistic expectations: "In just five short years, the Freedom Tower, Towers 3 and 4, the memorial, the Calatrava Transportation Hub, and the vibrant retail complex will be complete. In the coming months, we will see steel rising from the base of the Freedom Tower, major excavation for the basement of Towers 2, 3, and 4 and construction of the underground passageways that will link various modes of transportation." New Jersey governor Corzine's emphasis was more modest and nuanced given the reality of the situation: "This series of agreements culminates hundreds of hours of work and compromise…and will establish clear deadlines and accountability for getting these projects done responsibly so we can ensure the future economic strength of the region." Giving credit to the achievement of the lease renegotiation but being pragmatic, Mayor Bloomberg calibrated his praise to put the public on notice of what was still ahead: "Now we must all turn our attention to ensuring that the timetables and promises made today are adhered to and that they result in a fully rebuilt site of which we can all be proud." The agreements set forth financial plans for the commercial project, but they were not yet complete, which PA chairman Coscia seemed to signal when he said, "These agreements will provide us with a fiscally responsible road map that will help us expedite the redevelopment of the World Trade Center site."[60]

Under the terms approved by PA commissioners at the September 21 board meeting, the basic outline of the Conceptual Framework prevailed, with some notable adjustments. First, Silverstein's hands-on involvement as fee developer of the Freedom Tower was, in effect, terminated. He would be paid a "development fee" fixed at $21.5 million (payable in monthly installments of $500,000) in exchange for which a special-purpose affiliate of the Silverstein lessees "would make itself available only as and when specifically requested by the Port Authority." In other words, his investor group would not be acting as fee developer of the iconic tower, but rather the dollar amount of that projected development fee served as a break-up fee for being released from developing the uneconomic Freedom Tower. It was the opportunity cost of what the investors might have made if the firm had continued on as a fee developer. Silverstein would not actually be providing a service, but as in the corporate world, the breakup fee was a payment to walk away without suing after the breakup of a deal. The arrangement, the *Daily News* would note years later, was "costing bridge and tunnel commuters the equivalent of 2.7 million George Washington Bridge tolls or 12.3 million PATH fares." With the fee paid out in monthly amounts of $500,000, reporter Doug Feiden likened it to alimony payments.[61]

The Freedom Tower construction project would now go forward under the Port Authority's sole direction, but before they would commit to building the tower, the commissioners wanted a viable financial plan and firm irrevocable contracts from the state and federal governments for one million square feet of leases. Five months would pass before sufficient financial details were in place for the board to formally approve advancing implementation of the $2.877 billion Freedom Tower construction project at its February 2007 meeting.[62]

The second major adjustment to the Conceptual Framework had to do with the retail portion of the commercial program. As part of the December 2003 transaction in which the Port Authority acquired the WTC retail net lease from Silverstein's former partner in the July 2001 transaction, Westfield America held a right of first offer on future retail development on the Trade Center site. Under the master plan for rebuilding, the Transportation Hub offered exceptionally good retail space with strong long-term profit potential, and though concerned about the upper levels of retail integrated into the office buildings, Westfield was not about to give up its future rights in the retail development. As a result, the Port Authority could not resolve Westfield's right of first offer in a way that would allow a sale to the Silverstein lessees, so Silverstein was closed out of any opportunity to own or lease any retail space on the site and would formally have to release any such claims.

The macrolevel realignments of the 2006 deal shown in figure 14.2 created modest confidence among the stakeholders in the feasibility of the commercial program, yet the true meaning of the new arrangement of divided responsibility for rebuilding resided in the details, details embedded in some thirty-five legal documents necessary to execute the massive transactions of the Global Realignment Agreements.[63] These documents were either already complete or would be complete in the coming months as Port Authority staff worked through the layers of collaboration with the developer's professional staff and technical consultants, as well as additional counterparts from across as many as ten or more government offices. That's what it would take to document the details of how construction on multiple projects being undertaken concurrently or in sequence by several parties would advance. These projects were closely integrated to each other in every dimension: physically, structurally, operationally, and programmatically. The critical path of progress for both the Port Authority and Silverstein—critical to delivering *accelerated* results fundamental to the start of tower construction on the eastern portion of the site where a new bathtub had to be created—was built on the deal's time constraints.

The task of assuring results under the new and complex development plan would be governed by the Master Development Agreement (MDA) finalized two months later, on November 16. The 332-page document detailed the development responsibilities, obligations, and rights of the various parties with twenty-six supporting exhibits, forms of agreement, diagrams, and drawings covering, among other deal items, the scope of infrastructure development, allocation of spaces in the design for the East Bathtub, procedures governing site access, principles of cost allocation, and a month-by-month schedule of critical milestones for assuring accelerated delivery. This master development schedule laid out the set of "expected completion dates" by which Silverstein's towers would have to be substantially

Allocation of the 10.5 million sq ft to be built among 5 towers

Unified Financial Agreement 2006

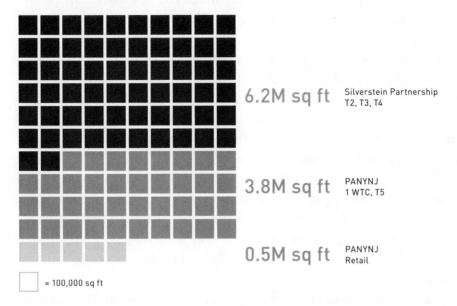

6.2M sq ft   Silverstein Partnership
T2, T3, T4

3.8M sq ft   PANYNJ
1 WTC, T5

0.5M sq ft   PANYNJ
Retail

☐ = 100,000 sq ft

Allocation of Remaining Insurance Proceeds

Unified Financial Agreement 2006

34.6%   PANYNJ
T1, T5

8.9%   PANYNJ
Retail

56.5%   Silverstein
Partnership
T2, T3, T4

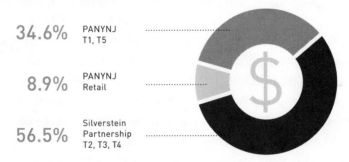

Other Financial Pieces of the Deal

a. Silverstein: $140 million fixed payment toward infrastructure in the East Bathtub;

b. PA: $100 million contribution toward construction of the Memorial;

c. New York State: $250 million toward development of the Freedom Tower;

d. Silverstein: commitment for $2.59 billion of Liberty Bonds ($1.67 billion from NYS and .92 billion from NYC).

FIGURE 14.2 *Realignment of development roles at Ground Zero, 2006.* C&G PARTNERS FOR THE AUTHOR.

complete—December 31, 2011, for Towers 3 and 4, and June 20, 2012, for Tower 2—with an option for a one-year extension in each case. For Silverstein to deliver on these dates, allowing for the four-to-five-year construction period needed to build big towers, the Port Authority would have to turn over the first two of three sites (sites 3 and 4) by December 31, 2007, and the third (site 2) by June 30, 2008. To meet the accelerated delivery schedule, the Port Authority planned to start running two ten-hour shifts at Ground Zero, but if it nonetheless failed to meet any of the turnover dates, it agreed to pay liquidated damages of $300,000 each day until the turnover failure was cured. The Port would, in fact, miss its turnover dates, but it undoubtedly moved more rapidly than might otherwise have been the case because of the time-focused structure of the MDA. Most important from Silverstein's perspective, any Port Authority failures to perform in line with the various agreements that impacted Silverstein's construction schedule would not create a contractual default or financial penalty for the developer because any such event would be considered "unavoidable delay" and create the basis for an adjustment in the expected completion date.[64] As a testament to its importance, a framed copy of the East Bathtub site turnover exhibit of the MDA (figure 14.3) was hung in the conference room adjacent to Janno Lieber's office at Silverstein Properties.

The construction obligations of the deal contractually tied Silverstein to the all-or-nothing penalty of "the cross," and gave the Port Authority the right to foreclose upon the partnership interests and cash of the Silverstein lessees in the event they failed to substantially complete their tower obligations by the expected completion date (as extended by unavoidable delay). The cross was an essential condition for the city—for Doctoroff; the investment banker in him wanted protection from the "walk-away" problem he had foreseen in the tenuous financial feasibility of the commercial project, but he also wanted a simultaneous buildout of the commercial sites. The Port Authority also wanted a full buildout to maintain its revenue stream. The cross was Doctoroff's solution. It was always a huge issue for Silverstein; he fought it as would any private developer rationally concerned about being hamstrung by such a demanding contractual economic obligation. "The city was actually surprised that Silverstein accepted the cross and not the check [for the alternative walk-away option: a flat payment of $50 million and ownership of site 5, valued at $300 million]," Janno Lieber told me. Silverstein, as a *Post* editorial remarked, "had called everyone's bluff and accepted the 'deal.'"[65]

The city's push for such tight strings on the deal might have been right at the time from a policy perspective. However, when the economic assumptions underlying a public-private development deal become unambiguously impossible, as would be the case only a few years later when the national economy sank into a severe recession, enforcing an uneconomic condition of performance becomes politically difficult, if not impossible. In such a situation, especially in a high-

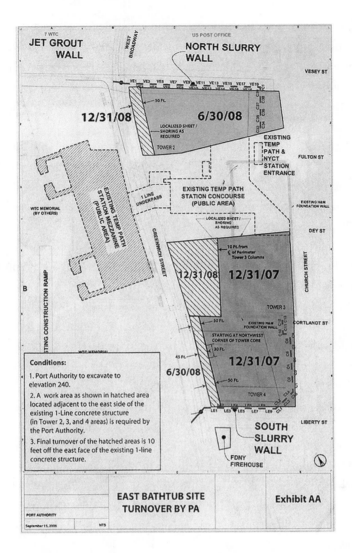

FIGURE 14.3 *Diagram of the Port Authority's contractual schedule for turning over development-ready sites in the East Bathtub to Silverstein Properties, agreed to as part of the 2006 realignment of development roles.* THE PORT AUTHORITY OF NEW YORK AND NEW JERSEY, MASTER DEVELOPMENT AGREEMENT FOR TOWERS 2/3/4 OF THE WORLD TRADE CENTER, NOVEMBER 16, 2006

profile development such as at Ground Zero, government officials are almost always forced into a political solution that leads to a revised deal. In other words, the developer is bound to return asking to renegotiate the deal.

WATERSHED

The 2006 deal uncorked the bottleneck of inaction at Ground Zero. With its compromises, adjusted responsibilities, financial carrots, and penalties for performance failures, the Realignment Agreements created a framework for moving rebuilding forward, specifically for allowing construction to start underground. On this point, a postevent consensus prevailed. The deal did not solve all of the economic issues—rapidly escalating construction costs, for one, were likely to put pressure on the delicate equation of rebuilding at Ground Zero. And it did not mean all the arguments and debates were over. But the agreements did enhance the feasibility of rebuilding in several ways:

They enhanced development capacity by dividing responsibility for delivering ten million square feet of office space between two developers, one public and one private, and redirecting funds from the insurance payout accordingly.

They enhanced economic value of the buildout with government commitments to lease 20 percent of the office space.

They enhanced debt financing with inducement resolutions for $2.593 billion of Liberty Bonds for the private towers and $702 million of Liberty Bonds for the Freedom Tower and retail program.

They enhanced equity funding for the Freedom Tower ($250 million) and the memorial ($100 million) with off-budget intergovernmental transfers that eased what could have been cash payments by the state of New York and the Port Authority to fund their respective commitments to these elements of the rebuilding program.[66]

They enhanced funding for the extraordinarily complex common-site infrastructure, then estimated to cost $1.529 billion, through a cost-sharing arrangement among the several project sponsors and direct stakeholders, though a balance of $183 million still had to be found to fill the financing gap. By sharing the costs of the foundation and base of the seven-story retail podium, which would also serve as the base for Tower 3 and house the mechanical floors for the PA's Transportation Hub, the PA's balance sheet would further support the economics of the Silverstein towers.

They enhanced the retail program by formally resolving the economics of land transfers between the city and the Port Authority involving Cortlandt and Dey Streets, again, through commonly used off-budget financing devices that would compensate the Port Authority for value lost with the elimination of an enclosed retail galleria on Cortlandt Street that the city, in pushing for street-facing retail shops, had insisted upon.[67]

The many avenues of enhanced feasibility brought into better alignment the economic interests of this uneasy public-private partnership. The sticking points in getting to this agreement had been many,[68] but they had been sufficiently resolved to give all principals enough confidence to finally move forward in a concrete manner with rebuilding. Loose ends remained. Ninety minutes after the Port Authority had formally voted on the plan, Bagli reported that the Port Authority and Silverstein were still working out their differences "through clenched teeth," just before the "celebratory, semi-secret news conference at the World Trade Center site with Gov. George E. Pataki, Deputy Mayor Daniel L. Doctoroff, Mr. Silverstein and members of the Port Authority."[69] Because the announcement of the press conference went out only minutes before it started, most of the press missed it.

As is common in complex public-private development projects, it is nearly impossible to resolve every detail of an uncertain future and contractually provide for every contingency that might arise throughout the development period. Partners often agree to resolve only what needs to be resolved and can be resolved, deferring other issues better resolved closer to when and if that issue emerges or when better information is at hand to understand and manage the full risks of implementing a complex development ambition. That type of arrangement, however, takes trust and a mutual alignment of interests—the missing part of the partnership dynamic between the Port Authority and Silverstein Properties. They were still wary adversaries with carved out areas of responsibility and a still unproven agreement to cooperate.

The dual-developer partnership would be tested. The Master Development Agreement demanded a lot of coordination among the stakeholders and their representatives, consultants, professionals, and contractors working concurrently or in sequence on various construction projects in the East Bathtub. Rebuilding Ground Zero remained technically complex. Coordination issues and unforeseen technical problems of construction would inevitably arise, and when these abutted or overlapped in the seventy-foot-depth of the East Bathtub, they would have to be worked out in a mutually satisfactorily way and on a timely basis. As time would reveal, this would not always be easy or amicable. Janno Lieber's assessment of the 2006 deal was restrained: "The new deal contained the germ of new progress because it created momentum for a new design of the East Bathtub. We liked the deadlines. It allowed us to design the East Bathtub in four months."[70]

The 2006 realignment marked a watershed for rebuilding. After five years of constant frustrations, nasty acrimonious disputes, and minimal tangible evidence of progress, resolutions about how to execute the ambitious plans for Ground Zero had been reached, finally. After pressure was brought to bear on Pataki, elected officials presented a united front to Silverstein; that type of political alignment happens infrequently but when it does, it is extraordinarily powerful. Facing that much authority, Silverstein had no place to turn for support and little choice but to swallow the terms of the Conceptual Framework. In public-private developments, developers are brilliant at exploiting the fissures among government actors; they know how to drive wedges between government partners. But in the rare instances when government entities are united, government control is formidable.

Coscia, in particular, played a crucial role mediating between strong personalities on all sides. Widely respected as a savvy, pragmatic leader possessing a nonpartisan mindset and a "Midas touch for finessing—as opposed to muscling—public-sector projects to fruition," Coscia was described in a *Times* Public Lives profile as "The Authority at the Authority." When appointed chairman of the Port Authority by New Jersey governor James E. McGreevey in April 2003, he had a reputation in New Jersey as a skilled financial expert and behind-the-scenes troubleshooter who was knowledgeable about the ways of government from his decade-long stint as chairman of the New Jersey Economic Development Authority. On the other side of the Hudson, he was unknown. He came to the chairmanship of the PA, he said, with "a great deal of interest in government and much less of an interest in politics," a perspective that was regularly tested as rebuilding at Ground Zero wore on in years. Though he would push to assure capital projects for his state, his viewpoint was more regional than others: "Looking at an artificial line drawn down the middle of the Hudson River in a global economy is naïve," he said. In the interview for the *Times*' 2005 profile, he went on record saying he wanted to see more aggressive building en masse at Ground Zero, as opposed to one piece at a time. "I'm happy to work *with* Silverstein Properties, and I'm happy to work *without* Silverstein Properties," he said. He was being pragmatic. He knew more about the subject than most other commissioners, having been on the board longer than most. And he was clear in his views. "He has a way of telling you what you don't want to hear, but in a polite and honest way," said James P. Fox, Governor McGreevey's chief of staff and later deputy executive director of the Port Authority when the 2006 negotiations with Silverstein were ongoing. "Everyone usually walks away saying how smart he is, but there are those who also say don't cross him."[71]

A self-professed deal junkie, Coscia had learned from years of experience as an attorney at Windels Marx Lane & Mittendorf how to pull all the pieces together to get a deal done. When he started at the Port Authority, though, he said what amazed him as a lawyer and nonpolitician was how the perception of a decision—and the politics of it—tended to shape the decision itself. Decisions, he believed, should be based first on an understanding of the engineering and economics of the situation. The 2006 agreement was a pivotal deal for the Port Authority. "The board had to come to grips with the decision of whether they would step up to the project, be players," he told me. "It was unclear if the return would be there for the risk the PA was taking. On the one hand, the risk was open-ended liability. Many said rebuilding was not the job the Port should be doing; it was a big economic development job, and that's not the PA's business." On the other hand, he believed if the Port did not play a principal role in the rebuilding effort, no one would. Could the LMDC have done it? "It took the PA ninety years of building and engineering to get where it is," he said. "If the LMDC had stepped up to do it, it would have been highly beneficial to the Port; it would have preserved its revenue stream." Ending the discussion on that topic, he added, "It's hard to be in this business."[72]

The LMDC was the odd player out when it came to carrying out the plans for the commercial program at Ground Zero. It was not purposed as an economic stakeholder but rather as an institutional agent, a facilitator; it was set up to plan and coordinate the rebuilding and revitalization of lower Manhattan, assure the development of a memorial, and manage the distribution of more than $2.7 billion of federal funds for the recovery and revitalization of lower Manhattan. Although it became an influence in lower Manhattan and a power base for its elected state representative, former State Assembly Speaker Sheldon Silver, the city-state development corporation had no role in the negotiations between Silverstein and the Port Authority, no control over any of the Liberty Bond allocations that would so impact rebuilding of the commercial portion of the site, and no political power to influence any outcome in the battles that were shaping up over money. In that sense, it was a "development corporation" in name only.

After the selection of the Libeskind master plan, the Arad-Walker memorial design, and the cultural programming decisions for the site, the LMDC's most essential work was done, but for approving contracts and dispensing the remaining millions in Department of Housing and Urban Development (HUD) funds, as a watchdog agency. In September 2003 when the agency amended the rebuilding plan to add the former Deutsche Bank Building (site 5) damaged by the 9/11 attacks and in August 2004 took title to the property at 130 Liberty Street, it became responsible for deconstructing the badly contaminated Deutsche Bank Building. Yet on July 26, 2006, even before the deconstruction had begun, the LMDC announced that its mission was nearing an end. The agency planned to shut its doors within months, surviving only as an entity for legal purposes with a skeletal staff, if any, to monitor its funded grants and manage the small amount of remaining HUD funds to be dispersed.[73] A protocol for transitioning the LMDC's functions to successor agencies followed in late summer, and in November the agency issued its *Final Report*.

"In many ways, the LMDC was the interloper," Rampe told me two years later. "The governor liked the LMDC because it was a 'pure way' to get involved; he didn't have to depend upon the Port Authority. The mayor, to some extent, he too liked it: It was a forum for getting together, for getting things done, a platform." An intermediary lacking in power to act with authority on the input it received, the LMDC was made powerless because Governor Pataki kept calling the shots after the LMDC had gone through elaborate public processes of inclusion and review. Still, the 2006 plans to shut down proved to be premature. The LMDC was given a new lease on life by Governor Eliot Spitzer soon after he took office in January 2007. The agency no one loved and everyone criticized, it played a politically valuable role. "If the Trade Center project was just one more economic development project, it would be hard to get the same attention, hard to get things done," said Rampe. "The LMDC provides a means to get things done, to bring attention to the issues if they are not getting done."[74]

The deconstruction of the heavily damaged forty-one-story Deutsche Bank Building, however, attracted constant negative news that spanned the tenure of four New York governors. It became a story unto itself. A sad story, a tortured tale. It did not start off well and it did not end well. It would be badly botched, beset by excessive regulation; insufficient oversight; continual delays due to the discovery of partial human remains from 9/11 on the roof of the building, injuries to workers from a fallen twenty-two-foot pipe, and injuries to two firefighters when a worker dropped a pallet jack; a lethal blaze that killed two firefighters and triggered a criminal investigation by Manhattan district attorney Robert M. Morgenthau; questions about criminal connections of some contractors; and wildly excessive costs. Every agency involved—an alphabet soup of federal, state, and local agencies—appeared to apply an ideal level of policy performance to the deconstruction of the building in order to prove that agency's purpose; everyone was getting into the act, another contributing factor to costs. In late 2004, the LMDC announced that it expected deconstruction would be complete by early 2006. In June 2005, it expected to start work during the coming summer but then the start date was fall 2005, with an expected completion date of September 2007. In August 2007, it became clear that the December 31, 2007, deadline set earlier that year by the Port Authority, which needed the site to start construction of the Vehicle Security Center, was not going to be met. The next completion goal was year-end 2008. A city work-stop order imposed following the fatal fire in August 2007 was lifted in April 2008, and work began again in May of that year. By January 2011, the building was nearly demolished to the ground, and on February 28, 2011, the last part of the building was taken apart. The deconstruction was done but there was no cheering. No LMDC press release. The LMDC filed lawsuits against the construction manager Bovis Lend Lease. Finally, "one of the nation's most expensive and long-running demolition projects" was no longer a newsmaker.[75]

The finalization of the 2006 Realignment Agreements triggered the long-awaited thrust of heavy construction excavators, bulldozers, cranes, delivery trucks, and hundreds of construction workers, consultants, and professionals in hard hats and safety gear moving in and out and about Ground Zero in a choreography of construction activity. Politically, something just as significant but less evident came into being at the same time: a power shift in the public-private partnership. Silverstein's decision not to walk away but rather to stay in the game and develop the three most valuable sites at Ground Zero from a real estate perspective foretold of an economic dynamic that would continually favor his interests as the economic and political stakes of ensuring completion intensified. Although the power shift would not fully reveal itself until Silverstein successfully achieved additional financial support for his towers in 2010, once again after a nasty public fight, the long-delayed start of construction and the approaching tenth anniversary of 9/11 would ultimately push the public sector, however reluctantly, to pledge more of its balance sheet to subsidize rebuilding the Trade Center site.

Though the united political alliance of 2006 gave Silverstein little wiggle room with those two take-it-or-leave-it options, he won in the court of commerce on many counts. He succeeded in continuing to hold his position and to control the bulk of insurance resources needed to rebuild. Despite the PA's serious considerations of displacing him by using its powers of eminent domain, he remained—single-minded on his position and doggedly in place. His ceaseless bargaining had proven its worth once again. The nasty "greedy" name-calling could not erase the underlying power he held through control of the insurance proceeds and the legal difficulties that would ensue in any efforts to dislodge him, and he knew it. "No matter who talked about, 'Let's get rid of Larry,' it was not something that could be done unless he was a willing participant or did not meet his contractual obligations," Ringler told *Times* reporter Deborah Sontag in 2006.[76] Others disagreed. "They could have gotten Larry out," said Roland Betts. It would have meant writing a check, said John E. Zuccotti, but it could have been done, he told Sontag. Governor Pataki would have had to agree, and when he was presented with the idea, his response was "no"—it would be too costly and too time consuming as discussed in earlier chapters.

In the political drama of rebuilding, Silverstein's role was straight out of central casting. As the profit-oriented developer, he was able to take positions that Governor Pataki could not or would have found difficult, politically. Keeping him on the stage and not condemning him provided political cover for the ambitions of the commercial program. "This is my right as well as my obligation to rebuild the commercial portion of the project," he could say and did, repeatedly. That was his mantra, and as his Wachtell attorney Robin Panovka said, "it turned out to be an important force in shaping the debate. It sounded short and simple, but was actually a carefully constructed position, backed by legal, moral, political and financial analysis and strategic thinking...to blunt arguments against Silverstein rebuilding."[77] With these lines, Silverstein could promote the commercial rebuilding agenda on the basis of his legal rights without any caveats, and in so doing counter early calls from the families and others who wanted less or no commercial activity on the site. Notwithstanding the fact that his role had been reduced by the realignment deal, his control over the critically important East Bathtub site was made sharper and stronger, and he had financial subsidies to support moving forward with his tower developments, as well as what remained of his insurance proceeds.

After 2006, rebuilding the Trade Center site became ever more dependent upon Larry Silverstein fulfilling his central-casting role. Completing the commercial program of rebuilding was always a unique platform of opportunity able to add a towering legacy-building coda to his long career. Even though Silverstein may have overplayed his hand at the eleventh hour of negotiations and was absent at the table when the two proposals were finalized and delivered to him on a take-it-or-leave-it basis, he had already secured a highly favorable deal in the option he finally selected. In the big picture, when the noise died down, he had not overplayed his hand, but had won brilliantly by being obstinate: Pataki still needed a deal done before he left office. Mayor Bloomberg wanted visible progress and a fast buildout. New Jersey wanted ARC. The Port Authority wanted its Transportation Hub. And they all got most of what they wanted—in slow, measured time, for the path forward was anything but assured.

The deal so celebrated by stakeholders in 2006 was a fragile one. It presented false assurances. Its economics were questionable. Its target completion dates, political fictions. It did, however, provide a foundation to move forward, to get beyond the stalemate of antiprogress. Within short order a sequence of troubles—soaring costs, inept construction management, promised site-turnover dates that came and went, arbitration proceedings—revealed its tenuous structure and exposed not just the project's weak underlying economics but the residue of smoldering distrust between its public and private developers. Both conditions had to be resolved before the parties seeking to rebuild the Trade Center site could possibly meet their rebuilding ambitions. This first realignment, though, was essential. Without it, the ambitions of the project surely would have been deeply, if not fatally, compromised. Those on the inside believed in the significance of the 2006 deal and its promise. From the outside, for the public at large and the victims' families, the only real benchmark of progress would be something tangibly visible, something other than the persistent seventy-foot-deep hole at Ground Zero. And that could only be the opening of the memorial on the tenth anniversary of the attack—a mandate of unquestionable symbolic priority. The Port Authority had taken over responsibility for building the memorial, furthering its ambition to control as much of the site's rebuilding as possible. It was collecting construction obligations in line with its hoped-for institutional resurrection as the region's major builder, but did it have the capacity to deliver?

July 7, 2010. BLOOMBERG/GETTY IMAGES

PART V
TROUBLED EXECUTION (2008–2010)

CHAPTER 15

Transportation Phoenix

FIGURE 15.1 *Federal, state, and local politicians, including U.S. senator Hillary Clinton (D-NY), join together at a groundbreaking ceremony for the Transportation Hub designed by Spanish architect Santiago Calatrava, September 6, 2005. The architect's ten-year-old daughter releases two doves as a symbol of the architect's design as a "bird in flight."* STEPHEN CHERNIN/GETTY NEWS/GETTY IMAGES

WHEN PORT AUTHORITY OFFICIALS unveiled Santiago Calatrava's design for the World Trade Center permanent PATH terminal in late January 2004, the acclaim for his "bird of flight" with its metaphoric image of a child releasing a dove was universal (figure 15.1). "Many of us have been waiting for a building that embodies grace and simplicity to fill the aching space tragically created on 9/11," said the *Times*, which nonetheless considered the "anticipatory architectural symbolism that has become familiar over the past few months" unnecessary. "Magnificent structure," said *Newsday*. It "will create a feeling of transcendent hope on a place where 2,749 people lost their lives." The station's $2 billion price tag was "a lot of money for a PATH station. . . . Whatever. The station is worth the price," the editorial board argued, because "to those who worry that New York doesn't build grand things anymore, this creation will be very grand." "On paper at least, the design reveals a lyrical buoyancy rare in so functional [a] structure," said the *Post*'s veteran voice of opinion, Steve Cuozzo. It seems "too good to be true in a city that still hasn't been able to get the forever-promised 'new' Penn Station off the ground." Only the *Daily News* believed the transportation priorities for lower Manhattan were misplaced, despite the fact that the "cathedral-like train station" was "stunning." "This is architecture for architecture's sake," the editorial said, "and a wasteful use of money the federal government sent to New York after 9/11. A pleasant, serviceable depot connecting PATH trains and downtown's subway spaghetti would do just fine, and cost a lot less.... A less expensive station would get the job done with money left over to invest in transportation projects that generate even more for the economy."[1] This lone and reasoned editorial voice of dissent relentlessly pursued for years would, in time, be joined by a chorus of others. But that was yet to come.

Architectural critics were effusive in their praise, thrilled that design was again center stage in plans for rebuilding Ground Zero. Their ovations vibrated in an echo chamber.[2] In his appraisal, Herbert Muschamp wrote in the *Times*, "public officials are not overstating the case when they describe a design as breathtaking." As with others, this most mercurial of critics saw in Calatrava's design something beyond a building: "It will cast out the defeatist attitude that has clogged New York's architectural arteries since the destruction of the old Pennsylvania Station." "It will deliver to New York City a phantasmagoric piece of urban theater," wrote *Newsday*'s Justin Davidson, who announced that the design "represents the arrival of a new, baroque architecture of waves and drama in a stodgily rectilinear city," and signals "New York City is once again prepared for architectural adventure." Michael Kimmelman of the *Times* saw in Calatrava's design "a metaphor and benchmark for the evolution of downtown as a place of cultural significance and symbolic weight."[3]

Even Ada Louise Huxtable, the venerated dean of architectural critics, waxed poetic about Calatrava's design. "His soaring bird is spot on for New York, where tragic circumstances and an unparalleled opportunity require a symbolic act of aesthetic daring." She understood better than most that well-worn visual clichés "can get dangerously close to kitsch," but a deep love for her city nevertheless brought her solidly into the camp that praised "the grace, ingenuity and dramatic power of these monumental functional follies." The lavish praise for Calatrava's design prompted lawyer Robert B. Tierney, the recently appointment chairman of the Landmarks Preservation Commission (which requires that a building be at least thirty years old to be eligible for landmark status), to half jokingly ask, "Should we preemptively landmark this?"[4]

Barely two years into the process of rebuilding, it was already quite clear that consensus about anything at Ground Zero was rare, which is one reason the widespread and fulsome celebratory applause for Calatrava's vision became an event of such an uplifting energy—and surprise. It was the only part of the project that was not generating controversy. Coming as it did after a bruising public battle over the design of the Freedom Tower, the consensus on the Calatrava vision for the transportation terminal offered welcomed political relief, not just emotional release.

Senior staff at the Port Authority desperately wanted to get in the lead with some aspect of rebuilding, and the train station would be the one project that would "indisputably" belong to the PA. They believed the agency had to make a statement of grandeur, and the world-famous Calatrava, age fifty-two and the recipient of much acclaim for his train stations, bridges, and cultural buildings, promised to bring grandeur to the project they hoped would revitalize the historic legacy of the institution. Over the decades, its reputation had suffered badly, and 9/11 provided an opportunity, however tragically, to repair the damage and at the same time improve upon the antiquated, chaotic transit infrastructure of lower Manhattan. "The trade center had been attacked twice," said Anthony G. Cracchiolo, the then powerful director of priority capital projects for the PA. "Our thinking at the time was we needed to make a statement. We wanted to create a Grand Central Terminal in Lower Manhattan. It could be a catalyst for development as Grand Central was in Midtown," he told *Times* reporter Deborah Sontag.[5]

The promise of institutional immortality behind this ambition was potent. The permanent WTC PATH Terminal, as the Transportation Hub was formally called, would serve the authority as a memorial to those of its own lost in the two terrorist attacks on the complex. At the same time, it would function as an institutional phoenix, a means to refurbish the Port Authority's legacy of engineering prowess. The duality of symbolic function bestowed institutional sanctity on the project— accompanied by something close to an indifference to its cost. "The Hub" was an unchallengeable institutional priority. The commitment was to build, in the words of the agency's January 22, 2004 press release, "A Glimpse of the Future in Lower Manhattan," "an enduring monument to the heroism of September 11, 2001...which will significantly improve mass-transit connections across Lower Manhattan." Calatrava called it "the Port Authority's gift to New York City." The designer was being politic—it was really the federal government's $2.2 billion gift to the city.

Officials were susceptible to criticism for being extravagant since a $323 million utilitarian temporary PATH station had opened just two months earlier, part of the $566 million program to restore PATH service as quickly as possible.[6] (See figure 6.3.) Other alternatives, for example restoring and reopening the old

Hudson and Manhattan Railroad Station at 30 Church Street on the eastern edge of the Trade Center site, closed since the 1970s, at a projected cost of $1.5 billion, had been briefly considered soon after 9/11. But why not think big and ambitious when Washington was picking up the full tab, or so agency officials reasoned at the time. Allocating $300 million from its insurance recovery proceeds along with the federal dollars, the Port Authority expected to provide transit riders with a new station for "free." Years later, as costs soared even beyond the Federal Transit Administration's expanded authorization of $2.872 billion (plus a $280 million reserve contingency), the Port Authority's funding plan was no longer a freebie; it was an open tab. By the fall of 2012, with its share of an even higher expected $4 billion cost for the Hub at $892 million, the project had become a direct hit to the agency's balance sheet. In 2006, Deborah Sontag had written, "Grand Central Terminal was built by the Vanderbilts. The new terminal in Lower Manhattan will be built by the taxpayers." By 2012, a coda was necessary: The new terminal will be built by the taxpayers *and* the toll payers on the Port Authority's bridges and tunnels.

Way before reality intruded upon the dream, though, the acclaim for Calatrava's design delivered the recognition Port Authority officials so avidly sought. "We can thank an enlightened patron," Kimmelman wrote. "The terminal might have been awful. But the authority acted civically. Everybody should be grateful." Among New Yorkers, the image of what the Port Authority was likely to build could have readily conjured up "charmless structures like the bus station near Times Square," Davidson wrote. That's why he and so many others were so surprised by its patronage of "a train station that might someday rival Grand Central Terminal in elegance and beauty." "The warm enthusiasm with which Calatrava's design was received certainly enhanced the image of the Port Authority, which for most of the time since September 11 had been viewed as an obstacle to progress. Now it seemed almost enlightened and self-assured," Paul Goldberger wrote in *Up from* Zero, even though he was not in the overenthusiastic camp of those showering accolades on Calatrava's design.[7]

Ever the architectural historian, Huxtable reminded readers of the *Wall Street Journal* that "the same kudos" marked the Port Authority announcement of Pier Luigi Nervi's design commission for the bus terminal at the George Washington Bridge, which was "also hailed as a visionary act in the early 1960s." Forty years later, again following the vision and persuasive advice of an aesthetically minded powerful senior engineering official, the Port Authority similarly awarded the prized commission to a Spaniard who like the Italian engineer Nervi had "an international reputation for turning engineering into art." This time the institutional inspiration at the Port came from Cracchiolo, a big fan of Calatrava's work for some time. It was Cracchiolo who helped convince Executive Director Joseph J. Seymour of the potential value of a serious act of architectural patronage, as did the agency's chief engineer, Frank J. Lombardi, and the two men made certain that Calatrava was on the PA's short list of designers for the project. "Often the authority's veteran architects and engineers have blocked innovative designs," wrote Goldberger, "but this time Cracchiolo managed to overcome his own agency's bureaucracy."[8]

The praise accorded Calatrava's design for the PATH terminal provided a strong political foundation in 2004, yet how soon might the underlying consensus begin to break apart and that political risk jeopardize the Port Authority's institutional ambitions? What would it take to turn the luminous sculptural vision into a constructible architecture program serving the functions of mass transit? How would the Hub fit within the master plan for Ground Zero and accommodate inevitable design adjustments? How could the Trade Center's physical historic artifacts be preserved and protected from adverse construction impacts, given their significant value to preservationists and their symbolic meaning to the families? Could the Port Authority manage to deliver the terminal on schedule and on budget? And when it was complete, would the institutional ambitions of building an architectural monument for a limited functional purpose meet, in Huxtable's words, "the traditional interdependence of art, structure and utility that has been the measure of architecture since antiquity?"[9] Answers to these would-and-could questions emerged only with time—and amid controversy that paradoxically helped generate some solutions to the endemic execution problems.

THE OCTOPUS BENEATH THE DOVE

The stunningly expressive iconic element of the Transportation Hub was the dovelike roof structure defined by a pair of parallel piggyback arches rising 150 feet from a central atrium 52 feet below ground and spanning 330 feet along the elliptical longitudinal axis of the transit hall. The arches would open as much as 30 feet to reveal a slice of the sky every September 11, as a symbolic gesture evocative of the city's vulnerability as well as its resilience. This vision was what captivated politicians, the public, design professionals, and the press once the rendered model came into view. The dramatic kinetic action promised to illuminate the vast central hall in a wash of natural light. "Ostensibly to control the light but guaranteed to knock your socks off," Huxtable wrote in her review of "Santiago Calatrava: Sculpture into Architecture" at the Metropolitan Museum of Art.[10] The "wow" effect created by the vision of a gigantic glass-and-steel-ribbed structure mechanically flapping its symbolic wings seemed even more impressive a technological

FIGURE 15.2 *Rendering of Santiago Calatrava's design for the WTC PATH Transportation Hub at its unveiling, January 2004. The "wow" effect of the design elicited immediate acclaim.* SANTIAGO CALATRAVA ARCHITECTS AND ENGINEERS

feat (or sleight of hand) when fit within the tight rectilinear grid that defines the street pattern of Manhattan (figure 15.2).

"Like an iceberg, only the 'tip' of the hub, the white dove, will be visible at street level," explained *Engineering News-Record*, the go-to publication for the construction industry.[11] Invisible from the street, the shape of the massive underground areas and concourse connections of the permanent PATH transportation terminal was impossible to judge by looking only at Calatrava's avian roof. The iconic vision inescapably diverted attention from what was to happen underneath—and what it would cost the Port Authority, in dollars and reputation—to follow through on its early staff-driven decision to rebuild the Trade Center site with an integrated, centralized system underground servicing the entire complex. Reverting back to what was there before the 9/11 destruction, the Port Authority was rebuilding the underground at Ground Zero in Disneyland fashion—with a central access point, common security, common utility service, and all of the circulation and back-of-the-house services out of sight—as it had done in 1962.

Only times had changed, dramatically. The original World Trade Center, built by the Port Authority for the Port Authority under semiautonomous powers that exempted the bi-state agency from local zoning and local building codes, rose with little political interference, once opposition to its eminent domain takings had passed. Those twin towers of gleaming metal soaring 110 stories and displacing the Empire State Building as the world's tallest building were built during a period of institutional power and self-regarding expertise. "Arrogance was always—is always—a danger for the Port Authority," Jameson W. Doig wrote in an influential 1987 essay on the entrepreneurial leader at the helm of the Port Authority, executive director Austin J. Tobin. "In planning and carrying out large projects, this large and able staff had long seemed to some observers too insulated, too unwilling to respond to the concerns of those who questioned its programs and policies." With the original World Trade Center, the agency had followed "a more cautious course"; nonetheless, the battles of an earlier decade over large projects had left "a legacy of wariness" toward the Port Authority and its leaders, "for they seemed intent on building gigantic, expensive projects even when those in the way, and some neutral observers, doubted that projects of such size were needed."[12] That legacy remained a constant.

The Hub became the linchpin of the PA's underground superblock. It is the only project connecting to all the other parts of the Trade Center's rebuilding program—and all the other stakeholders on the site (plate 14). Like an octopus, albeit an oddly shaped one, the tentacles of the Hub lead out in every direction to touch all the other Trade Center projects. They sprawl across four and a half city blocks from Battery Park City on the Hudson River east to Broadway as underground passageways connecting the Hub with seven subway stations serving eleven lines; they include a 350-foot-long pedestrian corridor leading east to the new Fulton Street Transit Center (Dey Street concourse), another 600-foot-long bilevel corridor leading west (east-west connector) deep under heavily trafficked West Street–Route 9A to Brookfield Place and the Battery Park City Ferry Terminal, and a 500-foot-long north-south passageway between Vesey and Liberty Streets, lined with retail stores, providing improved access and transportation connections for residents, workers, and visitors to lower Manhattan. The corridor-and-passageway tentacles were designed to rationalize a tortuous tangle of cross-town transit travel between subway connections in lower Manhattan accumulated in hodgepodge fashion "over decades of independent planning by competitive subway companies and other train lines that meant sometimes seven overlapping subway lines and the PATH system, none of which converged in a coherent way." This vastly intricate below-ground infrastructure was in the words of the PA's then executive director Kenneth J. Ringler Jr., the "world's largest three-dimensional jigsaw puzzle."[13] Within the octopus, the Port Authority planned revenue-generating retail space to replace what had been lost when the high-grossing retail mall of the original Trade Center crumbled into mounds of rubble.

The PATH station portion of the overall 800,000-square-foot Hub project lies just west of the main arrivals transit hall (and the No. 1 subway line's structural box running underneath Greenwich Street). It lays out in four levels: platform level to accommodate five PATH train tracks; mezzanine level, where commuters buy tickets and access stairs and escalators to the train platforms; and two concourse levels providing connections to the offices and retail on the Trade Center site, the Dey Street concourse leading to the Fulton Street Transit Center, the east-west connector leading to Brookfield Place in Battery Park City, and north-south corridors leading to several subway stations. The "Oculus," as the Port Authority chose to name the transit hall with its vast central space, is, in outline, an elliptical footprint of approximately 42,400 square feet, exceeding the size of the 33,000-square-foot Grand Central Main Concourse (figure 15.3); it sits regally at a strategic entrance to the Trade Center site—but at a distance from the PATH platforms. "An obvious place to put a station at ground zero would have been at the northeast corner of the former World Trade Center site, just above the PATH tracks and the No. 1 subway," *Times* critic Nicolai Ouroussoff wrote in 2009 when the luster of Calatrava's station design had worn off. "But by the time the Port Authority began planning the hub, this area had been declared scared ground, and the loaded politics surrounding the site made it impossible to rearrange any of the pieces." With the Hub sited east of Greenwich Street, where it could connect with subway lines and Fulton Street, "Calatrava was forced to create a second hall that serves the PATH platforms at one end."[14]

That quadrant of sacred ground complicated the transportation agenda in unforeseen ways. Because the Hub was literally a platform for the memorial, and a huge platform at that, its interface with the memorial program at the northeast corner of the site became a focal point of contention. It "has been the most troubling part of the project, the focus of most of the delay," said Kevin M. Rampe.

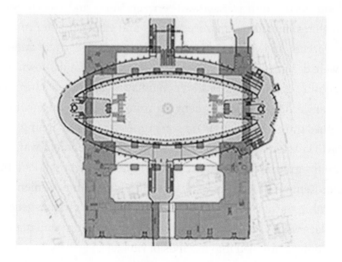

FIGURE 15.3 *The "Oculus" footprint of the transit hall shown superimposed on the footprint of the Great Hall of Grand Central Terminal. In line with the Port Authority's ambitions for a transportation terminal to rival the city's historic landmark in midtown Manhattan, the combined size of the transit hall and the PATH Hall exceeds it by 28 percent.* THE PORT AUTHORITY OF NEW YORK AND NEW JERSEY

"The problems revolved around the inability to resolve design issues. Designers, not engineers were in charge. Calatrava was chosen after the site plan had been laid out; it was one of the last pieces of the puzzle." Caught up with the design, "people might have fooled themselves on what engineering the structure would involve and cost," he told me. "It took a long time to understand how difficult the design-development issues would be: the ribs, the height and its relationship to the underground system, and the ground plane's height in relationship to the memorial."[15]

Hidden Complexity

Getting to street level ("grade" in construction parlance), where progress would be visible to the public, was going to be time consuming, technically tricky, and very costly, but in a city with two midtown transit hubs, Grand Central Terminal and Penn Station, both of which have numerous underground transit and pedestrian connections, it is hard for any underground environment to be labeled "unprecedented."[16] The vast size of the hole—an underground footprint of some five hundred thousand square feet—would be a big driver of costs. Five PATH train tracks and the No. 1 subway line ran into and through the site, and the governor had decided that the trains were to be kept running throughout the rebuilding process. The engineers knew it was going to be very slow and expensive to dig out the nearly seven-acre East Bathtub because it would have to be done by hand since the original bathtub was being extended *under* the No. 1 subway to the eastern boundary of the site at Church Street. A vast amount of reinforcement was needed, utilities put in place, decisions on underground uses made, details for the reopening Greenwich Street figured out, repairs to Route 9A completed, and the No. 1 subway line restored—all these things had to come first before a building could be put up. Underground, the design of everything to be built on the sixteen-acre site was interrelated in complex ways.

Was the complexity of this design and development process understood by the public? Was the process of getting to grade going to get the credit and attention it deserved? "If this had been surface construction, it would have had coverage as if it were the Hoover Dam," remarked Denise M. Richardson, executive director of the General Contractors Association. "The engineers were telling us we would be below ground for two to three years and that the public perception would be negative," Coscia recalled when we spoke; "people would not know that we're working and spending hundreds of millions of dollars. The site was a Rubik's cube for years." Several insiders tried to persuade Governor Pataki to let the agency shut down the No. 1 subway, but the governor was adamant about keeping it running, despite the cost of underpinning the subway to make continuous service possible. Temporarily taking the line out of service would have "cut an important transit link and angered commuters from Staten Island, a Republican stronghold, who use the No. 1 line after getting off the ferry," David W. Dunlap wrote years later in his assessment of how the train station's costs soared.[17]

Pataki's decision not to allow a temporary shutdown of the No. 1 subway line as the Port Authority's chief engineer and others had advocated exacerbated the technical complexity of construction and ramped up the costs of rebuilding. It impacted everything underground. The No. 1 subway bisects the Trade Center site north-south. Encased in a box-shaped concrete tunnel that runs for 975 feet under Greenwich Street, the Metropolitan Transportation Authority had built the "box" to replace the original tunnel destroyed on 9/11; construction crews had worked around the clock for nine months on the $100 million project to restore service to South Ferry a little more than a year after the 9/11 attack. (The Cortlandt Station at the World Trade Center would remain closed while plans for Ground Zero were being worked out.) The original poured-in concrete box built in 1914 was meant to lie on the ground, the surrounding soil providing structural reinforcement. It was never meant to be exposed, but would be if the subway line was to run continuously and be contiguous to the work of excavating soil to make way for new underground structures and program spaces. To keep the line running, the box would have to be underpinned to provide structural support. The engineers questioned how to do that, how to support the box, and what would happen if it was exposed to the elements.

The subway box would eventually be an integral part of the larger, multilevel underground complex at the site, but in the interim it would have to be supported on a solid but temporary structure while everything was built around it. "The spectacle of a supposedly subterranean railroad held up in midair and exposed to daylight will resonate with older New Yorkers who remember that the PATH tubes were disinterred and suspended during the construction of the trade center 40 years ago," Dunlap wrote in an article explaining the technical challenge of underpinning the box. The challenge was "daunting," recalled Charles J. Maikish, the first head of the Lower Manhattan Construction Command Center (LMCCC) and a former career professional at the Port Authority for twenty-seven years who had been responsible for repairing the tower damage after the 1993 bombing. "When the PATH tubes were suspended in the air in the 1960s, it was an innovative procedure; another innovative process would have to be developed again. This element was on the critical path and everything on the critical path involved risk."[18] Minipiles—so called, as Dunlap explained, because they are ten and three-quarters inches in diameter—450 of them, would have to be drilled through the soil into bedrock about forty feet below the subway (figure 15.4). The tolerances of the support system were tight: The box could not be allowed to move more than two inches under the weight of the passing subway cars.[19]

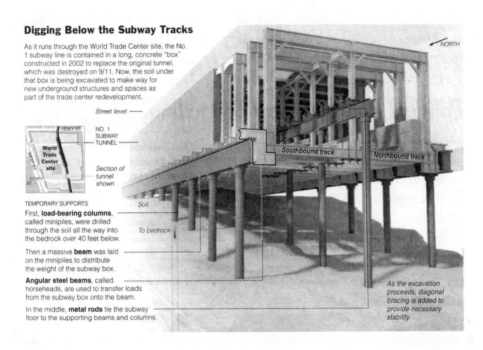

Digging Below the Subway Tracks

As it runs through the World Trade Center site, the No. 1 subway line is contained in a long, concrete "box" constructed in 2002 to replace the original tunnel, which was destroyed on 9/11. Now, the soil under that box is being excavated to make way for new underground structures and spaces as part of the trade center redevelopment.

Street level

NO. 1 SUBWAY TUNNEL

World Trade Center site

VESEY ST.

LIBERTY ST.

Section of tunnel shown

NORTH

Southbound track

Northbound track

Soil

To bedrock

TEMPORARY SUPPORTS

First, **load-bearing columns**, called minipiles, were drilled through the soil all the way into the bedrock over 40 feet below.

Then a massive **beam** was laid on the minipiles to distribute the weight of the subway box.

Angular steel beams, called horseheads, are used to transfer loads from the subway box onto the beam.

In the middle, **metal rods** tie the subway floor to the supporting beams and columns.

As the excavation proceeds, diagonal bracing is added to provide necessary stability.

FIGURE 15.4a *To keep the No. 1 subway line running while rebuilding the underground infrastructure at Ground Zero, the Port Authority had to engineer an elaborate and complex plan to dig below the train line's concrete box constructed in 2002 in order to replace the original 1914 tunnel, which was meant to lie on the ground, the surrounding soil providing structural reinforcement.* Mika Gröndahl/From the New York Times, May 8, 2008 © 2008 The New York Times

FIGURE 15.4b *Crews at work underpinning the No. 1 subway line.* FTA Lower Manhattan Recovery Office

Of all those reporting on the physical issues involved in rebuilding at Ground Zero, Dunlap has few peers. Writer, researcher, and editor, the veteran *Times* reporter grew up in Chicago loving both architecture and newspapers—he had his own, "The Daily Dunlap," at the age of twelve. Architecture was family conversation: His father was a student and colleague of Mies van der Rohe. After studying architectural history at Yale, the younger Dunlap joined the *Times* in 1975. As a metropolitan reporter, Dunlap has covered the broad gamut of city issues that shape the built environment: architecture, landmark preservation, urban history, public space, and city planning. An accomplished photographer, he spent nearly five years as graphics editor (1976–1981), during which time he helped the *Times* find new imaginative ways to better tell a news story. Since 2003, the rebuilding of the World Trade Center has been his chief beat, and the longevity with which he's been on the Trade Center story brings comprehensive depth and wisdom, along with sidebars of incisive humor and witty juxtapositions. With his well-honed understanding of planning and design and precise attention to detail, Dunlap has been able to intelligently draw out the implications and ramification of the rebuilding proposals and decisions, making the complications and compromises, as well as the mistakes, more comprehensive to policymakers, editorial boards, and readers alike. And the visual representations of complex relationships interwoven into his reporting have proved especially instructive to understanding the complex spatial puzzle and engineering of the underground at Ground Zero.

By the end of 2006, the Port Authority faced two major impediments on the critical path of rebuilding the underground: access to the site where the Hub was to be constructed and constructability of the Calatrava designs with the MTA No. 1 subway box in place. The site of the Hub was landlocked because of other projects under construction (Freedom Tower, east-west corridor, and the memorial). Access from the west would disrupt the memorial construction schedule in a major way, so the only practical construction access would have to be from the east using the Greenwich Street corridor above the No. 1 box, but that too presented problems. The MTA would not allow cranes to work directly on top of the subway box, and the Port Authority's general contractor would not build the PATH hall and transit hall without this access. One way to provide access for construction of the Hub was to build a trestle over the box for the length of the site, but the design, procurement, and installation of the trestle were not on any schedule; also, the PA had not committed to funding the trestle and was not offering any alternative plans. "The lack of a plan to construct the PATH Hall constituted a major risk with construction and design breakages of 9 months to more than 2 years," a team of experts wrote in a 2007 confidential risk assessment report commissioned by the Lower Manhattan Construction Command Center, which was responsible for coordination and general oversight of all construction projects south of Canal Street from the Hudson River to the East River. The East Bathtub excavation was also going to be impacted by the "problematic temporary underpinning approach," by the need to thread through a "jungle of interference from the slurry wall tie backs, temporary minipiles supports and bracing of the 1 Box, and the caissons supporting the trestle."[20]

From an engineering perspective, the constructability of the underground would have been simpler and delivery of Hub and the memorial faster if the No. 1 box could have been demolished, this portion of the subway line below Chambers Street shut down temporarily, and a new box built from the bottom up in sequence with the construction logistics of the underground. With the box in place, though, the Port Authority faced heightened risks to completing the complex work of the underground on schedule.[21] Greenwich Street was on the critical path to servicing the site since utilities for the site ran underneath. Delay risks were going to impact project budgets by triggering escalation costs and additional construction over-head costs, not to mention reputational costs to the Port Authority that were not susceptible to quantification. The engineering experts' conclusion was inescapable: The box was the "primary source of risk to the schedule"; if it could have been removed, it would have saved several years of technically demanding work and frustration. And costs: As reported by the *Wall Street Journal* in 2014, former PA officials estimated that the decision about the No. 1 box added between $300 million and $500 million to the cost of building the underground.[22]

Policy and practicality were on opposing ends of a decision-making spectrum. Planners always assumed the line had to be kept running because the disruption of service by shutting it down for years, busing displaced subway passengers to South Ferry Station, or forcing a transfer to the PATH at Thirty-fourth Street or another PATH station would have been too much, politically, for a major city like New York with a concentrated workforce in lower Manhattan. The MTA, I was told, did not want the line shut down because it would have disordered its transit-service logistics. Building top down from the Memorial Plaza by first underpinning the box was the alternative approach. That decision to underpin the box would be expensive, in both dollars and time. Before permanent underpinning could be put in place, the space under the box had to be completely hand-excavated, yet technical problems associated with completing the temporary underpinning remained unresolved throughout 2007 and most of 2008,[23] until the Port Authority shifted course under the leadership of a new executive director, Christopher O. Ward, who assumed the position with a clear mandate from a new governor, David A. Paterson (as explained in chapter 17).[24]

FIGURE 15.5 *The aesthetic demands of Calatrava's vision of the grand entrance for the PATH mezzanine required a massive and expensive truss.* THE PORT AUTHORITY OF NEW YORK AND NEW JERSEY

In a sense, this was an institutional failure. In many other cities, the line would have been shut down and rebuilt as quickly as possible. Yet the governor's insistence on keeping the No. 1 line running and the unwillingness of the MTA to play ball made construction of the underground octopus so much more difficult. The complications of rebuilding around the No. 1—in concert with the aesthetic demands of the Calatrava vision to create a grand entrance for the Transportation Hub—required expensive and massive girders under the No. 1 box to support the big truss (figure 15.5). It was all too costly and too complicated. The final roll-up cost for underpinning the No. 1 line, as revealed in the 2012 Revised Construction Agreement between the Federal Transit Administration (FTA) and the PA, totaled $355.5 million.

Risky Interdependencies

The decision not to shut down the No. 1 subway line was but one of several political parameters that configured the complex spatial puzzle of the multilevel underground into a warren of a basement. Below grade the competition for space—retail, mechanical and utility, parking, roadways, loading docks, and storage facilities—was fierce. Once Pataki declared that nothing could be built on the footprints of the twin towers, power feeds for the memorial and accompanying museum (as well as the rest of the site) had to be shifted east of the memorial quadrant into the basement of the closest commercial tower in the East Bathtub, Tower 2. Also, portions of the mechanical systems supporting the Hub's power, heating, cooling, ventilation, and plumbing were to be distributed throughout the Silverstein buildings for functional reasons and to meet security criteria. What would happen, though, if the timing of building Silverstein's three towers turned out to be uncertain, notwithstanding the 2006 realignment agreement with its "cross" provision obligating the developer to have all three complete by July 2013?[25] How would the site function with only some of the towers built? The transportation network would not work without all the office buildings in place, or at least built up to the structural level of the infrastructure systems and retail spaces that made up the lower seven stories of the two office towers—a problem in the making.

This was the build-it-all-at-once risk confronting rebuilding, and its complications and delays. No private developer of commercial real estate would build this way. Real estate is a very capital-intensive business; developers manage scarce capital so it can be deployed over time, not all at once. Large-scale projects are built out over time, in phases; to do otherwise is too risky, a bet on the project or the firm. Flexibility to time when to bring an office tower onto market is essential to control developers' financial exposure to the vagaries of the commercial market. How could a private developer when building a tower on spec, without tenants signed on to occupy it, put up the big dollars as the Port Authority was doing in building out the underground superblock all at once? In light of the final set of plans in the Innovative Design Study that might have been selected, one has to wonder about the reality of the integrated-building schemes that were being proposed.

The underground was a giant multidimensional puzzle, with layers of overlapping elements shared across many space users. The puzzle created by the superblock decision defined the problem of interdependencies—the Transportation Hub, for example, interfaced with twenty other Trade Center projects[26]—making a change in any one element was difficult without setting off a chain reaction of consequences almost everywhere else, much like the challenge in a game of pick-up-sticks, the metaphor Ward relied on to diagnose the challenge of construction at Ground Zero. The interdependencies made it hard to distinguish which use and stakeholder was responsible for which cost of the common infrastructure. Determining cost is easy; the issue is how you allocate shares to each use. What percentage of a column should be charged to what use? The slicing and dicing of infrastructure numbers could be endless. Elaborate and large graphic presentations with color-coded formulas were memorialized in diagrams.

Beyond formulas, however, the interdependencies demanded clear and consistent coordination of all stakeholders on the site, a decision-making structure to govern priorities, resolve conflicts, and decide on trade-offs so essential to skill-fully managing a complex and technically challenging construction project. Although the checkerboard of ownership was governed by a legal agreement, the stakeholders for these diverse projects were not united under a clear and com-monly accepted governing structure for dealing with technical issues and solving construction problems. "No one was talking to each other," said Maikish. To make the point concrete, he recounted how "the elevation of Greenwich Street was not the same on the plans of the Port Authority and Silverstein Properties. The PA's elevation was one foot higher to make the Transportation Hub more constructible, give it more head room. Silverstein wanted it one foot lower because one foot higher impaired the view down Greenwich Street. With that one-foot difference unresolved, one might have driven a car down Greenwich Street and hit a one-foot wall," he told me, without much humor.[27]

If the Port Authority was to make good on its aspirations, it needed skillful or-ganization to effectively manage engineering, design, construction logistics, cost and budget, delivery, and operations. The agency was not, however, set up to inte-grate and coordinate the many demands of this highly political and complex devel-opment project. It was simply not used to doing public-private projects. Rebuilding responsibilities were split between two departments, WTC construction and WTC redevelopment; WTC construction did not do leasing or engage with the business side of the project, yet, as in a private development project, these were critically interconnected with construction. Engineering was in a separate silo and brought in to the project only for code review and materials inspection. Described as a "crazy quilt of decision making" by one longtime staffer, questions about how the sitewide infrastructure elements would operate when complete—questions that should inform design and construction of facilities and would in a private-sector development project—could only be answered if there was cooperation between the two WTC departments. Instead, the lack of cooperation might find expression in a bureaucratic response: "It's not in our job description." "Great and constant pressure prevailed between WTC construction and engineering," recalled one former executive director. "The chief engineer is held responsible for safety and construction, but he has no control over the WTC construction process." Some of this is endemic to any large project, but the PA's organization for this project com-pounded the difficulties.

Year after year in its monthly monitoring reports, the Federal Transportation Administration detailed its concerns with the Port Authority's program manage-ment and project controls for the permanent WTC PATH Terminal. Did the WTC Construction Department have sufficient resources to carry out the job? Did it have people who knew how to put the project together or who had the credibility to raise concerns when critical bottlenecks arose? The integrated underground plan necessitating that everything be built all at once created problems because for years there were no clear priorities for what project should take precedence when conflicts arose. One insider suggested that the best way to think about the Port Authority was as a stack of CDs: All departments have their own information and don't communicate, and all are in competition with one another. Each department is a business unit, and all are at odds with one another, and no real mechanism existed within the agency to resolve the issues. This was the Achilles heel of the agency's ambition for rebuilding its Trade Center site. The lack of clear and continuous leadership made effective implementation impossible because there was no coordinated decision-making structure at the agency for this complex project. Though work on the underground was moving forward, the overall project was adrift until crisis hit in 2008.

The PA's decision to rebuild a centralized common infrastructure was at the heart of the construction crisis. It made rebuilding far more demanding and expensive than might otherwise have been the case. It created technical complexity and continuous complications that caused constant delays. The vast underground expanded the cost of the PATH transportation project. It made more difficult the delivery of Silverstein's three office sites. Building infrastructure simultaneously for many users—9/11 Memorial and Memorial Museum, commercial office towers, subway line and commuter train, security screening, bus and car garages, retail space, and back-of-the-house functions—inevitably engenders complicated cost-allocation issues that are contentious in any project with several uses, though they were ever more so at Ground Zero with its many different property interests who were generally not terribly cooperative.

The central integrated plan had never been a part of the elaborate public planning discourse; it was a dictate of the staff at the Port Authority. Once its limitations became apparent people started to ask, where did this come from? The Port Authority was thinking like the transportation agency it was, and about the lost revenue stream from the towers and retail spaces that comprised 20 percent of its combined 2000 income from operations. The centralized underground was a way to lock in rebuilding of ten million square feet of commercial space. As early as January 2002, the Port Authority released a graphic of its ambitious blueprint for rebuilding the transit network beneath lower Manhattan with a huge underground pedestrian network that would "connect the dots downtown."[28] In concept, it resembled what ultimately came to pass and reveals that the Port Authority was always thinking about the Trade Center site as a below-grade transportation and retail project.

The oft-cited $2 billion price tag for the transportation complex was an abstract number, "an order of magnitude cost estimate," prepared by the Port Authority in

January 2003—a number fit to the amount of federal funds available. "Right after 9/11, the Port Authority went down to Washington and when asked about the transportation needs—its wish list—and what it would cost, the agency priced the terminal as if in a 'normal world,'" recalled Rampe. "This was before Calatrava had been chosen; the project was to rebuild the PATH station, not a specific station design. In asking for $2 billion, agency officials believed they would have money left over. Then the Calatrava decision came after the failure of the first site design process when everyone was focused on design, design, and design, and the Port Authority wanted to be on the bandwagon as well. No one was focusing on the engineering issues. This was just a lack of focus, not a game of hide the ball."[29]

ACCOMMODATING HISTORY

Following removal of some 1.5 million tons of wreckage, the site became "the pit"—a deep, deep hole, seventy feet down, partially hallowed out, and surrounded by ninety-foot-high, three-foot-thick concrete perimeter walls—slurry walls held in place with steel-cable tieback pins anchored deep into bedrock (figure 15.6). The cavernous pit, however, was not empty in the most essential sense: It was packed with emotional content and physical remnants whose possible historic significance had to be carefully considered in the plans, processes, and designs for the rebuilding projects. Once the Trade Center site was determined eligible for inclusion on the National Register of Historic Places, those government agencies using federal funds for rebuilding were required to assess the potential impacts on cultural resources as part of their project's comprehensive environmental reviews and develop plans to mitigate any adverse effects that occur as a result of implementing those project plans, a process named after the provision in the National Historic Preservation Act of 1966, section 106.[30]

"The [historic artifacts] review may well liberate the site from the clutches of politicians, architects, their publicists and other unqualified figures who have presumed to speak in history's name," Herbert Muschamp wrote a month before the first findings were to come out. He wanted to believe that "[i]f done properly the review will be a pioneering undertaking in cultural archeology, for it will explore not merely the value that is inherent in urban artifacts but also the mechanisms a society uses to confer value on some artifacts and withhold it from others." But he also believed that historical significance "is in the memory of the beholder," which in the case of Ground Zero, "resides in the conflicts that arise when memories disagree."[31] Conflict did, in fact, adhere to the section 106 process and to a considerable degree shaped what visitors see at Ground Zero and in the 9/11 Memorial Museum.

FIGURE 15.6 *The remaining slurry wall of the original bathtub of the World Trade Center, which held back the waters of the Hudson River, one year after 9/11. The slurry wall with its exposed tie-backs gave powerful expression to the symbolism of resistance.* COURTESY ERIC ASCALON

"Exceptional tragedy, not time, justifies extra care where the towers fell," Dunlap wrote of the coordinated review by officials of three government agencies—the Federal Transit Administration, Federal Highway Administration, and the LMDC as recipient of funds from HUD—to determine eligibility of the site for listing on the National Register of Historic Places. Though its age was less than the customary half century, after 9/11 the World Trade Center site was of "exceptional importance" in the history of the nation, so determination of historic eligibility was only a question of when, not if. On February 6, 2004, when the LMDC issued the preliminary coordinated determination of eligibility, the site's location, setting, feeling, and association—not any particular physical remnants, although some possessed "integrity of materials"—rendered it historic. It was a distinction that enjoined a battle between preservationists and family members and rebuilding officials over the significance of the physical structural remnants. The slurry wall was the only structural part of the World Trade Center that survived the attacks; that it did not fail but held sentry-like through the destruction transformed the engineered walls into a symbolic touchstone of survival. Questions about it and other physical remnants left behind after the rubble had been cleared away triggered a fierce debate, one with "few precedents in American historic preservation."[32] What can you preserve? What do you preserve? What constitutes historical significance? These questions became the focal point of debate.

When the final coordinated determination of eligibility was issued on March 31, 2004, the finding had been amended, significantly: "Although the existing elements on the site do not fully express the scale or catastrophic nature of the events of the day, various remnants of the WTC's twin towers and other structures help convey in different ways the events of September 11 and their aftermath and, therefore contribute to the WTC Site's historic significance."[33] What significant remnants were called out for special treatment? The truncated box-beam column bases that help define the perimeter or "footprints" of the former twin towers—but not the footprints themselves—and the slurry walls that form the sides of the underground bathtub (figure 15.7). However much this represented an advance in position by the governmental agencies, it was not enough, not nearly enough to satisfy the demands of preservationists and a group of activist family members, who had just begun to fight for preservation of other physical remnants—in particular, those remnants jeopardized by plans for the WTC PATH Terminal that would occupy a portion of the footprint areas.

A long year later, with the signing of the section 106 memorandum of agreement (MOA) between the Port Authority and the Federal Transit Administration, the New York State Historic Preservation Office (SHPO), and the Advisory Council on Historic Preservation (ACHP), six specific historic assets of the Trade Center

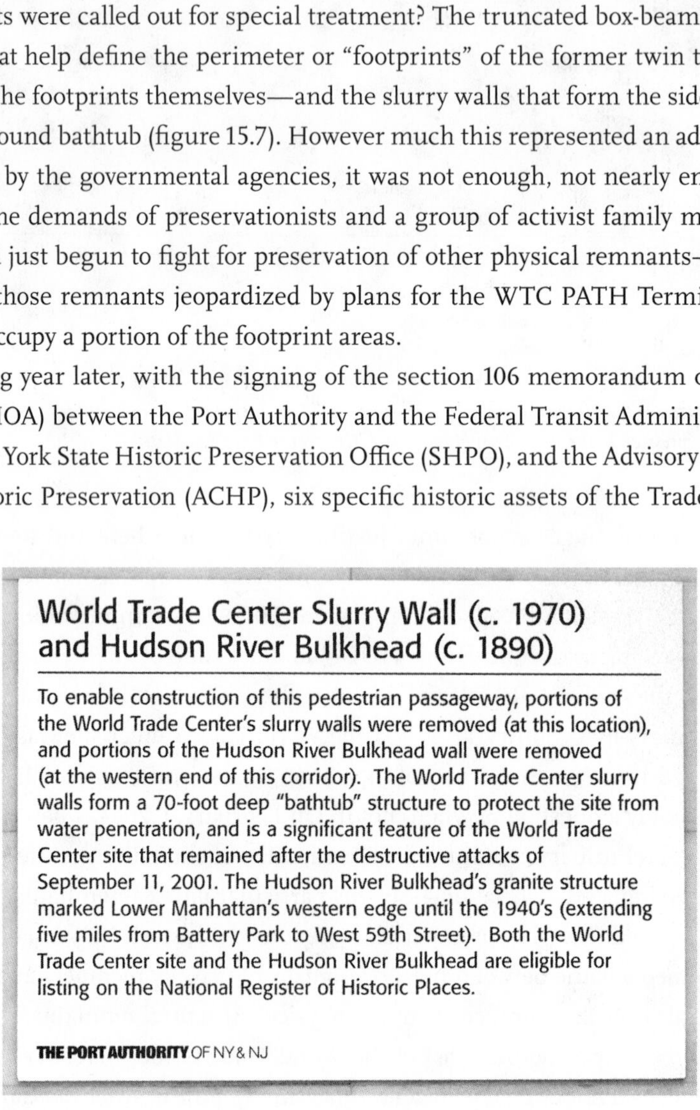

World Trade Center Slurry Wall (c. 1970) and Hudson River Bulkhead (c. 1890)

To enable construction of this pedestrian passageway, portions of the World Trade Center's slurry walls were removed (at this location), and portions of the Hudson River Bulkhead wall were removed (at the western end of this corridor). The World Trade Center slurry walls form a 70-foot deep "bathtub" structure to protect the site from water penetration, and is a significant feature of the World Trade Center site that remained after the destructive attacks of September 11, 2001. The Hudson River Bulkhead's granite structure marked Lower Manhattan's western edge until the 1940's (extending five miles from Battery Park to West 59th Street). Both the World Trade Center site and the Hudson River Bulkhead are eligible for listing on the National Register of Historic Places.

THE PORT AUTHORITY OF NY & NJ

FIGURE 15.7 *National Register of Historic Places marker of artifacts of the World Trade Center.* GARY HACK

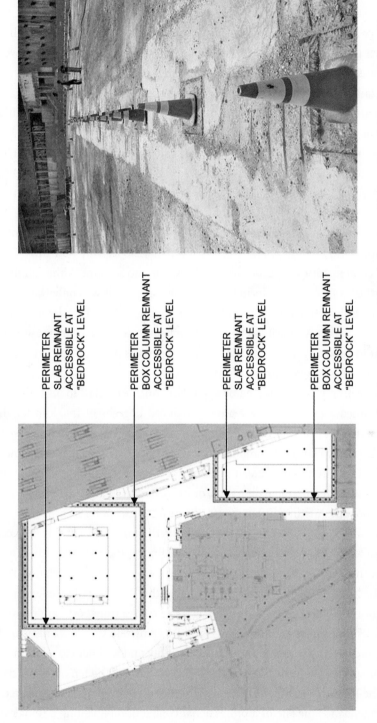

PERIMETER
SLAB REMNANT
ACCESSIBLE AT
"BEDROCK" LEVEL

PERIMETER
BOX COLUMN REMNANT
ACCESSIBLE AT
"BEDROCK" LEVEL

PERIMETER
SLAB REMNANT
ACCESSIBLE AT
"BEDROCK" LEVEL

PERIMETER
BOX COLUMN REMNANT
ACCESSIBLE AT
"BEDROCK" LEVEL

FIGURE 15.8a and b *Diagram of the plan to preserve the perimeter box-column remnants outlining the footprints of the twin towers (left) and on-site photo of the remnants in the northwest corner of the North Tower (right). As part of the federally mandated section 106 review, the truncated box-beam remnants were declared to be historic assets.* COURTESY LOWER MANHATTAN DEVELOPMENT CORPORATION

site entered the realm of history: the truncated box-beam column bases outlining the footprints of the North Tower and the South Tower serving "to poignantly delineate the areas where so many lives were lost" on 9/11 (figure 15.8a and b), the slurry walls with exposed tiebacks that give powerful expression to the symbolism of resilience (figure 15.6), the steel beams forming a cross erected by recovery workers, the E subway entrance, and the remnants of the Hudson Terminal and the H&M Railroad.[34] (The year had been long because of the difficulties in reaching consensus on what constituted historic assets.) The MOA was the definitive agreement of the environmental review governing the process by which the Port Authority committed to avoid, reduce, or mitigate adverse impacts of the Hub project by incorporating historic features of the Trade Center site into the PATH Terminal design, among other actions; the PA could not eliminate these mitigations from the project, except with written consent from the FTA.

In rebuilding of the Transportation Hub with federal funds, the Port Authority agreed to adhere to eight pages of detailed stipulations outlining how the effects of the project on historic properties were to be taken into account. Although finalizing the MOA completed the formal section 106 process, it was only the beginning of a precisely defined set of procedures for monitoring and implementation; it did not end the Port Authority's exposure to schedule delays, cost increases, and litigation from opposing parties challenging the agency's implementation actions regarding these historic resources. However much the complicated planning and review process might be considered by some Port Authority staff to be a "distraction,"[35] it defined a new reality, a reality of reduced degrees of freedom for the agency from its past practice. Rebuilding the Port Authority's institutional legacy was turning out to be far more complicated than the 1960s ground-up development of the World Trade Center on sixteen raw acres of a superblock, unfettered by any regulatory oversight, emotional demands, or historic significance. The rebuilding project was not one Austin J. Tobin would recognize—except for its ambition.

On September 6, 2005, just days before the fourth anniversary of 9/11, in a ceremony complete with the release of doves symbolizing the rebirth of the Trade Center site, the Port Authority launched construction of its Transportation Hub (figure 15.1). "This great transit facility will give the World Trade Center site a unique identity, and also will serve as the centerpiece of a transportation network that now links New Jersey and New York," said PA chairman Coscia. "This is truly a visionary project that will greatly enhance mobility and will help to address the region's transportation needs for decades to come." Each of the ten other officials quoted in the Port Authority's press release offered words of praise that reflected a particular agenda for the site or a professional contribution enabling a remaking of the transportation system in lower Manhattan. Since the actual construction work on site preparation would start days later, Dunlap called it a "rhetorical foundation."[36] Yet for the past nineteen months Port Authority staff had been clearing procedural hurdles of the section 106 process, as part of the overall environmental review of the WTC PATH Terminal project in order to get to the start line of construction.[37] Due to section 106 delays, the environmental impact statement had become a critical-path item in the overall PATH Hub project; over half of the comments received during July 2004 for the project's draft EIS were related to historic resources. The start of construction was therefore no little achievement for the agency and its funding partner, the FTA: The section 106 hurdling track had been a complicated one to traverse.

First up was an assessment of whether the Hub project would impact the historic assets identified in the MOA, specifically whether it would have an "adverse" effect or not. Under section 106, an adverse effect is found when a project "may alter, directly or indirectly, any of the characteristics of a history property that qualify the property for inclusion in the National Register in a manner that would diminish the integrity of the property's location, design, setting, materials, workmanship, feels or association."[38] When the LMDC issued its "proposed finding of no adverse effect" under section 106 for the WTC Memorial and Redevelopment Plan on February 9, 2004, it opened a breach of substantive significance with preservationists, a coalition of family members, and others among the designated section 106 "consulting parties." The "no effect" approach—which would have relieved the LMDC of any obligation to consider ways of reducing damage or destruction to the physical remnants on the site—was not what the FTA had recommended, and the March 2004 FTA monitoring report out of its Lower Manhattan Recovery Office (LMRO) emphasized that the LMDC's finding had "caused a delay of approximately three weeks prior to resolution." In the big scheme of things, however, that was not much of a delay.

As a general matter, delay was an expected condition of environmental review under the National Environmental Policy Act and of many state environmental statutes, yet ever more so the case at Ground Zero given the "high public profile of the project and the number of stakeholders" involved. The sharp criticism from the consulting parties, including the threat of litigation from the Coalition of 9/11 Families, that ensued from the LMDC's proposed finding of "no effect" forced the development agency to retreat from its position with a proposal to create a new review procedure that would guide the treatment of historical elements at the site for ten years. As codified in a "Programmatic Agreement," the SHPO and other consulting parties involved in the review process "would not have the power to stop or modify projects that would alter or destroy structural remnants," Dunlap wrote, but "they would be kept informed of those projects and their comments solicited."[39]

The ten-page Programmatic Agreement among the ACHP, SHPO, and the LMDC signed on April 22, 2004, did what the "no effect" proposed finding did not do: It identified as part of the development plan for the memorial specific physical remnants—portions of the western slurry wall on the Trade Center site and truncated box-beam column bases outlining portions of the lower "footprints" of the former twin towers at the World Trade Center site (but not the footprints themselves)—that the LMDC, in coordination with the Port Authority, "will preserve and provide for reasonable and appropriate access by Memorial visitors." In addition to defining these "Memorial Access Commitments," the Programmatic Agreement created an additional opportunity for the SHPO and the section 106 consulting parties, nearly sixty including seven well-established preservation organizations, to comment on plans for the memorial and the Trade Center site as they were developed; going forward, the Programmatic Agreement's main purpose was "to address any unanticipated or adverse effects on historic assets that may occur as a result of the Plan's implementation."[40]

The salvage list was growing. Though seemingly cleared, the site still held "many architectural features and structural outcroppings—some small and quite subtle—that speak to the site's history." The Coalition of 9/11 Families, said its ardent primary spokesperson Anthony Gardner, was "constantly, diligently, aggressively" pushing for the preservation of other physical remnants on the site. "Otherwise, the historic integrity of the World Trade Center would be destroyed," he said.[41] The group had been calling for a do-over of the memorial design ever since the jury's selection had been made public; it had long sought the maximum preservation of the footprints down to bedrock.

In late August, in an effort to stop demolition of slab and column remnants in the northwest corner of the site (figure 15.8b), the group brought suit in federal court, alleging that the LMDC's decision to allow the Port Authority to demolish the remnants had failed to comply with section 106 procedures and stipulations of the Programmatic Agreement; it sought to halt construction at Ground Zero until the agencies "adhere to their legally binding commitments to satisfy historic preservation requirements."[42] Technically, this particular issue was independent of the PA's Hub project, though the overlap and physical relationship between the Hub project and the Trade Center subgrade remnants fused in the reality of executing the plans for rebuilding.

In hopes of diffusing the near simultaneous announcement of this litigation, the Port Authority announced it would permanently preserve as part of the Hub project a sixty-six-foot-long, travertine-paved remnant of the original WTC concourse that it had planned to demolish.[43] It would also salvage a fluorescent orange memorial marker from the stairwell of the underground garage, uncover the remaining steel stubs of the twin towers' perimeter columns, and mark the edge of the North Tower outline on a planned additional PATH platform, Platform D, which would cover a corner, approximately 1,600 square feet, a small fraction of the 43,700-square-foot footprint of the North Tower. Although the federal court judge dismissed its claims in an opinion issued February 8, 2005, the coalition persisted in its efforts to preserve each and every one of the remnants that define the floor plans for the North Tower jeopardized by the Port Authority's plans for Platform D, and along with the Historic Districts Council, maintained its opposition to the Port Authority's final memorandum of agreement.[44]

Clearing the MOA hurdle marked a major milestone for rebuilding Ground Zero, and not just for the Port Authority's Hub project. At the time, amid the tremendous chaos and uncertainty that surrounded the prospects for moving beyond "the culture of inertia" that prevailed throughout 2005, it passed relatively unnoticed. The agreement, in great specificity, called upon the PA to preserve "to the maximum extent feasible" various historic architectural remnants of the twin towers, including column base remnants from the North Tower and the South Tower in such a way as to afford views of column bases though a glass wall that would otherwise be obscured by construction of a proposed terminal platform.[45] The MOA's mitigation measures were the result of an "extended consultation process." Reaching consensus among the section 106 consulting parties had been difficult, especially with respect to mitigating adverse impacts of the proposed Platform D. While a minority continued to disagree with the need for Platform D, the FTA's monitoring report said, "all Consulting Parties applauded the Port Authority's efforts and design modifications to Platform D to retain as much of the genuine North Tower footprint and column bases as possible while allowing for public viewing from the platform itself."[46]

The Port Authority was working hard to do the right thing, taking pains to accommodate history—its history—while rebuilding Ground Zero during this contentious period of regulatory review. The accommodations at Ground Zero were adding cost and complexity to an already demanding project, but the effort on the part of the PA staff to meet the concerns of the section 106 consulting parties (approximately sixty worked through the process) was genuine, even if, as one FTA official recalled, staff members would "blunder" into meetings and say, "there's no way we can save these elements; it's not feasible because of construction." After some back and forth during which they were advised "that will not fly," agency staff would come to the next meeting and say they had figured out a way to preserve the remnant or mitigate the adverse effect. The pattern repeated itself enough so that it worked by the end of the process, yet it took time and patience.

Some of the consulting parties praised the Port Authority: It had been "extremely responsive" by "repeatedly modifying the plans for the PATH Terminal to accommodate a number of unexpected ideas and suggestions that have emerged from consultation" wrote the deputy general counsel of the National Trust for Historic Preservation. It "had gone far beyond reasonable expectations to preserve the historic artifacts at the WTC site," said a Battery Park City residents group, BPC United. It had taken steps to preserve the historic artifacts from the Trade Center and house them in Hangar 17 at JFK Airport "long before the public took interest," listened carefully to all views at the meetings with consulting parties and addressed those concerns at succeeding meetings, and made modifications to plans that "demonstrated creativity and flexibility." As a set of actions, the agency had "treated the site with the respect," and the "results were evidence of their feelings for the old Trade Center, and the personal losses they all experienced." What the resident group took exception to was a "'preserve at all costs' mentality" that prevailed among some consulting parties who demanded preservation of artifacts of "secondary importance" and "disputed value" other than the column footings embedded in cement on the floor of the WTC bathtub.[47]

The extraordinary efforts by the FTA and the Port Authority to preserve the historic remnants of the World Trade Center, with their "evocative links with 9/11," achieved early recognition from the nation's leading preservation groups. In February 2009, the FTA received the Chairman's Award for Federal Achievement in Historic Preservation from the Advisory Council on Historic Preservation, an independent federal agency and advocate for historic preservation. The solutions to complex World Trade Center issues worked out in close partnership with the Port Authority, which received a "partnership commendation," were "exemplary." Eight months later the National Trust for Historic Preservation awarded the FTA's Lower Manhattan Recovery Office, and the Port Authority as a co-recipient, its National Trust/Advisory Council on Historic Preservation Award for Federal Partnership in Historic Preservation, citing the "exhaustive and sometimes contentious process of negotiation, collation and innovation" involved in preserving these artifacts, especially the Survivors' Staircase (discussed in chapter 20).[48]

ROLE REVERSAL

"Good architecture requires a good client"—that's the familiar adage in the development field, and by all indications the prospects for rebuilding Ground Zero to a higher aesthetic standard than what traditionally prevailed in New York seemed assured when the Port Authority selected Calatrava to design the WTC PATH Terminal. In turn, Calatrava had an institutionally committed, deep-pocketed patron, yet in their enthusiasm for his world-renowned artistic talent—"Our people call him the da Vinci of our time," former executive director Joseph J. Seymour told *Times* reporter Deborah Sontag in 2006—Port Authority officials, for years, allowed the architect to become, in effect, the client by not exercising effective control over design decisions that ultimately impacted the project's constructability and budget. Quickly, they all became enamored with Calatrava, charmed by his artistic persona and the promise of what his design could reliably deliver by way of institutional prestige. "I have become very, very fond of Santiago," said Kenneth J. Ringler, who followed Seymour as executive director of the Port Authority from 2004 until 2007. "The guy's a genius. But the first thing that hits you in the face—he gives you a hug."[49]

Calatrava's personal appeal, nearly a charismatic pull, was easy to comprehend, especially in the early chaotic years of rebuilding after 9/11. "Calatrava is courtly and gracious," wrote Paul Goldberger, "and he communicated his passion for his architectural mission, as well as for New York City, in general, with a sincerity that made him a refreshing presence amid the politicking of Ground Zero." Calatrava is also a master marketer, laid back, subtle, even seductive in delivering his vision, often sketching in public to convey his vision. When presenting his design for the Hub in January 2004, for example, he fluidly "drew in chalk a child releasing a bird from her hands, thus conveying the genesis of the design." With the best intentions of leaving the institution's mark on rebuilding, Port Authority officials were nonetheless operating beyond their range in this realm of world-class, high-profile architecture; neither Seymour nor Ringler had experience with large-scale development projects. But both were trusted members of the team operating in Albany and intensely loyal to the governor, who could, if he so chose, exercise hands-on control over Ground Zero through the Port Authority. But the governor's political ambition lined up well with the agency's institutional ambition for the Hub project. And the institutional ambition aligned all too well with Calatrava's architectural ambition. "We wanted to give the sense that it is not the tower that makes the place," he told journalist Andrew Rice, referring to the Freedom Tower, "but the station." In his design of a station at Ground Zero that could rival his "favorite space," the twentieth-century landmark achievement of Grand Central Terminal in midtown, Calatrava was after architectural immortality. The dual alignment of ambition between patron and client, client and patron, gave Calatrava commanding decision-making power for someone working as a subconsultant to the two big engineering firms in contract with the Port Authority. By early 2014, ten years later, it had rewarded him with $81 million in fees, 20 percent of the Port Authority's contract with the Downtown Design Partnership,[50] with more to come before the project was complete.

When conflicts between the complex design for the Hub and its constructability arose and created cost pressures, Port Authority officials were reportedly unable—and unwilling—to counter Calatrava's strong resistance to any change that threatened what he believed to be the project's design integrity. He was "amazingly charming, but difficult to work with," recalled another executive director of the Port Authority. He was able to hold on to an unusual degree of creative control over his commitment to the artistic and emotional statement of the PATH terminal hall even when it conflicted with the practical needs of the agency because Port Authority officials were reluctant to tie the hands of the man they considered an artist, as Ringler explained to journalist Rebecca Mead for her *New Yorker* profile, "Winged Victories," which described Calatrava's "soaring ambition": "My view was always, if we have to keep within budget, don't go and tell Santiago what to do; tell Santiago what is the problem. If you tell him what to do, it will conflict with his artistic desires; but he's a great problem solver."[51]

The NYPD's concerns about security, definitely not a possible pushback issue, triggered early design changes to the Hub. To make the structure more resistant to blasts resembling the terrorist bombings of Spanish commuter trains in Madrid in 2004 and the London Underground in 2005, the number of ribs for the Oculus was doubled, the amount of glass was reduced, and a solid wall more than three feet high was added as a ring at the base of the structure. Also, the length of the transit hall was reduced in order to pull the structure back from the street and reduce the potential for car-bomb damage. "The main transit hall," wrote Dunlap, "will almost certainly lose some of its delicate quality, while gaining structural expressiveness. It may now evoke a slender stegosaurus more than it does a bird." The cost of these security-driven changes, according to a report in *Bloomberg News*, added $591 million to the $2.221 billion project.[52] Some cost-conscious adjustments like substituting a different specification of concrete were not significant enough to threaten design integrity.

A serious conflict with the master plan had come to the fore in late 2004 when Calatrava objected to the placement of the 9/11 museum complex that was to rise over the PATH mezzanine, which "had been sold to the public as a luminous underground expanse."[53] When the cultural program fell apart in mid-2005, that objection turned moot and adjustments to the site plan to accommodate changes in the cultural program, Memorial Museum, and visitors' orientation center removed from the site the structure that would have intruded upon daylight filtering down into the mezzanine. In 2007, however, higher-order challenges to the execution of Calatrava's monumental ambitions for the Hub began to emerge, and by this time, a different set of political circumstances prevailed, one that altered the balance of power between the client and architect.

First up: a recurrence of the conflict between one of Calatrava's signature design elements—filtered natural light flowing down to the PATH mezzanine and platforms—and design plans for the northeast corner of the memorial precinct. That corner served as the roof of the enormous underground PATH mezzanine nearly fifty feet below. To achieve his light-filled mezzanine, Calatrava specified glass paving embedded in the Memorial Plaza above, yet this space was being designed by Peter Walker, one of the nation's most trusted and acclaimed land-scape architects, who was working for the Memorial Foundation; the quadrant, as he designed it, would hold swamp white oaks in east-west rows, as Dunlap ex-plained, "to create cathedral-like allées and clusters of trees to buffer the memo-rial voids and the parapets inscribed with victims' names." In this relatively small, three-quarter-of-an-acre corner roughly equivalent in size to the footprint of the central chiller plant on the site, the conflict between two professional giants, each of whom was intent upon preserving the integrity of his design, epitomized the type of programmatic tension common at Ground Zero where no formal frame-work had been set up to determine what priority ought to prevail when two proj-ects came into conflict. "More glass paving, fewer trees. More trees, less glass paving," as Dunlap succinctly put it.[54] If Calatrava's daylight-filled mezzanine was to prevail, Walker's memorial grove of trees was going to be abruptly interrupted by a bare area on the plaza with its own distinctive paving pattern.

The artistic tussle that ensued engaged the Bloomberg administration in strong opposition to the skylight plan. This was the Memorial Plaza, a sanctified area. At night, Calatrava's broad expanse of skylights set into the pavement would glow from below—"not unlike the disco dance floor in 'Saturday Night Fever,' one architect suggested." It was unseemly, and with that pejorative tag, the skylights disappeared from the Hub's blueprints. "Since the names of the victims are being brought above ground, we have to protect the sanctity of the area around the me-morial voids," explained Joseph C. Daniels, president and CEO of the Memorial Foundation. These careful words hid the vociferous behind-the-scenes dispute with the memorial designers. "The irresistible force" of Calatrava's Transportation Hub had, as Dunlap phrased it, "finally met an immovable object: the ground zero memorial." "What's baffling," the *Post*'s Steve Cuozzo wrote, "is why the PA didn't just say no to Calatrava in the first place."[55]

To anyone familiar with the role reversal that had thus far shaped the relation-ship, this wasn't terribly surprising. "Calatrava speaks of his client with courtly deference, dwelling on the Port Authority's more inspired projects—the construc-tion of the George Washington Bridge or the Holland Tunnel—rather than on its less impressive contributions to civic architecture, such as the Port Authority Bus Terminal," Mead wrote. Yet in an unusual moment of candor, in reference to the deletion of his glass paving blocks in the plaza, the architect told her, "I think it is absurd, but it is not my job to educate people." Years later when reconciled to the foliage substituting for his glass pavers on the plaza, he commented, "You have to live with the necessities of other people."[56]

When Eliot Spitzer was sworn in as governor on January 1, 2007, the political winds that had so favored Santiago Calatrava under the Pataki administration (1995–2006) might have shifted definitively. But Spitzer, too, became captivated by the architect and held fast to the Oculus without making visible changes, even as cost pressures were turning the purported $2.2 billion project into an out-of-control money pit that might cost as much as $3.4 billion, according to first estimates from the Hub general construction contractor, Phoenix Constructors. "We have notified Phoenix that costs so substantially above the original budget for the hub are simply unacceptable," said Anthony E. Shorris, Spitzer's appointee as executive director at the Port Authority. Shorris had served as the Port Authority's first deputy executive director from 1991 to 1995, and was thrilled to be back at the Port Authority. "This is our agency's moment," he was quoted as saying in the press release announcing board approval of his appointment. "We are engaged in the most epic construction project of our generation in Lower Manhattan."[57]

Dedicated to the institutional mission of the Port, he would try to put in place a cost-containing radical reengineering of the project without fundamentally altering Calatrava's iconic avian-inspired above-ground design for the terminal. But when Spitzer suddenly resigned from office in March 2008, on the heels of a call-girl sex scandal, Shorris resigned a few days later, and the options for radical cost-cutting change to the Hub project he had detailed in a seven-page memo a month earlier vanished. Considering that his resignation came a week after the newly installed Governor David A. Paterson signaled in a speech he was displeased with the pace of rebuilding the Trade Center site and would "revisit the issue at Ground Zero," some considered the resignation "forced." Whatever the reason, Paterson appeared to want his own person to gain full control over the high-profile project.[58]

Until this point, Calatrava had been successful in fighting off change to the signature element of his Hub design: the kinetic action of the roof—wings splitting open at the roof line for the entire length of the Hub to allow light to stream into the grand hall below. This was an expensive architectural gesture with a limited function. Only when Ward assumed the position of executive director of the Port Authority, the fourth executive director since 9/11 to occupy the fifteenth-floor office in the agency's nondescript executive offices at 225 Park Avenue South, did the architect-client reversal of roles that had so defined the PA's relationship with Calatrava from the time he was chosen for the Hub project nearly five years earlier revert to the norm, as explained in the next chapter.

The cocoon of unconditional praise that for years sheltered the complexity of the Hub's constructability and its architect from criticism was, by mid-2008, bursting open. There was not a lot of love behind the scenes for this very expensive institutional phoenix. Uncontrollable costs had eaten away at the illusion of a "free" new permanent PATH terminal. The bi-state agency's balance sheet would have to cover the extraordinary cost increases, and no one really knew how much the toll payers crossing the bridges and tunnels of the Hudson River would have to bear to cover the ever-spiraling cost of the Hub project. "Cost overruns are not uncommon in architecture, particularly for designs that depart from structural or technological norms, or demand a finer quality of execution than commercial schemes," Martin Filler explained in "The Bird Man," a 2005 review of Calatrava's works for the *New York Review of Books*.[59] "Budgets are exceeded for many reasons, not all of them within an architect's control." That certainly was the case at Ground Zero.

Filler was the rare critic not completely taken over by Calatrava's grandiose vision, and he was early in the game to caution that "[o]verspending to create a conspicuous work of architecture can have a damaging effect on other institutions." As a case in point, he cited Calatrava's first U.S. commission, a sculptural addition to the Milwaukee Museum of Art where the cost increase of his Quadracci Pavilion almost quadrupled from the original estimate of $35 million to $125 million, in part due to the museum trustees' mismanagement of the project, but also in part to technical problems in constructing the building's winglike machine sun-screen designed to open and close, similar to that at Ground Zero. "Fish gotta swim, birds gotta fly," he wrote, "but buildings do not have to move, at least not in the literal and often costly Calatrava manner," he wrote.[60]

As a designer of cultural buildings, bridges, and airports for governmental or cultural patrons, the Valencia-born engineer-architect, who thought of himself as an artist and sculptor, had acquired a reputation for not being on time or on budget, the two imperatives of commercial development. Even among institutional clients, the era of edifice building, of saying cost is no object, was long over, although this reality was slow to sink in at the Port Authority. There seemed to be no checks and balances on the project; people were just doing what Calatrava wanted, all of which, down to the design of door handles, was grandiose, recalled one insider.[61] When Ward took over as executive director of the agency, Silverstein's senior executive in charge of the Trade Center project, Janno Lieber, sent him a note cautioning him to get control of the Hub project. At the same time, a *Daily News* editorial, "Bust the Boondoggle," exploded with fury at the excessive gesture and slack management of the WTC Hub project. "The Federal Transit Administration report shows that the Port Authority has been fighting a losing battle to keep the revamped World Trade Center PATH station from becoming one of the all-time boondoggles." The editorial went on to say it was "time for the elected officials who control the bi-state Port Authority—Govs. Paterson and Corzine—to take firmer control on behalf of taxpayers."[62] The criticisms and complaints starting to emerge at a time of little visible progress tore apart the political consensus behind the one project of Ground Zero that had seemed immune to censure.

By early 2007, the Hub's soaring costs were making headline news, and the Port Authority's apparent inability to manage the demanding project had become a source of public embarrassment. The agency had lost control of the project as the engineering difficulties of the complex design repeatedly challenged conventional constructability, overran unrealistic budgets, and spawned scores of risk factors that the Transportation Hub's financial sponsor, the Federal Transit Administration, continuously detailed in its monthly monitoring reports. And all along, the architect's insistence on aesthetic specifications like column-free interiors and sculptural and curvilinear steel elements called for unique and expensive materials and fabrications that had to be manufactured abroad, further exacerbating the agency's financial exposure to its ungovernable ambition. Ironically, the centenary of the PATH system for which this symbolic "bird in flight" at Ground Zero was being constructed passed relatively unnoticed on February 25, 2008. On that day, only PATH's passengers riding free across the Hudson courtesy of the Port Authority had a reason to rejoice. By that time, the news about the Hub project had turned relentlessly negative.

The praiseworthy icon was well on the way to becoming a political pariah, an exorbitant folly. How did this happen? How did the transportation project morph from the most-heralded programmatic element designed by a celebrated architect-engineer into a constantly critiqued, overblown statement of the Port Authority's institutional self? The Hub was a terminal for one line, the PATH commuter system; prior to 9/11, the Trade Center PATH station serviced 67,000 riders each weekday (albeit facilitating connections underground to eleven subway lines and to the World Financial Center, later renamed Brookfield Place). Transit planners projected the station would service 175,000 riders by 2025. Sometime in the far future, perhaps it might include rail service to the LIRR and JFK. Its costly sculptural form overpowered its economic function: paraphrasing what John Zuccotti often said, "We're building a magnificent train station if only we had a magnificent train." Like the Trade Center's former high-grossing mall, though, it would provide the all-important building shell for several hundred thousand square feet for revenue-producing retail shops and restaurants.

Configured for multifunctional capacity, the Hub seemed to justify its scale and extravagance. But the powerful insularity and institutional hubris of the Port

Authority was undermining the agency's ambitions and its ability to act effectively in an area of legacy expertise. The proud institution could not hide the chaos engulfing the project from the public. How would it respond to the intense criticism it was receiving from all sides? How would it self-examine the issues thwarting timely construction and generating excessive costs of this extraordinarily high-profile eyes-of-the-world project? Could it change the narrative of institutional failure to deliver on the promise of a physical transportation icon for lower Manhattan? Taking on an ambitious agenda, not just for transportation but for rebuilding as much of the site as possible except for the three commercial towers, had exposed the institution's vulnerabilities and made it susceptible to reform-mongering political interference. What kind of a phoenix was this?

CHAPTER 16

Institutional Failure

THE DESIGN FOR A GRAND TRANSPORTATION Hub exposed the deeply rooted problems of the overdesigned site, even more so than the Freedom Tower. By 2008, the tide had begun to turn against the Port Authority's monumental ambition to build an icon to rival midtown's Grand Central Terminal. The Calatrava-designed PATH Terminal was too complicated, too delayed, too grandiose, and too expensive. Four years after the agency proudly unveiled the vision to an eager public, hype of expectation had turned into censure of excessive cost. Of the city's three dailies, only the *New York Times* continued to view the Hub project in a positive light; the *Times* believed in the model of a powerful regional authority, even if the patina of the 1920s progressive ideal behind the Port Authority's creation had long worn off. As one former executive director remarked, "In the end, it's all about risk, and the management of risk." Yet this is where the proud Port Authority failed, miserably.

The bi-state authority was designed to deliver regional transportation infra-structure with businesslike efficiency, and in failing to do so at Ground Zero, it was more exposed politically than perhaps at any other time in its past—this, less than a decade short of its centennial anniversary in 2021. The Port Authority's capacity to deliver on its institutional ambition was challenged, and if the capacity to execute the vision was flawed, then the agency was running the risk that a seemingly "free" rebirth might remain as mythical as the Greeks' phoenix. The public was still unaware of the chaos behind the scenes, though it was to learn of it soon enough. A crisis was in the making, but it was being kept under wraps, withheld from the public—until that unexpected shift in the seat of power in Albany put David A. Paterson in the governor's mansion and Christopher O. Ward in the executive director's seat at the Port Authority. Then the public would be told what many inside already knew: Chaos reigned.

SPOTLIGHT ON DELAY

The context of this chaos began in 2005, with an eighteen-month run of rampant confusion and continuous setbacks at Ground Zero that started with the redesign of the Freedom Tower. It captured the attention of the press, which typically went after stories of drama and principal (figure 16.1). As a general matter of journal-ism, the press was not prone to examine how institutions like the LMDC or the Port Authority actually operate and make decisions, unless a slashing of staff or scandal of one kind or another—blatant misappropriation of funds, egregious conflicts of interest, embarrassing high-profile mistakes or failures, as in the case of the deconstruction of the Deutsche Bank Building (described in chapter 14), the site of the proposed fifth office tower—came into play. As news, the business of government was a tiresome and boring read; it did not involve the fight of politics, especially its quadrennial electoral drama, as Edwin Diamond and Piera Paine argued in their 1990 classic analysis, "The Media in the Game of Politics." But that changed after the dramas surrounding the planning competition and design com-petitions had run their course.

The chaos at Ground Zero turned the governance factor into news, with much to cover in the way of government entities and public officials stumbling through the process of executing the plans for rebuilding. During this period, the press framed the story of rebuilding Ground Zero as a narrative of delay. That narrative, continuously repeated as setbacks, slowdowns, and interruptions impeding visi-ble progress at Ground Zero, became entrenched over time—even when actual progress, incremental and underground or necessarily procedural in nature, was being made. Repetition added meaning. It framed the context of action at Ground

Zero. By replaying that central message, the press affixed a narrative of delay onto the rebuilding story. By the calculus of informed and experienced players in the arena of large-scale complex development, however, the time trajectory of rebuilding these sixteen emotionally charged acres was relatively fast paced. Not to be interpreted as an excuse for the missteps, mistakes, and failures of purpose at Ground Zero, but "delay" is an unavoidable condition of any large-scale, complex, city-building project—and, most certainly, the handmaiden of false expectations of rapidly making a whole new place at Ground Zero. In New York, the typical timeline for big development projects to reach fruition is fifteen to twenty years, sometimes even longer as in the case of Battery Park City. (The *General Project Plan* for rebuilding the Trade Center site initially anticipated fifteen years, then inexplicably reduced the time frame to twelve years.)[1] The private sector needs this length of time to plan, finance, and build, and the real estate market needs this length of time to absorb large-scale speculative ventures. Ground Zero was vastly more complicated than the conventional big project, yet amazingly, Governor Pataki was publicly saying that the full buildout would only take five years! This false presumption stayed in place for years; no one was pushing back on the governor's assertion.

The issue of how the project was being governed became a priority issue of the city's editorial voices, replete with a long-running commentary of complaint. Each of the city's dailies took on the leadership issue at Ground Zero—its paucity, its missteps, and its failures—with gusto, albeit in different ways and with different points of criticism. The recurrent refrains about the "slow pace of rebuilding" began in earnest in the spring of 2005. Three and a half years after 9/11, "the only things rising on the Ground Zero site are projected costs and tensions between the many interested parties," reported the *Wall Street Journal*.[2] For the rest of 2005 and midway into 2006, incremental markers of progress were overshadowed by continual controversies played out in public. Economic uncertainties bedeviling the commercial program and headline-grabbing delays caused by the security-driven redesign of the Freedom Tower topped the list of troubles. Not long after, the focus of attention shifted to a rhetoric-driven fight over the International Freedom Center and Drawing Center and after that, the rapidly escalating costs surrounding the superexpensive memorial. The scars of those battles left deep imprints on the course of rebuilding and its chronicle by the press.

The persistence of conflict engulfed every element of the rebuilding program. Reading the headlines—headlines are supplied by editors, not reporters—stalemate appeared endemic: "A Deepening Gloom about Ground Zero's Future" (*NYT*), "Trying to Speed Ground Zero's Rebuilding" (*NYT*), "In Camera at Ground Zero, Still Shots of Slow Progress" (*NYT*), to name a few. In mid-April 2006 when

Governors Pataki and Corzine and Mayor Bloomberg announced a new accord between Silverstein and the Port Authority, the so-called Unified Financial Plan for Rebuilding Ground Zero, the plan promised to speed up rebuilding and open the door for construction starts by realigning roles and responsibilities for rebuilding. The *Times* editorial board praised "A Change of Course at Ground Zero" as some of the best news for lower Manhattan in the past four years. The *Daily News* voiced relief in "Building a Future at Ground Zero." The *Post*, ever skeptical that the public sector could do anything right and continuously promotional in its praise of the private developer, titled its snarky editorial "Small Steps at Pataki's Pit." Yet soon after, the hope for real progress dissipated quickly with regularly reoccurring headlines of new delays and escalating costs: "Pessimism Is Growing on Rebuilding of 9/11 Site," "Port Authority's Inability to Rebuild Quickly at WTC Site Will Cost Taxpayers," and "WTC Timeline Drags into '13." By 2008, deep doubt about the promise of rebuilding prevailed among politicians, stakeholders, and citizens alike. Work was proceeding on the underground superstructure, but the near invisibility of this work could not drown out the chorus of naysayers. The picture was static, and it was not pretty to the press or the public (figure 16.2).

FIGURE 16.2 *Construction workers and equipment excavate the southeastern corner of the Trade Center site, where developer Larry Silverstein would construct two office towers, January 2008. The near invisibility of this work proceeding underground out of sight could not drown out the chorus of project naysayers.* AP PHOTO/MARK LENNIHAN

The refrains of costly delays corresponded to revelation after revelation of real problems traceable to a trio of unforgiving political conditions impeding progress: a lack of communication among the public agencies responsible for rebuilding, flawed timetables driven by clouded political ambition instead of on-the-ground reality, and nonexistent budgets. The failings of the public entities in charge became targets of frustrated sarcasm and grist for a few editorial cartoonists willing to go beyond the conventional nonpolitical images of tribute, memorial, and remembrance (figure 16.1, figure 16.3). The LMDC was struggling with crisis after crisis in its appallingly difficult efforts to deconstruct the former Deutsche Bank Building, including a blaze in 2007 that killed two firefighters. The Port Authority was foundering, facing widespread criticism of its inability to manage its Trade Center responsibilities and withering scorn for its failure to deliver the sites for Silverstein's towers on the schedule established in the 2006 Master Development Agreement. The astronomical cost of its transportation phoenix was out-of-control. The holistic promise of the 2006 agreement had broken apart, and given the then $10 billion project's tumultuous history, few insiders or members of the public were surprised by the ensuing chaos. In late August 2009, 53 percent of New York City voters said that redevelopment of lower Manhattan is going "somewhat badly" or "very badly"—the highest negative score since the independent

FIGURE 16.3 Cox & Forkum

Quinnipiac University poll began asking this question in 2002. By a margin of up to two to one, they did not believe projections by the Port Authority that key redevelopment targets at Ground Zero—the Freedom Tower and the 9/11 Memorial—would be met.

Fatigue about rebuilding and its familiar story line—more delays—had set in. "For years, the World Trade Center occupied a prominent stage in New York politics, as elected officials jostled over questions of design, governance and delays before an engaged public audience," Eliot Brown wrote in the *New York Observer*. "But as the eighth anniversary of the terrorist attacks of Sept. 11 approaches and the redevelopment once again is tied up in delays and hurdles, it's become clear that the site has fully lost whatever place it once held, perhaps to the point where it has passed as a political issue of any strength at all."[3] An insightful journalist and urban policy buff who wrote with verve, Brown liked the interplay between the warring agencies and the private developer. He started covering the rebuilding story in 2007, while working at the *New York Sun* for nine months before moving to the *New York Observer* and after three years there moved to the *Wall Street Journal*. He was fascinated with the readers' attention to Ground Zero, the immediacy of the story readers could relate to, he told me. Well sourced and among the earliest to question the timetable of rebuilding, he was known for knowing how to ask a question, indirectly, by questioning around the question he was driving at, which made it difficult to dodge around the question, recalled one former deputy mayor. By his own account, Brown covered the story as a real estate story, rarely taking 9/11 emotionalism into account in terms of his critical approach.

Ground Zero's demise as a political narrative had been written earlier, in mid-2005, in a deeply penetrating op-ed by Frank Rich, "Ground Zero Is So Over." Rich called the vacant site not just "a poor memorial for those who died there," but "an all too apt symbol for a war on which the country is turning its back," the real focus on his opinion piece. For New Yorkers, however, "the pit," "the hole," "the void" remained a painful physical scar. The fallen cultural status of Ground Zero as a national narrative was irrelevant to the ongoing local saga he fittingly called a "raucous political narrative"—and more lay ahead. The raucous political narrative did not end any time soon, not with the Port Authority's new timetable put in place by Ward in October 2008 or with the resolution of the big conflict over how Silverstein's towers would be financed a year and a half after that in March 2010. Yet after construction of the office floors of the Freedom Tower began to rise in January 2010, a floor a week, the narrative had begun to change, albeit with an infusion of skepticism—"One WTC project actually on time."[4] But that is getting ahead of the story in this chapter.

Framing the story of Ground Zero as a narrative of delay indelibly shaped public perception of rebuilding at Ground Zero, in the negative. It was powerful and enduring—and limiting. It failed to explain why these sixteen acres could not get rebuilt immediately like Lego blocks rising in fast-moving video-frame motion as dictated by emotional need and political desire. "The narrative of delay was so tempting a story; it never goes away," a former chief of public affairs and government affairs for the Port Authority said. "It fits reporters."

THE FUNDING RELATIONSHIP

To build the Hub the Port Authority was being funded with $2.2 billion from the federal government, so how exactly did the Federal Transit Administration, lead agency for the grant funding, fit into the increasingly problematic picture at Ground Zero? The escalating costs, schedule slippages, and management problems with the Hub project were well known to the professionals monitoring the project for the FTA. Since the start of 2004, the federal agency's specially created Lower Manhattan Recovery Office had been closely monitoring the Hub project as well as other recovery projects on a monthly basis[5] (figure 16.4). Established in the summer of 2002 by FTA administrator Jenna Dorn as a separate office apart from the FTA's New York regional office, the LMRO was unique within the FTA. The dedicated office was set up with a "focused mission" to aid the city in rebuilding its lower Manhattan transportation network crippled by the attacks of 9/11 and to "expedite processes for the quick construction of these facilities."[6] President George W. Bush had issued an executive order designating the lower Manhattan transportation projects as priority projects (meaning they would receive an increased level of support at the cabinet level of the executive branch). Because the $4.55 billion appropriated by Congress in August 2002 was coming from the Defense Department and special antiterrorism legislation and not from the Department of Transportation, the LMRO started off with unusual flexibility to innovate in the way it conducted its grant oversight processes. It was not constrained by all of the usual FTA regulations and procedures, and for several years (2004–January 2007), the director of the office reported directly to the FTA administrator and deputy administrator in Washington rather than to the regional office, which had no direct responsibilities for these lower Manhattan projects.

The innovation mandate of the LMRO created a "unique experiment," said its first director, Bernard Cohen. Through its independent risk-based oversight process, the LMRO aimed to identify risks that would adversely impact its funded projects and work with the project sponsor, as a partner, to identify actions to minimize those risks before they became schedule delays or cost problems—at

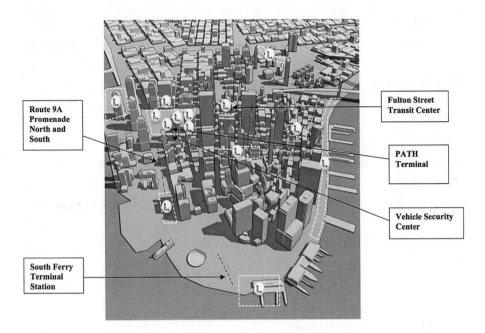

**Route 9A
Promenade
North and
South**

**Fulton Street
Transit Center**

**PATH
Terminal**

**Vehicle Security
Center**

**South Ferry
Terminal
Station**

FIGURE 16.4 *Locations of the five recovery projects funded by the federal government's grant of $4.55 billion to New York City.* FTA LOWER MANHATTAN RECOVERY OFFICE

least that was the theory. It pioneered a set of new project-delivery tools to expedite reconstruction of transportation projects. For its singular activities, the LMRO had an allocation of $90 million (from the $4.55 billion), allowing it to build a team of engineers, grant administrator, consultants for oversight of project development, and environmental planners for expediting the environmental review of the transportation projects in line with the requirements of the National Environmental Policy Act and review under section 106 of the National Historic Preservation Act. It was drawing on lessons learned from the U.S. Army Corps of Engineers and Pentagon officials following recovery from the 9/11 attacks on the Pentagon and operating with a twofold mission: to be a strong steward of the federal investment and streamline project delivery—though these were not necessarily symbiotic roles. "Every day we had to make decisions, and there was no clear dividing line. We had to invent as we went along," recalled Cohen.[7]

The scope of the permanent WTC PATH Terminal project ballooned quickly. Beyond the signature Oculus visible at ground level, it included a vast column-free mezzanine space connecting the PATH platforms below the mezzanine with the main transit hall defined by the Oculus, as well as other elements that were not a part of the initial proposal as presented in the Port Authority's request for expert professional architectural and engineering services for the PATH terminal. Included in the overall scope of the project were three connecting passageways designed to tie together the entire lower Manhattan transportation complex (east-west connector, north-south corridors, and Dey Street corridor) while offering transit riders and commuters convenient shopping opportunities. From the LMRO's perspective, pedestrian access was a legitimate rationale for including elements like the east-west connector (figure 16.5), though as the scope ballooned, the FTA became very critical, I was told by a senior PA staffer. All of it—the underground mezzanine, train platforms, and connecting concourses, as well as the Oculus—was being designed and promoted by Calatrava, who was a subcontractor to the Downtown Design Partnership entity (a consortium made up of STV Group Inc. and DMJM+Harris) providing the architectural and engineering services

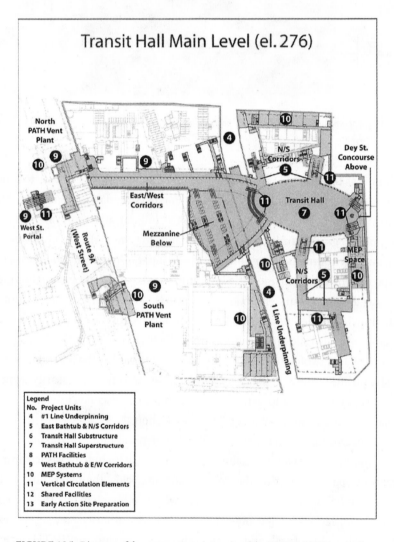

FIGURE 16.5 *Diagram of the numerous project units of the WTC PATH Terminal project, June 2008.* FTA LOWER MANHATTAN RECOVERY OFFICE

for the Hub project. "What concessions he could not gain with his considerable charm were often won by obstinacy," David W. Dunlap wrote in his review of how costs for the Hub eventually soared to $4 billion. The comprehensive scope of work directly related to the station initially represented approximately 77 percent of the $2.2 billion initial project breakdown; the Oculus, at $319 million, accounted for a small piece of the total, approximately 14 percent.[8]

Beyond those elements directly related to the PATH station, the rest of the project's funding grant covered several other components not directly tied to the Hub, including excavation work for the East Bathtub, where Silverstein would be building three towers. In a memo prepared for Governor Spitzer in March 2008 (by which time cost escalations had reached crisis proportions) executive director Anthony E. Shorris detailed the original project breakdown of $522 million for nonstation work: East Bathtub work clearing the land beneath the Silverstein office towers ($266 million), West Bathtub work constructing a permanent support structure for the MTA's No. 1 subway line ($31 million), work on elements of common site infrastructure needed for the whole site but not specific to the transportation program ($178 million), and general temporary work ($47 million). "It is worth noting," Shorris wrote, "that Federal transit funds were used for these 'non-station' elements with the explicit understanding of the FTA—they agreed these components could be linked to the transportation project in order to relieve the Port Authority of some of the burden of providing all of the general site infrastructure itself."[9] The Port Authority had every incentive to push as much of its related work on underground infrastructure for abutting sites and on common passageways and on shared mechanical, electrical, and plumbing systems into the Hub project as possible to maximize the dollars coming from the federal government (figure 16.6).

There was nothing unusual in the Port Authority's strategy. It was following a tried-and-true formula when the federal government is picking up the tab: load as much in the program as possible when the money is "free." That is what policy professionals mean when they talk about the "art" of giant infrastructure projects. It is a well-established behavior understood by every grant-writing professional and politician. The ever-pragmatic side of local politics includes a moral imperative to spend when money is given to you because there is never enough money to repair, maintain, or rebuild critical infrastructure. Cities have an insatiable appetite for capital investment dollars, and even though the federal spigot that had supplied a steady, well-lubricated stream of financial support for urban redevelopment had been turned off during the Reagan administration, cities never lost the touch of aggressively exploiting an opportunity for federal funding, especially when it required local treasuries to put up little or no cash themselves. Institutional memory had attached itself to this skill of grantsmanship absorbed during the

FIGURE 16.6 *A worker walks beneath the prefabricated arches adjacent to the Freedom Tower construction site, July 29, 2008. The arches will form an underground east-west pedestrian corridor connecting Battery Park City and Brookfield Place with the Trade Center Transportation Hub.* AP PHOTO/MARK LENNIHAN

liberal money-flowing decades of the federal urban renewal program. Besides being a rational policy strategy, ambition fueled by "free" money carried a New York pedigree: The city's legendary building czar, Robert Moses, had perfected the art. It just had been less in evidence since the Reagan-era cutbacks of federal funding for cities.

In approving these program elements, the FTA held a broad perspective on what was an acceptable scope for the permanent WTC PATH Terminal project. It was committed to the principle that creation of a more efficient transportation complex complete with pedestrian connections was consistent with the policy objectives of rapidly restoring transit service and enhancing the economic recovery of lower Manhattan through improvements capable of generating long-term benefits. Availability, convenience, and connectivity of mass transit have historically been essential elements of economic development, ever more so after 9/11 in the minds of elected officials and the downtown business community. Improved pedestrian access would be one of the dividends of the Hub program. Whether or not profit-making retail spaces lined the connecting corridors was not germane to FTA officials, who considered improved pedestrian access a legitimate rationale for including such elements in the program. They were also committed to the principle that creation of a highly visible street-level entryway for PATH was one of the project's benefits; pre-9/11, PATH was buried in the invisible basement of the twin towers—there was no "there" there for the PATH station. While possibly fine for commuters in a functional sense, a basement arrival space would hardly satisfy the ambitions of Governor Pataki, who wanted an iconic hallmark of lower Manhattan.

Just six months after the FTA signed a construction agreement[10] with the Port Authority on April 26, 2005, capping the total project cost for the Transportation Hub at $2.501 billion (inclusive of a $280 million reserve), independent monitoring reports coming into the LMRO office identified a series of troublesome "cost risks" and "major issues/problems" with the Port Authority's management of the complex Hub project. These were not new revelations; some had been identified in earlier 2005 reports. Over an eighteen-month period stretching into spring 2008, however, the lengthy reports prepared by its oversight contractor, Carter & Burgess, Inc., triggered ever-increasing tensions between the Port Authority and its funding agent as the detailed catalogue of identified impediments to the Hub's development and effective project management intensified. From the lengthy and detailed reports by its project management oversight contractor (PMOC), the Lower Manhattan Recovery Office knew almost as much about the projects as the Port Authority's project managers,[11] said its first director. If higher costs were estimated along the way, the construction agreement required the Port Authority to develop a recovery plan to find ways to keep costs within the funding allocations. That was the process, in theory.

By July 2007, the probability of meeting or underrunning the total project cost had slipped to 45 percent from 90 percent prior to signing of the construction agreement. Just three months later, that probability had dropped to less than 10 percent. From these reports, there could be little doubt that the FTA's restricted reserve of $280 million intended to cover cost overruns would fall short by more than $400 million under a 90 percent probability forecast that costs would not exceed $2.912 billion. The cost of the Hub project was escalating not only because of the complexity of the below-grade infrastructure and the fact that the Hub functioned as a huge platform for the memorial above, but because scope creep was playing a material role. As benchmarked by the FTA's midpoint cost-to-complete estimate in spring 2008, at $2.77 billion (an FTA figure Port Authority staff thought "prudent" to work off of, even though costs might come in lower, according to the Shorris memo), the nonstation elements accounted for some $350 million, or 61 percent of estimated cost increases since the 2004 estimate.

PA executive director Shorris was in a difficult position, as discussed more fully in the next chapter. Trying to explain why costs had escalated so much, he parsed the components of cost increases to argue, "These non-transportation related increases could well be considered as inflation in general site infrastructure (since they support elements like the Trade Center's chiller plant, excavation of the areas under SPI's towers, new watermains, and the like). If increases in these program elements were excluded, the cost of the transportation project itself (plus the other work in the original scope) could be considered as running about $2.4 billion."[12] In other words, scope creep was the culprit, even though it was a rational strategy when the money was "free."

Assessing the Port Authority's technical management capacities to execute on time and on budget constituted an important element of oversight, and on this front, the monthly oversight reports were particularly critical. A continuous chronicle of major issues and problems, estimated cost increases, schedule delays, and insufficient staff strength and project controls compelled the LMRO to intensify its oversight during 2007.[13] In an attempt to maintain the Hub construction cost budget and target schedule, the WTC Construction Department, headed by Steven P. Plate, had initiated a process of simplifying the design to facilitate construction; however, as the especially telling September 2007 oversight report noted, these in-house design changes "do not offset many of the current or forecast cost overruns."

Although Plate's department continued to hold to the position that it would finish the project within the $2.221 billion budget and the June 2011 schedule forecast, senior staff in the department believed otherwise and told the FTA that because this budget and schedule could not be met, it was preparing modifications to both. The track record of poor management undermined the credibility of this response. The Achilles heel of the Hub project was the PA's project management structure and insufficient staffing of its WTC Construction Department. The evident management issues stemmed from the WTC Construction Department's "disengagement" from the WTC Engineering Department's Construction Management Division, according to the FTA's consultants, and, as a result, "many program and project managers do not appear to have awareness and control of the project/contract budgets, cost estimates-at-completion and schedules for which they are responsible."[14]

Neutered bureaucratic prose could not hide the increasing tone of frustration filtering through the FTA's monitoring reports, particularly when it came to the assessment of cost risks. The WTC Construction Department "continues to provide old and unreliable data"; the PA's reported costs reflect "overly optimistic" projections or "do not include most likely costs for Contract Packages that are currently in Final Design and, in some case, under construction."[15] Forces other than the chaos inside the Port Authority's management of the Hub project were legitimately impacting all of the FTA-funded recovery projects in lower Manhattan— rising construction material and fuel prices and intense competition with other major projects in the New York City area, including two other projects being funded by the FTA (Second Avenue Subway and East Side Access, a $10 billion megaproject designed to bring the Long Island Railroad into a new East Side station to be built below and incorporated into Grand Central Terminal targeted for completion in 2022). But as the FTA's investigator general report of September 2008 noted, these were not enough to explain the big cost overruns and schedule delays at the Port Authority's Hub project.

By March 2008, the relationship between the FTA and the Port Authority was broken and close to a complete shutdown. For months, the monitoring reports had been replete with recommendations as to what the Port Authority needed to do to address the major issues and problems impeding its effective execution of the Hub project (many of which also impacted the Vehicle Security Center, a companion infrastructure project designed to provide centralized security for truck delivery and underground parking at the Trade Center, also funded by the federal government, and separately monitored). Since the PA was clearly not going to be able to meet the milestone dates and costs as agreed upon in the construction agreement, the LMRO twice requested the WTC Construction Department to submit a recovery plan, and twice the LMRO had found the submitted recovery plans "unacceptable"; it made a third request that March. The PA was apparently foot-dragging, bureaucratically pushing against the FTA funding requirements. The inspector general's report concluded that the recovery plans were not being used in line with their original intention—to identify actions that could enable grantees to "recover" the baseline cost and schedule estimates contained in the construction agreement. Rather, they had been "treated largely as a way to document the reasons for increases or delays."[16]

The semiautonomous agency was used to conducting its business its own way without oversight. It had "developed its own cost estimates and they were done professionally and independently," based upon 50 percent completion of the ultimate design documents and the project scope known at that time, staff in the WTC Construction Department stated in the PA's required response to the highly critical March 2008 report. Staff also "claimed that its construction schedule, although aggressive, reflected time frames that were realistic." The facts told a different story, as the inspector general reported: "The Port Authority's disagreement with the FTA, however, does not change the fact that its projects have experienced significant estimated cost increases and schedule delays." Port Authority staff weakly acknowledged that the FTA's risk process was "a good tool overall," but the staff was "at odds" with the FTA "on the degrees of risk assigned to certain areas of the project." A "better product" would result if PA staff members could be "more involved with the risk assessment process."[17] In disagreeing with the overall message of the March 2008 report and contending that the PA's management had been sufficient overall, the agency's executive director was protecting the institution he was so proud to be a part of, but this fiction of on time and on budget was about to explode.

However much pursued in the spirit of partnership, the FTA's intense oversight did not allow the agency to exercise authority over the ever-worsening situation—until the PA's lack of compliance ultimately threatened funding for both the Hub and the Vehicle Security Center. The major problems had been identified early and often, but the semiautonomous agency was unwilling, the FTA wrote in response to the inspector general's audit of its oversight management, "to take aggressive actions necessary to better control cost and schedule issues that were within their control." Its "failure to make effective use of this information" was leading down a path whereby the institution known for its past engineering prowess would be "found not to have the technical capacity to carry out the project, unless it took further action."[18] That was a serious threat, finally.

Although the FTA had a limited set of tools to "ensure" that its recommendations led to action, the Port Authority's lack of action to address project risks that had been identified over the course of nearly two years, its resistance to incorporating the FTA's risk-management process into its overall management of the project, and its reluctance to provide information jeopardized FTA officials' ability to perform the agency's fiduciary responsibilities. The situation, in typical bureaucratic language, was "disturbing." After more than four years of oversight, the grantor-grantee relationship had hit the extreme, and in the extreme the FTA had two options: It could withhold funds or declare a project in default. These were last-resort options because, inevitably, they would result in further cost increases and schedule delays, not to mention political embarrassment for both players. But FTA officials now considered "suspending the Port Authority's ability to draw down from the Federal funds provided for its two recovery projects."[19] Port Authority officials, including board chairman Coscia, got the message. Finally, the agency started to address many of the risk-based items on the FTA's list. By that time, however, many of the embedded cost and schedule problems were beyond radical rollback, and it was politically impossible for the PA to roll back its commitment to the transportation phoenix. Top management at the Port Authority was about to change, and repairing the frayed relationship with the FTA would be high on the to-do list for the agency's next executive director.

SPIRALING OUT OF CONTROL

A big problem hovered over the Transportation Hub. It was a problem rarely mentioned in the press, despite all the coverage of schedule delays and escalating costs.

It was rooted in the contracting relationship for building the Hub and became a bottleneck thwarting construction efficiencies and cost control. When the decision about how to contract for construction of the Hub was made in November 2004, it seemed to be the most rational approach, but by October 2006, it had become a monitoring concern and by March 2008, unworkable. However, it remained unresolved until April 2009. The approach, determined in conjunction with the FTA, combined construction management services and general contractor in a single contract relationship—abbreviated as CM/GC. It was an unusual approach. As memorialized in the deliberately dry language of the Port Authority's board meeting minutes, the "determination was reached, in part, due to the recognition that it would be advantageous to have construction manager services during the final design phase provided by the entity that will be responsible for the ultimate construction of the project."[20] A difficult reality would impair the intent of the complex contracting arrangement.

At the time the Port Authority signed the $1.1 billion contract with the joint venture of four major contractors in New York City—Fluor Enterprises, Slattery Skanska, Bovis Lend Lease, and Granite Halmar Construction Company—in late January 2006, the Hub design was incomplete and officially tied to Pataki's unrealistic schedule deadlines. A groundbreaking ceremony for the project had already been held almost five months earlier, in September 2005. There was urgency to push forward, even without final key design decisions for the project. This sowed seeds of future major problems. The contract with the joint venture working as Phoenix Constructors, a name with a symbolic resonance, was not structured with the built-in schedule or cost controls typical of large-scale construction contracts. According to one close insider to the project, had the Port Authority tried to impose such accountability measures, the bids would have skyrocketed because there was so much risk in bidding on complex designs that were not yet complete. The necessary early work packages were negotiated on an individual basis, with payment on a "time and materials" basis rather than "utilizing contracting arrangements that would most effectively limit the Port Authority's cost exposure and make sure the contractor's interests are aligned with the agency's interest in getting the job done promptly—such as guaranteed maximum price or 'lump sum' contract" (as Ward, who inherited the arrangement, later explained in his June 2008 assessment report laying out the many problems thwarting progress at the site). "These huge companies who are competitors," said Plate in early 2008, "are now forged into a team that has to share risk."[21] Actually, paying the bills under the "time-and-materials" contract made it full-risk to the Port Authority.

The arrangement remained problematic. The anticipated benefits of the PA's partnering relationship—beneficial construction management services prior to a guaranteed-maximum-price contract, efficient contract procurement, and appropriate self-performance of early contracts—"have not materialized," the FTA's PMOC consultants wrote in every monthly monitoring report from June 2006, just six months after the Phoenix consortium had been awarded the contract for work on the Hub, to December 2007, when the $200 million first phase of the CM/GM contract was nearing completion. Just eight months after Phoenix was on board, the trade magazine *Engineering News-Record* wrote of problems the joint venture was experiencing with cumbersome subcontractor procurement rules imposed by the FTA and the Port Authority that were "scaring away bidders, even in this early stage."[22]

Moreover, Phoenix could only recommend a subcontractor to the Port Authority, which had final approval—a fundamental difference between construction management in the public sector compared to practice in the private sector. In the private sector, a developer hires a construction manager (CM) who is paid to get the job done; the contract is structured for performance. The CM makes decisions for the developer, including hiring subcontractors, and brings the completed job to the developer, typically with incentive rewards for on-time and on-budget performance and penalties otherwise. In the public sector, the concept of a construction manager is different; it "lends" personnel to the public sector, which is still making all the decisions. As provided for in the first of two phases of the Phoenix venture's scope of work, the CM/GC would provide input and assistance to the Port Authority "in decision-making, constructability reviews, contract packaging, and budget and schedule control," as well as construction manager services to begin the construction of the WTC PATH Terminal's critical early action construction items.[23] This phase was supposed to lead to a second phase of construction for the remainder of the project (approximately $900 million), at a negotiated guaranteed maximum price. However, Phoenix and the Port Authority never got there. By March 2008, the Port Authority had an intensive plan to pull back from the Phoenix venture, although this did not happen for another year, until April 2009.

Phoenix could not get to the bottom line of what would be built, and that had financial implications for the venture. It was the other side of the story. Stakeholders were always changing the design of what would be built. Also, at some point, Phoenix was told for "integrity purposes," it could not self-perform project work (instead of subcontracting); it could only manage the project. "The Trade Center," explained Denise M. Richardson, executive director of the association for unionized heavy construction workers, the General Contractors Association of New York, "was supposed to be a design-build process," a method to deliver a project in which design and construction services are combined. That is not atypical of large-scale projects; it is the only way to get a project going immediately. "The

Phoenix venture had two of the best heavy construction firms, but they were hamstrung. The thing they do best, they were not allowed to do. If they had been able to self-perform, the project may not have had the problems it had," she told me. "Self-performing work is how a CM makes money—by being efficient, having a good set of plans and specifications. A construction manager does not make money by serving in an administrative capacity."[24] The combination of incomplete design work on a highly complex structure with constant changes being made along the way, the CM/CG arrangement with a weak contract structure, and the lack of self-performing work all undermined the chances for controlling costs and meeting schedule milestones for the Hub project. Internal relationship problems—the four contractors reportedly never got into a cooperative, working rhythm—further beset the venture. And these types of partnership problems undermined prospects for project performance.

The day-to-day work effort of Port Authority staff, the agency's dedication to the institution's reputation-redemptive project, and the memory of its own who were victims of the 9/11 attack easily got lost amid the mistakes and miscalculations of senior officials aired in news reports. There would always be critics of the authority, its lumbering bureaucratic ways, lack of accountability, and institutional hubris. But the critics of the Hub's "overblown extravagance" were late in coming out. When the project was conceived after 9/11, PATH was a commuter system of thirteen stations with over 67,000 riders boarding at the World Trade Center station each day (over 140,000 daily trips) and 15,000 pedestrians traveling through the terminal each day. In comparison, 458,000 combined Metro North commuters and subway riders moved in and out of Grand Central Terminal every weekday (not counting additional pedestrian pass-through). The Port Authority, under Governor Pataki's supporting directive, was building an edifice and projecting ridership of 80,000 passengers per day (over 175,000 daily trips) and 250,000 total pedestrians using the terminal, but its ambitious projections for the future still did not come close to the intense activity of Grand Central Terminal, or Penn Station, which handles through traffic of some 600,000 commuter rail and Amtrak passengers on an average daily basis. "We were all victims of group think," Richardson told me many years later. "We lost an opportunity, an opportunity to get past the psychological impact of 9/11 and send a message: 'We can come back bigger and better.' But with the Trade Center mired in so much constant controversy, rebuilding hasn't sent that message—at least not yet."[25]

Large-scale public-works projects are risky projects chronically prone to cost overruns. This has been true in the United States as well as abroad for as long as the public sector has been building infrastructure and transportation and economic development projects. Endemic economic and political forces inevitably impact cost escalation. As compellingly studied by academics for several decades, large and statistically significant cost overruns are rooted in systematic cost underestimations. The most extensive research has been done by Bent Flyvberg working with several colleagues. They carefully analyzed 258 large road and rail projects in twenty countries on five continents built between 1927 and 1998, and found cost underestimation to be a global phenomenon. Far from being an exception, cost underestimation occurred in 90 percent of the cases; on average, actual costs were 28 percent higher than estimated costs, and often much higher; the tendency toward underestimation did not diminish over the seventy-year study period; and transportation projects appeared no more prone to cost underestimation than other types of large-scale public-works projects. Based on their research as well as earlier study by others, cost underestimation resulted from tactics in the pursuit of project approvals rather than innocent technical forecasting mistakes or overly optimistic project outcomes. Their bottom-line conclusion straightforwardly put: "the cost estimates used in public debates, media coverage, and decision making for transportation infrastructure development are highly, systematically, and significantly deceptive."[26]

The $2.221 billion figure for the permanent WTC PATH Terminal project continuously cited by Governor Pataki, the Port Authority, and the media was never a "cost" or even an "estimate" in the true sense of being the product of analysis based on a design, engineering, or construction-pricing study. The federal government had allocated $4.55 billion to transportation recovery projects in lower Manhattan (much short of Governor Pataki's wish list of more than a dozen projects, including several that had little to do with 9/11, with a total price tag of $7.5 billion), and let the state decide which projects to finance with the award. The five projects eventually funded were sized to fit the money available. The $2.221 billion for the Hub was an allocation number; it became the "budget" for the project when the Port Authority's board of commissioners authorized the Hub project on July 28, 2005.

Between 2005 and 2007, construction costs throughout the United States increased dramatically, driven by rising global demand for essential construction commodities like steel and concrete as well as surging nonresidential construction spending. General contractors in New York City were reporting 12 percent construction cost increases in 2006 and 11 percent increases in 2007, according to a report of the New York Building Congress, but these general construction cost pressures would not suffice to explain the picture that was about to emerge when the Phoenix venture's cost estimate—between $2.7 billion and $3.4 billion, or some $1.2 billion or more over the original budget—made news headlines in early February 2007. Lulled by silence on what the Port Authority's ambitious Hub project would really cost, this first slug of reality came as a shock. In a memorandum to agency chairman Anthony R. Coscia and commissioner Anthony J. Sartor, chair of the WTC Redevelopment Subcommittee, Executive Director Shorris warned that "while approximately 20 percent of the project has gone to bid and has come in generally within budget, we have concerns that the project may be at risk of cost escalations." He questioned Phoenix's estimates because they "rely on outdated 2005 data using preliminary design drawings, rather than updated designs that factor in ongoing value engineering and bid schedules," and notified the joint venture that those cost figures were "simply unacceptable."[27] It was now unambiguously clear that the FTA's $280 million project reserve would be needed. Reining in costs to keep within the $2.5 billion budget was going to be exceedingly difficult, and involve an ongoing battle of trading off design elements, value-engineering practicality, constructability, and political considerations. Shorris pledged to preserve the "overall integrity" of Calatrava's iconic design, but time and further rapidly escalating costs would threaten even that.

CRISIS CONTROL

As soon as it became clear that the Port Authority was going to miss the deadlines memorialized in the Master Development Agreement for handing over two of the three development sites to Larry Silverstein, the press zoomed in on this newest episode of delay with headlines of what it would cost. "Port Authority Could Owe Larry Silverstein $12 M Plus for Delays" (NYO), "Deadline Dummies: Blown WTC Target Dates Costs PA 300G a Day" (NYP), "Port Authority's Inability to Rebuild Quickly at WTC Site Will Cost Taxpayers" (DN). For an institution defined by its legacy of engineering excellence, the continuous negative coverage hit hard; the wound to its professional pride was a high-profile public embarrassment.

For the former investment bankers who crafted the penalty provisions, Deputy Mayor Daniel L. Doctoroff and EDC president Seth Pinsky, the deadlines were functioning as intended: exerting public pressure for site delivery in a timely manner so the project could move forward in a predicable fashion. During 2006 negotiations the pair had insisted that the PA's plan for turnover of the East Bathtub sites include a real set of deadlines with financial consequences. "Even though the Port Authority missed the dates, it moved more rapidly than might have been the case," Pinsky told me in 2011; "the Port Authority had to get to the timelines." Shorris considered the missed-dates penalty approach embedded in the MDA naïve. "The situation is bigger and more complex than the sophisticated financial engineering structure can handle. There are many ways out of the situation without going to court," he said referring to the arbitration that resulted, but "the financing engineering set up pressures."[28]

From the authority's perspective, the financial net effect of this $14.4 million penalty—$4.4 million, after taking into account the $10 million incentive payment the authority did not have to pay the contractors for finishing on time—was relatively minor considering the total 6.7-acre excavation job tagged at $250 million; the daily cost of the $300,000 a day in liquidated damages was also nearly canceled out by the $215,726 a day in rent the developer was paying the Port Authority (out of insurance proceeds). If the authority missed the turnover deadline for the next site on the schedule (as marked in figure 14.3), the Tower 2 site (which it did), the penalty clock would start up again. When the penalties ended with the final site turnover for Tower 2 in late August 2009, the runup cost for being in the penalty box on all three sites, as reported in the Port Authority's 2009 Annual Report, had reached approximately $140 million, large in absolute size but relatively small considering the PA's overall financial exposure at the time across all its rebuilding projects at Ground Zero: approximately $11 billion. Though not quantifiable, the reputational cost to the Port Authority was near irreversible.

Despite the penchant of the press to constantly view conditions at Ground Zero in the negative, some slippage could legitimately be expected given the scope and complexity of the specific engineering task and the widely accepted fact within the world of real estate development that site conditions are typically the most unpredictable part of ground-up construction. The subterranean geology of Ground Zero was especially tricky. "It's a very complex, challenging area with a lot of unpredictable obstructions," remarked Guy Nordenson, a professor of structural engineering at Princeton, whose engineering firm was involved with the site. "You can do a lot of mapping there, and you'll still find the unexpected." The surprise was rock—lots of it, twice the amount of bedrock the construction managers expected. "Our initial estimates were based on test borings, but they're not really maps. You only find out when you're down there," said Shorris. And when they got down there, seventy feet below the street, the engineers hit quartz, a much harder rock than the Manhattan schist they expected. In one area, as reported in the *Times*, "the workers had to excavate down to 120 feet to reach bedrock because engineers encountered an ancient gorge in a former glacial streambed." The slippage of eleven days for the first turnover site (Tower 4) was "on time in a normal world," Shorris told me; the second (Tower 3), which was forty-eight days late, was also "pretty good."[29]

Other construction slippages reported by the press were not as easy for the Port Authority to explain away. First on the list was the completion of the memorial. In mid-December 2007, at a committee meeting of the authority's board of commissioners, Plate announced a revision of the schedule that pushed back the opening of Memorial Plaza to 2010 and the Memorial Museum and Visitors Center to

2011—two years past the 2009 originally scheduled opening. Not long after that, it was timeline setbacks and recurring cost-escalation problems for the Calatrava-designed Transportation Hub. In its January 2008 monthly report, the FTA's Lower Manhattan Recovery Office told federal administrators in Washington, D.C., that the consultant's forecast for the completion of the terminal was November 2013, four years past its originally planned opening in 2009; construction work to date, consultants Carter & Burgess noted, "has tended to take almost twice as long as originally anticipated."[30] Meanwhile, the official position of the Port Authority was that the terminal would open for passengers by the end of 2011, with all of its underground connectors ready by 2012.

The agency was also holding to its position that costs for the much heralded avian-like PATH Hub could be kept within a $2.5 billion budget by making design changes through value engineering. Value engineering aims to make a design more efficient, but it is also "a state of mind" about good management to control cost and create value by managing the architectural team, the contractors, and others involved in the building process. "If it comes too late in the process," said a highly experienced construction management professional, "it impacts too many things already done—for example, the sculptural steel elements already ordered—and limits the adjustments." It is an important tool, but the ability to create value, he emphasized, starts with strong management and clear leadership; it starts with the right program (right sized for what the structure will be used for) and the right design (designed efficiently), after which value engineering comes into the picture. It is the "icing on the cake" in a complex project such as the Transportation Hub. The message of the short lesson on value engineering in my off-the-record interview was clear: "Muddled silos of control" do not easily translate to control. The PA was evidently starting to value-engineer its train station at a late stage in the process. It had allowed itself to get locked into a "runaway train" going a hundred miles an hour with no conductor. It had hired a high-risk architect with a reputation for insensitivity to cost. And the program for the iconic train station was "wrong," because it was oversized for the limited ridership of the PATH station at the Trade Center. Like the Freedom Tower, it was a political project.

In telling the press that construction costs generally had been rising faster than the generation of value-engineering ideas to contain costs, Shorris was signaling what was about to come into view: "Right now," he said, "we don't think all of these changes get us all the way to where we need to go."[31] He had already informed Governor Spitzer and others in the governor's office of the financial challenges facing the agency on the Hub project; in a seven-page memo, he detailed the sources of increasing project cost, the dramatic (and likely controversial) changes that would have to be made to the Calatrava vision for the agency to keep within the initial budget for the PATH transit hall, and the likely consequences of those changes and reactions of various direct stakeholders—Calatrava, New Jersey board commissioners, FTA, and the lower Manhattan community, including Assembly Speaker Silver.[32] Worried that the risk of "large cost overruns would damage the agency's credibility as a builder and potentially (though unfairly) the Governor's as well," he recommended, "with some regret, that we proceed with the proposed changes."[33] Nothing came of this recommendation. A month after summarizing these options for cost control, Shorris was forced out by Governor Paterson and left in late April. The Transportation Hub would remain untouchable until Ward's assessment was completed in the fall of 2008. One did not need to be a confirmed skeptic of progress at Ground Zero to believe that the reported runaway costs and endless delays at the Transportation Hub were guaranteed to spill over to other parts of the big project—in particular, to the Silverstein tower sites because they shared the cavernous underground acres of the East Bathtub. The longest delay in site turnover would be that for Tower 2, late by some 419 days and a pivot point for the first of two formal conflicts between the Port Authority and Silverstein and triggering the arbitration procedure laid out in the 2006 re-alignment agreement.[34]

The December 2008 ruling on this first arbitration episode was revealing. In their opinion, not made public but which I obtained through a Freedom of Information request, the arbitrators said that the conflict over turnover delay was not the exclusive province of any one party, but rather symptomatic of a deep fault line between the Port Authority and the developer. The PA was found to be at fault on the majority of technical issues by the three-person panel, which also concluded that the two certificates of turnover completion the PA provided as of October 5, 2008, "represent an attempt by the PA to cut off the liquidated damages payments."[35] In retrospect, it seemed clear that the Port Authority had handed over the two sites too early, as I was later told by an agency insider at that time.

Although the panel cited the complexity of the task at hand and duly noted "admirable" cooperation of the PA and Silverstein Properties in resolving many of the conflicts and problems of the project, its discussion of the individual issues on which it was ruling repeatedly emphasized problems of communication and a lack of coordination between the PA and the developer. "Both parties must realize they are working in the real world," the ruling said with regard to site 4 issues. The panel directed—not just suggested—the parties "to cooperate and as rapidly as is reasonably possible to work out solutions to the problems presented by the change in plans for the underpinning of the subway box and the associated excavation." On site 2 issues, it emphasized "access" as a problem that was "obvious" when the MDA was entered into. Congested traffic filled lower Manhattan's narrow streets.

Plus, the simultaneous construction of three office towers, the Freedom Tower, and the Transportation Hub was "destined to be a major headache for everyone." Only if all parties cooperated "in dealing with conditions as they arise and change at the site" could a solution be found to the access problem. The panel rejected Silverstein's argument on the problem of access as being "too verbalistic and unrealistic" and pointed out that his argument "ignores the express provisions in the MDA about cooperating with the PA as conditions change." It admonished both sides that "the level of cooperation must increase, particularly in communicating with respect to problems as soon as they arise."[36]

The politically driven timetable of the Master Development Agreement pushed by the Pataki administration was a setup for failure. The dates were impossibilities because they were unmoored to the reality of what had to be accomplished in excavating the East Bathtub to deliver development-ready sites to Silverstein. Addressing the political origins of this timetable fell far afield of the arbitration panel's technical scope of review. And although the exact details of how the MDA dates were set remain murky, despite my queries of numerous players, not so the falsehood of expectations embedded in that timetable. Both the WTC Construction Department and the agency's Engineering Department might have put forth more conservative dates that never saw the light of day. By this time, however, Governor Pataki's speeches had laid out an aggressive and wishful timetable for construction that his loyalists hoped would provide evidence of tangible accomplishment at Ground Zero before the governor left office at the end of 2006.

The PA Engineering Department, which had been responsible for completing the foundation up to grade for the original World Trade Center complex, could not raise the issue to the level of awareness needed to flag the timetable issue because it was not involved with construction at Ground Zero, and it did not see the FTA monitoring reports. As efforts moved from rescue, recovery, and cleanup to rebuilding of the interim PATH station, the Port Authority chief engineer and his department had only a supportive role: primarily reviewing all work to ensure that any design and construction at the site conformed to applicable New York City building code standards, to which the agency had formally agreed in a memorandum of understanding with the City Department of Building in November 1993, months after the February 1993 terrorist bombing of the World Trade Center garage. Might the outcome have been different if the chief engineer and his department had been an integral part of the construction process instead of merely consigned to a role of code review and materials inspection? "The engineering department is cautious, and might not have agreed to many of those dates in the MDA," one former executive director told me. "It has always given itself long dates and large contingencies. It doesn't play the classic Robert Moses game: Once you've started, you're in and the rest of the money will have to come in. Steve Plate is much more a politician than those in the engineering department."

Insider Warnings

Less than two months after the PA and Silverstein signed the MDA documents, in January 2007, with the new Spitzer administration in Albany, a small set of pivotal players—Deputy Mayor Doctoroff, LMDC chairman Schick, and PA executive director Shorris—were briefed on the impossibility of meeting the completion date for the East Bathtub on time and on budget. (The same applied to other projects on the site.) The preliminary review initiated in fall 2006 by Governor Pataki's office and prepared by the Lower Manhattan Construction Command Center made explicitly clear "that project schedules and plans raised significant issues in terms of construction logic, activity durations, and constructability."[37]

The LMCCC was another new government entity operating in lower Manhattan. It had been established by executive orders of the governor and the mayor in November 2004, and charged with coordination and general oversight of all lower Manhattan construction projects, approximately $20 billion of infrastructure replacement and renewal. Downtown property owners and business interests had pushed for its creation. They had been suffering from the amount of work taking place on the streets of downtown, which were constantly being torn up, sometimes for weeks and months on end as a result of significant coordination problems among utility companies. The LMCCC was intended to be totally independent. It operated under executive orders, but was housed in the LMDC offices, which tended to produce tensions between the two government entities.

The LMCCC's task was something akin to "cat herding" players—and there were a lot of them—who were not well conditioned to working together: city and state transportation departments, the Port Authority, the Metropolitan Transportation Authority, the Battery Park City Authority, the LMDC, Silverstein Properties, Verizon, Consolidated Edison, cable and telecommunications companies, the city's design and construction department, the Economic Development Corporation, the city's police and fire departments, and at least five other agencies and bodies. It meant "getting people to put aside agendas" and focus on the greater objective of rebuilding lower Manhattan, "so we don't get weighed down in minutiae and weighed down in obstructions," said Charles J. Maikish, the LMCCC's first executive director.[38] Commanding the power to do what needed to be done, however, would be challenging. The big institutions with legacy and power would not want to give it away. Maikish was a perfect choice to head the new agency, well respected in the downtown community, but, as one insider remarked to me, "some institutional feathers were probably ruffled when the LMCCC was set up."

Born and raised in the Bronx, Maikish had spent the majority of his adult professional life in lower Manhattan and played an active role in several downtown organizations. Similarly, his association with the World Trade Center had been very long and very close. He joined the Port Authority in 1968 as a construction inspector and field engineer; one of his jobs, in the mud, was to "strike bedrock around the twin towers' foundations with an iron bar to determine from the sound, whether it was solid enough to build on." From engineering, he moved to law, and after finishing New York Law School at night, he worked as a trial attorney defending claims against the authority from 1974 to 1984. "I was fresh out of law school and got my own trials to manage; this never would have happened in a private law firm, where I would have been carrying someone's briefcase and working papers for years before getting my own trial responsibility," he told me. "The PA was good to me, sent me to Harvard Business School's mid-career program [the Advanced Management Program]," he added. From litigation, he moved into project management as director of ferry transportation, and, at the time of the 1993 terrorist bombing of the World Trade Center, he was heading the one department responsible for overall management of the World Trade Center—everything from operations, marketing, leasing, capital investment program, budgeting, and financial management to redevelopment. That also included spearheading the recovery and repair of the underground infrastructure that had been destroyed in the bombing. Maikish thought the repair job would take eight months. Governor Mario Cuomo believed people needed to get back to normalcy as soon as possible; he wanted the work done in three weeks! It got done in three weeks, Maikish said. "It was an incredible task that we had at that time; he was everywhere" said William H. Goldstein, the former deputy executive director for capital programs at the Port Authority. "He had the same suit on four days later. We declared him an environmental hazard."[39]

Afterward he and Frank J. Lombardi, the chief engineer of the authority, overhauled evacuation procedures; they removed stores and created new corridors in the shopping concourse so people could exit more quickly in case of emergency. "They had done underground what could not be done to the towers themselves: given more people chances to get out," wrote Jim Dwyer and Kevin Flynn in *102 Minutes: The Untold Story of the Fight to Survive inside the Twin Towers*. Maikish also privatized some business functions of the World Trade Center, selling the Vista Hotel before leaving the Port Authority in 1996, after twenty-eight years, for the private sector, where he held senior executive positions managing large-scale physical facilities, first for Columbia University and then for J. P. Morgan Chase.

Now he was returning to lower Manhattan, bringing well-honed skills, a tight emotional attachment to the place, and a deep understanding of the politics of the Port Authority. He was "the obvious choice," said Doctoroff. "We knew we had to find somebody who could establish credibility immediately."[40]

The LMCCC's mission, imprinted on its logo, was to facilitate, mitigate, and communicate. The way Maikish saw it, part of the mission involved looking at the timelines being told to the public—what they could expect to see rebuilt and when. "Our job was to bring discipline to the coordination effort of billions of dollars of construction work across more than one hundred public and private projects going on in lower Manhattan," he told me. "There were all sorts of problems and construction tie-ups" with so many government and private players operating in the same space. "And no one was talking to one another," Maikish said years later in a voice still full of exasperation.[41]

A committee of senior executives empowered to make decisions and working together toward a common goal without turf boundaries might—and the emphasis is on the word *might*—have been the kind of organization that could have gotten the job done from day one. But the LMCCC was not endowed with the structural power to coordinate. "It was a classic example of government overthinking the issue and putting to paper what sounded logical, but in practice made no sense," said one insider close to the issues. "The fundamental problem was that ultimately the Port Authority was on the hook for this project—certainly from a financial standpoint,[42] but also from a political one. So the idea that a separate entity was going to call the shots was DOA. The other problem was that the Port Authority and Silverstein held the contracts for all the major projects." The vacuum in central leadership gave Maikish the opportunity to position the LMCCC's mission in an expansive way, and the organization produced effective marketing materials that indicated it was pulling it all together, but with the layering of so many projects in lower Manhattan and so many conflicting priorities, it would become paralyzed politically, recalled another close insider.

Maikish organized a risk-assessment review, taking place in what was known as the Construction Coordinating Room (CCR), off-limits to all but a few, for obvious reasons. As described in the agency's 2007 report, the CCR was "a non-public locked facility that allows the parties to discuss openly their schedules and construction issues without fear that any issues identified would become public." It was set up after the LMCCC's initial review of the PA's August 2006 integrated schedule[43] revealed that "the outside influences on the project schedules" were "a major barrier" to developing an integrated schedule for coordination of site construction at Ground Zero. These outside influences—the financial and political milestones for the memorial, Goldman Sachs, and SPI—were linked to rebuilding's project schedules, and as the LMCCC's sterilized prose explained, the schedules "were not appropriate topics for public discussion by project personnel." Empowered by Governor Pataki and Mayor Bloomberg, both of whom had to sign off on the initiative because state and city agencies were involved, this technical review panel had as its goal bringing all stakeholders to the table to evaluate and assess the impediments to on-time, on-budget delivery of the projects.

After meeting twice weekly for two months, participants in the CCR process had gathered enough data from stakeholders to understand that the scope of significant issues and timeline implications clearly contradicted the false assurances being given the public. In its briefing in January 2007 to the small set of executive players (Schick, Doctoroff, and Shorris), the LMCCC identified "serious potential delays and construction breakages" and "pointed out that these issues could translate into significant additional costs—potentially exceeding available sources of funding." On the basis of that presentation, the executive group directed the LMCCC to assemble a team of "world-class, knowledgeable, mega project experts to confirm the magnitude of the problem" and authorized a budget up to $1 million for a two-week workshop to validate the results of the CCR process. With knowledge of the problems and cost-benefit program trade-offs, adjustments to scopes, schedules, and budgets could then be undertaken.[44]

The workshop brought together twenty-two world-class experts experienced in megaproject organization and construction, consummate professionals whose combined experiences tracked the world's largest, most complex high-profile developments, among them Britain's Channel Tunnel, Boston's Central Artery program, MTA's East Side Access program, JFK's redevelopment program, Hong Kong's Kowloon Station, and the only Calatrava structure built in the United States, the Milwaukee Art Museum Addition. Tasked with evaluating the scope, schedules, logistical, and construction interfaces between the many projects on the Trade Center site, they were asked to provide risk assessment and risk analysis, as well as mitigation scenarios that "could reduce regional cost impacts, increase benefits, and establish an optimal schedule for the program." This was a monumental task for a two-week workshop, even for world-class experts. As explained in a detailed description of the process appearing in a technical industry publication two years later by the person the LMCCC hired to lead and manage the process, Robert N. Harvey, "the design documents amounted to tens of thousands of drawing sheets at different design stages, and the combined project schedules amounted to approximately 20,000 activities, again at different development stages."[45]

Value planning may have been a standard practice used in the construction management industry, but the agencies involved nevertheless resisted the effort. The PA, in particular, did not want anyone looking over its shoulder. The Trade

Center was its site, and it had finally gained control over it. All of the agencies signed on to the review process, however reluctantly, on the condition that the work material would become confidential. "This could not be debated in the press," said Maikish; "that would have taken it out of the hands of the experts. The process would go public when the solutions were clear."[46]

As revealing as they were, the team's findings were not a huge surprise to insiders, but the review did serve a political purpose. "No one wanted to face reality," Avi Schick, then chairman of the LMDC, told me. "The report was a way of raising an alarm, a four-way alarm—to the city, the state, the PA, and the other stakeholders and contractors—a way to force people to address questions," he said.[47] After being told all along that the project could be delivered in 2009–2010, they were now being told it would be 2012, 2014, 2015, and 2016. The tenth anniversary of 9/11 was on everyone's mind. The memorial, however, was not going to meet its scheduled September 2009 completion date, according to the Workshop's risk-adjusted schedule; it would be delayed nearly two years and only the memorial pools would be complete by the estimated August 2011 completion date.

Fourteen projects were listed in the table of completion dates presented in the LMCCC summary, and each of four of those—the Memorial Museum, Visitor Orientation and Education Center, Visitor Security Center, and Transportation Hub—faced estimated delays of almost five years. The value planning report amplified the timetable issues. It gave credence to the LMCCC's initial assessment of the daunting obstacles and logistical issues of how these projects interfaced with one another in complex fashion. To deal with the issues it identified, the team made five proposals, each considered essential for forward success: One: put in place a governance structure representing all of the stakeholders to be led by the Port Authority in order to rapidly make decisions to advance progress the programs; two: remove the No. 1 subway box or make permanent a structure to support it, because the box was a "major impediment to the construction of the site"; three: revise the memorial opening date to September 11, 2011, to assure a "positive experience for those attending"; four: simplify the design of the Transportation Hub or reuse the existing PATH station, because "the Calatrava designs contain features which are straining the Port Authority's ability to construct and fund the program" and resulting in a "consistent pattern of schedule slippage"; and five: implement a risk management structure to keep the "revised (improved) programs on track."[48]

Following institutional protocol, the LMCCC turned the value planning process over to the Port Authority. As lead agency for the Trade Center projects, its job was to come up with engineering solutions to the problems. In this second stage of the site-coordination process, which ran from April to September 2007, the

LMCCC agreed not to "vet durations," but rather focus on near-site logistics and interfaces of the many projects. During these six months, CCR discussions continued on several topics, and the PA worked on solutions for several of the critical path problems, including design simplification of the Calatrava station, micropiling for the No. 1 subway box, and an integrated schedule for the memorial site. But because the PA did not agree with the projected schedule dates identified by the Value Planning Workshop, its unwillingness to confront the reality of the report would continue for nearly eighteen months, during which the public remained in the dark about the significant slippages in completion dates.

Ambitions in Conflict

Fissures in this false façade opened in early September, just before the sixth anniversary of 9/11, when Schick publicly repudiated the Port Authority's schedule predictions in a breakfast-meeting speech before the Alliance for Downtown New York. After first crediting Governor Spitzer's administration with many initiatives for furthering the revival of lower Manhattan, he went on to report that the LMDC was working with an independent engineering firm to establish "a rigorous, independently vetted master rebuilding schedule that sets forth realistic and accurate dates by which the public can expect completion of the key projects on the site." When the work was done, he promised, Governor Spitzer would announce dates that would "not be symbolic, but real"—"no more false promises and no more false starts."[49]

Doubts about anything happening at Ground Zero in predictable fashion amounted to general currency about town, which is why this statement wasn't really news, though Schick's short message marked the first public airing of the project's illusionary dates, key milestones, and commitments so out of whack that the project to rebuild Ground Zero, as one insider put it, was just drifting. If Schick's statement was not quite a press release, it did officially create a breach and expose to those in the know internal wrangling between the PA and the LMDC about how to handle the gap between fiction and reality of the project timelines for Ground Zero project completions.

Behind the scenes, intense personal rivalry and disagreement over political strategy for dealing with the contradictory evidence was at play, and not until David A. Paterson assumed the governorship would the surreal impasse to progress yield to reality. As executive director of the Port Authority, Shorris was making decisions to protect the institution. As loyal lieutenant, Schick was pushing to protect Governor Spitzer from the fallout of missing Pataki's dates. The Gordian knot of this conflict, so revealing of the ambitions swirling about Ground Zero, further exacerbated the distrust and disbelief lodged in the minds of the public about rebuilding. The seeds of this conflict take us back a few steps in time.

By early spring of 2007, only weeks into his position, Shorris figured out that Pataki's dates were all wrong, a giant lie. Called up to Albany, where he rarely went, by Spitzer's staff, he was told to refute all of Pataki's dates because they were not real. As a practical matter, he was not sure that approach would work. As former first deputy executive director of the authority from 1991 to 1995, someone with in-depth insider knowledge who understood its bureaucratic culture and engineering legacy, he was reluctant to expose the institution's internal issues. As a public policy professional, he didn't want the Trade Center project to absorb his entire leadership tenure at the helm of the Port Authority as it had his predecessor, Kenneth Ringler, whom he viewed as crushed by the process of rebuilding Ground Zero. Privately, he vowed that while in the executive director's office he would focus on more than the Trade Center project. In December 2006, the authority had adopted an aggressive ten-year capital plan that promised to "return the agency to historic investments in transportation infrastructure,"[50] and Shorris very much wanted to advance its implementation to reestablish the Port's core mission and enhance the region's economic and social power. He was modeling himself on other executive directors who had adopted a more regional, versus New York–centric, view of their role. Nevertheless, the Trade Center site commanded his front-and-center attention.

When Spitzer became governor, three big issues at Ground Zero were "re-litigated" by his administration: the No. 1 subway, the Freedom Tower, and the timetable and budgets. There were big sessions on each of these items. The analysis was political. As part of the new governor's team, Shorris found himself engaged in a top-to-bottom review of the Freedom Tower, the project candidate Spitzer had been on record as saying could become "a white elephant" because it seemed to lack "economic viability." Candidate Spitzer was now Governor Spitzer, and "the No. 1 priority of the governor," Shorris said at the time his appointment was announced, "is to get ground zero moving. The last thing that any of us wants to see is a slowing down of the progress."[51] Spitzer's review of the Freedom Tower went nowhere, once again validating the classic Robert Moses strategy for getting big things done: Start a project and the rest of the money will have to come from somewhere to complete it because, as a practical matter, it is too hard to pull the plug once a project is far along.

In Albany, the timetables at Ground Zero soon became a point of debate among senior officials and the newly installed governor. Schick, who held dual positions with money-controlling power as president of the Empire State Development Corporation and chairman of the LMDC, became a forceful personality on the issue. At forty, he was "an important public policy player," Robin Finn wrote in a *Times* Public Lives profile.[52] He had worked for Spitzer for eight years in the New York State attorney general's office as deputy attorney general. He was lead prosecutor in the lawsuit against former chairman of the New York Stock Exchange Richard A. Grasso, who was ordered to repay $100 million of a compensation package because, the attorney general's office contended, it was in violation of state laws regarding nonprofit institutions. He had also represented New York in the $206 billion master settlement agreement with tobacco companies. He was very loyal to Spitzer. He believed the governor would be better off by repudiating the Pataki deadlines, and he pushed for openness with the public about the inevitable delays.

By being open, the governor would be off the hook of past problems, shielded from delivering late, and able to move forward with a clean start. Shorris baulked at that approach and countered. He argued that the policy objective was to rebuild as fast as possible and as cheaply as possible. Saying the dates were all lies and it would take x more years, he argued, would not move the project forward. It would just ease the pressure on contractors, who at that point did not have penalties or bonuses in their contracts. Better to keep pressure on the job and on the contractors by using the dates as levers to get the work done faster, to at least come closer to hitting the original target dates. This is a special category of rationalization, what political theory would classify as the "noble lie," the lie done for the public interest, that is to save taxpayers (or in this case toll payers) money.[53] Coscia, too, was behind staying with the aggressive timelines as a way to keep pressure on the bureaucracy, give the rebuilding effort a "much-needed clarity and a sense of constructive urgency," and direct issues up the hierarchy to the board of commissioners, which had committed to these deadlines.[54] With Spitzer's family background in real estate, Shorris believed the governor understood that contractors, publicly given more time, were unlikely to move faster. His argument held the day—for the time being—but it set off a big fight that lasted for months. Yet another reason why Schick struggled to gain traction with the governor, as one insider noted in a confidential e-mail to me, was that his credibility was challenged by the fact that the agency he was 100 percent in charge of, the LMDC, was responsible for overseeing the remediation and deconstruction of the Deutsche Bank Building, and it had been disastrously managed.[55]

The big fight entangled Schick and Shorris, personally and professionally. They were rivals. As soon as he learned of Schick's ESDC appointment at the press conference in which the governor-elect announced eleven other senior appointments besides his, Shorris thought, "trouble." Others considered Schick dangerous and sneaky. Schick was not only very smart, ambitious, and closely aligned to

the governor, he was powerfully connected to the legislative side of state government as well through long-standing family ties to Assembly Speaker Silver, who
had been mentored by Schick's father and who, in turn, mentored him and would
repeatedly advocate on his behalf. Schick had risen fast in the world of economic
development. He was an imposing physical presence, with a reputation as a
"steamroller"; his critics considered him a forceful, uncompromising, and slow-
moving bureaucrat. In turf battles and other fights, his prosecutorial style reportedly led him to spar with other officials, notably, Shorris and Maikish. In short, he
was not among the well liked of those working on rebuilding.[56]

Shorris had come back to the Port Authority with a polished policy resume. He
was well respected for his insider skills and breadth of service over more than
twenty-five years in public and not-for-profit management. He was someone who
had experienced control tactics and power plays inside city government as deputy
chancellor of operations and policy at the City Board of Education, as the city's
commissioner of finance under Mayor Koch and prior to that, as deputy budget
director. (Under the current administration of Mayor William de Blasio, he is first
deputy mayor.) Outside of government, he had served as executive vice president
and chief operating officer of one of the region's largest health care organizations
and as a consultant. For several years, he taught in the academy and directed
Princeton University's Policy Research Institute at the Woodrow Wilson School of
Public and International Affairs, where I first met him. And just before returning to
the Port Authority as its executive director, he had been a senior policy advisor
to the Spitzer-Paterson 2006 campaign, and then in the governor-elect's transition
office. His view of the timetable issue was being filtered through the lens of the
lesson he drew from the public fiasco surrounding the city's botched renovation of
the Wollman Skating Rink in Central Park. The high-profile delay embarrassed
Mayor Koch, especially after Donald Trump took over the job and completed the
interminably stalled renovation job below budget and in record time.[57] Shorris did
not believe that going public with Pataki's timetable deceit would be good for the
city, the governor, or the Port Authority.

He was being loyal to the institution, perhaps too loyal. As an appointed official, he (as others in a similar position) had to balance loyalty to a bureaucracy
(where he may only be passing through), loyalty to his boss, and loyalty to service
in the public interest. The three-way balance, as one seasoned policy official explained, presents challenges because the three constituencies are driven by different
needs: the elected official motivated by ambition seeks change; the bureaucracy
operates with expertise but typically resists change; and the public interest is
served by forthright debate, transparency, and accountability. From the public-
interest perspective, why didn't Shorris clear the decks and get all the skeletons

out of the closet, especially since the Hub situation was unlikely to stay shielded as the schedule slippage worsened?

Persistent in his efforts to prove to Governor Spitzer that the timetable was way off the mark and seeking as well to wrestle control over the Trade Center site away from Shorris, Schick commissioned an update of the 2006 LMCCC study. This too was fraught with tension, institutional and personal. The LMCCC reports to the governor and the mayor, but as a practical matter Maikish and the LMCCC reported to the city's deputy mayor for economic development and the LMDC board. As chairman of the LMDC, Schick pushed Shorris hard, using the LMCCC, which had the technical staff needed to do the in-depth timetable risk analysis, until he let the cat out of the bag at that early fall breakfast speech to downtown interests. Meantime, Shorris was not giving up on the dates. Toward the end of 2007, when the first of the "magical" dates with their $300,000-per-day penalty neared and the press started asking questions, Shorris realized that this was going to be a career-threatening event. He restructured contracts to give the contractors bonuses to get the job done faster and put on the "squeeze."

Only weeks after the Port Authority delivered two of the East Bathtub sites, Shorris's tenure at the agency was suddenly vulnerable once Lieutenant Governor Paterson was sworn in as governor after Spitzer resigned in disgrace over extra-marital activities with paid call girls. Shorris was forced out. Paterson nominated Chris Ward, managing director of the General Contractors Association of New York, to be the agency's new executive director. Ward would be looking closely at all those unrealistic deadlines and budgets inherited from the Spitzer administration—he had been told by the governor's chief of staff to "clean it up; this project can't be Paterson's mess."[58] Truth time had arrived, finally.

The Port Authority continued to stick to its unrealistic dates and budgets—in the face of the LMCCC's confidential update assessment drafted two months earlier concluding that the PA's adjustments to schedule timelines aimed at maintaining "end dates" contradicted actual progress in the field.[59] Keeping the issue contained within the institution appeared to protect its signature contribution to the rebuilding program, the Calatrava-designed Hub, while the agency worked to reengineer its complicated design. In an internal e-mail dated April 22, 2008, sent to the agency's head of capital projects William Goldstein and WTC construction head Steven Plate, Coscia wrote, "I cannot support any prospective adjustment of the existing deadlines at this time." The board of commissioners had committed to these deadlines "because we recognized the critical need to accelerate redevelopment of the WTC site and to introduce accountability to the rebuilding process. The deadlines have given the rebuilding effort much-needed clarity and a sense of construction urgency, and provide comfort to the public at large that the site will be fully rebuilt within a reasonable timeframe." Coscia also would not support any increase in the overall construction budget. "As a public agency, we must explore all possible alternatives before committing additional funds to the redevelopment effort. Keeping to the existing budget, even in the face of rising expenditures in the construction industry, imposes upon the agency a discipline to spend public resources responsibly." To direct this exploration, Coscia charged New Jersey–appointed commissioner Anthony J. Sartor with "lead responsibility on an interim basis" for oversight of the major program components and for directing a panel of engineering and financial experts to investigate "all available options to meeting the existing construction timetable without expending additional funds."[60]

Among commissioners, Sartor may have been the one most familiar with the rebuilding project, but, as time would reveal, he lacked the necessary independence to oversee the situation and impose discipline over cost and schedule. First appointed to the PA board in March 1999 by then governor Christine Todd Whitman, a Republican, and reappointed by Governor Jon Corzine, a Democrat, Sartor had been serving as chair of the WTC Redevelopment Subcommittee for years. It was a position in which he exercised broad control over many of the decisions made in the rebuilding of Ground Zero, in particular those involving the Port Authority's prized multibillion-dollar Hub project. He was the only commissioner whose tenure at the Port Authority reached back prior to 9/11, and the others came to rely on his knowledge of the Trade Center project and familiarity with construction contract matters. "He could talk the contractor talk, and no one else on the board had that knowledge," one former executive director told me. That gave him power. A seasoned engineer with practical engineering credentials as well as a Ph.D., he was an engineer's engineer running a consulting-engineering business, Paulus, Sokolowski & Sartor. He had been influential in the hiring of Calatrava and a constant advocate on his behalf; that advocacy included a trip in 2005 with Calatrava to view his projects in Europe as doubts grew about the practicality of the design. "The PATH station became a pet project of the New Jersey faction on the board," journalist Andrew Rice wrote after extensive interviews with Calatrava about the Hub project, "and Calatrava gave its members special attention."[61]

Known to be intensely involved in making decisions and a micromanager, Sartor was devoted to the Trade Center project, "motivated by the pride and power of being able to be the guy who rebuilt downtown," said one insider. He was glued to the hip to Plate, who considered the commissioner to be "his mentor."[62] In an unusual arrangement for a commissioner, Sartor had an office next to Plate's in the historic and richly detailed Trinity Place building at 115 Broadway, between

Cedar and Thames Streets. "Everyone in the construction industry knew that Sartor was running the show," I was told by more than one Port Authority insider. He was a powerful player who only had to ask a question in a public meeting to make his point.

Just two weeks after Coscia's directive and two weeks before Ward moved into the executive director's office, Sartor sent an e-mail to Coscia, with copies to four of the New York commissioners and the agency's chief financial officer as well as Goldstein and Plate declaring victory on his "value-engineering" effort and affirming budgets and schedules that would blow up just a few weeks later. "We have developed a two-pronged approach for a final design that will help to ensure that this project will be built within the available budget of $2.5 billion, while maintain the Hub's iconic features and transformative role in Lower Manhattan," he said. He wanted "to assure" Coscia "that we will maintain the original completion schedule for the project. The Hub will be completed and functioning in 2011, with the portions of the project that connect to buildings scheduled for completion after 2011 completed in concert with those buildings."[63]

This was an astonishing statement, contrary to fact deeply documented by independent experts. The Calatrava Transportation Hub was not just wildly over budget, it was the linchpin of the Port's centralized underground infrastructure. Everything affecting the Hub would have a domino effect on other projects at Ground Zero. Even if Sartor's value engineering exercise brought costs within the budget, events percolating behind the scenes, specifically, the political mandate to assure opening of the Memorial Plaza on the tenth anniversary of 9/11, were about to blow the timeline out of the field of expectations. Ward was stepping into the quagmire.

CHAPTER 17

"It's a Construction Job Now"

FIGURE 17.1 *Construction cranes work above the Freedom Tower foundations at the Trade Center site, June 20, 2008.* AP PHOTO/MARK LENNIHAN

IT WAS A DOOMED PROMISE, the promise of progress heralded by the 2006 deal realigning responsibilities for rebuilding the Trade Center site. The highly promoted dates for when the office towers would be completed, when the transportation center would start receiving trains, and when the memorial would open for visitors were all fictions. The Port Authority was holding tight to its castle-in-the sky schedule and budget predictions until failure to meet the first of its deadlines for turning over two sites to developer Larry Silverstein forced the agency to issue a press release on the last possible day, January 1, 2008. At that point, a reluctant and defensive Port Authority acknowledged it was behind schedule, but only by two to four weeks. As long as the work remained incomplete the agency would be making payments of $300,000 each day.

The artfulness of that press release could not hide the financial calculations motoring in the minds of the press corps. In "Statistics Do Lie," the editorial board of the *Daily News* parried the agency's trumpeting of excavation work completed on the $250 million East Bathtub—"removal of nearly 300,000 tons, or enough concrete, soil and rock to fill Giants Stadium"; use of "fifty miles of trucks"; "installation of approximately 400 tiebacks, which if placed end-to-end would stretch down I-95 from Manhattan to Philadelphia"; and "pouring of enough concrete to pave a sidewalk from Wall Street to Rockland County"—with its own statistical interpretation of the estimated penalty: "If you laid 13,500,000 dollar bills end to end, they would extend 1,278 miles, the distance from New York to Hot Springs, Ark. Which is not a fact the Port Authority can be proud of."[1]

This was only the beginning of a full-throated bashing of the Port Authority that would spill forth once the full truth withheld from the public was exposed just six months later. As soon as senior state officials in the new administration of Governor David A. Paterson came to understand the deep reality of the problems at Ground Zero, they decided to publicly break with previous policy of protecting the institution of the Port Authority. Ground Zero was not going to be Paterson's mess; the new governor wanted the Port Authority to come clean and blow apart the repeated fiction of announced timelines and fantasy budgets, and he put Christopher O. Ward in charge at the PA with a mandate to do so. The formal charge came on June 11 when the governor called on Ward to assess the overall rebuilding effort at the Trade Center and publish a candid and transparent report of his findings. That was a good, if belated, trigger for accountability at Ground Zero. The three-week assignment took Ward and his team three months to complete.

Should the adjustments of completion dates even be labeled "delays" when the timelines set out by Governor Pataki amounted to political fantasy? Or when delays, whether due to extended litigation or market cycles, have been a predictable part of the city's largest development projects from Westway to Columbus Circle to Forty-second Street at Times Square? Because it was rooted in realistic doubts about the Port Authority's institutional capacity to manage the complexity of rebuilding the Trade Center site over which it had finally and proudly gained control by year end 2006, this situation was different—very different. In this instance, which the *Daily News* called "the most important rebuilding task in the city's history,"[2] there would be little forgiveness for misjudgment, mismanagement, or error and very little tolerance for "delay."

Following Ward's update to the PA Board of Commissioners about the delayed opening and the release of an "Assessment" report in June, Memorial Foundation president Joseph C. Daniels sent a letter to supporters refuting the Port Authority's report, saying "while aggressive, we believe it is both possible and essential that the memorial open to the public by the 10th anniversary of the attacks." Days later, fifteen family members, six of whom were members of the Memorial Foundation board, sent Ward an emotionally charged letter saying, "we do not accept the report's summary conclusion that the completion schedule for the Memorial should be delayed"; they believed "the Port Authority, together with other stakeholders at the site, must work to achieve a completed and permanently open Memorial in time for the 10th anniversary of the attacks."[3]

The morass at Ground Zero jeopardized the goal of opening the memorial to the public by the tenth anniversary of 9/11. The goal had slipped badly. When Ward first reviewed the situation on taking over as executive director in May 2008, he found out that the 9/11 Memorial and Memorial Museum was not going to open until September 2013. This was not politically acceptable, pure and simple. The need to meet that anniversary date was obvious to everyone. Governor Paterson told Ward to make it happen, whatever the cost. The mayor and the governor were on record saying opening the 9/11 Memorial on the tenth anniversary should be a priority, though each had stopped short of issuing a formal public mandate. Meanwhile, pressure on the Port Authority was rising.

Taking a high-profile route to express his strong and growing displeasure with events at Ground Zero, Mayor Bloomberg (also donning a second hat as chairman of the Memorial Foundation), penned a strongly worded op-ed for the *Wall Street Journal* that appeared on the eve of the seventh anniversary of 9/11: "No more excuses, no more delays. New York Gov. David Paterson and I are in complete agreement on this subject, and it's time for the PA to formally commit to the same goal." His real target was the excessively expensive marble-clad Calatrava Transportation Hub with its column-free mezzanine and its limited function: "The PATH's station design, including the underground hall, is too complicated to build and threatens to delay the memorial and the entire project. It must be scaled back." The mayor "may have simply jumped ahead of a conclusion that was likely to have been presented by the Port Authority as part of its much-anticipated report later this month on how to contain costs and shorten timetables at ground zero," wrote David W. Dunlap. "But he is also the first official to say publicly what had been whispered for weeks."[4]

At Port Authority headquarters, senior officials were focused on finding solutions to the crisis at Ground Zero. For four intense months Ward worked with staff and principal stakeholders to ensure a tenth anniversary opening of the memorial and deliver a new set of timetables and budgets intended to bring coherence and accountability to the process of rebuilding. It was a real achievement, finally. On October 2, 2008, Governor Paterson held a press conference to announce Ward's "roadmap for transforming 16 acres into a robust area ready for business, transportation, and tourism." The *Roadmap Forward*, in tandem with Ward's leadership, reenergized senior staff of the eighty-seven-year-old institution. A new regime determined to deliver results was in place; the change marked another watershed for rebuilding Ground Zero (figure 17.1).

CHRIS WARD: REFRAMING THE CRISIS

With tactical intent Ward set out to reframe the crisis, stripping away as much as possible of the emotions, politics, and complexities weighing down the Port Authority's efforts to rebuild the site. He wanted rebuilding to become a construction project and only a construction project, where decisions would reflect the reality on the ground. "It's a construction job now—the planning and the politics are over," he would say, repeatedly. A T-shirt could have been customized with this message (figure 17.2).

Ward was not walking in blind to the chaotic state of affairs at Ground Zero. He had known, for some time, that budgets and schedules were out of whack. As the managing director of the General Contractors Association of New York, he had heard from those working on the job about conditions at Ground Zero. The

FIGURE 17.2 *Christopher O. Ward, executive director of the Port Authority, on the Trade Center site.* www.picssar.com

surprise was how deep the fundamental flaws of the project had become, how the rush for a monumental vision had overtaken practical reality, and how "without a complete restructuring the project would fail on its own terms," he said. "Unfortunately, what we had were beautiful renderings, but very few blueprints."[5]

Seven years after the attack, the site was still a hole in the ground and every date of promised progress had been blown. Designs for the 9/11 Memorial, Memorial Museum, Transportation Hub, and Vehicle Security Center were incomplete, yet construction management for the entire Port Authority project was already under contract with no built-in schedules. In 2006, the inspector general of the U.S. Department of Transportation had launched an investigation into the Federal Transit Administration's monitoring of the five federally funded transportation projects for lower Manhattan, including the PATH Transportation Hub and the Vehicle Security Center. "Dysfunctional" was the best description of the PA's project management at Ground Zero, which was governed under a structure with potential conflicts of interest by a subcommittee chaired by New Jersey PA commissioner Sartor (discussed later in this chapter). Stakeholders were warring as infighting and lack of trust reached a fever pitch. In mid-2008, the real estate market was on the verge of collapse and, as Ward's chief of staff, Drew S. Warshaw explained, "the agreement that was the purported foundation for commercial development of the site—the 2006 Master Development Agreement—was a house of cards built on the flawed premise that 10 million square feet of office space could be financed and built on speculation all at once."[6]

At fifty-three, Ward possessed the right stuff to tackle the crisis at Ground Zero. A seasoned administrator with more than twenty years of public service, he came to the executive director position at the Port Authority—the fourth in seven years since 9/11—with a reputation for being able to navigate through thorny public projects. As the city's commissioner of environmental protection from 2002 to 2005 under the Bloomberg administration, he succeeded in gaining approval for a $1.3 billion water-filtration plant in the Bronx's Van Cortlandt Park over objections from community groups. As chief of planning and external affairs as well as director of port redevelopment from 1997 to 2002 at the Port Authority, he helped oversee execution of the $1.9 billion AirTrain service to JFK International Airport through low-income, minority communities in Queens, a project with lots of complex issues similarly subject to widespread opposition and in need of numerous regulatory approvals and skillful leadership. He was one of a handful of people in the city with experience in mastering these large complicated engineering projects, particularly the big bureaucracies that deliver them. He understood the city and the Port Authority, intuitively. And what would become especially important for managing the Trade Center, he was action oriented, "a force of nature" with a huge personality, a bit of a "cowboy."[7]

Praised by his friends and criticized by opponents still bruised by his forcefulness in pushing through both public projects, Ward came with skills as manager-politician, hardened taskmaster, pragmatic and decisive decision-maker—all of which were needed to put the Trade Center project on track. His resume included as well a master's degree in divinity from Harvard, a stint in the private sector as chief executive officer of a stevedoring and port-services company, American Stevedoring, Inc., and work on an oil rig in the Gulf of Mexico—an "incubator of personalities" as he put it, where he learned how to get along with a diverse group of oil riggers. His appointment was not one of political patronage. "I didn't know Ward before I interviewed him but he had lots of advocates," former governor Paterson said. "More than the advocates, he was very direct about what he wanted to do," and that was a persuasive point for Paterson.[8]

"Whether I had all the experience and skills needed, I was going to take this job," he told me. "It's a dream job, the number one public job in the country." He considered strategic project management—setting multiple goals, engineering and political, and managing to meet them—his strength. Passed up for the position by the Spitzer administration, he possessed a zeal for the complexities of the big projects, big challenges. Photographs of New York's two master builders—Austin J. Tobin, the legendary executive director of the Port Authority for thirty years, and his rival, Robert Moses, immortalized as *The Power Broker* by author Robert Caro—fashioned the otherwise bland walls on either side of his desk in the agency's headquarters on the fifteenth floor of 225 Park Avenue South. He claimed neither as his hero, but their portraits presented an object lesson for what it would take to rebuild the Trade Center site. "Here are two colossal egos that really did battle in shaping New York, and they should have been best of friends and partners because they were in some ways very similar," Ward told Alex Frangos of the *Wall Street Journal*. "But because they both felt they had to get their own way, they fought desperately."[9]

The push to reframe the crisis at Ground Zero began immediately. Only a few weeks later in mid-June the Port Authority released a statement announcing it was more than a month behind schedule for delivering the East Bathtub site for Tower 2 to Larry Silverstein, once again triggering a daily penalty of $300,000 (beginning July 1) until the 1.4-acre site could be turned over fully excavated. By the end of the day, Governor Paterson officially directed Ward to determine whether the current schedules and cost estimates for reconstruction of the trade center were "reliable and achievable." "If they are not," the governor wrote in his letter calling for a complete audit, "I would like an evaluation of what viable alternatives exist to get the project back on track or whether we need to alter our targets to meet the reality on the ground." He expected Ward to take an "aggressive but realistic approach" and provide him with an update on the status of the effort in short order, by June 30.[10]

This was an "unenviable task" in the words of a *New York Post* editorial, ever skeptical that anything positive could happen at Ground Zero. In more moderate language the *New York Times* worried that Governor Paterson "is setting the stage for adopting a less rigorous timetable. Politically, a new schedule makes sense," yet the editorial questioned "whether it makes sense on the ground. Easing the limits on costs and building time could also simply cause the whole project to take longer and cost more." For sure—as time would soon reveal and Ward would later confirm: "Make no illusion, 'save a lot of money' is not in the future for Ground Zero."[11] A realistic assessment would also take longer than the three weeks Governor Paterson had given Ward.

After a team analysis of the project's strengths, weaknesses, opportunities, and threats, known as a SWOT, revealed the state of current dysfunction, Ward and Warshaw were unwilling to go out with a set of dates uninformed by critical decisions yet to be made. They needed to buy time, several months' worth. Writing to the governor's office nine days before the assessment was due, they explained: "to forecast costs and dates before these decisions have been made and release them to the public will only send us down the same irresponsible path as before." They cautioned that any such release "will quite literally be not believable by the general public and, without having a clear and comprehensive way to fix them, could create such a destabilized environment that the stakeholders will be forced to bolt." Significant amounts of time would be lost, they reasoned, and political capital that did not exist would have to be spent picking up the pieces.[12] When Ward released the assessment report on June 30, the message was the same, only the tone was softer.

Ward was smart in his decision to hire Warshaw as his right-hand person at the Port Authority, a decision that came just one hour after they met in April 2008. Warshaw was finishing up in Albany as assistant secretary to the governor, where he had been an advisor to Governor Spitzer and his secretary (chief of staff) on all major policy matters and served as the secretary's representative to the budget office. After Spitzer resigned (with two weeks left in the fiscal year, in the middle of budget negotiations), he had been asked to stay on; after budget negotiations closed, he was planning to leave Albany. That was when Charles J. O'Byrne, secretary to newly installed Governor Paterson, suggested Warshaw and Ward should speak. Doing what any seasoned policy advisor would do, Warshaw studied the Port Authority's budgets, annual reports, and recent news, trying to anticipate any question Ward might ask. The Empire Service train down from Albany to Ward's office at the General Contractors Association in midtown Manhattan takes only two hours and thirty minutes, so Warshaw had a lot of cramming to do. Despite his earnest preparation, Ward's first question completely caught him off guard: "Who is your favorite band?" Warshaw answered, "The Band," which was a perfect answer as Ward had been to The Band's farewell concert, "The Last Waltz" (famously documented by film director and producer Martin Scorsese), so they spent the first fifteen minutes talking about the Canadian-American rock group. After that, Warshaw recalled, things seemed to flow pretty well. The chemistry so essential for the chief-of-staff position to work well clicked in that first-hour discussion. A partnership of complementary strengths and weaknesses formed, and, he said, they ran the Port Authority that way.[13] "When working for Chris," remarked one player close to the action, he was "a warrior."

At twenty-seven, Warshaw was coming to the Port Authority "battle tested." He knew what it was like to live in the 24/7 vortex of high-level government decision-making. He was comfortable in the vortex, so the pressure and stress of the job were not new. "Whether it was dealing with the World Trade Center, a hurricane, dueling governors, or a plane landing in the Hudson River, this was the kind of environment that got me up in the morning," he said. "I got into government to solve problems, and there was no bigger problem than rebuilding the World Trade Center, so there was no other place I wanted to be." His time in Albany had given him an up-close view of both the promise of power and its limits. The view he took away was that "the world is gray, not black and white, policies don't end up as simple triumphs or failures, and you must balance power with humility to effectively manage in any complex environment." He likened the management of the sprawling Port Authority bureaucracy and the World Trade Center project itself to a game of pick-up sticks: "Until you realize that if you move one thing, you have to anticipate how it's going to impact everything else, you're not going to be able to be very effective at managing. I think the Trade Center exemplifies that."[14]

Turning around the Trade Center project was a massive challenge for Ward and Warshaw, and they worked at the mission with a simple motto: "You cannot win if you do not play—but don't overreach." The motto was crafted from Ward's basic operating premise and modified with a corollary from Warshaw, after learning up close from his time with Spitzer.[15] Striking that balance was key to all of their negotiations and almost everything they did at the Port Authority, Warshaw said. Establishing himself quickly in the massive bureaucracy that did not look highly on new people, especially young, new people, the "gun and the badge" Ward gave him—that is, deputized to act on his behalf—helped, as did the fourteen-to-fifteen-hour days he was putting in. He would conceive and ultimately manage the

Trade Center assessment process, draft both assessment reports, and play a central role in all that followed.

Ward met Paterson's June 30 deadline with a thirty-six-page *World Trade Center Assessment* that positioned the project's problems as problems of construction management and logistics, not political fault finding. The time for blame had long passed. Political explanations for schedule and cost problems were at this point irrelevant. A clear task was at hand. In the first substantive paragraph of his cover letter to the governor, Ward made sure to acknowledge the cooperation of the project's key stakeholders, nine in number, whose genuine future collaboration was essential to his professional, civic, and personal ambition of assuring construction completion at Ground Zero. He promised "transparency, inclusiveness, and accountability." He sought not to overpromise. Rather he talked of tough decisions that had not been candidly addressed up to that point, "tough trade-offs that are necessary to getting WTC rebuilding on track." He labeled the task as a "challenge" and established its significance in terms of asserted construction magnitudes—"five major skyscrapers, which will house Class A office space comparable to all of downtown Atlanta; one of the world's most significant memorials and museums; the third-largest transportation hub in New York City; a world-class retail venue serving all WTC users; a major performing arts center; a state-of-the-art vehicle security center; two brand-new-city streets (Greenwich and Fulton) and two brand-new pedestrian ways (Cortlandt and Dey); and all of the critical infrastructure to support these projects (chiller plant, utility and communication networks, etc.)"—and institutional fragmentation—"19 public agencies, two private developers, 101 different construction contractors and subcontractors and 33 different designers, architects and consulting firms all in charge of one element of the project or another."[16]

This was a carefully constructed document. It sought to strip away as much of the emotion, politics, and complexity that weighed on the site and turn it into purely a construction project. It defined a set of fifteen "fundamental issues critical to the overall project"—a totality made up of seventeen major projects—"that had not yet been resolved,[17] many of which are in the control of stakeholders other than the Port Authority but impact our own schedule and budget." It acknowledged the need to establish "a more efficient, centralized decision-making structure—a steering committee—with authority to make final decisions on matters which fundamentally drive schedule and cost." The report's nine pages diagnosing the challenge and fifteen pages describing the decision points and mitigation options concluded with four pages laying out governance and organization issues. The whole was designed to show the Port Authority as being capable of a "clear-eyed assessment" of the situation, one that would provide a credible basis for putting forth a realistic schedule and acceptable budget in a second phase of the assessment process to be complete in three months' time, at the end of September. Politically, the report aimed to reposition the reputation of the much-maligned agency as an agency that "can do"—that can manage "the most important rebuilding effort in our city's history," a "construction challenge as complex as any in the world." Turning downtown into a construction project, Ward said in a 2010 speech, was necessary "to break the tension between vision and failure," to "put monumentalism aside."[18]

Ruffling Feathers

Ward's stark "truth assessment" of the problems at Ground Zero was not pretty but neither was it shocking or surprising. The dysfunction had been obvious for some time and known in detail to senior officials at the Port Authority and to insiders in government through the many risk assessments and monitoring reports. Port Authority commissioners, for example, most of whom had been on the board since 2003, had overseen and approved much of what became dysfunctional; deep down many may have known fundamental problems existed and may have felt relief that the issues were finally being tackled. Three weeks after the Ward report was published, board chairman Anthony R. Coscia upped board oversight of the rebuilding project by calling for new monthly meetings devoted to monitoring costs and schedules and overall progress at the site. The special meetings, to be held near the site, "will create an opportunity for the Board to give staff more policy direction regarding the rebuilding effort," he wrote in a memo to other commissioners.[19]

Commissioner Sartor's reaction to Ward's *Assessment* was bound to be more intense than that of other commissioners. In time and energy and professional commitment, he was heavily invested in the rebuilding of the site, especially the Transportation Hub. Not only had he been a staunch advocate of Calatrava's design, he had been a force behind setting up the Phoenix construction contract, and many other rebuilding contracts had been subject to his prior review and approval in his capacity as chair of the board's WTC site subcommittee since 2005. His long tenure as a commissioner meant he had outlasted several executive directors and had come to know more about the project than the several executive directors responsible for its execution. The constant shift in executive directors had worked to enhance his power. "What people don't understand," said a veteran senior PA professional, "is that with so many changes going on at the regional (governor, board) and local (PA staff, executive director) levels, it is hard to make decisions that are consistent with past regimes. Decisions are being made in a flux environment; everyone is trying to deal with their own agendas. In this type of leadership vacuum, Sartor gained a lot of control." His position of strength on the Trade Center project "filled a void left by both Seymour and Ringler," executive directors who were there to be "structurally protective of Pataki." Just four weeks before Ward issued his June *Assessment,* in the memo to Coscia and others cited in the last chapter, Sartor had declared the project to be on track and able to meet the $2.5 billion budget. His image of control had now been shattered; the embarrassment must have stung, and so too his partial downfall. Ward's take-charge position was resetting the power balance on the PA's Trade Center project.

Sartor's position in the decision-making at Ground Zero had acquired barnacle-like attachments. His connections to vendors closely involved with the Hub project were not totally unknown as much as publicly unexplored. In August 2008, Eliot Brown, writing at the time for the *New York Observer,* was the first to report on what he thought would become big news for Port Authority watchers: the potential conflict of interest, "or at least the appearance of it," in Sartor's role as president of KeySpan Services, which controlled his company, Paulus, Sokolowski & Sartor, a subsidiary of National Grid, and his role at the Port Authority. The giant engineering and architectural firm STV Incorporated, on retainer for jobs involving hundreds of millions (then billions) of dollars at Ground Zero, was in talks to acquire Sartor's company. STV had a long relationship with the Port Authority; also, it was where a number of former PA staff went after they retired. STV held a concentration of multiple contracts for rebuilding at Ground Zero through joint venture partnerships and subsidiaries—the PATH Hub (as part of the Downtown Design Partnership, with DMJM+Harris and Calatrava), the underground Vehicle Security Center (LibertyM Security Partners), foundation work for the WTC Performing Arts Center (LibertyM Security Partners), the Freedom Tower and September 11 Memorial (STV Engineers), and WTC infrastructure and streets (DowntownM Streetscape Partners)—as the *Daily News* emphasized weeks later in "Firm Gets WTC Gold."[20]

The FTA had contacted the bi-state authority about the potential conflict, and the PA's general counsel reportedly "put safeguards in place during the negotiation period." The safeguards did not allow Sartor to vote on approvals of STV's contracts, although as chair of the WTC site subcommittee, he was still able to exercise broad control over many of the decisions made at the site, including those that affected STV. He chaired the subcommittee meetings, took reports from his protégé, the director of WTC construction, Steven Plate, and called for votes on contract recommendations, even when records showed his recusal on the vote at board meetings. Moreover, those attending the open board meetings would not know of his or other commissioners' recusals because they were not announced;

they just appeared later in the minutes of the board meeting. Whether commissioners recuse themselves during closed-door meetings was unclear.

Sartor was "navigating an ethical minefield," Shawn Boburg of the the *Record* (Bergen County) would report years later. Indeed. Though STV dropped its interest in a deal for Sartor's company soon after the brief public flurry over the conflict, Sartor's business involvements with companies that did business at the Trade Center were so deep, he had had to recuse himself repeatedly from board votes on WTC projects, for years. Based on my inclusive analysis of all PA board authorization votes on Trade Center projects (and those of the Committee on Operations) from January 2008 through March 2014, Sartor recused himself on 119 of the 184 votes on monetary authorizations for Trade Center projects. In contrast, for the prior six-plus years from the start of the rebuilding effort following 9/11, his recusals amounted to only four votes out of forty-eight such votes.[21] When I asked Brown why the Sartor story never went further, he responded: "Where was the smoking gun?"[22]

However much Sartor's recusals appeared correct on paper, they were illustrative of a deeply flawed and dysfunctional culture of governance at the Port Authority. It took years, however, for that story to make front-page headlines and become a subject of public outrage. It was only by way of the scandal in 2013 involving the closure of access lanes from Fort Lee, New Jersey, to the George Washington Bridge, known as "Bridgegate." In an action long overdue in the minds of many, Sartor resigned from the Port Authority board in April 2014, amid speculation about his conflicts of interest and a new probe of the authority by Manhattan district attorney Cyrus Vance Jr. As "the driving force behind the vastly overdesigned, obscenely expensive PATH station at the trade center site," he was "[t]he man who blew billions," said the *Daily News* in an editorial that called his tenure at the PA "a horror show": "Good riddance to Tony Sartor and the cancer of wasteful arrogance and cozy dealing that he epitomized at the authority."[23]

Outrage

It was the tone of Ward's *Assessment*, its "unsparing candor," as *Times* reporter Charles V. Bagli recounted almost immediately upon its public release, that took beat reporters by surprise. Even those who had become pessimistically habituated to the travails of the Ground Zero story saw the report as a "stunning document," a "blunt revelation." What the papers really thought about the state of affairs was evident on the editorial pages. Here, the tabloids were unrelenting. "Grim truth," the *Post* pounced in characteristic style. "Port Authority Executive Director Christopher Ward confessed to the obvious yesterday: Six-plus years, two governors and hundreds of millions of dollars after 9/11, Ground Zero reconstruction has gone so far off the rails no one can say when—or even if—the project will be finished." Patting itself on the back for first calling attention "to the developing debacle in 2002," it castigated the institution of the Port Authority yet felt compelled to say that Ward "deserves a chance to try" and get the job done, and Governor Paterson, "credit for bringing the charade to a halt before he, too, was sucked into the hole in the ground."[24]

Indignant that the truth had been kept from the public, the *Daily News* let loose a broadside attack against the Port Authority for its "towering incompetence." "The PA has mismanaged the job on a monumental level and…said everything was fine. If that's not a lie, it's damn close." Just days before Ward's assessment report was released, the paper had scored an exclusive about the LMDC's risk-assessment reports, kept secret for more than a year, based on an internal memo it obtained that could have been leaked by LMDC chairman Avi Schick, sensing that this was his chance to say "I told you so."[25] As detailed in the previous chapter, Schick had lost the first round in the behind-the-scenes battle to repudiate the Pataki deadlines when Governor Spitzer acceded to the logic Shorris put forth, that the policy objective was to rebuild as fast as possible. Saying the dates were all wrong, Shorris argued, would just ease the pressure on the contractors. But Shorris was now out of the PA and Schick still in at the LMDC, ready to claim a policy victory. (The backstory of the Shorris-Schick infighting would not come to light until after Ward's "realistic schedules and budgets" had been memorialized in his *Roadmap Forward* report to Governor Paterson, which laid out his operational program for moving construction at Ground Zero forward.)

The *Times* took in the "grim news" dispassionately. As in so many of its Ground Zero editorials, it focused on the leadership factor: "[T]his frank declaration of problems gives Mr. Paterson a blank slate going forward." His appointment of Ward and demand for deadlines and cost estimates established the governor "as a prime mover in this crucial development. That means he will have to take control, making him first among equals with Gov. Jon Corzine of New Jersey and Mayor Michael Bloomberg." About Ward's conclusion that centralized decision-making needed to be established in the form of a steering committee consisting of all stakeholders at the site meeting regularly to resolve problems: "This is such a reasonable idea that it is distressing nobody tried it before." Notwithstanding its advice that the Port Authority "must fight its own bad habits of secrecy," the *Times* editorial board still held faith that the legacy-rich but reputation-damaged institution "is the right agency to rebuild ground zero," and called for oversight not just by the two governors but by the mayor, "who runs the city."[26]

Only *Newsday* captured the fundamental insight into the problem at Ground Zero: "To date, the rebuilding process has highlighted New York's weakness: too many players seeking credit, political gain, emotional release or professional glory." Ambition, the DNA of the city's economic and cultural success, was working in the negative against its "better qualities." New Yorkers might be forgiven for being cynical given how the "state" had created an international embarrassment by the way it handled the Trade Center site, the paper editorialized. But it was time "to put the finger-pointing behind us," face up "to the facts," rebuild "badly damaged public confidence," and restore "America's international image" by finishing the memorial by the tenth anniversary of 9/11.[27]

Dealing with the press was a big challenge for Ward. The press was "terribly cynical," he told me. With only a couple of exceptions, "it lacked an understanding of the complexity of the Trade Center site, of what the PA was building below-grade. It fed on the overlay of emotional dates, political dates, and groundbreakings that were at odds with what was realistic. The narrative was negative; reporting could be accusatory and inflammatory." Knowing the reporters and being candid with them was part of Ward's strategy for turning around the storyline. "His courting of the press did chafe at some of his subordinates, who felt Mr. Ward was claiming too much of the spotlight and misrepresenting some of the facts," Matt Chaban later wrote in the *New York Observer*. "Ultimately, it helped focus the agency's efforts." The editorial pages were very important, Ward said. He needed to convince the *New York Times* and the *Daily News* of the Port Authority's plans and its construction capability and slow down the negative reporting of the *Post*; the *Star-Ledger* and *Newsday* were also important. In working these papers, he sought to focus the editorial writers' understanding of the PA's ability to turn the project around. "When the press started to turn, it's amazing how much easier it gets," he recalled. "That's why you must be transparent and clear; they feed on you if they think you are hiding something."[28]

The pressure was on. Everyone was waiting for more than verbal promises.

THE LITMUS TEST

One benchmark of progress held meaning above all others: opening the memorial on the tenth anniversary of the 9/11 terrorist attacks. It was a litmus test of credibility for the institution, for the governor, for the mayor, the proof of commitment of a prideful city to the victims' families, its citizens, the nation, and the world at large. Its completion would be a watershed, pure emotion—every last detail of its design and execution embedded with deep associations and meaning, personal and civic, as had been the memorial ceremony on the first anniversary of the 9/11 terrorism attack (plate 4).

That first memorial ceremony at Ground Zero in 2002 held particular significance: It set the tone for recovery at the same time it set symbolic precedents of meaning. The Bloomberg administration spent months on preparing and planning, paying meticulous attention to every detail; no matter how small, every detail had to be right. The ceremony had to be dignified. The world was watching. The families were watching. Simple and powerful observances defined the unprecedented ceremony. No political speeches, only readings from Abraham Lincoln's Gettysburg Address, Thomas Jefferson's Declaration of Independence, and Franklin Delano Roosevelt's Four Freedoms speech. Rituals of simplicity to recall the losses were followed: the recitation of the names of those who perished—"So many names, there is barely room on the walls of the heart," U.S. poet laureate Billy Collins wrote in his poem of tribute, "The Names"; the chime of bells before moments of silence—8:46 A.M., 9:03 A.M., 9:59 A.M., 10:28 A.M.—moments poignantly endowed with emotion; and a trumpeter playing "Taps" after the last of the 2,801 names lost at Ground Zero remembered that morning—an enduring custom of honor. An air of universality inhabited the rituals, in which the victims' zones of origins were meaningfully edited out in deference to their shared final human condition. On anniversary after anniversary, as progress toward rebuilding stalled or inched forward, the pit at Ground Zero was home to the memorial service, the place to honor the losses through the rituals established at that first ceremony of remembrance. On anniversary after anniversary, Mayor Bloomberg quietly presided over the carefully choreographed ceremony for the families and first responders. The ceremony on the tenth anniversary had to be different: It had to take place on the Memorial Plaza in front of those massive memorial absences. It was a political imperative.

As years of endless controversies delayed visible progress at Ground Zero, the eyes of the world turned upon other global events, but they would very quickly return to those sixteen acres come September 11, 2011. On September 11, 2011, the fountains of the two largest man-made waterfalls in North America would have to flow perfectly, droplets of water cascading down each two-hundred-foot, black-granite-clad side of the memorial pools into a deep void where each of the towers once stood. The 2,982 names of those killed in the terrorist attacks of September 11, 2001, and February 26, 1993, would have to be inscribed perfectly on the bronze panels surrounding the pools, names backlit by a secure heating and cooling system designed to keep the panels warm enough in the winter to melt snow and ice and cool enough in the summer to be comfortable to the touch of loved ones and visitors. As many as possible of the 416 oak trees of the memorial grove had to be perfectly planted. And to ensure that the oaks would grow and thrive to maturity, substantial volumes of soil, some forty thousand tons in total buried beneath the Memorial Plaza, would need to be irrigated, aerated, and drained by maintenance crews through a specially designed network of maintenance tunnels to access these systems. And beneath everything visual on the Memorial Plaza would be 110,000 square feet of museum exhibition space at bedrock.

It wasn't just the technical requirements of the memorial program that made completion of its construction demanding; it was the "pick-up-sticks" interdependencies of the memorial program with the fifteen "fundamental issues" Ward had identified in his June assessment. Two were most critical: the Calatrava Transportation Hub and the No. 1 subway line. Both were contiguous with the Memorial Plaza and Memorial Museum. Both presented problems of structural complexity detailed by the experts of the LMCCC Value Planning Workshops. A compounding factor was the need for the roof of the PATH mezzanine to do structural double duty by serving as a ground plane for scores of trees that would be placed above on the Memorial Plaza. The final design and engineering of this northeast corner of the memorial quadrant was dicey. Both stakeholders involved held strong positions. The way the engineering of this corner interfaced with the demands of the landscape plan was complicated. At the same time, the complications revealed why it was so difficult to make decisions at Ground Zero that would result in certainty to schedules and budgets.

As Ward soon found out, the Port Authority and the Memorial Foundation had been negotiating for months over the final design details of the roof-plaza but were at loggerheads over the number of trees that could be accommodated on this section of the Memorial Plaza. It was not until mid-July that the Port Authority, the Memorial Foundation, and the Department of City Planning agreed to a final plan to place additional trees on the northeast section of the memorial quadrant. "While this may sound like a relatively trivial design element in the scheme of things," Ward wrote in October when describing the final resolution of this bottleneck, "each tree—with the tree itself, soil and planter—weighs 150 tons." At the time, fifty to sixty trees were to be planted in this corner and "that meant approximately 7,500 tons had to be factored into the design of the Hub's roof support—approximately the equivalent weight of 180 fully loaded tractor trailers," or to make a rhetorical point sure to resonate with New Yorkers, "half the weight of the Brooklyn Bridge." For the Memorial Plaza to open on the tenth anniversary, the interdependent issues of design, phasing, and construction of both transportation projects had to be reevaluated and, as in the case of the Hub, design details modified or reengineered. By fall of 2009, the quadrant's final tree count was eighty-six[29] (figure 17.3).

Meeting the tenth anniversary date was the only sure way the Port Authority could approach reestablishing institutional integrity while achieving its ambitions

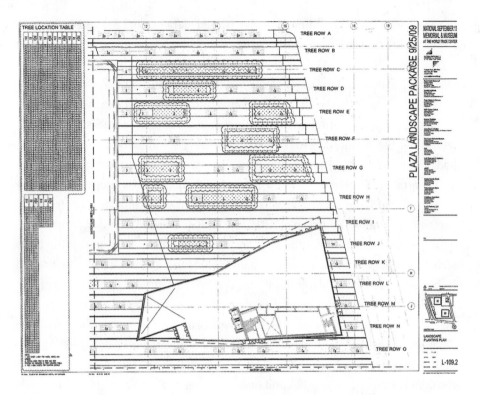

FIGURE 17.3 *Diagram of the tree pattern for the northeast quadrant of the Memorial Plaza.* THE PORT AUTHORITY OF NEW YORK AND NEW JERSEY/PWP LANDSCAPE ARCHITECTURE

for an iconic transportation hall. Yet the Port Authority had achieved only "limited construction progress" for the past year, according to the LMCCC, which had been receiving and reviewing periodic updates from the PA. When a majority of the participants from the 2007 Value Planning Workshop reconvened in March 2008 to update their earlier work, they could not report good news either. The team's second risk assessment indicated that "the overall risk dates for the projects had continued to push out due to the continued risks of the project." Construction coordination still remained a serious concern. As part of this two-week review, the Memorial Foundation had provided a presentation indicating that it was looking to a 2011 "complete" opening—Memorial Plaza, Memorial Museum, and Visitor Orientation and Education Center—however, the 2008 value planning update found this date "unachievable." "More significantly," it reported, "only a partial plaza opening is possible until the roof of the PATH Station is completed, which is not expected until 2015."[30]

Ward, his team, and the newly formed steering committee of direct stakeholders worked throughout the summer to bring order to chaos, doing a deep dive into the minutiae of what was impeding construction progress on the entire Trade Center site.[31] The deeper they dug, the scarier it got, Warshaw recalled. It was months before they reached the bottom of all the issues. They were working to isolate the agency's actions from the many layers of complexity bedeviling the project in order to get control of construction on the site. Through this process of establishing clear construction priorities, reviewing each project in depth, convening all stakeholders building on the site on a weekly basis, butting heads when need be, and rebuilding relationships frayed by past conflicts, pragmatic solutions emerged—a combination of engineering adjustments, design modifications, and construction management decisions—along with target completion dates, probabilistic completion dates, and budget estimates for each major milestone that emerged from resolving the fifteen foundational issues identified in Ward's June assessment. "Once people started to finally share information, there was a collective realization among all the stakeholders of the enormity of the challenge they were facing," recalled one participant. "Because people starting sharing information, collaborating, and rolling up their sleeves, there was also some sense of hope that they could tackle the challenges."

While they were excavating the details, analyzing the technical problems, and figuring out how to establish realistic schedules and budgets, what the public was reading from newspaper headlines did not offer much in the way of optimism. Ever-rising costs for the Memorial Museum, a slowdown in donations, and continual uncertainty over whether the Port Authority would be able to assure an opening of the Memorial Plaza on the tenth anniversary of the four attacks created ongoing public anxiety. The Port had already announced that Calatrava's ambitious design for the Oculus had to be trimmed back to deal with its soaring cost and difficult constructability. Different plans were in the works, but its fate and that of the cavernous underground mezzanine, which was the functional part of the Hub, still hung in the balance. The NYPD had gained control of security at the Trade Center, but its plan for a tightly controlled security zone—sally ports staffed by police in booths to control the movable barriers, security checkpoints, streets open to pedestrians and bicycles but closed to unauthorized vehicles, and bollards or other barriers—was arousing mixed feelings because it so threatened the long-sought goal of physically reweaving the Trade Center site into the fabric of the city. And Merrill Lynch had definitively ended talks on moving into new space in Silverstein's Tower 3 at Ground Zero, sending a wave of disappointment into lower Manhattan. (Yet, as notice of increasing office vacancy rates took hold in mid-2008, the real estate community embraced a delay in construction of the Trade Center towers.) Ward may have reframed the crisis as purely a construction problem, where decisions could reflect the reality on the ground, but he still had to provide a clear-and-certain strategy for delivering on that agenda if he was going to succeed in wiping away the prevailing negativism about the project. The way to do that only emerged at a point when he and his team seemed to be running out of time.

BUILD THE ROOF FIRST

Before the assessment process, the Hub was an untouchable project. That was about to change. It was late one evening in August, at a time when fourteen-hour days had become the norm for Ward and Warshaw; they had been working for months but had not gotten to a point where they could responsibly commit to opening the memorial by September 11, 2011. The complex engineering of the Hub was a growing concern, jeopardizing the ability of the Port Authority to complete the PATH mezzanine in time for the tenth anniversary. In the course of their discussion of the major challenges still be overcome, sitting in an un-air-conditioned Port Authority office on a hot summer evening, Ward decided to call in the senior WTC construction team from its offices at 115 Broadway.

As the team waited in one of the conference rooms on the executive floor of the Port's headquarters at 225 Park Avenue, Ward and Warshaw prepped in Ward's office; they knew it was going to be a defining moment. They needed more from their engineers. They walked into the conference room, and Ward simply told the engineers that if they could not figure out a way to deliver the memorial by the tenth anniversary, this effort would be viewed as a failure. Exhausted and strung out from the grind of the assessment process, the engineers were pretty upset. After about an hour of yelling and brainstorming, the idea to build the roof of the Transportation Hub—first—surfaced. Because the roof of the transportation center's PATH mezzanine doubled as the ground plane for the northeast corner of the Memorial Plaza, if they could get the roof up first instead of last, as in conventional construction, they would have a shot at meeting the anniversary date. Ward gave the team one week to test the feasibility of this "deckover" approach. Insistently, the engineers put forth a caveat: Without a conventional structure of permanent columns with steel plate girder supports replacing Calatrava's aesthetic choice of the Vierendeel trusses[32] (less efficient but allowing for long spans and cantilevers), the innovative deckover approach would not work (figure 17.4).

The engineering for the Oculus was very complex. The metaphoric artistic element of a continuous skylight with roof wings that would open and close like a dove in flight was risky to build, and risk means higher cost. Engineering issues dominated feasibility and the cost of the design. Two issues were paramount: constructability of the design and engineering the movement of the structure. On the engineering side, the aerodynamics of the flutter made the winged design problematic. This impacted the constructability. All of the mechanism to fabricate the

FIGURE 17.4 *Vierendeel trusses supporting the PATH hall roof.* THE PORT AUTHORITY OF NEW YORK AND NEW JERSEY

skylight had to be put into the arms of the support; there could be no structural members connecting the sides of the very long arched roof span. Calatrava wanted pure space, a 150-foot clear span without any structural cross beams and for this effect had specified use of Vierendeel trusses.

Before the 2008 review, there had been questions about the constructability of the design, but with the PA Engineering Department separated from responsibility for WTC construction these concerns were not heard until Ward came into the executive director's office and brought the engineering department into his assessment process. The chief engineer for the Port Authority, Frank J. Lombardi, had put in his papers for retirement, but when Ward came aboard with the intent of righting things on the Trade Center project, Lombardi was reenergized. Drawing on the Engineering Department, Ward uncovered a lot of things that were problematic. Lombardi, who had never been invited to WTC meetings, was now being asked, by Sartor's office, to attend. Why, what has changed, he asked himself? The answer: Ward wanted him there. Lombardi proposed an alternative to the giant truss-bearing ribs that involved a more conventional column-supported structural approach to the PATH mezzanine covered over with the sculptural design, but from Calatrava's perspective this would have violated the integrity of his design. From the Port Authority's perspective, the complication of building the Hub stemmed from the winged design. Eliminating these two elements, the birdlike wing movement and the column-free space in the mezzanine, would eliminate a major source of potential construction cost risk.

Four years of growth in the Calatrava program for the Hub had already led to $220 million in increased costs (nearly 40 percent of the total $570 million increase in the project's cost since the 2004 estimate of $2.2 billion), according to the 2008 Shorris memo on Hub cost-reduction options. Calatrava's unique design, Shorris reported to Governor Spitzer and others, had "created special cost pressures, some related to the unusual materials and structures his designs require, others related to the unfamiliarity of local contractors with the means and methods required to execute his vision." It was praised as a conceptual design, but had the costs and risks of constructability of Calatrava's design made the space "too extravagant for what is, basically, a commuter rail station"?[33]

The PA had been meeting with Calatrava's senior team throughout the assessment process, and Ward had met with Calatrava twice before at one of those informal meetings. But now, while the PA team went to work on testing the feasibility of the build-the-roof-first approach, it was time for a truth-telling meeting with the architect. As the story goes, Ward went to Calatrava's Upper East Side Park Avenue townhouse to get his engineers their columns. When he and Warshaw got there they were greeted by Mrs. Calatrava and Anthony Sartor, a surprise guest who was likely there to defend the design. After a tour of Calatrava's art collection, all his own work, and an explanation of his vision for the Hub, Calatrava walked them downstairs to his studio where he had a scale model of the Hub big enough for people to enter and view from inside the different sight lines of his design. Scale models are important devices for exploring and explaining architectural vision, and that evening Calatrava undoubtedly wanted his model to reveal the aesthetic elegance of the column-free space through personal experience and underscore why it was imperative that the PA preserve it (figure 17.5).

Ward is a big, burly six-foot two-inch man, and he could barely get into the small opening in the middle of the model. Warshaw could see his boss's blood pressure rising. Barely out of the room, Calatrava started talking again, and that is when Ward interrupted him. Flat out, Ward told the celebrated architect-engineer that the Hub was the Port Authority's project, and he was calling the shots now and there would, in fact, be columns in the Hub and anything else his design team felt was necessary to deliver schedule certainty and cost containment. Ward's message: He was the client, Calatrava was the architect. A different regime was in place now. There was no space for pushback. An executive director with conviction had arrived. This was not the message that either Calatrava or Sartor expected. Calatrava had every reason to expect that his relationship with the Port Authority would continue as in the past. Notwithstanding the changes that would come from Ward's direction, Calatrava would stay with the project—the Hub was still going to be his design.[34] Two minutes later, the men were out of the townhouse.

FIGURE 17.5 *Architect Santiago Calatrava posing next to the model of his design for the PATH World Trade Center Transportation Hub.* SANTIAGO CALATRAVA ARCHITECTS AND ENGINEERS

A week later, the Port Authority had a revised Hub design and initial drawings with the columns and plate girders necessary to implement its deckover approach and simplify constructability. (The details were then fully fleshed out and implemented by the Downtown Design Partnership, the joint venture between DMJM + Harris, STV, with Santiago Calatrava S.A., with support from the Phoenix venture.) The columns came to be known as "the Chris Ward columns" (figure 17.6).

The deckover solution was innovative. It made possible a tenth-anniversary opening of the Memorial Plaza with its waterfalls, reflecting pools, and parapets inscribed with the names of those killed on September 11 and in the 1993 bombing of the Trade Center, but it did not come cheap—it would cost an extra $75 million in additional construction costs and lost construction productivity, or roughly 2 percent of the Hub's newly reauthorized $3.2 billion budget (up from the initial $2.5 billion estimate). At least those were the estimates in the fall of 2008. With political symbolism and institutional credibility at stake, whatever it was going to take, the agency was committed to deliver the Memorial Plaza for an opening on September 11, 2011. "I understood that the Port Authority had lost its political constituency and needed to 'tie the wagon to the memorial,'" Ward told me. "Once that decision had been made, the decision-making got simpler. We knew how to proceed. The decision became a framework for setting priorities. The questions that followed from this decision led to redoing the scheduling for the entire project. The memorial decision was a game changer."[35] Finally, a priority was set.

FIGURE 17.6 *"Chris Ward columns."* The Port
Authority of New York and New Jersey

Working out the details for the tenth anniversary opening was a collaborative effort of the stakeholders on the site. Every Thursday from 8:30 A.M. to 10 A.M., the fifteen-person Memorial Oversight Committee met in the offices of the Memorial Foundation: six from the Port Authority (Chris Ward, Drew Warshaw, David Tweedy, Steven Plate, Alan Reiss, Tim O'Connor), three from the Memorial Foundation (Joe Daniels, Jim Connors, Allison Blais), five from City Hall (Robert Lieber or Robert Steel, Josh Wallack or Jeff Mandel, Seth Myers, Andrew Winters, Kate Levin), and the Memorial Foundation's construction manager (Frank Voci of Bovis Lend Lease). The scheduled meetings kept everyone's attention focused. "The most amazing thing about our meetings," Warshaw recalled, "is that by the early summer before the tenth anniversary, it became clear that we were going to make the anniversary commitment, and those meetings phased into what we called 'Day 2' meetings, in which the same group began tackling the operational challenges of opening the site to the public in the middle of the largest construction zone in New York City."[36]

INSTITUTIONAL RECAST

With release of *A Roadmap Forward* in early October, Ward promised "a new way of doing business, one in which openness and transparency will be at the forefront of our rebuilding effort, and we'll hold ourselves accountable for the results."[37] Under the new regime, the agency was committing to report openly on the construction milestones established as part of the report, to report on progress in reaching them, and, in cases where the targets were missed, to provide a clear explanation and a detailed plan to fix the problem.

Justly proud of the intense and massive effort of the last several months, Ward (and Warshaw) led off the seventy-page report to Governor Paterson with a summary of the four main results achieved by the resolution of the fifteen fundamental issues that had gone unresolved prior to the agency's June assessment. These included a simplified design for the Transportation Hub that promised to deliver schedule and cost savings without sacrificing Calatrava's iconic Oculus; the deck-over construction solution allowing for the opening of the Memorial Plaza on the tenth anniversary of the attacks; a more efficient approach to the complex and troublesome task of permanently underpinning the MTA's No. 1 subway line, which had to be completed before Greenwich Street was rebuilt on top of it; and a series of stakeholder agreements that would give the Port Authority greater control over delivery of the Vehicle Security Center, that part of the Port Authority's massive underground infrastructure serving as the key access point to all of the commercial development on the site.[38]

Getting to this point "was not an easy process," he said in a tone that might best be described as bureaucratic understatement. "There were few easy conversations and even fewer easy choices."[39] The all-consuming process had, in fact, been intense and excruciatingly fragile, not just because of the redesigns and hard work of executing the plans with their massive amounts of minutiae, but because the Port Authority had to repair relationships with the Memorial Foundation and the FTA, both of which were in tatters by the time Ward got to the agency in May.

The revamped plan for moving forward presented new, detailed schedules and new budgets with interim milestones. It showed "target dates" and "probabilistic dates," with most of the projects being completed between 2012 and 2014. It offered up budget estimates for the Port's four major projects, all but one significantly higher. (Reports at the time noted that the Port Authority was looking at a total increase in costs of about $1.5 to $1.7 billion, though as a 2011 audit would later reveal, the agency's overall exposure actually increased by some $3 billion between December 2006 and November 2008.)[40] It also laid out a new "functional decision-making model" designed to address the problematic lack of governance that had repeatedly bedeviled the PA's management of the Trade Center project. It detailed how a steering committee of stakeholders, Port Authority staff, and professional consultants had addressed every one of the June assessment report's fifteen fundamental issues to be resolved and presented fourteen detailed graphics illustrating the changes the Port Authority had made to achieve "certainty and control" over its projects.

The report's highly detailed descriptions and frequent numerical gauges referencing vast quantities were calibrated to point to the effort and complexity of the tasks ahead—thirty-seven hundred drawings for the complete design of the Hub, for example. In substance and style, the *Roadmap* document presented more than a blueprint for construction progress and performance. At the same time, tactically, it put forth the Port Authority's intense ambition to reestablish its reputation and reshape public expectations about its ability to deliver a completed rebuilt Trade Center site. Explanation of its realistic risk-based analysis and promise that the public could track its progress and hold "the Port Authority and its project partners" accountable aimed to instill confidence where none had existed before. It was a necessary institutional gamble as the falsehoods of the past had offered up plentiful evidence for doubting new promises, evidence that had seriously damaged the agency's credibility. Ward went so far as to acknowledge that "these new schedules and budgets will be met with a degree of skepticism." He wasn't wrong about the skepticism, though his reasoning for why these schedules and budgets were "markedly different from past ones" was sound. Still, it was going to be mighty hard to convince the public to put aside the past. Only clear and visible proof of performance would matter.[41]

The day after the report was released the *Post* penned an editorial dripping with cynicism: "Port Authority boss Chris Ward claimed yesterday that Ground Zero will indeed be rebuilt someday. That's encouraging. In fact, he's even distributed a seventy-page report detailing exactly how it's to happen, and when. Could it be that the end of the beginning is in sight? Alas, skepticism is warranted." In predictable fashion, the tabloid complained that the new schedule was "nothing to throw a party over.... [T]he Freedom Tower and palatial PATH station *still* won't be ready until 2013 and 2014." It railed against out-of-control costs—at $3.2 billion, the PATH station amounted to some $50,000 per average daily rider. It asked if "the new era of openness" would continue when inevitable schedule slippage began. It lambasted the agency's "double talk" upon learning that the tenth anniversary opening of the memorial would only be partial, that full, unrestricted access and the museum would not be ready at that time. The conclusion: "Ward & Co. may be headed down the same path as their predecessors—who fudged, fibbed and fiddled while the project stalled."[42]

The *Daily News* also restated its ongoing agenda of complaints of the Port Authority's cost-be-damned arrogance and zero accountability: The document was "impressive," the editorial admitted, but "[t]he Port Authority is beyond accountability in a realm unto itself." It doubted the agency could genuinely collaborate with the site's other stakeholders, always opting to do "just want it wants, as it wants, when it wants, the public be damned." It faulted the agency for failing to do anything substantial "to simplify and economize on the key engineering element and stumbling block in Ground Zero's reconstruction," for making "only minor adjustments in the palatial underground" of Calatrava's complex "masterwork." The public was "conned again," it said in another editorial days later, because Ward didn't deliver on "a plan for finishing the complete 9/11 memorial by the 10th anniversary of the terror attack…even if all of officialdom is pretending that he did."[43]

The *Times* penned no editorial, though veteran reporters Charles V. Bagli and David W. Dunlap wrote at length about "New Ground Zero Timetable Fails to Convert Some Skeptics." "Most telling," they reported, "was what was not said by some executives involved in rebuilding, like Larry A. Silverstein, a frequent critic of the authority, who did not embrace the report." In a statement, Silverstein said, "We are now going to study the report and back-up materials so that our construction professionals can evaluate the new dates…[and] gauge the impact on our part of the World Trade Center rebuilding effort."[44] Silverstein would issue no further comment, which was not surprising given what was going on between the Port Authority and Silverstein at this time, none of which was amicable.

The site-rebuilding partners were engaged in new, "already bitter" negotiation over the lease arrangement and the timetable for Silverstein's three towers, which he was contractually required to complete by 2013 or else run the risk of default and forfeiture of his development rights. Also ongoing between the two "partners" was a nasty construction dispute pertaining to the turnover of site 4, which would eventually go into arbitration (as discussed in the previous chapter). Neither Silverstein nor his project point person, Janno Lieber, showed up at the press conference Ward held with Mayor Bloomberg and Governor Paterson to announce the *Roadmap Forward*. The report said nothing about Silverstein's towers; it did not talk about the economics of that part of rebuilding. When asked about this, Ward said "the market will respond as it needs to respond. We will have available those sites and those foundations to Larry's team to meet the market."[45]

The lines of battle were being drawn anew in another nasty conflict over the private developer's ability to marshal the necessary financial resources to build his three towers and the market's ability to absorb 6.2 million square feet of new office space. The battle would rage for eighteen months. The Great Recession, as it came to be called in the United States, shuttered the window of development opportunity at Ground Zero and every other place across the globe where building cranes had been expected to populate city skylines. Financing was unavailable. Lending markets had collapsed dramatically fast when Lehman Brothers filed for bankruptcy in early September, just weeks before *Roadmap Forward* was issued. This critical context, however, runs ahead of the story laid out in the next chapter.

Ward found "no panaceas" for accelerating the project's timetables or radically scaling back its costs. The Hub project had been driven by both personal ambition (Pataki, Calatrava, Sartor) and institutional ambition, and once begun, the decisions that had made it so costly became irreversible. The grand vision had gotten out of control. Trimming the Hub's elaborate and complex design to make it easier and faster to build was the best that could be done at this point. The project was way too far down the road—way deep into design documents that detailed the size and shape of the Hub—for radical changes; radical changes would have created even greater risk to the completion schedule. The most visible change captured the full attention of the press: The building's wings—the roof canopy that Calatrava likened to a bird taking flight—would no longer fly. "This is a tough choice, but it's the right choice," Ward said. It had been lurking in the shadows all along, but Ward was the one to make the decision. "It's reflective of the kinds of choice we simply must make in the coming weeks and months if we are to establish priorities and milestones, to which we can be held accountable," he said.[46]

In place of movable wings, Calatrava substituted a less costly mechanism, an operable skylight spanning the nearly football-field length of the Oculus structure that would open on September 11 and other occasions to allow natural light to beam down into the vast elliptically shaped transit hall. Two other modest changes simplified the Oculus: The length of the south wing was cut back some, and the number of structural connections between wing elements (known as purlins) reduced from five to one. The Hub Working Group had recommended more substantial changes to the Oculus that would have reduced the above-grade structure by 25 percent in plan and by 50 in volume, making the Oculus floor space slightly smaller than that of Grand Central Terminal, but Port Authority staff working on the project pushed back on this and other recommendations of the group. It was unrealistic to think you could "shrink wrap" the Hub, Ward told me. The dynamic of the Working Group, he said, was heavily driven by the strong voices of Silverstein's people, who were always a few moves ahead on the chess board. He believed they were focused on reducing the PA's budget for the Hub because they wanted fewer dollars being swept up by the Oculus and presumably would benefit from a cutback in the Hub when the time came to press the PA for financial assistance in building out their towers. Nonetheless, they did not get the type of changes they sought.[47] The changes specified in *Roadmap Forward* promised hundreds of millions in cost savings for the $7.2 billion in estimated costs for Trade Center projects of the Port Authority. Still, the structure remained relatively close to its original design.

A radical redo as contemplated earlier in 2008 by a PA-assembled team had identified nearly $300 million of potential changes, changes that if implemented in their entirety were optimistically predicated to bring project costs within the available funding limits—at the cost of Calatrava's vision. The project would have been "dramatically changed, and one of the two great public spaces Calatrava proposed would be eliminated entirely," Anthony E. Shorris wrote. "The underground portions of the project would be new and serviceable, but more quotidian in design." The vision from the street would have been unaffected, with "great Oculus itself suffering only modest changes."[48] Those changes were no longer a discussion item after Shorris was gone from the Port Authority. And starting all over again with a new design (or making the temporary PATH station permanent) was also out of the question. In *Roadmap Forward*, Ward laid out ten detailed reasons why they could not simply scrap the current design and make the temporary PATH station permanent; prominent among them—squandering a significant portion of the $1.35 billion investment already spent on construction of the Hub and running afoul of its funding contract with the Federal Transportation Administration. The backstory of why the Port Authority was essentially locked into this overscaled symbolic statement designed to reestablish its institutional legacy, however, is more revealing.

The decision not to hit the reset button on the Hub came down to two major factors: the FTA and schedule risk. The FTA was the Port Authority's critical funding partner. It had "bought" a transportation facility that would check certain boxes of its funding criteria, and Ward and Warshaw reasoned the federal agency would have pulled its $2.65 billion had the Port Authority abandoned the fundamental design. The PA's relationship with the FTA was already strained from the federal agency's investigation of the Port Authority's oversight of the Transportation Hub and Vehicle Security Center and Tour Bus Parking Facility projects and the tensions of increasingly negative monitoring reports discussed in the prior chapter. By May 2008, conversations between the PA staff and the FTA had broken down. The relationship was in need of repair, not replacement. The PA also wanted something else from the FTA: $450 million of unspent funds from the VSC project, as well as $213 million "unprogrammed" FTA funds, reallocated to the Transportation Hub. The VSC was the critical below-ground passageway for the delivery of construction materials to the commercial towers and retail spaces, and the Port Authority was anxious to speed up its construction (figure 17.7). Consolidating the FTA's funding into the Hub from the Hub and the VSC would do that by removing a layer of federal oversight for the VSC project and giving the authority greater flexibility and control over the VSC's design, procurement, and construction.

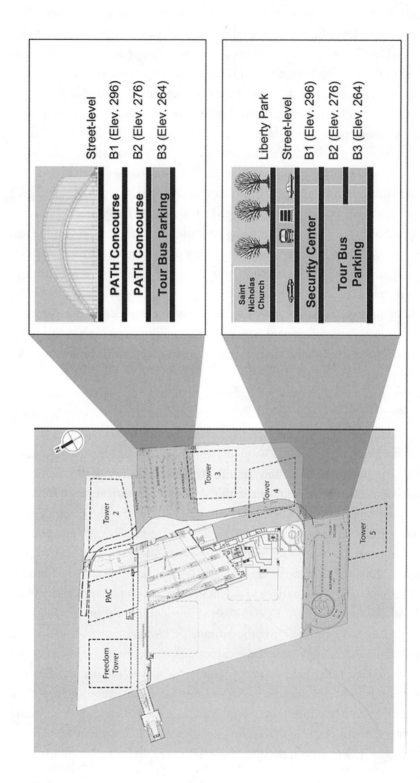

FIGURE 17.7 *Diagram of what is within the underground Vehicle Security Center at the Trade Center.* THE PORT AUTHORITY OF NEW YORK AND NEW JERSEY

Schedule risk was the second factor. The Hub had been in design since 2006 and hundreds of hours of coordination with the site's stakeholders—the Memorial Foundation, retail interests, Silverstein Properties, the NYPD, and the MTA—had gone into the Hub's thirty-seven hundred design drawings. The Hub touched every other project on the site. To completely redesign the transportation center would have meant restarting the entire design process, delaying the project for who knows how long—Ward figured at least eighteen months—and in a chain reaction, drag down every other project it touched. A totally new design would also have triggered the need for a new environmental impact review, a regulatory procedure that would undoubtedly not merely have subjected the project to lengthy review but set it on a potentially fatal course of opposition. In short, it was just too late to start over. Making the existing design more practical in terms of speed and simplicity and preventing impact on adjacent projects, rather than attempting a full-scale reset, would keep the peace with the FTA, would keep construction moving, and would avoid the major risk of a fundamentally new design that did not yet exist. It was an equation for institutional protection, though not without risk: The PA still had to deliver performance—on-time and on-budget results. Ward was not naïve. He knew rebuilding the Trade Center site was "an enormously difficult undertaking," that not all problems had been solved, and that the future would not be without "a new series of challenges," a rapidly deteriorating economy being one of them.[49]

One of the biggest issues seemingly but not definitively resolved by the *Roadmap Forward* was the "less-than-ideal" relationship with the Phoenix Constructors venture. The inefficiencies of the contracting relationship with Phoenix made Ward's list of the fifteen "fundamental issues critical to the overall project" in need of a firm resolution. It was also one of the few decisions under the Port Authority's control. Yet it was not a new issue. The agency had an earlier plan for change, which was lost to the political upheaval when Governor Spitzer abruptly stepped down from office. When Ward came on board the Port Authority, the problem with Phoenix was evident, but, he asked, was there a better alternative? The answer, at least for the time being, was no. The PA would stick with the Phoenix joint venture, with the FTA's concurrence, under a "modified relationship that provides the right incentives to control schedule, cost and risk." Keeping to the arrangement, Ward said "will avoid the lengthy delays and uncertainty of a whole new bidding process" that "would add schedule risk to the project without clear evidence that a lower cost could be achieved or that a new general contractor would improve performance."[50]

The major design changes for the Hub and Greenwich Street corridor (top-down construction of the No. 1 line) were not yet complete, so any rebidding of the work would have compounded the mistake the agency made in 2006 by bidding out designs that were not yet complete. Continuing with "builders who know the site and the project" held greater potential for reducing schedule risk than a new open-bid process that would take, at a minimum, six months, so PA officials reasoned. Not insignificantly, the FTA wanted to keep Phoenix on to maintain continuity, and the Port Authority needed the FTA's cooperation with other issues coming out of the assessment restructuring. Pragmatically, there was no point rocking that relationship when all of the other reasons pointed to keeping Phoenix on, at least for the time being. The fix, though, was temporary.

By early 2009, Ward realized the Phoenix arrangement would "never be right."[51] He was getting feedback from the General Contractors Association not to do it this way. Most important, he needed to get contracts moving to meet his milestones. By this time continuity was less of an issue. Ward and Warshaw believed they were in a much better position to make the move and restructure the relationship with Phoenix without risking schedule slippage or cost increases. Major designs for the Hub and the No. 1 line were complete. With the collapse of the construction market, the bidding environment became highly favorable. The Port Authority's relationship with the FTA was improving rapidly. Altogether, these factors made the time ripe to make the transition, so in April 2009, the PA modified the contract with Phoenix, which allowed the Port Authority to competitively bid future work on the Hub, while ensuring that Phoenix continued to work on and complete its existing work awarded to date.

The Port Authority was betting its institutional reputation on assuring completion of rebuilding the Trade Center site; the project was a bet-the-institution job. Under Ward's leadership, with the support of a new governor and a frustrated mayor seeking visible results on Ground Zero, it did an institutional about-face, a mea culpa, and adopted a strategy of disclosure. Only by coming clean with the fallacies of the past and reframing the rebuilding crisis as a construction project executed in an unbiased manner by construction professionals and development experts could the beleaguered agency, perennially criticized for its arrogance and autonomy, aim to neutralize the ever-ready force of politics. Politics had defined too many key rebuilding issues and irreversible decisions. In adopting the technical experts' frame of reference for the rebuilding project at Ground Zero, Ward was evoking the agency's founding Progressive Era roots of apolitical action. To be at all convincing, he also needed to change the press narrative from one of delay to one of progress.

The press is an enormous conduit: a weapon to some, a messenger to others, and perhaps the only one accessible to all stakeholders and different interests, including opponents, seeking to influence the political process. For getting the message out and shaping it or for positioning on political controversy, there was no other medium like it—for the mayor's office, the LMDC, and the Port Authority. The Port Authority, in particular, could look back on a powerful legacy of using public relations to great effect put in place by Austin Tobin's skillful director of public relations, Lee K. Jaffe, as soon as she was hired in 1944. All of the players at Ground Zero with information to share, official and unsanctioned, strategically moved it into the print media through press releases and statements, information leaks, and planted stories. They managed the message with orchestrated public-relations campaigns, and the twists and turns of the information had their own impact on the dynamics and events at Ground Zero.

Stephen Sigmund was the Port Authority's head of public affairs and government affairs for four and a half years, from February 2006 to September 2010, when the agency was constantly being attacked in the press for its bungling of its rebuilding efforts. Political communication is an art form, he explained in a 2011 media interview with the trade journal *Campaign and Elections*. "It changes with every situation. There are some general rules: You are in a fast-paced environment. The situation changes under your feet so you have to shift and adapt to the situation. You have to be smart about the situations you are facing and get smart quickly."[52] Sigmund indeed had to get smart quickly. Skilled at managing the message (part of his savvy at the job came from family familiarity: his mother was mayor of Princeton, New Jersey, and ran for the U.S. Senate, his grandfather was a member of the U.S. House of Representatives, and his aunt is National Public Radio reporter Cokie Roberts), he had been communications director for New York mayoral candidates Gifford Miller and Mark Green, and had temporarily served New Jersey governor Jon Corzine in that role, as well as having worked with large corporate clients in the private sector. He understood the business of crisis management, every bit of which was put to use at the Port Authority.

When he got there the bi-state agency was in the midst of a fierce and lengthy battle with Larry Silverstein over whether the developer was going to retain the rights to develop all five planned commercial towers. He was the agency's front-line spokesman in charge of a $22 million budget and a staff of sixty. Throughout his tenure at the helm of this multifaceted public relations operation, he served one Port Authority chairman (Anthony Coscia) but three executive directors (Kenneth Ringler, Anthony Shorris, and Christopher Ward). The 2006 realignment deal between the Port Authority and Silverstein did little to settle the deep frustrations with the agency's handling of its expanded rebuilding responsibilities. Repeatedly, it was being excoriated on the editorial pages of the dailies, blamed for stalled progress, delays in construction of the massive underground infrastructure, and missed deadlines for turning over sites to Silverstein. Sigmund spent 75 percent of his time on Trade Center issues, notwithstanding the myriad of other activities and projects the Port Authority was engaged in. Other stories were nowhere near as focused, complicated, or hot as the Trade Center story, he told me. "Ground Zero was all a political story because politics—the two states, the city, the families, and the developers—was the key issue of rebuilding."[53]

The storyline Sigmund crafted was simple and clear: "We're the only ones. The agency is taking responsibility for doing what others would not do: the Freedom Tower, the Memorial, and Tower 5." The initial messaging was all about responsibility, and the agency stayed with it for a long time, even over misses. It contrasted with the narrative of Silverstein as the profit-craving developer. The public storyline was pushed through by discussions with reporters; it was not driven by the editorial boards. But it was a very hard task to present a storyline of progress, he emphasized, especially when whatever was happening was underground, unseen. Seven years later, there still was no visible above-ground construction.

Resetting expectations with new timelines, new budgets, and new accountability reflected all the right policy responses—but would it work? It could turn out to be the agency's Achilles heel, yet, perhaps, only the Port Authority had the institutional arrogance to pull off rebuilding at Ground Zero. While it might not restore the agency's reputation, it gave it a chance of doing so—if it performed (plate 16).

CHAPTER 18

Stalemate over Subsidy

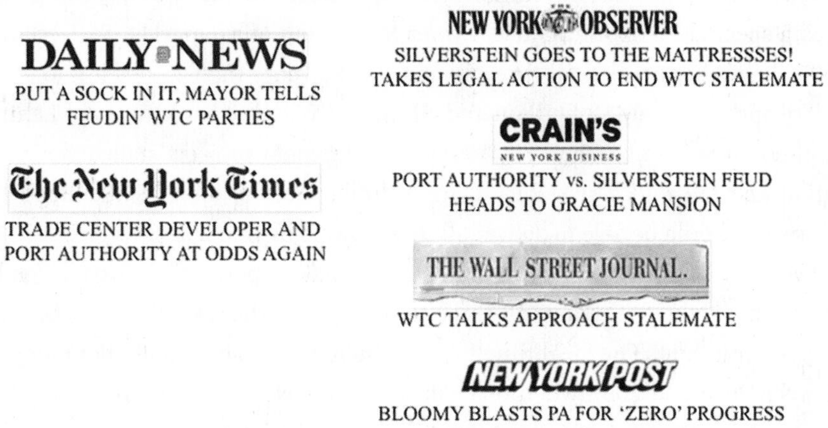

DAILY NEWS

PUT A SOCK IN IT, MAYOR TELLS FEUDIN' WTC PARTIES

The New York Times

TRADE CENTER DEVELOPER AND PORT AUTHORITY AT ODDS AGAIN

NEW YORK OBSERVER

SILVERSTEIN GOES TO THE MATTRESSSES! TAKES LEGAL ACTION TO END WTC STALEMATE

CRAIN'S NEW YORK BUSINESS

PORT AUTHORITY vs. SILVERSTEIN FEUD HEADS TO GRACIE MANSION

THE WALL STREET JOURNAL.

WTC TALKS APPROACH STALEMATE

NEW YORK POST

BLOOMY BLASTS PA FOR 'ZERO' PROGRESS

FIGURE 18.1 Author composite

The $250 million East Bathtub is where it came together, the public and the private spheres of development. This seven-acre commercial heartland of the master plan embodied economic promise for lower Manhattan. With the two parties together, yet apart in culture and style, the development partnership between the Port Authority and Larry Silverstein and his investors, codified in the 2006 Realignment Agreement and detailed in 332 pages of a Master Development Agreement, promised to bring physical shape to the vision, if not the literal form, of the master plan. The vision's state-of-the-art office towers comprised an ensemble of political compromises fused together through acrimonious public conflict and millions of public dollars. Although the 2006 deal pushed forward construction underground, it did nothing to resolve the weak economic equation of the three-tower program. Silverstein never believed the city's push to build out the project all at once was the correct approach, though he committed to a legally binding development schedule glued together by "the cross" of the 2006 Realignment Agreement, which tied the completion of all three towers to a defined time frame. It would take more than a contractual agreement, however well drafted, to move the commercial program from blueprints to towering physical presence by mid-2013 as called for in the 2006 agreement.

Time moved quickly. By 2008, Silverstein and his investors faced pressure from "the cross." Even in November 2006 at the time the agreement was signed, Silverstein did not have enough insurance funds left to build all three towers; he was short between $900 million to $1.2 billion, according to one inside source. Big lenders (and buyers of the $2.6 billion of Liberty Bonds pledged to the project) would insist upon a certain number of lease commitments before signing on to such a speculative exposure to the lower Manhattan office market. By December 2007, the cost to develop all three towers was up more than 35 percent to a total cost of approximately $5.4 billion and climbing.[1] With the bankruptcy of Lehman Brothers in September 2008, real estate development projects stalled across the nation and fell into a state of indefinite limbo; so too, did the likelihood that Silverstein would be able to deliver all three towers by mid-2013.

Even in a booming real estate market, real estate experts might have given low odds to his ability to finance all three towers within the time frame of his 2006 deal commitment. The ideal time for Silverstein to have begun development was between 2006 and 2007, when real estate markets were robust, but he could not line up the requisite anchor tenants. The Port Authority's site-delivery delays made more credible his continual charges of incompetence against the Port Authority; nevertheless, Silverstein was still bound by "the cross" that now dangled like the Sword of Damocles.

Although the cross was a severe test of financial ability, a default by the developer was far from a one-sided risk. In a downside scenario, the Port Authority would be exposed to the loss of $78.7 million in annual rent revenues and the need to still spend more millions to build the below-grade infrastructure underneath Silverstein's tower sites shared by the Transportation Hub and the memorial; also, its planned retail program would suffer significantly without the traffic generation of the office towers. Both sides understood that they needed the other to succeed. That, however, did not change the gamesmanship of the financial contest as each vied for negotiating leverage by galvanizing the public through the press (figure 18.1). Threatened with the potential loss of all of his development rights on Ground Zero, Silverstein played tough and true to his reputation, appealing to public opinion to get a concession on timelines, threatening to stop building in the East Bathtub, pushing his legal position, and invoking arbitration as he pressed hard and steady for deep financial support to build his towers. With little "skin in the game," it was all going to be upside for his investment partnership.

If the private commercial towers on Ground Zero were to get off the drawing boards, normative good-government policy needed to take second place to economic-development pragmatism. Whether or not the governor or the Port Authority commissioners or the mayor liked—and they did not—what Silverstein was doing, they would accede to providing financial support. The question was, how much financial support? Politically, how much choice was there of letting the commercial project remain in limbo, admitting to the world at large that the proud and powerful City of New York would just wait for the market to recover, wait in passive deference to the economics of the marketplace? This option was not coded into the city's DNA.

Again, using his bully pulpit, Mayor Bloomberg leveraged the moral imperative of rebuilding, asserting a need to prove the city's resilience in the face of calamity. He built an alliance with New York State Assembly Speaker Sheldon Silver, who represented downtown and was at the height of his power during a weak gubernatorial administration. It was an unusual alliance in the sense that Bloomberg and Silver had not agreed on much in the eight and a half years of Bloomberg's tenure in City Hall. Together, they aggressively advocated for the developer, pushing the Port Authority to use its balance sheet to assure commercial redevelopment of the site. As this high-profile conflict escalated into an ugly, eighteen-month, toxic public brawl, the politicians learned that Ward could play tough, too. With the support of the *Times*, Governor Paterson, and the city's influential civic groups, Ward persisted far longer than most observers could believe, holding to a disciplined policy position that sought to protect the Port Authority's balance sheet for regional capital investments beyond Ground Zero. In this all-too-familiar loggerheads scenario the money equation remained a contentious policy lever within the boardroom of the Port Authority and the bullpen of City Hall. In both governmental arenas, money equates with power, as it does in the corporate offices of private developers.

LARRY'S LOST OPPORTUNITIES

January 2007 ushered in a year of optimism for lower Manhattan. A resurgent uptick in residential population and new construction along with residential conversions of older office space was validating Mayor Bloomberg's 2002 *New York City's Vision for Lower Manhattan* (figure 18.2). Reports on the commercial real estate market were downright bullish: "Lower Manhattan: A Relative Bargain but Filling Up Fast" (*NYT*), "Demand Looks Good for Downtown Towers" (*NYO*), "Lower Manhattan's Revival Will Include New Hotels" (*NYT*).

As fit the historical pattern, the appeal of the downtown office market increased when office space in midtown Manhattan got pricey; after what *Crain's New York Business* called a "giddy run-up," midtown rents were "red-hot" in January 2007, on

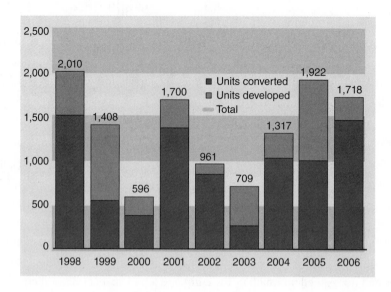

FIGURE 18.2 *Chart of residential growth in lower Manhattan—units converted and developed: 1998–2006.* ALLIANCE FOR DOWNTOWN NEW YORK AND NEW YORK CITY HOUSING AND PRESERVATION DEPARTMENT/CRAIN'S NEW YORK BUSINESS

average about $57 a square foot compared to $41 a square foot in lower Manhattan, and with limited new supply in the coming year, real estate experts foresaw continual rent increases in a market driven by strong demand for large blocks of space in short supply. Some of the city's largest financial-services firms, Merrill Lynch and J. P. Morgan Chase in particular, were in the market "shopping for towers with updated infrastructure and room for large trading floors," just the type Silverstein planned to build at the Trade Center. He was but one of three landlords "locked in a fierce battle" to win lease commitments from these potential anchor tenants; Brookfield Properties Corporation, owner of the four tower buildings of the World Financial Center across from the Trade Center, and Vornado Realty Trust, which was proposing to build a tower of 2.5 million square feet on the site of the Hotel Pennsylvania across from Madison Square Garden/Penn Station, were the other two.[2]

Silverstein needed at least one of these big financial tenants to solidify his plans for Ground Zero, yet his quest proved elusive. The first disappointment occurred when J. P. Morgan Chase directly approached the Port Authority, reportedly in November 2006, about building a tower of 1.3 million square feet for its investment banking headquarters on land at the corner of Cedar and Greenwich Streets. This was the location of the fifth tower site of the master plan, known as site 5, where the contaminated and vacant former Deutsche Bank Building was being deconstructed. The bank was not interested in Silverstein's sites at the Trade Center, according to Charles V. Bagli, who was reporting on the prospective deal; the giant financial-services firm preferred to control its own building even though site 5, the smallest footprint of the five office sites, could not easily accommodate the trading floors the firm needed.[3] To accommodate large and wide trading floors, the building would have to cantilever about one hundred feet over a planned park (Liberty Park) and church (replacement for St. Nicholas Church, destroyed in the 9/11 attack) on Liberty Street as well as over Cedar Street; that configuration would cast a permanent shadow over the one-acre park and require an adjustment to the recently amended project plan for the site, triggering a public review process that would surely stir up some amount of community opposition related, or not, to the proposed adjustment.

News of the negotiations sent a surge of adrenaline through the downtown market, seemingly substantiating the location as "ideal" for financial-services firms, said the president of the Alliance for Downtown New York, Eric J. Deutsch. "If the deal is completed," Bagli wrote, "it will represent a remarkable turnaround for a neighborhood whose future seemed so dismal after Sept. 11, when many experts predicted that the business district would never recover from the terrorist attack."[4] Ground Zero had lost the first potential big player to midtown in 2003 when Bank of America could not get comfortable with lower Manhattan and being in the Freedom Tower and instead chose to go with the Durst Organization and anchor its 2.1-million-square-foot tower, One Bryant Park. Two years later, Goldman Sachs also turned away from Ground Zero, although the bank stayed in lower Manhattan and built a new headquarters across the way on the last commercial office site in Battery Park City at 200 West Street (figure 9.7).

By 2007, the prospect of J. P. Morgan Chase moving its investment banking business back to the city's historic financial center was heady news indeed. The financial-services giant, eleventh on Fortune 500's annual ranking of America's largest companies in 2007, was close to a deal in April, having come to financial terms with the Port Authority on the right to develop a tower under a long-term lease. When Mayor Bloomberg and Governor Spitzer resisted the bank's demands for an incentive package on par with the lucrative package Goldman Sachs had received in 2005, the deal hit a roadblock, but not for long. Following the "routine game of corporate poker in which companies try to extract special benefits," the bank threatened to move to Stamford, Connecticut. Two months later it had a deal with the city and the Port Authority, "a very competitive deal from an overall cost perspective," said one executive who had been briefed on the deal. The bank's intended move carried double significance: It would be the first private company to commit to relocate to Ground Zero and it would represent a move back home for the successor to David Rockefeller's Chase Manhattan Bank, which had headquartered downtown before moving its executive offices to midtown in 1996. "Sweet Deal, Sour Price," said the *Daily News*.[5]

As could be expected, Larry Silverstein went on record saying the bank's decision was a "tremendous addition to the new Downtown."[6] It validated his unshakable belief in the area's resurgence, yet the euphoria of the announcement was short-lived. Less than a year later, in May 2008, two months after the bank's $240 million buyout of Bear Stearns Co., J. P. Morgan Chase CEO James "Jamie" Dimon told attendees at a financial conference that the bank would be able to save $3 billion because it no longer needed to build a new lower Manhattan headquarters for its investment bankers; instead, it would move into Bear Stearns's Manhattan headquarters at 383 Madison Avenue (completed in 2002) in midtown—a tower valued at approximately $1.5 billion or six times what J. P. Morgan Chase paid for the venerable but credit-starved eighty-five-year-old securities firm wiped out by mortgage-related losses that were similarly decimating many Wall Street banks.[7] The aspiration for a market-validating corporate commitment—gone.

Five office towers, two developers, one public and one private—when do the actions of one begin to undercut the other in competition for a shrinking number of potential corporate tenants that could create momentum for Ground Zero? This was the unspoken question when news of the J. P. Morgan Chase deal first circulated about town in November 2006. Was the Port Authority undercutting Silverstein by allowing the bank to buy another site whose footprint was too small to readily accommodate large trading floors that could more easily fit within the configuration of Silverstein's sites?

Next it was Merrill Lynch leveraging the power of its position to get the best deal possible from the three sophisticated competitors vying for its marquee when its lease at Brookfield's World Financial Center came to term in 2013. The investment bank had weathered the worst of the 9/11 attacks; its headquarters at 250 Vesey Street was not heavily damaged, and even though the firm had moved back into its offices by the end of 2001, given the magnitude of the tragedy, morale was low, recalled Martin J. Cicco, head of the firm's real estate investment banking at the time. By 2005, the issue of its expiring lease came up for discussion. The firm could stay at the World Financial Center, which had been a good home for Merrill since 1986, and negotiate for newly renovated space or go someplace else. The twenty-year-old space needed some renovation, said Cicco; the trading floors were no longer state-of-the-art, but the executive floor on thirty-two was beautiful, and senior executives had great quarters. Merrill was becoming quite profitable in '04, '05, and '06. The question was, "Where to go?"[8]

The jockeying for this top Wall Street player started in November 2006 with public whispers that downtown's largest employer might relocate out of town. Merrill let it be known that it was considering its options, including building on sites in New Jersey, building on the Hotel Pennsylvania site in midtown, and being an anchor tenant in Tower 2 or Tower 3 at Ground Zero. It had ruled out the Freedom Tower. CEO Stanley O'Neal, according to an investment banker on the inside, didn't want to be in the Port Authority's tower; reasoning that government would do whatever it needed to do to fill the space, he didn't want to be in that kind of building.

Silverstein's three towers were being designed by a trio of world-class architects: Fumihiko Maki, Tower 4 (150 Greenwich Street); Richard Rogers, Tower 3 (175 Greenwich Street); and Norman Foster, Tower 2 (200 Greenwich Street). All three gathered with the developer and city and state officials in early September 2007 to present refined designs and construction schedules for their towers (figure 18.3). The new addresses heralded the successful reintegration of Greenwich Street into the city street grid. Lower Manhattan was in the process of transformation and dual-rebranding these buildings was but one means of promoting the area's rebirth. "What's happening is that Greenwich Street is emerging as an identifiable corridor for Lower Manhattan," said Janno Lieber, Silverstein's executive directing the Trade Center project.[9]

As Merrill considered its options, city and state officials began lobbying heavily—working "like hell [Schick]," "doing everything we reasonably can [Doctoroff]," "whatever it takes [Silver]"—to keep the bank from relocating out of lower Manhattan,

FIGURE 18.3 *Larry Silverstein surrounded by the three architects chosen to design his towers. To the developer's right, Fumihiko Maki (Tower 4); to the developer's left, Lord Norman Foster (Tower 2) and Richard Rogers (Tower 3).* JOE WOODHEAD, COURTESY SILVERSTEIN PROPERTIES INC.

though the state was on record as saying that any additional subsides beyond incentives that were already in place were unlikely.[10] This factor may or may not have been the clincher in the bank's preference for Vornado's site on Seventh Avenue between Thirty-second and Thirty-third Streets, but Merrill did want especially large trading floors comparable to what it had in London and Tokyo, floors that would be competitive with what was being built by Goldman Sachs and planned by J. P. Morgan Chase. A building on the Hotel Pennsylvania site would accommodate trading floors of eighty thousand square feet, significantly larger than what Silverstein could accommodate in either of his Tower 2 or Tower 3 sites. Even though relocating to Vornado's midtown site was going to cost as much as $1 billion more than either of the two downtown options, Merrill's CEO had made up his mind. The unexpected, however, was about to radically reshape the firm's options.

The real estate decision was on the agenda of the firm's two-day board meeting the third week of October 2007. Standing outside the boardroom in the foyer waiting to make the midtown recommendation to the board was Mark E. Brooks, the managing director in charge of real estate planning and transactions. Inside the boardroom O'Neal was informing directors for the first time that he had had a conversation about selling the company! He had to explain to the board quarterly losses of $2.24 billion, the firm's first quarterly loss in six years. Hours later, still waiting to make his presentation, Brooks was told real estate was no longer on the agenda. Days later Merrill reported $7.9 billion in write-offs due to aggressive bets on mortgage-related securities. "The idea of Merrill popping the vault for its own Midtown skyscraper even as it revealed billions in subprime/CDO write-downs was a nonstarter," wrote real estate journalist Peter Slatin. "But the lure of the gleam of a new, eponymous building proved too great."[11] O'Neal had only a few more days before he would be forced out, having lost the confidence of his board. At that point, the clear uncertainty of the situation threw into question any decision to spend billions on a new headquarters building—in midtown or at Ground Zero.

Enter Governor Spitzer, somewhat last minute. In a letter dated October 26, addressed to the still-CEO O'Neal, the governor wrote, "instead of your negotiating with multiple parties, I have brought Silverstein Properties and the Port Authority together to agree on a single, much more competitive proposal.... Merrill's overall costs for the WTC site have now been reduced to $980 million." The proposal was for Merrill to make a one-time, lump-sum ground lease payment to the Port Authority of $680 million and a developer fee of $300 million to Silverstein Properties. Tower 3 could also be redesigned, he said, to accommodate the bank's business needs for a substantially larger trading floor than had been previously proposed; any change would require approvals by the Port Authority and LMDC, as signatories to the WTC Commercial Design Guidelines, but Merrill would have "my commitment" to work with Mayor Bloomberg to get the city's quick approval. "The Tower 3 site is already nearing complete excavation, and has received all of the necessary design and site approvals," the governor added. "That is simply not true of at least one of the options that Merrill is exploring [Vornado's site], which is contingent on air rights transfers, zoning changes and the future approval of governmental bodies and the New York City Council. I am certain you recognize the value that the certainty offered by the WTC site presents in comparison with some other sites."[12]

By year end, Merrill's new CEO, John A. Thain, former president and chief operating officer of Goldman Sachs and former CEO of the New York Stock Exchange, was in place with a heavy mandate to cure Merrill's shaky financial position. The pending decision to move to midtown was temporarily on hold as he reexamined Merrill's options; still, trading space remained a key consideration, and the competition remained fierce. Brookfield was offering to create three eighty-thousand-square-foot trading floors by expanding one of its buildings at the World Financial Center, and Silverstein was offering to adjust architectural plans to meet Merrill's needs. In short, it was still a heated competition to host Merrill, with a second round about to unfold just as the office market started to weaken.

Some good news on the money front came in mid-May: the final settlement of Silverstein's insurance payout—an additional payment of $2 billion on top of the $2.55 billion already disbursed. Although it was a little less than what Silverstein was awarded at trial, the settlement put to rest any further uncertainty about how much insurance money would be available for rebuilding the commercial towers at Ground Zero. Spitzer's new insurance commissioner, Eric R. Dinallo, "did what former Gov. George Pataki and his own insurance appointee should have done long ago," declared the *Times* editorial board. "He finally called all the warring parties into one room and prodded them to settle their differences." Although this settlement was far removed from solving the financial equation for the commercial program at Ground Zero, it "has provided new hope." In its continual promotion of Silverstein, the *Post* editorial was more presumptive in its assessment when it declared the settlement to be "the last financial roadblock to the redevelopment of Ground Zero."[13]

After Thain took over the helm, Merrill signaled that it would extend its lease at the World Financial Center. Nevertheless, in early May 2008, the firm restarted negotiations for the Tower 3 site with a counterproposal to the public-private partnership: $520 million to the Port Authority and $35 million to Silverstein Properties—a mere fraction of what Silverstein had proposed earlier and, ostensibly a statement that it wanted to buy the development rights but not necessarily the developer. Shortly thereafter, the Port Authority board authorized an amendment to the Master Development Agreement; the amendment extended by six months the development schedule for Tower 3 to give Silverstein Properties the time to design and construct a modified building foundation that could accommodate Merrill Lynch's trading-floor requirements and customized mechanical systems (design work already in progress for some months). The developer now had until June 2012 to deliver Tower 3 and a four-month extension of the deadline for the adjacent Tower 4 to April 2012. "We needed to move quickly to ensure that Merrill Lynch's plan downtown can in fact be realized," said Ward, adding, "We're working hand-in-glove with Larry Silverstein to see if that is possible."[14]

By this time, Merrill had abandoned the idea of moving to midtown but was still in serious negotiations with Brookfield over its contractual option for a five-year renewal of its space in the World Financial Center. On June 6, the Port Authority countered with an ask of $652 million; SPI maintained its ask of $300 million in developer profit and transaction fees, plus a $40 million cost reimbursement for design work it did in the fall of 2007 to accommodate trading floors, plus a developer fee of 2.5 percent of the construction cost for Tower 3. Six days later, Merrill rejected the offer and requested a revised proposal. On June 26, the Port Authority dropped its offer by 21 percent, to $513 million, but Silverstein refused to budge. The Port Authority's negotiators were stunned the developer would not move on price given that they had just gotten under the $520 million figure Merrill Lynch had proposed in early May. "Larry doesn't negotiate that way," they were told, said one of my sources.

Larry Silverstein's contrarian behavior had been evident before when he stood firm against heavy pressure from city officials who wanted him to drop his asking rents at 7 World Trade. "If there's no surplus, and there is massive demand for large blocks of space, there's no basis for reducing rents," he had told *Times* reporter Terry Pristin. Despite being pushed by the Port Authority, Silverstein would not budge on his Tower 3 offer. For Merrill Lynch, this was a game changer. It was over. "With no further movement on basic economic terms," the firm said in a letter to Lieber and Ward dated July 3, "We are too far apart to continue this process." The bank would renew its lease with Brookfield, presumably in a deal with very favorable terms. "That's just the marketplace working," said Mayor Bloomberg. At least Merrill was going to remain downtown, "a silver lining in all of this," said one person involved in the episode.[15]

Silverstein's posture on the Merrill offer rang true to his reputation as a tough and difficult negotiator who held out for every last dollar. In pricing high was Silverstein sending a message that he really didn't want to sell his development rights? Maybe. "It's not that he didn't want to capture Merrill as a tenant," one well-placed senior real estate executive told me, "but that he had a different view of the market. He thought it was hot and not a lot of options existed, so he could command his price. Silverstein always tries to shake the money tree."

Yet even if negotiations had continued, even if a deal could have been made, could Merrill have lasted long enough as a going concern to execute deal documents and actually perform on those commitments, given the firm's rapidly deteriorating financial position? Its financial problems were well known. In one year, the retail-banking giant lost $19.2 billion, or $52 million a day; its charges since the credit crisis first flared in the summer of 2007 totaled more than $41 billion— a staggering sum. The firm's stock price had plummeted to $50 a share by May 2008 (when Merrill reengaged in negotiations) from $90 a share in January 2007. Although Thain had made changes in top management and was selling off assets in an attempt to raise capital, the depth of its problems imperiled Merrill. As the U.S. credit crisis continued to roil capital markets and Lehman Brothers prepared to file for bankruptcy, on September 15, Bank of America announced it was acquiring Merrill, ending ninety-four years of its independence. By this time, Merrill's stock price had plummeted to $17 a share.

In the back-and-forth offers on Tower 3, Silverstein may have been thinking strategically. If a deal cratered because of Merrill's inability to perform, not only would he have lost the desired anchor tenant and been back at square one, he would have, essentially, bid against his own interest and set in place an unfavorable precedent on price. The developer's unwillingness to budge on price, however, appeared more consistent with his reputation than with a calculated refusal to take on the high credit risk of a Merrill Lynch deal, especially if the investment bank's ability to perform did not come up during the negotiations.[16] Could the surface of the situation also be covering something else more tactical? Was Merrill's unwillingness to continue negotiations because the developer would not budge on "economic terms" a corporate face-saving retreat? Could the Port Authority's initial price proposal to Merrill have been a veiled attempt to get even with Silverstein, cover its embarrassment over its payment of damages for being late in delivering sites to Silverstein? And was its concession to drop its price in June too late to make a difference to Merrill? A lot of collateral issues were swirling around this particular episode at Ground Zero, clouding any type of definitive conclusion. Any deal at the Trade Center "requires Merrill to come to agreement with both the Port Authority and Silverstein Properties, Inc.," Governor Spitzer had noted in his October 26, 2007, letter to CEO O'Neal. Coming to terms with both parties seemed impossible— revealing evidence of the ongoing, deep-seated tensions and misalignment of interests in this public-private partnership attempting to rebuild Ground Zero.

J. P. Morgan Chase and Merrill Lynch were the largest firms looking for the largest amount of space during the hot market of 2007, but they were not the only big-space users in the market at that time. By mid-2008, twelve lease transactions of more than 400,000 square feet in Manhattan had been signed, and all but two for midtown locations. Of the two downtown transactions, one was Moody's Investor Service, which had signed with Silverstein for nearly 600,000 square feet in 7 World Trade (the only large corporate transaction downtown since 9/11), and the second, a government lease. As a benchmark of market validation, only private-sector leases carry weight; they are the tenants the brokerage community views as having made an "elective decision." Government lease commitments of the type made for the Trade Center's Tower 4 and Freedom Tower are political decisions, and since 9/11, they had accounted for ten of the twenty-five biggest downtown transactions.

In terms of recovery, the office market of lower Manhattan was still waiting for a bona fide tenant of the likes of Goldman Sachs to validate the ambitions of public officials and private business. Whatever may have been the reason, Silverstein's failure to capture any of the three big financial firms—Goldman Sachs, J. P. Morgan Chase, Merrill Lynch—and any others the developer may have been quietly talking with represented a lost opportunity, with potential contractual consequences. With few corporate tenants in sight, the economy teetering on recession, and lenders reluctant to finance speculative office space, his construction deadlines loomed as an ever-present problem that no amount of optimism could ameliorate. The stage was set for a potentially acrimonious battle with the Port Authority. "There is no question that at some point he is going to sue. It is going to be a battle royal, and he is going to blame the Port Authority, the LMDC, and the city," predicted a source who had helped negotiate past agreements at Ground Zero on behalf of the state.[17]

News about the market turned negative quickly: "Fear WTC Could Be a Big Zero" (*DN*), "Manhattan Awash in Open Office Space" (*NYT*), "Recession Adds to WTC Troubles" (*WSJ*). New York did not need the 6.2 million square feet of office space—"not now, and possibly not even in four years, when the towers are slated to open," reported *Crain's* on what the brokers were saying, many of whom were relieved that Silverstein's towers at Ground Zero might be delayed. Financial-services firms were the big users of Manhattan's top-quality office space, and they were shedding it quickly due to pending layoffs, moves into new headquarters buildings planned years earlier, and dispositions of real estate inherited through acquisitions. Real estate experts expected the situation to be much bleaker in 2009, as the global financial crisis continued to take its toll on the financial industry and involuntary consolidation resulted in large blocks of space hitting the market. Lower Manhattan would be especially hard hit as Goldman Sachs vacated its space in four older buildings once it moved into its new headquarters in Battery

Park City, falling insurance giant AIG reduced its office footprint, and bankrupt Lehman Brothers and ailing Merrill Lynch surrendered large blocks of space. The combination of growing supply and low demand was bound to drive rents lower and vacancy higher. "The question is will we have a category one or category five" real estate hurricane, said Barry Gosin, chief executive for the commercial brokerage firm Newmark Knight Frank.[18]

Silverstein subscribed to the long view, as he did when he started 7 WTC in 2002 and the downtown vacancy rate was 17 percent. "The naysayers then and now don't seem to understand that we are building in anticipation of future demand, not based on today's market," he told the *Daily News*. A developer delivering into a future market, it is often said, has to have brains, foresight, and a lot of guts. Silverstein did not expect this downturn to be any different from development's earlier booms and busts: "New York City's economy has always absorbed every inch of office space that has been constructed. There is no reason now to expect this time to be any different," he wrote in an op-ed in *Downtown Express*, the newspaper of lower Manhattan, in November 2008. His confidence was based on his assessment of future demand— population growth from new residents and an economy "more and more dependent on high-value-added white collar jobs, which in turn require modern office space"— and great architecture and green design. "Building now, even if demand for offices either Downtown or anywhere else in the city softens temporarily, we will be ready when the New York and U.S. economies rebound. And have no doubt—they will. They always do."[19] These were logical arguments based on decades of personal experience, market intuition, and confidence in real estate fundamentals, but would the past inevitably forecast the future in downtown?

Historically, downturns in the office real estate cycle have been harsh, but something else was going on during this cycle: structural change. The state-of-the-art office towers proposed for Ground Zero were caught in the vortex of a shrinking landscape for financial services, and change would hit that business's historic home in lower Manhattan especially hard. Although it was not as obvious then as it would become only a few years later, media and communications companies were increasingly taking up residence in the financial district, accounting for 28 percent of the 4.7 million square feet of signed lease transactions in downtown between 2006 and 2008. This was a socioeconomic plus for downtown because many of the employees of these firms preferred to live near where they worked, and their lifestyle was creating a more vibrant round-the-clock, family-friendly neighborhood. But many of these firms producing television, movies, printing, publishing, and other forms of content wanted casual, open-space office environments. How would they view possible tenancy in towers specifically designed for button-down corporate giants in the financial-services industry?[20]

This was a question no one seemed to be asking at the time, at least out loud, perhaps because news of the financial crisis and its impacts demanded immediate and continual attention. Only six months earlier in March 2008, at a speech to members of the New York Building Congress, Silverstein had laid out a detailed construction schedule for his towers, optimistically projecting to be on schedule. He was not worried about lining up tenants. Somewhat glibly he remarked, "Between now and 2011 and 2012 we could be through three more cycles, so it's impossible to tell [referring to his ability to lease out space]. At the moment we are going through a much more difficult time, and presumably by the time these buildings are done those circumstances will be well behind us."[21]

In October 2007, when Merrill Lynch was in the midst of making a decision on a headquarters site, Janno Lieber confidently told a reporter from *Crain's New York Business*, "if we don't get tenants [before we open], that's OK"[22] (figure 18.4). This is a surprising admission for a developer to make, though perhaps not so for a developer with no "skin in the game"—exposure to downside risk as well as benefit from upside gain. And it reveals just how unlike a typical real estate deal it was. Confidence in opening without tenants in place may have been Silverstein's view for 7 WTC, which was financed with insurance proceeds and Liberty Bonds and without contractual constraints of a completion deadline, but the scenario for Towers 2, 3, and 4 at Ground Zero was completely different. Silverstein had a contractual commitment to build at least 6.2 million square feet by 2013 at an estimated cost of approximately $6 billion, and although his recently finalized insurance payout totaled $4.55 billion, reportedly, he had but $1.3 billion remaining insurance money.

FIGURE 18.4 *Janno Lieber of Silverstein Properties in front of models of the Trade Center office buildings.* COURTESY DOWNTOWN EXPRESS

The rate at which Silverstein was spending money to cover the carrying costs of maintaining position, prepare detailed plans and schematics for development, start foundation work on Towers 3 and 4, and pay management fees to the Silverstein investment partnership (as agreed upon in the 2006 realignment deal) was eating away at the insurance payout. Pre-development costs for a large project in a market like Manhattan run high, especially when the project comes about through a public-private partnership and is controversial, meaning likely to incur opposition, litigation, and delays—and time is money in the world of business. Developers typically structure deals to minimize the upfront costs of carrying a large-scale project; for example, rather than acquiring all at once the development sites in a project that will have several phases of construction, they aim to time the takedown of individual parcels to the start of building construction for individual sites. Under the terms of his ground lease, though, Silverstein was committed to paying a lump sum rent for his development rights on the three tower sites. He did have a Liberty Bond allocation of $2.59 billion to use for financing his towers, but the Liberty Bond program was due to expire at the end of 2009 unless Congress extended that sunset date a second time.[23]

Thinking forward, Silverstein was once again betting on the future upside possibility of the situation, confident that he would be able to finance the gap between his remaining insurance proceeds and the cost to build his towers, which had increased dramatically since the 2006 realignment deal.[24] He was preternaturally optimistic. The complete shutdown of global capital markets, however, made such financing indefinitely impossible. He needed access to money and particularly time extensions to meet his obligations and fulfill his ambition to rebuild the commercial stronghold of the Trade Center. He wanted to renegotiate the hard-fought Master Development Agreement and would argue that the difficulty he faced in financing his three towers was caused more by the significant delays at the site, that is, the Port Authority's failure to deliver "construction-ready" sites, and less by the collapse of real estate and financial markets. He had been doubted many times in the past seven years of conflicts and controversy, yet had firmly held onto his position. Despite the bleak prospects for development, who would bet against his abilities to prevail now when the seesaw of rebuilding was tipped in his favor? Still, the high-stakes battle about to erupt once again threatened the ever-tenuous ties of this public-private partnership.

POSITIONING IN THE PRESS

Renegotiation of the MDA hinged on the resolution of several main issues: the timing and phasing of when each tower would get built, how much rent Silverstein and his investors would continue to pay the Port Authority, how much the Port Authority would "backstop" the leases on the towers in order to finance their construction, and how the remaining insurance funds would be used to finance the towers. "Backstop" quickly moved into the lexicon of general reporting from the financial pages. It meant that because there was no tenant revenue that Silverstein could use to secure financing for his three towers (which combined with private equity is how private developers traditionally finance commercial development), the balance sheet of the Port Authority would take its place and guarantee the payments on the debt needed to build some or all of his towers. That is, the Port Authority rather than Silverstein would take the financial risk of completing and tenanting the buildings—directly exposing the agency to speculative development.

The Port Authority did not want a repeat of the 2006 bruising public battle that produced a new deal, yet it could not afford a complete backstop of the commercial towers. Even if Silverstein did not build his three towers, the agency still needed him to build the below-grade infrastructure in the East Bathtub other users would share. The Transportation Hub needed Silverstein's buildings for its utilities, ventilation system, entryways, and emergency exits. The memorial needed Silverstein's Tower 2 for its mechanicals. The potential for litigation loomed. "If SPI stopped building, there would be significant value loss for both public and private sectors," Seth Pinsky told me. "For the public, the PATH Hub, 1 World Trade Center, and the retail would have ground to a halt; all the systems were in the East Bathtub, which Silverstein controls."[25]

Silverstein did not have a weak hand. Although obligated under the cross to complete all three buildings within five years of final turnover of his sites by the Port Authority, his team knew they had leverage over the bi-state agency. The Port Authority needed Silverstein to keep paying lease rent and to build his three towers. Although it could wait out Silverstein by taking interim rents until the insurance funds run out, the agency would be more exposed in this downside scenario than if Silverstein went forward with construction but could not complete all three towers within the time frame of the cross obligation. "The PA would then have sites with no economic value, given the New York real estate cycle, which provides a fifteen-minute window in which to build an office building when you can get rents of $125 per square foot," said Janno Lieber.[26] Each side had obvious points of leverage over the other. Seasoned by the 2006 experience, each side also knew what to expect of the other in the ensuing battle: heavy rhetoric, forceful tactics, and stubborn tenacity.

Private negotiations started sometime toward the end of 2008. In its opening bid, the Port Authority sought to meet two objectives: first, to rationalize the commercial office development by changing the concept in the original 2006 master plan of building all ten million square feet of office space at once to phasing in the office space more closely to market demand. Second, to provide the basic sitewide infrastructure to ensure that the site had a sense of place and could function regardless of how much of the office space was built out. Thus, the Port Authority's original offer included support for Tower 4 with the rationale that it was the most economically viable of Silverstein's three towers because it was the smallest, it was the only tower among the three that had lease commitments—for two-thirds of the building (from the Port Authority for approximately one-third of the space and an option for New York City to take approximately another one-third of the building)— and it was already under construction. The proposal also called for construction of Tower 2 to grade and construction of Tower 3 to podium level to allow construction of critical sitewide infrastructure housed in those foundations, while pausing the full-scale development of the office towers until the private market demanded it.

Still, Silverstein was going to run short of funds to complete Tower 4, which he was funding with insurance proceeds, as the Liberty Bonds had not yet been issued. By April 2009, the *Times* reported that he had less than $1 billion remaining of the $4.55 billion in insurance proceeds. To advance completion of Tower 4, the Port Authority offered to provide financial support through a master lease that would backstop shortfalls on Silverstein's debt obligations. In exchange for taking on this new risk, the Port Authority wanted a commitment fee and agreement on its phased proposal. In addition to this basic structure, the agency outlined other ways in which it could provide additional support, including rent abatements meant to ensure the phased advancement of all three office buildings while protecting "within reason" the Port Authority's further exposure to risk.

For the Port Authority, the financial implications of the proposal depended upon the lease-up rate of Tower 4, but the downside estimate of its exposure was $1.4 billion (on a net present value basis accounting for the time value of money) if SPI failed completely and the agency lost its ground rent and was forced to absorb the full cost of the infrastructure buildout necessary for the site's operation. If SPI accepted the Port Authority's proposal, its losses would range anywhere from $280 million to $1 billion, depending on how quickly Silverstein could lease Tower 4. SPI countered with a proposal that asked the Port Authority to backstop all three towers—two of them upfront and the third once these buildings were financially stabilized. The PA viewed this proposal as unaffordable in the context of the Great Recession and the collapse of the J. P. Morgan and Merrill Lynch negotiations and out of tune with its broader regional transportation mandate. It sent back a list of questions to SPI to better understand the thinking behind its proposal.

In early January, before news of these private negotiations surfaced, Ward tactically signaled the authority's market-based approach to the development of Silverstein's three towers in an interview for *Downtown Express*. "It would be naïve to think real estate can respond in the same way it was expected to respond in 2006," he said, and the best way to ensure that Towers 2 and 3 are successful might be to phase them in over time. He also floated the possibility of building a retail-filled podium of stores on the sites of Tower 2 and 3, then adding skyscrapers when the economy improved, a placeholder idea that had been first mentioned in early spring of 2004 (see figure 12.4), when demand for the amount of office space contemplated by the master plan and construction of skyscrapers at Ground Zero other than the Freedom Tower appeared years away.[27] A few weeks later after testimony at a hearing before the State Assembly, Ward again mentioned the podiums as a fallback option until the market recovered.

This was a controversial option. However, it had been done before in Manhattan, in 1922 (the three-story Colonnade Building, completed five years later) and 1928 when William Randolph Hearst built the base of an intended skyscraper on Fifty-seventh Street and Eighth Avenue, which was postponed due to the Great Depression, only to be completed nearly eighty years later with a design by Lord Norman Foster. The Port Authority could also point to case studies of nine other precedents in U.S. cities and Shanghai. Silverstein said the plan was impractical: "It's almost impossible to get quality retail down below while you're building massive towers up above."[28] The opening round of the public fight had begun, at a relatively low decibel level compared to what was about to unfold over the next fourteen months.

Silverstein's proposal that the Port Authority backstop finance at least two of his three buildings entered the media arena around the third week of March. The two sides would not discuss the details of their private talks because they had reportedly signed confidentiality agreements. (Negotiations in public-private transactions rarely, if ever, take place in sunlight until the essential terms of a deal are in place.) In story after story, the players "declined to comment" on the negotiations, though they readily and repeatedly laid out their different positions on the stalled situation in the press.

"Unfortunately, the Port Authority has been unable to meet its obligations to deliver construction-ready sites or to maintain agreed-upon schedules for critical aspects of the World Trade Center rebuilding," a Silverstein spokesman said. "New Yorkers have been patient enough already, and tens of thousands of New Yorkers are counting on jobs that the rebuilding will produce." A spokesman for the Port Authority responded that the agency would continue discussing with SPI how best to meet a changed market and ensure the Trade Center site was rebuilt "while looking out for the public's interest." A few days later, when asked if there was a limit to the authority's capacity to financially assist Silverstein, PA chairman Anthony Coscia said, "Yes." "We have to deal with the economic reality today," Ward said the next month, after Port Authority officials offered a counterproposal that still kept to the agency's position of financing only one building, Tower 4. It would be "foolish" to finance more than one tower, he said. "Mr. Silverstein is asking the public sector to become his banker. That comes out of the Port Authority's balance sheet." In response, the developer evoked the image of an unfinished and unoccupied Trade Center site for years on end. "In 2006, all of the stakeholders—the city, the state, the Port and Silverstein—agreed that the best interests of both the city and downtown would be served by finishing the entire site simultaneously and as quickly as possible," said Janno Lieber. "One building surrounded by three half-finished blocks for the next 20 years does not make good on promises made to New Yorkers."[29]

The possibility of a deadlock in negotiations or litigation battle with each side claiming that the other missed timing deadlines presented a scenario, Eliot Brown wrote in the *New York Observer*, "likely to play poorly before a public already fatigued with changes to the timetable at the time, though that's more of a problem for the elected officials involved than for a private developer like Mr. Silverstein."[30] Correctly, he foresaw an opening for the governor or mayor to come in and broker a compromise.

Officials in City Hall were silent, publicly neutral on the situation, until March 23, when Mayor Bloomberg said, "What Larry did is take out all his equity at the beginning [in December 2003], so he really doesn't have a lot of skin in the game," the *Times* reported. "He has an enormous amount of upside potential, which doesn't leave the Port Authority with a lot of negotiating ability, because they're the ones who have to put up the money." The next day, the mayor offered to intervene: "The city has limited negotiating power, although we do have the bully pulpit, but I'll do everything I can to help all sides resolve their disputes and issues."[31] Governor Paterson had yet to say anything.

In the midst of an increasingly acrimonious situation, the Port Authority released a set of projections prepared by its real estate consultants Cushman & Wakefield based on anticipated market demand for office space at the Trade Center that predicted long-off dates of stabilized occupancy: 2019 for the Freedom Tower, 2014 for Tower 4, 2026 for Tower 2, 2037 for Tower 3 (based on a construction start in 2030). As reported in *Crain's*, the real estate consultant's study aimed to highlight that a full, simultaneous buildout of the towers would be "financially risky and have a potentially destabilizing effect on the real estate market" because it would flood the market with unneeded space, déjà vu for the original World Trade Center.[32] These were shocking, inflammatory estimates. "If you don't have commercial tenants demanding the space, I don't see it being developed," said Kathryn S. Wylde, chief executive of the Partnership for the City of New York. The 2030 start projection for the third tower was especially questionable; if history provided any guide to the viability of the city's office market, demand for office space in lower Manhattan was likely to return long before that. "It may take five years, it may take 10 years, but it's not going to take 21 years," she said.[33]

Silverstein Properties' response—a charge of "how can you doubt the city's resilience"—embellished the oratory Silverstein typically used to position his call for the public sector to carry the financial risk of his towers: "The Port Authority's position seems to be based on a totally pessimistic attitude about New York's economic future," said Janno Lieber in a statement. "Our view—and that of city leaders and many other experts—is that New York will bounce back strongly over the next five years while we are building these buildings. Nobody at Silverstein is ever going to give up on New York. The city desperately needs the 30,000 jobs that building these towers will provide—right now."[34] Silverstein offered up a compromise: Put Tower 3 (2.3 million square feet) on hold and build Tower 2 (2.8 million square feet) now, since that would make it easier to coordinate with the construction of Greenwich Street and the memorial (Tower 2 houses the power feed for the memorial). Was this a tactical "compromise"?

Not only was Tower 2 larger, but since Tower 3 housed the utilities, mechanicals, and emergency exits for the Transportation Hub, delaying its construction (until Tower 2 was fully leased) without building the podium would obviously put the Port Authority in a pickle of a position since that would mean Tower 3 would not open until 2030.[35] News stories subsequently mentioned rumors that the Port Authority wanted Silverstein to return the Tower 3 site so it could build the podium to house the Hub's infrastructure and retail spaces in exchange for helping him finance one tower. The PA did not literally want the site back, I was told by a close participant in the negotiations, as much as it needed the podium built to service the Hub and wanted the retail space to begin functioning as soon as possible, and Tower 3 was the best site for retail.

By mid-April, the behind-the-scenes fight had developed into a public battle of rhetoric and crossfire accusations. The Port Authority was taking a high-ground, principled policy position in line with its institutional vision of what was in the best interest of the region it was designed to serve: Financial prudence demanded that it not take on billions in speculative exposure to the real estate market and compromise its broader capital program for transportation improvements. Silverstein was free to build these buildings and speculate all he wanted, it said; since the public was being asked to shoulder 100 percent of the risk, the Port Authority had to be realistic about the real estate market.

In turn, Silverstein's position was calculated to appeal to civic pride and resonate with the emotionalism of Ground Zero: Financing a complete rebuild was in the best interest of New York City, as a symbol of its resilience as well as its recovery. This was not "spec" building, but rather, rebuilding what the terrorists destroyed. The Port Authority was at fault, the developer argued, because it had been unable to deliver construction-ready sites, and as a result of those delays, he now could not get financing for the towers because the financial markets were frozen in crisis. The city should not pay the penalty for this incompetence, he added. Going on record with its complaints against the Port Authority, on May 8, Silverstein Properties on behalf of its Trade Center private-investment partnerships filed a thirteen-page "Notice of Default" of the PA's "breaches of the schedule, consent and cooperation provisions of the Master Development Agreement for Towers 2/3/4 of the World Trade Center, as amended."[36]

The adversaries' positioning strategies were aptly captured by Eliot Brown when he raised the question, "Is the symbolism of completion and a bet on the future really worth multiple billions of dollars in public money, particularly when the most symbolic tower on the site, the Freedom Tower, is already going up?"[37] The editorial pages of the city's newspapers answered in predictable fashion. The Port Authority's offer to "bankroll Silverstein to the tune of $1 billion to build Tower 4" was "lunacy," fumed the Daily News. "The PA must withdraw its offer...and redraw plans for Ground Zero. The reasons are simple. First, that $1 billion is earmarked for transportation improvements in New York. That is how it must be spent. Second, trying to force development into Ground Zero would be futile and harmful." Rounding out its argument, the editorial concluded, "For a long time...Silverstein stood to make fabulous sums at Ground Zero while risking none of his own money. That was when times were good. Now they're bad, and he's asking the authority to put more public money at risk so he can stay in the game. But the game is up."[38] The owner of the News, Mortimer Zuckerman, was a prominent real estate developer in the city with interests in midtown Manhattan, and while his reasoned stance on the priority of infrastructure improvements was long-standing, he was not without some of his own interests when it came to commenting on public subsidies for new office development in Manhattan.

"The Port Authority is promising some additional support, but Mr. Silverstein is asking for too much," said the Times. "The authority, which was created to manage transportation and port facilities in the area, has limited resources, and it should not be getting deeper into the real estate business," and Silverstein's company "has already received billions of dollars in support: insurance, government bonds and subsidies, plus a handsome development fee for the Port Authority's construction of the 1,776-foot-tall tower at the site." Its editorial ended with a call for political leaders—the mayor and governor of New Jersey, "both successful businessmen who know the world of financial negotiation"—to get involved. "Those are the very skills needed right now."[39]

The *Post* took aim at its perpetual target, delay caused by the Port Authority: "The fact that the project has faltered yet again is an infamy. It is not only New York that is shamed by this; the nation stands humiliated before the world." Arguing to support the developer, who "is again at swords' points with the Port Authority," the editorial page continued its steady support of Silverstein. "He needs the agency's help with financing in a tough credit market. But the agency— a tool used expertly by New Jersey to aid that state at New York's expense—openly admits that it prefers projects like a new cross-Hudson commuter train tunnel to restoring Ground Zero to normalcy." *Newsday* simply said, if the Port Authority "gives in to developer Larry Silverstein's financing demands, New Yorkers will lose out on other good uses for this money."[40]

Where Silverstein might have expected support from the city's business paper, *Crain's New York Business,* none was forthcoming. A "WTC Solution Hinges on Larry Silverstein" was the lead on its editorial of May 3. While acknowledging that the Port Authority held "the high ground" and that it had "made many mistakes at the site, as have the city and the state," the past did not have "much bearing on the current situation." Rather, the business weekly argued that three considerations were paramount: First, Silverstein's optimism and the unique fact that the developer "has no money at stake" but had collected millions in fees;[41] "he will profit handsomely if he builds towers that succeed, and lose nothing if they fail." Second, the Port Authority was willing to finance one building and had committed to move its headquarters there and pay above-market rents,[42] and the city had committed to space there as well. Third, the question of an additional tower amounted to speculation: "If Mr. Silverstein believes that additional office towers will be a smashing success, he should be the one to put up the money to build them.... If others agree with him, like the city, they can put up money, too."[43]

The "no skin in the game" fact of Silverstein's position created a vulnerability in the negotiation dynamic that was easy for the public to understand and easy for politicians, Port Authority officials, and editorial page writers to exploit, which they all inevitably did as they had done before during the very public fight leading up to the 2006 deal. Without cash equity in the deal, all revenues from his engagement in rebuilding—management fees, development fees, leasing fees, and eventual profits from operating the three towers—amounted to an infinite return, only upside, with no downside exposure. The management fees were "gross," meaning SPI was using those monies to pay for "dozens of highly skilled professionals, equipment and overhead, as well as the cost of creating and occupying a state-of-the-art, 40,000-square-foot design and construction studio," Silverstein said in an exclusive *Daily News* article reporting on an analysis of "records."[44] The 2006 deal had set up a structure of administrative payments and fees to fund Silverstein's work at Ground Zero. In real estate projects, fees are always negotiated; it's a "black art," remarked one highly experienced Manhattan office developer. The payment of fees Silverstein was receiving for administration and management of his interests at the Trade Center had initially been put in place as part of the acquisition transaction in July 2001, and customized to meet the demands of the behind-the-scenes equity investors in the partnership. After the 2006 realignment deal with the Port Authority, these passive investors received 50 percent of the net fees, an increase from 25 percent.[45]

By 2009, the Port Authority's internal calculations based on its reading of the MDA revealed that Silverstein had already collected some $177.5 million in fees ($15 million in leasing fees, $60 million in management fees since 2004, and $102.5 million in development fees) and could expect to collect an additional $79.5 million, not including many millions in fees from leasing commissions on the three towers his firm would lease up. Silverstein was facing public pressure on the fee issue and his no-risk position from having gotten back all of his partnership's equity investment, and no amount of spin could counter the facts of the situation. The developer regarded the insurance funds "as his money," wrote Bagli, and, had not yet shown any intention of investing with his money in the buildings.[46] In his construction of the facts, the developer had already shared the insurance proceeds with the Port Authority when they realigned responsibilities for the commercial towers at Ground Zero.

Silverstein's reputation as a tough, tenacious, and inflexible dealmaker colored the volatile chemistry of the talks. The developer had been called a lot of things over the years of conflict, including "greedy," "public enemy #1," and "betrayer of public trust." He had been cast as private interest making private profit on a place that is public, hallowed by tragedy. This was a liability. Following the 2006 agreement, Silverstein needed to recast his professional and personal profile. Accordingly, his PR machine went into action. Howard Rubenstein of Rubenstein Associates, who had represented Silverstein as publicist and advisor for more than thirty-five years, Global Strategies Group, Mercury Communications, and MirRam Group, among others, plied their connections and skillfully honed a more positive profile that found its way into a stunning series of articles: "The Weekend Interview with Larry Silverstein" (*WSJ*), "Larry Takes a Bow on Ground Zero" (*NYO*), "Cometh the Tower, Cometh the Man: How Larry Silverstein Won the Battle to Build on New York's Most Hallowed Ground" (*Financial Times*), "The Optimistic (and Long) View of Larry A. Silverstein" (*NYT*), "Developer Creates Tower of Strength"

(*Crain's*). As the financing imbroglio of 2009 unfolded, he was aware, Theresa Agovino wrote in *Crain's*, "that he risks being depicted as obstructive in this latest round of talks, as he had been in the past, to which Silverstein said, 'When people need someone to blame, it is easy to blame the real estate developer. I've developed a thick skin.'"[47]

LOCKED IN POSITION

Talks between the two parties stalled sometime toward the end of April 2009, and it wasn't long before State Assembly leader Sheldon Silver intervened. "Seven years and eight months after the attacks, I am fed up with the stalling and I am exacerbated by the current state of the World Trade Center project," he said at a breakfast forum before the Downtown–Lower Manhattan Association, a membership organization of key downtown stakeholders founded by David Rockefeller in 1958. "It's an embarrassment to our city, our state and to the nation." He had grown "weary of the unfulfilled commitments, the recalcitrance, the slowing of progress at the World Trade Center site, and the absence of a clear and steady focus from leadership at the highest levels of government on the needs of Lower Manhattan." He wanted an end to the current impasse, no more stalled negotiations and no arbitration, so he was making public his offer expressed privately to bring the stakeholders together to facilitate agreement and move the rebuilding process forward. Despite rising vacancies and falling rents in the downtown financial district, he was "calling for the construction of at least two towers, with the provision that all of the stakeholders must share in the risk."[48]

Mayor Bloomberg immediately embraced Silver's proposal and invited Larry Silverstein and Port Authority executives to meet with him and other elected officials at Gracie Mansion "to find a way to align the incentives and keep progress moving at ground zero." "We'd like to see a better economic model in which all sides participate in both the upside or downside," said Deputy Mayor Robert C. Lieber, who had been appointed at the end of 2007 to succeed Daniel Doctoroff. Governor Paterson, too, was on board with the suggestion, though he was reluctant to provide government financing for the towers. "Moving forward, he said, "we must acknowledge that the public should not be the ones taking on all the risk for private development and that we should not repeat the mistakes of the past where unrealistic expectations get in the way of a practical path."[49]

If the adversarial positions were set, where the balance of power would settle on what *Downtown Express* called the "seesaw" was not. Ward and Silverstein were on opposite poles of this seesaw, and each needed "heavy friends to get more control." Governors Paterson and Corzine were expected to put more of their weight toward

Ward on the PA side of the seesaw, while Bloomberg and Silver were already leaning toward Silverstein on what was shown to be the lower side of the seesaw in the editorial cartoon in the article. Any possible movement would begin Thursday afternoon, May 21, at a meeting at Gracie Mansion. Two days before the summit, seven of the city's most active civic groups sent letters to Governor Paterson, Mayor Bloomberg, and Governor Corzine calling on them not to divert public funds to subsidize office construction on the site beyond the current commitments of the Port Authority. The funds were needed, they said, for transportation initiatives that would support new commercial activity; it was the responsibility of the private sector to absorb the risk of new construction.[50]

The question of how many towers should be built immediately spoke to the issue of critical mass and the success of rebuilding the site as a "place" of sufficient market strength to attract tenants and retailers. Positions aside, both parties understood that creating a sense of place at Ground Zero was important to achieving success in the eyes of the public as well as the commercial real estate market; they just differed on the immediacy of how much commercial space had to be built to accomplish that goal and who should pay for it. The site had been a hole for years. Port Authority officials needed at least one of Silverstein's towers up and operating by the time the Transportation Hub was expected to open in 2014, or else the site would lack a sense of place. Silverstein believed it was necessary to build two towers at once to meet his long-held view about the site's potential as part of a transformed downtown neighborhood. "The Port Authority doesn't yet recognize that two towers is [sic] better economically for them and a lot better for New York City and for downtown," Janno Lieber told the *Wall Street Journal* days later.[51]

Expectations for what could be achieved at the high-profile summit meeting, scheduled for only an hour, were low. "All sides have dug in deeper," Bagli reported on the day of the mayor's summit meeting. The day before, Silverstein had just taken another arrow out of his quiver, with the implied threat that the delays have given his investment partnership "the legal ammunition to demand repayment of the $2 billion in rent and insurance proceeds that the company has turned over to the Port Authority." Janno Lieber told the *Post*, "we are not asking the Port Authority for their money. But in order for us to justify letting the Port keep the $2 billion they have collected from us and continuing to pay many millions more in rent moving forward, we are asking for their assistance." Port spokesman Steven Sigmund responded: "The Port Authority shows its commitment to the site every day by actually doing the hard work of rebuilding, and we've reinvested the insurance money in downtown." The escalation of rhetoric and potential legal action had hardened into great antipathy between the two principals and their key people. They were barely talking to one another. "Officials involved in the negotiations

FIGURE 18.5 *Mayor Michael Bloomberg (right side of the table, second to the left) meets with PA chairman Anthony Coscia (to Bloomberg's right), State Assembly leader Sheldon Silver (left), Larry Silverstein (second from left), New York governor David Paterson (left), and New Jersey governor Jon Corzine (foreground right) in hopes of resolving an impasse over who will pay for new office towers to be constructed there.* AP PHOTO/FRANK FRANKLIN II

say that Deputy Mayor Robert C. Lieber has spent as much time trying to calm the warring parties as he has trying to come up with an acceptable compromise," Bagli reported. "The best outcome of the Gracie Mansion summit, many say, may be an agreement to meet again"[52] (figure 18.5).

Bloomberg was aiming modestly to defuse the situation, warning reporters in advance of the summit: "There will not be a grand announcement at the end of tomorrow afternoon that the days of wine and roses are here again." Given the "limited contact" between the Port Authority and Silverstein, the mayor's pragmatic goal was simply to serve as a "catalyst and provide a forum for them to get together." The one-hour meeting produced a news blackout and an agreement for each party to assign a key aide to enter intense negotiations behind closed doors and come up with a framework for a deal by June 11. Josh Wallack, a senior policy advisor for the deputy mayor for economic development, was standing outside the door of the meeting room along with other staffers, and his take on the meeting as he watched the actors exit was straightforward: "The implied threat was that the mayor would blame them publicly for the failure of Ground Zero, and no one wanted that hanging around their necks. The mood was tense." As the *Times* editorial board remarked the next week, "It was not exactly the quiet setting for complicated negotiations but it did emphasize the importance of resolving this latest disagreement quickly and fairly." All agreed, said Bloomberg, that "further delay is simply not acceptable."[53] Yet it would take ten more months before that framework came together. Why? What were the roadblocks toward an agreement on how to proceed? And what finally triggered a breakthrough to an agreement?

Another Formidable Alliance

The June 11 deadline failed to produce a new framework for rebuilding, and an extension of intense talks similarly delivered nothing but more sniping and frustration. Bloomberg and Silver issued a joint statement on the "WTC Site Development Talks," ratcheting up their campaign against the Port Authority and its persistent principled refusal to move off its position of financing only one tower at Ground Zero. On this one issue—pressuring the PA to deliver the financial package for Silverstein's towers—their interests were aligned. For anyone with a recall of the mayor's policy preferences—for an Olympics-oriented football stadium on the West Side (2005), congestion pricing (2008), retaining mayoral control of schools (2009)—this alliance of former adversaries undoubtedly seemed unlikely, if not startling. The Assembly leader's support was especially valuable insofar as he could apply pressure to influence outcomes on other projects or initiatives for which the mayor or governor needed his support in Albany. The new "cooperation might have some analysts questioning whether the mayor's change of heart had more to do with political prudence than real estate," Bagli wrote, though Silver was quick to say that the notion of a quid pro quo was "absurd."[54]

Whatever brought it about, in the détente between the mayor and the Albany leader, Silverstein was the beneficiary. Those two elected officials united together in common cause posed a formidable alliance and provided the cover Silverstein used to hold out. Insiders would say that the mayor had come around to see the incompetence and many problems the Port Authority had had in getting things done and in sinking so much money into the Transportation Hub, subordinating the entire project to Calatrava's vision. "The Port works for Calatrava, not the other way around," was a common perception. "The Port hasn't had the ability to manage the architect; it's not just a matter of cost and budget, but of functionality," a source told me. In time, Silverstein's key project leader said, the city grew uncomfortable with the PA's competency issues, which worked toward the mayor's switch in position. When linked to the PA's chronic delivery problems, the conclusion was clear: The private sector can do it better.[55]

The mayor's reversal of position from the developer's sharpest critic to Silverstein's outright advocate illuminated the tremendous change in the political dynamic and economics of the rebuilding effort that had taken place since the 2006 deal negotiations, when he formed a first formidable alliance with the Port Authority against Silverstein in order to push forward a realignment of roles and responsibilities for rebuilding the site. At that point, he was at war with Silver and ill disposed toward Silverstein. Five years later, the mayor and the developer were aligned.

Support for retaining control of the educational system, a Bloomberg priority, surely must have been a part of his new alliance, but only a part. City and state elected officials always have many points of needed cooperation, and in their joint statement on the Trade Center, it was notable that Bloomberg and Silver did not direct their criticism directly at the governors of New York and New Jersey (both weak governors facing reelection campaigns), but at the Port itself, as Eliot Brown emphasized in his write-up of the event. The mayor was at the end of his second term, contemplating a third—legacy time. He had come into office in the traumatic aftermath of 9/11 and nearly ten years later, what was there to show? "What's good for America and good for New York City may be slightly at odds with what's good for the Port Authority," the mayor told reporters the day after issuance of the joint statement. "We cannot leave a hole in the ground and the Port Authority just has to come to the party."[56]

The bully pulpit of the mayor of the city of New York, as noted earlier a position considered the second most powerful elected office in the nation by many, gave this especially strong incumbent a loud and influential megaphone. The city, however, was still without a legal interest in the site, yet as it was a signatory to the 2006 deal as well as many other program-related agreements for rebuilding the site, any change in terms required its approval. State and Port Authority officials were especially rankled that the city could push a pro-Silverstein position in deal negotiations without being directly exposed to a deal's financial impact because it too had no skin in the game. It was a continual point of contention. "Without a financial interest," Paterson said, "the city was just like any citizens group." At some point in pressure and counterpressure ping-ponging across officials involved in the negotiations, the secretary to the governor, Charles O'Byrne, asked the mayor how much the city would put into the project. "'Zero,' was the response in finger language, 'the number is zero,'" Paterson told me in interview. "'Zero is not a number, it's an integer,'" he said to the mayor. "This pissed off the mayor but when people play games with you, you should play games with them."[57] The small slights and bruises of battles fought were endless interplays in the Ground Zero saga.

"It's getting ugly," *Crain's* reported the day after the joint statement. Deputy Mayor Lieber "tried to put the best face on what was becoming a tedious effort, while seeming to scold both sides," Bagli reported. "The redevelopment of ground zero is no ordinary real estate project," Lieber said. "Rebuilding the site is a civic obligation of the highest order, and the people of our city rightly expect all those responsible for the site to work cooperatively to honor that obligation." As frustration mounted and tedium from stalemate set in, the mayor's campaign against the Port Authority moved into high gear. For the first time in near memory, Bloomberg was praising the developer: "I will say Larry Silverstein, while not turning over the keys to his family's net worth, has come up and has made a lot of progress." A few days later on his weekly radio show during what the *Daily News* called a "broadside" attack against the Port Authority for its five weeks of failed talks with the developer, he floated a plan to break the stalemate by taking millions of (federal) dollars from Moynihan Station, a long-stalled favorite project among the city's civic groups intended to compensate for the wanton destruction of the original McKim, Mead & White Pennsylvania Station masterpiece. It took but three hours for U.S. senator Charles Schumer to inject his strong, influential voice. "I would be totally opposed to robbing Peter to pay Paul." These federal funds, he warned, "should not be used as the basis for any compromise at Ground Zero."[58]

That all parties were still negotiating in the press was a sure sign that talks were going nowhere. On July 6, Silverstein released the arrow of arbitration, issuing a formal "Notice of Dispute" pursuant to the MDA with a three-page letter delivered to the Port Authority. The same day, in a four-page letter to the city (recipient redacted, presumably Mayor Bloomberg) and given to the press, Silverstein claimed, "If not for the Port's failures, the project clearly would be much, much further along—and we would have had the opportunity to finance in a much more positive economic climate." The Port was at fault, the developer said, for "repeatedly dragging its heels" in negotiating a new rebuilding agreement and because it "hasn't accelerated its key projects at the site," "has no realistic schedule for its construction work and no integrated logistics plan," and "has failed to establish the governance structure that the agency itself repeatedly said was necessary for proper decision-making and project management." The Port Authority "keeps taking millions and millions out of our insurance fund . . . while refusing either to address the consequences of its admittedly catastrophic delays and cost overruns on its own work, or to consider the compromise solutions offered by our elected leaders." This "latest move," Bagli wrote, "seems designed to pressure the authority to acquiesce to his demand that it guarantee as much as $3.2 billion in financing of two of the three office towers he is to build at the site."[59] Much as it might seem that Silverstein was looking to arbitration to break the Port Authority's resolve or to provide a solution to the stalemate, Port Authority officials had a different interpretation: "Silverstein was going political—positioning himself for missing the market," as one insider put it.

Within hours Ward issued a press release that laid the blame on Silverstein for "walking away from the negotiating table simply because the public has been unwilling to sacrifice critical infrastructure projects to subsidize private speculative office space." The threat of arbitration was not enough to move Ward off position: "We are certain that SPI understands that an arbitration decision under the MDA will not resolve when there will be a market for two private office towers on the site, and how this speculative private office space should be financed. A resolution to these issues can only be accomplished through good faith negotiations, not a legal fight." Bloomberg also issued a statement, weighing in with strong words consistent with his campaign against the Port Authority: "Not everyone worked as hard as necessary to find a solution" to the stalemate, he said. "No one disputes that the Port Authority is engaged in many projects important to our region, but pitting those projects against the development of the World Trade Center site creates a false choice."[60]

Silverstein had no pressing business reason to compromise, at least not yet. He still had enough insurance money to keep construction moving forward on Tower 4, which would help mediate the threat of the cross. The cross of the 2006 deal could work two ways. In the context of the current economic meltdown, the Port Authority was facing an uncertain value proposition. What kind of land value would there be at a time of depressed rents? "If Silverstein has money to build Tower 4, but no money for the other two, the cross may keep him in the game. What would he lose if he walked? He has no equity in the deal. He has extracted fees to sustain his overhead for the rebuilding effort and perform on his agreement with his investors. He would most likely have to disgorge the residual insurance funds, as they are for constructing the towers." That was the way a real estate finance expert interpreted Silverstein's position.

Unlike the dynamics prevailing in 2006, in 2008 the developer had a powerful alliance on his side. Silverstein's minimal downside financial exposure, strong political support, and well-known inflexible negotiating style combined to form impressive roadblocks to an agreement on anything less than his terms. If he stopped building, it would be significant value loss for all involved, and both sides knew it. If he defaulted because of a lack of economics, the prospect of a new developer stepping in was low. Who else would take the kind of risks that building out towers at Ground Zero presented? The established New York real estate family companies were unlikely to take this kind of risk. Only a few players—Boston Properties, Brookfield Office Properties, Tishman Speyer, Vornado Realty Trust, Forest City Ratner Companies (at the time, Related Companies was more of a residential developer)—have the development expertise and balance-sheet strength to even contemplate a project such as this. Would they put their equity at risk, especially when the economics of the lower Manhattan office market could not support a value of $1,000 a square foot and where rents, historically, had never been comparable to those in midtown?

On July 9, three days after Silverstein filed his arbitration notice, PA chairman Coscia and executive director Ward cosigned a letter to the developer with "a new proposal intended to break the impasse over the financing of private office space at the World Trade Center site." The agency would debt-backstop Tower 2 up to $1.2 billion of fixed-rate senior debt (in addition to its full backstop for Tower 4), as long as Silverstein Properties raised $625 million in subordinate financing for Tower 2. This "critical component" of the PA's proposal would "help insulate the public sector from unmanageable risk." Asking the developer to secure private funds for this "first-loss" risk, Coscia and Ward wrote, would "represent an important signal from the private market that this was a viable real estate transaction."[61] Silverstein viewed the Port Authority's financing condition as impossible in light of the deep distress in credit markets across the globe and "a step backwards" because the agency had shifted position from its early proposals.[62] There was no surprise five days later when the developer flatly refused to consider this proposal.

Persistent Counternarrative

Silverstein joined by Bloomberg and Silver had made the Port Authority the enemy. The fulsome alliance, however, underestimated Ward's willingness to play hardball and stand firm, to tactically deploy the arrows in his quiver, and to let the fight go into arbitration—and in the process create a public narrative of "influence" against them. As evident in his exchange with Calatrava on the Transportation Hub at the architect's townhouse (discussed in chapter 17), Ward was not an executive director easily pushed around. As some might have speculated, perhaps he wanted to show that he was tough compared to his predecessor and that he would not cave. That explanation would be too simplistic. His professional investment in the assessment process of 2008, his commitment to the institution of the Port Authority, and his stubborn personality kept him focused on a policy-based discipline protective of the PA's balance sheet and its broader regional transportation mandate. He did not want to mortgage the agency future to the open tab of rebuilding the Trade Center site. He needed to turn around the narrative.

Working with him was John P. L. Kelly, soon to be made head of media relations. Kelly had come to the agency in 2009 from the public information office of the NYPD. He was not a known quantity in the New York press world, so Ward had to learn to trust him enough and be convinced to hire him, Kelly told me.[63] He was familiar and comfortable with highly charged media environments. The bloated nature of the Port Authority—"Pork Authority," some called it—made it difficult to get a fair shake in the press. The agency was at a distinct disadvantage recalled a different former deputy director: There were few balanced stories. The storyline was that the PA was bureaucratic, foot-dragging. Less attention seemed to be paid to Silverstein, though the institutional memory of the 2006 negotiations remained in place: his constant coming back to ask for more or constant coming back to raise yet another issue, and his constant persistence in not budging from position.

Kelly's strategy in turning around the narrative of delay was to create communication "rules." Certain words were verboten: Ground Zero, for example; calling the site a cemetery had to stop, he said, and "pit" was out as well. In place of "rebuilding," they were "building"; "rebuilding," he said, boxes you in. To counter the negative impression that nothing was going on at the site—the nondisappearing narrative of delay—he brought people down there to see the construction, among them the comedian-activist Jon Stewart, who was deeply moved by the not yet finished memorial that even in outline conveyed emotional power (he knew people who were lost at the site in the attack) and later became a board member of the Memorial Foundation. Kelly wanted "to invite people into the excitement of the project, tell them we're winning." He believed he had a star—the project itself—and that it was his job to educate the public. He refused to accept the failure story, adopting the posture of: What are you talking about? With an engaging touch of irreverence, he pursued the messaging task at the Port Authority at a time he called "a Halley's Comet moment"—a brief period of time when both governors (Corzine and Paterson) happened to be non-politically motivated when it came to the agency. "They weren't interested in going after the candy," he said; "when politics leaves the building, things can get done. Ward had just enough time for the project to pick up momentum, to get the contracts out; the train left the station. He was there during a magic moment."[64]

Ward was right on principle, and that gained him backing by the editorial boards of the *New York Times, Daily News, Newsday, Crain's, Star-Ledger,* and the *Record* of Bergen County. The editorial boards were important because, with less leverage than the other side, the Port Authority needed to create its own by galvanizing the public. Even though it owned the sixteen-acre site, the Port Authority was disadvantaged because Silverstein's legal agreements with the agency gave the developer control of the East Bathtub, and in real estate, site control is always a commanding point of leverage. Ward's adamant position was a key counternarrative in the high-profile battle over Silverstein's demand for additional public subsidy in the form of credit support for his privately owned office towers. It took guts to take that position and hold it in a brutally political public fight.

Committing additional billions for rebuilding the Trade Center site threatened the Port Authority's ambitious capital plan. In December 2006 the PA Board of Commissioners had adopted its first ten-year capital plan to "return the agency to historic investments in transportation infrastructure" enabling "the entire region to grow."[65] The $8 billion for the reconstruction of the Trade Center site accounted for approximately 31 percent of the plan's total $26.1 billion ambitions. (The PA expected reimbursements of more than $4 billion from insurance and third parties, yet the lack of final reimbursement agreements had been a long-running issue of concern appearing in repeated FTA monitoring reports on the Permanent PATH Terminal project.) In actual capital spending, reconstructing the Trade Center site had been consuming larger and larger proportions of the total capital budget since 2005. By year end 2007, approximately 36 percent of the agency's capital budget was going into reconstruction at Ground Zero, up from 17 percent in 2006 and 10 percent in 2005. By 2009, this percentage had grown to 43 percent. Spending on its revered Transportation Hub dominated what the Port was spending on the site in 2005 and 2006, but the agency's other capital projects at Ground Zero quickly impacted how money was being spent at the site.

The PA executive director was in a tight spot. He faced intense political pressure from City Hall, which feared that a lengthy arbitration process would delay rebuilding for many more years. Also, he was unsure, at first, whether his governor would stay by his side when the fight went to the mat—which Paterson did. For months Ward had been making the argument against more financial subsidy for Silverstein's towers on principle. If he gave into Silverstein's demands for full financial support of two towers—as much as $3.2 billion—the agency might have to relinquish or at least postpone some of its goals for rebuilding the region's infrastructure. As City Hall's attack kept ratcheting up, Ward got specific. At a breakfast forum before an audience of the union-backed Business and Labor Coalition of New York, he discussed the agency's capital plan, laying out how the recession was shrinking what the agency would be able to do. "We had $29 billion [2007 updated capital plan] and now we're down to effectively a $25.5 billion plan." The implication was that committing to do more at Ground Zero was not possible. He ticked off the projects likely to be sacrificed: rebuild of the Central Terminal Building at LaGuardia Airport and a new Delta Terminal at JFK Airport, expansion of Steward Airport in Westchester County, and redo of the Goethals Bridge in New Jersey. "We are not doing those. We have no money in our budget right now for the Bayonne Bridge [spanning Kill Van Kull and connecting Bayonne, NJ, with Staten Island, NY]; we are not building an auxiliary bus garage in midtown Manhattan." The *New York Observer*'s Eliot Brown, who had been closely covering the intensifying financing imbroglio, reported, "The long list of cuts hadn't been made public or even approved yet—the Port Authority's 10-year capital budget isn't up for a revision until December—so one probably can't treat Mr. Ward's word with finality (the governors of New York and New Jersey make the final calls on these matters)."[66] Cuts, however, did materialize when the board of commissions announced on December 10, 2009, that its capital plan was being cut by $5 billion to $24.5 billion.

As the battle continued in the press with no letup and no resolution, the two governors who controlled the Port Authority remained silent. Considered politically weak, both Paterson and Corzine seemed to be protecting the agency's capital budget. Both wanted the Port Authority to fund their regional transportation projects. Corzine was facing a tough reelection and had much less political ownership of the project at this time compared to 2006, when he aligned with Mayor Bloomberg to foist a deal on Silverstein. Paterson was coping with leadership and budget crises in Albany (and had not yet pulled out of his 2010 campaign for reelection). State officials on the "second floor," political jargon for Albany, and the Port Authority were not acting together, though they were on the same side. Paterson's office wanted to get things moving but, reportedly, was still not willing to put hard-to-find state money on the table.[67]

After Silverstein rejected the Port Authority's July 9 offer, Paterson intervened, inviting the developer to the mansion to negotiate directly. He wanted to send "a message," that he didn't have anything personal against him. "I met with him for about four hours," the governor recounted in an interview with me. "Silverstein was so mad at my office.... [H]e had several issues, stumbling blocks: He didn't like the decision on the insurance [the May 2007 settlement], which was not my fault. He wanted the state to pay for everything. It was all about money." Paterson's intervention delayed for some weeks Silverstein's triggering a binding arbitration proceeding, but the governor did not move one inch off position. "Where private money is eschewing the opportunity, public money should not be used either," he said. "I insist that we cannot finance anyone else's project." "Exactly, Gov," said the editorial board of the *Daily News*.[68]

The environment was toxic. The situation was at a stalemate. The threat of binding arbitration was real, and though the arbitration process could not resolve the financial fight, the uncertainty of the outcome would create further delay. Behind the scenes, Ward and Warshaw had been crafting a second element of their "standing firm" strategy: a credible "Plan B." The idea behind Plan B was to move forward with construction of the public pieces of the master plan for Ground Zero independent of the construction of the developer's three office towers. It was a plan designed to free the agency from being held political hostage to Silverstein's demands for public financing of his office towers. It was a plan to meet its commitments at Ground Zero laid forth less than a year earlier in Ward's *Roadmap Forward*. It was a plan to push forward its institutional ambitions for the Transportation Hub. But more than anything else, Plan B was an "I-can-do-without-you" tactic in an increasingly acrimonious public battle, a tactic designed to increase the agency's leverage in the negotiations.

Although it was a second-best solution and not an outcome Port Authority officials wished for, to push through the political stalemate, they determined to make Plan B a credible plan and be prepared to move forward on it, if need be. To be credible, the threat of implementing Plan B had to be real. To construct the public components independent of Silverstein's control over the East Bathtub commercial sites, the Transportation Hub would have to operate without the planned mechanical infrastructure in the podium of Tower 3 (Plan B was different from the pejoratively labeled "stumps" plan previously put forth by the Port Authority to build only the podium pieces of Towers 2 and 3). Other parts of the massive underground infrastructure would have to be redesigned—in essence, physically cordoned off or severed from interdependencies with the three private office towers, while maintaining Silverstein's ability to commence construction of his three towers. Ironically, this would reverse-engineer the control-oriented interdependencies at the core of the Port Authority's rebuilding vision. All of this would take hundreds of millions of dollars, and on October 22, 2007, the Port Authority Board approved expenditures of $20 million for technical support services for "development of an alternative East Bathtub Construction Option."[69]

Next to enter on the scene, a white knight: Westfield Group. In a public bid to break the impasse, in mid-June, the Australian giant-mall company offered to build a $1.3 billion retail complex at the site—without using public money. An original partner with Silverstein in the July 2001 acquisition of the Trade Center leasehold, Westfield, as described earlier, had sold its interest back to the Port Authority in December 2003, but retained a right to come back into the project and had stayed involved, assisting the PA as an informal consultant on the retail component at Ground Zero. In early 2008, it had a tentative deal with the authority to co-develop the retail space, but talks were later suspended because of the uncertainty of how the East Bathtubs sites (where the majority of the retail space was located), would be developed.[70]

Two weeks after his meeting with the developer, Governor Paterson sent a letter proposal to Silverstein outlining a four-point framework that built on the foundation of Coscia and Ward's earlier July 9 proposal.[71] The Port Authority would fully backstop financing for Tower 4, but Towers 2 and 3 had to be market driven and backed by a significant amount of private money at risk before he would consider "a responsible amount of public participation." The developer would have to put at risk more than $75 million of conditional equity and the additional private sector money had to be in a position to be the first impacted if the project experienced losses. His development rights on all three towers would be preserved, and the governor would ask the Port Authority to offer rent relief on Towers 2 and 3 until the market returned. The governor recognized "the need to make appropriate revisions to the cross default provision in the 2006 Master Development Agreement (subject to the City's consent)." The fourth point concerned funds to complete the necessary underground infrastructure and assure provision of vibrant retail development; the PA would agree to provide financial support for the podium bases of Towers 2 and 3 but it would be contingent upon Silverstein applying the balance of his insurance proceeds on immediate construction of those towers.

If relenting on the cross was the newest "give" of this deal proposal, the governor's insistence that Silverstein apply the balance of his insurance proceeds to the construction of Tower 4 and the bases of Towers 2 and 3 was the "take." "This is a point where I know we have our differences," Paterson wrote. "Your proposal husbands a significant portion of insurance money for future office development that could be built many years from now. If we agree on the importance of completing the site as soon as possible and you have recognized the need to close the significant funding gap on your private development, then I cannot accept a proposal that does not put all insurance into the immediate construction of the site." He closed the letter by "directing the Port Authority to develop designs that will permit the complete construction of the public components of the site independent of your private development. This will ensure that, should you and the Port Authority not be able to reach an agreement, the site will no longer be subject to the fate of the real estate market or these negotiations."[72] In other words, Paterson was explicitly supporting the ultimatum threat of Plan B. The points of future negotiations were all in this letter: the amount of private capital put at risk, the extent of financial backstop for Tower 3, the amount and length of rent abatement, and the allocation of remaining insurance funds. The Port Authority believed Silverstein wanted a "kitty" as leverage for the future, fearing that if he had no insurance money left, he could be pushed out, said one insider to the negotiations.

Paterson had "intentionally" left out "hard and fast numbers and specific deal terms" to allow for negotiation within this framework. He wanted the parties to meet two days later, on August 5, and expected "a progress report from both sides on August 12th." The governor gained little traction. Silverstein quickly rejected his proposals. "Our initial review indicates that these ideas will not likely put us on a path to a two-building solution," Janno Lieber said in a statement issued the same day. "The path suggested by the governor will not get us there," said Sheldon

Silver. "From the beginning, we've said both parties would have to compromise to avoid stalemate and further delays on the site," said a spokesman for the mayor. The *Times* editorial noted that "Ground Zero might have been rebuilt today if former Gov. George Pataki had issued a similar warning [for Silverstein to 'get on board' with the program of rebuilding] eight years ago." Paterson's warning was "long overdue," but he was willing to ask the Port Authority "to move on its own to finish the victims' memorial, the transit hub, and other public portions of the site" if negotiations with Silverstein "did not proceed more quickly."[73]

The public responses, however, fail to reveal the intensity of pressure personally put on Ward. In particular, one story, related in confidence, was never public. In early August, while Port Authority officials had been negotiating in earnest with Silverstein and the mayor's office, they were asked to come down to City Hall to meet with the city's lead negotiators, Deputy Mayor Lieber and EDC president Pinsky. At that meeting, Ward and Warshaw heard the same Silverstein deal that the PA had rejected before, and in a private one-on-one conversation Ward was told by Lieber that he should settle because the PA was going to lose the arbitration. That was the nearly universal belief in real estate circles. Lieber was warning him that if the PA allowed this to go to arbitration, the recriminations of losing could drag him through the mud in the press. Ward may have been taken aback, but he was not to be cowed; he was not about to compromise. He was not going to settle.

On August 4, the day after Paterson's letter proposal, Larry Silverstein presented the Port Authority with a "Notice of Arbitration" letter, kicking off the process of binding arbitration. "We didn't have any choice," remarked Janno Lieber. "What were we going to do? Just keep paying them the money [lease payments] and not getting any rent?"[74] Under arbitration an independent three-member panel of experts would decide whether the Port Authority had breached its responsibilities under the 2006 MDA. Ward's press release in response to the letter of arbitration cited "four offers" rejected by Silverstein Properties "that put on the table significant amounts of public investment to move their private office towers forward." But, he said, Silverstein would not take on "the same risk he was asking of the public." The developer's contention "that delays have adversely affected the financing of his office towers completely ignores the reality," said Ward "that the single worst economic recession since the Great Depression" was forcing "developers all around the city to put their projects on hold and wait for the market to return. This is not something unique to the WTC site." The 2006 MDA, he noted to remind readers, "called for final turnovers by the end of 2008, well after major financial institutions contemplated as anchor tenants at the site were no longer in existence and after the economic recession fully set in. The bottom line is Silverstein didn't miss the market, the market missed Silverstein."[75]

The reaction by supporters for both sides was swift and predictably on message with their respective positions. In an op-ed penned for the *Post*, Silver verbally indicted the Port Authority for offering "only intransigence" and an avowed "willingness to see a standstill at the site rather than accept a middle ground." In his statement on "continued delays at the World Trade Center site," Mayor Bloomberg opened another line of blistering attack on the Port Authority consistent with Silverstein's charges of its actions impeding progress at the site detailed in his notice of arbitration. The results were "intolerable," said the mayor. He called for "genuine, independent and constant oversight of the Port Authority's progress" by delinking the Lower Manhattan Construction Command Center from the PA and the LMDC, and "hav[ing] it provide regular, public audits on what is happening at the site."[76]

In "Ground Zero Stalls Again," the *Times* editorial acknowledged that "Mr. Silverstein has a point when he says that the Port Authority's own delays have trapped him in an economic downturn that has made it hard for him to find either financing or tenants"; likewise, it noted, "he has also been getting penalty fees for these delays from the authority, and, in any case, all this complaining is not getting anyone anywhere." The developer should see Governor Paterson's offer for what it is, a "good deal." The *Daily News* said "trying to referee between developer Larry Silverstein and the Port Authority is like trying to score a fight between sewer alligators" and offered pointedly harsh words on a follow-the-money theme: "Silverstein's gambit is a naked attempt to muscle money out of the public in order to rescue his multibillion-dollar Trade Center dreams from the wreckage of America's economic meltdown."[77]

No words of exhortation, whatever the rhetorical pitch, could move either side off position, and there was no unambiguous event to trigger a change in negotiation leverage—until the arbitration panel issued its ruling on Silverstein's claims. Construction was still proceeding at Ground Zero. Workers for the Port Authority were continuing to prepare massive underground foundations, erect steel for the 9/11 Memorial, begin installation of the jumbo steel perimeter columns of the Freedom Tower, build structural support, and excavate under the No. 1 subway box in the East Bathtub. In his "Third Quarter 2009 Trade Center Progress Report" issued on November 6, Ward wrote that the Port Authority had hit twenty-one of its twenty-four milestones. But ahead, the agency faced several significant challenges related to the delays in the LMDC's problematic deconstruction of the former Deutsche Bank Building on site 5, where costly delays and a deadly fire in 2007 were responsible for holding up construction of the Vehicle Security Center. Crews and contractors for Silverstein Properties were doing foundation work on Tower 4, with the substructure expected to come up to grade

FIGURE 18.6 *Workers lift a steel bar into place at Tower 4 construction site, July 2009.* AP Photo/
Mark Lennihan

by September, while mechanical, electrical, and other trades were working below
grade (figure 18.6).

A key pressure point for Silverstein loomed on the near horizon, however. In late
July Port Authority officials announced they were four to eight weeks away from
complete turnover of the sites for Towers 2 and 3. Even more important than the end
to the daily penalty payment of $300,000 for being late in delivering these sites, the
full and final turnover of the Silverstein sites started the clock ticking on the 2006
MDA timetable requiring the developer to complete his three towers within five
years or, as Ward was quoted as saying, "he will be in default, and the conclusion of
that will be—and I emphasize the word conclusion—that the Port Authority would
take title to all three towers."[78] This trigger came on August 24, 2009, when the
agency announced the completion of its final turnover of the sites (figure 18.7).

The animosity between the public and private players was unconcealed and
raw. Scars remained from the 2006 deal negotiations that were all too evident in
the 2009 fight over financing the office towers. The Port Authority did not get to
take back the sites for Tower 3 and Tower 4 as it had aimed to do. Rather it emerged
with the Freedom Tower, the most expensive office building in the world, and site
5—whatever that would become sometime in the distant future. Had it been successful, those sites would have given the agency full control over the construction
inputs for its signature project, the Transportation Hub; as it turned out, control

FIGURE 18.7 *A construction crane works above the foundations of Tower 4, August 27, 2009. Heavy equipment, lower left, clears the site for the future Transportation Hub.* AP PHOTO/MARK LENNIHAN

had to be shared with a partner the agency considered difficult to work with. Silverstein emerged with the most valuable sites in the best locations with extraordinary views of the city's west-facing waterfront from high floors (others look at Battery Park City), views enhanced by the absence of high-density structures on the eight acres of the memorial program across Greenwich Street. However, he had to accept a continuation of steep rent payments. The developer believed he hadn't been treated well, according to at least one inside player and confirmed by another, and he couldn't stop talking about the past.

The escalating charges and countercharges of the press-focused verbal battle only exacerbated the festering anger of both parties. Forward movement was only possible if both sides moved out of their rigid positions. Silverstein would have to move beyond his anger at past treatment by the agency. The Port Authority would have to give some on its backstop position, and it had a significant financial incentive to do a deal: Without a deal, the agency would lose rental income and have to commit hundreds of millions of dollars in Plan B. By Labor Day, Coscia was talking to all the board members; there was no love lost for the developer, but they needed to make a deal. Silverstein was running low on funds to keep up construction of Tower 4, and he too would need to make a deal.

This "public-private partnership" was terribly broken. The partners' interests were aligned only in the most macro sense—to fulfill the ambitions of opportunity presented by rebuilding—and for that each needed the other. The Port Authority needed an experienced professional private developer to build out the three commercial towers that would feed ground rents into the agency's treasury and create synergy to enhance its retail venture. Silverstein needed the public sector to finance his development ambitions and because of the site's centralized underground infrastructure, his towers were dependent upon the PA's underground Vehicle Security Center. Bottom-line considerations, however, differed. For Silverstein, the project had always been a business proposition of risk and return, notwithstanding his avowed passion and personal commitment to the task expressed with great sincerity. For public sector officials, political perspective infused every decision; legacy credit, power and control, and avoidance of failure were central considerations. These different perspectives tend to work in complementary ways in successful public-private projects, but at Ground Zero, the essential components of a successful public-private project—mutual respect and cooperation—were missing, abysmally so. Rebuilding the Trade Center site was a development partnership by default of tragedy, not of choice. The question of whether relations could be repaired to the point of moving forward together would turn on the outcome of the arbitration proceeding and how that ruling would alter the leverage points of negotiation, if not its chemistry. Would it lead to a new deal or to continued stalemate and litigation? What Port Authority officials knew is that if they lost the arbitration, they would have a problem.

CHAPTER 19

The Gains of Brinkmanship

FIGURE 19.1 *After stalemate on the terms of financing for Silverstein's three towers, the stakeholders gather at a press conference following completion of the East Side Development Agreement, September 7, 2010 (left to right): PA chairman Anthony Coscia, developer Larry Silverstein, New York governor David Paterson, and Mayor Michael Bloomberg.* Joe Woodhead, Courtesy Silverstein Properties Inc.

W HEN THE ARBITRATION PANEL released its decision on January 26, 2010, Port Authority executive director Christopher O. Ward was at home, sick, under the weather. On a conference call, as his general counsel read the telltale first page of the decision, the outcome was not evident. "I've got to know, got to know," he said. So with a police alarm on top of his car, Ward raced down the West Side Highway in a record-breaking twenty minutes to read for himself the full opinion. By the time he got there, his staff had finished reading the twenty-two-page decision and knew they had won: There was no financial award to Silverstein.

"Winning was huge," said Ward. "Once we won the arbitration we were in a stronger position."[1]

Ward had been under pressure to settle for a very big number, but there was no way, he told me, he was going to do that because it would have been crippling for the agency. Battling through this binding arbitration proceeding for more than six months proved to be a tense turning point for the Port Authority. Now, with the decision in hand, Ward and his chief of staff, Drew Warshaw, walked across the street a short half-block to the Old Town Bar, one of the great late-nineteenth-century barrooms on East Eighteenth Street in the Flatiron district of Manhattan. Sitting in the bar's back room, both drinking Jameson's and beers, the two men stared at each other realizing what had just happened: They now had the leverage to rationalize rebuilding the commercial portion of the Trade Center site, not to mention the credibility that they believed would eventually win back over the mayor and others to rebalance the power between the Port Authority and Silverstein.

If reading the press release each party issued after the arbitration decision left doubt about who had won, the consistent message across news headlines dispelled any uncertainty: "Panel Rebuffs Trade Center Developer" (*WSJ*), "Arbitrators Rule against Silverstein at Ground Zero" (*Crain's*), "Ruling Sets Back Developer Trade Center Site" (*NYT*), "WTC Developer Denied $3.5B PA Payoff" (*DN*), "Why Silverstein Is Insecure" (*NYP*). Pivoting on the panel's technical ruling, the balance of the negotiation seesaw tipped toward the Port Authority and broke open the deadlock (figure 19.1).

The Port Authority's arbitration win, however, did not supply a resolution to the financing conflict. After reviewing scores of memos and reply memos submitted by both sides, examining hundreds of exhibits, listening to twenty-seven experts, and sizing up the dispute under the framework of the Master Development Agreement, the three-person panel set a forty-five-day deadline for the Port Authority and Silverstein Properties to resolve their dispute. If they could not resolve their differences, the panel would impose its own solution. Although it had broad powers and discretion to resolve disputes under the MDA's "unique form of arbitration," the arbitrators wanted to give the parties "one final chance to arrive at a solution mutually acceptable to them." Zeroing in on the essence of the situation, they wrote, "The specific issues in this arbitration involved a larger, more fundamental problem—how to reconcile and adjust the parties' interlocked construction obligations on this massive redevelopment project in view of the drastically changed economic conditions, and to do so in a way that would produce within a reasonable time a redeveloped WTC site that is comparable to that contemplated by the MDA and is consistent with its purposes." Succinct and ever pragmatic, Mayor Bloomberg said, "[O]ne thing is clear from the ruling: there is a deal to be made."[2]

In filing his "Notice of Arbitration" on August 4, 2009, Larry Silverstein assertively forewarned the Port Authority that once the "emergency interim relief" was secured and absent a settlement, a second arbitration was probable in which he planned to "seek an award of monetary damages, including rescission damages totaling at least of $2.75 billion," the amount paid to the Port Authority in rent and other payments. Furthermore, he planned to show "that the 2006 MDA itself was the product of the Port Authority's negligent misrepresentation and/or fraud."[3] Silverstein and his investment partners sought four items of "emergency interim relief": damages to offset ground rent until the project would be financially "stabilized" and able to generate sufficient rents to justify payment of ground rent to the PA, realignment of the construction schedule for his three towers, elimination of the cross-default provision, and a declaration that the Port Authority was in material breach of the MDA.

The panel, composed of a judge, lawyer, and construction executive, denied SPI three of its claims. It considered delays the fault of both parties, saying "there has been no proof that delay in these infrastructure projects has so far impacted construction of the Towers."[4] On ruling against the developer's claim of material breach, the panel cited changes in the Port Authority's performance—contracts let and work on infrastructure moving ahead—since Ward had taken over leadership of the agency. This was a key statement for the Port Authority because Silverstein had argued that the Port negotiated in bad faith, but the arbitration panel disagreed. "[T]he PA has committed or invested $2.3 billion to redevelopment of the WTC site, and in extensive and extended negotiations with SPI that have continued from mid-2008, the PA has made significant offers and concessions that go well beyond the PA's obligations under the MDA." The panel did not think it was "appropriate" to grant SPI any relief from its ground rent obligations at this time, and further denied its request for $2.75 billion in monetary damages. It did grant the developer's remaining claim for relief—elimination of the cross-default provision—something the Port Authority had already conceded in negotiations and agreed did not make sense in the present economic context— with language that explicitly conceded the impossibility of all the improvements at the site "suddenly bursting into full operation," that is, the build-it-all-at-once intent behind the MDA. "From today's perspective," it said, "such a vision seems strangely naïve."[5]

Five years—from 2005 to 2010—is what it took for political reality to catch up with the economic reality that rules real estate development. That is how long it took for the fiction of Governor Pataki's aspirational completion dates to vanish and for Mayor Bloomberg's push for an aggressive build-it-all-a-once timetable to finally give way to a phased approach for the development of office space at Ground Zero. The first step to economic reality came in October 2005, when city officials questioned Silverstein's financial capacity to deliver all five high-density, state-of-the-art office towers. After months of intense and acrimonious negotiations, there was a second step, in April 2006, when the Port Authority and Silverstein Properties signed a deal that realigned their responsibilities for rebuilding at Ground Zero. Because this agreement never resolved the intricacies of financing office development, rebuilding remained uncertain and full of risk. The arbitration ruling in January 2010 was a wake-up call to both, the third step to reality. The fourth step to economic reality—conclusive recognition that ambitious large-scale projects nearly always get built in phases, over time, in line with the amount of new office space the market can realistically absorb—would come out of the deal to be negotiated during the forty-five-day deadline set by the arbitration panel.

Absorption, the critical factor in the financial projections of a development project, was a word rarely uttered in the early debates about rebuilding; few officials had taken a developer's perspective and asked what was really possible in terms of absorption of new office space (just as no one appeared to rely on budgets for financial discipline on other rebuilding projects at Ground Zero). Real estate professionals seasoned by the vagaries of the cycle of development would have bet against a build-it-all-at-once approach. It was always going to be too much new speculative office space for the lower Manhattan market to absorb all at once, as was the case with the development of the original World Trade Center. That was why the Libeskind master plan for the Trade Center site assumed the ten million square feet of commercial space would be built out over time and across five discrete development sites.

Because the arbitration panel left many decisions about the eastern portion of the Trade Center site to be negotiated, its ruling was unlikely to force Silverstein to yield much ground. The developer considered the ruling indecisive and was still not about to acquiesce to Port Authority demands. With his having failed to gain full verification of his claims, it was plausible to think that he might be more willing to compromise in the negotiations to come. Given the pattern of negotiations to date, however, it seemed more likely that he would continue to push aggressively in order to get as many concessions as possible. Emboldened by the ruling, the Port Authority would also take an aggressive stance when negotiations resumed. How close to the brink of another collapse in negotiations these opponents would go in pursuit of their terms before one forced the other to back down and make final concessions was anyone's guess. It was, as one participant recalled, "guerrilla warfare."

THE ADVERSARIES FACE A DEADLINE

Immediately following the arbitration ruling, both sides retreated for approximately two weeks to interpret how they would use the decision to drive negotiations.[6] From a lawyer's perspective, Silverstein lost the arbitration, the Port Authority won. From a politician's perspective, it wasn't a win for either the city or the state. As one government insider to the negotiations wrote in a confidential memo, "At best, an extremely unfavorable capital position for the Port was avoided by a narrow decision that did nothing to resolve the scope of future development." Still, the "nonruling from the arbitrators contributed to the breakthrough," said EDC president Seth Pinsky; "it was a most helpful piece" because Silverstein became more willing to compromise than might otherwise have been the case.[7]

The warring parties had forty-five days to resolve what they had not been able to resolve for the past fifteen months—it was a deadline. And deadlines are important because they tend to get things done. Who would go first with a proposal? The arbitrators had found that the Port's August proposal, delivered through the letter from Governor Paterson,[8] went beyond the terms of the 2006 MDA. The agency did not believe it owed the developer anything, so it seemed highly unlikely that Ward would make the first move. Would the developer react to the postarbitration negotiating context by being the first to openly make a new proposal? Would his next proposal acknowledge that his stance of putting little equity in a deal would not pass the "smell test"?

After the arbitration ruling Silverstein faced intense political pressure, especially from the editorial pages, to do a deal. "Larry Must Start Dealing," said the *Daily News*, "to get real, finally, about getting the job done.…He must drastically scale back dreams of building three skyscrapers for which there is no demand." "Silverstein needs to end his appeals to arbitrators and political friends" and "get real," said *Newsday*. "He should build whatever the market will finance, but build it without any further grab for public money."[9] As holder of the ninety-nine-year lease, Silverstein always had the right to rebuild but not to demand that the public sector finance what market economics would not support. He would have to make concessions to the public's terms if he was to get the level of financial subsidy he desperately needed. His posture on the equity issue—that he and his investors would put up only $75 million of hard equity—did not pass policy scrutiny before the arbitration ruling; certainly, it would not pass the crucial political "smell test" now.

On February 14, the developer began to yield to reality. At a meeting in the governor's midtown Manhattan office at 633 Third Avenue, in a conference room on the thirty-ninth floor with its sweeping views to the south of Brooklyn, Silverstein offered a new proposal to shape negotiations. Dressed casually in a sweater and boots in deference to the day's weather following the second blizzard of the year, instead of his usual custom-tailored suit and tie, he offered to put more "skin in the game," between $150 million and $250 million of equity or mezzanine debt (subordinated debt that has rights to convert to equity if the loan goes into default) not backstopped by the PA. Although this proposed equity was substantially more than what he had offered before, it was still linked to achievement of mutually agreed upon milestones for infrastructure projects required for site development—a condition the PA had considered unpalatable since day one and had rejected in the past. Silverstein's proposal also shifted support for construction of a second tower to the smaller Tower 3 rather than Tower 2 to reduce costs.[10] The proposal was "broad and left many questions to be answered," according to an inside assessment, "but it was a useful start."

On February 26, 2010, Governor Paterson announced that he would not run for election. Still, he wanted a legacy at Ground Zero. A deal to get development started at Ground Zero would be a hallmark achievement for his administration, so the governor's people, principally his chief of staff, Lawrence S. Schwartz, and his point person on the negotiations, Timothy J. Gilchrist, a senior advisor to the governor, had every incentive to bargain toward a position that fit within the limits of the governor's August 3, 2009, letter proposal to SPI. The governor himself was not directly involved. State officials were surprised that the arbitration panel had not provided more guidance on who would do what to move the project forward. It was a frustration; four to five months were lost when work could have moved forward.

Mayor Bloomberg's well-known annoyance with the stalemate was intensifying, his patience with the lack of progress undoubtedly worn thin well before this latest impasse. Among the three elected executive officials with stakes in these negotiations, he had been in office the longest and rebuilding of the Trade Center site would constitute a major legacy of his mayoralty. "It's time to stop this craziness of everything and we just have to move forward here," he said on his weekly WOR radio show five days after Silverstein presented, in the mayor's words, "a very rational plan" at a meeting attended by the Port Authority and officials from the state and city. "I can tell you at this point it is the Port Authority who has to come back. And if they don't come back rationally with something that is doable and doable now, we are going to have a hole in the ground." He was urging Governor Paterson and newly inaugurated New Jersey governor Chris Christie to lean on the Port Authority to move forward. "And if we don't [move forward], you are going to see me out there beating the drums every day. I'm not going to leave this world with a hole in the ground ten years from now," Bloomberg vowed using his powerful bully pulpit. Saying that slow progress was impeding the development of lower

Manhattan, he challenged the agency to step up to the plate: "They should do it or just get out the way."[11]

The mayor's current lobbying for the developer did not get much support from the city's business press: "The City hasn't always helped the already complicated relationship between Mr. Silverstein and the Port," wrote *Crain's* op-ed columnist Greg David. "Officials claim to have consistently argued for a reasonable compromise, but in fact each time the mayor has distilled the city's position into sound bites, he has favored one party or the other. Lately, he had seemed to side with Mr. Silverstein, stiffening Mr. Silverstein's legendary unwillingness to give ground in negotiations."[12] The mayor had just won reelection to a controversial third term, and his staff was committed to achieving an agreement that delivered the majority of the public and private elements of the site before the end of his final year in office, 2013. The Port may have won the gamble on arbitration but the pressure on Ward to acquiesce to Silverstein's outsized demands for additional financial support remained intense.

On all sides, the pressure to come to terms on an agreement of what could be built and when was mounting, unabated. On February 21, a week after presenting his proposal to officials of the Port Authority, the city, and the state, Silverstein went on *60 Minutes,* carrying his case to the nation. "So when you look out on where this project is after eight years, how would you describe this?" television journalist Scott Pelly asked "the 78-year-old New York City real estate tycoon." "I describe this as a national disgrace," he responded. "I am the most frustrated person in the world." In the brief teaser for the show, Pelly related how the developer "shook his head slowly as we stood over the muddy pit known around the world as Ground Zero." Expanding on his frustration, Silverstein said, "It's hard to contemplate the amount of time that's gone by here, the tragic waste of time and what could have been—what could have been instead of what is today."[13]

If you were watching the segment "What Ever Happened to Ground Zero?" with little foreknowledge of the saga, it would have been hard not to conclude that Larry Silverstein was the victim of failure. "Well, failure has many architects," Pelly said in voiceover. "A hard-nosed businessman like Silverstein resisted building landmarks that didn't make sense to him commercially. The Port Authority didn't have the staff or management to lead the development of the grand master plan. And because the Port is a state agency, the nation's most powerful mayor, Michael Bloomberg, became a by-stander. Throw in egos, politics, and incompetence and you have a project that is still in a ditch." The thrust of Pelly's narrative, however, appears to have reflected his own strong opinions in editing the material. Ward had spent more than three hours walking the site with Pelly, explaining the complexity and interconnections of the rebuilding projects. It was a nice day, partly cloudy, somewhat warm, Ward recalled. Pelly asked all the right questions during the first half of the interview, and according to Ward, without a deal with Silverstein, Pelly knew Ward would not be able to answer his next questions: Could Ward could tell him when 1 World Trade would be completed? "No," Ward answered. Did he know when the second tower would be completed? "No." The second tower was Larry's tower, and at the time the footage was being shot, "we hadn't even gotten to arbitration," Ward said. "There was no way you could set a date for that tower. That was the set up. Pelly wanted those 'no' answers on the record," Ward told me.[14]

After reviewing the teaser for the upcoming show, the Port Authority lost no time in issuing a sharply worded statement. "It's really ridiculous for Larry Silverstein to stand on his empty sites, which he refuses to build without a public bailout, and bemoan the lack of progress when the only pit left on the World Trade Center site is his own," said agency spokesman Steven Sigmund. "The Memorial is taking shape and its steel is 95 percent complete, One World Trade Center is at 20 stories and rising, and the Transportation Hub and other public infrastructure the Port Authority is responsible for are moving forward, while Larry Silverstein squats on sites that are still holes in the ground." This too appeared to be the perspective of the arbitration panel. Work was crawling along. The developer's orchestrated performance on *60 Minutes* matched a lighthearted remark Governor Paterson made when I interviewed him: "I really like Larry; he should have been in Hollywood!"[15]

Silverstein was leveraging brinkmanship, expertly. With just nineteen days before the forty-five-day deadline for the parties to come to an agreement on how to proceed with development or risk letting the arbitration panel determine a solution, his public relations team managed to secure a sympathetic narrative broadcast to a national audience that set off fireworks in the governor's office. Just how much advance notice the governor's office had been given is unclear, but the upcoming *60 Minutes* segment, recalled an insider, had the governor's secretary literally screaming at Ward over the phone: "Tell me what you are going to do to get a deal with Larry Silverstein."

Media coverage was heating up as several of the city's influential interest groups added their strong voices to the roiling political caldron at Ground Zero. In early March the well-respected Regional Plan Association issued its second statement in support of the Port Authority's "new efforts to break the deadlock" with Silverstein Properties, reiterating its concern that "additional funds not be diverted" from the Port Authority's capital plan and its planned transportation improvements; "it should be the responsibility of the private sector to absorb the risks of new office space construction." The same week, the General Contractors

Association, whose members work on heavy construction projects, sided with the authority, "warning," as Bagli of the *Times* wrote, "that the city had to rebuild the trade center 'in a way that does not bankrupt the Port Authority and curtail critically needed investment in the port's transportation infrastructure.'" The next week, several thousand carpenters, iron workers, laborers, and unemployed members of the city's powerful construction unions came together at a lunchtime rally at Ground Zero. "We are not taking sides or assigning blame," said the president of the Building and Construction Trades Council of Greater New York, Gary Barbera. "We're making a public statement on behalf of the building trades that we're ready to build them [the towers]." Bagli was on point when he wrote, "But in this deeply politicized world of ground zero, things are not always what they seem." Citing one trade union official insisting on anonymity because he was not authorized to speak on behalf of the council, the reporter noted that Silverstein, a builder who used union labor, had urged the council to hold the rally to put pressure on the Port Authority. Not much prodding was needed, the union official added, "when you have 25 to 30 percent unemployment." Nor was that kind of media-focused demonstration in support of construction projects promising to employ thousands of union members an unusual tactic in political theater of New York City. "While we're cooperating with the sponsor of this rally," a spokesman for Silverstein Properties said, "the event was called for, belongs to and will be attended by the men and women of the construction unions."[16]

The arbitration panel's deadline was just one day away when a most unusual dichotomy of opinions appeared on the editorial pages of *Times*. In "What Ground Zero Needs," the *Times* endorsed the Port Authority's position, arguing that the agency "should not be obliged to provide what the market and Mr. Silverstein cannot." Opposite, on the op-ed page in "A Last Chance for the Trade Center to Rise Again," Mayor Bloomberg and State Assembly Speaker Silver accused the Port Authority of "continued intransigence." There was no new argument on either side of the newspaper's vertical fold, just a reminder that political brinkmanship was occurring.

Port Authority officials believed they had learned many lessons from the 2006 deal negotiations: learned that they needed to avoid Silverstein's "divide-and-conquer" strategy; learned that there should be a single representative deputized to negotiate with the developer, an extraordinarily skillful negotiator who would exploit any division if he sensed that the agency and the governor's office were not directly aligned and in sync; learned that things worked better when everyone was at the table. "When everyone was not at the table," Governor Paterson said, "Silverstein would go to people to get them to advocate for him—[real estate developer] Lenny Litwin, Mayor Bloomberg, Shelly Silver."[17] Negotiating in public intensified the pressure on both sides, however much the public might have perceived the back and forth as merely political posturing. Messy as it was, the public display of hardened conflict may have stopped some of the developer's maneuvering. That, at least, was Governor Paterson's perception. "Sunlight is a disinfectant," he told me, repeating the oft-noted quote of Oliver Wendell Holmes.

NO LONGER MONOPOLY MONEY

The circumstances for forging ahead with earnest negotiations between the warring parties presented vexing challenges in an environment still toxic. Senior staff for the governor and the mayor had to actively engage both parties in negotiations that would yield a new framework and financial equation for development of the eastern side of the site, yet do so in a way that protected the public's limited resources from exposure to a speculative real estate market.[18] Timothy J. Gilchrist was leading the negotiations for the governor and Robert C. Lieber for the mayor. Both were committed to getting a deal done. Both needed skill and perseverance to succeed because they were working against a difficult actuality: Silverstein's side did not trust the Port Authority's schedules and had continually questioned its competence over years of acrimonious exchanges. Having prevailed in the second arbitration, Port Authority officials believed they could set terms that would be best for the agency. When it came to information, each side believed the other was not forthcoming with dates, schedules, and data. Yet how forthcoming was information likely to be in an adversarial situation where each side was trying to get the most out of the other, where one felt irritated by a loss and the other, emboldened by a win? Both sides were likely to be cagey.

Second-floor officials in Albany did not trust Silverstein. They also harbored doubts about how much they could trust the Port Authority: Would the bi-state agency act in the interest of New York State or in accord with its institutional self-interests? They were unsure about the strength of Ward's loyalty to the governor; Ward, unlike his predecessors in the executive director's office, did not have any prior loyalty to or campaign relationship with the governor. Moreover, the New York governor was not able to deal as effectively with the Port Authority as had his predecessors because Paterson had only one appointee on the board of commissioners at the time and, as a group, the New York commissioners were not as well coordinated as their New Jersey counterparts. City officials also did not trust the Port Authority; based on historical conflict, an ever-present wariness of the bi-state agency's semiautonomous actions flowed from one mayoral administration to the next. And the public was skeptical of the Port Authority's promises. According to a Quinnipiac University poll taken in late August 2009, New York

City voters, by margins of up to two to one, did not believe projections by the Port Authority that key redevelopment targets would be met.[19] This was not an auspicious context for negotiations, to say the least.

Among the approximately twenty-five individuals engaged in the negotiations as principals or staff or advisors, at least eleven could draw upon their earlier experience with the 2006 realignment deal: at least five on the Silverstein team (Larry Silverstein, Janno Lieber, Mickey Kupperman, Jonathan Knipe, and James Worsley), three from the Port Authority (Anthony Coscia, Darrell Buchbinder, and Paul Blanco), and three from the city (Mayor Bloomberg, Robert Lieber, and Seth Pinsky). The biggest changes were in the governor's office, where no one came to the negotiations with institutional memory of that earlier negotiation experience.

Cultural, ideological, and personal divides further colored the negotiation environment. The people working on the private side of development and their counterparts in the public sector operated in distinctly different worlds. Timelines and tenets for making decisions differed, and an understanding of how to view the transaction from the other's perspective seemed to be missing. State officials, in particular, were disadvantaged by their limited experience with major real estate transactions. They did not have the same level of analytical familiarity with real estate finance, and even though they relied on Pinsky's EDC analyses, they were not negotiating from the same level of strength when it came to understanding positions on equity and exposure to risk. Gilchrist, the governor's representative, had been the person at the state's Department of Transportation in charge of rebuilding West Street after 9/11, and was familiar with the dynamics between the LMDC and the PA; he had been deputy secretary for economic development and infrastructure in the short-lived Spitzer administration. Ward had experience with major capital projects; staff principals leading the WTC Redevelopment Department at the PA were quite knowledgeable about commercial real estate; and the agency had experienced financial advisors in Cushman & Wakefield. Everyone knew that Bob Lieber was, by far, the most experienced dealmaker for the public sector in these negotiations.

Lieber had come to government service at the age of fifty-three, after twenty-three years at Lehman Brothers, where he was managing director responsible for a $2.8 billion private-equity real estate fund and after having served as global head of real estate investment banking. He was about to retire and looking for a new and engaging professional challenge. Several years earlier a serious bike accident had laid him up, stopped his incessant travel, and set him to thinking about what he was doing. "I had no political bent at all but thought the public sector might be able to use a private real estate geek's perspective," he told me; he liked the idea of being able to think long term and having an opportunity to make an impact that was more long-lasting than just from one transaction to another. He had worked in lower Manhattan for years and, he said, had "an instinct about the project." More directly, he had also been involved in pro bono work on the project. The first experience was in 2004, as part of a four-day Blue Ribbon Advisory Panel convened by the Urban Land Institute, the real estate development industry's most respected organization, in partnership with the Port Authority, the LMDC, Friends of Community Board 1, and the Alliance for Downtown New York, which had been charged with making recommendations for retail development as part of lower Manhattan's post-9/11 regeneration.

The second experience followed a year later, when Deputy Mayor Doctoroff asked Lehman Brothers to assist with a financial analysis of Silverstein's capability to rebuild all ten million square feet of office space. In 2007, Doctoroff recruited him to serve as head of the city's Economic Development Corporation, and when the announcement came that Doctoroff was stepping down after six years in City Hall, Mayor Bloomberg tapped Lieber to succeed him. Well known in business circles when he moved over to City Hall at the start of 2008, the new deputy mayor would become known for his low-key manner and straightforward approach to problem solving. "I am a deal-oriented person who aims to get things done," he said. His style was to ask, "What do you need to get done? What resources are needed? What are the execution issues, and what do you need to do to overcome them?" In City Hall, this would be "logarithmically more complicated and challenging" than he ever imagined.[20]

Lieber's dealmaking experience and determination to get things done would advantage Silverstein, who was looking to the mayor's office to ensure that the ultimate brokered deal would not set up SPI for failure and subsequent default. It would help that Lieber spoke the same real estate argot as the developer, but that would not be enough. Forthright by nature, Lieber told Silverstein he was only willing to work with him toward a deal if the developer would commit to move beyond his anger and frustration at past treatment by the Port Authority. Silverstein felt "irretrievably harmed," emotionally and economically, by the agency. Lieber was confident he could get a deal done, get the developer a legacy, but Silverstein would have to stop saying negative things about the Port Authority. "It's your choice," he told him. "You've been at this for ten years. Okay, the PA did all these things that you are angry about; we will stipulate this. But bickering and complaining and looking in the rear-view mirror is not going to get us anywhere. If we are going to make progress, you need to look out the windshield and envision what can be, the legacy of Larry Silverstein and what he did for New York City in the aftermath of a national tragedy, to see those four towers finally getting built." Characteristically, Lieber concluded: "This is no time for laments. You have to absolve yourself of this versus seeking revenge." Until Silverstein got past that condition, Lieber did not believe he could get a deal done.[21]

Proposals and counterproposals sallied back and forth over the course of intense behind-the-scenes negotiations leading up to the arbitrators' deadline. As each side sized up the risks inherent in each proposal, differences over how to advance progress on the site came into play, differences related to the many unknowns of moving forward with development of the three speculative office towers. Would the commercial real estate market continue to lag or worsen over the next twelve to thirty-six months? Would future market demand support this development and make the economics work in a manner that did not lead to insolvency for the public or private developer? The public sector needed to figure out what development benchmarks would be strict enough to encourage private market discipline, yet simultaneously flexible enough to make these towers financially feasible. This was an essential issue for the public sector because it needed to protect its investment in the speculative towers as best it could. The questions were not new, however, but essentially a reprise of the 2006 deal's negotiation dynamics.

In mediating the competing economic and political goals of the parties, Gilchrist and Lieber also needed to consider regional politics. A new Republican governor had just been inaugurated in Trenton. How would this change in leadership affect the Port Authority, its ability to raise tolls and fully fund its capital plan, and, in turn, the agency's commitment to rebuilding the Trade Center site? Looking across the Hudson River, the two New York officials would be forced to consider Governor Christie's agenda. What resources did New Jersey want from the Port Authority? How did the new governor and his PA commissioners view Silverstein? By the very complexity of the project's public and private ambitions, negotiating an agreement among the four principals in the room—New York City, New York State, Silverstein Properties, and the bi-state Port Authority—was going to turn on crafting a deal that allocated risk in politically feasible ways while assuring market-based discipline. Such a deal would reflect the political reality of compromise at Ground Zero in 2010.

In the parties' coming to terms with that reality, the drama of brinkmanship leading up to the 2010 deal was about to reveal a larger political story, a story of how public officials marshaled scarce public resources and reluctant private funds under great pressure to advance the ambitions of rebuilding at Ground Zero, and how their respective senior staffs moved mutually suspicious adversaries toward an overall agreement. The story would illustrate how financial risk was negotiated and shared, if not equally, in ways designed to assure that each of the four principals had "skin in the game." It would illuminate the art of political dealmaking, how "everyone got a fig leaf," as one powerful insider put it. Ultimately, it would become a story of how politics trumped policy, powerfully reasoned policy but, nevertheless, policy overpowered by a political imperative of seeing Ground Zero rebuilt as a symbol of New York's economic strength—as soon as possible. The money story behind this deal would also reveal the economic power of commercial real estate in New York, the city's patrimony in bricks and mortar, steel and glass.

TERSE AND INTENSE NEGOTIATIONS

For a compromise to emerge, the negotiations had to resolve at least six issues fundamental to what the Port Authority was being asked to do—that is, take on the risk of a banker and financially guarantee the debt on speculative development in the name of civic responsibility. On each fundamental issue, both sides held different positions. Alternatively put, between the PA and SPI, there were two sets of reality.

Issue no. 1: Market risk. Given current weak conditions in the commercial real estate market, particularly in lower Manhattan, what was the best timetable for the construction of Towers 2, 3, and 4, and in what order? The Port Authority agreed to build Tower 4 immediately but wanted to delay the other two until the market improved; Silverstein wanted to build Tower 2 and Tower 4 immediately and delay Tower 3 until the market improved.

Issue no. 2: Rent payments. If construction on particular towers was halted or delayed, should Silverstein's ground rent payments to the Port Authority be reduced or remain constant as set in the 2006 deal? The PA said the $78.7 million annual rent payment should continue because the revenue was vital to its capital capacity for borrowing power. Silverstein wanted ground rent adjusted to reflect current reality, with payments reset to market values and phased in as buildings were occupied.

Issue no. 3: Insurance dollars. How much was left, and how should the remaining dollars be treated—attached to one tower or spread across all three? The Port Authority viewed the insurance dollars as an offset to construction costs, not a new equity commitment; it wanted all of the insurance dollars put to work on a single tower to reduce the financing cost and risk of development. Silverstein viewed his insurance dollars as equivalent to equity and did not see the need to put in additional equity; he wanted to allocate the monies across all three towers, ostensibly to allow for future development. Furthermore, if he could use the funds as collateral for a guarantee of completion (required by any construction lender), this would bring down the cost of financing his towers.

Issue no. 4: Financial support. What level of debt guarantees, "backstop," should the Port Authority provide for each tower, if any, and for how many years? What percentage of profits, known as a "participation return," should the agency receive in exchange? The PA offered to fully backstop the debt on the first tower but offered no backstop for the remaining two, and in exchange, it wanted a limited participation in cash flow from operations and proceeds from a refinancing or sale of the asset, as well as a fee for using its balance sheet to enhance the debt on these speculative office towers. Silverstein initially asked the agency to fully backstop the first two towers built (and backstop the third once the two others were financially stabilized and the PA's backstop exposure became less risky) and agreed to give the Port Authority a limited participation only in capital events such as a refinancing or sale.

Issue no. 5: Development fees. Should Silverstein, as developer of Towers 2, 3, and 4, continue to receive market-rate development fees? If so, should all or part of these fees be kept in escrow as part of the Port Authority's backstop support or released to the developer? Silverstein had already received millions in fees, the Port Authority argued, and should cease receiving fees immediately, especially fees on a second tower; Silverstein argued the reverse, that standard market-rate development fees should continue.

Issue no. 6: Skin in the game. How much equity should Silverstein have to put into the deal to ensure private-market discipline in the development of the second tower? The Port Authority wanted the developer to commit $300 million of equity, upfront and unconditional. In his first postarbitration proposal, Silverstein offered to put in $150 million to $250 million conditional on the Port Authority reaching certain milestones for various infrastructure projects required for the successful development of the site.

Each of these economic issues was hard fought. Shuttling back and forth between the offices of these principals, Gilchrist and Lieber labored to find the sweet spot for a deal. The process, Gilchrist said, was one of cajoling and threatening—trying to understand when one or the other party had a legitimate concern and then saying to the other, "No, this is the reality."[22]

Governor Paterson's team layered in a corollary set of policy questions: Whose risk assessment mattered—the Port Authority's or the developer's? How much was the public sector going to commit in total and by entity—the Port Authority, New York State, New York City? What would be the timing order of those commitments? In a situation of distress, which slice of equity would be the first to absorb a loss? What benchmarks should be used to define "market discipline"? Running numbers on various financial scenarios required making assumptions, assumptions that would be considered conservative or aggressive or heroic given the deep uncertainty surrounding the timing and extent of a real estate market recovery. As noted in a confidential memo, Paterson's team was concerned about how to "overcome the fundamental distrust issues" of these warring parties, which that implied both SPI and the PA "will be deceptive" in the financial projections they developed and the term sheets they drafted. They assumed the documents each side produced would "suit the scenarios most beneficial to their respective positions."

The city's Economic Development Corporation led by Seth Pinsky faced an information quandary as well. Staff was running numbers all the time but staff members were operating in an information vacuum, and, therefore, did not have a full picture of the numbers. Without financial projections from either the PA or SPI, it was "little better than an academic exercise," according to a source familiar with the negotiations.[23] Similarly, the state's negotiating team was disadvantaged by a lack of full information as the Port Authority would only send PDF files of its financials, not the actual spreadsheets, which made it difficult to discern critical assumptions the agency was making to assess market viability and the public sector's risk exposure. Making the argument that his buildings would be the most technologically advanced and environmentally sophisticated in the city, Silverstein presented financial projections that incorporated aspirational assumptions: rent at $95 a square foot (a crazy number in the minds of real estate veterans), escalating at 3 percent annually, with one million square feet of space being absorbed each year in each of the three towers, which meant leasing more than six million square feet in two years!

These were aggressive assumptions that would make SPI's case for credit support stronger by showing that the agency's exposure would not be unduly excessive. SPI's actual underwhelming track record with 7 World Trade Center, however, suggested otherwise.[24] In sharp contrast, the Port Authority (working with consultants Cushman & Wakefield, who did an extensive historical analysis of the downtown market to arrive at a number that the PA could reasonably expect), were saying rents would run $60 to $65 a square foot, escalating at 3 percent, with 250,000 square feet being absorbed each year, figures SPI considered too conservative.[25]

Negotiating a deal during a market cycle when the timing of recovery and future leasing rents are highly uncertain, as was the case at the start of 2010,[26] calls for a firm view on near-term market dynamics. That was clearly missing in the chasm between SPI's and the PA's views of a 2013 future, and the implications for the public sector's exposure from its credit backstop ran into hundreds of millions. The Port Authority was running the numbers on an internal financial model that projected what its proposed support would cost and how it would impact the agency's capital capacity and credit rating. The total exposure was in the ballpark of $1.8 billion, according to a knowledgeable insider.[27] The parties were no longer playing with Monopoly money. The stakes were real.

The pace of negotiations, seemingly measured at the start, approached brinkmanship as the arbitrator's March 12 deadline came into immediate view and passed without a deal. The parties issued a statement saying they were unable to reach an agreement but were continuing to talk. They asked for an extension as they were getting close to a deal, and got one. It had been hard going until this point. The economics of each building were "brutal," recalled one PA negotiator; it was hard to make the numbers work and hard to figure on getting the occupancy and market rates needed for the developments to make financial sense.

Aligning Government Support

After the initial postarbitration meeting of all four parties on February 14 convened by the governor's secretary, Gilchrist worked with the Port Authority and Lieber with SPI. Although the parties had resolved most of the approximately twenty-two items included in the final term sheet proposal by March 11, they were still split on key issues: skin in the game, the extent of public-sector backstop for Tower 3 and prelease requirements, use of Tower 2 insurance proceeds, ground rents, and SPI's development fees. Some issues split public (city) to public (state), and others split public (PA, NYS, NYC) to private (SPI).

Reluctant to put hard money in the deal, each arm of government held its cards close. By mid-February, both finally realized that they would have to come up with subsidies of their own in order to get the Port Authority and Silverstein to compromise and get a deal done, otherwise the deadlock could prove fatal. Everyone had to be pragmatic. When PA chairman Coscia proposed that the city contribute its future PILOT from the project, payments the tax-exempt agency made to the city in lieu of property taxes, the city initially balked. "This dog doesn't hunt," said the deputy mayor, according to a senior PA insider at the meeting. Coscia's proposal basically built on the argument city officials had been making, that a stalemate would be a disaster for all parties, including the Port Authority: If SPI stopped building, both public and private sides would experience a significant value loss. Once the logic of this argument took hold and Port Authority officials "started acting in a manner consistent with this understanding of the situation," Pinsky later explained, the Port's request took on a different meaning. "When they asked us to participate in the solution by potentially foregoing revenues that we wouldn't receive but [that would be] a resolution to the deadlock, we agreed that this was a fair request and not a net loss to city taxpayers. In other words, in our minds, if the stalemate wasn't resolved, we would definitely lose the PILOT. So it was better for taxpayers to have a good chance to get the PILOT with some risk that they would not receive the PILOT than to have no chance of receiving it." This, Pinsky said, "took the excuse away from the city."[28]

City officials thus agreed to put in $130 million of future PILOT payments for fifteen years (originally thirty years). Committing future PILOT payments to fund the project that would generate property tax revenues is a well-honed off-budget mechanism (akin to tax-increment financing used in states and localities all over the nation), a politically painless source of funding for public-private developments because it is not hard cash taken away from budget priorities. In the press briefing on the deal weeks later, Mayor Bloomberg described it as an investment in the city: "What we've done is we've capitalized and invested the revenues that will only exist if Tower Three is built. We changed that into equity in the building."[29]

With the city's money in the deal, the state became the missing player on the public side of the equity slate. A day or so before the March 12 deadline, Lieber called the public parties into his office and during the meeting wrote on a napkin what each party was going to put in the deal, numbers that roughly conformed to what became the public positions. The state had been cautious in its financial commitment; the $200 million it was being asked to contribute ($80 million in equity and $120 million in backstop support) was not an easy sum to find at a time of big budget cuts. As state officials were in the midst of budget negotiations, the team considered whether the funds should come in the form of a budget authorization or from a pool of funds outside of the state's budget process. It chose the latter: $20 million in upfront equity would come through the state's Economic and Community Development Program (authorized in the 2008–2009 enacted budget); the remaining $180 million would come from a special ESDC fund (which captured payments from the Port Authority relating to space New York State had occupied at the original World Trade Center).

Once state and city officials ironed out what each entity would contribute to the equity stack and credit support for Tower 3 and agreed that Silverstein should increase his equity contribution to $300 million, they began to act in concert, submitting the first of several joint PA-NYS-NYC proposals to SPI on March 15. Relations between state and city offices were professional, but each had a different perspective. Not unexpectedly, the state saw a deal closer to the Port Authority's vision, and the city sided more closely with Larry Silverstein.

Insisting on $300 Million "Skin in the Game"

Silverstein was holding out on the equity issue. A lot of time had been spent on the difference between $250 million and $300 million in equity. Since its first postarbitration counterproposal (February 24), the Port Authority had been insisting that the developer put in a minimum of $300 million of unsupported, private-market capital that would be the first to be exposed to any loss of equity. Silverstein was likely to finance this piece by bringing together several investors in the form of a syndicate to provide the necessary capital as he had done in the past. His professional legacy was going to be defined by this historic rebuilding project known across the globe. What else mattered? Unquestionably, the developer needed a deal, the prospects for which had been made possible by the city's and the state's commitments—without which a very different scenario would have unfolded—but Silverstein held fast to his position and did not acquiesce to the $300 million figure—until March 15, three days into the extended deadline for a deal. His concession finally broke the deadlock.

Capping Credit Support

Backstop support for Tower 3 was one of the last big items to get resolved. Providing full credit support for Tower 4, the smallest of Silverstein's three towers, was always the minimum the Port Authority was going to do; with two-thirds of the space already preleased to the Port Authority, agency officials considered the risk of providing this forty-year credit enhancement to be relatively modest. Tower 3 presented greater credit risk, however, and the PA agreed to support this second tower[30] only on the condition that the developer was able to meet two private-market triggers: a significant prelease commitment (of several hundred thousand square feet) and a substantial equity commitment ($300 million). These construction triggers had become sticking points between the city and state negotiators.[31] Getting both governments to commit equity *and* additionally contribute to the credit backstop proved essential to closing the negotiations on this item. Without these financial assists, the Port Authority would be left to backstop the debt based on the strength of its balance sheet alone, divorced from underlying economics that typically inform a private-sector transaction. In such a full-backstop scenario, the public sector would be in the first-loss position, exposed to all losses on the project while Silverstein would share upside potential, effectively, at no cost.

Port Authority officials reasoned that unless the public sector imposed some of its own market-based requirements for funding the project, development would go ahead regardless of its economic viability—bleeding the agency of public dollars meant for regional transportation and infrastructure investment and dragging down the downtown office market with a vast oversupply of empty office space. PA chairman Coscia, in particular, did not want the PA to abandon its core transportation mission while rebuilding the Trade Center site. He had made "a 'box' around transportation," he told me, which "allocated time to spend on transportation and worked to make sure the PA was strong financially." He had been a powerful driver behind the PA's highly ambitious ten-year 2006 capital plan. When the Great Recession hit and adjustments had to be made to that plan, he believed this almost helped because it kept the agency focused on its transportation mission. That mission, in his view, wasn't all roads and bridges, but also included investment in mass transit. "We had to get the PA into the twenty-first century and transform it into a proponent for a more sustainable transportation network than the systems that had supported the agency's balance sheet in the past," he said.[32]

From the very start of the financing battle, Port Authority officials questioned how they could provide backstop support for a second tower, given the authority's capital capacity and required debt coverage for its consolidated bonds. In its assessment of a forthcoming PA debt issue in October 2009, Fitch Ratings raised concerns about "the authority's very large financial commitments for the improvement and expansion of its existing assets, along with the development at the World Trade Center (WTC) site and the Access to the Region's Core Project [the commuter rail project to increase passenger service capacity between New Jersey and Manhattan]." The Trade Center commitment, then at $9.5 billion, represented 32.2 percent of the 2007–2016 capital plan. The "ah-ha" moment on credit support for a second tower, an insider recalled, came when the agency realized that if Silverstein delivered an anchor tenant in fulfillment of the preleasing requirement, provided private lender financing, and put up cash equity, then it could limit its credit support to a "cap," as long as the city and the state put money into the project as grants, which would reduce the size of the loan needed for construction.[33]

In stark contrast to the open-ended exposure of the full backstop Silverstein had demanded at the very start of the financing fight in 2009, public-sector executives now worked in concert to limit their risk exposure on the $2 billion Tower 3 at $390 million and allocate it across all public entities.[34] As a result, Port Authority officials would not be carrying the full burden of risk and, consequently, did not view their role in credit support for a second tower as "trading off" other capital priorities of the agency. After the deal was announced and the agency went to market with another bond issue, Fitch Ratings concurred, saying, "Importantly, it remains unclear how the potential agreement will exactly affect the authority's financial position; yet Fitch does believe the authority's level of risk exposure, at this stage of the negotiations, is minimal."[35]

Trapping Silverstein's Fees

Fees were a sticky issue for both sides, for different reasons. The 2006 agreements allowed Silverstein and his investors to continue collecting management fees from the insurance payout as they had been doing since 2004,[36] as well as specific fees for development services for his towers. Over the years, the investment partnership had taken in millions. The press made much of these fees over the years of delay and inaction at Ground Zero and later, during the fight over financing. Silverstein's lack of skin in the game and continual draw down of "out-sized" fees remained a political embarrassment for the public entities. The developer was thick-skinned about the issue. By contract, he was entitled to the fees; he claimed to be carrying big overhead for the project. How much in excess of those costs no one outside the partnership could know because the exact amounts and the terms under which fees are paid are private to the investment partnership agreement.

Politically, however, privacy of fees paid on a public-purpose project supported by public subsidies was not a defensible explanation. Each time the existing development agreement came to be renegotiated, the fee issue emerged anew. During the 2010 negotiations, much horse-trading ensued. In its first postarbitration proposal, the Port Authority proposed a cessation of the management fees on all three towers once definitive documents on a restructured development agreement were signed, and a suspension of development fees until the actual start of construction. Not unexpectedly, SPI rejected this item, saying the 2006 MDA fee structure should continue in place. In the proposals and counterproposals between March 15 and the final draft terms, SPI gained ground on what the PA initially proposed. It prevailed on maintaining its fees for Tower 4. For Tower 2, to be developed sometime in the future in line with market demand and without support from the public sector, SPI would not be able to take fees out of the insurance proceeds. On Tower 3, the negotiators put in place a structure to "trap" the fees, color coded to ease understanding of its complexity (plate 20).[37]

Closing In

The negotiators were closing in on a full draft of terms when the tail-end negotiations shifted from the financial details of Tower 3 to the economics of Tower 4. The PA thought it almost had a deal, but Silverstein started talking about all the things on the arrangements for Tower 4 that bothered him. His wear-you-down technique in strung-out negotiations seemed to be having an effect. City and state officials were frustrated; they thought Tower 4 issues had been settled. Everyone was exhausted. Port Authority officials argued that the agency would lose at least $100 million (adjusted for the time value of money) over the term of the ground lease if it gave into the proposal Silverstein was now making to lower rent payments on Tower 4. They held firm to their positon. In the process of resolving this last item, however, the state, wanting to see a deal done, gave up half of its potential profit participation in Tower 3, which would only generate a return in the event of a capital transaction triggered by SPI.[38] Finally, the parties were in agreement on the funding of development costs, the details of debt financing and credit support, and other related financial items.[39]

The last major negotiation involved the "Construction Partnership" between the PA and SPI. Poor coordination of work, lack of communication, and fragmented decision-making between the two developers on the site had long been a heavy drag on effective and efficient construction management at Ground Zero. The problems had been costly in time and resources. They had frustrated stakeholders and hampered the achievement of their ambitions. The same set of problems had surfaced repeatedly in various third-party professional evaluations of the project—the LMCCC risk assessments, the Value Planning Workshops, the first arbitration ruling, and the FTA monitoring reports on the Transportation Hub project. Moving forward with real progress demanded certainty of off- and on-site construction coordination, as well as real schedules in order to assure each party, potential lenders, and investors of "reliable commitments" that would assure "timely delivery" of the elements essential to the rebuilding of the Trade Center site.[40]

The Construction Partnership called for SPI and the PA to jointly develop a plan to better integrate construction teams working on all of the interrelated work in the East Bathtub within sixty days of execution of the final term sheet. The intent of the plan was to resolve construction issues meaningfully, not punitively. Reflecting on the reality of this achievement, Janno Lieber told me shortly after the plan was completed: "There is a project schedule now. This is a project schedule that, for the first time, is professionally and logically valid. This is a schedule that SPI can trust; we had our people and experts review it in detail." This was, he said, "an enormously important milestone." It would make the PA accountable for delivering on its construction on schedule because if the PA fell behind on a particular element of the schedule, "it can't hide it in the end date [of construction completion], as before."[41]

On March 25, in a joint press statement, the four stakeholders announced "an outline of a development plan" for the east side of the Trade Center site. It was a tentative agreement, with details and secondary issues still to be worked out. Ward had presented this general agreement earlier in the day at the commissioners' monthly board meeting. He expected to return before the commissioners for review and approval of the definitive documents in four months, though given the history of this project and what it typically takes to finalize a complex public-private agreement among multiple parties, some slippage was probable, if not inevitable. To reach agreement on this "final framework," as one executive official called the March 25 deal, it had taken seven proposals and counterproposals, four of which were transacted in the last twelve days after the initial March 12 deadline—and intense behind-the-scenes political pressure on both parties, especially from Mayor Bloomberg. Governor Corzine, Bloomberg said, "has been pushing" PA chairman Coscia "to find a solution to the problem."[42] The solution was to pay the price of getting to a deal.

"This Is the Best Deal You Will Get"

The night before the deal was to go to the PA board, Governor Paterson called the developer, whose reputation for never wanting to close negotiations had become an invariant aspect of his professional persona, and asked him to stop bargaining and accept the deal. The mayor followed in the morning, telling the developer to accept it, that "[t]his is the best deal you will get." As early as that morning, however, Silverstein had not yet given the final pencils-down sign-off. Until the very last hours before the meeting, the parties were still negotiating limits on the developer's fees.[43]

Disquiet prevailed among the commissioners. Many were upset about approving the deal. "In a private session before the public meeting," Andrew Ross Sorkin of the *Times* wrote in his column DealBook, "the board insisted that Mr. Ward get strong language limiting Mr. Silverstein's development fees while public money was at risk in the second tower and providing the authority with a percentage of any profits coming from the first building." When a commissioner does not agree, going to the media is always a possibility. This quickly became reality on March 27, the day after the board meeting, when Bagli reported on the public airing of vice chairman Henry R. Silverman's "blistering" e-mail note. "The notion that a private developer and/or his investors profit while the public sector is at risk for billions of dollars is unacceptable," Silverman wrote to his eight fellow commissioners and Ward.[44]

Appointed by Governor Pataki in 2002 and reappointed by Governor Spitzer in 2008, the private-equity investor was best known for his role in building Cendant Corporation into a multibillion-dollar provider of business and consumer services, principally within the real estate and travel industries. He had approved earlier actions the agency had taken, including the 2006 realignment deal, but was firmly opposed to any Port Authority financing of private commercial towers and indignant about the little-spoken reality of subsidizing Silverstein, who would be competing with the PA for office tenants at Ground

Zero: "By enabling the construction of Towers 3 and 4, we are further crystallizing" a loss of $1 billion to $2 billion on 1 World Trade Center, Silverman wrote in the e-mail note. "If we owned a losing McDonald's at 18th and Park, would we build two more restaurants on the block?" Silverman, Bagli reported, also thought that the PA should have gotten a bigger return for its investment if the buildings proved to be successful. When asked for a comment on the deal, Coscia said, "much work needs to be done to hammer out all the details in a complex agreement."[45]

With the announcement of a general deal framework, the editorial pages expressed skepticism as well as relief at the promise of a breakthrough in this latest impasse holding up progress at the site. First up was the *Daily News*: Ward deserved "major credit" for insisting that the developer "prove the projects were commercially viable by delivering hundreds of millions of dollars in private backing." The pill for progress was "bitter" but "a world better than a hole in the ground." In "'Breakthrough' Baloney," the *Post* once again pounced on "Ground Zero's sorry record," saying, "New Yorkers can sure be excused for not popping the champagne quite yet." *Crain's* said the parties had "reached a sensible compromise" and that the tentative agreement "vindicates the tough negotiating stance" that the PA had taken with Silverstein. The *Times* wasn't quite convinced it was time to "break out the confetti." Admonishing the developer and the Port "to make sure that the agreement does not fall apart yet again, as they fill in the remaining details," it had "questions about [the] development fees for Mr. Silverstein and the interest rate for the authority's financing" that needed to be settled in order to "get things moving."[46]

THE DEAL, FOR REAL

On August 26, in a nondescript room at the northwest corner on the fifteenth floor of 225 Park Avenue South, a room distinguished only by its views north toward midtown and the Empire State Building, seven of the ten Port Authority commissioners (two of the twelve seats were unfilled at the time) convened in a special meeting, open to the public. They were there to consider and, as expected, authorize actions to effectuate the 2010 restructured development agreement between Silverstein and the agency, the deal now known as the "East Side Site Development Plan." They were seated on simple faux-leather chairs around a long wooden conference table capable of seating twenty to twenty-five people, at which they had met in a private executive session immediately prior to the public session. Others seated at the table and present in the room to answer any questions: Executive Director Chris Ward, New Jersey–appointed deputy executive director

William Baroni Jr., and thirty-four other staff members, plus one guest from the Office of the Governor of New Jersey.

The meeting lasted all of eighteen minutes. No suspense. The vote was baked in beforehand. It would not have been put on the agenda otherwise. The private executive session was the place for candid discussion and questioning of "matters involving ongoing negotiations or reviews of contracts or proposals...where public disclosure may impact property values," as explained in formal board language.[47] Probing questions may have been raised because the deal was "hair-hurting complex," as the *Daily News* noted, and the financial logic linking its many component parts especially intricate. The all-important preparatory work of briefing commissioners on the deal had already taken place. In the many weeks between March 25 and August 26, the negotiating teams had hammered out the essential details necessary to give legal meaning to the deal's business terms. What had been succinctly summarized in three single-spaced pages was now forty single-spaced pages of closely worded text (and hundreds of pages when the definitive documents were later signed on December 16, 2010). Experienced real estate finance professionals would need to subject it to multiple readings in order to fully comprehend the detailed linkages and overall financial significance of the deal. The complexity of it was mind-numbing.

Getting all of the board commissioners to agree does not appear to have been easy. Coscia, into his eighth year as chairman of the board, had extracted experiences from the Trade Center project that shaped his view of leadership. "When you take on a big project like this, you have to get comfortable with the fact that the project is the project and it's not about you, it's not about ego. It's a matter of being pragmatic. I could chart a graph about when people subordinate themselves to the project," he told me. "I learned that you have to have this to get everyone on the same page." On the Trade Center project, he had worked through three ego-subordinating events: the 2006 realignment agreement, "when the board commissioners came together"; the chaos of 2008, when things "started to go sideways, and the board had to toughen up"; and the 2010 deal, which called for the board to do a deal with Silverstein.[48]

As was his style, Coscia worked the board, giving individual commissioners a lot of one-on-one time, briefing them on the situation, and listening to their suggestions. He was hands-on with deals, diving into the weeds. He was on good terms with a wide circle of people, respected as skillful and likeable. He was the consummate professional, a quality act, as one civic leader remarked, who liked to work behind the scenes. He was someone who could be political, but also navigate the politics to get a substantive deal done. He was a real survivor in the trenches of politics, and if any deal tested his métier, this was it. The commissioners had been prepped, and those who did not agree with the Port Authority's position would not show up for the meeting where the vote would be taken. That was the custom. For whatever reason, on August 26, there were three no-shows: Michael Chasanoff (NY), Henry Silverman (NY), and David Steiner (NJ)—all experienced with commercial real estate transactions.

Assurance of certain policy principles was essential, and they appeared on the first page of the report on the deal PA staff presented to the board: "It continues to ensure the immediate restoration of the eastern portion of the site, secures a long-term revenue stream for the Port Authority, and shares development risk among all stakeholders." The Port Authority's credit would fully support development of Tower 4. For Tower 3, New York State, New York City, and the Port Authority would each put in $200 million in a combination of equity grants (NYC, $130 million of PILOT; NYS, $80 million) and backstop credit support (NYC, $70 million; NYS, $120 million; PA, $200 million). The $390 million of public-sector credit support would be accessed when the private-market triggers for development had been achieved and only after all of the portion of SPI's fees for the development of Tower 3 held in escrow had been used in full. In accord with its financing role, the Port Authority would have audit rights for Tower 3 and Tower 4. Silverstein was obligated to raise $300 million of private capital and put all of his remaining insurance funds into construction of the two towers. Since Tower 3's financial viability would be evaluated by private investors and lenders plus a major anchor tenant, the PA believed its money in the project would be short-term, to cover potential problems with debt coverage in the early years. Development of Tower 2 had to stand on its own financially: The PA would only support construction of what was needed to build out the infrastructure for its Transportation Hub and bring the structure to grade; construction of the office tower would be "deferred until market demand allows it to proceed without further financial support."[49]

The deal assured the commissioners, elected officials, business and civic interests, and the public of "a baseline level of certainty—certainty over what will be built, how it will be paid for, and when it will be delivered." With overall financial support of $1.65 billion from the public sector, Silverstein would be able to complete the first and smallest office tower, Tower 4 (sixty-four stories, 1.8 million square feet), which was already rising out of the ground and expected to be complete by 2013. Construction of the two other office towers would be driven by market demand. No one was projecting completion dates for these towers, but the certainty of a development plan created confidence in the market about the Port Authority's other in-the-works transactions, namely the Condé Nast anchor-tenant lease for 1 World Trade Center and the joint-venture agreement with Westfield for development and ownership of the retail program on the Trade Center site.

The starting point for the East Side Site Development Plan, "the premise that private office space should be phased in, as opposed to built all at once," brought the Trade Center's commercial rebuilding program back to where it should have started—with the realistic assumption of phasing the full buildout. This assumption had been built into the redevelopment master plan and made a part of the project's 2004 environmental impact statement. As a premise of economic development, the lesson of past large-scale projects, particularly those built under public-private arrangements, was unequivocal: Phasing large-scale development is fundamental to the successful execution of big-city building ambitions; it is the only economically viable way to proceed in a market economy. Whether in New York (at Battery Park City and Forty-second Street–Times Square), Los Angeles (at California Plaza and Grand Avenue in downtown), or San Francisco (at Yerba Buena and Mission Bay), to name a few cities (and projects), the lesson always repeated itself. Yes, development needs a certain critical mass to effectuate a transformation, but lower Manhattan did not need ten million square feet of replacement office space delivered all at once. The PA's early decision to re-create a centralized underground infrastructure system, in concert with the city's drive for a rapid rebuild of the Trade Center, created the build-it-all-at-once requirement. Attempting to force an all-at-once full buildout was a gamble that amounted to economic suicide. Finally, and with no small touch of irony, the costly 2010 deal for the east side sites put an end to the flawed political mandate that the Trade Center site had to be completely rebuilt all at once. However, it did not change and could not reverse the Port Authority's deterministic decision to rebuild with a vast centralized underground infrastructure, which created the technically complex and problematic physical interdependency between the public infrastructure and the private office towers. That too was part and parcel of the build-it-all-at-once fallacy.

The Port Authority succeeded in securing certainty over its new phased approach to development of the east side sites by winning the negotiation over the allocation of SPI's remaining insurance funds. It was a big win, recalled one of the staff principals. The PA had pushed for all of the remaining insurance funds to go into Tower 4. Silverstein wanted to distribute the proceeds across his three towers, but the agency would not give on leaving any insurance money for construction of Tower 2. In the end, the proceeds were allocated to Tower 4 and Tower 3.[50] All of the liquidated damages previously paid by the PA for late delivery of the three sites ($140 million) and SPI's entire allocation of New York Liberty Bonds (approximately $2.593 billion in total) went toward construction of these two towers as well. Though he had ardently negotiated, Silverstein could make no credible economic argument for holding back insurance funds for Tower 2.

To secure project certainty and enhance economic feasibility in the context of a risky market, the PA made an "essential" financial trade-off when it agreed to abate the ground rents for Tower 3 and Tower 2 during pre-development and construction phases. This type of subsidy comes straight out of the standard toolbox of public-private development assistance. Along with other technical adjustments to the rent schedule, this was a very significant win for the developer.[51] On Tower 4, the original rent structure was left in place to support the financial strength of the planned issuance of Liberty Bonds, specially authorized by Congress for rebuilding, and to maintain the PA's credit rating, though the developer's net lease was economically enhanced some by other adjustments.[52] In exchange, the PA got "a significantly increased" upside in any Tower 4 future sale or capital transaction, 17.5 percent (instead of the 5 percent participation in the 2006 deal).

Without the public-sector credit supports, selling $2.593 billion of Liberty Bonds to private investors would have been impossible. The triple-tax-exempt Liberty Bonds offered the advantage of low-cost debt, but carried no assurances of marketability. They had to be made to fit the investor market by stripping out the real estate risk. What kinds of risk? Development risk—completion timing; completion cost, including funding of construction cost overruns; delivery risk. Market and occupancy risk—operating deficits during tenant lease-up and sufficiency of operating cash flow to service the debt, as well as ongoing capital costs to maintain tenant occupancy. The structure of the Liberty Bond offering, including the critical credit support from the three public entities, had to insulate the bondholders from all those risks. The buyers of these bonds would be retail buyers, high-net-worth individuals who seek tax-exempt income. The development risks being covered by the deal's credit-support agreements are typically those a developer or equity investor would take in the normal course of development. But at Ground Zero, a developer and equity investor would never willingly take on these risks because they would not have the control over the project as in a conventional development situation.[53] There was nothing conventional, however, about the financial-support agreements of the East Side Site Development Plan—it was breaking new ground, even in the sophisticated Wall Street world of credit enhancement.

The last element giving certainty to the development deal was Silverstein's ever-reluctant commitment to provide $300 million in equity to Tower 3. Since under the technical terms of the agreement, other private parties willing to invest in the project could supply up to $250 million of the $300 million, it is possible to make the argument that Silverstein's direct skin in the game was essentially only $50 million, his starting number at a far earlier point in the negotiations.

The way the Port Authority became comfortable with this deal provision speaks to the financial politics of what made the replacement of office space at Ground

Zero possible. First, the agency asked, what is equity? Equity is the riskiest money of all of the funding sources for a project because it only earns a return after all the debt holders are paid and, hence, it is the first to absorb losses when funds from the project are insufficient to pay all of the project's obligations. Equity is a simple concept—the first money in and the last money out—but little understood. The return to equity increases as the value of a property grows.

The equity going into the "capital stack" for the development of Tower 3 (and Tower 4) is shown in figure 19.2. Any third party in the market willing to supply deeply subordinated mezzanine debt that is not guaranteed (credit-supported by the Port Authority) was going to do its own due diligence on the risk and return of investing in Tower 3, which was still substantial because the project would be highly leveraged and the income produced through a lot of public subsidy. The mezzanine debt for the tower was unlikely to be paid back for quite some time (unless the project was refinanced), meaning it would have to be very patient capital, which is not typical of mezzanine debt. From the Port's perspective, patient third-party investment would be a definite positive for the project, a clear sign of private-market validation, and the authority would have approval rights over this third-party source of capital. Allowing for such flexible sourcing for the "equity" requirement had another benefit: It took away the emotion of insisting that Larry Silverstein personally or SPI have hard cash in the deal. At the same time, it assured the Port Authority that it was "just not going to fund another white elephant," as one senior agency official explained. Equally important, it would pass the political "smell test" of providing deep subsidies for a private development project because the PA was less likely to be criticized for "giving away the store."

If in the fall of 2009, after the Port Authority had completed its turnover of the east side sites, Ward had caved to the demands of the Silverstein-Bloomberg-Silver alliance, a different deal would have resulted. Exactly how different in monetary terms is impossible to say, but at a minimum, the Port Authority would have been fully backstopping not one but two towers, including Tower 2, the largest of the three at 2.8 million square feet, larger than the PA's own 1 World Trade at 2.6 million square feet. Rather than cave, Ward chose to gamble and take the Port Authority into arbitration, "despite a nearly universal belief in real estate circles that it would lose," remarked *Crain's* columnist Greg David.[54]

In an e-mail *WSJ* reporter Eliot Brown sent to me, he wrote, "I think people miss just how much guts it took to take (and hold) the position Ward did with the renegotiations with Silverstein. The mayor, Shelly, and Silverstein were putting an extraordinary amount of pressure against Ward, who was even unsure if his governor would stay by his side when things went to the mat. So, from that perspective, he did quite well for the health of the agency." The same could be said for

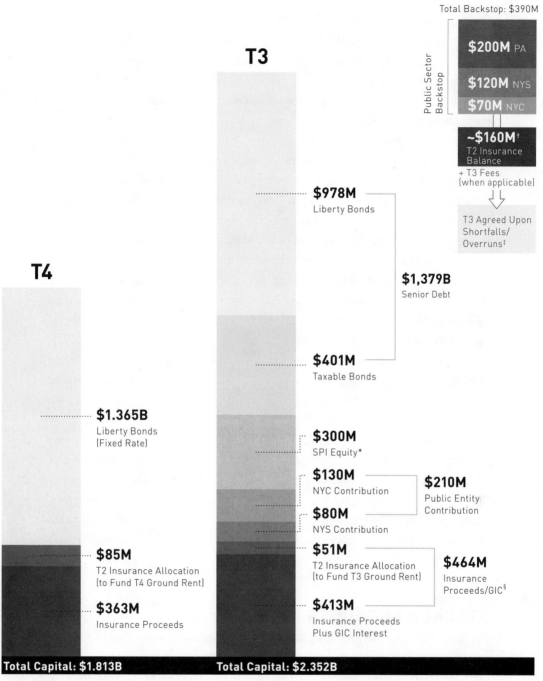

Total Backstop: $390M

Public Sector Backstop

$200M PA

$120M NYS

$70M NYC

~$160M[†]
T2 Insurance Balance
+ T3 Fees
(when applicable)

T3 Agreed Upon Shortfalls/ Overruns[‡]

T3

$978M
Liberty Bonds

$1,379B
Senior Debt

$401M
Taxable Bonds

$300M
SPI Equity*

$130M
NYC Contribution

$210M
Public Entity Contribution

$80M
NYS Contribution

$51M
T2 Insurance Allocation (to Fund T3 Ground Rent)

$464M
Insurance Proceeds/GIC[§]

$413M
Insurance Proceeds Plus GIC Interest

T4

$1.365B
Liberty Bonds (Fixed Rate)

$85M
T2 Insurance Allocation (to Fund T4 Ground Rent)

$363M
Insurance Proceeds

Total Capital: $1.813B   Total Capital: $2.352B

* Subject to review of bond sizing and financing sources and uses

† T2 insurance is first loss for T3 construction cost overruns. After T3 is substantially completed, remaining funds are applied to T4 construction cost overruns and then shared between T3 and T4 for leasing overruns and operating deficits as provided in the respective Tenant Support Agreements (TSAs).

‡ Includes operating deficits beyond operating reserve, 5% of hard costs, and 5% of leasing cost overruns for public sector backstop

§ GIC = Guaranteed Investment Certificate

Source: PANYNJ Minutes of Special Board Meeting, August 26, 2010.

FIGURE 19.2 *The sources of funding for financing the East Side Development Plan for Tower 3 and Tower 4, August 2010.*
C&G PARTNERS FOR THE AUTHOR

Coscia, Brown added, "but the pressure wasn't being directed at him." Ward's "obstinate position was really key to the narrative of the renegotiation with Larry down there, and I felt I should emphasize this."[55]

Over the course of negotiations, some of the Port Authority's risk exposure was siphoned off. Under the final agreement, the risk of moving forward with development of the two office towers was shared by all of the four stakeholders, not just the Port Authority. The key element to executing the deal's protections for the public sector was the "trapping" of any excess revenues (specifically, net cash profits from operating the building and net proceeds from any refinancing or sale events and certain fees attributable to Tower 3) until all of the public-sector credit-support payments were repaid. The cash-trap structure did not allow SPI to profit immediately from the deep levels of public support; a detailed hierarchy controls the release of funds in the cash-trap lockbox and directs when Silverstein can access that cash; it also provides a "significant incentive" for the developer to refinance the debt with a private institution once the towers reach profitability and remove all of the public-sector backstops from the two towers.[56] The cash trap would provide a structure for financial accountability.[57]

The four-way negotiations challenged all of the stakeholders. They were "quite difficult," Janno Lieber said; "there was only one real issue—would the PA become a partner for one or two buildings, this was the big dispute." Tim Gilchrist spoke of the "two sets of reality." The negotiations, said Chris Ward, became "brutally political," but essential. "Until you solved the Silverstein building issue, you never solved the downtown issue. Tower 2 and Tower 3 [built at least to grade] were necessary to get the Transportation Hub built." Pinsky took a macrolevel perspective: "The way government works it is more likely to lead to stalemate than progress. There are layers of government entities with many different interests. It is hard to get them aligned, and the window to move forward for development is short and so hard."[58]

STACKED SUBSIDIES

For more than eighteen months, Silverstein had been single-minded in his pursuit of financing from the Port Authority. It was essential to his ambition—without it there would have been no way to complete construction of even one tower at Ground Zero, let alone a second, until the private financing market recovered and real estate demand reemerged, and no one had any idea of that timeline under the economic duress of the Great Recession. Many times since September 12, 2001, the developer had said he was in for the long haul, and he had shown he had the patience to weather the process and all that the past nine years of contention and controversy had entailed. He had been frustrated as much as other players. "One problem with rebuilding," he told the audience at the RealShare New York real estate conference in midtown Manhattan in November 2009, "has been the revolving door of New York and New Jersey governors, who share control of the Port Authority. Every time there's a change of executive, there's a change of agenda," he said. "And every time there's a change of agenda it wreaks havoc with everything you're trying to accomplish if you're trying to hold a specific timeframe" (i.e., the time frame of the cross). The impediment to progress was cultural, his comments implied. "You know," he continued, "the attitude [in the public sector] is, 'I'll get back to you for the decision.' Construction doesn't wait for people who say, 'I'll get back to you.' You need the decision now."[59] Nonetheless, Silverstein was equally at fault for delays in rebuilding.

He was right about what the lack of continuity at the highest political executive level can do to undermine complex, risky projects. Continuity of governance had been a significant element in the final success of the redevelopment of Forty-second Street–Times Square, but even so that large-scale transformation took some twenty years. During the Pataki administration, Silverstein had been incredibly adept at pushing the governor's office to see his point of view. After its departure at the end of 2006, he had less influence in Albany and with the ever-changing leadership wielding power at the Port Authority post-9/11: three New York governors (who appointed four executive directors of the Port Authority) and four New Jersey governors (who appointed two PA chairmen). Silverstein and Bloomberg were the only two constant parties for twelve years, until 2014, when a new mayor entered City Hall.

Silverstein's single-minded approach and tenacity ultimately paid off brilliantly with a deep and broad set of subsidies, more extensive than anything revealed in the press. And he hadn't given up very much to get that highly favorable deal. The septuagenarian developer was fond of saying that he did not have time for "green bananas." It had become his signature line since he first deployed it in 2003. Years later, he was still saying, "I feel time passing. I want to build the towers while I can still enjoy them."[60] With the 2010 deal signed and sealed on December 16, 2010, Larry's green bananas had ripened, fully. He was seventy-nine (figure 19.3).

The subsidies negotiated as part of the 2010 deal transformed the impossible into the probable. By adjusting the economic equation of feasibility in multiple ways, almost all of them through off-budget mechanisms, the subsidies assured construction of one tower and made possible a second. The subsidy package is striking for the breadth in which it reshaped the economics of just about every layer of a ground-up development project: development funding, equity investment, preleasing commitments, construction cost, land cost, accessibility to

FIGURE 19.3 *Developer Larry Silverstein poses for a portrait in his office overlooking the Trade Center site in May 2007, when an analysis prepared for the Port Authority predicted that Silverstein would not be able to finish building all three towers until 2030.* AP Photo/Mark Lennihan

low-cost debt financing, tenant rents, operating deficits, and future capital improvements. Stripped of any policy judgment, it stands as an impressive illustration of how the financial power of the public sector can be harnessed in response to an emotional mandate to show resilience in the face of massive destruction and determination to fulfill large-scale rebuilding ambitions. Yet it is hard, very hard, to strip away policy judgment because the size and scope of the benefit package is so extraordinary. Voices that might otherwise comment on the subsidies to the Trade Center have been silent, whether because a rigorous analysis calls for making many assumptions about the public sector's future risk exposure or because the long imbroglio has exhausted the attention of policy analysts and scholars.

The "layering of subsidies at the trade center site," Eliot Brown wrote soon after the final deal framework was made public, "has been a vacuum for government assistance." The subsidies had accumulated in installments of "a recurring series," he wrote, "as the desire to rebuild the World Trade Center has proved a dominant force in public decision-making, often at the expense of rational fiscal policy."[61] The package of subsidies, eleven by my count, as shown in table 19.1, grew over time and in response to what it was going to take to make construction of these towers economically viable. It grew, as well, from Silverstein's persistence and skill in politically leveraging the emotional call of the "gaping hole" at Ground Zero.

Table 19.1 Financial Assistance for the Silverstein Towers, as of August 2010.

Type of Financial Assistance	Source	Impact on Project Economics	Tower
Abatement of ground rent	PANYNJ	Reduces up-front cost during the construction period and/or predevelopment phase; also provides phase-in during tower construction.	T2
Modification of ground rent payments	PANYNJ	Escalations delayed by two years (T4) and phase-in once construction starts (T3).	T4, T3
Fixed payment for infrastructure	PANYNJ	Provides certainty for a highly variable cost of construction and likely to be less than final actual cost on a pro-rata basis.	T4, T3, T2
Deferred payment for pro-rata share of substructure podium work	PANYNJ	Acts as an interest-free loan until financial obligation to pay commences.	T3, T2
Public-sector tenancy preleasing commitment	PANYNJ NYC (option)	Enhances developer's ability to secure financing for a speculative building project. Tenant rent increased over 2006 deal figures.	T4
Liberty Bonds	Federal Government	Triple tax-exemption of interest reduces the cost of debt financing to developer.	T4, T3, T2
Bond support payments	PANYNJ NYS NYC	Credit backstop guarantees "efficient and cost-effective" execution of project financing. Broad coverage of support: debt service obligations, construction cost overruns, leasing cost overruns, operating deficits, as well as capital expenditures.	T4 (full) T3 (capped)
Synthetic bond swap	PANYNJ	Protects developer against volatility of floating-rate interest rates during construction period with a hedging contract.	T3
Direct tenant rent subsidy	NYS	Enhances a building's competitive market position with tenant subsidy.	T4, T3 (limited, most went to 1 WTC)
Permanent commercial rent tax abatement for towers on WTC site	NYC	Relieves tenants of the 3.9 percent tax on their rent, directly reducing the total rent burden.	T3, T2
Public-sector equity	NYS NYC	Reduces the amount of construction debt required and enhances the overall financial security of the project.	T3

Source: Author

"Patriotism played a role in this heavily charged political environment," remarked one player, "and there's nothing wrong with that, but there's a price [to be] paid." As the developer's negotiating leverage increased over the years, Silverstein captured the favorable updraft of the public sector's limited appetite for continued brinkmanship.

As with any complex transaction, there were gives and takes between the parties. An early subsidy came in the form of the Port Authority's commitment to reestablish its headquarters in Silverstein's first-up building, Tower 4. As part of the 2006 realignment deal, the agency agreed to pay a starting rent of $59 a square foot (then a few dollars above the prevailing weighted average of $56.56 for class A space in the WFC-WTC submarket) for the 600,000 square feet it would occupy in the tower. Later, in a boost to the economics of Tower 4, the agency increased the starting rent it was willing to pay to $65 a square foot as part of its July 2009 prearbitration offer to SPI. It also agreed to shift its occupancy to the low-rise portion of the tower, floors 7 through 21, from floors 22 through 36, to give the developer "the ability to consolidate a larger block of space" on higher-level floors for lease to private tenants, "allowing the building potentially greater revenue," which would reduce the agency's risk and increase its future overall capital participation.[62] Market rents were falling during the Great Recession, and by the time the final 2010 deal framework was in place, the PA's rent figure was substantially above the weighted average of $51.08 a square foot for class A office space in this submarket. Somewhat offsetting the rent increase, the PA would benefit economically from other adjustments to the conditions of its space lease.[63] To successfully market the Liberty Bonds for Tower 4, the two prelease commitments made by the PA and New York City for two-thirds of the tower were essential because they reduced the speculative risk of development when the demand for new office space in lower Manhattan was so uncertain. And because they were from credit-worthy tenants, what the finance world considered "bankable" leases, they were more important than the general rent subsidy of $5.00 a square foot New York State offered to tenants who signed qualifying leases for the first 750,000 square feet at the Trade Center site.[64]

Abating the annual ground rent dramatically changed the economic equation for Tower 3 and Tower 2 because it reduced immediately the cash expenses of the project until the start of tower construction through the time it took to achieve stabilized occupancy, anywhere from three to five years, depending upon how quickly Silverstein was able to lease the office space. In its July 2009 offer letter to Silverstein, the agency said it would be "giving up approximately $770 million in rent over the next twelve years." In its report to the commissioners, staff justified the abatement by explaining that if SPI had a greater chance of developing the building, then the Port Authority had a greater chance of generating revenue from that building. Silverstein could only benefit from the rent-abatement subsidy for a set period, though; the developer had to begin construction of both towers within six years of the opening of the Transportation Hub.[65] Trading off immediate cash flow for future long-term benefits flowing from a project's success is a tried-and-true financial mechanism in public-private developments, typically more important to the policy calculus of ensuring success than the give of extra dollars up-front. The trade-off embodies a present-value arbitrage in which the private developer benefits from the immediate and certain value of saving upfront dollars in exchange for giving up a share of future and uncertain capital gains, and the public sector benefits in the long term from stronger project performance.

The physical interdependency of the project's ambitions remained a part of the new phased approach to development brought about by the 2010 deal. To house mechanical spaces for the Hub and some PA facilities, as well as the retail spaces programmed for both buildings, construction of the podiums for Tower 2 (to street level) and Tower 3 (seven stories) could not wait until development met the test of market feasibility. Even though the retail economics in all three towers belonged to the joint venture between the Port Authority and the Australia-based Westfield Group, the retail program's share of the costs for the office-tower bases would help keep SPI's economics rational. Since the vast integration of underground services and the re-creation of revenue-generating retail space reflected the Port Authority's ambitions, the 2010 deal, in turn, incorporated a nearly hidden subsidy to bring Tower 2 to street level: a commitment from the Port Authority to fund that cost (not to exceed $200 million), including SPI's share of such subgrade costs. SPI would reimburse the PA for its share (estimated at approximately $100 million) when it started construction of Tower 2 sometime in the future. In the meantime, the PA's full funding would serve as an interest-free loan for SPI.[66]

Other details of the deal created financial benefits for SPI. To shield it against the volatility of floating interest rates typically used to finance construction, the Port Authority agreed to absorb the cost of providing the developer with the equivalent of a fixed interest rate at a cost of approximately $136 million. Tenants in SPI's buildings would benefit from a permanent abatement of its commercial rent tax to the Trade Center area, which the city put in place in 2005, relieving tenants of a would-be 3.9 percent effective tax on their rent. Under certain and specific conditions SPI would be allowed to sell its full or partial interest in Tower 4 and Tower 3 with its backstop support agreements in place, which added future financial value to the buildings as investment assets. Plus, $2.6 billion of subsidized triple-tax-exempt Liberty Bonds were financing the two towers. And SPI's payment for the Trade Center's common infrastructure, fixed at $140 million under the 2006 realignment deal, represents a small fraction of the overall $1.6-billion cost estimate as of May 2010.

"EVERYONE GOT A FIG LEAF"

Silverstein and his investors were not the only beneficiaries of the 2010 deal. "There was the sandbagging by the New Jersey side of the Port Authority," Governor Paterson told me. "Spend what you want, we'll get the same money, was their attitude. What's a regional project? What's a national project, I ask? Some of the federal money went to New Jersey and beyond the WTC site." At the tail end of the negotiations—and like many issues determined by politicians, the merits of the deal itself were not the final determining factor of whether to authorize the new deal—"New Jersey was horse-trading for days at the end over what they would get. [It was] not about the WTC; New Jersey wanted a commitment from the [Port Authority] to raise the Bayonne Bridge so cargo ships could dock in Newark," a senior city official remarked in a tone of deep irritation and frustration once out of office. Governor Christie was the newest governor from the other side of the Hudson River to appear on the scene, and the Trade Center project was not on his agenda. His March 25 statement in response to the financing proposal for the site put distance between his office and the agreement with language positioning his responsibility to "protect the taxpayers, commuters, and toll payers of New Jersey and New York" and "a fiduciary duty...to make sure that our final agreement is financially sensible and fair."[67] Far from a ringing endorsement of the deal, the statement did speak the truth about the state's bargaining for a piece of the action.

New Jersey commissioners were experienced at creating a stalemate situation. Over the years, the Port Authority had become a more important institution to New Jersey than New York when it came to funding big economic-development projects. Because of its relatively weak board presence during the 2009–2010 Trade Center negotiations, Ward faced a big problem—New Jersey's price: $1 billion for rebuilding the ninety-year-old steel-arch Bayonne Bridge, a water crossing between Bayonne, New Jersey, and Staten Island, New York, to accommodate larger container ships' access to the marine terminal facilities of the Newark Bay port area. The project was a top priority for the Garden State. As revealed just one day after the August board vote on the two deals, Christie had threatened to block the agency from supporting the Trade Center deal if the Port Authority board did not approve funding for the bridge project. This was parity politics in action.[68]

Beyond the horse-trading on spending for their respective states, Port Authority commissioners wanted more power and more oversight of approvals for Trade

Center projects. Before they authorized the 2010 deal, they demanded that the chair of the board would have to approve the adequacy of the benchmarks SPI was to meet for the agency to produce its financial support. This marginalized the staff, which usually brought fully baked deals to the board. "It was an odd dynamic that wasn't publicized much," Coscia told me.[69]

Concluding the 2010 financing deal without a hiccup in the all-important schedule for opening the Memorial Plaza on the tenth anniversary of the attack assured Mayor Bloomberg a legacy. Other reputations were made and images recast by the 2008–2010 financial episode. Ward finally got credit, from the editorial page of the *New York Post*, which was not one to find much to praise at the bi-state agency, for his promise that there would be more results than "deadline announcements" under his leadership. "The financing deal is a sign that Ward is keeping his word. Kudos to him." Ward, in turn, gave the credit to Governor Paterson: "He's the unsung hero of the story. He got us through this; he didn't grandstand. He backed us up with Shelly Silver and Mayor Bloomberg. He let us negotiate on the public policy merits of the issue."[70] Personal recognition of achievement through the drama and complexity came to Bob Lieber and Seth Pinsky, as well as others who did not garner the same media attention but were essential players: Drew Warshaw, Tim Gilchrist, and Janno Lieber. And Larry Silverstein—by succeeding in this latest seemingly impossible quest—reframed his image as an obstructionist developer only out for more monetary benefits to "The Man Who Is Rebuilding Ground Zero" for whom it was "Time to Celebrate." These were certainty better headlines than "Silverstein Won't Budge," "Butt Out, Larry: Silverstein Must Quit WTC Site, Says Mike," and "World Trade Center Developer Larry Silverstein Wants Own Bailout."

In terms of moving forward with construction at Ground Zero, Albany and City Hall got what their political leaders wanted, at a price. The political pain of paying the cost of a very favorable deal for the developer lingered on in conflict between the states across the Hudson—in controversy over the sharp increases in bridge and tunnel tolls that came in August 2011, and the comprehensive audit of the entire agency that the governors jointly initiated as a condition for these toll and fare increases. In 2011, the Trade Center projects consumed $1.94 billion, more than half of the agency's $3.22 billion capital-budget spending for the year. Even though the threat of a potential downgrade had spooked the authority into raising its tolls and fares, in the fall of 2012 Moody's Investors Service downgraded the Port Authority's bond rating to Aa3 from Aa2, citing "the increased financing needs of nearly $2 billion through 2016" identified in the audit report of the PA by the business consulting firm Navigant Consulting, Inc.; the Trade Center development was a primary driver of the credit downgrade. Analysts further warned the agency that it was reaching the limit of its ability to turn to toll payers to cover its debts, especially in a period of slower economic recovery.[71]

The new financing demands of the 2010 deal deepened the political fissures at the Port Authority as New Jersey interests on the board fought hard about what their state would get in dollars equivalent to the additional dollars being spent at the Trade Center. As close to home as the 9/11 losses were to New Jersey families of the victims and its citizens, in the offices of its elected officials, the rebuilding effort continued to be viewed as a New York project, a New York responsibility. It was the same hard lesson the 9/11 Memorial Foundation had learned in its fund-raising effort years earlier—despite the city's taking the brunt of the terrorist attack on the United States, rebuilding Ground Zero was a New York project.

The repercussions of the authority's management of projects at Ground Zero and its uncontrolled spending on its rebuilding effort were not singularly financial. The large toll hikes prompted the late U.S. senator Frank Lautenberg (D-NJ), an outspoken critic of the Port Authority, to request an investigation by the U.S. Government Accountability Office, and when the report came out in August 2013, the bi-state authority's process for fast-tracking the toll hikes came under sharp criticism. The Navigant audit of the Port Authority produced for the two governors and widely viewed as a political effort to discredit past leadership opened with strong words of censure. It characterized the agency as "a challenged and dysfunctional organization suffering from a lack of consistent leadership, a siloed underlying bureaucracy, poorly coordinated capital planning processes, insufficient cost controls, and a lack of transparent and effective oversight of the World Trade Center program that has obscured full awareness of billions of dollars in exposure to the Port Authority." It rebuked the historically proud agency for being out of control, especially when it came to mismanagement of the $14.8-billion Trade Center project, and cast another blemish on its reputation. "The audit caused considerable pain in the organization," *Crain's* quoted a top insider as saying.[72] A top-to-bottom shake-up, including governance reform, was not far off, and Governor Andrew Cuomo was reportedly interested in bringing the quasi-independent authority under control. Surely, exposure of deep fissures in the governance structure of the bi-state Port Authority was an unintended consequence of the institution's quest to control and rebuild the site of its iconic home, making its future somewhat uncertain.

As a public-private development project, the rebuilding the Trade Center site was crippled by conflict stemming from a number of fundamental conditions: the particulars of the players, the institutional structure inherited from the 2001 privatization and leasehold transaction, and the emotional mandate of 9/11. More than anything else, though, the mistrust between the Port Authority and Silverstein, who acted as competitors more than partners even though they needed one another to push forward progress on the site and succeed in their respective ambitions, was crippling—and not typical of voluntary public-private ventures. No amount of rhetoric to the contrary could whitewash the evident adversarial relationship. In sharp contrast, the Port Authority's other Trade Center public-private partnerships—with Westfield for the retail program, the Durst Organization for ownership of 1 World Trade (discussed in the next chapter), and Legends Hospitality for the Observatory Deck—have been created with greater alignments of interest as straightforward business transactions without high-profile controversy and consummated in relatively short order.

For a public-private partnership to succeed, both sides need to be sophisticated in negotiation and real estate finance; if not, one side will benefit to the advantage of the other. Often the imbalance is rooted in the quality of negotiators and the political constraints bearing down on the options facing each party. The private sector may get a better deal, and the public sector may not realize it until some things go wrong, as was the case with the 2006 realignment deal. On the 2010 financing deal, until the full costs are tallied, the final assessment is still to come. When a final tally is done, the cost is going to be extraordinarily high, far more than anticipated when the plan for rebuilding was laid out and far more than the public was ever given to understand. The incremental process by which this came about, however, is "an emblem of a flaw so common to public-private partnerships," Eliot Brown wrote with words that aptly captured the essence of what it means for the public sector to commit to these partnerships. Over the course of development "conditions change, costs increase, the market worsens, and once it seems too late to turn around and scrap a deal, a developer needs more aid, and the public sector is in a tough place to refuse."[73] This is what is meant by the phrase "lying down in a partnership."

Public-private partnerships are rarely as perfectly balanced as the word "partnership" suggests, and this one was no exception. Once the emotional issues of building the memorial had been settled and above-ground construction on the site became visible, the balance of power in this volatile public-private partnership shifted, definitively, to favor the private developer as the economic and political stakes of assuring accelerated completion intensified. The extended period of delays and conflicts had increased the stakes of the partnership and made the costs for either side of walking away near to impossible. Ward held the line on advancing deep subsidies to the developer as long as it was possible and the PA won the arbitration gamble, which enhanced the public sector's negotiating position. Ultimately, the public sector paid a price for progress because political forces were aligned against letting the market determine the fate of the most important rebuilding task in New York City's history.

May 5, 2011. Timothy A. Clary/AFP/Getty Images

PART VI
DELIVERANCE
(2011–2016)

CHAPTER 20

Reckoning Anew

FIGURE 20.1 *1 World Trade Center: The new polestar of lower Manhattan, opened November 2014.* PISAPHOTOGRAPHY/SHUTTLESTOCK

I N PHOTOS AND NEWS STORIES, videos and tweets, media all around the world sent out reports for over two weeks in the spring of 2013 as the finishing touch—a silver spire rising as high as forty stories and weighing in at 785 tons—was installed atop New York City's newest landmark, the 1,776-foot tower at Ground Zero (figure 20.1). Few words were needed to convey the symbolic significance of this event. The message was clear in the not-to-be-missed photo images and the bold-typeface headlines: "Crowning Achievement at Ground Zero" (*NYT*), "Tallest Building in the West Rises from the Ashes of the Twin Towers" (*Daily Telegraph* [London]), "On Top of the World 4,259 Days Later, WTC Rises Again" (*DN*). "One World Trade Center has risen over the sacred ground as the symbol of resolve and resurgence that it was designed to be," the *Daily News* editorialized in an effusive expression of civic pride. It "will reflect the strength of this city, the only city in the world capable of the feats of engineering entailed in the rebuilding of Ground Zero, the only city resilient enough to rebound from the depths into an era of safety and prosperity, the only city tough enough to erect its own defenses against domestic and international attack." In "Towering over Terror," the editorial board of the *New York Post* said "the building means New York did not allow the terrorists to have the last word."[1]

The messages of this long-awaited event reprised the themes of patriotism and civic renewal that had so infused the post-9/11 months of planning for the rebuild of Ground Zero and helped calm deep-set anxieties triggered by the trauma of the attack. The completion of 1 World Trade Center offered tangible, inconvertible affirmation that after all the angst and controversy, a new place was materializing, a place that balanced remembrance of the past with optimism for the future. The many goals public officials set out to achieve were settling into place. After more than a year of uncertainty, the Chicago-based Council on Tall Buildings and Urban Habitat officially ruled the 1,776-foot landmark tower to be the tallest in the Western Hemisphere, taller than Chicago's 1,451-foot tall Willis Tower (formerly known as the Sears Tower), which had captured the title from the twin towers in the 1970s. "Oh, perfect," the *Daily News* editorialized days before the ruling, "[t]he Second City is passing judgment on the first." New York had reclaimed the tallest in the United States title, "bragging rights" as messaged in the *Wall Street Journal* storyline.[2] It was the tallest, yet not the first completed tower on the skyline of the Trade Center site; that ribbon-cutting distinction ceremoniously took place six months earlier at Larry Silverstein's 4 WTC, a subtly designed building by a respected master who believes in understatement, Pritzker Prize–winning Japanese architect Fumihiko Maki.

Other milestones were piling up: Workers were replacing the long-sought missing blocks of city streets—Greenwich, Cortlandt and Fulton—eradicated some fifty years earlier to create the World Trade Center's superblock despised by urban planners and architects and lovers of civic spaces. When the World Trade Center stub of Greenwich Street was rejoined to the city's street grid, it fulfilled the goal of creating connectivity with the Financial District and Tribeca neighborhoods for pedestrians. The three blocks of Cortlandt Street, renamed Cortlandt Way, were on their way to becoming an open-air pedestrian lane lined with retail shops, achieved after a long and unshakable effort by City Planning Commissioner Amanda M. Burden to ensure that the site would be integrated into the fabric of lower Manhattan; the Port Authority had sought to re-create Cortlandt as an enclosed galleria for retail space.[3] Even the bollards, those short vertical posts positioned to obstruct the passage of motor vehicles and apt to trigger ever-present security concerns, did not dampen the sense of openness beginning to take hold

FIGURE 20.2 *Openness of the Trade Center site despite the ever-present security bollards, a dramatic change from the original WTC.* GARY HACK

of the site by fall 2013 (figure 20.2). More openness emerged at the start of 2014 when after more than a decade of construction barricades, workers started to dismantle parts of the blue fencing around the site. Although full integration into downtown did not come until the Port Authority completed the Transportation Hub designed by Santiago Calatrava in 2016, with the fences partially down, people could now walk back and forth freely between the Memorial Plaza and parts of downtown. The podium on which the original World Trade Center had been built was gone and with it, the impeding walls on three sides of the sites.

The opening of the Memorial Plaza happened as scheduled on the tenth anniversary of the attacks, September 11, 2011. It was a day of collective sadness and united remembrance, public observance and private reflection, national commemoration and worldwide awareness, a symbolic day to honor from near and afar those who perished tragically on that strikingly clear but fateful day in September when the crystalline blue skies brought forth terror, so unexpectedly, so brutally, so horrifyingly. It would not have happened on the tenth anniversary without the push and determination of Michael Bloomberg. He was the sole elected official whose continuity of public service marked New York City's traverse from cataclysmic tragedy to determined defiance to triumphant rebound as the global city of the twenty-first century. He did not always make the right calls on rebuilding throughout the process, but he assured completion of the priority of priorities: the memorial.

The eight-acre memorial quadrant, filled with about four hundred swamp white oak trees softly buffering the two memorial pools, was becoming more of a park day by day, and New Yorkers who are used to small, tight spaces were reveling in its vast openness (plate 22). (In Manhattan, only Central Park offers such an experience of vast open space; by comparison, the plaza at Rockefeller Center is relatively small.) The long-awaited National September 11 Memorial Museum opened in May 2014 and completed the remembrance program by memorializing the site as well as those who perished. It accommodated the World Trade Center's history with large artifacts from the complex, including portions of the Vesey Street staircase, now known as the Survivors' Staircase, which on that fateful day became the exit to life for hundreds. By immediately attracting thousands of visitors to downtown, the museum was being heralded by the business community as a "further catalyst for growth." That long-sought-after growth seemed to be on the horizon as office rents started to "show downtown's rising cachet," condos started to "stack up," and "the area's retail scene began to revive" in anticipation of thousands of new office workers, tourists, and residents.[4] At long last, downtown was acquiring a new positive profile, standing for the creative class and the moneyed flocking to neighboring Tribeca and surrounds. The transforming neighborhood was no longer Ground Zero, though the moniker for the Trade Center site would be hard to let go for many citizens and the media alike.

For so many years, political language served as a stand-in for substance. Rhetorical language in particular had become a form of political action throughout the stages of planning and in the troubled interlude of controversy and conflict before construction on the site transformed the sixteen acres into a new urban place populated with daily activity. Far from inactive, the interlude could only deliver promises and more promises but now it had ended. The interlude was over. Enough was in place so the future rebuild of the whole was foreseeable, even though several pieces of the master plan were yet to come, and even though what was delivered was not the exact vision that had been promised, and even though the full urban fabric of the place was still evolving and the security issues of this twice-targeted site had yet to be tested. The complaints about interminable delays and the repeated editorializing about the lack of leadership, in retrospect, tended to obscure for the populace at large the progress that was being made on the ground—and the dedication of thousands of individuals who "committed themselves, in many ways, and for many reasons, to one of the most complicated, scrutinized, demanding, exhausting, frustrating and emotionally charged projects in history."[5] It was, however, also quite plausible to argue that the continual narrative of delay served to goad the principal actors toward more expedient action than otherwise might have been the case. Almost twelve years had passed between the total cataclysmic collapse of the World Trade Center and the milestone openings—record time when set against the city's decades-long redevelopment of Forty-second Street–Times Square or Battery Park City, both far less complex and emotionally contested large-scale projects than the rebuild at Ground Zero.

In terms of time, the evidence contradicted the conventional belief that rebuilding the Trade Center site was irredeemably undermined by conflict and controversy. For sure, less conflict and controversy would have been far better for the body politic and less costly in terms of dollars spent and political reputations sullied. Less delay on Silverstein's part could have changed the timeline. A less complex program could have changed the timeline. More coordination and clear direction among the public entities could have done this too. Even if complete smooth sailing had been possible (a scenario never realistically in the cards), is it possible to say for certain what was tangibly and irrevocably lost during the interlude? What might have been? Within the achievements to date lie lost opportunities and mistakes, the still uncertain cultural program for the site for one. Rebuilding took place in a heavily charged political environment, naturally and legitimately, and that environment exacted a price beyond excessive costs. Under intense pressure to rebuild fast, public officials made decisions that were sometimes at odds with what might have been viewed as most needed for New York City's long-term growth and continued global preeminence, in particular when it came to choices of how to spend the $4.55 billion of transportation dollars granted to the city. As with the 9/11 event itself, time has yet to deliver the full meaning of rebuilding at Ground Zero and an understanding of how the long-term identity of the place will be shaped by future use. In the interim, the experience of rebuilding leaves a legacy that will grow as the leaves of those swamp oaks unfurl each spring and die back each winter, naturally dormant before the cycle of life restarts anew.

UNDISCIPLINED COSTS

Twenty-five billion is a very big number. That is the projected cost for rebuilding Ground Zero, as shown in the tabulation in table 20.1 (not including rebuilding 7 World Trade Center or St. Nicholas Greek Orthodox Church). It is a gigantic number, especially when benchmarked against other twenty-first-century, high-profile, big-ticket projects in the United States: Boston's Big Dig ($14.5 billion), New York City's East Side Access Project ($10.2 billion), Chicago's O'Hare International Airport Modernization ($8.8 billion), New Jersey's Access to the Region's Core ($8.7 billion before cancellation), Washington, D.C.'s Dulles Corridor Metrorail Project ($6.2 billion), or New York City's long-deferred Moynihan Station project ($3.2 billion), to name just a few. In terms of order of magnitude, the big number

Table 20.1 The Direct Costs of Rebuilding Ground Zero.

WTC Site Rebuilding Component	Approved Cost (Millions)
Transportation:	
Permanent PATH Transportation Hub[1]	$3,995
Dey Street passageway[2]	219
Cortlandt Street subway station[3]	210
Site infrastructure:	
Underground infrastructure[4]	1,965
Streets, utilities, open spaces[5]	327
Additional finance expense & contingency[6]	705
Security & centralized servicing:	
Vehicle Security Center, roadways, Helix[7]	1,340
PANYNJ sitewide management facilities & projects[8]	240
NYPD campus plan[9]	300
Commercial development:	
1 WTC (PANYNJ-Durst)[10]	3,949
Towers 4, 3, 2 (Silverstein)[11]	6,796
130 Liberty Street (site 5)[12]	1,696
Retail development (Westfield)[13]	2,060
Memorial Plaza and Memorial Museum[14]	1,024
Performing Arts Center [15]	482
LMDC site and memorial planning[16]	8
LMDC other site acquisiton[17]	61
TOTAL REBUILDING ESTIMATE[18]	**$25,506**

Compiled by the author from the following sources:
1. PA-FTA Project Authorization, September 6, 2012.
2. Connector of PATH Hub complex to Fulton Street Station, FTA project authorization, 4Q13.
3. MTA No. 1 subway station on Trade Center site, PA project authorization, February 6, 2013.
4. PA Navigant audit report, estimate at completion, current estimate, January 31, 2012.
5. PA project authorization, December 4, 2013, April 23, 2014.
6. PA Navigant audit report, estimate at completion, current estimate, January 31, 2012.

for the Trade Center is on par with the Ten-Year Capital Plan the Port Authority put forward for 2014–2023 ($22.7 billion), after taking out the cost to complete the agency's Trade Center projects ($4.9 billion). It takes on a more modest fiscal context only when benchmarked against the enormous need for continual public capital investment of the nation's largest city, evident in its Ten-Year Capital Strategy Plan for 2014–2023 ($53.7 billion). Still, $25 billion is a humbling figure, more than double the LMDC's earliest estimate in 2003 for rebuilding Ground Zero ($10 billion), and far in excess of the $6.7 billion the Federal Reserve Bank of

7. PA project authorizations, phase 1, August 5, 2010; phase 2, September 18, 2013; phase 3, July 23, 2014.

8. PA project authorizations, September 17, 2014, October 22, 2014.

9. PA Navigant audit report, estimate at completion, current estimate, January 31, 2012.

10. PA Navigant audit report, estimate at completion, current estimate, January 31, 2012.

11. T4 Liberty Bond offering, October 29, 2014; T3 Liberty Bond offering, November 2, 2011; T2 estimate from SPI; all towers include financing cost and standard tenant improvement bridget for fit-out procided by landlord.

12. LMDC acquisition and deconstruction costs ($292 million) in addition to settlement dollars of $103.8 million; NYC Independent Budget Office, *The Aftermath: Federal Aid 10 Years after the World Trade Center Attack*, August 2011; plus, assumption on construction of high-density space; program unspecified at this time but the Amended General Project Plan allows for up to 1.3 million square feet; assumed future cost, $1,100 per square foot.

13. PA-FTA project authorization (not including tenant fit-out work), December 4, 2013.

14. Memorial and Memorial Museum ($718 million), plus PA infrastructure for the site, as per 2012 cost settlement between the PA, NYC, and the Memorial Foundation, PA project authorization, September 20, 2012.

15. PA Navigant audit report ($182 million), plus assumed future construction cost ($300 million).

16. NYC Independent Budget Office, *The Aftermath: Federal Aid 10 Years after the World Trade Center Attack*, August 2011.

17. LMDC acquisition of 155 Cedar Street (site of St. Nicholas Greek Orthodox Church) and 140 Liberty Street, which when combined with 130 Liberty, complete the assembly for the southern site and provide for construction of the underground VSC facility. NYC Independent Budget Office, *The Aftermath: Federal Aid 10 Years after the World Trade Center Attack*, August 2011.

18. Does not include the cost of rebuilding 7 WTC, St. Nicholas Greek Orthodox Church, Fiterman Hall of Manhattan Community College; repairs and realignment to Route 9A (West Street); and restoration of other structures heavily damaged in the 9/11 attack on the World Trade Center (two buildings at World Financial Center/Brookfield Place and Winter Garden and Verizon Building, among others).

Note: Due to data limitations, no attempt has been made to adjust figures for inflation.

New York had conservatively figured in 2002 would be needed to replace the destroyed buildings of the World Trade Center complex along with $3.7 billion in public infrastructure (subways and utilities) to "essentially duplicate what existed before the attack."[6]

With the private sector paying for three office towers, the retail shops, a portion of the 9/11 Memorial and Memorial Museum, and the PAC (sometime in the future), approximately 35.5 percent of the overall projected cost will be borne by the private sector, albeit with heavy public subsidies from every level of government. Ironically, the projected cost of Silverstein's three office towers (6.7 million square feet) at $6.8 billion almost equals what the developer sought in his two-occurrence insurance claim to rebuild all 10 million square feet of lost office space in *five* towers. At this point in accounting, rebuilding the five towers will run to $12.6 billion.

Getting a handle on rebuilding costs mirrors the complexity of the task itself: many projects with interwoven elements, some public and some private, stretched out over time and subject to innumerable delays, plan adjustments and design changes, and engineering challenges. Some costs are too speculative to estimate because they are contingent liabilities—for example, the credit backstops of the 2010 deal to finance two of the three Silverstein towers. It is close to impossible to definitively document the all-inclusive costs for rebuilding the Trade Center site; costs would have to be comprehensively traced across the many different direct stakeholders, and even an ex post analysis of historical costs would likely bump up against the limits of "supporting detail and source documents," as noted by the comprehensive audit of the Port Authority conducted by Navigant Consulting for the Special Committee of the Port Authority Board of Commissioners in 2011.[7] How much of the cost might be attributed to complexity, constantly changing plans arising from controversy, or pragmatic adjustments to changing market conditions or political mandates certainly dwells in the realm of speculative discourse.

There should be no surprise in the fact that the costs of rebuilding were undisciplined. Carefully prepared cost estimates and project budgets did not govern decisions at Ground Zero, many of which were politically driven, for a long time. At the Port Authority, costs were out of control for years until Chris Ward moved into the executive director's office. Even at that point, the work already in progress for the Transportation Hub and 1 World Trade Center precluded radical adjustments in response to escalating costs. As reporters David W. Dunlap of the *Times* and Eliot Brown of the *Wall Street Journal* explained in 2014, multiple forces were driving the transportation center to a $4 billion price tag far beyond the initial $1.9 billion figure. Ambitiously sized at 800,000 square feet with a transit hall to rival

Grand Central Terminal, the cost for the Hub comes to a startling $5,000 for each square foot. As a visit will quickly reveal, the interiors everywhere—top, sides, bottom, and columns—are clad with enormous quantities of white Italian marble, on rainy days a slippery surface capable of exciting attorneys specializing in slip-and-fall claims. What would it take to keep this pristine surface looking clean and bright against the demanding wear and tear (and ubiquitous remnants of chewing gum) of commuters? Only the *Daily News* editorial board dared to question how "this disaster in the making" would be maintained by the PA.[8] How many millions would it take? Ten million annually was one answer I got from an insider. Project direction and administration for the Hub amounted to an astounding $820 a square foot and project design, another $206 a square foot. These two cost elements alone exceeded the full cost to develop the seventy-two story 4 WTC ($928 a square foot).

The expense of the eight-acre Memorial Plaza with its emotion-packed voids and 110,000-square-foot memory museum similarly ballooned from a loose estimate of $350 million to nearly $1 billion before being trimmed back to a budget of $560 million (not including site infrastructure costs); in time, however, costs once again escalated over $1 billion. More or less, the memorial program had unlimited money. Who was going to put a limit on what could be spent on the emotion-driven memorial and its museum of memory? Costs ballooned beyond the $90 million of approved budget overruns that had been built into the July 2006 agreement between the PA, the LMDC, the Memorial Foundation, and the city. By summer 2011, a dispute over $156 million in cost overruns the Port Authority claimed it was owed by the foundation erupted in public. The agency slowed work on the museum and stopped approving contracts and extensions of existing contracts[9] (figure 20.3). Like other conflicts at Ground Zero, this one involved powerful egos and competing agendas in a tug of war for political control of events, other decisions, and overall stewardship of the 9/11 Memorial. Collateral issues, including the projected $60 million annual cost for operating the Memorial Museum, also shaped the context of negotiations and the drift in time before all parties reached agreement on costs. The official cost for the 9/11 Memorial and Memorial Museum settled in at $718 million, not accounting for the more than $300 million for the site's infrastructure. As with nearly every project at Ground Zero, the costs were extraordinary.

Deconstruction of the former Deutsche Bank Building at 130 Liberty, where another high-density tower will rise at some time in the future, also proved to be extraordinarily costlier than anticipated and, following the deadly fire in 2007 that killed two firefighters and injured 115 others, tragic. The LMDC acquired the site for $90 million and the remediation and deconstruction, initially budgeted at $74

FIGURE 20.3 Jimmy Margulies/The Record

million, ultimately was reset at $292.1 million *in addition* to over $103.8 million in settlement costs received from Deutsche Bank and third-party insurers. Massively botched, it stands as a "prime example of certain things the government should not be involved with," said a savvy policy professional. Government became the repository of all public policy, forced to make rational policy decisions with contradictory forces: the Environmental Protection Agency, New York Fire Department, the LMDC, and the community. Each agency and stakeholder insisted on pushing public policy in its jurisdiction beyond where it had ever been before, a story deserving of its own separate account.

Certain policy decisions at Ground Zero turned out to be financially costly. Governor Pataki's decision to keep the No. 1 subway line in continuous service, for example, meant underpinning the line at a cost of $355.5 million, according to the FTA's accounting. The PA's decision to centralize underground servicing and management of the complex produced an extensive program for a Vehicle Security Center and underground roadway system built out in three phases. "The Rodeo," was how LMDC director Roland Betts, chair of the development corporation's site planning committee, described the underground servicing system snaking southeast to northwest in a counterclockwise manner, in and out and under the No. 1 subway line, PATH train tracks, utilities, and the Freedom Tower.[10] Though not visible to the public, this engineered wonder-world underground built to blast-proof standards of robustness was authorized at a cost of $1.34 billion, with an additional $240 million authorized for the Port Authority's sitewide management facilities in the underground, along with other related projects. By comparison, the expense to build the superstructure for the signature Oculus of the transit hall seems modest: $279.3 million and $203.6 million for its substructure, all of which was detailed in the FTA's 2012 Revised and Restated Construction Agreement with the Port Authority.

The rebuilding objectives being served at Ground Zero go beyond policy mandates, beyond commercial objectives, and beyond the accommodations for history (stabilization and reinforcement of the slurry-wall remnant) and the demands of activist family members (preservation and presentation of the truncated box-beam columns or integration of the Survivors' Staircase into the Memorial Museum). Though high-profile conflicts, these political accommodations would reflect relatively small sums in the overall tally.[11] Money was no object in showing the world that New York City could rebuild better than before, in defiance of the terrorists' intent. Hewing to the aesthetic demands and engineering challenges of the Hub's star architect, who was not concerned with cost-conscious decision-making, the Port Authority allowed costs for its phoenix project to escalate beyond any reasonable number. While the result may be seen as a significant addition to Manhattan's architectural heritage, as discussed in the epilogue, whether it will exceed the globally acknowledged grandeur of Grand Central Terminal's Grand Hall and its most meaningful role as a place of public assembly only time will tell.

How was it that the cost issue became a secondary consideration in rebuilding Ground Zero? Politics superseded budgets. Priorities were not established. Everything on this sixteen-acre site, seventy feet deep, was to be built all at once, Lego-like. Authority for decision-making was fragmented over numerous stakeholders, public and private. No fiscal barometer existed and no local tax hike to raise the ire of citizens, only a series of controversial steep toll increases on the Port Authority's bridges and tunnels connecting the metropolitan region. Accountability was missing in no small part because the information was deftly obscure. Political intervention and bureaucratic competition turned out to be costly. An enormous amount of capital was invested in the future of the city, yet how much money was squandered will never be known. Undoubtedly, some but not all of the cost-elevating decisions will prove to be salutary. Other decisions might not turn out to be so salutary in light of what other development objectives, for example, regional transportation beyond PATH into lower Manhattan and capital allocated to the larger region, might have been achieved with the enormous pot of opportunistic dollars that flowed into the city post-9/11.

MUSEUM OF MEMORY

The 9/11 Memorial Museum is a profoundly moving experience. It is an emotional journey, overwhelmingly meaningful and at the same time painfully difficult to take in all at once, like the 9/11 event itself. It is a site of cultural memory, and the power of this skillfully orchestrated place comes on gradually in a gentle descent to bedrock seventy feet below the ground plane of the Memorial Plaza. Called "the Ribbon," the descent on a processional ramp serves as "a symbolic reminder of the ramp used in the recovery," said Steven M. Davis, partner in Davis Brody Bond, the architects for the Memorial Museum. That utilitarian haul ramp had become "a bridge to memory, a fixed conduit in an upended realm, a link to that day in September 2001," Dunlap wrote in a report just before it was dismantled after seven years of logistical and ceremonial duty. Used as a kind of funerary path whenever remains were found and a processional route for effects like the laying of the Freedom Tower cornerstone and a rite of observance for relatives of the victims on successive anniversaries of the terrorist attack, the 460-foot-long ramp had taken on meaning over time. It "gave you time to approach," said Paula G. Berry, whose husband was killed in the attack. "That length of time was very important. It prepared you for what you were about to go into."[12] So too, the Ribbon ramp in the 9/11 Museum (plate 19).

The museum architects wanted the progression down into the depths to be a constant revelation, a "progressive disclosure." The concrete pathway unfolds with switchbacks and overlooks. On reaching the first overlook, the raw slurry wall with its engineered tie-backs comes into view, and the impact of the Trade Center's enormous scale is dramatic and commanding. On the second overlook twenty-seven feet in descent, the visitor is perched between the two aluminum-sheathed tower voids. The finish point of the Ribbon leads to the Foundation Hall, a vast cathedral-like volume of space reached by descending a wide set of stairs alongside the whole sixty-four-foot length of the fifty-seven-ton Survivors' Stairs, which was moved three times before being permanently installed in the museum. The monumental space of the Foundation Hall, unadorned but for the sixty-ton, thirty-six-foot steel "Last Column" covered with inscriptions, mementos, and missing posters placed there by ironworkers, rescue workers, and others, is arresting in its simplicity, a place of quiet contemplation. It is inspirational in its vastness and volume (figure 20.4). At bedrock level, housed within the spaces of the tower footprints are exhibitions (in the north void, a historical exhibition chronologically retelling the events of the day and galleries recording narratives before and after 9/11; in the south void, the *In Memoriam* exhibition commemorating the lives of those who perished in the two attacks on the Trade Center).

FIGURE 20.4 *Foundation Hall of the Memorial Museum, opened May 2014.* Photo Amy Dreher, Courtesy 911 Memorial.org

The immediacy of perspective and collection of bent steel artifacts—some so sculpturally beautiful and displayed with such refinement that they could be mistaken for conscious artistic creations—and other talisman items of the towers' destruction convey the physical enormity and fuel-scorching violence of the attack. There are discreet backdoor exits throughout if the experience gets too difficult and, carefully placed, boxes of tissues throughout. A repository for the unidentified human remains of 9/11 victims (some 7,930 remains of 1,115 people of the 2,753 missing on that day had yet to be identified) under the jurisdiction of the Office of Chief Medical Examiner of the City of New York lies behind a wall faced with 2,983 individual squares of Fabriano Italian paper—one square for every person killed in the 9/11 attacks and February 1993 attack—each hand-painted by the artist Spencer Finch in different shades of blue, "Trying to Remember the Color of the Sky on That September Morning." This private space lies between the two twin tower footprints.

In descent and in tandem, the path traces out episodes of conflict and controversy that beset the memorialization process itself. The sixty-five-foot-high by sixty-foot-wide section of the exposed slurry wall accessed at bedrock in the West Chamber became but a derivative of the idea put forth in Libeskind's master plan as *the* memorial site, symbol of resilience. The scale of the Memorial Museum itself grew to a monumental 110,000 square feet after the controversy triggered by the proposed International Freedom Center led to its eviction from Ground Zero. The amount of exhibition space at bedrock was significantly increased and placed *within* the two tower-footprint areas after security concerns pushed Arad's concept of underground memorial structures up to the street level. Preservation of key artifacts—the cut-off remnants of the original box columns that supported the exterior walls of the twin towers visible through a glass-floor covering and the Survivors' Staircase—reflect prolonged protest by activist family members resolute in their determination to prevent anything from encroaching upon the sanctity of the towers' footprints they wanted to remain empty. Each of these elements marks a turning point in the political history of rebuilding at Ground Zero. Each evidences how accommodation to the many competing ambitions in the political vortex at Ground Zero came to define the terms and conditions of rebuilding of the Trade Center site.

Designed and executed abiding by a process deeply respectful and emotionally responsive to the memorial mission, the creation of this experience was a huge effort. It was led with exquisite sensitivity by Alice M. Greenwald, director of the 9/11 Memorial Museum. Greenwald arrived at the position in April 2006, age fifty-four, after nineteen years at the U.S. Holocaust Museum in Washington, D.C., where she was associate museum director for museum programs. Though the atrocity of the 9/11 attack was different, it raised the same kinds of questions for a memorial museum setting, if not answers, she told me. The time factor compounded the inherent challenges of the task. The museum would be responsible for codifying the narrative of 9/11 without the scholarship that would typically be available in a longer time frame of museum planning. Planning would also take place while families of the victims were still grieving.

From the beginning, Greenwald was firm on focus: "The museum would be a platform to tell the story of what happened on 9/11; the museum would not be a platform for a comparative analysis of terrorist acts." The Memorial Museum's mission was to preserve the memory of loss, collective loss and individual loss. The narrative of 9/11 as told in the museum would be through the lens of memory. "A central premise of the design direction" would be "about encounter, and as much about 'feeling' the history as about knowing it,'" she later wrote in "Passion on All Sides: Lessons for Planning the National September 11 Memorial Museum," and given the history of 9/11, this meant that the information and documentation could be at times "graphic in its violence and provocative in its implications."[13]

Being true to what happened on 9/11 needed to be carried out without traumatizing visitors. Yet telling the truth—and how much truth—presented many difficult decisions. How much horror and graphic carnage should be shown? Which artifacts of destruction should be displayed? How many of the "thousands of harrowing first-person recollections, photographs, and videos from survivors and witnesses, many of them raw," should be made public? Should the "composites," chunks of compressed floors, be exhibited as "objects that perhaps best capture the destructive force unleashed that day"? How much of "a factual presentation of what is known about the terrorists, including their methods and means of preparation," a museum guideline formally adopted by the Memorial Foundation, should be explored? Did it mean including photographs and some of the words of the hijackers? It was not possible for the museum to preserve the history of what happened on 9/11 without documenting the perpetrators of this mass murder, controversial as it might be, but what were the right parameters for doing so? As detailed by *Times* reporter Patricia Cohen, during eight years of museum planning "every step has been muddied with contention," and the task of figuring out how to tell the story of 9/11, "an undertaking pockmarked with contradictions."[14] Massive loss turned out not to be easy to document.

The painstaking challenge of carrying out the museum's remembrance mission on the site of the 9/11 World Trade Center attack that many venerated as hallowed ground was unlike that faced by other commemorative museums. It was further compounded by the physical contours of the subterranean space, "hemmed in by the undersides of the memorial pools and by the abutting PATH station, 1 World Trade Center, vehicle security center and central cooling plant." The deep pit itself is an artifact first identified by Libeskind in his master plan for rebuilding. As a consequence of the emotional and physical conditions, the museum became the "inverse of a traditional museum," Davis said.[15] Unlike a traditional museum itself considered to be the icon, with the 9/11 Memorial Museum, the commanding physical presence of the site became the icon. Davis and his team would use the archeology of the big hole—its scale, authenticity, memory, and emotion—as "conceptual vectors" to shape the walk-through experience of the museum.

The documentary aspirations of the museum shaped the process of planning. Greenwald coordinated planning discussions among an enormous team of experts from every conceivable curatorial and conservation field, exhibit designers, and architects to give visual, spatial, and sound shape to the telling of the 9/11 history and its traumatic losses. They left no detail unexplored; every decision, small or large, was handled with the same level of care, debate, discussion, and balance between accommodating the desires of stakeholders and the conceptualized narrative for the museum. "The process was long, very long. There were so many questions on the table, decisions about which pieces were relevant to the story," she told me. "Figuring out how to lay out a coherent story that was not obviously sequential—it took a long time to figure out the narrative sequences for these spaces."[16]

September 11 was new history; the event was still proximate in time. Over a period of seven years beginning in the summer of 2006, Greenwald and her staff convened a diverse group of constituents to engage in a "Conversation Series." This series was meant to be "inclusive"; decisions about the museum, she said, "could not be isolated from the other components of the memorial; the museum had to be a part of a unified conversation." There were dozens of conversations; they were "robust, at times contentious," according to the series' summary reports, but "always productive." Feelings were raw; five years later, people were still processing the event. The museum needed a long-term vision, and the Conversation Series allowed Greenwald and her staff to test their assumptions about the conceptualized narrative they were developing. At times, the complexity of the challenge created something of "an identity crisis"—"a tug of war between memorializing and documenting."[17]

Serendipity is the path by which the most prized artifact—the two immense rusted steel columns in the form of tridents salvaged from the original towers standing as sentinels in the entryway pavilion designed by Snøhetta—came to be preserved. In December 2001, as the last remaining standing portions of the twin towers were being dismantled and removed, Peter L. Rinaldi, a long-serving engineer at the Port Authority involved in the emergency response and recovery efforts at the site after 9/11, looked out at the site and saw the last remaining standing portions of the towers—the eight column sections standing about ninety feet tall that formed the northeast corner of the building at the lobby level of the North Tower. "I guess that's when I had that 'curatorial impulse' in that I thought this was the last opportunity to save a portion of the building to allow for the possibility of maybe a future reconstruction and display," he wrote in an e-mail to Dunlap. Following that impulse, he had the site contractors doing the demolition and removal mark and save all eight columns (which had to be cut into three pieces each due to the size and weight of each) and transport them all to the hangar at JFK, where the Port Authority was storing various artifacts from the site.[18] They stand as the iconic memory of the twin towers.

In a ceremony marked by quiet dignity and humanistic grace, the September 11 National Memorial Museum was officially dedicated on May 15, 2014, every piece of the program perfectly choreographed to touch in remembrance that combination of collective and individual loss evocative of the museum's mission. Stories of heroism and survival, music of strength and resolve, and words of gratitude and compassion filled the cavernous underground museum. Getting to this point had been trying. The museum had been fought over hard, its construction halted over cost overruns and a protracted financial dispute over who would pay for the cost overruns. And while it was still under construction, its completion had been set back by massive flooding—seven feet of water at bedrock—caused by Hurricane Sandy.[19]

In celebrating the opening, the *Daily News* editorial heralded the spirit of common humanity and tireless effort that "transformed Ground Zero into the exact opposite of what the World Trade Center destroyers intended," and made this place "a historical victory." It was a day for reflection, a day for unity, a day to put aside the difficult politics of the past—"the years of skirmishing among museum leaders, politicians and family members," as the *Times* editorial said. "And saved for later were the pleas from museum officials about the need for more federal money from the president and his colleagues in Washington to support this national memorial. Instead, it was a day remembering extraordinary people," extraordinary acts of sacrifice.[20] When the museum opened its doors to the public the next week, they came by the thousands, undeterred by the $24 entrance fee, long a frustrating issue that ceased to be an issue, at least for the time being.

Commentary and criticism mixed with circumspect praise and professional respect tinged with disappointment came quickly, as was to be expected with such a high-profile memorial undertaking of international significance. The power of the exhibits was evident, but did everything have to be preserved to bear witness to the truth? Or evil? Is the museum too much of a shrine, a 9/11 reliquary, the personal items of lost lives enshrined under Plexiglas too close to the feel of a religious pilgrimage and ritual? Troubled by the museum's grand public ambition of monumentality and its devotion to personal and immediate memory, critic at large Edward Rothstein wrote that "in keeping with its devotion to experience, it tries to become an experience itself." This was an inversion of a museum's usual role and the result was questionable. Though the 9/11 museum "may be breaking new ground both in its ambition's scale and the ways it falls short," he went on to say, "it left little room for more elaborate and public considerations; it doesn't even try to offer a rough first draft of history." He objected to the "almost fetishistic" preoccupation with the private, to the exclusion of the public, yet considered this flaw as part of a broader context common to contemporary memorials "having become democratic signposts demanding attention for the dead in a crowded political marketplace where there is no clear notion of a public realm."[21] With so little time for historical reflection having passed before the embarking on the memorial mission, the vaulted scale of the museum was open to criticism among those who were not yet ready to unquestionably agree that it matched the horrific scale of the event.

Architectural critics too were uneasy with the results. Pulitzer Prize–winning Inga Saffron thought reviewing the building as architecture did not even seem right since "we are still living in history, still trying to come to terms with emotions whose shelf life has yet to expire." As a memorial, history exhibit, and mausoleum for unidentified remains, the museum "actually does a heroic job of straddling the competing demands.... And yet, for all its lurid hold, the museum offers no reckoning, no lessons, no real insights into why those planes fell from that brilliant-blue autumn sky.... [I]t is content to re-create the day and replay it in an endless loop."[22] The *Washington Post*'s art and architectural critic Philip Kennicott considered the museum "structured like our memories of the day, a hellish descent into a dark place." The experience, he wrote, "overwhelms—or more literally undermines—the dignified power of Arad's memorial by inviting visitors to re-experience the events in a strangely, obsessively, narcissistically repetitious way."[23] Did everything have to be choreographed?

Revealing a common professional bias, Christopher Hawthorne of the *Los Angeles Times* considered the museum "an overstuffed answer to the appealing minimalism of the 9/11 memorial." The crushed fire trucks, mangled steel artifacts, personal items, and other pieces of "dark memorabilia" within the two tower footprints were "profoundly moving, to the point of emotional exhaustion." The "unrelenting literalism" of the chosen curatorial approach was "crushing." Writing for *Architect*, Karrie Jacobs found the level of exhibition detail "so conscientious that it's overwhelming," "simply too much," "numbing." She considered the bedrock space itself the architectural highlight and the Foundation Hall, "DBB's best architectural moment." It is a "compelling open space where Libeskind's 68-foot-tall slurry wall actually fulfils its symbolic destiny." But even here, in this dramatic space that "borders on sacred," the questions remain: Why did the curators have to add interactive information displays projected on adjacent walls? Would not this space have been even more profound an experience if visitors were given room to simply reflect?[24] After visiting the 9/11 Memorial and Museum, Adam Gopnik writing in the *New Yorker* did not give high marks to either expression of commemoration. He too questioned the intent of what had been so fastidiously accomplished, what lessons were held within. "Museums first preserve, and then teach, and, although a few grimly eloquent objects are preserved here—a half-crushed fire engine, a fragment of the pancaked floors from one tower—nothing is really taught." He was distraught over profuse documentary evidence presented by designers who "seem engaged in curatorial white-water rafting, struggling to keep the displays afloat while in constant peril from the enormous American readiness to be mortally offended by some small misstep of word or tone." Whether this was the result of a lack of priorities or a sincere intention to present something for everyone, he felt the designers to be "navigating the requirements of interested parties at every turn."[25]

Gopnik chose to evaluate the 9/11 memorial expressions through the lens of historical commemoration, explaining how the language of minimalism in America had become "the most potent language of the elegiac and the evocative, the one common basis with which to build a memorial." Yet it was "limited as a language of representation. It feels, but it cannot show." Hence, the personal ephemera on display. The displays could succeed in showing, but to what effect? There is something heavy, almost artificial, he was saying, in the scope and scale of such profuse and orchestrated displays of documentary evidence—in contrast to "the simplest memorials of the first days after the disaster, those Xeroxed hand-bills with 'Missing' emblazoned on them." The spontaneity of those handbills, he argued, provided a simple lesson: "that life is tragic and precious and fragile, that there is an irreducible core of violence in the world, and of fanatics in love with it, and that we failed once in our responsibility to protect ourselves from them, and from it." As to architectural memorials, he wondered whether any would be "half as moving, or as fitting" as those two violet columns of lights where the towers had once been. "Fragility and resilience, loss and persistence, spire and substance—all that was expressed by the two luminous pillars in a way that drains and benches and wall labels can't."[26]

The purpose of what was happening in that deep hole, that crypt turned memorial artifact, was still being debated by the critics. More subdued but nevertheless evident, a central disappointment with the 9/11 Memorial Museum reprises the controversy over culture at Ground Zero that led to the eviction of the International Freedom Center in 2005. The eviction ended that site-specific cultural controversy, but it did not resolve the larger societal debate about how to consider the impact of 9/11 at Ground Zero in a way capable of educating future generations not yet born for whom 9/11 would always be history. Is the name "Memorial Museum" a contradiction in terms, as *Times* reporter Patricia Cohen had probingly asked years earlier? "Museums are about understanding, about making meaning of the past," the overseer of the nation's legislative archives, presidential libraries, and museums, James Gardner, had told her. "A memorial fulfills a different need; it's about remembering and evoking feelings in the viewer, and that function is antithetical to what museums do."[27]

The lack of historical perspective and the prospect that the 9/11 Museum's time-bound in-memoriam concept might freeze its potential to function as a true museum became especially troubling to these U.S. critics. (Critics from across the pond were snarkier in their commentary.) Likening its prevailing narrative to "a story of angels and devils," the *Times*' Holland Cotter concluded, "is not so much wrong as drastically incomplete. It is useful history, not deep history; news, not analysis." He saw this approach as "probably inevitable in a museum that is, to an unusual degree, still living the history it is documenting." Still, he was holding out hope that the museum, regarding "itself as a work in progress, involved in investigation, not summation," would "tackle the reality that its story is as much about global politics as about architecture, about a bellicose epoch as much as about a violent event." If in time it did, he concluded, "it could deepen all our thinking about politics, morality and devotion."[28]

The true test of the 9/11 Memorial Museum will come over time, by how it delivers educational meaning, by how it holds the attention of future generations, and by how it tells the bigger story of 9/11. This is what we all have to hope for because a deep understanding of the event is too fundamental to America's historical trajectory to limit its consideration to individual loss and architectural memory. Because it is still too early to tell this bigger story, because the process of understanding it has barely begun, the most appropriate way to interpret the meaning of the 9/11 Memorial Museum is to view it as the first stage of a series that will unfold over time as the country comes to grips with the historical impact of the terrorist attacks on America and its way of life.

ENTROPY CONTINUES

It has been hard to make culture happen at Ground Zero. In 2004, after a high-profile process, four cultural entities were chosen with the expectation that their residence, in two specially designed structures at Ground Zero, would make the place a new and vital cultural destination. A year later, the number dropped to two, and eighteen months after that, to one. Then, after six more years of plans, designs, cost estimates, and political tussles, the cultural program changed once again—for the fourth, and then again, for a fifth, though not necessarily the last, time. In the place of the remaining cultural anchor that was to make the proposed center a home for dance, the Performing Arts Center (PAC) would "instead be a multidisciplinary space that includes theater, music and film, as well as dance," its president, British-born Maggie Boepple, told the *Times*' veteran arts reporter Robin Pogrebin.[29] What should the arts at Ground Zero stand for? For lower Manhattan? For 9/11? For New York City? What could be there that would make the PAC unique? These are questions still in the process of being answered. Boepple is experienced in the arts and believes that distinctive cultural offerings of a type to draw a big everybody public to Ground Zero will happen.

Over the course of years, the quest for culture at Ground Zero had followed steps of an erratic dance: one step forward, one or two steps back, another step forward and another step back. Each step forward was important, each step back, disillusioning. Money for the PAC was authorized by the LMDC ($55 million), but the estimated cost for the one building grew exorbitant ($668 million). Ambitions had to be cut back. Then political power struggles threw into question even the location for the proposed PAC, designated in the Libeskind master plan as site 1B, just sixty feet east of 1 World Trade Center. After much sustained effort, the Bloomberg administration secured an institutional victory that finally propelled the LMDC in February 2010 to authorize release of up to $50 million for the Port Authority to construct the underground elements and common infrastructure for the complicated PAC site. This early-action commitment seemed to rule out the public efforts by the LMDC president and its chairman to move the PAC to the site of the former Deutsche Bank Building (site 5), but nothing about culture at Ground Zero was ever assured. The estimate for the structure designed by Frank Gehry was still very high ($540 million).[30]

On the other side of the economic ledger, the proposed PAC agenda gained significant momentum when the LMDC supported the allocation of an additional $100 million in federal funds later that year. And with the Bloomberg administration's creation of a six-person board (at the last possible moment in December 2011), the proposed PAC remained eligible for the LMDC's $155 million funding. The cultural agenda continued to move forward with the hiring of a director and a small staff. The size of the proposed cultural center, however, had to be dialed back once more because the cost estimate for the Gehry building was still too high ($469 million), and fundraising as uncertain as the program for which the building was being designed. After a year of deep thinking, the PAC board came to the conclusion that it needed to scuttle the Gehry design and start over with another architect; parting with Gehry caused some agita. Year after year, uncertainty was the storyline of culture at Ground Zero: Culture was "in limbo," "wilting," "stuck."[31] More than a decade after planners heralded an agenda for culture at Ground Zero, the proposed PAC still faced an uphill battle.

Without institutional leadership or fundraising, culture at Ground Zero was adrift. The Memorial Foundation had split its fundraising into two phases, or in the view of some, abandoned the cultural part of its mandate. "Whether the foundation is willing to take up the performing arts center next remains an open question," remarked Pogrebin. A political void existed. "The Pataki administration didn't stand up to the role at all," said Tom Healy, president of the Lower Manhattan Cultural Council. "He abdicated it, and the city stepped in."[32] Through the summer of 2006, the city worked on a detailed review of the engineering cost and programmatic issues of the proposed PAC's viability. Would the PAC work? A detailed nine-page confidential memo presenting an "honest assessment" was on Doctoroff's desk by the end of August and finalized just before Thanksgiving.

From an engineering point of view, building what had been proposed "appears to be technically feasible," the memo said, but the assessment brought into focus "a more complex series of questions raised by the other aspects of the project's feasibility." The design for the proposed building conflicted with the need for a temporary entry to PATH during construction of the permanent PATH Terminal, which would significantly impact when construction could start and add nearly a hundred million dollars to the cost of the facility. The building would be built over the PATH train tracks and "a series of intertwined service functions located directly below," which would make building on this site more expensive than it would be elsewhere. The adjacent Freedom Tower added another complication. Security concerns had significantly reduced the amount of program space, "which is already very tight." Because of the limited footprint of the site, the multiple theaters planned for the building would have to be stacked; when combined with political demands for a world-class building, the ambitions of the proposed project led to a prohibitively expensive building. The projected cost reached an extraordinary $668 million, or more than $2,650 a square foot, and "far beyond any comparable projects throughout the United States or in New York, even in the current expensive and inflationary construction climate." The conclusion was clear: "It just wasn't going to happen," said Doctoroff, at least not as initially envisioned. The only viable option was to scale back ambitions in a significant way by eliminating the Signature Theater[33] and focusing on the creation of a single large performance hall for the Joyce Theater (with possible ancillary spaces for rehearsal, administrative, and similar functions). City Hall had no trust in the LMDC, I was told by one insider, and thought the proposed PAC design was a "crazy" building.

The many changes in the program triggered by removal of the Signature Theater involved another eighteen months of new planning and construction documents to engineer the new design. The changes had "big spillover effects," said Andrew Winters, who sat in the mayor's office as director of capital projects and, as a former LMDC vice president for planning, design, and development, was very familiar with the site. "The new design had to be best-in-class, no compromises. When the Joyce and Signature were to occupy the same structure, it was too compromised. Gehry changed the look of the building with the new design."[34] This was before the decision to break with him.

The PAC was always next year's issue. It would take years to complete the permanent PATH Hub, and above-ground construction could not begin until the PAC site became available, 2011 at the earliest—at first. As the Port Authority shifted the Hub completion date forward to sometime in 2013, then 2015, and then again 2016, the pressure for progress on the PAC appeared far from immediate. Even if the active pursuit by senior LMDC officials to shift the proposed PAC to the site of Tower 5 succeeded in gaining traction, the Vehicle Security Center had to be completed first and that too would take several years. The LMDC completed a feasibility study of the site 5 alternative that purported to support the case for the Liberty Street site, though it was not released publicly.

The site 5 proposal put forth by LMDC president David Emil and its chairman Avi Schick, both appointed by Governor Spitzer, signaled another round of the power struggle between the state and the city for decision-making control at Ground Zero. It was linked to a four-way MOU signed years earlier in February 2006 involving a swap of sites between the LMDC and the PA, which was intended to happen when the former Deutsche Bank Building deconstruction was complete. The logic of the swap was about the value of future development: With the PAC on site 1B the parcel had been made economically worthless to the PA because without commercial uses on the site, there would be no future financial gain. The swap in combination with the LMDC footing the bill for the acquisition and deconstruction of site 5 would compensate for that value dilution. Although the city took over responsibility for the creation of the PAC at the start of 2007, the state's senior appointees to the LMDC were not content to delegate this issue to the city. They did not want the LMDC to give up the site, which is a major development site with approximately 1.3 million square feet of development rights—a highly valuable asset in the real-estate-centric world of Manhattan. The Port Authority was not about to change its mind on the swap. At the beginning of 2016, the issue still remained in limbo, but, I was told, the squabbling in public had been quashed by officials in Albany.

Once again, the political tussle raised the familiar question about Ground Zero: Who was in charge? "Without the city's involvement, the PAC would be dead. It's been hard to stay at the table, though," Winters said in July 2011. "There's been a lot going on at the PA. The proposed PAC had to have an advocate, and the city did a lot of things to keep it alive. We let the PA know the mayor cares about the cultural agenda. The mayor kept it alive."[35] What happens to the PAC under the administration of Mayor de Blasio is evolving. The new deputy mayor for housing and economic development, Alicia Glen, is on the board and solidly behind the effort. The issue is: How can it be built in a more economical way? With a new programmatic agenda and hundreds of millions to raise, the PAC WTC, as it has been renamed, faces a fresh set of hurdles in an increasingly crowded landscape of cultural venues in Manhattan, including two new major venues: the $400 million Culture Shed underway at Hudson Yards and the $130 million park on Pier 55 near Fourteenth Street being underwritten by businessman Barry Diller. All are competing for donor dollars, and at this time the PAC shows no evidence of fundraising success.

The PAC at the Trade Center will have to differentiate itself from the city's many other cultural offerings, and this may turn out to be the silver lining of past entropy because the competition may lead to a distinctive set of cultural offerings. The something different could involve a building open from morning to evening, a building for more than live performances. The something different could be technology driven. The building could be designed with one main entrance, an "everyone opening," Boepple told me. It could include a "producing house," a place where cultural productions in conjunction with local and global partners are brought in, something that is missing in New York.[36]

In July 2015, an LMDC review of finances led to the conclusion that the PAC had to be scaled down yet again (to about eighty thousand square feet) and brought within a $200 million budget—about half of the cost of the scaled-back design for the Gehry building. This was a "serious blow," wrote Pogrebin. On the other hand, the smaller budget would reduce the amount of private funds the PAC board needs to raise for the project and increase the likelihood of success. Boepple is convinced that this can be done, that it has to be done. "It may be smaller," she said; "there may be things that you might have liked to see, but that's how it is."[37] The forthcoming new design will still allow for multiple theaters that can be flexibly configured. Several months later, in October, Boepple announced the new architects for the project: REX, a Brooklyn-based firm led by Joshua Prince-Ramus, a former protégé of Dutch architect Rem Koolhaas, with the firm Davis Brody Bond as executive architect.

The indeterminate state of culture at Ground Zero is a microcosm of the issues that have bedeviled every project at Ground Zero, the proposed cultural agenda more so. The political hurdles have been grueling, even for those who have worked around government for years. The original proposal to bring the arts to Ground Zero was to make sure that the development site wouldn't be monopolized by grief or commerce, because culture brings meaning to life. The notion of a "living memorial" was a promise to the downtown community. It still is. Culture is likely to happen around the Trade Center site because the demographic changes reshaping lower Manhattan will support new offerings, but when and how the PAC happens will depend on whether the entropy—"the momentum of attrition"—can be transformed into momentum of action. Let's hope so.

TOWER OF AMBITION

Over the passage of twelve turbulent years of rebuilding, the symbol of New York ascendant, the symbol of national defiance, the symbol of global position, and the symbol of political ambition materialized into a big version of the New York developer's commercial office tower. Singular in concept, 1 World Trade Center is something much less inspiring than the early conceptual designs presented to the public. The readily identifiable tower with a globally recognized address reaches the symbolic height of 1,776 feet and carries emotional meaning as a memorial marker in the sky of 9/11. It looks best with a long perspective.

Viewed not from afar or from the air but at the immediate street level only one particular difference sets it apart from other supertall skyscrapers: its security-conscious fortification designed into a 186.5-foot-high, reinforced concrete, blast-resistant base with concrete walls twenty-eight-inches thick—the "concrete bunker" to many critics of the reimagined design—camouflage-clad with a scrim of 4,232 glass fins and 8-inch-wide stainless-steel slats (figure 20.5). The $35 million fins are illuminated from behind so that the façade will glitter twenty-four hours a day. Critic Justin Davidson called them "the architectural equivalent of Swarovski crystals." They lightened the tower's defensive base presence, wrote Blair Kamin, Pulitzer Prize–winning architectural critic for the *Chicago Tribune*, but "only mitigate its massiveness." This crystalline facade represents the second design go-around to embellish the base, the first having been abandoned after a $10 million effort because of technical difficulties in fabricating the clear prismatic glass panels and welded aluminum screens David Childs initially specified to create, in his words, "a dynamic shimmering glass surface."[38]

Finding a solution to disguise the robustness of a concrete base so massive that the office space does not begin until what is the twentieth floor proved to be a struggle between safety and elegance. "The problem with the glass," wrote Charles

FIGURE 20.5 *The glass fins of 1 World Trade Center hiding the massive security-required foundation walls.* Gary Hack

V. Bagli of the *Times*, "illustrates the tension inherent in the entire [then] $3.2 billion project: how to create a skyscraper that is at once iconic and defended against terrorism, while also containing costs." Will the tower withstand an attack? "Who knows what terrorists will do?" remarked Childs. "Do you design for a small bomb, dirty bomb, small aircraft? Yes, if a plane flew into the new building the building would respond differently [than] the twin towers.... But the place to solve these problems is at airports, not in buildings, or all we'd have would be concrete towers."[39]

Downtown had regained its "polestar." The tapering tower, Childs told Dunlap, played "a necessary civic role of being the 'answering spire' to the skyscrapers of Midtown." That was all Childs or anyone else was saying publicly about the building. The firm had had "too many run-ins" with the Port Authority and was "banned from doing interviews," according to a news article.[40] The architectural critics remained unimpressed. "It's going to be a good building, but no more than that," said Paul Goldberger. "We lost the opportunity to build a great building by being overly conservative in the design, overly concerned with security." It was a missed opportunity "to reassert American leadership."[41]

The tower "tries to maintain an equilibrium between ferocity and elegance, brawn and poise," Davidson wrote late in 2012 after he toured 1 World Trade. It was "a strange griffin of a building," he concluded, "with its armored base, its lean glass torso, and its elaborate ceremonial headgear [the spire]. The divisions reflect a culture struggling to integrate transparency and security." Kamin called the tower "a bold but flawed giant," "a new version of the trade center's old gigantism—a tower that stands free in space instead of shaping it as does the gracefully tiered, street-hugging base of the Empire State Building." Given the "myriad forces that buffeted this building," he said, it was "an achievement of a sort and, on balance, a step forward." But the tower did not have "the artistry it could have had. It's solid, occasionally scintillating, yet it's no masterpiece." "It is far too dull for the most important new building in America," said John Arlidge, writing in the *Sunday Times* of London. Like the Shard Tower in London, to which it was compared, 1 World Trade was so much higher than anything else around it that "it reconfigures the cityscape, creating a new trig point." That is its pole-star quality. Being gigantic is about all that the critic thought is good about the new landmark. "The tower may be big but it boasts none of the proud, two-fingered, dollar-sign of self-confidence of the twin towers," Arlidge wrote. "Those two rectangles may have looked rather plain but they captured something of the American psyche—optimistic, stupendous and, frankly, little concerned with what others think. What's there now looks like a clumsy, bloated American in a shiny suit." His closing comment: "Britain beats New York at blocks! Ha! It feels good. But only a bit. This time, for once, it would have been nice if it had been a draw."[42]

The critics wrote less of distaste for the tower than of deep disappointment. Over the passage of time, this political project—this tower of ambition—arrived at Ground Zero as an enormous commercial real estate venture, as had its twin-tower predecessor. In ways both big and small, adjustments to its design, its name, and its ownership reflect the inevitable accommodations to the realities of the commercial office marketplace—after all, at nearly $4 billion (not including land value), 1 World Trade stands as the world's most expensive skyscraper, more expensive by far than even the world's tallest tower, the 2,717-foot Burj Khalifa in Dubai constructed (2004–2010) at a cost of $1.5 billion. The cost of each square foot of 1 World Trade's 3.5 million square feet (comprising office space, observatory deck, parking, and broadcast and antenna facilities) was nearly two and a half times what it cost to build the Burj's 3.3 million square feet of space ($1,128 versus $455 a square foot). Critics like *Times* op-ed columnist Joe Nocera were outraged at the costs of 1 World Trade, saying it "will be a cash drain for decades to come," another white elephant for the Port Authority, which under the "complicity" of the two governors approved "onerous" toll increases. "Where's the Tea Party when you need them?" he asked.[43]

Similarly, it is more expensive than the more comparable tower built by the Durst Organization, 1 Bryant Park. Completed in 2010, the fifty-one-story sustainable tower, certified LEED Platinum, built to serve as headquarters for Bank of America's global corporate and investment banking businesses, as well as its own corporate headquarters, was developed at an approximate cost of $1.3 billion, or $568 a square foot, according to the project's 2004 Liberty Bond offering. Given 1 World Trade's market status, tenants (who would have other options in Manhattan) have always been the essential factor for filling its 2.6 million square feet of office space. (By the time the building was being widely marketed to tenants, the rentable area had been "remeasured" in line with the standards of the Real Estate Board of New York at 3.0 million rentable square feet.)[44] As important as the continuous lofty rhetoric was for civic renewal, a steady stream of cash flowing from the rental of the vast amount of office space was critical for the bi-state transportation agency and the investors holding its consolidated bonds. With a $4 billion cost basis, however, it is likely to take longer for 1 World Trade to make a return than was the case with the original World Trade Center complex.

The shift to a new market-based narrative began in early 2007, with the change-over in the New York governor's office and not long after the Port Authority gained full responsibility for the tower in 2006. By 2009, the Port Authority had swapped out the patriotic Freedom Tower moniker for a more straightforward, marketable name: 1 World Trade Center. Unnoticed except by Dunlap's City Room blog post, the changeover first appeared in a regular news release of actions taken by the Port Authority Board of Commissioners at its July 26, 2007, meeting, in which the tower was referenced as "1 World Trade Center, the Freedom Tower." Twenty months later, on the day the Port Authority signed a commercial lease with its first private-sector tenant, the Beijing-based real estate firm Vantone Industrial Co., for five floors of "One World Trade Center (the Freedom Tower)" after three years of stop-and-start negotiations, agency officials acknowledged that the informal moniker had been dropped. It had never been the official name, a spokesman said; the brand change would make the building more marketable. "One World Trade Center is its address. It's the address we're using. It's the one that's easiest for people to identify with and frankly we've gotten a very interested and warm reception to it," remarked Port Authority chairman Coscia. "It had to be 'depoliticized,'" said the agency's real estate broker, Tara Stacom, vice chairwoman of Cushman & Wakefield. "This building needed to be about commerce, it needed to be about exciting the interest of corporations."[45] As was to be expected, former governor Pataki took strong exception to the name change.

The editorial boards of both the *Daily News* and the *Post* immediately seized on the name change. Employing sharp words, the *News* attacked the "imperious, unaccountable" Port Authority for "taking license with freedom," breaking "promises on everything else to do with redeveloping Ground Zero," engaging "in massive schemes to lie about costs," and failing "to meet every solemnly pledged construction deadline," all of which made "tossing a name like Freedom Tower...child's play." To strip the iconic name from the tower, the *Post* said in "Nothing Left to Lose," "is to degrade the true intent of the project—to mark enduring resistance to terrorism." On the opposite end of the opinion spectrum, the *Times* editorial board said the agency had "Freedom to Name That Tower." The iconic name had become "its burden" and the agency is "sensibly" promoting the place by its legal address. The change was pragmatic: "any prospective tenants worried about another terrorist attack," it explained, citing Dunlap's news report of the same day, "'might well balk at a name with such potent ideological symbolism.'" As has been the case with name changes to other landmark towers, Chicago's Willis Tower (née Sears Tower) and Manhattan's Met Life Building (née Pam Am Building), "Ultimately, people will call the building whatever they like." "That there is a debate at all suggests how much has changed since the first years after 9/11," Dunlap emphasized, "when no official pronouncement was complete without an assurance that the attacks, the victims, the rescuers and the survivors would never be forgotten; and when any use of patriotic motifs seemed to be beyond public reproach, no matter how cynical or sentimental."[46]

Private Capital Alters the Equation

Landmark or icon, political project or commercial investment, 1 World Trade signifies different things to different people, perspective once again depending on position more than passion. "Tourists and city dwellers will first assess the overall design (do I like the way it looks?) and its urbanism (does it work in the neighborhood?)," wrote critic Sarah Williams Goldhagen. "Users will value the location, access to public transportation, and the quality and flexibility of its spaces. Design and engineering professionals will note advances in technology and materials. Developers will see the bottom line."[47]

"It's an office building and not a memorial and not a monument," said the Port Authority's new equity partner in the tower's development and operation, developer Douglas Durst, chairman of the Durst Organization, which bought into the project in August 2010, three years after the name change. The third-generation scion of one of the city's fabled real estate families, Durst won the bid for an expected 10 percent ownership interest in the landmark tower, beating out six other major well-capitalized competitors to invest $100 million, the minimum the Port Authority had required of any partner and a tiny slice of the big tower's development cost. His family-based firm had what the Port Authority needed if the landmark tower was to produce results as an economic venture: "a strong track record of large-scale office development in New York City" and a sophisticated organization with "the ability to deliver a full suite of real estate services."[48]

For sure, the bi-state authority needed a private-capital player to help generate a cash-flow return from the building. More critically, it needed a New York real estate player with a premier reputation, a player who could counter the problem of negative image—who wants to do a lease with the Port Authority?—that had crippled its leasing effort for the original World Trade Center complex for so many years. Government commitments from the 2006 deal would fill only so much of the space in the gigantic tower; the Port Authority still needed tenants for approximately 1.5 million gross square feet of uncommitted space. To pursue its ambition of running the tower as a commercial real estate project, the agency needed a business-minded operator. Indeed, when the PA took back the tower project from Silverstein, Durst and others suggested to the PA that it bring in someone familiar with office building development to finish the building and lease it up.

The Durst family stake in 1 World Trade held the promise of being the harbinger of a turnaround in marketability for the symbolic but often-scorned tower. All along agency officials had reasoned that a private-sector player who had equity at risk as an investor in the building would have a greater incentive to manage the asset to its highest possible performance than someone operating the building only for a fee. This public-private development situation was unlike any other: The building was valued at $2 billion at the time of the equity sale but its then estimated cost at $3.2 billion was growing and would reach $3.949 billion (not including land value). And this "in a marketplace where rents can barely support $500 a foot," remarked PA chairman Coscia. "It's half memorial, half office building, and tenants don't pay you for their building to be a memorial."[49]

The Port Authority first tried to sell a piece of equity in the 1,776-foot tower early in 2007, informally approaching Brookfield Properties and the Related Companies in exploratory talks. At the time, the agency was also talking to J. P. Morgan Chase about selling the development rights on site 5. It was an ideal time for the Port Authority to test the appetite of investor interest, even though the 104-story tower, with construction beams just being welded to the building's base, was years away from completion. In 2007, the Manhattan office market was red hot, flooded with capital from a broad range of investors—private equity firms, pension interests, and sovereign wealth funds—all looking to acquire Manhattan office property, especially trophy buildings. It is "welcome news," editorialized the *Wall Street Journal*. "The twin towers were underoccupied and underutilized for at least two decades after their construction. Letting private capital take on the risks of turning a profit" on the tower "would ensure that history does not repeat itself at taxpayer expense."[50] But the PA's early efforts at bringing in private capital failed to gain traction, and when the financial crisis hit the next year, the opportunity disappeared. Had the Port Authority been able to bring a major private developer or premier corporation into the project, it would unquestionably have altered the subsequent dynamic of negotiations with Larry Silverstein and his campaign for public financial support to fulfill his obligations to construct three office towers at Ground Zero.

In late 2009, the Port Authority resumed its sale initiative, this time pursuing a more formal process.[51] The *Journal*'s assumption that bringing in private capital would mean sharing the risks of ownership, however, was not part of the bid package. Although the competition to buy into the project was real, the Manhattan office market was nothing like what it had been in 2007. Over the intervening period, as a consequence of the global financial crisis, distress had reconfigured the economic landscape, dramatically. Finding tenants for class A space being built for financial service firms was going to be far more challenging since far fewer of them populated the new economic landscape; the disappearance (and forced merger) of several brand-name investment banks (Bear Stearns, Lehman Brothers, Merrill Lynch) had reduced the ranks of potential large-space users.

The Manhattan office market was hit especially hard. Commercial property values plummeted. Rents dropped dramatically, in midtown Manhattan and in downtown. "Glutted" was the best descriptor of office space availability in the Manhattan market at the time. With a recovery so uncertain, buying into 1 World Trade necessitated a long-term perspective. "You have to take a patient approach to your capital on this," said Tommy Craig, a senior executive at Hines, one of the bidders. "It's possible to structure the investment so that the risk that's inherent is potentially offset by the return possibilities." Still, the buy-in bet on 1 World Trade pivoted on bringing in private market-rate tenants. "The developers wouldn't be interested in the building if they thought it was going to be all government," said Cushman & Wakefield's Stacom. "They, too, are convinced that this building will lease to private companies, professional and financial services."[52]

Coming off the development of 1 Bryant Park, as much a comparable real estate development to 1 World Trade as possible, the family-directed firm had the professional team, the operational scale, and the experience the Port Authority wanted in a business partner, as well as a long-term perspective. The Dursts had been buying, managing, and later developing property since 1915 when the family patriarch, Joseph Durst, purchased his first building in Manhattan, a short twelve years after arriving in the United States from Gorlice, Austria (present-day Poland), with three dollars to his name. Its property bona fides included control of ten million square feet of commercial space across ten midtown Manhattan office towers and a proud reputation for paying close attention to its tenants' needs and for cultivating loyalty through well-established relationships. It had won out over Stephen Ross's Related Companies, developer of the Time Warner Center at Columbus Circle in Manhattan, which acutely wanted to win this trophy bid.

The compelling factor that most likely clinched the selection was the more advantageous deal structure Durst offered the Port Authority. The $100 million Durst was investing in the joint venture would be valued at the time of stabilization, 2018; that was atypical. The typical way to value the investment in the joint venture would have been to do a valuation at the time Durst was buying in, but at stabilization, he said, "you are dealing with actual numbers rather than a projection, so it is a stronger basis and fact for a valuation." The firm had the statistics to show that this had been the case with 4 Times Square and 1 Bryant Park. In addition, unlike other bidders who were said to offer a conventional flat management fee for real estate services, Durst's final bid proposed something the agency could hardly refuse as it confronted the tower's ever-escalating cost: an incentive-based management fee linked to construction cost savings for the Port Authority. The agency did not relinquish its control over construction and financing—staff held a propriety view of rebuilding—and Durst was not taking on any of those risks. The private developer was taking over the leasing, marketing, management, and day-to-day operations of 1 World Trade. The big risk, Douglas Durst told me, was "reputational risk," which for the Durst Organization is huge. "Money was not the big risk, not in the way the investment was set up," said his longtime attorney, Gary Rosenberg, cofounding partner of Rosenberg & Estis. "The reputation risk was in completion, if the building did not get completed in a rational fashion, like in seven years. They did not have control over that timing."[53]

The deal came before the Port Authority Board of Commissioners twice, and between its initial approval on August 5, 2010, and amendment on May 25, 2011, the joint venture with the Durst Organization underwent material revisions as the partners negotiated the transaction documents. In its final form, the deal provided Durst with an initial 6.5 percent preferred return on its investment and a base construction-related services fee of $15 million. These were the starting points. Because the PA sought to reduce the overall construction cost of the tower, if the actions Durst took in managing the final buildout achieved cost savings, his firm stood to benefit from incentive payments. In addition, the firm's return on its investment was protected against construction delays, and any further increases in construction cost would not trigger additional investment capital from the private partner. Once the building was completed, Durst could capture additional returns for exceeding an agreed-upon baseline projection of operating income. Staffing costs and expenses would be reimbursed, and as the in-house broker, Durst would earn market-rate leasing fees (shared with the Port Authority's broker, Cushman & Wakefield).

A particularly attractive feature of the deal gave Durst a competitive advantage over other landlords in the market in renting out space in the big tower: The Port Authority would be absorbing the leasing expenses of attracting tenants for the first 92.5 percent of rentable office space in the building, regardless of cost. These expenses might include buying out a tenant's existing lease in another building to allow a move to the new tower, paying a tenant's moving costs, and providing generous allowances for fitting out tenant space, among other concessions.[54] This arrangement gave Durst an edge over Silverstein in the quest for private tenants. Silverstein had been bought out of the tower's development as part of the 2006 realignment deal, and as part of that deal, the Port Authority and City of New York had signed leases for space in his first tower. But in 2010, he had still not landed a private-sector tenant for Tower 4, and had no comparable subsidy for lease-up costs, which typically runs into tens of millions for class A office towers.

Both New York family-based owner-developers were courting the same type of tenants (law firms, media firms, and general business-service firms), although the physical characteristics of their buildings differed, and the buildings' different floor configurations might better serve a certain type of tenant than the other. Durst was confident, however, of the desirability of the space in 1 World Trade, which would be "well above the height" of any of Silverstein's towers.[55] So were they competitors, these two publicly subsidized towers with private owner-operators? "Yes and no," one New York–appointed PA commissioner told me when I asked. "Yes, because they are both going for law firms and general business tenants. No, because 1 World Trade can't compete on trading operations; the Silverstein buildings have bigger floor plates in the base of those towers. Each wants and needs the other to succeed," he added. This was in 2012. As time would reveal, the new Trade Center towers were slowly filling up, not with the financial companies that factored into the plans for these glass-and-steel skyscrapers, but with technology, media, and advertising companies, and that change in tenant mix would make for greater competition between the two developers.

From a public-private development perspective, 1 World Trade is a very complicated joint venture. On the one hand, the Port Authority could not let a $100 million minority partner control the then $3.2 billion project. On the other, the Port Authority saw the need to give Durst protections against ever-increasing construction costs and building delays that would impact tenant occupancy, among other items that would expose the private developer to risks not under its control. The business deal also had to pass the all-important political smell test, of course, as the Port Authority did not want to be pilloried in the press for giving away the store. Still, in final form, it was a highly favorable deal for Durst.[56]

Durst's selection resonated with irony, nearly mimicking the scenario of what had transpired in the 1990s during the stalled redevelopment of Times Square when he bought the rights to develop the largest and most desirable office site of the Forty-second Street Development Project (now known as 4 Times Square) from the joint venture between Prudential Insurance Company and George Klein's Park Tower Realty. In both instances, his buy into a publicly sponsored project came after staunch, well-publicized opposition to its development. Similarly, in both instances, his buy-in became a bellwether of the project's reputational transformation, which he smartly leveraged to financial advantage. At Ground Zero toward the end of 2005, when one crisis after another continued to bedevil progress, Durst told Bagli of the *Times*, "If they abandoned the Freedom Tower, the market downtown would do just fine."[57] Meaning—let the market operate on its own and supply new space when there is demand for new space.

Fifteen months later in a reprise of public opposition their family patriarchs had taken to the original World Trade Center project forty-three years earlier, Durst and his cochair of the Continuing Committee for a Reasonable World Trade Center, Anthony E. Malkin, owner of the Empire State Building, took out full-page ads in the city's major papers calling upon Governor Eliot Spitzer to "reevaluate" the tower's design and schedule. "The economic recovery of Downtown is evident everywhere," they argued. "Why now is the government planning to pay for the construction of an overly expensive design to be occupied by government agencies at overly expensive rents, all at the expense of taxpayer's money which could be put to better uses?" In this open letter, they were asking the new administration to reverse "the legacy of poor planning and decision-making by the Pataki administration." They thought the Freedom Tower should be the last built, not the first, so that it might capitalize on the success of the others, and that its "frenetic redesign" after the NYPD's security review was too rushed, and would be "extraordinarily expensive to build and cumbersome for tenants"[58] (figure 20.6).

Three years later, Douglas Durst was bidding for the largest building in the redevelopment of the World Trade Center site he had so publicly criticized. Over the intervening years as 1 World Trade rose higher and higher in the sky, as its cost overruns became a matter of sunk costs, and as the rancor of past disputes was rendered meaningless to its completion trajectory, the landmark tower had become an "object of desire," "a much-sought-after trophy for a who's who of New York real estate figures." He wanted into the project and had approached the Port Authority even before the RFP had been issued, just as Ward was coming on board at the PA in mid-2008. "Timing is everything in real estate, and we think now is the time for 1 World Trade Center. It is going to be the only new building downtown and possibly the only new building in the city at the time," Durst told a reporter during the bidding season. "The building is going ahead no matter what anyone says. Similarly, with the Times Square redevelopment, we bitterly opposed that, but once the decision was made to go forward, we were a part of it. That is," said the generally taciturn developer whose actions often reveal the skillful tactics of a wise contrarian, "in the past, we've been against something before we were for it." At Ground Zero, another ripe opportunity was waiting, and for Durst, the pattern of the deal unfolding with its limited risks struck an uncanny resemblance to how the scenario played out in Times Square. "If there's going to be subsidies handed out they should come our way," he told a reporter from *Forbes* years later.[59]

As has been the case earlier, Durst would bring something to the deal that was more important than the $100 million of cash equity. He had a long and strong relationship with a big-name tenant that he knew from experience would be the key to transforming the marketability of this ambitious but heavily burdened project, a tenant that would seed its future success as a commercial venture: Condé Nast. By bringing this particular tenant, the swank and trendy media company renowned for its influence in style and famous for its perks, to the Trade Center site, Durst reprised the game-changing move he had scored in Times Square—a business transaction whose significance cannot be overstated. The publishing giant's commitment to move to the Trade Center site from Times Square to occupy

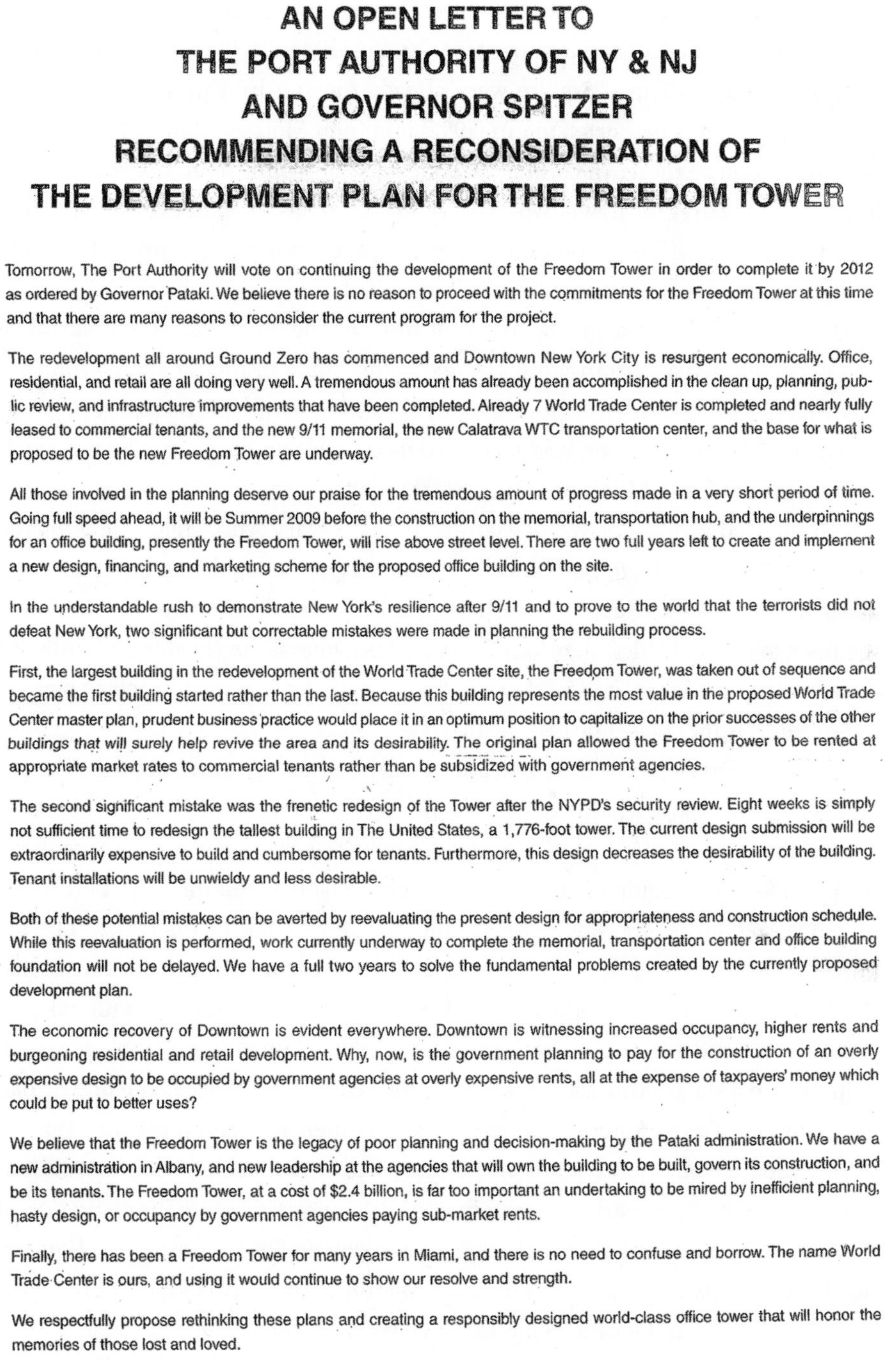

AN OPEN LETTER TO
THE PORT AUTHORITY OF NY & NJ
AND GOVERNOR SPITZER
RECOMMENDING A RECONSIDERATION OF
THE DEVELOPMENT PLAN FOR THE FREEDOM TOWER

Tomorrow, The Port Authority will vote on continuing the development of the Freedom Tower in order to complete it by 2012 as ordered by Governor Pataki. We believe there is no reason to proceed with the commitments for the Freedom Tower at this time and that there are many reasons to reconsider the current program for the project.

The redevelopment all around Ground Zero has commenced and Downtown New York City is resurgent economically. Office, residential, and retail are all doing very well. A tremendous amount has already been accomplished in the clean up, planning, public review, and infrastructure improvements that have been completed. Already 7 World Trade Center is completed and nearly fully leased to commercial tenants, and the new 9/11 memorial, the new Calatrava WTC transportation center, and the base for what is proposed to be the new Freedom Tower are underway.

All those involved in the planning deserve our praise for the tremendous amount of progress made in a very short period of time. Going full speed ahead, it will be Summer 2009 before the construction on the memorial, transportation hub, and the underpinnings for an office building, presently the Freedom Tower, will rise above street level. There are two full years left to create and implement a new design, financing, and marketing scheme for the proposed office building on the site.

In the understandable rush to demonstrate New York's resilience after 9/11 and to prove to the world that the terrorists did not defeat New York, two significant but correctable mistakes were made in planning the rebuilding process.

First, the largest building in the redevelopment of the World Trade Center site, the Freedom Tower, was taken out of sequence and became the first building started rather than the last. Because this building represents the most value in the proposed World Trade Center master plan, prudent business practice would place it in an optimum position to capitalize on the prior successes of the other buildings that will surely help revive the area and its desirability. The original plan allowed the Freedom Tower to be rented at appropriate market rates to commercial tenants rather than be subsidized with government agencies.

The second significant mistake was the frenetic redesign of the Tower after the NYPD's security review. Eight weeks is simply not sufficient time to redesign the tallest building in The United States, a 1,776-foot tower. The current design submission will be extraordinarily expensive to build and cumbersome for tenants. Furthermore, this design decreases the desirability of the building. Tenant installations will be unwieldy and less desirable.

Both of these potential mistakes can be averted by reevaluating the present design for appropriateness and construction schedule. While this reevaluation is performed, work currently underway to complete the memorial, transportation center and office building foundation will not be delayed. We have a full two years to solve the fundamental problems created by the currently proposed development plan.

The economic recovery of Downtown is evident everywhere. Downtown is witnessing increased occupancy, higher rents and burgeoning residential and retail development. Why, now, is the government planning to pay for the construction of an overly expensive design to be occupied by government agencies at overly expensive rents, all at the expense of taxpayers' money which could be put to better uses?

We believe that the Freedom Tower is the legacy of poor planning and decision-making by the Pataki administration. We have a new administration in Albany, and new leadership at the agencies that will own the building to be built, govern its construction, and be its tenants. The Freedom Tower, at a cost of $2.4 billion, is far too important an undertaking to be mired by inefficient planning, hasty design, or occupancy by government agencies paying sub-market rents.

Finally, there has been a Freedom Tower for many years in Miami, and there is no need to confuse and borrow. The name World Trade Center is ours, and using it would continue to show our resolve and strength.

We respectfully propose rethinking these plans and creating a responsibly designed world-class office tower that will honor the memories of those lost and loved.

FIGURE 20.6 *Full-page ad placed in New York newspapers by the Continuing Committee for a Reasonable World Trade Center, cochaired by Douglas Durst and Anthony E. Malkin, February 21, 2007.* THE CONTINUING COMMITTEE FOR A REASONABLE WORLD TRADE CENTER

one-third of the landmark tower was even more significant a market maker for downtown than its decision to move from east midtown to Times Square in 1996. In 1996, trends in Times Square were already moving in a new direction with corporate decisions by Bertelsmann (1992) and then Morgan Stanley (1993) to establish a presence there. In contrast, Condé Nast's commitment to 1 World Trade became *the* catalyst for downtown's subsequent market momentum. It validated the marketability of the Trade Center towers at a low point in the real estate cycle when deep doubts about downtown still prevailed.

Ground Zero was a major construction site, and the press's continual narrative of delay remained a discouraging market factor. Many in the brokerage community thought of downtown as "another city," and they were not interested in going there. Condé Nast, however, was about to defy convention once again and sign the largest lease in lower Manhattan in more than twenty-five years. The media giant hadn't internalized the biases of Manhattan, said Mary Ann Tighe, CEO for the New York Tri-State Region of CBRE; the company set its own standard and acted in accord with its individualist internal logic. As a private company, it did not feel the need to justify its decisions other than to its owners, the Newhouse family. In acting on its own ideas, it is fearless, said Tighe. It takes comfort in acting beyond the norm. It wants to be ahead of fashion.[60]

The transformative deal at 1 World Trade was the culmination of "Project Hedgehog," the name Condé Nast chairman Si Newhouse had given to the firm's search for a new headquarters. The code name was a reference to a favorite essay by the Oxford philosopher Isaiah Berlin, "The Hedgehog and the Fox." Berlin had pulled the title from the saying of the ancient Greek poet Archilochus: "The fox knows many things, but the hedgehog knows one big thing." Newhouse, like Durst, considered business decisions from a long-term multigenerational perspective. Stewardship being a guiding principle, he wanted to leave the next generation with a stable, affordable real estate structure, as low cost as the one he had achieved at 4 Times Square. When its lease expired in 2019, the firm's rent in Times Square would price it out of the market given how rents were trending in the Manhattan office market. Begun in 2004, fifteen years before the expiration of its lease, Project Hedgehog took Newhouse to downtown only after all other options had been exhausted (Hudson Yards, Atlantic Yards in Brooklyn, addresses in Long Island City, and locations along the New Jersey waterfront).

At first, company executives would not consider the Trade Center site with its "negative drumbeats" constantly reappearing in press headlines. That was in 2008. In 2009, the company's real estate brokers, Tighe and her colleague Gregory Tosko, took Condé Nast executives to the top of the Winter Garden to show them the changes taking place downtown and at the Trade Center. Retailers like Tiffany's were opening stores downtown. More of the publishers' editors were living downtown, in Tribeca and the West Village. Condé Nast's move downtown would accelerate these social changes, but if the broader trends in these neighborhoods had not been already in place, senior executives like Anna Wintour might not have been persuaded, and the storyline would have been different. In the fall of 2009, Newhouse asked for a tour of Ground Zero. By 2010, Condé Nast was in discussions with the Port Authority on the outlines of a deal and doing deep due diligence on 1 World Trade; at that point, the company was not yet aligned with Durst in his bidding for the tower, Tighe and Tosko later told a class of graduate students at Columbia Business School.

The Port Authority was thinking only in economic terms, renting one million square feet of office space to a "tenant" paying a market rent. Tighe, who has a special skill in finding the right spot for her tenant clients, was saying this is one million square feet of space *of Condé Nast*. To make the argument as to why the Port Authority should "covet Condé Nast as a tenant," she emphasized how the media giant had been a catalyst for Times Square's recovery. In a letter with a formal bid for the space sent to Executive Director Ward, she attached a twelve-page 1998 *Vogue* spread, "Corporate Chic," which featured on the front page of the magazine and within of models on the steel beams of 4 Times Square. This, she said, is what Condé Nast did for Times Square.[61]

Durst and Newhouse are focused bottom-line thinkers. With the business model of media companies strategically threatened by electronic media, the opportunity available at the Trade Center meshed extremely well with long-term business prudence, if not sheer necessity. In laying out the logic to students of how they successfully persuaded the media executives to consider the Trade Center site, Tighe and Tosko never discussed or revealed the economics of the Condé Nast deal. Once the deal was approved by the Port Authority, the minutes of the special interim meeting of the Committee on Operations revealed that the term sheet Condé Nast executives put forth was aggressive: Take over financial responsibility for the remainder of their lease at 4 Times Square and give them the same economics as at 4 Times Square.[62] The publisher did not even consider Silverstein's Trade Center buildings because a privately developed building adhering to a bottom line could not deliver the same advantageous tenant deal. There was no economic sense to 1 World Trade, which made it possible for Condé Nast to get the kind of deal it wanted. Only the Port Authority using its balance sheet could absorb this kind of cost. The company's willingness to sign a term sheet quickly, while the Port Authority was interviewing potential development partners, gave it additional leverage in the negotiations with the Port Authority; the details, Tighe told Condé Nast executives, could be worked out later. Capturing this anchor tenant, Port Authority officials would later say, improved the economics of their investment. "What they fail to point out," said critic Joe Nocera, "is that Condé Nast's rent is less than half the break-even cost of the 1 million square feet it will occupy. In other words, a company that publishes high-end magazines aimed at rich people will be getting an enormous government subsidy for the foreseeable future."[63]

One week after they had agreed on most of the terms for Condé Nast's twenty-five-year deal for more than one million square feet of space, the Port Authority selected Durst as a partner in 1 World Trade. Two streams of independent activity overlapping in time had come together. Although Durst had not played a role in the Condé Nast talks, he was the publisher's landlord at 4 Times Square, and bringing in a world-class owner-operator was essential to the Condé Nast decision. Announcements of each bellwether transaction followed one after the other, only days apart. Among those involved, many had worked on the Times Square deal[64] and a sense of déjà vu prevailed. Less than eight months after signing a lease estimated to be worth $2 billion, the publisher said it planned to take an additional 133,000 square feet of space in the tower.

Bringing private capital into the ownership of 1 World Trade meant buying into the calculus of a private-market operator, even though the Port Authority retained "ultimate responsibility" for its construction and development. Legally speaking, the Durst Organization was an equity member of the joint venture. It was not co-developer of the tower and was "prohibited from holding itself out, or describing itself as, the developer" for the tower "to anyone under any circumstances." It did not need that official label to exert influence within its customary domain as an experienced private developer building for profit. It was the managing partner, "the de facto controlling interest in the joint venture," said Durst.[65] Also, the deal was structured with powerful "incentive payments" for construction cost savings that might still be possible at this juncture in construction (plate 17). When Port Authority commissioners first approved the partnership deal on August 5, 2010, the tower's superstructure had just reached 320 feet above street level—tall enough, a *Times* reporter noted "that the word 'looming' is becoming appropriate." Plans for the building were complete, so form and shape were set in place, but it was not past the point where changes to design details could be made, and with the firm's investment tied to market-driven bottom-line performance, professional staff in Durst offices would undoubtedly be carefully reviewing the construction plans with laser-like focus on how the design would impact marketing, leasing, maintenance, and operations. As a construction manager, Durst would be providing project services broad in scope,[66] and when it came to coordination of tenant requirements with base building construction, that meant servicing tenant needs, especially those of the big anchor tenant, Condé Nast, publisher of eighteen titles, including the *New Yorker, Vanity Fair, Vogue, Bon Appétit,* and *Architectural Digest.*

When I spoke with Douglas Durst about the firm's role in the project, it became clear that the firm inherited a large residue of unresolved issues in the design of the Freedom Tower.[67] The fiberglass-and-steel enclosure called a radome was one of the first things the firm looked at while it was working under an interim contract with the Port Authority. With a focus on operations and cost control, Durst staff asked the PA, what was the function of this $20 million element? The building had been designed under the Silverstein leasehold and after the 2006 realignment value engineered before Durst came into the venture; during that process the radome had been redesigned in a way that Durst concluded made its maintenance near impossible. Radome is a material transparent to radio waves and is used to protect broadcast equipment mounted to an antenna mast inside, but the PA had decided not to include a broadcast facility, so at the time the firm reviewed the building's plans, the radome was "strictly decorative," said Douglas Durst. "It was not structural." Moreover, the earlier cost-cutting exercise eliminated the doors on the radome to outside. To maintain the radome, which by law had to be inspected, someone would have to go to the top, go out a hatch, and rappel down. "There are people who do this," Durst told me, "but you don't want to consider what it would cost. What about lightning?" he added. "How would you replace one of these huge forty-foot panels of radome? A climber would have to attach a cable to the top, lower the cable about 2,000 feet to the ground at a forty-five-degree angle over the Memorial Pool, which would require closing down the Memorial, and then use it to hoist a 2,000-pound piece of fiberglass back to the top," explained Jordan Barowitz, a spokesman for Durst. "This is the stuff of 'Mission Impossible,' not skyscraper construction," he said.[68]

Could the building's owners take a chance on this design element? No one had a clue about how to maintain it, said Durst, whose firm was responsible for maintaining the building. The designers reportedly refuted this claim, yet it was not yet a part of the maintenance manual SOM had prepared, according to Durst. The quest for the 408-foot spire carried symbolic meaning: It was designed to bring 1 World Trade to the height of 1,776 feet (topping the roof height of 1,368 feet, the same height as the North Tower of the original World Trade Center). The Port Authority's decision in mid-2012 to eliminate the rooftop mast and replace it with "an exposed latticework structure" caused much consternation among the design community. Eliminating the spire might jeopardize the building's status as the tallest in North America under the criteria set by the international arbiter of skyscraper height, the Council on Tall Buildings and Urban Habitat. David Childs was not happy about this, to say the least, nor with other changes that would come about.

The other design revisions came incrementally. An intended cascade of stainless-steel steps on the building's west plaza down to Vesey and West Streets, bound to be slippery in bad weather conditions, was replaced with a landscaped terrace, and a skylight to have been set in the plaza to bring daylight to the below-ground observation deck lobby was eliminated. With the squaring off of intended chamfered corners, the tower lost what was to be a "gentle but distinctive outward slope." "Taken together," Dunlap noted, "the design revisions will probably not much alter the presence of 1 World Trade Center on the city's skyline. But they may change its place in the civic consciousness, if the tower is perceived as too isolated or fortified at its base, or as having too little of a symbolic spire at its summit."[69]

Durst maintained that the changes were not made "to save money, but were made in order to construct the building," as suggested by the details of what it would take to maintain the sculptural radome. The monetary benefits to the firm from the millions of dollars in construction savings, construction savings the PA also wanted, were real. In the case of the radome, the expected construction cost savings when Durst made its proposal was $20 million but by the time the Port Authority accepted it, it was $12 million, only 25 percent of which would accrue to Durst.[70] The impact of remeasuring the rentable space of the building would also benefit his capital account in the investment partnership. He also negotiated with the federal government to cut back more than 50 percent of the space the U.S. General Services Administration committed to occupy (at preset rents capped at $59.05 a square foot under the 2006 agreement) to 270,104 square feet; the adjustment increased the tower's potential market-rate space for lease and enhanced the firm's potential upside, which is based on cash flow exceeding a baseline figure agreed upon by the partners. In a separate arrangement with the Port Authority, Durst would be overseeing the construction and operation of a broadcast facility atop the tower.

For Durst as a long-term owner—the firm prefers not to sell assets—the investment in 1 World Trade Center was a generational investment. For a developer of high-density buildings facing escalating land values in Manhattan, it was going to be hard to do a next project without land at a reasonable cost basis. Prices were outpacing underlying fundamentals, especially for office buildings. "The odds of assembling a site for an office building were small, and office development with rents at $70 a square foot was not their idea of opportunity," Rosenberg said. "The profile of 1 World Trade helped them maintain commercial development activity. The price was tying up $100 million for a long time."[71]

Selling the Sky-High View

On March 20, 2013, the PA Board of Commissioners approved the selection of Legends Hospitality to develop and operate an observation deck at the top of 1 World Trade Center. The action layered in a second private player in the PA's anxious quest for new sources of revenues to recoup some of the extraordinary capital cost of building the political monument. The authority had taken the lead in negotiating a fifteen-year lease with Legends, which was expected to produce total revenues of $875 million over the term of the lease. This would be a net return to the PA as Legends would also be billed for building expenses attributable to the Observation Deck. Moreover, the PA had structured the deal so that it would not be putting in any additional capital. Also, in specifying a defined number of years for the lease, it had retained long-term sponsorship of the potential moneymaker. The deal did not give Legends Hospitality, a company owned by the New York Yankees, the Dallas Cowboys, and the Checketts Partners Investment Fund, any renewal rights. The sports and entertainment company anticipated investing approximately $62.5 million according to the presentation to the board of commissioners, and at the end of the fifteen years, all of the property used in the operation of the Observation Deck, including trade names and trademarks and technology, would become the property of the Port Authority. Recalling the not-so-great state of repair of the observation deck in the South Tower of the original World Trade Center, the PA staff negotiating the deal required Legends to put aside 2 percent of annual gross revenue for renewing and upgrading the space (approximately 120,000 square feet) to assure continuing visitor appeal of the ticketing areas, dining spaces, arrival theater, and event areas over the term of the lease—a mechanism that would ensure Legends continually maintained and improved the experience. In addition, Legends provided a substantial performance guarantee to back its obligations in the lease.

As an operator running marketing, merchandising, and skyboxes for stadiums, Legends brought expertise in managing big-volume entertainment events. Although the firm did not have specific experience operating an observatory, it brought in professionals who were experts in this area, among them, Phil Hettema of the Hettema Group, who had developed the Amazing Adventures of Spider-Man and other theme park attractions for Universal. The PA also brought in its own expert consultants, the entertainment and attractions group of AECOM, to assist and advise during the extensive due diligence and selection process. Among the three finalists, Legends "provided the best proposal, as it offered an attractive combination of an experienced and well-capitalized partner, an exciting design concept, and a compelling financial proposal," according to the minutes of the PA board meeting.[72] It was, the PA concluded, the one bidder who best understood the people dynamics of creating a three-level theatrical sky-high experience.

When One World Observatory—New York's tallest observatory (1,268 feet, 102nd floor) outranking the sightseeing height of the Empire State Building (1,250 feet, 102nd floor) and the Top of the Rock at 30 Rockefeller Center (850 feet, 70th floor)—opened a little more than two years later on May 29, 2015, the sky-high attraction started to deliver immediately. Thirteen days after opening, the digital display in the building lobby that counts scanned tickets as visitors entered showed more than 106,000 visitors had come to experience the "Skypod" multimedia time-lapse history of Manhattan Island (as high-speed elevators whisked them to the 102nd floor in forty-eight seconds), take in unobstructed views of the entire New York City region on level 100 (on a clear day presenting itself in a fifty-mile panorama), and watch a two-minute video on New York City life at the "See Forever" theater on level 102. Perhaps they might stop to sample some food at one of the dining options and purchase 1 WTC books, videos, apparel, or souvenirs at the gift shop. Adults were paying $32 (seniors $30 and children $26). By the end of that opening year after seven months of operation, the observatory had attracted 1.6 million visitors. According the PA's Fact Sheet as of January 2016, Legends expects 3.8 million annual visitors. At an average ticket price of under $25, the gross take (without considering sales from food and beverage, events, and the gift shop) would ring up to a projected $90 million. What was not as clear as the stunning 360-degree view from this high perch was how One World Observatory would fare over time in the intensely competitive world of New York popular attractions, which includes the Statue of Liberty and Ellis Island and Broadway Theater productions, among many others, including existing Manhattan sky observatories and a new one at 1,100 feet atop one of the newest skyscrapers in the city, 30 Hudson Yards. As an entertainment attraction, the "step-right-up showmanship," David W. Dunlap remarked in his description of the observatory experience, "does credit to the memory of P. T. Barnum."[73]

Observatories today are big business, money-minting machines. When a tower's height and iconic branding permit, they can bring in extraordinary amounts of cash. In the case of the Empire State Building, its two observatory decks (open-air on the 86th floor and enclosed on the 102nd floor) visited by 4.3 million people in 2014 brought in $111.5 million in revenues and accounted for 40 percent of the iconic skyscraper's revenues, according to the company's annual report. This record amount was 55 percent more than in 2010. The observatory's "eye-popping income growth," wrote a securities analyst, resulted from the Empire State Building's "near-monopoly position in the past decade." With the opening of One World Observatory, however, that position would be challenged. Analysts who follow these market trends expect One World Observatory to capture market share from the Empire State Building (and to a lesser extent from Rockefeller Center's Top of the Rock). The original Trade Center observatory attracted nearly two million visitors a year, perhaps a 40 percent market share at the time. Because of Ground Zero's place in history and the 9/11 Memorial and 9/11 Memorial Museum on the site, One World Observatory is likely to be a more significant destination than the pre-9/11 World Trade Center observatory. While it is too soon to know how much market share it will capture, past trends suggest that the size of the market for observatory visits is not fixed, but rather grows with the number of venues. New York City is a tourist mecca, with over 55 million visitors in 2014, and the number of tourists taking in an observatory visit has grown steadily, from 3.4 million in 2005 to an estimated 6.9 million in 2014.[74]

The PA's cash intake from One World Observatory depends on the number of visitors and how much of the observatory-visitor market it captures. Under the terms of its deal with Legends, the annual rent paid to the Port Authority is made up of two elements: a fixed base rent and a variable rent component based on profitability of Legends' operations from a combination of ticket sales and revenues from food and beverage, gift shop purchases, and event-space rentals. Legends' response to the PA's request for proposals for bids on the observatory lease provides an order-of-magnitude estimate of potential cash flow to the PA. In this 2012 response, Legends proposed a base rent of $14 million, and a 65–35 percent split in profits in favor of the PA. Its base-scenario financial projection for the first year, assuming 3.2 annual visitors, showed the variable portion ($21.8 million) to be 61 percent of total payments to the Port Authority. Under an optimistic assumption of 4.5 million visitors, variable rent might reach $40.4 million, or 74 percent of total annual dollars flowing to the PA from the observatory space. And as with other retail lease arrangements, the variable rent portion would grow over time with increasing sales and inflation. This is serious money, especially when benchmarked against the annual rent of $78.7 million the Port Authority receives from Silverstein for the three commercial office sites. "If all goes according to plan," Bagli reported, Port Authority officials expected One World Observatory "to account for a hefty 40 percent of the revenue" from the tower by 2020 when the building reaches economic stabilization.[75]

The actual final terms of the deal's economics are not available to the public. Why? How can it be that financial information on the most high-profile publicly owned office tower in the county developed by a public entity is shielded from public review? As Eliot Brown wrote, "the agency has taken the position that a tenant's rent is private information, and should be withheld given that it could impair the agency." (It was the same with the Condé Nast transaction.) Presentation of "select terms of the lease" as described in a bare two pages of the minutes of the board meeting was high level, economically light. The oft-cited revenue intake of $875 million over the life of the fifteen-year lease was in nominal dollars, unadjusted for the time value of money. The day before the transaction went before the board of commissioners, Governors Cuomo and Christie issued a joint statement announcing the selection of Legends and called on the board to approve the agreement. In the lease with Legends, now available online through a FOI request, the rent payment arrangements as well as any other specifics on the economics of the transaction were redacted.[76] Ironically, as Brown pointed out, there is far more financial information publicly available for many privately owned towers than there is for 1 World Trade. Silverstein's towers "were being financed with hundreds of millions in debt by bond buyers who need detailed financial information to evaluate the strength and performance of their investments.[77] But even for the Port Authority's joint ventures with Westfield Group and the Durst Organization, there is far more detailed financial information in the minutes of the board meetings where these transactions were approved.

This was a much-needed deal. The Port Authority needed to take out the risk of developing and managing the observatory space itself. It did not have the expertise to do this, and neither did the Durst Organization since it had never built an observation deck. It needed the economics that would flow from leasing out the observatory space. Turning around the perception of the PA as an institution run amok was the other much-needed objective of this transaction. The authority had been under searing attack for years for its mismanagement of projects at Ground Zero, its organizational dysfunction, and its lack of transparency. Changing the perception of the agency would be difficult, even when it made a mark with this economic deal. Its aspirations for control over rebuilding Ground Zero and the largess of its spending of billions and billions to achieve that goal had exposed its vulnerabilities on all fronts—political, financial, and institutional—to become a troublesome legacy shaping the future of the Port Authority.

CHAPTER 21

Ambition and Legacy

FIGURE 21.1 *The new skyscrapers on and around the Trade Center site seen in reflection on the glass facade of the Memorial Pavilion, November 2015.* GARY HACK

B Y THE THIRTEENTH ANNIVERSARY of the 9/11 attack, the forward trajectory at Ground Zero was clear. The city was riding high on economic adrenalin, powered by diverse social energy. With dynamic job growth higher than the national average, robust business investment, population at an all-historic high, tourism hitting record-breaking levels, and residential and commercial real estate attracting capital from all over the world, New York's position as a global city of the first order was unquestionable. Facing off against London, it ranked above other global cities in its attractiveness to business and jobs and people. And that status extended beyond the centricity of Manhattan. Brooklyn was a global brand for youthful creative cool and in a diffusing catalytic arc, economic growth had traversed the East River to Long Island City and other neighborhoods in Queens. Its historic economic trajectory renewed, by 2014 the city had proven its resilience once again. It had not been changed forever by 9/11, as many had feared in the aftermath of trauma. It had met the challenge and opportunity of rebuilding after massive tragedy with characteristically vast ambition and impatience and written its own chapter on resilience for the book of history.

The momentum in lower Manhattan outpaced the city's story of resilience. The statistics on population growth (62,000 residents, or nearly three times that in 2000), private-sector jobs (227,069), public and private investment ($30 billion), construction activity ($4.8 billion, or 13.4 percent of the citywide total for 2014), and fiscal power ($2.4 billion in New York City tax revenues for fiscal year 2014) spoke to a "radical transformation" since the dark days following 9/11. As the Alliance for Downtown New York enthusiastically reported, the economy of lower Manhattan "had reached a level not seen since before September 11," and the future was "even more promising."[1] In the fifteen years since 9/11, lower Manhattan had benefited from three big infusions of federal money unlike anything in the past: $20.5 billion to repair and rebuild from the 9/11 attack, billions to the bailout Wall Street banks, and additional billions to repair the disaster damage from Hurricane Sandy. The revived economy downtown was now built on a more diverse foundation that reflected a shrinking financial-services industry's footprint and a rising "TAMI" sector—jobs in technology, advertising, media, and information. In their move from midtown or midtown south attracted by lower costs, these companies had leased over three million square feet of office space in lower Manhattan since 2008—61 percent of it at the Trade Center: 1 World Trade (Condé Nast, 1.6 million square feet), 3 World Trade (Group M, 520,000 square feet), and 4 World Trade (MediaMath, 106,000 square feet). Alongside, the shift in the economy fueled a flourishing of restaurants, cultural facilities, hotels, and parks. In short, lower Manhattan "healed more quickly around its gaping wound that anyone would have thought possible"[2] (figure 21.1).

Ambition had been the driving force shaping rebuilding at Ground Zero: Ambition to be historically enduring and mark New York as a great city of strength. Ambition to majestically remember massive loss on the site at the same time the city rebuilt a strong commercial platform for the future. Ambition to advance a visionary urban agenda for the twenty-first century that would reenergize lower Manhattan. Ambition to define a better paradigm for large-scale development in the twenty-first century. Ambition tied to political agendas and business interests, civic and cultural agendas, and institutional prestige. Ambition manifested itself in the vision of the master plan, the scope of each memorial project and each commercial tower, and the aspirations for a transportation terminal to rival that of midtown's Grand Central Terminal. Ambition in the quest for high-profile choices in architecture and design, even in undisciplined costs. Ambition served as a platform for aspirational achievement and was later recognized by numerous awards and honors in nearly every professional sphere.[3] The accompanying competition and ego-driven actions that emerged at Ground Zero were not invented there; they are familiar age-old conditions. They are not unique to New York or its culture. Large-scale opportunity quickens ambition, wherever.

The other face of ambition fueled the drive to move forward quickly, to grab opportunity before it might dissipate. The haste to deploy "free" federal funds produced a selection of transportation projects from an ever-present wish list of waiting projects as opposed to systematically prioritizing what the city might need most. Almost alone among the world's big cities, New York still lacks a direct link to its international airport (JFK). With its allocation from that pot of money, the Port Authority was building a great train station—"if only there was a great train to put in it," a targeted rebuke repeated often by those invested in the future of downtown. The rush into a second planning process for Ground Zero suffered from a similar fault line to that of the botched first process: Officials were never clear about what the process was really about, what would really result from the selection of a winning design plan. In the press and town hall meetings people weren't being told what they were looking at, that the architectural images put into these plans were there to give a sense of dimension and style to the land-use arrangements, that they did not preordain specific architecture that was going to get built. The process set up unrealistic expectations. No single person determined the move-fast pressure; it came from all sides: public officials, stakeholders, citizens, editorial boards. Moving fast appeared to be the way to cauterize the pain as fast as possible.

In the rapidity of the planning process and the conflicts of implementation that followed, specific ambitions were lost or preempted by other decisions: Potential investments with money lost to tactical grandstanding, inefficiency, and competition among agencies and stakeholders rather than cooperation. The collection of individual and institutional ambitions undermined the possibility of consensus at Ground Zero—with one exception: the reintegration of the site into the city, restoring former streets and allowing easy-flowing pedestrian movement across the site unimpeded by physical barriers. But even here, it is hard to know what impact required security measures will have on the site over time. Unified action in the public interest solidified by broad-based comity over the many years it takes to implement a large-scale urban project is an ideal rarely achieved. As it played out over the years, the ambitions of rebuilding Ground Zero revealed a number of paradoxes that have shaped the legacy of each direct stakeholder, those who won and those who lost. In these paradoxes ironies reside.

IRONIES OF POWER

The authority to make decisions and fulfill the ambitions of rebuilding seemed to be the essence of power in this highly wrought situation bounded on one side by catastrophic loss and on the other by unique opportunity. In implementing the rebuilding plans for Ground Zero, however, state government with its concentrated power over the apparatus for rebuilding under the governor's control squandered its power. Although it seemed only logical to many (but not all) that the city should have had more formal powers over Ground Zero, in the deal made with the Port Authority in the 1960s for development of the original World Trade Center, the city traded its ownership over those sixteen acres for future economic benefits. Having no formal power on the site, the Bloomberg administration maneuvered to find strategic points whereby it could effectively intercede in the rebuilding process and push the project forward in line with city priorities when other actors with formal power were not willing or able to set priorities. The rebuilding legacy Mayor Bloomberg achieved was an unlikely and belated political success. It was belated because during his first term in office many believed he "abdicated responsibility for reviving it [the Trade Center], instead centering on the West Side where he would have less layered competition from the state, a bi-state New York–New Jersey agency and the emotions of 9/11 survivors." Once Pataki was no longer in the governor's mansion in Albany, however, the tacit agreement between the mayor and the governor—Bloomberg attending to the development of the West Side while Pataki took charge of the Trade Center—ceased to have effect.[4] And the quest for a New York Olympics had been lost in the summer of 2005. By the end of Bloomberg's third term at midnight on the turn of 2013, the mayor's bully pulpit and his presence at Ground Zero as chairman of the 9/11 Memorial Foundation had served his ambition for a grand gesture in the physical realm of the city.

After more than twenty years of debate and delay, the Port Authority had finally privatized its biggest venture in the real estate business in 2001. Not long after that, the agency reversed course on that strategic policy mandate with the 2006 realignment deal with Larry Silverstein and willingness to take on the responsibility for construction of the 9/11 Memorial and Memorial Museum. In tandem with its construction of the underground infrastructure and Transportation Hub, the Port Authority was back in control—and at risk. Central decision-makers at the Port Authority believed that the agency was the only government entity with the execution capability to carry the responsibility. Their logic: No one else had a better infrastructure to do it, not the LMDC, not Silverstein Properties, not the state of New York, not the city of New York. It was a big gamble for the institution and a big financial risk for sure, but no one at the Port Authority was on the ballot, as one insider noted, unlike the governor and the mayor. Nevertheless, project complexity undermined the agency's ability to perform in line with its rebuilding ambition and legacy of institutional prowess. In the spotlight of a high-profile symbolic project exposed to unmitigated political pressure and constant monitoring by a federal funder, the staff-driven agency struggled to manage the ambitions of the project in a complicated intergovernmental context. The rebuilding of the Trade Center site stretched its institutional capacity. It also revealed the institutional limits of the 1920s Progressive ideal of an autonomous, seemingly apolitical, business-like public authority governed under the aegis of two governors. In so doing, the Trade Center crisis at the bi-state Port Authority eventually—ironically—opened a potential path toward structural reform (abetted by investigations related to the closing of the George Washington Bridge by New Jersey–appointed officials at the Port Authority, known as "Bridgegate")—or dissolution.

Larry Silverstein was the consummate economic actor at Ground Zero. He possessed the right to rebuild, as long as he could continue to perform under the terms of his ninety-nine-year lease with the Port Authority. Having his contractual property rights to the Trade Center site subject to an elaborate public process circumscribed his decision-making rights under his lease, though not his ability to tactically maneuver around those constraints. Ultimately, he triumphed in holding on to the brass ring (albeit smaller), to harvest millions in fees, and, someday in the future, profits, with little to no personal equity at risk. The changing market dynamic of lower Manhattan helped Silverstein. His speculative office towers at Ground Zero have been among the very few being delivered to the marketplace at a time when residential development was capturing the highest-and-best-use activity everywhere across the city landscape. They may take many years to fill up with tenants, but his patience is being heavily subsidized by the public sector. He was in the right place at the right time (figure 21.2).

Had the Silverstein investor partnership been bought out, or able to exit with hundreds of millions or several billion in funds without rebuilding, the wealthy developer would have missed the opportunity to create a lasting professional legacy that far surpasses what he had accomplished in his five decades of wheeling and dealing in Manhattan real estate before that fateful September day. When in March 2014, he overreached once again and asked for additional financial support for Tower 3—"For Ground Zero Developer Seeking Subsidies, More Is Never Enough"—his maneuvering finally failed to deliver the desired result. New York–appointed Port Authority commissioner Kenneth Lipper, a prominent figure in the world of finance who served as deputy mayor under Mayor Edward Koch among many other professional roles, led a charge against board approval of additional subsidies for the developer's second tower. After months of debate among

FIGURE 21.2 Gary Hack

a sharply divided board and three postponements of a vote on a proposed new deal for Tower 3, the Port Authority board said no, finally, at its June 25, 2014, meeting.[5] The seemingly unbridled power of commercial real estate as a political driver at Ground Zero had finally hit a limit—almost.

Silverstein came back again, as developers in a complex public/private project are prone to do, for financial assistance on Tower 2 when he was close to bringing in as anchor tenants News Corporation and Fox News, giant media companies controlled by billionaire Rupert Murdoch. Supposedly, this was the one office tower at Ground Zero that was to be developed under market discipline without further public support, as agreed to in the 2010 deal between Silverstein and the Port Authority. In 2014, the Port Authority had promised not to use any more public dollars to subsidize Tower 2, the largest office tower on the site at 2.8 million square feet. But on December 10, 2015, the board of commissioners agreed to more subsidies to help jump-start construction, under the argument the subsidies would "catalyze the development of Tower 2," "bring significant financial benefits" to the Port Authority (compared to a "no build" scenario), and "accelerate the Port Authority's "strategic intent" to "exit the real estate development business and refocus on its core transportation mission." The subsidies were controversial to a certain set of critics and some industry watchers. It seemed unwise from a policy perspective, if not economically suspect, to provide additional subsidies for a corporate relocation from midtown to downtown when the New York economy was so robust. According to the Port Authority's clarification of the subsidy structure as presented in a *Politico* news article, the proposed public support (including support from New York State) would "total approximately $23 per square foot for Tower 2, below the $30 per square foot provided Group M at Tower 3 and the $250 per square foot for Condé Nast" in 1 World Trade. Was this relatively lesser amount of subsidy, which some real estate executives thought might be understated, supposed to make the deal more acceptable? Despite the public support, the proposed corporate relocation fell through five weeks later when Murdoch announced the companies were dropping plans to relocate to 2 World Trade Center. Saying it would be "too distracting in the near-term" and that "our resources could be better directed elsewhere," they would stay in their offices at 1121 and 1185 Avenue of the Americas.[6] Without execution of leases with Twenty-first Century Fox and News Corporation by the end of the first quarter of 2016, the modifications to the terms of Silverstein's lease for Tower 2 as authorized by the board became "null and void."[7]

THE PRESS GAP

The drama at Ground Zero included the press as a player, not just a chronicler of news. In selective disputes like the tabloids' heated interventions over culture at Ground Zero or the *New York Times Magazine*'s bold venture into the vision arena with an elaborate spread on ideas for rebuilding Ground Zero that would celebrate "the power of architecture to inspire, to dazzle—and to spur furious debate," the city's three dailies took on an advocacy role beyond that of their editorial pages. The press also elevated the issues of the 9/11 families, gave them a collective voice, though the families never spoke in one voice. The ink flowed over thousands of stories reporting on delays, conflicts, ego battles, and political skirmishing (figure 21.3).

The scale of press coverage was the critically important tool for shaping public opinion of what was going on at Ground Zero. However, the public would have benefited from more news analysis. There were strong reporters who struck with the project over the years and knew what was going on, knew more perhaps than they ever were able to write about, including Charles V. Bagli (*NYT*), Eliot Brown (*NYO, WSJ*), Steve Cuozzo (*NYP*), David W. Dunlap (*NYT*), Douglas Feiden (*DN, WSJ*), Maggie Haberman (*NYP*), William Neuman (*NYP, NYT*), and Lois Weiss (*NYP*). They explained the disputes between Silverstein and his insurers. They explained his difficulties with the Port Authority. They explained the outlines of his financial interests in rebuilding—the 2003 deal that returned most of the partnership's equity without diminishing its development rights, the 2006 deal reallocating development rights for the office towers with Silverstein getting the three best sites and the Port Authority left holding the noneconomic Freedom Tower and site 5, and the 2010 deal providing the developer with more subsidies

FIGURE 21.3 Author composite

and financial support to move forward with two of his three speculative towers. These were but fragments of a bigger business story that all but went untold: the shaky cost foundation for rebuilding, the bottom line of rebuilding, the levers of control over the insurance escrow that gave Silverstein the power to spend vast sums of it before a spade hit the ground to rebuild the towers, and the resultant call on the public fisc to make up the deficit of funds necessary for rebuilding through one mechanism or another, all while Silverstein and his partners were collecting millions in management fees. When reporting turned on criticism of the subsidies Silverstein was getting, access could become difficult, I was told by one reporter.

Rebuilding Ground Zero was not an easy project to cover. To begin with, it was not a single project, but a fusion of numerous discrete projects—approximately thirty-two of them—each fraught with many interests and many physical, emotional, economic, and political components. (See list of individual projects in table 21.1.) The whole was complicated, easily watered down. It included a lot of inside baseball, specialized knowledge of bureaucratic and political spheres of action. Many stories, particularly those about the business transactions, infrastructure plans, and issues of ownership responsibility, were technical and hard to translate

Table 21.1 Individual Projects in the Rebuilding of the World Trade Center Site.

	Project	Stakeholder
Transportation	Interim PATH Terminal	PANYNJ
	Terminal Transportation Hub:	
	WFC Underpass	Brookfield
	East/West Connector	PANYNJ/FTA
	North Temporary Access	PANYNJ/FTA
	Utility work at Church Street	PANYNJ
	Oculus	PANYNJ/FTA
	PATH Facility	PANYNJ/FTA
	Eastside North/South Connectors	PANYNJ/FTA
	Dey Street Passageway and Fulton Street	MTA/NYCTA
	Subway stations (FTA funded)	MTA/NYCTA
	Route 9A Realignment	PANYNJ/FTA
Infrastructure	West Bathtub	PANYNJ/FTA
	VSC Phase 1 - VSC and Tour Bus Parking	PANYNJ/FTA
	VSC Phase 2 - Eastside Tour Bus Parking Facility	PANYNJ/FTA
	VSC Phase 3 - West Bathtub Vehicular Access (helix)	PANYNJ/FTA
	Street, Utilities and Related Infrastructure	PANYNJ/FTA
	Central Chiller Plant and Water River System	PANYNJ/FTA
	Common Electrical System	PANYNJ/FTA
	Common Infrastructure - Temporary Underpinning of #1 Subway	PANYNJ/FTA/MTA
	Common Infrastructure - Permanent Underpinning of #1 Subway	PANYNJ/FTA/MTA
	Site-Wide Security / Operations Center	PANYNJ/FTA
	Vent Structure	PANYNJ/FTA
	Master Manager Facility	PANYNJ/FTA
Commercial	Commercial Infrastructure - East Bathtub Incremental Construction	PANYNJ/FTA
	1 WTC/ Freedom Tower	PANYNJ
	Tower 2	SPI
	Tower 3	SPI
	Tower 4	SPI
	Tower 5	LMDC/PANYNJ
	Deutsche Bank Building Deconstruction	LMDC
	Retail Development	PANYNJ/Westfield
	Commercial Infrastructure - Parking	SPI/PANYNJ
Cultural	Memorial Plaza	Memorial Foundation/PANYNJ
	Memorial Museum and Memorial Pavilion (VOEC)	Memorial Foundation/PANYNJ
	Performing Arts Center	LMDC/NYC
	St. Nicholas Greek Orthodox Church	St. Nicholas Church
	Liberty Park	PANYNJ

Source: Author

to the general public. The underlying technical explanations required hundreds of words, and getting enough column space for these kinds of stories was difficult.

Rebuilding Ground Zero was also a challenging story to cover. It was challenging because the power of the city's real estate interests makes it difficult to unravel the financial relationships, personal connections, and collateral interests underlying the observed outcomes. "Business is hard to report on because its officials, by and large, don't have to talk to reporters," Elinore Longobardi of the *Columbia Journalism Review* wrote in her preface to "The Remarkable Larry Silverstein Story" in fall of 2007. "This is particularly true of closely held businesses, and triply true of real estate companies."[8] As a consequence, gaps existed between actions taken by players and the story the public received, further increasing the confusion about what was going on at Ground Zero and why events were unfolding as they were. Sometimes the gaps reflected the choices made about what to cover; other times gaps arose because of the pullback in beat reporting on big institutions such as the Port Authority and a general decline in investigative reporting stemming from economic pressures on the business model of print media. And still other times, they existed because the behind-the-scenes action, especially on the private side of business at Ground Zero, was just unavailable or only available months later when it was no longer news.

Silverstein was able to control the message surprisingly well, for years. Even in 2010, during one of the most intense months of negotiations over a financial deal for his towers, Silverstein went on CBS's *60 Minutes* and laid out his position for national television viewers: "I describe this as a national disgrace," he told Scott Pelly, who said the developer "shook his head slowly as we stood over the muddy pit known around the world as Ground Zero." By way of emphasizing the scope of his view of the dysfunction, Pelly added: "It took three cameramen from '60 Minutes' to photograph the expanse of the 16-acre hole that was once the basement of the World Trade Center." He could see that some construction had begun, but, Pelly said, "as I stood there with Silverstein looking at the rainwater pooling down below, I thought, 'Nobody's gonna believe this.'"[9] This was brilliant staging. With an affect of great sincerity and some light laughter at the situation, Silverstein was once again presenting himself as the victim of the Port Authority's bureaucratic bungling and obstruction, as if there was only one player at fault.

It is possible to say that the press let itself be misled. It is also possible to criticize the coverage as "pack journalism at its worst" as did *Columbia Journalism Review*'s The Audit.[10] Yet that line of commentary misses the bigger problem in media coverage of the rebuilding process and its political history. There was little digging into what did not happen and almost no investigative reporting. If

Silverstein was, in the image he put forth for the public, a private steward of the $4.55 billion of insurance payouts whose sole purpose was to "rebuild and honor," how should he be held accountable for that stewardship in the absence of investigative reporting? Was it enough that the towers just get built, that is, for the ends to justify the means, with little public scrutiny? In this gray area of private property rights imbued with a clear and compelling public interest, a protocol for accountability from private-sector beneficiaries of the public's largess was missing. Where, for example, was the counterbalance to Silverstein's argument that the insurance payout dollars represented his partnership's private equity contribution to rebuilding, a rebuilding made possible by an undergirding of massive public investment? Isn't the probing of such questions the role of the fourth estate?

Throughout the years, Silverstein proved that he was something quite different from a plucky underdog: He proved to be a savvy player often a few steps ahead of his public-sector counterparts. Throughout the years, he tacked from A to B, B to C, C to D, moving in ways that enabled him to get much of what he wanted by being doggedly persistent and thick-skinned, by using the press to advance his case (though not always successfully) and recast his image, and by building a sophisticated organization with the capacity to rebuild on a scale demanded by the city's ambitions for the Trade Center site. He did not always win every battle but he survived as a beneficiary and emerged with a new persona known around the world as the man who rebuilt Ground Zero. And he achieved a new legacy—a legacy endowed with financial capacity provided by the public sector.

For New York City and its residents who have borne the physical burden as well as the emotional scars of the destruction on 9/11, the physical reality of a new Trade Center will trump the messy political process of how it all came about. When fully rebuilt and defined by the city's dynamic energy of activity, the intense conflicts, high-profile controversies, and exorbitant costs of rebuilding the Trade Center site will likely be forgotten. Some observers, though are likely to see in the troubled storyline verification of government incompetence. Within the achievements are lost opportunities and failures of purpose, mistakes, irrevocable decisions that were at odds with what was needed for the long term. There were many talented and experienced and certainly dedicated people at work on this historic project, but their talents were often undermined by the fragmentation of power and inability to make decisions that would survive some higher political purpose. While it is not possible to say what might have been if such decisions had not been made, the experience of rebuilding Ground Zero leaves a legacy of lessons.

THE LEADERSHIP FACTOR

It was a constant refrain—rebuilding was taking too long. In editorial after editorial, the culprit—lack of leadership. The complaints were many: Focus was missing. Attention was wandering. Politicians were distracted. Rebuilding wasn't a priority. Progress was not being made. Bureaucratic turf fighting was the only action evident at Ground Zero. Action needed to match promises. Sustained energy had to be put behind the convictions. A sense of urgency was necessary. Everything was a priority, so there were no priorities. Everyone was in charge, so no one was in charge. Someone had to take command, establish firm priorities and clear direction.

Leadership did not mean a single autocratic hand manipulating the strings of power to serve a single vision in the power-broker style of Robert Moses. Rather, the type of leadership needed at Ground Zero called for a consensus builder who could skillfully meld together the various factions amid the many ambitions. Across all of the city's print editorial boards, the prevailing perception was that no one was in charge at Ground Zero. And that was the painful truth.

The early optimism and heady expectations for a big vision accompanied by immediate tangible evidence of rebuilding had rapidly dissipated into a series of recriminations as conflict and controversy consumed public enthusiasm and frustration came to dominate, especially among those in the business and real estate communities. With each setback, disappointment came into sharp focus. And it was Governor Pataki—the only one with the power to exercise executive leadership over the Trade Center site—who was repeatedly called to task for his lack of leadership. The governor had set up the organization for public decision-making over the site, but regularly overrode the LMDC's decisions. He had been a steadfast champion of the Freedom Tower, yet was caught unawares in a high-profile debacle when the NYPD voiced security concerns and forced a redesign of the symbolic tower. He appointed the executive directors of the bi-state Port Authority, yet was strategically disadvantaged when it came to controlling critical decisions at Ground Zero that only the landowning PA could make because he could not corral the New York commissioners, some of whom, he said, were "not visionary." At the end of "The George Pataki Era," the governor was faulted less for his decisions than for his executive style—an "ebb and flow" focus on the city's rebuilding and slow rise to action at Ground Zero, as the *Times* said on the governor's last day in office. "He was not always there when he was needed. As criticism mounted, he would eventually appear and often do the right thing. But the lag time hurt."[11]

"It goes with the turf," Governor Pataki told me when I interviewed him early in January 2015 and asked about the years of harsh editorial criticism. "If you are leader and willing to do things that are right, you do them. What matters is the result. I got criticized in Albany too, for the process. You always listen." The most difficult issue, he said, was that "you had to take a long-term view. At the same time, there was a sense of immediacy because lower Manhattan was struggling even before 9/11. This was, after all, the second attack." Restoring a sense of normalcy and doing it right, were "two competing priorities that were somewhat inconsistent," he said. "When you go down there today, I think we did the right thing—1 World Trade, the memorial, the museum."[12]

The promise of leadership was implied in the dedicated mission of the LMDC—"the entity that drives the train of Lower Manhattan," Pataki said at the time he created the agency. Its initial blueprint for rebuilding drew praise, as did its early staff and board appointments. And in its early period, led by John Whitehead, it was more independent than other New York State public authorities. Also, it was charged, implicitly, with managing issues of symbolic importance and to attend to what the public wanted. Yet the development corporation was never empowered to take on the role suggested by its name. Rather, from the start, it was a political vehicle set up to assure the state's control over federal funds for the recovery and rebuilding of lower Manhattan being sent directly to the LMDC as a result of Whitehead's efforts; at the same time those he put in charge of the agency would shield the governor from criticism that might damage his future aspirations. The LMDC managed the early planning process, but it did not have the legal power or political influence to manage the complications that flowed from the split ownership of the Trade Center site. It ran the process and, as one board member told me, "contributed moral probity to the process." But even in exercising its planning role, the LMDC was dramatically shut out of making a lasting impact at Ground Zero, eviscerated by the hand that created its mission because Governor Pataki was always the final political arbiter of the big decisions: the master plan for the site, the set-aside of the footprints from development, and the eviction of the International Freedom Center and consequential exclusive memory focus of the 9/11 Memorial Museum. Thoroughly marginalized by those decisions, the agency faded into the shadow of its initial promise. By late fall 2005, even its oversight role was being questioned, and in the summer 2006, its chairman Kevin M. Rampe announced that the LMDC would be laying off many of its fifty-four employees and shutting the lights in a few months. "We're nearing the end of the mission," he said.[13]

A prescient notice of its shutdown appeared in *Crain's* some two years before. Having disbursed most of the $2.7 billion of federal funds, the corporate shell still had to endure as an entity for legal purposes to meet HUD reporting requirements. Unfinished jobs would be passed on, most significantly, in the case of the

Performing Arts Center to the city, which was ever-eager for control at Ground Zero. "The greatest accomplishment of a public agency such as ours is to successfully work itself out of existence," said Stefan Pryor, then president of the corporation and its first employee.[14] The LMDC issued a "2001–2006 Final Report," but the sunset announcement turned out to be premature—more than once.

The LMDC was a big symbol of state control and a power base for the then leader of the State Assembly, Sheldon Silver. As a source of grants, it still had some $200 million to dispense in Silver's lower Manhattan district. When Eliot Spitzer moved into the governor's mansion in Albany in 2007, he decided to keep the agency alive, as did his successor, David Paterson. City politicians and downtown residents continued to call for its demise—in 2008 and 2010—and by 2011, even state officials had joined the chorus to disband what was left of the agency. Still in existence in 2014, albeit with only twenty-five employees and nearly all of its funds obligated, a spokesperson for the new administration of Mayor Bill de Blasio said, "We're looking at the LMDC with fresh eyes. Even though its functions have become more limited, it still has responsibilities to fulfill before its work is complete." Having been a longtime opponent of this government agency, the *Post* editorialized, "When you translate this into plain English, it means: 'Just keep it going. We'll come up with a justification later.'" Silver refused to sign off on dismantling the agency, arguing that the agency had not "finished overseeing the allocation of these [federal] funds."[15] Having been politically eviscerated, the LMDC, nevertheless, used its control over the pot of federal dollars to disburse money throughout lower Manhattan in incremental actions less susceptible to the governor's overriding power and more in line with Mayor Bloomberg's broad agenda for downtown. Ironically, its failure to exert a commanding political influence on planning decisions at Ground Zero may have allowed the agency to quietly pursue a different political agenda from that of the governor in distributing federal dollars for recovery and rebuilding.

By the end of 2006, after the Port Authority consolidated construction control over much of the site, the leadership complaint ceased to settle on the governor's office. At that time, the major decisions shaping the scope and character of rebuilding were in place, and the lens of attention self-adjusted onto the job of executing those decisions, to the "logistical leadership" of coordinating the "snarl of public agencies, private developers, contractors, architects, and consultants on the site" to get it done.[16] That job belonged to the Port Authority and so did the criticisms for repeatedly failing to deliver results on schedule and on budget. Logistical leadership failed, too. Under the divided-power arrangement that defined decision-making at the bi-state bureaucratic behemoth, control proved to be an elusive political goal; the agency was effectively beholden to no one.

In point of fact, the type of assertive directed leadership editorialists and others kept calling for at Ground Zero was crippled from the start, structurally. The public-private ownership interests of the World Trade Center that had been so proudly finalized just six weeks prior to 9/11 created a flawed structure for rebuilding once the complex lay in ruins. Fragmented ownership raised thorny issues of control. What the teams of lawyers had so assiduously structured as a complementary public-private real estate transaction between the ground-owning Port Authority and the private leaseholders who would operate the towers somersaulted into a dysfunctional adversarial relationship. At Ground Zero there was no alignment of interest, no trust, no shared vision between these adversaries. The multiple different parties were "literally at war with one another," said Doctoroff. "The site taught me more than anything else how difficult it is to manage a set of government entities when no one is in charge," he said in a retrospective interview.[17]

The lack of alignment among stakeholders would make any large-scale public-private project difficult to execute; indeed, it is antithetical to the idea of a public-private venture. But in this fraught endeavor it was a crippling handicap. Although the transparency of the fragmented situation was well known, it was left in place under the pragmatic logic that reversing the site's split ownership would precipitate a costly and contentious process that would tie up the site in unknown years of litigation; at the same time, the governance issue was left unresolved. Any force of leadership had to fight against the politics of the complicated structure and its four central stakeholders—the Port Authority, the Silverstein Investor Partnership, the 9/11 families, and the City of New York—all of whom by dint of their position became adversaries as they pushed their individual ambitions for rebuilding Ground Zero. It was all a fight, a fight with its own set of costs and lost opportunities.

Rebuilding lacked a protocol. It was being figured out on the fly, and that proved to be not just imperfect, but inadequate. It was the structural flaw in the elaborate rebuilding effort. Public-private real estate ventures need to incorporate a protocol for the contingency of catastrophe, for determining who will be in charge and how major decisions will be made, including exiting the partnership. They need more than ideals, more than plans, and more than deals. The improvised protocol for rebuilding Ground Zero was left to the selective interference of the governor, whose executive leadership style conflicted with the imperative for clear direction and consistent leadership. So the public lost. The contractual obligations of the lease agreement gave the Port Authority legal control as owner of the land, but in the political and emotional exigency of the situation that control had to be renegotiated—and it was improvised. It was all very messy and very ugly. Mayor Bloomberg's control over the Memorial Foundation gave him a formal claim to decision-making at Ground Zero, and in combination with his political power and influence, leadership emerged, however belatedly. It was an important adjustment in the landscape of power, but it could not remediate the structural flaw that continued to bedevil the rebuilding process.

BEYOND REBUILDING

The experience at Ground Zero defined collective rights to symbolic territory. With the whole world watching, it legitimized a new set of voices claiming a right to influence decisions about what should happen on a site transformed by collective tragedy, sanctified by extraordinary loss. The rights were political. First accorded to citizens through a deliberate participatory planning process, they were then aggressively asserted by a vocal chorus of opposition to anything that threatened to overshadow the memory of those who perished. These political rights exerted enormous influence on the course of events, not just at the margins. The collective experiences proved that Ground Zero did not belong solely to those players whose property rights could be enforced in courts of law, but rather that the site, in the most fundamental sense, belonged to the city and its residents, the nation and its citizens.

Whether the public should have built under the footprints of the twin towers remains an issue for the historians of memory to debate. Perhaps we have should have waited until time presented an opportunity for deeper reflection on the meaning of 9/11 and what to memorialize, but patience in the throes of civic pain is an idealist virtue. Patience, moreover, is not what one thinks of as New York's compelling civic trait, not for a New York minute. In decades to come, the National September 11 Memorial together with the Memorial Museum may come to be seen as an outlandish planning gesture. We cannot know; its purpose now is well served. And meaningful to the millions of visitors who come to pay homage to the losses of that day. Surely, we cannot know what would have been different if the footprints had not been eliminated as development sites. Conversely, we know that the decision to build an entire servicing underground integrated into the site complete with a circulatory road system was an expedient decision from a security perspective, but whether it will prove to be wise in the long term is far less certain.

To a considerable degree, the experience at Ground Zero presents elected officials and policymakers with a question they are likely confront in future urban situations: What kind of governance structure is best suited for resolving conflicts across fragmented property rights and fragmented government power? Protocols are essential to fair and effective policy governance in situations of extreme civic distress, especially those that execute rebuilding through a formal public-private arrangement. Without a governance protocol, the ability to set priorities is absent.

At Ground Zero, the decision to reconstruct the site all at once, codified in plans and contractual agreements and promoted to the public at large, meant that politicians did not need to set priorities. It was both misleading and naïve. Strong positive leadership matched to a clear protocol for decision-making would have gone a long way to ironing out much angst and confusion, especially in a context as fragmented as that at Ground Zero.

To resolve the anomalous situation of a private player in a highly symbolic public space—a real estate partnership that held a contractual interest in the World Trade Center complex for only a short six weeks, then by default of tragedy became the developer at Ground Zero—public officials chose the pragmatic path. The lease agreement provided no structure for unwinding the relationship; that was a critical loose end of the 2001 transaction. Whether the long and litigious road of exercising eminent domain to take out the Silverstein partnership would have produced a better outcome stands as a hypothetical. Yet once the towers collapsed, the interests of the Port Authority and the Silverstein partnership at Ground Zero were misaligned. With Silverstein, the civic body had a developer not known for architectural creativity overlaid with a bureaucracy also not known for its architectural creativity. Could the LMDC have done it better? No. The city? Maybe.

There is a genuine set of reasons to applaud what has been achieved at Ground Zero. Yet that is not to say that the rebuild has delivered the same accolades that greeted the first images of what could be on those sixteen acres. What was built at Ground Zero reflects the Libeskind master plan only in the placement of buildings and the symbolic height of 1 World Trade Center. The composition of the whole has been lost to a collection of competing buildings, each fighting for attention (none of which were designed by the architect of the master plan). This is not totally unexpected, given the city's pattern of negotiated design guidelines and the Port Authority's overriding decision-making over the commercial agenda. "Silverstein asked various architects to build skyscrapers on the site, none of whom," remarked architectural critic Paul Goldberger, "have produced anything close to their best work." From the start, however, the planning evidenced a "determined rejection" of the mixed-use model, said the *Financial Times* critic Edwin Heathcote.[18] Except for the memorial mandate, for Silverstein and the Port Authority, Governor Pataki, and the downtown business community, it was always about maintaining the site as a commercial center, even as the area around it continued its transformation into a live-work-play district.

Is the public sector ever on a level playing field with an experienced private developer in complex property negotiations? No. But that is not really the issue. Government and the private sector work in different cultures, with different time horizons, different levels of information, different skill sets, and different bottom lines. There are projects that are too significant and too complex to allow private developers to control such a critical position as was the case at Ground Zero. Conversely, the business acumen of private development supplies a necessary economic discipline typically lacking in the public sector. Rebuilding at Ground Zero might have been privatized even further, by having a private entity take on building the transportation station and other elements of the master plan under the aegis of a strong set of governance arrangements. But that—ironically, given the mandate of privatization that resulted in Silverstein's ninety-nine-year leasehold position at the World Trade Center—was never given consideration.

In situations demanding extraordinary sensitivity, wisdom, and prescience for long-term planning, elected officials play critical roles, especially when matched against cumbersome bureaucracies bound by institutional prerogatives and calcified cultures. These government entities too have important roles to play in executing complex public initiatives, but they should not become substitutes for elected officials on big decisions, especially if strong accountability and transparency mechanisms are missing. At the same time, when elected officials delegate decision-making to these public entities, their powers should not be undermined by unilateral ad hoc decision-making.

New York City has thrived on making places a success, on maintaining its hold on the urban imagination through its panoply of diverse neighborhoods, as well as its skyline (plate 23). The historic lessons of rebuilding lower Manhattan will emerge more slowly than have the physical elements that now define the new World Trade Center. When the sixteen-acre precinct is fully populated and people build their daily patterns around it, it will be time to judge the results. The legacy of the place lies in how it becomes a vibrant part of lower Manhattan and how it contributes to New York City's historic economic trajectory. As policymakers, elected officials, and scholars consider how a great city responded to tragedy, there will be time to consider the deep and rich legacy of this rebuilding project.

EPILOGUE

THE PORT AUTHORITY'S SIGNATURE architectural contribution to lower Manhattan—the Oculus, centerpiece of its $4 billion Transportation Hub conceived as a "bird in flight" by Santiago Calatrava—opened to the public on March 3, 2016, in unusually quiet fashion (plate 21). No great fanfare, no public ceremony, no majestic banner of achievement heralded the long-awaited opening of this institutional phoenix. No politicians were on hand to offer praise. No doves of peace were released as at the project's groundbreaking in September 2005. The Hub's excessive cost and seven-year delay in opening checked the idea of a ribbon-cutting celebration of what the Port Authority's executive director, Patrick J. Foye, deemed a "symbol of excess." This was an odd position for the agency to take for such a high-profile project of civic significance. Reportedly, it appeared to reflect internal friction and was quickly reversed the next day when the chairman of the bi-state agency, John J. Degnan, announced that an opening ceremony would take place after all, in the coming spring with completion of the Oculus and its complement of access points. Then, he said, it would be time to express gratitude to the thousands who worked to build the complex and to highlight the Hub's symbolic significance in rebuilding in the wake of the 9/11 terrorist attack.

The March debut of the Oculus (with its underground passage to 4 World Trade Center) was the third in a sequence of partial openings of this vast and sprawling complex of concourses, mezzanines, and train platforms. The West Concourse, formerly the east-west connector, an elegant and cavernous 600-foot-long pedestrian underpass to Brookfield Place framed by a run of white columns joined to slanting white ceiling ribs, opened on October 24, 2013. Four months later, on February 15, 2014, it was Platform A for the Hoboken PATH, the first of four new island platforms for the WTC PATH station currently serving fifty thousand weekday commuters. The 365,000 square feet of retail space designed into the 800,000-square-foot Hub as a replacement for the mall destroyed on 9/11 was not scheduled to open until August 2016. The eastern part of the Oculus was still under construction as were connections to the eleven subways through the northern connector to the Dey Street passageway and the Fulton Street Transit Center. A quarry of beautiful Italian white marble cut with precision clads surfaces both horizontal and vertical as far and as wide as the eye can see, and beyond. All of that interior whiteness reflecting natural light flooding into the Oculus from the ribbon-of-glass skylight 160 feet above speaks to the ambition and extravagance of New York's newest civic monument—a civic cathedral for the twenty-first century. The absorbed stillness of this pure space is not yet inhabited by thousands hurrying to offices or connecting to subways or traversing to the Memorial Plaza. Yet even in this interim period of partial use, with children gliding on the buffed marble floors and adults quietly talking and teens lying about looking upward or taking selfies, the special place the Oculus is destined to occupy in the realm of the city is readily apparent.

Grand railway stations have been significant historical place makers for cities all over the world. Monuments to rail travel, they have always served a broader civic function, even when built by private railway corporations. The grandest of them—New York's Grand Central Terminal and its long-lost Penn Station, St. Pancras in London, Atocha Estachion in Madrid, Chhatrapati Shivaji Terminus in Mumbai, or Flinders Street Station in Melbourne, to name a few—captured the public imagination. They combined architectural design and engineering prowess on a monumental scale. They celebrated the importance of transportation in the life of a city, enabling it to thrive and grow. They anchored a locale and catalyzed development of its surrounding area. They established a centralizing place for gathering and created an urban crossroads. Notably, they stood majestically as a symbol of a city's power.

A visibly grand rail station like New York City's Penn Station was "unnecessary," wrote architectural historian Hilary Ballon. "The train tracks were four stories underground. Nothing above street level was needed for railroad operations. Functional requirements could have been met by covered entrances to the lower depths, like those to the subway. In short, a big station above ground was superfluous. From a real estate perspective, the optimal solution was to bury the station and build a skyscraper above it since rental income from the tower could finance the station's operating expenses." That was the economic approach, she observed, adopted twice on the West Side of lower Manhattan: first for construction of the original Hudson Terminal Buildings and again for their successor, the World Trade Center, which sat above the renamed PATH station.[1] The possibility of building atop a new PATH station at Ground Zero surfaced briefly in mid-2003; under prodding by Larry Silverstein, the *Times* reported, the Port Authority asked master planner Daniel Libeskind to consider adding an office tower above the new transit Hub train. The idea died quickly, however, as did Silverstein's efforts to move the Freedom Tower to the eastern portion of the site closer to the planned Transportation Hub. Both adjustments to the master plan would undermine the symbolic mandate of rebuilding Ground Zero.

None of the journalists and critics commenting on the opening of the Oculus missed the intent of its mandate. The winged structure was "brazenly spectacular," an "extravagantly idealistic creation unlike any in New York," "a unique and singular structure," "a product of hope and idealism." It was an expression of "aspiration and grandeur," "an architectural moment," "breathtaking from the inside—luminous, intricate, uplifting, and tranquil," a structure that "draws its real power from an unusual mixture of infrastructural scale and commemorative emotion."[2] Overall, however, the reactions were emphatically mixed, many severely critical. Where some saw "a monument to perseverance," others saw "a monument to excess." Where some saw "beauty" others saw "an epic boondoggle," "unconscionable waste," "a void in search of a purpose other than to connect a bunch of subways and pedestrian corridors and concourses with one another," "more of a shopping destination than a transport hub," "a monstrosity offensive both inside and out." Still others saw "a debacle of extraordinary scale," or what Calatrava built for Manhattan, "a little too similar" to his works in Lyon (1994), Milwaukee (2001), and Valencia (2009). The Hub was "structurally overwrought and emotionally underwhelming," "the apogee of a kind of architecture that wows rather than elevates."[3]

The sharply divergent reactions present a striking contrast to the universal acclaim that first greeted the images of Calatrava's vision for the Hub in January 2004, when the concept design promised a healing vision and inspired civic hope. Eleven years later the reactions to the Oculus encapsulate the many tensions surrounding rebuilding of the Trade Center site: the push for an architectural vision of civic resilience, the strained balance between commercial renewal and memorial remembrance, the excessive costs of ambition, and the disappointing performance of government in executing the master plan. Eleven years later, a lot has changed in lower Manhattan and the city at large. The emotionally charged atmosphere following 9/11 in which this project was conceived has passed, making it is impossible not to be more skeptical of what $4 billion delivered. By 2016, New Yorkers needed less symbolism and wanted greater functionality.

Every review raised the question of cost versus value. Yet when the $4 billion price tag is emphasized, most commentators implicitly assume that is the cost of the Oculus and PATH Hall. Construction of these two visible public spaces totaled nearly $1.1 billion, or 27 percent of the overall cost, according to the itemized list in the Port Authority's 2012 Revised and Restated Construction Agreement with the FTA; adding in the $451 million for customized structural steel brings this subtotal to $1.53 billion, a little more than 38 percent of the total. The rest of the cost went into the not-so-evident functional components of the total project—construction of the octopus-like pedestrian connections between PATH and eleven subway stations, mechanical and electrical systems, the East and West Bathtubs, and other unglamorous underground elements to service the site and create raw spaces for 365,000 square feet of retail stores. Line items in this accounting also include architectural engineering, design, project management, construction management, project administration, and program contingency, among others that make a project of this scope and architectural ambition hugely expensive.

The reviews are incomplete at this stage because they have focused only on particular elements—the Oculus, the West Concourse to Brookfield Place, and the PATH Hall—without giving credit to the sense of the whole and its contribution to transit connectivity downtown when the rest of the completed project becomes operational. So the critics are right—it is an outrageous amount of money for a relatively small number of people transiting through the Hub when compared to Penn Station or Grand Central Terminal. And they are wrong—the price tag includes the full scope of what makes for transit interconnectivity throughout lower Manhattan and beyond—decisions made by the Port Authority in the early stages of project conception—and that is no small achievement in a dense city like New York. Still, the cost for marble-clad connectivity is outrageously high.

Several critics put forth the position that if you can get yourself past the "insanely expensive" cost of the Oculus, "you can have an architectural experience there that may renew your faith in the potential of the public realm in New York." The Oculus, wrote Paul Goldberger, "is the exhilarating nave of a genuine people's cathedral." Hedging on the side of ambivalence, he went on to say that for all the billions of public money, "it's still a shrine to the commercial marketplace," but that "doesn't destroy the impact of the architecture, or negate the fact that this is the first time in half a century that New York City has built a truly sumptuous interior space for the benefit of the public." Echoing a similar line of argument in the concluding remarks of his overall laudatory review, design critic Justin Davidson wrote, "Cost is an objective fact; value isn't."[4]

If, however, you cannot overlook the cost issue and the opportunities forgone to improve and expand the capacity of New York City's transportation system—the lifeblood of its economic engine—the cost of the Calatrava Hub has implications for how one judges whether it is a success, whether it is a "boondoggle," "functionally vapid," or an exceptional twenty-first-century civic monument that embodies resolve, elevates the spirit, and instills optimism about the future. All the critics brought up issues with the design of the Oculus, but as Karrie Jacobs emphasized in her review, "the real problem has nothing to do with the design. Rather, it's the notion that some of those billions of dollars would be better spent elsewhere."[5] And there is no shortage of worthy transportation projects that would enhance the power of the New York City economy. It is both obvious and long-standing: rebuilding the "universally detested" Penn Station serving more than six hundred thousand daily commuters, completing the Second Avenue Subway line under discussion for nearly a century, redoing the "third-world" conditions of LaGuardia Airport, rebuilding the congested sixty-five-year-old Port Authority Bus Terminal, and joining all the other global cities with one-stop mass transit to a regional airport.

As a piece of civic sculpture, the WTC PATH Transportation Terminal will undoubtedly become a much-photographed city landmark. It will undoubtedly also become a collecting spot for people to enjoy the flood of light and unobstructed open space of the Oculus, to rendezvous with friends, to see others, and to be seen. That is the timeless element of being in a big urban public space. But as *Times* critic Michael Kimmelman cautioned in an intense conclusion to his review of the Oculus, "If the takeaway lesson from this project is that architects need a free pass, a vain, submissive client and an open checkbook to create a public spectacle, then the hub is a disaster for architecture and cities."[6]

It is too early to understand the full meaning of the Hub's civic value and to judge what kind of enduring role it will have in the cityscape. The mixed reviews that have accompanied its opening represent a search for meaning—first-draft thoughts about ways in which we might calibrate the unbridled cost of this civic structure against its limited functionality at this time when the missed transportation opportunities still sting. A full assessment of what $4 billion has produced lies in the future—by the way citizens and visitors regularly use the vast public space of the Oculus (which can be used for private events under the control of the Port Authority's retail operator, Westfield Group), how the enhanced transportation nexus impacts surrounding neighborhoods, and whether the structure itself becomes a beloved and timeless icon of the city. In that regard, the future of this particular piece of the new World Trade Center complex stands as a metaphor for the whole. As much as has been accomplished at Ground Zero by way of physical rebuilding, the enduring quality of what these sixteen acres will mean to the city and its citizens remains for time to reveal.

DRAMATIS PERSONAE

Positions and Roles during the Storyline of Rebuilding

MICHAEL ARAD, architect and designer of the 9/11 Memorial pools at Ground Zero.

CHARLES V. BAGLI, veteran *New York Times* reporter with an eye on the real estate business and its politics.

ROY BAHAT, policy staffer to Deputy Mayor Doctoroff credited with coming up with the idea for a swap of land between the Port Authority (site of the World Trade Center) and the city (land under LaGuardia and JFK Airports).

TOM A. BERNSTEIN, cofounder of the proposed International Freedom Center (with Peter W. Kunhardt), president of Chelsea Piers recreational complex, business partner of Roland Betts, and a longtime human rights advocate.

PAULA GRANT BERRY, former publishing executive, 9/11 family member, and LMDC board member, active in LMDC Family Advisory Committee, who served on the memorial design jury.

ROLAND W. BETTS, LMDC board member and chair of its site-planning committee; entrepreneur and developer of Chelsea Piers on the West Side of Manhattan.

MICHAEL R. BLOOMBERG, 108th mayor of the City of New York, serving three terms (2002–2014) as a Republican; presided over the city's economic recovery after 9/11; philanthropist entrepreneurial businessman who founded Bloomberg LP.

MAGGIE BOEPPLE, president of the WTC Performing Arts Center.

J. MAX BOND JR., architect and partner in Davis Brody Bond (DBB), associate architects for the memorial and design architects for the Memorial Museum at Ground Zero.

LEONARD BOXER, New York real estate attorney, lawyer for Larry Silverstein on the July 2001 transaction to acquire the ninety-nine-year lease on the World Trade Center.

ELIOT BROWN, journalist reporting on real estate for the *New York Observer*, then the *Wall Street Journal*.

AMANDA M. BURDEN, commissioner of city planning (2002–2013), during mayoral administration of Michael R. Bloomberg.

Debra Burlingame, writer of op-ed "The Great Ground Zero Heist" and the sister of one of the pilots whose hijacked American Airlines Flight 77 crashed into the Pentagon on 9/11.

John P. Cahill, top advisor and chief of staff for Governor Pataki and point person on Ground Zero for the governor.

Santiago Calatrava, architect-engineer designer of the World Trade Center Transportation Hub.

David M. Childs, Yale-educated architect, chairman emeritus of the architectural firm Skidmore, Owings & Merrill (SOM) best known for his design of 7 World Trade Center and 1 World Trade Center.

Christopher J. Christie, Republican governor of New Jersey (2010–2014), reelected to a second four-year term in 2014.

Bernard Cohen, first director of the Lower Manhattan Recovery Office (LMRO) specially created by the Federal Transit Administration (FTA) to monitor the federal government's grant funding of the five recovery transportation projects for lower Manhattan.

Anita F. Contini, LMDC vice president responsible for developing a process and implementation plan for the 9/11 Memorial, cultural, and civic programs at Ground Zero, and for managing the jury process to select a designer of the 9/11 Memorial.

Alexander Cooper, Yale-educated urban designer, architect, and partner in Cooper, Robertson & Partners, who worked with Brookfield Properties on ideas for rebuilding lower Manhattan after 9/11.

Jon S. Corzine, Democrat governor of New Jersey (2006–2010), former investment banker and CEO of Goldman Sachs (1994–1999), and U.S. senator (2001–2006).

Anthony R. Coscia, attorney and longtime-serving chairman of the Port Authority (April 2003–February 2011), appointed by successive New Jersey governors; presided over the board during the most turbulent periods of rebuilding the Trade Center site.

Steve Cuozzo, veteran journalist and op-ed writer for the *New York Post*.

Joseph C. Daniels, president and CEO of the private nonprofit National September 11 Memorial and Museum.

Steven M. Davis, architect and partner in Davis Brody Bond, associate architects for the 9/11 Memorial and design architects for the Memorial Museum.

Daniel L. Doctoroff, deputy mayor for economic development and rebuilding (2002–2008) during administration of Michael R. Bloomberg; managed the city's negotiations culminating in the 2006 realignment deal.

Robert R. Douglass, attorney, civic leader, chairman emeritus of the Alliance for Downtown New York and longtime associate of the Rockefeller family.

David W. Dunlap, veteran reporter for the *New York Times* covering issues of planning, preservation, and the built environment.

Douglas Durst, developer and scion of the family real estate firm, the Durst Organization; bought into ownership of 1 World Trade Center in 2010.

Stanton Eckstut, urban designer, architect, and partner in Ehrenkrantz Eckstut & Kuhn Architects hired by the Port Authority to do in-house transportation, infrastructure, and urban design planning for Ground Zero.

David Emil, president of the LMDC (April 2007–April 2015) and former owner of Windows on the World restaurant at the top of the North Tower, destroyed on 9/11.

James P. "Jamie" Fox, PANYNJ deputy director (November 2004–July 2007) appointed by New Jersey governor James McGreevey.

Patrick J. Foye, PANYNJ executive director (November 2011–), appointed by New York governor Andrew Cuomo.

Alexander Garvin, Yale-educated urban planner, educator, and author; LMDC vice president (February 2002–May 2003) in charge of coordinating planning for the Trade Center site.

Timothy J. Gilchrist, long-serving public-sector professional. At the state Department of Transportation, he was in charge of the rebuilding of West Street after 9/11. Involved in Ground Zero as deputy secretary for economic development and infrastructure in the short-lived Spitzer administration and a senior advisor to Governor Paterson.

Rudolph W. L. Giuliani, 107th mayor of the City of New York (1994–2001), Republican; gained international recognition for his leadership in the aftermath of the 9/11 attacks, sometimes referred to as "America's Mayor."

Alice M. Greenwald, director of the 9/11 Memorial Museum, appointed to that position after nineteen years at the U.S. Holocaust Museum as associate director for museum programs.

Edward Hayes, lawyer and journalist who represented Daniel Libeskind during the master plan competition, who was able to call Yale Law School classmate Governor George Pataki on his behalf.

Matthew Higgins, director of communications then chief operating officer at LMDC (November 2001–February 2004), former press secretary under Mayor Rudolph Giuliani, managing the global media response to the 9/11 attacks for New York City.

Thomas S. Johnson, banking chief executive (GreenPoint Financial Corporation and GreenPoint Bank, 1993–October 2004), 9/11 family member, and the first family member appointed to the LMDC board, who acted as a liaison to the families; also a board member of the 9/11 Memorial Foundation.

John P. L. Kelly, public affairs and communications professional, director of media relations at the Port Authority during the 2010 intense negotiations with Larry Silverstein; he had previously served as spokesman for the NYPD.

Daniel Libeskind, architect, selected winner of the competition to design a master plan for the Trade Center.

Nina Libeskind, wife and business partner of Daniel Libeskind, cofounder of Studio Daniel Libeskind.

John N. "Janno" Lieber, real estate executive at Silverstein Properties, responsible for the World Trade Center project.

Robert C. Lieber, former deputy mayor for economic development in the Bloomberg administration (January 2008–June 2010) and former investment banker with Lehman Brothers, managed the city's negotiations with Larry Silverstein culminating in the 2010 East Side Development Plan.

Frank J. Lombardi, PANYNJ chief engineer (August 1995–November 2010), who started work at the Port in 1971 as an engineering trainee.

Charles J. Maikish, first head of the Lower Manhattan Construction Command Center, long-serving former Port Authority employee, who was head of the WTC Department that managed the recovery after the 1993 terrorist attack.

Ira M. Millstein, attorney and nationally recognized expert in corporate governance.

Cherrie Nanninga, former director of real estate at PANYNJ and chief operating officer, CBRE.

Barry R. Ostrager, trial attorney (Simpson Thacher) and lead counsel for Swiss Re in the insurance-coverage battle with Larry Silverstein.

Robin Panovka, real estate attorney, Wachtell, Lipton, Rosen & Katz, a part of Silverstein's legal team.

George E. Pataki, three-term Republican governor of New York (1995–2006), who presided over the first five-plus years of the process of rebuilding Ground Zero.

David A. Paterson, Democrat governor of New York (March 2008–2010), during the turbulent period of battle between Silverstein and the Port Authority over subsidies for the commercial towers.

Seth Pinsky, president, New York City Economic Development Corporation (2008–2013, first hired as vice president in 2003), who played a key role in the 2006 and 2010 negotiations over the commercial program for rebuilding.

Steven P. Plate, deputy chief of capital planning and director of WTC Construction Department (2004–present), PANYNJ.

Max Protetch, New York gallery owner and dealer in contemporary art and architecture, curated a show of concepts for rebuilding the World Trade Center site from architects worldwide in 2002.

Stefan Pryor, LMDC executive director (May 2005–September 2006), appointed by Governor George Pataki.

Kevin M. Rampe, LMDC president (February 2003–May 2005), LMDC chairman (May 2006–April 207), appointed by Governor George Pataki; Memorial Foundation board member.

Kenneth J. Ringler Jr., PANYNJ executive director (October 2004–January 2007), appointed by Governor George Pataki.

E. John Rosenwald Jr., finance executive, philanthropist, and 9/11 Memorial Foundation board member.

Anthony J. Sartor, PANYNJ commissioner (NJ, 1999–2014, resigned), appointed by Republican governor Christine Whitman in 1999 and reappointed by Governors Donald DiFrancesco (R) and Jon Corzine (D).

Avi Schick, LMDC chairman (April 2007–April 2015), appointed by Governor Eliot Spitzer.

Charles E. Schumer, New York senior U.S. senator.

Frank J. Sciame Jr., construction management expert appointed by Governor George Pataki and Mayor Michael Bloomberg to lead effort to ensure a buildable WTC memorial by taking hold of a budget spiraling out of control.

Joseph J. Seymour, PANYNJ executive director (December 2001–October 2004), appointed by Governor George Pataki.

Anthony E. Shorris, PANYNJ executive director (January 2007–April 2008), appointed by Governor Eliot Spitzer.

Stephen Sigmund, chief of public affairs and government affairs (January 2006–October 2010), PANYNJ, and acting communications director for former Governor Jon Corzine.

Sheldon Silver, former New York State Assembly leader (1994–February 2015), representing Assembly District 65 in lower Manhattan (1976–November 2015).

Larry A. Silverstein, New York developer and holder of the ninety-nine-year lease on the World Trade Center in a partnership with other private investors.

Eliot L. Spitzer, Democrat governor of New York (January 2007–March 2008).

Nikki Stern, 9/11 family member and member of the LMDC Families Advisory Council, public relations and communications specialist.

Mary Ann Tighe, commercial real estate professional, CEO of New York Tri-State Region of CBRE.

Richard J. Tofel, president and chief operating officer of the International Freedom Center, former assistant publisher of the *Wall Street Journal*, and founding general manager of ProPublica, a nonprofit investigative journalism organization in New York.

LOUIS R. TOMSON, first president of the LMDC (January 2002–February 2003), appointed by Governor George Pataki.

HERBERT WACHTELL, founding partner of Wachtell, Lipton, Rosen & Katz, a part of Silverstein's legal team, and Larry Silverstein's friend since high school.

PETER WALKER, internationally known landscape architect asked to work with Michael Arad on the 9/11 Memorial.

CHRISTOPHER O. WARD, PANYNJ executive director (May 2008–October 2011), appointed by Governor David Paterson.

DREW S. WARSHAW, PANYNJ chief of staff (May 2008–November 2011) to executive director Chris Ward, intensely involved with the assessment review and strategy for reframing the implementation problems at Ground Zero.

CARL B. WEISBROD, long-serving LMDC board member appointed by Mayor Michael Bloomberg and president of the Alliance for Downtown New York during the early years of rebuilding, formerly president of the city's Economic Development Corporation and the Forty-second Street Development Project, among many other roles in both the public and private sectors.

JOHN C. WHITEHEAD, first chairman of the LMDC (November 2001–May 2006), appointed by Governor George Pataki, and founding chairman of the 9/11 Memorial Foundation (December 2004–May 2006).

MADELYN G. WILS, chair of Community Board 1 in lower Manhattan (2001–2005) when she was appointed to the LMDC board by Governor George Pataki; played an active role in the rebuilding process at Ground Zero and served as advocate for the downtown resident community of which she was a part.

KATHRYN S. WYLDE, long-serving president and CEO of the nonprofit Partnership for the City of New York, the city's leading organization for the business community.

ROBERT D. YARO, president of the Regional Plan Association (2001–2014), who was an active force behind the Civic Alliance, strategizing its role in the planning dialogue for lower Manhattan after 9/11.

JOHN E. ZUCCOTTI, chairman of Brookfield Properties, attorney, advocate for lower Manhattan, and respected former public official, who served as the first deputy mayor of New York City (1975–1977) and chairman of the City Planning Commission (1973–1975), among many other professional positions.

LIST OF SOURCE ABBREVIATIONS

ABNY	Association for a Better New York
ACHP	Advisory Council on Historic Preservation
AP	Associated Press
BBB	Beyer Blinder Bell
CA	Construction agreement
CM/GC	Construction manager/general contractor
Crain's	*Crain's New York Business*
DBB	Davis Brody Bond
DCP	Department of City Planning, City of New York
DLMA	Downtown–Lower Manhattan Association
DN	*Daily News* [New York]
DOT	Department of Transportation
EDC	Economic Development Corporation, City of New York
EIS	Environmental impact statement
ESDC	Empire State Development Corporation
FEMA	Federal Emergency Management Agency
FHWA	Federal Highway Administration
FOI	Freedom of Information
FRBNY	Federal Reserve Bank of New York
FTA	Federal Transit Administration
GAO	Government Accounting Office
GPP	*General Project Plan*
GSA	Government Services Administration
LMCCC	Lower Manhattan Construction Command Center
LMDC	Lower Manhattan Development Corporation
LMRO	Lower Manhattan Recovery Office
MAS	Municipal Art Society
MDA	Master Development Agreement
MOA	Memorandum of agreement
MOU	Memorandum of understanding
MTA	Metropolitan Transportation Authority
NEPA	National Environmental Policy Act

NYC	New York City
NYC IBO	New York City Independent Budget Office
NYFD	New York Fire Department
NYNV	New York New Visions
NYO	*New York Observer*
NYP	*New York Post*
NYS	New York State
NYS	*New York Sun*
NYSHPO	New York State Historic Preservation Office
NYT	*New York Times*
PA	Port Authority
PANYNJ	Port Authority of New York and New Jersey
PATH	Port Authority Trans-Hudson
PBS	Public Broadcasting System
PILOT	Payment in lieu of taxes
PMOC	Project manager oversight contractor
REBNY	Real Estate Board of New York
RFP	Request for Proposals
RPA	Regional Plan Association of New York
SOM	Skidmore, Owings & Merrill
SPI	Silverstein Properties, Inc.
UPI	United Press International
VSC	Vehicle Security Center
WFC	World Financial Center [Brookfield Center]
WSJ	*Wall Street Journal*
WTC	World Trade Center

SELECTIVE CHRONOLOGY OF THE REBUILDING OF THE WORLD TRADE CENTER SITE: 2001–2016

2001

July   The Port Authority of New York and New Jersey (PA) net leases the office towers and retail areas of the World Trade Center (WTC) to an investment partnership led by New York developer Larry A. Silverstein in a historic transaction valued at $3.21 billion.

September   Two hijacked jets ram into the twin towers of the WTC causing the death of more than twenty-eight hundred people and widespread destruction in lower Manhattan.

President George W. Bush pledges $20 billion in federal funds to help the city of New York recover and rebuild.

November   Silverstein initiates litigation with his insurers over insurance payouts for business interruption and casualty destruction, claiming that the 9/11 terrorist attack constitutes two "occurrences," which if successful would mean a maximum payout of $7.1 billion to finance his rebuilding obligations.

Governor George E. Pataki creates the Lower Manhattan Development Corporation (LMDC), a subsidiary of the Empire State Development Corporation (ESDC), to oversee the rebuilding of the Trade Center site and the revitalization of lower Manhattan.

December   Work crews pull down the last standing piece of the twin towers, four stories of steel known as "the shroud."

2002

May   The PA and LMDC choose Beyer Blinder Belle (BBB) (assisted by Parsons Brinckerhoff and eleven other specialty and engineering firms) to conduct an integrated urban design and planning study for the Trade Center site.

The WTC recovery operation comes to a ceremonial end, marking the completion of the removal of more than one million tons of concrete and steel.

June   Governor Pataki says that no building will occur where the twin towers stood, thereby declaring the footprints of the twin towers sacred ground.

July   The LMDC and PANYNJ unveil BBB's six concept plans for the Trade Center site. Approximately forty-five hundred attending "Listening to the City" at the Jacob Javits Convention Center give a clear thumbs down to these plans. LMDC officials respond by saying they will consider new options for the site, including scaling back on the amount of commercial space.

August   Deputy Mayor for Economic Development and Rebuilding Daniel L. Doctoroff publicly proposes to trade the city-owned land occupied by LaGuardia and Kennedy Airports in exchange for the PA's ownership of the WTC site. After much discussion, the proposal dies eight months later.

Federal, state, and city officials announce success in securing $4.55 billion in federal funds for transportation projects for lower Manhattan.

LMDC officials launch a second attempt to select a plan for rebuilding at Ground Zero with a new worldwide "innovative design study" for the site.

September   LMDC officials select 6 out of 406 architectural teams who submitted responses to the "innovative design study" RFP.

November   Silverstein announces plans for the first major rebuilding project, 7 World Trade Center adjacent to the sixteen-acre site.

December   Mayor Michael R. Bloomberg unveils his *Vision for the 21st Century for Lower Manhattan*.

2003

February   The LMDC announces the selection of Studio Daniel Libeskind's *Memory Foundations* as the master plan design concept for the site.

March   City officials propose a broad revamping of the LMDC that would give it more authority over the reconstruction of the site, as well as control over the federal recovery money.

April   Governor Pataki announces his commitment to an "aggressive timetable" for rebuilding.

July	The PA chooses Santiago Calatrava to design a transportation hub for the site.
September	The LMDC expands the site for rebuilding with the inclusion of blocks south of Liberty Street.
November	After a renovation effort that took sixteen months and cost $323 million, the PA opens the temporary PATH station at the WTC site.
December	After a bitter public dispute between architects David Childs and Daniel Libeskind, a compromise design for the Freedom Tower is unveiled at the Federal Hall National Memorial in lower Manhattan. The PA completes a series of transactions to buy out the WTC interests of Host Marriott, Westfield America, and the federal government's GSA; repay Silverstein's acquisition mortgage on the Trade Center; and pay out nearly all of the equity to Silverstein and his investors that they had invested to gain ninety-nine-year control of the World Trade Center office towers.

2004

January	The memorial jury chooses *Reflecting Absence* by Michael Arad and Peter Walker, after the young unknown architect was required to add a leading landscape architect to his team and make revisions to the design for the memorial.
	Architect Santiago Calatrava unveils his design for the WTC Transportation Hub.
February	Officials of the LMDC and Federal Transit Administration and Federal Highway Administration determine that the WTC site is eligible for listing on the National Register of Historic Places.
April	A win for insurers in the WTC insurance litigation results in a maximum insurance payout of $4.675 billion for Silverstein, if the developer wins every subsequent legal battle.
June	The LMDC announces the selection of four groups for the WTC cultural complex: the Joyce International Dance Center, International Freedom Center (IFC), Signature Theater, and Drawing Center.
July	A symbolic cornerstone-laying ceremony for the Freedom Tower is held at Ground Zero.
November	Stakeholders enter into formal agreements on the details of a master plan for rebuilding the Trade Center site.
December	Silverstein gains his first insurance victory in his thirty-eight-month battle with insurers.

2005

April   The NYPD formally raises security issues about Freedom Tower. In June, a revised design for the tower is released with unprecedented life safety and security features.

May   Rebuilding officials unveil the design for the WTC Cultural Center, which will house the site's visitor center, IFC, and Drawing Center.

June   The *WSJ* publishes "The Great Ground-Zero Heist," an op-ed by Debra Burlingame, which sets off a high-profile controversy over plans for the cultural program at the site.

Governor Pataki lays out content criteria for the "sacred ground" of the memorial quadrant, saying, "We will not tolerate anything on that site that denigrates America, denigrates New York or freedom, or denigrates the sacrifice and courage that the heroes showed on Sept. 11."

July   The families of the 9/11 victims call for a memorial fundraising boycott until the International Freedom Center and Drawing Center are eliminated from the site.

The PA Board of Commissioners authorizes the $2.221 billion WTC Transportation Hub project, and construction begins in September.

September   Governor Pataki evicts the IFC from the WTC site.

October   Running for his second term, Mayor Bloomberg stakes out a public position, vowing a bigger role in Ground Zero rebuilding.

December   A high-profile dispute breaks out between Governor Pataki and Mayor Bloomberg over the allocation of tax-exempt Liberty Bonds to be used to rebuild the office towers at Ground Zero.

Silverstein is under pressure to cede part of the Trade Center site. Pataki gives Silverstein and the PA ninety days to resolve their differences and come to an agreement on rebuilding. The deadline does not produce a deal until April 2006.

2006

February   Several hundred police officers, firefighters, emergency workers, and 9/11 families rally to oppose the memorial's underground location.

City Hall goes public with its financial analysis of Silverstein's ability to rebuild all ten million square feet of office space and its doubts that the developer can fulfill his obligations to rebuild.

March   Governor Pataki's senior advisor for counterterrorism, James K. Kallstrom, concludes that the memorial design leaves it vulnerable to a terrorist attack and offers suggestions to reduce the risks.

April	Governor Pataki of New York, Governor Jon Corzine of New Jersey, and Mayor Bloomberg reach accord on a "Unified Financial Plan" for rebuilding at Ground Zero—without Silverstein at the negotiating table—after three weeks of behind-the-scenes negotiations.
	The PA begins construction on the Freedom Tower.
	Mayor Bloomberg visibly takes charge of the memorial cost crisis, which has been simmering since the fall of 2005.
May	7 World Trade Center opens.
	The Memorial Foundation indefinitely suspends fundraising until the costs of the memorial project are resolved.
June	The LMDC approves a scaled-back, less expensive plan for the 9/11 Memorial. The new design brings the display of victims' names up to the street level and shrinks the size of the underground museum. The PA agrees to take responsibility for construction of the 9/11 Memorial and Memorial Museum.
July	LMDC announces to its staff that its work will soon end and its duties allocated to other authorities, but as it is a big symbol of state control, this does not come about.
September	The PA and Silverstein finalize a series of agreements formally re-aligning roles in rebuilding the site. Under the Master Development Agreement, the PA will build the Freedom Tower and Tower 5, and Silverstein Properties will build Towers 2, 3, and 4.
	Governor Pataki announces start of deconstruction of 130 Liberty Street to be carried out in two phases and completed by the end of 2006. Several events intervene, including a tragic fire that kills two firefighters, and the deconstruction is not complete until February 2011.
	The city assumes responsibility for the ongoing planning, design, development, and construction of the Performing Arts Center at the site in an agreement with the LMDC.
October	Mayor Bloomberg is named chairman of the World Trade Center Memorial Foundation.
December	The controversy over the arrangement of names on the parapets surrounding the memorial pools is resolved.

2007

| February | News report discloses that the projected cost for the Calatrava-designed Transportation Hub has soared to $3.4 billion, which is beyond the estimated range of $2.2–$2.5 billion approved by the PA Board of Commissioners. |

May	The administration of Governor Eliot L. Spitzer announces a final settlement of all Silverstein's insurance claims at Ground Zero.
June	The PA Board of Commissioners authorizes the agency to enter into a long-term subnet lease with J. P. Morgan Chase to develop Tower 5 as a 1.3-million-square-foot skyscraper, but this deal fails to materialize after the financial-services giant acquires Bear Stearns and its newly constructed headquarters in midtown Manhattan.
July	The PA Board of Commissioners authorizes a preliminary agreement with the Hellenic Orthodox Church St. Nicholas for a new location and the construction of a new church building on the southern WTC site, but talks collapse in March 2009.
August	Governor Spitzer's office announces a solution to the "Survivors' Staircase" issue: all thirty-eight stairs will be moved off the Tower 2 site and set into a flight of steps in the Memorial Museum.

2008

January	The PA begins paying penalties of $300,000 per day to Silverstein Properties for missing its contractual deadline to complete site excavation and preparation for two of the developer's office towers.
	The Westfield Group and the PA agree to a $1.45 billion partnership to develop and operate about 500,000 square feet of shops and restaurants at Ground Zero.
June	Newly appointed PA executive director Christopher O. Ward presents his initial report on construction problems at the site and promises a detailed review of delays and cost overruns and a new schedule in ninety days.
July	Merrill Lynch ends talks on moving to Ground Zero.
September	New design by Snøhetta for the Memorial Museum pavilion is unveiled.
October	The PA releases *A Roadmap Forward*, laying out a new timetable for construction at Ground Zero. Reconstruction of the site is expected to take up to two years longer than last projected and likely to cost an additional $1.5 billion.
November	Silverstein serves the PA with notices of arbitration to resolve disputes over construction-ready delivery of the sites for Tower 2 and Tower 4.

December	Silverstein's plans for rebuilding are interrupted by the Great Recession.

2009

March	Silverstein asks the government to finance the development of at least two of his three tower obligations; the PA considers helping with one.
	The PA changes the name of the Freedom Tower to 1 World Trade Center, saying this will make the building more marketable for commercial tenants.
May	Mayor Bloomberg holds a "summit" meeting at Gracie Mansion attended by the stakeholders. The summit produces another deadline, June 11, for a solution-resolution to the financing conflict, but this deadline comes and goes without a resolution.
June	Negotiations between Silverstein and the PA reach a stalemate.
August	Silverstein initiates binding-arbitration proceedings with the PA to resolve the financing dispute and schedule for the development of Towers 2, 3, and 4.
October	Following a request from Governor David A. Paterson, the PA Board of Commissioners authorizes $20 million to allow consultants to modify certain components of the WTC Hub and permit the PA to complete the construction of the public components of the site independent of Silverstein's construction of Towers 2, 3, and 4.

2010

January	After a three-month process, arbitrators issue their ruling that favors the PA's claims and give both sides forty-five days to come up with a new schedule for erecting Towers 2, 3, and 4.
March	Both sides inform the arbitrators that they have been unable to reach an agreement but are continuing to talk.
August	Plans for an Islamic cultural center and mosque in the vicinity of Ground Zero ignite intense controversy.
	After eighteen months of dissension and negotiation, officials of the states of New York and New Jersey, the City of New York, the Port Authority and Silverstein Properties announce agreement on a development plan for the east side of the World Trade Center site.

The Durst Organization, a New York–based family real estate company, buys into the 1 World Trade Center partnership with the PA, with a $100 million investment, becoming its managing partner.

October   The LMDC agrees to fund $100 million for the Performing Arts Center at Ground Zero.

2011

February   The PA Board of Commissioners reauthorizes the World Trade Center Transportation Hub project at a total estimated project cost of $3.44 billion, an increase of $180 million over the previously authorized project.

May   A watershed transaction for rebuilding, Condé Nast signs a twenty-five-year lease for one million square feet at 1 WTC, approximately one-third of the tower.

September   The Memorial Plaza opens at Ground Zero on the tenth anniversary of 9/11.

October   The PA and the Hellenic Orthodox Church St. Nicholas reach agreement on a series of transactions that will result in the construction of a new church on a portion of the site at 130 Liberty Street.

November   The dispute over cost overruns between PA and the Memorial Foundation delays the intended 2012 opening of the 9/11 Memorial Museum.

2012

February   The PA Board of Commissioners approves a joint venture with Westfield Group to develop, lease, and operate more than 450,000 square feet of retail and dining space at the site.

2013

March   The PA Board of Commissioners approves the selection of Legends Hospitality to develop and operate the observation deck at the top of 1 World Trade Center.

November   Tower 4 developed by Silverstein opens.
Chicago-based Council on Tall Buildings rules the 1,776-foot 1 World Trade Center to be the tallest tower in the Western Hemisphere.

December   The PA Board of Commissioners approves the sale of the remaining interest in the retail joint venture to Westfield Group; the venture is now valued at $1.6 billion.

2014

May   The National September 11 Memorial Museum opens.
November   1 World Trade Center opens.

2015

May   One World Observatory opens.
July   The Performing Arts Center is scaled back yet again and a $200 million budget established.

2016

March   The Permanent PATH Transportation Hub at the World Trade Center opens.

NOTE ON THE AUTHOR'S SOURCES OF INFORMATION

Following convention typical of trade books, I have built sources into the text for much of the material used in my research. For attributed quotes, full citations are in chapter notes. Many people spoke to me off the record and requested confidentiality, and I have honored their requests. The chapter notes also contain much of the more technical explanations of real estate finance and deal-related considerations, as well as contextual descriptions and expansions.

Listed below are the most pertinent primary documents related the rebuilding story. It is by no means a complete record of all the works and sources I consulted in my research. Of note, the thousands of newspaper articles, hundreds of editorials, and scores of press releases, RFPs, public hearing testimonies, public-dialogue reports, economic reports, speeches, design statements, and other documents I reviewed have been excluded from this listing; when used for quoted material, specific citations are in the chapter notes. Also excluded are complete lists of the monthly or quarterly board minutes of meetings of the LMDC (as well as its advisory councils), PANYNJ, and WTC Memorial Foundation, all of which were essential to understanding these decision-making bodies. In addition, numerous civic organizations issued reports and summaries of public events (Civic Alliance, Municipal Art Society, Partnership for the City of New York, and the Regional Plan Association, among others) that were important to understanding the public dialogue on rebuilding, especially in the first years after 9/11 when planning was in flux. Important data are also available in the offering documents for the Liberty Bonds used to finance the development of the office towers. To secure the documents needed for this research, Freedom of Information requests to the PANYNJ, the LMDC, and City Hall were essential.

The primary documents listed below are organized by project, in chronological order within. The list is intended to serve as a starting point for those who wish to pursue the study of public policy for city building and the politics of urban development, especially the politics of New York City. A complete bibliography is available on my personal website.

SELECTIVE PRIMARY DOCUMENTS

Planning for Rebuilding

PANYNJ and LMDC, "Cooperation Agreement," May 10, 2002.

LMDC, *Principles and Revised Preliminary Blueprint for the Future of Lower Manhattan*, June 5, 2002.

LMDC, *Request for Qualifications, Innovative Design Study for the World Trade Center Site*, August 2002.

New York City Office of the Mayor, *New York City's Vision for Lower Manhattan*, December 2002.

LMDC, *World Trade Center Site Memorial Competition Guidelines*, April 2003.

PANYNJ and LMDC, "Memorandum of Understanding" [regarding cooperation to implement the Studio Daniel Libeskind master plan], June 16, 2003.

LMDC, *Invitation to Cultural Institutions for the World Trade Center Site*, June 30, 2003.

FTA, FHWA, and LMDC, "Coordinated Determination of National Register Eligibility—World Trade Center Site, New York City, New York," March 31, 2004.

Letter to John Whitehead and Kevin Rampe [LMDC] from City Planning Commissioner Amanda Burden, ACIP, regarding review of the *General Project Plan for the World Trade Center Site*, March 8, 2004.

LMDC, *World Trade Center Memorial and Redevelopment Plan: Final Generic Environmental Impact Statement*, April 2004.

PANYNJ and City of NY, "World Trade Center Redevelopment Agreement," including "Attachment A: World Trade Center Design and Site Agreement," November 24, 2004.

LMDC, *World Trade Center Memorial and Cultural Program, General Project Plan*, June 2, 2004, as amended February 14, 2007.

WTC Memorial and Memorial Museum

NYSHPO and LMDC, "World Trade Center Memorial and Redevelopment Plan Programmatic Agreement" [section 106], April 22, 2004.

LMDC, PANYNJ, and WTC Memorial Foundation, "Memorandum of Understanding" [regarding three-way exchange and transfer of property interests to accommodate redevelopment plan for the WTC site], February 1, 2006.

Frank J. Sciame, "World Trade Center Memorial Draft Recommendations and Analysis," n.d. [June 20, 2006]

PANYNJ, LMDC, WTC Memorial Foundation, and City of NY, "World Trade Center Memorial/Cultural Project Agreement," July 6, 2006.

PANYNJ and WTC Memorial Foundation, "Memorandum of Understanding" [regarding memorial construction cost overruns], September 10, 2012.

Cultural Program

LMDC, "Report on the Memorial Center and Cultural Complex at the World Trade Center Site," February 10, 2004.

International Freedom Center, "Content and Governance Report," September 23, 2005.

Infrastructure / Construction / PATH Transportation Hub

FTA and PANYNJ, *Permanent WTC PATH Terminal Project Development Agreement*, February 14, 2004.

FTA, NYSHPO, ACHP, and PANYNJ, "Memorandum of Agreement Regarding the WTC Transportation Hub" [related to section 106 review], April 2005.

FTA, PANYNJ, and PATH, *Permanent WTC PATH Terminal Final Environmental Statement*, May 2005.

PANYNJ, *WTC Report Assessment* ["Ward Report No. 1"], June 30, 2008.

PANYNJ, WTC Design and Construction Analysis, HUB Working Group, *Steering Committee Report*, September 25, 2008.

PANYNJ, *WTC Report: A Roadmap Forward* ["Ward Report No. 2"], October 2, 2008.

PANYNJ and FTA, "Permanent WTC PATH Terminal Construction Agreement," May 2006; Revised and Restated Construction Agreement, September 2012.

Commercial Towers

PANYNJ, Letter agreement regarding the use of insurance payments and advances ["swap agreement"] with WTC leaseholders c/o Silverstein Properties, December 1, 2003.

WTC Arbitration No. 1, "Decision," December 11, 2008.

WTC Arbitration No. 2, "Decision, Interim Award, and Supplemental Order," January 22, 2010.

1 World Trade

PANYNJ, "Freedom Tower Project Authorization," staff presentation and minutes of the board meeting, February 22, 2007.

PANYNJ, Minutes of the board meeting authorizing joint venture with the Durst Organization, August 5, 2010; update, June 25, 2011.

PANYNJ, Minutes of the board meeting authorizing joint venture with Westfield, February 9, 2012; December 4, 2013.

PANYNJ, Minutes of the board meeting authorizing lease agreement with Legends for Observation Deck Space, March 20, 2013, and slide deck presentation.

Silverstein Towers

NYC EDC, "World Trade Center Site Summary of Financial Analysis," presented to the New York City Council, March 2006.

SPI, Letter to Anthony R. Coscia and Kenneth J. Ringler [PANYNJ], re WTC revised "Conceptual Framework" ["2006 deal"] for the redevelopment of the WTC site, April 26, 2006.

PANYNJ, Minutes of the Board of Commissioners meeting authorizing the "Conceptual Framework" agreement ["2006 deal"], September 21, 2006.

PANYNJ and SPI, "Master Development Agreement for Towers 2/3/4 of the World Trade Center," November 16, 2006.

PANYNJ, Minutes of the Board of Commissioners special meeting authorizing the WTC East Side Development Plan ["2010 deal"], August 26, 2010; update, November 18, 2010; Tower 4 Liberty Bonds Update, October 20, 2011; Tower 3 update, June 25, 2014; December 10, 2015.

LIST OF INTERVIEWS

Position listed in reference to roles in the rebuilding of the World Trade Center or other expertise relevant to the story; also see "Dramatis Personae." In addition to those listed, several interviews, conducted in complete confidence, are not listed. Because of their untimely passing, I missed interviews with Louis R. Tomson (first president, LMDC) and Max Bond (architect, 9/11 Memorial Museum). Informal conversations were held with many others involved with rebuilding the WTC site, including Peter Walker (landscape architect) and Robin Panovka (real estate lawyer, Wachtell, Lipton, Rosen & Katz, for Larry Silverstein). Others declined to speak with me (Michael Arad, Santiago Calatrava), and though I tried several times through several high-level channels, I was unable to secure an interview with former mayor Michael Bloomberg.

Charles V. Bagli, veteran reporter, New York Times.

Roy Bahat, senior policy director, Office of Deputy Mayor Daniel Doctoroff (February 2002–November 2003).

Tom A. Bernstein, cofounder of the proposed International Freedom Center, 9/11 Memorial Foundation board member (2005).

Paula Grant Berry, LMDC board member, 9/11 family member.

Roland W. Betts, LMDC board member (November 2001–October 2005) and chair of its site planning committee.

Jack Beyer and John Bell, architects and cofounders, Beyer Blinder Bell Architects and Planners, LLC, consultants for the first set of plans for Ground Zero.

Maggie Boepple, president of the WTC Performing Arts Center.

Leonard Boxer, New York real estate attorney (partner, Stroock & Stroock & Laven LLP) for Larry Silverstein on the July 2001 WTC transaction.

Eliot Brown, reporter (New York Observer, Wall Street Journal) covering commercial real estate.

John P. Cahill, senior advisor to the governor, then secretary–chief of staff to Governor George Pataki (February 2001–2007), attorney (Chadbourne & Parke LP), WTC Memorial Foundation director (2006–present).

David M. Childs, architect and chairman emeritus, Skidmore, Owings & Merrill LLP, designers of 1 World Trade Center and 7 World Trade Center.

Martin J. Cicco, investment banker, former head of real estate at Merrill Lynch.

Bernard Cohen, first director of the FTA Lower Manhattan Recovery Office (January 2004–December 2006).

Anita F. Contini, LMDC vice president and director, memorial, cultural, and civic programs (August 2002–July 2005).

Kevin S. Corbett, operating officer and executive vice president, ESDC, and executive deputy commissioner of the NYS Department of Economic Development (1999–December 2005); executive director of PA affairs, acting for the governor's office (1995–1999).

Anthony R. Coscia, PANYNJ chairman (April 2003–June 2011), attorney and partner (Windells Marx Lane & Mittendorf, LLP).

Steve Cuozzo, longtime op-ed columnist and reporter, New York Post.

Joseph C. Daniels, lawyer, and president and CEO, National September 11 Memorial and Museum (formerly WTC Memorial Foundation) (October 2006–present), previously general counsel and acting president and CEO.

Peter W. Davidson, executive director (2009–2011), ESDC.

Steven M. Davis, architect and partner, David Brody Bond LLP, designers of the 9/11 Memorial Museum.

Daniel L. Doctoroff, NYC deputy mayor for rebuilding and economic development (2002–2008, Bloomberg administration).

Robert R. Douglass, civic leader, chairman of the Alliance for Downtown New York, LMDC board member (November 2005–present), director emeritus, former secretary to Governor Nelson Rockefeller.

David W. Dunlap, veteran reporter for *New York Times*.

Douglas Durst, New York real estate developer, chairman and third-generation head of the Durst Organization, partner with PANYNJ in 1 World Trade Center.

Craig Dykers, architect and founding partner, Snøhetta, designers of the 9/11 Museum Pavilion.

Stanton Eckstut, architect and urban designer, consultant for the PANYNJ on a master plan for rebuilding the site.

Martin Edelman, real estate attorney and commercial real estate business expert (of counsel, Paul, Hastings, Janofsky & Walker LLP).

David Emil, president LMDC (April 2007–April 2015) and former owner of Windows on the World, restaurant at the top floors of the North Tower of the WTC destroyed on 9/11.

James P. "Jamie" Fox, deputy executive director (November 2004–July 2007), PANYNJ.

Patrick J. Foye, executive director (November 2011–present), PANYNJ.

John Gallagher, director of communications: LMDC (May 2005–May 2006), office of Mayor Bloomberg (February 2006–May 2008), Tishman Construction (September 2008–July 2012).

Alexander Garvin, urban planner, LMDC vice president and director of planning and design (February 2002–May 2003).

Timothy J. Gilchrist, senior advisor for transportation and infrastructure, Governor David Paterson (February 2009–July 2010).

Patricia Goldstein, real estate finance expert, vice chair and head of commercial real estate, Emigrant Savings Bank.

Barry M. Gosin, New York real estate professional, CEO Newmark Grubb Knight Frank; testified at City Council March 2006 hearings on WTC rebuilding.

Lawrence F. Graham, executive vice president, development, Brookfield Office Properties (1996–2011).

Jeffrey Green, general counsel (July 2991–October 2004), special counsel (October 2004–October 2009), PANYNJ.

Alice M. Greenwald, executive vice president for programs and director of the 9/11 Memorial Museum (April 2006–present).

Jordan Gruzen, architect, actively involved with New York New Visions.

Gary Hack, urban designer and city planner on the Libeskind Master Plan team.

Craig Hatkoff, real estate professional and entrepreneur, Tribeca Film Festival.

Woody Heller, real estate professional, executive managing director, capital transactions group head, Savills Studley.

Matthew Higgins, vice president of communications (November 2001–February 2004), LMDC.

Erik Horvat, director, WTC redevelopment department (July 2011–July 2014), PANYNJ.

Kenneth T. Jackson, Jacques Barzun Professor of History and the Social Sciences and director, Herbert H. Lehman Center for the Study of American History, Columbia University; editor in chief, *Encyclopedia of New York City*.

Todd D. Jick, consultant facilitator on memorial issues for LMDC.

Thomas S. Johnson, LMDC board member (May 2002–present), 9/11 Memorial Foundation board member, family member.

Hugh Kelly, real estate market expert, consultant to Silverstein Properties on insurance and arbitration issues.

John P. L. Kelly, director of media relations and acting chief, public affairs (2009–2011), PANYNJ; media relations and writer, NYPD (December 2003–2009).

Marcie Kesner, city planner and leadership participant, New York New Visions.

Jenna LaPietra, WTC manager—retail redevelopment (July 2002–November 2006), PANYNJ.

Peter M. Lehrer, construction management expert in large-scale complex construction projects, cofounder of Lehrer McGovern and founder of Lehrer, LLC.

Daniel Libeskind, architect, winner of the Innovative Design Study competition (master plan).

John N. "Janno" Lieber, president of World Trade Center Properties, an affiliate of Silverstein Properties, Inc.

Robert C. Lieber, NYC deputy mayor for economic development (January 2008–June 2010, Bloomberg administration).

Frank J. Lombardi, long-serving engineer, chief engineer (August 1995–November 2010), PANYNJ.

David Lombino, reporter, New York Sun.

Joseph Macnow, real estate professional, executive vice president and chief financial officer, Vornado Realty Trust.

Peter Madonia, former chief of staff for Mayor Michael Bloomberg (2002–January 2006), senior advisor to the Bloomberg campaign for mayor.

Charles J. Maikish, first executive director, Lower Manhattan Construction Command Center (2005–2007), long-serving staff, PANYNJ (1968–1995), including director of the WTC Department and manager of the recovery after the 1993 terrorist bombing on the WTC.

Jeffrey Mandel, senior policy advisor to Deputy Mayor for Economic Development Robert K. Steel (June 2010–December 2013, Bloomberg administration).

Marvin Markus, municipal finance expert and managing director, Goldman Sachs.

Charles McCafferty, former chief financial officer (1994–2003), PANYNJ.

Benjamin McGrath, real estate finance professional, managed Chemical Securities 1995 analysis of WTC privatization.

Robert A. McNamara CEO of Lend Lease America, construction manager for the 9/11 Memorial and Museum.

Dara McQuillan, chief marketing officer, Silverstein Properties, Inc.

Julie Menin, chair of Community Board 1 (June 2005–June 2012).

Michael Mennella, construction manager expert and executive vice president, Tishman Construction.

Ira M. Millstein, attorney (Weil, Gotshal & Manges LLP), pro bono counsel to the LMDC board of directors, and 9/11 Memorial Foundation board member.

Jeffrey A. Moerdler, attorney (partner, Mintz, Levin, Cohn, Ferris, Glovsky and Popeo, PC), PANYNJ board commissioner appointed by Governor David Paterson (April 2010–June 2015).

Mitchell Moss, urban planning professor (NYU), policy advisor to the Bloomberg administration.

Cherrie Nanninga, director of real estate (1998–2002), PANYNJ; chief operating officer (July 2002–April 2014), CBRE TriState.

Barry R. Ostrager, attorney (partner, Simpson Thacher & Bartlett LLP), lead counsel for Swiss Re in the WTC insurance battle.

Coburn Packard, real estate associate at Lehman Brothers (1998–2009), worked on the pro bono analysis of rebuilding feasibility for NYC.

Anne Papageorge, landscape architect, senior vice president, and memorial design director (July 2004–September 2006), LMDC.

Governor George E. Pataki, politician, former governor of New York (1995–2006).

Governor David A. Paterson, politician, former governor of New York (March 2008–2010).

Seth Pinsky, president (2008–2013), NYC EDC.

Steven P. Plate, director, WTC Construction Department (2004–present), PANYNJ.

Stephen D. Plavin, commercial real estate finance professional, CEO, Blackstone Mortgage Trust.

Kevin M. Rampe, executive vice president and general counsel (January 2002–2003), president (February 2003–May 2005), chairman (May 2006–May 2007) LMDC; 9/11 Memorial Foundation board member.

Lynn Rasic, executive vice president external affairs and strategy (January 2012–June 2015), public affairs and communications positions (July 2005–January 2012), 9/11 Memorial Foundation; press secretary to Governor Pataki (2003–2005).

Denise M. Richardson, executive director, General Contractors Association of New York.

Gary Rosenberg, attorney (cofounder Rosenberg & Estis) for the Durst Organization, commercial real estate business expert.

E. John Rosenwald Jr., vice chairman emeritus, J. P. Morgan, philanthropist, 9/11 Memorial Foundation board member.

Michael Rotchford, real estate professional, Cushman & Wakefield.

William Rudin, civic leader, Association for a Better New York, real estate developer.

Tom Saylak, former co-head, Blackstone Real Estate (held debt on original 7 WTC).

Avi Schick, chairman LMDC (April 2007–April 2015).

Peter Schwartz, senior executive vice president and general counsel, Westfield.

Frank J. Sciame, construction management expert (memorial cost review and evaluation), real estate developer.

Joseph J. Seymour, executive director (December 2001–October 2004), PANYNJ.

Linda Shelton, executive director, the Joyce Theater.

Anthony E. Shorris, executive director (January 2007–April 2008), PANYNJ.

Stephen Sigmund, chief of public affairs and government affairs (January 2006–October 2010), PANYNJ.

Henry R. Silverman, PANYNJ commissioner (NY: June 2002–June 2012) appointed by Governor George Pataki.

Larry A. Silverstein, New York real estate developer, leaseholder WTC.

Joseph Simenic, director for downstate infrastructure and economic development, Office of the governor (April 2009–April 2011); executive director, LMCCC (April 2013–May 2014).

Josh Sirefman, chief of staff (May 2004–June 2006) for Deputy Mayor Daniel Doctoroff and interim president NYC EDC (June 2006–January 2007).

Edward Skyler, deputy mayor for operations (January 2002–April 2010), Bloomberg administration; press secretary to Mayor Michael Bloomberg.

Peter Slatin, journalist, founder and editor of the business magazine GRID.

Dean Starkman, Wall Street Journal staff reporter (June 1996–December 2004); editor, Columbia Journalism Review (April 2007–September 2014).

Nikki Stern, LMDC Families Advisory Council, 9/11 family member.

Mary Ann Tighe, real estate expert and vice chair, CBRE TriState Area; commercial broker for Silverstein Properties, Inc.

Daniel R. Tishman, real estate executive and chairman and CEO of Tishman Construction (construction managers for many projects on the WTC site), 9/11 Memorial Foundation board member.

Richard Tofel, president, International Freedom Center; founding partner and general manager, ProPublica.

Philippe B. Visser, director, WTC Redevelopment Department (January 2009–September 2013), PANYNJ.

Christopher O. Ward, executive director (May 2008–October 2011), PANYNJ.

Drew S. Warshaw, chief of staff to executive director Christopher Ward (May 2008–November 2011), PANYNJ.

Carl B. Weisbrod, president of the Alliance for Downtown New York, LMDC director (April 2007–present), president of the real estate division of Trinity Church, founding president of NYC EDC, 9/11 Memorial Foundation board member.

Lois Weiss, veteran reporter, New York Post.

James Whalen, chief of staff for Deputy Mayor Daniel Doctoroff (spring 2007–December 2008).

John C. Whitehead, first chairman (November 2001–May 2006); LMDC, founding chairman, 9/11 Memorial Foundation.

Carol Willis, architectural historian and founder, the Skyscraper Museum.

Madelyn G. Wils, chair (2001–2005), Community Board 1.

Andrew Winters, founding director, Office of Capital Project Development, Office of Deputy Mayor for Economic Development and Rebuilding (Bloomberg administration).

Howard Wolfson, deputy mayor for governmental affairs (2010–2013, Bloomberg administration).

Tom Wright, president (2015–present), Regional Plan Association (RPA).

Kenneth Wong, real estate professional, former president, Westfield America.

Katherine S. Wylde, civic leader and president, Partnership for New York City.

Robert D. Yaro, president (2001–2014), Regional Plan Association (RPA).

John E. Zuccotti, civic leader, real estate professional, chairman Brookfield Properties, LMDC director (February 2008–2015).

NOTES

Prologue

[1] Charles V. Bagli, "An Agreement Is Formalized on Rebuilding at Ground Zero," *NYT*, September 22, 2006.

[2] Ground Zero presented the media with an extraordinary opportunity for extensive coverage, which it took up with extraordinary effort, extraordinary care, and extraordinary resources. Eight of the fourteen Pulitzer Prizes awarded for journalism in 2002 recognized the exceptional public service news reporting on the 9/11 attacks and the war on terrorism; six of the eight went to the staff of the newspapers primarily involved in coverage—the *New York Times*, the *Washington Post*, and the *Wall Street Journal*. Ground Zero and what was happening there—or not—was in the glare of the 24/7 news cycle. Stories on the rebuilding effort ran for years, and then more years, still a commanding worldwide saga despite the fact that the fervor of the earliest coverage had notably abated. The tenth anniversary of the attacks and the opening of the Memorial Plaza at Ground Zero rekindled international coverage, as did the long-awaited opening of the Memorial Museum nearly three years later in the spring of 2014. A major design announcement or a new deal between the Port Authority and Larry Silverstein also could still trigger ongoing coverage even if these repetitive narratives were taking on tiresome age.

[3] Alex Frangos, "Pact May Mean Rebuilding Delay at Ground Zero," *WSJ*, September 17, 2001.

[4] E. B. White, *Here Is New York* (New York: Harper & Row, 1949; Warner Books ed., 1988), 11, 18.

[5] Joyce Purnick, *Mike Bloomberg: Money, Power, Politics* (New York: Public Affairs, 2009), 203.

[6] My interviews with various players in the drama began as early as 2003, when I first started the research for this book, and carried into 2015, altogether, in total, some 180 interviews and conversations. I was personally involved in the earliest discussions about rebuilding in 2002 organized by New York New Visions, a coalition of civic and design professionals pulled together shortly after 9/11 to consider foundational principles for rebuilding.

Chapter 1

[1] Marita Sturken, "Memorializing Absence," unpublished essay (2001), http://essays.ssrc.org/sept11/essays/sturken_text_only.htm.

[2] I owe this point to my Columbia University colleague, political sociologist Saskia Sassen.

[3] Mike Wallace, "The Fragile City: 'These Fantasies Have Been Horribly Realized,'" *NYT*, September 16, 2001.

[4] Editorial, "The Pilgrimage to Lower Manhattan," *NYT*, September 14, 2001; Joyce Purnick, "In a Crisis, the Giuliani We Wanted," *NYT*, September 13, 2001.

[5] Jennifer Steinhauer, "After the Attacks: The Mayor; Giuliani Takes Charge, and City Sees Him as the Essential Man," *NYT*, September 14, 2001; Jennifer Steinhauer, "After the Attacks: The Mayor; in Crisis, Giuliani Overflows City," *NYT*, September 20, 2001.

[6] Mayor Michael Bloomberg, inaugural address, January 1, 2002, http://www.gothamgazette.com/searchlight/bloomberg_inaug.shtml.

[7] Jason Bram, James Orr, and Carol Rapaport, "Measuring the Effects of the September 11 Attack on New York City," FRBNY *Economic Policy Review* (November 2002): 5–20, at 2.

[8] In the months ahead, federal regulators would begin working on a draft disaster-contingency plan that urged major financial firms, most with headquarters or key operations in Manhattan, to consider development of out-of-the-region backup sites as much as two hundred to three hundred miles away. When the federal plan was released in August 2002, New York's elected officials quickly attacked the idea, saying that such a policy would lead to massive job losses and corrode the city's already-vulnerable tax base. The regulators eventually backed off their proposed plan after Senator Charles E. Schumer (D-NY), who called the plan a "dagger pointed at the heart of New York," and other New York officials demanded that it be scuttled. Maggie Haberman, "Chuck: Fed's Plan 'Big Trouble' for Wall St.," *DN*, November 22, 2002.

[9] Mei Fong and Peter Grant, "Giuliani Says American Express Seeks Extra Security to Return Downtown," *WSJ*, November 29, 2001; George E. Pataki author interview, January 14, 2015.

[10] The net job losses represent the marginal effect of the attack on employment in New York City, that is, the difference between what the path of New York's employment would have been in the absence of an attack and the actual path of employment in the city on a monthly basis. As a result of a national and local business slowdown, the number of private-sector jobs in New York City had begun to decline at the beginning of 2001. From the peak in employment in December 2000 to the trough in March 2002, the Federal Reserve Bank study reported that the number of people working in New York City's private sector fell by 147,000, or 4.6 percent, with more than one-third of the job losses, 55,000, occurring between January and September 2001. Bram et al., "Measuring the Effects," 7.

[11] Michael L. Dolfman and Solidelle F. Wasser, "9/11 and the New York City Economy: A Borough-by-Borough Analysis" (hereafter cited as "BLS Report"), New York Regional Office, Bureau of Labor Statistics, *Monthly Labor Review* (June 2004): 6, 4, 6.

[12] Saskia Sassen, *The Global City: New York, London, Tokyo* (Princeton, NJ: Princeton University Press, 1999); Saskia Sassen, "Global Financial Centers," *Foreign Affairs* 78 (1999): 84.

[13] Mitchell Moss, "Why New York Will Flourish in the 21st Century," *NYO*, January 20, 2000.

[14] Jameson W. Doig, *Empire on the Hudson: Entrepreneurial Vision and Political Power at the Port of New York Authority* (New York: Columbia University Press, 2003), 390.

[15] When Chase's new sixty-story corporate home at One Chase Manhattan Plaza on Liberty Street, designed by Gordon Bunshaft of Skidmore, Owings & Merrill (SOM), opened in 1961, it became the largest bank building in the world.

[16] James Glanz and Eric Lipton, "The Height of Ambition," *NYT Magazine*, September 8, 2002.

[17] James Glanz and Eric Lipton, *City in the Sky: The Rise and Fall of the World Trade Center* (New York: Times Books, Henry Holt, 2003), 30.

[18] See www.nysm.nysed.gov/wtc/about.

[19] See *Smithsonian*, Smithsonian.com/history/Helen-gurley-brown-the-world-trade-center-and-nobel-prizes-109966716/?no-ist.

[20] David W. Dunlap, "After the Attacks; the Icon; Towers Lend City a Lift, Adding Postcard Panache and an Air of Resilience," *NYT*, September 13, 2001.

[21] Kirk Johnson, "A City Changed Forever? Maybe Not," *NYT*, October 7, 2001.

[22] Editorial, "Rebuilding Downtown," *NYT*, September 24, 2001; editorial, "Making Downtown Whole Again," *DN*, September 28, 2001; editorial, "From the Ashes: Beyond the Grieving New York Must Build Anew," *Newsday*, October 7, 2001.

[23] John Mollenkopf, "New York: Still a Resilient City?" paper prepared for Thematic Panel on Tenth Anniversary of 9/11: Assessing the Impact on Communities, Eastern Sociological Society, Philadelphia, February 26, 2011, 5.

[24] Mollenkopf, "Still a Resilient City?" 7. Known for its high-paying jobs, "Manhattan became unique in the number of jobs it supported," the BLS economists noted in their 2004 report on 9/11 and the New York City economy. In Manhattan, "the relationship between jobs and wages was different from that experienced in the Nation as a whole. For the country as a whole, wages had remained relatively flat between 1978 and 2000, while employment growth was marked and consistent. For Manhattan, the converse was true: employment growth had remained essentially level, while wages increased substantially." "BLS Report," 4, 5.

[25] Thomas Kessner, *Capital City: New York City and the Men behind America's Rise to Economic Dominance, 1860–1900* (New York: Simon & Shuster, 2003), xvi, cited in BLS Report, 29. As the BLS 2004 report emphasized, for decades, the financial industry was Manhattan's driving economic force, with Manhattan-based security and commodity brokers representing about 25 percent of the financial industry's nationwide employment and about 40 percent of its nationwide payroll.

[26] The nine major studies are the Regional Plan Association (RPA), *The Regional Plan for New York and Its Environs* (1929); the New York City Planning Commission's preliminary master plan (1940), which was never adopted; two plans by the Downtown–Lower Manhattan Association (DLMA, a business group led by David Rockefeller), *Lower Manhattan: Recommended Land Use, Redevelopment Areas, and Traffic Improvements* (1958), and *Major Improvements, Land Use, Transportation, Traffic* (1963); two plans for lower Manhattan from the New York City Planning Commission (1966, 1969); another plan from the RPA, *The Second Regional Plan* (1969); a joint public-private effort between the DLMA and the New York City Department of City Planning and Economic Development Corporation, *The Plan for Lower Manhattan* (1993); and a third regional plan by the RPA, *A Region at Risk* (1996).

[27] Although fewer in number than in midtown, on average, the new skyscrapers in downtown were larger. From 1967 to 1973, the average size of new buildings constructed in lower Manhattan was an astonishing 1,448,000 square feet, while the average size of new towers in midtown was significantly smaller, 985,000 square feet. See the virtual exhibit of the Skyscraper Museum, *Big Buildings*, http://www.skyscraper.org/EXHIBITIONS/BIG_BUILDINGS/bb.htm.

[28] O&Y carried their success at Battery Park City across the Atlantic Ocean to Canary Wharf, where the firm became overextended and eventually filed for bankruptcy in 1992. See

Walter Stewart, *Too Big to Fail: Olympia & York: The Story behind the Headlines* (Toronto: McClelland & Stewart, 1993).

[29] Mark McCain, "Commercial Property: The Downtown 'Empty States'; Two Behemoths with 3 Million Square Feet to Let," *NYT*, March 22, 1987.

[30] Eric Lipton and Michael Cooper, "City Faces Challenge to Close Widest Budget Gap since 70's," *NYT*, January 4, 2002.

[31] Bloomberg, inaugural address.

[32] Jennifer Steinhauer, "City Agencies Are Struggling with Cutbacks," *NYT*, November 23, 2001.

[33] The city's economy was in virtual shutdown for days after the attack. The New York Stock Exchange was closed for four days, flights were suspended at the region's three airports, tourism dropped dramatically, and businesses in lower Manhattan not destroyed either closed, relocated, or suffered major losses from a suspension of business. Assuming the economic downturn persisted through the first half of the next calendar year, the IBO initially predicated the shortfall in tax revenues for the city's current fiscal year at $935 million less than anticipated in the budget that had been adopted, or a shortfall of 4.2 percent. This November 2001 projection of revenue at risk was even larger than what the city comptroller's office had foreseen in its October preliminary assessment of "The Impact of the September 11 WTC attack on NYC's Economy and Revenues" issued a month earlier. The City of New York Office of the Comptroller, "The Impact of the September 11 WTC Attack on NYC's Economy and Revenues." Both reports offered a detailed look at the city's revenue intake, and the picture was not pretty: less income from property tax receipts (from destroyed property), business taxes (from loss of businesses that moved out of the city), sales and hotel taxes (from loss of tourism and related retail sales), personal income tax (from lost wages net of those companies relocating elsewhere in NYC), and revenues from parking garage taxes and motor-vehicle violations, and airport fees.

[34] NYC IBO, "Confronting the Budget Shortfall: How Bad Are the Gaps?" January 7, 2002, 3; David Saltonstall, "Mayor's Defining Crisis, Mike Faces Historic Budget Woes with No End in Sight," *DN*, February 17, 2002; editorial, "The Gathering Storm," *NYP*, December 10, 2001.

[35] The prime candidates Bloomberg named were "The Hub" in the Bronx; Red Hook and downtown Brooklyn; Harlem, Governors Island, the World Trade Center, the Javits Convention Center, and former Con Ed Waterside Steam Plant site in Manhattan; Long Island City and Jamaica in Queens; the Home Port and Fresh Kills Landfill on Staten Island. Mike Bloomberg, "My Economic Blueprint: Part 2," undated; www.gothamgazette.com/ searchlight 2001/feature19.html.

[36] "Text of Mayor Giuliani's Farewell Address," December 27, 2001, reprinted in *NYT*.

[37] Daniel Doctoroff author interview, July 1, 2014.

[38] Bloomberg, inaugural address.

[39] City and state officials would lobby Washington hard for coverage of revenue losses from corporate and personal taxes (as part of the $20 billion aid package promised by President Bush), losses typically not covered by the Federal Emergency Management Agency, making the case that the terrorist attack was an attack on the country and, therefore, the federal government should take up more of the bill. It would be an uphill struggle, as described in chapter 4.

[40] Felix Rohatyn, "Fiscal Disaster the City Can't Face Alone," *NYT*, October 9, 2001.

[41] Moss, "Why New York Will Flourish."

[42] The creation of superblocks emerged as part of city planning orthodoxy during the early and mid-twentieth century and became especially prevalent during the mid-1960s era of urban renewal with its wholesale clearance of slum areas. Based on modernist ideas in architecture and urban planning, which disregarded streets (and pedestrians) in favor of freestanding towers in open space, the superblock sought to create a large building site protected from the noise and congestion of the automobile at the same time it sought to rationalize automobile circulation. "The demapped streets contributed to the open space of the site, while the bounding streets were sometimes enlarged to handle the displaced traffic," Hilary Ballon wrote in *The Greatest Grid: The Master Plan of Manhattan, 1811–2011* (New York: Columbia University Press, 2010), 185. The 16-acre WTC superblock may be among the most notable, yet superblocks are evident in many areas of New York City, including Grand Central Terminal, as Ballon notes, "the only building to obstruct a grid avenue and force a detour around itself"; the 18-acre United Nations campus; the 16.3-acre Lincoln Center for the Performing Arts; the sprawling Stuyvesant Town–Peter Cooper Village apartment complex covering approximately 80 acres, bisected only by East Twentieth Street running from First Avenue to Avenue C; and numerous housing projects throughout Manhattan and other boroughs, as well as campus areas for New York University, Columbia University, and Fordham University.

[43] The condemnation of commercial and industrial tenants, small businesses, and approximately one hundred residents, many of whom actively protested dislocation, on the stated public purpose of "world trade" was challenged and upheld in *Courtesy Sandwich Shop, Inc. v. Port of New York Authority*, 190 N.E.2d 402, 404–405 (N.Y. 1963). Including 7 WTC, a surplus parcel of the original project developed by Larry Silverstein under the auspices of the Port Authority but not a part of the sixteen acres of the Trade Center, increases the count to fourteen blocks combined into two superblocks.

[44] Edith Iglauer, "The Biggest Foundation," *New Yorker*, November 4, 1972.

[45] David W. Dunlap, "In a Space This Sacred, Every Square Foot Counts," *NYT*, March 29, 2004.

[46] State of New York Office of the State Comptroller, "Analysis of World Trade Center Occupancy and Rentals," Audit Report NY-AUTH-26-81, February 6, 1981.

[47] "This Month in Real Estate History," *Real Deal*, January 31 2010; Glanz and Lipton, *City in the Sky*, 134.

[48] Doig, *Empire on the Hudson*, 384–385, endnote citation 29, 546–547.

[49] Doig, *Empire on the Hudson*, 384, note 26, 546; Glanz and Lipton, *City in the Sky*, 60, 61, 90. See Doig, *Empire on the Hudson*, 379–385 for the complete story of the planning.

[50] Alexander Garvin, "Negotiating the Mega-Rebuilding Deal at the World Trade Center: The Historical Context," *Transactions: The Tennessee Journal of Business Law* 10 (Fall 2008): 15–26, at 16.

[51] As described in a *Times* article, to construct the slurry wall, the engineers first dug a three-foot-wide trench seventy feet deep, down to Manhattan's bedrock of mica schist, "a hard, unyielding rock, 700 million or 800 million years old, left over from an ancient mountain range," according to Christopher J. Schuberth, a professor at Amstrong Atlantic State University in Savannah, Georgia, and author of a book on New York geology. The geology

of Manhattan's mica schist is "the bedrock of what defines high-rise real estate." With the trench work proceeding in twenty-two-foot sections, as each was dug it was filled with "slurry, a mixture of clay and liquid that can withstand the pressure of soil trying to close the trench. Then a cage of reinforced steel was dropped into the slurry and concrete pumped into the trench from the bottom, pushing the slurry out the top, where it was captured and used in the next section. After a year of work, the bathtub—"a waterproof wall more than 3,000 feet long encircling the oblong excavation site"—was complete. Dennis Overbye, "A Nation Challenged: Engineers Tackle Havoc Underground," *NYT*, September 18, 2001; also see George J. Tamaro, "World Trade Center 'Bathtub': From Genesis to Armageddon," *Engineering and Homeland Security* 32 (Spring 2002).

[52] Charles Maikish author interview, November 4, 2010; Angus Kress Gillespie, *Twin Towers: The Life of New York City's World Trade Center* (New Brunswick, NJ: Rutgers University Press, 1999), 63–68.

[53] Overbye, "Engineers Tackle Havoc Underground."

[54] Glanz and Lipton, "The Height of Ambition."

[55] Eric Wanner, introduction to *Contentious City: The Politics of Recovery in New York City*, ed. John Mollenkopf (New York: Russell Sage Foundation, 2005), x.

[56] Adam Nagourney, "Political Memo: Tenuous Grip on Rebuilding May Hurt Mayor's Term," *NYT*, January 30, 2002.

Chapter 2

[1] Peter Grant, "Trade Center Leaseholder Is Determined to Rebuild, but Will Wait to Make Plans," *WSJ*, September 14, 2001; Alessandra Stanley, "Trade Center Leaseholder Pledges to Rebuild," *NYT*, October 5, 2001; Larry Silverstein, letter to the editor, *NYT*, October 26, 2001.

[2] Eric Herman, "Developing Plan for WTC: 4 New Buildings Seen for Twin Towers Site," *DN*, September 21, 2001; Glen Thompson, "Silverstein: 'If We Don't Rebuild It, We Give In,'" *Globe St.com*, September 18, 2001; Herman, "Developing Plan for WTC."

[3] Amanda Hall, "Towering Determination," *Sunday Suteleaph* (London), September 16, 2001; Steve Cuozzo, "Larry Lusts for Twin Towers; Silverstein Has an Eye on WTC's Untapped Retail Potential," *NYP*, January 30, 2001; Catlin Kelly, "Who Is the Silverstein Guy? Real Estate Tycoon Builds Nothing but Anger at WTC; Larry's Got to Go!," *DN*, April 23, 2006.

[4] Ronald Smothers, "As It Turns 80, Port Authority Looks to Roots for Its Future," *NYT*, April 30, 2001. To enable the deal to go forward, the Port Authority had to subordinate a piece of the annual rent payment to the lenders: $13.75 million, or 12.8 percent of the total base rent for the office component of the deal during the first thirty lease years. This tranche of rent was subordinate to many other obligations: senior debt obligations, capital improvement reserves, tenant improvements and leasing commission reserves, a rollover reserve, payment in lieu of taxes (PILOT) and insurance escrows, operating expenses, capital expenditures, and mezzanine debt service and principal payments at maturity. The PA director of real estate, Cherrie Nanninga, was strongly criticized by the board commissioners for this subordination, but she said it was the only way the deal was going to get done. In addition, the Port Authority would receive a percentage of rent based on gross revenues.

[5] One big issue remained unresolved: tax payments to the City of New York. Because of its tax-exempt status, the Port Authority paid a negotiated PILOT, $28 million a year, a sum

that was way below what would be the full tax bill. Mayor Giuliani was aggressively pursuing full taxes with any privatization of the World Trade Center complex. Under the deal signed on April 26, 2001, the Port Authority would cover any increases in property taxes. For discussion of the resolution of this issue, see note 55 of chapter 4.

[6] "Silverstein Scrambles to Resolve Financing of Trade-Center Deal," *WSJ*, April 26, 2001; Kathryn House, "Westfield Takes over World Trade Center," *Australian Financial Review*, April 28, 2001; Larry Silverstein interviewed by Charlie Rose, *The Charlie Rose Show*, PBS, show transcript, DVD, February 27, 2003.

[7] Peter Grant and Jim VandeHei, "A Developer's Struggle to Rebuild the WTC Is Making Some Strides," *WSJ*, November 2, 2001; Julia Levy, "WTC Partners Keeping Low Profile," *NYS*, August 27, 2002; Alex Frangos and Peter Grant, "Meet the Other Trade Center Builder; Larry Silverstein's Deep-Pocketed Partner, Lloyd Goldman, Is Likely to Take Over the Office Towers One Day," *WSJ*, November 11, 2008; Christine Haughney, "Real Estate Scion on Buying Binge; Goldman Leaves Shadows to Snap Up Trophy Buildings," *Crain's*, August 16, 2004. Before Lloyd Goldman, the Dutch institution ING had signed a letter of intent to become Silverstein's partner in the purchase of the Trade Center, but the deal fell apart over details of management.

[8] Frangos and Grant, "Meet the Other Trade Center Builder." Boxer had brought Goldman into the investment partnership that built the Montana, an Upper West Side apartment building, in the mid-1980s when additional capital was needed to cope with financial distress brought on by double-digit interest rates. Haughney, "Real Estate Scion on Buying Binge." During the course of final negotiations, the lease transaction was split into two contracts, with the Silverstein investor group agreeing to make payments on the office portion and Westfield America agreeing to make payments on the retail portion (427,000 square feet in the concourse mall). With Westfield's $12 million deposit, the office share of the $100 million deposit was $88 million.

[9] Grant, "Trade Center Leaseholder Is Determined to Rebuild"; Leonard Boxer author interview, September 23, 2014. According to the PA board meeting minutes of April 26, 2001, Westfield "indicated that it would provide $146.7 million" for the retail component of the Trade Center; after final negotiations, it invested $127 million, financed with a $100 million mortgage from UBS and $27 million of equity (6). *Westfield America Trust Annual Report 2001*, 6.

[10] Vornado CEO Roth was the first person to call Silverstein, who was in a car riding back to his office from the signing, and congratulate him on completing the deal. As part of his 2001 annual report to shareholders, Roth wrote, "Everyone tells me how lucky we are not to have owned the World Trade Center. We won the bidding but were unable to complete the deal. In the end we were happy to lose the business deal. But as history, the attack on the World Trade Center and on the Pentagon, really the attack on America, is as important as Pearl Harbor and maybe even any event in the last one hundred years." *Vornado Annual Report 2001*, 2.

[11] As explained by Jameson Doig in an e-mail, the veto power was a demand of New Jersey's then governor Harry Moore that arose during a debate over the George Washington Bridge; specifically, his goal was to allow him to block the awarding of contracts for the bridge construction to any firm outside New Jersey. Governor Al Smith reluctantly agree to veto power. The New York statue originally allowed the governor only five days to veto, and in 1972, was

amended to ten days. For New Jersey, the statute is chapter 333, Laws of New Jersey, 1927, and for New York, section 7152 in McKinney's Unconsolidated Laws, amended 1972.

[12] Leonard Boxer author telephone interview, November 20, 2014.

[13] Peter Grant, "Control of World Trade Center Towers Moved to Private Hands Just Months Ago," *WSJ*, September 12, 2001; Andrew Rice, "Silverstein Recovers: Dark Horse May Win World Trade Center," *NYO*, April 9, 2001. After the official announcement, there was a quiet period during which Silverstein's public relations team had asked that there be no publicity. During this period Grant was preparing an exclusive story on the transaction scheduled to appear as the lead story on the front page of the paper on September 13, 2001. Needless to say, other news consumed the front page that day.

[14] Charles V. Bagli, "Developer Scrambles to Save World Trade Center Deal," *NYT*, April 26, 2001.

[15] Tom Shachtman, *Skyscraper Dreams: The Great Real Estate Dynasties of New York* (Boston: Little Brown: 1991), 298.

[16] Sarabeth Sanders, "Interview with Larry Silverstein," *Real Deal*, September 2011; Albert Scardino, "A Realty Gambler's Big Coup," *NYT*, July 11, 1986.

[17] Thomas J. Lueck, "New York Developers Feel a Chill," *NYT*, September 19, 1990; James Kim, "Realty Baron Blues," *USA Today*, August 8, 1990. Silverstein and partners Melvin Simon and William Zeckendorf Jr., lost their equity position in the one-million-square-foot mall A&S Plaza, which they had redeveloped out of the old Gimbels department store at Herald Square, when they turned back the asset to the bank in an uncontested foreclosure; Silverstein was the managing partner and had the largest partnership interest. The partnership was similarly forced to cede its interest in Park Avenue Court (at Eighty-sixth and Lexington Avenue) to its lender in another uncontested foreclosure. Both deals were a financial disaster for the partners, who lost 100 percent of their equity. In another distressed development project during this period, Silverstein was forced to sell his Embassy Suites hotel in Times Square, built with financing from the General Electric Pension Fund.

[18] Robert Guenther, "New York Developer Follows New Tack at Trade Center Site," *WSJ*, November 21, 1984.

[19] Peter Grant, "New Act on 42d St. Mammoth Apt. Complex at Hudson," *DN*, February 24, 1997.

[20] Kelly, "Who Is the Silverstein Guy?"; Barbara Martinez, "Name Dropping: A Real-Estate King Sees a Legacy Unravel as Creditors Move In," *WSJ*, March 21, 2000.

[21] Stanley, "Trade Center Leaseholder Pledges to Rebuild."

[22] Jonathan Berke, "GMAC Powers World Trade Center Deal," *Daily Deal*, April 30, 2001.

[23] In 1981, an audit by the office of New York State comptroller Edward Regan criticized the PA's long-term leases (fifteen–twenty years) "at rates substantially below the present market [which] tend to limit the Authority's ability to increase substantially and quickly the revenue potential of the complex." Also, the PA "did not maintain an ongoing record of leases and space to become available by rental date," as is best practice in private commercial property management. State of New York Office of the State Comptroller, "Analysis of World Trade Center Occupancy and Rentals," Audit Report NY-AUTH-26-81, February 6, 1981, 5, 10. Unsurprisingly, the agency was susceptible to political influence: The many banks in the mall space would close at 4 P.M., and when they closed, the space was dead, dark. The PA had a plan that would enhance the retail mall's performance with a new tenant mix, part of

which involved moving the banks up to the concourse space. All of a sudden every banker with a friend on the board was called. Eventually, the PA was able to move the banks to the plaza level shortly before 9/11. Charles McClafferty (former PA CFO) author interview, March 29, 2012.

[24] Fitch Ratings, "GMAC Commercial Mortgage Securities, Inc., Series 2001-WTC," August 2, 2001, 4.

[25] Eric Herman, "Sky's Limit for WTC Retailing," *DN*, September 10, 2001.

[26] Ben English and Michael Beach, "Bite into Big Apple—Lowy's Westfield in Shopping Triumph," *Daily Telegraph*, April 28, 2001.

[27] Eric Herman and Michael Saul, "New Apts. at Ground Zero? Bloomberg Envisions Apts. on Part of the Site," *DN*, November 30, 2001; Paul Goldberger, "The Skyline: Groundwork: How the Future of Ground Zero Is Being Resolved," *New Yorker*, May 20, 2002, 92; *Rebuilding the World Trade Center*, Cornell Real Estate Council Meeting, DVD, March 8, 2012; Eric Herman, "Revving Up; WTC Rebuild Developer Sees Work on '7' Starting within a Year," *DN*, November 8, 2001.

[28] Stanley, "Trade Center Leaseholder Pledges to Rebuild." On the eve of September 11, as I was told by an insider to the insurance litigation, Silverstein called his lawyer and public relations expert to discuss the attack and how they should frame the insurance claim, debating whether it should be four occurrences, for the four buildings lost, or two occurrences, for the twin towers.

[29] Robin Finn, "Public Lives: Undaunted and Planning the Next Great Skyline," *NYT*, February 15, 2002.

[30] Paul Goldberger, *Up from Zero: Politics, Architecture, and the Rebuilding of New York* (New York: Random House, 2004), 81.

[31] Editorial, "Starting at Ground Zero," *NYT*, February 2, 2002; Editorial, "Don't Start Trade Center Rebuilding without a Plan," *Newsday*, February 22, 2002.

[32] Alex Garvin, "Reflections and Choice," n.d. [2003], http://alumninet.yale.edu/classes/yc1962/garvinview03.html; Eric Herman, "Setting New Path for 7 WTC Redesign Opens Greenwich to Traffic," *DN*, January 23, 2002.

[33] Goldberger, "How the Future of Ground Zero Is Being Resolved," 86; Dean Starkman and Peter Grant, "Consuming Debate: A Mall Magnate Shapes Rebuilding of Trade Center," *WSJ*, June 5, 2002.

[34] Goldberger, "How the Future of Ground Zero Is Being Resolved," 93.

[35] Lisa Goff, "New York's Hometown Architect Faces a New World Order," *Crain's*, July 31, 2006. Silverstein at first wanted to rebuild 7 WTC as it had been; that would be the way to proceed fast, and he needed to move fast to replace the ConEd substation, according to his insurance documents. He had the plans; rebuilding it as before would also save him architectural and engineering fees and no approvals would be necessary. "That's Larry," remarked one of my sources. After thirteen or fourteen models, it became obvious that two million square feet was not possible on that site, the developer told me.

[36] Julie V. Iovine, "The Invisible Architect," *NYT*, August 31, 2003.

[37] Iovine, "The Invisible Architect"; John Gendall, "AIArchitect Talks with David Childs, FAIA," *Practicing Architecture*, September 9, 2011, http://www.aia.org/practicing/aiab090856. Childs told a journalist that as an architecture graduate student at Yale, "we'd march against skyscrapers like that, we felt they were destroying our cities." The towers, he added, "didn't

take any clues from New York, apart from being 200 sq ft" [200 feet is the length of a Manhattan block].... They were not interactive with the pedestrian and were a touchstone of what not to do with urban design." Tim Teeman, "All Eyes Turn to the New York Skyline; A Decade after 9/11, the World's Most Awaited Building Is Finally Taking Shape, but Has Its Architect Got It Right?" *The Times* (London), August 13, 2011.

[38] Goldberger, "How the Future of Ground Zero Is Being Resolved," 94; Sylvia Lewis, "Mr. Precedent: When Alexander Cooper Leads, All Sorts of People Tend to Follow," *Planning* 62 (August 1996): 10–15, at 14.

[39] Goldberger, "How the Future of Ground Zero Is Being Resolved," 94. Cooper's plan included a cultural center just south of the memorial, which would have required "the demolition of 90 West Street, a landmark office building designed by Cass Gilbert that was seriously damaged on 9/11 and which preservationists wanted to see repaired." Childs was working with SOM partner and urban designer Marilyn Jordan Taylor, who was a leading force in the establishment of New York New Visions and intensely involved with selecting artifacts from among the rubble at the WTC site to be temporarily stored in Hanger 17 at JFK Airport until permanent placements were determined. Their plan, according to Goldberger, put a new opera house placed northeast of the Cass Gilbert building, "which saves the landmark but cuts slightly into the south tower's footprint."

[40] David W. Dunlap, "A Through Street Restored, Looking Thinner," *NYT*, July 10, 2003.

[41] Starkman and Grant, "Consuming Debate."

[42] Herman, "Developing Plan for WTC"; Peter Grant, "Silverstein Wants to Build 4 Smaller Towers at Trade Center Site, Owner Sees No Rush," *WSJ*, September 21, 2001; Stanley, "Trade Center Leaseholder Pledges to Rebuild."

[43] Stanley, "Trade Center Leaseholder Pledges to Rebuild"; Herman and Saul, "Bloomberg Envisions Apts."; Greg Grittich, "Silverstein: Gimme Space; Wants WTC Office Area Rebuilt, but Concedes 'Footprints,'" *DN*, October 9, 2002.

[44] Steven Brill, *After: How America Confronted the September 12 Era* (New York: Simon & Schuster, 2003), 228–229.

[45] Standard & Poor's Structured Finance, "GMAC Commercial Mortgage Securities Inc. $563 Million Commercial Mortgage Pass-through Certificates Series 2001-WTC," August 2, 2001, 3. For example, all cash flow from the buildings would be retained after Silverstein and his partners in the office component received a return of 10 percent on equity.

[46] Anthony Coscia author interview, October 5, 2010; Mike Kelly, "Ground Zero's Obstacle," *The Record* (Bergen County, NJ), December 13, 2005.

[47] Brill, *After*, 231.

Chapter 3

[1] Eric Lipton and Charles V. Bagli, "A Nation Challenged: Turf Battles, Conflicting Visions of How to Rebuild Lower Manhattan," *NYT*, September 21, 2001.

[2] Charles V. Bagli, "The Reconstruction: A Nascent Effort, Still in Need of a Plan," *NYT*, October 29, 2001; Lipton and Bagli, "Turf Battles, Conflicting Visions." The "real estate industry leaders had a deep desire to prevent the New York City Council from playing a serious role in the rebuilding effort," according to urban planner Mitchell Moss, "Redevelopment of Lower Manhattan: The Role of the City," in *Contentious City: The Politics of Recovery in*

New York City, ed. John Mollenkopf (New York: Russell Sage Foundation, 2005), 95–111, at 101. On October 4, the Real Estate Board of New York sent a delegation to then deputy mayor for economic development Robert Harding, with a proposal for organizing recon-struction; days later, the Partnership for the City of New York adopted a resolution calling on the governor and the state legislature to create an authority to manage reconstruction of lower Manhattan.

[3] Lipton and Bagli, "Turf Battles, Conflicting Visions."

[4] Editorial, "Rebuilding Downtown New York," *NYT*, October 20, 2001; Robert Douglass author interview, March 19, 2012; Moss, "Redevelopment of Lower Manhattan," 103.

[5] George E. Pataki quoted in Elizabeth Greenspan, *Battle for Ground Zero: Inside the Political Struggle to Rebuild the World Trade Center* (New York: Palgrave Macmillan, 2013), 46.

[6] Of the initial eleven LMDC board members, Governor Pataki appointed John C. Whitehead (chair), Roland W. Betts, Lewis M. Eisenberg, Edward J. Malloy, Madelyn G. Wils, Deborah C. Wright, and Frank G. Zarb; and Mayor Giuliani appointed Paul A. Crotty, Richard Grasso, Robert M. Harding, and Howard Wilson. Governor Pataki appointed Thomas S. Johnson as his eighth board member; Mayor Bloomberg appointed Sally Hernandez-Pinero, Stanley O'Neal, Billie Tsien, and Carl B. Weisbrod as his four additional board members.

[7] John C. Whitehead, *A Life in Leadership: From D-Day to Ground Zero* (New York: Basic Books; New American Books, 2005), 4, 9.

[8] Andrea Bernstein, "A Jostled Czar, John Whitehead Roiling His Foes," *NYO*, November 25, 2002; Andrew Rice, "Goldman's Ex-Chief, John C. Whitehead, Is Downtown's Czar," *NYO*, December 24, 2001.

[9] Whitehead, *A Life in Leadership*, 2.

[10] Bernard J. Frieden and Lynne B. Sagalyn, *Downtown, Inc.: How America Rebuilds Cities* (Cambridge, MA: MIT Press, 1989), 20–27.

[11] By 2011, the distribution of CDBG funds between economic recovery and long-term re-building had changed significantly, as revealed in a crosswalk analysis prepared by the IBO. Whereas long-term rebuilding allocations had been expected to amount to some 54 percent of the total CDBG dollars going to the city, by 2011, the distributions for business assistance ($496.8 million), programs for utilities ($323.6 million), residential grants ($236.2 million), the WTC 9/11 Memorial ($319.5 million), affordable housing ($54 million), and other LMDC projects and administrative costs ($1.3 billion), plus not yet allocated funds ($35.4 million), amounted to 78 percent of the total CDBG funds going to the city ($3.5 billion). NYC IBO, "The Aftermath: Federal Aid 10 Years after the World Trade Center Attack," August 31, 2011, webtable, 1. Of the total CDBG dollars, some $842 million, or 24.2 percent, would be spent on the World Trade Center site.

[12] Carl Weisbrod author interview, March 5, 2013.

[13] Greg Sargent, "City Is 'Favorite' for Convention, Republicans Say," *NYO*, November 25, 2002; Andrew Rice, "Who's Top New Yorker in Bush White House? Chelsea Piers' Betts," *NYO*, January 29, 2001.

[14] Robin Finn, "Public Lives: A Role at Ground Zero for the Master of the Piers," *NYT*, April 4, 2003.

[15] Eric Herman, "Legal Advice for Lower Manhattan Redo," *DN*, January 15, 2002; Ira Millstein author interview, June 21, 2011.

[16] LMDC board meeting minutes, February 21, 2002, 13.

[17] Louis Tomson, "Testimony before New York State Assembly," October 8, 2002; Whitehead, *A Life in Leadership*, 8; John Whitehead author interview, February 12, 2008.

[18] The eight advisory councils covered the following constituencies: arts, education, and tourism; development; families; financial-services firms; professional firms; residents; restaurants, retailers, and small business; and transportation and commuters.

[19] William Neuman, "Rebuild Panels in the Dark," *NYP*, February 1, 2002.

[20] Whitehead author interview, February 12, 2008; Dean Starkman and Peter Grant, "Rebuilding New York: A Consensus Forms—Mixed Use Plan Envisions Memorial, Fewer Offices, Improved Transportation," *WSJ*, December 19, 2001.

[21] Editorial, "A First Rate Choice," *DN*, January 14, 2002; editorial, "Rebuilding New York; How to Fill the Hole at Ground Zero," *NYT*, January 13, 2002.

[22] Eugenie L. Birch, "U.S. Planning Culture under Pressure: Major Elements Endure and Flourish in the Face of Crises," in *Comparative Planning Cultures*, ed. Bishwapriya Sanyal (New York: Routledge, 2005), 352.

[23] The fourteen goals included: preserving an area of the WTC site for one or more permanent memorials; facilitating the immediate revitalization of lower Manhattan to ensure its viability, restoring a portion of the street grid to reintegrate the site into downtown, eliminating West Street as a barrier for Battery Park City, better integrating mass transit services with the rest of the city and region, creating a distinctive transit gateway to lower Manhattan, creating facilities to accommodate the anticipated surge in charter and tour buses, expanding the residential population, promoting retail opportunities to serve the residential community, providing new cultural and civic institutions, creating more parks and open space, using sustainable design and green building technologies, preserving outstanding historic structures, and diversifying the area's economy beyond financial services. LMDC, *Principles and Preliminary Blueprint for the Future of Lower Manhattan*, April 9, 2002.

[24] Paul Goldberger, "Groundwork: How the Future of Ground Zero Is Being Resolved," *New Yorker*, May 20, 2002.

[25] Editorial, "Turning to Renewal," *NYT*, May 31, 2002.

[26] LMDC, *Principles and Preliminary Blueprint for the Future of Lower Manhattan*, 4.

[27] Josh Sirefman author interview, February 2, 2012.

[28] Millstein author interview; "A Conversation with Lou Tomson," *Gotham Gazette.com*, n.d. [July 24, 2002]; Joseph Seymour author interview, September 25, 2014; "A Conversation with Lou Tomson."

[29] Charles Maikish author interview, November 4, 2010; Seymour author interview.

[30] Anthony Coscia author interview, October 5, 2010.

[31] Daniel Machalaba, "Low-Profile Actor Takes Center Stage at Trade Center," *WSJ*, October 23, 2002; editor, "Jeffrey Green: Corporate Counsel Stands Tall with New York," *Metropolitan Corporate Counsel*, May 2002.

[32] Fueled by criticism that big real estate projects had distracted the agency from its core mission of easing the region's transportation bottlenecks, in 1995 the PA redirected its strategic focus back to investments in improving regional transportation facilities. From the viewpoint of regional transportation groups and downtown business interests, the PA faced two pieces of unfinished business considered by many to be central to the future of lower Manhattan: addressing its long-standing failure to build a rail-freight tunnel between New

York and New Jersey and providing a commuter-rail link to the suburbs of Long Island. Tom McGeveran, "Port Authority Reasserts Grip on Towers Site," *NYO*, May 6, 2002.

[33] Eric Herman, "Developer May Face Detour; Condemnation Powers Threaten WTC Rebuild," *DN*, July 31, 2002.

[34] Seymour author interview; Pataki quoted in Greenspan, *Battle for Ground Zero*, 86.

[35] Deborah Sontag, "The Hole in the City's Heart," *NYT*, September 11, 2006.

[36] Eric Herman, "Developer May Face Detour; Condemnation Powers Threaten WTC Rebuild," *DN*, July 31, 2002.

[37] Birch, "U.S. Planning Culture," 351.

[38] Alan Altshuler, private communication, October 1, 2004; Douglass author interview, March 19, 2012.

Chapter 4

[1] James Sanders, "Ideas and Trends: Thinking Big; in New York Seeking a Grand Vision of Public Works," *NYT*, September 1, 2002.

[2] Sanders, "New York Seeking a Grand Vision."

[3] Sanders, "New York Seeking a Grand Vision."

[4] "Grid Symposium; Ground Zero: Renewing New York," *Grid* 3:8 (October 2001): 20–29, at 26.

[5] Joyce Purnick, "Metro Matters: Yes, New York Will Prosper Again, but It Needs More Than Moral Support," *NYT*, September 17, 2001.

[6] "Text of Bush's Act of War Statement," September 12, 2001, news.bbc.co.uk/2/hi/americas /1540544.stm; "Negotiating the Future of Ground Zero," meeting of the Program on Negotiation at Harvard Law School, November 18, 2002, http://www.pon.harvard.edu/ news/negotiating-the-future-of-ground-zero.

[7] "NY Gets More WTC Aid from Congress," UPI, November 17, 2001; Purnick, "Yes, New York Will Prosper Again."

[8] Sam Roberts, "Infamous 'Drop Dead' Was Never Said by Ford," *NYT*, December 28, 2006.

[9] Shannon McCaffrey, "New York Lawmakers Battle for Buck, but Does the City Need More Money?" AP State and Local Wire, December 15, 2001.

[10] A compromise was reached in the early morning hours just before "a pair of symbolic deadlines—members of Congress and the president planned to attend a noon memorial service at the Washington National Cathedral on Sept. 14, with Bush scheduled to depart for New York immediately afterward." Daniel J. Parks, "Quiet Tension over Spending," *Congressional Quarterly Weekly*, September 14, 2001. Half the $40 billion in Congress's over-all appropriation would be used for disaster relief and response (including security) related to the destruction in Manhattan, the Pentagon, and rural Pennsylvania where the attacks occurred. The president would be allowed to use $10 billion without any congressional authorization, and Bush could spend another $10 billion after giving Congress a fifteen-day prior notification. The other half would be made available in the fiscal year starting October 1, with Congress directing the use of that money for rebuilding through the regular appro-priations process. David Masci, "Emergency Funds to Be Divided between Recovery and Retaliation," *Congressional Quarterly Weekly*, September 14, 2001.

[11] Sara Kugler, "Lawmakers from New York Vow to Fight for Billions in Federal Dollars for City's Recovery," AP State and Local Wire, October 10, 2001.

[12] Editorial, "New York to Feds: Show Us the Money," *DN*, October 22, 2001; editorial "Federal Help for New York City," *NYT*, October 11, 2001; Charles V. Bagli, "The Reconstruction: A Nascent Effort, Still in Need of a Plan," *NYT*, October 29, 2001.

[13] James C. McKinley Jr., "City and State Ask the U.S. for $54 Billion for Recovery," *NYT*, October 10, 2001.

[14] "Billions Separate New York and Bush," UPI, November 15, 2001; Timothy J. Burger, "Veep Axes 10B in Aid—for Now," *DN*, November 15, 2001; Frank Lombardi, "Rudy Says Pols Should Stop Pestering Feds for All $20B," *DN*, November 17, 2001.

[15] Editorial, "Vital Help for New York," *NYT*, December 15, 2001; Raymond Hernandez, "A Nation Challenged: The Federal Aid; Negotiators Back $8.2 Billion in Aid for New York City," *NYT*, December 19, 2001; Raymond Hernandez, "The President's Budget Proposal: New York Perspective; Bus Budget Renews Battle over Pledge of Aid to City," *NYT*, February 5, 2002.

[16] Raymond Hernandez, "$20 Billion? Sure, Maybe, and Not So Fast; Debate on Aid Package Reflects the Nation's Ambivalence toward New York," *NYT*, February 17, 2002.

[17] Editorial, "New York's $20 Billion," *NYT*, March 8, 2002; Raymond Hernandez, "A Nation Challenged: Federal Aid; Bush Offers Details of Aid to New York Topping $20 Billion," *NYT*, March 8, 2002.

[18] For details on these tax benefits, see US GAO, *Tax Administration: Information Is Not Available to Determine whether $5 Billion in Liberty Zone Tax Benefits Will Be Realized*, September 2003, appendix 1, 12–15.

[19] NYC IBO, "World Trade Center Assistance: Aid Received, Aid to Come," July 31, 2003, 4; city officials were most concerned about the unused allocation of commercial capacity. By mid-August 2004, the city and state had awarded $1.3 billion for twelve residential projects (out of the $1.6 billion pool for residential projects) and $1.5 billion for ten commercial projects (out of the $6.4 billion for commercial projects). NYC IBO, "Three Years After: Where Is the $20 Billion in Federal WTC Aid?" August 11, 2004, 6.

[20] The value of the tax benefit package soon became a source of tension between the Bloomberg administration and Washington. A report prepared for the administration by PriceWaterhouseCoopers estimated the tax benefits were worth less than $3.8 billion, not the $5.029 billion projected by federal officials on the basis of estimates by the Congressional Joint Committee on Taxation. Accounting for their actual use was difficult, because of the seven different types of Liberty Zone tax benefits available, the Internal Revenue Service only collects information on one, business employee tax credits ($864 million), and usage was not collected or reported by state or local agencies. The federal government estimated that the $8 billion of Liberty Bonds authorized (and eventually issued) resulted in a tax expenditure (loss of taxes collected) of $1.2 billion. Neither Congress nor the White House was willing to convert the tax credits to cash when the Bloombereg administration pressed on the issue in the fall of 2003, but some part of the $5.029 billion did end up being converted to general budgetary relief ($937 million). NYC IBO, "The Aftermath: Federal Aid 10 Years after the World Trade Center Attack," August 2011, web table 1.

[21] NYC IBO, "World Trade Center Aid: Too Much for Some Needs, Not Enough for Others?" May 28, 2002, 1.

[22] Editorial, "Foundations for Lower Manhattan," *NYT*, April 29, 2002.

[23] Edward Wyatt, "Rebuilding Transit in Lower Manhattan Will Take More Money, or a Narrower Scope," *NYT*, August 13, 2002. Alternatively described as America's most ambitious infrastructure project or a gold-plated boondoggle, the Central Artery Project had a full cost that tallied $14.6 billion at completion in December 2007—a cost overrun of about 190 percent in 1982 dollars, the starting year for the official planning phase—but a 2000 agreement codified into law by Congress capped the federal funding at $8.55 billion. The engineering was masterful, but the project, a high-profile story of mismanagement. Rick Klein, "Big Dig Failures Threaten Federal Funding; Future Projects May Be Shortchanged," *Boston Globe*, August 6, 2006, http://www.boston.com/news/local/articles/2006/08/06/big_dig_failures_threaten_federal_funding/?page=full. Also see Alan Altshuler and David Luberoff, *Mega-Projects: The Changing Politics of Urban Public Investment* (Washington, DC: Brookings Institution Press, 2003).

[24] Charles V. Bagli and Randy Kennedy, "Old or New? Debate Rages over Transit Downtown," *NYT*, October 12, 2002.

[25] Bagli and Kennedy, "Old or New?"

[26] The debates about how best to spend the $4.55 billion of federal money for transportation and the politics of setting priorities for spending those funds in lower Manhattan deserve greater treatment than can be given in this book. The issues reprise long-standing debates among transportation professionals and advocates for different modes of transport. See Pataki's February 6, 2003, letter to FEMA and FTA officials and consistent post-9/11 coverage in the *Times* until the final projects were defined in mid-July 2005.

[27] Kenneth T. Jackson, foreword, Jameson W. Doig, *Empire on the Hudson: Entrepreneurial Vision and Political Power at the Port of New York Authority* (New York: Columbia University Press, 2003), xvi, xvii.

[28] Doig, *Empire on the Hudson*, 1.

[29] World Trade Center Task Force, *The Future of the World Trade Center, a Report to Governor Hugh L. Carey*, April 1981 (hereafter cited as the Zuccotti Report), 1; Doig, *Empire on the Hudson*, 55; James Glanz and Eric Lipton, *City in the Sky: The Rise and Fall of the World Trade Center* (New York: Times Books, Henry Holt, 2003), 55.

[30] Doig, *Empire on the Hudson*, 379; Glanz and Lipton, *City in the Sky*, 56.

[31] For the full story, see Glanz and Lipton, *City in the Sky*, 38–61; and Doig, *Empire on the Hudson*, 379–384.

[32] The bond covenant Goldberg drafted formally guaranteed that the Port Authority's reserves would not be drained away by the rail projects (thereby jeopardizing its ability to repay its bondholders) by limiting the agency to the H&M, plus other rail activities *only* if the total annual deficits from all rail operations did not exceed 10 percent of the agency's General Reserve Fund.

[33] Zuccotti Report, 36; "Biography: Tightrope between the Towers," *American Experience*, PBS, http://www.pbs.org/wgbh/americanexperience/features/biography/newyork-tightrope/; editorial, "Tag Sale at the Trade Center," *NYT*, September 19, 1980.

[34] Zuccotti Report, 3. The Port Authority had experienced years of difficulty in leasing out the mammoth amount of office space of the complex. The long-term leases the agency signed at rents "substantially below the present market," according to a critical managerial audit by the office of New York State comptroller Edward V. Regan, represented competition that most

real estate professionals could not be happy about, especially Olympia & York, as developers of the adjacent Battery Park World Financial Center. The annual square foot rental for 1981, according to the Regan audit, averaged $13.19 a square foot compared to the going rate of $20.00 a square foot for downtown office space. The impact a disposition would have on the downtown office market was a consideration; the task force believed that it "might actually have a beneficial impact on the rental market. Private ownership," the report said, "would eliminate the special privilege aura of the Trade Center, and the price would have a positive influence on the value of future transactions." State of New York Office of the State Comptroller, "Analysis of World Trade Center Occupancy and Rentals," Audit Report NY-AUTH-26-81, February 6, 1981 (hereafter cited as the Regan Report), 10, 23.

[35] Regan's audit analysis of the WTC's operations did not paint a pretty picture. Given the difficulty of slow lease-up, the PA was "leasing space to firms involved in international business but not extensively or directly related to world trade." Except for the Trade Center's large size, its operation was not that different from similar properties operated by private enterprise—which led the comptroller to recommend sale of the complex and Governor Carey's appointment of the Zuccotti task force to determine the feasibility of a sale. The audit's major observations were telling: Based on current projections, 1983 would be the first year the WTC complex broke even, financially; net deficits, from 1972 through the first six months of 1980, totaled $135.5 million. By the end of May 1980, occupancy had only reached 84 percent, and government offices accounted for 3.9 million square feet, or 47.6 percent of the occupied space in the complex. Long-term leases "substantially below the present market" would limit the PA's ability to quickly increase the complex's revenue potential. The PA had written several leases in 1979, at a time when a sale of the Trade Center complex was a target of outside investors (for example, Prudential Insurance, Deutsche Bank, and Donald Trump) with a cap provision limiting the pass-along of increases in real estate taxes should the WTC be transferred to private ownership, which, the audit noted, "serves as a disincentive to potential buyers." Regan Report, 1, 2, 3, 4.

[36] "World Trade Center Sale Urged," *Washington Post*, April 11, 1981.

[37] Joyce Purnick, "It's Still No Sale at the Trade Center," *NYT*, May 31, 1981.

[38] Earlier, in May 1982, Governors Kean and Carey had appointed a blue-ribbon panel of six to study the revenue-generating capability of the Port, including the question of whether the World Trade Center should be sold. The panel called for greater involvement by the states in the Port Authority's budget-making process and suggested that the Trade Center be sold.

[39] Joseph F. Sullivan, "Kean to Seek More Influence over Port Authority Policies," *NYT*, January 10, 1984.

[40] The value of net revenues over the period of the New York State move-out (based on twenty years of incremental lease revenue and after covering the cost of its move-out) dedicated to economic development activities within the Port district was, at the time, estimated to be $350 million to $400 million, or three to four times the net revenues going to the Port Authority in 1983. Bear Stearns, *Options for the Disposition of the World Trade Center, a Report to the States of New Jersey and New York and the Port Authority of NY and NJ*, June 1984, 13.

[41] David Bird, "Use of Trade Center Rentals for Transit Urged," *NYT*, May 30, 1982.

[42] Intended as a temporary vehicle, a precursor to the legislatively approved Bank for Regional Development, which failed to materialize, the fund attained a permanent status. Focused on getting higher property tax revenues, New York City declared itself against the

bank unless the World Trade Center was sold. Although a "bank" per se did not come into being, the Port Authority set up a series of additional "regional development programs," non-revenue-generating to the Port Authority, none of which were related to its own programs. By year end 2012, a total of approximately $2.1 billion had been spent on the following nine "regional" programs: Regional Development Facility; Regional Economic Development Program; Oak Point Rail Freight Link; New Jersey Marine Development Program; New York Transportation, Economic Development and Infrastructure Renewal Program; Regional Transportation Program; Hudson-Raritan Estuary Resources Program; Regional Rail Freight Program; and Meadowlands Passenger Rail Facility. *PANYNJ Annual Report 2012*, note H to the financial statements, 71. In this way, Doig remarked, "a substantial chunk of the Port's surpluses would be allotted to meet the governors' perceived needs, whether to stimulate economic development in a creative way or simply to finance pork-barrel operations." *Empire on the Hudson*, 400.

[43] The money in this special fund would continue to grow since New York State's lease for the space, signed in 1967, was effectively ninety-nine years in duration. In 1990, New York and New Jersey agreed to terminate the fund by being bought out by the Port Authority (at a present value of $430.5 million at the time of the termination agreement). In turn, the Port would make a series of fifty-nine semiannual payments, equally divided between New York and New Jersey, beginning on March 1, 1992, at approximately $14 million and increasing thereafter to approximately $26.6 million, with the last payment approximately $53.6 million. In other words, this special fund would keep on giving through 2021. See Office of the State Comptroller, *The Port Authority of New York and New Jersey Fund for Regional Development*, Report 88-S-30, March 29, 1990, for the managerial audit of the fund, and *PANYNJ Annual Report 1990*, note I to the financial statements; and subsequent annual reports, note D to financial statements.

[44] Doig makes the point that the decision calculus had already changed at the executive director level with Governor Carey's appointment of Peter Goldmark from outside the staff to the position. Previously, staff leadership had been determined by the commissioners. Whether selected by the New York governor or the commissions, the position had been filled based on proven leadership skills and experience—until Governor Pataki appointed George Marlin to head the agency.

[45] Doig, *Empire on the Hudson*, 400.

[46] Editorial, "Mr. Pataki's Mediocre Choices," *NYT*, January 12, 1995, and "Mr. Pataki's Port Authority Problem," February 7, 1995; as cited in editorial, "Managing the NY-NJ Port," *Journal of Commerce*, January 25, 1995; Richard C. Leone, "Pataki's Politics; Everyone's Port Authority," *NYT*, January 7, 1995; Kevin Sack, "Conservative Party Leader Picked to Run Port Authority," *NYT*, January 10, 1995.

[47] Editorial, "Mr. Pataki's Port Authority Problem," *NYT*, February 7, 1995; Doig, *Empire on the Hudson*.

[48] Under Marlin, the Port Authority undertook several actions to "increase private-sector involvement" at the Trade Center. The Vista Hotel was put up for sale. Private developers were sought to participate in the redevelopment and management of the retail mall plaza. New private management would reopen the Windows on the World restaurant in early 1996. The Observation Deck was to be turned over to a private operator for redevelopment and management.

[49] Chemical Securities Inc., *Options for Maximizing the Value of the World Trade Center to the Port Authority of New York and New Jersey* (hereafter cited as the Chemical Securities Report), 3 vols., October 26, 1995, vol. 1, 8; Chemical Securities Report, vol. 2, 46.

[50] Chemical Securities Report, 2; 13. My source on the Chemical team explained, still with some amazement years later, that the Port Authority had no professional accounting system for the WTC. The data was sparse. The agency could not give the Chemical team cash flow numbers. The team had to build a financial model to get cash flow numbers. It went through every lease and built what it said was the first full model of the office and retail complex. It helped that two of the Chemical team members had worked on the 1984 study while at Bear Stearns.

[51] Charles Gasparino, "Management of Trade Center Is Called Poor," *WSJ*, November 17, 1995; Al Frank, "Agency to Consider Report on Trade Center Sale," *New Jersey Star-Ledger*, December 6, 1995. After the PA board had finally discussed the findings of the Chemical study for the first time in late January 1996, Eisenberg announced a series of steps "to test the reaction of the marketplace to three specific options—sale of the complex, net lease of the complex, or private asset management." "Port Authority Chairman Lewis M. Eisenberg Today Announced a Series of Steps to Test Marketplace Response to Options for Maximizing the Value of the World Trade Center to the Port Authority and to the People of the Region," press release, January 25, 1996. Months later, when the *Daily News* finally secured a copy of the Chemical report the agency had refused to release (rejecting a Freedom on Information law request on the basis that releasing "sensitive financial information" would put the towers at a "competitive disadvantage"), the PA said it would "go slow" on the Chemical recommendations. "There is no gun to our head saying you have to do this now, so we intend to be very deliberate and very prudent," said PA chairman Eisenberg, a Whitman appointee. Douglas Feiden, "PA Has Double Trouble: Sell or Lease Ailing Twin Towers, Hush-Hush Study Sez," *DN*, May 5, 1996; also see editorial, "Twin Towers of Waste," *DN*, May 7, 1996.

[52] The Port Authority told Chemical it was conflicted out. Chemical had taken the job as an entrée for being the sales agent for a possible transaction; the $550,000 fee was but a quarter of the real cost of conducting its study.

[53] Peter Grant, "Gov Turns Up Heat for Sale of WTC by Port Authority," *DN*, December 22, 1997.

[54] There were also rumors that Whitman didn't want to make any commitment during the year of her reelection campaign. Al Frank, "Trade Center Sale Seen as Worst Option," *New Jersey Star-Ledger*, March 2, 1997.

[55] The city sued the PA three times on the PILOT issue. The Silverstein leasehold acquisition of July 2001 went forward before resolution of the city's claims, with the transaction documents providing that in the event there was a final, nonappealable determination that property taxes were payable with respect to 1, 2, 4, and 5 World Trade Center, and the retail components of the complex, the Port Authority would be responsible for payment of such amounts. Finally, in November 2002, at the same time the city and the PA reached a deal on the extension of the LaGuardia and JFK airport leases, the parties reached an agreement on future WTC PILOT payments (beginning January 1, 2004), which was approved by the PA Board of Commissioners. Upon execution of the amended agreement, all pending litigation with respect to the PILOTs was terminated. *PANYNJ Annual Report 2003*, note 6 to the financial statements.

56 Sea-Land–Maersk was the world's largest container-ship operator and supply-vessel operator with ports all over the world, including Port Elizabeth. The stakes riding on this lease deal were extraordinarily high—jobs, growth in the maritime economy, and the region's status as the premier port on the East Coast. Within the region's $20 billion shipping industry, the giant operators accounted for about a quarter of the cargo moving annually through the harbor. Together they accounted for one thousand employees and a $100 million payroll. Maritime executives and union leaders feared a devastating effect on the maritime economy if these two anchors left the region, and they layered on political pressure. Despite their "profound differences in how to run the Port Authority," Governors Whitman and Pataki "have an obligation to put them aside and conduct themselves likes allies for the sake of the regional economy," the *Times* editorial board said. "Saving New York's Shipping," *NYT*, April 13, 1999. A deal had been made with a Denmark-based business conglomerate when the lines threatened to leave and move to Baltimore, which was wooing them with increased subsidies while the two states bickered. As reported in the *Times*, "an original offer made to the companies by the Port Authority included a host of subsidies," and Governor Whitman "sweetened the deal by also offering $120 million in state funds." Jim Yardley, "A Port with a Political Storm; as Governors Feud, Dockworkers Fear for Their Jobs," *NYT*, April 26, 1999. It was a big deal, with much-disputed valuation of subsidies ranging from "$180 million to $1 billion depending on which side is talking." Owen Moritz, "Port Authority Projects in Limbo, N.Y. Commissioners Shun Meeting," *DN*, December 17, 1999.

57 Yardley, "A Port with a Political Storm."

58 Linda Sandler, "World Trade Center Lease Documents Sit as Governors Spar," *WSJ*, November 24, 1999.

59 Ronald Smothers, "Port Authority Rift Revealed States' Competitive Instincts," *NYT*, June 6, 2000.

60 Editorial, "Peace across the Hudson," June 6, 2000; editorial, "No End of a Stalemate," *The Record* [Bergen County, NJ], June 5, 2000.

Chapter 5

1 Kirk Johnson and Charles V. Bagli, "A Nation Challenged: Architects, Planners and Residents Wonder How to Fill the Hole in the City," *NYT*, September 26, 2001.

2 Eric Lipton, "A Nation Challenged: Ground Zero: Cleanup's Pace Outstrips Plans for Attack Site," *NYT*, January 7, 2002.

3 Kirk Johnson, "A Plan without a Master, Rebuilding by Committee? Robert Moses Would Cringe," *NYT*, April 14, 2002.

4 Ada Louise Huxtable, "In the Fray: New York's 9/11 Site Needed Not a Moses but a Logue," *WSJ*, August 27, 2008. In "More Than Zero," architectural critic Martin Filler earlier cited Logue's "benign influence in shepherding huge architectural and infrastructure projects to completion." *New Republic*, September 9, 2002, https://newrepublic.com/article/66451/more-zero.

5 Paul Goldberger, "After the World Trade Center: The Struggle to Make a City for Our Time," lecture delivered to the Architectural Foundation of Cincinnati, May 6, 2004, http://www.paulgoldberger.com/lectures.

6 Edward Wyatt, "The Proposals: Everyone Weighs in with Rebuilding Ideas," *NYT*, January 12, 2002.

[7] Cathleen McGuigan, "Up from the Ashes," *Newsweek*, November 12, 2001; Andrew Rice, "Developers, Pataki Making Huge Plan for New Skyline," *NYO*, September 24, 2001.

[8] See Eugenie L. Birch, "U.S. Planning Culture under Pressure: Major Elements Endure and Flourish in the Face of Crises," in *Comparative Planning Cultures*, ed. Bishwapriya Sanyal, (New York: Routledge, 2005), 337–346.

[9] Rice, "Developers, Pataki Making Huge Plan"; editorial, "Rebuild Downtown from Bottom Up," *DN*, September 30, 2001.

[10] The task force was organized into ten subcommittees focusing on energy, transportation, building codes, and planning and zoning. For expertise in planning and zoning, it reached out to the city's deep architectural community; as the architects reached out to professionals in allied professions, the subcommittee grew to become a twenty-member coalition of the design, planning, and development communities that became so large, it formed its own entity, separate from the partnership, New York New Visions (NYNV). I was a participant in the NYNV Growth Strategies Subcommittee.

[11] Partnership for New York City, *Working Together to Accelerate New York's Recovery* (2001), 16; Kathryn S. Wylde, "The Old Downtown Economy Won't Return," *NYT*, March 29, 2002.

[12] Charles V. Bagli, "A Nascent Effort, Still in Need of a Plan," *NYT*, October 29, 2001.

[13] "Grid Symposium; Ground Zero: Renewing New York," *Grid* 3:8 (October 2001): 20–29, at 21.

[14] Carl B. Weisbrod, "Downtown Must Be Rebuilt," *Gotham Gazette*, December 31, 2001.

[15] During 2000, rental revenues from the Merrill Lynch tenancy at the World Financial Center alone accounted for 10 percent of the company's $732 million consolidated revenue from its commercial property operations in both the United States and Canada. Brookfield's other Manhattan commercial properties included 245 Park Avenue in midtown and two development sites, 300 Madison Avenue (where a 1.2-million-square-foot tower was under development for CIBC World Markets) and a site on West Thirty-first Street at Ninth Avenue. Brookfield Properties Corporation, "Annual Information Form," May 18, 2001, 4.

[16] "Grid Symposium; Ground Zero," 22; Dean Starkman and Peter Grant, "Brookfield and Silverstein Hold Talks on Future of World Trade Center Site," *WSJ*, October 16, 2002.

[17] "Grid Symposium; Ground Zero," 22, 23; Johnson and Bagli, "A Nation Challenged: Architects, Planners and Residents Wonder How to Fill the Hole in the City."

[18] After the 2001 attacks on the World Trade Center, Graham organized and supervised the $140 million restoration of the company's buildings, including the World Financial Center and its Winter Garden, and received the 2002 Building Trades Employers' Association Leadership Award.

[19] The idea of burying West Street was not new; it was part of a plan put forth by the Urban Development Corporation to bring West Side Highway up to interstate standards. It was re-named "Westway" in 1974; the idea was to bury the highway in new landfill south of Fortieth Street (requiring about two hundred acres of the Hudson River to be landfilled) and place development atop the land so created along with a ninety-three-acre park; the 1981 price tag was $2.1 billion. Controversy and lawsuits erupted, and when Judge Thomas Griesa of the U.S. District Court ruled against a needed dredge-and-fill permit filed by New York State because the proposed road would harm striped bass (and therefore violated the National Environmental Policy Act and the Clean Water Act) and the U.S. Court of Appeals for the Second Circuit upheld the decision, the project was essentially dead; in September 1985, New

York City officials gave up on the project. A gulf of 260 feet separating Battery Park City from the rest of Manhattan remained in place. Fast forward to 2002 WTC rebuilding: The resuscitated idea of burying West Street, this time from Chambers Street south to Battery Place, would free up sixteen acres of land for other uses. The cost was prohibitive, roughly in the vicinity of "a billion and a half dollars because water mains and power conduits would have had to be relocated, and the new street constructed in the form of a watertight tunnel, since West Street is on landfill that is above the water table." Paul Goldberger, "The Skyline: Groundwork: How the Future of Ground Zero Is Being Resolved," *New Yorker*, May 20, 2002.

[20] Trained as a nuclear engineer and whose career took a turn to transportation planning, Forman was thinking out of the box about using existing transit lines to bring the Long Island Railroad (LIRR) into the Trade Center site. Seven of the nine LIRR lines went through Jamaica and proceeded to either Penn Station in west midtown Manhattan or Atlantic Avenue (now Barclay Center) in downtown Brooklyn, where passengers could transfer to numerous subway lines to downtown Manhattan. Regardless of what train passengers boarded in Long Island, they could always change at Jamaica to board a train for their ultimate destination in either midtown or downtown Manhattan.

Forman was leading the engineering team designing East Side Access, which would bring trains from Jamaica through a new tunnel under the East River and down Park Avenue to Grand Central Terminal in east midtown Manhattan. As part of this project, the Brooklyn branch of the LIRR would need to be turned into a shuttle. Trains could not originate on Long Island and pass through Jamaica and continue on to three separate destinations in Manhattan. The track crossings would be too complex. The solution would be to convert the Brooklyn branch into a shuttle. Then trains originating on Long Island would continue to pass through Jamaica and only proceed to two locations. However, in the new configuration the two destinations would be in midtown Manhattan. If one wanted to go to lower Manhattan by way of Brooklyn, one would have to transfer to a shuttle to downtown Brooklyn and then transfer again to the subway. Lower Manhattan would now always be a three-seat ride through Brooklyn. Mass transit to lower Manhattan was going to be worse, not better. Forman believed that if the Brooklyn branch could be connected to the underutilized A/C subway tunnel to Manhattan, the new shuttle could run directly from Jamaica to the WTC site. The new shuttle would be express to the Barclay Center, connect to the A/C line, stop at the Barclay Center, and three stops later be at the Trade Center. It could either be run as an LIRR shuttle or a subway express. As a subway express, it would have the added benefit of relieving the overcrowded Queens subway lines, which all went to midtown, by creating a new, unique express to lower Manhattan.

[21] Lawrence Graham author interview, March 29, 2012; John Zuccotti author interview, November 13, 2013; editorial, "Under the Surface Downtown," *NYT*, November 26, 2002.

[22] Alex Garvin author interview, March 29, 2013.

[23] NYNV's subcommittee report, *Growth Strategies Team Report: Possible Futures* (May 2002), won the New York Chapter Project Award from the American Institute of Architects; Christopher Choa, letter to John Whitehead, April 26, 2002.

[24] The eight working groups covered these specific topics: economic development; transportation and mobility; social, economic, and environmental justice; the memorial process; green buildings and sustainable systems; civic amenities; urban design; and the regulatory framework.

[25] The six principles in the document were: focus public funds on infrastructure and civic amenities; integrate the memorial design process with planning for lower Manhattan and the WTC site; plan for all of lower Manhattan, not just the WTC site; make the process fair; develop all plans in an open and inclusive process; and adopt green building and sustainable development principles. In addition, the framework put forward twenty-one recommendations from its eight working group areas. Civic Alliance, *A Planning Framework to Rebuild Downtown New York* (2002), 4; Philip Lentz, "Coalitions Seek Downtown Say," *Crain's*, December 10, 2001.

[26] R.Dot's development objectives embraced eight principles: self-determination and inclusion, memorialization, livability and balance, arts and culture, productivity, decentralization, sustainability, diversity, efficient transportation, and pride of place. Rebuild Downtown Our Town, *Toward a Sustainable City: Rebuilding Lower Manhattan*, n.d. [2002].

[27] See David W. Woods, *Democracy Deferred: Civic Leadership after 9/11* (New York: Palgrave Macmillan, 2012), 1–3; Charles V. Bagli, "Developer's Pace at 7 World Trade Center Upsets Some," *NYT*, January 31, 2002.

[28] Arielle Goldberg, "Civic Engagement in the Rebuilding of the World Trade Center," in *Contentious City: The Politics of Recovery in New York City*, ed. John Mollenkopf (New York: Russell Sage Foundation, 2005), 112–139, at 123.

[29] Birch, "U.S. Planning Culture under Pressure," 344. LCAN's five principles were as follows: The rebuilding decision-making process must be broad-based, transparent, and inclusive; rebuilding must be linked to all the people, business, and communities damaged by September 11, not just to those in lower Manhattan or in high-wage industries; redevelopment resources should be concentrated on infrastructure, not on corporate subsidies; rebuilding should be done to ensure maximum social, economic, and environmental sustainability; public revenue must match public needs, even if this means raising taxes. Goldberg, "Civic Engagement in the Rebuilding of the World Trade Center," 121.

[30] Birch, "U.S. Planning Culture under Pressure," 337.

[31] Richard Ivy, editor-in-chief letter, *Architectural Record*, January 18, 2002; Deyan Sudjic, "Review: Critics: Architecture: Can Anyone Do Justice to Ground Zero? Of Course, the World Trade Center Will Be Redeveloped; the Problem Is How Best to Replace One of New York's Most Remarkable Landmarks," *The Observer* [London], January 26, 2002.

[32] Nobel quoted in Clay Risen, "Book Review: Rebuilding Ground Zero," *NYT*, January 30, 2005; Alexander Garvin, *The Planning Game: Lessons from Great Cities* (New York: W. W. Norton, 2013).

[33] Benjamin Forgey, "Visions to Fill an Aching Void; Architects Image a Future for the Twin Towers Site," *Washington Post*, January 31, 2002; Goldberger, "After the World Trade Center."

[34] Max Protetch, *A New World Trade Center: Design Proposals from Leading Architects Worldwide* (New York: Regan Books, HarperCollins Publishers, 2002), viii; Benjamin Forgey, "World Trade Center Plans, Rising above the Squabbles," *Washington Post*, April 18, 2004; Protetch, *A New World Trade Center*, xi.

[35] Gary Tuchman, "Six Months Later: The WTC Attack," *People in the News*, CNN.com, March 9, 2002, www.cnn.com/TRANSCRIPTS/0203/09/pitn.00.html.

[36] Sudjic, "Review: Critics: Architecture: Can Anyone Do Justice to Ground Zero?"; Forgey, "Visions to Fill an Aching Void."

[37] Herbert Muschamp, "Thinking Big: A Plan for Ground Zero and Beyond," *NYT Magazine*, September 8, 2002.

[38] Muschamp, "Thinking Big," 45. With the exception of some notable icons and a few extraordinary buildings, Manhattan's architectural portfolio presented a conservative profile considerably short of the historical quality that defined Chicago's exceptional architectural history, so the goal of elevating the city's architecture certainly resonated widely. Whether what Muschamp presented as "a celebration of the power of architecture to inspire, to dazzle—and to spur furious debate"—was going to meet the challenge, however, remained open to a lot of speculation.

[39] Muschamp, "Thinking Big," 48–49.

[40] Herbert Muschamp, "Appraisal; Marginal Role for Architecture at Ground Zero," *NYT*, June 23, 2002. That BBB was not being asked to design buildings but rather was charged with defining a plan for the district of lower Manhattan, including Ground Zero, was beside the point that Muschamp wanted to make. To many professional colleagues who wrote letters to the principals of the firm expressing outrage at Muschamp's unsubstantiated bashing, it was "vitriolic nastiness," "high-handedness," "out-of-line and ill-timed," "gratuitous and unwarranted public criticism." The firm mounted a counteroffensive by talking to the *Times* editorial board and soliciting letters from supporters. On May 29, the *Times* printed one of who knows how many letters that might have been sent. In his letter to the editor, Ernest W. Hutton Jr., urban designer and chairman of the communications committee of New York New Visions, the collaborative civic group formed after 9/11 that was influential in shaping the planning process for Ground Zero and lower Manhattan, wrote that Muschamp "would seemingly have us renounce rational urban planning in favor of an unrealistic approach to city design in which an architecture of narcissism trumps all other considerations of program, use, context and public interest." The firm defended its position after the summer 2002 Listening to the City event; see John H. Beyer and John Belle, "A New Downtown: More Ideas Wanted," letter to the editor, *NYT*, August 17, 2002.

[41] Mayor Bloomberg could register his position at LMDC board meetings through the city's eight appointees and Deputy Mayor Doctoroff, who attended most LMDC board meetings. The mayor was also in constant communication with Roland Betts about site-planning issues. Neither, however, equated with formal decision-making power.

[42] Deborah Sontag, "The Hole in the City's Heart," *NYT*, September 11, 2006.

[43] Liz Robbins and Mike McIntire, "A True Champion of Grand Plans and Tiny Details," *NYT*, May 16, 2004; Michael O'Keefe and Luke Cyphers, "Political Games: Doctoroff Makes Play in City Sports Plans," *DN*, January 13, 2002.

[44] The Port Authority took several financial actions to protect itself against the risk of not being able to repay the bondholders of its long-term debt. After issuing a statement to calm bondholders, the agency's chief financial officer set in motion a plan to accelerate retirement of the $1.8 billion of debt that matured after 2015. It also reduced the maturity of its debt issued for airport construction to twenty years from thirty-five years. The faster twenty-year amortization schedule did constrain the agency because it meant higher debt-service payments and a lower coverage ratio, but it did not immobilize the issuance of debt. The agency also went back and reworked its public-private deal with LCOR and Schippipool for the international terminal at JFK Airport, shortening the term of the agreement to twenty-five

years, with a kick-out if the city lease did not get renewed; it then issued $934 million of special project bonds for redevelopment of the outdated terminal. As I was told by a senior PA financial officer, this transaction made it difficult for Giuliani to claim that the PA was failing to adhere to its capital obligation under the lease, and enabled the PA to keep doing deals at the airport—and outlast Giuliani.

[45] Anthony Coscia author interview, October 5, 2010.

[46] Sontag, "The Hole in the City's Heart"; Michael Saul and Greg Gittrich, "Won't Let Airports Go, Must Keep Control in Any WTC Swap, Mike Says," DN, August 9, 2002.

[47] Editorials: "A Good Deal for Lower Manhattan," NYT, August 6, 2002; "Let's Make a Deal? Okay. If It's Fair," DN, August 7, 2002; "Questionable Swap: A Lot of Loose Ends Must Be Tied Up Tight before the Port Authority Is Given City Airports," Newsday, August 8, 2002; "WTC Swap Is Right for City," Crain's, August 12, 2002; "Not a Job for City Hall," NYP, August 8, 2002.

[48] The dispute over airport rents was in arbitration initiated by the Giuliani administration. The PA had already rejected the city's claim that it was owed about $660 million in back rent, but based on projections in its budget documents, the city was still expecting to collect that sum. The lease agreement had guaranteed the city only $3 million a year, but delivered more depending upon annual revenues after accounting for capital investments; over the past ten years, the PA had paid an average of $23 million a year.

[49] Initially, the PA could not see how the swap would make sense; then the financial staff began to crunch numbers on what it would cost, how long it would take to rebuild the Trade Center site, what the rents would be, what the PILOT payments were, what insurance proceeds would result; staff members did lots of sensitivity analyses. They looked at the revenues from the airport and what the PA would have to pay the city. They used a 9 percent discount rate, approximately; their hurdle rate cost of capital was between 8 percent and 8.5 percent, but this potential transaction was riskier. It started to seem like a positive proposal, that a swap would make a lot of sense. Senior staff and their consultant went to Trenton to brief Governor James McGreevey around April 2003. They were not far into their briefing when McGreevey asked, "What are we talking about? What is this?" The proposal died.

[50] Charles V. Bagli, "Bloomberg Administration and Port Authority Get Closer on Possible Land Swap Deal," NYT, April 1, 2003.

[51] In a sizable ad printed on August 12 in the Times, developer Douglas Durst called the land swap "an ingenious approach to gaining control of the WTC redevelopment process," but argued that "the economics of the swap must take into account other economics like the taxes due on the WTC land," specifically, the city's claim for "additional annual taxes of $73 million going forward and at least $105 million in total for previous years." Not doing so would "shortchange" New York City. "The easiest way for the City to get control of the World Trade Center land," he said, "is to have a negotiated condemnation of the lease by the LMDC.... The Port Authority could receive its rent net of real estate taxes and the lessee could maintain its position while the City gains control of the process." Durst's position was curious. Staking out a position favoring the use of condemnation held no small amount of irony since his family-based company had long maintained a philosophical position against government exercise of its powers of eminent domain. However, Durst would soon seek such government assistance against a couple of longtime holdouts frustrating his firm's quest to assemble the remaining parcels on the block of West Forty-second Street and Sixth

Avenue for development of a new headquarters tower for Bank of America. Construction of the tower started in 2004, after Durst completed a deal to purchase the two holdout parcels for what was then one of the highest ever prices paid, $348 a square foot, completing an effort begun thirty-six years earlier by his father, Seymour Durst. Behind the holdout's ultimate settlement loomed the state's initiation of condemnation action against the property owners. Drawing upon $650 million of tax-exempt Liberty Bonds that many, including LMDC chairman Whitehead, thought should only be used for the recovery of lower Manhattan, the fifty-seven-story tower in midtown was very controversial.

52 Saul and Gittrich, "Won't Let Airports Go."

53 A recent deal cut with New Jersey governor McGreevy and Mayor James Sharp of Newark preemptively renegotiating the Port Authority's Newark Airport lease, extending it thirty-four years, gave Newark an immediate cash windfall of $265 million. In exchange, Newark agreed to drop a long-standing lawsuit against the Port Authority over $1.3 billion in disputed rent payments. This angered Doctoroff for two reasons: First, it created a new precedent-setting starting point; second, the terms of the precedent gave Newark most-favored-nation status, meaning, this is what I get now, and if New York City gets something "better," I get that too. The definition of "better" was ambiguous, said an insider to the Port Authority's negotiations.

54 Saul and Gittrich, "Won't Let Airports Go."

55 Bagli, "Bloomberg Administration and Port Authority Get Closer on Possible Land Swap Deal"; William Neuman, "Jersey Barrier to WTC Land Swap," NYP, March 2, 2003.

56 Tom McGeveran, "W.T.C.-Airports Swap Unsheathes Conflict with Gargano, City," NYO, August 12, 2002; Anthony Coscia author interview, May 8, 2015.

57 Joseph Seymour e-mail to author, April 1, 2015.

58 Daniel Doctoroff author interview, January 23, 2008.

59 David Seifman, "9/11: The Road Back; Bloomy Bids for Control," DN, June 28, 2003; PA board meeting minutes, November 20, 2003, 555–558.

60 Charles Butler, "Feature: The Right Person at the Right Time, Lou Tomson '61 Played a Key Role in the Development of Plans for the World Trade Center Site," Columbia College Today, July 2003, http://www.college.columbia.edu/cct_archive/jul03/features2.php; "Head of Downtown Rebuilding Agency to Leave," NYT, January 17, 2003.

61 Under the city's proposal, LMDC would be restructured with the city assuming more direct control over planning for the Trade Center site, in particular, PAC and the cultural program, and lower Manhattan generally; with the state assuming more direct control over the memorial; and the LMDC remaining in place only to run any programs already underway, such as the residential grant program, and to approve funding decisions jointly recommended by the city and the state. The LMDC would continue to cover all planning costs. No role for the Department of City Planning appears in the four-page summary of proposed change. "Proposed Changes to New York State and New York City Roles in Lower Manhattan Rebuilding," sent to John P. Cahill from Daniel Doctoroff, confidential document sent to author under a FOI request, n.d. [2003]; William Neuman, "City Hall Makes Push to Control WTC Rebuild," NYP, March 7, 2003.

62 Sam Roberts, "The Legacy of Westway: Lessons from Its Demise," NYT, October 7, 1985; Chicago too had its elite business group, the Chicago Central Area Committee, formed in 1956 to seize control of a redevelopment program in which neighborhood actors had begun

to play a significant role. Pittsburgh had its Allegheny Conference on Community Development and Baltimore, its Greater Baltimore Committee.

[63] It was his mantra, urban designer Gary Hack (my husband), who worked with Leventhal on several projects, told me. "He repeated it many times during a meeting."

[64] Edward Wyatt, "Ground Zero: Planning: Many Voices, but Little Dialogue on Memorial for Trade Center Site," *NYT*, January 26, 2002.

[65] Diane Cardwell, "In Final Address, Giuliani Envisions a Soaring Memorial," *NYT*, December 28, 2001.

Chapter 6

[1] Dan Barry, "Mournful Task Ending, Forever Unfinished," *NYT*, May 3, 2002. The somber thirty-minute ceremony attended by the families of the victims, members of the city's uniformed services, and top local politicians began at 10:29 A.M., the moment the second of the two towers collapsed. It was distinguished by the ringing of fire department bells, bagpipes playing "America the Beautiful," and a ceremonial casket containing a fifty-eight-ton steel beam from one of the towers (the "last beam" now in Foundation Hall of the 9/11 Memorial Museum), driven out of the site on a flatbed truck shrouded in black and covered with an American flag and a bouquet of flowers. Jennifer Steinhauer, "Tribute Will Signal the End of Search," *NYT*, May 17, 2002.

[2] Tom McGeveran, "Port Authority Reasserts Grip on Towers Site," *NYO*, May 6, 2002.

[3] PANYNJ, "Statement from Joseph J. Seymour Executive Director The Port Authority of New York and New Jersey Regarding Today's FEMA Announcement," press release (#86–2002), August 12, 2002; Edward Wyatt, "Rebuilding Transit in Lower Manhattan Will Take More Money, or a Narrower Scope," *NYT*, August 13, 2002; Jack Lyne, "Week of August 19, 2002, Snapshot from the Field, New York Will Build WTC-Area Transit Hub with $4.55B in Federal Funds," *Snapshot from the Field*, siteselection.com/ssinsider/snapshot/sf020819.htm.

[4] Robert Douglass author interview, April 18, 2012.

[5] David W. Dunlap, "Blocks: For Construction at Trade Center, the Future Is Now," *NYT*, October 10, 2002; David W. Dunlap, "Reopening Soon, a Spartan Gateway Downtown," *NYT*, October 31, 2002.

[6] Scott Raab, "Good Days at Ground Zero," *Esquire*, October 2010, part 6 of an eight-part series, http://www.esquire.com/features/new-world-trade-center-towers-1010.

[7] Avi Schick author interview, May 10, 2010.

[8] Christopher Bonanos, "The Complex: The Politics at Ground Zero Have Been Painfully Difficult. But Its Construction Demands May Be Even Worse," *New York Magazine*, May 16, 2010, 28; Schick author interview.

[9] GMAC turned most of the $563 million mortgage loan into securities. The August 2001 securitization sold off all but $80 million of the mortgage to a large number of investors. Despite the terrorist bombing of 1993 and the complex nature of the ground lease between the PA and Silverstein, the offering was well received by investors, who looked to the high quality of the asset and the likely upside in net income as Silverstein Properties worked to increase the operating efficiency of the buildings and bring rents up to market levels as leases expired. Though GMAC committed to an additional $200 million mezzanine loan to finance specific capital improvements required by the Port Authority, those plans were made moot by the 9/11 attack.

[10] Joseph Seymour author interview, September 25, 2014.

[11] William Neuman, "Ground Zero Snag—Mall Rebuilder Rejects Winning Design," *NYP*, April 3, 2003; Edward Wyatt, "Retail-Space Developer Balks at the Design for Ground Zero," *NYT*, April 4, 2003.

[12] Tom McGeveran, "Libeskind's Plan Hits First Wall with Mall Giant," *NYO*, April 14, 2003; Wyatt, "Retail-Space Developer Balks at the Design for Ground Zero."

[13] David W. Dunlap, "Marriott Ceding Property Where Hotel Stood on the World Trade Center Site," *NYT*, October 24, 2003. When it brought the Vista from the Kuo Hotel Corporation of Hong Kong in 1989, the Port Authority saw it as a strategic decision to enhance the competitive stature of the WTC, which it believed needed a four-star hotel to support the commercial activities of the complex. It was, a PA official said, "An opportunity to expedite the renovation of the hotel, which was being forestalled by the weakening relationship between Kuo and Hilton International [the operator of the hotel]." David W. Dunlap, "Commercial Property: Downtown Hotels; Bond, Vista, Marriott—Now Come the Millennium," *NYT*, June 30, 1991.

[14] PA board meeting minutes, July 31, 2003, 352.

[15] In a letter from Westfield to the PA dated March 14, 2003, reported in Neuman, "Ground Zero Snag"; Dean Starkman, "Silverstein and Port Authority Are Sued by Lender GMAC," *WSJ*, September 4, 2003.

[16] Peter Grant, "Property Report: Friction at Ground Zero," *WSJ*, September 4, 2002.

[17] Grant, "Property Report: Fiction at Ground Zero." Buying out the creditors of 7 WTC was complicated by a situation that did not exist with GMAC: a contractual obligation obligating Silverstein to share increases in the building's value over $475 million. This "equity kicker" provision was a part of the $450 million construction financing Silverstein had obtained from Teachers Insurance and Annuity Association (TIAA); when the developer ran into financial difficulties in the early 1990s, as a consequence of the severe real estate downturn, and had to restructure his debt on this asset, as part of that transaction, he agreed to give TIAA the 40 percent equity kicker. Along with the TIAA debt, Blackstone purchased the kicker. To buy out the mortgage, Silverstein and Blackstone would have to agree on the value of the kicker, which was not going to be as easy as the asset no longer existed. Finally, in March 2005, when Silverstein's allocation of Liberty Bonds for 7 WTC were issued, this prior debt was discharged for $508.8 million.

[18] "Westfield America to Sell World Trade Center Retail Interest to Port Authority of New York and New Jersey," Westfield America press release, September 15, 2003; Charles V. Bagli, "Pataki Seeks Insurance Settlement So Work Can Begin on Trade Center," *NYT*, October 10, 2003.

[19] Charles V. Bagli, "Time Granted in Dispute over Insurance for 9/11 Site," *NYT*, September 26, 2003; "WTC Leaseholder Working to Fashion Loan-Repayment Plan," Dow Jones International News, September 25, 2003.

[20] The $570 million cost of the GMAC buyout included the expense associated with early repayment of the interest-only securities of the GMAC loan; investors who had bought these riskier securities, including GMAC, stood to lose the most financially if they were repaid earlier than expected when they priced the purchase of that security.

[21] The Port Authority allowed Silverstein to use funds in the insurance escrow rather than the reserve account (maintained under the loan agreement) for the entire $563 million to

pay off GMAC, including associated prepayment costs under the interest-only portion of the GMAC loan, thereby freeing up the $98.5 million in the reserve account as a return of equity to Silverstein and his investors. In an exchange, the terms of the agreement gave the PA the ability to reconfigure the premises to be developed by Silverstein. By removing from the net leased premises the portions designated as "Public Transit, Streets and Open Spaces" (consistent with the WTC Site Diagram dated November 26, 2003), the agency regained control over the location of the Transportation Hub and its related infrastructure and the memorial and cultural facilities. It was also able to define the amounts and uses of funds Silverstein was allowed to withdraw from the funds on deposit in the insurance escrow. On the other side of the ledger, the agreement kept in place payment of management fees to Silverstein as provided for in "the existing Management and Leasing Agreement dated July 24, 2001" between the Silverstein investors and Silverstein's property management entity, Silverstein WTC Mgmt. Co. LLC., which was consistent with post–September 11, 2001, practice. Letter Agreement between the Port Authority of New York and New Jersey and 1 WTC LLC, 2 WTC LLC, 4 WTC LLC, and 5 WTC LLC, c/o Silverstein Properties, Inc., December 1, 2003 [FOI Request #13209] hereafter cited as PA 2003 Letter Agreement.

[22] PA 2003 Letter Agreement.

[23] PA 2003 Letter Agreement; Tom McGeveran, "Downtown 2.0: Politics Makes Big Redesigns," *NYO*, September 22, 2002; "Rebuilding the World Trade Center," *Cornell Real Estate Review* 10:1 (July 2012): 29–53, at 46.

[24] Jody Shenn, "GMAC on WTC—No Grudge, but Lessons," *American Banker*, December 29, 2003, 1.

[25] Shenn, "GMAC on WTC—No Grudge, but Lessons"; Charles V. Bagli, "Silverstein to Get Back Most of Cash from Trade Center Bid," *NYT*, November 22, 2003.

[26] McGeveran, "Port Authority Reasserts Grip on Towers Site"; William Neuman, "WTC Planners Mend Fences," *NYP*, April 23, 2002; William Neuman and Maggie Haberman, "Rebuild Boss: Everybody Has Final Say," *NYP*, April 25, 2002.

[27] McGeveran, "Port Authority Reasserts Grip on Towers Site."

[28] Cooperation Agreement between the Port Authority of New York and New Jersey and the Lower Manhattan Development Corporation [to develop and coordinate long-terms plans for the development of lower Manhattan, including the World Trade Center Site], May 10, 2002; editorial, "Rebuilding New York; How to Fill the Hole at Ground Zero," *NYT*, January 13, 2002.

[29] William Neuman, "Mike Aide Raps Slow Motion on Memorial," *NYP*, April 24, 2002.

[30] Editorial, "The Revival of Lower Manhattan," *NYT*, November 24, 2001); All NYT editorials, "Immediate Needs at Ground Zero," December 26, 2001; "Rebuilding New York: How to Fill the Hole at Ground Zero"; "Starting at Ground Zero," February 2, 2002; "Rebuilding Downtown," April 3, 2002.

[31] Paul Goldberger, *Up from Zero: Politics, Architecture, and the Rebuilding of New York* (New York: Random House, 2004), 111.

[32] Seymour author interview.

[33] Edward Wyatt, "Rebuilding May Expand Beyond Site," *NYT*, June 20, 2002.

[34] David W. Dunlap, "Redevelopment Pact Is Sought for World Trade Center Site," *NYT*, April 21, 2004.

[35] McGeveran, "Port Authority Reasserts Grip on Towers Site"; Roland Betts author interview, November 24, 2004.

[36] Frank Rich, "The De Facto Capital," *NYT*, October 6, 2002.

[37] Edward Wyatt, "Further Designs Are Sought in Rebuilding Downtown," *NYT*, August 15, 2002.

[38] PA board meeting minutes, December 12, 2002, 543.

Chapter 7

[1] James C. McKinley Jr., "The 2002 Elections: The Governor; Pataki Coasts to a 3rd Term; McCall Is a Distant Second," *NYT*, November 6, 2002; editorial, "Under the Surface of Downtown," *NYT*, November 26, 2002; editorial, "Downtown Needs Pataki," *Crain's*, November 11, 2002.

[2] Deborah Sontag, "The Hole in the City's Heart," *NYT*, September 11, 2006.

[3] Edward Wyatt, "Pataki's Surprising Limit on Ground Zero Design," *NYT*, July 2, 2002; Paul Goldberger, *Up from Zero: Politics, Architecture, and the Rebuilding of New York* (New York: Random House, 2004), 212; Edward Wyatt, "Blueprint for Ground Zero Begins to Take Shape," *NYT*, May 4, 2002; Wyatt, "Pataki's Surprising Limit."

[4] Steve Cuozzo, "Damage and Delay," *NYP*, March 31, 2003.

[5] George Pataki, "Governor's Remarks at ABNY Lunch," April 24, 2003.

[6] The controversy stemmed from questions about the process for picking a consultant, in particular about Garvin's favorable scoring of BBB over Ehrenkrantz Eckstut & Kuhn and four other finalists, and whether his scoring unfairly skewed the process. See Edward Wyatt, "Doubts on Bid Rankings Spur Redevelopment Review," *NYT*, May 22, 2003, and "Design Firm Chosen to Oversee Rebuilding of Lower Manhattan," *NYT*, May 23, 2002, for reliable reports on the episode.

[7] LMDC, "The Lower Manhattan Development Corporation and the Port Authority to Hold Public Hearing Tomorrow on Future of the World Trade Center Site, Adjacent Areas and Related Transportation Infrastructure," press release, May 22, 2002.

[8] Charles V. Bagli, "6 Plans for Ground Zero Share Striking Similarities," *NYT*, July 11, 2002; Alan J. Wax, "Starting at Ground Zero: Architectural Firm Known for Historic Renovations Faces Its Greatest Challenge—Planning Lower Manhattan's Future," *Newsday*, June 2, 2002; Alexander Garvin, "Reflections and Choice," http://alumninet.yale.edu/classes/yc1962/garviniview03.html.

[9] Edward Wyatt, "Six Plans for Ground Zero, All Seen as a Starting Point," *NYT*, July 17, 2002; Edward Wyatt, "Bloomberg Pushes More Housing at Site," *NYT*, July 20, 2002.

[10] Editorial, "The Downtown We Don't Want," *NYT*, July 17, 2002; editorial, "Talk to the Man in Charge," *NYT*, July 20, 2002.

[11] Editorials, *DN*: "Rent Controls Ground," July 17, 2002; "Port Authority: Flawed by Design," July 20, 2002; "PA Backs Off, but Not Far Enough," July 23, 2002; "Just Say 'No' to Port Authority," July 31, 2002.

[12] Editorial, "None of the WTC Proposals Is Good Enough," *Newsday*, July 21, 2002; editorial, "A Fair First Draft," *NYP*, July 17, 2002.

[13] Ada Louise Huxtable, "Another World Trade Center Horror," *WSJ*, July 25, 2002.

[14] Though these other schemes were not public, they were known to an "inner sanctum" of professionals. Shortly before the six schemes were publicly revealed, a *Daily News* story on July 10, 2002, identified the provenance of these two developers' plans. Although BBB did not disagree with the approach, the firm expected the other plans would have individual

authorship, not that all would be labeled BBB. The six plans and their underlying authors were Memorial Plaza (BBB), Memorial Square (BBB), Memorial Triangle (Cooper-Robertson), Memorial Garden (SOM), Memorial Park (Peterson-Littenberg), and Memorial Promenade (Peterson-Littenberg). For fuller renditions of this episode, see Goldberger, *Up from Zero*, 94–97; Philip Nobel, *Sixteen Acres: Architecture and the Outrageous Struggle for the Future of Ground Zero* (New York: Metropolitan Books, Henry Holt, 2005), 109–115.

[15] Maggie Haberman and William Neuman, "Low Marks: Approved Designs Were Rejected," *NYP*, July 26, 2002.

[16] Josh Rogers, "Tomson to Leave LMDC in February," *Downtown Express*, January 21–27, 2003; Roland Betts author interview, November 22, 2004.

[17] Goldberger reported that Betts and Garvin saw the design study as a way to get inspired designs from architects more creative than BBB: "They had long go accepted the notion that a truly visionary plan for Ground Zero stood no chance of surviving the political process. They saw their roles as trying to squeeze as much design quality as they could out of that process, not of bypassing it altogether." *Up from Zero*, 128.

[18] In a speech before the New York State Assembly in November, Garvin articulated six main themes that would be incorporated into new planning guidelines: restoring the skyline with a tall structure or symbol; preserving the footprints of the twin towers; improving transportation infrastructure in downtown; creating a grand promenade to connect the WTC site to Battery Park City, burying a portion of West Street; restoring the street grid; and creating more program flexibility by reducing the minimum amount of required office space to 6.5 million square feet.

[19] Paul Goldberger, "The Sky Line: Designing Downtown," *New Yorker*, January 6, 2003, 62–69, at 62.

[20] Betts author interview.

[21] Marcie Kesner author interview, April 3, 2002.

[22] William Neuman, "Building Resentment over PA's Ground Zero Wish List," *NYP*, October 28, 2002.

[23] Goldberger, "Designing Downtown"; Glenn Thrush, "World Trade Center Officials to Choose Single Site Design," *Bloomberg News*, January 9, 2003.

[24] Dean Starkman and Ryan Chittum, "Silverstein Asserts His Rights in Project at Twin Towers Site," *WSJ*, February 3, 2003; letter from Larry Silverstein to John Whitehead, January 31, 2003.

[25] Edward Wyatt, "Trade Center Leasehold Says Officials Are Ignoring His Right to Rebuild as He Wants," *NYT*, February 1, 2003; Starkman and Chittum, "Silverstein Assets His Rights."

[26] The THINK team led by Rafael Vinoly submitted three designs, making for a total of nine designs from the seven teams.

[27] Maggie Haberman and Greg Gittrich, "PA to Skip Show of Plans for WTC," *DN*, November 22, 2002.

[28] Anthony Flint, "WTC Site Designs to Be Unveiled: Second Round of Ideas on Rebuilding Sires Lively Debate," *Boston Globe*, December 18, 2002; editorial, "Port Authority's Downtown Scam," *DN*, December 29, 2002.

[29] Maggie Haberman, "PA No-Show for WTC plans," November 23, 2002.

[30] As part of his work for the Port Authority, Eckstut (with ten consultants) undertook a comparative analysis of the LMDC's design proposals.

[31] Edward Wyatt, "Ground Zero Plan Seems to Circle Back: Compromises behind the Scenes Echo a Proposal Rejected Earlier," *NYT*, September 13, 2003.

[32] Memorandum from Joseph J. Seymour and Louis R. Tomson to members, Joint Working Group, Port Authority of New York and New Jersey/Lower Manhattan Development Corporation, "Reaching Agreement on an Integrated/Master Plan for the WTC Site," [PANYNJ FOI #13267], December 5, 2002.

[33] Editorial, "Port Authority's Downtown Scam."

[34] A first scheme, reported in the *Daily News*, called for an underground transit concourse cutting through the North Tower footprint. Paul H. B. Shin and Maggie Haberman, "Secret PA Plan Cuts thru WTC Footprint," December 27, 2002.

[35] Libeskind Design Team Statement, December 2002; Gary Hack author interview, October 19, 2003.

[36] The eight steering committee members were LMDC board member and chair of the site subcommittee Roland Betts, LMDC chairman John Whitehead, LMDC president Louis Tomson, New Jersey–appointed PA commissioners Charles Kushner and Anthony Sartor, PA executive director Joseph Seymour, Governor Pataki's deputy secretary Diana Taylor, and Deputy Mayor Daniel Doctoroff.

[37] Joseph Seymour author interview, September 15, 2014.

[38] Edward Wyatt, "Panel Supports 2 Tall Towers at Disaster Site," *NYT*, February 26, 2003.

[39] Betts author interview.

[40] The nine finalist designs of the Innovative Design Study were Foster and Partners; United Partners (Foreign Office Architects, Greg Lynn FORM, Kevin Kennon Architects, Reiser+Umemoto RUR, UN Studio); Studio Daniel Libeskind (with Gary Hack, urban planner, Hargreaves Associates, landscape architect, Jeff Zupan, traffic engineer); THINK: Ban, Schwartz, Smith, Viñoly—three schemes; Peterson-Littenberg Architecture and Urban Design; Meier Eisenman Gwathmey Holl; and SOM, which later withdrew from the competition.

[41] Betts author interview.

[42] Edward Hayes (with Susan Lehman), *Mouthpiece: A Life in—and Sometimes Just Outside—the Law* (New York: Broadway Books, Random House, 2006), 272.

[43] Hayes, *Mouthpiece*, 273, 274. The comfort factor had been facilitated by Hayes's advance work in sending the governor images of Libeskind's proposal, in particular, a framed picture of the view of New York Harbor from Libeskind's planned iconic tower. Included in that packet was a picture of Libeskind with a haystack. By itself the haystack was meaningless to what was going on at Ground Zero, except for the fact that it forged a connection with the governor, whose autobiography included a photo of him standing next to a haystack in Hungary, the kind of haystack Libeskind said he grew up with in Poland. After the selection was final, Hayes received a call from Pataki's office. "You tell those people they owe you a lot. It was those goddamned haystacks. I couldn't get those haystacks out of my mind." Seems a bit implausible, but many things were converging in the governor's selection of Libeskind's proposal. George Pataki author interview, January 12, 2015.

[44] Sontag, "The Hole in the City's Heart." Betts focused on the technical aspects of how the latticework towers would get built. Clean factories would be built on the site. He

figured construction should move right along, hoisting modules month after month, every thirty days another module lifted into place; it would become an event every month for eighteen months. Nobel, *Sixteen Acres*, 175; Betts author interview; Goldberger, *Up from Zero*, 167.

[45] Daniel Libeskind, "Statement on Selected Design for the WTC Site as of February 2003," http://www.renewnyc.com/plan_des_dev/wtc_site/new_design_plans/selected_libeskind/default.asp.

[46] Goldberger, *Up from Zero*, 166.

[47] LMDC, "Governor Pataki and Mayor Bloomberg Unveil Design for the Tallest Building in the World—the Freedom Tower—to Rise on the World Trade Center Site," press release, December 19, 2003.

[48] Karen Matthews, "City Official Urges Developer Not to Move Freedom Tower," Associated Press Worldstream, August 1, 2003; Andy Soltis, "City's View on WTC Spire: Love at First Site," *NYP*, August 1, 2003.

[49] Alex Frangos, "Property Report: Uncertainties Soar at Ground Zero," *WSJ*, October 20, 2004; Frank Rich, "Ground Zero Is So Over," *NYT*, May 29, 2005; Elizabeth McBride, "WTC Deal Doesn't Allay Fears," *Crain's*, May 1, 2006; Frangos, "Uncertainties Soar at Ground Zero."

[50] Editorial, "Rethinking the Future of Rebuilding," *DN*, May 5, 2004; editorial, "Rebuilding Lower Manhattan," *NYT*, May 6, 2004; John Heilmann, "Poker at Ground Zero; Larry Silverstein, George Pataki, and a Few Other Big Bettors Are Playing a High-Stakes Game Downtown. Who Loses? Probably Us," *New York Magazine*, March 27, 2006.

[51] State of New York Executive Chamber, "On July 4th, 2004, We Will Break Ground on the Freedom Tower," press release, May 5, 2004.

[52] David W. Dunlap, "This Is Not a Traditional Groundbreaking," *NYT*, June 3, 2004; "A 9/11 Cornerstone, Chiseled With a New York Accent," July 8, 2004.

[53] David W. Dunlap, "One Cornerstone, but Many Loose Ends," *NYT*, July 4, 2004.

Chapter 8

[1] Adam Gopnik, "Critic at Large: Stones and Bones," *New Yorker*, July 7, 2014; Marita Sturken, "Memorializing Absence," n.d., http://www.essays.ssrc.org/sept11/essays/Sturken_text_only.htm, 3. See Marita Sturken, *Tourists of History: Memory, Kitsch, and Consumerism from Oklahoma City to Ground Zero* (Durham, NC: Duke University Press, 2007), 226–227.

[2] The idea for this conceptual memorial arose immediately, in the week following the attack. The art installation of eighty-eight searchlights was independently conceived by architects John Bennett and Gustavo Bonevardi of PROUN Space Studio ("Project for the Immediate Reconstruction of Manhattan's Skyline") and Richard Nash Gould, and artists Julian LaVerdiere and Paul Myoda ("Phantom Towers," commissioned by the *New York Times Magazine* to create an image of the project for its September 23, 2001, cover), with lighting consultant Paul Marantz. Initially, it was to be named "Towers of Light," but in deference to the families of the victims, who emphasized that the project should remember the people killed, not the buildings destroyed, it was named Tribute in Light. A second temporary memorial was created in March 2002 at Battery Park, the centerpiece of which was *The Sphere*, a sculpture created in 1971 by Fritz Koening under commission by the Port Authority for the open plaza at the World Trade Center as a monument to fostering world peace through

world trade. One of the few public art treasures recovered from the attack, albeit with a large gash through its center, *The Sphere* became a symbol of hope.

3 LMDC, "Joint Meeting of Memorial Competition Jury and the Families Advisory Council" (hereafter cited as "Joint Meeting Memorial Jury and FAC"), transcript, May 7, 2003, 20.

4 Dinitia Smith, "Hallowed Ground Zero: Competing Plans Hope to Shape a Trade Center Memorial," *NYT*, October 25, 2001; Edward T. Linenthal, *The Unfinished Bombing: Oklahoma City in American Memory* (Oxford: Oxford University Press, 2001).

5 Lauren Sandler, "Terrorism in the Heartland," *Newsday*, December 16, 2001, cited in Lawrence J. Vale and Thomas J. Campanella, eds., *The Resilient City: How Modern Cities Recover from Disaster"* (Oxford: Oxford University Press, 2005), 58.

6 Interview with Edward T. Linenthal by James S. Russell, "Who Owns Grief," *Architectural Review*, July 2002, 120–123; Linenthal, *The Unfinished Bombing*, 181.

7 Smith, "Hallowed Ground Zero."

8 Anita Contini author interview, April 11, 2012; Julia Levy, "Contini on Contini—Weighing Culture and Memory," *NYS*, January 27, 2003; Robin Finn, "Public Lives: A Delicate Challenge for the 'Voice of Organization,'" *NYT*, August 23, 2002.

9 Contini author interview.

10 The memorials visited included Tompkins Square Park memorial to the victims of the 1891 *General Slocum* steamboat disaster in the East River in which an estimated 1,021 people on board died; the Prison Ships Martyrs Monument in Brooklyn's Fort Greene Park commemorating the more than 11,500 men and women held captive by the British during the country's 1776 Revolution who died on ships anchored in the East River; and the *Maine* Monument at the entrance to Central Park in Manhattan, commemorating the 260 American sailors who died when their battleship exploded in the harbor of Havana, Cuba, in 1898.

11 Paul Goldberger, *Up from Zero: Politics, Architecture, and the Rebuilding of New York* (New York: Random House, 2004), 213–214.

12 The sites visited included Shanksville Flight 93 impact site and temporary memorial, the Pentagon outdoor and indoor memorials, Vietnam Veterans Memorial, Lincoln Memorial, Jefferson Memorial, World War II Memorial (under construction), Korean War Memorial, National Law Enforcement Memorial, Japanese American Internment Memorial, John F. Kennedy Memorial, Pentagon Memorial and Grave Site, Tombs of the Unknown Soldiers, Franklin Delano Roosevelt Memorial, Marine Corps (Iwo Jima) Memorial, Arlington National Cemetery, U.S. Holocaust Memorial Museum, Oklahoma City National Memorial, Civil Rights Memorial, and Rosa Parks Museum.

13 LMDC, "Memorial Research Tour, October 1–5, 2002, Summary and General Observations," n.d. [October 2002], PowerPoint slides available at renewnyc.com/The Plan/memorial.asp.

14 Goldberger, *Up from Zero*, 216.

15 The ten members of the Mission Statement Drafting Committee included Kathy Ashton, Lt. Frank Dwyer, Tom Eccles, Capt. Steve Geraghy, Meredith Kane, Michael Kuo, Julie Menin, Dr. Antonio Perez, Nikki Stern, and Elizabeth Thompson. The eleven members of the Memorial Program Drafting Committee included Diana Balmori, Frederick Bell, Paula Grant Berry, Max Bond, Albear Capsosuto, Christy Ferer, Father Alex Karloutsos, Richard Kennedy, Tom Roger, Jane Rosenthal, and Christopher Trucillo.

16 The LMDC had already solicited broad input into these preliminary draft statements through various means: a public meeting (August 20, 2002), mailings to the families of the

WTC victims (which garnered 480 responses as of October 21, 2002), and a meeting of New Jersey families of the 9/11 Trade Center victims convened by Governor James McGreevey.

[17] Todd D. Jick, "Memorializing That Day," *Boston Globe*, September 11, 2003.

[18] Contini author interview.

[19] The others were James Young, professor of English and Judaic studies at the University of Massachusetts, Amherst; Tom Finkelpearl, executive director of the Queens Museum of Art; Sara Bloomfield, director of the U.S. Holocaust Memorial Museum; Kirk Varnedoe, former chief curator of painting and sculpture at the Museum of Modern Art, who was a professor of the History of Art at Princeton's Institute of Advanced Study, prior to his passing; and Kenneth Jackson.

[20] Paul Goldberger, "Talk before the Families Advisory Council," Lower Manhattan Development Corporation Memorial speaker series, December 2, 2002.

[21] LMDC, "Public Dialogue Draft Memorial Mission Statement and Program for the WTC Memorial," March 12, 2003; Contini author interview; Goldberger, *Up from Zero*, 217.

[22] Levy, "Contini on Contini—Weighing Culture and Memory"; Goldberger, *Up From Zero*, 213.

[23] George Pataki author interview, January 12, 2015.

[24] I owe this point to David Dunlap, author interview, May 23, 2011.

[25] Kevin Rampe author interview, May 23, 2008.

[26] Robin Finn, "Public Lives: A Consensus Builder for Ground Zero's Renewal," June 17, 2004.

[27] Finn, "A Consensus Builder."

[28] Christy Ferer, "Lives Lost and the Renewal of Downtown," *NYT*, May 18, 2002.

[29] LMDC, "Joint Meeting Memorial Jury and FAC," 23.

[30] David W. Dunlap, "Marking Off Sacred Ground at the Trade Center," *NYT*, October 6, 2005; Philip Nobel, *Sixteen Acres: Architecture and the Outrageous Struggle for the Future of Ground Zero* (New York: Metropolitan Books, Henry Holt, 2005), 177; Ferer, "Lives Lost and the Renewal of Downtown."

[31] Nobel, *Sixteen Acres*, 253.

[32] Contini author interview.

[33] Contini author interview.

[34] Karen Alschuler, "The Competition Craze," *Planning* 70 (9) (October 2004), 28–33, at 28.

[35] Edward Wyatt, "Panel, Not Public, Will Pick Final 9/11 Memorial Design," *NYT*, April 9, 2003; Glenn Collins and David W. Dunlap, "The 9/11 Memorial: How Pluribus Became Unum," *NYT*, January 19, 2004.

[36] LMDC, "World Trade Center Site Memorial Competition Guidelines," n.d. [April 28, 2003].

[37] James Young, "The Memorial Process: A Juror's Report from Ground Zero," in *Contentious City: The Politics of Recovery in New York City*, ed. John Mollenkopf (New York: Russell Sage Foundation, 2005), 140–162, at 149, 150; Edward Wyatt, "In 9/11 Design, Rules Are Set to Be Broken," *NYT*, April 29, 2003; Neil Graves and William Neuman, "No-Rules Memorial Contest," *NYP*, April 29, 2003.

[38] Christine Hughney, "Competition to Design 9/11 Memorial Starts," *Washington Post*, April 8, 2003.

[39] Paul Goldberger, "After the World Trade Center: The Struggle to Make a City for Our Times," lecture before the Architectural Foundation of Cincinnati, May 6, 2004; Allison Blais and Lynn Rasic, *A Place of Remembrance: Official Book of the National September 11 Memorial* (Washington, DC: National Geographic Society, 2011), 136; LMDC, "WTC Memorial Jury Statement for Winning Design," January 13, 2004.

[40] *Garden of Lights: Last Light* (Pierre David, Sean Corriel, Jessica Kmetovic); *Votives in Suspension* (Norman Lee and Michael Lewis); *Suspending Memory* (Joseph Karadin with Hsin-Yi Wu); *Lower Waters* (Bradley Campbell and Matthais Neumann); *Passages of Light: The Memorial Cloud* (Gisela Baurmann, Sawad Brooks, Jonas Coersmeir); *Inversion of Light* (Toshio Sasaki); *Dual Memory* (Brian Strawn and Karla Sierralta); and *Reflecting Absence* (Michael Arad). The eight were greeted with more criticism than praise. Critics complained that the designs were too minimalist and elitist; others complained that they were "generic" and "impersonal." Still others, including Mayor Bloomberg, questioned the financial feasibility of building and long-term feasibility of maintaining some of the proposed designs. New Yorkers remained deeply split over the memorials' most basic outlines: What is its purpose? Who is it for? And when should it be done? As carefully orchestrated as it was, the competition failed to please the public.

[41] To ensure that the jury's wishes were followed, the LMDC required Arad to agree to other conditions before he won the designation: The architect would have no control over where the cultural buildings would be placed, and he would also have to cede control over the placement of other infrastructure elements.

[42] Editorial, "An Appropriate Memorial," *NYP*, November 20, 2003.

[43] Editorial, "New York Demands Proper Memorial," *DN*, December 21, 2003.

[44] Editorials, *NYT*: "The Memorial Finalists," November 20, 2003; "Toward a Final Design," December 13, 2003; "The Winning Memorial," January 8, 2004; "Reflecting Absence," January 15, 2004.

[45] Kevin Rampe author interview, November 7, 2008.

[46] Martin C. Pedersen, "The World Trade Center: Goodbye Memorial Foundations, Hello Reflecting Absence," *Metropolis*, January 21, 2004.

[47] Paul Goldberger, "The Sky Line: Slings and Arrows: The Architectural Machinations at Ground Zero Can Be Treacherous," *New Yorker*, February 9, 2004; David W. Dunlap and Eric Lipton, "Revised Ground Zero Memorial Will Include an Artificial Center," *NYT*, January 12, 2004.

[48] Quoted from Nobel, *Sixteen Acres*, 253; LMDC, "WTC Memorial Jury Statement."

[49] Glenn Collins and David W. Dunlap, "Fighting for the Footprints of Sept 11; Families Renew Call for a Memorial That Includes Traces of Towers Themselves," *NYT*, December 30, 2003.

[50] Collins and Dunlap, "Fighting for the Footprints."

[51] In February 2004, three government agencies, including the LMDC, determined that the WTC site's location, setting, feeling, and association rendered it eligible for the National Register of Historic Places. Without the site having to be actually nominated for the register, the determination had the same practical effect of requiring, where possible, ways to avoid or reduce any damaging impacts redevelopment might have on the site's historic nature. Following section 106 of the National Historic Preservation Act, the agencies identified sixty-nine "consulting parties" to the rebuilding process, eight of which were preservation

groups. One of these consulting parties observed that "a footprint can be something that is written on the psyche or in the soul and on the heart and not necessarily always in steel and cement and concrete." LMDC, "World Trade Center Memorial and Redevelopment Plan, Proposed Finding of No Adverse Effect under Section 106 of the National Historic Preservation Act," February 9, 2004.

[52] David W. Dunlap, "Critics Say Memorial Plan Imperils Towers' Remnants," *NYT*, March 2, 2006.

[53] David W. Dunlap, "Memorial Pools Will Not Quite Fill Twin Footprints," December 15, 2005.

[54] LMDC, "Joint Meeting Memorial Jury and FAC," 22–23.

[55] LMDC, "Joint Meeting Memorial Jury and FAC," June 5, 2003, 26, 53.

[56] David W. Dunlap, "At 9/11 Site, Balancing Reverence and Retailing," *NYT*, March 29, 2004.

[57] David W. Dunlap, "Mayor's Office Seeks More Retail Space at Ground Zero," *NYT*, October 29, 2003.

[58] Letter from Daniel Doctoroff to Joseph Seymour, [Re: Issues That Must Be Resolved for the City of New York to Approve the Site's Master Plan], October 17, 2003.

[59] Dunlap, "Mayor's Office Seeks More Retail Space at Ground Zero."

[60] Letter from Amada Burden to John Whitehead and Kevin Rampe, March 8, 2004, 3; David W. Dunlap, "Planners Seek More Streets through Trade Center Site," *NYT*, March 2, 2004. The basis for the Department of City Planning's review of the *GPP* was tied to the LMDC's override local law or regulation stemming from the expansion of the site through the proposed acquisition and redevelopment of two city blocks south of the Trade Center, one bounded by Liberty, Washington, Albany, and Greenwich Streets, and the other bounded by Liberty, West, Cedar, and Washington Streets, as well as a portion of Liberty Street between those parcels and the WTC site. These blocks would come to be known as Site 5, or the Southern Site.

[61] Michael Saul, "City Pushes WTC Role," *DN*, April 21, 2004. Doctoroff's April 5, 2004, letter to Seymour and Rampe called for a formal agreement. Following the Department of City Planning's recommendations, the administration wanted the agreement to cover five planning areas: the public realm and open space (reintegrating the site with lower Manhattan), commercial and cultural programs (creating a pedestrian environment), traffic and transportation (lower Manhattan street management), infrastructure (managing user needs), and below-grade concourses and related above-grade infrastructure. Ongoing management issues such as security, city services, airport access, and compliance with building code standards requiring city approval would also need to be covered in an agreement.

[62] Attachment 2 of the *GPP* detailed the Department of City Planning's participation in "Certain Design Guidelines." The scope of the four areas of participation—street-level requirements (first setback requirements, retail frontages, ground floor retail space, and ground-floor transparency requirements for all commercial buildings other than Tower 1 [Freedom Tower]); exterior retail signage; design standards and configurations for security devices installed in streets, sidewalks, or other open spaces; and maximum slope, elevation, and other grade controls for streets and sidewalks—spoke to the city's goals for enlivening

the streets of the Trade Center site with retail and pedestrian activity and Burden's particular well-known focus on the details of urban design. In a May 19, 2005, amendment to the *GPP*, the language was simplified but the intent of detailed participation remained the same.

[63] The full text of the letter laid out "a host of management, operations and other matters critical to redevelopment.... [that would] need to be embodied and reflected in a more comprehensive and detailed Redevelopment Agreement" with the Port Authority. In addition to the property issues, the "non-exhaustive" list covered issues including streets, curbside usage, building codes, security, city services, airport access, public open spaces, and construction coordination. The last important issue the city wanted the proposed Redevelopment Agreement to address was "how decisions will be made regarding the use of federal funds for the rebuilding effort." Letter from Daniel L. Doctoroff to Joseph Seymour and Kevin Rampe, "Re: Proposed Redevelopment Agreement for the Redevelopment of the World Trade Center, April 5, 2004"; David W. Dunlap, "Blocks: The Fine Print on the Trade Center Site," *NYT*, April 22, 2004.

[64] Deborah Sontag, "The Hole in the City's Heart," *NYT*, September 11, 2006; Roland Betts author interview, May 12, 2005; Sontag, "The Hole in the City's Heart."

[65] In the ten-page (plus appendices) of the World Trade Center Redevelopment Agreement, the PA, the city, and the LMDC agreed to execute a series of documents to effectuate various land transfers necessary for the *GPP*. The city would own the at-grade areas of all streets and sidewalks within the Trade Center site (as specified on the Dimensioned Site Plan) and areas immediately below the surface of such streets and sidewalks (to a specific level below curb grade), and the PA would own all other areas within the Trade Center site. The streets issue was finally put to rest with the February 2007 amendment to the *GPP* and settlement of the formal property interests, including use restrictions for Cortlandt Street and Dey Street rights of way, on December 5, 2007.

[66] William Neuman, "Libeskind's Lousy Rules," *NYP*, November 5, 2003; David W. Dunlap, "Master Plan for World Trade Center Gets Down to the Finest Detail," *NYT*, November 8, 2003; Richard Ivy, "Libeskind Isn't Finished," *NYT*, November 14, 2003; Gary Hack, "A Houston on the Hudson?" *NYT*, November 15, 2003.

[67] David. W. Dunlap, "At 9/11 Site, No Guidelines? No Problem. Design Away," *NYT*, December 29, 2005.

[68] PANYNJ and the City of New York, "World Trade Center Design Guidelines Administration Agreement," November 16, 2006; LMDC, *World Trade Center Memorial and Cultural Program, General Project Plan*, June 2, 2004, as amended February 14, 2007, 11. The February 2007 amendments to the *GPP* narrowed the scope of the design guidelines as applicable only to the commercial structures on the site; they eliminated application of design guidelines to the Memorial Program (Memorial, Memorial Museum, and Visitor Orientation and Education Center) because the designs had advanced to a point at which design guidelines were no longer necessary. The change removed the LMDC from formal adoption and administration of the commercial design guidelines, though all parties (the LMDC, the city, the PA, and the PA's net lessees) were expected to "work together in a cooperative manner" on their formulation; Charles V. Bagli, "Architect's Proposals May Inspire, but Have Little to Do with Reality," *NYT*, December 19, 2002.

Chapter 9

[1] Benjamin Forgey, "At Ground Zero, a Plan Worth Building On; Studio Daniel Libeskind's Design Is a Winner," *Washington Post*, February 28, 2003.

[2] James Traub, "The Way We Live Now: Public Building: New York's Engagement in the Redesign of the W.T.C. Site May Be the Best Memorial—if It Lasts," *New York Times Magazine*, September 7, 2003, 17–18, at 17.

[3] Editorial, "The Future at Ground Zero," *NYT*, February 24, 2003.

[4] In May 2003, the architect Eli Appia, who had been a frequent critic of the rebuilding process, published a study showing that much of the time the "Wedge of Light" would be in shadow cast from the Millennium Hilton Hotel across the street. Libeskind defended his position by saying the Wedge of Light is created by "the effect of the facades of the buildings reflecting the light back into the plaza." The effect would be "a three-dimension phenomenon...about the ambience of light and the reflections of light between the buildings." Edward Wyatt, "Shadows to Fall, Literally, over 9/11 'Wedge of Light,'" *NYT*, May 1, 2003.

[5] Tom McGeveran, "The Libeskinds: His Bronx Story Fused with Hers," *NYO*, March 10, 2003, 15.

[6] Frank Rich, "Group Therapy at Ground Zero," *NYT*, January 4, 2003.

[7] Paul Goldberger, "The Sky Line: Slings and Arrows: The Architectural Machinations at Ground Zero Can Be Treacherous," *New Yorker*, February 9, 2004; David W. Dunlap, "The New Look at Ground Zero May Be the Oldest," *NYT*, December 11, 2003; Justin Davidson, "Primary Plan for Redoing Towers Begins Wobbling," *Newsday*, September 11, 2003.

[8] Edward Wyatt, "Libeskind to Control Design of Trade Center's Terminal," *NYT*, June 19, 2003.

[9] Robin Pogrebin, "The Incredible Shrinking Daniel Libeskind," *NYT*, June 20, 2004; Deborah Sontag, "The Hole in the City's Heart," *NYT*, September 11, 2006.

[10] Nicolai Ouroussoff interviewed by Charlie Rose, "A Look at the World of Art and Architecture," *The Charlie Rose Show*, PBS, transcript, December 28, 2005.

[11] Ada Louise Huxtable, "In the Fray: The Death of the Dream for the Ground-Zero Site," *WSJ*, April 20, 2005; Ada Louise Huxtable, "The Next Great Center of the City: Daniel Libeskind Envisions Ground Zero," *WSJ*, March 19, 2003; Ada Louise Huxtable interviewed by Charlie Rose, "A Conversation With Architects Renzo Piano and Frank Gehry; Discussion with Architecture Critic Ada Louise Huxtable," *The Charlie Rose Show*, PBS, transcript, August 5, 2005.

[12] Paul Goldberger, "Profiles: Urban Warriors," *New Yorker*, September 15, 2003, 72–81, at 74.

[13] George Pataki, "Governor's Remarks at ABNY Lunch," April 24, 2003; George Pataki, "Remarks Laying of the Cornerstone for Freedom Tower," July 4, 2004. No one I asked seemed to know where the stone had been put until journalist Douglas Feiden, writing for the *Wall Street Journal*, reported in August 2014 that it resided "in the grassy front yard of a stone manufacturing plant in an industrial precinct in the Long Island hamlet of Yaphank...on private property with limited public viewing." Douglas Feiden, "Freedom Stone Is Far from Ground Zero," *WSJ*, August 28, 2014. The Port Authority did not see a place for it and the National September 11 Memorial and Museum also passed on accepting the stone. Orphaned from the WTC site, the Freedom Stone became the private property of Penn Fabricators, which purchased it for about $10,000 as a result of the original manufacturer's bankruptcy. Governor Pataki responded to the news by calling for the stone to be

returned to downtown, ideally in the lobby of 1 WTC, *Crain's* reported as part of its same-day reader poll: "Should the Freedom Stone Go Back Home?" *Crain's*, August 28, 2014.

[14] David W. Dunlap, "Deal Leads Architect to Lower His Sights, and the Trade Center Tower," *NYT*, December 17, 2003.

[15] David W. Dunlap and Glenn Collins, "Freedom Tower Sheds the Look of Bulky Armor," *NYT*, June 29, 2006; David W. Dunlap, "After a Year of Push and Pull, 2 Visions Met at 1,776," *NYT*, December 26, 2003; "Sacred Ground," *Frontline*, PBS, produced by Nick Rosen, directed by Kevin Sim, aired September 7, 2004, transcript; David Childs interviewed by Charlie Rose, "Revisiting 9/11: A Talk with [the] Architect Who Designed Freedom Tower," *The Charlie Rose Show*, PBS, transcript, August 16, 2005.

[16] David W. Dunlap, "1,776-Foot Design Is Unveiled for World Trade Center Tower, *NYT*, December 20, 2003.

[17] John Costonis, *Icons and Aliens: Law, Aesthetics, and Environmental Change* (Urbana: University of Illinois Press, 1989), 18; Kevin Lynch, quoted in Costonis, *Icons and Aliens*, 49.

[18] "Sacred Ground," *Frontline*, PBS, www.pbs.org/wgbh/pages/frontline/shows/sacred/etc/script.html; Edward Wyatt, "Architect and Developer Clash over Plans for Trade Center Site," *NYT*, July 15, 2003.

[19] "Sacred Ground."

[20] Edward Wyatt, "News Analysis: Building Teamwork: By Grasping the Developer's View, Forging a Ground Zero Compromise," *NYT*, July 17, 2003; "Sacred Ground"; Wyatt, "Building Teamwork."

[21] Editorial, "The Basic Rift in WTC Plans," *Crain's*, July 21, 2003.

[22] "Sacred Ground." Developer logic led to placement of the big tower east of Greenwich, on top of what would be a transportation center. The northwest corner where Libeskind had placed his tall tower was the most heavily damaged area of the sixteen-acre WTC site; it was over water and over the PATH tracks, which would complicate construction. Also, Fulton and West Streets in that corner had been destroyed on 9/11. That northwest corner was the hardest site for rebuilding: Constructing a tall building on a curving heavy railroad involved a lot of maneuvering underground. It was an "island" location. Staging would be difficult because it would be a construction zone for years. From a planning perspective, it was far from other infrastructure on the site. It was going to be more expensive to build in that location; although no cost estimates had been done, one informal number suggested to me was that building on the northwest corner site would involve at least a 25 percent surcharge.

[23] Edward Wyatt, "Downtown Rebuilding Officials Try to End Conflict," *NYT*, July 16, 2003; "Sacred Ground."

[24] Childs and SOM staffers began working informally on an idea for the WTC tower immediately after 9/11. The idea for a torqued design had been proposed by architect Richard Dattner in sketches of a linked pair of twisted towers made on September 17, 2001. "He refined the design and sent out about 50 booklets describing the proposal," one of which went to Silverstein, who was "most intrigued by them," and forwarded the booklet to Childs. Dunlap, "The New Look at Ground Zero May Be the Oldest." With credit given to Dattner and other architects who had designed precedents, Guy Nordenson also presented a torqued tower concept in *New York Times Magazine* in September 2002.

[25] "Sacred Ground."

[26] As reported in a long article in the *NYO*, Childs and SOM were concerned about the cost implications of Libeskind's tower concept. "Structural engineering programming had not been carried out on either tower," and SOM was concerned that "an asymmetrical tower would require immense internal structural steel to resist the lateral movement of the wind at its tremendous height, especially near the top." Considerations pertaining to how to create stability for the asymmetrical spire "made the structural guts of the building appear to be extremely expensive," which was no small item for Silverstein. Tom McGeveran, "Zero Catfight: Big Architects in Twin Suits," *NYO*, November 3, 2003.

[27] Sontag, "The Hole in the City's Heart"; Maggie Haberman and Greg Gittrich, "PA Dodging Ground Zero Tower Feud," *DN*, October 24, 2004; "Sacred Ground."

[28] Haberman and Gittich, "PA Dodging Ground Zero Tower Feud"; editorials: "Let the Public See the Plans," *NYT*, October 24, 2003; "Show Us the Plan, Larry," *NYP*, October 29, 2003.

[29] "Sacred Ground."

[30] "Sacred Ground."

[31] Maggie Haberman and Greg Gittrich, "City in Sour Note on PA's WTC Plan," *DN*, October 29, 2003; McGeveran, "Zero Catfight"; Dunlap, "After a Year of Push and Pull"; "Sacred Ground."

[32] "Sacred Ground."

[33] Blair Golson, "Two Architects Whip Up Tower in Mad Frenzy," *NYO*, December 1, 2003; Dunlap, "After a Year of Push and Pull."

[34] Dunlap, "After a Year of Push and Pull"; David W. Dunlap, "Trade Tower to Reflect Compromise," *NYT*, December 20, 2003; Huxtable, "In the Fray: The Death of the Dream."

[35] David W. Dunlap, "Scenes from a Forced Marriage," *NYT*, November 16, 2003.

[36] Daniel Doctoroff interviewed by Charlie Rose, "New York City's Deputy Mayor Discusses New Design for Freedom Tower," *The Charlie Rose Show*, PBS transcript, June 29, 2005.

[37] Sontag, "The Hole in the City's Heart." Silverstein Properties had been copied on the NYPD's October 2004 letter sent to the Port Authority. With engineering documents for the substructure underground and a conditional building permit from the Port Authority, Silverstein could have begun drilling but knowing of the police department's concerns, he held back. Janno Lieber author interview, October 19, 2010.

[38] Sontag, "The Hole in the City's Heart"; Patrick D. Healy and William K. Rashbaum, "Security Issues Force a Review at Ground Zero," *NYT*, May 1, 2005.

[39] Editorial, "Get Ground Zero Back on Track," *DN*, May 6, 2005.

[40] Quoted in Elizabeth Greenspan, *Battle for Ground Zero: Inside the Political Struggle to Rebuild the World Trade Center* (New York: Palgrave Macmillan, 2013), 103; Sontag, "The Hole in the City's Heart"; "Rebuilding the World Trade Center," *Cornell Real Estate Review* July 2012, 39–53, at 52.

[41] A shorter-than-typical turnaround on the redesign was perhaps possible because Childs and his SOM team had designed many a blast-resistant structures, including a building already designed for the site adjacent to the New York Stock Exchange, 33 Wall Street. The NYPD had signed off on this particular SOM design when it was being considered for the Wall Street site. Indeed, after the 1993 bombing of the World Trade Center, most buildings of note would have been blast-tested, said Carol Willis, founder of the Skyscraper Museum.

[42] Sontag, "The Hole in the City's Heart."

[43] Glenn Collins, "A Freedom Tower Restarted from Scratch; for Design Team, a Desperate Rush," *NYT*, July 10, 2005.

[44] Healy and Rashbaum, "Security Issues Force a Review at Ground Zero"; James Gardiner, "Freedom Tower Security Issues Worry Police," *NYS*, November 19, 2004.

[45] Healy and Rashbaum, "Security Issues Force a Review at Ground Zero"; "Get Ground Zero Back on Track"; Healy and Rashbaum, "Security Issues Force a Review at Ground Zero"; Tony Sclafani and Adam Lisberg, "Tower Warning Is Year Old, NYPD Says," *DN*, May 2, 2005.

[46] Michael Cooper, "Delay at Ground Zero, Bad Timing for Pataki," *NYT*, May 6, 2005; Patrick D. Healy and William K. Rashbaum, "Meeting about Ground Zero Finds Security at Forefront," *NYT*, April 27, 2005.

[47] Ray Kelly, *Vigilance: My Life Serving America and Protecting Its Empire City* (New York: Hachette Books, 2015), 257–269, at 261.

[48] Leonard Levitt, *NYPD Confidential*, www.nypdconfidential.com, August 10, 2009.

[49] David W. Chen and Charles V. Bagli, "Goldman Plans at Ground Zero Are in Doubt," *NYT*, April 5, 2005; Pataki, "Governor's Remarks at ABNY."

[50] Charles V. Bagli, "Despite Its Jersey City Tower, Goldman Sachs Commits to One in Lower Manhattan," *NYT*, April 17, 2004; Patrick D. Healy and Charles V. Bagli, "Pataki and Bloomberg Endorse Changes in Ground Zero Tower," *NYT*, May 5, 2005; Matthew Scheuerman, "Childs Told to Straighten Out the Zero Mess," *NYO*, May 16, 2005.

[51] David W. Dunlap, "State Gives Up Plan for Tunnel at Ground Zero," *NYT*, April 14, 2005; William Rudin author interview, September 6, 2011.

[52] Senator Charles Schumer, "Speech before *Crain's* Business Breakfast Forum" ("Culture of Inertia" speech), May 3, 2005.

[53] Alfred P. Doblin, "Maybe No Tower Is the Right Choice," *Herald News* [Passaic County], May 9, 2005; Glenn Collins and Patrick D. Healy, "A Top Official at Ground Zero Quits His Post," *NYT*, May 3, 2005.

[54] Editorials: "Do Something, George," *NYP*, April 7, 2005, "Get Ground Zero Back on Track"; editorial, "Manhattan's Mayor Ahab," *NYT*, May 2, 2005.

[55] Michael Cooper, "Picking Up the Pace at Ground Zero," *NYT*, May 14, 2005.

[56] Martin Z. Braun, "New York's Post-9/11 Liberty Bond Program Gets Mixed Grades," *Bloomberg.com*, September 11, 2006. The sweetened deal consisted of an additional allocation of $650 million in tax-free Liberty Bonds for a grand total of $1.65 billion, with an estimated annual cost savings of $9 million on the thirty-year bonds; up to $25 million in cash grants under the Federal World Trade Center Job Creation and Retention Program (federal funds to companies with more than two hundred employees who committed to lower Manhattan); state and city sales tax exemptions on construction costs and equipment purchases (through the fourth year of occupancy of the building), which were not expected to exceed $60 million in value; utility cost savings; $5 million of landscape work paid for by New York State; and in-lieu-of-property-tax payments (arranged when a developer is building on publicly owned land) capped at $10.71 per square foot, or $21.4 million annually, which represented $9 million in annual savings over the previously negotiated amount of $15.11 per square foot, or $30.2 million. To make up the lost revenue from the lower cap, the

state agreed to reimburse the city for the difference, expected to be about $40 million between 2012 and 2026. Charles V. Bagli, "Board Approves Deal for Bank Tower in Lower Manhattan," *NYT*, August 24, 2005; Charles V. Bagli, "Negotiations underway to Ease Ground Zero Deal," *NYT*, May 13, 2008. Also see exhibit M, "Term Sheet," in the "Agreement of Lease between Battery Park City Authority and Goldman Sachs Headquarters LLC," August 23, 2005.

[57] Editorial, "The Rich Got Richer," *DN*, August 25, 2005; editorial, "A Golden Goldman Sachs," *NYT*, August 25, 2005; Daniel Doctoroff author interview, January 23, 2008.

[58] The specific projects to be completed included: Route 9A–West Street Reconstruction; WTC Transportation Hub, including PATH Concourse; 9A underpass and associated retail shops; construction of streets in and adjacent to the WTC site; construction of Vesey and Murray Streets, memorial and cultural buildings (Memorial Museum, Cultural Center, and Performing Arts Center to grade), and East Bathtub to grade and aesthetically treated; security program and construction of Vehicular Network and Security Center; and Vesey Street Ferry Landing.

[59] Matthew Schuereman, "Goldman Goes for Money-Back Deal Based on Safety," *NYO*, August 22, 2005.

[60] The NYPD would not be reviewing the security of the other towers, which would look and feel like the rest of the city, but for the underground system. While the department reviewed the design and security guidelines for the other buildings, it would not be asked to sign off on the buildings. This would be akin to having the department review all buildings being constructed in the city. The Real Estate Board of New York was against the NYPD getting involved, against the department's growing power, according to one insider, and the department did not press the issue.

[61] Letter from James K. Kallstrom to Edward C. Forst, "Re: World Trade Center Site and Environs Security Plan," July 29, 2005, included as part of exhibit 3 in the "Agreement of Lease between Battery Park City Authority and Goldman Sachs Headquarters LLC."

[62] Douglas Feiden, "Sachs-ful of Cash, PA's Inability to Rebuild at WTC Site Quickly Enough Will Cost Taxpayers...," *DN*, May 12, 2008; editorials: "Give It Up, Goldman," *DN*, July 20, 2009; "Goldman's Extreme Makeover," *DN*, November 20, 2009;"Good as Goldman," *DN*, December 9, 2009.

[63] PA board meeting minutes, July 24, 2008, 203.

[64] Collins, "A Freedom Tower Restarted from Scratch"; David W. Dunlap and Glenn Collins, "New Design for Freedom Tower Calls for 200-Foot Pedestal," *NYT*, July 29, 2005; John King, "New York's Freedom Tower Fails to Live Up to Its Lofty Name," July 7, 2005, *San Francisco Chronicle*, http://www.sfgate.com/entertainment/articles/New-York-s-Freedom-Tower.

[65] David W. Dunlap and Glenn Collins, "Redesign Puts Freedom Tower on a Fortified Base," *NYT*, July 30, 2005; Collins, "A Freedom Tower Restarted from Scratch."

[66] Blair Kamin, "Tower of Banal," *Chicago Tribune*, July 3, 2005; Blair Kamin, "New Look for Ground Zero's Freedom Tower: Too Much Fortress, Not Enough Beauty," June 30, 2005.

[67] Justin Davidson, "Review: Tower Still Needs Work," *Newsday*, June 29, 2005.

[68] James S. Russell, "Freedom Tower's Redesign Substitutes Dullness for Inspiration," *Bloomberg.com*, June 29, 2005; Nicolai Ouroussoff, "An Appraisal: A Tower of Impregnability, the Sort Politicians Love," *NYT*, June 30, 2005.

[69] Healy and Bagli, "Pataki and Bloomberg Endorse Changes in Ground Zero Tower."

[70] Kevin Rampe author interview, November 7, 2008.

[71] Sontag, "The Hole in the City's Heart"; editorial, "Adrift Downtown," *DN*, April 11, 2005; "Get Ground Zero Back on Track."

[72] Alex Frangos, "Showdown at Ground Zero: Beset by Politics, Safety Issues, the World Trade Center Site Suffers a 'Culture of Inertia,'" *WSJ*, May 4, 2005.

[73] "Adrift Downtown," "Get Ground Zero Back on Track"; editorial, "Building on Ground Zero," *NYT*, May 7, 2005; editorial, "Trump's Towers," *WSJ*, May 10, 2005; "To-do List for Fixing Downtown," *Crain's*, May 9, 2005.

[74] Steve Cuozzo, "Ground Zero: Ground to a Halt," *NYP*, April 7, 2005.

Chapter 10

[1] LMDC, "Joint Meeting of Memorial Competition Jury and the Families Advisory Council" (hereafter cited as "Joint Meeting Memorial Jury and FAC"), transcript, June 5, 2002, 21; LMDC, "Report on the Memorial Center and Cultural Complex at the World Trade Center Site," February 10, 2004.

[2] Julie Salamon, "Following a Trend, Downtown Looks to the Arts," *NYT*, September 15, 2003.

[3] To put the 500,000 square feet of cultural space in perspective, the *General Project Plan* adopted in June 2004 provided for up to 1 million square feet for retail uses in the office and hotel structures, which was far more than the 450,000 square feet of shops of the original Trade Center, which at the time was among the highest grossing retail space in the United States. This was later reduced to 500,000 to 600,000 square feet in the amended *GPP* of February 2007. The PAC site was a complex and expensive one, situated atop underground service ramps and PATH transit lines, and would be among the last to be developed.

[4] Robin Pogrebin, "Is Culture Gone at Ground Zero?" *NYT*, September 30, 2005.

[5] Pogrebin, "Is Culture Gone at Ground Zero?"; LMDC, "Invitation to Cultural Institutions for the World Trade Center Site" (hereafter cited as "Invitation Cultural Institutions"), June 2003, 3; Robin Pogrebin, "Back to Square One at Ground Zero," *NYT*, June 6, 2004.

[6] Miriam Kreinin Souccar, "Arts Groups Line Up for WTC Site," *Crain's*, July 21–27, 2003; LMDC, "Invitation Cultural Institutions," 7.

[7] Philip Nobel, "The Downtown Culture Derby Begins…," *NYT*, August 31, 2003; Robin Pogrebin, "4 Arts Groups Chosen for Lower Manhattan," *NYT*, June 11, 2004; Robin Pogrebin, "News Analysis: Worries Rise over the Loss of Arts Focus at Ground Zero," *NYT*, May 26, 2004; "LMDC Announces Vibrant Cultural Mix of Dance, Theater, and Fine Arts for the World Trade Center Site," press release, June 10, 2004; LMDC board meeting minutes, July 8, 2004, 10, 14.

[8] Robin Pogrebin, "Arts Groups Call for Openness at Ground Zero," *NYT*, June 3, 2004.

[9] Pogrebin, "4 Arts Groups Chosen." In addition to the chosen four, the other short-listed institutions included the Children's Museum of the Arts, New York Hall of Science, New York City Opera, Orpheus Chamber Orchestra, Tribeca Film Festival, and the Ninety-second Street Y. The list also included institutions that might develop the curatorial approach or content for the memorial center: the Museum of the City of New York, New-York Historical Society, New York State Museum, Project Rebirth, and Sound Portraits Productions/Story Corps.

[10] Miriam Kreinin Souccar, "$300 Million Set for WTC Arts Centers; 15 Finalists May Face Dark Horses," *Crain's*, March 1, 2004.

[11] Souccar, "$300 Million Set for WTC Arts Centers"; Pogrebin, "Arts Groups Call for Openness at Ground Zero"; "LMDC Chooses WTC Cultural Components," *Backstage*, June 18, 2004.

[12] Terry Teachout, "In the Fray: At Ground Zero, Culture by Committee," *WSJ*, June 15, 2004; Frederick M. Winship, "Commentary: Hodgepodge Plan for 9/11 Site," UPI, June 17, 2004.

[13] Anthony Tommasini, "Rejection Won't Stop City Opera's Quest," *NYT*, June 12, 2004; John Rockwell, "Critic's Notebook: What Impact Will Art Center at Ground Zero Have (if Any)?" *NYT*, June 15, 2004.

[14] Edward Wyatt and Robin Pogrebin, "Trade Center Cultural Decisions Affected by What's Best for Lincoln Center," *NYT*, June 15, 2004.

[15] Ada Louise Huxtable, "In the Fray: The Death of the Dream for the Ground-Zero Site," *WSJ*, April 20, 2005.

[16] Robin Pogrebin, "Plans for Cultural Complex at Ground Zero Take Form," *NYT*, March 31, 2002; Robin Pogrebin, "Freedom Center Is Still a Somewhat Vague Notion," *NYT*, June 24, 2004.

[17] LMDC, *Principles and Preliminary Blueprint for the Future of Lower Manhattan*, 2002, 4; Nobel, "The Downtown Cultural Derby Begins..."

[18] LMDC, "World Trade Center Site Cultural Institution: The International Freedom Center Fact Sheet," May 19, 2005; "World Trade Center Site Cultural Institution: Drawing Center Fact Sheet," May 19, 2005.

[19] Debra Burlingame, "The Great Ground Zero Heist," *WSJ*, June 7, 2005; Theresa Ann Donofrio, "Ground Zero and Place-Making Authority: The Conservative Metaphors in 9/11 Families' 'Take Back the Memorial' Rhetoric," *Western Journal of Communication* 74:2 (March–April 2010): 150–169, at 157.

[20] Just two days prior to the Memorial Foundation board meeting on April 7, the cultural facilities were also discussed at the LMDC Families Advisory Council. Members expressed their "confusion with the titles and locations of the Memorial, the Cultural building, and the Performing Arts Center" and wanted to understand how the cultural facilities would enhance the memorial. Rampe seemed to be on the defensive, reminding the group about the process ("nearly a year long" and "open to the public" and, as stated in the minutes of the meeting, "that the institutions were selected in a public hearing"), the master plan role played by the Cultural Center ("a filter that separates the reflective nature of the Memorial Complex from the hectic commercial towers surrounding the site"), and the logic of the memorial's location below grade ("to convey the significance of the sacred ground"). LMDC Families Advisory Council, "Brief Summary of Minutes," April 5, 2005.

[21] David W. Dunlap, "Heavyweights Assemble for Inaugural Meeting," *NYT*, January 5, 2005.

[22] Robin Finn, "Public Lives: Fighting for the Underlying Meaning of Ground Zero," *NYT*, August 12, 2005; Debra Burlingame, "Our 9/11; The 'Families of September 11' Don't Represent Me," *WSJ*, March 8, 2004; Jarrett Murphy, "Memorial Plots," *Village Voice*, June 28, 2005.

[23] Donofrio, "Ground Zero and Place-Making Authority," 154, citing Burlingame, "The Great Ground Zero Heist."

[24] Robert Kolker, "The Grief Police: No One Says the 9/11 Families Aren't Entitled to Their Pain. But Should a Small Handful of Them Have the Power to Reshape Ground Zero?" *New York Magazine*, November 28, 2005, 46–56, at 51; Richard Tofel author interview, April 12, 2011.

[25] Burlingame, "The Great Ground Zero Heist."

[26] Burlingame, "The Great Ground Zero Heist."

[27] Julia Levy, "Victim Groups Don't Speak for Everyone," *NYS*, September 6, 2002.

[28] Kolker, "The Grief Police," 52.

[29] Kolker, "The Grief Police," 51.

[30] Levy, "Victim Groups Don't Speak for Everyone."

[31] Richard Tofel, "A Fitting Place at Ground Zero," *WSJ*, June 9, 2005; Gretchen Dykstra, letter to the editor, *WSJ*, June 20, 2005; Janon Fisher, "Relatives Protest Plan for Museum at 9/11 Memorial Site," *NYT*, June 21, 2005; Nancy Dillion, "WTC Museum Panned. Focus on Attack, Kin Urge," *DN*, June 21, 2005.

[32] Fisher, "Relatives Protest Plan for Museum at 9/11 Memorial Site."

[33] Patrick D. Healy, "Pataki Warns Cultural Groups for Museum at Ground Zero," *NYT*, June 25, 2005; Kenneth Lovett, "Pataki Finally Agrees: 'Blame America' Trash Has No Place at Ground Zero," *NYP*, June 25, 2005.

[34] Healy, "Pataki Warns Cultural Groups for Museum at Ground Zero"; Douglas Feiden, "WTC Museum Not Anti-U.S., Boss Vows," *DN*, July 7, 2005; Tom Topousis, "WTC Center's Change Bids for Museum Peace," *NYP*, July 6, 2005. Eric Foner, Columbia University DeWitt Professor of History, considered this to be a "general stance of surrender" and re-signed from the IFC's committee of scholars and advisors. David W. Dunlap, "Blocks: How a Cultural Building Divides the Trade Center," *NYT*, July 28, 2005; Topousis, "WTC Center's Change Bids for Museum Peace."

[35] Burlingame: "Do we really want to entrust the meaning of Sept. 11 to a man who is calling our secretary of defense, in a time of war, dishonorable and dishonest?" Fisher, "Relatives Protest Plan for Museum at 9/11 Memorial Site"; "If you want to debate, go to Columbia or NYU. Don't do it on the ashes of all these people," Douglas Feiden, "Violated...Again'. Kin Slap Art Center's 9–11 Pieces," *DN*, June 21, 2005; "This kind of ploy [Pataki's ultimatum] completely undermines our confidence in the governor's ability to do the right thing, or even know what the right thing is," Healy, "Pataki Warns Cultural Groups for Museum at Ground Zero"; "It is dishonest and despicable to use the 9/11 artifacts and 9/11 heroes as window dressing to mislead the public. So long as there is but one square inch housing dialogue, debates, artistic impressions, or exhibits about extraneous historical events, the IFC is inappropriate and a slap in the face," Michael Weissenstein, "Freedom Museum at WTC Site to Shrink, Focus More on 9/11 Victims," AP, July 6, 2005; " 'The underground museum,' Ms. Burlingame likes to say, prompted one family member to say the museum will be 'down there with the rats,' " Matthew Schuerman, "Embattled Libeskind Defends Controversial W.T.C. Museum," *NYO*, August 15, 2005; "They outsourced the problem of the memorial to someone who knows nothing about what is going on. It's a complete sham to make the public think they are acting in good faith, and they are not," David Lombino, "Conflict Resolution Specialist Is Hired to Mediate Dispute over Freedom Center," *NYS*, September 9, 2005; "They don't belong there," David W. Dunlap, "Freedom Museum Is Headed For Showdown at Ground Zero," *NYT*, September 22, 2005.

[36] LMDC, "Statement by John C. Whitehead," June 20, 2005; WTC Memorial Foundation board meeting minutes, July 12, 2005, 5; LMDC board meeting minutes, July 14, 2005.

[37] Paul D. Colford, "Push for New WTC Arts Center Site," *DN*, July 15, 2005; Dunlap, "How a Cultural Building Divides the Trade Center."

[38] David W. Dunlap, "Critics Call for Boycott of Memorial Fund-Raising," *NYT*, July 26, 2005.

[39] LMDC board meeting minutes, August 11, 2005; David W. Dunlap, "Freedom Center's Place at 9/11 Site Is in Question," *NYT*, August 12, 2005. At the same meeting, to show its support for the cultural agenda, the chairman announced that the LMDC intended to earmark $50 million in LMDC funds toward the creation of the Performing Arts Center. This is but "a drop in the bucket," noted the *Times* weeks later, given that a Frank Gehry building would "cost eight times that amount." Pogrebin, "Is Culture Gone at Ground Zero?"

[40] LMDC board meeting minutes August 11, 2005; The September 11th Fund collected $534 million from more than two million donors and designed programs that were implemented through 559 grants totaling $528 million. Upon completing its mission, it dissolved in December 2004.

[41] Dunlap, "Freedom Center's Place at 9/11 Site Is in Question"; State of New York Executive Chamber, "Statement from Governor George E. Pataki," press release, September 28, 2005.

[42] David Lombino, "LMDC Condemns Pataki's Move to Kill Freedom Museum Plan," *NYS*, October 7, 2005; Vito Fossella, Peter King, and John Sweeney, "Quit the IFC Games; Federal Funds at Risk," *NYP*, July 15, 2005.

[43] At the time, Clinton was considering a run for the Democratic presidential nomination. Presumably, support from Rupert Murdoch, publisher of the *Post*, would have been beneficial. Bernstein had been told she would not be out front on this. Then the big front-page headline: "Hill No! Nix 9/11 Freedom Center."

[44] Celeste Katz and Paul D. Colford, "Mike's Ground Zero Flip-Flop?" *DN*, September 28, 2005.

[45] IFC, "Statement of the International Freedom Center," September 28, 2005.

[46] Editorials: "The Governor's Proxy," *NYT*, August 16, 2005; "Ground Zero Plan Unravels, Gov. Pataki Fails to Stand Up for His 9/11 Master Plan at WTC site," *Newsday*, September 30, 2005; "Pataki's Mess at Ground Zero," *DN*, September 29, 2005; "The Freedom Center: Good Riddance," *NYP*, September 29, 2005.

[47] LMDC board meeting minutes, October 6, 2005.

[48] David W. Dunlap, "Downtown Board Criticizes Pataki for Barring Museum," *NYT*, October 7, 2005; David W. Dunlap, "In the Politics of Redeveloping Ground Zero, a Lone Critical Voice," *NYT*, February 11, 2015.

[49] David Lombino, "LMDC Condemns Pataki's Move to Kill Freedom Museum Plan," *NYS*, October 7, 2005.

[50] Deborah Sontag, "The Hole in the City's Heart," *NYT*, September 11, 2006.

[51] The Drawing Center later received $10 million as a Cultural Enhancement Funding Grant from the LMDC to set up in a new location, yet after several announcements of possible new locations and five years of search and assessment, it decided to stay in its SoHo home even though that meant walking away from what had become $20 million of government support. Building a new home had become just too expensive, plus the organization was suffering from real estate fatigue. Carol Vogel, "Drawing Center Won't Move to Seaport,"

NYT, March 14, 2008. In February 2011, it announced plans to expand and make permanent its space at 35 Wooster Street in SoHo, where the institution had been located since 1986. Funding for the $8.6 million project included a $3 million allocation from the LMDC.

[52] Robin Pogrebin, "Signature Plans Move to Space in Midtown," *NYT*, October 22, 2008. The new complex would greatly expand the Signature's production capability. In place of its one 160-seat auditorium in midtown Manhattan, the new seventy-thousand-square-foot facility, designed by Frank Gehry, would operate with three theaters: one with 299 seats and two with 199 seats. In addition, the new space would contain two rehearsal studios, a café, a bookstore, and offices.

[53] Craig Dykers author interview, February 12, 2016.

[54] Dykers author interview.

[55] Kevin Rampe author interview, May 23, 2008.

[56] Tofel author interview; Tom Bernstein author interview, November 10, 2011.

[57] David W. Dunlap, "Pataki Solution on Museum Flies in Face of Planning," *NYT*, September 29, 2005; David W. Dunlap, "Varying Boundaries of Hallowed Ground," *NYT*, September 8, 2005.

[58] Nikki Stern telephone author interview, December 3, 2009.

[59] Stern telephone author interview.

[60] Burlingame, "Our 9/11; The 'Families of September 11' Don't Represent Me"; Stern telephone author interview.

[61] Kolker, "The Grief Police," 50; Julia Levy, "Victim Groups Don't Speak for Everyone," *NYS*, September 6, 2002.

[62] Stern telephone author interview.

[63] Bernstein author interview.

[64] Todd Jick author interview, March 5, 2014.

[65] The flash points were numerous: opposition demonstrations and a letter-writing campaign to politicians; Governor Pataki's demand of an "absolute guarantee" that the two cultural players would not mount exhibitions that "denigrate...America, denigrate...New York or freedom, or denigrate...the sacrifice or courage that the heroes showed on Sept. 11"; statements of elected officials who threatened "appropriate legislative action and remedies," responses of LMDC officials, and statements and counterresponses from select family members; a call for a boycott of fundraising for the memorial; the police union's public opposition; the Drawing Center's voluntary decision to look for space elsewhere in lower Manhattan; and the announcement of Senator Hillary Rodham Clinton in opposition to the IFC's location at Ground Zero.

[66] Editorials, *DN*: "The Gov Got the Picture," June 25, 2005; "Get the Picture, Governor?, June 24, 2005; "Taking Back Ground Zero," July 31, 2005; "Pataki's Mess at Ground Zero," September 29, 2005.

[67] Editorials, *NYP*: "No Place for Politics," June 9, 2005; "Send 'Em Packing," August 12, 2005; "Hit 'Em in the Bank Account," July 27, 2005; Matthew Schuerman, "Bloomberg Evades on Freedom Museum as Founders Lobby," *NYO*, October 3, 2005.

[68] Editorials, *NYT*: "Freedom and Ground Zero," June 27, 2005; "Keeping Ground Zero Free," July 12, 2005; "A Sense of Proportion at Ground Zero," July 29, 2005; "The Governor's Proxy," August 16, 2005; "Freedom or Not?" September 23, 2005.

[69] Kolker, "The Grief Police," 50, 56.

70 Tofel author interview.

71 Paul D. Colford, "Memorial Donation Lagging—WTC Big," *DN*, July 13, 2005.

72 Matthew Schuerman, "Spiked by Pataki, Museum Vanishes without a Space," *NYO*, October 10, 2005.

73 Dunlap, "Downtown Board Criticizes Pataki for Barring Museum."

74 David W. Dunlap, "An Unclear Role for an Oversight Agency at Ground Zero," *NYT*, November 10, 2005.

75 Jacob Gershman, "Sides Dig in over Ground Zero Mosque," *WSJ*, August 2, 2010; editorial, "A Monument to Tolerance," *NYT*, August 4, 2010; editorial, "Unmask the Mosque," *DN*, August 3, 2010.

76 Sharon Otterman, "Developer Shrinks Plans for Muslim Center," *NYT*, April 30, 2014.

Chapter 11

1 Martin Filler, "At the Edge of the Abyss," *New York Review of Books*, September 21, 2011; Inga Saffron, "9/11 Memorial Stirring—but Backdrop Fails to Impress," *Philly.com*, August 28, 2011; Inga Saffron, "Absence of Feeling," *Philadelphia Inquirer*, January 13, 2004.

2 Joseph Daniels author interview, April 16, 2013.

3 The memorial design jury had awarded Arad the prize for breaking the rules, but before he would be announced as the winner, the young New York City architect had to submit to a number of impositions. First, as described in chapter 8, the jurors insisted that the inexperienced architect join up with an experienced landscape designer. He was then told that the design team would also include associate architects, who would work with Arad and Walker in "the realization of the design for the memorial," projected to cost between $175 million and $200 million. Arad further had to agree to give up control over the placement of the cultural buildings as well as cede control over infrastructure elements like the location of a truck ramp. Notwithstanding the conditions of design collaboration and minimal control, Arad fought constantly with everyone for absolute control. "Lower Manhattan Development Corporation Selects Associate Architect for World Trade Center Site Memorial," press release, March 13, 2004.

4 Philip Nobel, "Soaring Modesty," *Metropolis*, August 1, 2004.

5 See *PWP Landscape Architecture*, http://www.pwpla.com/national-911-memorial/landscape-design.

6 Philip Nobel, *Sixteen Acres: Architecture and the Outrageous Struggle for the Future of Ground Zero* (New York: Metropolitan Books, Henry Holt, 2005), 255 ("this place made sacred through tragic loss," language of the Memorial Mission, www.911memoiral.org/mission-statements).

7 Whereas it took decades before memorials were created for Abraham Lincoln (1922, Washington, DC), Franklin D. Roosevelt (1997, Washington, DC; 2010, FDR Four Freedoms Park, NYC), and World War II (2004, Washington, DC), to name a few, the memorialization process has since accelerated. The celebrated Vietnam Veterans Memorial (1982, Washington, DC) was built seven years after the end of U.S. involvement in that war, and the Oklahoma City National Memorial open five years after the April 1995 bombing.

8 Pedersen noted, as did other commentators, that the competition's 5,201 submissions came mostly from youthful designers, which might explain why none of the designs were fully realized: "They all feel provisional, like ambitious first drafts." The more experienced

ones, he noted, most likely did not think the odds were favorable to justify the costs involved. Each design study team would only be paid $40,000, only a fraction of what an entry would cost to develop and submit. Martin C. Pedersen, "Urban Journal: The Impossible Burden of the WTC Memorial," *Metropolis*, November 25, 2003. Also, see Martin Filler, "I Wept But About What I Cannot Say," *Arch Daily*, August 13, 2013.

[9] Justin Davidson, "Design Improved, but Still Incomplete," *Newsday*, January 15, 2004; jury quoted in Michael Kimmelman, "Architecture: Ground Zero's Only Hope: Elitism," *NYT*, December 7, 2003.

[10] Christopher Hawthorne "The Voids: An Interview with Peter Walker," *Landscape Architecture Magazine*, September 2011, 116–127, at 120; Christopher Hawthorne, "Growing Up," *Slate Magazine*, January 16, 2004, www.slate.com/articles/arts/architecture/2004/01/growing_up.html; Blair Kamin, quoted in "The Chosen Memorial Design: Reflecting Absence," *Gotham Gazette*, http://www.gothamgazette.comartice/20040107/202/825.

[11] Arad's initial design showed a narrow cultural building on the West Street side of the site, but the memorial jury requested its removal; it was replaced by a barrier wall, but the LMDC was forced to remove that too because the adjacent community viewed it as a barrier; Hawthorne, "The Voids," 120; Michael Arad and Peter Walker, "Reflecting Absence: Design Statement," n.d. [January 2004], www.wtcsitememoria.org/fin7.html.

[12] Urban Land Institute, "Peter Walker, FASLA—2012 Laureate of the ULI J.C. Nichols Prize Visionaries in Urban Development," press release, October 1, 2012; Robin Finn, "Public Lives: A Landscaper's Presence in 'Reflecting Absence,'" *NYT*, January 22, 2004. His firm's own entry in the competition—a glassy wall with the victims' and heroes' names etched within—did not, Walker said, "make it past first base."

[13] Finn, "A Landscaper's Presence"; Hawthorne, "The Voids," 123.

[14] Benjamin Forgey, "Making a Design More Winning; Revisions Add Strength to the Final Choice for Trade Center Memorial," *Washington Post*, January 15, 2004; "Reflecting Absence Design Statement."

[15] Nobel, *Sixteen Acres*, 252.

[16] Martin C. Pedersen, "The World Trade Center: Goodbye Memory Foundations, Hello Reflecting Absence," January 24, 2004. Davidson, "Design Improved, but Still Incomplete."

[17] The Council of the City of New York, Committee on Lower Manhattan Redevelopment, "Rebuilding Ground Zero—Status of the World Trade Center Memorial," briefing paper of the Infrastructure Division (hereafter cited as NYC Council briefing paper), March 29, 2006, 9–10.

[18] See http://aiweiwei.com/projects/5-12-citizens-investigation/remembrance. From a Twitter campaign to commemorate students who perished in the earthquake in Sichuan on May 12, 2008.

[19] David W. Dunlap, "Random List of Names at Ground Zero Memorial Angers Families," *NYT*, February 19, 2004.

[20] No transcript, only a briefing paper, which Gerson's committee had prepared, "Status of the World Trade Center Memorial"; Deborah Sontag, "The Hole in the City's Heart," *NYT*, September 11, 2006.

[21] Glenn Collins, "Protesters Step Up Calls to Put 9/11 Memorial above Ground," *NYT*, February 28, 2006.

[22] Letter from James Kallstrom to Stefan Pryor, March 3, 2006; David W. Dunlap, "Security Concerns Raised About Memorial at Ground Level," *NYT*, April 21, 2006.

[23] In response to family member concerns, the plan to keep the thousands of unidentified remains of 9/11 victims in a chamber with a large stone vessel was removed from the memorial design and the medical examiner's private repository for the unidentified remains was moved to a space between the two tower footprints so as "not to privilege one footprint over the other." Allison Blais and Lynn Rasic, *A Place of Remembrance: Official Book of the National September 11 Memorial* (Washington, DC: National Geographic, 2011), 152.

[24] The Spitzer administration's resolution of the problematic location of the Survivors' Staircase in 2007 triggered a material adjustment to the memorial program. Following a high-profile campaign by preservationists that succeeded in getting the symbolic remnant listed on the National Registry of Endangered Artifacts, Spitzer and his chairman of the LMDC, Avi Schick, intervened. The solution they proposed kept just the seven-foot-wide stairway proper (not the concrete structure around the thirty-eight steps) and moved it out of the way of the commercial tower for temporary storage, at an estimated cost of $2 million, before it could be permanently set into a long flight of stairs leading from the Visitor Orientation and Education Center to the underground Memorial Museum.

[25] Memorial Foundation, "WTC Memorial Foundation Chairman Mayor Bloomberg Announces Major Progress in Effort to Build the Memorial," press release, December 13, 2006. As explained in the press release, 1,518 names at the north pool would include two groupings: those who worked at or were visiting the North Tower on 9/11 and the individuals who lost their lives on American Airlines Flight 11, which crashed into that tower. At the south pool, 1,461 names would include eight groupings: those who worked at or were visiting the South Tower; individuals who died on United Airlines Flight 175, which hit the South Tower; those who died in the United Airlines Flight 93 crash in Shanksville, PA; those who died on American Airlines Flight 77, which crashed into the Pentagon; those who died at the Pentagon on September 11; those killed in the February 26, 1993, bombing of the World Trade Center; the first responders; and those whose specific location when they perished is not known. (In the final arrangement, the 1993 bombing names were moved to the north pool parapets and there was no specific grouping for those without a specific death location. By May 5, 2011, the final arrangement included 2,982 names; the names of those killed in the 1993 bombing were moved to the parapets surrounding the north pool. See Memorial Guide, National September 11 Memorial & Museum, names.911memorial.org.) and plate 18.

[26] Joe Hagen, "The Breaking of Michael Arad," *New York Magazine*, May 22, 2006, 5 of 15 printed out, nymag.com/arts/architecture/features/17015/; David W. Dunlap, "Discontent Spills into Open on Way Names Will Be Listed," *NYT*, February 20, 2004.

[27] "WTC Memorial Foundation Chairman Mayor Bloomberg Announces Major Progress in Effort to Build the Memorial."

[28] Started in 2003, this ad hoc group met about twenty times over the course of some eighteen months during which people developed personal relationships, and through them, a tolerance for the different cultural perspectives brought to the discussion. The advocacy group prepared a plan that it thought would satisfy everyone. "It was a peace covenant when a peace covenant was needed," Johnson told me in an interview. Although rejected at the time (October 2004), the Bloomberg plan eventually adopted shared two similarities:

location identification—the names of those who died at the Trade Center would be arranged on parapets around the memorial pool that corresponded to their tower—and clustering of the uniformed rescue workers, who would be arrayed by company or unit. The main differences were in personal details (age, company affiliation, and rank), which many family members said were important to telling the full story of 9/11; these individual stories of and tributes to every victim of the attacks would be included in the program of the Memorial Museum. See David W. Dunlap, "Relatives' Groups Use TV and Internet to Call for More Details with Names on 9/11 Memorial," January 25, 2007, for a comparison of the mayor's plan for the arrangement of names and an alternative put forth by some family groups; David W. Dunlap, "9/11 Memorial Faces Setback over Names," *NYT*, June 27, 2006, for a graphic of the families' plan; and for the museum program, NYC Council Briefing Paper, 10–11.

[29] Dunlap, "9/11 Memorial Faces Setback over Names"; David W. Dunlap, "Plan Is Changed for Arranging Names on Trade Center Memorial," *NYT*, December 14, 2006.

[30] Elizabeth Greenspan, *Battle for Ground Zero: Inside the Political Struggle to Rebuild the World Trade Center* (New York: Palgrave Macmillan, 2013), 185, 186, 185.

[31] Dunlap, "Plan Is Changed for Arranging Names on Trade Center Memorial."

[32] Editorials, *NYT*: "Naming Names at Ground Zero," July 5, 2006; "Names on the Memorial," September 23, 2006; "A Public Memorial," January 29, 2007; editorial, "Thanks, but No Thanks," *DN*, October 22, 2006.

[33] "Names on the Memorial," *NYT*; editorial, "2,979 Names Placed in Fitting Honor," *DN*, December 15, 2006; editorial, "Downtown, Little Steps," *NYP*, December 18, 2006; Blais and Rasic, *A Place of Remembrance*, 157.

[34] Charles V. Bagli and David W. Dunlap, "Memorial's Cost at Ground Zero Nears $1 Billion," *NYT*, May 5, 2006; David W. Dunlap, "Companies Are Weighing in on Financing for Memorial," *NYT*, April 19, 2006.

[35] Editorial, "Wanted: Leadership at Ground Zero," *DN*, March 31, 2006; editorial, "Too Many Zeroes at Ground Zero," *DN*, May 10, 2006.

[36] Alex Frangos, "Memorial Mess," *WSJ*, May 5, 2006.

[37] Editorials: "A Memorial Amiss," *NYT*, May 6, 2006; "Too Many Zeroes at Ground Zero"; "The Memorial Mess," *NYP*, April 6, 2006; World Trade Center Memorial Foundation, "Confidential Memorandum" (hereafter cited as Bovis memo), May 2, 2006, 4, http://www .nytimes.com/packages/pdf/nyregion/20060505_memorial.pdf. The Memorial Foundation argued that it could not be responsible for infrastructure costs not only because it needed to use all its fundraising capacity for the memorial and the Memorial Museum but because the three-way contemplated land swap transaction, which would provide the foundation with a lease or ownership of the memorial site, was structured for parity: "LMDC is expending its funds to deliver to the Port a site ready to build on by undertaking the expensive deconstruction of the Deutsche Bank building; LMDC has not asked for the Port Authority to contribute to such deconstruction. Similarly, the Foundation must have a site ready to build on." Bovis Memo, 5.

[38] Charles V. Bagli, "Mayor Chastises Foundation over Memorial's Costs," *NYT*, May 6, 2006; David W. Dunlap, "9/11 Group Suspends Fund-Raising for Memorial," *NYT*, May 9, 2006; David W. Dunlap, "Memorial Chief Quits as Plans Grow Confusing," *NYT*, May 27, 2006; Paul D. Colford, "More Tumult as WTC Leader Calls It Quits," *DN*, May 12, 2006;

Dunlap, "Memorial Chief Quits as Plans Grow Confusing"; Tom Topousis, "WTC Memorial Bigs BLA Chief," *NYP*, April 11, 2006.

[39] David W. Dunlap, "Port Authority Says It Can Build 9/11 Memorial," *NYT*, November 19, 2005.

[40] Dunlap, "Port Authority Says It Can Build 9/11 Memorial"; David W. Dunlap, "Ground Zero Memorial Cost Put at About $490 Million," *NYT*, November 23, 2005.

[41] Bagli, "Mayor Chastises Foundation over Memorial's Costs."

[42] Tom Stabile, "Rescue Mission: Sciame Takes a Major Detour to Make Sept. 11 Memorial Feasible," *New York Construction*, November 2006.

[43] Frank Sciame author interview, February 2, 2011; Stabile, "Rescue Mission: Sciame Takes a Major Detour to Make Sept. 11 Memorial Feasible."

[44] Charles V. Bagli and David W. Dunlap, "Memorial's Cost at Ground Zero Nears $1 Billion," *NYT*, May 5, 2006; David W. Dunlap, "News Analysis: Timing Down to a Less Costly Design at Ground Zero," *NYT*, May 6, 2006; David W. Dunlap, "Cost and Safety Put Memorial's Striking Vision at Risk," *NYT*, May 11, 2006.

[45] Sontag, "The Hole in the City's Heart"; LMDC board meeting minutes, November 10, 2005, 10.

[46] Tom Topousis, "9/11 Memorial Towers over $800 M," *NYP*, November 11, 2005.

[47] David W. Dunlap, "Every Week, a Meeting Pursues the Quest for a $500 Million Memorial for 9/11," *NYT*, April 26, 2006.

[48] Hagen, "The Breaking of Michael Arad."

[49] Hawthorne, "The Voids," 122, 123.

[50] Robin Finn, "Public Lives: Breaking Molds, and Then Designing New Ones," *NYT*, April 21, 2004.

[51] David W. Dunlap, "Unheard Voices on Planning New Trade Center," *NYT*, October 16, 2003.

[52] Hawthorne, "The Voids," 123.

[53] As Arad had conceptualized the memorial, the four-ramp arrangement was fundamental to the integrity of the design. Reducing the ramps to two would alter the experience. The change would destroy "his notion of drawing visitors through a distinct walking narrative that focused on the experience of the pools, especially the initial breathtaking view at the bottom." The loss of the ramps was a painful accommodation to reality for Arad. Hagen, "The Breaking of Michael Arad."

[54] Hagen, "The Breaking of Michael Arad."

[55] Robert Douglass author interview, April 18, 2012.

[56] LMDC, "Governor Pataki and Mayor Bloomberg Announce Frank Sciame to Lead Effort to Align Memorial Vision with $500 Million Budget," press release, May 17, 2006; Sciame author interview.

[57] Sciame author interview; Stabile, "Rescue Mission." Sciame's advisors included Bob Douglass, chairman, Alliance for Downtown New York (business relations); Jack Rudin, chairman, Rudin Management Company (who had called Sciame soon after the appointment to brief him on the players and political relationships) (community relations); Richard DeMatteis, president, and Scott DeMatteis, senior executive vice president and COO, the DeMatteis Organizations, and Chris Larsen, principal, Halmar International (construction consultants); Anthony D'Auria, partner, Winston and Strawn (legal); Marvin Mass, chairman,

Cosentini Associates (mechanical engineer); Richard Kennedy, senior director, Cushman & Wakefield (real estate consultant); Richard Tomasetti, chairman, Thorton-Tomasetti Group (structural engineer); Tom Mayne, principal, Morphosis Architects; Richard Cook, principal, Cook + Fox Architects; Peter Claman, principal, SLCE Architects; and Rick Bell, executive director, American Institute of Architects (vision alignment consultants).

[58] Dunlap, "Every Week, a Meeting Pursues the Quest." Of the costs Sciame shaved from the Port's infrastructure estimate, $74.1 million came from value-engineering adjustments and $49 million by refining the figure for the slurry wall and eliminating the cost of relocating the river water line.

[59] The steps included: review of budgets and cost reconciliation reports prepared by the LMDC, the foundation, and the Port Authority, along with the construction manager Bovis Lend Lease and consultants Faithful + Gould and URS Corporation; review of current design; reduction of cost through traditional value-engineering methods; exploration of further cost-effective design refinements and options with the designers that remained in keeping with the *Reflecting Absence* vision; analysis of the impact of common infrastructure on the memorial and Memorial Museum; identification of the most promising design refinement options; analysis, evaluation, modification, and prioritization of design refinement options; and presentation of draft recommendations to the governor and the mayor. Frank J. Sciame, "World Trade Center Memorial Draft Recommendations and Analysis" (hereafter cited as Sciame Report), n.d. [June 20, 2006], 5. Sciame author interview.

[60] Sciame author interview. In addition to the elimination of the underground waterfall, they analyzed several other options that were not considered consistent with the *Reflecting Absence* vision: bringing the reflecting pools up to plaza level (making them shallow versions of the original), reducing the landscaping on the Memorial Plaza, eliminating the Visitor Orientation and Education Center, and relocating the Memorial Museum to the inside of the adjacent Freedom Tower. On the latter, which Mayor Bloomberg had publicly proposed, the contribution of one advisor, Richard Kennedy, a senior director at Cushman & Wakefield, proved crucial in pointing out the problematic real estate issues that would have been created. See Sciame Report, 7–8, for further explanation, and Stabile, "Rescue Mission."

[61] LMDC, "Governor and Mayor Release Sciame Report on WTC Memorial and Museum," press release, June 20, 2006; James Gardner, "Value Engineering Comes to Ground Zero," *NYS*, June 21, 2006.

[62] Sontag, "The Hole in the City's Heart." By the tenth anniversary opening of the Memorial Plaza, Arad was reconciled with his anger. As he told Charlie Rose on his PBS show: "At the end of it, yes, I got everything that was important, I think. And it changed as it had to change." Then he said, "these changes that came out of this process of unexpected constraints, unexpected obstacles actually in some way distilled the design down to its most essential elements." "Rebuilding Ground Zero," *The Charlie Rose Show*, PB, transcript, September 13, 2011.

[63] Charles V. Bagli and David W. Dunlap, "Revised Design for 9/11 Memorial Saves Many Features and Lowers Cost," *NYT*, June 21, 2006; Stabile, "Rescue Mission." The LMDC decided not to make the comments public as was its custom on other occasions of public input, even though 80 percent of the 523 comments specific to the design refinements expressed support.

[64] Editorial, "9/11 Memorial, Version 2.0," *NYT*, June 22, 2006; editorial, "Memorial Madness," *NYP*, June 22, 2006.

[65] Ken Lovett and Frankie Edozien, "Eliot Spits Venom at 'Failed' LMDC," *NYP*, May 30, 2006.

[66] Charles V. Bagli, "Eight Plans to Cut Costs at Ground Zero," *NYT*, May 25, 2006.

[67] In the wake of Whitehead's departure, the chairman of the executive committee, Tom Johnson, assumed interim leadership of the foundation. According to an anonymous source, he was next in line for the chairmanship, but he was considered by some to be controversial. He would also not have had the fundraising power that the mayor brought to the task.

[68] E. John Rosenwald author interview, October 24, 2011.

[69] Rosenwald author interview.

[70] Matthew Schuerman, "Bloomberg Hits Up Real-Estate Bigs for WTC Memorial—$5M. Apiece!" *NYO*, March 5, 2007.

[71] Diane Cardwell and Charles V. Bagli, "Bloomberg Is Set to Take Reins of 9/11 Memorial Foundation," *NYT*, October 4, 2006.

Chapter 12

[1] Swiss Reinsurance Co., Sigma Catastrophe database, September 24, 2013.

[2] Marc Hochstein, "Muddy Water," *Grid*, November 2001.

[3] SR International Business Insurance v. Silverstein, Westfield, and PANYNJ, U.S. Court of Appeals 2nd Circuit, 345F.3d 154; 2003 U.S. App. LEXIS 19944, Decided, September 26, 2003; Alison Frankel, "Feature: Indemnity," *American Lawyer*, September 4, 2002.

[4] The Council of the City of New York, "Transcript of the Minutes of the Committee on Lower Manhattan Redevelopment" (hereafter cited as City Council Hearings October 2006), transcript, October 19, 2006, 55; Ben Hallman, "Up from the Ashes," *American Lawyer*, September 2007, 84–91, at 90.

[5] As quoted in Frankel, "Indemnity"; Steven Brill, *After: How America Confronted the September 12 Era* (New York: Simon & Schuster, 2003), 112.

[6] Timothy Hia, "Note: Que Sera, Sera? The Future of Specialization in Large Law Firms," 2002 *Columbia Business Law Review* (2002), 541–571, at n. 63.

[7] Frankel, "Indemnity."

[8] Charles V. Bagli, "Judge Rules for 3 Insurers on Coverage of Twin Towers," *NYT*, September 26, 2002. The two insurers, ACE Bermuda Insurance Ltd. and XL Insurance (Bermuda) Ltd., agreed to pay $298 million and $67 million respectively to settle all claims with the Silverstein group in cash. Both carriers had signed binders expressly referencing the "WilProp" policy form and had not been advised of any different form. One trade journal editorial complained that Silverstein and the PA have been "skimming off the top of all funds going to rebuilding.... when will New Yorkers get our buildings?" "ACE, XL Reach Accord with Silverstein on WTC Claims," *Insurance Journal*, February 18, 2002, http://www.insurnacejournal.com/news/east/2002/02/18/15749.htm; Bagli, "Judge Rules for 3 Insurers on Coverage of Twin Towers."

[9] Brill, *After*, 228–229.

[10] Brill, *After*, 229.

[11] Charles V. Bagli, "U.S. Jury Limits Payout of Trade Center's Biggest Insurer," *NYT*, May 4, 2004.

[12] Bagli, "U.S. Jury Limits Payout of Trade Center's Biggest Insurer." In pursuing this storyline, I reached out to Martin Polevoy, but he did not respond to my request for an interview. Alex Frangos and Dean Starkman, "Trade Center Jury Foils Silverstein," *WSJ*, April 30, 2004; David W. Dunlap, "News Analysis: How a Verdict Could Change the Future of Downtown," *NYT*, May 1, 2004.

[13] Editorials: "Ground Zero Fund Cut," *Newsday*, May, 4, 2004; "Rethinking the Future of WTC Rebuilding," *DN*, May 5, 2004; "Rebuilding Lower Manhattan," *NYT*, May 6, 2004.

[14] Errol A. Cockfield Jr, "Getting Ground Zero off Ground; Critics Are Saying That Silverstein's Plans for the Area Are the Biggest Gamble of the Developer's Career," *Newsday*, May 24, 2004.

[15] William Neuman, "Ground Zero Rebuild Cost to Hit $11B," *NYP*, January 30, 2004.

[16] By June 2006 when the state's Liberty Development Corporation gave preliminary approval to formally finance Silverstein's three towers, the estimated cost of this space was $706 per square foot.

[17] Amy Westfeldt, "$7BN Question: Was 9/11 One Attack or Two?" *Independent on Sunday* [London], February 8, 2004; editorial, "Downtown Funds Go Pfft," *DN*, May 11, 2004. On the breakdown of the $1.3 billion of insurance payments already spent, see Dean Starkman and Alex Frangos, "Before Ground Zero Rebuilding, $1.3 Billion Has Already Been Spent," *WSJ*, February 25, 2004.

[18] Blair Golson, "$1.1 Billion Award Elates Silverstein, Stuns Downtown," *NYO*, December 13, 2004. The Port Authority settled with its insurers for something more than the once-occurrence amount but less than two occurrences. Charles McClafferty e-mail, February 24, 2012. In May 2008, the Southern District of New York ruled that PA insurance was not secondary to Silverstein's and could not be called upon to fund shortfall in Silverstein coverage. See Clausen Miller, www.clausen.com/index.cfm/fa/firm_pub.article/article/bb1429ff-5232-40c8-893a-03935bbe6547/ThirdParty_Indemnity_Clause_Precludes_Coverage_For_WTC_Claim.cfm.

[19] Golson, "$1.1 Billion Award Elates Silverstein, Stuns Downtown."

[20] David W. Dunlap, "Developer at Ground Zero Has Twice the Capital and Extra Clout," *NYT*, December 8, 2004; Dean Starkman and Janet Morrissey, "Jury Rules for Silverstein on Trade Center Insurance," *WSJ*, December 7, 2004; Golson, "$1.1 Billion Award Elates Silverstein, Stuns Downtown."

[21] Brill, *After*, 192.

[22] Suzanne Kapner, "Taken for a Spin; Publicist Rubenstein Celebrates 50 Years of Cosmetic Surgery," *NYP*, June 6, 2004; Blaine Harden, "Image Spinner at the Center of a Web; Rubenstein, 'Dean of Damage Control' for New York's Powerful," *NYT*, September 30, 1999.

[23] Ken Auletta, "Annals of Communication: The Fixer, Why New Yorkers Call Howard Rubenstein When They've Got a Problem," *New Yorker*, February 12, 2007, www.newyorker.com/magazine/2007/02/12/the-fixer.

[24] Howard Rubenstein, "WTC Insurance Issue Isn't Settled," letter to the editor, *Crain's*, July 29, 2002; Brill, *After*, 113.

[25] Elinore Longobardi, "The Audit: The Remarkable Larry Silverstein Story, How the *FT* (and Others) Were Had by a Huckster," *Columbia Journalism Review*, October 30, 2007;

and "The Audit: The Larry Silverstein Story, Continued.... *Esquire* Joins the *Financial Times* in Fantasyland," *Columbia Journalism Review*, November 1, 2007; Dean Starkman, "Esquire vs. The Audit on Ground Zero Coverage, Raab, Longobardi Trade Shots on Silverstein, Rubenstein, the Port Authority and Lack of Progress," *Columbia Journalism Review*, November 19, 2007.

[26] Hugh F. Kelly, "The New York Regional and Downtown Office Market: History and Prospects after 9/11," report prepared for the Civic Alliance, Economic Development Working Group, August 9, 2002, 5. Also see Franz Fuerst, "The Impact of 9/11 on the Manhattan Office Market," in *Resilient City: The Economic Impact of 9/11*, ed. Howard Chernick (New York: Russell Sage Foundation, 2005), 62–96.

[27] Kelly, "The New York Regional and Downtown Office Market," 69.

[28] Edward L. Glaeser and Jesse L. Shapiro, "Cities and Warfare: The Impact of Terrorism on Urban Form," *Journal of Urban Economics* 51 (2002): 205–224, at 222. The policy stimulus behind the steady conversion of buildings to residential use, the so-called 421-g tax incentive program of real estate tax exemptions and abatement, in effect from 1995 to 2006, spurred more than 15 million square feet of conversions, producing 8,225 apartments (rental and condominium units) by the end of 2006. Another 3,371 units were converted by the end of 2010 for a total of 11,596 converted units, and the transformation of lower Manhattan to greater residential use generated new construction of 4,995 units. Data supplied to the author by the Alliance for Downtown New York.

[29] Kelly, "The New York Regional and Downtown Office Market," 69; Eric Herman, "Coming Home to New Downtown," *DN*, September 8, 2003.

[30] James Glanz and Eric Lipton, *City in the Sky: The Rise and Fall of the World Trade Center* (New York: Times Books, Henry Holt, 2003), 216; State of New York Office of the State Comptroller, "Analysis of World Trade Center Occupancy and Rentals," audit report NY-AUTH-26-81, February 6, 1981, 2.

[31] Fuerst, "The Impact of 9/11 on the Manhattan Office Market," 69.

[32] Charles V. Bagli, "Plans to Use Tax-Exempt Bonds for Midtown Cause a Stir," *NYT*, September 5, 2003; Charles V. Bagli, "Bank of America Is Scouting Midtown as Site for New Headquarters," *NYT*, March 12, 2003. Administered by the New York City Economic Development Corporation, the Industrial Development Agency acts as a conduit agency to provide financing assistance to businesses, including small industrial and manufacturing companies and not-for-profit organizations. Charles V. Bagli, "Bank of America Nears Agreement with Developer to Build 42nd Street Skyscraper," *NYT*, May 27, 2003.

[33] Charles V. Bagli, "Bonds for a Midtown Skyscraper Bring Out Supporters and Critics," *NYT*, September 30, 2003; Michael McDonald, "N.Y.C. IDA to Green-Light $650 Million of Liberty Bonds for Midtown Project," *Bond Buyer*, September 30, 2003.

[34] Carl Weisbrod author interview, April 5, 2016.

[35] Office of State Assembly Speaker Sheldon Silver, "Remarks of Speaker Sheldon Silver before the Association for a Better New York/Downtown Alliance Breakfast," May 20, 2005; Charles V. Bagli, "Silver Demands 'Marshall Plan' for Downtown," *NYT*, May 21, 2005. This was not Silver's first attempt to support his business constituency downtown with financial incentives aimed at enhancing the downtown office market relative to its midtown competition. In the fall of 2003, at a time when the investment firm Cantor Fitzgerald was negotiating a return to lower Manhattan following its catastrophic loss on 9/11 when 658 of its 960

employees at the World Trade Center were killed, Silver supported the company's efforts, saying it would send a powerful message to the world about downtown's rebound. Toward that goal, the State Assembly leader was reportedly blocking reinstatement of expired legislation that provided city benefits known as the Relocation and Employment Assistant Program over details of specific provisions. The legislation would benefit Cantor, and other companies, with benefits worth $3,000 per employee for twelve years if they moved to certain locations in the city. The program was eventually reinstated. Cantor wanted $12 million more in subsidies, which the Bloomberg administration was not willing to provide, and in July 2004, the firm announced it had signed a lease for new headquarters in midtown, at 499 Park Avenue at Fifty-ninth Street.

[36] CBRE, *World Trade Center Feasibility Study*, October 21, 2005, 8–9.

[37] Charles V. Bagli, "As Companies Scatter, Doubts on Return of Financial District," *NYT*, September 16, 2002.

[38] The unsettled issues at the start of construction in fall 2003 included ongoing disputes about his insurance recovery amounts and still-to-be-completed legal work with the city and Port Authority on reinserting Greenwich Street. On the land issues, "a series of complex regulations needed to be addressed by having the required strip condemned, which was a court process that could be challenged and which carried various risks." "Rebuilding the World Trade Center," *Cornell Real Estate Review*, July 2012, 39–53, at 47. There was no certainty on Liberty Bond financing, which did not come through until two years later, when the building was nearly three-fourths complete. Until that point, insurance money sustained the development and construction. The most unconventional aspect was the complexity of building with the ConEd power substation in the first seventy-seven feet of the building with the office tower directly above it. With construction fast-tracked before plans for the structure were complete, it was not possible to allocate costs between Silverstein and ConEd prior to construction. Instead, both parties agreed to proceed on the basis of week-by-week agreements, allocating costs for the past week's construction and agreeing upon what was to happen the next week. As his lawyer, Wachtell real estate partner Robin Panovka related the story at a retrospective public discussion of the project on August 1, 2011, "Rebuilding 7 World Trade," remarking how it foretold of stakeholder issues and bedeviling regulatory obstacles that would have to be overcome in rebuilding the towers at Ground Zero. Without the emotion of the lives lost on the site and the complications of adhering to a sitewide master plan, development of 7 World Trade still confronted hurdles.

[39] Christine Haughney, "Leaders Call for Cut in 7 WTC Asking Rent," *Crain's*, May 9, 2005.

[40] CBRE, *World Trade Center Feasibility Study*, 9; Haughney, "Leaders Call for Cut in 7 WTC Asking Rent"; CBRE, *World Trade Center Feasibility Study*, 9; Alex Frangos and Christine Haughney, "Lots of Space, Few Tenants," *WSJ*, December 14, 2005.

[41] Eric N. Berg, "Talking Deals; Developer Plays a Waiting Game," *NYT*, April 7, 1988; Mark McCain, "Commercial Property: Empty Offices; Pegging Rents High, and Waiting for 'Right Tenants,'" *NYT*, December 11, 1988.

[42] Haughney, "Leaders Call for Cut in 7 WTC Asking Rent."

[43] The $1.37 billion of funds would be used to repay $508.8 million of prior indebtedness, $189.8 million in prior indebtedness carry costs and other expenses of the original 7 WTC, and $670.8 million to construct the new 7 WTC. See pages 15–16 of the New York City

Industrial Development Agency, *Liberty Revenue Bonds Offering Prospectus for 7 World Trade Center LLC Project*, March 15, 2005; David W. Dunlap, "More Borrowing Clout for Ground Zero Developer," *NYT*, January 12, 2005.

[44] Josh Sirefman author interview, February 2, 2012; Seth Pinsky author interview, April 5, 2011.

[45] Pinsky author interview.

[46] Daniel Doctoroff author interview, January 23, 2008.

[47] Editorial, "How to Build at Ground Zero," *DN*, October 23, 2005; David Saltonstall, "Butt Out, Larry: Silverstein Must Quit WTC Site, Says Mike," *DN*, October 23, 2005.

[48] Julia Levy, "Bloomberg Meets Ground Zero Backlash," *NYS*, October 25, 2005. Those technicalities would be of reasonable concern to the PA's in-house lawyers. As one former general counsel at the authority explained it to me, the PA can only do that which it is statutorily authorized to do, unless the statute can be fairly read to include that activity not explicitly mentioned. And, he went on to say, he did not believe anyone would be understanding housing to fall within the statutory definition of what the Port could do. However, time and purpose matters. If, in the case of the rebuilding of the Trade Center site, there had been a consensus to do anything that required legislation, he believed such bi-state legislation could have been successful. Whereas the PA was involved in the development of housing over the George Washington Bridge, it did not build that housing; it only undertook repairs to infrastructure related to the housing. Real estate interests, he said, would have opposed the PA being allowed to build money-making luxury housing.

[49] "How to Build at Ground Zero."

[50] Janno Lieber author interview, June 6, 2012.

[51] Alison Gregor, "Profile: Larry Silverstein's Right-Hand Man," *Real Deal*, May 1, 2006.

[52] Gregor, "Larry Silverstein's Right-Hand Man"; Lieber interview.

[53] Silverstein statement, October 2005, confirmed by Dara McQuillan e-mail, July 2, 2013.

[54] Paul D. Colford, "Space for WTC Retailers Taking Shape," *DN*, October 3, 2005.

[55] Tom Topousis and David Seifman, "Gov Incensed over Mike's WTC Betrayal," *NYP*, October 25, 2005; editorial, "Lights Out for Downtown," *NYP*, October 25, 2005.

[56] Joe Mahoney and David Saltonstall, "Mike's WTC Apt. Talk Galls Silver," *DN*, October 25, 2005.

[57] Saltonstall, "Butt Out, Larry."

Chapter 13

[1] Charles V. Bagli, "Hearing Yields No Accord on Liberty Bonds for Trade Center," *NYT*, December 9, 2005. Twenty speakers testified at the December 8 public hearing. In addition to Andrew Alper, nine Industrial Development Agency members and twenty agency staff members and over sixty-five members of the public attended the hearing. Representatives of elected officials (four) as well as community and downtown interests (four) who spoke or submitted written testimony wanted assurances that the bonds would be used solely for downtown or, more specifically, for the Trade Center and that conditions such as an accelerated schedule and a requirement for above-ground retail space, among others, should be tied to the allocation of Liberty Bonds. They also wanted some of the remaining bond allocation to be reserved for other projects in lower Manhattan.

The venerable Trinity Church, whose property holdings downtown went back to a 1705 "Church Farm" land grant from Queen Anne of England, was still one of its largest real estate landholders, and it had a clear vested interest in the future viability of downtown. Carl Weisbrod, who was then president of the church's real estate division, believed that the time was premature to allocate all the remaining Liberty Bonds to the WTC site. Given market conditions in lower Manhattan, especially the lack of tenants, several speakers considered allocating all remaining bond to the site risky, but in their written responses to these comments IDA staff argued that "there could be no more appropriate use of the Liberty Bonds than the replacement of the commercial and retail space lost at the WTC on that horrible day."

Several speakers voiced concerns about the plans for retail space on the site, especially that it be built out as quickly as possible, while others criticized the city for being more interested in residential development than commercial development, arguing that the WTC site should be developed for a mix of uses including retail shops, hotel, schools, and cultural institutions. Industrial Development Agency, "Public Testimony Present Critical of the Project and Agency Responses for World Trade Center Liberty Bonds," public hearing of December 8, 2005, n.d., received from NYC Economic Development Corporation, Freedom of Information request, February 23, 2012. In short, these and other opinions expressed at the public hearings echoed many of the issues of earlier planning debates about how the Trade Center should be rebuilt.

[2] Katheryn Wylde author interview, December 10, 2009.

[3] PANYNJ, "Pre-Negotiation Agreement between the Port Authority of New York and New Jersey and World Trade Center Properties LLC [Silverstein]," December 8, 2005 [FOI #13043]. In the short nonbinding agreement, the parties agreed that "[t]he Negotiation Communications shall be exempt from public disclosure by the Port Authority to the fullest extent permitted by the Port Authority Freedom of Information policy." In essence, a public agency was saying, let's agree to keep as much of our business as possible out of the public purview.

[4] "The chiller plant decision is a long story," Janno Lieber told me. The type of chiller plant that the PA planned to use, a so-called river-water plant, is far more energy efficient than those drawing water from the city's drinkable water system. More efficient it may be, but river-water plants also consume aquatic micro-organisms (fish eggs and larvae), which caused consternation for environmental groups.

The original WTC chiller system was designed before the passage of the Clean Water Act of 1972, and apart from the United Nations and a couple of hospitals, few such systems still exist in New York City. Whether from inattention or automatic expiration because it was out of use, the permit for the existing WTC water-river chiller plant had expired. To build and operate a new plant, the PA needed a new permit from the New York State Department of Conservation, which opened up the issue to environmental challenges. As first envisioned, the new plant would have cooled the entire new Trade Center complex, as the earlier system did, but the amount of river-water usage was viewed as excessive by environmentalists, who were prepared to do battle over the larger plant.

Without the same capacity, the question for the PA became how much less water could be used; the solution to the scale problem was to eliminate the Silverstein towers from the system. The PA's chiller would supply central air conditioning and water cooling to the 9/11 Memorial and Memorial Museum, the Transportation Hub and its passageways and shopping concourses, the Vehicle Security Center, and the proposed Performing Arts Center.

For the private developer, the decision to cast off the office towers from the central chiller plant begat yet another negotiation, this one with the New York State Energy Research and Development Authority. To qualify for LEED certification, Silverstein's towers needed another path to energy efficiency, so Lieber asked the agency to "cough up enough money to buy fuel cells to offset being thrown off the central chiller plant." One year later with a deal in hand, the Port Authority announced plans for a drastically smaller WTC chiller plant, though few seemed to notice the end of this environmental controversy and significance of the programmatic change. State officials, reported David W. Dunlap of the *Times*, regarded the change as a logistical and environmental victory. Silverstein Properties chalked it off as another time-consuming but essential step in the complex process to rebuild the site. "We agreed to this approach in order to maintain the schedule," Janno Lieber told the press, "and the government agreed to help us address the significant costs and environmental impact of this switch." By spring 2009, the $200 million chiller plant with a drastically reduced intake of Hudson River water was nearing completion. David W. Dunlap, "Ground Zero Cooling Plant Shrinking from XL to S," *NYT*, November 16, 2005. Janno Lieber author interview, June 6, 2012.

[5] Bagli, "Hearing Yields No Accord on Liberty Bonds for Trade Center"; Deborah Sontag, "The Hole in the City's Heart," *NYT*, September 11, 2006.

[6] Editorial, "WTC Quarrel Deconstructed," *Crain's*, December 12, 2005.

[7] Charles V. Bagli, "Pataki Offers Liberty Bonds to Keep Tower on Schedule," *NYT*, December 15, 2005.

[8] Michael Barbaro, "The Bullpen Bloomberg Built: Candidates Debate Its Future," *NYT*, March 22, 2013; Ester Fuchs, e-mail to author, March 2, 2015.

[9] Jennifer Steinhauer and James C. McKinley Jr., "Political Memo: These Men Don't Brawl or Bicker; How Odd," *NYT*, February 1, 2003; Andrea Bernstein, "Mike and George Are Speaking—but Not Much," *NYO*, September 29, 2003.

[10] Steinhauer and McKinley, "These Men Don't Brawl or Bicker"; Jennifer Steinhauer and Al Baker, "For Pataki and Bloomberg the Rift Is Becoming Visible," *NYT*, August 8, 2003.

[11] Office of the Mayor of the City of New York, "Mayor Michael R. Bloomberg Delivers 2006 State of the City Address, "A Blueprint for New York City's Future," press release (#030-06), January 26, 2006.

[12] Sontag, "The Hole in the City's Heart." The roots of this political alliance trace back further in time, to late 2003, when discussions to buy out Silverstein's mortgage lender, GMAC, and partner for the retail portion of the lease arrangement, Westfield America, heated up. Westfield wanted out, but Silverstein wanted the retail component as did the Port, though their reasons for questing after it differed. The developer wanted to design his towers for maximum appeal to corporate financial-services tenants and minimize the presence of retail shops in his towers. The Port wanted at least as much retail space as had been there before 9/11, when the WTC mall ranked as one of the highest grossing shopping centers in the nation. It wanted to bring that level of retail space back as soon as practical for financial considerations. The city wanted street-level retail shops for planning purposes, to activate street life and help revitalize lower Manhattan, also as soon as practical.

[13] Matt Chaban, "Let's Make a Deal: How Mild-Mannered Seth Pinsky Got the City Building Again," *NYO*, April 4, 2012; Seth Pinsky author interview, April 5, 2011; Chaban, "Let's Make a Deal."

[14] Michael Saul, "Mike Turns Up Heat on WTC's Silverstein," *DN*, February 7, 2006.

[15] Whether Silverstein and his partners had "underinsured" their leasehold position proved to be a point of contention during the insurance litigation. The background on this controversial issue came from memos Ostrager's associates found in the broker's files during pretrial discovery. In a lengthy article on the insurance issues surrounding the 9/11 attacks, law professor Lucien J. Dhooge explained the controversy over coverage. "According to SR International Business Insurance Company (Swiss Re), one of the participating insurers in the World Trade Center, Willis estimated the replacement value of One, Two, Four and Five World Trade Center and the retail complex at $3.9 billion and the accompanying loss of rental income for a three-year period at an additional $1.1 billion. However, according to Swiss Re, the Lessees initially instructed Willis to obtain coverage totaling $2.32 billion." Lucien J. Dhooge, "A Previously Unimaginable Risk Potential: September 11 and the Insurance Industry," *American Business Law Journal* 40 (Summer 2003): 687–778, at 700. Steven Brill reported that the Ostrager team had found a second memo in the files that revealed that when Silverstein got a price quote for the $5 billion of insurance, he rejected it because it had cost too much. Steven Brill, *After: How America Confronted the September 12 Era* (New York: Simon & Schuster, 2003), 389. Silverstein subsequently increased the coverage to approximately $3.55 billion at the insistence of his lenders. "Regardless of the exact amount, Swiss Re claimed that '[t]he amount of coverage ultimately purchased was far below the $5.05 billion necessary both to replace the buildings and cover [the Lessees'] rental income losses in the event of a catastrophic loss.'" Dhooge, "A Previously Unimaginable Risk Potential," 700.

[16] NYC Economic Development Corporation, "World Trade Center Site: Summary of Financial Analysis," presented to the New York City Council, March 2006.

[17] Pinsky author interview.

[18] Charles V. Bagli, "5 Weeks Left for Decisions on Rebuilding," *NYT*, February 6, 2006.

[19] Charles V. Bagli, "Disputes over 9/11 Site Simmer On," *NYT*, November 9, 2005.

[20] Bagli, "5 Weeks Left for Decisions on Rebuilding."

[21] SPI, "Silverstein Properties Responds to City's Flawed Analysis of World Trade Center Plan," press release, February 9, 2006.

[22] SPI, "Silverstein Properties Responds to City's Flawed Analysis of World Trade Center Plan."

[23] SPI, "Silverstein Properties Responds to City's Flawed Analysis of World Trade Center Plan." The incentives for tenants to locate in downtown were substantial: rental subsidy from New York State of $5.00 a square foot for the first 750,000 square feet of space rented at the Trade Center, excluding 7 WTC; at 7 WTC, $3.80 a square foot for the first 750,000 square feet; permanent elimination of the 3.9 percent New York City commercial rent tax; a ten-year exemption from the sales tax on purchases of office furniture, equipment, and construction materials for tenant improvements; and for businesses relocating employees to the downtown area or creating new jobs in the downtown area, an annual $3,000 tax credit for each qualifying employee for twelve years. Letter from Ronnie Lowenstein to Hon. Scott M. Stringer, "The Need for Office Space and Rebuilding the World Trade Center Site" (hereafter cited as IBO March 2006 Report), March 13, 2006, 5.

[24] The Council of the City of New York, "Transcript of the Minutes of the Committee on Lower Manhattan Redevelopment" (hereafter cited as City Council Hearings March 2006), transcript, March 9, 2006, 215–216.

[25] City Council Hearings March 2006, 10.

[26] Office of the Borough President of Manhattan, "Borough President Scott Stringer Calls for Impartial Analysis of Economic Picture for Rebuilding Ground Zero," press release, February 17, 2006; IBO March 2006 Report, 1, 3, 5.

[27] As quoted in Elizabeth Greenspan, *The Battle for Ground Zero: Inside the Political Struggle to Rebuild the World Trade Center* (New York: Palgrave Macmillan, 2013), 147.

[28] Tom Topousis, "Livid Larry Sticks to Guns on WTC," *NYP*, February 10, 2006; David Lombino, "Schumer Plan Increases Pressure for a Compromise at Ground Zero," *NYS*, February 28, 2006.

[29] Daniel Doctoroff author interview, January 23, 2008; Julie Satow, "Mayor's WTC Revamp Plan Roils Execs," *Crain's*, February 13, 2006; editorial, "Ground Zero by the Numbers," *DN*, February 8, 2006.

[30] Editorial, "Down to the Wire at Ground Zero," *NYT*, February 13, 2006; editorial, "Mike at Ground Zero," *NYP*, February 10, 2006.

[31] Satow, "Mayor's WTC Revamp Plan Roils Execs."

[32] Anne Michaud, "Ground Zero Showdown," *Crain's*, February 20, 2006; Satow, "Mayor's WTC Revamp Plan Roils Execs"; City Council Hearings March 2006, 68.

[33] Anne Michaud, "Politicking Imperils Progress at Site; Jockeying over Mayor's, Governor's, Landlord's Goals Leaves Area Languishing," *Crain's*, February 20, 2006; Charles V. Bagli and Sewell Chan, "In Tug of War at Ground Zero, Schumer vs. Bloomberg," *NYT*, February 28, 2006; U.S. Senator Charles Schumer, "World Trade Center Speech before Breakfast Meeting of the Association for a Better New York," February 27, 2006.

Chapter 14

[1] Deborah Sontag, "The Hole in the City's Heart," *NYT*, September 11, 2006.

[2] Paul D. Colford, "Pataki Says Ground Zero Developer 'Has Betrayed the Public's Trust,'" *DN*, March 15, 2006; Charles V. Bagli and David W. Dunlap, "Developer Told to Build 9/11 Site or Stand Clear," *NYT*, March 16, 2006; David Seifman and Tom Topousis, "Silverstein to Gov: Lead Us to Table," *NYP*, March 17, 2006. Calling Silverstein "greedy" evoked an unfortunate stereotype for Jewish people. I owe this point to Herbert Sturz.

[3] Alex Frangos, "Ground Zero Rebuilding Is Set Back as Talks Falter," *WSJ*, March 16, 2006.

[4] Editorial, "Greed vs. Good at Ground Zero," *NYT*, March 17, 2006.

[5] Editorial, "Larry Silverstein's Duty to New York," *DN*, March 16, 2006.

[6] Editorial, "Pataki's Permanent Pit," *NYP*, March 22, 2006.

[7] Editorial, "Ground Zeroes," *WSJ*, March 18, 2006.

[8] SPI, "Statement by Larry A. Silverstein," March 15, 2006, at 7 World Trade Center; Charles V. Bagli, "Expressing Eagerness to Build, Developer of 9/11 Site Asks Pataki to Revive Talks," *NYT*, March 17, 2006.

[9] Charles V. Bagli, "Port Authority Rejects Silverstein's Offer to Talk," *NYT*, March 18, 2006.

[10] Charles V. Bagli, "Talks at Ground Zero Construction Approach the Deadline," *NYT*, March 14, 2006.

[11] Neil MacFarquhar, "Port Authority Chief to Leave, after Cutbacks and Criticism," *NYT*, January 18, 1997.

[12] Jameson Doig cited in Bob and Barbara Dreyfuss, "Inside the Port Authority, Governor Christie's Vast Patronage Machine," *The Nation*, February 14, 2014.

[13] John Heilemann, "The Power Grid: Poker at Ground Zero," *New York Magazine*, March 27, 2006, 22; Charles V. Bagli, "Master of Slow and Deliberate at Ground Zero," *NYT*, March 24, 2006.

[14] Martin Gottlieb, "The Region; the Sky Is No Limit for New York's Master Builders," *NYT*, November 24, 1985.

[15] Sontag, "The Hole in the City's Heart."

[16] Charles V. Bagli, "Master of Slow and Deliberate at Ground Zero," *NYT*, March 24, 2006.

[17] Sontag, "The Hole in the City's Heart."

[18] Daniel Doctoroff author interview, January 23, 2008.

[19] Kevin Rampe author interview, November 15, 2011; Janno Lieber author interview, March 1, 2010.

[20] Bagli, "Port Authority Rejects Silverstein's Offer to Talk"; Doctoroff author interview.

[21] Diane Cardwell and Charles V. Bagli, "Handshake across Hudson Is Forged at Ground Zero," *NYT*, April 7, 2006.

[22] Charles V. Bagli, "Pataki and Silverstein Inch Closer to a Deal on the Trade Center Site," *NYT*, March 28, 2006; Paul D. Colford, "Freedom Tower May Get 250M Boost From Pataki," *DN*, March 29, 2006.

[23] Charles V. Bagli, "Ground Zero Still Lacks an Agreement on Rebuilding," *NYT*, March 30, 2006.

[24] "NY, NJ Governors Weigh in on Ground Zero Talks," AP, March 29, 2006.

[25] Bagli, "Ground Zero Still Lacks an Agreement on Rebuilding"; Charles V. Bagli, "Ground Zero Still in Limbo as Talks Fail," *NYT*, March 31, 2006.

[26] Fredric U. Dicker, "Corzine a 'Nickel & Dimer': Pataki Aide," *NYP*, April 2, 2006; Tom Topousis, "Hevesi & Thompson Slam Jersey," *NYP*, April 4, 2006; Tom Topousis, "N.Y. to Jersey: Mind Your Own Biz on WTC," *NYP*, March 31, 2006.

[27] Editorials, *NYP*: "Corzine's Blackmail," March 29, 2006; "Bi-State Bandits," March 30, 2006; "Calling Jersey's Bluff…," March 31, 2006; editorial, "Wanted: Leadership at Ground Zero," *DN*, March 31, 2006; David Lombino, "Mayor Sides against N.Y. in Face-off with Jersey," *NYS*, April 3, 2006.

[28] The 2007–2016 ten-year Capital Plan authorized by the PA Board of Commissioners on December 19, 2007, included an additional $1 billion for the ARC project as part of an increase of $3.4 billion since the initial adoption of the Capital Plan in 2006. PANYNJ, "Port Authority Board Takes Action on Several Items," press release (#113-2007), December 19, 2007.

[29] Bagli, "Ground Zero Still in Limbo as Talks Fail."

[30] Charles E. Schumer, "Rebuilding Roadblocks: To End the Impasse," *NYP*, April 3, 2006; Lombino, "Mayor Sides against N.Y."

[31] Seth Pinsky author interview, April 5, 2011.

[32] Kevin Rampe author interview, November 7, 2008.

[33] Charles V. Bagli, 'Political Chiefs Iron Out Plans for 9/11 Site," *NYT*, April 6, 2006.

[34] Charles V. Bagli, "Time for Talk Is Over, Silverstein Is Told," *NYT*, April 21, 2006; Michael Saul, "Silverstein, See Ya in Court. 'I'm Not Going to Negotiate Anymore,' Bloomberg Says," *DN*, April 22, 2006.

[35] Sontag, "The Hole in the City's Heart."

[36] SPI's proportionally reduced rent payments to the PA for each tower, as detailed in the PA board meeting minutes of September 21, 2006 (229–232), are composed of three tiers of rent: (1) a base rent, increasing gradually over the term of the lease beginning in the eleventh year following the amendments to the net leases, 2017 (according to the schedule presented in the Conceptual Framework), the increase being approximately 1.7 percent in 2017 and 3 percent per year thereafter; (2) a percentage of gross revenues; and (3) "additional base rent," payable over forty years, beginning January 1, 2017. The additional base rent component is subordinated "to the payment of all other rentals, operating expenses, certain reserves and monthly capital costs, and debt service on SPI's financing for each Tower (but not in excess of approximately $3 billion in total aggregate amount of Liberty Bonds and construction mezzanine/junior loans" for the three towers. If cash is insufficient to pay the additional base rent, the amount due would accrue interest at a rate equal to 10 percent per year and 12 percent while any construction mezzanine or junior loans are outstanding. In the aggregate, the new base rent to the PA would be $78,740,000 per year. The PA would receive a 15 percent participation on the occurrence of a capital event (determined on a tower-by-tower basis) until it received $193 million (with this benchmark growing at 8 percent interest beginning January 1, 2006, and compounded annually), and thereafter a 5 percent participation in any capital events. SPI could pay all or any portion of the $193 million prior to December 31, 2016.

[37] The remaining insurance proceeds would be distributed proportionally; a commitment of $250 million from the Pataki administration would go toward construction of the Freedom Tower; Silverstein's towers would get $2.5935 billion of inducement resolutions for Liberty Bond allocations ($1.673 billion from New York State and $921 million from New York City, with what remained in the city's pot going to the Freedom Tower); and $100 million would support the Memorial Foundation's buildout program. Also, pledges were being made to secure long-term government leases for space in the Freedom Tower (about one million square feet from federal agencies) and Tower 4 (1.2 million square feet from New York City and the Port Authority).

[38] Charles V. Bagli, "Unified Financial Plan Is Presented for Ground Zero," *NYT*, April 20, 2006.

[39] Editorial, "Don't Go Away Mad, Larry...," *DN*, April 25, 2006; letter from Larry A. Silverstein to Anthony R. Coscia and Kenneth J. Ringler Jr., Re: World Trade Center (hereafter cited as Silverstein April 2006 letter), April 25, 2006 (PA FOI #13192); editorial, "Don't Go Away Mad, Larry...."

[40] Silverstein April 2006 letter.

[41] They were "prepared to give the PA this new and very substantial economic interest," which he claimed "would put the PA on an equal footing with all current equity partners"; however, he wanted clarification that the profit sharing element of the deal would be subordinate to debt financing and would not "adversely affect the financing required to get the project built." This is typical of public-private deals. Silverstein April 2006 letter.

[42] Silverstein April 26 letter. The seventeen points of the Conceptual Framework attached to the letter included provisions related to (1) Towers 1 and 5; (2) Towers 2, 3, and 4; (3) retail space; (4) a hotel; (5) parking; (6) the development schedule; (7) the development plan; (8) insurance; (9) the Liberty Bonds; (10) rent; (11) infrastructure; (12) developer fees; (13) the memorial; (14) a space lease option; (15) Silverstein lessees' work plan for Freedom Tower construction; (16) PA participation; and (17) the completion process, which included seven items subject to resolution in the sole discretion of the Port Authority, and eleven items subject to resolution in a mutually satisfactory basis to the Silverstein lessees and the Port Authority.

[43] The details would fill in just how the net leases would be amended to reflect the new rents and other terms and conditions of the rebuilding realignment, how the land transfers would be executed, how each partner would access the site, how the space lease option for both the PA and the city would work, and how the Freedom Tower and the infrastructure complex would be financed. The teams of counterparts would also have to prepare a mutually acceptable development agreement for the design and construction of the Freedom Tower and a development plan for the East Bathtub Development Project.

[44] The agency had refused to take space in the Freedom Tower, which is where Governor Pataki wanted the agency to be housed, citing the employees' emotional trauma of losing eighty-four colleagues in the twin towers on 9/11; asking them to work there, "would simply carry too much emotional weight," said a spokesman for Coscia. Patrick McGeehan, "Prospective Employees Say No to Freedom Tower," *NYT*, September 19, 2006.

[45] Janno Lieber author interview, June 6, 2012.

[46] Charles V. Bagli, "Silverstein Says Insurers Might Not Pay $4.6 Billion," *NYT*, May 19, 2006. Seven of the insurers failed to provide any assurances that the implementation of the Conceptual Framework would not have an impact on their obligations. The Port Authority and Silverstein then took legal action; at the time the commissioners authorized the 2006 deal, declaratory judgment action continued against four remaining insurers with coverage of approximately $1.1 billion. See PA board meeting minutes of September 21, 2006, 243; editorial, "Assurances for Ground Zero," *NYT*, July 24, 2006.

[47] Editorials, "Small Steps at Pataki's Pit," *NYP*, April 27, 2006; "A Change of Course at Ground Zero," *NYT*, April 27, 2006; "Get Lost, Larry," *DN*, April 21, 2006.

[48] Lieber author interview, June 6, 2012.

[49] Charles V. Bagli, "Amid Talk of Three Impressive Buildings, Silence on One Crucial Issue," *NYT*, September 8, 2006.

[50] Bagli, "Amid Talk of Three Impressive Buildings."

[51] Bagli, "Amid Talk of Three Impressive Buildings."

[52] As specified in the April 26, 2006, Conceptual Framework, the Silverstein lessees had a "continuous right" to require the Port Authority to lease approximately 600,000 square feet of space in Tower 4 and the City of New York to lease approximately 600,000 square feet of space in Tower 4 for a term (mutually agreeable to both parties) of between fifteen and twenty-five years, at a fair market value net rental rate, based on rental rates for class A office space in lower Manhattan, taking into account applicable free rent periods, tenant improvements, and leasing commission costs and governmental benefits available to tenants.

[53] Accounting for $3.80 a square foot of state and local incentives reduced Moody's rent to $37.70, before taking into account free rents and other inducements such as tenant improvements offered by Silverstein as developer-owner.

[54] Vacancies had dropped to 8 percent by September from 12 percent in April, and for the Ground Zero submarket, the drop in vacancy was even more dramatic, down to 10.4 from 20.2 percent and a high of 27 percent in March 2003.

[55] Pinsky author interview.

[56] In connection with the development of the original WTC, the Port Authority leased approximately 2.14 million square feet in the South Tower building to the state of New York under a long-term agreement for successive five-year terms totaling one hundred years. As of August 1980, prior to the first of several studies to analyze the potential privatization of the complex, New York State paid an average rental of $8.50 a square foot, which was substantially below market. State of New York Office of the State Comptroller, "Analysis of World Trade Center Occupancy and Rentals," audit report NY-AUTH-26-81, February 6, 1981, 3.

[57] Charles V. Bagli, "U.S. and State Pledge to Rent at Ground Zero," *NYT*, September 17, 2006. U.S. Customs had previously occupied 6 World Trade Center, and following the 9/11 destruction, the Port Authority and U.S. General Services Administration (GSA) had entered into a series of memorandums of agreement regarding the agency's future occupancy at the rebuilt site. The first was on July 29, 2003; the second, June 28, 2006; and the third, which pertained to leasing space in the Freedom Tower, laid out the conditions necessary for final execution of an amended and restated lease between the Port and the agency, and the key terms of that lease. Under the GSA's memorandum of agreement, the federal government would commit to more than six hundred thousand square feet in the Freedom Tower. See PA board meeting minutes, September 21, 2006, 224–225.

[58] Sewell Chan, "2 Vying for Governor Back Plan for Public Agencies as Anchor Tenants in Freedom Tower," *NYT*, September 18, 2006.

[59] Bagli, "U.S. and State Pledge to Rent at Ground Zero."

[60] LMDC, "Governor Pataki, Governor Corzine and Mayor Bloomberg Announce World Trade Center Site Global Realignment Agreement and New Milestones," press release, September 21, 2006.

[61] Douglas Feiden, "Port Authority Paying Larry Silverstein $21.5 Million but Has Yet to Seek 'Development' Tips," *DN*, April 14, 2009.

[62] PA board meeting minutes, September 21, 2006, 235. The commissioners were briefed on the preliminary financing plan, which identified five sources of funding (WTC insurance coverage, Liberty Bonds, PA recoveries for property damage allocated to 6 WTC [the former U.S. Customs House], the PA's commitment to New York State under the PA's Regional Transportation Program, and the issuance of debt by the PA), but neither specific figures nor an estimate of project cost was recorded in the minutes of the meeting. The minutes, however, detailed the procedures being followed to establish a financial plan and duly recorded the conventional caveats about pro forma projections of returns being dependent upon varying assumptions regarding final project costs and economic conditions. "Inevitably, as in any other financing of this type, some assumptions will not be realized, and unanticipated events and circumstances may occur. . . . Additionally, there are likely to be differences between the forecasts underlying the plan and actual results, and those

differences may be material." After the base case assumptions were stressed to project various potential outcomes and the lease commitments factored into the analysis, the Port's Freedom Tower pro forma projections revealed a positive net present value return (but no discount rate was specified) in a range of $285 million to $478 million, depending upon the iconic tower's costs. The last comment in the minutes on this item would be the most revealing of the unknown risk: "In addition, the Freedom Tower financing plan indicates a range of debt service coverage ratios which suggests that it could be financially self-sustaining, *although* [emphasis added], applying any number of stressing assumptions, the rent under the Net Lease would have to be subordinated to maintain acceptable coverage ratios" (223).

[63] The thirty-five legal documents of the November 16, 2006, restructuring addressed five elements of the mega transaction: redevelopment of the WTC site documents (Conceptual Framework, April 26, 2006, and the Master Development Agreement for Towers 2, 3, and 4 of the WTC with its accompanying twenty-five exhibits), deposit account and security agreement, and collateral assignment of membership interests, net lease and reciprocal easement and operating agreement documents (amended and restated agreement of lease and second amended and restated reciprocal easement and operating agreement of the East Bathtub of the WTC), Freedom Tower documents (agreement for purchase and sale of membership interest assets), city and LMDC documents (two letter agreements re: the Design and Site Plan Agreement), and Liberty Bond application in the amount of $2,593,500,000 (June 26, 2006). List is courtesy of Silverstein Properties, received from Robin Panovka, August 5, 2014.

[64] Certain parcels on each site required for the PA to perform underpinning work for the No. 1 subway running through the WTC site were to be held back an additional six months. Site 4 turnover would be fully complete June 30, 2008, and sites 2 and 3, December 31, 2008.

[65] Lieber author interview, June 6, 2012; editorial, "Pirates of the Port Authority," *NYP*, April 26, 2006.

[66] As detailed in the September 21, 2006, minutes of the PA board meeting, the $250 million pledged by Governor Pataki's administration for the construction of the Freedom Tower would offset 100 percent of the Port Authority's commitment for the state of New York under the PA's Regional Transportation Program, dollars that represented New York's share of a previous toll increase on PA-owned bridges and tolls. Allocating these funds to the Freedom Tower replaced the governor's earlier letter decision to use these funds for certain security features of the Freedom Tower (226–227). As part of the Sciame cost-cutting review of the Memorial project, the PA's $100 million contribution increased to $150 million.

[67] The city had long pushed for street-level retail shops on the Trade Center site, as discussed in chapter 5, and in her role as planning commissioner, Amanda Burden was able to stop the Port Authority from building a glass-enclosed mall over Cortlandt Street (now Cortlandt Way). As compensation for the Port Authority's consent to eliminate plans for an enclosed galleria on Cortlandt Street, the city agreed to transfer, subject to certain use restrictions, the property interests in the Cortlandt Street and Dey Street rights-of-way. As additional compensation for this adjustment, the city agreed to provide $34 million in *credits* to be applied toward the PA's PILOT payments to the city, credits that would be further adjusted to take account of "certain matters relating to the City's space lease in Tower 4," as stated in the September 21, 2006, minutes of the PA board meeting. The city further

allowed the Port Authority to increase by one hundred thousand square feet the amount of developable space for Tower 5. At an approximate value of $100 per square foot of air rights (the figures embedded in the zoning resolution governing the purchase of additional FAR [floor area ratio] in the Hudson Yards Special District), the additional buildable area could be said to carry an opportunity cost of approximately $10 million but far more in investment value to the Port Authority's future balance sheet for Tower 5 (229). All of these arrangements are common off-budget financing devices.

[68] These included the distribution of remaining insurance proceeds—the Port Authority would not take responsibility for the Freedom Tower without a major portion of the insurance money; the amount of rent the Silverstein lessees would be charged for reduced development rights—the PA had made concessions to reduce the rent and limit the size of the rent increases over time; the allocation of common-site infrastructure cost, a point on which the parties had been in discussion for a very long time—according to press reports, the Port was asking for $250 million and Silverstein was offering $60 million; tenancy of the Port Authority, whether in the Freedom Tower (Governor Pataki's preference) or Tower 4 (the PA's preference); the PA's contribution to the memorial; the PA's right to participation in a capital event for Towers 2, 3, and 4; and the question of Silverstein's development fees.

[69] Charles V. Bagli, "An Agreement Is Formalized on Rebuilding at Ground Zero," *NYT*, September 22, 2006.

[70] Janno Lieber author interview, October 19, 2010.

[71] Robin Finn, "Public Lives: The Authority at the Authority, Embracing Dullness," *NYT*, November 4, 2005; Ronald Smothers, "At Helm of Port Authority, behind-the-Scenes Outsider," *NYT*, July 16, 2003.

[72] Anthony Coscia author interview, October 5, 2010.

[73] The LMDC planned to pass other unfinished jobs to the city and the Port Authority. In the case of the Deutsche Bank Building, the most likely handover candidate was the Lower Manhattan Construction Command Center, an entity set up by the governor and mayor in 2004 to coordinate rebuilding efforts downtown. The Memorial Foundation was in place to fundraise for the 9/11 Memorial and Memorial Museum, which was to be constructed by the Port Authority.

[74] Rampe author interview, November 7, 2008.

[75] Charles V. Bagli, "$100 Million Suit Planned over Former Deutsche Bank Building," *NYT*, January 25, 2011.

[76] Sontag, "The Hole in the City's Heart."

[77] "Rebuilding the World Trade Center," *Cornell Real Estate Review*, July 2012, 39–53, at 46.

Chapter 15

[1] Editorial, "Santiago Calatrava's Contribution," *NYT*, January 24, 2004; editorial, "PATH Station, of All Things, Will Enrich WTC Site," *Newsday*, January 25, 2004; Steve Cuozzo, "WTC Hub: A Winner," *NYP*, January 23, 2004; editorial, "Beautiful Monument, Waste of Money," *DN*, January 23, 2004.

[2] In *Up from Zero: Politics, Architecture, and the Rebuilding of New York*, Paul Goldberger, architectural critic for the *New Yorker* at the time, praised the "gifted Spanish architect and engineer" for his "spectacular and lyrical bridges, train stations, airports, and museums," but questioned whether the hype would deliver. "The major above-ground hall holds forth

the promise of being one of New York's most exhilarating public interiors, although it also seems to suggest some of Calatrava's shortcomings," including "overly symmetrical designs" that, he believed, "promise more in striking exterior shapes than what would be delivered in interior space. He is as gifted in the translation of structural ideas into dramatic form as any architect alive, which is why his buildings are deservedly popular. They are exciting, however, more than they are profound" (237). The winged structure that Calatrava compared to a dove released by a child was not a new motif, Philip Nobel wrote in *Sixteen Acres: Architecture and the Outrageous Struggle for the future of Ground Zero*, though when the architect had proposed similar structures in the past in his native Spain, "he said they were inspired by a charging bull" (256).

[3] Herbert Muschamp, "An Appraisal: PATH Station Becomes a Procession of Flight," *NYT*, January 23, 2004; Justin Davidson, "*Newsday*'s Justin Davidson Finds a Soaring Icon," *Newsday*, January 23, 2004; Michael Kimmelman, "Architecture: Ground Zero Finally Grows Up," *NYT*, February 1, 2004.

[4] Ada Louise Huxtable, "A Landmark Destination: The Bus Station," *WSJ*, June 15, 2004; Ada Louise Huxtable, "Too Much of a Good Thing?" *WSJ*, December 8, 2005; David W. Dunlap, "A PATH Station That Honors 9/11, and Opens Wide, Too," *NYT*, January 23, 2004.

[5] Andrew Rice, "The Glorious Boondoggle," *New York Magazine*, March 9–22, 2015, 46–54, at 52; Deborah Sontag, "The Hole in the City's Heart," *NYT*, September 11, 2006.

[6] The sixteen-month process of rebuilding PATH was an incredibly proud moment for everyone at the Port Authority. In rebuilding service, they had kept a remnant of the old WTC concourse: Fifty feet of travertine flooring and six shallow travertine steps were visible in the vestibule between the station and E train platform. It was "the right thing to do," said Robert I. Davidson, chief architect of the PA. David W. Dunlap, "Again, Trains Put the World in Trade Center," *NYT*, November 24, 2003.

[7] Kimmelman, "Ground Zero Finally Grows Up"; Davidson, "Soaring Icon"; Goldberger, *Up from Zero*, 238.

[8] Huxtable, "A Landmark Destination"; Goldberger, *Up from Zero*, 181, 182.

[9] Huxtable, "Too Much of a Good Thing?"

[10] Huxtable, "Too Much of a Good Thing?"

[11] Nadine M. Post, "Team for WTC 'Bird of Peace' Tries to Remain Unflappable; Future Neighbors Slow Design, Contracting Rules Hamper Awards," *Engineering News-Record*, September 11, 2006.

[12] Jameson W. Doig, "To Claim the Seas and the Skies: Austin Tobin and the Port of New York Authority," in *Leadership and Innovation: A Biographical Perspective on Entrepreneurs in Government*, ed. Jameson W. Doig and Erwin C. Hargrove (Baltimore: Johns Hopkins University Press, 1987), 162, 163.

[13] Randy Kennedy, "Transit Plan Would Connect Dots Downtown," *NYT*, January 23, 2002; David W. Dunlap, "Coordinated Rebuilding Efforts Speed Progress at Ground Zero," *NYT*, November 16, 2006.

[14] Nicolai Ouroussoff, "Architecture: Post-9/11 Realities Warp a Soaring Design," *NYT*, May 11, 2009.

[15] Kevin Rampe author interview, November 7, 2008. Calatrava had designed the Transportation Hub for a level ground plane, yet there was a substantial grade change across the

whole Trade Center site; there was an extensive debate about the elevation of the intersection of Vesey and Greenwich Streets where the Hub was sited, according to several sources.

[16] David Dunlap author interview, May 23, 2011.

[17] Denise Richardson author interview, July 22, 2013; Anthony Coscia author interview, October 5, 2010; David W. Dunlap, "How a Train Station's Price Swelled to $4 Billion," *NYT*, December 3, 2014.

[18] David W. Dunlap, "Ground Zero's Train in a Box above a Forest of Steel," *NYT*, May 8, 2008; Charles Maikish author interview, February 2, 2013.

[19] To dig beneath the subway tracks, as Dunlap explained in the graphic accompanying the article, "[f]irst, load-bearing columns, called minipiles, were drilled through the soil all the way into the bedrock over 40 feet below. Then a massive beam was laid on the minipiles to distribute the weight of the subway box. Angular steel beams, called horseheads, are used to transfer loads from the subway box onto the beam. In the middle, metal rods tie the subway floor to the supporting beams and columns. As the excavation proceeds, diagonal bracing is added to provide necessary stability." Dunlap, "Ground Zero's Train in a Box above a Forest of Steel."

[20] LMCCC, "Value Planning Risk-Based Analysis Study to Validate Results of the Construction Coordination Room Process (CCR)," February 20, 2007, through March 2, 2007, New York City, n.d. [2007], 8, 24. The Port Authority subsequently decided to proceed with the construction of the trestle, but this would not be a definitive resolution of the challenge of unpinning the No. 1 subway box.

[21] The risks included delays for excavation under the box, very slow rates of excavation and construction of program space under the box, delays for the start of construction of the PATH hall, and delays to the completion of a finished Greenwich Street—removal of the box would save up to 4.5 years from the risk-adjusted schedule, according to the LMCCC's 2007 risk-analysis team.

[22] LMCCC, "Value Planning Risk-Based Analysis Study," 40–41; Eliot Brown, "Complex Design, Political Disputes Send World Trade Center Rail Hub's Cost Soaring," *WSJ*, September 3, 2014.

[23] A second LMCCC report a year later found that "significant constructability challenges" still remained because the presence of minipiles and cross bracing severely limited the available work space under the subway box, while construction to the east by Silverstein Properties and the PATH construction to the west limited access to deliver and move the materials. LMCCC, "Value Planning Risk-Based Analysis Study to Validate Results of the Construction Coordination Room Process (CCR), Addendum A: 2008 Update," April 30, 2008, 6.

[24] Under the FTA-approved construction budget, $63.9 million was the estimate for the temporary underpinning of the No. 1 box as of March 2006; by October 2008, after Ward's *A Roadmap Forward* for rebuilding the WTC site, the new approved budget number was $82.1 million. In Ward's report, a permanent support structure for the box was estimated at $325 million; in terms of schedule, the projected completion date of September 2014 meant that Greenwich Street could not be completed until as late as 2015 or 2016.

[25] Substantial completion of Towers 3 and 4 was to be achieved by December 31, 2011, and Tower 2, by June 30, 2012; in each case, the Silverstein lessees had a one-year extension option.

[26] The twenty projects and their stakeholders included: Towers 2, 3, 4 (SPI); Towers 1 and 5 (PA); Performing Arts Center (NYC); 9/11 Memorial, Memorial Museum, and Memorial Pavilion (Memorial Foundation); central chiller plant (PA); WTC Retail (Westfield-PA joint venture); Dey Street (MTA); temporary PATH station (PA); Route 9A (NYS DOT); No. 1 Subway Line (MTA-PA); Vehicle Security Center (PA); streets and utilities (PA); Fulton Street (MTA); commercial infrastructure (PA-MTA); and WFC Pavilion (PA-NYC). PANYNJ, *World Trade Center Assessment*, June 2008.

[27] Charles Maikish author interview, February 1, 2013.

[28] Kennedy, "Transit Plan Would Connect Dots Downtown."

[29] FTA Project Management Oversight Program, "Permanent World Trade Center Port Authority Trans-Hudson Terminal, Monthly Report" (hereafter cited as FTA-LMRO Monitoring Report), January 2004, I-8; Rampe author interview.

[30] Normally the section 106 process, named after the provision in the National Historic Preservation Act of 1966 that requires federal agencies to identify historic properties (e.g., buildings, other structures, sites, objects, and districts) eligible for inclusion in the National Register of Historic Places, involves a single agency and a single project, but due to the close proximity of three federally sponsored projects—WTC Memorial and Redevelopment Plan, WTC Permanent PATH Terminal, and the Route 9A Project—the Federal Transit Administration, Federal Highway Administration, and the LMDC, as recipient of funds from the U.S. Department of Housing and Urban Development, coordinated the section 106 processes at Ground Zero. Once the determination of eligibility was complete, the coordinated process effectively ended, with each lead agency responsible for meeting the remainder of its section 106 responsibilities separately as appropriate to its project. With regard to the permanent WTC PATH project, the FTA, as the lead agency for the project, began its section 106 process in September 2003, concurrent with scoping for the project, issued its final environmental review in May 2005, and released its record of decision in June 2005.

[31] Herbert Muschamp, "Critic's Notebook: A Chance for Scholars to Assess Ground Zero's Historical Significance," *NYT*, January 6, 2004.

[32] David W. Dunlap, "In Depths of Ground Zero, Historic Notice Can't Wait," *NYT*, February 8, 2004; LMDC, "Coordinated Determination of National Register Eligibility—World Trade Center Site, New York City, New York," February 6, 2004, 15; David W. Dunlap, "Opinions Vary on Treating Remnants at Ground Zero," *NYT*, March 6, 2004.

[33] LMDC, "Coordinated Determination of National Register Eligibility—World Trade Center Site, New York City, New York—Revised," March 31, 2004, 15.

[34] LMDC, "Coordinated Determination of National Register Eligibility—Revised," 15; "MOA among the FTA, the NYSHPO, ACHP, and the PANYNJ Regarding the World Trade Center Transportation Hub (WTC PATH Terminal and Pedestrian Connections) in New York City, New York," April 19, 2005, 2.

[35] Daniel Machalaba, "Low-Profile Actor Takes Center Stage at Trade Center," *WSJ*, October 23, 2002.

[36] PANYNJ, "Governors Pataki [NY] and Codey [NJ] Joined by Mayor Bloomberg and U.S. Transportation Secretary Mineta to Launch Construction of WTC Transportation Hub," press release (#98-2005), September 6, 2005; David W. Dunlap, "Looking Back to Move Forward with a New Rail Terminal at the World Trade Center Site," *NYT*, September 7, 2005.

[37] Under the terms of the development agreement between the PA and the FTA, no construction of the Hub project, or any project segment, could begin "before completion of the appropriate environmental evaluation under the National Environmental Policy Act, execution of a Construction Agreement, and preparation of a final scope, budget and schedule for the Project or applicable project segment, which will be agreed to and reflected in the Construction Agreement." "Permanent WTC PATH Terminal Project Development Agreement between the Port Authority of New York and New Jersey and the Federal Transit Administration," February 17, 2004, 5.

[38] 36 CFR 800.5 ([a][1]).

[39] FTA-LMRO Monitoring Report, March 2004, 1–14; David W. Dunlap, "New Process Is Proposed for Remnants at 9/11 Site," *NYT*, March 26, 2004.

[40] LMDC, "World Trade Center Memorial and Redevelopment Plan Programmatic Agreement," April 22, 2004, 4, 3.

[41] David W. Dunlap, "Transit Hub to Include Ground Zero Remnants," *NYT*, August 27, 2004.

[42] The August 2004 lawsuit was dismissed by the court because plaintiffs were deemed to have no standing to enforce the Programmatic Agreement of the section 106 procedures. The coalition subsequently brought at least two additional lawsuits in pursuit of its mission, one in October 2005 in U.S. District Court and another in March 2006 in Manhattan Supreme Court, both of which came to naught as well.

[43] The concourse was still being used daily by hundreds of commuters walking between the Eighth Avenue subway platforms and the PATH station; the PA intended to remove it to eliminate a fourteen-foot difference in floor levels. A PA spokesman said that the decision to preserve it had resulted from suggestions during the section 106 consultations. The entire segment would be joined to the new building by stairs or escalators, and it would still serve as a conduit between the PATH station and the subway.

[44] The coalition filed a second lawsuit in federal court after the Port Authority issued a final resource protection plan for the construction of the WTC PATH Terminal project, alleging that as called for under stipulation F of the MOA the Port Authority was in violation of section 4(f) of the Department of Transportation Act in determining to build the WTC PATH terminal at a location that uses the historic site (historic support beams) when other feasible and prudent alternatives exist that would avoid such use. In March 2006, the coalition filed a third lawsuit in Manhattan Supreme Court to block the start of construction of the memorial at Ground Zero. Again, the conflict turned on different interpretations of what constitutes the tower's footprint; in seeking to enjoin the LMDC and the PA from pouring a concrete slab on the footprint of the North Tower, the coalition was insisting that the whole of the footprints—inside which the LMDC planned to use as memorial space, exhibition galleries, and mechanical equipment—not just the perimeter truncated box-beam column remnants, were the meaningful footprints. On May 16, 2006, the court dismissed this article 78 proceeding.

[45] Other mitigations included incorporating historic features of the E subway platform, providing visibility from within the terminal to a portion of the east or west slurry wall, relocating the steel column and crossbeam pending final resolution of the artifact (along with others in Hangar 17 at JFK Airport under the PA's custody and control), preparing a resource protection plan for construction at the WTC site, and performing an analysis to address unanticipated

cumulative adverse effects on the historic resources during the design (as requested by several consulting parties and endorsed by others), implementation, and testing of the project, among other things. See MOA, 6–20.

[46] FTA-LMRO Monitoring Report, I-6. Adopting language that addressed the adverse cumulative effects of the WTC PATH Terminal project in conjunction with adverse effects of other projects at the Trade Center site proved to be complex and time consuming, and was a material factor in the time it took to reach agreement. According to the FTA-LMRO report, delays in finalizing language in the MOA centered around "striking a balance" between the interests of LMDC as a concurring party to the Programmatic Agreement for the WTC memorial and redevelopment project at the WTC site that does not recognize the potential for adverse effects and a stipulation in the MOA that outlined a satisfactorily cumulative effects analysis approach.

[47] FTA and PANYNJ, *Permanent WTC PATH Terminal, Final Environmental Impact Statement*, May 2005, vol. 6, 349, 6, 392.

[48] Advisory Council on Historic Preservation, "Federal Transit Administration Receives Chairman's Award for Federal Achievement," news release, February 2009, http://www.achp.gov/news_award_chairmans.html; National Trust for Historic Preservation, "National Trust for Historic Preservation Presents Its National Trust/Advisory Council on Historic Preservation Award for Federal Partnerships in Historic Preservation for the Preservation of the Last Remnants of the World Trade Center Site," news release, October 15, 2009.

[49] Sontag, "The Hole in the City's Heart."

[50] Goldberger, *Up from Zero*, 237; Rebecca Mead, "Winged Victories: The Soaring Ambition of Santiago Calatrava," *New Yorker*, September 1, 2008; Rice, "The Glorious Boondoggle," 50. The fees to the Downtown Design Partnership, greatly enhanced by the enlarged scope of the project, were considerable. As of September 19, 2014, the Downtown Design Partnership had received $405.6 million in payments from the Port Authority. "Records of Payments to the Downtown Partnership," http://www.panynj.gov/corporate-information/foi/15481-WTC.pdf.

[51] Mead, "Winged Victories."

[52] David W. Dunlap, "Approval Expected Today for Trade Center Rail Hub," *NYT*, July 28, 2005; James S. Russell, "Calatrava's $3.2 Billion Hub to Brighten Ground Zero," *Bloomberg News*, August 20, 2008.

[53] David W. Dunlap, "Fearing That Museum Will Cast Shadow on PATH Hub," *NYT*, November 18, 2004.

[54] David W. Dunlap, "The Intersection of Two Designs and Two Purposes," *NYT*, November 30, 2006.

[55] Dunlap, "How a Train Station's Price Swelled to $4 Billion"; Dunlap, "The Intersection of Two Designs"; Steve Cuozzo, "The Next PA Fiasco," *NYP*, January 30, 2008.

[56] Mead, "Winged Victories." From a practical standpoint, the liabilities of glass paving tiles were not absurd to the citizens and town officials of Bilbao, Spain, nor were they a matter of education. In that town made a compulsory destination by a Guggenheim Museum designed by Frank Gehry, Santiago Calatrava's steel and glass Campo Volantin footbridge became a distinctive part of the city skyline upon its completion in 1997. The beautiful footbridge with its "limpid glass floor tiles, designed to reflect the grey-green waters of the river Nervión that flow beneath," became a liability. For ten years, residents and visitors

reportedly complained of skidding and tumbling on the slippery surface. The weather of Bilbao was not kind to the glass tiles, either, "all 560 of which cracked over the years, ravaged by the extremes of climate [Bilbao is 43.25 degrees north latitude] and had to be replaced at a cost to taxpayers of €200,000" or approximately $285,000. Elizabeth Nash, "Architect Sues for 'Violation of Copyright' over Bridge Changes," *The Independent*, October 26, 2007. Rice, "The Glorious Boondoggle," 53.

[57] PANYNJ, "Anthony E. Shorris Elected Executive Director of the Port Authority of New York and New Jersey," press release (#7-2007), January 25, 2007.

[58] Joe Mahoney, "PA Boss Tapped by Eliot Bows Out," *DN*, April 18, 2008; Eliot Brown, "In Dropping Port Authority Chief, Paterson Putting His Stamp on Development," *NYO*, April 17, 2008.

[59] Martin Filler, "The Bird Man," *New York Review of Books*, December 15, 2005.

[60] Filler, "The Bird Man." To cover the last $25 million in cost overruns, the museum launched an emergency fundraising drive. According to Filler, this set off "a chain reaction that has brought several of the city's older cultural institutions close to bankruptcy because of increased competition for local donations."

[61] One particular detail illustrates the lack of checks and balances: door handles designed by Calatrava in the sculptural form of nude men and women intended for the Oculus and the mezzanine. Although the use of nudes harkens back in grand artistic fashion, what were people thinking? Nude sculptures parading as door handles in the Transportation Hub at Ground Zero—it was inappropriate, and after some to-do, this design detail disappeared from the drawings.

[62] Editorial, "Bust the Boondoggle," *DN*, April 16, 2008.

Chapter 16

[1] In laying out the methodology for its Final Generic Environmental Impact Statement, the LMDC came a tad closer to historical reality by assuming a two-phase buildout over eleven years with the Silverstein towers completed several years later in 2015. Only the Freedom Tower, memorial, museum, cultural facilities, open spaces, and retail uses (as well as the below-grade bus parking and service facilities) were expected to be completed within the five-year window, by 2009. Ambition was committed to paper, though few would ever read this three-volume document covering thousands of pages of analysis.

[2] Alex Frangos, "Showdown at Ground Zero: Beset by Politics, Safety Issues, the World Trade Center Site Suffers a 'Culture of Inertia,'" *WSJ*, May 4, 2005.

[3] Eliot Brown, "The Biggest Shrug," *NYO*, September 8, 2009.

[4] Frank Rich, "Ground Zero Is So Over," *NYT*, May 29, 2005; Miriam Kreinin Souccar, "One WTC Project Actually on Time," *Crain's*, March 29, 2010.

[5] By 2007, the major transportation projects approved by the FTA being overseen by the Lower Manhattan Recovery Office included the Permanent WTC PATH Terminal ($2.2 billion), Fulton Street Transit Station ($847 million), South Ferry Terminal Station ($420 million), Route 9A–West Street Reconstruction ($287 million), and WTC Vehicle Security Center and Tour Bus Parking Facility ($478 million). In addition, the office also was monitoring its grant funds to the Lower Manhattan Construction Command Center, which it had begun funding in October 2005 ($17 million).

[6] Bernard Cohen, U.S. Department of Transportation, FTA LMRO, "Report on Program Innovations," August 2004, 1. The innovative oversight program was constructed by two of the FTA's most senior staff members, Susan Schruth and David Vozzolo. In addition to the risk-based oversight, the new project-delivery tools included a single grant in place of the FTA's typical incremental grant awards, a project development agreement, and a construction agreement. The LMRO also hired its own consultants, which had not been done before for DOT transportation projects.

[7] Bernard Cohen author interview, July 17, 2013.

[8] The original FTA grant was for $1.7 billion, but in response to a request by Governor Pataki for an additional $221 million to cover hardening of the east-west corridor (following the terrorist bombings of Spanish commuter trains in Madrid in 2004 and the London Underground in 2005) and work on the East and West Bathtubs, the FTA approved a grant amendment that brought the total grant to $1.921 billion; a $280 million contingency was also allocated, bringing the total federal allocation to $2.21 billion. The PA's $300 million insurance payout allocated to this project set the total budget at $2.5 billion.

[9] "Memorandum from Tony Shorris to Governor Eliot Spitzer, Paul Francis, Tim Gilchrist, Avi Schick, RE: WTC Hub Cost Reduction Options" (hereafter cited as Shorris 2008 memo), March 7, 2008, 2.

[10] The construction agreement (CA) was one of the three innovative tools instituted by the FTA for the Lower Manhattan Recovery projects; the others were a single grant process and a development agreement. Signing the CA allowed the Port Authority to access the federal funds for construction; in turn, it allowed the FTA to reevaluate the project prior to release of any funds for construction and assured the FTA that funding coming from sources other than the federal government was in place. Most critically, the CA contained a "recovery plan" requirement in the event of project schedule delays or over-budget cost increases. Cohen, "Report on Program Innovations," 13.

[11] To implement its risk-assessment mandate, the LMRO hired project management oversight contractors, who were charged with regularly monitoring the project and reviewing costs and schedules to validate the project sponsor's budget and schedule, and these assessments were then summarized in detailed reports to the LMRO. PMOC consultants were hands-on. They attended Port Authority meetings, conducted on-site reviews several times a week to look at construction materials, and reviewed quality assurance on the project. To benchmark project risks, PMOC professionals employed a 90 percent probability analysis to determine whether the Port Authority's WTC Construction Department would meet or underrun the baseline FTA grant budget ($2.221 billion), project reserve ($280 million), and schedule milestones as established in the construction agreement.

[12] Shorris 2008 memo, 3.

[13] The five most frequently cited cost risks and major issues and problems identified in monthly monitoring reports from June 2006 to September 2007 included "cost contributions for shared infrastructure costs from third parties to project may be less than currently anticipated"; "construction manager/general contractor's guaranteed maximum price contract procurement format, in which the grantee entered into negotiations with a single entity, may result in a cost premium"; "schedule delays result in a direct cost impact to project (in addition to escalation) in the form of extended contractor overheads"; "estimated costs may continue to increase during final design due to interdisciplinary design integration, design/concept

changes, additional work done for others, and specific technical concerns"; and "lack of management approvals and timely decisions causing delays, lack of firm schedule, slow processing of change orders, delays in construction package awards, and lengthy subcontractor procurement process." Author's tabulations based on PMOC monthly monitoring reports.

[14] FTA Project Management Oversight Program, "Permanent World Trade Center Port Authority Trans-Hudson Terminal, Monthly Report" (hereafter cited as FTA LMRO Monitoring Report), December 2007, 37. As early as August 2005, the LMRO's general engineer had raised concerns about the lack of staffing on the PATH Terminal project. With the PA's assumption of additional responsibility for program and construction management of the 9/11 Memorial and Memorial Museum and Freedom Tower work in 2006, the "already overburdened" staff and project control resources of the WTC Construction Department were insufficient for the amount of required program, design, and construction management functions involved in the agency's increased WTC construction portfolio. Cost-cutting redesign work on the Hub was putting additional demands on the WTC Construction Department's limited resources, and its technical capacity to manage the Hub project was being "significantly threatened by insufficiently experienced Project Controls staff, the long period without an experienced Project Controls Manager, and the lack of an integrated project controls strategy." FTA-LMRO Monitoring Report, September 2007, 6–7.

[15] FTA-LMRO Monitoring Report, September 2007, 3.

[16] In its March 2008 report, the LMRO reiterated many of these recommendations, requested more timely critical cost and schedule data—a problem the investigator general report noted was more persistent with the Port Authority than other FTA grantees—and wrote that the Port Authority "needed to make significant changes in its management approach to completely demonstrate its technical capacity and capability to effectively manage its two Lower Manhattan Recovery Projects" (permanent WTC PATH Terminal and WTC Vehicle Security Center). At the end of March 2008, the Port Authority began providing monthly reports "with more explanatory and specific forecasts for the PATH Terminal's progress; the reports, however, did not include the data needed to meet FTA requirements." U.S. Department of Transportation, Office of the Secretary of Transportation, Office of Inspector General, "Baseline Report on the Lower Manhattan Recovery Projects" (hereafter cited as the FTA IG Report) September 26, 2008, 12, 19.

[17] FTA IG Report, 14, 19–20.

[18] FTA IG Report, 20; FTA "Response" to the IG Report, appendix, management comments, 25, 31.

[19] As noted in its response to the IG report, "Two of FTA's most useful tools are requiring the grantee to fund any costs exceeding the Federal commitment, and precluding the grantee from reducing project scope to save costs without FTA approval. However even these tools are not always effective at keeping projects on budget and schedule, particularly when external factors such as cost increases in materials, exert a substantial impact on the project." FTA "Response," 33.

[20] PA board meeting minutes, July 28, 2005, 308.

[21] Janice L. Tuchman, "Making 'Cooperation' Work on Trade Center Projects," *Engineering News-Record*, February 26, 2008.

[22] Nadine M. Post, "Team for WTC 'Bird of Peace,' Tries to Remain Unflappable," *Engineering News-Record*, September 11, 2006.

[23] PA board meeting minutes, July 28, 2005, 309.

[24] Denise Richardson author interview, July 22, 2013.

[25] Richardson author interview.

[26] Bent Flyvberg, Mette Skamris Holm, and Soren Buhl, "Underestimating Costs in Public Works: Error or Lie?" *Journal of the American Planning Association* 68:3 (2002): 279–295, at 290.

[27] "$1-Billion Overrun Is Not Acceptable," *Engineering News-Record*, February 19, 2007; David W. Dunlap, "Rising Costs Prompt Changes in Transit Hub at Ground Zero," *NYT*, February 9, 2007.

[28] Seth Pinsky author interview, April 5, 2011; Anthony Shorris author interview, December 10, 2009.

[29] Glenn Collins, "Between Rock and the River, the Going Is Slow, and Costly," *NYT*, January 13, 2008; Shorris author interview.

[30] Collins, "Between Rock and the River"; FTA-LMRO Monitoring Report, January 2008, 3.

[31] David W. Dunlap, "Citing Budget Concerns, Port Authority Plans for More Modest Hub at Trade Center Site," *NYT*, April 16, 2008.

[32] Shorris anticipated that such changes as were being contemplated would dramatically alter the Calatrava vision (even though "the only portion of his vision that would be visible from the street would be unaffected"), and therefore, Calatrava, who "has never feared from protesting changes to his often over-budget designs," would oppose these changes and possibly turn to the design community to protest them. New Jersey, on the other hand, was likely to support the changes, since that side of the river "has traditionally viewed WTC expenses as benefitting New York at the expense of the financial health of the bi-state agency and has already expressed concern through our Board about rising costs of the project." He believed the FTA would also support the changes because "[t]hey are institutionally traumatized by their 'Big Dig' experience in Boston, and under great pressure to show Congress they can deliver projects closer to budget, even in cases such as this where the additional costs are borne locally." Speaker Sheldon Silver was also likely to support the changes being contemplated, "as long as the visible architectural statement created by the Oculus does not change." Shorris 2008 memo, 6.

[33] Shorris 2008 memo, 6.

[34] Disputes in complex redevelopment projects are inevitable and the mechanism in the MDA (article 9) called for, in the words of the arbitration opinion, "an unusual form of arbitration" in the event mandated negotiations failed to resolve a dispute: "Before any disputes had arisen, the PA and Silverstein jointly selected a panel to be available to hear, on short notice, any dispute under the MDA, with a tight timetable for resolving the disputes." "Decision in the Matter of the Arbitration between 2 World Trade Center LLC and 4 World Trade Center LLC and the Port Authority of New York and New Jersey, WTC Arbitration No. 1, before John A. Cavanagh, Harry P. Sacks, Esq., and Hon. George C. Pratt, Decision" (hereafter cited as Arbitration Decision No. 1), 5.

[35] Arbitration Decision No. 1, 10.

[36] Arbitration Decision No. 1, 21, 25, 26, 32.

[37] LMCCC, "Value Planning Risk-Based Analysis Study to Validate Results of the Construction Coordination Room Process (CCR)," February 20, 2007–March 2, 2007, New York, n.d [2007], 2–3.

[38] David W. Dunlap, "An Overseer Is Chosen for All Work Downtown," *NYT*, February 15, 2005.

[39] Dunlap, "An Overseer Is Chosen"; Charles Maikish author interview, November 4, 2010; Teri Karush Rogers, "A Career That Revolves around the Trade Center," *NYT*, October 9, 2005.

[40] Jim Dwyer and Kevin Flynn, *102 Minutes: The Untold Story of the Fight to Survive inside the Twin Towers* (New York: Time Books and Henry Holt, 2005), cited in Dunlap, "An Overseer Is Chosen for All Work Downtown"; Rogers, "A Career That Revolves around the Trade Center."

[41] The elevation of Greenwich Street, for example, was not the same on the Port's plans and Silverstein's plans, as described in chapter 15.

[42] Funding for the LMCCC came from multiple sources: the Federal Transportation Agency through the LMDC, the Port Authority (most reluctantly), the MTA, and in-kind allocations from the city in police, building inspectors, and transportation traffic enforcement personnel. All were institutionally suspicious of each other.

[43] As became obvious, one of the problems stemmed from the fact that the PA only integrated those projects for which it had direct responsibility.

[44] LMCCC, "Value Planning Risk-Based Analysis Study," 5.

[45] Robert Harvey, Tarek Bahgat, David Gerber, James Kotronis, and David Pysh, "BIM as a Risk Management Platform Enabling Integrated Practice and Delivery," *Journal of Building Information Management* (Fall 2009): 14–17, at 15.

[46] Maikish author interview, February 1, 2013.

[47] Avi Schick author interview, May 10, 2010.

[48] LMCCC, "Value Planning Risk-Based Analysis Study," 7–9, 5.

[49] Avi Schick, chairman, LMDC, "Remarks at the Alliance for Downtown Breakfast," September 6, 2007; Amy Westfeldt, "WTC Rebuilders Show New Tower Designs, Promise New Deadlines," AP Financial Wire, September 7, 2007.

[50] PANYNJ, "Port Authority Approves 10-Year Capital Plan Outlining Critical Regional Transportation Needs," press release (#109-2006), December 14, 2006.

[51] Patrick Healy and William Neuman, "Spitzer Names Port Authority Head and Fills 11 Other Top Positions," *NYT*, December 16, 2006.

[52] Robin Finn, "Public Lives: Juggling a Pair of Policy Jobs, to the Music of Hammers," *NYT*, December 16, 2007.

[53] Flyvberg et al., "Underestimating Costs in Public Works," 288.

[54] Anthony Coscia e-mail to William Goldstein and Steve Plate, cc: to Anthony J. Sartor [Subject left blank], April 22, 2008 (hereafter cited as Coscia 2008 e-mail).

[55] The LMCCC struggled with credibility too, given that it was supporting the remediation and demolition efforts.

[56] Shorris author interview; Eliot Brown, "Meet Avi Schick, New York's New Steamroller," *NYO*, March 25, 2008; Eliot Brown, "Avi Schick Leaves ESDC," *NYO*, January 6, 2009.

[57] The Wollman Skating Rink episode became an enduring symbol of government inefficiency and a lesson in the comparative efficacy of public and private sector contracting. Situated in the middle of Central Park, Wollman Rink had been closed since 1980, when its concrete floor buckled. After more than five years of errors and nearly $13 million, in June 1986, the city was back to where it started: without a functioning skating rink. Before it took

another try at repairs, Donald Trump stepped in with an offer to take over the project with city monies and finish it within six months (nine less than the Parks Department officials were estimating it would take) by mid-December (1986). The mayor reluctantly accepted his public offer and agreed to pay $2.975 million for the work. "Mr. Trump's only profit was to be favorable publicity," but that was a good return for replacing earlier professional setbacks with successfully rescuing "a highly visible and well-loved landmark." Samuel G. Freedman, "Trump Feud: Barns Show Deeper Split," *NYT*, July 6, 1987. We do not know what Trump may have told his contractors to get them to get the job moving and finish it at the $3 million price, but it would not be surprising if he told them he would make it up later, in the next contract. For more on this episode, see Alan Finder, "Wollman Rink: 6 Years of Errors and Delays," *NYT*, June 17, 1986; editorial, "Lessons of the Wollman Rink," *NYT*, November 13, 1986; "New York Hopes to Learn from Rink Trump Fixed," *NYT*, November 21, 1986.

[58] Christopher Ward author interview, September 21, 2010.

[59] LMCCC, "LMCCC Assessment—2/13/08 Latest Schedule MS 37 (12/31/07)."

[60] Coscia 2008 e-mail. What was so strange about this memo, remarked an insider, was that this came after the board had already established a special WTC committee headed by Sartor. It was not as if the board was not fully involved in the project at that point.

[61] Andrew Rice, "The Glorious Boondoggle," *New York Magazine*, March 9–22, 2015, 46–54, at 52.

[62] Nadine Post, "Stepping Up to the Plate at the World's Most Visible Project," *Engineering News-Record*, January 23, 2012.

[63] Anthony Sartor memo to Anthony Coscia, copy to Commissioners Bruce Blakeman, Virginia Bauer, Christine Ferer, David Steiner; A. Paul Blanco, [PA] CFO; William Goldstein, DED-Capital Programs; Steven Plate, director, WTC Construction, "Subject: WTC Transportation Hub Budget," May 7, 2008.

Chapter 17

[1] Editorial, "Statistics Do Lie," *DN*, January 3, 2008.

[2] Editorial, "Towering Incompetence," *DN*, July 1, 2008.

[3] Amy Westfeldt, "NY-NJ War Brewing over New Ground Zero Costs," AP, July 2, 2008; letter from fifteen 9/11 family members to Christopher Ward, July 10, 2008.

[4] Michael R. Bloomberg, "There Should Be No More Excuses at Ground Zero," *WSJ*, September 10, 2008. Bloomberg also called for the dismantling of the LMDC, whose responsibilities, he said, should be transferred to the city and for a different city-state agency (the existing Lower Manhattan Construction Command Center) to take responsibility for demolishing the former Deutsche Bank building at 130 Liberty, which had been plagued by long delays and extraordinary cost overruns due to mismanagement, among other problems. David W. Dunlap, "Bloomberg Shakes Up Trade Center Planning," *NYT*, September 10, 2008.

[5] "Chris Ward, *Crain's* Speech" April 28, 2010, unpublished.

[6] Drew Warshaw author interview, December 19, 2012.

[7] Matt Chaban, "Cowboy Chris: Port Authority Chief Chris Ward's Outlaw Antics Alienating Albany," *NYO*, June 20, 11.

[8] Diane Cardwell, "Port Authority, Often Tangled, Gets an Infusion of Philosophy," *NYT*, July 7, 2008; Governor David Paterson author interview, December 6, 2012.

[9] Christopher Ward author interview, September 21, 2010; Alex Frangos, "Cultural Conversation: Can His Agency Repair the Ground Zero Debacle?" *WSJ*, September 11, 2008.

[10] "Governor Paterson Calls on Port Authority to Assess World Trade Center Site Reconstruction Timeline and Budget," reprinted in Eliot Brown, "Paterson Officially Launches Review of Trade Center Timetable," *NYO*, June 11, 2008.

[11] Editorial, "Downtown Debacle," *NYP*, June 23, 2008; editorial, "A Real Schedule for Ground Zero," *NYT*, June 18, 2008; Frangos, "Can His Agency Repair the Ground Zero Debacle?"

[12] Warshaw author interview.

[13] Warshaw author interview.

[14] Warshaw author interview; Laura Nahmias, "LMDC Will Go Out of Business…Someday," *City and State.com*, September 19, 2011.

[15] Warshaw author interview.

[16] PANYNJ, *World Trade Center Assessment*, June 2008, 3, 6, 4.

[17] The fifteen decision points and mitigation options identified in Ward's June 2008 reports are as follows: WTC Hub design alternative, construction of a permanent underpinning for the MTA's No. 1 subway line, St. Nicholas Greek Orthodox Church—land rights claim, final design and engineering of the northeast corner of the memorial quadrant, owner-builder management coordination for the memorial and museum, 130 Liberty Street abatement and demolition, potential redesign of Tower 3 to accommodate Merrill Lynch lease requirements, contracting strategy for the WTC Transit Hub, procurement and contracting inefficiencies, temporary PATH station early removal, Route 9A staging and funding, WTC police and security plans, Cortlandt Street subway station—design and schedule issues, below-grade engineering at the Performing Arts Center site, and site logistics.

[18] "Chris Ward, *Crain's* Speech."

[19] David W. Dunlap, "Port Authority to Intensify Its Ground Zero Role," *NYT*, July 28, 2008.

[20] Eliot Brown, "At WTC, Conflict of Interest Concerns," *NYO*, August 5, 2008; Douglas Feiden and Greg N. Smith, "Firms Gets World Trade Center Gold," *DN*, September 28, 2008.

[21] A count of *all* votes on WTC matters during these years revealed showed a similar frequency of Sartor recusals: 147 out of 229 votes (64 percent) from January 2008 to March 2014 (last vote before Sartor resigned from the board) compared to 9 out of 69 (13 percent) from post-9/11 to year end 2007. Author's calculations.

[22] Eliot Brown author interview, February 24, 2012.

[23] Editorial, "The Man Who Blew Billions," *DN*, April 16, 2014.

[24] Charles V. Bagli, "Higher Costs and Delays Expected at Ground Zero," *NYT*, June 30, 2008; Daniel Henninger, "The Politics of Can't-Possibly-Do," *WSJ*, July 4, 2008; Cardwell, "Port Authority, Often Tangled, Gets an Infusion of Philosophy"; editorial, "Ground Zero: Grim Truth," *NYP*, July 1, 2008.

[25] Editorial, "Towering Incompetence," *DN*, July 1, 2008; Greg B. Smith, "Port Authority Ignores Secret World Trade Center Construction Report," *DN*, June 28, 2008. As reported, at the end of 2007, the LMDC warned Governor Spitzer, "Before we can even consider these options, we need to do a rigorous analysis, but before we do the analysis, we have to acknowledge that we have a problem." This, as noted earlier in this chapter, was Schick's long-held position on how to handle the schedule slippage and how best to protect the governor

from the inevitable fallout from his predecessor's politically driven and illusionary time-lines for rebuilding Ground Zero.

[26] Editorial, "A Cleareyed Look at Ground Zero," *NYT*, July 2, 2008. The editorial board of the *Record* (Bergen County) did not print an editorial, but the paper's longtime columnist Mike Kelly similarly complained that there was "no single coordinator. No boss." Citing the "cour-age" of the Port Authority to admit the mistakes at Ground Zero, he argued that the agency "needs to accept—finally—that it should be in charge," and called upon Governor Corzine to take a position on "the big picture at Ground Zero." "Ground Zero Reconstruction in Disarray," July 6, 2008.

[27] Editorial, "Finally, Some WTC Realism and with It, Some Optimism Too. The New Head of the Port Authority Inspires Confidence That the Ground Zero Site May One Day Be Built," *Newsday*, July 6, 2008.

[28] Christopher Ward author interview, November 4, 2010; Chaban, "Cowboy Chris"; Ward author interview.

[29] PANYNJ, *World Trade Center Report: A Roadmap Forward*, October 2, 2008, 25; National September 11 Memorial and Museum at the World Trade Center, "Plaza Landscape Package (L-109.2), 9/25/09" (PA FOI #13550).

[30] LMCCC, "Value Planning Risk-Based Analysis Study to Validate Results of the Construction Coordination Room Process (CCR) Addendum A: 2008 Update," 3, 5.

[31] In July 2008, the Port Authority formed four working groups to study options for improv-ing the schedule and cost performance of four key elements of the WTC project: Greenwich Street corridor, Transportation Hub, memorial, and Vehicle Security Center. The working groups included representatives of all the major stakeholders in these projects and utilized outside consultants to provide expert design and construction input. Working throughout the summer and into the early fall, the working groups developed specific technical recom-mendations that were presented, along with supporting materials and detailed drawings, to the steering committee for decision-making. These reports and additional analyses by the PA's engineering department provided Ward with the data he needed for his report to Governor Paterson at the end of September. PA, "WTC Design and Construction Analysis: HUB Working Group Steering Committee Report, September 25, 2008," 4.

[32] For a technical description of a Vierendeel truss, see *A Roadmap Forward*, 20 n3. To create 150-foot clear spans, Calatrava had proposed using Vierendeel trusses on either side of the PATH mezzanine to support the arched roof structure.

[33] "Memorandum from Tony Shorris to Governor Eliot Spitzer, Paul Francis, Tim Gilchrist, Avi Schick, RE: WTC Hub Cost Reduction Options" (hereafter cited as Shorris 2008 memo), March 7, 2008, 3; David W. Dunlap, "Rising Costs Prompt Changes in Transit Hub at Ground Zero," *NYT*, February 9, 2007.

[34] Calatrava cooperated with the Port Authority on the design changes and, according to Rebecca Mead's *New Yorker* profile, "in laying the groundwork for this sobering announce-ment [that the wings of the Oculus would not open]." He issued a statement saying the revi-sion was "just the latest example of many changes we have recommended" to save time and money "while preserving the integrity of the original design." David W. Dunlap, "Design for Ground Zero Transit Hub Is Trimmed Back," *NYT*, July 2, 2008. His outward acceptance of the changes, however, differed from his underlying belief that the decision was short-sighted. Mead recounts that when these changes were in process, Calatrava told her, "In

terms of the users, the project is better now than it was before." Yet on a flight with him from France to Spain in April, "he had argued that it was wrongheaded to believe that economic belt-tightening calls for a less extravagant architectural statement. 'It's like someone says, "I have to save, I must sell my car"—and then you can't go anywhere.'" From his conversation in which he commented that the form the station eventually took would be an expression of the city's priorities, she concluded that "he did not seem convinced that New York would have the self-confidence necessary to hold fast to its vision, and his." Rebecca Mead, "Winged Victories: The Soaring Ambition of Santiago Calatrava," *New Yorker*, September 1, 2008.

[35] Ward author interview, September 21, 2010.

[36] Drew Warshaw responses to author question, July 10, 2013.

[37] PANYNJ, "Port Authority Launches New WTC Web Site with First List of Key Milestones," press release (#111-2008), October 3, 2008.

[38] The fifteen issues resolved fell into five categories: (1) Transportation Hub design: design alternatives and final design and engineering of the northeast corner of the memorial quadrant; (2) Greenwich corridor: construction of a permanent underpinning for the MTA's No. 1 subway line, temporary PATH station reconfiguration, and Cortlandt Street subway station design and scheduling issues; (3) Vehicle Security Center: construction sequencing and funding of the VSC, St. Nicholas Greek Orthodox Church land-rights claims, 130 Liberty Street abatement and demolition, and WTC police and security plans; (4) contracting performance and efficiencies: contracting strategy for the WTC Transportation Hub, procurement and contracting efficiencies, and owner-builder management coordination for the memorial and Memorial Museum; and (5) other significant issues: Route 9A–West Side Highway staging and funding, below-grade engineering at the Performing Arts Center, and site logistics.

[39] PANYNJ, *A Roadmap Forward*, 7.

[40] Navigant, "Phase I Interim Report," presented to The Special Committee of the Board of Commissioners of The Port Authority of NY and NJ, January 31, 2012, 37.

[41] For three years, the PA under Ward's leadership did not hold a single press conference at the site until the agency announced the successful completion of the Condé Nast lease negotiation. Held on the thirty-ninth floor of 1 World Trade Center, it was "the new way of doing business" as a "construction project," remarked Drew Warshaw in an e-mail to the author, January 31, 2016.

[42] Editorials, *NYP*: "Ground Zero Promises," October 3, 2008; "PA Double Talk," October 12, 2008.

[43] Editorials, *DN*: "Zero Accountability," October 4, 2008; "Conned Again," October 9, 2008.

[44] Charles V. Bagli and David W. Dunlap, "New Ground Zero Timetable Fails to Convert Some Skeptics," *NYT*, October 3, 2008.

[45] Eliot Brown, "City and State: Market Will Determine Silverstein's Schedule at WTC," *NYO*, October 2, 2008.

[46] Dunlap, "Design for Ground Zero Transit Hub Is Trimmed Back."

[47] Christopher Ward author interview, January 12, 2015. The Hub Working Group included representatives of all the major stakeholders: City of New York, Port Authority, FTA, Memorial Foundation, MTA, and Silverstein Properties. The developer had long considered

the Hub to be massive in size relative to its transit function; because of Calatrava's design demands for column-free space, Silverstein's office towers had to carry structural loads from the wings of the Oculus and utilities for the transit hall. His team engaged in the Hub Working Group had suggestions about the complex structure of the PATH hall, suggestions that would have put in columns at the ends to carry the loads instead of the expensive and custom-fabricated structural members for the cantilever. However, PA staff, I was told, did not want to redesign their project, which put Ward in the middle, since this was his process. At the time of Ward's assessment review, the office market was in free fall, and the developer's evident shortfall in insurance funds to meet his rebuilding obligations would soon lead him to aggressively and publicly press the Port Authority for financial support. Beyond technical reasons for simplifying the construction of the Oculus, reducing the scope of the Hub might also reduce its call on the finances of the Port Authority.

[48] The changes proposed by PA staff to shave costs from the Hub project fell into two categories: technical changes ($40 million) to the mechanical and other systems and reductions in hardening requirements, and changes to the Calatrava vision ($222 million) through simplification of the north-south connectors, changes to the PATH platform and mezzanine and related actions, and the addition of two retail floors underneath the main transit hall to simplify construction of the hall itself and add revenue-generating space. Other smaller changes would bring the value of the potential savings to nearly $300 million in project costs. Shorris 2008 memo, 4–5.

[49] PANYNJ, *A Roadmap Forward*, 7.

[50] PANYNJ, *A Roadmap Forward*, 38, 39.

[51] Ward interview, September 21, 2010.

[52] Noah Rothman, "Stephen Sigman Sets Sail from Port Authority, Lands at Global Strategy Group," *Campaigns and Elections*, January 2011.

[53] Stephen Sigmund author interview, April 12, 2012.

Chapter 18

[1] Confidential data given to the author by an insider.

[2] "Q&A: Forecasts from Five New York Real Estate Experts," *Crain's*, January 15, 2007; Julie Satow, "Sites Vie for Finance Firms; 3 Big Landlords with Prime Sites Go after Merrill, Lehman, J. P. Morgan HQs," *Crain's*, February 5, 2007.

[3] Charles V. Bagli, "Chase Is Said to Plan Tower Near 9/11 Site," *NYT*, April 4, 2007.

[4] Bagli, "Chase Is Said to Plan Tower Near 9/11 Site."

[5] Charles V. Bagli, "Chase Says It Will Move to Stamford if City Balks," *NYT*, April 25, 2007; Charles V. Bagli, "Chase Bank Set to Build Tower by Ground Zero," *NYT*, June 14, 2007. As presented in PA board meeting minutes of June 21, 2007 (120–122), the deal called for J. P. Morgan to pay $290 million for the development rights to site 5 until "substantial completion of the construction of the core and shell of the tower," after which it would be reimbursed for $250 million of the costs of the tower's construction. Net, the bank would be paying $40 million for the development rights (plus up to $10 million in reimbursement to the PA for design and construction of foundation work performed by the PA to secure the site), in addition to contributing $10 million to the capital costs of constructing St. Nicholas Greek Orthodox Church or the World Trade Center 9/11 Memorial and making monthly ground rent payments to the PA and related site payments (transfer taxes, site-wide operating

cost charges). The bank would receive discounted electric power rates and the as-of-right rent subsidy from New York State ($5 per square foot) that tenants in 7 WTC got. The board authorized the deal, but it was never consummated. Editorial, "Sweet Deal, Sour Price," *DN*, June 16, 2007.

[6] John Koblin, "Larry Lovers Chase's Ground Zero Move," *NYO*, June 14, 2007.

[7] "JPMorgan Sees Bear's Midtown NY Site Saving $3Bln," Reuters, May 14, 2007. There were other hurdles to the intended deal even before the mortgage-related losses decimated Wall Street firms. The cantilever over part of Liberty Street—a swell from 32,000 square feet at the base of the building to as much as 56,000 square feet beginning 190 feet above the ground—necessitated a change in the master plan for the project, which could open up the door to an untold number of opposition concerns. Moreover, the Port Authority did not actually own site 5, yet; the LMDC was the owner of record and the party responsible for the demolition of the former Deutsche Bank building (130 Liberty Street), which was not going well. The PA's eventual ownership of site 5 was part of the planned three-way land swap among the LMDC, Port Authority, and the Memorial Foundation conceptualized in the MOU of February 1, 2006.

[8] Martin Cicco author interview, November 29, 2012.

[9] Matthew Schuerman, "Ground Zero Rebranded with Tribeca Patina," *NYO*, September 12, 2007.

[10] Eliot Brown, "How N.Y. State Woos Merrill on Downtown," *NYS*, September 7, 2007.

[11] Peter Slatin, "Merrill's Midtown Move Another O'Neal Casualty?" *Forbes*, November 2, 2007.

[12] Office of Eliot Spitzer, Governor of the State of New York, letter to Mr. E. Stanley O'Neal, [Re: Conversation about Merrill Lynch's Corporate Headquarters Location Decision], October 26, 2007, 1, 2. After months of resistance, Silverstein finally proposed selling a site and reconfiguring the existing design (though not enough to accommodate extra-large trading floors), according to Bagli's reporting for the *Times*, but at a price Merrill's executives considered especially high and one well-sourced broker called "outrageous." Bagli reported that Silverstein cut his price by $400 million late in the negotiations; in conjunction with the $300 million (approximately $414 a square foot based on a building of 2.365 million square feet) offer cited in Governor's Spitzer's letter, Silverstein's starting offer would have been in the range of $700 million (approximately $584 a square foot), a figure still well above prevailing transactions in Manhattan at that time. Charles V. Bagli, "Merrill Lynch Is Expected to Quit Downtown for Midtown," *NYT*, October 25, 2007. The Port Authority's figure, $680 million ($288 a square foot), was quite close to a valuation in line with conventional real estate finance practice, which would value the rent-payment income stream ($12.69 a square foot) by a relatively low cap rate appropriate to the fee position (5 percent), yielding a value of $600 million ($253 a square foot) for the land. In selling his position to develop site 3 for $300 million, Silverstein was asking for a development fee that was 3.8 times the midpoint of the industry fee range for large-scale projects (3.75 percent) based on a March 2009 estimated cost of $900 a square foot (author's calculations).

[13] Editorial, "Ensuring Progress at Ground Zero," *NYT*, May 26, 2007; editorial, "Ground Zero: Good News," *NYP*, May 24, 2007.

[14] Charles V. Bagli, "Merrill Lynch Weighs Putting Headquarters at Ground Zero," *NYT*, May 23, 2008.

[15] Terry Pristin, "As a Weaker Office Market Looms, Landlords Bargain," *NYT*, April 2, 2008; letter from Mark E. Brooks of Merrill Lynch to John Lieber and Chris Ward, July 3, 2008 (hereafter cited as Brooks letter); Kenneth R. Bazinet and Adam Lisberg, "Mike Sees No Peril in Exit by Merrill. Says WTC Site Will Still Be Thriving Area for Biz," *DN*, July 18, 2008.

[16] Although the possibility exists that Merrill might have been negotiating with Silverstein to get more leverage with Brookfield, it does not seem likely. The Merrill team spent a lot of time on the negotiations and were even in touch with the governor, so "it would have been a pretty bold ruse had they just been playing us," recalled an insider to the negotiations. Also, Merrill and Silverstein Properties had signed an agreement dated March 14, 2008, regarding the sharing of certain design costs for modifications to the proposed WTC tower. Brooks letter. In October 2011, Brookfield Office Properties announced that Bank of America/Merrill Lynch had renewed its lease for 767,000 square feet (down from 2.3 million square feet) in Brookfield's World Financial Center, retaining space in both 4 WFC and 2 WFC. As part of the same transaction, Brookfield agreed to purchase Bank of America–Merrill Lynch's remaining 49 percent interest in 4 WFC for $264 million. Before doing so, however, Bank of America–Merrill Lynch moved much of its banking, sales, and trading from downtown to midtown into its 1 Bryant Park tower, further exacerbating the worse commercial property slump in more than a decade.

[17] Peter Kiefer, "Merrill Lynch Move Could Spark Silverstein–Port Authority Battle," *NYS*, July 18, 2008.

[18] Theresa Agovino, "Real Estate Market Embraces WTC Delay," *Crain's*, September 22, 2008.

[19] Douglas Feiden, "Fear WTC Could Be a Big Zero. Financial Woes Rattle Dreams for New Towers," *DN*, September 21, 2008; Larry A. Silverstein, "Progress Report 2008: Downtown Will Rise Again. It Always Does," *Downtown Express*, November 21–27, 2008.

[20] Eventually, the PA did have Silverstein value-engineer Tower 3 and eliminate the massive utilities needed for trading floors after the developer lost the opportunity of a Merrill Lynch tenancy, a PA inside source told me.

[21] Peter Kiefer, "Towers 3 and 4 to Start Rising at Ground Zero," *NYS*, March 13, 2008.

[22] Theresa Agovino, "Merrill Nears Decision on Headquarters Site," *Crain's*, October 15, 2007.

[23] Charles V. Bagli, "Merrill Lynch Ends Talks on Moving to Ground Zero," *NYT*, July 17, 2008. The first extension in 2004 was for five years; it expired at the end of 2009, and the second extension sought by Port Authority, state, and city officials passed the House of Representatives in December 2009, but stalled in the Senate. Just before the legislation expired, Silverstein opted to pay a small premium to sell his $2.59 billion in Liberty Bonds and place them in an escrow account, rather than risk losing out on the special tax-exempt financing.

[24] Confidential data given to me shows that by December 2007, the costs of building the three towers had increased dramatically—by over $2 billion—since the 2006 realignment deal. Such a sharp increase in such a short period suggests that the 2006 budget number may have been understated. As of March 2009, the budget number was up to $6.6 billion.

[25] Seth Pinsky author interview, April 5, 2011.

[26] Janno Lieber author interview, March 1, 2010.

[27] Julie Shapiro and Josh Rogers, "Port: Recession Could Change W.T.C. Timeline," *Downtown Express*, January 16–22, 2009.

[28] Douglas Feiden, "WTC Towers Might Look More like Towers. Plan Is to Cut Size Till Economy Turns Around," *DN*, January 30, 2009.

[29] Sam Goldsmith and Rich Schapiro, "World Trade Center Developer Larry Silverstein Wants Own Bailout," *DN*, March 21, 2009; Ray Rivera, "Port Authority May Help Financing of Tower," *NYT*, March 22, 2009; David M. Levitt, "Port Authority Said to Seek Cash from Silverstein in WTC Deal," *Bloomberg.com*, March 26, 2009; Theresa Agovino, "Port Authority Draws the Line at Ground Zero," *Crain's*, April 16, 2009; Charles V. Bagli, "As Finance Offices Empty, Developers Rethink Ground Zero," *NYT*, April 15, 2009.

[30] Eliot Brown, "Port, Silverstein at Odds over Last Two Towers; Bloomberg to the Rescue?" *NYO*, April 20, 2009.

[31] Bagli, "As Finance Offices Empty, Developers Rethink Ground Zero"; Agovino, "Port Authority Draws the Line at Ground Zero."

[32] Agovino, "Port Authority Draws the Line at Ground Zero."

[33] Amy Westfeldt, "Talk of Delaying 2 WTC Towers for Years," AP State and Local Wire, April 16, 2009.

[34] Douglas Feiden, "Over the Rainbow for WTC. Gloomy PA Predicts Project Won't Be Finished until 36 Years after 9–11," *DN*, April 16, 2009.

[35] Julie Shapiro, "Facing Decades of W.T.C. Delay, Silverstein Firm Blasts Port," *Downtown Express*, April 17, 2009.

[36] 2 World Trade Center LLC, 3 World Trade Center LLC, 4 World Trade Center LLC, c/o Silverstein Properties to the Port Authority of New York and New Jersey, "Notice of Default," May 8, 2009.

[37] Eliot Brown, "Location: Are the World Trade Centers Worth It?" *Observer.com*, April 27, 2009.

[38] Editorial, "Square One, Ground Zero," *DN*, April 19, 2009.

[39] Editorial, "Ground Zero Saga Continues," *NYT*, May 8, 2009.

[40] Editorial, "Speaking Power to Jersey," *NYP*, May 12, 2009; editorial, "Silverstein's $$ Grab; Other Projects Need Higher Priority," *Newsday*, May 18, 2009.

[41] On April 13, *Crain's* real-estate reporter Theresa Agovino penned "The Trouble with Larry," in which she argued that the developer was under little pressure to reach a deal quickly because of the fees the firm had already collected from the site since 2006 (an estimated $150 million) and expected to collect in the future (rising to $200 million in total). In a letter to the editor, Dara McQuillan, vice president in charge of communications and public relations for the firm, took the newspaper to task for what the firm believed were "inaccuracies" and "misinformation" in the article. With regard to the fee issue, "The Silverstein organization will ultimately receive $21 million in fees for the Freedom Tower (not the $150 million you cite). But that is only after giving the Port $1.2 billion of its insurance proceeds, turning over $100 million worth of design and construction work on the Freedom Tower, and paying more than $800 million in rent to the Port Authority since Sept. 11 for sites Silverstein hasn't been able to build on." Letter to the editor, "Nothing to do with WTC Memorial," *Crain's*, May 11, 2009. Actually, the fees received to date by its WTC investment partnership were a combination of management fees, development fees, and the $21.5 million breakup fee agreed upon in connection with the 2006 realignment agreement.

[42] Interpreting reports in the papers on aspects of the deal proposals going back and forth between the Port Authority and Silverstein during this time period could be confusing. The *Crain's* editorial of May 3, "WTC Solution Hinges on Larry Silverstein," for example, said that the Port Authority's lease agreement with Silverstein Properties for six hundred thousand square feet was at an "above-market rent." A May 11, *Daily News* story reported the PA "would pay below-market rent" and that the agency was offering to "hike its payments as part of the deal." As presented in the *Daily News* story, May 2009 downtown office rents averaged $44.58 a square foot, down from 11 percent from the prior year, according to Cushman & Wakefield. At the time of the 2006 deal, the Port Authority's rent agreement, starting at $59 a square foot, was, in fact, marginally above market; average market rents for class A space in the WFC-WTC market averaged $56.56 in September of 2006 and had been trending upward. Perspective matters a lot in drawing comparisons. In response, SPI's spokesperson Dara McQuillan said, "The Port's starting rent is actually $20 a square foot below the most recent lease at 7 World Trade Center (which was signed in December 2008, in the middle of the financial sector meltdown)." "Nothing to do with WTC Memorial," *Crain's*. As broker turned developer, Silverstein was focused on what the industry calls "trended rents," the rents expected to prevail when the building finally opened. The Port was also pressing Silverstein to exercise his option requiring the city to lease six hundred thousand square feet in Tower 4, but Silverstein was resisting doing so because he believed rents would be higher when the building was finished, which was then slated to be 2014.

[43] "WTC Solution Hinges on Larry Silverstein."

[44] Douglas Feiden, "Port Authority Paying Larry Silverstein $21.5 Million but Has Yet to Seek 'Development' Tips," *DN*, April 14, 2009. As noted in the discussion of the 2006 realignment deal, this "development fee," the paper noted, was "costing bridge and tunnel commuters the equivalent of 2.7 million George Washington Bridge tolls or 12.3 million PATH fares." Financial benefits accruing to the investment partners also included sizable complicated tax benefits from the loss of operations from its leasehold investment.

[45] Alex Frangos and Peter Grant, "Meet the Other Trade Center Builder; Larry Silverstein's Deep-Pocketed Partner, Lloyd Goldman Is Likely to Take over the Office Towers One Day," *WSJ*, September 11, 2008. Development fees turn on the issue of control. If the developer is putting its own capital at risk, the fee is higher than if a pure third-party source is providing capital. Development fees (based on hard and soft costs, excluding land in New York instances) run in a range of 4 percent to 4.5 percent; on a large-scale project, the fees tend to be lower, 3 percent to 3.5 percent. Development fees, in general, are a return on capital invested in a project. Once a project is up and going, by contrast, management fees are the monies necessary to sustain the operating side of the development business.

[46] Confidential document given to author. Also see Feiden, "Port Authority Paying Larry Silverstein $21.5 million but Has Yet to Seek 'Development' Tips"; Charles V. Bagli, "Getting Trade Center Parties in a Room, if Not on the Same Page," *NYT*, May 21, 2009. In the midst of the escalating battle over tower financing and charges that Silverstein had "no skin in the game," a little-noticed item appeared in the *Wall Street Journal*'s Plots and Ploys section of its weekly Property Report. "In the meantime, Mr. Silverstein has another project to watch after: his new yacht," Alex Frangos reported. The 174-foot twin-diesel-engine-powered boat, under development and set to deliver in 2010, would replace the developer's 131-foot, 1987-vintage *Silver Shalis*, according to *Super-YachtTimes.com*. As Frangos wrote, "it isn't

clear what he is paying, but industry observers point to similar-size vessels that cost in the $30 million to $40 million range. Mr. Silverstein declined to comment." "The Property Report: Plots and Ploys," *WSJ*, April 15, 2009.

[47] Agovino, "The Trouble with Larry."

[48] Sheldon Silver, "Speaker Silver Calls for Leadership Summit on World Trade Center Reconstruction," speech before the breakfast forum before the Downtown Lower Manhattan Association, May 8, 2009.

[49] Charles V. Bagli, "Assembly Speaker Urges End of Impasse on New Skyscrapers at Ground Zero," *NYT*, May 9, 2009.

[50] Josh Rogers, "The Ups and Downs of the W.T.C. Talks to Come," *Downtown Express*, May 22, 2009; letter from Peter W. Herman [RPA chairman] and Robert D. Yaro [RPA president] to NY governor Paterson, NJ governor Corzine, and Mayor Bloomberg (May 19, 2009), that emphasized the need to restore "street life and connections to the rest of Lower Manhattan as quickly as possible."

[51] Christina S. N. Lewis, "Silverstein and Officials Talk Trade Center—Again," *WSJ*, May 20, 2009.

[52] Bagli, "Getting Trade Center Parties in a Room, if Not on the Same Page"; Tom Topousis, "Larry Holds $2B Sword over Port in WTC Fight," *NYP*, May 20, 2009; Bagli, "Getting Trade Center Parties in a Room, if Not on the Same Page."

[53] Bagli, "Getting Trade Center Parties in a Room, if Not on the Same Page"; Elizabeth Greenspan, *Battle for Ground Zero: Inside the Political Struggle to Rebuild the World Trade Center* (New York: Palgrave Macmillan, 2013), 173; editorial, "Stalemate at Ground Zero," *NYT*, May 28, 2009; Charles V. Bagli, "Pledge to End Impasse at 9/11 Site," *NYT*, May 22, 2009.

[54] Charles V. Bagli, "Once at Odds, Bloomberg and Silver Pressure Port Authority on the Trade Center," *NYT*, June 23, 2009.

[55] Undoubtedly, this was the belief behind Silverstein's offer to the Port Authority in a June 4 proposal to assume responsibility for much of the work at Ground Zero, with the developer claiming that the arrangement would save between $300 million to $400 million, as well as provide "certainty that the entire East Bathtub will be completed by 2014–2015." (Silverstein's firm was already doing work in the East Bathtub for the PA and earning a contractually set margin on the cost for this work.) The developer did not offer to guarantee those savings, Bagli reported, but said he would invest $75 million, a paltry sum state officials were quick to say was inadequate. Bagli's story also noted that "[t]he arrangement would allow him to make an estimated $120 million in fees." Charles V. Bagli, "Little Progress Is Seen in Talks on Ground Zero," *NYT*, June 9, 2009.

[56] Eliot Brown, "Bloomberg and Silver: Strange Bedfellows in WTC Offensive against Port Authority," *NYO*, June 17, 2009.

[57] Paterson author interview. The struggle between the city and state was a constant theme Governor Paterson brought up in my interview with him. Recounting the to-do surrounding the wreath-laying event for the September 11 ceremony in 2009, he said both New York and New Jersey governors wanted to go down to Ground Zero, but the mayor said he was the only one who was going to do so. Paterson was told security would not let him go down to the site, but he said, "Let them stop me!" Then Corzine decided he would go down as well since Paterson was going to do so, but Paterson said "no," reasoning that if he didn't have

the courage to go first, he shouldn't go. In another incident in 2010, when Queen Elizabeth of England was coming to the site, the mayor wanted to escort her there, but Buckingham Palace protocol said that the governor is the only local government official to escort her. And the protocol runs as follows: the government whose land it is stands first, then other government officials, and only then the mayor. As Paterson recounted the story, New Jersey's heavy-set governor Christopher Christie told Paterson, "If the mayor stands in front of you, you trip him, and I'll sit on him!" Paterson author interview.

[58] Charles V. Bagli, "Still No Breakthrough in Ground Zero Talks," *NYT*, June 16, 2009; Theresa Agovino, "Port Authority on Hot Seat at Ground Zero," *Crain's*, June 17, 2009; Doug Feiden, "Use Station Funds for Ground Zero—Mike," *DN*, June 20, 2009.

[59] Letter from 2 World Trade Center LLC, 3 World Trade Center LLC, 4 World Trade Center LLC [signed by John N. Lieber, president] to the Port Authority of New York and New Jersey, "Re: Dispute Notice to Article 9.1 of the Master Development Agreement Notice of Default Dated May 8, 2009," July 6, 2009; WTC stakeholder letter attached to Eliot Brown, "Silverstein Goes to the Mattresses! Takes Legal Action to End WTC Stalemate," *NYO*, July 6, 2009; Charles V. Bagli, "Port Authority Is Blamed for Trade Center Delays," *NYT*, July 7, 2009.

[60] PANYNJ, "Statement by Christopher O. Ward, Executive Director of Port Authority of New York and New Jersey, in Response to Silverstein Properties Notice of Dispute," press release (#84-2009), July 6, 2009; Office of the Mayor of the City of New York, "Statement of Mayor Michael R. Bloomberg on Developments at World Trade Center Site," press release, July 6, 2009.

[61] Letter from Anthony Coscia and Chris Ward to Larry Silverstein, "Re: [New Proposals to Break the Impasse over the Financing of Private Office Space at the WTC Site]," July 9, 2009, 2. As part of this deal proposal, the PA offered to waive any prelease requirement on Tower 2, "leaving the determination of specific leasing requirements, if any, to the private real estate market." Silverstein would have to apply the balance of "the site's insurance proceeds ($530 million) and its Guaranteed Investment Contract Income ($70 million)" to the overall development cost of Tower 2 ($2.4 billion). The agency also offered to abate the developer's ground rent—"giving up approximately $770 million in rent over the next twelve years."

[62] Letter to Anthony R. Coscia and Christopher O. Ward, "Re: World Trade Center," July 16, 2009, 2. In this four-page letter to Coscia and Ward, among several other strong objections to the PA's July 9 proposal, Silverstein identified two backward-sliding financial elements: the reduction of the PA's backstop for Tower 2 to less than $1.2 billion (compared to the PA's May proposal, which nominally contemplated a full $1.9 billion backstop) and the requirement that Silverstein Properties raise $625 million of new subordinated financing (compared to the PA's May proposal of $370 million of funds) over and above the amount of available insurance. Under Silverstein's proposals, the developer would put up to $75 million toward the towers, an amount, reporter Eliot Brown pointed out, "that is less than he would receive in development fees." "Silverstein Rejects Port's Latest WTC Financing Plan; Arbitration Could Start Monday," *NYO*, July 17, 2009, which also included a link to the SPI rejection letter.

[63] John P. L. Kelly author interview, October 25, 2013.

[64] Finally, he "won" when the *New Yorker* in its June 14, 2010, issue published "Rising" by Lauren Collins in its Talk of the Town section, which in 792 words positively framed the

story of 1 World Trade Center's construction progress under Ward's leadership. "This was a tide change in perception," he said. "The task was a constant march of fighting the wall of perception to get people to see the reality." Kelly author interview.

[65] PANYNJ, "Port Authority to Build World Trade Center Memorial; Authorizes Lease for Freedom Tower Office Space," press release (#108-2006), December 14, 2006.

[66] Eliot Brown, "Port Authority Chief Fires Back at Mayor; for First Time, Names the Names of Projects Sacrificed to WTC Financing," *NYO*, June 18, 2009.

[67] Eliot Brown, "Mike vs. Larry vs. Jon and David," *NYO*, June 16, 2009.

[68] Paterson author interview; Eliot Brown, "Paterson (Finally) Jumps into WTC Mess, Delays Arbitration for Now," *NYO*, July 20, 2009; editorial, "Exactly, Gov," *DN*, July 19, 2009.

[69] PA board meeting minutes, October 22, 2009, 236–237. The $20 million authorized increases in compensation to existing agreements with various architectural, engineering, and other firms for services related to the following public components of the project: WTC Transportation Hub ($6.5 million), WTC streets program ($865,885), 1 World Trade Center ($4 million), WTC VSC and Tour Bus Parking Facility ($1.9 million), WTC retail LLC ($4 million), and other miscellaneous work ($2.7 million).

[70] Some weeks before the June announcement, Peter S. Lowy, global co-managing director for Westfield, presented his plan to Governors Paterson and Corzine. Westfield's June 2009 plan for 540,000 square feet of retail development at Ground Zero required "modifications in the site's master plan to make room for more prominent retail space," changes that also required approval by Silverstein, who would undoubtedly have objected. Christina S. N. Lewis, "Westfield Pitches Retail Plan for WTC," *WSJ*, June 10, 2009.

[71] Letter from Governor David A. Paterson to Larry Silverstein [Re: Proposed Framework to Resolve Issues of Financing Towers 2, 3, and 4], August 3, 2009, 2. In sympathy with Ward's goals and position, ten civic, environmental, business, and transportation planning groups issued a statement on July 16, reacting to the Port Authority's "latest attempt to break the impasse between the agency and Silverstein Properties' planned commercial towers," urging Silverstein to accept the offer so construction of the site could continue—to no avail. "Statement from Civic, Environmental, Business, Transportation and Planning Groups on Latest Proposal to Resolve Impasse at the World Trade Center Site," July 16, 2009. This was a second statement urging the parties to resolve the impasse without further public funding beyond the Port Authority's current commitments to the development of speculative office space at Ground Zero; the first written two months earlier was signed by seven groups, including the Regional Plan Association, the Fiscal Policy Institute, and the Tri-State Transportation Campaign. For the second effort, the coalition of civic, environmental, business, transportation, and planning groups gained four new signatories—Environmental Advocates, Environmental Defense Fund, General Contractors Association of New York, and Natural Resources Defense Council; the Fiscal Policy Institute did not sign this second statement issued on July 16, so there were ten in the July 2009 coalition effort.

[72] Paterson, "Re: Proposed Framework," 3.

[73] Charles V. Bagli, "Developer Rejects Paterson's Proposals for Ground Zero Towers," *NYT*, August 4, 2009; Sheldon Silver, "Snarling Up Ground Zero—WTC Parties Must Share Risks," *NYP*, August 5, 2009; Bagli, "Developer Rejects Paterson's Proposals for Ground Zero Towers"; editorial, "Ground Zero Stalls Again," *NYT*, August 10, 2009.

[74] Greenspan, *Battle for Ground Zero*, 173.

[75] PANYNJ, "Statement by Chris Ward, Executive of the PANYNJ, in Response to Letter of Arbitration from Silverstein Properties," press release (#99-2009), August 4, 2009.

[76] Silver, "Snarling Up Ground Zero"; Office of the Mayor of the City of New York, "Statement of Mayor Michael R. Bloomberg on Continued Delays at Work Trade Center Site," press release, August 4, 2009.

[77] Editorial, *NYT*, "Ground Zero Stalls Again"; editorial, "Larry's Last Stand," *DN*, August 6, 2009.

[78] Michelle Kaske and Ted Philips, "Northeast Bond-Watch: WTC Site Agreements," *Bond Buyer*, July 27, 2009; Douglas Feiden, "Port Authority Puts Screws to Developer Silverstein on Ground Zero Construction," *DN*, July 24, 2009.

Chapter 19

[1] Christopher Ward author interview, September 21, 2010.

[2] In the Matter of the Arbitration between 2 World Trade Center LLC, 3 World Trade Center LLC, and 4 World Trade Center LLC and the Port Authority of New York and New Jersey, WTC Arbitration No. 2, before Eugene McGovern, Harry P. Sacks, Esq., Hon. George C. Pratt, Arbitrators, "Decision, Interim Award, and Supplemental Order" (hereafter cited as "Arbitration No. 2 Decision"), January 22, 2010, 6, 21, 6; Office of the Mayor of the City of New York, "Statement of Mayor Michael R. Bloomberg on World Trade Center Development Arbitration Ruling," press release, January 27, 2010.

[3] 2 World Trade Center LLC, 3 World Trade Center LLC, and 4 World Trade Center LLC c/o Silverstein Properties, Inc. "Arbitration Notice Pursuant to Article 9.2 of the Master Development Agreement Seeking Emergency Interim Relief to Remedy the Port Authority's Material Breach of the Master Development Agreement," August 4, 2009, 14, 12–14.

[4] "Arbitration No. 2 Decision," 12. The arbitration ruling listed fourteen delays and events mentioned during the hearings by one or both parties. This list, which the panel remarked was "not all-inclusive," would have made a tough and complex equation for sorting out causality. The list's most notable items included time extensions requested by SPI and granted by the PA in connection with the Merrill Lynch negotiations; delays in the demolition of the former Deutsche Bank Building; relationship, if any, between delays in connection of the VSC and construction of the towers; delays in completion of the Hub, Greenwich Street utilities, and other infrastructure elements, and their impact on construction of the towers; delays in the PA's turnover of the towers' sites; consequences of the credit squeeze and inability to obtain financing; increases in budgets for the towers and their effects on SPI's financing problems; promptness and diligence with which SPI proceeded when the sites of the towers were turned over to it; consequences, if any, of the termination of Phoenix Constructors by the PA and introduction of Tishman/Turner as construction managers; delays, if any, caused by third parties other than SPI or the PA, which impacted or would impact the progress of the project; and finally, whether various delays were unavoidable under the terms of the MDA (11).

[5] The panel ruled that "SPI may be entitled to have the schedule for completion of the Towers adjusted to make an appropriate accommodation for any construction problems created by the PA's delays in completing the infrastructure," but it could not at the time determine the extent of adjustment, if any. "Arbitration No. 2 Decision," 18, 15, 16, 13.

[6] Much of the material on the postarbitration negotiations comes from confidential sources or interviews with those who have spoken on background or off the record. I have been

privileged with their confidences and have used the material without attribution in a non-prejudicial manner to tell the negotiation story in candor and to present the complexity of trade-offs that shaped the results of intense negotiations.

[7] Seth Pinsky author interview, April 5, 2011.

[8] The guidelines of Governor Paterson's letter, written by PA executives, were as follows: preservation of SPI's development rights on all three towers and an extended timeline that took into consideration the current limits of the real estate market; Tower 4 was economically viable; Towers 2 and 3 must be market driven; SPI must be willing to invest enough private capital ($75 million was inadequate), whether in the form of equity, subordinated debt, or some combination of the two, to make certain that the deal would contain private-market discipline and real private-sector risk; SPI must be willing to assume a first loss; and financial support for the Towers 2 and 3 podiums must be contingent upon spending insurance funds on immediate construction and acceptance of retail development.

[9] Editorial, "Larry Must Start Dealing," *DN*, January 31, 2010; editorial, "Stop Fighting and Build the World Trade Center; Site Has Been Mired in Litigation for Too Long," *Newsday*, February 12, 2010.

[10] The other key elements of SPI's proposal included the application of all SPI Liberty Bonds to the first two towers to further reduce financing costs; immediate resumption of construction of the subgrades and podiums for the entire East Bathtub to allow for the structural and mechanical needs of the Transportation Hub; use of the remaining insurance proceeds allocated to Tower 2 for lender completion-guarantee requirements in order to support financing of Towers 3 and 4; and a scaled-back public-private partnership proposed earlier, rather than the full partnership mechanism previously suggested and rejected by the Port Authority. Confidential memo.

[11] "NYC Mayor Urges Push to Rebuild Ground Zero," *AP Online*, February 19, 2010; Theresa Agovino, "Silverstein Offers More Money for Ground Zero Site," *Crain's*, February 19, 2010; Douglas Feiden, "Silverstein Nixes Plans for Tower 2," *DN*, February 19, 2010.

[12] Greg David, "Larry and the Port: A Dispute Unraveled," *Crain's*, February 1, 2010.

[13] Scott Pelly, "What Ever Happened to Ground Zero?" *60 Minutes*, CBS, transcript, aired February 21, 2010.

[14] Pelly, "What Ever Happened to Ground Zero?"; Christopher Ward author interview, January 12, 2015.

[15] Eliot Brown, "Silverstein to *60 Minutes*: Ground Zero Is a 'National Disgrace,'" *NYO*, February 18, 2010; Governor David Paterson author interview, December 6, 2012.

[16] RPA, "Statement by Regional Plan Association on Latest Proposal for Moving Development Ahead at the WTC Site," press release, March 5, 2010; Charles V. Bagli, "Unions to Rally to Build Towers at Ground Zero," *NYT*, March 9, 2010.

[17] Paterson author interview.

[18] Under this broad umbrella of protecting public dollars, the governor's senior staff was instructed not to allow the Port Authority to be a "parochial obstructionist" to the private development; on the other hand, Silverstein was not to proceed without skin in the game, and he was not to profit off the backs of the public sector. Confidential source e-mail.

[19] "New Yorkers Don't Believe Ground Zero Promises," Quinnipiac Poll, August 27, 2009.

[20] Robert Lieber author interviews, August 3, 2010, April 23, 2014.

[21] Robert Lieber author interview, October 23, 2013.

[22] Timothy Gilchrist author interview, September 27, 2013.

[23] Both the PA and EDC ran numbers on SPI's February postarbitration proposal. Pinsky's staff ran a stalemate scenario as a downside exercise. This scenario assumed that SPI stopped construction at the site but continued to pay ground rent until it defaulted in 2012, at which point insurance funds were assigned to the PA; the PA redesigned and completed development of the East Bathtub sites with the Hub and three retail podiums. According to an inside source, Pinsky was attempting "to sell the balance sheet—not the cash flow [of the project]." He was arguing that the master lease agreement enabled the Port to take over both towers if SPI defaults, and that the PA should consider SPI's February postarbitration proposal because the East Bathtub sites were real assets with "some intrinsic value, whether or not they create a positive cash flow for the Port in the short or long term." But as the confidential memo given to me by an inside source pointed out, "the negative externality imposed by not completing Towers 2, 3, and 4 may be just as challenging a disposition as completing SPI's two towers and facing the proposition of losing WTC1 tenants to T3 and T4." Moreover, there was the long-term problem of how the PA would find the capital capacity to build speculative towers. In addition, if the purpose of public-private development is to bring in private expertise because the PA is not good at commercial real estate development, as the past proved, then why would the PA want to take on this tremendous capital obligation, other than to hold its position for future disposition?

[24] Marketing for 7 WTC began in July 2004. The projected lease-up schedule included as part of the NYC Industrial Development Agency Liberty Bond Offering Memorandum of March 15, 2005, projected stabilized occupancy at 95 percent in two years, at year end 2006. The actual lease-up was not even close to that optimistic forecast. By year-end 2006, the lease-up achieved had reached 22.6 percent; after five years, the building was still 19 percent vacant versus the 5 percent vacancy rate, which SPI forecast would be achieved in less than three years. 7 WTC had several advantages that should have led to a very successful lease-up. During initial lease-up, the downtown vacancy rate was at historically low levels, and there was virtually no competition with similar new high-quality, class A office buildings downtown. The economy was strong and financial firms, in growth mode, were experiencing record profits. SPI, however, could not declare full lease-up until September 2011.

[25] Cushman & Wakefield expressed concern about a number of aspects of SPI's February 14 proposal. In particular, SPI's $250 million contribution, at less than 4 percent of the total cost of SPI's three towers, was unacceptably low. The SPI proposal was ambiguous with regard to responsibility for beginning construction of the tower podiums immediately, so the PA could only assume that it was being asked to carry the full cost of this $300 million construction. Also, the advisors did not think it wise to use the Tower 2 insurance allocation for a completion guarantee; rather, it sought to persuade the agency that the best approach for the PA was to have these funds applied directly to construction, which would lower the total debt needed to finance the project. Confidential memo.

[26] During this real estate cycle rents had fallen faster than in any such period in the past forty years. By January 2010, average rental rates in the downtown market had dropped 17 percent, to $42.75 a square foot from $51.55 a square foot, according to data collected by Cushman & Wakefield; total vacancy had shot up to nearly 9 percent, with a cycle trough nowhere in sight. The trough in the real estate cycle hit in the third quarter of 2010, with nearly 12 percent vacancy. Data courtesy of Cushman & Wakefield.

²⁷ The PA's analysis of the cost of Silverstein's proposal for a full backstop of two buildings, including lost ground rent, ran to $4.5 billion. Under this proposal, Tower 3, in competition with 1 World Trade and Tower 4, would be bleeding cash for years.

²⁸ Seth Pinsky email to author, March 11, 2015.

²⁹ Office of the Mayor of the City of New York, "Remarks of Mayor Bloomberg at Briefing on World Trade Center Rebuilding Agreement," press release, March 25, 2010.

³⁰ At 2.3 million gross square feet, Tower 3, designed by Richard Rogers, was smaller than Tower 2 (2.8 million gross square feet), designed by Norman Foster, but because it was going to be the most expensive tower to construct on a square-foot basis, the PA wanted it to be value-engineered to reduce costs. The agency also wanted a redesign of the tower to incorporate a sky lobby to accommodate an enhanced retail program. Silverstein balked; he had steadfastly refused to have sky lobbies in his towers; it was even a part of his legal development agreement with the Port Authority. The developer was proposing giant trading floors for Tower 3, but the Port Authority was saying this was not where the market was, that there was no demand for them. Silverstein eventually agreed to the sky lobbies and the retail spaces, but there was great skepticism at first, according to a senior PA official. Confidential source.

³¹ The PA sought to impose an $80 per square foot prelease requirement for 25 percent of the tower; SPI argued that the equity financing would impose market discipline and obviate the need for a specific rental dollar requirement. Lieber basically agreed with SPI; he was more interested in setting the total prelease square footage. The state wanted to know the break-even rent for Tower 3 and then scale back the total square footage to some percentage lower than the PA's ask and higher than SPI's offer. As the sides got closer and closer to a deal, the preleasing requirement and minimum rent level kept coming down, getting closer and closer to a break-even rent for Tower 3. They settled on four hundred thousand square feet at $60 a square foot (with CPI escalation beginning from 2012 onward). To avoid tenant swapping, no preleasing could involve tenants moving from other buildings in SPI's portfolio, other than in connection with regularly scheduled lease expiration.

³² Anthony Coscia author interview, October 5, 2010.

³³ "Fitch Rates Port Authority of New York and New Jersey $300 MM Consolidated Bonds Series 162 'AA-'; Affirms Outstanding Debt," Business Wire, October 20, 2009. Tower 3 would still bleed operating deficits for three years (projected at approximately $300 million), but the risk to the agency was manageable as long as there was a strong "cash trap" ("lockbox" on the funds coming out of the building) available to ensure that the developer would not start pulling money out of Tower 4 until he paid off the backstop on Tower 3.

³⁴ An anecdote on the backstop sheds more light on the dynamics leading up to a final resolution of the Tower 3 backstop issue. At a meeting of all the stakeholders and their staff principals at 7 WTC, as the story was related to the author, Silverstein was handing out cookies and Marvin Markus of Goldman Sachs, the deeply experienced maven of public-sector financing transactions, was asked if he could finance Tower 3 with the $200 million capped backstop from the Port Authority. When he quickly responded, "yes," it was then a done deal.

³⁵ "Fitch Rates Port Authority of New York and New Jersey Series 162 'AA-'"; Affirms Outstanding Debt," Business Wire, March 29, 2010.

³⁶ As it related to fees going forward, the 2006 agreement allowed the Silverstein investor partnership to withdraw management fees of approximately $10 million annually up to a

$50 million cap for the five-year period beginning July 1, 2007. PA minutes of special board meeting, August 26, 2010 (hereafter cited as PA August 26 special board meeting), 240.

[37] An exception to the PA's proposal for a suspension of management fees would apply if SPI constructed the podium using insurance proceeds, in which case it would earn a to-be-negotiated development fee. For Tower 3, the developer would be paid only 50 percent of the remaining development fees and allocable share of its management fees provided for in the 2006 MDA; the remaining 50 percent would be frozen and escrowed in the cash trap until release of the Tower 3 backstop and satisfaction of any outstanding Tower 4 support payments. The escrowed fees would be used first to pay construction overruns and leasing overruns and other costs that might otherwise be covered by the PA's support payments. As long as the tenant support agreement was in place, whether drawn or not, all unused Tower 3 escrow fees would be trapped in the system.

[38] The net rent (then $22.86 million) on Tower 4 stayed in place because the Port Authority was credit-supporting the tower; however, PA negotiators allowed that the scheduled escalations to this rent would be delayed by two years, to 2019, "in recognition of the need for initial lease-up in a difficult market." "Proposed Terms of Restructured Development Agreement and Net Leases with SPI, March 25, 2010 Briefing Paper, Privileged and Confidential (Updated for Negotiations through August 3, 2010)," August 3, 2010.

[39] Beyond the funding of development costs and financing (senior and mezzanine), the list of other items on a final term sheet of concern to any private developer in this situation would have included the terms and conditions of the tenant support payments, repayment, and termination; lockbox setup and release of funds; public participation in capital proceeds; sales and transfers; rents and conditions of the space leases to New York City and the PA; and completion guarantees.

[40] "Proposed Terms of Restructured Agreement and Net Leases with SPI March 25, 2010 Briefing Paper (Updated for Negotiations through August 3, 2010)."

[41] Janno Lieber author interview, October 19, 2010.

[42] Josh Rogers, "Mayor Says New Jersey Might Solve World Trade Center Stalemate," *Downtown Express*, July 10–16, 2009.

[43] Eliot Brown, "With $600 M. in Public Pledges, Trade Center Stalemate Nears an End," *NYO*, March 25, 2010; Charles V. Bagli, "Two New Towers May End the Impasse at Ground Zero," *NYT*, March 25, 2010.

[44] Andrew Ross Sorkin, "Tentative Deal Struck for 2 Ground Zero Towers," *NYT*, March 26, 2010; Charles V. Bagli, "Port Authority Official Criticizes Towers Deal," *NYT*, March 27, 2010.

[45] Bagli, "Port Authority Official Criticizes Towers Deal."

[46] Editorials: "Ground Zero Rising," *DN*, March 27, 2010; "'Breakthrough' Baloney," *NYP*, March 29, 2010; "Trade Center off the Ground," *Crain's*, March 29, 2010; "A Deal at Ground Zero?" *NYT*, April 3, 2010.

[47] PA board meeting minutes, February 3, 2010, 2.

[48] Coscia author interview.

[49] The public-sector support payments for Tower 3 would cover capped amounts for the following items: construction cost overruns prior to substantial completion, leasing cost overruns for first-generation leases, and building operating shortfalls, including debt service; they could not cover any remedial or other capital expenditures. They would be made in

the following order of priority: first, $80 million by the PA; second, $50 million by NYS and $50 million by the PA; third, $70 million by NYC, $70 million by NYS, and $70 million by the PA. PA August 26 special board meeting, 170.

[50] Based on the summary of the special board meeting on August 26, the remaining insurance proceeds were allocated as follows: Tower 4 construction ($363 million), Tower 4 ground rent payments ($85 million, including credited payments), Tower 3 construction ($404 million), Tower 3 ground rent payments ($51 million, including credited payments), and Tower 3 "first-loss" source of funds for construction overruns, the completion guarantee deposit ($159 million).

[51] When initially set by the Port Authority as part of the bidding process for the 2001 privatization of the WTC towers, the net rents were above market and, most notably, contained big escalations beginning in 2006 and continuing every five years thereafter. These rents were maintained in the PA's 2006 deal with Silverstein. By 2021, the base rent was scheduled to have more than doubled; ten years later, by 2031, rent would have almost quadrupled, to $390 million from $93.5 million at the start of the leasehold. With those escalations in place, some thought it was conceivable that Silverstein could default decades before the ninety-nine-year lease reached its term. That was the optionality of the original deal. As part of the 2010 renegotiated deal, Silverstein was able to renegotiate the net rent schedule for Tower 3 and Tower 2, eliminating the original 2001–2006 base rent structure for these two towers along with its tranche of additional base rent and percentage rent provision. As stated in the minutes of the August 26 special board meeting, after twenty years, the base rent would be reset "based on a determination of the then fair market value of the land by an appraiser." The new base rent would be determined by multiplying the appraised fair market value by either 6.25 percent for the first two twenty-year reset periods or 6.5 percent for each reset period thereafter (207).

[52] These adjustments included deferral of base-rent escalation, additional base rent, and percentage rent for two years, until 2019.

[53] For example, the timing of delivery of the development sites had depended upon the Port Authority completing the East Bathtub and the infrastructure necessary for Silverstein's buildings to function, including the VSC, and it still depended upon the agency meeting its construction schedules. Moreover, in this project public and private construction teams needed to work in partnership, in a coordinated fashion, sharing information, decision-making, schedule development, and a host of other technical demands that go into constructing a complex project in a high-density urban environment.

[54] Greg David, "Larry and the Port: A Dispute Unraveled."

[55] Eliot Brown e-mail to author, March 2, 2012.

[56] Tenant-support payments for Tower 4 fully wrapped Silverstein's risk exposure. They covered credit support for Liberty Bond financing (except for rent payable by New York City under the city's space lease) and capped amounts of the following items: construction cost overruns prior to substantial completion, leasing cost overruns for first-generation leases, capital expenditures for necessary maintenance and repairs (not covered in support payments for Tower 3), and building operating shortfalls, including debt service. At the time the deal was being negotiated, the break-even rent for Tower 4 was in the low $60s. The Port Authority's support of operating deficits for Tower 4 releases pressure on SPI to make deals with tenants at less than its optimal leasing rental rate, that is, it gives SPI optionality in

holding out for the highest possible rents much as the developer did in the case of 7 WTC. Still, SPI cannot afford to bleed too much because the tenant-support payments for Tower 4 accrue interest at 7.5 percent (with no indexing), a number that would not inhibit SPI from using the credit facility (and deliver a reasonable return to the Port Authority), but high enough that SPI would be unlikely to use it excessively. At the time this accrual rate was negotiated, it was a reasonable figure for a junior subordinated bond and an attractive rate for Silverstein. As interest rates change over time, the benefit changes; by 2012, with lower rates prevailing, it became an attractive rate for the PA. On coverage of the Tower 3 credit support, see note 49 in this chapter. The cash trap terminates only when the Tower 3 public sector backstop is terminated and all amounts advanced under the backstop provisions are repaid, all Tower 4 PA support payments have been repaid, and in respect of Tower 4 only, so long as a 1.25 minimum debt service coverage ratio is achieved for Tower 4. PA August 26 special board meeting, 173–174.

[57] For Tower 4, eleven sources of funds for five different uses flow linearly into ten separate accounts that will disburse funds for specific purposes (necessary building purposes and public support payments), release funds for particular taxes, or transfer excess revenues under explicit conditions, as depicted through a graphic dance of dotted-line arcs and directional arrows. For Tower 3, the traps are greater in number and more complex: Fourteen sources of funds for six different uses flow into thirteen separate accounts that will disburse funds for specific purposes, release funds for particular taxes, or transfer excess revenues under explicit conditions similarly depicted in a graphic dance.

[58] Janno Lieber author interview, October 22, 2013; Gilchrist author interview; Ward author interview, September 21, 2010; Pinsky author interview.

[59] Julie Shapiro, "Silverstein Breaks the Silence in WTC Dispute," *Downtown Express*, November 6, 2009.

[60] Theresa Agovino, "The Trouble with Larry," *Crain's*, April 13, 2009.

[61] Eliot Brown, "Subsidy City: The Real Public Costs of the World Trade Center Towers," *NYO*, April 5, 2010.

[62] PA August 26 special board meeting, 209.

[63] Between the final framework of March 25 and the terms delivered to the PA board for authorization on August 26, the agency "also gained substantial annual rent savings resulting from a technical remeasurement of its space without reducing the actual space to be occupied, an allotment of fifteen additional parking spaces in the subgrade from SPI's parking spaces, and the consolidation of its space all in one elevator bank." "Proposed Terms of Restructured Agreement and Net Leases with SPI March 25, 2010 Briefing Paper (Updated for Negotiations through August 3, 2010)."

[64] The World Trade Center Rent Reduction Program was first adopted January 18, 2006, and amended as of November 15, 2007, and December 18, 2008. The subsidy would run for the term of the tenant lease not to exceed twenty years, or a shorter period of time if the total amount of program funding set ($115 million) had been expended. The funding for this program traces back to payments the Port Authority had agreed to make to the state of New York (and that the state had assigned to the Empire State Development Corporation) as part of a 2003 transaction set in motion by Governor Pataki. See Empire State Development, World Trade Center Rent Reduction Program (WTC RR), esd.ny.gov/businessprograms/wtc_rr.html.

[65] If SPI did not start construction by that deadline, the base rent would automatically escalate to 100 percent of the 2010 base rent until it started construction.

[66] The Tower 3 podium would be built with the $404 million of SPI insurance funds; if SPI did not succeed in securing tenants to meet its prelease hurdles by December 31, 2013 (including the one-year extension), the podium would be capped at its seventh-story retail and mechanical level on a 50:50 cost-share basis.

[67] Paterson author interview; State of New Jersey, Office of the Governor, "Governor Chris Christie Responds to New Development Proposal for World Trade Center Site," press release, March 25, 2010.

[68] Tom Davis, "N.J. Gets a Piece of the Action," *The Record* (Bergen County), August 27, 2010; PA board meeting minutes, September 14, 2010, 229.

[69] Coscia author interview.

[70] Editorial, "Ground Zero Build-out," *NYP*, August 28, 2010; Christopher Ward author interview, November 4, 2010.

[71] "Moody's Lowers Port Authority Credit Rating," *Bloomberg News*, September 24, 2012.

[72] Navigant, "Phase I Interim Report," presented to the Special Committee of the Board of Commissioners of the Port Authority of New York and New Jersey, January 31, 2012, 1; Jeremy Smerd, "Port in a Storm: Revamp in Works; Top-to-Bottom Shake-up Will Oust Senior Managers, Cut Benefits and Speed Projects," *Crain's*, March 5, 2012.

[73] Brown, "Subsidy City."

Chapter 20

[1] Editorial, "The Tower and the Glory," *DN*, May 11, 2013; editorial, "Towering over Terror," *NYP*, April 30, 2013.

[2] As David Dunlap noted, 1 World Trade Center was deemed the tallest "even though it has six fewer floors and its roof is more than 100 feet lower than the top side of the [1,451-foot tall] Willis Tower." Up for debate among the twenty-five members of the council's height committee was whether the top mast of the tower was a "spire" or an "antenna," which the council does not count in calculating the height of a building. The issue became clouded when in May 2012, the Port Authority and its partner in the tower, the Durst Organization, said they had decided to remove an architectural shell for the mast because of maintenance and cost concerns—a decision that riled its chief architect, David Childs. In their presentation before the council, Childs and the Port Authority argued that the 408-foot-long mast atop the tower was a permanent element of the overall design and always essential as an embodiment of the building's symbolic height of 1,776 feet. They convinced the council, but with Chicago's architectural pride of place stung, its mayor, Rahm Emanuel, thought otherwise: "If it looks like an antenna, acts like an antenna, then it is an antenna," he said after announcement of the decision. "At the Willis Tower, you have a panoramic view that is unmatched. You can't get a view like that from an antenna." David W. Dunlap, "By a Spire, Manhattan Regains a Title from Chicago," *NYT*, November 13, 2013; editorial, "A Tall Tale," *DN*, November 9, 2013; Eliot Brown, "World Trade Tower Wins 'Tallest' Bragging Rights," *WSJ*, November 13, 2013.

[3] To compensate the Port Authority for the elimination of the enclosed galleria, the city agreed to transfer, subject to certain use restrictions, the property interests in the Cortlandt and Dey Street rights-of-way. As additional compensation for the loss of real estate value,

the city would provide credits in the approximate amount of $34 million to be applied toward the Port Authority's PILOT payments and also allowed the development potential of Tower 5 to expand by 100,000 square feet for a total of developable space of 1.3 million square feet. Conceptual Framework Realignment Agreement, September 21, 2006, PA board meeting minutes, 229.

[4] Theresa Agovino and Lisa Fickenscher, "Museum to Boost Downtown," *Crain's*, May 19, 2014; Keiko Morris, "Rents Show Downtown's Rising Cachet," *WSJ*, April 5–6, 2014; Josh Barbanel, "Condos Stack Up Downtown," *WSJ*, May 17, 2014; Alison Gregor, "Rise of World Trade Center Spurs a Retail Revival," *NYT*, July 6, 2011.

[5] Nadine M. Post, "Witness to 9/11, Devoted to Rebuilding World Trade Center," *Engineering News-Record*, September 12, 2011.

[6] Jason Bram, James Orr, and Carol Rapaport, "Measuring the Effects of the September 11 Attack on New York City," FRBNY *Economic Policy Review* (November 2002): 5–20, at 13.

[7] Navigant, "Phase I Interim Report," presented to the Special Committee of the Board of Commissioners of the Port Authority of New York and New Jersey, January 31, 2011, 37.

[8] Editorial, "They Lost Their Marbles," *DN*, February 27, 2014.

[9] As the sparring and rhetoric over who was to pay continued, by the end of the year foundation chairman Mayor Bloomberg announced what had been known since the dispute eruption: "There is no chance of its being open on time." AP, "Sept 11. Museum Won't Open on Time, Bloomberg Says," *NYT*, December 30, 2011. The museum was originally scheduled to open on the eleventh anniversary of the attack, but construction work on it was frozen in the fight over financing. More than nine months passed before Governor Andrew M. Cuomo and Mayor Bloomberg announced that a memorandum of understanding on the cost dispute had been reached—on the eve of the twelfth anniversary of 9/11. A deal fashioned by the governors of New York and New Jersey reportedly had been reached earlier, by summer 2012, but the mayor dismissed it.

[10] Roland Betts author interview, November 22, 2004.

[11] Likewise, the economic importance of rebuilding extended beyond the site to all of lower Manhattan, as was evident in how the $20.5 billion from Washington, DC, for the city's recovery and rebuilding was spent: $8.8 billion or 43 percent went to long-term rebuilding; the rest of the funds went to emergency response, business assistance, utilities, housing, streets and transportation, community and culture, education, and planning and administration and spread broadly across all of lower Manhattan. Just $3.4 billion went specifically to the Trade Center site (including the PATH Transportation Hub), and of the $2.7 billion of Community Development Block Grant funds, the LMDC budgeted $841.6 million or 31 percent for the WTC. NYC Independent Budget Office, *The Aftermath: Federal Aid 10 Years after the World Trade Center Attack*, August 2011, 5.

[12] David W. Dunlap, "Dismantling Ground Zero's Bridge to Bedrock," *NYT*, December 9, 2008.

[13] Alice Greenwald author interview, April 12, 2012; Alice Greenwald, "'Passion on All Sides': Lessons for Planning the National September 11 Memorial Museum," *Curator* 53:1 (January 2010): 117–125, at 117.

[14] For example, the people who jumped to their death: The museum gives visitors a choice as to whether to go into this alcove exhibit. The curators used still shots, not video of the jumpers, which exists, and it used images where people could not be identified; Patricia Cohen, "At Museum on 9/11, Talking through an Identity Crisis," *NYT*, June 2, 2012.

[15] David W. Dunlap, "In 9/11 Museum to Open Next Spring, Vastness and Serenity, and Awe and Grief," *NYT*, June 29, 2013; Steven M. Davis author interview, April 19, 2013.

[16] Greenwald author interview.

[17] Greenwald author interview; 9/11 Memorial Museum, "2013 Museum Planning Conversation Series Report." From 2006 through 2013, the Conversation Series solicited fifty-five nearby residents and business, community, and government representatives; seven preservationists; twelve uniformed rescue and recovery workers; nine interfaith and multicultural representatives; seventy-eight museum and educational specialists; eight social service and counseling processionals; and sixty foundation staff members. The detailed lists are published in individual summary reports of each series; Cohen, "At Museum on 9/11, Talking through an Identity Crisis."

[18] Peter L. Rinaldi e-mail to David W. Dunlap, July 5, 2013, cited with permission.

[19] The flood from Hurricane Sandy reopened opposition from those victims' relatives who objected to the unidentified remains being placed at bedrock level.

[20] Editorials: "Rising from the Ruins," *DN*, May 16, 2014; "The Man in a Red Bandanna," *NYT*, May 16, 2014.

[21] Edward Rothstein, "A Memorial to Personal Memory: Recalling Sept. 11. by Inverting a Museum's Usual Role," *NYT*, May 22, 2014.

[22] Inga Saffron, "Changing Skyline: 9/11 Museum Is an Immersing Experience," *Philly.com*, May 25, 2014.

[23] Philip Kennicott, "Depth of Despair: The 9/11 Museum Doesn't Just Display Artifacts, It Ritualizes Our Grief on a Loop," *Washington Post*, June 8, 2014.

[24] Christopher Hawthorne, "Architecture Review: At 9/11 Memorial Museum, a Relentless Literalism," *Los Angeles Times*, May 26, 2014; Karrie Jacobs, "Letter from Ground Zero: Delirious World Trade," *Architect*, July 30, 2014.

[25] Adam Gopnik, "A Critic at Large; Stones and Bones: Visiting the 9/11 Memorial and Museum," *New Yorker*, July 7, 2014.

[26] Gopnik, "Stones and Bones: Visiting the 9/11 Memorial and Museum."

[27] Cohen, "At Museum on 9/11, Talking through an Identity Crisis."

[28] Holland Cotter, "The 9/11 Story Told at Bedrock, Power as a Punch to the Gut," *NYT*, May 14, 2014.

[29] Robin Pogrebin, "Plans for Ground Zero Arts Hub Shift Again," *NYT*, March 26, 2013.

[30] The program for the PAC at this time included a seven-story building of approximately 180,000 square feet containing a one-thousand-seat theater, rehearsal halls, a café, retail space, and a four-hundred-seat catering hall. The footings, foundations, and shear walls supporting the PAC were integral with the Port Authority's West Bathtub Vehicular Access Project foundations, and especially important because if this early-action work for the PAC was not set in motion in a timely fashion, it would be too late (and too costly) to provide for the PAC since the structural plan was intricately embedded in the substructure.

[31] Robin Pogrebin, "Arts Funds in Limbo Downtown after Demise of Lower Manhattan Development Agency," *NYT*, August 1, 2006; Miriam Kreinin Souccar, "Culture Wilting at WTC," *Crain's*, August 16, 2010; Matt Chaban, "The Never-Ending Story—Ground Zero Cultural Center Stuck at Square One," *NYO*, May 18, 2010.

[32] Robin Pogrebin, "News Analysis: State's Back at the Table in Planning Downtown," *NYT*, April 23, 2007.

[33] Office of the Deputy Mayor for Rebuilding and Economic Development, "Confidential Memo on the PAC," November 21, 2006; Robin Pogrebin, "Ground Zero Arts Center Won't Have Theater Company, Only Dance," *NYT*, March 28, 2007. The Signature Theater was "an obvious choice" to go because it had other alternatives: It wanted two theaters of different sizes, whereas the Joyce needed a one-thousand-seat theater, and there were few other sites in Manhattan that could meet this need. Still, the decision to eliminate the Signature Theater did not come easily, city official Andrew Winters recalled. "This came at a time right after the IFC controversy, and with the Signature going, the cultural program had lost three of its four-selected entities." Andrew Winters author interview, July 18, 2011. The off-Broadway theater company eventually built a new home with three theaters, an informal gathering space, and administrative offices, as part of a tower being constructed by the Related Companies on West Forty-second Street, near its current home and in the heart of the theater district. The new space, modestly designed by Frank Gehry, was expected to cost $60 million. "We worked rigorously to try to make that happen," said James Houghton, the company's artistic director, of the PAC project. But "sometimes you end up right where you should." Robin Pogrebin, "Signature Plans Move to Space in Midtown," *NYT*, October 23, 2008.

[34] Winters author interview.

[35] Winters author interview.

[36] Maggie Boepple author interview, April 17, 2015.

[37] Robin Pogrebin, "Art and Design: Ground Zero Arts Center to Shrink Further," *NYT*, July 23, 2015.

[38] As the tower was rising, Childs countered the critics who said it would look like a fortress, saying it will look "democratic" and "accessible" but with a concrete and steel frame "robustness greater than the typical skyscraper." Tim Teeman, "All Eyes Turn to the New York Skyline; A Decade after 9/11, the World's Most Awaited Building Is Finally Taking Shape, but Has Its Architect Got It Right?" *Times* [London], August 13, 2011. The tower's life-safety features are another distinguishing feature rooted in the legacy of 9/11 new to New York City skyscraper design. There is "a stair for use only by first responders and a 'fireman's lift'—an elevator used as a service elevator during the building's day-to-day operations but equipped with water-resistant controls and a second door that opens into a pressurized, dedicated fireman's lobby," among other features. Joann Gonchar, "A Controversial Tower Rises at Ground Zero," *Architectural Record*, September 2011; Justin Davidson, "A Visit to the Top of the World Trade Center," *New York Magazine*, December 20, 2013; Blair Kamin, "One World Trade Center 'a Bold but Flawed Giant,'" *Chicago Tribune.com*, October 18, 2014; Charles V. Bagli, "In Design Shift, Trade Center Base Won't Be Covered with Special Glass," *NYT*, May 12, 2011.

[39] Bagli, "In Design Shift, Trade Center Base Won't Be Covered with Special Glass"; Teeman, "All Eyes Turn to the New York Skyline."

[40] John Arlidge, "Twin Towers: Two Skyscrapers. In Two Rival Cities. Built at the Same Time, and Taller Than Ever. Can London Beat New York in the First Transatlantic Battle of the Skies?" *Sunday Times* [London], September 2, 2012.

[41] David W. Dunlap, "With a Column of Steel, a Tower Can Reclaim the Sky," *NYT*, April 30, 2012; Ed Pilkington, "Front: 9/11 Ten Years On: From the Rubble of the Twin Towers: Long-Delayed Monument to US Resilience Rises from the Ashes," *Guardian* [London], September 5, 2011.

[42] Davidson, "A Visit to the Top of the World Trade Center"; Kamin, "One World Trade Center 'a Bold but Flawed Giant' "; Arlidge, "Twin Towers: Two Skyscrapers."

[43] Joe Nocera, "9/11's White Elephant," *NYT*, August 20, 2011.

[44] The SOM design included four-foot by one-hundred-foot vent shafts running for the whole height of the tower up to the roof for kitchens in the tenant spaces. Because the shaft was built in, the shaft was not rentable area, according to Durst, and so was lost rental space. When Condé Nast looked at the space, the tenant with test kitchens for its media publications, and realized it was going to cost $4 million to vent its kitchens 1,000 feet, it refused to pay for this. The solution, much to the chagrin of David Childs, was to create vent holes out the north side of the tower. Gary Rosenberg author interview, February 19, 2016.

[45] The Vantone commitment had been helped along by the New York City Investment Fund, the economic development arm of the Partnership for New York City, which pledged up to $3 million in funding to support the China Center and had worked with Vantone to gain the support of the Chinese government for one of the first authorized offshore real-estate investments. PANYNJ, "Port Authority and Vantone Industrial Sign First Lease for One World Trade Center (the Freedom Tower)," press release (#39-2009), March 26, 2009; Tom Topousis, "Port Authority Doing Away with Freedom Tower Name," *NYP*, March 26, 2009; Andrew Rice, "The Saving of Ground Zero," *Bloomberg Businessweek*, August 3, 2011.

[46] Editorials: "Taking License with Freedom: Port Authority Is Imperious in Renaming Ground Zero Tower," *DN*, March 27, 2009; "Nothing Left to Lose," *NYP*, March 28, 2009; "Freedom to Name That Tower," *NYT*, March 28, 2009; David W. Dunlap, "A Debate at Ground Zero over Which Name Will Last," *NYT*, March 28, 2009.

[47] Sarah Williams Goldhagen, "Symbol in the Skyline: With Opening of One World Trade Center, Ground Zero's Fraught Icon Is Finally Complete," *Architectural Record*, January 2015.

[48] Sarah Rose, "NY Real Estate Commercial; No, That Isn't Freedom Tower," *WSJ*, June 23, 2013; PA board meeting minutes, August 5, 2010, 128.

[49] Rice, "The Saving of Ground Zero."

[50] The tower is actually less than "104 stories," variable floor counts being a fairly common practice in the numbering of high-rise towers. In 1 WTC, floors 94 to 99 do not exist and not all floors are of equal height. The seventy-one office floors end at the ninetieth floor, and the floors that hold mechanical equipment (91, 92, 93) have higher than normal ceilings. The lobby at the top of the base structure is located on the nineteenth floor. One World Observatory occupies floors 100, 101, and 102. Editorial, "Freedom for Sale?" *WSJ*, February 14, 2007.

[51] The Port Authority prequalified nine firms and sent an RFP package to each; six responded: Boston Properties, Brookfield Properties, the Durst Organization, Hines Interests, the Related Companies and L&L Holding Company, and Vornado Realty Trust. The Rudin Management Company, Rockefeller Group Development Company, and the Trump Organization declined to submit proposals. PA staff together with the agency's consultants, Cushman & Wakefield and Jones Lang LaSalle, evaluated the proposals; the "least competitive proposals," from Brookfield and Vornado, were eliminated. Hines was dropped because it would not put up the $100 million threshold amount of equity, and (without an explanation) Boston Properties subsequently dropped its bid in May, leaving Durst and Related as the two final bidders. After a six-month process, on July 7, the Port Authority announced it had selected Durst "because

its proposal best aligned with the agency's interests in the long-term success of the office tower and because of the firm's prior success in developing premier, 'green' office buildings." PANYNJ, "The Durst Organization Selected to Negotiate Equity Membership Interest in One World Trade Center," press release (#48-2010), July 7, 2010.

[52] Charles V. Bagli, "As Tower Rises at Ground Zero, So Does Competition to Buy In," *NYT*, April 24, 2010.

[53] Douglas Durst author interview, February 22, 2016; Rosenberg author interview.

[54] The deal structure, particularly as it pertains to the initial lease-up period, was remarkably favorable to Durst. The Port Authority would fund 100 percent of all first-generation leasing costs until the building reached 92.5 percent occupancy; hence, Durst faced no lease-up cost in this most critical period when the task of attracting tenants would be most difficult. This element in the deal essentially enabled Durst to attract Condé Nast since the huge buyout cost for the media giant to leave 4 Times Square would be picked up by the Port Authority. The firm receives a "promote" if leasing results outpaced the projected lease-up (excluding the Vantone and Condé Nast leases) and for leasing more than 92.5 percent before the scheduled stabilization year. Based on how the promote works, Durst would be motivated to offer high upfront concessions (lease buyouts, high tenant-improvement allowances) in exchange for actual rents that exceeded the pro forma projections. (For the remaining 7.5 percent, the agency and Durst would split leasing costs 90/10.)

[55] Eliot Brown, "Developer Sees Pricey Market," *WSJ*, May 31, 2011.

[56] Durst's ownership percentage depends upon the tower's economic performance, and will not be determined until occupancy is stabilized and the tower revalued in line with an agreed upon process; he receives a "promote interest" for outpacing the projected lease-up (excluding Vantone and Condé Nast leases) as noted in the previous note. His share of the tower's cash flow follows a pattern of "waterfall" distribution common to private-equity deals, but is more complex. The other essential terms of the deal can be found in the minutes of the PA board meeting of August 5, 2010, 127–156, and May 25, 2011, 110–120 detailing updates to the deal structure.

[57] Charles V. Bagli, "Disputes over 9/11 Site Simmer On," *NYT*, November 9, 2005.

[58] Douglas Durst and Anthony Malkin, "An Open Letter to the Port Authority of New York and New Jersey Recommending a Reconsideration of the Development Plan for the Freedom Tower," *NYT*, February 21, 2007.

[59] Bagli, "As Tower Rises at Ground Zero, So Does Competition to Buy In"; Eliot Brown, "Durst Once Dissed Freedom Tower—but Now He Wants a Piece!" *NYO*, April 6, 2010; Erin Carlyle, "Sky Scrappers: World Trade Center Is a Risk for Everyone Involved—Except the Durst Family," *Forbes*, July 21, 2014.

[60] Mary Ann Tighe author interview, October 21, 2014.

[61] Mary Ann Tighe and Gregory Tosko lecture, Columbia Business School, March 22, 2012.

[62] Newhouse wanted to preserve the full benefit from his earlier sweetheart deal in Times Square, and the deal with the Port Authority did so for the remaining five years of that lease. See the minutes of the PA Board Committee on Operations, special interim meeting, May 25, 2011, 5–7.

[63] Nocera, "9/11's White Elephant."

[64] Many professionals working on the 2010 Condé Nast transaction with the Port Authority were also at the table for the publishing giant's headquarters deal fifteen years earlier: Gary

Rosenberg (Rosenberg & Estis, Durst attorney), Jonathan Mechanic (Fried Frank attorney), Mary Ann Tighe (CBRE CEO, New York Tri-State Region), Greg Tosko (CBRE, vice chairman), Robert Safran and Lauren Slifer (Patterson Belknap), Douglas Durst and Jody Durst, among others. "There are a couple of new parties—[Cushman & Wakefield vice chairman] Tara Stacom, the Port Authority—but it's fascinating to be arguing the very same things 15 years later." Jonathan Sederstrom, "Gary Rosenberg Has a Feeling He's Been Here Before," *NYO*, November 22, 2010. It was an unusually "crowded negotiating table," Tighe told the class of Columbia Business School students in her lecture.

[65] Brown, "Developer Sees Pricey Market."

[66] PA board meeting minutes, August 5, 2010, 150. As provided under a Freedom Tower Development Agreement entered into as part of the realignment deal struck in 2006, Silverstein remained the fee "developer" of the tower, on a "call for services" basis, until ten days following substantial completion of the core and shell. Michael Pollak, "F.Y.I.," *NYT*, August 15, 2010. The services Durst would be providing included: "assistance with base building construction oversight, assistance with change order review and management, recommendation of design and engineering alternatives, preservation of construction budget and schedule, reporting, financial structuring (to the extent specifically requested by the Port Authority), coordination of tenant requirements with case building construction, and coordination of tenant move-in." PA board meeting minutes, August 5, 2010, 140.

[67] These trouble-shooting items included the lack of a loading dock by the time Condé Nast was supposed to move into its tenant spaces, program issues with the GSA space, and problems with the prismatic glass intended for the base of the building (it could be fabricated but kept breaking), among others.

[68] Durst author interview; "WTC Change Raises Question of Height," *Berkshire Eagle* (Pittsfield, MA), May 10, 2012.

[69] David W. Dunlap, "As Trade Tower Rises, It's Not Quite What Was Planned," *NYT*, June 13, 2012.

[70] Under the first agreement, to the extent it "initiates and recommends base building changes that result in net economic benefit to the project," Durst would receive 75 percent of the first $12 million of realized savings and 50 percent of any cost savings above $12 million. The revised agreement benefited Durst by giving the firm 75 percent of the first $24 million in cost savings, 50 percent of the savings between $24 million and $30 million, 25 percent of the cost savings between $30 million and $70 million, and 15 percent of the cost savings in excess of $70 million. PA board meeting minutes, May 25, 2011, 113–114. Durst had first sought a construction management fee of $30 million for what it envisioned would be five years of work, but the Port Authority was unwilling to pay the amount. Instead, the deal incorporated an incentive portion as an add-on to a base management fee of $15 million.

[71] Rosenberg author interview.

[72] From an initial field of six bidders, the two other finalists were GSM Projects, a Canadian company working with restaurant-entrepreneur Danny Meyer, and Montparnasse 56 USA, an affiliate of the French firm that runs an observatory and restaurant at the Montparnasse Tower in Paris, as well as observatories in Berlin and at the John Hancock Tower in Chicago. The three dropped bidders were Aramark, a national food services company; Ripley Entertainment, operator of museums and aquariums; and the Empire State Building Company,

which operates the observatory atop that building. PA board meeting minutes, March 20, 2013, 76.

[73] David W. Dunlap, "The View from Manhattan's New Summit, Taking in the City 100 Floors Up at the World Trade Center Observatory," *NYT*, May 21, 2015.

[74] Empire State Realty Trust, *2014 Annual Report*; Green Street Advisors, "Empire State Realty Trust: 'Observations' on a High-Profile IPO," September 23, 2013.

[75] Legends Hospitality, LLC, response to Port Authority's "Request for Proposal, Observation Deck Development and Management One World Trade Center, New York, NY," May 3, 2012, "Financial Proposal to Owner"; Charles V. Bagli, "Port Authority, with Eye on Income, Will Pick Firm for Trade Center Observatory," *NYT*, March 19, 2013. At one point in its planning process the Port Authority considered re-creating a high-end restaurant at the building's summit as a replacement for Windows on the World, destroyed on 9/11. It was a major debate for many years, I was told. Ultimately, the economics of incorporating an observatory at the top of this world-known tower proved far more compelling. It would become, in the words of critic Ed Pilkington, "a paean to height." Ed Pilkington, "The Observatory: One World Trade Center Looking Squarely to the Future," *TheGuardian.com* (London), May 27, 2015.

[76] Eliot Brown, "One World Trade Center: Public Building, Private Information," *WSJ*, January 6, 2015; PA board meeting minutes, March 20, 2013, 76.

[77] Brown, "One World Trade Center: Public Building, Private Information."

Chapter 21

[1] Alliance for Downtown New York, *Surging Ahead: Lower Manhattan's Economic Impact and What It Means for New York*, n.d. [2015], 2.

[2] Paul Goldberger, "The Sky Line: Shaping the Void: How Successful Is the New World Trade Center?" *New Yorker*, September 12, 2011.

[3] So many awards. Among them: Memorial: 2012 American Society of Landscape Architects Honor Award; 2012 Liberty Award from the Lower Manhattan Cultural Council; 2014 A+ Award in Typology Memorials. Memorial Museum: 2015 AIA Institute Honor Award for Interior Architecture; 2015 AIA New York Chapter Design Award Honor Award for Architecture; 2014 AIA New Jersey Design Award; 2015 Chicago Athenaeum American Architecture Awards; 2015 *Building Design + Construction* Building Team Gold Award; 2015 Society of American Registered Architects NY Council The Gold Award of Excellence; 2015 *The Architects Newspaper* Annual Best of Design Awards Building of the Year, Honorable Mention; *Contract* Interiors Award Public/Civic Category; 2014 *Interior Design* Best of the Year Award Winner in the Museum/Gallery Category; 2012 *Architect* Honorable Mention Annual Design Review, Bond (Cultural) Category. 1 World Trade Center: 2014 American Institute of Steel Construction Presidential Award of Excellence in Engineering and 2015 IDEAS2 Award; New York State Society of Professional Engineers 2014 PEC Project of the Year; 2014 American Council of Engineering Companies NY Diamond Award in Structural Systems; 2013 National Council of Structural Engineers Excellence in Structural Engineering Award; 2015 Lighting Controls Association Innovation Award; American Concrete Institute 2015 Excellence in Concrete Construction Honorable Mention; 2011 Real Estate Board of New York Most Ingenious Deal of the Year Award (the Henry Hart Rice Award) to the Lease of One World Trade Center first and second place winner. Preservation of the last remnants

of the WTC site: 2009 National Trust/Advisory Council on Historic Preservation Award for Federal Partnerships in Historic Preservation.

4 Joyce Purnick, *Mike Bloomberg: Money, Power, Politics* (New York: Public Affairs, 2009), 146.

5 Michael Powell, "For a Ground Zero Developer Seeking Subsidies, More Is Never Enough," *NYT*, April 1, 2014; Scott Pelly, "What Ever Happened to Ground Zero?" *60 Minutes*, CBS, transcript, aired February 21, 2010. Though the board rejected Silverstein's ask for additional subsidy, it revised the 2010 deal for PA support of Tower 3 by allowing the use of $159 million of previously escrowed funds that had been intended for use on Tower 2 to be used for Tower 3; this would "minimize SPI's amount of senior debt to levels that allow it to move forward with construction under current market conditions," as stated in the PA press release on board approvals of the modification to the 2010 deal. PANYNJ, "Port Authority Commissioners Approve Modification to 2010 Agreement for 3 World Trade Center," press release (#135-2014), June 25, 2014. What the press release did not mention are three other adjustments that would ease the pressure on the building's cash flow, especially what is still likely to be a slow lease-up of the 2.8-million-square-foot building: provisions for significant rent payment deferrals and an adjustment to the calculation of the amount of base tax space tenants would have to pay; the latter adjustment would also be made to apply to Tower 4 and Tower 2. PA board meeting minutes, June 25, 2014, 114, 115.

6 "The World Trade Center—East Side Site Development Plan—Authorization of Agreements and Related Documents," PA board meeting minutes, December 10, 2015, 244–247. PA board member Kenneth Lipper, who successfully argued against further subsidies on Tower 3 in 2014, had to recuse himself from the vote and did not participate in the consideration of this 2015 deal. On the financial deal, see two articles in *Politico* by Dana Rubinstein, "Port and New York State Consider Subsidizing News Corp. Lease," December 7, 2015, and "Critics Question the Need, Size of Subsidies at World Trade Center," December 9, 2015. News of the prospective move first surfaced in April 2015. Shortly thereafter, Silverstein announced that the Danish architect Bjarke Ingels, age forty, had been brought in to redesign the tower, replacing Pritzker Prize–winning architect Lord Norman Foster, age eighty. Reportedly, Ingels was the choice of James Murdoch, Rupert's son. At first reluctant to agree to the selection of Ingels, who had never designed an office building (déjà vu of the developer's rejection of Libeskind designing the Freedom Tower), Silverstein called upon the others who had designed towers on the site (David Childs, Richard Rogers, and Fumihiko Maki) to vet the design. They all approved.

7 PA board meeting minutes, December 10, 2015, 244–246, at 246.

8 Elinore Longobardi, "The Remarkable Larry Silverstein Story: How the *FT* (and Others) Were Had by a Huckster," *Columbia Journalism Review*, October 30, 2007.

9 Pelly, "What Ever Happened to Ground Zero?"

10 Elinore Longobardi, "The Larry Silverstein Story, Continued.... Esquire joins the Financial Times in Fantasyland," *Columbia Journalism Review*, November 1, 2007

11 Editorial, "The George E. Pataki Era," *NYT*, December 31, 2006.

12 George Pataki author interview, January 12, 2015.

13 Ryan McKaig, "Lower Manhattan Redevelopment Corp. to Oversee Future of WTC Site," *Bond Buyer*, November 5, 2001; David W. Dunlap, "Downtown Rebuilding Agency Says It Is No Longer Needed," *NYT*, July 26, 2006.

[14] Dunlap, "Downtown Rebuilding Agency Says It Is No Longer Needed."

[15] Editorial, "Shut It Down," *NYP*, August 10, 2014; Annie Karni, "Life after 9/11 Blaz: Save Agency That Aids Downtown Biz," *DN*, August 6, 2014.

[16] Justin Davidson, "Why We Need a Hero at Ground Zero," *New York Magazine*, July 14, 2008.

[17] Eliot Brown, "Doctoroff Unfiltered," *NYO*, November 6, 2008; Daniel Doctoroff author interview, July 1, 2014.

[18] Goldberger, "Shaping the Void"; Edwin Heathcote, "Planners, Architects and Developers Promote Mixed-Use Property Projects," *Financial Times*, March 10, 2014.

Epilogue

[1] Hilary Ballon, *New York's Pennsylvania Stations* (New York: W.W. Norton, 2002), 17.

[2] Rebecca Mead, "The Best Part of Calatrava's World Trade Center Plan," *New Yorker*, March 10, 2016; Justin Davidson, "Boondoggle or Beauty? A First Walk through Calatrava's Transportation Hub," *New York Magazine*, February 19, 2016; Martin C. Pedersen, "Opinion: 10 Excuses for Santiago Calatrava," commonedge.org/10-excuses-for-santiago-calatrava/, March 2, 2016; Jimmy Stamp, "New York's Oculus Transit Hall Soars, but It's a Phoenix with a Price Tag," *Guardian*, March 4, 2016; Alastair Gordon, "Visual Arts: Ground Zero's New Transport Hub: Crash Landing or 'Dove of Peace'?" *Miami Herald*, March 11, 2016; David W. Dunlap, "Oculus, Centerpiece of Transit Hub and Selfie Magnet, Is Set to Open," *NYT*, February 24, 2016; Christopher Hawthorne, "Review: The Newly Opened $4-Billion World Trade Center Transit Hub Is Overwrought and Underwhelming," *Los Angeles Times*, March 23, 2016.

[3] Stamp, "New York's Oculus Transit Hall Soars"; Michael Kimmelman, "Architectural Review: A Soaring Symbol of a Boondoggle," *NYT*, March 3, 2016; editorial, "They Lost Their Marbles," *DN*, February 27, 2014; Steve Cuozzo, "World Trade Center's $4B Transit Hub Is a Lemon," *NYP*, February 21, 2016; Mikkel Rosengaard, "Is Santiago Calatrava's WTC Transportation Hub in New York Worth the Hefty Price Tag?" *Architectural Review*, August 7, 2015; editorial, "$4 Billion PATHway to Nowhere," *NYP*, February 24, 2016; Stamp, "New York's Oculus Transit Hall Soars"; Hawthorne, "Review: The Newly Opened $4-Billion World Trade Center Transit Hub"; Julie V. Iovine, "Architecture: Dazzle over Details," *WSJ*, March 2, 2016.

[4] Paul Goldberger, "Beyond the Hype, Santiago Calatrava's $4 Billion Transportation Hub Is a Genuine People's Cathedral," *Architecture*, March 2, 2016; Davidson, "Boondoggle or Beauty?"

[5] Karrie Jacobs, "Transit: Calatrava's Transportation Hub Finally Takes Flight," *Architect*, March 3, 2016.

[6] Kimmelman, "A Soaring Symbol of a Boondoggle."

ACKNOWLEDGMENTS

The 9/11 attack on the World Trade Center in lower Manhattan hit New Yorkers with a visceral force. It was an emotional tsunami. Everyone had stories of where they were on that fateful day. Too many people knew someone who had perished. Disbelief prevailed as the seemingly imperishable twin towers collapsed with the world watching on television in real time. The next day and for weeks afterward a comforting civility permeated the city as residents looked around with a new-found awareness of community, searching for ways to help. Few were thinking about rebuilding. The immediate was all about recovery. Conversations about how to rebuild and what to rebuild started soon enough—in some circles, only days later. My craft as a scholar was writing about how cities revitalize themselves through physical renewal, but this story was too raw and too close to home for me to contemplate at the time. I had just spent ten years on *Times Square Roulette*, and the story of rebuilding Ground Zero was sure to take longer. I wasn't ready. My good friend Carl Weisbrod, however, foresaw otherwise as early as November 2001.

The task of telling the story of rebuilding Ground Zero started as a single essay on the politics of planning the site's redevelopment, but the scope of the story expanded beyond any reasonable expectation I held at the start. It became a marathon. At first I thought a series of essays might contain the story; that was in 2006, but the ever-expanding and contentious story broke out of that construct. By 2011, I finally realized that this epic story demanded a big book. I have long believed that city building is a story of implementation for which plans are but the foundation for debate and action, and that action is driven by politics, big and small. In cities such as New York, those politics are more complicated than they appear on the surface. In telling this story, I aimed for breadth—to tell the full story—and for depth—to explain why things happened as they did. I wanted readers to understand how the forces of ambition and money and ego shaped the varied strands of this epic story.

I was fortunate to start this research during the early stages of rebuilding, in 2002, while the actions and recall of events by those engaged in decision-making were fresh in their minds and before time inevitably cast a different hue on events. I hoped to capture the history of city building in the making. The revitalization story of Times Square turned out to be a warm-up for this endeavor. Analyzing the dynamics of rebuilding on Ground Zero was of a completely different order, far more complex and far more challenging. Moreover, I did not know when the research and interviewing would end. And as the last pieces of the story are yet to be resolved, it is continuing.

The quest to cover so much territory could have been a lonesome endeavor but for all the support I received. During the many years of research and writing, I benefited handsomely from the continual encouragement of longtime colleagues and friends within and outside of the academy. So many gave generously of their time and were available for conversation when I needed to draw on their particular expertise or test out my understanding of events shaping the complicated path of rebuilding. I am especially grateful to Jim Doig, Carl Weisbrod, Betsy Blackmar, and Meredith Kane for reading the entire manuscript and offering insightful and invaluable comments. John Mollenkopf brought me into the fold of the Russell Sage Foundation 9/11 Recovery Project in 2002, and remained supportive for many years after that three-year study project concluded. As I worked to figure out the big picture from the many episodes of controversy and the myriad details of each and the complexity of motives across the many players at Ground Zero, many others offered wisdom and insight. My thanks go to Alan Altshuler, Hilary Ballon, Alicia Glen, Kenneth Jackson, Herb Sturz, and Carol Willis, among many others, including anonymous peer reviewers. My appreciation extends to Tim Mennell at the University of Chicago Press for early guidance helping me sort out how to present the big theme of the story to a general audience. And to Rafe Sagalyn who offered wise advice on what I would face in seeking a publisher for such a large manuscript. Daniel Rayner and Ralph G. De Palma III graciously eased my way through the legal aspects of the publication process.

My position at Columbia Business School developing and leading the MBA Real Estate Program for the past two decades has led to extensive relationships in the real estate industry. I have been fortunate to have many friends in the industry who were never too busy to talk with me, answer my questions, or help me source needed information. So many professionals gave of their expertise and helped me get access to others who were a part of the story. The late John Zuccotti, Marty Edelman, Robin Panovka, and Cherrie Nannigna were particularly helpful, and ever ready with one or more suggestions of others I needed to speak with.

This book was made possible by access to the many players at Ground Zero. On the public side, officials at every level of government offered their inside stories and opinions without ever asking how I viewed or would record these events in which they figured so prominently. At City Hall, Dan Doctoroff and Bob Lieber in their respective tenures as deputy mayor for economic development and Seth

Pinsky at EDC; Tony Coscia, Tony Shorris, Chris Ward, Drew Warshaw, and Pat Foye at the Port Authority; Kevin Rampe and David Emil at the LMDC, and Charles Maikish at the LMCCC; and Governors George Pataki and David Paterson, Tim Gilchrist, Joe Simenic at the state level—all made significant contributions to my understanding of how decisions were made at Ground Zero. On the private side of the rebuilding process, my many conversations with Janno Lieber were crucial; he was always ready to expand on an episode and even when frustrated with the seemingly interminable delays, he could deliver the story with a light touch. Roland Betts, Tom Bernstein, Dick Tofel, Frank Sciame, and John Gallagher offered accounts of central episodes in the rebuilding saga. Several family members spoke honestly and candidly about their involvement in the painful process of memorialization. Without all of these interviews as well as my confidential sources, this book would have had far less color.

No book such as this would have been possible without access to primary documents and supporting data, for which I have many to thank: Dara McQuillan, Silverstein Properties; Louis D'Avanzo, Cushman & Wakefield; the Alliance for Downtown New York; FOI officers at the Port Authority; reporters David Dunlap, Charles Bagli, Eliot Brown, Lois Weiss; Lynn Rasic, while at the 9/11 Memorial Foundation. The density of the rebuilding story is offset, I hope, by the inclusion of images that give visual form to the story or offer editorial commentary on high-profile episodes. I am grateful to all, but especially appreciative of those who generously supplied their work as a professional courtesy. For the crisp maps and infographics, I thank Maya Kopytman and Amy Siegal at C&G Partners; all of us strived for perfection.

I was fortunate to have many able and committed research assistants: Paul Aylesworth, Kate Crosby, Meghan Cunningham, Laura Dunn, David Gest, Arielle Goldberg, Joshua Grossman, Lea Guberina-Sulc, Zip Inayat, Stephanie Jennings, Alice Kamens, Ben Kornfeind, Jonathan Lemle, Matthew Mickstin, Andrea Nair, Andrea Olshan, Taylor Ott, Christopher Reynolds, Michael Tillman, Andrew Turco, Phillipe Visser, and Andrea Wong. In the time it has taken for this book to come to fruition, all have become professionals in the fields of real estate or city planning.

The behind-the-scenes support was substantial. I am grateful for financial support from the Russell Sage Foundation; the Regional Plan Association; and the Dean's Office, the Paul Milstein Center for Real Estate, and Robert Berne Research Fund at Columbia Business School. My staff at the Milstein Center, Kate Kerrigan, Kristin Svenningsen, Maricel Piriz, and Angela E. Lee, provided fantastic support beyond the normal course of their responsibilities in order to do everything they could to free up time for me to focus on this book in addition to my teaching and administrative responsibilities. With an award from Furthermore grants in publishing, the J. M. Kaplan Foundation has supported my work for a second time, and I owe Joan Davidson a special thank you.

When it came time to select a publisher, Niko Pfund at Oxford University Press was obviously persuasive, and all that he promised, the Press has delivered and then some. The care and attention of Gwen Colvin, senior production editor for my book, and the amazing skill of my copyeditor, Robert Milks, enhanced the finished manuscript. I am also thankful for the detailed attention of Kathleen Weaver, editorial assistant, who could answer every question I posed rather quickly. I benefited greatly from substantive guidance from my consummate editor, Dave McBride. The clarity of this complex story owes much to his intelligence and experience—and persuasion to go the extra distance whenever I questioned my stamina.

I am deeply indebted to my family for their support during the many years it has taken me to produce this book. "The book," they would ask, how is it going? Their understanding and patience in listening to the trials and tribulations of my research offered continual sustenance. I owe the most to my husband, Gary Hack. The unique combination of his love, professional perspective, and critical intelligence were essential to the task, as was his photography and wizardry adjusting images.

New York, New York
February 22, 2016

INDEX

Figures and tables are indicated by "f" and "t" following the page numbers.

Performing Arts Center (PAC), 298, 300, 321, 682–686, 720, 804n39, 858n30. *See also* Cultural program

Permanent PATH Transportation Hub. *See* PATH Transportation Hub

Peterson-Littenberg Architects, 197, 198

Petit, Philippe, 36, 120

Phoenix Constructors, 506, 525–529, 555, 567, 575–576, 849n4

Pier 55 park, 685

Pilkington, Ed, 863n75

Pinsky, Seth, 408, 422–423, 425, 431, 452, 459, 529, 594, 615, 624, 630, 635, 637, 650, 657, 734, 851n23

Pittsburgh, Pennsylvania, 784n62

"Plan for New York and Its Environs" (1929), 37

A Planning Framework to Rebuild Downtown New York (2002 report), 146

Planning process
Commercial Design Guidelines, 586
design alternative for "podium" scenario, 390, 390*f*
Design and Site Agreement (2004), 410
design guidelines, 185, 223, 247–252, 261, 264
environment impact statements, 211, 426, 499, 575, 646, 831n47, 832n1
expanding the site, 186–187
first concept designs (BBB), 93, 154–155, 193–200, 206–207, 260
General Project Plan, 183, 219–220, 247–249, 252, 801n3
Greenwich Street reinsertion, 63–67
master plan competition/Innovative Design Study, 199–210
public debate, 38–44, 431–436
too many players, 709

Plate, Steven P., 418, 522, 525, 530–531, 534, 543–545, 568, 734

Pogrebin, Robin, 262, 299, 303–304, 309, 320, 682, 683, 686

Polevoy, Martin D., 389–390, 813n12

Port Authority of New York and New Jersey (PANYNJ). *See also* Coscia, Anthony R.; Foye, Patrick J.; Shorris, Anthony E.; Ward, Christopher O.

Annual Report, 31, 393, 530, 774n42, 775n43, 776n55

audit, 57, 766n23, 773n34, 774n35

backstop financing from, 594–596, 609, 613–614, 618, 634, 636, 638–639, 649*f*, 650–656, 653*t*, 670, 852n27, 852n34

BBB plan, 154, 193–199

as bi-state entity, 10, 45, 76, 89, 92, 99, 108, 112–119, 127, 157, 187, 207, 280, 441–442, 446, 449, 482, 507–508, 510–511, 556, 577, 594, 629, 632, 657–658, 689, 691, 710–711, 718, 720, 835n32

Bloomberg's view of Ground Zero plan for, 420–422, 446

Board of Commissioners, 46, 49–51, 113–114, 119, 126, 162, 189, 360*f*, 390, 441, 528, 543, 547, 555, 557, 611, 670, 690, 694, 703, 706, 712, 776n35, 821n28

budget effects of Ground Zero reconstruction, 611–612

buyout transaction with, 174–182, 408, 424, 440, 785n20

Capital Plan (2007–2016), 821n28

chiller (river-water) plant and, 417, 522, 817–818n4

city vs. state power struggle and, 77–80, 82, 87–90, 210–212

civic organizations and, 149, 150

Committee on Operations, 557

Conceptual Framework deal and realignment transaction, 452–465, 463*f*, 823n52, 824–825nn62–63

condemnation powers, 92–94, 395, 397

construction progress, 546, 548–554, 549*f*, 556, 558–559, 561–564, 566–578, 574*f*

costs, 525–527, 668*t*, 671–673, 725–729. *See also* PATH Transportation Hub

crisis control, 529–534, 834n16, 836n43

cultural program, 683–686